Politics UK

Visit the Politics Chamber at **www.pearsoned.co.uk/politicschamber** to access a wealth of valuable politics resources, including:

- Guides to studying politics
- Short essays on the political process, from speech-writing to committee work
- Information on careers in politics
- An archive of updates and essays on various aspects of the contemporary political scene

From the Politics Chamber, click through to the Companion Website for *Politics UK*, Sixth Edition or visit the website directly at **www.pearsoned.co.uk/jones**. Here you will find:

- Regular updates on developing aspects of British Politics
- Revision notes
- Extensive links to relevant sites on the web

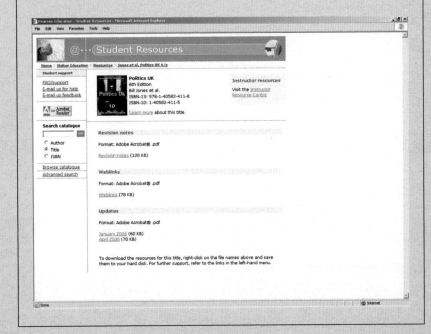

PEARSON
Education

We work with leading authors to develop the
strongest educational materials in politics,
bringing cutting-edge thinking and best
learning practice to a global market.

Under a range of well-known imprints, including
Longman, we craft high quality print and electronic
publications which help readers to understand and
apply their content, whether studying or at work.

To find out more about the complete range of our
publishing, please visit us on the World Wide Web at:
www.pearsoned.co.uk

BILL DENNIS MICHAEL PHILIP
JONES KAVANAGH MORAN NORTON

With additional material by: Barrie Axford, Simon Bulmer, Peter Byrd, Colin Copus, Andrew Flynn, Robert Pyper and Jonathan Tonge   **And concluding essays by:** David Denver, Simon Jenkins, Michael Moran, Kenneth Newton, Andrew Rawnsley and Kevin Theakston

Politics UK

SIXTH EDITION

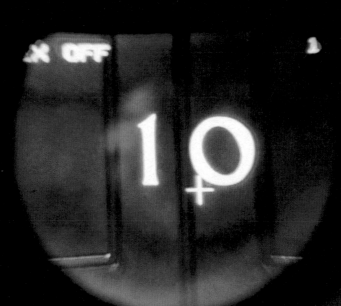

Pearson Education Limited
Edinburgh Gate
Harlow
Essex CM20 2JE
England

and Associated Companies throughout the world

Visit us on the World Wide Web at:
www.pearsoned.co.uk

First published 1991
Second edition 1994
Third edition 1998
Fourth published 2001
Fifth edition 2004
Updated fifth edition 2006
Sixth edition 2007

© Philip Alan Ltd 1991
© Prentice Hall 1994, 1998
© Pearson Education Limited 2001–2007

ISBN-13: 978-1-4058-2411-8
ISBN-10: 1-4058-2411-5

British Library Cataloguing-in-Publication Data
A catalogue record for this book is available from the British Library

Library of Congress Cataloging-in-Publication Data
Politics UK / Bill Jones (editor) . . . [et al.]; with additional material by Barrie Axford . . .
   [et al.]; and concluding comments by David Denver . . . [et al.].—6th ed.
      p. cm.
   Includes bibliographical references.
   ISBN-13: 978-1-4058-2411-8
   ISBN-10: 1-4058-2411-5
   1. Great Britain—Politics and government—1997–   I. Jones, Bill, 1946–

   JN231.P69 2007
   320.941—dc22

                                                                    2006051538

10 9 8 7 6 5 4 3 2 1
11 10 09 08 07 06

Typeset in 10/12.5pt ITC Century by 35
Printed and bound by Mateu Cromo, Artes Graficas, Spain

The publisher's policy is to use paper manufactured from sustainable forests.

POLITICS UK

Brief contents

Contents

Part 2   Defining the political world

Part 3   The representative process

Part 4 The legislative process

Part 5 The executive process

Supporting resources

Visit **www.pearsoned.co.uk/politicschamber** to find valuable politics resources

Politics Chamber

- Guides to studying politics
- Short essays on the political process, from speech-writing to committee work
- Information on careers in politics
- An archive of updates and essays on various aspects of the contemporary political scene

Companion Website

Visit **www.pearsoned.co.uk/jones** for

- Regular updates on developing aspects of British Politics
- Revision notes
- Extensive links to relevant sites on the web

For instructors

- Complete downloadable Instructor's Manual

For more information please contact your local Pearson Education sales representative
or visit **www.pearsoned.co.uk/politicschamber**.

Contributors

Bill Jones joined the Extra-Mural Department at the University of Manchester as Staff Tutor in Politics and was Director of the Department from 1987 to 1992. His books include *British Politics Today* (7th edn, 2004 with Dennis Kavanagh) *Debates in British Politics Today* (2001, with Lynton Robins), *Political Issues in Britain Today* (5th edn, 1999), and *The Russia Complex* (1978). He undertakes regular consulting work for publishers, radio and television and also writes books and articles on political and continuing education. He was Chairman of the Politics Association from 1983 to 1985 and became a Vice-President in 1993. In 1992 he retired from full-time work on medical grounds but still maintains his undergraduate and adult teaching as well as his writing and consultancy interests. He is currently a Research Fellow in the Department of Government, University of Manchester.

Dennis Kavanagh is Professor of Politics at the School of Politics and Communication Studies, University of Liverpool teaching courses in British Politics, Political Parties and Political Marketing. He is the author of numerous books and some of his recent publications include *The British General Election of 2001* (2002), *The British General Election of 2005* (2005), 'British political science between the wars: the role of the founding fathers' *British Journal of Politics and International Relations*, 2003, and *The Blair Effect 2001–2005* (2005), co-editor with Anthony Seldon.

Michael Moran is Professor of government in the Department of Government, Politics and International Relations at the University of Manchester.

He has written widely on British politics and comparative public policy. He currently teaches an undergraduate course on Business and Politics in Britain, a graduate course on Business and Politics in the New Europe as well as an undergraduate introduction to political analysis and methods. He is Chairman of the editorial board of Government and Opposition and was editor of *Political Studies* from 1993 to 1999. His most recent major publications are: *Governing the Health Care State: A Comparative Study of Germany, the United States and the United Kingdom* (1999), *States, Regulation and the Medical Profession* (1993, with Bruce Wood), and *The Politics of the Financial Services Revolution* (1990).

Philip Norton (Lord Norton of Louth) was appointed Professor of Government at the University of Hull in 1986, making him – at the age of 35 – the youngest professor of politics in the country. In 1992 he also became Director of the Centre for Legislative Studies. In 1998 he was elevated to the peerage, as Lord Norton of Louth. He chaired the Conservative Party's Commission to Strengthen Parliament, which reported in 2000, and from 2001 to 2004 he was Chairman of the House of Lords Select Committee on the Constitution. Lord Norton is an internationally recognised expert on the British Parliament and on comparative legislatures. He has been described in *The House Magazine* – the journal of both Houses of Parliament – as 'our greatest living expert on Parliament'. His many publications include *Parliament in British Politics* (2005), *Parliaments and Citizens in Western Europe* (ed.) (2002), *The British Polity* (4th edn, 2001),

Parliaments and Pressure Groups in Western Europe (ed.) (1999), *The Conservative Party* (ed.) (1996) and *National Parliaments and the European Union* (ed.) (1996).

Additional material has been supplied by the following:

Barrie Axford is Head of the Department of Politics and International Relations, School of Social Sciences and Law, Oxford Brookes University. He is also a visiting Fellow at the ESRC Centre for the Study of Globalisation and Regionalisation, University of Warwick, and at the University of California Santa Barbara. His publications include the forthcoming *Theories of Globalization* (2007), 'Global civil society or "networked globality": beyond the territorialist and societalist paradigm', *Globalizations* Vol. 1, No. 2, December 2004, *Telematics and Informatics – special issue on the Internet and Local Governance: Issues for Democracy* (ed.) (2003, with R. Huggins), 'Globalization and the prospects for cosmopolitan world society', in V. Lerda (ed.): *Which Global Village?* (2002), 'Political transformation or Anti-Politics?' (ed.), 'The New Media and Politics' (2001, with R. Huggins).

Simon Bulmer is Jean Monnet Professor of European Politics in the School of Social Sciences at the University of Manchester. He teaches an undergraduate module on Britain in the European Union as well as postgraduate courses on the European Union and on EU-member state relations. His most recent books are: *British Devolution and European Policy-Making: Transforming Britain into Multi-Level Governance* (2002, with Martin Burch, Caitriona Carter and Patricia Hogwood) and *The Member States of the European Union* (2005, co-edited with Christian Lequesne). His forthcoming books are: *Policy Transfer in European Union Governance: Regulating the Utilities*, for publication in 2007 (jointly authored with David Dolowitz, Peter Humphreys and Stephen Padgett) and *Mandarins, Ministers and Europe* (with Martin Burch), submitted autumn 2006. He was joint editor *of Journal of Common Market Studies* from 1991 to 1998.

Peter Byrd is the Senior Tutor at Warwick University. His publications include *British Foreign Policy under Thatcher* (1998) and *British Defence Policy: Thatcher and Beyond* (1991).

Colin Copus is Senior Lecturer in Local Politics at the Institute of Local Government Studies, School of Public Policy, University of Birmingham. He has written widely about politics of local government having spent ten years working for a number of London Boroughs and having served for 16 years as a local councillor, sitting on four different authorities. His recent publications include *Leading the Localities: Executive Mayors in English Local Governance* (2006).

David Denver is Professor of Politics and International Relations at Lancaster University. A leading figure in the fields of elections and electoral behaviour, he is the author of numerous books, including, most recently, *Elections and Voters in Britain* (Palgrave, 2003), and *Central Debates in British Politics* (joint editor, Pearson Education, 2003). He frequently comments on electoral matters in the press and broadcast media.

Andrew Flynn is Senior Lecturer in Environmental Policy and Planning at the School of City and Regional Planning at Cardiff University. He has worked on a number of projects funded by the Economic and Social Research Council and European Regional Development Fund and his recent publications include 'Ecological modernization as a basis for environmental policy: current environmental discourse and policy and the implications on environmental supply chain management' *Innovation: The European Journal of Social Science Research*, Vol. 14, No. 1, pp. 55–72, 2001 (with G. Berger, A. Flynn, F. Hines and R. Johns), 'The regulation of food in Britain in the 1990s', *Policy and Politics*, Vol. 27, No. 4, pp. 437–48, 1999 (with T. Marsden and M. Harrison), *Consuming Interests* (2000, with T. Marsden and M. Harrison) and 'The National Assembly for Wales and the Promotion of Sustainable Development: implications for collaborative government and governance', *Public Policy and Administration*, Vol. 14, No. 2, pp. 62–76, 1999 (with K. Bishop).

Simon Jenkins is one of most distinguished figures in British journalism. A former editor of the *Evening Standard* and *The Times*, he was knighted for services to journalism in 2004. He is the author of many books, including, most recently, *England's Thousand Best Houses* (Allen Lane, 2003) and the forthcoming *Thatcher & Sons: A Revolution in Three Acts* (Allen Lane, 2006). After a long association with *The Times*, he is currently a columnist for *The Guardian*.

Kenneth Newton is Professor of Comparative Politics at the University of Southampton. His recent publications include academic articles on the mass media and politics, mass attitudes and behaviour in Western democracies, and trust and social capital. Recent books include *Foundations of Comparative Politics* (2005, with Jan van Deth), *The New British Politics* (3rd edn, 2003 with I. Budge, I. Crewe, and D. McKay) *The Politics of the New Europe* (2nd edn, 2001), *The Politics of the New Europe: From the Atlantic to the Urals* (1997, with Ian Budge), *Beliefs in Government* (1995, Max Kaase).

Robert Pyper is Professor of Government and Public Management at Glasgow Caledonian University. He was Director of the Centre for Public Policy and Management between 2000–2005, and has been Head of Globalisation and Public Policy since 2005. His publications include *New Public Management and Modernisation in Britain* (2005, with Andrew Massey), *The New Public Administration in Britain* (2002, with John Greenwood and David Wilson), *Aspects of Accountability in the British System of Government* (ed.) (1996), and *The British Civil Service* (1995).

Andrew Rawnsley is a political journalist, author and broadcaster. He is Chief Political Commentator at *The Observer* and presents *The Westminster Hour* on BBC Radio 4. His highly-praised account of the early years of New Labour, *Servants of the People*, was published in 2000.

Kevin Theakston is Professor of British Government at the University of Leeds. His books include: *Winston Churchill and the British Constitution* (2004), *Bureaucrats and Leadership* (ed.) (2000), *Leadership in Whitehall* (1999), *The Civil Service Since 1945* (1995), and *The Labour Party and Whitehall* (1992).

Jonathan Tonge is Professor of Politics at the University of Liverpool. He co-edits *Irish Political Studies* and sits on the editorial board of *Parliamentary Affairs*. He was recently elected Chair of the Political Studies Association of the United Kingdom, the national representative body for Politics academics with 1,600 members. He is a regular writer and broadcaster on Northern Ireland and his books include *Sinn Fein and the SDLP* (2005, with Gerard Murray), *The New Northern Irish Politics* (2005), *Northern Ireland: Conflict and Change* (2nd edn, 2002) and *The New Civil Service* (1999).

Guided tour

The sixth edition of **Politics UK** is packed with features expressly designed to enhance your understanding and enjoyment of British politics. Here are just a few:

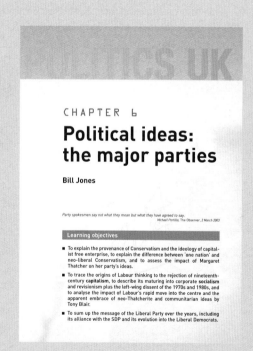

Each chapter opens with a set of **Learning objectives**, which list the topics covered and outlines what you should understand by the end of the chapter.

Biography boxes, found throughout the book, focus on particular individuals who have helped develop our understanding of what politics is, or who have played a significant role in British politics.

Ideas and Perspectives boxes focus in on specific questions, events or issues and suggest a range of responses.

Fact boxes feature throughout the text to help delineate your understanding of the developing themes.

Towards the end of each chapter you will find the new **Britain in Context** feature, which looks at the issues covered within a chapter in the context of global politics and provides a useful comparative angle on the key issues in British politics.

Chapter summaries come at the end of each chapter, to provide a resumé of the issues that have been under the microscope; this feature can be useful when it comes to doing that all important revision, or, simply, vision, for those of you who haven't been paying attention. **Discussion points** are listed at the end of each chapter, prompting you to consider and develop your own responses to the issues at hand. You will find annotated suggestions for **Further reading** at the end of each chapter. This feature will help you to navigate the minefield of secondary sources and suggest further areas of study.

Each chapter also ends with a list of **Useful websites** and, sometimes, **Blogs**. While the web should be approached with caution it can be a tremendous tool for deepening your understanding of politics.

Throughout the text you will find certain terms and phrases highlighted in bold; you will find definitions for these terms and phrases in the **Glossary**, which comes towards the end of the book.

And another thing . . .

The marriage of true minds?
The Blair/Brown relationship

Andrew Rawnsley

And another thing . . . is a feature that you will find at the end of each of the six parts of the book. These interpretive essays by leading political thinkers take a sideways glance at some of the key issues under debate in contemporary British politics.

Preface

Politics is an exciting subject. We, the authors, are naturally biased in thinking it offers students very special attractions. It is a subject you digest with your breakfast each morning; its complex canvas unfolds with the daily papers, the *Today* programme, the broadcast news, not excluding possible viewings of blogs; by the evening new details have been painted in and the picture subtly, sometimes dramatically, has changed.

Politics is unpredictable, dynamic; it affects us, it is about us. In one sense the canvas *is* us: a projection of ourselves and our aspirations, a measure of our ability to live together. Politics, despite the dismal image of its practitioners, is arguably the most important focus there is in the study of the human condition. We hope that this volume on the politics of the United Kingdom does the subject some kind of justice.

This book is designed to provide a comprehensive introduction to British politics for both the general reader and the examination candidate. With the latter group in mind, we fashioned a text for the first edition that was unusual by British standards. When we studied A-level politics, all those years ago, the transition from O-level to A-level was quite difficult. This was hardly surprising, because many of the A-level texts were the same as those we went on to study at university, partly because of shared assumptions about A-level and university students. It was believed that we should be treated as mature intellects (good), but also that it was up to us to extract meaning from the texts which, in the name of standards, made few concessions to our possible unfamiliarity with the subject (not so good). In these circumstances it is hardly surprising that so many aspiring university students gave up before the intrinsic interest of the subject could capture them.

Things have improved since then, in the field of textbooks remarkably so. Syllabuses have become much wider and now embrace stimulating new areas such as political sociology and current political issues. This has helped authors produce more interesting work but a revolution has also taken place on the production side. *Politics UK*, when it came out in 1990, was arguably the first book to embrace the American approach of providing a comprehensive course textbook with a plethora of new features such as photographs, diagrams, tables and illustrative figures.

Since then most of our rival textbooks on British politics have adopted similar styles, and if imitation is the highest form of flattery then we are greatly flattered. The book has moved through five successful editions and this is the sixth. The key features of this new edition are as follows.

■ The Fourth Edition was comprehensively 'Europeanised': each chapter was looked at and amended to take account of the EU impact and influence – all this material has been accordingly updated for the Sixth Edition. 'Updating' means covering developments over the three years since the last edition, of course – including the 2005 election – but older examples are still cited in some cases; there are continuities in British politics and the whole of the postwar period is used as a kind of laboratory in which political behaviour is observed.

■ In addition to the chapters on devolution, globalisation and the record of the Blair government new to the fourth edition, we have added another on Blair's overall record since 1997.

■ Many of the chapters have been completely rewritten, and all chapters not rewritten have been comprehensively updated up to summer 2006.

■ The sixth edition includes extensive coverage and assessment of New Labour and Tony Blair's nine years or more in power.

■ The book contains an alphabetical glossary defining all the key terms highlighted in the text.

■ The comparative approach to politics has become increasingly popular over the last decade and, while this is not expressly a comparative text, we have introduced a 'Britain in context' box for each chapter which provides a limited version of this kind of input.

■ *Politics UK*'s Companion Website contains the best available guide to useful websites, as well as many other additional features, including a specially written set of revision notes for each chapter.

■ The book's presentation has been augmented by the inclusion of many new and up-to-date cartoons (see below).

With one exception (for Part 2), the comment and debate sections at the end of each major part have been written, as before, by distinguished guest writers. This time they are:

■ **Professor David Denver** – famous among politics teachers for his books and articles, not forgetting his witty lectures at student day schools.

■ **Simon Jenkins** – for some the doyen of current columnists, he now writes for *The Guardian* and the *Sunday Times*.

■ **Professor Ken Newton** – distinguished former Essex political scientist, now at Southampton University.

■ **Andrew Rawnsley** – another heavyweight columnist and broadcaster, he writes regularly for *The Observer*.

■ **Professor Kevin Theakston** – expert on the civil service, from the University of Leeds.

The original line-up of principal authors has diminished from six to four; we were sorry to lose Andrew Gray and Anthony Seldon both through pressure of work. Barrie Axford, Simon Bulmer, Peter Byrd, Colin Copus, Andrew Flynn, Robert Pyper and Jonathan Tonge all contribute towards this volume with discrete chapters or shares of one.

The chapters on parliament in this book have always been authoritative and up-to-date; they are even more so since Philip Norton became a member of the House of Lords himself in 1998. Thanks are due to all the contributors and to the staff at Pearson Education who have proved remarkably helpful and professional, especially Janey Webb, and Philip Langeskov who piloted the book through its later stages. We have to thank Chris Riddell for his brilliant cartoons, borrowed from his weekly contributions to *The Observer*. Special thanks are offered to those reviewers who commented so usefully on draft chapters of this book and thereby helped to improve them. Lecturers and teachers are reminded that if they adopt the book they will receive, free of charge, the Instructor's Manual, written by Bill Jones and Graham Thomas. We hope readers find the book as useful and stimulating as previous editions.

Bill Jones
Michael Moran
Philip Norton
Dennis Kavanagh
November 2006

Foreword

■ Labour's transition of Power

> 'The public will let you have what you deserve but seldom what you really want.'
>
> (Lord) Cecil Parkinson on his personal version of Parkinson's Law, interview with author, 2001

Authors and publishers of books on politics often think of Harold Wilson's famous line about 'a week is a long time in politics' as a book approaches its final stages. The problem of course, every time, is that by the time the book comes out aspects of it are already out of date. As this book is being 'proofed' in September 2006, the unusual circumstances which currently obtain regarding the Labour leadership have moved me to write this foreword. As I write Tony Blair is still Prime Minister but if the book is read, either soon after publication or during the following two years, there will be a different Prime Minister from the one who has ruled since May 1997 when he was 43 years old. It is a thorny problem for textbook authors and publishers, but a useful reminder to any student of politics that ours is a fluid, dynamic subject. It moves quickly, and that is a part of its excitement. The importance of keeping an ear (or an eye) to the ground – be that through newspapers, websites (not least our own) or the *Today* programme – cannot be over-emphasised. All scraps of information you can glean will be useful to your developing understanding of politics.

■ The alleged 'coup' and its provenance

It was alleged in the autumn of 2006 that Gordon Brown, frustrated after years of waiting to inherit the premiership, had instigated a 'coup' to bring Tony Blair down. The details were briefly as follows: on Tuesday 5 September 2006, a letter signed by 15 Labour MPs led by Sion Simon and Chris Bryant, formerly bywords for slavish loyalty to their leader, asked him to step down. It seems their letter had been sparked off by an interview Blair gave to *The Times* in which he refused to be specific about when he was going to go. The next day seven of the signatories resigned their unpaid positions as parliamentary private secretaries, the lowest rung on the ministerial ladder but one for which ambitious politicians vigorously compete in order to show their paces and progress higher. The apparently timed nature of their going – one every thirty minutes – made some commentators suspect choreography by some guiding hand. As Brown kept eloquently silent during a period of intense media activity, many suspected that hand was his. Why was Labour, only elected for its third term just over a year earlier, suffering a nervous breakdown over its most successful ever leader? The reasons are complex and go back to the very beginnings of New Labour's provenance.

1. The Granita 'Agreement'

In 1994, shortly after John Smith, the previous Labour leader died, the two leading 'modernisers' in the party and obvious candidates for Smith's crown, met to discuss the situation in the (now defunct) Granita restaurant in Islington. No notes were kept from this meeting so much speculation surrounds its content but clearly the subject of the succession was on the agenda. Supporters of Brown claim that, while Brown agreed not to stand, Blair agreed that, if becoming PM, he would step down after a while to allow Brown, the 'senior partner' in the young tyros' friendship, to take his turn. What does seem to have been decided was that, as Blair's Chancellor, Brown would have virtual free rein over the domestic agenda. In practice of course Blair did not stand down although, rumour has it, Brown constantly reminded him of his obligation and bore him considerable ill-will. The resultant 'feud' between the two men is said to have caused many internal problems with 'the most economically-illiterate Prime Minister since Alec Douglas Home' according to Simon Jenkins, (*Sunday Times*, 17 September 2006) and a man who transformed Treasury control into a kind of *de facto* domestic premiership. Blair, not to mention his wife Cherie, was said to have hated the peremptory way Brown treated him in front of colleagues and maybe this helps explain why he kept Brown hanging on for so long. The brooding Scot was said to have been incensed when Blair apparently reneged on an agreement to go at the end of 2004, in the autumn of which, possibly as a compensatory sop to Brown, Blair announced that he would not contest the next election expected in 2009. However, this placatory move did not stop the sniping or the rumblings among supporters of both men, especially when Labour began to plummet in the polls. Most commentators assumed this meant he would go well before that date and he later agreed in 2006 that he would leave 'ample' time for his successor to establish himself before fighting the coming election. But there were many reasons why elements in the party wanted him to go earlier or at least to state a timetable for his departure.

2. David Cameron makes Conservatives electable again

In December 2005 David Cameron won the contest to lead the Conservatives on a centrist, reforming ticket. Dealing in generalities rather than policy specifics, he shifted the direction of policy away from traditional Tory concerns like tough approaches to law and order and immigration and towards a more liberal attitude to issues like gay rights and ethnic minorities as well as a concern for the disadvantaged.

By September 2006 his party had established a lead of 9 points according to one ICM poll. The older Labour MPs had seen the Conservatives fall 25 points behind Labour in 1992 yet still come through to win the election but more recent recruits to the chamber began to worry their seats might be at risk and that their prime minister was no longer the magician who had won three elections for Labour in succession but a serious liability. Several of the 2001 intake were to sign the Simon-Bryant letter.

3. John Prescott related scandals

John Prescott was at the centre of an unlikely scandal in April 2006, when it transpired he had been engaged in a two year affair with his diary secretary, Tracey Temple. The details of assignations, illicit couplings and sundry betrayals of his wife and family, were assiduously relayed to the public who pored over them, mostly with delighted disbelief. It was reminiscent of the last days of John Major when it seemed every Conservative MP was having an affair with his secretary. But politically the publicity was harmful in that it held the government up to ridicule.

The second scandal was less entertaining but more serious. While on a trip to the US in July 2005, the deputy Prime Minister, with his civil servants, stayed at the ranch of billionaire casino owner, Philip Anshutz, and received various gifts. Not declaring the stay was bad enough but the fact that Prescott could have conceivably assisted his host in obtaining UK government approval to open a controversial mega-casino on the site of the Millennium Dome, bought by Anshutz some years before, ratcheted up the affair to a resignation issue. Tony Blair refused to sack one of his very few working class Labour ministers because his post of deputy leader of the party was an elected one and would raise the vexed issue of when Blair was going to stand down too. However, the two scandals attracted much odium which naturally attached themselves to the government and damaged its standing.

4. Foreign prisoners scandal

Again in April 2006 it became known that some thousand foreign criminals – some of them rapists and murderers – had been allowed to finish their sentences and re-enter society instead of being deported as intended. Home Secretary Charles Clarke, struggled to explain such astonishing inefficiency and eventually resigned, with marked ill grace. Together with related rows about immigration running way ahead of predictions and others related to failings of government agencies like the Child Support Agency (June 2006), Clarke's departure seemed to reinforce an impression that Labour was not very skilled at the business of government. The new Home Secretary John Reid, scarcely helped matters by declaring that the department was 'not fit for purpose', an implicit criticism of his previous colleagues in the post.

5. Loans for peerages scandal

On top of all these other woes, in July 2006, it became known that Labour's election funding in May 2005 had been raised substantially through loans from rich businessmen whose names turned up later recommended for honours, including peerages. It seemed this was strictly a Downing Street affair and the Treasurer of the party was astonished and angry when he found out about it. According to a 1925 law the selling of peerages is against the law and the police were called in. Assistant Chief Commissioner Yates was placed in charge of the investigations and soon prominent people were questioned and in some cases – for example Lord Levy, Blair's tennis partner and fund raiser – arrested. It seems natural that such activities would involve the person at the head of the party and at the time of writing it is still not known if Tony Blair will be questioned, implicated or even tried for breaking the law.

6. Tony Blair's foreign policy

This issue had been a running sore within the Labour Party ever since Blair's decision to follow the lead of George Bush, hugely unpopular in the party, in his responses to the 9/11 attacks. Blair pledged to stand 'shoulder to shoulder' with Bush. He sent forces into Afghanistan to defeat the Taliban but much more controversial was Iraq which Britain jointly invaded with the US on the grounds that Saddam Hussein had weapons of mass destruction (WMD). Blair's attempts to win a legitimising resolution from the UN, failed and when to the dubious legality of the war was added the total absence of WMD, Blair's position and credibility was fatally undermined. His alleged deference to Bush was hilariously reinforced when a private conversation with Bush at a conference in July 2006 was recorded and published. His subordinate status – Bush greeted him with the words 'Yo Blair' – was palpable and his offer of diplomatic help was humiliatingly dismissed.

7. The Lebanon war

This happened slightly later in July. This was set in motion when the guerilla force based in Lebanon, Hezbullah, widely believed to be an instrument if Iranian foreign policy, breached the Israeli border to kill some soldiers and kidnap two. When they were not returned, Israel began a fearsome aerial bombardment of suspected Hezbullah positions as well as Lebanese infrastructure to impede possible rearmament via Syria. It soon became clear that Israel, which also initiated a land invasion, was seeking to destroy what it saw as a centre of terrorism close to its borders. Most EU nations condemned the response as a brutal over-reaction and called for an instant cease-fire but Blair stuck rigidly to the Bush line, to the fury of his party critics who believed he was complicit in a delay designed to allow Israel time to destroy completely an enemy which was raining rockets on Israeli cities. This issue of Lebanon, with hundreds of innocent civilians killed via the heartless realpolitik of US-backed Israeli policy, acted as a lightning rod to elements in the Labour Party and helped crystalize inchoate discontent into action – via the letter sent on 5 September 2006.

■ Brown and the 'coup'

When Blair's response was brusquely negative, the PPSs resigned, during the afternoon of 6 September 2006 and the Labour Party lurched to the brink of civil war. Brown and Blair had two rancorous meetings in which Brown demanded conditions which Blair rejected. For a while it seemed as if Blair might be gone in matter of days not several months as he had intimated, but in the end the party backed off from ditching its three-time election victor in the kind bloodbath of recrimination which had attended Thatcher's departure in 1990. Blair eventually accepted he would go earlier than he would have wished – maybe February 2007 – with a new leader in place by the summer, but at the time of writing some echoes of the febrile atmosphere remains as the Labour conference in Manchester approaches. Speculation continues that Gordon Brown knew of the plot and, while not actively sponsoring it, was tacitly supportive.

The irony was that Brown's suspected role and his refusal publicly to disavow the plotters, probably left him as much if not more damaged than Blair by the feuding. Former Home Secretary bruiser, Charles Clarke, weighed in on 8 September 2006 with a withering attack on the Chancellor accusing him of being 'stupid' to come out of a crucial meeting with Blair grinning in triumph while also accusing him of being 'un-collegiate', 'autistic' and poor at managing colleagues. While Clarke was no Blairite, he was clearly paying off some old scores with someone who had not been the easiest colleague. Clarke's outburst was criticised by those who wanted to maximise Labour unity but few denied that the Chancellor suffered from handicaps likely to make his role as premier more problematic than easy. In consequence Alan Johnson, the Education secretary, with a 'back story' of overcoming a poverty stricken orphaned childhood, suddenly was thrust into the limelight. He admitted being interested in the Deputy Leader post but was soon being fancied for the leader's job, as Blairites preferred him to Brown as someone easy to work with; his communication skills were said to be superior to Brown's; and his Englishness was held to play better with English middle class voters than the dour and somewhat charmless Scot. On 19th September Brown's hopes for a free run at the top job once Blair stood down were further dashed when Home Secretary John Reid, no friend of his fellow Scot, made signals that he might well stand as well. So at the time of writing, it looks as if there might be more than one competitor for Gordon Brown when he finally comes to contest the top job in British politics. However, the excellent extended *Economist* article on the subject – 16 September 2006 – predicted the ingrained loyalty of the party, combined with a sense of gratitude to someone who had maintained such astonishing economic growth since 1997, would eventually see Brown installed in Downing Street.

Readers of the book will know much more how the story unfolded during the autumn of 2006 and whether the eventual transition of power within Labour was as 'smooth' as spokespeople proverbially said it was going to be, or more like a bloodbath with Blairite and Brownite factions doing battle. You can say a lot about politics – that it's rancorous and sometimes puerile – but you can't say it isn't interesting.

Bill Jones
Autumn 2006

POLITICS UK

Acknowledgements

We are also grateful to the following for permission to reproduce copyright material:

■ Illustrations and figures

Figure 2.1: Foreign and Commonwealth Office (2003) *UK International Priorities: A Strategy for the FCO*, FCO command paper, 2 December 2003, Chapter 3, Chart 5, p. 6 (www.fco.gov.uk/Files/kfile/Chapter3IntSystem,0.pdf). © Crown Copyright 2003. Crown copyright material is reproduced with the permission of the Controller of Her Majesty's Stationery Office (HMSO); Figure 2.2: From Hamish McRae (2005) 'They're young, overpaid and over here. And that's why London is thriving', *The Independent on Sunday*, 13 November 2005, p. 15. Copyright © 2005 Independent News and Media Limited, reproduced with permission; Figure 3.1: From *The Economist*, 20 June 1992, p. 155. Copyright © 1992 The Economist Newspapers Limited, London. Reproduced with permission; Figure 3.2: From World Bank (2004) World Development Indicators (www.worldbank.org/data). Copyright 2006 World Bank. Reproduced with permission of World Bank in the format Other Book via Copyright Clearance Center; Figure 3.3: Office of National Statistics (2005) *Social Trend*, No. 35, 2005 Edition, p. 46. © Crown Copyright 2005. Crown copyright material is reproduced with the permission of the Controller of Her Majesty's Stationery Office (HMSO); Figure 3.5: From *The Economist*, 20 February 1993. Copyright © 1993

The Economist Newspaper Limited, London. All rights reserved. Reproduced with permission; Figures 3.6, 3.7 and 3.8: From Office of National Statistics (2005), *Social Trends*, No. 35, 2005 Edition, p. 55 and p. 15. © Crown Copyright 2005. Crown copyright material is reproduced with the permission of the Controller of Her Majesty's Stationery Office (HMSO); Figure 6.2: From R. Tressell (1965) *The Ragged Trousered Philanthropists*, Allen and Unwin (Panther, first published 1914). Reproduced with permission of HarperCollins; Unnumbered figure in Box 11.1: From the *Road Traffic Reduction Campaign*, reproduced with permission of the Friends of the Earth; Figure 11.1: From W. Grant (1998) 'Pressure groups and the policy process', *Social Studies Review*, Vol. 3, No. 5. Reproduced with permission from the California Council for Social Studies; Figure 11.2: From W. Grant (1985) 'Insider and outsider pressure groups', *Social Studies Review*, Vol. 1, No. 1. Reproduced with permission from the California Council for Social Studies; Figure 11.4: From A. McCullough (1998) 'Politics and the Environment', *Talking Politics*, Autumn 1998. Reproduced with permission of The Politics Association; Figure 14.1: From *The Daily Telegraph*, 20 September 1997. Copyright © Telegraph Group Limited, 1997, reproduced with permission; Figure 14.2: From *The Guardian*, 7 November 1999. © Guardian Newspapers Limited 1999, reproduced with permission; Figure 14.3: From 'How devolution is changing our identity' in *The Guardian*, 29 March 2002 (Opinion Research Services for the BBC). © Guardian Newspapers

■ Tables

University Press; Table 13.3: Adapted from the Inter-Parliamentary Union website: www.ipu.org/wmn-e/classif.htm. Reproduced with permission; Table 13.4: From W. Maloney, G. Smith and G. Stoker (2000) 'Social capital and urban governance: adding a more contextualized "top-down" perspective', Political Studies, 48:4, pp. 802–20. Reproduced with permission of Blackwell Publishing; Tables 14.7 and 14.8: From *The Economist*, 6 November 1999. Copyright © 1999 The Economist Newspaper Limited, London. All rights reserved. Reproduced with permission; Part 3 'And another thing . . .' (p. 347): Tables 1, 3 and 4: Adapted from the *British Election Study, 2005–06*. Reproduced with permission of Department of Government, University of Essex; Table 16.1: From MORI, *British Public Opinion*, 25 (1), Spring 2002 and www.mori.com. Copyright © Ipsos MORI, reproduced with permission; Tables 17.1 and 17.2: From B. Criddle (2005) 'MPs and candidates', in D. Kavanagh and D. Butler (eds) *The British General Election of 2005*. Reproduced with permission from Palgrave Macmillan; Table 17.3: From A. Somit and A. Roemmele (1995) 'The victorious legislative incumbent as a threat to democracy', Legislative Studies Newsletter, Vol. 18, No. 2, July. Reproduced by permission of A. Somit; Table 17.4: From the *House of Commons Sessional Information Digests, 2001–2005*. © Parliamentary Copyright 2005. Parliamentary copyright material is reproduced with the permission of the Controller of Her Majesty's Stationery Office (HMSO) on behalf of Parliament; Table 17.5: Calculated based on data from the *House of Commons Sessional Information Digests, 2003–2004*. © Parliamentary Copyright 2004. Parliamentary copyright material is reproduced with the permission of the Controller of Her Majesty's Stationery Office (HMSO) on behalf of Parliament; Table 17.8: From MORI, *British Public Opinion*, 21 (6), August 1998 and www.mori.com. Copyright © Ipsos MORI, reproduced with permission; Table 17.9: From S. Coleman (1999) *Electronic Media, Parliament and the Media*, p. 20. Reproduced with permission from The Hansard Society; Table 17.10: From MORI, State of the Nation Poll, 1995; ICM Research, State of the Nation Poll, 2000. Copyright © Ipsos MORI, reproduced with permission; Table 18.1: From House of Lords (2006) *House of Lords Annual Report and Accounts 2005–2006*. © Parliamentary Copyright 2006. Parliamentary copyright material is reproduced with the permission of the Controller of Her Majesty's Stationery Office (HMSO) on behalf of Parliament; Part 4 'And

another thing . . .' (p. 482) Table 1: From MORI and the University of Leeds. Copyright © Ipsos MORI, reproduced with permission; Box 19.5, unnumbered table: From Richard Rose and Tony J. Pitcher (2001) *The Prime Minister in a Shrinking World*, p. 242. Reproduced with permission of Polity Press Ltd; Table 21.1: Office of Public Services Reform (2002) *Better Government Services. Executive Agencies in the 21st Century*. © Crown Copyright 2002. Crown copyright material is reproduced with the permission of the Controller of Her Majesty's Stationery Office (HMSO); Table 21.2: Next Steps Team (1998) Next Steps Briefing Note, September 1998, pp. 64–5. © Crown Copyright 1998. Crown copyright material is reproduced with the permission of the Controller of Her Majesty's Stationery Office (HMSO); Table 22.1: C. Rallings and M. Thrasher (1997) Local Elections in Britain. Oxford: Routledge. Reproduced with permission; Table 22.2: From the New Local Government website, nlgn.org.uk, April 2003. Reproduced with permission of the New Local Government Network; Table 22.3: From the New Local Government website, nlgn.org.uk, October 2002. Reproduced with permission of the New Local Government Network; Table 23.1: Adapted from the Department of Constitution Affairs website, (www.dca.gov.uk/judicial/2004salfr.htm). © Crown Copyright 2005. Crown copyright material is reproduced with the permission of the Controller of Her Majesty's Stationery Office (HMSO); Table 23.2: Adapted from the Department of Constitution Affairs website, (www.dca.gov.uk/judicial/ethmin.htm). © Crown Copyright 2005. Crown copyright material is reproduced with the permission of the Controller of Her Majesty's Stationery Office (HMSO); Table 26.1: Office for National Statistics (1999), *Social Trends*, No. 29, 1999 Edition, Table 3.13, p. 61. © Crown Copyright 1999. Crown copyright material is reproduced with the permission of the Controller of Her Majesty's Stationery Office (HMSO); Table 30.1: Adapted from Royal Ulster Constabulary (1999) *The Royal Ulster Constabulary Chief Constable's Report, 1999*. © Crown Copyright 1999. Crown copyright material is produced with permission of the Controller of Her Majesty's Stationery Office (HMSO); Tables 30.2 and 30.3: ARK (2004) *Northern Ireland Life and Times Survey, 2004* (www.ark.ac.uk/nilt). Reproduced with permission of ARK social and political archive; Table 30.7: Police Service of Northern Ireland (2002), *Report of Chief Constable 2001–02*. © Crown Copyright 2002. Crown copyright material is produced with permission of the Controller of Her Majesty's Stationery Office (HMSO); Table 31.3: From the European Parliament website (www.elections2004.eu.int/ep-election/sites/en/results1306/turnout_ep/turnout_table.htm). Reproduced with permission of the European Communities; Tables 31.5, 31.6 and 31.7: From *The Economist*, 6 November 1999. © The Economist Newspaper Limited 1999. All rights reserved. Reproduced with permission.

■ Photos and cartoons

Page 14: Getty Images; 22: Steve Allan / Brand X pictures; 32: Cartoon Stock / John Morris; 33: J. Vella; 35: Getty Images / National Geographic; 45: Copyright © Peter Macdiarmid / EPA / Corbis; 59: Copyright © David Simonds. From *The Economist*, 7 February 2002; 72: PA Wire / Empics; 75: Janine Wiedel Photolibrary / Alamy; 93: Copyright © Chris Riddell. From *The Observer*, 2 June 2002. Reproduced with permission from Guardian Newspapers Limited; 99: Mary Evans Picture Library / Alamy; 109: © Bettman / Corbis; 110: © Bettman / Corbis; 115: Getty Images; 130: Courtesy of the Conservative Party (www.conservatives.com); 137: Copyright © David Parkins. From *The Guardian*, 29 December 2005; 138: Courtesy of the Labour Party (www.labour.org.uk); 147: Courtesy of the Liberal Democrats Party (www.libdems.org.uk); 160: Neil Tingle / Action Plus; 168: Courtesy of *The Socialist Worker*; 172: Gareth Copley / PA / Empics; 182: Copyright © Chris Riddell. From *The Observer*, 20 February 2005. Reproduced with permission from Guardian Newspapers Limited; 185: Copyright © Chris Riddell. From *The Observer*, 6 March 2005. Reproduced with permission from Guardian Newspapers Limited; 186: Copyright © Peter Nicholls / Pool / Reuters / Corbis; 212: Getty Images; 213: Copyright © Chris Riddell. From *The Observer*, 8 May 2005. Reproduced with permission from Guardian Newspapers Limited; 223: Copyright © David Bebber / Reuters / Corbis; 233: Copyright © Toby Melville / Reuters / Corbis; 236: Rex Features / Nils Jorgensen; 250: Copyright © Chris Riddell. From *The Observer*, 17 November 2002. Reproduced with permission from Guardian Newspapers Limited; 258: Chris Radburn / PA / Empics; 275: Copyright © Chris Riddell. From *The Observer* 21 November 2004. Reproduced with permission from Guardian Newspapers Limited; 284: Copyright © Chris Riddell. From *The Observer*, 12 September 2004. Reproduced with permission from Guardian Newspapers Limited; 290: PA Wire / Empics; 295: Copyright © Chris Riddell. From *The Observer*, 7 January 2001. Reproduced with permission from Guardian Newspapers Limited; 299: Rex Features; 308: Philip Langeskov; 313: © Tim Graham / Corbis; 322: Copyright © Chris Riddell. From *The Observer*, 12 March 2000. Reproduced with permission from Guardian Newspapers Limited; 324: Copyright © Chris Riddell. From *The Observer*, 21 September 1997. Reproduced with permission from Guardian Newspapers Limited; 329: PA Wire / Empics; 361: PA Wire / Empics; 369: Empics Sports Photo Agency; 383: Copyright © Pool / Tim Graham Picture Library / Corbis; 393: Empics / Associated Press; 418: Copyright © Adam Woolfitt / Corbis; 427: PA / Empics; 430: From the Foreign and Commonwealth Office (www.fco.gov.uk/Files/kfile/FACresponse029899,0.pdf). © Crown Copyright material is reproduced with the permission of the Controller of Her Majesty's Stationery Office (HMSO); 455: one-image photography / Alamy; 458: Rolf Richardson / Alamy; 472: Copyright © Chris Riddell. From *The Observer*, 23 January 2000. Reproduced with permission from Guardian Newspapers Limited; 491: Empics Sports Photo Agency; 492: Copyright © Chris Riddell. From *The Observer*, 18 February 2001. Reproduced with permission from Guardian Newspapers Limited; 505: PA Wire / Empics; 519: Empics Sports Photo Agency; 520: Empics Sports Photo Agency; 539: PA wire / Empics; 547: Copyright © Chris Riddell. From *The Observer*, 24 January 2001. Reproduced with permission from Guardian Newspapers Limited; 557: Copyright © Steve Bell. From *The Guardian*, 18 January 2005. Reproduced with permission; 564: Copyright © Tim Hawkins; Eye Ubiquitous / Corbis; 576: Copyright © Chris Riddell. From *The Observer*, 30 April 2000. Reproduced with permission from Guardian Newspapers Limited; 580: Empics Sports Photo Agency; 584: PA Wire / Empics; 597: Ian McKinnell / Alamy; 599: Copyright © Corbis Sygma; 601: Empics Sports Photo Agency; 608: Copyright © Chris Riddell. From *The Observer*, 19 December 2004. Reproduced with permission from Guardian Newspapers Limited; 635: Associated Press; 649: Copyright © Chris Riddell. From *The Observer*, 10 September 2000. Reproduced with permission from Guardian Newspapers Limited; 651: Copyright © Steve Bell. From *The Guardian*, 28 June 2005. Reproduced with permission; 656: From

The Observer, 9 July 2000; 658: Copyright © David Simonds. Reproduced with permission; 665: Courtesy of The Stephen Lawrence Charitable Trust (www.stephenlawrence.org.uk); 667: Copyright © Cordaiy Photo Library Ltd / Corbis; 684: Copyright © Bettmann / Corbis; 687: PA Wire / Empics; 689: Copyright © Chris Riddell. From *The Observer*, 11 July 2004. Reproduced with permission from Guardian Newspapers Limited; 691: Copyright © David Simonds. From *The Observer*, 3 August 2003. Reproduced with permission; 696: Copyright © Chris Riddell. From *The Observer*, 2 July 2000. Reproduced with permission from Guardian Newspapers Limited; 699: Copyright © Angelo Hornak / Corbis; 707: Copyright © Chris Riddell. From *The Observer*, 5 December 2004. Reproduced with permission from Guardian Newspapers Limited; 715: Sang Tan / AP / Empics; 727: Copyright © Chris Riddell. From *The Observer*, 14 November 2004. Reproduced with permission from Guardian Newspapers Limited; 732: Copyright © Chris Riddell. From *The Observer*, 10 October 2004. Reproduced with permission from Guardian Newspapers Limited; 737: NASA / Science Photo Library; 760: PA Wire / Empics; 763: Copyright © Chris Riddell. From *The Observer*, 3 July 2005. Reproduced with permission from Guardian Newspapers Limited; 768: Shout / Alamy; 774: Copyright © Martin Rowson. From *The Guardian*, 20 May 2005; 778: Copyright © Oliver Kugler. From *The Guardian*, 22 February 2005; 788: Reuters / Yves Herman; 794: Courtesy of the European Communities, 2006; 796: Reuters / Yves Herman; 797: Copyright © Chris Riddell. From *The Observer*, 12 June 2005. Reproduced with permission from Guardian Newspapers Limited; 822: Empics Sports Photo Agency; 824: Empics Sports Photo Agency; 827: Copyright © Chris Riddell. From *The Observer*, 1 November 2004. Reproduced with permission from Guardian Newspapers Limited; 830: Copyright © Chris Riddell. From *The Observer*, 31 August 2003. Reproduced with permission from Guardian Newspapers Limited.

■ Text

Page 5: From *1984* by George Orwell (Copyright © George Orwell, 1949) by permission of Bill Hamilton as the literary executor of the estate of the late Sonia Brownell Orwell and Secker & Warburg Ltd; 94: Roy Hattersley (1989) 'Endpiece: nous and nostalgia', *The Guardian*, 30 September 1989. © Guardian Newspapers Limited 1989, reproduced with permission; 96: John Sutherland (1999) 'How Blair discovered defeat by definition', *The Guardian*, 25 October 1999. © Guardian Newspapers Limited 1999, reproduced with permission; 183: Peter Kellner (1996) 'Never mind the ballots', *The Observer*, 24 March 1996. © Guardian Newspapers Limited 1996, reproduced with permission; 198: Patrick Barkham, Oliver Burkeman, James Meek and Ed Vul (2005) 'Stage-managed rings of confidence', The Guardian, 5 May 2005. © Guardian Newspapers Limited 2005, reproduced with permission; 224: Walter Cronkite (1996) *A Reporter's Life*. Copyright © 1996 by M and SA, Inc. Reproduced by permission of Alfred A. Knopf, a division of Random House Inc.; 227: Simon Hoggart (1999) 'Commons Sketch: No joke for No. 10 when Hague gag hits the target', *The Guardian*, 11 November 1999. © Guardian Newspapers Limited 1999, reproduced with permission; 239: Nick Cohen (1999) *The Observer*, 24 October 1999. © Guardian Newspapers Limited 1999, reproduced with permission; 244: Simon Hoggart (1999) 'Commons Sketch: Blair lays on the therapy for the terracotta army', *The Guardian*, 3 November 1999. © Guardian Newspapers Limited 1999, reproduced with permission; 302: P. Mair (1996) 'Party systems and structures of compeitition', in L. Le Duc, R. Niemi and P. Norris (eds) *Comparing Democracies*. Reprinted by permission of Sage Publications; 307: Excerpt from an editorial in *The Guardian*, 17 June 1999. © Guardian Newspapers Limited 1999, reproduced with permission; 663: Polly Toynbee (2002) 'What really causes crime?' *The Guardian*, 12 June 2002. © Guardian Newspapers Limited 2002, reproduced with permission; 668: Excerpt from *The Observer*, 28 February 1993. © Guardian Newspapers Limited 1993, reproduced with permission.

We are also grateful to the Financial Times Limited for permission to reprint the following material:

Figure 3.9: From the *Financial Times*, 22 June 2005, p. 21. Copyright © 2005 The Financial Times Ltd, reproduced with permission.

In some instances we have been unable to trace the owners of copyright material, and we would appreciate any information that would enable us to do so.

PART 1
CONTEXT

CHAPTER 1

Introduction: explaining politics

Bill Jones and Michael Moran

Learning objectives

- To explain and illustrate the concept of politics.
- To discuss possible reasons why politicians become involved in their profession.
- To explain the nature of political actors and the essence of decision making in political situations.
- To discuss the kind of questions that political science addresses and the variety of approaches that exist.
- To introduce some of the main political relationships between the state and the individual.
- To look at the rationales for studying politics together with some of the major themes and issues in the study of British politics.
- To provide a brief overview of topics covered in the book.

Introduction

There has never been a perfect government, because men have passions; and if they did not have passions, there would be no need for government.

Voltaire, *Politique et legislation*

The love of power is the love of ourselves.

William Hazlitt

I love fame; I love public reputation; I love to live in the eye of the country.

Benjamin Disraeli

This opening chapter is devoted to a definition of 'politics' and the way in which its study can be approached. In the first section, we discuss decision making and identify what exactly is involved in the phrase 'political activity'. In the second section, we examine the critical political questions. We then go on in the third section to describe how the more general activity called 'politics' can be distinguished from the workings of 'the state'. In the fourth section, we describe some of the most important approaches used in the study of politics and examine the chief reasons for its study in schools and colleges. We conclude by sketching in some of the themes raised in the study of British politics and finish with a brief comment on multi-level politics.

■ Definitions and decision making

Is politics necessary, and is power the motivation of politicians?

'A good politician', wrote the American writer H.L. Mencken, 'is quite as unthinkable as an honest burglar'. Cynical views of politics and politicians are legion. Any statement or action by a politician is seldom taken at face value but is scrutinised for ulterior personal motives. Thus, when Bob Hawke, the Australian Prime Minister, broke down in tears on television in March 1989, many journalists dismissed the possibility that he was genuinely moved by the topic under discussion. Instead they concluded that he was currying favour with the Australian electorate – who allegedly warm to such manly shows of emotion – with a possible general election in mind.

Given such attitudes it seems reasonable to ask why people go into politics in the first place. The job is insecure: in Britain elections may be called at any time, and scores of MPs in marginal seats can lose their parliamentary salaries. The apprenticeship for ministerial office can be long, hard, arguably demeaning and, for many, ultimately unsuccessful. Even if successful, a minister has to work cripplingly long days, survive constant criticism – both well and ill informed – and know that a poor debating perform-

ance, a chance word or phrase out of place can earn a one-way ticket to the back benches. To gamble your whole life on the chance that the roulette wheel of politics will stop on your number seems to be less than wholly rational behaviour. And this is just in democratic politics; in authoritarian systems being a politician is a much more hazardous occupation involving risk to life itself. Why, then, do politicians put themselves into the fray and fight so desperately for such dubious preferment?

In some political cultures, especially those undemocratic ones, it seems clear that politicians are struggling to achieve and exercise **power**, power for its own sake: to be able to live in the best possible way; to exercise the power of life and death over people; to be in fact the nearest thing to a god it is possible for a human being to be. We see that some early rulers were actually deified, turned into gods either in their lifetimes or soon after their deaths.

To support such an idea, take the example of President Saparmurat Niyazov of Turkmenistan in Central Asia. This autocrat, in a region characterised by autocracies, was brought up in humble circumstances as an orphan but climbed the ladder of advancement offered by communism, becoming Gorbachev's choice as General Secretary of the Turkmenistan Communist Party, the traditional position, under a Stalinist system, of dominant power.

When the USSR began to collapse Niyazov repositioned himself as a nationalist and when independence came he became President, Prime Minister and Chairman of the Council of Ministers. He assumed the name 'Turkmenbashi' (Father of Turkmenistan) and set about establishing a degree of power over his people to which Stalin could only have aspired. Rather like Qadhafi of Libya – another self-regarding and prolix autocrat – he wrote *The Rukhnama*, a book of philosophy 'on a par', suggests the modest author, 'with the bible or the Koran . . . to remove the spiritual anxieties from day to day living'. Schoolchildren are required to learn sections of this work and familiarity with it is necessary to qualify for a wide range of jobs. While the people of this oil-rich country live in poverty, Niyazov lives like an old-fashioned absolute monarch, surrounded by his images in the form of statues, posters, even on vodka bottles. Most absurd of all, he has declared that the month of January is to be named after him. If left unchecked, it would seem that the worst kind of politician will continue to accumulate power in pursuit of such godlike status.

George Orwell, in his famous novel *Nineteen Eighty-Four*, suggested that the state had potentially similar objectives. Orwell suggested that for the totalitarian **state**, power was potentially an end in itself. Towards the end of *Nineteen Eighty-Four*, the dissident Winston Smith is being interrogated under torture by O'Brien, a senior official of 'the Party'. O'Brien asks why the Party seeks power, explaining:

Now I will tell you the answer to my question. It is this. The Party seeks power entirely for its own sake. We are not interested in the good of others; we are interested solely in power. Not wealth or luxury, or long life or happiness: only power, pure power. What pure power means you will understand presently. We are different from all oligarchies of the past, in that we know what we are doing. All the others, even those who resembled ourselves, were cowards and hypocrites. The German Nazis and the Russian Communists came very close to us in their methods, but they never had the courage to recognize their own motives. They pretended, perhaps they even believed, that they had seized power unwillingly and for a limited time, and that just round the corner there lay a paradise where human beings would be free and equal. We are not like that. We know that no one ever seizes power with the intention of relinquishing it. Power is not a means, it is an end. One does not establish a dictatorship in order to safeguard revolution; one makes the revolution in order to establish the dictatorship. The object of persecution is persecution. The object of torture is torture. The object of power is power.'

Later on he offers a chilling vision of the future under the Party:

There will be no loyalty, except loyalty towards the Party. There will be no love, except love of Big Brother. There will be no laughter, except the laugh of triumph over a defeated enemy. There will be no art, no literature, no science. When we are omnipotent we shall have no more need of science. There will be no distinction between beauty and ugliness. There will be no curiosity, no enjoyment of the process of life. All competing pleasures will be destroyed. But always – do not forget this, Winston – there will be the intoxication of power, constantly increasing and constantly growing subtler. Always, at every moment, there will be the thrill of victory, the sensation of trampling on an enemy who is helpless. If you want a picture of the future, imagine a boot stamping on a human face – for ever.

Source: From *1984* by George Orwell (Copyright © George Orwell, 1949) by permission of Bill Hamilton as the literary executor of the estate of the late Sonia Brownell Orwell and Secker & Warburg Ltd

BIOGRAPHY

George Orwell (1903–50)

Political writer. Born in India and served in the Burmese Imperial Police 1922–7 but moved back to Britain to try to become a successful writer. He eventually succeeded with *Down and Out in Paris and London* (1933). He went on to do a stint fighting in the Spanish Civil War in 1937. After this experience he found his true métier in political writing – novels and journalism. *The Road to Wigan Pier* (1937) was the first, *Homage to Catalonia* (1938, based on his Spanish experiences) the second. His best-known books appeared after the Second World War: *Animal Farm* (1945), a biting satire on the USSR; and *Nineteen Eighty-Four* (1949), an attack on totalitarian tendencies in the postwar world. He died of tuberculosis, almost certainly before his full promise had been revealed.

In developed **democratic** countries the answer is more complex than just pursuit of power, although one somewhat cynical school of thought insists that it is still the chief underlying motivation (see below: Ambition and the career politician). These countries have realised the dangers of allowing politicians too much power. Checks and balances, failsafe **constitutional** devices and an aware public opinion ensure that politicians, however much they may yearn for unlimited power, are unable to expect or enjoy it. We have instead to look for more subtle motivations.

Biographies and interviews reveal an admixture of reasons: genuine commitment to a set of beliefs; the desire to be seen and heard a great deal; and the trappings of office such as the official cars, important-looking red boxes containing ministerial papers, and solicitous armies of civil servants. Senator Eugene McCarthy suggested that politicians were like football coaches: 'smart enough to understand the game and dumb enough to think it's important'. A witty remark, but true in the sense that politics is an activity that closely resembles a game – with sudden rushes forward followed by reverses – and that similarly exercises an addictive or obsessive hold on those who play it. Tony Benn cheerfully admits to being consumed with politics, and one of this chapter's authors (BJ) remembers once asking an exhausted Labour ex-Cabinet minister, David Ennals, why he continued to work so hard. 'Ah, politics', he replied, spreading his hands helplessly, 'is just so *fascinating*, you see'. Writing in *The Guardian*, 11 March 2006, Michael Heseltine, the famously ambitious Conservative politician who narrowly missed gaining the top prize, probably spoke for all those bitten by the political bug when he said: 'Politics is a life sentence. It's an obsessive, all demanding, utterly fascinating, totally committing profession – stimulating, satisfying, stretching.' But is the game worth playing? Words like 'betrayal', 'opportunism', 'exploitation', 'distortion' and 'fudge' are just some of the pejorative terms frequently used in describing the process. Would we not be better off without politics at all?

In his classic study *In Defence of Politics* (see 2000 edition), Bernard Crick disagrees strongly. For him politics is 'essential to genuine freedom – something to be valued as a pearl beyond price in the history of the human condition'. He reminds us of Aristotle's view that politics is 'only one possible solution to the problem of order. It is by no means the most usual. **Tyranny** is the most obvious alternative, **oligarchy** the next'. Crick understands

BIOGRAPHY

Michael Ray Dibdin Heseltine (1933–)

Conservative politician. Born Swansea and educated at Shrewsbury School and Oxford. Made money from property before becoming an MP in 1966, ending up in the safe seat of Henley in 1974. Served as junior minister under Heath, where his energy was noted. He was originally somewhat too liberal for Mrs Thatcher but served her at Defence and Environment before resigning over the Westland dispute in 1986. Encouraged by Geoffrey Howe's resignation speech in November 1990, he stood against Thatcher for the leadership. He brought her down but failed to win, though winning office under John Major and becoming Deputy Prime Minister in 1995. His enthusiasm for things European won him enemies in the Euro-sceptical Conservative Party in the mid-1990s, but it was heart problems that prevented him from contesting the leadership in 1997. Since then he has become an elder statesman, offering advice and consistent support for the more liberal form of Conservatism.

'politics' as the means whereby differing groups of people with different, often conflicting, **interests** are enabled to live together in relative harmony. For him 'politics' describes the working of a **pluralist** political system 'in advanced and complex societies' that seeks to maximise the freedom and the power of all social groups. The system may be far from perfect, but it is less imperfect than the various authoritarian alternatives.

This line of thinking provides a valuable antidote to overly cynical analyses of politics. The compromises inherent in the process tend to discredit it: few will ever be wholly satisfied, and many will feel hard done by. Similarly politicians, as the imperfect practitioners of an imperfect system, receive much of the blame. But without politicians to represent and articulate demands and to pursue them within an agreed framework we would be much the poorer. Whether Crick is right in reminding us to count our democratic blessings is a question that the reader

BIOGRAPHY

Bernard Crick (1929–)

Educated at London, Harvard and McGill Universities. Lectured at LSE, professor at Sheffield. Founded Politics Association, 1969, the professional body of politics teachers dedicated to improving political literacy. Biographer of Orwell (1980); wrote classic book on nature of politics: *In Defence of Politics* (1962). Chairman of Labour government's Working Party on Citizenship 1997–8. He was knighted in 2001.

must decide, and we hope that this book will provide some of the material necessary for the making of such a judgement.

Andrew Rawnsley in *The Observer*, 5 December 1999, expressed a very Crickian view of the then recently announced Northern Ireland settlement. First he quoted the British Social Attitudes Survey, which revealed that 91 per cent of the public cynically expect a politician to 'lie in a tight corner'. He then moved on to review the settlement, acknow-

ledging the brave role played by Mo Mowlam, when Secretary of State, in visiting prisoners in the Maze Prison in December 1997. Next he expressed admiration that David Trimble, the hardline leader of the Ulster Unionists, had 'displayed the special courage to change himself and then persuade others to follow'. He went on to say that 'The final victory of politics in Northern Ireland will be when it has become too mundane for the rest of the world to be bothered with', and he concluded, memorably, with the words 'In the toughest of crucibles, politics has demonstrated that it does not have to be the art of the futile. It can even be a calling with a claim to nobility.'

Ambition and the career politician

'Politics is a spectator sport', writes Julian Critchley (1995, p. 80). An enduring question that exercises us spectators is 'Why are they doing it?' Dr Johnson, in his typically blunt fashion, said politics was 'nothing more nor less than a means of rising in the world'. But we know somehow that mere self-interest is not the whole truth. Peter Riddell of *The Times*, in his wonderfully perceptive book *Honest Opportunism* (1993), looks at this topic in some detail. He quotes Disraeli, who perhaps offers us a

BOX 1.1 IDEAS AND PERSPECTIVES

What does government do?

If politics is largely about government then what are the things that governments do? Anthony Giddens, in his *The Third Way*, provides the following analysis:

- provide means for the representation of diverse interests;
- offer a forum for reconciling the competing claims of those interests;
- create and protect an open public sphere, in which unconstrained debate about policy issues can be carried on;
- provide a diversity of public goods, including forms of collective security and welfare;
- regulate markets in the public interest and foster market competition where monopoly threatens;
- foster social peace through the provision of policing;
- promote the active development of human capital through its core role in the education system;
- sustain an effective system of law;
- have a directly economic role, as a prime employer, in macro and micro intervention, plus the provision of infrastructure;
- more controversially, perhaps, have a civilising aim – government reflects the widely held norms and values, but can also help shape them, in the educational system and elsewhere;
- foster regional and trans-national alliances and pursue global goals.

Source: Giddens (1998), pp. 47–8

more rounded and believable account of his interest in politics to his Shrewsbury constituents: 'There is no doubt, gentlemen, that all men who offer themselves as candidates for public favour have motives of some sort. I candidly acknowledge that I have and I will tell you what they are: I love fame; I love public reputation; I love to live in the eye of the country.'

Riddell also quotes F.E. Smith, who candidly gloried in the 'endless adventure of governing men'. For those who think that these statements were merely expressions of nineteenth-century romanticism, Riddell offers the example of Richard Crossman's comment that politics is a 'never ending adventure – with its routs and discomfitures, rushes and sallies', its 'fights for the fearless and goals for the eager'. He also includes Michael Heseltine, whom he heard, irritated, asking at one of Jeffrey Archer's parties in 1986: 'Why shouldn't I be Prime Minister then?'

The tendency of politicians to explain their taste for politics in terms of concern for 'the people' is seldom sincere. In the view of Henry Fairlie this is nothing more than 'humbug'. William Waldegrave agrees: 'Any politician who tells you he isn't ambitious is only telling you he isn't for some tactical reason; or more bluntly, telling a lie – I certainly wouldn't deny that I wanted ministerial office; yes, I'm ambitious.' As if more proof were needed, David Owen once said on television – and 'he should know', one is tempted to say – that 'Ambition drives politics like money drives the international economy.' Ambition, of course, is good for society only if it works for the general good; if it is purely self-inclined we end up with the likes of Saddam Hussein. As Edmund Burke noted: 'Ambition can creep as well as soar.'

Riddell goes on in his book to analyse how the ambitious political animal has slowly transformed British politics. He follows up and develops Anthony King's concept of the 'career politician', observing that a decreasing number of MPs had backgrounds in professions, or 'proper jobs' in Westminster parlance, compared with those who centred their whole lives on politics and whose 'jobs' were of secondary importance, merely supporting the Westminster career. In 1951 the figure was 11 per cent; by 1992 it was 31 per cent. By contrast, the proportion of new MPs with 'proper jobs' fell from 80 per cent to 41 per cent. Many of this new breed begin life as researchers for an MP or in a party's research department, then proceed to seek selection as a

candidate and from there into parliament and from then on ever onwards and upwards. The kind of MP who enters politics in later life is in steep decline; the new breed of driven young professionals has tended to dominate the field, proving firmer of purpose and more skilled in execution than those for whom politics is a later or learned vocation. The kind of businessman who achieves distinction in his field and then goes into politics is now a rarity rather than the familiar figure of the nineteenth century or the earlier decades of the twentieth.

Some less sensible quotations by politicians

I would have made a good Pope.

Richard Nixon

OK we've won. What do we do now?
Brian Mulroney on being re-elected Prime Minister of Canada

Outside the killings we have one of the lowest crime rates in the country.
Marion Barry, former mayor of Washington, DC

I have opinions of my own – strong opinions – but I don't always agree with them.

George Bush (Snr)

I didn't go down there with any plan for the Americas or anything. I went down to find out from them and learn their views. You'd be surprised. They're all individual countries.
Ronald Reagan on how his Latin American trip had changed his views

The real question for 1988 is whether we're going forward to tomorrow or past to the – back!

Dan Quayle

What a waste to lose one's mind – or not to have a mind. How true that is.

Dan Quayle

I never make predictions. I never have and I never will.

Tony Blair

and finally (though there are many more):
I stand by all the mis-statements.

Dan Quayle
all quotations from Oliver, 1992

Politicians pride themselves on being fluent and always in control, but however powerful and mighty they might be, they can say some seriously stupid things, as the examples above illustrate.

Defining politics

Politics is difficult to define yet easy to recognise. To some extent with the word 'politics' we can consider current usage and decide our own meaning, making our own definition wide or narrow according to our taste or purposes. From the discussion so far, politics is obviously a universal activity; it is concerned with the governance of states, and (Crick's special concern) it involves a conciliation or harmonisation process. Yet we talk of politics on a micro as well as a macro scale: small groups such as families or parent/teacher associations also have a political dimension. What is it that unites these two levels? The answer is the conflict of different interests. People or groups of people who want different things – be it power, money, liberty, etc. – face the potential or reality of conflict when such things are in short supply. Politics begins when their interests clash. At the micro level we use a variety of techniques to get our own way: persuasion, rational argument, irrational strategies, threats, entreaties, bribes, manipulation – anything we think will work. At the macro level, democratic states establish complex procedures for the management of such conflicts, often – although famously not in Britain's case – codified in the form of written constitutions. Representatives of the adult population are elected to a **legislature** or parliament tasked with the job of discussing and agreeing changes in the law as well as exercising control over the **executive** – those given responsibility for day-to-day decisions in the running of the country.

Is the political process essentially peaceful? The answer is usually, but not exclusively, yes. If violence is involved on a widespread scale, e.g. war between states, it would be fair to say that politics has been abandoned for other means. But it must be recognised that:

1. Political order within a state is ensured through the implicit threat of force, which a state's control of the police and army provides. As nineteenth-century US President John Adams pointed out, 'Fear is the foundation of most government'. Occasionally passions run high and the state's power is explicitly exercised – as in the 1984–5 miners' strike.

2. There are many situations in the world, for example in Palestine, Afghanistan or Iraq, where violence is regularly used to provide both a context for and an alternative to peaceful political processes. And, though politicians tend to deny this, it can be successful. One might persuasively argue, for example, that the underlying threat of violence succeeded in bringing the terrorist IRA from the streets to the highest conference tables in the UK.

So, while political activity is peaceful for most of the time in most countries, the threat of violence or its reality are both integral parts of the political process.

We should now be able to move towards a definition:

Politics is essentially a process that seeks to manage or resolve conflicts of interest between people, usually in a peaceful fashion. In its general sense it can describe the interactions of any group of individuals, but in its specific sense it refers to the many and complex relationships that exist between state institutions and the rest of society.

Peaceful political processes, then, are the alternative, the antidote to brute force. As the practitioners of this invaluable art, politicians deserve our gratitude. It was interesting to note that in July 1989, when Ali Akbar Rafsanjani emerged as the successor to the extremist Iranian religious leader Ayatollah Khomeini, several Iranians were quoted in the press approving him as 'a political man': someone who would be likely to steer the country away from the internal violence that religious conflicts threatened at the time. Such a comment would be less likely to be made in connection with the current hard-line Iranian president, Mahmoud Ahmadinejad.

Does this mean that cynical attitudes towards politicians should be discouraged? Not exactly, in our view. It is wrong that politicians should be widely undervalued and often unfairly blamed, but experience suggests that it is better to doubt them rather than trust them unquestioningly. After all, politicians are like salesmen and in their enthusiasm to sell their messages they often exaggerate or otherwise distort the truth. They also seek power and **authority** over us, and this is not a privilege we should relinquish lightly. Lord Acton noted that 'all power tends to corrupt', and history can summon any number of tyrants in support of this proposition.

We are right to doubt politicians, but, as John Donne advised, we should 'doubt wisely'.

Decision making

Much political activity culminates in the taking of decisions, and all decisions involve choice. Politicians are presented with alternative courses of action – or inaction – and once a choice has been made they have to try to make sure their decisions are accepted. Two examples follow that illustrate the micro and macro senses of politics and that also introduce some important related terminology.

Decision making I: micro-politics

When the outgoing school captain of chess goes to university a struggle ensues between three candidates for his position: Mary is a little short of things to cite as 'other activities' on her application forms to university, especially as she is not very good at more traditional sports; David is something of a 'chess prodigy' and wants to convince his father he can go on to become a grandmaster and earn his living from the game; Sarah is already captain of hockey but enjoys the status of being in charge and thinks the addition of this more cerebral title might clinch the position of Head Girl for herself.

On the face of it, this commonplace situation has little to do with politics – yet it is an example of politics with a small 'p' or 'micro-politics', and political science terms can fruitfully be used to analyse the situation.

Interests in politics are defined as those things that people want or care about: usually financial resources but other things too such as status, power, justice, liberty or the avoidance of unwanted outcomes. In this example one person (Sarah) is interested mainly in the prestige and status of the office and the possible knock-on effect it may provide for an even more sought-after goal, while the other two are interested for future educational and career reasons.

Political actors in this instance include the three pupils, the headteacher and Mr Stonehouse, the master with responsibility for chess in the school. Other actors, however, might easily be drawn into the political process as it develops.

Power in politics is the ability to get others to act in a particular way. Typically this is achieved through the exercise of threats and rewards but also through the exercise of *authority*: the acceptance of someone's right to be obeyed (see below for fuller explanation).

The *power relationship* in this case might be seen in the following terms. The pupils are bereft of any real power: all the cards are held by the master in charge, who has been given authority by the head to choose the person for the job. Conceivably the two disappointed candidates might exercise a threat of disruptive behaviour if their claims are overlooked, but this threat, if it existed, would lack any real credibility and would be unlikely to affect the outcome. Moreover, all three pupils accept the authority of Mr Stonehouse to make the decision and are likely to accept his verdict. The outcome of this conflict of interests will depend on a number of factors:

1. *Political will*: How prepared are any of the pupils to advance their cause? David, for example, arranges to play a public simultaneous game against a visiting grand master to give his candidature some extra weight, but such a strategy could backfire – if he loses too easily, for example.

2. *Influence*: How open are any of the actors to rational argument, appeals to loyalty and so forth? Mr Stonehouse, for example, was once employed by David's father to give him extra chess lessons. Will this former contact create a sense of loyalty that will tip the balance in David's favour?

3. *Manipulation*: How effectively can the candidates involve the other actors? Mary's mother is a close friend of Mr Stonehouse, and her father is a school governor. Could ambitious parents be mobilised to pull these possible levers of influence?

The *political process* would take place largely through face-to-face contacts, nods and winks in the case of Mary's father, for example (lobbying for his daughter could scarcely be done openly – such **influence** is not after all thought to be 'proper'). David, however, could advance his claim through a good performance against a grandmaster. The whole political process could therefore take place virtually unseen by anyone except the actors themselves as they make their moves. Open discussion of their claims is unlikely to occur between candidates and Mr Stonehouse (not thought to be good form either). How did it pan out? (This is only a hypothetical situation, but the reader may have become interested by now so I'll conclude the mini-drama.)

Well, David did well against the grand master and was the last to be beaten after an ingenious defensive strategy that actually put him in difficulty after he lost a rook. David's ambitious father made an excuse to ring up Mr Stonehouse and at the end of the conversation just 'happened' to raise the subject of his son's chess prowess and his great commitment to the school team. Despite his efforts, however, the approach was a little unsubtle and Mr Stonehouse was unimpressed. Mary's father (the school governor), however, had heavier guns to fire. He met Mr Stonehouse at a parents' evening and contrived to meet him afterwards in the pub for a quiet drink. There he was able to suggest in oblique but unmistakable terms that he would support Mr Stonehouse's interest in becoming head of his subject in exchange for Mary becoming head of chess. I would like to say that Mr Stonehouse was above such petty manoeuvring, but he too was ambitious and was being urged by his wife to be more so. After some wrestling with his conscience, he ignored both David and Sarah and appointed Mary. Moral: justice is often not meted out by the political process, and human frailties often intervene to ensure this is so.

Decision making II: macro-politics

A major national newspaper breaks a story that Kevin Broadstairs, a Conservative cabinet minister, has been having an affair with an actress. The PM issues a statement in support of his colleague and old friend from university days. However, more embarrassing details hit the front pages of the tabloids, including the fact that the same actress has also been carrying on with a senior member of the Opposition. The 1922 Committee meets, and influential voices call for a resignation.

This by now somewhat familiar situation is quintessentially political.

■ *Interests*: The PM needs to appear above suspicion of 'favouritism' but also needs to show that he is loyal and not a hostage to either groups of back-benchers or the press. Broadstairs obviously has an interest in keeping his job, retaining respect within his party and saving his rocky marriage. The governing party needs to sustain its reputation as the defender of family values. The press wishes to sell more newspapers.

■ *Actors*: In this situation are potentially numerous: the PM, Broadstairs, the actress, her former lovers, back-bench MPs, editors, television producers, the Opposition, Mrs Broadstairs and (unfortunately) her children, the Church, feminists and anyone else willing to enter the fray.

■ *Power*: The power relationship in these circumstances is naturally influenced by the ability of each side to enforce threats. The PM has the power of political life or death over the minister but would like to show his strength by resisting resignation calls; Broadstairs effectively has no power in this situation and is largely dependent on the PM's goodwill and possible press revelations.

■ *Authority*: No one questions the PM's right to sack Broadstairs. However, the press's right to force resignations is very much resisted by politicians. The ultimate authority of the governing party to call for the minister's head is also not questioned.

■ *Political process*: Will Broadstairs survive? Our minister in this situation is a hostage to the discretion of his mistress and other people either involved or perceiving an interest in the affair.

The outcome will depend on the following:

■ *Political will*: How prepared are the PM and Broadstairs to stand firm against resignation calls? How long could he hold out once the 1922 Committee has given the thumbs down? How long would this committee stay silent as it saw the issue eroding voter support? How effective would Broadstairs' enemies in his own party be in hastening his downfall?

■ *Influence*: How much influence does the PM have in Fleet Street? The evidence suggests that political sympathies of a paper count for nothing when a really juicy scandal is involved. Even right-wing papers carried full coverage of sleaze stories relating to John Major's government. Does Broadstairs have a body of support on the back benches, or is he a 'loner'?

■ *Manipulation*: How good is the minister at coping with the situation? Can he make a clean breast of it, like Paddy Ashdown regarding his extramarital affair in January 1992, and survive with reputation arguably enhanced? Can he handle hostile press conferences and media interviews (as David Mellor did with aplomb – though much good it did him)? Can the minister call up old favours on the back benches?

Let's suppose that things quieten down for a few days, the PM defends his friend at Question Time and the wife says she'll stand by her man. If this was all there was to it, Broadstairs would survive and live to fight again, albeit with his reputation and prospects damaged. We saw that in the somewhat similar David Mellor case the revelations kept on coming (much to public amusement and his embarrassment), but the crucial revelations concerned acceptance of undeclared favours by the minister. After this, back-bench calls for a resignation and an excited press ensured that Mellor had to go.

The political process in this case is a little haphazard and depends to some extent on each day's tabloid headlines. It will also depend on the PM's judgement as to when the problem has ceased to be an individual one and has escalated to the point when his own judgement and the political standing of his party are in question. Alastair Campbell, Blair's famously powerful Press Secretary, reckoned that if public criticism of a minister continued after fourteen days then, even if blameless, the minister would have to resign as such publicity prevents the minister from functioning as the government requires. Once that point has been reached it is only a matter of time before the minister's career is over. There was much in ex-Prime Minister Harold Wilson's tongue-in-cheek comment that 'much of politics is presentation, and what isn't is timing'.

■ The critical political questions

Because politics studies the making and carrying out of decisions, the student of politics learns to ask a number of important immediate questions about the political life of any institution:

1. Who is included and who is excluded from the process of decision making? It is rare indeed for all the members of a community or organisation to be allowed a part in the decision-making process. Mapping the divide between those taking part and those not taking part is an important initial task of political inquiry.

2. What matters are actually dealt with by the political process? This is sometimes called 'identifying the political agenda'. Every community or body has such an agenda – a list of issues that are accepted as matters over which choices can be made. In a school the agenda may include the budget and the curriculum; in a church, the religious doctrine of the institution; within the government of a country such as Britain, the balance of spending between defence and education. But the range of subjects 'on the political agenda' will vary greatly at different times and in different places. In modern Britain, for instance, the terms on which education is provided by the state are a major item of political argument. But before 1870, when compulsory education was first introduced, this was a matter that did not concern decision makers.

3. What do the various individuals or groups involved in the political process achieve? What are their interests and how clearly can they be identified?

4. What means and resources do decision makers have at their disposal to assist them in getting their way? When a decision is made, one set of preferences is chosen over another. In practice this means that one person or group compels or persuades others to give way. Compulsion or persuasion is possible only through the use of some resources. These are highly varied. We may get our way in a decision through the use of force, or money, or charm, or the intellectual weight of our argument. Studying politics involves examining the range of political resources and how they are employed.

■ Politics, government and the state

Every human being has some experience of politics, either as the maker of decisions or as the subject of decisions, because politics is part and parcel of social organisation. An institution that did not have some means of making decisions would simply cease to be an institution. But this book is not long enough to deal with the totality of political life in Britain; it concentrates on politics inside government and the organisations that are close to it.

The best way of understanding the special nature of macro-politics (or politics with a capital 'P') is to begin by appreciating the difference between the state and other institutions in society.

In a community like Britain there are thousands of organisations in which political activity takes place. By far the most significant of these is that body called 'the state', which can be defined as follows:

That institution in a society which exercises supreme power over a defined territory.

Three features of the state should be noted:

1. *The state is more than the government.* The state should not be equated with 'government', let alone with a particular government. When we speak of 'a Conservative government' we are referring to the occupancy of the leading positions in government – such as the office of Prime Minister – by elected politicians drawn from a particular party. This in turn should be distinguished from 'government' in a more general sense, by which is meant a set of institutions, notably departments of state such as the Treasury and the Home Office, concerned with the conduct of policies and everyday administration. The state certainly encompasses these departments of state, but it also embraces a wider range of institutions. Most importantly, it includes the agencies whose role it is to ensure that in the last instance the will of the state is actually enforced: these include the police, the courts and the armed forces (for a view of the functions of the state see Box 1.1).

2. *Territory is a key feature of the state.* What distinguishes the state from other kinds of institution in which politics takes place is that it is the supreme decision maker in a defined territory. Other institutions in Britain take decisions that their members obey, but power in a family, a school or a firm is ultimately regulated by the will of the state. In Britain, this idea is expressed in the notion of **sovereignty**. The sovereign power of the state consists in the ability to prescribe the extent and limits of the powers that can be exercised by any other organisation in British society.

   It follows that this sovereignty is limited territorially. The British state lives in a world of other states, and the extent of its rule is defined by its physical boundaries, which inevitably abut onto the boundaries of other states.

   Disputes about the physical boundaries of state sovereignty are among the most serious in political life. It might be thought that an 'island

state', which is how Britain is conventionally pictured, would have no difficulty in establishing its boundaries. In practice, identification is complicated and often leads to fierce disputes with other states over claims to territory. In 1982, a rival sovereign state, Argentina, had to be expelled by force when it occupied territory (which Britain claims for its own) in the Falkland Islands of the South Atlantic. Another source of dispute arises from the fact that the boundaries of a state are not identical with its land mass: states like Britain also claim jurisdiction over the air space above that land mass and over territorial waters surrounding the land. In recent decades, for instance, Britain has extended its 'territorial limits' – the area of sea over which it claims sovereignty – from three miles to 200 miles beyond the shoreline, in order to possess the fishing and mineral exploration rights of those waters. This extension has often caused disputes between rival claimants.

The fact that there exists on Earth only a finite amount of land, sea and air space means that the sovereignty of a particular state over territory is always subject to potential challenge from outside. Occasionally the ferocity of this challenge may actually lead to the destruction of a state: in 1945, for instance, the defeat of Germany at the end of the Second World War led to the destruction of the German state and the occupation of all German territory by its victorious opponents.

However, a state's sovereignty is not only subject to external challenge; it can also be disputed internally. In 1916, for instance, the boundaries of the British state encompassed the whole island of Ireland. Between 1916 and 1921 there occurred a military uprising against British rule, which ended in agreement to redraw territorial boundaries, creating an independent Irish state covering most of what had hitherto been British sovereign territory.

3. *State power depends on legitimacy.* As the example of the Falklands, the destruction of the German state after 1945 and the creation of an independent state in Ireland all show, control of the means of coercion is an important guarantor of sovereignty. But the sovereign power of a state depends not only on its capacity to coerce; it also rests on the recognition by citizens that the

state has the authority or right to exercise power over those who live in its territory. This is commonly called **legitimacy**. It would be extremely difficult for a state to survive if it did not command this legitimacy. Britain, like most other large communities with sophisticated and advanced economies, is far too complex a society to be governed chiefly by force. This is why the state in Britain, as in other advanced industrial nations, claims to be not only the supreme power in a territory but also the supreme legitimate power.

This right to obedience is asserted on different grounds by different states at different times. The German social theorist Max Weber offered a famous distinction between three types of legitimacy: *traditional*, *charismatic* and *rational–legal*. The first of these rests on custom and appeals to continuity with the past. It is the principal ground, for instance, by which rule through a hereditary monarchy is justified. The second appeals to the divine-like, 'anointed' quality of leadership: in our century many of the greatest dictators, such as Adolf Hitler, have commanded obedience through their charismatic qualities. Rational–legal legitimacy rests on the ground that in making decisions agreed rules and agreed purposes are observed.

Although in any state elements of all three sorts of legitimacy can be identified, they will be emphasised in different ways. In Britain, **charisma** is relatively unimportant. Although some politicians are occasionally described as 'charismatic' personalities, this is no more than a journalistic way of saying 'exciting' or 'appealing'. Political leadership in Britain does not rest on a claim that governors are 'anointed' with divine-like qualities. Tradition in Britain, by contrast, does have some importance. The crown is the symbol of political authority, and the Queen's right to that crown of course rests on inheritance – she was born to the succession, like the monarch who preceded her and the one who will follow her. However, the legitimacy of the state in Britain rests only in part on tradition; for the main part it is rational–legal in character: its actions are taken in accordance with agreed procedures, in particular laws passed by Parliament. It is an absolute principle of the exercise of state authority that the state cannot legitimately command the obedience of citizens if its demands do not carry the backing of legislation, or the force of law (see also Chapter 5 on concepts).

Power and authority

Also central to the study of politics as well as to the concept of 'the state' are the concepts of 'power' and 'authority'.

Power is one of the founding organising concepts in political science. We talk of a government being in 'power', of Margaret Thatcher being a 'powerful' Prime Minister. We talk of people with the 'power to make decisions'. In essence the concept means a quality, the ability of someone or some group to get

Keep off the grass! The notion of compulsion in the face of threats lies somewhere close to the heart of power
Source: Getty Images

others to do what they otherwise would not have done. In crude terms this can be achieved by coercion: a man with a gun can induce compliance through the fear that people naturally have of the consequences.

In real-life politics this rarely happens outside brutal tyrannies like Iraq when under Saddam Hussein, but the notion of compulsion in the face of threats lies somewhere close to the heart of political power; after all, when the chips are down, states go to war either to impose their will on other states or to prevent this happening to them. Normally, though, power is exercised by recognised politicians acting within an established system making important decisions on behalf of communities or nations.

Bachrach and Baratz (1981) argued that decisions *not* made by politicians were just as important as those actually made. If a matter can be marginalised or ignored completely through the ability of someone to exclude it, that person can be said to exercise power. For example, it could be argued that cars have been choking our cities for decades, that this problem has been recognised but that remedial action has been postponed for so long because the motor industry is so important to the economy and voters themselves have a potent relationship – more love than hate – with their cars.

It can also be argued that power can be exercised through the ability of some groups to induce people to accept certain decisions without complaint. Marx believed that the ruling class was able to permeate the institutions of the state with its values so that the exploitation of capitalism was fully accepted and approved and consequently perceived as simultaneously natural, unavoidable and 'common sense'. With the advent of the modern media other theorists such as Antonio Gramsci argued that the exploited masses had been induced through a ruling class-permeated culture to 'love their servitude'.

Authority is closely associated with power but is crucially different from the crude version of, say, a man with a gun. Authority entails a degree of acceptance that someone else has a right to give orders. When our politicians announce new laws we accept them and obey them even if, say, we disagree with them, because we accept the right of politicians to discuss and pass legislation through a popularly elected chamber. In other words, MPs have 'authority' to pass laws on our behalf. Something similar occurs when a traffic warden gives us a ticket: we may be furious but we pay up as we respect his or her authority, backed up as it is by statute law.

> I think the critical difference between a dictatorship and a democracy is that in a dictatorship there are only two people out of every hundred who take a personal interest in politics; in a democracy there are three.
>
> Healey (1990), p. 156

■ Approaching the study of politics

We now have some idea of the nature of politics as an activity and some familiarity with the central ideas of state, power and authority. Politics, then, is the process by which conflicting interests are managed and authoritative choices made in social institutions as different as the family, the school and the firm. The most important set of political institutions are conventionally called 'the state', and it is the state that is one of the main focuses of the discipline called 'political science'.

Political science is now a large and well-established academic discipline in both Europe and North America. For instance, the American Political Science Association has 12,000 members, and in Britain the Political Studies Association and the Politics Association combined have over 2,000 members. However, this is a relatively recent development. The emergence of political science as a separate discipline organised on a large scale in universities and colleges first developed in the United States in the early decades of this century. Even now, the overwhelming majority of people called 'political scientists' are American. Before the emergence of political science the subject was divided between specialists in different disciplines (see Figure 1.1). Constitutional lawyers studied the legal forms taken

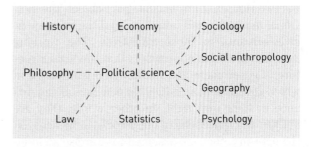

Figure 1.1 Some of the disciplines contributing to political science

Table 1.1 Summary of important approaches to the study of politics

Approach	Focus	Main assumptions	Examples of characteristic evidence examined
Institutional	Formal machinery of government	Formal structures and legal rules are supreme	Structure of parliaments, cabinets, civil services
Policy cycle	Choices made by government	Government action shaped by mix of demands and resources; policy affects wider society	Kinds of resources (money, etc.); patterns of policy making and implementation
Socio-political	Social context, links between government and society	Structure and production of government shaped by wider society	Economic and class structure; organisation of interest groups

by states. Historians studied the relations between, and the organisation of, states in the past. Philosophers discussed the moral foundations, if any, of state authority. In large part, the modern discipline is the heir to these earlier approaches. It is important to be aware of the main approaches, because the approach employed in any particular study influences the kind of questions it asks, the evidence it considers relevant and the conclusions it draws.

Three important approaches are sketched here: the *institutional*, the **policy cycle** and the *socio-political* (see Table 1.1 for summary). These, it should be emphasised, are not mutually exclusive. They are indeed complementary approaches; and just as we usually gain an appreciation of a physical object like a work of art if we look at it from a variety of angles, so we understand a system of government better if we examine it in a similarly varied way.

The *institutional* or *constitutional approach* to the study of politics was, up to some forty years ago, dominant in the study of government in Britain. It has three distinctive features: its focus, its assumptions and its choice of evidence. The focus of the institutional approach is on the formal institutions of government. In Britain, this means a concentration on the bodies at the heart of what is sometimes called 'central government' in London: the two Houses of Parliament, the Cabinet, the individual ministries and ministers, and the permanent civil servants in those ministries. The working assumption of this approach is that the legal structure of government and the formal organisations in which government activities happen have an importance in their own right. In other words, they are not just the reflections of other social influences; on the contrary, they are assumed to exercise an independent influence over the life of the community. In practical terms, this means that the approach is

dominated by an examination of the legal rules and the working conventions that govern the operation of these formal institutions.

It is sometimes objected that this approach is static, that it has a tendency to stress the character of government at one fixed moment and to neglect the fact that political life is characterised by constant cycles of activity.

The *policy cycle approach* tries to capture this cyclical quality. Government is examined as a series of 'policy cycles'. It is pictured as a system of inputs and outputs, as shown in Figure 1.2. Political activity is pictured as a series of stages in the making and execution of decisions about policy. At the stage of policy initiation there exist both demands and resources. At any one moment in a community there will be a wide range of views about what government should do, which will manifest themselves as demands of various kinds: that, for instance, government should provide particular services, such as free education for all under a certain age; that it should decide the appropriate balance of resources allocated to different services; or that it should decide the exact range of social activity that is appropriate for government, rather than other social institutions, to regulate. Making and implementing

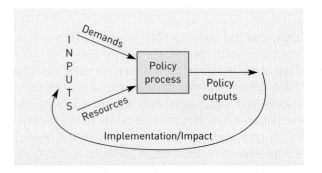

Figure 1.2 The policy cycle

policy choices in response to these demands requires resources. These are the second major input into government and include people, like the administrators and experts necessary to make policy choices and to implement them, and money, which is needed to pay government personnel. These resources can be raised in a wide variety of ways: for example, revenue can be raised by taxation, by borrowing or by charging for the services that governments provide.

After examining the initial stages of resource raising and allocation, the policy cycle approach describes the processing of inputs, in other words how the balance of different demands and the balance between demands and resources is allocated to produce policy choices. Finally, the process of what is sometimes called policy implementation and policy impact (see Figure 1.2) studies how government policies are put into effect and what consequences they may have for the subsequent balance of demands and resources. It is this emphasis on the linked nature of all stages in the policy process that leads us to speak of the policy cycle approach (see also Chapter 24). This approach is also distinguished by its particular focus, assumptions and choice of evidence. Although it resembles the institutional approach in concentrating attention on the institutions of government, its focus is primarily on what these institutions do rather than on how they are organised, because the most important assumption here is that what is interesting about government is that it makes choices – in response to demands and in the light of the scarce resources at its command. In turn this affects the sort of evidence on which the policy cycle approach concentrates. Although much of this evidence concerns practical functioning and organisation of government, it also involves the wider environment of government institutions. This is necessarily so because the demands made on government and the resources that it can raise all come from that wider society. In this concern with the wider social context of government institutions, the policy cycle approach shares some of the concerns of the socio-political approach.

The *socio-political approach* has two particularly important concerns: the social foundations of the government order; and the links connecting government to the wider organisation of society. Close attention is paid to the wider social structure and to the kinds of political behaviour that spring from it. It is a working assumption of this approach that government is indeed part of a wider social fabric, and

that its workings can be understood only through an appreciation of the texture of that wider fabric. Some versions make even stronger assumptions. For instance, most Marxist scholars believe that the workings of government in a community are at the most fundamental level determined by the kind of economic organisation prevailing in that community. The focus and assumptions of the socio-political approach in turn shape the kind of evidence on which it focuses. This includes information not only about the social structure but also about the social influences that shape important political acts, such as voting and the kinds of economic and social interests (like business and workers) that influence the decisions taken in government.

■ Themes and issues in British politics

Britain's system of government is one of the most intensively examined in the world; not surprisingly, therefore, there is no shortage of issues and themes. We conclude this introductory chapter by selecting four that are of special importance and that recur in different ways in the chapters following. These themes are democracy and **responsibility**, efficiency and effectiveness, the size and scope of government, and the impact of government on the wider society.

Democracy and responsibility

British government is intended to be democratic and responsible: it is meant to be guided by the choices of citizens, to act within the law and to give an account of its actions to society's elected representatives. The issue of how far democracy and responsibility do indeed characterise the political system is central to the debates about the nature of British government. Defenders of the system point to a variety of features. Democratic practices include the provision for election – at least once every five years – of the membership of the House of Commons by an electorate comprising 43 million from Britain's 60-odd million inhabitants. The membership of the Commons in turn effectively decides which party will control government for the duration of a parliament, while all legislation requires a majority vote in the Commons. In addition to these formal practices, a number of other provisions support democratic political life. Freedoms of speech, assembly and publication allow the presentation of a wide variety of opinions, thus offering the electorate a choice when they express a democratic preference. The existence of competing political parties similarly means that there are clear and realistic choices facing voters when they go to the polls in elections.

Democracy means that the people can decide the government and exercise influence over the decisions governments take. *Responsibility* means that government is subject to the rule of law and can be held to account for its actions. Those who think British government is responsible in this way point to a variety of institutions and practices, some of which are formal in nature. They include the right to challenge the activities of government in the courts and to have the actions of ministers and civil servants overturned if it transpires that they are done without lawful sanction. They also include the possibility of questioning and scrutinising – for instance in the House of Commons – government ministers over their actions and omissions. In addition to these formal provisions responsibility rests on wider social restraints that are intended to hold government in check. The mass media report on and scrutinise the activities of politicians and civil servants, while a wide range of associations and institutions, such as trade unions and professional bodies, act as counterweights in cases where government threatens to act in an unrestrained way.

Against these views, a variety of grounds have been produced for scepticism about the reality of responsible democratic government in Britain. Some observers are sceptical of the adequacy of democratic institutions and practices. Is it possible, for instance, to practise democracy when the main opportunity offered to the population to make a choice occurs only in a general election held once every four or five years? It is also commonly observed that the links between the choices made in general elections and the selection of a government are far from identical. The workings of the British electoral system (see Chapter 8) mean that it is almost unheard of for the 'winning' party in a general election to attract the support of a majority of those voting.

Even greater scepticism has been expressed about the notion that government in Britain is 'responsible'. Many observers argue that the formal mechanisms for restraining ministers and civil servants are weak. Widespread doubt, for instance, has been expressed about the notion that the House of Commons can effectively call ministers and civil servants to account.

Indeed, some experienced observers and participants have spoken of the existence of an 'elective dictatorship' in Britain: in other words, of a system where government, although it requires the support of voters every four or five years, is able in the intervening period to act in a more or less unrestrained way. There have also been sceptical examinations of the wider mechanisms intended to ensure restraint and accountability. Some insist that the mass media, for instance, are far from being independent observers of the doings of government; that, on the contrary, they are systematically biased in favour of the powerful and against the weak in Britain. Similar claims have been made by observers of the judiciary – a key group since, according to the theory of responsible government, judges are vital in deciding when government has acted in a way that is not sanctioned by law. Finally, some radical observers go further and argue not merely that 'democratic responsibility' is defective but that there is a 'secret state' in Britain, in other words, a system of unchecked power that operates outside the scrutiny of public institutions and that is able to act systematically outside the law. Some quite respectable opinion (e.g. Jonathan Freedland, *The Guardian*, 14 March 2006) argues that in the late sixties sections of the security services plotted a coup to overthrow Harold Wilson and install Lord Mountbatten in his place.

Efficiency and effectiveness

Arguments about democracy and responsibility touch on the moral worth of the system of government in Britain, but government is to be evaluated not only by its moral credentials. It is also commonly judged by its working effectiveness – and justifiably so, for the worth of a system of government is obviously in part a function of its capacity to carry out in an effective way the tasks that the community decides are its responsibility.

Until comparatively recently it was widely believed that British government was indeed efficient and effective in this sense. Britain was one of the first countries in the world, for instance, to develop a civil service selected and promoted according to ability rather than political and social connections. In the last quarter-century, however, the efficiency and effectiveness of British government have been widely questioned. Critics focus on three issues: the skills of public servants, the evidence of the general capabilities of successive British governments and the evidence of particular policy failures.

The most important and powerful public servants in Britain are acknowledged to be 'senior civil servants' – a small group of senior administrators, mostly based in London, who give advice about policy options to ministers. This senior civil service is largely staffed by what are usually called 'generalists' – individuals chosen and promoted for their general intelligence and capabilities rather than because they possess a particular managerial or technical skill. However, critics of the efficiency of British government have argued that the nature of large-scale modern government demands administrators who are more than generally intellectually capable; it demands individuals trained in a wide range of specialised skills (see Chapter 20).

The absence of such a group, drawn from disciplines such as engineering and accountancy, at the top of British government is often held to explain the second facet of poor effectiveness – the general inability of British government to manage its most important tasks effectively. In recent decades the chief task of government in Britain has been to manage the economy. That task, measured by the standards of Britain's major competitors, has been done with conspicuous lack of success. In the 1950s, Britain was one of the richest nations in Western Europe; by the 1980s it was one of the poorest. (Though to be fair to both Conservative and Labour governments since, some recovery occurred from the mid-eighties onwards.)

The debate about the general competence of British government has been heightened by a series of more particular instances of policy failure in recent decades. One observer, surveying the history of British policy initiatives, concluded that there existed only one instance of a major policy success (the introduction of 'clean air' legislation in the 1950s). On the other hand, every observer can produce numerous instances of policy disasters: the Concorde aeroplane, which should have assured the country a first place in modern aircraft manufacture, and which turned out to be an expensive commercial failure; a series of financial and technical disasters in the field of weapons development; the comprehensive disaster in the building, during the 1950s and 1960s, of uninhabitable high-rise tower blocks in the effort to solve the country's housing problems; and the ill-starred Millennium Dome built by New Labour at Greenwich as a symbol of its inclusiveness and 'newness'.

The belief that the efficiency and effectiveness of British government have been defective has dominated debates about the organisation of the system in the last thirty years and has produced numerous proposals for reform in the machinery. A few of these have even been implemented. Local government, for instance, was reorganised in the early 1970s into larger units which, it was believed, would deliver services more efficiently. Within the last decade, however, a new argument has entered the debate. The belief that the problems of efficiency and effectiveness were due to a lack of particular skills, or lack of an appropriate organisational structure, has been increasingly displaced by a more radical notion: that the failings of the system were intrinsic to government, and that more efficient and effective institutions could come only when government itself was reduced to a more manageable size and scope. In other words, there is a link between the debates about efficiency and effectiveness and our third theme – the size and scope of government.

Size and scope of government

British government is big government. Major public services – the provision of transport, healthcare, education – are performed wholly or largely by public institutions. Many of the institutions are, by any standards, very large indeed – for example, the National Health Service. As we will see in Chapter 3, Britain has a 'mixed' economy. In other words, goods and services are produced by a combination of private enterprise and public institutions. Nevertheless, an astonishing variety of goods and services are provided by what is commonly called 'the **public sector**'. What is more, until very recently this sector was steadily growing at the expense of the **private sector**.

The growth of government to gigantic proportions has prompted two main debates, about its efficiency as a deliverer of goods and services, and about the impact of a growing public sector on the wider economy. The efficiency debate we have already in part encountered. In the last decade, however, many free-market economists have argued that government failures are due to more than the failings of particular people and structures. They are, it is argued, built into the very nature of government. According to this view, the public sector lacks many of the most important disciplines and spurs to effectiveness under which private firms have to work. In particular, say its critics, the public sector rarely has to provide services in competition with others. Because the taxpayer always stands behind a public enterprise, the discipline exercised by the possibility of losses and bankruptcy, which guides private firms, is absent in the case of government. Thus government has an inherent tendency towards wastefulness and inefficiency. Defenders of the public sector, on the other hand, while not denying the possibility of waste and inefficiency, argue that failures also happen in the private sector and that, indeed, one of the most important reasons for the growth of government is the failure of private enterprise to provide vital goods and services on terms acceptable to consumers.

A more general argument about the problems of having a large-scale public sector concerns the resources that are needed to maintain this sector. In the 1970s, perhaps the most influential explanation of the failings of the British economy rested on the claim that Britain had 'too few producers'. It was argued that non-productive services had grown excessively at the expense of the sector of the economy producing manufactured goods for the home market and for export. A large proportion of the excessive expansion of the 'service' sector consisted in the growth of public services such as welfare, health and education. These were in effect 'crowding out' more productive activities. Against this view, it has been argued that the growth of 'services' is more a consequence than a cause of the contraction of manufacturing in Britain, and that in any case 'non-productive' services, such as education, are actually vital to sustaining a productive manufacturing sector.

Whatever the rights and wrongs of these arguments, we will see in succeeding chapters that critics of 'big government' have, in the 1980s and 1990s, enjoyed much influence over policy. Many activities once thought 'natural' to the public sector – such as the provision of services such as a clean water supply and energy for the home – have been, or are being, transferred to private ownership. Arguments about 'privatisation', as these transfers are usually called, have also cropped up in the final major theme we sketch here – the impact of government.

The impact of government

We already know from our description of the policy cycle approach that government has powerful effects on the wider society. Modern government takes in society's resources – money, people, raw materials – and 'converts' them into policies. In turn, these policies plainly have a great effect on the lives of us all. On this there is general agreement, but there is great disagreement about the precise impact of government. This disagreement has crystallised into a long-standing argument about the extent to which the effects of government activity are socially progressive or regressive – in simpler terms, whether the rich or poor get most out of the policy process.

The most important way in which government raises resources in a country like Britain is through taxation. The taxation system in Britain is guided by the principle of 'progression': in other words, the wealthier the individual or institution, the greater the liability to pay tax. On the other hand, the services provided by government are consumed collectively (e.g. national defence), are consumed individually but are freely available to all (e.g. free art galleries) or are designed for the poor (e.g. supplementary welfare payments). By contrast, it is difficult to think of a public service that is designed to be consumed only by the rich. These considerations should ensure that the impact of government is redistributive between rich and poor. At the extremes of poverty, for instance, the poor should contribute nothing to taxation but nevertheless be eligible for a wide range of benefits paid for from the general taxes paid by everyone else in the community.

Critics of the view that the impact of government is redistributive in this way rest their case on several arguments. First, some services of government, while not designed for the benefit of the better-off, may nevertheless be worth more to the rich than to the poor. An efficient police service, for instance, which deters theft, is correspondingly desirable according to the amount of property one stands to lose to thieves. Second, some services, while again designed to be universally enjoyed, may in practice be almost totally consumed by the better-off. In the arts, for example, opera attracts large public subsidies but is rarely patronised by the poor and is highly fashionable among the rich. Third, some services, while designed actually to ensure equality of treatment for all, or even preferential treatment for the deprived, may nevertheless in practice be more widely used by the better-off than by the poor. It is widely alleged, for instance, that the National Health Service in Britain actually disproportionately devotes its resources to caring for the better-off. This is partly because the poorest in the community are least knowledgeable about the services available and least willing to make demands for these services, and partly because the actual distribution of resources inside the Health Service is alleged to be biased towards the more vocal and better-off groups in society.

Most of the arguments about the redistributive effects of government focus on where the services provided by the public sector actually end up, but some observers also question how far the formally 'progressive' character of the taxation system is realised in practice. It is commonly argued that the very richest are also the most sophisticated at

minimising their taxation obligations by the use of skilled advisers like accountants and tax lawyers, whose speciality is to arrange the financial affairs of a company or an individual so as to minimise the amount of tax that must legally be paid.

Multi-level government

A final introductory point to be made about British government would be true of most complex

---

BOX 1.2   BRITAIN IN CONTEXT

Types of government

It is sometimes easy to forget that Britain's political system is only one of a particular type, albeit a very influential one which has been copied worldwide. In addition there are a huge variety of government types, within the democratic category and the authoritarian one as well.

Democracies

In 1900 not a single country had what we would today consider a democracy: a government created by elections in which every adult citizen could vote. Today 119 do, comprising 62 per cent of all countries in the world. What was once a peculiar practice of a handful of states around the North Atlantic has become the standard form of government for humankind . . . For the vast majority of the world, democracy is the sole surviving source of political legitimacy.

Zakaria (2004), p. 13

Democracies are governments removable by free elections. The British system is a representative democracy, of course, based on an elected parliament and an executive based on the majority elected group in that parliament. So it provides an example of a 'parliamentary democracy' of which there are scores, including Canada and all of the members of the European Union. But there are many varieties among democracies. The USA has a presidential system with a legislature and executive which are separately elected. France has a separately elected president too, but one who serves a term of seven years and who, while less powerful than the US president, still wields considerable powers, including the ability to appoint

or dismiss the nation's prime minister. Many of the European democracies use a proportional system of electing their legislatures, creating a greater chance of coalition governments comprising a group of political parties rather than the single one which as a rule holds power in the UK.

Former colonial governments

Some democracies, however, are nowhere near as democratic as they seek to appear. For example, several former British colonies were bequeathed Westminster-style democracies when Britain conceded self-rule. None survived without difficulties but some flourished, for example India, which represents the biggest democracy in the world. Others, like that of Zimbabwe, retained the outward appearance of democracy but were in reality dominated by a dictatorial figure such as Robert Mugabe. Other governments in Africa fared better, but Kenya's democracy is criticised for its corruption and disregard of human rights. Some parliamentary governments began democratically but then morphed into single-party states once one ruler was able to establish his dominance.

Communist governments

These have often been described as 'totalitarian', based upon a single official ideology of Marxism–Leninism or communism; a single dominant (communist) party controlling not just government but most aspects of economic and social life; a ubiquitous secret police which acts effectively as the 'terrorist' arm of the government using arbitrary arrest, execution and exile; and a single dominant ruler, often the General Secretary of the communist party, who enjoys the power of a virtual dictator. These were not popular governments and during the 1980s and 1990s those in Russia and Eastern Europe imploded in the face of popular uprisings. Most of them now fall into the category of 'flawed democracies' as they seek to adjust to the post-communist world with elections and political parties. However, some, like those in Central Asia, for example Turkmenistan, have seen a former communist official suborn the political process and install himself as a Stalin-like autocrat. Cuba, China, North Korea and Vietnam retained their communist governments but all, except North Korea, have introduced modifications.

Military governments and dictatorships

Within poorer, less developed countries the military are often the most powerful force and it is unsurprising that military strongmen have seized control and installed themselves as dictators. Latin America used to provide a procession of such rulers, each deposed by the next one able to organise the *coup d'état* necessary to seize power. The military, for example, took power in Brazil in 1964, ruling with the help of torture and death squads. However, in 1984 civilian rule was restored and in 2003 a left-wing president, 'Lula', was elected. Uruguay suffered a similar period of military rule from 1974 until 1984 when civilian rule returned. Even European countries such as Spain and Portugal experienced military rule for long periods; in Greece the 'Colonels' took control in 1967 and remained until 1974. However, the number of governments controlled by the military has diminished in recent decades, especially in Latin America, and those which remain, as in Burma, are much reviled by international opinion.

The Mother of Parliaments: a model for many other legislatures
Source: Steve Allan/Brand X Pictures

developed countries: it operates on a number of different levels. At the lowest level government of sorts is delivered by parish councils – very active in some parts of the country but virtually defunct in others. Next in the hierarchy of importance comes local government which provides essential services like sanitation, rubbish collection and disposal, planning and environmental health (Chapter 22). Then comes a degree of regional government – where regions coincide with separate national histories there are devolved assemblies for Wales and Northern Ireland plus a parliament for Scotland (Chapter 14). Westminster in London provides the parliament which has the ultimate power to change things as well as the complex machinery of government bureaucracies (Chapters 15–23). Finally, there is the supranational level of the European Union (Chapter 31) involving contacts at the legislative levels of the twenty-five member states, as well as at the executive and bureaucratic levels.

A level above that of the regional collectivity of states can be discerned involving international bodies like the United Nations and the World Bank, non-governmental organisations such as Médecins sans Frontières, and human rights groups such as Amnesty International. In addition to the levels employing elected bodies and bureaucrats, pressure groups seek to apply influence to policy made in other bodies. Skilled bureaucrats and politicians commute regularly and naturally through these levels, enabling them to interact in new and complex ways.

■ Plan of the book

This opening chapter has discussed the meaning of politics, the characteristics of the state, approaches to the study of politics, reasons for studying the subject and some important themes and issues in British politics. The rest of the book, organised in six parts, follows directly from the definition we adopted on page 9.

Politics is about conflicting interests: Part 1 provides the historical, social and economic contexts from which such conflicts emerge in Britain; Part 2, on ideology, examines the intellectual basis of such conflicts.

Politics is centrally concerned with how state institutions manage or resolve conflicts within society: Parts 3, 4 and 5 deal respectively with the representative, legislative (law-making) and executive (law-implementing) processes whereby such management takes place or is attempted. Finally, Part 6 examines how these institutions handle the major policy areas.

Chapter summary

This introductory chapter has explained that politics is about the management and resolution of conflicts by what people want to do and achieve. The study of the subject focuses on how this process is performed, especially the way individuals relate to the state. Three approaches – institutional, policy cycle and socio-political – are outlined, and it is suggested that we study politics for understanding and improved citizenship. Major themes include the control citizens have over their government, the efficiency of the system and the extent of its intervention in everyday lives.

Discussion points

■ Why do you think people go into politics and make it their life's work?

■ Think of a typically political scenario and analyse it in the way demonstrated in the chapter.

■ Which approach to politics, from the ones outlined, seems to be the most interesting and helpful to you in explaining political phenomena?

Further reading

Crick's classic work (2000) is essential reading, as is Duverger (1966). Leftwich (1984) is worth reading as an easy-to-understand initiation, and Laver (1983) repays study too. Renwick and Swinburn (1989) is useful on concepts, though Heywood (1994) is by any standards a brilliant textbook. Axford *et al.* (1997) is also well worth looking into. Riddell (1993) is both highly perceptive and

▶

very entertaining – a must for anyone wondering if the subject is for them. O'Rourke (1992) is a humorous but insightful book. Oliver (1992) is an amusing collection of silly quotations from politicians. Michael Moran's book (Moran, 2005) offers the best current analysis of multi-level governance.

References

All, A.R. and Peters, B.G. (2000) *Modern Politics and Government* (Macmillan), Chapter 1.

Axford, B., Browning, G.K., Huggins, R., Rosamond, B. and Turner, J. (1997) *Politics: An Introduction* (Routledge).

Bachrach, P. and Baratz, M. (1981) 'The two faces of power', in F.G. Castles, D.J. Murray and D.C. Potter (eds), *Decision, Organisations and Society* (Penguin).

Crick, B. (2000) *In Defence of Politics* (Continuum).

Critchley, J. (1995) *A Bag of Boiled Sweets* (Faber and Faber).

Dearlove, J. and Saunders, P. (2000) *Introduction to British Politics* (Polity Press), Chapter 1.

Duverger, M. (1966) *The Idea of Politics* (Methuen).

Gamble, A. (2000) *Politics and Fate* (Polity Press).

Giddens, A. (1998) *The Third Way* (Polity Press).

Hague, R., Harrop, M. and Breslin, S. (2000) *Comparative Government and Politics* (Palgrave).

Healey, D. (1990) *The Time of My Life* (Penguin).

Heywood, A. (1994) *Political Ideas and Concepts* (Macmillan).

Jones, B. (2005) *The Dictionary of British Politics* (Manchester University Press).

Kingdom, J. (1999) *Government and Politics in Britain* (Polity Press).

Lasswell, H. (1936) *Politics, Who Gets What, When, How?* (McGraw-Hill).

Laver, M. (1983) *Invitation to Politics* (Martin Robertson).

Leftwich, A. (1984) *What is Politics? The Activity and its Study* (Blackwell).

Minogue, K. (2000) *Politics: A Very Short Introduction* (Oxford University Press).

Moran, M. (2005) *Politics and Governance in the UK* (Palgrave).

Oliver, D. (1992) *Political Babble* (Wiley).

O'Rourke, R.J. (1992) *Parliament of Whores* (Picador).

Orwell, G. (1955) *Nineteen Eighty-Four* (Penguin).

Renwick, A. and Swinburn, I. (1989) *Basic Political Categories*, 2nd edn (Hutchinson).

Riddell, P. (1993) *Honest Opportunism* (Hamish Hamilton).

Robins, S. (2001) *The Ruling Asses* (Prion).

Zakaria, F. (2004) *The Future of Freedom* (Norton).

Useful websites

British Politics page: www.ukpol.co.uk

Euro Consortium for Political Research: www.essex.ac.uk/ecpr

International Political Science Association: www.ipsa-aisp.org/

Political Science resources: www.socsciresearch.com/r12html

UK Political Studies Association: www.psa.ac.uk

Blogs

Bill Jones's blog: http://skipper59.blogspot.com/

Norman Geras: http://normblog.typepad.com

Guido Fawkes: http://5thNovember.blogspot.com/

CHAPTER 2

The historical context: globalisation

Barrie Axford

Learning objectives

- To describe the nature of **globalisation** as an historical process affecting the UK and to identify some recent key trends that are shaping British politics and society.

- To illustrate the particular sensitivity and vulnerability of the UK to globalising and regionalising forces by looking at some areas of public policy increasingly subject to global and European constraints.

- To explore the ways in which internal political debates and national political agendas condition UK responses to both globalisation and Europeanisation.

- To assess the extent to which globalisation and Europeanisation are effecting a transnationalisation of domestic politics.

Introduction

For part of the eighteenth and much of the nineteenth century Britain was a global power. Indeed by the middle of the nineteenth century it was the dominant power on the world stage, and its 'Great Power' status remained a given for national policy makers until after the Second World War (1939–45). In recent decades Britain has ceased to be an economic and a military giant in a world that is more and more interconnected and in which there have been seismic changes in the balance of economic and strategic might. In the period of intense globalisation since the early 1970s, weak or fluctuating economic performance, loss of empire and world role and a chronic ambivalence on European integration have all made the UK especially sensitive to global forces and trends. In line with other nation-states, successive British governments have adopted a variety of strategies to manage globalisation, and these reveal the ways in which domestic factors are affected by and in turn qualify the impact of global forces and trends.

■ What is globalisation? Why is it important?

Globalisation is a convenient shorthand for processes that are making the world more interconnected and interdependent. More fundamentally, globalisation challenges the borders around both territorial jurisdictions and identities. Despite the fact that globalisation is not a new phenomenon, it is only in recent decades that the concept has captured the attention of politicians, businesses and political activists across the world. Among such constituencies globalisation generates feelings of disquiet and enthusiasm in almost equal measure. On the one hand there is a feeling that the current phase of globalisation is wreaking a profound transformation in the nature of states and societies, cultures and economies around the world. Speaking in Washington, DC, in February 1998, early in his first term of office, Tony Blair said 'We on the centre-left must try to put ourselves at the forefront of those who are trying to manage change in the global economy', sentiments he has repeated at intervals since then. This pronouncement hardly endorses the thesis that nation-states are powerless in the face of global pressures, only that they need to address them to prosper. In his continuing attempts to galvanise other EU economies to embrace market values, Blair has often invoked globalisation as the main challenge to what he sees as over-regulated European business. But some sceptics believe that there is little new in the current phase of globalisation and that nation-states remain, or can remain, in charge of their destinies.

For Michael Porter, a writer on international business competition (1990), states are still crucial to corporate and sectoral economic success, if only as the providers of the **supply-side** resources necessary to ensure global competitiveness. In another version of the 'states matter' thesis, the novelty and power of current 'globalising' forces is questioned and the capacity of states to exercise political controls over both capital flows and labour markets is seen (largely) as a matter of political will. Broadly this is the position of the revisionist left, principally in the groves of academe, but also on the part of such noted commentators as Will Hutton (1995, 2002). People like Mr Hutton tend to put their faith in state investment in knowledge and people – sometimes called human capital – to ensure national competitiveness, or if they can abide the whiff of Americanism, some version of ex-president Bill Clinton's **Competition State**. To some extent being sceptical about the power of globalisation, or enthusiastic or pessimistic about its promise, misses the point, or reduces the argument to a polemic about good and bad effects. More interesting for an analysis of contemporary British politics is the manner in which such complex processes are mediated and possibly shaped by the agency of states and other sub-global actors.

At its most visible globalisation is a process that makes for greater depth, extent and diversity in cross-border connections and processes. Money, goods, technologies, images, communications and people are moving across national frontiers at an accelerating rate. Distance is no longer an obstacle to interaction, and many social relationships have been 'stretched' across time and space. In a world made up of independent nation-states, the most obvious impact of all these movements and connections is to make national borders less coincident with the organisation of economic life and, increasingly, with the conduct of **governance**. For many observers and not a few practising politicians, the growing integration of markets and the homogenising effects of cultural commodities signal the demise of the independent authority of the nation-state and the erosion of separate national cultures and identities. In the United Kingdom, the chronic debate about the scale of national commitment to the European Union reflects these concerns, especially over ambitious projects such as monetary union and European collective security. These major concerns and others with a more visceral feel, such as terrorism, immigration and asylum-seeking, global warming, GM foods, fear of possible pandemics such as Asian bird flu and the cross-border traffic in drugs and people, are firmly on the UK political agenda. They presage seminal changes in domestic policy and politics. In fact, such issues already have eroded the conventional distinctions between domestic and foreign affairs, leading to a **transnationalisation** of domestic politics.

Globalisation is often discussed as just an economic phenomenon, seen in the spread of the ideology and practices of the market, in the increased extent and intensity of trade as practised by multinational corporations and in the power of global financial institutions. But globalisation is a multidimensional process, and, even where the driving force is economic, the consequences are often felt most in other areas of life. For example, the easy availability of what might be called 'global products', such as McDonald's and ipod, have transformed the eating and leisure habits of young people the world over. Global branding of the sort perfected by Nike, Apple, Microsoft, Tommy Hilfiger and Starbucks not only increases the volume of transborder exchanges, but globalises the definition of what it takes to be cool (Klein, 2001). Curiously, icons of global cool sometimes owe everything to fashion and music styles which are entirely local in origin, like *gangsta rap*. In addition, the huge growth in relatively cheap intercontinental air travel exposes most parts of the world to the mixed blessings of the tourist gaze. The now remote possibility of tying the United Kingdom into a single European currency would involve surrendering control over monetary policy (for example, setting interest rates) to European institutions,

notably the European Central Bank. For some Britons such a departure would at least compromise the ability of British governments to act in the national interest, while others fear deleterious consequences for the UK economy. Still others lament the potential loss of sterling as a symbol of national pride and identity.

Fears about globalisation extend to the allegedly deleterious effects of market forces upon, for example, the poor in Africa, Brazil, Thailand and India, but also take in Third World migrants in the UK, other marginalised Britons such as the unemployed, those without the skills to prosper in the job market and those on welfare benefits. Nowadays, this litany extends to the newly insecure middle classes, whose jobs are now more precarious and whose pension schemes have been eroded by the drop in world stock prices driven by the slow-down in America's end of millennium boom, uncertainties after the events of 11 September 2001, and an ageing population in many core states. Of course, such effects might be seen by some as a failure to achieve real economic globalisation, rather than a necessary or direct consequence of it.

These are matters of current concern, but of course globalisation is not a new phenomenon, even if its scope and intensity have varied over the centuries (Ferguson, 2003). In the eighteenth century, the world was a patchwork of empires, some of them 'global' in reach or ambition (the British, Dutch, Spanish, French and Portuguese), others largely regional (the Japanese, Chinese and Russian). Indeed, the expansion of European empires from the middle of the nineteenth century was one of the primary mechanisms of globalisation during this period. With possessions that eventually covered almost one-quarter of the world's land surface, Britain was the pace-setter in this respect, with British advocates of *laissez-faire* deeply committed to the **liberalisation** of world trade.

This period is also remarkable for the growth in the number of intergovernmental organisations charged with regulating trading and commercial activities, and notable too for some major breakthroughs in communications technologies, whose effect was to 'compress the world' still further. For instance, from the 1840s, advances in telegraphy began to remove distance as an impediment to easy communication across borders and between continents. Between 1865 and 1910 thirty-three world organisations were established, including the Universal Postal Union (1874), the International Bureau on Weights and Measures (1875), the International Labour Office (1901) and the International Court of Justice (1907). In 1930, when opening the London Naval Conference, King George V made what amounts to the first global radio broadcast, when his message was relayed simultaneously to 242 stations across six continents.

Since the end of the Second World War, in addition to the United Nations and its agencies, which claim a universal competence, a rash of regional organisations has arisen. These include superpower-led military alliances (such as the North Atlantic Treaty Organisation or NATO and the now defunct Warsaw Pact), anti-colonial groupings aimed at fostering national independence (for example, the Organisation for African Unity, now called 'African Union') and a variety of sub-regional frameworks for collective security (e.g. the Gulf Co-operation Council and the Association of Southeast Asian Nations). As well as regional attempts at collective security, whose main purpose was to protect state sovereignty from external threat, there emerged in Western Europe a different sort of regional body, the European Economic Community (1957). Originally the EEC had no strict security function, but it did have institutions that possessed or claimed jurisdiction over member states. The extent to which nation-states are now part of a dense fabric of world, regional and sub-regional groupings is conveyed in Figure 2.1 which shows the numbers and overlapping memberships of defence and collective security organisations.

In the last four decades or so it is arguable that the pace and scope of globalisation and regionalisation have increased dramatically, along with a growing awareness on the part of politicians, activists, businesses and more and more citizens of the threats and opportunities thus posed. As we have noted above, this claim is not uncontested and globalisation is sometimes portrayed as little more than a myth or just an intensification of existing trends. Somewhere between the claims of those convinced that globalisation is transforming the conduct of governance and economic affairs and the belief that the world is still given shape and order by territorial states, lies a more complex zone for analysis. In this zone, states and societies are required to come to terms with the demands of a period of more intense globalisation, but one in which they still retain considerable autonomy. This period of more intensive globalisation is characterised by seven major trends, all of relevance to the United Kingdom.

The closer integration of the world economy

Flows of capital, goods, communications and, to a much lesser extent, labour across borders are on the increase. About $1.9 trillion (US) flows through the world's foreign exchange markets on a daily basis (April 2004 figures), an amount that is hugely in excess of the combined foreign exchange reserves of all the world's richest nations. Since the 1980s there has been a massive growth in global financial activity, with more currencies and more financial assets being traded at much greater speed than ever before. In this world of 'footloose' capital, as it is sometimes called, the City of London occupies a key position as the world's largest foreign exchange market and 'knowledge centre' for the banking industry, a status it has reclaimed after several decades of decline earlier in the twentieth century. An indication of how well the UK does in key areas of the global finance business is provided in Figure 2.2. This resurgence looks reasonably secure and supports the argument that globalisation may not always work against the interests of individual nation-states, as some commentators argue, but that states are vulnerable and sensitive to global pressures to varying degrees. Of course, London's dominance in sectors of the financial markets is not entirely secure and over the next decade challenges to its position may well come from the Asian time zone and from Shanghai in particular. Dominance or not, the periodic volatility of exchange rates and interest rates, along with the dramatic impact wrought by speculative trading in currencies and other financial assets, makes it increasingly difficult for all national governments to conduct macro-economic policy without regard to the consequences in global currency markets.

Trade too has become increasingly important to the world economy and has reached unprecedented levels, both absolutely and in relation to total world output. In 2000, trade in merchandise was up on 1999 by 12 per cent and world output was up by 4.5 per cent over the same period. But in 2001, the uncertain international situation led to a slowing of growth in the volume of merchandise traded to an estimated 2 per cent. Figures from the World Bank for 2004 show strong growth in trade, with expected increases in 2005 and 2006 (World Bank: *Global Prospects*, April 2005). Almost all of the world's nations are part of the global trading system, although some 80 per cent of trade in finished goods

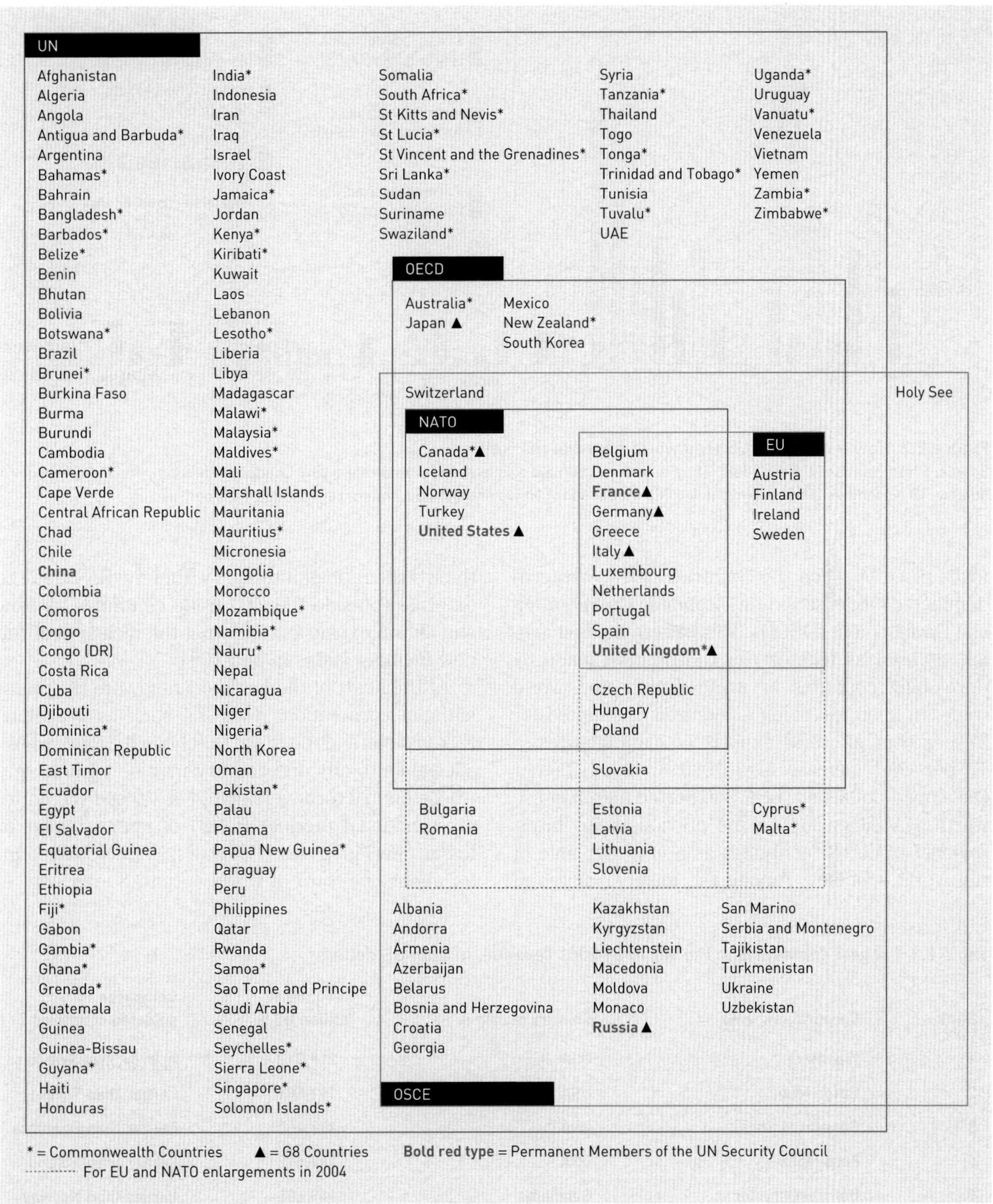
UN
Afghanistan
Algeria
Angola
Antigua and Barbuda*
Argentina
Bahamas*
Bahrain
Bangladesh*
Barbados*
Belize*
Benin
Bhutan
Bolivia
Botswana*
Brazil
Brunei*
Burkina Faso
Burma
Burundi
Cambodia
Cameroon*
Cape Verde
Central African Republic
Chad
Chile
China
Colombia
Comoros
Congo
Congo (DR)
Costa Rica
Cuba
Djibouti
Dominica*
Dominican Republic
East Timor
Ecuador
Egypt
El Salvador
Equatorial Guinea
Eritrea
Ethiopia
Fiji*
Gabon
Gambia*
Ghana*
Grenada*
Guatemala
Guinea
Guinea-Bissau
Guyana*
Haiti
Honduras
India*
Indonesia
Iran
Iraq
Israel
Ivory Coast
Jamaica*
Jordan
Kenya*
Kiribati*
Kuwait
Laos
Lebanon
Lesotho*
Liberia
Libya
Madagascar
Malawi*
Malaysia*
Maldives*
Mali
Marshall Islands
Mauritania
Mauritius*
Micronesia
Mongolia
Morocco
Mozambique*
Namibia*
Nauru*
Nepal
Nicaragua
Niger
Nigeria*
North Korea
Oman
Pakistan*
Palau
Panama
Papua New Guinea*
Paraguay
Peru
Philippines
Qatar
Rwanda
Samoa*
Sao Tome and Principe
Saudi Arabia
Senegal
Seychelles*
Sierra Leone*
Singapore*
Solomon Islands*
Somalia
South Africa*
St Kitts and Nevis*
St Lucia*
St Vincent and the Grenadines*
Sri Lanka*
Sudan
Suriname
Swaziland*
Syria
Tanzania*
Thailand
Togo
Tonga*
Trinidad and Tobago*
Tunisia
Tuvalu*
UAE
Uganda*
Uruguay
Vanuatu*
Venezuela
Vietnam
Yemen
Zambia*
Zimbabwe*
OECD
Australia*
Japan ▲
Mexico
New Zealand*
South Korea
Switzerland
Holy See
NATO
Canada*▲
Iceland
Norway
Turkey
United States ▲
Belgium
Denmark
France▲
Germany▲
Greece
Italy ▲
Luxembourg
Netherlands
Portugal
Spain
United Kingdom*▲
EU
Austria
Finland
Ireland
Sweden
Czech Republic
Hungary
Poland
Slovakia
Bulgaria
Romania
Estonia
Latvia
Lithuania
Slovenia
Cyprus*
Malta*
Albania
Andorra
Armenia
Azerbaijan
Belarus
Bosnia and Herzegovina
Croatia
Georgia
Kazakhstan
Kyrgyzstan
Liechtenstein
Macedonia
Moldova
Monaco
Russia ▲
San Marino
Serbia and Montenegro
Tajikistan
Turkmenistan
Ukraine
Uzbekistan
OSCE
* = Commonwealth Countries
▲ = G8 Countries
Bold red type = Permanent Members of the UN Security Council
For EU and NATO enlargements in 2004

Figure 2.1 Membership of international organisations as at 31 December 2003
Source: Foreign and Commonwealth Office (2003) *UK International Priorities: A Strategy for the FCO*. FCO Command Paper, 2 December 2003, Chapter 3, Chart 5, p. 6. © Crown Copyright 2003, Crown copyright material is reproduced with permission of the Controller of Her Majesty's Stationery Office (HMSO)

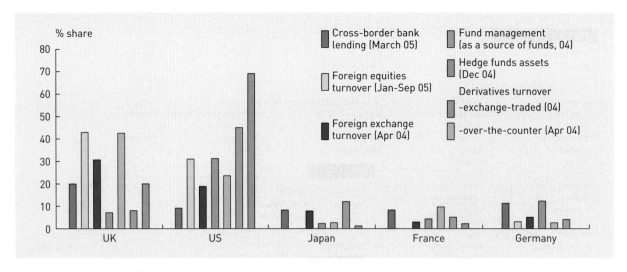

Figure 2.2 How the UK and US lead world financial markets
Source: From Hamish McRae (2005) 'They're young, overpaid and over here. And that's why London is thriving', *The Independent on Sunday*, 13 November 2005. Copyright © 2005 Independent News and Media Limited, reproduced with permission

takes place between the countries of the Western-dominated Organisation for Economic Co-operation and Development (OECD). This pattern too is changing, at least as regards the contribution made by developing countries to world output and world trade. In 2000, developing countries accounted for 27 per cent of world exports of manufactures, a 10 per cent increase over 1990. In 2004, Lesser Developed Countries (LDCs) exported merchandise worth \$71 billion, up on the previous year. Intra-regional trade too continues as a core dynamic of the world economy. Among the member states of

the EU the ratio of internal (within the EU) trade to external (outside the EU) trade continues to grow and shows expansion following the inclusion of ten new member states in mid-2004.

At the heart of the world economy are the multinational corporations (MNCs), such as Wal-Mart, Exxon Mobil and the Royal Dutch/Shell Group, whose allegiance to any one country may be tenuous and whose annual turnovers match or exceed the entire gross national product (GNP) of many smaller or lesser developed states (Table 2.1). MNCs account for about one-third of world output, 80 per cent of

Table 2.1 Largest companies in the world by 2001 revenue, million US dollars[a]

Rank	Corporation name	Country of origin	Revenue in million US $	Compared to selected countries
1	Wal-Mart	USA	219,812	Approx. size Sweden
2	Exxon Mobil	USA	191,581	Larger than Turkey
3	General Motors	USA	177,260	Larger than Denmark
4	Ford Motor	USA	162,412	Larger than Poland
5	DaimlerChrysler	Germany	149,608	Larger than Norway
6	Royal Dutch/Shell Group	Netherlands/Britain	149,146	Larger than Norway
7	BP	Britain	148,062	Larger than Norway
8	Mitsubishi	Japan	126,629	Larger than Finland
9	General Electric	USA	125,913	Larger than Greece

[a] Excludes banking organisations and *Enron*, which went bankrupt in 2003 but would have been ranked eighth in this table.
Source: From *New Internationalist*, Issue 347, July 2002. Copyright © 2002 New Internationalist Publications Ltd. All rights reserved. Reproduced with kind permission of the New Internationalist (www.newint.org)

international investment and 70 per cent of world trade. Their economic clout is facilitated by the growth of inter-firm networks, strategic alliances, joint ventures and sub-contracting to achieve economies of scale and maximum efficiency in the supply chain. It is also enhanced by the ability of MNCs to relocate production in parts of the world where labour and infrastructural costs are lower and where state regulation is light or absent. For example, in the expanded EU, Slovakia, a new member since 2004, is rapidly deregulating its economy and reforming its welfare provision to attract foreign direct investment, and to a lesser degree so are other accession states.

Another area of significant growth in the world economy is international tourism. In 2000 there were in excess of 697 million tourist journeys compared with only 70 million in 1960. Figures for 2001 showed a drop to 639 million, due to a slowdown in the world economy and the repercussions of September 11th. By 2004, the global flow of tourists had reached a new record level with 763 million journeys between countries recorded.

Over the past thirty years the balance of power in the world economy has also shifted. Until the early 1970s the USA enjoyed economic dominance, but since then the global economy has become much more pluralistic and regionalised, with powerful trading blocs operating in Western Europe, the Americas and – in a rather less developed form – on the Pacific Rim. The burgeoning Indian and Chinese economies will further skew the balance of global economic power over the next decade.

The dominance of market forces

Since the middle 1970s **neo-liberalism** has become the global economic orthodoxy, so that by the 1990s it was fashionable to talk about the success of a **Washington Consensus** on the way to conduct successful management of an economy. Many countries, including Britain, have partly restructured their economies in line with neo-liberal dogmas. These include deregulating most aspects of economic activity, privatising public enterprises and at least trying to cut back on state expenditures. In the middle decades of the twentieth century, many of the richer member states of the OECD followed a 'welfare nationalist' policy, by which they aimed to promote full employment and a large measure of social protection through welfare. Following the oil crises of the early and mid-1970s and a series of

Table 2.2 Government spending as a percentage of gross domestic product

	1960	1980	1998	2004
Australia	21.2	31.4	32.9	36.2
Britain	*32.2*	*43.0*	*40.2*	*43.9*[a]
Canada	28.6	38.8	42.1	41.1
France	34.6	46.1	54.3	53.4
Germany	32.4 (FRG)	47.9 (FRG)	46.9 (all)	46.8
Italy	30.1	42.1	49.1	48.5
Japan	17.5	32.0	36.9	38.2
Sweden	31.0	60.1	60.8	57.3
USA	26.8	31.4	32.8	36.5

[a] In 2002 the UK-based Institute of Fiscal Studies (2002) estimated that spending by the British government as a proportion of GDP would rise to 42 per cent of GDP by 2005–6, still rather lower than under Mrs Thatcher's strict monetarist regime between 1979 and 1990, when public expenditure averaged 43 per cent. In fact, expenditure rose to 43.9 per cent.

Source: Organisation for Economic Cooperation and Development (OECD) (2004)

recessions in the 1980s, these countries introduced cutbacks in welfare provision and invoked the disciplines of the market to make national economies more prosperous and competitive in the global marketplace. In some cases this discipline has imposed a harsh period of adjustment on individual states, but we should not overestimate the extent to which the power of market forces and the mobility of capital have diminished the authority of nation-states, or their capacity to make policy. A quick glance at patterns of government spending across some of the major economies in the past forty years or so reveals modest increases in the amount of gross domestic product (GDP) taken up by public expenditures in many countries, rather than the opposite (Table 2.2). While the overall tendency in these figures is to increase spending, they also show evidence of substantial national variation. In the global age there is still room for national diversity, and this was true even during the heyday of the Washington Consensus in the 1990s when economic liberalisation and market principles were taken as icons of prudent macroeconomic management, and held up as models for developing countries.

In the UK, government investment is much lower as a proportion of GDP than in most European countries. OECD and European Commission figures for 2004 reveal that the UK spent 1.8 per cent gross of GDP on public investment, while Italy spent 2.6 per cent, France 3.2 per cent, the Netherlands 3.1 per cent and Portugal 3.1 per cent. The current Chancellor, Gordon Brown, has increased the contribution year-on-year between 1999 and 2004. Major increases in capital investment are the prerequisite to delivering continued improvements in areas such as health, education, transport and housing, but these changes still leave the UK well behind many other member states of the EU. Public sector net investment is set to rise to 2 per cent of GDP by 2005–6.

The transformation of production systems and labour markets

In general the effects of globalisation on the organisation of industrial production have been to introduce smaller and more flexible production systems, where flexibility means rapid production cycles, computer-based design systems and accounting software and new patterns of working, including part-time contracts, multi-skilling and de-unionisation of the workforce. While some of these changes are driven by innovations in information and communications technology, they are also the fruit of massive and rapid movements of investment capital around the world as foreign direct investment (FDI). Innovations in the ways that companies are organised and conduct business have been made easier by the liberalisations of controls on FDI and on the movement of capital in general, making it less costly to invest in other countries. The result is a significant expansion in international production since the 1970s, driven by MNCs and dispersed across a growing number of countries. The UK has a very successful track record in attracting FDI, and accounted for 28.02 per cent of all European FDI projects in 2004 (taking into account the enlarged EU). In the period since 1998, the UK has averaged 17.5 per cent of all inward investment, compared with France on 11.7 per cent and Germany on 12.4 per cent. In the early years after the introduction of the euro, FDI in the UK fell, prompting fears that the UK was starting to suffer from its voluntary exclusion from the euro-zone, but these now look unfounded.

Indeed, since the passage of the Single European Act in 1986 and the formal completion of a European Single Market in 1992, Britain has been the major European recipient of inward FDI from both

"A Japanese company will deliver them to us for £6.75 a thousand."

Ironies of a global economy?
Source: Cartoon Stock/John Morris

Japan and the USA, as well as from companies in other EU countries. Companies with headquarters in those countries have been anxious to take advantage of UK membership in the European 'domestic' market and of the fact that the UK workforce is relatively highly skilled and relatively low paid. Should the UK remain outside the single currency, some observers still suggest a long-term sharp downturn in its attractiveness to investors, but this too is far from certain.

The attractiveness of Britain in general and of London in particular as locations for inward investment was enhanced under the Thatcher governments (1979–90) by far-reaching legislation that severely proscribed the power of trade unions and the incentives for workers to join them. Under 'New' Labour much of this legislation remains intact, witness to the Blair administration's commitment to keeping Britain open to continued high levels of inward investment. The rhetoric of free trade and open markets has been central to British economic policy for the past twenty years, the latest iteration of a much longer engagement with the global political economy through the doctrines of free trade and open investment, such as occurred at the turn of the nineteenth century. Of course, the downside of open investment and fluid capital is that FDI can be withdrawn as easily as it was put in place, especially in the UK, where regulation is permissive and

Legislation introduced under the Thatcher government – and continued under New Labour – made London an attractive location for the global investor, and helped sustain Britain's influence on the economic stage
Source: J. Vella

penalties on employers generally lighter than in some other EU member states. On the ground, whether in Luton (where Vauxhall Cars, a subsidiary of General Motors, ended car production in 2002) or Llanwern (where steel giant Corus closed most of the plant as part of a massive restructuring of its UK business following a worldwide drop in demand for steel), the costs of internationalising production may be counted higher than the benefits. The vulnerability of domestic manufacturers to market forces was further demonstrated in 2005, when Shanghai Automotive, a Chinese holding company with a controlling stake in the ailing British auto firm MG Rover, refused to invest in major car manufacture in Birmingham and, taking the intellectual copyright for Rover models with it, announced that it would begin production in the Far East. At the same time it should be noted that when the pharmaceutical giant GlaxoSmithKline threatened that it might have to pull some production out of the UK if the govern-

ment did not make its costly new flu drug available on the NHS, the then Health Secretary, Frank Dobson, called its bluff and the company backed down. Overall, it might be said that these examples demonstrate that the distinction between domestic and foreign capital has become blurred in this period of intensive globalisation. But arguments remain about the willingness and ability of national governments to resist pressures from mobile capital even where the costs may be measured in terms of lost jobs and lost votes.

The speed of technological change

In the last couple of decades there have been significant innovations in information and communications technologies (ICTs). The rapid spread in usage of personal computers, mobile phones and PDAs, along with the appeal of the Internet as a medium of information and communication, linking the personal and the global, are key aspects of this technological 'revolution'. The Internet has caught on faster than any technology in history, passing 50 million users worldwide in just four years. By comparison, personal computer use took thirteen years to reach the 50 million mark, television sixteen years, and radio thirty-eight years. According to research conducted by the pollster MORI in the summer of 2001, in the UK 25 million adults use the Net regularly, whether in work or in their own time. Numbers admitting to regular use had increased by 6 percentage points over the previous six months. By 2005 nearly 36 million people, or almost 60 per cent of UK homes, have a PC, and 88 per cent of these have Internet access. Such changes are treated as seminal by some observers, heralding a new type of 'informational' or 'knowledge-based' economy, quite unlike the economy based on the mass production of goods that marked earlier periods of capitalism. New Labour is completely wedded to this version of the global future. In government, the party is attempting to apply a raft of ICT initiatives to the creation of **social capital** in the UK and to improving human capital as a supply-side resource in global economic competition (Hudson, 2002). At the EU Barcelona summit in March 2002, Tony Blair earmarked the promotion of broadband Internet access across the EU by 2005 as one of the six key objectives on which the summit had to make progress. In addition to their actual use by governments to facilitate economic performance and improve representative democracy, developments in ICTs also challenge the ability of the same national governments to police their cultural and, of course, their digital borders.

The media revolution and consumerism

Global media in the form of multi-media giants such as Time-Warner, the News International Group and Vivendi-Universal now produce and market products for world consumption, tailoring their output for local and niche audiences. While the fortunes of these multi-media giants took a fall in 2002 and the early part of 2003, the longer-term prospects for the marriage of 'old' media (films, television and newspapers) and 'new' media (digital technologies, Internet service providers) now look bullish. Despite initial concerns, the EU gave backing to the successful merger of Sony and BMG. Their combined market share of the music industry is now just over 25 per cent. Eighty per cent of this market is controlled by four media conglomerates: Sony-BMG, Vivendi-Universal, EMI and Warner Music.

Digital and satellite television, as well as the Internet, reduce the cultural distances between countries, and the ready availability of luxury and other exotic goods in local supermarkets and stores has revolutionised the eating habits of substantial sections of national populations. Digital TV is estimated to have reached 63 per cent of UK households. Fear about the sanctity of the TV licence fee in the face of growing commercialisation and the advent of digital television in the UK is an interesting case of the debates around global media and the impact of new technologies on customary behaviour and local traditions. The BBC's fabled status as a public service broadcaster is only possible – so its advocates insist – through the provision of some £5 billion of public funds per annum in the form of the licence fee. Critics argue that a publicly funded BBC will become impossible in the face of the accelerating take-up of digital TV and broadband entertainment services. In the end, they argue, consumer choice will out.

More generally, global brands such as Starbucks are all selling lifestyle choices and aspirations constructed around and realised through acquiring brands. The evidence on whether consumers discriminate between goods with different national origins or whether they identify 'national' products at all is mixed. It is also very hard to say what effects media outputs have on traditional values and cultures, but probably too simplistic to argue that these are simply being eroded. Again, the key point is likely to be the degree to which a national culture is vulnerable to global forces and how far these same forces are used by locals to change only the material conditions of their lives, leaving local cultures and identities intact. Hostile reactions to branded capitalism are visible in the spate of protests seen since 1999 in London, Seattle, Prague, Nice, Genoa, Barcelona, Johannesburg, Davos at the World Economic Forum and Gleneagles in Scotland when **G8** leaders met in July 2005.

In the UK, as elsewhere, reactions to 'branded globalisation' and 'transnational capitalism' have taken a number of forms and been driven by a variety of motives, not all of them consonant. Resistance to American hegemony in various forms and its alleged imperialism (Stop the War Coalition), the depredations of transnational corporations in the Global South and the whole 'global capitalist' agenda are all powerful motifs (Globalise Resistance, Dissent). At

The power and influence of global brands has changed the way people live the world over
Source: Getty Images / National Geographic

the same time, and certainly since 9/11, there has been much talk of the need for 'global solidarity' between civil society organisations across the world and a growing emphasis on alternative models of globalisation informed by the pursuit of global justice (e.g. World and European Social Forums, Live8).

The spread of democracy

Globalisation has facilitated the spread of democratic values and practices around the world. Global ideologies stressing human rights and the necessity for regimes and societies to democratise have been important features of world politics in the last forty years. The fall of state socialism after 1989 provides the most dramatic evidence of this process, but there are other important features. Major Western European powers such as the UK and France have decolonised and international migration flows challenge the concept of citizenship as a purely national status. Of course, the picture is not entirely benign. In the 2002 French presidential election, a strong first round showing by the ultra-nationalist

candidate Jean-Marie Le Pen distilled the anxieties felt all across Western Europe about loss of identity, immigration and the intrusion of American culture, or in Le Pen's convenient shorthand, about 'Euro-globalisation'. Perhaps the most visible and widespread evidence of this anxiety is the response to immigration in general, and to asylum seekers in particular, that was seen across much of Europe during 2002 and that intensified in 2003. In the UK, the issue focused both on the reception of asylum seekers and on the plight or threat (depending on your point of view) of illegal entrants trying to enter the UK from the (now closed) Sangatte refugee camp in France. In May 2002, Tony Blair and his then Spanish counterpart, Jose Maria Aznar, pleaded for tougher immigration controls across the EU. The UK's Nationality, Immigration and Asylum Act, passed in 2002, seeks to clamp down on people-smuggling and introduced an 'entitlement card' system to check up on who have the right to work in the UK. Under the new measures people applying for asylum well after they have arrived in the UK were deemed ineligible for state support. In February 2003, the High Court ruled that this measure breached the provisions of the Human Rights Act. In March of the same year, the Court of Appeal rejected this interpretation, but ruled the policy over-zealous. When Algerian asylum seekers were charged with possible terrorist offences in January 2003, calls for Britain to abjure its 'soft' approach to the management and policing of asylum reached a new pitch in the tabloid press. In 2004, the government set a new target for the removal of failed asylum applicants to the effect that by the end of 2005 removals must exceed the number of applicants whose claims are unfounded. Asylum and immigration were mentioned by all parties in the 2005 general election campaign and the Tories discussed the possibility of quotas for refugees and economic migrants. Their tough stance did not attract the voting public.

The dilemma of the Blair government over this issue is palpable. On the one hand, immigration is, once again, a hot political topic often linked to fears about terrorism, with the far right British National Party (BNP) trading on public anxieties to win the odd local government seat and feelings still running high in the opinion polls. On the other hand, the UK still wishes to reap the benefits migrant workers bring to the economy and to be seen as a haven for genuine asylum seekers. Labour's election platform of awarding points to potential immigrants on the basis of their possession of skills in short supply in the UK was enshrined in a new Asylum and Immigration bill announced in the Queen's speech following the general election of 2005. In March 2006, these clauses were being discussed in the House of Commons.

Humanitarian interventions in the world's trouble spots by regional and global organisations are treated as a much more legitimate feature of the world order after the fall of state socialism. In a speech to the Chicago Economic Club in April 1999, Tony Blair unveiled his 'Doctrine of the International Community', which outlined the circumstances in which intervention in the affairs of independent states would be legitimate. The US-led intervention in Afghanistan in 2001 is, in some measure, an endorsement of this ideology. But Afghanistan under the Taliban was, at best, a quasi-state and doubts remain about the feasibility, let alone the legitimacy, of the doctrine when applied to Iran, Zimbabwe, and the chronic conflict in Chechnya, but no longer, of course, to Iraq. Where military intervention is not on the agenda of, or an option for, the international community or 'willing coalitions' are not formed from it, the emphasis

these days is on applying 'conditionalities' to long-term support from Western governments and international organisations. Regimes in LDCs and also in the former Soviet and North African 'near neighbourhood' of the recently enlarged EU are being constrained to speed up democratisation and marketisation as signifiers of their modernising intent. All of this amounts to a globalised system of governance without government.

Common cause apart, the weight of national interests and pure expediency still govern the external relations of states despite protestations to the contrary. Early in its first term of office New Labour espoused the idea of an ethical foreign policy, with the then Foreign Secretary, Robin Cook, establishing *de facto* criteria by which to judge Britain's dealings with other states on the basis of their respect for human rights. The actual record is patchy. Britain has championed the setting up of an International Criminal Court, and in East Timor and Sierra Leone, for example, its actions have gone well beyond narrowly defined national interest. At the same time, in January 2000 Tony Blair overruled Robin Cook by giving the go-ahead for the sale to Zimbabwe of spare parts for British Hawk fighter jets being used in an African civil war in which Zimbabwe had intervened and which has cost tens of thousands of lives. The removal of Cook as Foreign Secretary early in Blair's second term was a recognition that, as a major platform of foreign policy, an avowedly ethical dimension was always going to be a hostage to fortune.

Blair has become an even more visible figure on the world stage, particularly in the wake of the September 11th atrocities in New York and Washington. Engaging in a frenetic brand of shuttle diplomacy, he travelled the world in late 2001 and throughout 2002 trying to build, or at least shore up, support for the war on terrorism and possible military intervention in Afghanistan. In 2003, his efforts on the world stage were directed to influencing international opinion on bringing Saddam Hussein to account. Subsequently his efforts have included a visit to Libya in 2004 to celebrate Colonel Qadhafi's renunciation of weapons of mass destruction and his seeming coopting to the Western cause of the global 'War on Terror'.

National involvement in regional and international regimes

These days most, if not all, nation-states operate in a dense weave of regional, international and global regimes and authorities, such as the UN, the EU and the Council of Europe. After the end of the Second World War, the division of the world into two ideological blocs each dominated by a superpower decisively shaped the contours of the world order, and **bi-polarity**, as it was known, restricted a state's capacity to conduct independent foreign and defence policies. The ending of the **Cold War** has increased the involvement of states in a wide variety of security, humanitarian and economic organisations and groupings, reflecting the growing complexity of what are now **multi-polar** world politics. The proliferation of regional and international bodies follows from an awareness of the need for collective solutions to problems of world order and the uncertainty many states feel in a world where their scope for independent action has been limited. In recent years, the threats to national, regional and even world security have become more diffuse. The danger in what are called 'asymmetric threats' has increased massively as challenges to an American-brokered world order come not just from rogue states and failed states, but from non-state actors such as terrorist networks and their cohorts in drug trafficking and cyber-crime. Greater volatility also springs from the partial withdrawal of Russia from a geo-strategic world role and the extent to which the USA is now seen less as a global policeman subject to international constraints, and more as an aggrieved protagonist. In other respects uncertainty reflects the globalisation of defence industries and the threat of the proliferation of weapons of mass destruction. All of these are now key issues in the search for more robust mechanisms of regional and world security.

Of course, most states are still concerned to maintain effective control of public policy, including defence policy, by national governments. At the same time, almost all recognise the prohibitive costs involved and the power of what by now is a global standard: namely the need to avoid inter-state conflict where possible. As a result, multilateral frameworks for collective security and the growth of international military and intelligence cooperation are on the increase. It may be that the Iraq crisis and tensions over how to deal with Iran's nuclear ambitions compromise these trends, but it is still too soon to judge. Of course, providing for the defence of national territory is one of the defining features of an independent state and loss of autonomy in this area of policy sometimes wounds national pride. The same may be true of cooperation and loss or surrender of autonomy in other areas of policy. In the case of Britain and the EU such issues run very deep.

The EU has also assumed a greater presence in key policy areas, all of which challenge or may press upon the decisional freedoms of national government. These include its growing significance as a trading bloc, the economic and political implications of Economic and Monetary Union (EMU), and the engagement with foreign policy and security matters, as well as social issues such as immigration and labour flexibility. Such issues now inform the conduct of domestic party politics and the national policy agenda. During 'New' Labour's first term in office they failed to catch fire as electoral issues, thanks to careful agenda management by the government and the failure of the Conservative Party to make a fist of its role as official opposition. Riven by doubts over Europe throughout the Thatcher and Major terms of office, the Tories remained vulnerable to a terminal crisis over the issue of the single currency right up to the general election of 2005. Indeed, membership of the EMU touches deep questions of identity for many Conservatives. In a speech to the Conservative Party annual conference in October 1999, the then party leader, William Hague, offered a strong line on the virtues of things British when set against the shortcomings of Europe and Europeans. Paradoxically, Tory divisions over Europe were part of the generally negative image that dogged the party into the 2001 and 2005 general elections, despite the fact that poll data continued to show a majority of the electorate opposed to UK entry into the single currency. Hague's successor as party leader, Iain Duncan Smith, trod a more cautious and apparently less jaundiced line over some aspects of Europe and Europeans than his immediate predecessor. While still immune to the appeal of the single currency, Duncan Smith was more agnostic on the virtues of European systems of funding healthcare and supporting education than would have been countenanced in a party still influenced by Margaret Thatcher's legacy. Under the short-lived stewardship of Michael Howard the divisive nature of Europe led to a rather muted treatment of the issue during the 2005 general election campaign, with talk of renegotiating the various European treaties and saving the pound absent from the hustings.

The globalising and regionalising trends noted above, and their reverberations in national politics, are all contemporary, but we should note that globalisation and the discourses through which it is mediated are historical phenomena. By turns, British political and business élites have embraced the world or sought protection from its wiles.

■ Britain in the world

All the trends identified above raise serious questions about the ways in which and the extent to which the United Kingdom is addressing the current phase of globalisation. Some observers have argued that New Labour accepts the view that in the global age there is no alternative to the full acceptance of neo-liberal canons, to curbing welfare provision and to a pro-business stance in industrial relations. As a means of coming to terms with what Mr Blair has called 'the way of the world', these shifts in the policy agenda of national government appear quite radical, a deliberate attempt to undo history and ideology as a way of managing the present. The criticisms levelled against New Labour's stance on globalisation display an interesting twist. At one remove, Blair has been accused of accepting the neo-liberal framework altogether, but notably in relation to the idea of the global marketplace and its inexorable constraints on national autonomy. In addition, he has been condemned for lacking the vision and the conviction of Margaret Thatcher (Hall, 1979, 1998). Whereas the 'Iron Lady' presided over the 'Great Moving Right Show', Blair is just 'Nowhere Man', or in another guise, 'Bush's poodle'. It is hard enough to answer claims that you are delinquent on basic socialist (or social democratic) principles; attracting calumny for not out-Thatchering Thatcher might be a little hard to swallow, even for a 'modernising' politician like Blair.

But the relationships between global forces and domestic policy and politics are very complex. Having to come to terms with globalisation is not and never has been just a matter of dispensing with the legacies of the past or with the constraints of national culture and the domestic political agenda, however much policy makers might like to do this. In this section we will examine some of the key features of the international and global environment as these have emerged in the past 150 years or so, and discuss how Britain has been affected by, and in turn has affected, such changes. Over the period as a whole the motif is one of relative decline in terms of Britain's standing in the world. From being an imperial power and a manufacturing giant towards the end of the nineteenth century, by the early years of the new millennium Britain has followed a path which leaves it increasingly bound to Europe but still very ambivalent about this tie. Its world role now depends on the status of multilateral bodies such as the UN and NATO, on the vitality of the City of London as a financial centre and on its ability to give the external relations of the EU a distinctly British gloss. Of course, Britain's standing also depends on the quality of its 'special relationship' with the United States. That relationship remains a source of tension within British politics and between Britain and some of its European partners.

Shifting global balances in the nineteenth century: Britain as hegemon

In 1750, the UK accounted for 1.9 per cent of world manufacturing output. By 1880, this proportion had risen to 22.9 per cent, with its nearest single rival, the United States, a long way back on 14.7 per cent. It is worth underlining the depth of this comparative advantage. In 1860, Britain produced 53 per cent of the world's iron and 50 per cent of its coal. Britain's success as the first industrial nation only served to consolidate its already dominant position as a maritime, commercial power and world centre for financial credit. In the 1860s, it was responsible for two-fifths of world trade in manufactured goods and fully one-third of the world's merchant marine flew under the British flag, a proportion that continued to rise for some decades. In other words, the Victorian age saw Britain at the centre of the world's manufacturing and trading economy, and Victorians, eminent or otherwise, usually rejoiced in this position of dominance.

The interesting thing about Britain's economic dominance during these years is that it was not matched by its military capacity. Naval power remained an article of faith for Victorians, but expenditure on military hardware and the maintenance of large standing armies were deemed by many politicians and statesmen as costly and unproductive. This perception was due to the success of the ideology of *laissez-faire* political economy, first propounded by Adam Smith in 1776, which championed the cause of low government expenditure and the reduction of state control over both individuals and the economy as a whole. For proponents of this doctrine, peace was a necessary condition for prosperity, and war a means of last resort to prevent any violation of national territory and to secure the conditions of trade. Of course, both in Parliament and outside, *laissez-faire* was always a contested doctrine. But its appeal to the political and business classes can be measured by the steady dismantling of those **mercantilist** dogmas and institutions that had characterised much of the eighteenth-century trading economy, and which were based on the principle that national security and national wealth were inextricably linked. Tariffs which protected domestic producers were abolished, bans on the export of high-tech machinery lifted and a variety of imperial 'preferences' on designated goods were outlawed.

The upshot was that, by the middle decades of the nineteenth century, Britain was a very reluctant player in international, and especially European, conflicts where engagements went beyond diplomatic interventions and the judicious appearance of a naval squadron. Direct involvement in the Crimea in the mid-1850s under the premiership of Palmerston was considered a costly disaster, and Britain sat out other important European conflicts, such as the defeat of Austria by Prussia in 1866 and the Franco-Prussian war of 1870. Even in the non-European empire, Britain was miserly in its deployment of British regiments and government personnel, including to the Indian sub-continent, the jewel in Britain's imperial crown.

Apart from its industrial capacity and commercial clout, the factors that underpinned British hegemony in the century following the Napoleonic Wars were threefold:

■ *Naval power*: No other country, and critically no other maritime power, came near to matching British strength.

■ *An expanding colonial empire*: With no serious threats from other European powers, and only the beginnings of American rivalry in the western hemisphere, the British empire grew without much hindrance. Anti-imperial and protectionist sentiments flourished occasionally at home, but did little to check the expansion of the land empire. Apart from the economic benefits that accrued to Britain, the sheer scale of British possessions guaranteed that British influence and the British way of life were spread across the globe.

■ *Financial power*: Vast sums of British investment capital were exported during the mid- to late nineteenth century. Between 1870 and 1875, an average of £75 million per annum was invested abroad annually, remarkable sums when translated into current numbers. Much of the lavish return on this investment was promptly reinvested, so contributing to a virtuous spiral whereby national wealth creation in turn contributed to the growth in world trade and communications infrastructures.

But the strengths of the British empire and trading economy during the nineteenth century were also potential weaknesses. For one thing, the law of comparative advantage eventually worked against British dominance, as competitor nations narrowed the technology gap and became thoroughly industrialised. In this regard the wealth-producing efforts of British inventors and investors overseas contributed in no small measure to the developments in American, Russian and central European manufacturing capacity. For another, the British economy was heavily reliant on international trade and finance. *Laissez-faire* liberals argued that the more Britain and other countries became integrated with the burgeoning world economy, the less likely it was that wars would ensue. However, ran the dogma, in the event of a war between the great powers British export markets would be disrupted, the flow of imports restricted and financial markets damaged. Whether a mature economy like Britain's could survive such an upheaval, let alone retain its dominance, was open to doubt.

Post-hegemony, 1900–45

In Queen Victoria's Diamond Jubilee year of 1897, Joseph Chamberlain, the British Minister for the Colonies, could still tell a conference that 'the tendency of the time is to throw all power into the hands of the greater empires, and the minor kingdoms – those which are non-progressive – fall into a secondary and subordinate place'. The next fifty years proved Chamberlain to be wrong, as the old empires fell apart and would-be new ones arose. A pacific world, so central to *laissez-faire* models of prosperity, also went up in flames, as a more realist and bloody order took Europe and some other parts of the world into desolation and ruin.

In 1900 Britain still possessed the largest empire the world had ever seen along with a mighty navy and huge industrial strength. But there were strong challenges to British interests, and these were most pronounced in the Caribbean and Latin America (from the USA), in the Near East and Persian Gulf (Russia) and in China, where Great Power interest in carving up the Celestial Empire threatened Britain's domination of China's foreign trade. Such challenges were not new, but by the end of the century were being posed by countries that were stronger and less inclined to accord Britain the privileges of rank. The British economy was also less competitive than in the recent past, with a decline in the share of world production in key commodities such as coal, textiles and iron goods. For two decades up to 1894, industrial production grew at no more than 1.5 per cent annually, far below the growth of its keenest rivals. Increasingly Britain's open home market was flooded by lower-cost foreign manufactures, while British exports were subject to high tariff barriers in protected markets in North America and industrialised Europe. In 1880, the UK had 23.2 per cent of world trade; by 1914 this proportion was down to 14.1 per cent. During this critical period, when Britain was under sustained challenge from its economic rivals, the doctrine of free trade began to give way to the ideas of **social imperialism** and national protectionism, especially in the Conservative Party. These doctrines advocated the enlargement of the British empire, or at least much closer integration of the colonial economies with that of the metropolis, as a way of holding on to Britain's status in the world economy.

Of course, decline was relative, and on other indicators the UK remained an economic giant. The shipbuilding industry, on which Britain's trade and defence depended, was still producing 60 per cent of the world's merchant tonnage in 1914, and 33 per cent of its warships. Britain still marshalled 43 per cent of the world's foreign investments, with $19.5 billion (US) invested overseas. On the eve of the First World War in 1914, Britain was hardly in a parlous state, but had lost out industrially to both the USA and Germany and was subject to growing pressure in commercial and maritime affairs, as well as over its imperial interests. For all this, in the prewar international order Britain remained the major player.

The postwar world order that emerged was quite different from its predecessor. In many respects it was still a Eurocentric world, but some of the main protagonists of the old order, notably Britain, France and Germany, had been badly hurt materially and pyschologically by the war, while Russia had undergone a social revolution. In other respects the war simply accelerated trends that were already visible.

Perhaps the most significant of these was the fact that the USA overtook Europe in terms of total industrial output by 1919, confirming its position as the new economic hegemon. During the 1920s the 'Gold Standard', the world's first real international monetary system, was being restored in most countries. But it was a much less stable financial and commercial basis for the world economy than it had been before the First World War. The great fragility of the new commercial and financial order led to the Wall Street crash of 1929 and the Great Depression of the early 1930s, and this was echoed in the precariousness of the whole postwar security settlement based on the Versailles Treaty and the League of Nations. By the mid-1930s, the **cosmopolitan** world order envisaged in the Versailles settlement had all but splintered into rival currency blocs – sterling, dollar, yen and gold – and into forms of national protectionism.

Dreams of world peace and internationalism, built around the League of Nations and on the horror of total war, also began to fragment in the late 1920s and early 1930s, giving way to a politics based on national security and spheres of influence. In Germany, the ravages of the Depression fanned the discontent left by the draconian peace settlement at Versailles and contributed to the appeal of those that counselled national reconstruction through martial action and imposed order. Other fascist movements in Europe and the brand of militaristic nationalism that dominated Japanese politics echoed these sentiments. The 'revisionist' states of Germany, Italy and Japan were antagonistic not only towards the Western democracies that had brokered the peace in 1919, although Italy was a victor nation then, but also towards the Bolshevik Soviet Union, keeper of a new truth. In other respects the world was becoming much less Eurocentric. For Britain perhaps the most obvious and far-reaching example of this trend was the growing opposition to British rule in India, centred on Gandhi, which intimated imperial demise.

The slide into another European and then world war in 1939 stemmed from the failure to solve the German question after 1919. The 'twenty-year truce' between 1919 and 1939 saw Germany relinquish its tenuous grip on democracy under the Weimar Republic and embrace National Socialism. Throughout this period the USA remained outside the League of Nations and wedded to its doctrine of hemispheric isolation. Britain and France could not agree on the proper role for the League and so it never really developed teeth as a means of collective security. In 1939, the Western democracies were not well equipped to face the aggressive territorial ambitions of Hitler's new Reich. Of course, Britain was still a substantial power in the 1930s, but not one ready, in any sense of the word, to halt the German challenge. In many ways the policy of appeasement under Neville Chamberlain was recognition of Britain's weakness and a mechanism for preserving what remained of British power. Rises in defence expenditure (from 5.5 per cent of GNP in 1937 to 12.5 per cent in 1939) placed severe pressure on industries already depleted by lack of investment and skills shortages. As a result government had to purchase arms from overseas, thereby eroding foreign currency reserves and threatening balance of payments difficulties. The decision to shore up Britain's 'continental commitment' and give the Mediterranean theatre priority over Singapore in the way of naval resources, weakened the British military presence in the Far East, soon to be faced by Japanese expansionism. Over-stretched and under-resourced, Britain made the decision in 1939 to abandon appeasement of Hitler and his territorial ambitions and go to war.

Stable bi-polarity and unstable multi-polarity, 1945–89

The 'proper application of overwhelming force', made possible by US entry into the war in 1942, sealed the long-term fate of the Axis powers (Germany and Japan). It also set the seal on the old balance of power and of the key role played in it by the European Great Powers. The bi-polar world now emerging owed everything to the geo-military strength of the two superpowers and to the unrivalled economic clout of the Americans. In the 'free world' American influence was everywhere and a whole new world economic and strategic order was constructed in the image of American capitalism and commitment to Western democratic values. All the international economic institutions which grew out of the Second World War – the International Monetary Fund (IMF), the International Bank for Reconstruction and Development and the General Agreement on Tariffs and Trade (GATT) – were apologists for a liberal world order based on open competition and the free convertibility of currencies. Countries wishing to reconstruct their economies (and this included most European states) were obliged to sing from the same hymn sheet as the Americans. The Soviet Union, at first invited to be a participant in this American-brokered renaissance, backed off when it became apparent that the price was to surrender socialist controls on economic activity. The USSR went its own way, constructing a defensive wall in east-central Europe to rival the North Atlantic Treaty Organisation (NATO) of 1949. A socialist version of the economic cooperation that began to develop in western Europe in the early 1950s was called the Council for Mutual Economic Co-operation (COMECON). In the style of many previous empires, the USSR also began to build a military capacity that was well beyond its economic means, and which swallowed a massively disproportionate amount of GDP.

Britain emerged from the war intact, but with its status as a global power depleted. Of course it was still an imperial power and, through its seat as one of the Permanent Members of the United Nations Security Council, ostensibly still in the front rank of world powers. When possession of nuclear weapons became a potent symbol of national virility and a means of retaining some trace of Great Power independence in the early 1950s, Britain was anxious to be a member of the nuclear club. On the surface, as well as in the minds of many British people and politicians, the UK was still at the centre of the world politically and holding its own in economic affairs. The reality was rather less flattering and destined to get worse. For one thing, Britain's long-term industrial decline had been accelerated by the war and it no longer enjoyed primacy in the areas of financial services and invisible exports. The empire and Commonwealth were increasingly important to Britain in economic terms, but also burdensome because of the demands for overseas bases and the pressures of various anti-colonial movements. Europe and European reconstruction figured much less prominently in the world-views of British policy makers than did the empire and British Commonwealth, the Atlantic relationship with the USA and the exigencies of economic decline. Early on in the Second World War, Churchill had spoken of the three 'circles' that defined British policy and interests: the empire, the 'special relationship' with the United States and, on the outer rim, Europe. Let us look more closely at these three relationships.

Empire and Commonwealth

The British Empire was renamed the Commonwealth in the light of postwar decolonisation. The process of decolonisation was begun in 1947 with the withdrawal from India and Burma, and in the next twenty-five years led to the dismantling of all but the residual outposts of empire. Nationalist pressure, American opposition and cost were the primary factors behind the withdrawal from empire, rather than any hint of drawing closer to Europe. The Suez fiasco of 1956 demonstrated Britain's inability to act independently of the USA and speeded up the process of decolonisation. Britain, France and Israel were forced by American and world pressure to withdraw their 'protective' military force from the Suez Canal Zone, where it was trying to wrest control of the strategic waterway from President Nasser's Egypt with its then unacceptable message of secular, pan-Arab nationalism. Paradoxically, years later, during the Falklands crisis of 1982 the militarily audacious expedition to reclaim the islands from Argentine forces relied on American diplomatic goodwill and satellite intelligence.

In the wake of empire, Britain turned to the Commonwealth to preserve its waning influence in former colonies and around the world. But the burgeoning Commonwealth was not in any sense a power bloc in world politics, still less a vehicle for enduring British influence. Where Britain was America's firm partner in the conduct of the Cold War, many Commonwealth states declared themselves to be 'non-aligned'. Britain also lost markets in the Commonwealth to more aggressive European and Far Eastern rivals, and some Commonwealth members, such as New Zealand, had to redirect their patterns of trade when Britain's entry to the EC in 1973 cut off or severely curtailed Commonwealth preference agreements for many agricultural products. At meetings of Commonwealth Heads of State and government, Britain has often found itself in a minority, accused of bolstering racist regimes in South Africa and Southern Rhodesia (now Zimbabwe), or failing to broker conflicts between Commonwealth states.

For example, since the independence of Zimbabwe in 1980, the ruling party, ZANU-PF, and its leader, Robert Mugabe, have been the focus of chronic diplomatic wrangling and recrimination. Strained relations have stressed the continued 'imperialist' pretensions of Britain on the one hand and the contentious land redistribution policies and dubious election tactics of the Zimbabwean ruling party on the other. Britain retains a strong interest in African affairs generally, but these days set in the context of a global policy agenda concerned with lifting Africa out of what Tony Blair has called its 'disastrous decline'. Speaking at the George Bush Snr Presidential Library in Texas on 2 April 2002, Blair couched the issue of Africa's regeneration in terms of the need to draw the continent more fully into global processes, such as trade. He insisted that 'What the poor world needs is not less globalisation but more. Their injustice is not globalisation, but being excluded from it. Free enterprise is not their enemy, but their friend.' At the Johannesburg World Summit on Sustainable Development in September 2002, he noted of the persistence of world poverty that 'What is truly shocking is not the scale of the problems. The truly shocking thing is that we know the remedies.'

These sentiments informed Blair's decision to set up a 'Commission for Africa' in 2003, which included the campaigner Bob Geldof as one of its members. Geldof had made the original suggestion for such a body. With a very wide remit, including HIV/AIDS, governance and economic issues, the Commission reported in March 2005 as follows:

■ It recommended an immediate £13 billion per year increase in international aid to Africa, followed by a further £13 billion annually after 2010.

■ It recommended that debts to the World Bank, IMF and African Development Bank of poor countries in sub-Saharan Africa should be written off, but that recipients must be committed to good governance, economic growth and poverty reduction.

■ The Commission recommended that donor countries should aim to spend 0.7 per cent of GDP on development aid.

■ It endorsed a British proposal to raise money for Africa on world capital markets.

■ It called on Western nations to agree to eliminate trade-distorting support for cotton and sugar growers and by 2010 to end all trade-distorting support in agriculture.

■ It called on African governments to ratify the UN Convention against Corruption.

■ It recommended that negotiations on an arms trade treaty should open no later than 2006.

■ It called on Western nations to fund at least 50 per cent of the African Union's peacekeeping budget.

Few people in Brussels and in the USA believe that there is much chance of getting farm subsidies dismantled by 2010, and for all its pious commitment to African economic and social development the UK has been one of the worst poachers of African health workers to meet its own skilled labour shortages.

In the run-up to the G8 conference at Gleneagles in July 2005, the Chancellor, Gordon Brown, echoed some of the Commission's recommendations and upped the ante by calling for 100 per cent debt relief to pay for education and health. The USA remains sceptical about the feasibility of some targets and anxious not to pour more development aid money into venal African regimes. The global importance of issues about poverty, debt relief and free trade was underlined by the massive demonstrations and events, including the Live8 concert in London, which attended the G8 meeting.

Relationship with the United States

By the early 1940s the UK recognised that it was incapable of holding on to its empire and its world role without help – or more to the point, without American help. Only the USA could oversee the conditions necessary to recreate a liberal world order and had the muscle to protect Europe by kick-starting its economic recovery. Relations with the USA had been poor during the prewar years, but wartime cooperation improved them, giving the British, at any rate, a false sense of their importance to Washington. Britain now set out to support the American version of the new world order, a stance which has scarcely varied across successive governments. Over the years, Washington has been both cavalier and solicitous by turns in its dealings with Britain. In 1946 the US peremptorily cut off collaboration with the British in nuclear research, and the Suez affair demonstrated that if there was a 'special relationship' it was not between equals. At the same time, the US has been willing to supply nuclear arms only to Britain and has benefited from the willingness of the British governments to legitimate and subvent its actions as a global policeman. When the new Labour government in the person of Prime Minister Harold Wilson refused to commit British troops to support the US-sponsored government of South Vietnam in 1964, the Americans were not only outraged, but baffled by British reluctance to get involved.

The more routine response of British governments has been to play the good neighbour. During the Thatcher–Reagan years, between 1980 and 1988, the leaderships of both countries shared a goal to liberalise the world economy, and a fundamentally realist and aggressive stance on confronting the enemies of the West. In 1983 the UK offered full diplomatic support for the US invasion of Grenada, to oust its Marxist regime, and in 1986 the US made use of British air bases to launch its bombing raid on Libya in reprisal for Colonel Qadhafi's support for international terrorism. In both these cases the unequal nature of the relationship between the UK and the United States was revealed. Over Grenada, Margaret Thatcher complained to President Reagan about invading an island that was still a British dependency, and on the Libyan raid, the UK was only informed rather than asked for permission about using US air bases on British soil during the mission. During the Iran–Iraq war of the late 1980s British and American warships patrolled Gulf shipping lanes endangered by the conflict.

These excursions were taken by some in the British foreign policy community as evidence of the ability of the UK to play an effective world role, and to 'punch above its weight' in conflict situations. More critical responses questioned the value of such commitments to Britain and expressed unease at the overstretching of British military resources and defence budgets to suit American interests. These fears were exacerbated by more lavish and potentially long-term interventions in the 1990s. The ending of the Cold War between 1989 and 1991, when the Soviet Union collapsed, left the USA as the only superpower worth the name, but still in need of a little help from its friends in a world that was, if anything, more dangerous and volatile.

As part of the Gulf War coalition against Iraqi aggression in Kuwait in 1990, Britain contributed the second largest contingent to the **multilateral** force and has been a mainstay of UN and NATO interventions in parts of the former Yugoslavia. In 1999, under New Labour, Tony Blair was outspoken in his calls for NATO military action to reverse the forced expulsion of ethnic Albanians from Kosovo. The USA under President Clinton was seen as laggard in its commitment to intervention on humanitarian grounds, allowing Britain to take the moral high ground. The use of NATO as the chosen instrument of intervention was a calculated move to thwart any Russian veto on the UN Security Council against military action. The issue also allowed Blair to demonstrate his credentials as an international statesman and a committed European by reinforcing claims that New Labour was determined to be 'at the heart of Europe', if not in the first tranche of states to join a single currency, then in matters of defence and foreign policy. Even here, the British stance is complicated. At St Malo in 1998, Tony Blair and French president Jacques Chirac signed an accord approving the establishment of a European Rapid Reaction Force (RRF) to cater for the changing security needs of the post-Cold War era in Europe. The French, following their own security agenda, wanted such a force to operate independently of NATO, while Britain favoured maintaining strong links with the Alliance. An apparent commitment to entanglements in one key area of policy and continued ambivalence about another is characteristic of Britain's demeanour over Europe, but looks increasingly uncomfortable as the stakes get bigger.

The continued ambivalence that marks Britain's stance towards European integration reveals a number of tensions in its image of itself as a world player, only one of which is its 'special relationship' with the United States. The first is the extent to which domestic politics prevent a wholehearted embrace of the European project in the shape of grand projects such as the single currency. Party loyalties have been strained by upping the ante over membership of the single currency, over possible tax

harmonisation and in the debates over a constitutional treaty for the EU. Overall, public opinion remains sceptical of the European project. In the wake of what supporters hoped would be a summer of love for the new euro as holiday-makers made its acquaintance, public sentiment in 2003 remained unconvinced that 'ditching' the pound would bring anything but grief, a sentiment still apparent in 2005. Second, the traditions of British foreign policy are decidedly globalist, a legacy of empire, no doubt, but also reflected in the pronounced Atlanticist slant of recent years. That Britain still has a sense of itself as a global player is clear, and it views the inability or unwillingness of the EU to act decisively and collectively as a regional, let alone a global, actor with irritation and concern. Equivocation by some EU member states and by the EU itself in prosecuting the war on terrorism and the outright opposition of France and Germany to intervention in Iraq were taken by the British government as evidence of this lack of resolve and as one more instance of an endemic anti-Americanism.

By the late summer of 2002, Blair's role as the broker of both American and European interests in the war against terrorism was compromised by the

BOX 2.1   IDEAS AND PERSPECTIVES

Defending the realm: Britain, global terrorism and the rights of citizens

The prosecution of the global 'war on terror' has pushed its most active protagonists – the United States and Britain – to review existing laws and policies that bear on the security of their respective realms and their citizens. Both countries, as well as others such as Australia and the Netherlands, are debating the balance between what might be seen as competing claims and interests. These are the rights and freedoms of individuals on the one hand, and the rights of the community as a whole to take protective measures for its own security. These debates focus on grave moral issues including, at least in the USA, whether or not there is a 'liberal' case for torture as a last resort when the lives of many people could be saved by its use on terrorist suspects.

In the UK the current government has proceeded by trying to amend UK law to deal with the danger of terrorist attacks. Legislation to cope with terrorism was already on the statute book before the events of 11 September 2001 in the form of the 1974 Prevention of Terrorism Act, passed at the height of the IRA bombing campaign on mainland Britain and renewed annually, and the Terrorism Act of 2000. The latter made permanent the 'temporary measure' of the 1974 Act whereby suspects could be held for up to seven days without charge. It also extended the definition of terrorism to include any act designed to 'intimidate the public for the purpose of advancing an ideological cause'.

The first response of the British government following 9/11 was the Anti-Terrorism, Crime and Security Act of 2001. It allowed foreign nationals thought to be a threat to national security to be held indefinitely without charge, and because of this the UK was required to 'derogate' from its obligations under part of the Human Rights Act. In 2003 the Criminal Justice bill, proposed by the then Home Secretary David Blunkett, doubled the time that terrorist suspects could be held without charge to 14 days.

During 2004, the law lords ruled that the indefinite detention without trial of foreign nationals was discriminatory, thereby attacking a major tenet of the government's response to the terrorist threat. Instead the government pushed through a new Prevention of Terrorism Act giving the Home Secretary the power to impose 'control orders' on suspects, UK nationals or not. Such orders allow surveillance of suspects, even house arrest and restrictions on communication. The measure has to be renewed annually by Parliament.

The July 2005 bombings in London triggered a new bill now in contested passage through Parliament. The bill originally proposed that police would be able to hold suspects for 90 days without charge. In early November 2005 an adverse vote in the House of Commons cut that period to 28 days. The bill also proposes making indirect incitement to terrorism an offence, banning the glorification of terrorism, introducing an offence of acts preparatory to terrorism, and outlawing of the giving or receiving of terror training.

These issues, along with the heated debate about whether identity cards are a useful weapon in the fight against terrorism or a further manifestation of the 'surveillance state', go to the heart of key issues about human rights, civil liberties, rights of citizenship and the power of the state *vis-à-vis* its citizens and others resident in the UK. In particular, the detention without trial measures undermine the principle of *habeas corpus*, and for some critics signal a slide into state extremism and authoritarian behaviour. At the same time, even campaigners for civil liberties recognise that 'there is a serious terrorist threat' (Shami Chakrabarti, Director of *Liberty*). Where do you stand in this debate? What sort of argument would you advance?

The attacks on London in July 2005 demonstrated terrorism as a global weapon
Source: Copyright © Peter Macdiarmid / EPA / Corbis

growing reluctance of some EU partners to countenance the use of force against Iraq and from domestic opinion less and less willing to endorse intervention. Franco-British relations suffered a further setback during the early months of 2003, when President Chirac intimated that he would veto any new US- or UK-sponsored resolution before the UN Security Council that sanctioned the use of force against Iraq. French opposition to a so-called 'second' UN resolution in March 2003 was interpreted in UK and US government circles as signalling the end of diplomatic attempts to secure a UN-brokered disarmament process in Iraq. Apart from its impact on the UN, the Iraq issue had and continues to have profound implications for the prospects of an EU common foreign and security policy despite, perhaps because of, Blair's successful attempt to divide France and Germany (both publicly anti-war) from some other European states more inclined to adopt a hard line over intervention. Third, the global dimension of British foreign policy is informed by a strong sense that the world is not only more interconnected and interdependent, but also more fluid and more dangerous than at the height of the Cold War, when a brittle stability obtained. International terrorism, the threat of the proliferation of weapons of mass destruction and risks from global pandemics such as AIDS are felt to disfigure the prospects for global peace and security and to present challenges for the conduct of domestic governance.

In the wake of September 11th such concerns translated easily (some commentators argue, too glibly) into calls for integrated responses and the protection of common values through the application of armed force. Speaking in London at the Lord Mayor's Banquet in April 2002, Labour's then Foreign Secretary, Jack Straw, reiterated Blair's doctrine of the international community as consisting of four principles:

I suggest that there are four principles which need to underpin the modern idea of a global community:

First, that international relations must be founded on the idea that every nation has an obligation properly to meet its global responsibilities;

Second, that the global community has the right to make judgements about countries' internal affairs, where they flout or fail to abide by these global values;

Third, that because our interests are now more entwined than ever, the global community must make renewed efforts to resolve those persistent conflicts which threaten the security of us all;

And fourth, that the global community must play a more active role in dealing with conflicts within states, which in the past it has overlooked until it is too late.

Speech given by the Foreign Secretary, Jack Straw, at the Lord Mayor's Banquet, Mansion House, 10 April 2002

For critics, this vision of a global order is still too reliant on the good offices of the USA and its continued willingness to engage with the world in pursuit of globalisation with a human face. Events provide support for both arguments. Some opinion saw America's willingness to tough it out against Iraq, alone if necessary, along with President Bush's hard line on national missile defence and the Kyoto climate protocols, as aspects of a 'new realism' in US foreign policy, sometimes called the 'Bush Doctrine'. Others find it hard to believe that the USA wants to disengage from collective solutions to the problem of world order, or that – in this period of intense globalisation – that it can do.

American policy towards Iraq provides evidence for both interpretations. On the one hand, the administration's determination to eliminate threats from rogue or failed states by a pre-emptive strike was a radical, though not unprecedented, departure from the mantra of collective security and consensual multilateral solutions to international crises. On the other hand, Bush's attempts to build a coalition to pursue the 'war on terrorism' and to require Saddam to implement the will of the UN over the manufacture and possession of weapons of mass destruction was, to some degree, multilateralist in intent.

In all this, Blair no doubt saw himself, and may still be seen, as the link between the USA and Europe, perhaps the means whereby the USA remains tied into a global cosmopolitanism, even if this is not the version sanctioned by the UN. But much commentary in Britain and Europe continues to depict Blair as President Bush's poodle. While there is no doubt that Britain's support for America's world-view is strong and enduring, there are substantial areas of disagreement. These include British support for the International Criminal Court, a body shunned by the USA, and British backing for EU sanctions against discriminatory US tariffs on imported steel. At the Johannesburg Summit on Sustainable Development in 2002, Mr Blair reiterated his support for the Kyoto climate protocols, saying that they are 'right and should be ratified by us all', sentiments not echoed in Washington. By the time of the Montreal Summit on climate change in December 2005, there was little evidence that core positions on either side had changed. Evidence leaked in the autumn of 2005 suggested that Blair persuaded President Bush not to bomb the offices of the Al-Jazeerah Arabic-language television station when it was seen by the Americans as a mouthpiece for international terrorism. At the same time, the British government's seeming acquiescence in America's policy of detaining 'war criminals' and terrorist suspects without charge at Guantanamo Bay in Cuba for some makes a mockery of its independent status and of its duty of care towards its citizens. However, the Prime Minister did make successful overtures to Mr Bush for the return to the UK of nine British detainees, and Britain has always opposed the US decision to try detainees through military tribunals, with the Attorney General Lord Goldsmith saying that such devices will not offer 'sufficient guarantees of a fair trial'. On Guantanamo itself, British ministers seem opposed to its continued existence in principle, but more agnostic in practice, preferring to interpret the US action as 'anomalous' rather than issue a forthright condemnation. In March 2006, it was reported that the USA was seeking Britain's advice on possible closure of Guantanamo.

But the charge that Blair is Bush's poodle is most pronounced over UK support for direct military action against Iraq. During the summer of 2002 and into 2003 his position over a possible invasion was subject to a growing volume of complaint from within his own party, and public opinion polls demonstrating a majority against invasion. A massive anti-war protest in London on 15 February 2003 and parliamentary revolts by 122 Labour MPs on 26 February 2003 and by 139 on 18 March provided more evidence of anti-Americanism in Labour ranks. Following the invasion of Iraq in March 2003, the parliamentary party tempered its opposition in order to show support for British troops in the field. Public opinion was reassured by the Prime Minister's claims about the need to eliminate the real threat posed by Saddam's weapons of mass destruction, as evidenced in his continued refusal to accede to UN Resolutions. In the difficult postwar reconstruction of Iraq, the USA and Britain have been at greater pains to bring other countries and the UN on board as partners in the peace-keeping and anti insurgent coalition, while still consigning the UN to a role subordinate to the powerful US Office of Humanitarian and Reconstruction Assistance (OHRA). The failure to find weapons of mass destruction or the research facilities needed to manufacture their components has wounded the credibility of Blair and Bush in both world and domestic opinion. As insurgency in Iraq has mounted, so the calls for withdrawal or an exit strategy have become more pronounced. Nonetheless in December 2005, Iraq held elections for a national legislature and its first full-term government, having approved a federal constitution at a referendum earlier in the year. With the 'War on Terror' still being prosecuted in Afghanistan and Iran a cause of tension between the EU and the United States, the success and legitimacy of the doctrine of military intervention for humanitarian ends remain in doubt.

Like all British prime ministers, Blair carries a good deal of historical baggage along with him concerning relationships with the USA and Europe. Some of this baggage is courtesy of the long-term hostility to things American shown by sections of his own party and its ambivalence over the EU, which is still unresolved despite the fact that New Labourites are officially born-again Europeans. Some of it is the product of historical and cultural factors that still make Britons appear reluctant Europeans.

Over the years the perception of British subservience to the United States and its relative aloofness from developments on the mainland of Europe have made it difficult for governments to appear anything like sold on European integration. Britain's first two attempts to join the then European Economic Community (EEC) in 1961–3 and 1967–8 foundered, in part, on the fears of France that Britain would be a 'Trojan horse' for American influence, as much as on the antipathy of the British for supra-national institutions. During these years, a grudging recognition that the fledgling EEC was becoming increasingly important to Britain's trading economy gradually overcame the reluctance to join a Western European economic order, but never extinguished the sense that almost any movement towards partnership would compromise British sovereignty. Britain finally joined the renamed European Community on 1 January 1973.

Britain and Europe

In many ways, the image of Britain as a reluctant European rings true, but many states in postwar Europe were also ambivalent about surrendering decision-making autonomy and abandoning national identity. As states recovered from their wartime travails, they became more selective in their commitment to cooperation but, as we have noted, increasingly drawn into collaboration. From the early

1950s, economic cooperation prospered through such bodies as the European Coal and Steel Community (ECSC), founded in 1952. At Messina in 1955, the six members of the ECSC took the decision to extend 'functional cooperation' to a much wider range of economic activity. The result was the EEC (1957). No such agreement existed over defence matters and the European Defence Community (EDC), bruited as one of the three strands of a European Political Community (EPC) in 1952, proved abortive. The plans to amalgamate the ECSC, the EDC and the Council of Europe (the latter body first proposed by Churchill in 1945 with the aim of promoting dialogue about human rights and freedoms) were far too ambitious in what was still a quite fragile climate of cooperation. Although Britain was a founder member of the Council of Europe, it remained just an interested spectator as the momentum for greater economic collaboration built up in the 1950s. Following rebuffs in the 1960s, Britain secured membership of the EC in 1973 under the government of Edward Heath, only to have the new Labour administration (1974) under Harold Wilson promise the electorate that it would renegotiate more favourable terms of entry. This promise was directed at internal party divisions over Europe as much as anything else. In 1975, the British people endorsed membership in a referendum, but largely on the premise that it would be inconvenient to undo what had been done, rather than because of any great enthusiasm for the European venture.

During the Thatcher years, between 1979 and 1990, a more pronounced and systematic '**Euroscepticism**' came to dominate British policy towards the EC. During this period, the Prime Minister was committed to Atlanticism, especially to the role of the USA as guarantor of Western security. In language increasingly reminiscent of the older liberal discourse, free trade and freer markets became the economic orthodoxy, along with the need to adapt domestic policies and practices to meet global competition. Until 1987, the Labour Party's alternative economic strategy was no more than unreconstructed national protectionism, consisting of withdrawal from Europe, controls on capital and imports, and a greater degree of national self-sufficiency. If Labour's stance was consistently anti-European and anti-global, the Conservative position was more nuanced, almost paradoxical, despite the abrasive rhetoric often used (for example in 1984, when Mrs Thatcher argued successfully for a reduction in the UK contribution to the EC budget, and in her

landmark speech to the College of Europe in Bruges in 1988). Thatcher herself was a supporter of an open world economy, and this is still an article of faith for many Conservatives who are either strongly pro- or anti-EU. Belief in the virtues of the open market goes some way to explain Mrs Thatcher's support for the radical Single European Act (SEA) of 1985. This was a measure that opened the way for a single internal market in goods, services, capital and people in the EC by 1992, but which also curtailed the veto power of national governments in Community decision-making through the introduction of qualified majority voting in some areas of policy. For Thatcher, the EC was a barrier to the sort of globalisation she advocated (free trade between independent states) because it was (or was seen as) protectionist, bureaucratic and willing to countenance profligate levels of public spending. As an economic venture, it would be acceptable only if it could embrace the shock of competition and the discipline of market forces. At the same time, the SEA and the internal market promised a type of regionalism which would function as an integral and dynamic part of the open global economy, rather than as a hedge against it.

But the relaunch of European integration through the SEA was not just an acknowledgement of the need to be competitive in global markets. It was also the signal for a renewed commitment to economic and monetary union and political integration in Europe. Negotiations over the Maastricht Treaty on European Union in 1991–2 intensified British ambivalence over the shape of Europe and the UK's role in it. The treaty created a European Union, although in deference to British sensitivities the word 'federal' was deleted. This sop apart, the treaty once again threw into bold relief the tensions between a Europe based on the concept of ever closer union, requiring the 'deepening' of institutions and practices, and the preferred British model in which the EU would develop as an association of states, growing in number to accommodate entrants from the 'new' Europe to the east and south.

The compromise solution was to allow Britain and Denmark to 'opt out' of certain treaty provisions and postpone decisions on others. Thatcher's successor, John Major, did not share her antipathy to Europe *per se*, but was sensitive to divisions within his own party and pressured by sections of British business anxious about being left behind in the push for a more integrated Europe-wide economy. At Maastricht Major negotiated a separate protocol to the treaty that dealt with social affairs and labour relations (the Social Chapter) and exempted Britain from its very general remit. In the other key area of agreeing a timetable for the final stages of monetary union, Britain was allowed to choose whether and when it wanted to join the single currency. In the event, the UK did not join the third stage of EMU on 1 January 1999, preferring to wait until the 'proper' conditions for entry become available.

Since 1987, the Labour Party has gone through a process of reinvention, not least in terms of where it stands on Europe. Under Tony Blair, it has endorsed almost all the changes enacted by the Thatcher government, notably on the need to make British labour relations and working practices fit for the rigours of a global economy. The post-Maastricht agenda for economic and monetary union and for greater cooperation in foreign and security policy is still being played out in Britain. In other EU member states, with the exception of Denmark and Sweden, monetary union is now in place, with hard currency in circulation since January 2002. The impact of monetary union on the domestic politics of each state is likely to be considerable, not least on domestic political cleavages and on the ideological framework of party politics, as the deflationary pressures of monetary union force countries to reassess their pattern of spending in areas such as employment protection and social welfare.

New Labour's conviction is that, in a world of increasing globalisation, the European Union is becoming even more relevant to national and regional success. At the same time, the momentous process of monetary union and Britain's continued hesitancy about membership fuel unease on the Continent about its level of commitment to the EU project. Other recent and long-term developments in the EU demonstrate the UK's ambivalent relationships with Europe. Britain was a firm supporter of the expansion of the EU by 2004 to include ten new member states, eight from central and eastern Europe, whose accession was confirmed at the EU's Copenhagen summit in December 2002. Since these new members formally entered the EU on 1 May 2004, Britain has remained at the forefront of member states, arguing that this landmark expansion should not signal closure on further EU membership. Writing in *The Times* on the eve of the 2004 expansion, Mr Blair said 'I believe . . . that the accession tomorrow will be a catalyst for change in the EU, helping to give a new push to Britain's agenda.' Enlargement of the EU to the east has been an article of faith for both Conservative and Labour adminis-

trations. For the UK the modernising agendas and Anglo-American world-view of new member states is an important counterweight to Franco-German dominance in the EU and a plank in Britain's strategy for turning the EU into a liberal, competitive economic space and a firm supporter of the Atlantic Alliance. During its presidency of the **European Council** from July to December 2005, Britain looked to gain approval for a review of the role of EU institutions, including its budget, which is skewed heavily towards agricultural subsidy through the Common Agricultural Policy (CAP). In the final weeks of its presidency, these aims looked rather threadbare as the Union struggled to agree a budget and Britain's 'allies' among the new accession states became alarmed by its continued defence of the UK 'rebate', first agreed under Margaret Thatcher in 1984. In the event, a compromise was reached on 17 December 2005. European leaders agreed the next seven-year EU budget after two days of tense talks. The UK gives up 10.5bn euros (£7bn) of its rebate, some 20 per cent, while the budget grows to 862.4bn euros, helping to fund the development of new member states. In return, France has agreed to a budget review in 2008–9, which could lead to cuts in farm subsidies. Critics suggest that this deal leaves the UK as an overall loser, but such a judgement will turn, no doubt, on the ability of the EU to bring France and Ireland to the table on agricultural review in a few years and on the way in which Germany under a new Chancellor behaves towards Britain, France and the USA.

On the positive side, during the presidency the UK did broker the agreement whereby Turkey (an aspirant member for some 24 years) could start formal membership talks, and pushed for an accord on the mutual recognition of evidence, a key part of the new European arrest warrant.

Controversial among policy-making circles in Britain, because they tend to inflame fears about an emerging European 'superstate' run from Brussels, were the EU Commission's White Paper on European Governance (2001) and the deliberations of a Constitutional Convention, whose task was to draft a constitution for the EU by mid-2003. The latter was quickly labelled by opponents in the UK and in some other member states as a charter for a strong integrationist, even a federal model of EU development. The UK's official response was more muted. In February 2002, in a speech at The Hague, Jack Straw endorsed reform of EU institutions and procedures, but his gloss on the direction of change was to give priority to those aspects of reform most favoured by the UK. These included underlining the role of member states in the operation of the Community principle of **subsidiarity**, overcoming apathy among EU citizens, and reforming both the Council of the EU (made up of heads of national governments) and the Council of Ministers (of which there are currently sixteen, for example, in agriculture and finance). The Convention itself had a very wide remit: how to accommodate ten new members into the decision-making machinery of the Union, how to make the EU more democratic and open, and how to make the machinery of EU governance more efficient.

Straw's speech in February 2002, cautious on the use of the phrase 'EU constitution', nevertheless entertained the merit of a 'statement of principles, which would set out in plain language what the EU is for and how it can add value, and establishes clear lines between what the EU does and where the member states' responsibilities should lie'. When he made much the same plea at a meeting of business leaders in Scotland in August 2002, calling for a written constitution, or a 'basic rulebook', he was accused by his Conservative counterpart Michael Ancram of having 'caved in to the European integrationists, to the people who want to see full political union'. Ian Davidson, a **Eurosceptic** Labour MP, lamented the fact that Straw was really just 'trying to drum up support for the Euro'.

Until February 2003, the deliberations of the Constitutional Convention were hardly calculated to ruffle the surface of official and public opinion in the UK. Then, the first draft of the constitution, consisting of sixteen articles, was published by the Convention's presidium and immediately drew criticism from Peter Hain, a member of Blair's cabinet and one of the UK representatives on the Convention. The old spectre of a European super-state, so troubling to UK opinion, was revealed in the draft's first article which used the dread word 'federal' to describe the division of powers between the EU and its member states. Hain emphasised that there was no chance of a federal super-state being set up in Brussels, but Eurosceptics in the UK and elsewhere in the EU saw all the hallmarks of a Franco-German vision of European unity on display at a crucial point in the institutional development of the Union. By the autumn of 2003, New Labour were under some pressure from opponents of the draft constitution at home to hold a referendum on the subject. At the same time they faced similar pressure from some

Continental opinion in favour of the constitution, anxious that Blair should declare his European credentials. The rejection of the Constitutional Treaty by Dutch and French voters in 2005 now means that the project is on ice, probably for some years, thus sparing Mr Blair's blushes. As we have noted above, the initial fillip provided by this rejection to Britain's standing in the hierarchy of EU major powers may be short-lived.

Within British political parties there remain widely opposed, but also highly nuanced positions on Europe. Blair's own position on the EU is itself open to a variety of interpretations. Wanting to see Britain 'at the heart of Europe' now seems to mean operating outside the single currency. When Blair steps down as leader of the Labour Party, his heir apparent, Gordon Brown, is unlikely to countenance any flirtation with membership of the euro-zone, at least in the foreseeable future. This change, along with the demise of the constitutional treaty, has let Labour off the hook of holding a referendum on the single currency and of campaigning for a 'yes' vote it is likely to lose. Of course, Iraq apart, Mr Blair remains a pragmatist, and being more positive about EU constitutional reform and enthusiastic about enlargement always meant little while the British electorate remained hostile to monetary union and anxious about 'uncontrolled' immigration. In the meantime, at the 2001 general election, the Conservatives failed to talk up a storm about the dangers to national sovereignty posed by monetary union. Once *the* party of Europe, the European and especially the euro dispute splits the Tories, and the victory of Iain Duncan Smith in the leadership race put anti-Europeans firmly in charge of the party. Michael Howard was a root-and-branch opponent of joining a single currency and wanted to renegotiate the treaties which took Britain into Europe in the first place. On the constitution his views were robust. Howard told *The Times* newspaper on 29 April 2004 that 'we don't want to be a part of a country called Europe'. His successor, David Cameron, is not likely to depart from this mantra despite his modernising intent. Internal weaknesses in the Conservative Party over Europe meant that it had to play a cautious hand during the 2005 general election campaign just to offset the claim that its leadership was deeply divided on the single currency. While it tried to play a stronger hand over controlling immigration and combating crime, both valence issues for the electorate, its lack of unity on Europe did not play well on the hustings.

■ Sensitivity to globalisation

The EU dimension of British policy is itself part of the transnationalising of domestic politics and policy linked to the processes of globalisation (Krieger, 1999). Transnationalisation is apparent in the growing importance of transnational forces and actors in world politics. These include *transnational structures* of production and finance (MNCs and money markets), *transnational problems* such as terrorism, SARS, and global warming, which are outside the control of any one state, and *transnational organisations*, such the EU and the UN. These days no state in the mainstream of world politics and economics is immune from globalising processes. The transnationalisation of politics also refers to the extent to which 'domestic' actors now take regional and global matters as a significant frame of reference, affecting their behaviour and even their rationale for certain types of policy initiative.

As we have noted, states are more or less sensitive and vulnerable to global forces. In part this variability is explained by material factors such as economic strength or military capacity, but it is also affected by the secureness of national institutions and practices, by all manner of cultural legacies and by the vagaries of the domestic political agenda. In other words, the processes of globalisation do not simply write on states and societies as if they are blank pages. Yet much of the rhetoric on the relationships between states and globalising forces adopts one of two main positions. The first depicts states as losing out to irrevocable global economic forces; the second portrays them as resisting, or needing to resist, these same forces in the interests of national traditions of resource allocation and cultural autarky, though with varying prospects of success. In fact a third discourse has also informed the hackneyed debate about domination or resistance and, in the UK at least, provided a contested intellectual underpinning for a different sort of engagement with global forces. The so-called 'Third Way' is ostensibly a doctrine about social-democratic renewal, but at its core it is a coping strategy for a globalised world (Giddens, 1998, 2001).

Much ridiculed by 'old' Labourites and opponents on the right, the 'Third Way' is said to chart a path between the radical neo-liberalism of the 1980s under President Reagan and Margaret Thatcher and the **statist-corporatism** of postwar European social democracy. New Labour has set aside much of its own ideological past and has distanced itself from many social democratic parties on the Continent because it does not see the globalisation of financial markets, setting limits to welfare statism and the national race for competitiveness, simply as unwelcome constraints on the realisation of true social democracy. Instead, they are seen as salutary reminders of the need to 'modernise' entrenched economic and social structures and practices. Globalised money and capital markets mean that the scope for independent national monetary and fiscal policies, for macro-economic employment policy and other forms of government intervention in the economy, is much more circumscribed than during the 'golden era' of social democracy (1945–73). In other words – and this is critical to an understanding of the extent to which Third Way discourse transcends the language of domination or resistance – New Labour accepts globalisation as both a constraint *and* a resource. During Blair's second term of office and into his third term, this tenet is a cardinal element of New Labour's view of the world, but its translation into actual policies is not always pristine. We can illustrate the complexities of the interaction between the local and the global by reference to two key areas of policy – welfare provision and finance (including the EMU) – and some reflection on the ways in which the constraints of **Europeanisation** and globalisation result in a paradox for policy makers.

Erosion of the welfare state?

The welfare states built after the Second World War were intended to protect some aspects of economic life and some categories of people from the impact of market forces. For the most part this meant shielding the poor and other vulnerable groups in the population by providing benefits of various sorts, including security of income. It also meant pursuing full employment and investing in programmes of public health. Mainstream thinking on industrial policy allowed the business cycle to be regulated, encouraged cushioning of strategic industries and national champions from the harsher climates of competition, and advocated cooperative arrangements between employers and organised labour to promote wage stability. There was, of course, significant national variation in the ways in which these policies were applied, although the existence of a generic 'European social model' is often acknowledged. The broad aims of the postwar systems of welfare capitalism were to remove obstacles to the efficient functioning of markets but, crucially, to guard against and compensate for market failures.

In the UK before 1979 there was a large public sector and a great deal of state investment in major UK-based manufacturing enterprises, such as Rolls-Royce and Ferranti (an electronics and weapons systems manufacturer). Governments of both left and right periodically sought to control prices and incomes, and trade unions enjoyed important rights to immunity from civil damages in many trade disputes. However, the social and political conditions in which welfare states and managed economies were established have changed since the 1970s. International recessions early in the decade and later, in the 1980s, forced the Western industrial nations (then other parts of the world) to reassess some of the basic tenets of welfare nationalism. As we noted earlier (Table 2.2), during this period some national governments increased the level of public spending as a proportion of GDP. Nonetheless, it became routine to blame the social model for at least some of the economic difficulties besetting countries like the UK. Labour market regulation was blamed for restricting the efficient use of labour, the high social charges of social protection were blamed for making businesses uncompetitive and stifling the entrepreneurial spirit, and high public spending was charged with precipitating fiscal crises and fuelling inflation. To make matters worse the 1970s were years of 'stagflation', that is, the phenomenon of economic stagnation and rising unemployment, coupled with rising inflation. Previously, **Keynesian** thinking had it that serious inflation was something that only happened to immature economies and that judicious state intervention could promote both growth and social justice.

Keynesian economic policies that accorded priority to growth and full employment were now seen as profligate and likely to lose the confidence of financial markets, leading to a massive exodus of capital. In 1976, a crisis produced by government spending promises and a slide in the value of sterling on the money markets saw the IMF impose a deal on the Labour government of Harold Wilson. It is possible that the Labour government was not too reluctant to accept this deal, as it made the introduction of harsh policies seem to be the outcome of pressures from external forces. Indeed a promise of cuts in government spending signalled a shift in the direction of national policy, from investment in public and social services and full employment to tighter controls on public expenditure and inflation. While 'crises' with a remarkably similar script were not uncommon, 1976 was symbolic of the shift to an era when it was becoming unacceptable for British governments to increase spending if this unbalanced the budget. Raising taxes as a way of achieving balance also became suspect, as this caused capital to flee the country and unsettled the financial markets.

In an attempt to make the economy competitive, since the late 1970s UK governments have adopted strategies that are much more market led. These include the reduction of taxation as a goal of public policy, greater flexibility in labour markets, the removal through deregulation of various obstacles to competition, and a commitment to reducing the size of the public sector. Over taxation, at any rate, the gap between intention and implementation has widened under both the Major and Blair governments, both of which increased the weight of indirect taxation. Under Gordon Brown's direction the burden of direct taxes has also gone up, a progressive strategy seen by some commentators as giving the lie to his espousal of free market economics. Governments have also placed great weight on the need for the acquisition of skills and training relevant to an enterprise culture in a global economy. In this sea-change, the Conservative Party under Margaret Thatcher was the driving force, embracing the disciplines of the market, where the Labour governments of Wilson and Callaghan had been reluctant converts to limiting government spending and controlling the money supply.

Under Thatcher, the rhetoric of the global marketplace flourished and became a canon of economic policy. In the midst of these changes, basic welfare provisions remained or were subject to only limited 'rollback'. At the same time, data for the 1980s show that all of the countries that adopted neo-liberal formulas experienced deepening inequality and rising poverty. In the UK, between 1980 and 1990, earnings in the lowest decile of the workforce lost ground relative to the median by some 14 per cent. There was also a substantial rise in what has become known as 'child poverty', because of the low earning capacity of many single-parent families and the limited, but real, decline in some state benefits. During this period, the Labour Party adopted its radical *alternative economic strategy* but remained unelected and, on some accounts, unelectable. In its guise as New Labour, the party in government after 1997 has sought a notional 'third way', a means of 'combining economic dynamism with social justice in the modern world', as Mr Blair said at a dinner in The Hague in 1998.

New Labour is as committed to an open economy as were the Conservatives. Its preferred methods – fighting inflation, trying to ensure macro-economic stability in part through control of the money supply, and relaxing controls on financial markets and the movement of capital – are classic neo-liberal tenets. It is also attempting to address what are known as 'supply-side' weaknesses in the UK economy through skills training, education reform, technology developments and reviews of the transport infrastructure. In the broadest sense of the term, Tony Blair is keen to make Britons employable in what he now sees as a global economy. At the same time, the government has been engaged in a modest reinvestment in social protection, including:

- increasing public sector spending on health and education;

- the restoration of some rights for trade unionists;

- the establishment of a national minimum wage;

- a modest redistribution of wealth through charges levied on the 'better-off' for university education and changes to the rates of National Insurance;

- the adoption of the European Social Chapter;

- passing a Human Rights Act; and

- means testing applied to a system of tax credits for the less well-off.

For some observers these measures pit New Labour policies against the received global wisdom from bodies like the IMF, whose recipe for good governance is still profoundly neo-liberal. Instead of the Thatcherite mantra that macro-economic parsimony will produce 'trickle down' social benefits, New Labour's stance intimates a renewed flirtation with state-sponsored capitalism, or perhaps a form of 'globalisation with a human face'. However, we must be cautious about such interpretations, since in Mr Blair's own words, such measures still leave the UK 'the most lightly regulated labour market of any leading economy in the world'. But this claim tells only one side of the story, since business leaders in the UK continue to bemoan the stricter regulatory regimes imposed by the Labour government and by Brussels in areas such as the length of the working week and maternity leave. As if to

reaffirm his longer-term commitment to free markets, in February 2002 Blair and right-wing Italian prime minister Silvio Berlusconi declared an 'absolute convergence' of views on the need to achieve genuine structural reform of the EU economy by introducing greater flexibility of labour markets and opening up relatively closed national markets in energy to Europe-wide competition. These declarations look somewhat threadbare when judged by the course of subsequent events. In 2006, sharp increases in fuel prices in the UK were partly caused by the failure of some other EU countries to deregulate their energy markets to allow energy suppliers to engage in price fixing.

Before the 1997 general election, New Labour said that if elected it would abide by Tory spending plans. So, despite presiding over an expanding economy, Mr Blair's first administration (1997–2001) was extremely parsimonious. Total public spending, as a proportion of national income, was lower than it had been under either Major or Thatcher. But at the outset of Blair's second term in office, Chancellor Gordon Brown's April 2002 budget promised significant rises in welfare spending, including an additional $6.1bn from April 2003 for the NHS and $2.5bn extra support for families. As we have noted (Table 2.2), by 2004 these increases left the overall level of public spending slightly higher than the average for the Thatcher years. Despite his continued adherence to a policy of monetary prudence based on healthy public finances and buoyant tax revenues, a downturn in British manufacturing output in the summer and autumn of 2002 and the global erosion of the recent stock market boom left Brown's big budget 'giveaway', as some commentators dubbed it, exposed.

Elements of a worst-case scenario were apparent in 2004 and it still appeared valid at the end of 2005 when the Chancellor was forced to amend his optimistic statement about growth in the economy, made in November 2004. Instead of growth in the region of 3–3.5 per cent, Brown lowered his forecast for 2005–6 to a relatively miserly but still respectable 1.75 per cent. Lower growth than expected and increased public expenditure funded out of increased direct taxes and a growing body of indirect (stealth) taxes, as well as through borrowing, are all hallmarks of the kind of 'crises' that dogged the British economy in the 1970s. By the summer of 2002, the financial institutions and markets were still willing to believe that Gordon Brown was being sufficiently prudent to sustain their belief in him. A report by the Organisation for Economic Co-operation and Development (OECD) in 2002 noted that 'while sound monetary and fiscal policies have contributed to greater macroeconomic stability, and should continue to do so, . . . some deep-seated structural problems remain to be settled. It is important for . . . policy to succeed in enhancing human capital and work incentives, raising competitive pressures and improving public infrastructure'. Early in 2003, the Institute for Fiscal Studies predicted that taxes would have to rise by £11 billion to allow Brown to stay within his own rule about borrowing only to fund investment. In the same week the European Commission also warned that the impending British budget deficit may well exceed its own rule for prudent economic management and climb above 3 per cent of GDP. By the autumn of 2003, Britain looked stronger than many of its EU partners on key economic indicators, but hardly on track to stay within borrowing limits or to halt the rise in the tax burden on individuals and corporations.

In 2006, the economy still looked much more buoyant than many of its European rivals, but growing costs and shrinking tax revenues now hamper Gordon Brown's vision for the continuing reform of public services, particularly the Health Service, education, and the alleviation of child poverty. Speaking to the International Monetary Fund (IMF) in September 2005, the Chancellor signalled a slowdown in the UK economy, but blamed this on oil price increases and generally slow growth in Europe and the world economy. While this may be true in part, the problem for the government is that the slowdown has coincided with a number of other problems. These include the reduced extent of the government's borrowing capacity in order to stay within the Chancellor's self-imposed 'golden rule' that borrowing should only fund investment and not subvent day-to-day or current spending, a budget deficit of 3.2 per cent in the previous fiscal year, and the sheer cost of the ambitious social programmes in train. More radical redistributive changes would certainly run counter to free-market ideology, and will require redistribution through the tax system at a time when the boom years of increasing revenue are coming to an end. At the same time, a Labour government under Blair or Brown looking to cut back on public spending by imposing job cuts in the public sector (for example, the 40,000 jobs cut in the Civil Service bruited by the Chancellor in 2005) may well trigger a resurgence in confrontational trade union politics that many thought buried by Thatcherite reforms and the changed nature of the global economy.

Global finance

From the end of the Second World War up to the early 1970s the economic system of the Western world was based on the Bretton Woods agreement. In July 1944, as the war was drawing to a close, the world's leading politicians – mostly from northern countries – met in conference to reorganise the world economy. The Conference opted for a system based on the free movement of capital and goods with the US dollar as the international currency. By the late 1960s, the Bretton Woods dream of a stable monetary system of fixed exchange rates with the US dollar as the only international currency was collapsing under the strain of US trade and budgetary deficits. In the early 1970s, British governments of both main parties jumped on board the roller-coaster of floating exchange rates, borrowing heavily to finance expenditure on the welfare state, letting sterling fall in value to stimulate exports and pegging interest rates as low as possible. Such moves only served to mask the UK's deterioration in the world economy. Eventually, rising inflation and loss of foreign reserves pushed the government into the arms of the IMF in 1976.

The increased openness and vulnerability of the British economy to the global economy after 1976 required national government to exercise fiscal prudence and to control inflation, in earnest with their neo-liberal credentials. In October 1979, the new Conservative government abolished exchange controls, just as the USA had done. The boost to inward investment encouraged Mrs Thatcher to support the Single European Act in 1985 in the expectation that this trend would continue. Once exchange controls had been abandoned in 1979, government efforts were directed at encouraging both inward and outward investment and accepting (at least in principle) the policy constraints imposed by the financial markets. In practice, in the mid- to late 1980s, the Conservatives pushed ahead with expansion of the economy and cuts in income tax, showing a blithe disregard for the ways in which the markets would react. The upshot was a growing balance of payments deficit and high inflation. By the autumn of 1990 the government was presiding over an overheated economy moving into recession, an exchange rate that was unsustainably high and a loss of confidence in sterling.

To counteract these debilitating factors and to ease pressure from the markets by stabilising sterling, Mrs Thatcher took Britain into the Exchange Rate Mechanism (ERM), a device which linked the exchange rates of the currencies of all participating member states in the EC to each other and to the European Currency Unit (ECU). The ERM was a mechanism of the European Monetary System (EMS), which was set up in 1979 as the basis on which to build monetary cooperation and eventual monetary union in the EC. The UK (along with Spain and later Portugal) was allowed a margin of fluctuation of up to 6 per cent above or below the central rate. The underlying rationale of the ERM was that, if currencies reached their tolerances, the central banks of other member states would intervene to support them. By 1992, under the premiership of John Major, the bankruptcy of this policy and the fragility of British membership was exposed owing to massive instabilities in the currency markets and heavy speculative activity against some of the weaker currencies. On 'Black Wednesday', 16 September 1992, the UK suspended its membership of the ERM and allowed sterling to float. Italy followed suit on 17 September. In response to all these movements of 'hot money', members of the ERM had already agreed on 2 August 1992 to widen the bands within which currencies could float, to plus or minus 15 per cent.

Since then, governments in the UK have pursued policies intended to please the markets. These involve tight control over inflation, with a preference for monetary policy (manipulating interest rates and money supply) rather than fiscal policy (taxation) as the means to achieve this end. In this respect the Major and Blair governments have been at one, although, as we have noted, both have increased the overall burden of taxation. In fact the success of these measures in removing the sobriquet 'sick man of Europe' from the UK was contingent on factors beyond the direct control of the government. Chief among these were the strength of the US dollar between 1995 and 2000 and Britain's more favourable position in the economic cycle relative to rivals Germany and Japan. Conditions in 2002, especially with regard to the continued health of the American economy, were less propitious, but on some indicators the UK appeared to have weathered the global recession in train for some 18 months and exacerbated by September 11th. In the face of less flattering judgements about the soundness of his economic strategy, Mr Brown remained bullish. Speaking to the Social Market Foundation on 3 February 2003, he again argued that the 'fundamentals' of British economic management remained sound and that the UK economy 'is better placed than we have been in the past to deal with economic shocks . . . and the ongoing risks to the global recovery'. As we have already noted above, this optimism took something of a knock during 2005.

New Labour's claim to be financially prudent was accompanied by a minor revolution carried out by Tony Blair and his Chancellor of the Exchequer, Gordon Brown, that went beyond the Thatcherite mission simply to roll back the state in the area of macro-economic management. Early in the new administration's first term, the Bank of England was given operational freedom to set interest rates, a clear sign to global markets that the government intended to stick to the anti-inflationary core of its economic policy. On almost all accounts this reform has been a success. For some commentators, however, the change was a clear indication that Britain was willing to join European monetary union sooner rather than later. Events have given the lie to this prediction.

Britain and the EMU

The decision to join or not to join the process of Economic and Monetary Union (EMU) in Europe once again reveals the tensions in UK–EU relationships, because monetary powers are seen as central to a state's independence and authority. It also highlights some of the ways in which regional and global trends in finance are influencing national policy-making arrangements. Finally, the process offers pointers to the repositioning of the main political parties and other actors in what it is increasingly hard to call domestic politics.

In ratifying the Maastricht Treaty on European Union during 1992–3, most member states of the EU committed themselves to the 'irrevocable' locking together of their currencies from 1 January 1999 in line with the EU's convergence criteria. Britain, Denmark, Sweden and, initially, Greece were not among the first tranche of countries to create what has become known in the UK as 'Euroland' (Figure 2.3), but, of the then fifteen member states, only the UK and Denmark have not committed themselves to joining as soon as possible. Greece was admitted in time for the official launch of the new currency in January 2002. In September 2003, Sweden held a referendum on membership of the EU currency and rejected the proposal to join by 56 per cent of the votes cast to 42 per cent.

The Maastricht Treaty provides the legal underpinning for EMU and identified three main stages through which the goal of monetary union would be achieved. The first, already in train when member states met at Maastricht in December 1991, concerned the free movement of capital; the second, starting on 1 January 1994, dealt with preparations for the single currency, including the creation of a European Monetary Institute, to be dissolved in the third stage, and certain convergence criteria against which potential members could be judged. These criteria, still in operation, are:

■ The annual government budget deficit must not exceed 3 per cent of GDP.

■ Total outstanding government debt must not exceed 60 per cent of GDP.

■ The rate of inflation must fall within 1.5 per cent of the three best-performing EU countries.

■ The average nominal long-term interest rate must be within 2 per cent of the average rate in the three EU countries with the lowest inflation.

■ Exchange rate stability, meaning that for at least two years the country concerned has kept within the 'normal' fluctuation margins of the ERM.

The third stage, beginning on 1 January 1999, established an independent European Central Bank and formally introduced the single currency (the euro). Euro banknotes and coins were introduced in 2002, when they replaced the national variety.

The policy of the Blair government was and remains to prepare to join the EMU, subject to five economic tests announced in October 1997. These tests are intended to judge membership in relation to whether it is good for jobs, trade, investment and industry in Britain. The tests are:

■ sustainable convergence between Britain and the economies of a single currency;

■ whether there is sufficient flexibility to cope with economic change;

■ the effect of entry on investment in the UK;

■ the impact on British financial services;

■ whether entry is good for employment in the UK.

In a speech delivered on 14 October 1999 at the launch of the pro-euro 'Britain in Europe' campaign, the Prime Minister reiterated his European sympathies but, with an eye on public opinion, stated only that he 'would not rule out' British membership of EMU. On 6 June 2001, in an interview with the *Sun* newspaper, he said that 'even if it (going into the euro) is unpopular, I will recommend it if it is the right thing to do'. The government sees some possible economic obstacles to membership, and some political hurdles to overcome, but no constitutional barrier to participating. It is committed, or apparently so, to holding a referendum on the subject of entry, but by autumn 2003 the date had not been fixed. An earlier commitment to pronounce on the five tests no more than two years into the new parliament (June 2003) put some pressure on the government to name the date for the referendum and formulate the question. On 12 December 2002, in response to a parliamentary question, Mr Blair reiterated that there would be no referendum until the five tests had been passed. In reality, British public opinion is deeply divided about the merits of a single currency, with a majority against entry but with some signs of growing acceptance of or aquiescence in eventual British membership. At this time a public campaign on the published question would probably have entrenched the anti-vote and the government's stance on a referendum was always tempered by this knowledge. Meanwhile it was estimated by the market intelligence agency Mintel in 2003 that more than 50 per cent of Britain's leading retailers have already accepted or will soon accept the euro, perhaps acclimatising the public to its use.

In opposition, the Conservative Party, fractured by feuds over Europe, opposes a decision to join EMU on both economic and constitutional grounds, either in the current parliament or in the next. Although William Hague was agnostic on never joining the single currency, under its next leader, Iain Duncan Smith, even the get-out clause 'a decision to join is not ruled out' was, well, ruled out. Under Michael Howard there was a softening of the tone, if not the policies of the party, aimed at downplaying the Thatcherite legacy in the run-up to a general election. At a speech in Berlin in February 2004, he told his audience that the Community should be more flexible and less interfering in the affairs of member states and that it should abandon plans for its own constitution. Britain, he said, might never join the single currency.

Control of money has always been closely linked with national sovereignty, but, as we have suggested above, sovereignty over monetary policy is quite

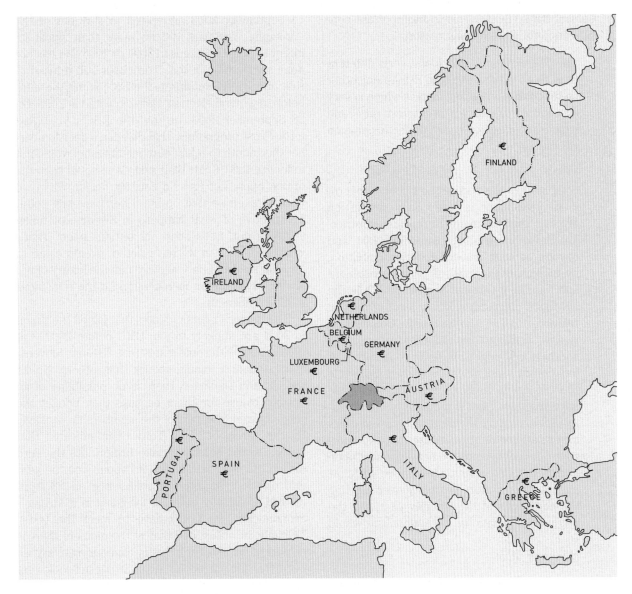

Figure 2.3 Euroland on 1 January 2005

limited in an era of global finance. Indeed, one of the underlying justifications for EMU is that in recent years it has become less possible to exercise national power over monetary policy. That said, political debate within the UK still rehearses familiar arguments about looking for some more 'natural' grouping through which to manage currency issues, such as the G7 group of leading industrial and trading nations. The arguments for joining EMU turn on the extent to which the UK would be marginalised in EU decision making if it stayed out and pushed into the second rank of European states. At the same time, it may be that the UK is still a big enough economy in world terms to chance its arm and stay outside.

The complexity of economic arguments about the merits of entry is daunting. Mr Brown's five tests are clearly important, though hard to quantify and thus to take seriously as objective measures in what is, after all, as much a political judgement as an economic one. But economic considerations are important. In addition to Brown's criteria are the convergence rules laid down by the EU itself for entry to the euro – its stability and growth pact. These also raise some problems for the UK economy. A number of issues arise:

■ Could the UK economy prosper under the 'one size fits all' interest rate set by the European

Central Bank (ECB)? This is an important consideration for the following reasons:

- The UK economy still looks very different from those in the rest of the EU. Among other factors, it has a housing market which is very susceptible to changes in interest rates and which might suffer badly under a common EU rate.

- Britain's public infrastructure is still poor compared to the rest of the EU and government investment is lower as a proportion of GDP than in many European countries. Mr Brown's spending plans for 2004 and beyond at least ameliorated this condition, by increasing the level of public investment and funding it through borrowing. While the UK has a comparatively low level of debt in relation to GDP, the European Commission is now insisting that countries reduce debt and balance budgets, in order to ensure that inflationary tendencies are curbed. So, while the UK needs higher investment in public infrastructures (and is required by the stability pact to produce them), the EU also counsels lower national debt to ensure that the euro-zone does not become too heavily reliant upon borrowing. One solution would be to allow member states more flexibility over meeting the conditions of the stability pact, but the argument for national exceptionalism would seem to undermine the whole rationale for monetary union.

In addition to the five tests, the UK Treasury commissioned eighteen supplementary studies to investigate the impact on the British economy of joining the euro. These included its impact on prices and a comparision between the UK housing market and those in the rest of Europe. In February 2003, Brown was rumoured to be set against British entry and ready to pronounce on the five tests as early as his main budget statement in March (actually postponed until April). On 9 June 2003 the government published the assessment of the five economic tests, the eighteen supporting studies and the third outline national changeover plan.

This assessment counselled a 'not yet' verdict on the tests. Even without the cautious tone of the studies, some flexibility was available to Mr Blair. Denmark still had to put the issue to its people. As we noted above, Sweden held a referendum on 14 September 2003 and voted to stay out of the euro-zone. Denmark did no more than signal its intent to poll its citizens in 2004 or 2005 and has not done so. Despite all this, Tony Blair still refused to rule out a referendum on the UK joining the euro before a general election, then expected in 2005. On 28 September 2003, he told the BBC's *Breakfast with Frost* programme that Sweden's decision earlier this month to reject euro membership would not influence the UK. Mr Blair said: 'We should keep the option open. Let us as a country decide when we want to exercise that option. I don't see any point, irrespective of what happens in Sweden, of ruling anything out. Let's keep our options open. That's what we'll do.' As we have noted, events came to Mr Blair's aid and have allowed him the luxury of not having to decide on membership for the remainder of his premiership.

The ten new member states that joined the Union in 2004 are unlikely to join EMU before 2007–8 at the earliest, with some states (e.g. Estonia, Slovenia and Lithuania) joining sooner than others. Unlike the UK and Denmark, there is no possibility of an opt-out clause for them because they bought the single currency as part of the membership package. By the spring of 2005, Tony Blair indicated that Labour would not try to take Britain into the euro during the next parliament, if Labour won the general election. At a press conference on 28 April he said 'Politically the case for going in is strong – economically we (still) have to meet the tests.' Tellingly, he also stated that 'at the moment there is no part of business or industry clamouring to say we need this for our economy, so it doesn't look very likely.' Moreover, the general tone of comment about the euro economies is that they remain uncompetitive, even stagnating. Dissatisfaction with economic performance undoubtedly affected the outcome of the Dutch and French referendums on the EU Constitutional Treaty, and (admittedly anecdotal) evidence from some leading politicians in Germany and Italy suggests a root-and-branch disillusion with euro membership.

Of course, for many people in the UK, the biggest question about the euro is not economic gain or loss, or the threat of isolation, but whether it will lead to fiscal union and then full political union. A single European currency will probably encourage a European economy that is at least as integrated as national economies are now, but there remains a large element of uncertainty about whether it will be successful. The prospects for the euro being no

Britain

Britain and the euro
Fit to join?

Europe's fiscal straightjacket: How difficult will it be for Britain to squeeze into Europe's fiscal straightjacket in order to join the euro?
Source: Copyright © David Simonds. From *The Economist*, 7 February 2002

more than a 'soft' currency in world terms, and subject to the same sorts of speculation it was designed to inhibit, remain extant more than three years after its introduction. Early signs remain difficult to read. Over the three months up to June 2002 sterling weakened against the euro in the foreign exchange markets, and the latter achieved near parity with the US dollar. Both sterling and the dollar have strengthened against the euro in 2004 and 2005, more obviously since the decision of the European Central Bank in late 2005 to cut interest rates in the euro-zone. Of course, a strong pound is also a barrier to UK entry to the single currency, making British exports less competitive. By weakening against the euro, the exchange rate[1] appears to make entry viable as it would not damage exports nor fuel inflation.

In the absence of any mitigation for national circumstances or traditions, it is not clear how far monetary union will necessitate closer integration in other matters deemed critical to national autonomy and sovereignty. When the UK government passed the Bank of England Act 1998, which gave the Bank independent powers to set interest rates, this was widely interpreted as paving the way for EMU. But in a world of deregulated currency markets and

[1] 1.53 euros to the pound in June 2002, 1.47 in December 2005. To monitor changes visit: http://newsvote.bbc.co.uk/1/shared/fds/hi/business/market_data/overview/.

global financial flows, both governments and central banks have relatively little influence, although they can affect the climate in which changes take place. The creation of independent central banks is symptomatic of this era of global finance, because they are seen usually as the guardians of financial probity and committed to low inflation. For the financial markets, banks are more likely to preach the disciplines of the market than are politicians. While the Bank of England Act looked like a prelude to membership of EMU, the independence of central banks is in accord with the ethos of globalisation. At the same time, the deepening of economic integration which is at the heart of monetary union, and the deflationary impetus derived from it, are peculiarly European constraints on national autonomy, although still ones that are hard to separate from the impact of global processes and global dogmas about sound national economic management.

In the midst of very technical discussions about EMU, other issues contribute to a richer politics of monetary union and Europeanisation. These issues include whether the European Central Bank can be held accountable, the fight to avoid relegating key items on the national political agenda, such as social protection, to the status of mere 'technical' data, and the impact of shared sovereignty on the decision-making autonomy and political culture of the UK. In the absence of British membership of EMU it is wrong to speculate too much on future constellations of politics in the UK. However, strains within political parties over EMU may yet result in new cross-party groupings, and in a fully integrated European economy and an EU with a constitution there may well be transnational political parties and interest groups: perhaps a truly Europe-wide public. The neo-liberal agenda which has dominated UK politics and policy for two decades continues as a major constraint on policy makers. As we have noted, it is reflected too in the EU's 'Stability and Growth Pact' which acts as a benchmark for potential members of EMU. Regionalisation and globalisation now inform the very core of British political life.

Paradoxes in British visions of Europe and the World

As David Marquand (1998) has said, like the Thatcher and Major governments before it, New Labour still looks across the Atlantic for much of its inspiration, not across the Channel. 'Its rhetoric is American; the intellectual influences which have shaped its project are American; its political style is American' (Marquand, 1998, p. 2). The Iraq crisis brought these sentiments into sharp focus. With the possible exception of Guantanamo, Tony Blair is convinced that any moral high ground visible in this issue is occupied by the USA. In a speech to British ambassadors in January 2003, he noted that Britain would support the Americans over Iraq, not because the UK is a client state of the US, but because America is right. In the protracted and difficult aftermath to the war, he remains convinced of this position and reiterated his conviction to the Party's annual conference in October 2003. Grass-roots opinion in his own party and sections of the Parliamentary Labour Party begged to differ. The revolt of 139 members of the Parliamentary Labour Party in the 18 March 2003 Commons division on the legitimacy of war in Iraq was significant because of its size, but more so in that it offered the first serious challenge to Blair's world-view.

On a broader canvas, New Labour still endorses the prevailing American view of the global economy, which is highly contested in some respects in the middle of the first decade of the new millennium. Like Bill Clinton's New Democrats, New Labour takes globalisation as a given and is concerned to be an active player in the global marketplace. And that is why, says Marquand, it remains suspicious of the European social model, sharing its predecessor's commitment to flexible labour markets and low social costs, and why it sees other European social democrats as off-message. Changes in the leadership of the party are unlikely to affect this world-view. When Gordon Brown and other government luminaries, including the then Foreign Secretary Jack Straw, spoke in the run-up to Britain taking over the EU presidency and the Chair of the G7 and G8, the burden of their messages was to criticise EU economies for their long-term inattention to prudent economic management, affordable welfare and general flexibility and competitiveness and their failure to curb rising unemployment.

Of course, Tony Blair still takes the European Union as a given, and looks to influence the pattern of European integration, including monetary integration. New Labour under Gordon Brown or Britain under a Conservative government led by David Cameron may well take a more jaundiced view of the European project. But the paradox for all of them is that part of the rationale of the EU is to Europeanise – an elastic term but here taken to mean underwriting a solidaristic model of society and economy,

drawn partly from the European social democratic tradition and partly from strains of Catholic social thought. As we have noted above, there may be signs that the elusive convergence between British and Continental patterns of social provision may be taking place as the result of the pressures created by EMU, so that a kind of globalised practice is achieved almost by default. If this argument carries any weight, the failure of the EU constitution and the budget crisis played out at the end of 2005 could be seen as part of a necessary catharsis in the development of the Union and its model of regional integration. Such a catharsis may have the effect of producing a more globalised (market-orientated) Europe rather than strengthen the solidaristic model based upon European exceptionalism. None of these outcomes is certain. By early 2006, evidence of 'economic patriotism' by France with regard to attempts to block 'foreign' takeovers of key French industries, including the food company Danone, seems to place the UK in the unusual role of being the champion of the European Commission's policy of freeing up the internal market in Europe. With Poland siding with France, and the Netherlands with the UK, new alignments on core EU policy areas are emerging.

At the same time, part of the purpose of monetary union is to defend the older European social model against the pressures of the global marketplace, to create a supranational space in which to protect the European social market from creeping Americanisation and globalisation. Of course, for some Europeanists in the UK, the main purpose of monetary union is not to protect against but to facilitate globalisation, regional integration being seen as a facet of a dynamic global political economy. The upshot is that New Labour is in something of a quandary. It endorses much of the American worldview (not least in its desire to entrench a Western model of international security), and it is also wooed by aspects of integrationist Europe (though it avoids such language, having preferred a studied equivocation over EMU). It is also strung out on the vagaries of UK public opinion and the (remote) possibility that various opposition forces will be able to talk up issues of national autonomy and even sovereignty into an electoral barnstorm. Following the 18 March 2003 revolt, it must also recognise that anti-Americanists, anti-globalists and the rump of 'old' Labour in the Commons will work to undermine the modernising credo central to 'new' Labour's identity. In public, senior British politicians continue to use the metaphor of the link or the bridge to summarise the role of the UK in Euro–Atlantic relations. Thus, Gordon Brown on 5 November 2001 noted that: 'We in Britain do not have to choose – as some would suggest – between America and Europe, but are instead well positioned as a vital link between America and Europe.' In early 2006, with the recon-struction of Iraq still in difficulties and some European partners aghast at Britain's attempts to redirect Europe's future, that aim looks more necessary than ever, but somewhat harder to deliver, despite the less francophile demeanour of Germany's new Chancellor, Angela Merkel.

BOX 2.2	BRITAIN IN CONTEXT

How globalised is the UK?

This is a difficult question to answer because it assumes a number of things. First, that complex processes of globalisation are measurable; second, that indicators of the extent and intensity of globalisation can be agreed, and finally that reliable comparative data exist on the basis of which we can say that Britain is more or less globalised than Morocco, Thailand or the Republic of Ireland. As we shall see there are serious attempts to measure the extent and depth of globalisation on a country by country basis, but that does not mean we can generate a detailed and subtle picture of how globalisation processes affect a particular country and its people. All indexes of globalisation should be treated as useful, but often rather simple devices to capture complex processes.

Nor is this just a problem of what to measure and how to measure it. It is also a matter of understanding the nature and extent of what might be called 'global consciousness', or the ways in which various sectors of the British population, as well as individuals, experience and evaluate globalisation. This is not an easy task. British people are 'conscious' or aware of globalisation to varying degrees. When they are aware, just how they evaluate its impact on them as individuals and on the UK may differ markedly with age, political persuasion, sense of job security, as well as a host of other factors. It is unlikely, though not impossible, that networks of young people in higher education, business and the professions feel the same way about globalisation as those who are elderly, dependent and poorly educated. Even where all kinds of people enjoy 'global' products of one sort or another (some movies and music, food, intercontinental travel) just how this fare impinges upon their lives and outlook cannot be read off from a list of what they consume. Even protestors set on 'resisting' globalisation may be agitated about different facets of the phenomenon.

With these health warnings in mind consider these data from the *A.T. Kearney/Foreign Policy Globalization Index* (published 2005 using 2003 data). You may also wish to look at the *Globalisation Index* constructed by the Centre for the Study of Globalisation and Regionalisation (CSGR) at the University of Warwick in the UK and the *UNDP Human Development Index* (HDI). Each index uses a slightly different methodology to achieve its scores. The result is that on the Foreign Policy Index, the UK is listed as the 12th most globalised country in the world, the same as in the previous year, while data from Warwick for the two pevious years has it ranked 6th. On the Foreign Policy index Singapore tops the league, with Britain's near neighbour, the Republic of Ireland, coming in a close second. Morocco and Thailand are 40th and 46th respectively. China, touted as the coming global power of the 21st century, at present ranks only 54th, despite its massive growth in GDP of 9.1% in 2003 and 8% in 2002.

The Index is constructed by gathering data on a number of variables or dimensions. These are economic, personal contacts, technological and political. Each dimension yields a number of items, so that *economic integration* includes trade and foreign direct investment; *personal contact* covers telephone contact, travel and financial remittances from one country to another; *technological* refers to the number of internet users, internet hosts and secure servers, while *political* embraces membership in international organisations, contributions to UN peacekeeping forces, ratification of international treaties and government transfers between states. Numerical values are assigned to each item to determine country rankings and averages are used to give an overall globalisation index.

The UK is more globalised in some areas than in others. Overall it ranks 5th for political engagement, but only 32nd for degree of economic integration. Go deeper into the data and it is 12th for personal internet connections, but just 45th for trade and 20th for foreign direct investment.

The relationships between being more-or-less open to globalisation and other factors is also hard to assess. On the face of it 'globalised' countries such as the UK, with relatively open borders, sophisticated communication networks and cultural and legal traditions which respect dissent and individual liberties might appear more vulnerable to terrorist attacks than those less open to the world. In fact comparing the Foreign Policy Index with the U.S State Department's 'Patterns of Global Terrorism' for 2003, reveals that countries strongly integrated with the wider world were no more likely to suffer attacks than those with many fewer links. Clearly, such patterns may be modified in a short space of time by a small number of dramatic events such as occurred on the London Underground in July 2005.

■ Conclusion

For much of the past 200 years the United Kingdom has been involved in global matters, principally because of economic factors but also through its status as a colonial power and key player in global geo-politics. Even during those periods when certain anti-global or protectionist sentiments characterised domestic politics, for example between 1914 and the late 1970s, Britain never ceased to be deeply involved in the global economy and embroiled in regional and global conflicts. Over this period the language or discourse of what we now call globalisation has informed much of national policy and been the context for a good deal of domestic politics. This includes both the 'high' politics of international diplomacy and the 'low' politics constituted by party conflict, organised interests and, occasionally, public opinion. It is accurate to say that, over the whole period, Britain has declined as a global power, so that at the beginning of the new millennium it is largely shorn of the trappings of greatness, though still a player on the world stage. As a key part of the 'coalition of the willing' which carried the war against Saddam Hussein, Britain again occupies a highly visible, if uncomfortable, position on the world stage. So the UK is not a clear-cut example of an allegedly modal phenomenon – the demise of the nation-state – but it demonstrates many of the pressures now visited on states. All nation-states have been weakened by the forces of globalisation and some forms of regionalisation, but they are far from demise. Rather, there is a long-term transformation of the political architecture of world politics, in which states continue as important actors in a rich weave of formal and informal organisations, local, national, international and transnational. It follows from what we have said above that an awareness of and accommodation to global constraints has been an enduring feature of UK politics over the years, and that while these constraints seem to be intensifying, rather than the opposite, their impact on individual states is variable. As the official Foreign Office website notes, '. . . today's world is a small place. What happens across the globe can directly affect the lives of every one of us in Britain.' While this is true, this chapter has revealed that from the standpoint of national experience there are many globalisations and many ways of interpreting them.

Chapter summary

- The UK was a global power for much of the last 200 years.
- Globalisation has been a major feature of British policy and political debate for all of this period, and in the last thirty years its significance has been on the increase.
- Britain's engagement with the global political economy can be conveniently periodised into hegemonic stability, post-hegemonic instability, bi-polar stability, and multi-polar flux.

- Periods of *laissez-faire* liberalism and global neo-liberalism have been separated by interludes of national protectionism, but openness to the world economy has been an underlying theme.
- After the Second World War, Britain, a much diminished power, still clung to a global role through empire and was firmly Atlanticist rather than European. Trying to behave as a link between Europe and America produces an element of policy ambiguity and confused identity.
- Grudging engagement with European integration has introduced an important regional dimension to British politics, the parameters of which are still emerging.
- Global and regional constraints have had impacts on welfare policy and on financial policy.
- The EMU process exemplifies many of the issues about national autonomy and sovereignty that lie at the heart of debate on globalisation.

Discussion points

- Is globalisation a process that affects you? For example, could you name any global factors which influence the way you, or people like you, live?

- Thinking about the impact of globalisation upon the UK, what sort of advantages and disadvantages are apparent? How would you weigh the balance?

- Do you think that Britain made the right choice in the early postwar years in giving European integration a low priority?

- Will regional and global pressures eventually push the UK into membership of EMU, or is there still room for manoeuvre?

- Would staying out of EMU be a good or a bad thing?

- Does Britain have to choose between Europe and America?

- In what ways do you see British domestic politics changing because of European and global pressures?

Further reading

Gamble, A. (2003) *Between Europe and America: The Future of British Politics* (Palgrave). An informed and readable account of the ways in which domestic politics have to be understood in the light of geo-strategic considerations.

Giddens, A. (1998) *The Third Way* (Polity Press). Much discussed and much criticised volume from 'Tony Blair's favourite guru' on the meaning of the Third Way.

Hirst, P. and Thompson, G. (1999) *Globalization in Question*, 2nd edn (Polity Press). An iconoclastic account of the misuse of the concept of globalisation, in which the authors contend that nation-states remain key actors in global politics and economics.

Kennedy, P. (1988) *The Rise and Fall of the Great Powers* (Fontana). An account of the factors contributing to the rise and fall of the Great Powers since 1500. A book which had a great impact in academic and governmental circles on both sides of the Atlantic.

Krieger, J. (1999) *Britain in the Global Age* (Polity Press). A case for the renewal of social democracy in an age of intense globalisation.

Young, J.W. and Kent, J. (2003) *International Relations Since 1945: a Global History* (Oxford University Press). Up-to-date and comprehensive – deals with the whole period from 1945 to the present day and is organised by both region and subject.

References

Axford, B. (2002) 'The processes of globalisation', in B. Axford, G.K. Browning, R. Huggins and B. Rosamond (eds), *Politics: an Introduction*, 2nd edn (Routledge), pp. 524–60.

Beck, U. (2000) *What is Globalization?* (Polity Press).

Calvocoressi, P. (2000) *World Politics: 1945–2000* (Pearson).

Coates, D. (1994) *The Question of UK Decline* (Harvester Wheatsheaf).

European Commission (2005) *A Constitution for Europe* (Official Publications of the European Union).

Ferguson, N. (2003) *Empire: How Britain Made the Modern World* (Allen Lane).

Foreign and Commonwealth Office (2003) *UK International Priorities: A Strategy for the FCO* (HMSO).

Giddens, A. (1998) *The Third Way* (Polity Press).

Giddens, A. (ed.) (2001) *The Global Third Way Debate* (Polity Press).

Hall, S. (1979) 'The great moving right show', *Marxism Today*, Vol. 23, No. 1, pp. 23–41.

Hall, S. (1998) 'The great moving nowhere show', in Jacques, M. (ed.) *Marxism Today, Special Issue*, pp. 143–56.

Halliday, F. (2001) *The World at 2000* (Palgrave).

Hay, C. (1999) *The Political Economy of New Labour* (Manchester University Press).

Held, D., McGrew, A., Goldblatt, D. and Perraton, J. (1999) *Global Transformations: Politics, Economics and Culture* (Polity Press).

Hudson, J. (2002) 'Digitising the structures of governance', *Policy and Politics*, Vol. 30, No. 4, pp. 515–31.

Hutton, W. (1995) *The State We're In* (Cape).

Hutton, W. (2002) *The World We're In* (Little, Brown).

Institute of Fiscal Studies (2002) *Trends in British Public Investment*, Fiscal Studies Press Release, 29 September 2002.

Klein, N. (2001) *No Logo: No Space, No Choice, No Jobs* (Flamingo).

Krieger, J. (1999) *Britain in the Golden Age* (Polity Press).

Marquand, D. (1998) *The Blair Paradox* (*Prospect* magazine, May).

McRae, H. (2005) 'They're young, overpaid and over here. And that's why London is thriving', *The Independent on Sunday*, 13 November 2005, p. 15.

New Internationalist (2002) *New Internationalist*, Issue 347, July 2002.

Ohmae, K. (1995) *The End of the Nation-State* (Free Press).

Organisation for Economic Cooperation and Development (OECD) (2004) *Enhancing the Cost Effectiveness of Public Spending: Experience in OECD Countries* (Paris, OECD).

Porter, M. (1990) *The Competitive Advantage of Nations* (Macmillan).

Useful websites

A.T. Kearney / Foreign Policy Measuring Globalisation Index: http://www.foreignpolicy.com
Annually produced globalisation measures for 62 countries.

Warwick Globalisation Index: http://www2.warwick.ac.uk/soc/fac/csgr/index
Produced by the ESRC Centre for the Study of Globalisation and Regionalisation at the University of Warwick.

European Commission: A Constitution for Europe (2005):   http://europa.eu.int/constitution/
Guide to the draft Constitutional Treaty for the EU produced by the European Convention on the Constitution.

Global Transformations: http://www.polity.co.uk/global/links.htm
Produced by Polity Press to provide links to some of the most significant resources relevant to the study of globalisation.

Open Politics: http://news.bbc.co.uk/hi/english/static/in_depth/uk_politics/2001/open_politics/foreign_policy/globalisation.stm
A BBC News and Open University site dedicated to British politics. These pages deal with the question of whether globalisation spells the end of British foreign policy.

The Globalsite: http://www.theglobalsite.ac.uk/
University of Sussex. Good links to various aspects of globalisation, plus commentary on current world events and problems.

Foreign and Commonwealth Office: http://www.fco.gov.uk/servlet/Front?pagename=OpenMarket/Xcelerate/ShowPage&c=Page&cid=1007029391674
Official government site for all aspects of UK foreign policy. This page links to British relations with the European Union.

House of Commons Foreign Affairs Committee – Second Report, 2001: http://www.publications.parliament.uk/pa/cm200102/cmselect/cmfaff/327/32702.htm
The Proceedings of the Foreign Affairs Committee on UK–USA relations. The published report was ordered by the House of Commons to be printed on 11 December 2001.

CHAPTER 3

The social and economic contexts

Michael Moran

Learning objectives

- To sketch the social and economic settings of British politics.

- To explain how the national setting is part of a wider global and European system.

- To identify the main patterns of change in the social and economic contexts.

- To show how the wider global and European setting is continuing to reshape British politics and society.

Introduction

No political system operates in a vacuum. Everything that happens in politics is affected by the social and economic context within which institutions have to operate. Part of that context is internal to Britain and consists of the social hierarchies and economic structures of British society. Part is external to Britain and consists of the wider global economy and the developing European economy and political system of which Britain is a part. This chapter introduces both the internal and the external aspects of the social and economic settings.

This connection between the 'internal' and the 'external' social settings is of growing importance. The United Kingdom is an island, or rather a group of islands. But in today's world no state is an island: we cannot make sense of British politics, or of the social context of British politics, by looking at domestic society alone. That is why in the pages that immediately follow substantial attention is given to Britain in a global setting. To take only a single example that emerges shortly: in a world of great poverty Britain, whatever its short-term economic ups and downs, is a privileged island of wealth – and this fact, about which most of us never think, deeply affects the working of British government both at home and abroad.

■ Britain in a global setting

The best way to start is with the geography of the United Kingdom, because this is both the most basic aspect of the social and economic setting and the most obvious way to appreciate the significance of Britain's location in a wider world. Viewed in this way, several features of the UK become clear:

1. *It is small*: Only 244.1 thousand square kilometres.

2. *It is densely populated*: The number of persons per square kilometre is 244, against an average

for the 25 members of the European Union of 118.

3. *It is industrial*: Barely 1 per cent of employment is in agriculture.

4. *It is rich*: We live in one of a small number of rich countries in a largely poor world. Viewed internationally, the arguments about the allocation of resources in Britain are arguments between comparatively well-off groups of people. Figure 3.1 illustrates Britain's long-term position in the 'league table' of world wealth. Despite long-term

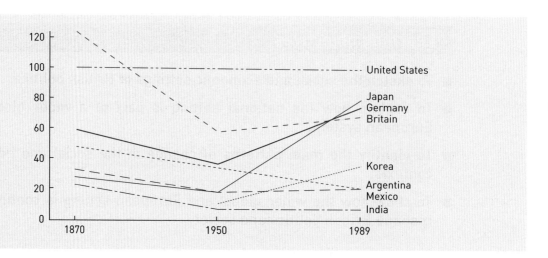

Figure 3.1 The wealth of Britain, compared over the historical long term with other countries
Source: From *The Economist*, 20 June 1992, p. 155. Copyright © 1992 The Economist Newspaper Limited, London. All rights reserved. Reproduced with permission

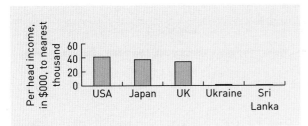

Figure 3.2 The UK is still in the premier league of wealth, 2004
Note: Figures are for per head income, to nearest thousand dollars, for selected rich and poor countries.
Source: World Bank (2004) *World Development Indicators*, (www.worldbank.org/data). Reproduced with permission from the World Bank

decline we remain in the 'premier league' of wealth, as Figure 3.2 illustrates; our secure position in the 'premier league' has not altered for over a century. Indeed in the last decade that historical decline has reversed: in the mid-1990s the UK was the poorest of the big economies in the European Union; now she is the richest. (For more discussion of the recent economic performance, see Chapter 27.) That prosperity is reflected in the life chances of the British people compared with those of other inhabitants of the globe: life expectancy in the United Kingdom is 75 for men and 80 for women; in Africa, the comparable figures are 52 and 55.

5. *It is capitalist*: '**Capitalism**' is a word often used offensively or defensively in political argument. Here it is neutral: it describes a system where property is privately owned and where goods and services are traded for a price by free exchange in markets.

Viewed from the 'outside', therefore, British society can look uniform. But when we examine it more closely, variety appears.

One of the most striking sources of variation is geography. Britain is a 'multinational state': that is, it is a political unit ruled by a single sovereign authority but composed of territories that historically were different nations, and whose populations still retain distinct national identities.

There are at least five different historical national groupings in the United Kingdom: the English, Welsh, Scottish, Irish and those (mostly Protestants in Northern Ireland) who identify with 'Ulster'. Identity has been further complicated by another feature, which reflects the fact that Britain is part

of a wider global system: immigration. The United Kingdom has periodically received waves of immigrants from abroad and in the 1950s and 1960s received particularly large numbers from what is conventionally called the 'new Commonwealth' – notably from our former colonial possessions in the West Indies and the Indian subcontinent. But this wave of migration was only one episode in a history that has seen perpetual migration: at the end of the nineteenth century, large numbers of Jewish refugees fled to Britain from persecution in Eastern Europe; at the end of the twentieth century, as we shall see later, large numbers of refugees arrived from numerous war-torn parts of the world. We look later in the chapter at the complex connection between ethnic identity and national identity.

The question of national identity in Britain is therefore more complicated than the simple existence of a political unity called the United Kingdom would suggest. But there is a further aspect to territorial differences. Even the most casual traveller in Britain soon realises that within national areas striking variations exist – differences ranging from the most profound cultural and economic matters to the most mundane aspects of everyday life. Even inside the biggest nation in the United Kingdom, England, striking regional differences also exist.

Although the actual figures change with time, for several decades real income in the southeast of England, and accompanying measures of well-being such as employment, have been more favourable than in any other part of the United Kingdom. The southeast is the powerhouse of the United Kingdom economy and – another sign of the impact of the wider global setting – in many ways has more in common with rich regions on the continent of Europe than with the poorest parts of the United Kingdom. Conversely, areas such as Northern Ireland and the northwest of England have been among the most deprived. The scale of this is illustrated in Table 3.1.

The regional differences identified here have been widely noticed in recent years and have given rise to the argument that in Britain there exists a 'north–south divide' between the more prosperous and the poorer parts of the United Kingdom. But despite the undoubted gaps in the wealth of different regions, such characterisations are, at best, only a part of the truth. There exist numerous prosperous communities in the north of Britain. In the heart of the prosperous south, in parts of London for instance, there are by contrast greatly impoverished

Table 3.1 Regional inequality in Britain, 2002–3

	Southeast	West Midlands	East Anglia	Southwest	East Midlands	Wales	Northwest	Yorkshire and Humberside	Northeast	Scotland	Northern Ireland
% of working age with a degree	19.9	12.7	16.2	16,2	13.0	14.6	13.3	13.4	11.3	15.4	13.1
Gross average weekly earnings per head (£, rounded)	497	427	460	422	413	400	427	410	399	427	390
Unemployed rate (%)	3.9	5.9	4.2	3.9	4.3	4.6	5.1	5.5	6.6	5.4	7.3
% of households with no car	17	25	21	18	21	25	29	31	35	35	27

Source: Calculated from Office for National Statistics (2004) *Regional Trends*, 2004 Edition. The figures are for various dates in 2002–03. © Crown Copyright 2004. Crown copyright material is reproduced with the permission of the Controller of Her Majesty's Stationery Office (HMSO)

communities. Part of the reason for this is that overlaying any divisions between regions are important differences between various parts of urban areas in Britain.

■ Urban problems and the city

It is common to speak of the 'urban problem' in Britain or, in the same breath, of 'the problems of the **inner city**'. But a wide array of social features is actually summed up in a single phrase like the 'urban problem'. Similarly, although the 'inner city' has become a byword for poverty and misery, many areas of inner cities (witness parts of London) are the homes of the rich and fashionable, while in outer suburbs and even in rural areas there are, especially on public housing estates, areas of deep poverty. Nevertheless, a number of long-term social changes have combined to alter the character of the giant cities that were the characteristic creation of Britain's **Industrial Revolution**. Two should be noted.

First, long-term shifts in population have changed both the numbers living in many inner city areas and the social balance of the remaining population. The figures of movement tell the story. Take a single instance, covering the two decades 1982–2002: deprived and declining inner-city Liverpool lost 13.7 per cent of its population; at the other end of England, rich suburban Barnet gained 9.3 per cent in the same period (*Regional Trends*, 2004, Chapter 14.)

This shift of population out of established areas of cities to suburbs and small towns reflects a second change: population decline is commonly a reflection of economic decline and social crisis. Often the white

middle classes leave and the poor plus new immigrants tend to remain. The cities of the Industrial Revolution have seen their economic foundations decay as the traditional industries have decayed, with important consequences for prosperity and financial stability. In the biggest cities, especially London, 'averages' conceal huge inequalities in wealth, health and life chances. We may now be seeing a reverse of these long historical trends, at least as far as the cores of old industrial cities are concerned: formerly declining industrial centres like Leeds and Liverpool have 'reinvented' themselves to attract new generations of apartment dwellers and have invested in services designed to cater for conspicuous consumption by the well-off, such as bars, restaurants and art galleries. How substantial a difference this is making to the underlying story of deprivation and decline we need more time to tell.

■ Work and unemployment

Work is a central part of each individual's life – whether the worker is the unpaid homemaker or the company chief executive earning $500,000 a year. But the nature of work is also important for wider social reasons. Occupation is the single most important influence on the social structure. The kind of work done is a key determinant of the material rewards and the status an individual enjoys. Indeed, the class structure in Britain closely corresponds to the occupational structure. Definitions of class commonly mean **occupational class**: 'working class', for instance, usually refers to those people – and their families – who earn a living from 'manual' jobs. The central place of occupation in the political life of the country is well illustrated by the case of voting and elections, where occupational class has been, and remains, a key influence on the way people vote. Work is central to the life of the individual, but it is also central to the economic structure. Four aspects of this centrality are notable.

Most people in Britain live by selling their labour

Britain is a market economy in which the only significant tradeable resource controlled by the majority of the population is labour. There are indeed exceptions: a small minority of the wealthy control sufficient productive property to be able to live on the returns of that property; a larger group – pensioners, the unemployed – live off state-provided benefits. But most individuals either live by selling their labour to others, or – as in the case of children – are dependent on 'breadwinners'. Figure 3.3 shows that the British are not, as Napoleon once said, a nation of shopkeepers; they are a nation of employees.

Most people sell their labour to private firms

Because Britain is a capitalist society, only a minority of the workforce is employed in the public sector. Until the beginning of the 1980s, there had been a long-term increase in the size of this minority – so marked that some observers argued that excessive growth of public sector employment was the main cause of Britain's economic difficulties. This trend has been reversed. A combination of cuts in numbers employed in public services and the **privatisation** of many important industries means that the dominance of private firms as employers has been reinforced in recent years.

Women are becoming more important in the workforce

Women have always worked, but they have not always been paid for working. For example, until the beginning of the last century 'domestic service' was a major source of paid employment for women. Social change has since almost eliminated domestic servants, and their jobs are now done for nothing by mothers, wives and daughters. In recent decades women – especially married women – have taken paid employment in large numbers. The trends are illustrated in Figure 3.4.

Three features of women's work should be noted. First, it is disproportionately concentrated in the 'service' sector and in what is sometimes called 'light manufacturing' – work involving, for instance, assembling and packing components. Second, while just over half the population are women, far more than half of working women are in jobs with low pay and status and far less than half are in high status jobs: a disproportionately high proportion of women are cleaners in universities, and a disproportionately low number are teachers in them. Third, women occupy a disproportionate number of casual and part-time jobs in the workforce.

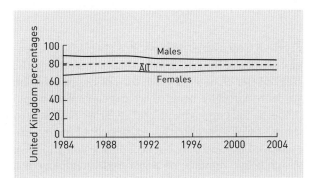

Figure 3.3 The British are a nation of employees: economic activity rates 1984–2004
Note: Figure measures percentage of population aged 15–69 in employment.
Source: Office for National Statistics (2005) *Social Trends*, No. 35, 2005 Edition, p. 46. © Crown Copyright 2005. Crown copyright material is reproduced with the permission of the Controller of Her Majesty's Stationery Office (HMSO)

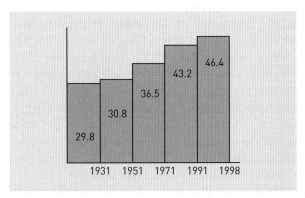

Figure 3.4 The rise of female employment (percentage of workforce female)
Source: Gallie (2000), p. 293

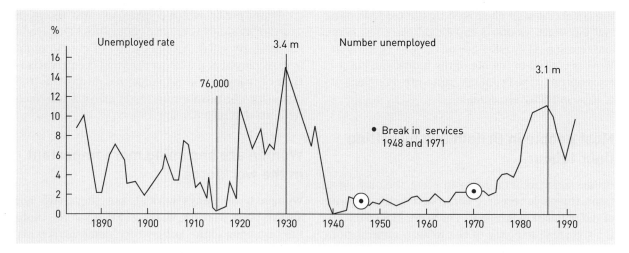

Figure 3.5 The history of unemployment
Source: From *The Economist*, 20 February 1993. Copyright © 1993 The Economist Newspaper Limited, London. All rights reserved.
Reproduced with permission

Full employment has returned

For virtually the whole of the twentieth century, unemployment was the single greatest immediate economic problem confronting governments in Britain. As we can see from Figure 3.5, there were very big long-term swings in the levels of measured unemployment over the course of the century. Discussion in earlier editions of this book was dominated by the shape of the graph for the second half of the twentieth century, which as far as unemployment was concerned was divided into two quite distinct periods. From the 1940s to the 1970s unemployment was at historically low levels. This era of what is usually called full employment contrasted with the mass unemployment of the 1930s, but it also contrasted with what came afterwards: from the early 1970s unemployment was on a rising trend, and by the middle of the 1980s – around the time when most readers of this book were born – it had topped three million, almost matching the levels reached in the worst times of the 1930s. A new age of mass unemployment had dawned. This new mass unemployment also had a distinctive social distribution: it was the poor, those with little or no formal education or skills, and those who lived in traditionally declining economic areas – like the northwest of England – who were most likely to suffer.

As Figure 3.6 shows, the period since the middle of the 1980s, and especially since 1992, has shown a very different pattern. (You should compare the two figures with care: Figure 3.5 measures percentages;

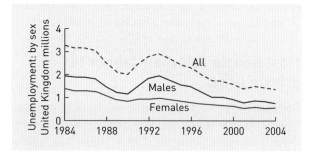

Figure 3.6 The return of full employment
Source: From Office for National Statistics (2005) *Social Trends*, No. 35, 2005 Edition, p. 55. © Crown Copyright 2005. Crown copyright material is reproduced with the permission of the Controller of Her Majesty's Stationery Office (HMSO)

Figure 3.6 measures millions. It is therefore the general shapes of the two graphs that help in telling the story of the change.) By the turn of the millennium we were virtually back to what economists would define as full employment, and so far we have stayed there. ('Full' despite the existence of many unemployed because any big economy is going to have a significant number of registered unemployed: a minority who for health or other personal reasons just cannot hold down a job; a minority who at any one moment are between jobs.) The old social distribution of unemployment was still there: the unskilled, those living in depressed regions, were more likely to be out of a job. But even when we look beyond the overall figures the transformation is striking. For example, anyone who took the trouble to compare Table 3.1 in this book with the same table in the third edition of *Politics UK* would notice that the unemployment rate now for a traditionally high-unemployment area, Northern Ireland, is actually lower than the unemployment rate for the boom region of the southeast in 1995: unemployment in Northern Ireland now is 7.3 per cent; in the southeast in 1995 it was 7.9 per cent.

The causes of this dramatic change in the history of unemployment are greatly debated, and they go to the heart of the wider debate about how to manage the British economy. Some of the change is due to government measures that take the unemployed – especially the young unemployed – off the unemployment register and put them into various forms of education and training: the worth of these measures is discussed more fully in Chapter 26. But these direct government measures are in any case not the main cause of the turnaround. In the last fifteen years the British economy has been strikingly successful in creating new jobs to replace the old ones destroyed in earlier decades of industrial decline. And it is the significance of this history of new job creation that is the great issue in debates about the new age of full employment.

We can illustrate the arguments by sketching two opposing positions. A sceptical view of the recent transformation would run as follows. An international economic boom began in the early 1990s, mostly driven by a boom in the US economy, the biggest in the world. Britain was just the lucky beneficiary of this boom, and it led to the creation of large numbers of 'Mcjobs' – in other words low-skilled, badly paid, temporary, part-time jobs of the kind allegedly typified by those offered in the McDonald's hamburger joints, which, coincidentally, sprang up almost everywhere in Britain during the 1980s and 1990s. The creation of low-paid, low-skilled jobs together with the persistence of a core of the impoverished unemployed in turn raised a debate about the meaning and causes of social exclusion – an issue with which we also deal in Chapter 26.

The counter to the argument that the age of full employment is an illusion comes in two parts. One is simply that almost any job is better than unemployment, even if it is badly paid, and not all the old industrial jobs were self-evidently desirable. How many readers of this book would swap serving in McDonald's for working in deep coal mining – one of the occupations that virtually disappeared in the 1980s and 1990s? But the second part of the response is that there was much more to the new job creation than 'Mcjobs': there was also an expansion in important areas of skilled, often professional employment in the 'service' sector, for example in financial services and in healthcare. However, these debates do alert us to an important consideration: simple measures of job numbers conceal important changes that are occurring in the structure of the workforce. To an increasing degree, large employers are dividing their workforce into a 'core' and a 'periphery'. The 'core' consists of workers in secure, long-term employment. There is also a tendency for these to be the better qualified and to enjoy the best pay and fringe benefits. The 'periphery' consists of a shifting group of temporary employees who can be taken on, and laid off, according to demand. There is a corresponding tendency for these workers to be disproportionately women, to work at less-skilled jobs, and to be comparatively poorly rewarded. The 'dual' labour market, as it is sometimes called, offers considerable advantages to employers. Temporary and casual workers are comparatively cheap, most of them are poorly organised in unions, and legal protection against such eventualities as dismissal is more limited than in the case of the permanent workforce. Thus employers can use their 'peripheral' workforce in a highly flexible way to respond to changing market conditions.

For most people in Britain, their labour amounts to the only serious economic asset at their disposal. But for a minority economic resources come in the form of a considerable stock of wealth. This is examined next.

■ Wealth, property and the social structure

Only one thing can be said with certainty about the distribution of wealth in Britain: it has long been, in statistical terms, highly unequal. But the meaning and even the accuracy of the bald statistics are perhaps more uncertain here than in any other area of British society. Beyond the general proposition that a statistically small group owns an arithmetically large amount of the nation's wealth, there exists little agreement.

Debate starts with the very significance of inequality. For some, the existence of a minority of very wealthy people in Britain is a good thing and any diminution of the wealth of the few a bad thing. According to this argument, great wealth is desirable

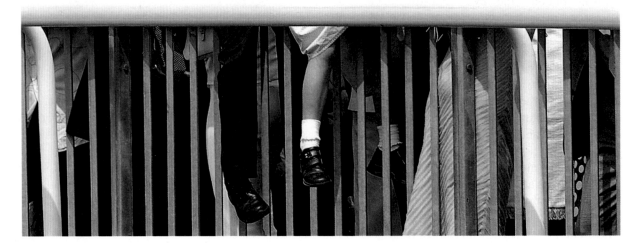

Great displays of wealth such as Royal Ascot illustrate the ongoing divide between the haves and the have nots: the 'poor' punters have a separate enclosure
Source: PA Wire / Empics

BOX 3.1 **FACT**

Labour as an economic resource

The vast majority of employees in Britain are united by one single important feature: their labour power is their only significant economic resource. But otherwise employees in Britain are fragmented into numerous groups:

1. Public-sector and private-sector workers
2. Manual and non-manual workers
3. Workers in service and manufacturing sectors
4. Part-timers and full-timers.

because it shows the ability of the market system to reward the enterprising with great incentives, thus encouraging innovation and risk taking in the economy. In addition, the wealthy are a socially important group, because although a minority they are still, in absolute terms, large in number. This means that they support social diversity by, for example, sponsoring a variety of political causes, charities and artistic activities: the classic example, often cited, is the financial support given to the nineteenth century revolutionary Karl Marx by his rich capitalist friend and collaborator, Friedrich Engels. Without the wealthy, according to this view, society would be dull, uniform and dominated by the state. On the other hand, critics of the social order in Britain maintain that control of great wealth by a minority is illegitimate. It appropriates what is properly the wealth of the community for a few and contradicts the aim of democracy by lodging wealth – and thus power – in the hands of a minority.

These arguments are, in the long run, inconclusive because they involve competing notions of what a just social order should look like. But they have also proved inconclusive for a more mundane reason: nobody can agree on how to measure wealth and its distribution definitively. Most of us think we could recognise the existence of great wealth – but we would soon disagree about what exactly to include as a measure of wealth, and how to value what is actually included. We could probably agree, for instance, that the great landed estates still owned by some aristocrats are a form of wealth and should be counted as such: for instance, in most tables of the super-rich in Britain the Duke of Westminster tops the league principally because his family have for several hundred years owned fabulously valuable property in the most fashionable parts of London. But should this also be said of even the most humble

property, such as the family terraced house? In an age when domestic houses often fetch high prices, and where virtually 70 per cent of dwellings are owner-occupied, this decision can make a big difference to estimates of the distribution of wealth. Similarly, there would probably be general agreement that ownership of shares in a large business corporation is a form of wealth. But should this also be said of more indirect stakes in ownership? In many of the largest corporations in Britain a substantial proportion of shares are owned by **'financial institutions'** – organisations such as insurance companies and pension funds, which invest the proceeds of the contributions of individual policy holders or those paying into pension schemes. Since an individual making such contributions is entitled to a return on the investments, just as certainly as the direct shareholder is entitled to a dividend, it may be thought that participants in insurance schemes and pension funds should be counted as owning some of the wealth of the economy. If this is indeed so, it suggests not only that wealth is quite widely distributed but also that it has become more equally distributed in recent decades, because the beneficiaries of life insurance and pension schemes have grown greatly in number. For instance, in 1936 only two million people were in an occupational pension scheme; by the early 1990s the figure was over ten million (Webb, 2000, p. 567). Table 3.2 shows how sensitive the figures can be to the definition of wealth, by comparing the results when we include or exclude the value of dwellings.

An additional complication is introduced by the difficulty of actually valuing wealth, even when we agree on what is to be included in a definition. The values of shares in companies, for instance, are decided on the open market. Falls in share prices can thus drastically reduce estimates of the riches of

Table 3.2 Distribution of marketable wealth in Britain (Inland Revenue estimates)

	1976	2002
Marketable wealth: percentage of wealth owned by		
Most wealthy 1%	21	23
Most wealthy 5%	38	43
Most wealthy 10%	50	56
Most wealthy 25%	71	74
Most wealthy 50%	92	94
Marketable wealth less value of dwellings: percentage owned by		
Most wealthy 1%	29	35
Most wealthy 5%	47	62
Most wealthy 10%	57	75
Most wealthy 25%	73	88
Most wealthy 50%	88	98

Source: Office for National Statistics (2004) *Social Trends*, No. 34, 2004 Edition, p. 80. and (2005) *Social Trends*, No. 35, 2005 Edition, p. 102. © Crown Copyright 2004, 2005. Crown copyright material is reproduced with the permission of the Controller of Her Majesty's Stationery Office (HMSO)

the (mostly wealthy) groups of large shareholders – as discovered by the 'dot com' millionaires in the Internet company stocks boom of the late 1990s, who saw their suddenly acquired wealth disappear almost as quickly when the market in their companies' shares collapsed.

It is important to bear these cautionary remarks in mind when discussing arguments about wealth distribution and in interpreting the figures presented in Table 3.2. Nevertheless, three observations seem beyond reasonable doubt. First, there is indeed a minority that owns a statistically disproportionate amount of the community's total wealth. Second, there is a very large group at the other end of the social scale that is virtually propertyless. Third, some redistribution of wealth is occurring over time away from the very richest, but the trickle of resources down the social scale is slow and uneven.

■ Multi-ethnic and multi-cultural Britain

In a famous introduction to the social fabric of British politics, published forty years ago, Jean Blondel summarised Britain as a homogeneous society (Blondel,

1963). By this he did not mean that social divisions were absent but that Britain, when compared with the United States or with other important European nations, was marked by comparatively few important lines of division. Whereas religion, race and territory were important lines of division elsewhere, the social context of British politics could be pretty fully understood by reference to class divisions alone: the most important 'blocs' in British society were classes, identified by their occupation. The key division was between manual and 'white-collar' workers, often expressed in everyday language as a divide between a 'working' and a 'middle' class.

That line of division remains important, and more generally the divisions between the rich and poor remain significant in British society, but two developments have combined to make this line of division less crucial.

First, the unity of the two big class 'blocs' has declined. This is most obvious in the case of the manual working class: the numbers of manual workers have fallen; they have been internally divided between those in permanent, full-time jobs and those in temporary and/or part-time work; and there has been a growth in unemployment among those who would formerly have done manual work. Conversely, there has been a big increase in the numbers of white-collar workers, but this increase has also brought more internal variety: a wider span of jobs, and important divisions between those in fairly secure permanent work and those on short-term and temporary contracts.

But the second development has become increasingly important: this consists in the rise in new kinds of social identification and a strengthening of old ones. Of the first of these, perhaps the most important has been the rise of different ethnic identities. In the last fifty years Britain, especially England, and even more especially London, has been transformed into a multi-ethnic society. The most important cause of this development is the large-scale migration, especially from the West Indies and the Indian subcontinent, that took place into Britain, notably in the 1950s and 1960s. These groups had very distinct racial identities; many also brought a very strong sense of religious identity to a society where religion had been, for most of the population, a comparatively unimportant matter. In the 2001 census, which for the first time asked a question about ethnic identity, 4.6 million people (8 per cent of the population) described themselves as belonging to a minority ethnic group, of whom the largest (nearly 2 per cent)

In the last fifty years Britain, especially England, and even more especially London, has been transformed into a multi-ethnic society
Source: Janine Wiedel Photolibrary / Alamy

described themselves as Indian. The census only provides a single snapshot, albeit a comprehensive and authoritative picture of Britain's social mix. In a world of rapid population movement the picture is constantly changing. Figure 3.7 therefore provides a more up-to-date supplement: it documents the proportion of those accepted for settlement in more recent years. The most obvious implication of this figure is a change in the character of immigration. Where once we drew immigrants mostly from our old empire, now immigrants come from a much wider range, especially from parts of the world affected by wars and economic collapse.

The rise of ethnic diversity has created an extended public debate about 'British' identity, with some public figures arguing that it has created a serious problem of national loyalty and identity. The former Conservative Cabinet Minister Lord Tebbit has argued that failing the 'Tebbit test' – do you support England at cricket? – is a sign of this problematic

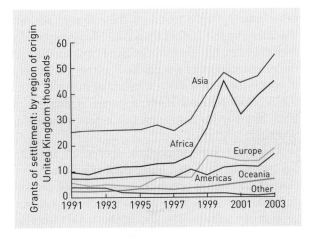

Figure 3.7 Immigrants to Britain: acceptances for settlement by selected region of origin
Source: From Office for National Statistics (2005) *Social Trends*, No. 35, 2005 Edition, p. 15. © Crown Copyright 2005. Crown copyright material is reproduced with the permission of the Controller of Her Majesty's Stationery Office (HMSO)

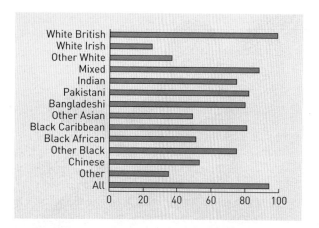

Figure 3.8 Passing the Tebbit test: national identity in multi-ethnic Britain (percentage of Great Britain population who consider their identity to be British, English, Scottish or Welsh, by ethnic group: national surveys, 2002–3)
Source: From Office for National Statistics (2005) *Social Trends*, No. 35, 2005 Edition, Figure 1.6. © Crown Copyright 2005. Crown copyright material is reproduced with the permission of the Controller of Her Majesty's Stationery Office (HMSO)

nature of identity in multi-ethnic Britain. But what Figure 3.8 suggests is that this 'problem' – if it is a problem – is greatly exaggerated. The overwhelming majority of members of ethnic groups identify with some kind of British identity. And the only really 'disloyal' group are the white Irish who (like this writer) comprehensively fail the 'Tebbit test'.

Alongside these new identities 'imported' by migration there has been a revival of traditional identities, notably those based on the different nations that make up the 'United Kingdom'. This is especially noticeable in the case of Scotland, culminating in the establishment of a separate Scottish Parliament in which there now sits a substantial minority from the Scottish National Party, a party committed, at least formally, to achieving full independence for Scotland.

A second very important source of identity beyond ethnicity is that based on gender. There is a close connection between changes in the job market and change in both perceptions of women and perceptions by women. The rise of the (paid) working woman, the figures for which we saw earlier, has had important consequences even beyond the labour market itself. It undoubtedly lies at the root of a new sense of self-confidence and self-consciousness among many women, reflected in, for instance, a heightened sense of dissatisfaction with long-established inequalities within and outside the workplace between men and women. It has greatly affected the culture and the structure of family life. In many groups – notably in traditional working-class communities – the spread of paid employment among women has accompanied a decline in the very occupations where manual workers were traditionally employed. The result is that the historical role of 'breadwinner' now lies with women rather than men in many instances, inevitably enforcing changes in power and authority within the family.

■ The economic structure: the public and the private

The United Kingdom, as we have seen, is a capitalist country: private ownership of property dominates; most people rely on the sale of their labour to make a living. But this capitalist country, like most others, also has a large public sector: the state is important in economic life. State involvement in economics is often thought of as meaning 'public ownership'; in fact, that is only one way among many by which the state shapes economic structures, and these ways are summarised below.

The government as owner

Public ownership is the most visible form of state participation in the economic structure. Government has long been a major owner of productive property: for instance, the crown was already a great property holder when land was the main source of wealth in the community. In the nineteenth century, government established a public monopoly in a major new industry of the time, post and telecommunications. In modern Britain, government is still a major owner of society's natural resources, such as coal, oil and gas. (The right to exploit these is only given by licence to private firms.) However, the best-known instances of public ownership are the result of what is usually called **nationalisation**. The nationalised industries were the product of conscious political choices. For most of the century until the start of the 1980s the nationalised sector grew, with successive governments of different political outlooks adding to the range. In the years between the two world wars, for instance, industries as different as broadcasting and electricity supply were nationalised (by the creation of, respectively, the British

Broadcasting Corporation and the Central Electricity Generating Board). The years immediately after the Second World War saw a substantial increase in public ownership: coal, steel and railways were all taken into the state sector. The main reason for the postwar growth of public ownership was the belief that the enterprises, if left in private hands, would be run inefficiently or would even fail. This motivation also explains many of the important pieces of nationalisation accomplished in the 1960s and 1970s. These included shipbuilding and important sections of the aircraft and motor vehicle production industries.

Until the mid-1970s, it seemed that the continued expansion of public ownership was an irreversible trend in Britain. However, Mrs Thatcher's Conservative administrations of the 1980s destroyed this assumption. Through a programme of 'privatisation' they sold into private hands about 40 per cent of what was in public ownership at the start of the decade. The 'privatised' concerns include many once thought 'natural' to the public sector, such as the gas supply and telecommunications industries. Privatisation marks a radical shift in the balance between the state and the market in Britain. However, the retreat of state ownership does not necessarily mean that total public participation in the economy is in decline. On the contrary, in most of the other five cases that we will consider the importance of government is apparently growing.

The government as partner

The state can act as a partner of private enterprise in numerous ways. Publicly controlled institutions in the financial sector commonly provide investment capital to allow private enterprises to set up or to expand. The major area of growth in partnership in recent years, however, has been at the local level. Faced with the need to redevelop declining and derelict areas of the cities, local authorities and local development corporations have embarked on numerous joint developments with private firms. Some of the best-known examples of policy initiatives at the local level – such as the redevelopment of London's docklands – are the result of precisely such partnerships.

A substantial attempt to boost the 'partnership' model was made in the 1990s by the then Conservative government by its Private Finance Initiative (PFI), a scheme for raising the investment cost of large public projects like hospitals from the private sector, and licensing private firms to run the projects once completed. In opposition, the Labour Party criticised PFI; but since 1997 it has embraced and extended the scheme, rebranding it as the Public–Private Partnership.

The government as regulator

Although most debate about public intervention in the economy concerns ownership, it is arguably the case that the structure of the market economy in Britain is less influenced by ownership than by public regulation – in other words by sets of rules either contained in law or otherwise prescribed by the government. Public regulation is of three kinds. First, the state sets a general framework for the conduct of life, including economic life. Criminal and civil law defines and enforces commercial contracts, identifies what constitutes honesty and dishonesty and provides a means for detecting and preventing fraud. Corporate law defines the nature of the most important economic institution in the private sector – the individual company. Without this general framework of enforced rules, the market economy could not operate.

A second category of regulation is directed at particular industries or sectors of the economy, governing the conduct of affairs inside individual enterprises. For instance, there now exists a large body of law governing relations in the workplace. Industrial relations law places obligations on both employers and trade unions in industrial bargaining. Health and safety legislation prescribes rules safeguarding the life and health of employees.

Finally, there is regulation governing the relations between firms in the private sector and the rest of society. The importance of this kind of regulation has grown greatly in recent years. Two of the most important instances concern pollution control and consumer protection. Pollution regulations govern the nature of industrial processes and restrict the emissions that firms can allow into the atmosphere. Consumer protection regulates the content of many products (in the interests of safety), how they can be advertised (in the interests of honesty and accuracy) and the terms of competition between firms (in the interests of ensuring fair prices).

One important form of regulation is sometimes called 'self-regulation'. Under this system, an industry or occupation determines its own regulations and establishes its own institutions for policing and enforcement. Some important professions (such as the law) and major industries (such as advertising) are organised in this way. But most self-regulation should more accurately be called regulation under public licence, because what happens is that the state licenses a group to regulate itself – thereby saving the difficulty and expense of doing the job directly. This links to our next instance of public participation in the market economy.

The government as licensee

When the government does not wish directly to engage in a particular economic activity but nevertheless wants to retain control over that activity, it has the option of licensing a private firm to provide goods and services under prescribed conditions. This method is historically ancient: in the seventeenth and eighteenth centuries, for instance, governments often granted monopolies to private corporations to trade in particular products or in particular regions of the world. In the modern economy, licensing is used extensively. The exploitation of oil reserves in the North Sea has largely been accomplished by selling licences to explore for oil to privately owned companies. The service of providing commercial radio and commercial television is handled in a similar way. In the wake of privatisation this system of licensing, or 'franchising', has become even more important. For instance, the provision of rail services since privatisation has been controlled in this way. The 'franchise' to run the inter-city train service from Manchester to London, for instance, is held by Virgin Trains.

One of the most common ways of allocating licences is through a system of competitive bidding for the award of the franchise; the government, of course, can also use the competitive system by going to the private sector as a customer for goods and services.

The government as customer

We saw in the opening chapter that governments can use a variety of means, including coercion, to raise goods and services. But government in Britain in fact normally uses the market. In other words, it employs the state's revenues (from such sources as taxation) to buy the goods and services it needs. A glance around any classroom or lecture theatre will show the importance of the public sector as a customer. The room itself will almost certainly have been built as the result of a contract with private firms of builders and architects. The teacher at the front of the room is a private citizen hired on the labour market. Virtually every piece of equipment in the room will also have been bought from private firms. This simple example is illustrated on a wider scale throughout government. Take the example of national defence. Although we usually think of government as providing the defence of the country, it actually buys most of the means of defence in the marketplace: soldiers, sailors and airmen have to be recruited from the labour market in competition with other recruiters of labour, such as private firms; most defence equipment is bought under contract from the private sector; and the everyday necessities of the forces – from the food eaten in the regimental mess to the fuel used by a regimental staff car – are bought in the marketplace.

The government is a customer in the market economy, but it is a very special kind of customer. Because government is the biggest institution in British society, it is also the biggest customer. In some important areas it is to all intents and purposes the only customer. To take the example given above, in the supply of most important defence equipment – rockets, military aircraft, warships – the public sector is the sole purchaser. Here the 'producer–customer' relationship is obviously a very special one. Firms producing defence equipment, while nominally in private ownership, operate in such close contact with government agencies that they are in practical terms often indistinguishable from public bodies.

That the state is a customer of the private sector is well recognised; but in understanding the country's economic structure it is as important to emphasise the role of the public sector as a supplier of goods and services.

The government as supplier

Until recently, government had a major role as a direct supplier of goods and services in Britain. Housing (council dwellings), transport (bus and rail services), energy (coal, gas, electricity), healthcare (NHS hospitals), education (schools and universities): these were just some of the important goods and services that were provided directly by central or local government, or by nationalised corporations. Perhaps the biggest change in the role of government produced by Conservative governments after 1979 was to shrink its importance as the direct supplier of goods and services. Even where the state has retained some responsibility in this area it has

BOX 3.2   FACT

Roles of government in the economic structure: changing, not declining

Forms	Examples
Ownership	Minerals, land
Partnership	Development schemes in inner cities
Licensing	Oil exploration, commercial radio and television
Regulation	Health and safety at work
Purchase	Defence contracting
Supply	Healthcare, education

become a 'contract state', contracting out the delivery of services to private agencies. Nevertheless, the state retains a residual importance in this area, notably in the fields of education and healthcare.

The list in Box 3.2 is significant both because it shows how important is the state and because it shows how far the issues that are argued about in British politics concern the balance between its various roles. Take the single example of ownership. In the 1980s, the government 'privatised' many enterprises such as gas supply and the telephone service. At the same time it set up public bodies to regulate the newly privatised concerns: to fix prices and other conditions under which services are supplied to customers. Arguments between supporters and opponents of privatisation are not, therefore, arguments about whether or not government should be present in the economic structure; they turn on differences about whether, in particular cases, it is better for the state to be an owner or a regulator.

■ The economic structure: the balance of sectors

The role of public institutions is obviously a key aspect of a country's economic structure, but just as important is the balance between what are sometimes called 'sectors'. We often speak of Britain as an 'industrial' economy, but the industries dominant in the economy have changed greatly in the recent past and continue to change. These alterations have momentous wider consequences: they affect the social structure, noticeably the class structure, and thus feed through to politics. For instance, the declining proportion of manual workers in the economy has been a cause of declining votes for the Labour Party, once the party of most manual workers.

It is conventional to make a distinction between 'primary', 'secondary' and 'tertiary' (or 'service') sectors. The primary sector extracts the basic raw materials of production from nature: obvious examples include mining, forestry and agriculture. The secondary sector is most closely identified with manufacturing – in other words, with turning raw materials into finished goods, be they cars, refrigerators or aeroplanes. The tertiary (or service) sector refers to activities designed neither to extract and process materials nor to manufacture goods, but to deliver services; hence the alternative, commonly used name. We saw earlier in this chapter that many important services – such as health and education – are provided by public institutions, but others, ranging from catering and tourism to financial services, are provided by privately owned firms operating in the market.

The three categories of sector are extremely broad, but their changing importance illuminates aspects of the developing economic structure. The decisive historical event in the evolution of the British economy was the Industrial Revolution. It began in the latter half of the eighteenth century and within 100 years had transformed the country. This revolution involved a shift in the balance between sectors. The key change was the decline in agriculture as a source of wealth and a source of jobs. At the same time, the economy began to depend increasingly on the production and sale of finished goods – at first cotton, then a wide range of manufactures based on the iron and steel industries. Thus the Industrial Revolution coincided with the rise of the secondary or manufacturing industries. But in recent decades a further stage in structural change has occurred: the decline of manufacturing and the rise of service industries in the tertiary sector. In part this change is not specific to Britain. It reflects the characteristic development of most industrial economies. The reasons for the expansion of service industries are various. Technical advance has made the activities of extraction and manufacture much more efficient than in the past: in agriculture, for instance, a workforce that is the tiniest in Britain's history produces more food than ever before because of the use of advanced technology

Phases of economic development

1. Before the Industrial Revolution, most economic activity involved agriculture.
2. After the Industrial Revolution, manufacturing was supreme.
3. In recent decades, service industries have become increasingly important. This is changing the class structure from one dominated by manual workers to one dominated by non-manual workers.

on the farm. At the same time, growing prosperity has created an increased demand for services of all kinds, ranging from education to catering and tourism. Britain, because it is a classic example of an advanced industrial economy, has shared in this common experience of economic change.

In Britain, 'sectoral' change has been especially marked. The great industries on which Britain's nineteenth-century industrial might were built have almost universally declined – both in world markets and as components of the British economy. Coal, shipbuilding, iron and steel – all once major centres of economic power and employment – have become much less significant. This decline can be traced back over a century in the case of many industries, but in recent decades it has accelerated: the scale of recent change is illustrated in Table 3.3, simply by reference to some historically important sources of employment for men. Behind these summary figures are some striking and little noticed changes that graphically illustrate the scale of change in the structure of the economy. Employment in curry houses is now greater than employment in steelmaking: the economy owes more to balti than to Bessemer.

The important changes in the balance between the sectors are also reflected in another important feature of the economy – the structure of ownership.

Table 3.3 Changing balance of selected economic sectors, 1984–2004 (% of male employees)

	1984	2004
Financial and business services	12	21
Manufacturing	28	18
Agriculture	2	1

Note: percentages do not sum to 100.
Source: Office for National Statistics (2005) *Social Trends*, No. 35, 2005 Edition, p. 2. © Crown Copyright 2005. Crown copyright material is reproduced with the permission of the Controller of Her Majesty's Stationery Office (HMSO)

■ The structure of ownership

We have already examined one aspect of ownership in Britain's economy – the balance between enterprises owned and controlled in the public and private sectors. But the simple phrase 'private ownership' is complex and deserves close scrutiny. The legal vesting of the ownership of productive property – factories, equipment and so on – in private hands is an important feature of the British economy. The changing structure of that ownership has implications for the functioning of the whole social system and for the kinds of policy that governments can pursue.

In the early stages of the Industrial Revolution Britain, like many other capitalist economies, was marked by what is sometimes called *the unity of ownership and control*: firms were for the most part small by modern standards; they were controlled by families or by partnerships; and the legal owners were usually those who took the main part in daily management. Like much else in Britain, this pattern has changed in modern times.

Three developments are important: the separation of the managerial function from the role of ownership; the changing structure of legal ownership in the most important enterprises; and the changing size and scope of firms' activities.

The development of a division of functions between those responsible for the daily control of firms and those vested with legal ownership actually began in the nineteenth century; it is now predominant among larger firms in the economy. It has been prompted by the growing complexity of the task of running a large business enterprise, which has resulted in the emergence of a wide range of specialised managerial jobs covering finance, production, personnel, sales and so on. No-one seriously disputes that a separation now exists in most large corporations between, on the one hand, individuals responsible for the daily running of the enterprise

> **BOX 3.4** **FACT**
>
> ## Changing structure of firms
>
> The structure of private enterprise in recent decades has been marked by three great changes:
>
> 1. the rise of a specialised group of salaried managers responsible for the main functions inside firms;
> 2. the concentration of share ownership in the hands of institutional investors such as insurance companies;
> 3. the domination of many sectors by giant multinationals organising their markets on a world scale.

and, on the other, groups vested with legal ownership. However, there is a serious argument about the implications – including the political implications – of this shift. Some argue that Britain is only one of a range of advanced capitalist nations where a 'separation of ownership from control' has occurred. In other words, real power in firms is no longer exercised by owners but by salaried managers. The consequence is that one of the traditional characteristics of the capitalist system – the concentration of economic resources in the hands of private individuals motivated largely by the desire for profit – has been modified. Salaried managers, it is argued, have a wider set of motivations than pure profit and are responsive to the needs and wishes of the community. Others argue that, by contrast, the rise of the manager has only allocated traditional tasks in a new way. Managers, it is claimed, run firms in the traditional interests of owners – with profits in mind above all. They do this because many managers are also in part owners; because owners who are not managers still retain the power to dismiss managers who ignore the pursuit of profits; and because in any case most managers accept the philosophy that the point of a firm is to make profit.

The original notion that owners were no longer powerful in big firms arose because of changes in the legal nature of firms. Most big enterprises in Britain are no longer family-owned firms or partnerships. They are 'joint stock' companies – which means that ownership is vested jointly in a multiplicity of individuals who own the stock, or shares, in the firm. Where the owners are many and scattered, and managers are few and concentrated, it is natural that the latter should more effectively control decisions inside the company.

This connects to the second main development identified at the beginning of this section – the changing form of legal ownership. The largest and most important firms in the economy are typically owned jointly by many people scattered around the country – and in some cases around the world. Since important decisions – such as contests for membership of the board of directors – are decided by majority votes, with shareholders allotted votes in proportion to the number of shares owned, it is virtually impossible for numerous small shareholders to combine together in sufficient number to control decisions.

In recent years, however, changes in the nature of share ownership have altered this state of affairs. Although the number of individuals owning shares in Britain grew in the 1980s – principally because of widespread buying of the stock of newly privatised concerns such as British Telecom and British Gas – the proportion of total shares owned by private individuals has shown a long-term fall over recent decades. The facts are illustrated in Figure 3.9. In place of the private shareholder, ownership is increasingly in the hands of what are conventionally called 'institutions', notably insurance companies and pension funds; increasingly these are foreign owned.

This change has an important implication for the debate about the separation of ownership from control. The institutions' shareholdings are concentrated in the biggest and most important firms. Hence, the argument that managers have the power to wield influence over a dispersed mass of owners no longer holds. Indeed, there have been striking cases in recent years where the institutions have wielded their numerical resources to control and discipline managements of individual firms. But recent developments add an extra twist to this debate. As Figure 3.9 shows, the globalisation of economic life – discussed in Chapter 2 – has had a profound effect on ownership: a growing proportion of shares are owned by foreign institutions and individuals.

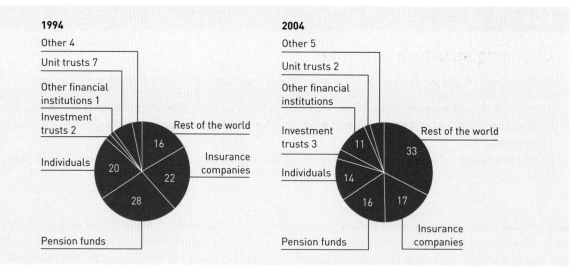

Figure 3.9 Changing patterns of share ownership (percentage of UK equities owned by different institutions, 1994 and 2004)
Source: From *Financial Times*, 22 June 2005, p. 21. Copyright © 2005 The Financial Times Ltd, reproduced with permission

The rise of the giant firm is the third important feature of the structure of ownership in the private sector. Most firms in Britain are tiny, but a small number of giant enterprises nevertheless dominate the economy. This is the result of a long-term trend: the domination of big firms increased greatly in the twentieth century, a change mirrored in other advanced industrial economies. The giant firms

---

BOX 3.5   BRITAIN IN CONTEXT

British society in international context

All societies are special. The characteristics of British society, viewed comparatively, both link her to some societies, and differentiate her from others. Compared with the other big states of the European Union, notably Germany and France, Britain has a distinctive economic structure: she relies less on manufacturing for employment, and more on services; she has labour markets which are much less regulated and which, at least in the last decade, have been much better at creating jobs; and she has more social inequality. By comparison with the Scandinavian members of the European Union – Sweden, Finland and Denmark – she places much less emphasis on the provision of services by the state, and is strikingly more unequal. This had led to the common claim that the nearest model for Britain is the society of the United States: we share a common language and, to some degree, a common popular culture; like the United States we have heavily deregulated labour markets, a good recent record on job creation, and high levels of inequality. Our governments are also more likely to agree with the United States on key foreign policy controversies. And British governments often picture the UK as a model of Anglo-Saxon liberalism which other members of the European Union should follow. But British society is far from being a clone of the United States. There is inequality, but much less marked inequality. The state has a large role in the provision of services: contrast the virtually universal free healthcare provided by the NHS with the American reliance on the market in this field. And since the general election of 2001 the Labour government has radically increased the scale of public spending on services like education and health; for more on this see Chapter 27. Increasingly, therefore, British society looks like a complex fusion of many elements – drawn from German, Scandinavian and American influences. This fusion fittingly reflects the way Britain is positioned at a junction between many of the great competing national social systems in the world today.

dominant in the economy are also usually **multi-national** in scope. A multinational is a firm that produces its goods in different nations and sells them in different national markets. The most sophisticated firms have an international 'division of labour': it is common, for instance, for different components of a motor car to be produced in factories in a variety of countries and then to be assembled in yet another country. In the years since the Second World War the significance of multinational companies has grown greatly. Many of the biggest British concerns have taken on a multinational character. British markets have also themselves been deeply penetrated by foreign multinationals. Britain is one of the most popular locations for American firms expanding abroad, and even when firms are not located in Britain there are whole markets – for instance in motor cycles, electrical goods and automobiles – where the products of foreign multinationals either dominate or are a substantial part of the supply.

These observations connect to what is the most important theme of this chapter: the way the social and economic context of the political system is itself part of a wider context – of Britain as a global and European society.

■ British society in the wider world

That British society exists within a wider global and European context is obvious. But what implications does this have for the society, particularly in so far as the social context helps to shape the kind of political system we have?

The answer lies in two 'contextual' developments – in other words, developments not special to the United Kingdom but those providing a wider setting for British politics and society:

1. *Globalisation*: An ever more closely enmeshed global system is being developed. Although many of the features of the modern global economy can be found in the past, what is unique in the last generation is the combination of factors that all intensify global connections: greater ease of international human transportation; rapidly developing telecommunications and electronic communication; growing world trade, especially between the rich countries of the world, of which Britain is one; and the growing global organisation of

markets for the production and sale of goods and services. These developments are important for all countries on the globe, but for Britain they are especially important. The United Kingdom is especially sensitive to globalisation because we have a uniquely 'international' economy: we both export and import to an unusual degree, and we provide the location for foreign multinationals to an unusual degree.

2. *Europeanisation*: The development of the European Union, since its original foundation as a 'common market' uniting only six countries in the late 1950s, has transformed, and continues to transform, European economy and society. This transformation takes many forms, most of which are examined in later pages of this book. In the realm of government, for example, European political institutions must now be considered an integral part of the decision-making system in Britain – they are not just important 'external' institutions. Socially and economically, Britain has become a much more obviously 'European' society in recent decades. Economically, the United Kingdom is now increasingly integrated with the economy of the rest of the European Union.

These two forces – globalisation and Europeanisation – are bound together. The development of a more integrated European economy has been connected to the development of a more integrated global economy: European multinationals have penetrated beyond Europe, and American and Japanese multinationals have established an often dominating presence in Europe. What have these two powerful contextual features to do with British politics? Much of that question is properly answered in the chapters that follow, but it is sensible to alert ourselves to the momentous consequences. Among the more important are the following:

■ Thatcherite economic reforms, which dominated politics throughout the 1980s, were a sustained response to globalisation – and in part, also, one of the forces that helped to accelerate the globalisation revolution. Thatcherism was an attempt to cope with the fact that, in a world of increasing global production and competition, the British economy as traditionally organised could not perform as effectively as the economies of some other leading industrial nations. Without globalisation we would not have Thatcherism;

and without Thatcherism, in turn, globalisation would have been that much less pronounced.

■ The way the response to globalisation was organised in the 1980s has had long-term consequences for the distribution of power and resources in society and the political system. Some groups have suffered badly. The most obvious case is the miners. In the 1970s, the miners were a great political and economic power, partly responsible for the fall of the Conservative government of Edward Heath in 1974. By the 1990s, after a comprehensive defeat in a landmark strike in the 1980s, privatisation of their industry and a programme of pit closures, they had all but disappeared as an occupation and had completely disappeared as a political force. By contrast, the response to globalisation has greatly enriched some groups who worked in financial markets and has made the markets themselves important arbiters of the economic policy of governments.

■ Britain's experience as a member of the European Union was an important contributory factor to one of the most significant institutional innovations of the 1990s: the introduction in 1999 of devolved government, together with elected assemblies, in Scotland and Wales, for the notion that the two Celtic nations could operate successfully through the EU institutions to secure resources has undoubtedly been an important impetus behind the pressure for devolved government.

■ More directly still, membership of the EU has had profound effects on the system of interest representation in the United Kingdom. A quarter of a century ago, all important pressure groups directed their main activities to central government in Whitehall. Now, there is not a single important group that does not devote a large amount of its time and money to lobbying European institutions, especially the policy makers in the European Commission in Brussels. Many have their own offices in Brussels and belong to Europe-wide interest groups. In short, the growing salience of Britain as a European society has been matched by the 'Europeanisation' of the system of interest representation (see Chapter 11).

■ Finally, the European dimension is clear in its impact on political parties and political debate. In the new millennium, attitudes to Europe – for instance, on the issue of how much deeper should be the integration of Britain into the EU – are a key line of division, both between the political parties and within them.

We can thus see the twin impacts of globalisation and Europeanisation at four levels of the political system: at the highest level of changes in the constitution; at the level of government policy making, as in the integration of government decision making in Whitehall with the European system; at the level of the representation of interests; and at the level of debates conducted within and between the political parties.

Chapter summary

This chapter has described the context of British politics in several ways:

■ It has described how Britain looks from a global context. We have emphasised that Britain belongs to a special 'family' of nations. This family has very specific characteristics: in particular, its economic system is based on the principles of the market, and it is fabulously richer than most other families of nations across the globe. Britain, in short, is capitalist and rich.

■ The chapter has described a range of domestic social hierarchies, relating to occupation, gender and wealth. Here we have seen a mixture of persistence and change. In many ways inequalities, notably in the distribution of income and wealth between classes, have remained remarkably untouched by successive governments intent on lessening inequality during the twentieth century. Indeed, in some respects inequality, especially income inequality, increased towards the end of the century. But substantial changes have taken place in other kinds of inequality, notably gender inequality. Above all, Britain has become a more diverse, plural society in the last generation, and this is a key change in the setting of the system of government.

■ The chapter has described the economic structure, stressing the role of government in that structure. However, it has also shown that revolutionary changes have taken place in some spheres, notably public ownership.

■ Finally, the chapter has described how the global and European setting of British society has to a growing extent helped to shape politics. Thus the chapter returns at the end to one of the key themes announced at the opening: the increasing importance of the wider international setting of the British system of government.

Discussion points

■ Who do you think have been the main winners and losers in the decline of manufacturing industry?

■ What political problems have been caused by the impact of globalisation on British politics?

■ Why has government become less important as an owner, and more important as a regulator, in recent years?

Further reading

By far the best overview of British economy and society is contained in the collection edited by Halsey and Webb (2000). It assembles all the leading experts to cover succinctly all the topics surveyed in this chapter, and much more. The two most valuable sources of up-to-date information are published annually by The Stationery Office for the Office of National Statistics: *Social Trends* charts changing social trends over time; *Regional Trends* compares the regions of the United Kingdom along the main social and economic measures and also provides summary comparisons between the United Kingdom and regions elsewhere in the European Union. Various editions are used for the tables in this chapter, but at the time of going to press the latest available edition of *Social Trends* was for 2005 and for *Regional Trends* was 2004 – both downloadable at www.statistics.gov.uk/statbase. Perkin (1989), though not easy going, is invaluable in describing historical evolution.

References

Adonis, A. and Pollard, A. (1996) *A Class Act* (Hamish Hamilton).

Blondel, J. (1963) *Voters, Parties and Leaders* (Penguin).

Gallie, D. (2000) 'The labour force', in Halsey and Webb, pp. 281–323.

Halsey, A.H. and Webb, J. (eds) (2000) *Twentieth-Century British Social Trends* (Macmillan).

Office for National Statistics (2004) *Regional Trends*, 2004 Edition.

Office for National Statistics (2004) *Social Trends*, No. 34, 2004 Edition, p. 80.

Office for National Statistics (2005) *Social Trends*, No. 35, 2005 Edition, pp. 2, 102.

Perkin, H. (1989) *The Rise of Professional Society: England Since 1888* (Routledge).

Webb, J. (2000) 'Social security', in Halsey and Webb, pp. 548–83.

World Bank (2004) *World Development Indicators* (www.worldbank.org/data)

Useful websites

The range of online sources is increasing in diversity and richness with every passing day. They are particularly important as a source of original material for any student projects, and they also have the advantage of often supplying much more up-to-date figures than it is possible to make available in 'hard copy' form.

For an overview official site: www.statistics.gov.uk/

For employment and economic structure: www.employment.gov.uk/

For income and wealth an official site is: www.inlandrevenue.gov.uk/

An important independent site is provided by the Institute for Fiscal Studies: www.ifs/org.uk/

And another thing . . .

Civil societies: social capital in Britain

Kenneth Newton

Social capital is a new idea with a long history. It goes back to Alexis de Tocqueville (1805–59), the French writer whose classic work *Democracy in America* argued that the society and government of the USA in the mid-nineteenth century rested on the organisation of civil society and its rich and diverse variety of voluntary associations. Americans, de Tocqueville claimed, were particularly active in forming and running voluntary associations, community groups and clubs of all kinds. These not only nurtured the 'habits of the heart' of civic virtue and community participation, but they taught people the art of government, especially self-government.

Alexis de Tocqueville's insight into the importance of voluntary associations has been echoed by almost every major social and political theorist of the nineteenth and twentieth century, but has been given new and powerful form in recent years by Harvard Professor of Government, Robert Putnam. In his books on Italy (Putnam, 1993) and the United States (Putnam, 2000), he argues that 'social capital' is vital for democratic stability, political participation and good government. According to him, social capital is a mixture of three things:

■ *Trust*: Trust between citizens is a powerful bonding agent of society. It helps citizens to cooperate in order to achieve common goals and it is associated with the trust in politicians necessary for democracy.

■ *Norms*: Norms are the cultural expectations of reciprocity (mutual help and respect), civic engagement and community participation. These, in turn, encourage political participation and recognition of the public good.

■ *Networks and social connectedness*: The face-to-face relations produced by a dense network of

clubs and voluntary associations helps to bind society together by creating common identities and interests. Voluntary associations, especially those bridging different social groups, are said to create trust, facilitate cooperation and encourage community engagement and political involvement.

Social capital is about a sense of community, about being able to rely on friends and neighbours and trust strangers, and about community involvement and civic engagement. Social capital, it is claimed, has all sorts of beneficial effects for society and for politics (some bad ones as well): communities with high levels of social capital, it is said, have lower crime rates, better schools, and happier, healthier and wealthier people. Most of all, social capital is necessary for democratic health. Putnam argues that regions with high levels of social capital in Italy are more democratic, and their governments more effective and less corrupt. He argues that many of the problems of American democracy in the late twentieth century – declining voting turnout, lower trust in politicians, less confidence in democratic institutions, political alienation and disillusionment, cheating in tax matters – are due to declining membership of voluntary associations, and the erosion of social capital and community participation. Whereas Americans once went to bowling alleys in teams and clubs, they now 'bowl alone'.

The mass media, especially television, are said to be a prime cause of the decay of social capital. TV pulls people out of their community, isolates them in their living rooms and turns them into couch-potatoes. TV is said to feed us a diet of bad news about corruption, lies, incompetence, war, famine and crime. This is thought to generate the symptoms of 'video malaise', including distrust, political alienation, low confidence in democratic institutions and a general fear and suspicion of the world – the 'mean world' effect.

What relevance does this have to modern Britain? It is true that Britain is suffering from some of the signs of political malaise found in the USA: fears of rising crime, falling voting turnout, declining confidence in political institutions, less trust in politicians and increasing political alienation (Bromley *et al.*, 2001, pp. 203–25). Party identification and membership have fallen, and so has trade union membership. Young adults are more turned-off from conventional politics than any previous generation since the 1950s (Electoral Commission, 2002).

Is a decline of social capital responsible for this? Probably not. Research shows not a decline but a modest growth in voluntary organisations and membership since the 1950s (Hall, 1999; Maloney *et al.*, 2000; Institute for Volunteering Research, 1997). Some groups have declined (traditional women's organisations, trade unions and religious organisations), but others have increased (environmental groups, pre-school play groups and charities). About two-thirds of adults are members of at least one voluntary association, and a third of two or more. An estimated three million people in the UK are activists on voluntary committees, and 22 million are volunteers. The number of charities is growing, their income is rising, they employ more people, and voluntary workers are increasing (National Council for Voluntary Organisations, 2006).

There are no clear indications that social trust is declining in the UK. The evidence shows that most of us still feel able to ask friends and neighbours for help when we are ill, or when we need to borrow something. Most of us would not hesitate to rely on strangers to give directions, or to change a £5 note for the phone (Johnston and Jowell, 2001, pp. 180–6).

The evidence we have about the effects of television also suggests that it does not have particularly malign effects. On the contrary, it is an important source of political information because the average adult watches so much television (21–22 hours a week) that they also watch a lot of TV news as well. More than half the adult population watches TV news every night of the week, but there is little evidence that they suffer from 'video malaise', nor a lot to suggest that those who watch a lot of entertainment TV suffer from 'video malaise' either. In other words, TV viewing, even though a lot of people do a lot of it, does not seem to account for declining levels of political involvement and interest. It is, however, exceedingly difficult to judge the effects

of TV, simply because it is all around us. In the same way that fish may be the last forms of life on earth to discover water, so we may not be able to detect the effects of TV in a world that is totally permeated by it.

Although social capital in postwar Britain has not declined, and has probably increased in some respects, it is not equally distributed between different social groups. By and large the middle-class, middle-aged, white and better educated sections of the population have greatest access to the resources of social capital. This group is well connected, and therefore more likely to be surrounded by a supporting social network that provides help with information, jobs, health, schools, housing and opportunities of many different kinds. They can use their social networks and contacts and their trustworthy friends and colleagues to improve their life chances and quality of life. It is not the same for minority groups and the socially excluded.

The idea that governments can do something about social capital may, at first sight, seem implausible. One cannot improve levels of social trust by passing laws that say people should trust each other. At the same time there is also evidence that social capital is strongly affected, in a top-down manner, by government and its operations. Social trust is higher in countries with just and fair laws, honest and incorruptible public officials, democratic and egalitarian politics and high quality public services.

What can we conclude from all this? In the first place it seems that modern Britain does suffer from many of the forms of democratic malaise that characterise the USA. Election turnout, political alienation, social and political trust, confidence in the institutions of democratic government, and political engagement of many (not all) kinds, are all a cause for concern, although perhaps the trends are not as worrying as in the USA. At the same time, social capital in Britain does not appear to be the main explanation for this. On the contrary, social capital is no worse and perhaps even better than it was in the 1960s and 1970s. The mass media, television in particular, do not seem to have the effect of undermining social capital in Britain.

What, then, explains the problems of democratic malaise? We are certainly not sure of the answer but quite a lot seems to depend on political rather than social factors. In the long run democracy depends upon a well-founded civil society, but in the short and medium term democratic attitudes and behaviour probably rest, as much as anything else, on honest and effective government that seems to have the public interest at heart, maintains good public services and retains the confidence of the voters. What seems to undermine confidence in government and democratic institutions is not a decline of social capital, but a widespread belief that the political system is not working well or democratically, that politicians are not to be trusted, and that economic performance and public services are not good enough. In the long run, a decline of social capital is likely to undermine the best efforts of politicians to do these things, and the result will be a vicious circle in which both social capital and democratic performance will go into decline. But in the short run the causes of political alienation seem to lie mainly in the performance of the political system and of politicians themselves.

References

Bromley, C., Curtice, J. and Seyd, B. (2001) 'Political engagement, trust, and constitutional reform', *British Social Attitudes, The 18th Report* (Sage/National Centre for Social Research, London), pp. 199–225.

Electoral Commission (2002) 'Voter engagement and young people', http://www.electoralcommission.gov.uk/templates/search/document.cfm/6188

Hall, P. (1999) 'Social capital in Britain', *British Journal of Political Science*, 29: 417–61.

Institute for Volunteering Research (1997) http://www.ivr.org.uk/nationalsurvey.htm

Johnston, M. and Jowell, R. (2001) 'How robust is British Civil Society?', *British Social Attitudes, The 18th Report* (Sage/National Centre for Social Research, London), pp. 175–97.

Maloney, W., Smith, G. and Stoker, G. (2000) 'Social capital and associational life', in *Social Capital: Critical Perspectives* (Oxford: Oxford University Press), pp. 212–25.

National Council for Voluntary Organisations (2006) http://www.ncvo-vol.org.uk/

Putnam, R. (1993) *Making Democracy Work: Civic Traditions in Modern Italy* (Princeton, NJ: Princeton University Press).

Putnam, R. (2000) *Bowling Alone – The Collapse and Revival of American Community* (New York: Simon and Schuster).

POLITICS UK

PART 2
DEFINING THE
POLITICAL WORLD

CHAPTER 4

Ideology and the liberal tradition

Bill Jones

Learning objectives

- To clarify the concept of ideology.

- To trace the transition of new ideas from their 'revolutionary' inception to accepted orthodoxy.

- To show how classical liberalism developed into new liberalism, the creed that set the social agenda for the next century.

Introduction

This chapter begins by discussing what we mean by the term 'ideology'. It goes on to explain how 'liberal' ideas entered the political culture as heresies in the seventeenth and eighteenth centuries but went on to become the orthodoxies of the present age. Classical liberalism in the mid-nineteenth century is examined together with the birth of modern liberalism in the early twentieth century. So-called 'liberal' ideas therefore provide the architecture of our beliefs in a democratic society. We may be Labour, Conservative, Liberal Democrat or something else, but we hold these views, discuss and debate them within the framework of ideas acquired hundreds of years ago.

■ What is ideology?

For up to two decades after 1945 it seemed as if ideology as a factor in British politics was on the wane. The coalition comradeship of the war had drawn some of the sting from the sharp doctrinal conflicts between the two major political parties, and in its wake the Conservatives had conceded – without too much ill grace – that Labour would expand welfare services and nationalise a significant sector of the economy. Once in power after 1951, the Conservatives presided over their socialist inheritance of a mixed economy and a welfare state. Both parties seemed to have converged towards a general consensus on political values and institutions: there was more to unite than to divide them. By the end of the 1950s, some commentators – notably the American political scientist Daniel Bell – were pronouncing 'the end of ideology' (see Bell, 1960) in Western societies.

However, the faltering of the British economy in the 1960s, exacerbated in the early 1970s by the rise in oil prices, industrial unrest and raging inflation, reopened the ideological debate with a vengeance. A revived Labour Left hurled contumely at their right-wing Cabinet colleagues for allegedly betraying socialist principles. Margaret Thatcher, meanwhile, Leader of the Opposition after 1975, began to elaborate a position far to the right of her predecessor Edward Heath (Prime Minister, 1970–4 – see biography). The industrial paralysis of the 1978–9 'winter of discontent' provided a shabby end for Jim Callaghan's Labour government and a perfect backcloth against which Thatcher's confident assertions could be projected. From 1979 to 1990, ideology in the form of Thatcherism or the New Right triumphed over what has subsequently been labelled the 'post-war consensus'.

BIOGRAPHY

Edward Heath (1916–2005)

Conservative Prime Minister. Educated at Oxford in the 1930s, when he was deeply concerned about unemployment and the threat of fascism. He fought with distinction in the war and entered politics in its wake. He was a prominent younger member of Macmillan's governments and became leader of the Conservatives a year after their defeat of 1964. He became Prime Minister in 1970 on a right-wing ticket but resorted to 'left-wing' reflation when unemployment began to soar. During his four years in power, his greatest achievement was taking the country into Europe. He was replaced by Margaret Thatcher as leader in 1975 and could not hide his resentment at her 'disloyalty' (i.e. to him) or her extreme right-wing policies. He remained a bitter critical figure, defending his record and Europe, attacking his successor until the end of his career.

Ideology as a concept is not easy to define. It is to some extent analogous to philosophy but is not as open-ended or as disinterested. It shares some of the moral commitment of religion but is essentially secular and rooted in this world rather than the next. On the other hand, it is more fundamental and less specific than mere policy. Perhaps it is helpful to regard ideology as 'applied philosophy'. It links philosophical ideas to the contemporary world, it provides a comprehensive and systematic perspective whereby human society can be understood, and

Critics say Tony Blair is too flexible with Labour ideas and principles
Source: Copyright © Chris Riddell. From *The Observer*, 2 June 2002. Reproduced with permission from Guardian Newspapers Limited

it provides a framework of principles from which policies can be developed.

Individuals support ideologies for a variety of reasons: moral commitment – often genuine, whatever cynics might say – as well as self-interest. It is quite possible for a businessman, for example, to believe that a pro-business set of policies by a party is good not only for him but for the nation as a whole. Clearly, ideology will mean more to political theorists active within political parties, elected representatives or the relative minority who are seriously interested in political ideas. It has to be recognised that most people are ill informed on political matters, nor especially interested in them. It is quite possible for large numbers of people to subscribe to contradictory propositions – for example, that welfare services should be improved while taxes should be cut – or for non-rational reasons like voting for a party out of sentiment while disagreeing with its major policies. But the broad mass of the population is not completely inert. During election campaigns they receive a crash course in political education,

and leaving aside the more crass appeals to emotion and unreason, most voters are influenced to some extent by the ideological debate. The party with the clearest message that seems most relevant to the times can win elections, as Labour discovered in 1945, the Conservatives in 1979 and Labour again in 1997.

Classifying ideologies

This is a difficult and imperfect science, but the following two approaches should help to clarify it.

The horizontal left–right continuum

Left	Centre	Right

This is the most familiar classification, used and abused in the press and in everyday conversations. It arose from the seating arrangements adopted in the French Estates General in 1789, where the aristocracy sat to the right of the King and the popular movements to his left. Subsequently the terms have come to represent adherence to particular groups of principles. Right-wingers stress freedom, or the right of individuals to do as they please and develop their own lives and personalities without interference, especially from governments – which history teaches are potentially tyrannical. Left-wingers believe that this kind of freedom is only won by the strong at the expense of the weak. They see equality as the more important value and stress the collective interest of the community above that of the individual. Those occupying the centre ground usually represent varieties of compromise between these two positions.

The implications of these principles for economic policy are obviously of key importance. Right-wingers champion free enterprise, or capitalism: the rights of individuals to set up their own businesses, to provide goods and services and to reap what reward they can. Left-wingers disagree. Capitalism, they argue, creates poverty amid plenty – much better to move towards collective ownership so that workers can receive the full benefit of their labour. Politicians in the centre dismiss both these positions as extreme and damaging to the harmony of national life. They tend to argue for various combinations of left and right principles or compromises between them: in practice a mixed economy plus efficient welfare services. The left–right continuum therefore relates in practice principally to economic and social policy.

Left	Centre	Right
Equality	Less inequality	Freedom
Collectivism	Some collectivism	Individualism
Collective ownership	Mixed economy	Free enterprise

The vertical axis or continuum

The inadequacies of the left–right continuum are obvious. It is both crude and inaccurate in that many people can subscribe to ideas drawn from its whole width and consequently defy classification. H.J. Eysenck suggested in the early 1950s that if a 'tough' and 'tender' axis could bisect the left–right continuum, ideas could be more accurately plotted on two dimensions. In this way ideological objectives could be separated from political methodology – so tough left-wingers, e.g. communists, would occupy the top left-hand quarter, tough right-wingers, e.g. fascists, the top right-hand quarter, and so on.

The vertical axis can also be used to plot other features:

1. An authoritarian–libertarian axis is perhaps a more precise variation on the tough and tender theme.

2. A *status quo*–revolutionary axis is also useful. The Conservative Party has traditionally been characterised as defending the established order. However, Margaret Thatcher was a committed radical who wanted to engineer major and irreversible changes. It was Labour and the Conservative 'wets' who defended the *status quo* in the 1980s. This approach produces some interesting placements on our two-dimensional diagram.

Political parties and the left–right continuum

Despite its inadequacies, the left–right continuum is useful because it is commonly understood (though see Box 4.1). It will be used as a guide to the following sections, but first a word on the way in which political parties relate to the political spectrum.

For most of the postwar period, the major ideological divisions have not occurred between the two big parties but within them. The Labour Party has covered a very wide spectrum from the revolutionary Left to the cautious social democrat Right. Similarly, two major Conservative schools of thought developed in the late 1970s: traditional ('wet') conservatism and the New Right or Thatcherite conservatism. The centre ground was dominated for many years by the Liberal Party, but during the 1980s it was first augmented by the Social Democratic Party (which split off from the Labour Party in 1981) and then was fragmented when the merger initiative following the 1987 general election resulted in the awkward progeny of the Social and Liberal Democrats plus the rump Social Democratic Party led defiantly by David Owen until May 1990, when the party formally folded.

Ideas and values in politics

In politics, ideas and values cannot exist in isolation. They need a vehicle by which they can be transformed from abstract ideology into practical legislative effect. The vehicle is the political party . . .

It is more than nostalgia that justifies the party system. It is essentially the belief that some of the 'ideas and values' of politicians have a permanent importance. The policies by which those ideas and values are implemented may change with time and circumstance but the ideology abides.

Roy Hattersley, 'Endpiece: nous and Nostalgia', *The Guardian*, 30 September 1989. © Guardian Newspapers Limited, reprinted with permission

| BOX 4.1 | IDEAS AND PERSPECTIVES |

Left and right discussed

In his book *The Third Way* (1998), Anthony Giddens suggests left and right are less than adequate terms. He points out that what was once left can now be right – such as nineteenth-century free-market views. He quotes the Italian writer Bobbio, who argues that politics is adversarial and that 'left and right' encapsulates the familiar idea of bodily opposites, i.e. the left and right arms. He goes on to say that when ideas are evenly balanced most people accept the dichotomy, but when one ideology seems 'the only game in town' neither side finds the terms suitable. The strong ideology seeks to claim it is the 'only' alternative, while the weaker tries to strengthen its position by absorbing some elements of the stronger side and offering them as its own, producing a 'synthesis of opposing positions with the intentions in practice of saving whatever can be saved of one's own position by drawing in the opposing position and thus neutralising it'. Both sides then present their views as beyond the old left/right distinction and as something totally new and exciting. Giddens comments that 'the claim that Tony Blair has taken over most of the views of Thatcherism and recycled them as something new is readily comprehensible from such a standpoint'. Giddens insists that the 'left' is not just the opposite of 'right': the core of the former is concerned with social justice or 'emancipatory' politics, while the right has shifted to anti-global and even racist positions.

He goes on to accept that socialism is no longer valid as a 'theory of economic management' and that in consequence the right/left distinction has lost relevance. Now people face 'life politics' decisions such as those connected with nuclear energy, work, global warming, devolution and the future of the EU, none of which fits easily into the old dichotomy. By talking of the 'radical centre', Giddens suggests that 'major gains' can be derived as it 'permits exchange across political fences which were much higher'. So to look at welfare reform, it is not merely an argument about high or low spending but comprises 'common issues facing all welfare reformers. The question of how to deal with an ageing population isn't just a matter of setting pension levels. It requires more radical rethinking in relation to the changing nature of ageing'.

Source: Giddens (1998), pp. 37–46

■ The liberal tradition

Since then, like so many other political labels coined as forms of abuse ('tory' was once a name given to Irish outlaws), the word 'liberalism' has lost its derogatory connotations and fully traversed the ground between vice and virtue. Now liberalism denotes opinions and qualities that are generally applauded. Most people would like to think they are liberal in the sense of being open-minded, tolerant, generous or rational. This is partly because the ideas of the English liberal philosophers from the mid-seventeenth to the mid-nineteenth centuries became accepted as dominant elements in our political culture. These were the ideas that helped to create our liberal democratic political system in the late nineteenth century and since then have provided its philosophical underpinning.

Interestingly, in the USA the term came to assume a pejorative meaning in the early 1980s, when the Republicans successfully linked it to being 'soft on communism' and therefore anti-American (see Box 4.2); in March 2006 the film actor George Clooney's statement that he was indeed a 'liberal' consequently contained a note of defiance.

An important distinction clearly has to be made between liberal with a small 'l' and the Liberalism associated with the party of the same name until the 1987 merger. The Liberal Party always claimed a particular continuity with liberal philosophical ideas; but so deeply ingrained have these views become that most political parties also owe them substantial unacknowledged philosophical debts. For their part, liberals have made contributions to political, social and economic thinking that have been hugely influential and have been plundered

BOX 4.2	IDEAS AND PERSPECTIVES

The demonising of the word 'liberal' in US politics

Guardian columnist John Sutherland meditated on Tony Blair's attacks on the 'forces of conservatism' at the 1999 Bournemouth conference. He wondered whether Blair was not trying to do for the 'c' word what had been done to the 'l' word in the USA.

Up to the mid eighties, 'liberal' was one of the blue chips of American political discourse. There was a negative side to liberalism. But it was the endearing quality of being so open-minded – so small 'l' liberal – as to be 'wishy washy'. . . Some behind the scenes mastermind set up his masters to demonise the term. Liberals were not henceforth to be portrayed as weak kneed, well intentioned guys. They were powerful, cunning, and ruthless Machiavels. They had a sinister agenda and long term anti American goals. As Secretary for Education William Bennett's mantra was that 'liberalism has brought America to its present crisis'. . . The demonisation of the word 'liberal' was a triumph for the right. On talk shows Rush Limbaugh nowadays spits out the word as venomously and repetitively as McCarthy did 'reds'. And it always hits the mark. Democrats became terrified of the term of which they had been the proud possessors. Clinton's presidency has been one long lame duck and weave against any charge of liberalism. The L word now frightens the hell out of the liberals.

Source: John Sutherland, 'How Blair discovered defeat by definition', *The Guardian,* 25 October 1999.
© Guardian Newspapers Limited, reprinted with permission

shamelessly by other parties. It makes sense, therefore, to begin with some consideration of the liberal tradition of both the philosophical 'l' and party political 'L' variety.

Philosophical liberalism

Bertrand Russell attributes the birth of English liberal thought in part to the French philosopher René Descartes (1596–1650). His famous proposition 'I think, therefore I am' made 'the basis of knowledge different for each person since for each the starting point was his own existence not that of other individuals or the community' (Russell, 1965, p. 579). To us such propositions seem unexceptional, but in the mid-seventeenth century they were potentially revolutionary because they questioned the very basis of feudal society. This relied on unquestioning acceptance of the monarch's divine right to rule, the aristocracy's hereditary privileges and the Church's explanation of the world together with its moral leadership. Feudal society was in any case reeling from the impact of the Civil War (1642–9), the repercussions of which produced a limited constitutional monarchy and the embryo of modern parliamentary government. Descartes had inaugurated a new style of thinking.

BIOGRAPHY

Bertrand Russell (1872–1970)

British philosopher and mathematician. *Principia Mathematica* was his most influential philosophical work but he wrote many popular books as well, including *The History of Western Philosophy* (1946). A radical member of the Liberal Party, he opposed the new creed of communism and after the Second World War threw himself into opposing nuclear weapons as a passionate pacifist.

Rationality

John Locke (1632–1704) did much to set the style of liberal thinking as rational and undogmatic. He accepted some certainties, such as his own existence, God and mathematical logic, but he respected an area of doubt in relation to most propositions. He was inclined to accept differences of opinion as the natural consequences of free individual development. Liberal philosophers tended to give greater credence to facts established by scientific enquiry – the systematic testing of theories against reality – rather than to assertions accepted as fact purely on the basis of tradition.

Toleration

This lack of dogmatism was closely connected with a liberal prejudice in favour of **toleration** and compromise. Conflicts between crown and Parliament, Catholicism and Protestantism had divided the country for too long, they felt: it was time to recognise that religious belief was a matter of personal conscience, not a concern of government.

Natural rights and the consent of the governed

This idea emerged out of the 'contract' theorists of the seventeenth and eighteenth centuries. These thinkers believed that each individual had made a kind of agreement to obey the government in exchange for the services of the state, principally 'security' or protection from wrong-doing. The logical extension of this mode of thought was that if a contract of this sort had been somehow agreed, then the citizen had a right to reject a government that did not provide services up to the requisite standard. It was not suggested that anything had actually been signed; the idea was more of an application of the legal concept of rights to the philosophical realm. It was all a far cry from Sir Robert Filmer's doctrine that the divine authority of monarchs to receive absolute obedience could be traced back to Adam and Eve, from whom all monarchs were originally descended (see also Chapter 5 on the concept of rights).

Individual liberty

The idea of natural rights was closely allied to the concept of individual **liberty**, which had already been established by the eighteenth century:

These liberties included the freedom from arbitrary arrest, arbitrary search and arbitrary taxation; equality before the law, the right to trial by jury; a degree of freedom of thought, speech and religious belief; and freedom to buy and sell.

Gamble (1981), p. 67; see also Chapter 5 on the concept of freedom

Such liberties in practice were protected by constitutional checks and balances, limited government and representation. John Stuart Mill established the classic liberal view on liberty when he argued that anyone should be free to do as they wish unless their actions impinge on the freedom of someone else (see Box 4.3).

Constitutional checks and balances

Locke argued something destined to influence all future democratic government: that to ensure that executive power was not exercised arbitrarily by the monarch, the law-making or legislative arm of government should be separate, independent and removable by the community. This doctrine of the 'separation of powers' informed liberal enthusiasm for written constitutions (although, ironically, Britain has never had a written constitution or, indeed, an effective separation of powers).

Limited government

Instead of the absolute power that Filmer argued the monarch was free to exercise, liberal philosophers, mindful of past abuses, sought to restrict the legitimacy of government to a protection of civil liberties. It was held to be especially important that government did not interfere with the right to property or the exercise of economic activity.

Representation

It followed that if the legislature was to be removable then it needed to be representative. Many liberal Whigs – inclined to support parliament rather than the monarch – in the eighteenth century believed that Parliament was generally representative of the nation, even though the franchise was small and usually based on a highly restrictive property qualification. However, such positions were destined to be eroded by the inherent logic of natural rights: if everyone had equal rights then surely they should have an equal say in removing a government not of their liking?

The influence of the liberal philosophers perhaps seems greater in retrospect than it was because they were often seeking to justify and accelerate political trends that were already well under way. Nevertheless, such liberal notions were of key importance and provide ideas still used as touchstones in the present day.

BOX 4.3	IDEAS AND PERSPECTIVES

Libertarianism

For some people the central aim of political activity should be the defence of freedom. These 'libertarians' argue, like Sharon Harris, President of a US group called Advocates for Self-Government, 'that each person owns his own life and property and has the right to make his own decisions as to how he lives his life – as long as he simply respects the rights of others to do the same.' This is essentially the J.S. Mill position, but the assertion of the individual right to freedom above all else leads to some unusual political positions. For example, some argue that the state needs to defend the freedom of others to certain rights – welfare support, for example – but for libertarians this involves an unacceptable imposition of taxes by the government, demands backed by force.

They also argue against any kind of censorship, the military draft, the minimum wage, laws on sexual behaviour, drug use and immigration controls while supporting free trade and prostitution. Robert Nozick's much admired 1974 work, *Anarchy, State and Utopia*, elaborated some of these positions including the view of taxation as 'forced labour'. Translated into the more conventional political world, libertarianism appeals partly to the anarchic left who resent any controls but perhaps more powerfully to the right and, because it implicitly entails disobedience to the law and a complete 'rolling back' of the state, the far right. In the USA some groups have established themselves as libertarian enclaves in conventional society, seeking to be true to their visions and in the process rejecting the whole concept and machinery of government with its controls, regulation and impositions. At this point left-wing anarchism and right-wing libertarianism meet in a variety of intriguing ways.

Some commentators, such as Eccleshall (1984, 1986) and Gamble (1981), see liberalism as providing the philosophical rationale for modern capitalist society. Certainly the idea of individual freedom, property rights and limited government suited the emergent entrepreneurial middle classes destined to come of political age in the next century. However, liberal views on government have enjoyed a general acceptance not just in Britain but also in the USA, Western Europe and elsewhere. They have provided the commonly accepted ground rules of democratic behaviour, the 'procedural values' of toleration, fair play and free speech that Bernard Crick argues should be positively reinforced in our society via our classrooms (see Chapter 1). They have provided in one sense an 'enabling' ideology that all major parties have accepted. Indeed, it is in some ways surprising that a creed originating in an agrarian, largely non-industrialised country should have provided a political framework that has survived so tenaciously and indeed triumphantly into the present day (see also Chapter 5 on this concept).

Classical liberalism

The American and French Revolutions applied liberal principles in a way that shocked many of their more moderate adherents. The Napoleonic interlude caused a period of reaction, but during the mid- to late nineteenth century classical liberalism took shape. Claiming continuity with the early liberals, this new school was based on the economic ideas of Adam Smith and the radical philosophers Jeremy Bentham, James Mill and his son John Stuart Mill. Liberalism with a capital 'L' then took the stage in the form of the Liberal Party, a grouping based on the Whigs, disaffected Tories – the group in the eighteenth-century parliament which supported the king – and the Manchester Radicals led by Richard Cobden and John Bright. Classical liberalism was characterised by:

An acceptance of the liberal conception of the independent, rational and self-governing citizen as the basic unit of society.

For liberals, this concept now represented a goal or vision to be worked for. Liberals hoped that through the erosion of aristocratic privilege and the moral transformation of the working class, social differences would give way to a new society of equals.

Human nature

The liberal view of human nature was fairly optimistic. John Stuart Mill, for example, doubted whether working for the common good would induce citizens to produce goods as efficiently as when self-interest was involved. His awareness of human selfishness perhaps underlay his advice against too rapid a rate of social progress. However, at the heart of liberal philosophy was a belief in the potential of human nature to change into Locke's civilised reasonable human being, capable of being educated into responsible citizenship. Many liberals felt that such

an education would take a great many years but that it was possible, especially through direct involvement of citizens in the economy and the political system.

Freedom

Classical liberalism retained the emphasis on freedom. In his essay *On Liberty*, for example, Mill felt: 'It was imperative that human beings should be free to form opinions and to express their opinions without reserve.' The only constraint should be that in the exercise of his freedom, an individual should not impinge upon the freedom of others (again see Chapter 5).

Utilitarianism

Jeremy Bentham (1748–1832) took the rationality of liberal philosophy to new levels with his science of utilitarianism. His approach was based on what now seems an extraordinarily simplistic view of human psychology. He argued that human beings were disposed to seek pleasure and avoid pain. While they sought what was best for themselves they frequently made mistakes. The role of government therefore was to assist individuals in making the correct choices, in enabling the achievement of the 'greatest happiness for the greatest number'. While Bentham embraced the *laissez-faire/capitalist* economic system as highly utilitarian, he believed that most laws and administrative arrangements reflected aristocratic privilege and therefore were in need of reform. His ideas were criticised as simplistic and his Panopticon – a model prison based on his philosophy – was generally seen as risible, but he had a pervasive influence on Liberal legislators in the nineteenth century.

Minimal government

Bentham's influence paradoxically led to far-reaching legal and administrative reforms: for example, the regulatory framework for mines and factories. However, other liberals were strongly opposed to such regulation both as a violation of *laissez-faire* principles and as an interference in the moral education of the poor. Liberals such as the social Darwinist Herbert Spencer (1820–1903) argued that welfare provision was wrong in that it sheltered the poor from the consequences of their behaviour. 'Is it not manifest', he argued, 'that there must exist in our

---

BIOGRAPHY

John Stuart Mill (1806–73)

John Stuart Mill, 1806–73, the father of British representative democracy
Source: Mary Evans Picture Library / Alamy

British philosopher. Influenced by his father, James, he became a leading advocate of representative government. Sat as an MP in the 1860s and supported votes for women. Wrote *Principles of Political Economy* (1848), *On Liberty* (1859), *Representative Government* (1861) and *Utilitarianism* (1863).

midst an immense amount of misery which is a normal result of misconduct and ought not to be dissociated from it?' State support for the poor was therefore a dangerous narcotic likely to prevent the right lessons being learned. The stern lesson that classical liberals wished to teach was that the poorer classes would face the penalties of poverty unless they adopted the values and lifestyles of their economic superiors: thrift, hard work, moderate indulgence and self-improving pastimes.

Representative government

Bentham and James Mill (1773–1836) introduced arguments in favour of representative government. Bentham dismissed the natural rights argument as 'nonsense on stilts'. His own utilitarian reasoning was that such a form of government was the most effective safeguard for citizens against possibly rapacious rulers or powerful 'sinister interests'. As both men believed individuals to be the best judge of where their own interests lay, they favoured universal franchise (although Mill sought to restrict it to men over 40). His son, J.S. Mill (1806–73), is probably the best-known advocate of representative government. He urged adult male and female suffrage, but to guard against a 'capricious and impulsive' House of Commons he advised a literacy qualification for voting and a system of plural voting whereby educated professional people would be able to cast more votes than ill-educated workers. Mill also believed that a participatory **democracy** and the sense of responsibility it would imbue would contribute towards the moral education of society: 'Democracy creates a morally better person because it forces people to develop their potentialities'.

Laissez-faire *economics*

Laissez-faire economics was predicated on the tenet of individual freedom: it asserted that the ability to act freely in the marketplace – to buy and sell property, employ workers and take profit – was central to any free society. Adam Smith's (1723–90) broadsides against the trade protection of the eighteenth-century mercantilist system provided the clearest possible statement of the case for economic activity free from political restrictions. According to Smith, producers should be allowed to supply products at the price consumers are willing to pay. Provided that competition was fair, the 'invisible hand' of the market would ensure that goods were

produced at the lowest possible price commensurate with the quality consumers required. Producers would be motivated by selfish pursuit of profit but would also provide social 'goods', through providing employment, creating wealth and distributing it in accordance with the energy and ability of people active in the economic system. Smith believed that government intervention and regulation would impede this potentially perfect self-adjusting system. Liberals were not especially worried by the inequalities thrown up by *laissez-faire* economics; nor did they waste any sleep over the socialists' claim that the wage labour system enabled the middle-class property owners to exploit their workers. Classical liberals were opposed to inherited financial advantages but not so concerned with the differences created by different performances in relation to the market. They favoured the meritocracy of the market: they were the high priests of capitalism.

Peace through trade

Liberals, especially the so-called Manchester Radicals, also applied their free-trade principles to foreign affairs. Richard Cobden, for example, regarded diplomacy and war as the dangerous pastimes of the aristocracy. His answer to these perennial problems was 'to make diplomacy open and subject to parliamentary control', eliminate trade barriers, and encourage free trade worldwide. Commerce, he argued, was peaceful and beneficial, and it encouraged cooperation and contact between nations. If the world were a completely open market, national economies would become more integrated and interdependent and governments would be less likely to engage in conflicts or war.

The new liberalism

The emphasis of classical liberalism was on *laissez-faire*, wealth production, toleration of inequality, minimal welfare, individual responsibility and moral education. Towards the end of the nineteenth century, however, liberals themselves began to move away from their own ascetic economic doctrines. John Stuart Mill had argued that government was only justified in intervening in society in order to prevent injury to the life, property or freedom of others. To some liberals it appeared that capitalist society had become so complex and repressive that the freedom of poor people to develop their potential was being restricted: even if they were inclined to emulate their middle-class betters their capacity to do so was held back by poverty, poor health and education, and squalid living and working conditions. Liberal thinkers began to shift their emphasis away from 'negative' freedom – freedom from oppression – towards providing 'positive' freedom – the capacity of people to make real choices regarding education, employment, leisure and so on.

State responsibility for welfare

T.H. Green (1836–82) helped to initiate this movement for positive action to assist the poor by calling for a tax on inherited wealth. Alfred Marshall (1842–1924) believed that capitalism now provided such material plenty that it had the capacity to redistribute some of its largesse to the disadvantaged so that they would be able genuinely to help themselves to become self-reliant. But it was L.T. Hobhouse (1864–1929) who perhaps marked the key shift of Liberals towards paternalism:

The state as over-parent is quite as truly liberal as socialistic. It is the basis of the rights of the child, of his protection against parental neglect, of the equality of opportunity which he may claim as a 'future citizen'.

Hobhouse insisted that his version of paternalism should not be oppressively imposed; he favoured a basic minimum standard of living that would provide 'equal opportunities of self development'. He followed Green in proposing taxation to finance such welfare innovations as health insurance and pensions. The great Liberal victory of 1906 enabled the government to implement many of these new measures. Thereafter Liberals became firm advocates of **welfarism**; in 1942, the Liberal William Beveridge produced his famous blueprint for the postwar welfare state.

The mixed economy: Hobsonian and Keynesian economics

Government intervention of a different kind was proposed by J.A. Hobson (1858–1940). He was the first major liberal economist (he later became a socialist) to argue that capitalism was fatally flawed. Its tendency to produce a rich minority who accumulated unspent profits and luxury goods meant that the full value of goods produced was not consumed by society. This created slumps and, indirectly, the phenomenon of economic imperialism. Capitalists were forced by such under-consumption to export their savings abroad, thus creating overseas interests

---

BIOGRAPHY

John Maynard Keynes (1883–1946)

Born in Cambridge, Keynes was the son of an academic. He was educated at Eton and King's College, Cambridge, where he mixed in *avant-garde* intellectual circles, such as the 'Bloomsbury group', and taught sporadically. He served in the India Office (1906–8) and later wrote his first book on this subject. In the First World War he advised the Treasury and represented it at the Versailles Treaty negotiations but resigned over the terms proposed. His essay *The Economic Consequences of the Peace* (1919) brought his powerful radical intellect to the notice of the country's ruling élite. He attacked Churchill's restoration of the gold standard in 1925, and the unemployment caused by the Depression inspired his most famous work, *A General Theory of Employment, Interest and Money* (1936). His views won support on the left and in the centre as well as helping to inspire the New Deal policies of Roosevelt in the USA.

Keynes married a Soviet ballerina and with her father founded the Vic-Wells ballet. In 1943 he established the Arts Theatre in Cambridge. In the same year he played a leading role in the Bretton Woods agreement, which set up a new international economic order, the establishment of the International Monetary Fund and negotiations following the ending of lend-lease (a financial agreement whereby aid was channelled to the UK during the war) after the war to secure a major loan to help Britain to survive the rigours of the immediate postwar world. Most people achieve only a fraction in their lifetimes of what Keynes managed to do. He was one of the truly great figures of the century, and his influence lives on today.

with political and colonial consequences. Hobson argued that the state could solve this crisis with one Olympian move: redirect wealth from the minority to the poor via progressive taxation. The section of society most in need would then be able to unblock the mechanism which caused overproduction and unemployment, thus making moral as well as economic sense.

J.M. Keynes (1883–1946) (see biography, page 101) completed this revolution in liberal economic thought by arguing that demand could be stimulated not by redistribution of wealth to the poor but by government-directed investment in new economic activity. Confronted by a world recession and massive unemployment, he concentrated on a different part of the economic cycle. He agreed that the retention of wealth by capitalists under a *laissez-faire* economic system lay at the heart of the problem, but he believed the key to be increased investment, not increased consumption. Instead of saving in a crisis, governments should encourage businessmen to invest in new economic activity. Through the creation of new economic enterprises wealth would be generated, consumption increased, other economic activities stimulated and unemployment reduced. He envisaged a mixed economy in which the state would intervene with a whole range of economic controls to achieve full employment and planned economic growth. Keynes was not just concerned with the cold science of economics: his view of the mixed economy would serve social ends in the form of alleviated hardship and the extension of opportunity. But while Keynes was unhappy with capitalism in the 1930s he did not propose to replace it – merely to modify it. He was no egalitarian, unlike socialist economists, and disagreed with Hobsonian calls for wealth redistribution, which he felt would adversely affect the incentives to achieve that human nature required: 'for my own part I believe there is social and psychological justification for significant inequalities of income and wealth' (Keynes, 1985, p. 374).

Internationalism

Radical liberals such as J.A. Hobson, Norman Angel, E.D. Moorel, C.R. Buxton, H.N. Brailsford, Lowes Dickinson and Charles Trevelyan produced an influential critique of the international system, arguing that the practice of secret diplomacy, imperialist competition for markets, haphazard balance-of-power policies and the sinister role of arms manufacturers made war between nations tragically inevitable. The First World War appeared to vindicate their analysis and encouraged them to develop the idea of an overarching international authority: the League of Nations. The idea was picked up by political parties and world leaders, including the US President, Woodrow Wilson, and through the catalyst of war was translated into the League of Nations by the Versailles Treaty. Most of the radical liberals joined the Labour Party during and after the war, but the Liberal Party subsequently remained staunchly internationalist and in favour of disarmament proposals throughout the interwar period. Despite the failure of the League, Liberals passionately supported the United Nations which emerged in the wake of the Second World War.

Further development of democratic government

The New Liberals were no less interested than their predecessors in the development of representative democracy through extension of the franchise and the strengthening of the House of Commons. Lloyd George's device of including welfare proposals in his 1909 Budget – a measure that the House of Lords had traditionally passed 'on the nod' – precipitated a conflict between the two chambers that resulted in the House of Lords' power being reduced from one of absolute veto over legislation to one of delay only. In the early 1920s, the Liberal Party gave way to Labour as the chief opposition party, returning 159 MPs in 1923, fifty-nine in 1929 and only twenty-one in 1935. The dramatic decline in the party's fortunes coincided with its support for a change in the electoral system from the 'first-past-the-post' system, which favoured big parties, to alternatives that would provide fairer representation to smaller parties, such as the Liberals, with thinly spread national support.

This chapter has sought to emphasise the centrality of the liberal (note small l) tradition in the evolution of modern British political thought. In the eighteenth century, it helped to establish reason, toleration, liberty, natural rights and the consent of the governed in place of religious dogma, feudal allegiance and the divine right of monarchs to rule. In the nineteenth century, it added representative, democratic government with power shared between various elements. Having provided key guidelines for our modern system of government, classical liberalism argued for minimal government intervention in social policy and an economy run essentially in harmony with market forces.

BOX 4.4 BRITAIN IN CONTEXT

Liberal values

It is seductively easy to believe that the beliefs underpinning one's own system of government are somehow 'natural', 'universal' and superior to those of other cultures. Probably the most famous statement of liberal values is enshrined in the Declaration of Independence made by the 'thirteen united states of America' in 1776, beginning:

We hold these truths to be self-evident, that all men are created equal, that they are endowed by their Creator with certain unalienable Rights, that among these are Life, Liberty, and the pursuit of Happiness. That to secure these rights, Governments are instituted among Men, deriving their just powers from the consent of the governed.

These few words embody much of the liberal thinking of Hobbes (his views were a mixture of the liberal and illiberal), Locke, Paine, Rousseau and other thinkers associated the impending French Revolution. 'Life, liberty and the pursuit of happiness' were considered to be 'self evident' truths, reflecting universal rights owned by all humans. At the time, when it was believed monarchs ruled with the authority of God who had decreed a natural order and social hierarchy, such views were wholly unorthodox and revolutionary; as much as the armies of Napoleon they unseated the established order in Europe and set the movement towards democracy in train.

As the new order took shape, what once was heretical became at first acceptable and then, by degrees, the new unchallenged orthodoxy. Citizens in Britain and the USA do not question these 'inalienable rights' which are enshrined in law and constitution; though in the USA the term 'liberal' has acquired pejorative overtones through the efforts of Republicans to identify Democrats with 'UnAmerican' (and hence unpatriotic) socialist ideas.

However, elsewhere in the world, such liberal values did not pass unchallenged. Communist countries claimed such beliefs were merely one of the means whereby property-owning capitalists fooled the exploited working classes into accepting gross inequalities. In more recent times fundamentalist Muslim movements have condemned Western liberalism as a sign of the West's decadence and corruption. They do not subscribe to notions of free speech but believe government should be a direct extension of their religion. This has given birth to a 'theocracy' in Iran, powerful internal movements in Muslim states and worldwide movements like al-Qaeda which seek to destroy the West, all this reinforcing the analysis of Samuel P. Huntington's exceptional book *The Clash of Civilizations and the Remaking of World Order* (Touchstone Books, 1997).

We should not, therefore, assume that liberal values are automatically right, and we should remember that:

1. Even cherished values – such as freedom of speech – are not absolute; Western countries all legislate to place limits of some kind.
2. Some Muslim countries do not accept liberal values but regard religious values as absolute, thus producing powerful conflicts with secular views of government (read Orhan Pamuk's novel *Snow* for excellent insights into these conflicts).
3. Before we reject such opposing views we should remember that even in 1776 (our Christian) God's name was invoked as the source of liberal values.

The New Liberals, however, engineered a new intellectual revolution. They argued for government intervention to control an increasingly complex economy that distributed great rewards and terrible penalties with near-random unfairness. They also saw commerce not as the healing balm for international conflicts but as the source of the conflicts themselves. The irony is that the Liberals Keynes and Beveridge proved to be the chief architects of the postwar consensus between Labour and Conservatives, while, as we shall see, Margaret Thatcher wrought her revolution not through application of traditional conservatism but through a rediscovery of classical liberalism.

■ Fukuyama and the end of history

No account of the development of the liberal tradition in politics can end without some reference to Francis Fukuyama, the formerly obscure official in the US State Department who argued in articles and a book (1992) that the liberal tradition had developed to the extent that, allied to free-enterprise economics, it had eclipsed all its rivals on the left and right – communism, fascism, socialism – thus producing the 'universalisation of Western Liberal democracy as the final form of human government'.

He founded his reasoning on the Hegelian notion that civilisations successively develop, resolve internal conflicts and change for the better. The 'end of history' is when a point is reached whereby conflict is eradicated and the form of society best suited to human nature has evolved.

The importance of the article lay partly in its timing. The British Empire took a couple of decades to expire, but Stalin's collapsed in a few years at the end of the 1980s. The intellectual world was deafened by the crashing of rotten regimes and astonished by the apparent vibrancy of their democratic successors. Moreover, after decades of defending liberal values against a grey and predatory communist bloc, the Western intelligentsia responded warmly to a thesis that appeared to say 'we've won'. Fukuyama's bold thesis fitted the facts and suited the mood of the times. Even in Britain the triumph of Thatcher in three successive elections between 1979 and 1987 seemed to reflect the thrust of the argument and her stated resolve to destroy socialism in her country. However, Fukuyama's thesis seems to ignore the exponential forces for change that are transforming society at breakneck speed: computer technology and the information revolution; the huge pressure on finite world resources; the spread of nuclear weapons; and the increasing concentration of wealth in a few hands, leading to the huge and growing gap between rich and poor. Who is to say that these forces will not undermine the liberal consensus and positions and possibly usher in a new authoritarianism? Moreover, as Samuel P. Huntington's book, *The Clash of Civilizations and the Remaking of World Order*, suggested, the world could now be engaged in a struggle between the values of the West and the more traditional and narrow values of Islam.

To assume that the liberal underpinnings of many of the world's political systems will survive can be seen as at best naive and at worst complacent.

Chapter summary

Ideology is a kind of applied philosophy. It can be classified on the right–left continuum, a flawed but still much-used form. The liberal tradition, based on rights, freedom and representation, developed from the seventeenth century and set the ground rules for political activity during the nineteenth and twentieth. Classical liberalism elevated the market economy, but the New Liberalism, which was concerned to protect society from its excesses, still provides the rationales for the welfare state and the mixed economy.

Discussion points

■ Are there better ways of classifying ideology than the left–right continuum?

■ What are the grounds for thinking that all human beings have rights?

■ Should government resist interfering in the economy?

■ Have the Liberals been exploited/robbed in ideological terms by the other two big parties?

■ Defend the Fukuyama thesis that the evolution of political systems has reached its end-point in liberal democratic free enterprise.

Further reading

Two excellent books are available that introduce politics students to ideology: Adams (1999) is well written and subtly argued, while Heywood (1998) is also essential reading. Useful in general terms are Eccleshall (1984) and Gamble (1981). Plant (1991) is more difficult but no less rewarding. On utilitarianism and liberalism, the texts by J.S. Mill (1971, 1975, 1985a, 1985b) are as good a starting point for understanding liberalism as any. Eccleshall (1986) lays some claim to be the definitive text, but Arblaster (1984) and Manning (1976) address wider readerships. Fukuyama (1992) elaborates the 'end of history' theory. Fareed Zakaria's *The Future of Freedom* (2004) is a quite brilliant book on threats to liberal democracy.

References

Adams, I. (1999) *Political Ideology Today*, 2nd edn (Manchester University Press).

Arblaster, A. (1984) *The Rise and Fall of Western Liberalism* (Blackwell).

Bell, D. (1960) *The End of Ideology* (Free Press).

Eccleshall, R. (1984) *Political Ideologies* (Hutchinson).

Eccleshall, R. (1986) *British Liberalism* (Longman).

Fukuyama, F. (1992) *The End of History and the Last Man* (Hamish Hamilton).

Gamble, A. (1981) *An Introduction to Modern Social and Political Thought* (Macmillan).

Giddens, A. (1998) *The Third Way* (Polity Press).

Hattersley, R (1989) 'Endpiece: nous and nostalgia', *The Guardian*, 30 September 1989.

Heywood, A. (1998) *Political Ideologies: An Introduction*, 2nd edn (Macmillan).

Huntington, S.P. (1996) *The Clash of Civilizations and the Remaking of World Order* (University of Oklahoma Press, also in paperback published by Touchstone Books, 1997).

Keynes, J.M. (1985) *A General Theory of Employment, Interest and Money*, Vol. VII of his *Collected Works* (Macmillan; first published 1936).

Manning, D.J. (1976) *Liberalism* (St Martin's Press).

Mill, J.S. (1971) *Utilitarianism* (Everyman; first published 1863).

Mill, J.S. (1975) *Representative Government* (Oxford University Press; first published 1861).

Mill, J.S. (1985a) *On Liberty* (Penguin; first published 1859).

Mill, J.S. (1985b) *Principles of Political Economy* (Penguin; first published 1848).

Nozick, R. (1974) *Anarchy, State and Utopia* (Blackwell).

Pamuk, O. (2004) *Snow* (Faber and Faber).

Plant, R. (1991) *Modern Political Thought* (Blackwell).

Russell, B. (1965) *The History of Western Philosophy* (Unwin).

Sutherland, J. (1999) 'How Blair discovered defeat by definition', *The Guardian*, 25 October 1999.

Zakaria, F. (2004) *The Future of Freedom* (Norton).

Useful websites

http://libertarianism.com

CHAPTER 5

Political ideas: key concepts

Bill Jones

Learning objectives

- To introduce the conceptual approach to understanding political ideas as an alternative to the ideology-centred perspective traditionally employed.

- To identify and explain the essence of some key concepts in the study of political science.

- To explain how these concepts are employed in the real world of politics.

Introduction

Chapter 1 dealt with the concepts central to political science, 'power' and 'authority'; Chapter 4 touched on some more key concepts; this one takes the examination a step or two further. It examines the field of political ideas through the perspective of concepts, and it goes on to discuss some of the most familiar and most used ones, relating them to broader questions concerning political ideas. The most obvious starting point is with the notion of a concept itself.

■ What is a concept?

A concept is usually expressed by a single word or occasionally by a phrase. Concepts are frequently general in nature, representing a specific function or category of objects. For example, the word 'table' usually refers to an individual human artefact, but it also embodies the whole idea of a table, which we might understand as a flat platform usually supported by legs and designed to have objects rested upon it. Without this definition a table would be a meaningless object; it is the concept that gives it purpose and function. As Andrew Heywood (1994, p. 4) explains:

a concept is more than a proper noun or the name of a thing. There is a difference between talking about a chair, a particular and unique chair, and holding the concept of a 'chair', the idea of a chair. The concept of a chair is an abstract notion, composed of the various features which give a chair its distinctive character – in this case, for instance, the capacity to be sat upon.

It follows, therefore, that the concept of a 'parliament' refers not to a specific parliament in a given country but to the generality of them – the abstract idea underlying them. By the same token, as we grow up, we come to attribute meaning and function to everyday objects through learning the appropriate concepts – plates, cups, windows, doors and so forth. Without these concepts we would be totally confused, surrounded by a mass of meaningless phenomena. In one sense concepts are the meaning we place on our surrounding world, impose on it, to enable us to deal with it. Similarly, we come to understand the political world through concepts that we learn from our reading, the media and our teachers. Over the years we come to extend them and refine them in order to achieve a sophisticated understanding, to become 'politically literate'. To

use a slightly different analogy, concepts are like the different lenses opticians place in front of us when attempting to find the one that enables us to see more effectively. Without them we cannot bring a blurred world into focus; with them we achieve, or hope to achieve, some clarity and sharpness.

Some political concepts are merely descriptive, for example 'elections', but others embody a 'normative' quality – they contain an 'ought'. 'Representation' is both descriptive, in that it describes why MPs sit in legislatures, and normative, in that it carries the message that states ought to base their political system on some kind of electoral principle.

Ideologies are composites of complex concepts, and one way we can seek understanding of them is by focusing on these constituent elements. This chapter will proceed to examine briefly eleven key concepts in political science: human nature, **nationalism**, **class**, freedom, **representation**, democracy, **equality**, social justice, rights, markets and planning.

■ Human nature

We must soften into a credulity below the milkiness of infancy to think all men virtuous. We must be tainted with a malignity truly diabolical, to believe all the world to be equally wicked and corrupt.
Edmund Burke, *Thoughts on the Present Discontents*, 1770

It is appropriate to refer again to the quotation by Voltaire that opens Chapter 1: 'There has never been a perfect government, because men have passions; and if they did not have passions, there would be no need for government.' Voltaire sums up the concern of the political scientist and philosopher with the vexed subject of human nature. Many other thinkers have been concerned with our relationships, individually and collectively, with political institutions, and it is understandable that they should focus on the nature of what is being organised and governed: ourselves. Many seek to identify something that explains what 'mankind is all about', a central core to our natures. Martin Hollis (cited in Plant, 1991, p. 28) writes:

All political and social theorists . . . depend on some model of man in explaining what moves people and accounts for institutions. Such models are sometimes hidden but never absent. There is no more central or persuasive topic in the study of politics.

Often these models will be the template of the related philosophy. Thomas Hobbes, for example, believed man outside society, in a 'natural' state, was disposed towards pleasure and against pain but in each case would be impelled to make individual choices. This would mean that agreement on what was desirable or undesirable would be lacking, resulting in a kind of perpetual state of war; life, in his famous description, would consequently be 'solitary, poor, nasty, brutish and short'. There would be no security of property, 'no thine and mine distinct; but only that to be everyman's, that he can get; and for so long as he can keep it'.

He points out, to those who may doubt his pessimistic analysis, that a man already arms himself when taking a journey, locking doors and chests at night, even when he knows there are officers whose job it is to protect him. 'Does he not . . . as much accuse all mankind by his actions?' Hobbes goes on to argue the need for a sovereign power, a Leviathan, to impose order on society, to quell the inherent civil war of 'all against all'. Rousseau similarly predicated a state of nature in his philosophy based on man's nature in which the 'savage' was uncivilised although basically kindly. It was only the effects of organised modern society that made him bad. Already in this discussion it is possible to discern a pessimistic view of human nature, like that of Hobbes, and a more optimistic one, as in Locke and Rousseau (see biographies, below and page 110).

In the nineteenth century the same tendencies can be seen. Marx was an optimist, believing mankind was much better than it appeared because of the corrupting effects of the harsh economic system of privately owned capital. Marx believed that human nature was a rogue product of a sick society: 'Environment determines consciousness'. It followed that to change the social environment for the better would be to improve human nature too. However, experience has tended to disappoint Marxist expectations. The Soviet Union was established after the 1917 revolution as a new experiment in political organisation. Progressive intellectuals and the working class the world over rallied to its cause, confidently expecting it to transform human nature, as, according to Marxist reasoning, the underlying capitalist economic system had been abolished. Rightwing politicians opposed it and sought to expose it

BIOGRAPHY

John Locke (1632–1704)

Source: © Bettman / Corbis

Locke was one of the founding fathers of the English empirical approach and of liberal democracy. Born in Somerset and educated at Oxford, he was fascinated by medicine and science and became the personal physician of Lord Shaftesbury. After a spell in government service he retired to France (1675–9), where he made contact with the country's leading intellectual figures. When his patron fell from power he fled to Holland, where he supported, presciently enough, William of Orange, who was invited to take the English crown in 1688. Locke's *Two Treatises of Government* (1690; see Locke, 1956) were intended as a riposte to the divine right ideas of Robert Filmer and the 'total sovereignty' of Hobbes. Locke's works are characterised by tolerance and moderation and a less pessimistic view of human nature, sentiments often perceived as typically English.

BIOGRAPHY

Jean-Jacques Rousseau (1712–78)

Source: © Bettman / Corbis

Rousseau's mother died giving birth in Geneva, and he had little family life or any formal education. In 1728, he ran away to Italy and became the lover of a baroness before moving to Paris in 1741, where he made a living from secretarial work and copying music. He established a lifelong relationship with an illiterate servant girl, Thérèse le Vasseur, with whom he had four children. Despite his expressed concern for children, he eventually delivered them all to orphanages. He was a friend of famous intellectuals like Voltaire and Diderot, writing music and contributing articles to the latter's *Encyclopédie*, but his first famous work was his prize-winning essay on arts and sciences, which argued that civilisation was corrupting man's natural goodness. He developed these ideas in a further essay on inequality in which he attacked private property. In 1762, he published his classic *Du Contrat social* (see Rousseau, 1913), which begins with the famous line: 'Man is born free but everywhere he is in chains'. This work, plus his slogan 'Liberty, Equality, Fraternity', became the founding text of the French Revolution. See also Chapter 4.

as a harsh police-supported tyranny disguised by stirring rhetoric and naive left-wing support.

The debate continues, but it is hard to deny that the pessimists were proved right. Through skilful manoeuvring and ruthless opportunism Joseph Stalin moved himself into a position of total power and exercised a bloody hegemony over a huge state for over two decades. Far from transforming human nature, the Soviet Union merely demonstrated that, in Herzen's phrase, 'we are not the doctors, we are the disease'.

In the late nineteenth century, Charles Darwin formulated his theory of evolution, which argued that all species did not replicate themselves perfectly on all occasions; they sometimes developed exceptions or mutations in their bodily form. Those mutations that suited the environment survived and thrived and went on to establish a new strain, which carried the banner for the species while the remaining strains faded into extinction. This notion of the 'survival of the fittest' was used by a number of classical liberal thinkers – such as Herbert Spencer – to justify capitalism as the way in which the species was developing itself and to argue against government interference with the 'natural order' of things.

Despite their differences, these philosophies were united in assuming the basic rationality of man, that

BIOGRAPHY

Herbert Spencer (1820–1903)

English philosopher. A teacher, journalist and engineer before becoming a full-time writer. Usually seen as the author of 'social Darwinism', that there is a natural process in human society whereby only the fittest survive.

humans make rational decisions about their lives and act in accordance with reason for most of the time. However, the later part of the century saw the emergence of a revolutionary new approach, which had widespread repercussions for many kinds of thinking: the ideas of Sigmund Freud. Freud argued that man is driven by instinctual urges underlying the pleasure principle and the, often conflicting, need to adjust to social reality.

To live any kind of ordered life excludes the continuance of the pleasure principle, so drives are repressed and sublimated into socially useful activities like work and achievement:

Sublimation of instinct is an essentially conspicuous feature of cultural development: it is what makes it possible for the higher psychical activities, in [the] scientific, artistic or ideological, to play such an important part in civilised life.

Freud (1963), p. 34

But whereas Freud applauds the constructive consequences of repression, others, such as Fromm and Marcuse, believed it to be harmful. Fromm argued that it created an alienated person who was in one sense mentally ill. To achieve 'mental health' he called for a number of reforms, many of them socialist in form. Critics such as Thomas Szasz pointed out shrewdly that 'mental health and illness are new ways of describing moral values'.

Marcuse agreed with Freud that some degree of repression – he called it 'basic repression' – is necessary for a society to function acceptably, but he believed that in Western society the degree of what he called 'surplus repression' based on class domination was unjustifiable and that a revolution was necessary to correct the imbalance. His ideas were destined to inspire many of the youthful revolutionaries of 1968.

Another variety of idea is based on a biological approach. Racialists, for example, posit different characteristics for different races. Nazis believed the Aryans to be the 'master race' and others to be inferior; others argue that some races are genetically inferior in terms of intelligence. Radical feminists also perceive huge irreconcilable 'essential' differences between the sexes, based on the male sex's disposition to dominate through rape or the fear of rape and violence (Brownmiller, 1975).

A final item under this heading is the degree to which we are rational. In 'rational choice theory' social theorists posit individual actors facing different choices and extrapolate results based on their exercising choice in a rational way. It could be, however, that choices are not made on such a basis but on irrational grounds. Do voters make rational choices in the polling booth? It depends: we know that many voters favour politicians on the basis of how they look and sound, not the content of their policies. Do leaders make rational choices? We hope so but we are told that Ronald Reagan was heavily influenced by his wife's astrologist. There are many other examples of leaders being influenced by emotional or venal factors or, in the case of the likes of Hitler or Idi Amin, by the wayward workings of an unbalanced mind.

■ Nationalism

Nationalism derives from the view that the world is divided naturally into national communities, all of which have the right to independence and the right to govern themselves. Nations often, although not necessarily, coincide with state frontiers; the notion of 'national territory' is potent, often stimulating countries to resort to war in its defence or reacquisition. Argentina's military rulers attempted to win popularity by invading the Islas Malvinas, as

---

BOX 5.1   IDEAS AND PERSPECTIVES

Milgram's experiment

The experimental psychologist Stanley Milgram conducted a historic experiment which suggested that – even though we might think it's the last thing we might do – everyone is capable of being sadistically cruel in response to presumed authority. He set up a situation in which people – more or less at random – were invited to join an alleged test involving someone tied to a chair. The participant was asked by a man in a white coat who appeared to have scientific authority to ask the pinioned person some questions and to administer electric shocks if the answers were wrong. The subject of the test was in fact an actor who shouted and writhed in response to the shocks. The participant, however, was told to continue with the shocks notwithstanding the subject's screams right up to an allegedly fatal level of 450 volts. Most of them did so without serious complaint. This experiment, essentially into human nature, showed, somewhat bleakly, that most of us are capable of behaving like guards in concentration camps if we accept the authority of the person directing us to apply the sadistic or even fatal force.

they called the Falkland Islands, in 1982, but were resisted and defeated by Britain, which defended the islands not essentially because they were part of the British state but more for a mixture of national pride, principle and, perhaps, political expedience.

States usually contain a dominant ethnic type, but most have minorities living within their borders too, either indigenous or immigrant. Well-established countries usually have a sense of 'community', a combination of shared history, language and culture. In these circumstances it is normal for citizens to share a patriotic love of their country, to feel a sense of duty towards it and, ultimately, a willingness to die for it.

Such devotion to nation was not always so powerful. True, it was not unusual for people to feel strong attachments to their country, as far back as the Ancient Greeks and Romans. In Shakespeare's time patriotism was acknowledged in, for example, Henry V's stirring address at Harfleur ('Cry God for Harry, England and Saint George!'), but it was quite possible for royal houses to be 'borrowed' from other countries or imported by invitation, as in the case of George I in 1714 from Hanover.

Modern nationalism, the notion that nations have the right to be in charge of their own destiny, was a product of the French Revolution. Here the liberal idea of natural rights, with its accompanying right of citizens to reject governments, was allied with Rousseau's idea of the general will, that nations had a sense of what they wanted that could be interpreted and which endowed both freedom and 'sovereign' power: the first appearance of the idea that the will of the people was superior to any other, including the head of state and ruling class.

So the French, always patriotic and intensely proud of their country, acquired an additional mission: to carry the idea of national self-determination into the wider world. A further element was added through the Romantic movement in the late eighteenth century, which idealised national myths and heroes. In Germany, Gottfried von Herder (1744–1803) attacked the tendency of the German ruling class to ape French customs and culture in an attempt to appear sophisticated. He believed that a nation's language was the repository of its spirit; that it should be nurtured and artists working within it revered.

During the nineteenth century nationalism grew in two ways: first, through nations developing the will to unite, as in the cases of Germany and Italy; and, second, within the large multinational empires of Austria-Hungary and Turkey. In 1848, a number of revolutions erupted based on emergent nationalism.

Towards the end of the century, the major European powers embarked on a kind of 'super'-nationalism – **imperialism** – whereby they colonised huge tracts of Africa and Asia, extracting wealth and brutally denying the native populations the same rights to self-determination they insisted on for themselves and other European peoples. Nationalism in parts of Europe took on an ugly complexion, combining authoritarianism with ideas of racial superiority.

The emergent doctrine of socialism appeared initially to be the antithesis of nationalism when the Second International at Stuttgart in 1906 passed a resolution committing the working classes in the event of war to intervene to 'bring it promptly to an end'. And yet in the summer of 1914 the military machines of Europe proved firmer of purpose, more swift in motion than the ponderous political armies of socialism. One by one the major socialist parties accepted the *fait accompli* of the war and rallied to their respective national causes. On Saturday, 2 August, over 100,000 British socialists demonstrated against the war, but on 15 October a Labour Party manifesto duplicated the Liberal view of the war as a struggle between democracy and military despotism. Shortly afterwards, Labour took its place in the wartime coalition government. Socialism had briefly stood up to nationalism, but the result had been a walkover.

At Versailles in 1918 a number of states were invented (Czechoslovakia) or reinvented (Poland) as the notion of self-determination reached its high-water mark. But by this time the colonial possessions of the imperial powers had begun to imbibe some of the ideas of their masters. In India and Africa, independence movements began to emerge and gained much impetus when Europe was weakened by the Second World War, itself initiated by the murderously aggressive nationalism of Nazi Germany, supported by that of Italy as well as Japan. In its wake India gained its freedom (1947) and during the 1950s and 1960s the map of the British Empire was effectively rolled up as the anti-colonial 'wind of change' – to use Macmillan's phrase – gathered storm force.

The establishment of the United Nations in 1945, followed by many other international organisations such as the North Atlantic Treaty Organisation (NATO) and the Organisation of Petroleum Exporting Countries (OPEC), marked the advance of internationalism at the expense of nationalism. This was especially true of the European Economic Community, set up in the 1950s and rapidly perceived as spectacularly successful. However, nationalism is still very much a motivating force in world politics, and in places such as the former Yugoslavia, Russia, the Middle East and the Indian subcontinent is capable of a sustained and virulent expression.

English people like to portray themselves as not especially nationalistic – theirs is a long-standing and confident arrangement – but occasions like the Euro '96 soccer championships and other sporting events reveal the English to be as fervently supportive of their country as any other. As Chapter 14 on devolution shows, Britain as such does not receive as much identification as its constituent national entities: within British politics nationalism also has an important role to play.

■ Class

The danger is not that a particular class is unfit to govern. Every class is unfit to govern.

Lord Acton

Every society becomes divided into groups over time. Those who are in authority over others tend to be replaced by younger family members and/or their friends. Those who do not have power also tend to form a coherent group with subgroups forming according to a variety of criteria. Greeks and Romans and early plantation owners in the southern states of the USA actually *owned* a group of people: slaves. It is quite easy to see how society became divided into 'classes' of people, distinguished mainly through their economic power. In Britain such considerations scarcely entered the thinking of the dominant group during the seventeenth to early nineteenth centuries. It was taken as given that the poor, and women, had no role in the government of the country and precious little say in anything else either. The Church was happy to endorse a world in which people were happy with their lot. The popular hymn *All Things Bright and Beautiful* sums it up succinctly:

The rich man in his castle, the poor man at his gate
God made them high or lowly and ordered their estate.

However, all this contentment was about to change in the middle of the nineteenth century. Reading and writing voraciously in the British Museum, Karl Marx launched his revolutionary analysis of capitalist society at about this time. He argued that those people in power at any one time were the rich and powerful, those with the resources to advance themselves and make their way in a world where wealth spoke volumes and poverty earned little but contempt and neglect. This produced a ruling class who owned the means of producing wealth and a subordinate class of those who actually did the work to provide the wealth in the first place. He discerned a conflict between these two classes: the bourgeois owners of wealth seeking to perpetuate their exploitation of the proletarian mass of the population who toiled but the fruits of whose labour were purloined by the owners of property. Marx went on to argue that in the age of capitalism the rich would so exploit the poor that in the end the latter would rise up, strike down their rulers, cast off their shackles and commence a process whereby members of the working class would seize control of their own destinies.

But it did not quite work out that way. At the turn of the twentieth century society was stratified into:

■ a recognisable ruling élite, emerging from the aristocracy and the rich middle classes, who could educate their children in expensive schools and then send them to Oxbridge;

■ the working class comprising the bulk of the rest of the population.

But the polarisation Marx predicted did not happen, nor did the revolution, and where it did occur, in Russia, the resultant dictatorship by Stalin, masquerading as communism, fooled nobody except those few on the far left who wished to be fooled. Milder forms of reformist socialism took over in Europe which introduced state-funded services to help the poor: benefits, pensions, education. Soon the middle classes were being joined by a new breed of working-class children and the structure of society was changing.

In the present day the working class has halved in size since the early twentieth century and the middle class has burgeoned. John Major, when he became Prime Minister in 1990, tried to argue that Britain was now 'classless', but few accept this complacent analysis which so favours the group in power. Andrew Adonis and Stephen Pollard, in their book *A Class Act* (1997), show how a new 'super class' has emerged on US-style salaries and how another group

– sometimes called an 'underclass' – has emerged at the bottom, living in poverty. Attempts by New Labour since 1997 to remove class inequalities have entailed huge expenditures on welfare services but the evidence is that the inequalities remain huge: only the rate of change has been arrested. Class is still very much a live political issue in the UK.

■ Freedom

The sense of liberty is a message read between the lines of constraint. Real liberty is as transparent, as odourless and tasteless as water.

Michael Frayn, *Constructions*, 1974

Freedom, as the above quote suggests, is not easy to define or describe, partly because it is so emotive: most politicians declare commitment to it or its synonym, 'liberty', and it is generally held to be a 'good thing'. To explore some of the intricacies and difficulties of this concept, consider the five cases listed below:

1. A man is locked in a cell for twenty-four hours a day; his fellow prisoners are beaten when they break the rules of the prison.

2. A girl is left on a desert island, where she can walk around but not escape.

3. A woman lives in Toxteth on social security, unable to support her children or fulfil her ambition of becoming a professional musician.

4. A man is held up by a mugger and told to hand over his money or be attacked with a knife.

5. A woman lives in a comfortable house in East Grinstead and fulfils her dream of becoming a successful novelist.

If the question is put 'are these people free?' then what can we conclude? Clearly the first man is not free in any sense; his movements are wholly restricted and he is prevented from leaving his cell by the locked door – he is the archetype of the person denied freedom. The second person is free to walk around but not beyond this to leave the restricted space of the island; she is effectively exiled or imprisoned. The third is free to walk wherever he wishes and in theory to do anything she pleases, but in practice he is prevented by lack of money/resources and is unable to fulfil her desire or

life goal. The fourth man faces a dilemma: he can refuse to hand over his money, but if he does he will face the prospect of being badly wounded, even killed, raising the question of whether he has any kind of choice. The final woman is the archetypal successful person: she has the ability to move freely according to choice; she can holiday abroad and has the resources to do so; she has fulfilled her ambitions regarding her career. It seems fair to conclude that there are degrees of freedom, with the first example the least free, the last, most so.

The cases discussed above reveal the range of debate about this elusive concept. The first and fourth people face physical coercion: if they refuse to obey what they are told, force will be used against them. They are classic victims of loss of freedom. Marginally close behind them is the occupant of the desert island: she is free from physical fear, but is not free to leave a restricted space. The argument gets difficult with the third woman, who lives in poverty. She is free from coercion but the problem is this: can she be said to be free if she has no resources to leave her less than salubrious living area, is poorly educated and unable to become the person she wants to be?

These cases demonstrate the difference between freedom *from* and freedom *to*: 'negative' and 'positive' freedom. Philosophers might say that in cases 1, 2 and possibly 4 the subjects were unfree in the negative sense: they are the victims of coercion; they are oppressed in one way or another. The third person is free, although in the negative sense: free to improve herself, 'get on her bike' and look for a job. This sort of freedom is seen by certain thinkers, including nineteenth-century classical liberals and politicians, as the real core or 'essential' definition. Poverty, they argue, is not necessarily restrictive; it might even be the spur to prosperity and hence the route to more viable choices. Such thinkers defended the *laissez-faire* economic system and opposed regulatory government intervention as unjustifiable incursions into the freedoms of factory owners and other employers, not to mention the best interests of the individuals concerned.

It was the liberal philosopher T.H. Green (see Green, 1988 [1911]) who first argued, in modern times, for 'positive freedom'. He believed that anyone prevented from realising his or her full potential was in a real sense unfree. He defined freedom as the ability of people to 'make the best and most of themselves'. If they were not able to do this then they were not free. This definition, so attractive to

'Man is born free and is everywhere in chains' . . . freedom – and its opposite – is a mental condition as much as it is physical
Source: Getty Images

socialists, in theory opened up the whole field of government intervention, especially via welfare services. Such a formulation of the concept also carries with it the clear implication that wealth should be redistributed to give more chances to more people.

Opponents of this approach, echoing classical liberals, claim that it is self-defeating: the government takes away the individual's freedom to improve his or her lot; it takes away the freedom of employers to employ workers at rates the market requires; it is part, in fact, of a subtle, incremental tyranny. In the twentieth century, Friedrich Hayek (1979) and the economist Milton Friedman (Hayek and Friedman, 1994) argued this case passionately, insisting that such a position was the 'road to servitude'. Sir Keith Joseph, a disciple of both thinkers, stated flatly that 'poverty is not unfreedom'.

Defenders insist that unless individuals are empowered to realise their personal potential, then they are not truly free. They also argue that the kind of freedom right-wingers and classical liberals want is the freedom of the strong to dominate the weak, or, as R.H. Tawney (1969) vividly put it, 'the freedom of the pike is death to the minnows'.

Some dictatorial regimes claim to be 'free' when they are not. Fascist regimes, for example, claimed that the only 'true' freedom occurred when people were obeying the will of the national leader, i.e. total subjugation, not freedom as we in Western European countries would understand it. We tend to believe that we are not free from government oppression unless it can be removed via unfettered elections.

Anarchists argue for a much wider kind of freedom; in fact, they believe there is no need for

BIOGRAPHY

R.H. Tawney (1880–1962)

Socialist economist and philosopher. Educated at Oxford, where he became a fellow and author of many works on economic history. Active in the Workers' Educational Association; also active as a Christian and a passionate advocate of equality. Professor at LSE 1931–49. His major works were *The Acquisitive Society* (1926), *Religion and the Rise of Capitalism* (1926) and *Equality* (1931).

any kind of authority and advocate complete freedom. This is generally not thought to be desirable, for it would give licence to murderers, child molesters, robbers and the like. J.S. Mill tried to solve this problem by advocating that people should be allowed all freedoms except those that were harmful to others: the 'harm principle'. According to this approach, personal harm – like suicide or addictive drugs – would be acceptable as others would not be involved. Modern libertarians use similar arguments to urge the legalisation of harmful drugs such as heroin and cocaine.

■ Representation

Your representative owes you, not his industry only, but his judgment; and he betrays, instead of serving you, if he sacrifices it to your opinion.

Edmund Burke, speeches at his arrival at Bristol (November 1774)

Representation is a fundamental concept in politics and not exclusively to democracies; many a dictator has seen himself as the only true 'representative' of his people. The idea originated in the arts where painters 'represented' scenes and actors played characters. According to Wyn Grant, in the sixteenth century it then came to acquire the usually legal sense of 'representing' someone for a specific purpose. Then it became politicised to mean someone deputed to represent a number of people in a legislative or deliberative assembly. In other words 'representation' provides a crucial nexus between

the governed and the government: we give someone the right to speak for us in some important context. It seems quite simple but in practice there is more than one interpretation and each is freighted with its own difficulties.

1. *'Altruistic representative'*: This view sees a representative as primarily concerned with protecting and advancing the interests of those he or she represents. But experience tells us this view is naive. People who claim to be altruistically committed to the public good often find that access to the levers of power eventually persuades them to operate them in their own favour, corruptly lining their own pockets.

2. *'Delegate representative'*: This implies that the person representing us takes our views into account and speaks up for them, having a 'mandate' from us to do so, possibly via an election. But what if our views are not consistent with the general good, e.g. they favour our interests to the exclusion of other groups?

3. *'Judgement representative'*: Edmund Burke, in his quote above, felt strongly that a representative in parliament was there to exercise his judgement on behalf of his constituents. But this is implicitly an élitist sense of the concept: who is to say such a person knows what is in the interests of their constituents better than they themselves?

4. *'Revolutionary or class representative'*: Marx and Lenin believed that people were blinded by the institutions of capitalism and the people who benefited from them – government, companies, bureaucracies – as to the true nature of their exploitation. Because they did not perceive where their own best interests lay, a vanguard group of revolutionaries had the duty of smashing the present system and installing a vastly superior one.

5. *'Educated representative'*: John Stuart Mill, often described as the father of representative government, believed education to be crucial to the business of representation. He thought public affairs so complicated that anyone lacking in education would be unsuitable not only to represent his fellows, but also as a voter electing such a person to office. But, as Andrew Heywood points out, this, at root élitist, view is to some extent contradictory. If people are too ill-educated to

know their own interests, surely they cannot be trusted to select people to act on their behalf? And if education is to be the criterion for representation, then why not select those who excel in competitive exams to represent us in government, like the mandarins of imperial China? (Heywood, 1994, pp. 178–9).

6. *Representation as microcosm*: American President John Adams (1735–1826) argued that the legislature should be as exactly as possible 'a portrait in miniature of the people at large, as it should think, feel, reason and act like them'. This somewhat statistical view suggests contentiously narrow possibilities of representation: for example, that a man cannot represent a woman or vice versa, or that working-class people cannot represent the middle classes. It also suggests – a very thorny area of debate – that voting systems should select in proportion to groups in society.

In the British system representation is accepted as a fundamental requirement but no single interpretation is entrenched. Rather – perhaps in tune with Britain's pragmatic traditions – aspects of several of the above can be discerned. Apart from the occasional exceptions, British politicians are relatively non-corrupt and take their representative duties seriously; Tony Benn has argued for the delegate approach to representation, but for his fellow parliamentarians the Burkean view is the more accepted; the revolutionary approach has never been widely supported in Britain; and, whilst most MPs are well educated, it is not thought that a high level of education is an essential prerequisite either for an MP or for a voter.

◼ Democracy

There are no wise few. Every aristocracy that has ever existed has behaved, in all essential points, exactly like a small mob.

G.K. Chesterton, *Heretics*, 1905

As with freedom/liberty, democracy is a universally regarded 'good thing', with many oppressive regimes claiming the title for propaganda purposes.

Rousseau's conception of democracy was based on his unusual idea of what constituted freedom; for him it had to be small-scale and 'direct'. Citizens had to contribute personally to the formation of a

'general will' of the community by participating constantly in its governance. They could only be truly 'free' when they obeyed the imperatives that they themselves had helped to create. It followed that those who failed to obey this general will were not obeying their 'true' natures and should be impelled to conform or be 'forced to be free'. Bertrand Russell believed this doctrine to be pernicious and the thin end of what eventually became the totalitarian wedge. Rousseau's idea of direct democracy hearkened back to the Greeks, but it must be clear to most enthusiasts for democracy that such a form of governance is not possible in the context of large nation-states. Even small groups find it hard to agree on simple things, so it is stretching credence to the limits to believe that large groups in open discussion can agree on big issues, at least to any meaningful degree.

To maximise direct democracy, one of the aims of the Left, some advocate the introduction of more and more referendums, but such devices would surely introduce unacceptable delays into government when decisions often have to be made quickly and emphatically. Some point out that today computer technology enables government to be carried out in theory on an 'interactive' basis, and some experiments along these lines have been tried in the USA and elsewhere. From one point of view our existing system is superior to any direct method, whether using ballot boxes or new technology, as many popular attitudes are authoritarian and illiberal. For example, on penal policy (see Chapter 25) the public tend to favour harsh sentences for criminals and the death penalty for murderers. They can also be illiberally nationalistic and xenophobic. At least our existing system allows these extremes to be filtered out in favour of views that are the result of rational debate and intensive research. Still others accept the difficulties of scale and number and advocate instead the devolution of decision making down to the lowest level compatible with efficiency.

As a result of the inadequacies of direct democracy, an indirect form of it has been developed, as we have seen above, called 'representative democracy', whereby people are elected to serve the community for a space of years; they become more or less full-time professional politicians, experienced in understanding the complexities both of public affairs and of interpreting the public mood. Most importantly, they are also accountable to the public at election times and hence removable if they are deemed ineffective or unsuitable. This has also been called liberal democracy, the triumph of which some have discerned with the demise of communism in the late 1980s (see the section on Fukuyama at the end of Chapter 4). Churchill famously said that this was the worst kind of government except for all the rest, but this should not blind us to its manifest imperfections.

On democracy

No one pretends that democracy is perfect or all wise. Indeed, it has been said that democracy is the worst form of government, except for all the others that have been tried from time to time.

Winston Churchill

The task of parliament is not to run the country but to hold to account those who do.

William Ewart Gladstone

We close this section with six considerations of democracy.

1. Most people are bored by politics and functionally politically illiterate. This makes them a prey to unscrupulous politicians who can use the freedom of the system to abuse its fundamentals. As an extreme case, Hitler subverted the Weimar Republic to seize power in the early 1930s.

2. Politicians, as already suggested, cannot be trusted to be wholly disinterested servants of the community. Dr Johnson once declared that politics was 'nothing more nor less than a means of rising in the world'; and the Nolan Committee's investigations in 1995 revealed that the cupidity of politicians remains a danger to the independence and honesty of our elected representatives.

3. Voting is an occasional ritual whereby the citizen briefly has the chance to change the government; as Rousseau dismissively pointed out, the electorate in Britain have power only on election days; once they have voted, their power is vested in a body that is essentially able to do what it likes. He was right to the extent that majority voting is a fine principle, but majorities can be as tyrannical as minorities; for example, the Protestant voters in Northern Ireland used their position to disadvantage the Catholic minority over a

number of decades. Lord Hailsham in the mid-1970s declared that the British system of government had become an 'elective dictatorship' for the five years that parties were allowed to govern before the next election (although, ever the politician, he seemed to lose his indignation when his party came to power in 1979).

4. As the German sociologist Robert Michels (1949) argued, there is a tendency for any democracy to be subverted by small élite groups: his so-called 'iron law of oligarchy'. Interestingly, Sir Anthony Eden supported this theory in the British case when he told the House of Commons in 1928 that 'We do not have democratic government today ... What we have done in all the progress of reform and evolution is to broaden the basis of oligarchy'. Marxists tend to agree with Michels and argue further that the liberal democratic system is merely a decoration; behind the façade of elections and democratic process, the richest groups in society take all the major decisions in their own interests and against those of the masses.

5. In the modern era issues have become increasingly complex: for example, the arguments over the desirability of a unified European currency. This has meant that the natural reluctance of voters to involve themselves in political issues has been accentuated through an inability to absorb their complexities.

6. The political process is now dominated by the media – elections are essentially media events – and the politicians have been able to use their skills in manipulating the media, via the infamous **spin doctors** and others, to disguise and obfuscate the real issues. Often issues are abandoned altogether in favour of 'negative campaigning'; a good example is the ploy of character assassination, as in the case of Neil Kinnock in the 1992 general election, who was the object of a highly personal campaign by the Murdoch-owned *Sun* newspaper.

■ Equality

What makes equality such a difficult business is that we only want it with our superiors.

Henri Becque, *Querelles Littéraires*, 1890

Equality is yet another hotly disputed concept. There is 'equality of opportunity' and 'equality of outcome'. The Left prefer the latter, the Right the former. Equality of opportunity is agreed now by all shades of opinion as a desirable thing; the liberal view has prevailed. Even South African supporters of the National Party now claim to have renounced their old apartheid attitudes, which caused so much suffering and injustice. (Whether they have or not is hard to tell, but at least they no longer claim racist views are correct, fair and God-given.)

The problems arise when the equality of outcome argument is considered. For many on the left any inequality is deemed to be bad and remediable through government action. If the analogy of a race is employed, then everyone stands on the same starting line when embarking on their lives. The right-winger tends to say that how far and fast individuals progress in the race of life is a function of their ability, their energy and their will to succeed: 'winners' will strive and achieve and be admired; 'losers' will fall behind, be looked down on and make excuses. While the consensus after the war in Britain was that inequality was something to be deplored and reduced, Margaret Thatcher asserted the right of people to be 'unequal', to excel, be better. In March 1995, John Major was asked in the House of Commons if he believed inequality should be reduced; perhaps surprisingly, he replied 'Yes'. Nevertheless, Major would not have accepted the left-wing argument regarding the extent of the state's obligation to help those who fall behind in life's race. He would have been more likely to argue that some differences in outcome were the consequence of 'natural inequalities', which are likely to affect anyone: some can run faster, others have exceptional memories, musical gifts and so on. To interfere with 'nature' in this way is harmful, say right-wing theorists, likely to distort the internal dynamics of society. Moreover, too much help tends to sap initiative – to encourage dependency, which is bad for giver and recipient alike.

The left-winger tends to interpret the 'equal start in life' argument as an illusion: most people carry handicaps; for some it might be a broken home, resulting in emotional turmoil and underachievement in school; for others it might be lack of resources, poverty, lack of adequate role models and so forth. To maintain that everyone has an equal chance in present society is to say, according to the Left, that the fleet of foot have a clear opportunity to excel without any impediment over others less gifted or blessed by birth.

So the Left tends to argue for a system that helps the slower to catch up, for their poverty to be alleviated, their special needs met, in some cases for special 'affirmative action' whereby those groups regularly excluded from success, such as racial minorities and women, are given some preference, perhaps in the form of 'quota' allocations for university entrance, as in the USA, or all-women short-lists for parliamentary candidates in certain constituencies, as in the Labour Party.

The Right claims that, to work effectively, people need to be given an incentive. If wages are equalised, for example, then the lazy will have no incentive to work and will be idle while the industrious are exploited and denied proper reward for their effort. They claim that this is fundamental for the effective functioning of the economy, which is fuelled by incentives: when a role needs performing in society the market puts a price on filling it; when it is a freely available skill, like sweeping the streets, the rate is low, but when the skills are rare and dependent on years of study plus high intellectual ability – as in the case of running a major company or becoming a brain surgeon – the rates are high and rightly so. This argument was also employed by the Conservatives in the 1980s when they cut taxes for high earners. A corollary of this argument is that a hierarchy of reward stimulates effort: if someone desires advancement in the form of riches or status they are prepared to work for it and strain every effort. In the USA this is part of the so-called 'American Dream', whereby immigrants often arrived with nothing except their clothes yet within a generation or two had accumulated large fortunes or won respected positions in society. Similarly, Sir Keith Joseph was making the same point when he stated the apparent paradox that for 'the poor to become richer, we have to make society more unequal'.

Finally, right-wing polemicists claim that remedial intervention by the state is implicitly tyrannical as it involves taking away from the able – sometimes through the law, backed up by force – some of their just rewards produced by their talent and honest labour. They also point to the former communist regimes, where 'equality' was imposed on society through the agency of an oppressive regime complete with police powers, labour camps and punitive prison sentences.

■ Social justice

Justice is the right of the weakest.
                    Joseph Joubert, *Pensées*, 1842

Who should get what in society? The Left tends to favour an approach based on 'needs' and the Right one based on 'rights' or 'deserts'. In his book *Modern Political Thought* (1991), Raymond Plant investigates this by positing the problem of the just distribution of 100 oranges in a society of 100 people. The obviously fair approach, especially if all members have been involved in the production process, is to give one orange to each person. However, if some people have a particular physical need for vitamin C, then the question arises whether their needs justify an unequal distribution. Maybe these special needs people need two each? Or three, or even more? This is the kind of debate that social justice discussions stimulate, and it obviously has wider implications for the way in which income and wealth are distributed together with other material goods like welfare benefits, taxation and housing.

Karl Marx declared that in a communist society the principle of material distribution would be 'From each according to his ability, to each according to his needs!' A charming fictional version of what life might be like in a truly socialist society is found in William Morris's novel *News from Nowhere* (1891; see Morris, 1993), in which the main character finds himself in a future socialist England in which money has been abolished, people work happily for the community and take what they need for basic consumption and leisure purposes. In reality this utopian vision would probably remain a mere vision, but some vestige of its moral force still informs current thinking on the Left.

At the heart of this notion of social justice is that large accumulations of wealth, juxtaposed by poverty and ill health, are not justifiable. It follows, according to this approach, that wealth should be redistributed in society and, indeed, between nations. On the other hand, even left-wing theorists agree that some economic inequality is necessary to make the economic system work, so the real debate concerns how much redistribution is needed to achieve justice.

One influential thinker on the Left has been John Rawls, whose book *A Theory of Justice* (1971) has occasioned much debate. He asked us to consider what distribution of goods we would endorse if we were rational people planning a society but, crucially, were unaware of our own capacities. In this way it would be possible to prevent people from favouring their own talents and strengths, for example preventing a clever person from advocating a meritocracy or a physically strong person a free-for-all society. This ensures that any decisions reached would be neutral. Rawls argues that all would agree on the greatest possible degree of liberty in which people would be able to develop their talents and life plans. In addition, however, Rawls posits the 'difference principle', whereby he maintains that social and economic inequalities – differences in wealth, income and status – are only just if they work to the advantage of the most disadvantaged members of society and only if they can be competed for fairly by all. Rawls argues that in such a situation rational people would choose, through a sense of insecurity, a society in which the position of the worst-off is best protected; this would be a market economy in which wealth is redistributed through tax and welfare systems up to the point when it becomes a disincentive to the economic activity. It has to be said, however, that some poor people oppose high taxation and the benefits public expenditure can give to the poor because they hope one day to be rich and do not wish their bounty to be reduced by the depredations of the taxman.

Right-wing theorists tend to ignore this notion of needs; indeed, the very notion of social justice is denied by some (e.g. Friedrich Hayek). The Right tend to favour 'rights'-based approaches: for example, the fact that someone has made an artefact endows a property right upon the craftsman or woman. Similarly, if a person has bought something, the same right is presumed to be in place, as money can be seen as a symbolic exchange for labour. Work, or the exercise of talent, is held to establish a right to material reward: 'well, he's earned it' is often said about wealthy, hard-working people. Alternatively, if someone is rich through unusual talent, as a writer maybe or an exceptional entertainer, the usual response is that 'he's worth it'. Robert Nozick (1974) has been an influential theorist on the Right, arguing that wealth is justifiable if it is justly acquired in the first place – for example has not been stolen – and has been justly transferred from one person to another. He goes on to argue that if these conditions have not been met the injustice should be rectified. Nozick rejects the notion of 'social justice', the idea that inequality is somehow morally wrong. If transfers of wealth take place between one group in society and another, it should be on the basis of private charity, made on the basis of personal choice. But

BOX 5.2　BRITAIN IN CONTEXT

Conceptual dissonance

The former publisher and infamous fraud, Robert Maxwell, once wrote a series of hagiographic studies of East European leaders which sold extremely well in their own countries but showed a strange disinclination to fly from the shelves anywhere else. In the book he wrote about the notorious Romanian leader, Nicolae Ceauşescu, Maxwell, in an interview incorporated into the text, asks 'Mister President, tell me, why do your people love you so?' This question and its unperturbed reply illustrate the fact that different people have different takes on commonly understood ideas. Maxwell, driven by self-interest, probably knew the man was a vicious autocrat; Ceausescu in turn probably genuinely believed he was loved, as his famous look of incomprehension indicated when crowds in front of his palace began angrily to interrupt one of his interminable speeches in 1989, a short time before he was deposed and shot. Both men, totally absorbed in their own false worlds, no doubt perceived the world differently from the people they exploited. But such 'conceptual dissonance' tends to occur between nations as well as between different kinds of people.

In many cases this flows from the vastly different histories experienced by countries. France, for example, has never quite recovered from its 1789 revolution founded upon the great ideas of 'Liberty, Equality and Fraternity'. Consequently new arrivals to France have become citizens of the republic on an equal standing with everyone else. Such legal even-handedness is wholly admirable, one might think, but in the autumn of 2005 its limits were exposed when French leaders, especially Jacques Chirac, seemed to refuse to believe that the young men of the Muslim faith, many of North African provenance, who were rioting in the suburbs of Paris and other big cities, suffered from severe racial discrimination and disproportionate economic hardship. So deeply ingrained was this belief in equality that no separate social statistics were available regarding France's constituent minorities. They were just the same so there were no separate figures.

Another example of conceptual dissonance is provided by the difference between Western and Muslim societies. In the West free speech is a hallowed principle, defended even if it offends some people holding deep religious beliefs. For fundamentalist Muslims such tolerance is not possible. Anything which reflects what they see as disrespect for the prophet Mohammed they interpret not as merely a difference of viewpoint or maybe satirical humour, but as unforgivable blasphemy. The case of the Danish cartoons published in a right-wing newspaper in November 2005 well illustrated this difference in perception, only one of many between the two cultures.

In Japan, still influenced by its ancient culture, the world is also perceived in a way different from in the west. For example, social hierarchy is deemed in some situations to be as important as equality, so that people seated at a dinner table will place the person believed by a group to be the most senior and important in the place of honour while other guests will be placed according to their perceived rank and place in society.

The USA, created in the heat of a revolution against the perceived tyranny of George III, places huge stress on the need for democracy. This helps explain why the USA elects far more public officials than the UK; for example, dog and rat catchers, as well as mayors and sheriffs, are elected in America but not in the UK. It might also explain why President George W. Bush and his advisers believed so passionately in disseminating democracy in the Middle East. They believed it would lead to greater moderation, acceptance of the west and happiness for the Arab citizens concerned. At the time of writing, this assumption seems to have tragically misfired in the case of an Iraq on the verge of civil war.

Nozick's views do not necessarily bolster right-wing views on property as the rectification principle could imply the redistribution of much wealth, especially when it is considered that so much of the wealth of the West has been won at the expense of plunder and slavery in Third World countries.

Right-wing thinkers are also attracted by social Darwinism. Herbert Spencer (see Spencer, 1982) argued that material circumstances were merely the reflection of differing innate abilities and talents: people are rich because they are more able than others and therefore deserving of reward. In his view, this reflected the 'natural' order of things and as such should not be disturbed. He also believed it was wrong to intervene to assist people who had fallen on hard times: 'If we protect people from the consequences of their own folly we will people the world with fools'.

■ Rights

Rights that do not flow from duties well performed are not worth having.
Mohandas K. Gandhi, *Non-Violence in Peace and War*, 1948

Human 'rights' embodies the idea that every human has certain basic entitlements and gives rise to a number of questions:

■ What is the basis of these rights? Are they legal? Some are embodied in the law, but others are not.

■ Are they related to religious ideas? To some extent but not necessarily.

■ What are the sources of human rights?

Their origins lie more in moral than in political philosophy. They were implicit in the notion of the social contract, popular in the seventeenth century and revived in a singular form by Rawls in the 1970s, as mentioned above. Before the seventeenth century, political ideas were dominated by God and feudalism. All authority was vested in the monarch, sanctioned by God via the 'divine right of kings' theory. There were no thoughts of individuals having any rights beyond those invested by the law. Hobbes's theory was so unorthodox because it rested on the notion of a contract between individuals and the state whereby allegiance was given in exchange for protection from the anarchic disorder of an ungoverned society. However, if the state failed in its duty of providing protection then the obligation of

citizens would 'last as long, and no longer, than the power by which he is able to protect them'. In other words, according to Hobbes, citizens retain a right of independence even under an all-powerful ruler. This notion of a social contract and fundamental rights was revolutionary in his time; it gathered strength during the century and in the thought of John Locke became a means whereby 'equal and independent people' in a state of nature could decide whether or not 'by their own consent to make themselves part of some political society'. It followed that everyone had rights independent of the state; and the authority of the government depended on the consent of the governed. Nearly a century later – in 1776 – these ideas were neatly and wonderfully summarised in the American Declaration of Independence:

We hold these truths to be self-evident, that all men are created equal, that they are endowed by their Creator with certain unalienable Rights, that among these are Life, Liberty and the pursuit of Happiness. That to secure these rights, Governments are instituted among Men, deriving their just powers from the consent of the governed.

There is a clear distinction to be made between moral and legal rights. Legal or 'positive' rights are included in the law and can be enforced in the courts. Such rights can be a right to do something should one choose – such as walk on the highway – or a right not to be treated in a certain way – such as not be the victim of violence – or they can be the empowering right to vote in an election. In Britain, basic rights such as freedom of speech and worship are not enshrined in law but instead are not excluded – so they are therefore allowed. In contrast, in the USA such rights are included in the constitution and are more easily defended (although similar legal safeguards in despotic regimes, such as the former USSR, have not protected human rights). Internationally, human rights are held to exist as the basic conditions for a tolerable human existence. The United Nations issued its Universal Declaration of Human Rights, which 'set a common standard of achievement for all peoples and all nations'. Similar declarations exist in relation to economic, social and cultural rights. The European Union has its own set of declarations along very similar lines. Interestingly, the European Convention on Human Rights was the source of rulings made by virtue of Britain being a signatory that overruled domestic law, as in the case of corporal punishment in schools. In 1998 the Human Rights Act embodied the Convention into British law. The United Nations and other international bodies associated with rights have done much to extend consensus on them.

As in the case of freedom and justice, there is a familiar left–right dichotomy over rights that relate to the operation of the economy. The Right tends to stress 'negative' rights: the right to be left alone, not to be imprisoned or attacked by the state. The Left stresses 'positive rights', such as the UN's 'right to work' (Article 23) and 'right to education' (Article 26). Such rights are denied by the Right; this conflict can also be seen in the Labour Party's adherence to the Social Chapter of the Maastricht Treaty and the Conservatives' opposition to it (see also Figure 5.1 in the chapter summary).

Some thinkers champion animal rights. Logically, if humans have rights by virtue of being alive, then other forms of life must have rights too. This makes vegetarianism a difficult philosophy to refute. True, animals cannot think and express themselves, but their very helplessness offers a reason why humans should protect and not exploit them through killing and eating them. The Animal Liberation Front feels especially strongly about experiments inflicted on animals for medical or, much worse, cosmetic research.

■ The market

You can't buck the markets.

Margaret Thatcher

At first sight this concept, central to how an unfettered economic system works, might seem closer to economics than politics and, while this may be true, anything that determines, as the market does, how shares of scarce resources are allocated must be highly political. At the heart of the 'free-market' model is the idea of a public market in which goods are offered for sale by a variety of producers who seek to sell their products or produce to consumers. Using the model we can see how such an economy works. Producers create their goods, whether manufactured or grown, and seek to make a profit on their sale. Within the market a subtle kind of communication occurs. People wishing to buy, for example, cotton shirts will probably survey what is available, making judgements about quality and tempering them with calculations of price. Those stalls offering good quality at low price will find trade brisk, while those offering poor quality at high prices will find it slow to non-existent. The favoured stalls will soon become well known, and shirt purchasers will tell friends who also wish to buy such products about the key options available in the market. The result will be, over time, that the recommended stalls will prosper, while the others will face failure unless they change their mode of operation. They will need to rethink their production techniques, cutting down on costs wherever possible, introducing new equipment perhaps and experimenting with new styles. With this done satisfactorily, they can re-enter the market and, provided that the word gets around, will trade again but this time with success.

Adam Smith, already mentioned in Chapter 4, was the first influential theorist on the working of the market. He pointed out that the dynamic of the market is provided by the consumers who wish to buy and the providers who wish to sell: 'supply and demand'. Smith believed that any regulation of these complex processes, for example by government, would hinder their efficient working as they worked best when left alone. Edmund Burke too declared 'The moment that government appears at market, all the principles of the market will be subverted'. The French term *'laissez-faire'* – let be – is used to describe this approach to economics.

There is, therefore, according to *laissez-faire* advocates, a 'natural' or 'magic' quality to the market that, if left to its own devices, works perfectly. Enoch

BIOGRAPHY

Adam Smith (1723–90)

Scottish economist born in Kirkcaldy and educated in Glasgow and at Oxford. He became one of the brilliant Edinburgh circle which included David Hume. His *Wealth of Nations* (1776) explained, analysed and advocated the system of modern capitalism, unhindered by government intervention. He perceived that division of labour was at the heart of economic efficiency and became the prophet of classical liberalism during both the nineteenth and the twentieth centuries. His lesser known *The Theory of Moral Sentiments* (1759) reveals that Smith was far from being the supporter of a pure and unfettered market which he is sometimes depicted.

Powell, a great advocate of unfettered markets, wrote of 'this wonderful silent automatic system – this computer' and 'the subtlest and most efficient system mankind has yet devised for setting effort and resources to their economic use'. The role of government should be strictly contextual or supportive, according to free-marketers. It should sustain an inflation-free currency, maintain frontiers from external attack and provide a peaceful and safe environment in which business can flourish, together with a framework of law in which business transactions can be legally validated and pursued in the courts if violated. The beauty of the market to its supporters is that:

1. It does not depend on qualities that 'ought' to be present in mankind but accepts what qualities there are and makes the best of them. So by pursuing his profits and becoming rich the businessman provides employment for his workforce, who also become consumers whose money helps to keep other businesses and thence the whole of society prosperous.

2. It provides the possibility of personal development for employers and workers alike: they can become the people they wish to be through hard work, savings and creating opportunities for themselves.

3. It enables individuals to influence via their purchases the future of the market or the economy. Purchases are likened to voting; if enough people 'vote' for a particular product it becomes established as a part of social life; if they reject it the product disappears. So electrical goods have become standard, computers are becoming so too; and it is all the product of thousands of individual choices freely made. Similarly, products which are deemed inadequate soon disappear: consider how the VHS video-recorder eventually triumphed over its rivals in the 1980s.

4. The market is wholly egalitarian. It cares nothing for the sex, religion or race of the producer or retailer; the only qualities that count are hard work, dedication and the talent to provide society with what it requires and wants.

However, critics of the market point out that it is far from perfect:

1. The national and international markets can undergo rapid periods of growth, which are then followed by slumps in which millions can be made unemployed and consigned to destitution.

2. The ability of those who supply or control the market to make large profits creates huge disparities of wealth and hence chronic inequality in which the producers of wealth, the workers, receive scant reward for their efforts. This inequality can also produce social unrest and political instability.

3. The emphasis on individual effort can encourage selfishness and a callous attitude towards those who fail in the market.

4. Unregulated markets produce fallouts that can harm society, for example environmental pollution.

5. Markets do not provide for all the requirements of a successful society. For example, governments have to step in to provide mechanisms to dispose of garbage or sewage or, in the example cited by Heywood (1994, p. 280), provide lighthouses.

6. The existence of so many producers creates wasteful duplication of effort by workers and management alike.

7. The market is dependent on demand and may find it is merely serving those with money, producing luxury goods and neglecting the needs of society as a whole.

The dependence of successful business on individuals and entrepreneurs has tended to concentrate its support in the ranks of those who have benefited from the system. Accordingly, opponents have tended to spring from those who have not benefited or those who have chosen to champion the cause of those who have not benefited.

■ Planning

Make no small plans: they have no power to stir the hearts of men.

Daniel H. Burnham, motto of city planners

Planning is to an extent, say the opponents of *laissez-faire*, its antidote. It is lack of regulation that creates the unjust excesses of capitalism, and planning offers a means of distributing scarce or even plentiful resources on a more equitable and efficient basis. Planning is a rational means of achieving economic goals; it presupposes a defined goal and route to its achievement. However, planning as a concept has suffered from the close relationship it has in the popular imagination with the economic and political system of the former USSR. Here an ancient system was overthrown and replaced by one that aimed to change the basis of human nature itself. Initially, however, it had to compromise with reality as it existed in the early 1920s. Lenin's New Economic Policy in 1921 allowed the activity of free enterprise in certain areas, but ideological imperatives soon took over once Stalin had tightened his grip over the embryonic new state. He set up a complex system of ministries that served Gosplan, the State Planning Committee, which itself took its orders from the highest political authority, the Politburo. Planning sometimes resembled that employed successfully in capitalistic enterprises – the techniques of mass production, for example, and the time and motion studies of the American management guru F.W. Taylor. For a while such planning was applauded in the west and tribes of observers, of left and right, trailed around the Soviet Union seeing very much what the Communist Party wished them to see. Certainly planning laid the foundations of heavy industry in the country and established the strength that helped to see off Hitler and his armies. For a while it seemed after the war that maybe Stalin did represent the wave of the future and that the *laissez-faire* economics had been superseded by a superior system. The launch of the orbiting Soviet Sputnik in the 1950s seemed to confirm Soviet ascendancy, but it probably marked a high tide from which it subsequently retreated. By the 1980s, it had become clear that the Soviet economy was imploding, with net GDP actually shrinking in the early part of the decade. Once its economy had ceased to function the USSR had to opt out of the arms race, and when Mikhail Gorbachev abandoned the Soviet economic and political system its days as a superpower were over; without economic efficiency no country can stay powerful politically for long. But this unhappy experience of planning should not blind us to its successes and advantages.

1. During the Second World War Britain introduced a centrally planned economic system that proved highly efficient and was arguably superior to the German equivalent.

2. Since the war Britain has introduced planning into policies affecting the environment with some success. Here the policy is not imposed from the centre but is open to scrutiny and democratic debate (although some claim that what is available is insufficient).

3. Other countries such as the Netherlands, Germany and the Scandinavian countries, especially Sweden, have embraced a substantial degree of economic planning with results that are reflected in their high standards of living.

4. The activities of the EU are founded on the notion of careful planning in all policy areas, the aim being to encourage a Europe that is prosperous without its many existing areas of low economic performance. The EU has generally been judged a success in its economic and environmental policies.

5. The above successes prove that political authoritarianism is not the inevitable concomitant of planning.

6. Planning is a way of maintaining the dynamism of the free enterprise system while guarding against its unacceptable side-effects. Planning is accountable not to businessmen or shareholders but to elected politicians, who can be called to account in the public interest.

7. Planned economic activity is more likely to be democratic, reflecting values of justice and fairness; its advocates claim that such unselfish social policies and institutions inspire loyalty and greater effort by those involved.

One of the first attempts to develop a critique of planning was undertaken by Friedrich Hayek in *The Road to Serfdom* (1944). In an analysis elaborated in later writings, Hayek suggested that planning was inherently inefficient because planners were confronted by a range and complexity of information that was simply beyond their capacity to handle. Central planning means making 'output' decisions which allocate resources to them. However, given that there were well over 12 million products in the Soviet economy, some of which came in hundreds if not thousands of varieties, the volume of information within the planning system was – according to economists – exceeding the number of atoms in the entire universe.

Heywood (1994), p. 272

While planning can boast some successes, it is obvious that it has its downside:

1. It is almost impossible to plan an economy efficiently for a whole nation. To do this planners must know exactly what consumer demand is,

how much of each product will be required and when. The amount of data required for such planning is impossible to collect, let alone compute (see quotation above). Consequently planners make educated guesses and frequently make mistakes, creating shortages and queues. The Soviet Union was so beset by queues that some people used to make a living out of hiring themselves out to stand in queues for scarce products. Even when people earned reasonable salaries it was of little benefit to them as there was little to buy in the shops.

2. Some goods were completely unavailable in the Soviet Union and consequently could only be bought on the huge black market.

3. Because goods were in short supply, shop assistants became key people in communist countries as they exerted some control over the flow of goods, rather as they did in Britain during the war, when rationing was in place.

4. Planned economies tend to be sluggish and to deter innovation. They may provide full employment, but there is no incentive to work hard, to get ahead, as in capitalist countries. Workers tended to serve their time in communist economies. Moreover, managers tried to keep planning targets low and, once they were achieved, tended to relax.

5. The idea that planning can inspire workers to work harder for the 'community' or the nation is not borne out in practice. Nationalised industries in the UK after the war were famous for being overmanned, inefficient and staffed by workers who resented their managers every bit as much as they had former private employers. Furthermore, such workers were more than willing to hold the country to ransom in the 1970s for more pay, even if the whole nation suffered as a result.

6. In planned economies a class of bureaucrat emerges in charge of the process. They tend to fix things so that they benefit from the system, creating, in the words of Yugoslav communist dissident Milovan Djilas, a new class, privileged and able to exploit advantages rather like the upper middle classes in capitalist countries.

7. Political opponents such as Hayek argued that planning was the thin end of a wedge that could become totalitarian in character; when people objected to being planned – as Soviet farmers made it clear they did not wish to be collectivised in the 1930s – they were imprisoned or executed.

8. Some critics of planning claim it acts as an asphyxiating blanket on enterprise by laying down what will happen as opposed to what could or might have been possible: in other words, it takes the dynamism out of capitalism. Conservatives, once back in power, tend to dismantle the planning structures created by Labour, for example the National Economic Development Council (set up by Macmillan and supported by Labour) which John Major abolished in 1992.

Chapter summary

A concept is like a lens placed in front of one's perception of the world and can be descriptive and/or normative. Many key concepts are interpreted differently according to the political perspective (see Figure 5.1 for summary of left and right versions of key concepts). Power is a crucial organising concept used in analysing why people do the bidding of politicians, and authority is essentially power plus legitimacy.

Apart from 'representation' and 'nationalism', all the above concepts display a 'negative' and 'positive' variation which are placed at opposite ends of a left–right spectrum as Figure 5.1 illustrates.

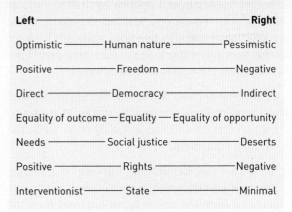

Left		Right
Optimistic ———— Human nature ———— Pessimistic
Positive ———— Freedom ———— Negative
Direct ———— Democracy ———— Indirect
Equality of outcome — Equality — Equality of opportunity
Needs ———— Social justice ———— Deserts
Positive ———— Rights ———— Negative
Interventionist ———— State ———— Minimal

Figure 5.1 Concepts and ideology

Discussion points

■ In what ways does the study of concepts tell us more about political ideas than approaches based on looking at different ideologies?

■ Of the eleven concepts studied in this chapter, which three are the most central to the study of politics?

■ Is the left-wing interpretation of concepts more defensible than that of the right?

Further reading

The best book on political concepts is Andrew Heywood's simply excellent *Political Ideas and Concepts* (1994). Also very useful are Plant (1991), Russell (1965) and Plamenatz (1963). McLean's (1996) *The Concise Oxford Dictionary of Politics* is very useful for clear and simple definitions of political concepts.

References

Adonis, A. and Pollard, S. (1997) *A Class Act: The Myth of Britain's Classless Society* (Hamish Hamilton).

Brownmiller, S. (1975) *Against Our Will: Men, Women and Rape* (Simon and Schuster).

Freud, S. (1963) *Civilisation and its Discontents* (Hogarth Press; first published 1930).

Green, T.H. (1988) *Works*, ed. R. Nettleship (Oxford University Press; first published 1911).

Hayek, F. (1979) *The Road to Serfdom* (Routledge; first published 1944).

Hayek, F.A. and Friedman, M. (Introduction) (1994) *The Road to Serfdom: Fiftieth Anniversary Edition* (The University of Chicago Press).

Heywood, A. (1994) *Political Ideas and Concepts* (Macmillan).

Locke, J. (1956) *The Second Treatise on Government*, ed. J. Gough (Blackwell; first published 1690).

McLean, I. (1996) *The Concise Oxford Dictionary of Politics* (Oxford University Press).

Michels, R. (1949) *Political Parties* (Free Press).

Morris, W. (1993) *News from Nowhere* (Penguin; first published 1891).

Norton, P. and Aughey, A. (1981) *Conservatives and Conservatism* (Temple Smith).

Nozick, R. (1974) *Anarchy, State and Utopia* (Blackwell).

Plamenatz, J. (1963) *Man and Society* (Longman).

Plant, R. (1991) *Modern Political Thought* (Blackwell).

Rawls, J. (1971) *A Theory of Justice* (Harvard University Press).

Rousseau, J.-J. (1913) *The Social Contract and Discourses* (Dutton; first published 1762).

Russell, B. (1965) *A History of Western Philosophy* (Unwin).

Smith, A. (1759) *The Theory of the Moral Sentiments* (published as *The Theory of Moral Sentiments* by Cambridge University Press, 2002).

Smith, A. (1776) *An Inquiry into the Nature and Causes of the Wealth of Nations* (published as *Wealth of Nations* by Oxford Paperbacks, 1998).

Spencer, H. (1982) *The Principles of Ethics*, ed. T. Machan (Liberty Classics; first published 1887).

Tawney, R.H. (1969) *Equality* (Allen and Unwin; first published 1931).

CHAPTER 6

Political ideas: the major parties

Bill Jones

Party spokesmen say not what they mean but what they have agreed to say.
Michael Portillo, *The Observer*, 2 March 2003

Learning objectives

- To explain the provenance of Conservatism and the ideology of capitalist free enterprise, to explain the difference between 'one nation' and neo-liberal Conservatism, and to assess the impact of Margaret Thatcher on her party's ideas.

- To trace the origins of Labour thinking to the rejection of nineteenth-century **capitalism**, to describe its maturing into corporate **socialism** and revisionism plus the left-wing dissent of the 1970s and 1980s, and to analyse the impact of Labour's rapid move into the centre and the apparent embrace of neo-Thatcherite and communitarian ideas by Tony Blair.

- To sum up the message of the Liberal Party over the years, including its alliance with the SDP and its evolution into the Liberal Democrats.

Introduction

In the aftermath of the Second World War, some commentators felt that the two major political parties in Britain were 'converging' ideologically. Daniel Bell, the American sociologist, wrote of 'the end of ideology', and in the 1970s a postwar 'consensus' was discerned between the two parties on the desirability of a welfare state and a mixed economy. Britain's relative economic decline inclined both parties to adopt more radical remedies that drew on their ideological roots. Margaret Thatcher swung the Conservatives violently to the right, while Labour went radically to the left in the early 1980s. Once Thatcher had gone, Major adopted a less overtly ideological stance, while Labour, following the failed experiment of Michael Foot as leader, successively under Neil Kinnock, John Smith and Tony Blair moved rapidly into the centre. This chapter analyses the evolution of the ideas of the major parties and brings up to date their most recent changes.

■ The Conservative Party

Source: Courtesy of the Conservative Party
(www.conservatives.com)

Key elements of Conservatism

Conservatism has a long history stretching back before its formal emergence in the 1830s. Critics have doubted whether the party has ever possessed a coherent philosophy, and indeed Lord Hailsham (1959) has described it as not so much a philosophy as an attitude. However, it is possible to discern a number of key tenets on which this attitude and Conservative policies have been based:

1. *The purpose of politics is social and political harmony*: Conservatives have traditionally believed that politics is about enabling people to become what they are or what they wish to be. They believe in a balance, a harmony in society. They have avoided too much ideological baggage in favour of measured **pragmatism** that has always kept options open. Like Edmund Burke, they have tended to believe that 'all government . . . is founded on compromise'.

2. *Human nature is imperfect and corruptible*: This quasi-religious notion of 'original sin' lies at the heart of Conservatism, leading its supporters to doubt the altruism of humankind beyond close family, to perceive most people as more interested in taking rather than giving, and to see them as fairly easy to corrupt without the external discipline of strong government.

3. *The **rule of law** is the basis of all freedom*: Law restricts freedom, yet without it there would be no freedom at all, but instead – given humanity's selfish, aggressive nature – anarchic chaos. Accepting the authority of the law is therefore the precondition of all liberty.

4. *Social institutions create a sense of society and nation*: Social and political institutions help to bind together imperfect human beings in a thing called society. Living together constructively and happily is an art, and this has to be learned. At the heart of the learning process lies the family and the institution of marriage. The royal family provides an idealised and unifying 'micro-model'. At the macro level is the idea of the 'nation', ultimately a cause worth dying for.

5. *Foreign policy is the pursuit of state interests in an anarchic world*: States exhibit all the dangerous characteristics of individuals plus a few even more unpleasant ones of their own. A judicious defence of national interests is the best guide for any country in the jungle of international relations.

6. *Liberty is the highest political end*: Individuals need freedom to develop their own personalities and pursue their destinies. Conservatives agree with Mill that it should entail freedom from oppression and be allowed to extend until

it encroaches upon the freedom of others. It should not embrace the 'levelling' of wealth, as advocated by socialists, as this redistribution would be imposed upon a reluctant population by the state (see also Chapters 4 and 5).

7. *Government through checks and balances*: 'Political liberty', said Lord Hailsham, 'is nothing else than the diffusion of power.' This means in practice institutions that divide power between them, with all having a measure of independence, thus preventing any single arm of government from being over-mighty. Hailsham also argued that political factions should balance or alternate with each other, each taking a turn at government rather than allowing it to be the preserve of one party alone.

8. *Property*: Conservatives, like David Hume, believe that the right to property is the 'first principle of justice' on which the 'peace and security of human society entirely depend'. Norton and Aughey (1981) take this further, arguing that it is an 'education. It enlightens the citizens in the value of stability and shows that the security of small property depends upon the security of all property' (p. 34). The Conservative policy of selling council houses is in line with this belief in that it is assumed, probably rightly in this case, that people will cherish their houses more once they enjoy personal ownership.

9. **Equality of opportunity** *but not of result*: Conservatives believe everyone should have the same opportunity to better themselves. Some will be more able or more motivated and will achieve more and accumulate more property. Thus an unequal distribution of wealth reflects a naturally unequal distribution of ability. Norton and Aughey (1981) maintain that the party is fundamentally concerned with justifying inequality in a way that 'conserves a hierarchy of wealth and power and make[s] it intelligible to democracy' (p. 47). To do this, Conservatives argue that inequality is necessary to maintain incentives and make the economy work; equality of reward would reward the lazy as much as the industrious (see also Chapter 5).

10. *One nation*: Benjamin Disraeli, the famous nineteenth-century Conservative Prime Minister, added a new element to his party's philosophy by criticising the 'two nations' in Britain, the rich and the poor. He advocated an alliance between the aristocracy and the lower orders to create one nation. His advice was controversial and has come to be seen as synonymous with the liberal approach to Conservatism.

11. *Rule by élite*: Conservatives have tended to believe the art of government is not given to all; it is distributed unevenly, like all abilities, and is carefully developed in families and outside these most commonly in good schools, universities and the armed forces.

12. *Political change*: Conservatives are suspicious of political change as society develops organically as an infinitely complex and subtle entity; precipitate change could damage irreparably things of great value. Therefore they distrust the system builders such as Marx, and the root-and-branch reformers such as Tony Benn. But they do not deny the need for all change; rather they tend to agree with the Duke of Cambridge that the best time for it is 'when it can be no longer resisted', or with Enoch Powell that the 'supreme function of a politician is to judge the correct moment for reform'.

The impact of Thatcherism

This collection of pragmatic guides to belief and action was able to accommodate the postwar Labour landslide, which brought nationalisation, the managed Keynesian economy, close cooperation with the trade unions and the welfare state. The role of Harold Macmillan was crucial here. In the 1930s he wrote *The Middle Way*, a plea for a regulated *laissez-faire* economy that would minimise unemployment and introduce forward planning into the economy. He was able to accept many of the reforms introduced by Labour and reinterpret them for his own party.

The postwar consensus continued with little difference over domestic policy between Macmillan and Gaitskell, Wilson and Heath. But when the economy began to fail in relation to competitors in the late 1960s and early 1970s a hurricane of dissent began to blow up on the right of the Conservative Party – and the name of the hurricane was Margaret Thatcher. She had no quarrel with traditional positions on law, property and liberty, but she was passionately convinced of a limited role for government (although not necessarily a weak one); she wanted to 'roll back' the socialist frontiers of the state. She was uninterested in checks and balances but wanted to maximise her power to achieve the things she wanted. She was opposed to equality and favoured the inequalities caused by a dynamic economy. She had scant respect for the aristocracy as she admired only ability and energy, qualities she owned in abundance. She was not in favour of gradual change but wanted radical alterations now, in her lifetime. She was a revolutionary within her own party, which still, even in 2006, had not stopped reverberating from her impact.

Thatcherite economics

1. Margaret Thatcher was strongly influenced by Keith Joseph, who was in turn influenced by the American economist Milton Friedman. He urged that to control inflation it was merely necessary to control the supply of money and credit circulating in the economy.

2. Joseph was also a disciple of Friedrich von Hayek, who believed that freedom to buy, sell and employ, i.e. economic freedom, was the foundation of all freedom. Like Hayek, he saw the drift to collectivism as a bad thing: socialists promised the 'road to freedom' but delivered instead the 'high road to servitude'.

3. Hayek and Friedman agreed with Adam Smith and the classical liberals that, if left to themselves, market forces – businessmen using their energy and ingenuity to meet the needs of customers – would create prosperity. To call this 'exploitation' of the working man, as socialists did, was nonsense as businessmen were the philanthropists of society, creating employment, paying wages and endowing charities. When markets were allowed to work properly they benefited all classes: everyone benefited, even the poor: 'the greatest social service of them all', said Mrs Thatcher, 'is the creation of wealth.'

4. Thatcher believed strongly that state intervention destroys freedom and efficiency through taking power from the consumer – the communist 'command' economies were inefficient and corrupt, protecting employment through temporary and harmful palliatives, and controlling so much of the economy that the wealth-producing sector becomes unacceptably squeezed.

5. Trade unions were one of Thatcher's *bêtes noires*. She saw them as undemocratic, reactionary vested interests that regularly held the country to ransom in the 1970s. She was determined to confront and defeat them.

6. She believed state welfare to be expensive, morally weakening in that it eroded the self-reliance she so prized, and in addition monopolistic, denying choice as well as being less efficient than private provision.

7. Her defence of national interests was founded in a passionate patriotism, which sustained her support for the armed forces and the alliance with the USA. During the Falklands War she showed great composure and courage in taking risks and ultimately triumphing. The reverse side of this was her preference for the US link over the European Union, which she suspected of being a Trojan horse for German plans to dominate the whole continent.

Margaret Thatcher therefore drove a battering ram through traditional Conservatism, but economically it was in effect a return to the classical liberalism of the early to mid-nineteenth century (see Chapter 4). Andrew Heywood (see Further reading) discerns another thread in Thatcherism, that of a pre-Disraelian emphasis on duty, responsibility, discipline and authority, although in her it was a reaction to the permissiveness of the 1960s, the defining decade of postwar socialistic culture. Many claimed to have been converted to her ideas, but the 1980s witnessed a tough internal battle, which the Prime Minister eventually won, between her and the so-called 'wet' wing of the party, which still hearkened back to the inclusive 'one nation' strand of the party's thinking.

The Major years

When John Major succeeded her following the virtual 'coup' in November 1990, many thought he would be the best hope of stern and unbending Thatcherism, but he seemed much more conciliatory, more concerned with achieving unity even at the cost of compromise, a very un-Thatcherite course of action. As the years passed, however, it became apparent that this initial analysis is far away from what happened. Major's government was almost wholly circumscribed by the ideas of his predecessor. As Heywood has pointed out, the Major government accepted her ideas; there was no conflict with 'wets', and even Heseltine, Clarke and Patten had accepted the supremacy of markets by the mid-1990s. Moreover, he took her ideas further even than she dared in her day, privatising British Rail and introducing the market principle into many hitherto forbidden areas of the welfare state.

Heywood (1998) points out that the changes have been in style rather than substance. In the 1980s, Thatcherism adopted a 'heroic' mode, smashing socialism and the power of the trade unions; it was like a continuous war or revolution as the Prime Minister tried to change 'the hearts and minds of the nation'. Major replaced that style with a 'managerial' version. However, he also added another element: a return to 'neo-conservatism' with a renewed emphasis on morality (the 'back to basics' campaign), obligation and citizenship. Conservatives have long been worried by the downside of market forces: growing inequality, the emergence of an underclass, insecurity at work and the loss of the 'feel-good factor', or the sense of the nation 'being at ease with itself' to use Major's phrase. There was a feeling in the mid-1990s that the nation's social fabric was in dire need of repair. Added to this market individualism plus neo-conservatism had been a shift towards a 'Little Englandism'. Most commentators did not believe Major was this kind of politician by instinct, but that he was forced to adjust his position on Europe quite drastically by the determined Eurosceptic minority, empowered in the early 1990s through their removal – through dissent – of the Conservatives' overall majority and thus elevated into a position of great influence and potential power.

Major was criticised for being too weak on ideology and a poor leader. The *Sun* editorials attacked him as showing 'poor judgement and weak leadership'. Lord Rees-Mogg, a pillar of the right-wing establishment, wrote: 'He is not a natural leader, he cannot speak, he has no sense of strategy or direction'. Kenneth Clarke frankly stated that when he was first mooted as leader he thought him 'a nice bloke but not up to the job'. Norman Lamont applied the cruellest cut when he said the government gave the 'impression of being in office but not in power'. Major's predecessor wrote in her memoirs that he was prone to compromise and to 'drifting with the intellectual tide'.

Hague's new start

As soon as the Conservatives lost the 1997 election so calamitously Major resigned and a contest was held for a new leader. Kenneth Clarke, genial and successful former Chancellor, was the popular choice in both the country and the party, but the Conservative Party in Parliament, entrusted with

BIOGRAPHY

William Hague (1961–)

English Conservative politician. Made his debut with a precocious speech at the 1977 conference. After Oxford, worked as management consultant and then became MP for Richmond in his native Yorkshire. Was seen as suitably opposed to Europe in 1997 and was preferred to Kenneth Clarke as leader. His early years were difficult with successes inside the Commons but rarely in the country. In the election of 2001 he stuck to his Eurosceptic guns throughout the campaign but could only persuade the nation to return one more Conservative MP. He resigned, with remarkably good grace, shortly after the election defeat. After that he busied himself with after-dinner speaking, an acclaimed biography of the Younger Pitt and occasional broadcasting. David Cameron, however, in December 2005 summoned him back to his party's front bench as Shadow Foreign Secretary.

choosing the new leader, had shifted decisively to the right; Clarke's pro-Europeanism just would not do. In the end the MPs chose the relatively unknown and untested William Hague, known to most politics watchers as the precocious sixteen-year-old who had impressed Thatcher with a right-wing speech at a 1970s party conference: it won plaudits at the time but in retrospect seemed excruciatingly embarrassing. He was at least, for those who regretted the demise of Thatcher, firm on the subject of Europe: he would have very little of it and would not join the emergent European single currency for at least a parliamentary term, if ever. Those who mocked this narrow, Little England perspective were checked when his party won the European elections handsomely in June 1999. At the party conference in October 1997, many of the deposed party leaders spoke contritely of how the party had been guilty of arrogance and indifference to the needs of the disadvantaged; a 'Compassionate Conservatism' – although ill defined – was the result. Subsequently Michael Portillo, the right-winger many felt would have won the leadership had he not astonishingly lost his huge majority to novice Labour candidate

Stephen Twigg, had effectively reinvented himself as the quintessence of such a notion. However, this flirtation with a softer image did not last for the party as a whole. It seems the Conservative High Command – alarmed by polls flat-lining at one-third of the vote – were worried that the party's core vote was about to crumble. In October 1999 Hague unveiled his 'Commonsense Revolution', a bundle of right-wing measures focusing on five 'guarantees': to cut taxes as a share of the national income; to keep out of the single currency until at least the end of the next parliamentary session and to demand opt-outs on measures not in the national interest; a 'parents guarantee' whereby inefficient heads could be dismissed; a 'patients guarantee' setting maximum times for treatment; and a get-tough guarantee on work dodgers, who would lose all benefit if refusing work after eight weeks. In fact the conference represented a surprising swing back towards Thatcherism. The lady herself appeared and was cheered to the echo by the ageing delegates as well as praised in speeches that pointedly and hurtfully ignored the contributions made by the premier of seven years, John Major. Most of the right-wing press applauded the party's rediscovery of its identity – being right-wing, Eurosceptic and proud of it. But others were not so sure. That shrewd commentator Peter Riddell wrote that 'The more William Hague roused his party faithful in Blackpool, the more he led them away from power . . . [his] main achievement . . . may have been to deepen the divisions within his own party and to reduce still further its chances of winning the next election' (*The Times*, 12 October 1999).

Riddell, not for the first time, proved remarkably prescient as Labour's second landslide in June 2001 illustrated. Hague resigned and a contest for the leadership of the Tories took place amid some acrimony. According to the new rules for electing a leader, the parliamentary party held a series of ballots to find the two candidates between whom the party faithful would choose. Portillo soon fell by the wayside, foundering, it seemed, on his admission of homosexual experience when a student at Cambridge. It was left to Kenneth Clarke, again, to battle it out with the inexperienced right-winger Iain Duncan Smith. The latter's Euroscepticism, tough line on crime and general Thatcherite orthodoxy proved much more attractive, in the judgement of the ageing party membership, compared with the liberal one-nation approach of Clarke, who went down by a two-to-one majority.

The Iain Duncan Smith effect

'IDS', as he is known, began his tenure as leader by striving to make an impression in the Commons, but Blair proved too dominant and his opponent too unsure of his ground to 'win' even a few of the weekly Prime Minister's Question Time encounters. What made it worse was that so many of the well-known Conservatives either had retired (e.g. Tebbit, Baker, Fowler), had not been keen on serving under Duncan Smith (e.g. Clarke, Hague), or were still stigmatised by association with the 'bad old days' of the Conservative's eighteen years in power (e.g. Howard, Gummer). Despite his defeat for the leadership, Portillo's influence remained as a voice calling for 'modernisation' of the Conservative message: a more inclusive attitude to women, gays and ethnic minorities; a distancing from anything resembling racism; an acceptance of the need to modernise and improve public services; and a less dogmatic hostility to all things European. Duncan Smith's ineffectual orthodoxy was soon found in the polls to be out of touch, and in the spring of 2002, at the party's Harrogate conference, IDS effected a neat *volte-face* on policy, calling for a compassionate attitude towards the 'vulnerable' in society, a decentralisation of power to the regions and a supportive attitude towards the public services. However, shifting towards a new policy position is one thing; communicating it, via an unknown Shadow Cabinet, is another: the polls still flat-lined at just over 30 percentage points. The new leader faced immense difficulty in convincing voters that his party was not, as he complained, 'nasty, extreme and strange' (*The Observer*, 2 July 2002). At the party conference later in the year, the new party chairman, Theresa May, urged the party to lose its 'nasty' image: evidence of her support for the modernisation camp. However, the *éminence grise* of this tendency featured again in February 2003 when Michael Portillo complained bitterly at the peremptory sacking of the chief executive of the party, Mark MacGregor – an alleged Portillo supporter – and his replacement with an IDS supporter, the right-wing MP Barry Legg. The outbreak of war against Iraq the following month enabled Duncan Smith to occupy familiar Conservative territory – pro-armed forces and pro-USA – although such a position precluded political exploitation of Prime Minister Blair's discomfort in prosecuting a war unpopular in the country and even more so in his own party. The Conservative leader's fate, it was agreed, lay with his party's fate

BIOGRAPHY

Michael Portillo (1953–)

Conservative politician. Educated at Cambridge. Worked for the Conservative Research Department, 1976–9, and as junior minister in various departments until he became a Cabinet minister in the early 1990s. Was defeated in the 1997 election and missed his chance to lead the party then. Worked hard at being an advocate of 'caring Conservatism' before becoming adopted as a candidate in the safe seat of Kensington. Made Shadow Chancellor in late 1999. 'Reinvented' himself as a caring inclusive one-nation Conservative with speeches, television programmes and an admission of student-day homosexual experience. This last caused trouble with older Conservatives; when Portillo stood for the leadership after Hague's resignation, Norman Tebbit made a thinly veiled attack on his sexuality, and the modernisers' hope was defeated at the Commons stage (according to the new procedure) before party members were able to vote on the two nominees.

in the May local elections, an event that saw his party win over 500 seats. Most commentators concluded that the figures were good enough to enable IDS to survive; Kenneth's Clarke's backing of an 'anti-war' horse over Iraq also helped to strengthen the embattled leader's position. Discontent with Iain Duncan Smith grew in the run-up to the 2003 party conference and soon afterwards he lost a crucial party vote of confidence. Michael Howard, the right-wing former Home Secretary, was selected in his place.

The era of Michael Howard

On Thursday 6 November 2003 the man who came sixth in the 1997 leadership challenge was elected unopposed to the leadership of his party. Despite his reputation for being a right-winger, Howard stressed his desire to continue IDS's emphasis on social justice with policies aimed at helping the disadvantaged. This was accompanied by calls for zero tolerance policing, more spending on drug treatment for addicts and an increase in the basic state pension. His concerns regarding Europe were underlined by renewed calls for a referendum on the proposed new constitution for the EU.

Losing Conservative themes

The truth is that the European debate will not subside. It is at the heart of our economic and constitutional traditions. It will proceed into the next parliament with a vitality that challenges loyalties.
John Biffen, *The Guardian*, 17 February 1996

We are unpopular, above all, because the middle classes – and all those who aspire to join the middle classes – feel that they no longer have the incentives and opportunities they expect from a Conservative government.
Margaret Thatcher's attack on 'one nation' Conservatism, 11 January 1996

'Nasty, extreme and strange.'
Iain Duncan Smith's view of how his party was perceived by voters, *The Observer*, 2 July 2002

From the outset, Howard proved reasonably effective at Prime Minister's Questions but found it hard to resist the need to bolster up the core vote and did little to move the party into the electorally crucial centre ground. The party continued to languish in the polls as the general election approached in 2005. The party continued to lack a distinctive message right up to polling day on 5 May and duly paid the price when the votes were counted. The Conservatives won thirty-three more seats but had to sit back and watch an unpopular government led by a gifted but mistrusted Tony Blair maintain its hold on the Commons to the extent of an overall majority of sixty-six. Howard, the old professional seasoned politician, had hoped to lead a renaissance of Toryism but had proved to be merely a stop-gap leader of a party which some perceived to be in terminal decline. Howard resigned quite soon but stayed on to preside over the election of his successor. This period – May to October – saw much soul searching during which most party members came to realise that drastic change was necessary. The Conservative Policy Exchange think tank produced a devastating report on the party highlighting its unpopularity, lack of contact with modern society and hopeless image as a party favouring middle-class people in the shires and the southeast. Figure 6.1, drawn from the report, reveals how people viewed

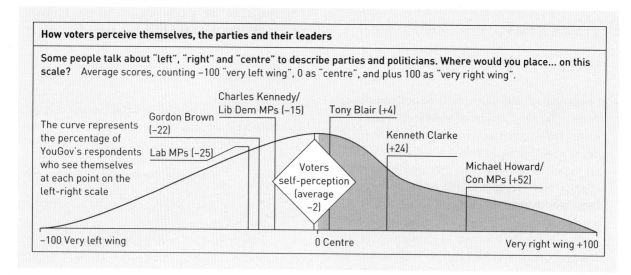

Figure 6.1 How voters perceive themselves, the parties and their leaders
Source: From Policy Exchange (2005) *The Case for Change*, May 2005. Reproduced with permission

their own political position on the left–right continuum and then superimposed their estimates of where leading politicians stood. Inevitably the majority of people occupy the centre ground, indicating where any party wishing to win an election needs to project its messages. Howard was perceived as being quite far to the right – his MPs also. Kenneth Clarke, on the other hand, was seen as substantially closer to the centre. Gordon Brown was located slightly to the right of Labour MPs and to the left of Charles Kennedy. And Tony Blair? His brilliant sense of where the centre of political gravity lies enabled him to sit astride the middle of the graph, four points to the right of dead centre.

The election of David Cameron, December 2005

The Conservative Party conference in October 2005 at Blackpool indicated that the party had finally realised that major change to the party and its thinking was necessary before an election win could be contemplated. The declared leadership candidates were able to address the delegates and make an initial pitch. Howard had influenced his own succession by placing members of the new young liberal or 'moderniser' group in his party to major positions in the Shadow Cabinet – George Osborne (34) to Shadow Chancellor and David Cameron (39) to Education – and allowing them to make an impression before the leadership contest in the autumn. Osborne, it seemed, had already decided not to run

but to manage the campaign of his friend, the old Etonian, Cameron. Parallels with Tony Blair's rise to power were already being made before Cameron delighted the conference with a speech he had learnt by heart and delivered without notes, giving the impression of spontaneity as he walked around the stage. David Davis, the former minister in his mid-fifties, who had assembled what many thought to be an impregnable lead among MPs who had declared their support, tried to follow suit but, compared with the sparkling, inspiring rhetoric of his rival, appeared lack-lustre and dull. Cameron went on to win easily the MPs' ballot and then to win over the party for the membership ballot on 5 December which he won by a margin of two to one. On 6 December he took on Blair at PMQs and, in an excellent, witty debut performance, told him 'you were the future once'.

Cameron, while copying the informal, media-friendly style of the younger Tony Blair, was careful to steer clear of specific policy commitments, though it was clear his period in power would see a jettisoning of the party's much beloved positions on a number of issues. Cameron and his coterie of 'Notting Hill Set' colleagues were very keen to change the brand image of the party. During the 2005 election, focus groups had revealed that members who liked a policy position when it was explained to them changed their mind when they discovered it was a Conservative party policy. Concerted efforts were made to banish the notion of the 'nasty party', the idea of a bigoted, intolerant group of richer, older

Bob Geldof helps accelerate the Conservatives' new momentum by agreeing to become a consultant for them on world poverty
Source: Copyright © David Parkins. From *The Guardian*, 29 December 2005. Reproduced with permission

people who wanted power merely to advance their own interests and outdated way of life. Consequently Cameron let it be known his name was not David but 'Dave'; that he cared deeply about special-needs child-care (with a disabled son this was clearly true); that he cared about the environment (cycling to the Commons, appointing environmentalist Zac Goldsmith to an advisory position); that he cared about world poverty (Bob Geldof's turn to be corralled); and that the party no longer hated gays and opposed civil partnerships.

In late December Oliver Letwin declared his party to favour redistribution of wealth, and shortly afterwards Cameron shifted its position on immigration from opposition to qualified support for those incomers essential to the economy. Cameron also addressed the key area of tax cuts. It seemed Conservatives now would basically accept the 4 per cent increase in basic taxation since 1997 as necessary to

sustain public services at requisite levels. He also declared that cuts would have to come in the wake of economic stability, a reversal of the Thatcherite view that the latter is a condition for the achievement of the former. And the party would no longer be the natural adjunct of the free enterprise economy: henceforward, the party would 'stand up to as well as for business'.

The new boy was careful, however, to keep the core vote onside with a judicious dash of Euroscepticism. True, he wished to bury the party's civil war over the EU, which he deemed irrelevant now that the proposed new constitution had been rejected by France and Holland. But he nevertheless wanted the Conservative party to end its membership of the European People's Party, a right-wing grouping which nevertheless favoured rather too much integration. Perhaps his biggest break with the past, however, was to declare that the litmus test for social policies should be what they could do for the disadvantaged: many older Tories must have done a double-take on that one.

Like Blair in the mid-nineties he set up a number of study groups to review policy areas. Opinion polls almost immediately registered a lead for Labour, albeit a slender one at that early stage. Blair must have realised at once that the political situation had been drastically changed and that he no longer could expect a free ride in his domination of the centre ground. But Cameron too does not, at the time of writing, face an easy ride. By swinging his party back from the Thatcherite end of the spectrum, he faced no little opposition within his own party. After his declaration just after the turn of the new year in 2006 in favour of alleviating world poverty, reducing social and economic inequality and industrial emissions of greenhouse gases, Melanie Phillips wrote in the *Daily Mail* on 2 January 2006:

This leaves millions of natural conservatives effectively disenfranchised – and even worse demonized as dinosaurs by the party that is supposed to represent them, but is now telling them to go hang while it tears up everything they believe in.

Wise old commentators judged such opposition to be precisely what Cameron needed. Blair had risen to public prominence over his brilliant defeat of party traditionalists over Clause 4. Lacking any similar dragons to slay, Cameron needed to overcome opposition from the older cohorts as represented for example by Lord Tebbit, one of Thatcher's most loyal and true-blue Conservative followers. For it would be by overcoming such opposition that his party would be seen to have changed.

■ The Labour Party and socialism

Source: Courtesy of the Labour Party (www.labour.org.uk)

Socialism

Socialism developed as a critique and alternative to capitalism and its political expression, Conservatism.

It focused on economics as the key activity, but the full sweep of its message provided guidance on virtually all aspects of living. Perhaps the clearest statement of the idea is still provided in Robert Tressell's *The Ragged Trousered Philanthropists* (1965, first published 1914), when the hero, Owen, addresses his scornful workmates on the subject by drawing an oblong in the dust with a charred stick to represent the adult population of the country: 'all those who help consume the things produced by labour'. He then divides the oblong up into five to represent five classes of people (Figure 6.2):

1. All those who do nothing, e.g. tramps, beggars and the aristocracy.

2. All those engaged in mental work that benefits themselves and harms others, e.g. employers, thieves, bishops, capitalists.

3. All those engaged in unnecessary work 'producing or doing things which cannot be described as the necessaries of life or the benefits of civilisation'. This is the biggest section of all, e.g. shop assistants, advertising people, commercial travellers.

4. All those engaged in necessary work producing the 'necessaries, refinements and comforts of life'.

5. The unemployed.

Underneath the oblong he then draws a small square, which, he explains, is to represent all the goods produced by the producing class: group 4. The crucial part comes next: how are all these goods shared out under the 'present imbecile system'?

As the people in divisions one and two are universally considered to be the most worthy and deserving we give them two-thirds of the whole. The remainder we give to be 'shared out' amongst the people represented by divisions three and four.

Tressell (1965), p. 272

Owen then proceeds to point out that it is groups 3 and 4 that battle most ferociously for their third, while 'most of the people who do nothing get the best of everything. More than three-quarters of the time of the working class is spent making things used by the wealthy.'

Despite his eloquence, Owen's workmates are reluctant to listen, so, as playwright Alan Sillitoe observes in his introduction to the 1965 edition, he calls them:

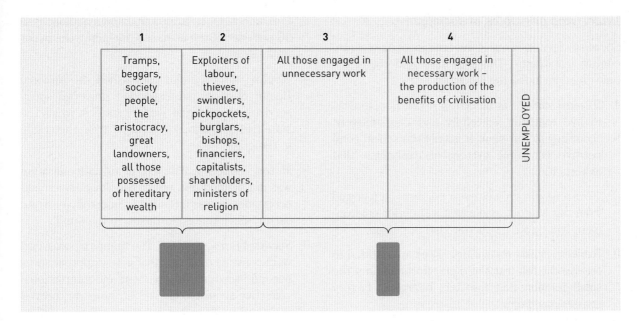

1	2	3	4	
Tramps, beggars, society people, the aristocracy, great landowners, all those possessed of hereditary wealth	Exploiters of labour, thieves, swindlers, pickpockets, burglars, bishops, financiers, capitalists, shareholders, ministers of religion	All those engaged in unnecessary work	All those engaged in necessary work – the production of the benefits of civilisation	UNEMPLOYED

Figure 6.2 How the things produced by people in division 4 are 'shared out' among the different classes of the population
Source: R. Tressell (1965) *The Ragged Trousered Philanthropists*, Allen and Unwin (Panther, first published 1914). Reproduced with permission of HarperCollins

philanthropists, benefactors in ragged trousers who willingly hand over the results of their labour to the employers and the rich. They think it the natural order of things that the rich should exploit them, that 'gentlemen' are the only people with the right to govern.

Tressell (1965), p. ii

Towards the end of the book another character, Barrington, orates his vision of a socialist society: nationalisation of land, railways and most forms of production and distribution; the establishment of community culture and leisure facilities; the ending of unemployment; the abolition of the now redundant police force; equal pay; good homes for all; automation of industry and consequent reduction of the working day to four or five hours; free education to 21 and retirement at full pay at 45; and the ending of military conflict worldwide.

This classic account of socialism issues from a fundamental set of assumptions, provides a critique of capitalism and its related ideology, and offers a superior form of society as an achievable objective.

Critique of capitalism

Socialism asserted that capitalism 'exploited' the working masses by selling the fruits of their labour, taking the lion's share of the revenue and paying only subsistence wages. This produced huge disparities in income between the suburban-living rich and the urban-based poor. Because the ruling capitalists dominate all the institutions of the state, argued socialists, they subtly intrude their values into all walks of life, and a complex web of mystifications produces a 'false consciousness' in which the working class believes wrongly that its best interests are served by supporting capitalist values. Capitalist championing of 'individualism' and 'freedom' are mere cloaks for the exploitation of the weak by the strong. The ruthlessness of the system induces similar qualities within society. Wage labour merely relieved employers of any residual obligations they might have felt towards their workers. By living in large urban settlements working men were alienated from each other, while the automating of industry denied workers any creative satisfaction. A final criticism was that capitalism with its booms and slumps was inevitably inefficient and inferior to a planned economy.

Socialists argued that two large antagonistic classes emerge in capitalist societies: a small wealthy ruling class and a large impoverished proletariat living in the cities which actually created wealth.

Underlying principles of socialism

Socialism developed out of this critique of nineteenth-century capitalism. The principles underlying the new creed included the following:

1. *Human nature is basically good*: People wish to live together peacefully and cooperatively, according to this view; it is only the selfish competitive economic system of capitalism that distorts it.

2. *'Environment creates consciousness'*: It followed from this Marxist axiom that a superior environment will create a superior kind of person.

3. *Workers create the wealth*: They are entitled to receive the full fruits of their efforts and not the small fraction that the rich, bourgeois factory owners pay them.

4. *Equality*: Everyone has the right to start off in life with the same chances as everyone else; the strong should not exploit their advantage and impose themselves on the weak.

5. *Freedom*: The poor need more resources for the playing field of life to be level and thus be truly free.

6. *Collectivism*: Social solidarity should take the place of selfish individualism.

The Labour Party

Labour in power

Labour held power briefly in the 1920s and began to formulate a more pragmatic, less emotional and more coherent version of socialism. During the 1930s and the war years socialist thinkers such as Hugh Dalton (1887–1962) and Herbert Morrison (1888–1965) developed what has since been called 'corporate socialism', comprising:

1. *Keynesian economics*: Management of the economy, using investment to cure slumps and squeeze out unemployment.

2. *Centralised planning of the economy*: This was the corollary of the Keynesian approach; it had worked brilliantly during the 1939–45 war and would do the same for the peace, promised Labour.

3. *Nationalisation*: Morrison devised this approach based on bringing an industry out of private and into public control via a board accountable to Parliament. Once in power, Labour nationalised 20 per cent of the economy, including the major utilities.

4. *Welfare state*: Labour established the National Health Service and expanded universal social services into a virtual 'welfare state' in which the state had obligations to citizens 'from the cradle to the grave'.

5. *Mixed economy*: The extent of nationalisation was not defined but, unlike the Soviet command economies, it was intended to maintain a private sector, albeit one subordinate to the public.

6. *Socialist foreign policy*: The trauma of two world wars convinced Labour that a new approach was needed based on disarmament and international collective security. The USSR, however, proved resistant to fraternal overtures from a fellow left-wing government, and ultimately Labour's combative Foreign Secretary, Ernest Bevin (1881–1952), was forced to attract the USA into the NATO alliance.

Revisionism

Some Labour intellectuals – such as Hugh Gaitskell (1906–63), Hugh Dalton, Roy Jenkins (1920–2002), Denis Healey (1917–) and, most importantly, Anthony Crosland (1918–77) – were not content, like Morrison, to declare that 'socialism is what the Labour government does'; they looked for a new direction after the huge achievements of Clement Attlee (1883–1967) and his government. Crosland's book, *The Future of Socialism* (1956), asserted that Marx's predictions of capitalist societies polarising before revolutions established left-wing government had been proved hopelessly wrong; the working class had ignored revolutions and had been strengthened by full employment. The business class had not fought the advance of socialism but had been tamed by it. Crosland argued that the ownership of the economy was no longer relevant, as salaried managers were now the key players. He attacked another sacred cow by maintaining that nationalisation was not necessarily the most effective road to socialism and that other forms of collective ownership were more effective. He concluded that Labour should now concentrate its efforts on reducing inequality through progressive taxation and redistributive benefits and – the key proposal – reducing class differences through an end to selection in education.

In practice, revisionism was Labour's policy for the next thirty years, but when in government in the 1970s its fatal flaw was exposed: it was dependent on an expanding economy, and when this fell into decline cuts in public expenditure became inevitable. With the cuts came the end of socialist advances, dependent as they were on the availability of resources.

The left wing of the party never accepted revisionism, and first Aneurin (Nye) Bevan, then Michael Foot, opposed the new drift towards a diluted ideology. In the 1960s, Wilson defied the Left in the parliamentary party, but when it teamed up with the trade unions trouble was in store for the 1970s administrations under both Wilson and Callaghan. Led by Tony Benn, the Left now offered an alternative economic strategy based on workers' control, extended state control of the economy, **participatory democracy** at all levels of national life, fresh injections of funds into the welfare state, encouragement of extra-parliamentary activity, and unilateral abandonment of nuclear weapons. The revisionist leadership tried to ignore the Left, but when the 1979 general election was lost to a new and militantly ideological leader, Margaret Thatcher, the Left insisted that a similar return to the roots of socialist ideology was necessary. With the revisionist leadership defeated and discredited, the Left made its move, managing to translate its candidate, Michael Foot, into leader in 1980, plus imposing a radically left-wing set of policies on the party, which resulted in the 1983 manifesto being dubbed by Gerald Kaufman 'the longest suicide note in history'. More significantly, the Left's ascendancy led to the defection of an important wing of the party to form the Social Democratic Party (see Box 6.1). The conventional view is that the new party split the anti-Tory vote and helped to keep Thatcher in power for a decade. However, the party's history as written by Ivor Crewe and Anthony King (1995) concluded that this transient new force, if anything, reduced the Tory majority.

Neil Kinnock, elected as Foot's successor, was a child of the Left but soon recanted, dismissing its prescriptions as 'Disneyland thinking'. He assiduously began to nudge his party towards the centre ground via a series of policy reviews, which essentially accepted the 'efficiency and realism' of the market

BOX 6.1　EXAMPLE

The brief, eventful life of the Social Democratic Party

On 1 August 1980, Shirley Williams, David Owen and William Rodgers published an open letter to the Labour Party in *The Guardian*: the famous 'Gang of Three' statement. It followed in the wake of Roy Jenkins' Dimbleby Lecture, in which he had suggested that a new party might 'break the mould' of British politics. Members of the 'gang' had opposed previous proposals on the grounds that a centre party would 'lack roots and a coherent philosophy'; they warned, however, that if Labour's drift to the left continued, they would have to reconsider their position.

After the Wembley Conference in January 1981, which pushed through measures strengthening the control of left-wing party activists over the election of the leadership and the reselection of MPs, the three ex-Cabinet ministers joined Jenkins in creating the Social Democratic Party (SDP). Over the ensuing months twenty to thirty centre-right Labour MPs made the journey over to the new party, plus a fair number of peers and other figures, not forgetting the solitary Conservative MP.

The Guardian article had called for a 'radical alternative to Tory policies . . . rejecting class war, accepting the mixed economy and the need to manage it efficiently'. The SDP fought the 1983 election in tandem with the Liberals, gaining 26 per cent of the vote, but their high hopes were dashed in 1987 when they mustered only 22 per cent. The resultant merger negotiations split the SDP into 'Owenite' and 'mergerite' camps and appeared finally to disperse the heady optimism that had attended its birth.

During its brief life, did the SDP truly offer a 'radical alternative'? Certainly SDP members elaborated on *The Guardian* manifesto in a spate of articles and books. Shirley Williams in *Politics Is for People* drew heavily on the ideas of Robert Owen and Tawney, while Owen's *Face the Future* drew on Mill, William Morris and G.D.H. Cole. Both authors acknowledged their debts to the Fabians and Anthony Crosland.

The SDP was formed in a blaze of publicity and 'breaking the mould' rhetoric, but a genuine alternative was probably not on offer. In one sense its message represented an amalgam of policies picked up across the political spectrum. Decentralisation was close to the Liberal, Bennite and Green position; SDP views on the market economy and trade unions were close to Margaret Thatcher's position – she actually praised Owen for being 'sound' on both – and on social policy and defence the SDP was close to the position of the Callaghan government, to which the SDP leaders had once belonged. This is not to say that the SDP lacked a carefully worked out and detailed programme, merely that it lacked a distinctive alternative or even radical quality. History will judge the SDP as a party of protest with a limited appeal outside the middle classes.

When the party's twelve-point plan was announced in March 1981, *The Times* concluded that this 'new beginning' was no more than a modern version of **'Butskellism'** that was 'seeking essentially to bring that consensus up to date'. In other words, the SDP was merely developing Labour revisionist policies free of the political and rhetorical restrictions caused through working within the Labour Party. In Samuel Beer's (1982) view: 'What had happened was quite simple: the Labour Party had been a socialist party . . . [and] many of its adherents ceased to believe in socialism.'

In August 1980 the Gang of Three had written that a 'Centre Party . . . would lack roots and a coherent philosophy.' The final irony of the SDP is that its leaders succeeded in writing its obituary before its birth had even taken place. However, defenders of the SDP argue that its formation was crucial in reminding Labour of where the electoral ground for a reformist party lay and in providing the agenda eventually adopted by New Labour under Blair.

as the best model of economic organisation. It was implicit in this new analysis – although hotly denied – that socialism was no longer relevant, and even the word disappeared from policy documents and manifestos. When he lost the crucial 1992 election, he resigned and John Smith continued this 'desocialising' work. When Smith died tragically of a heart attack in May 1994, Tony Blair was elected leader and soon placed his stamp on a party denied power for nearly fifteen years.

Views by Labour leaders past and present

As for Tony Blair, I still think, as I thought when I first met him, we're lucky to have him – both the Labour Party and the nation. He might have gone off and joined the Social Democrats and no-one would have heard of him again.

Michael Foot, *The Observer*, 6 September 1996

My view of Christian values has led me to oppose what I perceived to be a narrow view of self-interest that Conservatism – particularly in its modern, more right-wing form – represents.

Tony Blair, September 1995

Having already abandoned its former policies of opposition to the European Community/Union, unilateral nuclear disarmament and nationalisation, Blair shifted the party even further to the right by attacking the power of trade unions in the party. He waged a spectacularly successful war against the 'collective ownership' Clause Four in the party's constitution, drafted by Sidney Webb in 1917:

To secure for the workers by hand or by brain the full fruits of their industry and the most equitable distribution thereof that may be possible upon the basis of the common ownership of the means of production, distribution, and exchange, and the best obtainable system of popular administration and control of each industry or service.

The iconic clause, so fundamental that it was inscribed on membership cards, was replaced in April 1995 by a massive majority at a special conference.

Clause Four rewritten

Philip Gould records the meeting in Blair's bedroom in March 1995 when the new Clause Four was drafted:

In the end Blair wrote it himself . . . I liked the last draft and said so. The main sentence is long but has power. 'The Labour Party is a democratic socialist party. It believes that by the strength of our common endeavour we achieve more than we achieve alone, so as to create for each of us the means to realise our true potential and for all of us a community in which power, wealth and opportunity are in the hands of the many and not the few, where the rights we enjoy reflect the duties we owe, and where we live together freely, in a spirit of solidarity, tolerance and respect.' This is the essence of what Tony Blair has always believed: individuals should be advanced by strong communities, in which rights and responsibility are balanced.

Gould (1998), p. 229

The clause went on to endorse a 'dynamic economy, serving the public interest'; a 'just society which judges its strength by the condition of the weak as much as the strong'; 'an open democracy, in which government is held to account by the people'; and where 'decisions are taken as far as practicable by the communities they affect'.

Not content with this he drew the party away from the social democratic heartland of full employment and welfare spending. This was for two reasons. First, it was deemed that the requisite high taxation would never be endorsed by middle-class voters – remember that Labour was caught out badly by the Conservatives over tax in 1992. Second, it was believed that the world's economy had changed. With modern technology the economy has become globalised so that flows of capital can break companies and even currencies in minutes. To maintain policies of high taxation risks massive withdrawals of capital by speculators and investors from any economy contemplating such socialistic measures.

'New Labour' has effectively embraced the economic side of Thatcherism: tax cuts, low inflation, a market economy plus encouragement of entrepreneurial activity and some privatisation. Tony Blair has even felt able to praise aspects of Thatcher's legacy and to endorse some of them as worth keeping. He has tried to strike out, however, and to devise some distinctive policies for his party. He eschewed a major 'big' idea but came up with some middling-sized ones instead, for example a 'stakeholder society', that everyone, individuals and groups, should have some investment in society, and everyone should feel part of their community at all levels, economic, cultural and social; the idea withered through business opposition to any wider role. The other biggish idea supported by Blair has been constitutional reform; Labour has embraced devolved assemblies for both Scotland and Wales plus reform of the House of Lords and a referendum on the electoral system. However, the changes are pitted with flaws, none more so than the unresolved so-called 'West Lothian question', whereby Scottish MPs would have the ability to vote on English issues but English MPs do not have the ability to reciprocate as the internally elected assembly would assume this role (see Chapter 14). The Lords reform agenda stalled after the abolition of hereditary peers and the chamber continues in its half-reformed way with everyone, except Blair, urging a degree of elected representation but no-one really knowing how much. As for reforming the voting system, the results of the Jenkins Report continue to gather dust and the referendum seems indefinitely postponed.

It is often said that Blair has moved Labour so far to the centre that he is now even to the right of some 'one nation' Tories. Figure 6.1 shows there is some-

---

BOX 6.2   IDEAS AND PERSPECTIVES

Blair's project

We worked our way towards our new political project. Slowly Blair gave substance to his ideas, fleshing them out. By the end of it, he would have priorities for government based upon his analysis of the problems facing Britain: lack of a first class education system for the majority of children; community disintegration leading to crime and pressure on families; the poor performance of the economy, and the unstable relationship between government and business; a centralised and secretive political system; and isolation and lack of influence overseas.

Source: Gould (1998), p. 244

thing in this; certainly his approach bears comparison with this strain of Conservatism, and it must be significant that he happily uses the phrase 'one nation' socialism. The tactical purpose of the term is evident in that it implies that the party which once claimed it as its own is arguably now the party of a narrow, nationalistic and divided collection of people. Cameron will seek to reclaim the term for the Conservatives.

The massive endorsement of New Labour in the general election of 1 May 1997 was fulfilment of the strategy conceived and implemented by Tony Blair and his close collaborator Peter Mandelson to move the Labour Party into a position where it embraced the market economy and removed the fear of old-style socialism felt by the middle-class occupants of 'Middle England'. 'Blairism' is vaguely expressed and lends itself to wide interpretation, but sceptical commentators wonder whether he has a framework of belief strong enough to survive the vicissitudes of several years in office and to resist the atavistic influences of the union-based old Labour ideology. Others disagree and claim that Blairism can boast a coherent philosophical framework and a well worked-out 'project'. Socially it is based on the idea of communitarianism. This derives from Blair's studies at university, where he was very interested in the ideas of John McMurray, a Scottish philosopher who took issue with the modish idea of 'individualism', that the individual has choices and freedoms and is an autonomous unit. McMurray argued the contrary, that, as Adams puts it:

People do not exist in a vacuum; in fact, they only exist in relation to others. The completely autonomous self of liberal theory is a myth. People's personalities are created in their relationships with others, in the family and the wider community. By pursuing the interests of society as a whole we benefit individuals including ourselves.
Adams (1998), pp. 148–9

Blair believes that people should build communities based on the idea of responsibility, a sense of duty towards others maybe less fortunate and a recognition that one's actions have repercussions and may require reparation. Old Labour tended to see poor people as 'victims of the system'; to speak of them having responsibilities is to borrow from another right-wing lexicon. Blair has also subscribed to the idea of a Third Way. Apart from being an alternative to socialism and pro-capitalist ideology, it is not clearly defined. Another participant has been the eminent sociologist Anthony Giddens, highly regarded by Blair, who has written a book, *The Third Way: The Renewal of Social Democracy*. This argues that the old definitions of left and right are obsolete (see Chapter 4) and that in the world of globalisation a new approach is required. He defines the overall aim of Third Way politics as helping citizens to:

pilot their way through the major revolutions of our time: globalisation, transformations in personal life and our relationship to nature . . . One might suggest as a prime motto for the new politics, 'No rights without responsibilities'.
Giddens (1998), pp. 64–5; see also Box 6.3

Blair in power

Tony Blair has been Prime Minister since 1997 and has seemed, on balance, to be a strong and decisive premier. But has his tenure in power altered the basic outlines of New Labour ideology? Constitutional change has been advanced successfully, although the implications of the measures have yet to be thought through and completed, as in, for example, the House of Lords. However, the biggest departure from the cautious initial agenda has been over taxation and spending on the public services. For his first two years in office Chancellor Gordon Brown exerted tight control over spending to reassure middle-class voters that New Labour was not the same as tax-and-spend Old Labour. However, plentiful evidence was showered on the government that the public was deeply unimpressed with health, education and transport and felt disappointed that the incoming government had not achieved any real improvements. Consequently Blair and, perhaps more importantly, Gordon Brown decided to embark on a massive reinvestment programme in the public services, in 2002 proposing to spend over £100 billion over the next few years. Arguably such spending marked a return to Old Labour values, something that Brown was always regarded as being closer to than the focus group based New Labourism. Certainly Labour's former deputy leader Roy Hattersley, once seen as right-wing but now – because Blair has swung so far right – a left-wing critic of Tony Blair, welcomed the return to the traditional socialist agenda of publicly funded, universally available public services.

However, the event that transformed Labour during the early months of 2003 was the threatened and

BOX 6.3   IDEAS AND PERSPECTIVES

How 'new' is New Labour?

A number of scholars have considered this question but the approach of Steven Fielding of Salford University (2003) is perhaps the most useful for this chapter's purposes. Fielding argues that New Labour is in reality part of the continuous development of social democratic thinking over the last century and a half. He denies the claim, associated with Roy Hattersley for one, that New Labour was a kind of 'coup' involving Blair, Mandelson and Gould and also denies the idea that New Labour was, in fact, all that new. His case is that New Labour is less to do with high-profile personalities and more to do with social democratic adaptations to the constantly fluid nature of international economics.

Socialism, he observes, has always been about relating the needs of the many to the productive bounty of the economy and, in the absence of any alternative, that has been the capitalist system. There is therefore a built-in contradiction between an ideology which preaches equality and a system which produces winners and losers: inequality. Politicians of the left, throughout the twentieth century, have sought to reconcile this conflict. After the Second World War, Keynesian demand management techniques seemed to be the answer: Attlee nationalised chunks of the economy and installed the welfare state; there was full employment and economic growth, and Labour politicians claimed the goal of equality had been brought substantially closer. The myth of the 'golden age of social democracy' was established in the minds of many Labour supporters.

However, efficiency, the other major socialist goal, was another matter. Nationalised industries proved disastrously inefficient as the economy generally declined. Labour began to view the economy not so differently from the Conservatives: as something whose growth was to be encouraged and facilitated. During the pivotal decade of the seventies international competition caused growth to decline and unemployment to rise. As inflation soared during the seventies, public spending was placed under a critical microscope by Labour's Chancellor, Denis Healey. The unions, bedrock supporters of Labour, rebelled at proposed cuts and restrictions on wage increases. The Conservatives came into power, in consequence, with policies that hurt but that many people recognised as necessary to turn the economy around.

Some of those who felt this were Labour supporters, but the dominant reaction in the party was to swing violently back to basic principles: more state control of the economy. Such an approach was emphatically rejected by voters in 1983 and 1987, and Labour under Neil Kinnock began to make adjustments which recognised the new economic, social and political realities. When his changes were still not deemed sufficient by voters in 1992, Tony Blair took over in 1994. He was less bound by traditional beliefs and vigorously urged adoption of those Thatcherite tenets he believed were needed to run an efficient economy in a globalised world and to reassure middle-class voters that Labour could rule effectively; meanwhile he sought to assure traditional supporters that the basic values of the movement would still be served.

As long as public expenditure was on the leash, as it was for some years after the 1997 victory, those who equated New Labour with Conservatism and yearned for a return to the golden age of 'Old Labour' had some purchase for their arguments, but once the funds began to flow into health and education, this position was less viable. Fielding concludes:

The party at the start of the twenty first century may be a highly cautious social democratic organization; but recognizably social democratic it remains. If the state has advanced modestly and in novel ways since 1997 Labour's purpose in office is the same as it ever was: to reform capitalism so that it may better serve the interests of the majority.

Source: Fielding (2003), p. 217

then the actual war on Iraq. Tony Blair had decided to stand 'shoulder to shoulder' with George W. Bush after the horrific attacks on the World Trade Center on 11 September 2001, but the extent of his loyalty to a right-wing president advised by Republican hawks was not to the liking of many Labour MPs, and in February 2003 over 100 rebelled against Blair's support for the impending war. When it proved impossible to muster a United Nations Security Council majority for the war in March, 139 MPs supported a hostile motion and Robin Cook resigned from the Cabinet. Left-wing critics, already angry at their leader's slavish support for business and the government's enhanced participation in public services, scented blood, and there was talk of a special conference to elect a new leader. Such speculation proved premature, but Blair's obsession with Iraq and blind support for US foreign policy was exacting a severe price in terms of political support in his own New Labour power base (see also Chapter 28).

Having won a third term in May 2005, albeit with a reduced majority and with few fanfares, Blair found his authority beginning to slide. Late in 2004 he had sought to end the feud with Gordon Brown over when he would stand aside, by declaring he would not stand in the next election. This imparted a 'lame duck' quality to his third term in Downing Street and his attempts to secure 'legacy' achievements acquired a somewhat desperate and even vainglorious quality. Apart from the ongoing quagmire of Iraq, Blair lost much support in his own party for being:

■ over-zealous in proposing *allegedly illiberal anti-terrorist measures*. In November 2005 his suggestion that suspects could be held without trial for 90 days was defeated by a whopping 31 votes;

■ overly keen on introducing *market forces and privatisation into his reform of public services*. The proposed freedom for schools from local authority control in the autumn education White Paper was criticised bitterly from the Left whose consciousness was still rooted in municipal control of education and who suspected schools would use their new freedom to reintroduce the hated selection of pupils by ability. David Cameron cleverly exploited Blair's discomfort by offering votes to help overcome the PM's internal party opposition. Blair's desire to keep Middle England happy was finally coming home to inflict damage on his drive to leave reformed, efficient public services as a monument to his years in

power. For the Labour Party faithful, Blair's vision for the public services seemed to confirm the suspicion of some that he was never really part of the party but from the outset was a 'closet' Tory who, along with Thatcher, believed in the classic right-wing syllogism: 'private sector good: public sector bad'. His supporters in the party argue that his huge diversion of spending into public services prove this accusation to be false.

Blair's legacy

Tony Blair became obsessed with his 'legacy' as his period in power approached an end that he himself had ordained in autumn 2004 by announcing he would not contest the next general election. With Gordon Brown constantly snapping at his heels and keen to step into the PM's shoes, Blair manoeuvred for time, saying there was much still he wanted to achieve. It became a commonplace of politics that he wanted to leave something, an array of things maybe to rank with Attlee's welfare state or Thatcher's turning around of the economy. Public service reform was known to be high on his list of priorities – a shiny new modernised health and education service would be a lasting achievement which would go down in history associated with his name. However, public services offered a contradictory set of pressures. They became black holes for investment of taxpayers' money but Blair's Conservative-style market reforms infuriated union leaders and Labour MPs and hampered progress towards genuine reform. Throughout, the public remained massively unconvinced that any substantial improvements in the public services had taken place. However, one legacy which Blair can arguably say he has achieved is the death of Thatcherism. When he came to power, Thatcher had changed the political culture. She had declared war successfully on union power, over-manning, secondary picketing, high tax-and-spend politics and inefficient nationalised industries. Blair came to lead Labour just when it had began to adjust to the new realities of a globalised form of capitalism. He recognised that legalised union restraint had to be retained, that inflation had to be sat on firmly, and that changes needed to improve competitiveness had to be encouraged. He worked hard to edge his party away from its traditionally held positions and succeeded. He did not mind inviting Margaret Thatcher around to her old home in Downing Street in a symbolic sign to his party that there would be continuity.

One result was the absolute clampdown he and Brown declared on expenditure during their first two years in power. In retrospect this time can be seen, perhaps, as the high tide of Thatcherism. Once he won his second term and Brown began to deploy the billions of accumulated treasure his skilful stewardship of the economy had garnered, New Labour slipped back into the social democratic traditions of what has become known as Old Labour. The public were not convinced he was working any magic in schools and the NHS but most could see that, at the very least, the decline had ceased. Meanwhile the Conservatives stewed in their fratricidal juice, mourning their own assassination of their great leader and failing to rise in the polls above their one 30 per cent core vote. Each attempt at a 'compassionate Conservatism' was soon followed by a reversion to the hallowed tenets of Thatcherism, the gaunt, familiar features of Norman Tebbit serving as her mouthpiece. Blair had stolen their clothes but had subtly reattired his party as liberal, tolerant and dedicated to improving the place of the less well-off majority. As leader followed leader the Conservatives finally got the message: they would have to change, just as Labour did from the mid-eighties. David Cameron was the result. Now the litmus test for a new policy is what it can do for the disadvantaged. Homophobia is out; environmentalism is very much in; pro-business yes, but at a distance; tax cuts maybe but not until the economy can sustain them. Already the signs of Blair's greatest legacy perhaps are evident in our present politics: Thatcher finished off left-wing socialism but Blair has put paid to right-wing Conservatism. Now that is a legacy of which any left-leaning politician can be exceedingly proud.

■ The Liberal Democrats

Source: Courtesy of the Liberal Democrats Party
(www.libdems.org.uk)

After the war the Liberal Party continued to decline politically but still offered an alternative to voters

in the centre of political ideas. At heart the party still adhered to the ideas of 'new liberalism' covered in Chapter 4, with emphases on individual liberty, equality, a mixed economy, a developed welfare state and a reformed, democratised system of government. Under the skilful successive leaderships of Jo Grimond, Jeremy Thorpe and David Steel, the party survived the postwar decades but hardly prospered. Then in 1981 it joined forces with the breakaway SDP to form the 'Alliance'. It was not difficult to unite on policies, which were very close; rather it was personalities who caused the foundering of this short-lived collaboration (see Box 6.1). In 1987, the two elements of the Alliance formally merged and fought the 1992 election as the Liberal Democrats. Its manifesto, *Changing Britain for Good*, called for a shift of power to the consumer and ordinary citizen, the development of worker shareholding and a market economy in which the market is the 'servant and not the master'. In addition, the party repeated the traditional call for reform of the voting system and **devolution** of power to the regions. Following the 1992 general election its new leader, Paddy Ashdown (elected in 1988), made steady progress, and the Liberal Democrats' policy of 'equidistance' between the two big parties was replaced by one of open cooperation. Iain McWhirter, writing in *The Observer* (17 April 1995), suggested, interestingly, that if indeed the Lib-Dems come to support a Labour government, they can find a role to the left of Labour, acting as its conscience on constitutional reform and the welfare state. In 1996, a joint Labour/ Lib-Dem committee was set up to liaise on constitutional reform, a notoriously time-consuming set of proposals over which Labour felt it wise to maximise agreement in case votes from the smaller party were needed.

The strong showing by the Liberal Democrats in the 1997 general election buttressed the claim of that party to be the *de facto* left-of-centre conscience of the new Blair order regarding constitutional reform and the nurturing of the welfare state, especially the educational system. The Lib-Dems joined a Cabinet committee tasked with studying the future of constitutional reform – a tempting whiff of power perhaps for a party starved of it since the paltry sniff provided by the Lib–Lab pact of 1977–9. In 1999, Paddy Ashdown stood down after a distinguished period as leader of Britain's third party. His successor was the amiable Charles Kennedy, popular on quiz shows and a witty, clubbable man. He faced a problem, however: how could he put his stamp on the party in a way different from that of his predecessor? In the event he chose not to. He rejected suggestions to take up a left of Labour stance as the kind of *cul de sac* that had ruined Labour in the early 1980s. Instead he chose a 'business as usual' policy of 'constructive opposition' to Tony Blair with a view to replacing the Conservatives as the official opposition to the Labour government. *The Guardian* commented (24 September 1999) that Kennedy's conference speech was a 'thin bowl of porridge' and that he had too little new or exciting to say, especially compared with Ashdown's inspiring valedictory address. Some commentators warned that his party stood on a knife edge; a small swing to the Conservatives at the next election would rob the Lib-Dems of many of their seats in England. Some of the party's middle-class (some three-quarters), middle-aged (average age 58) members still do not trust Labour and fear that a backlash will hurt them at local and national levels if things go wrong for the government party. According to *The Guardian* in September 2001, Kennedy's 'vision remained some form of centre left coalition which was pushed aside by the 1997 victory'. In an interview with the US magazine *Talk*, Blair said that his biggest mistake in May 1997 had been not to ask Ashdown to join his Cabinet, although with such a huge majority it was politically impossible to deny even a single post to his own party. The Lib-Dems found it hard deciding what attitude to take to Blair

as they supported many of his policies such as devolution and his pro-EU stance.

In the 2005 election Kennedy fought his usual relaxed campaign, offering an anti-war stance over Iraq, increased taxation for the very rich, and no tuition fees for university students. This worked well in constituencies where Labour was the Lib-Dem target, and twelve seats were won in this way. However, what attracted former Labour voters did not work the same magic in the close Lib-Dem–Conservative seats: only three were won while five were lost. Peter Riddell in *The Times*, 7 May, felt the third party should have done better, given 'a very unpopular government and prime minister, a bitterly divisive issue in Iraq and a largely unappealing opposition party'. Instead they won only eleven extra seats on the back of a 4 per cent rise in their vote.

This feeling of a missed opportunity, plus a sense that the party was losing what momentum it had gained at the election, contributed towards a whispering campaign against Kennedy. Complicating the situation, by the time of the autumn party conference a new wing was identified in the expanded 62-strong ranks of the Lib-Dems: a group leaning more to the right, epitomised by *The Orange Book* of essays written by MPs and activists favouring a greater acceptance of market forces. Kennedy found his attempts to keep both factions happy were failing and by November senior party colleagues were said to be briefing against him.

After extreme pressure was placed on Kennedy, he admitted the chief accusation against him – that he had a drinking problem – and a few days later, when the pressure did not abate, stood down. In the resultant, chaotic contest Simon Hughes and Chris Huhne waged a lively campaign, but the veteran Sir Menzies (Ming) Campbell won quite easily in the end. He is generally regarded as a reliable performer in debate and on the media but in the early months after his election showed little sign of moving his party in a new direction. However, psephological predictions of a hung parliament in the 2009–10 election raised much talk of which side he would swing in any resultant coalition negotiations. The political positions of the Lib-Dems have never seemed to matter very much as power has always seemed so far away. However, the prospect of a hung parliament, at the time of writing, has made their evolving policy positions for once into matters of intense interest.

BOX 6.4   BRITAIN IN CONTEXT

Mainstream ideas and the political spectrum

As explained in Chapter 4, the political spectrum is usually represented from left to right, with unregulated free enterprise on the right and an anarchic or a communally owned economy on the left. Many of the ideas on the fringes – anarchism on the left or fascism on the right – would be regarded as extreme in the present day and unlikely to hold centre stage. Ideas likely to feature in the 'main-stream' of politics will usually be in the centre ground, that group of ideas which at any one time represents the general consensus of what people believe to be reasonable or legitimate political objectives.

Objectives which fall outside the mainstream are not automatic lost causes: repeated advocacy or changed circumstances can draw them into the centre – like anti-union legislation and privatisation during the early eighties in the UK. During that same period the political spectrum was at its broadest in Britain with a near command economy being urged on Labour's left and a minimalist free enterprise state on the Thatcherite right. Since then ideological differences have narrowed significantly but they are still wider in Britain than in the USA.

Naturally right-wing pro-capitalist ideas are powerful in the USA, often seen as the 'headquarters' of world free enterprise thinking. By the same token 'left-wing' ideas, together with the US mainstream, are further to the right than in the UK. Americans have traditionally regarded any left-wing idea as the thin end of a communist wedge and therefore to be resisted as 'unpatriotic', not sufficiently 'American'. So even state-funded health services, commonplace in Europe, are seen from across the Atlantic as 'socialist' and therefore slightly sinister. Some theorists explain the weakness of US left-wing thinking as the consequence of 'hegemonic' right-wing ideas: ideas so deeply ingrained and powerful they squeeze the life out of any alternatives. It is certainly true that both major parties in the USA stoutly support free enterprise economics: even the Democrats urge economic growth and support business, though not with the passion of the true believing Republicans.

Within Europe political spectrums, as in Britain, have tended to shift rightwards. Capitalism is no longer seen as a system which necessarily disadvantages large groups of people, but rather as the motor of dynamic economic growth from which all can benefit. Consequently communism has faded away in the wake of the Cold War and most brands of left-wing socialism have tended to follow suit. Former communist countries display a fascinating mix of ideas in their spectrums. During communism, as in most authoritarian regimes, the political spectrum was very narrow, containing virtually no options for genuine change.

But once the old pro-Moscow regimes imploded they were replaced by volatile new democracies in which, as in Russia, wild nationalism was present together with some surviving residual old-style communism. Many Russians, relieved at the passing of communism, were alarmed by their new combustible democracy and associated social dislocation. They gratefully accepted the promise of security which the former KGB chief Putin offered as president, even if political choices were once again heavily circumscribed. It would seem to be the case that a wide political spectrum, offering the chance of usually limited change at any particular time, is a characteristic of democracies. Authoritarian regimes do not tend to offer much choice and seek to shrink their spectrums into an unchanging narrowness.

Chapter summary

Conservatism is more than mere pragmatism in the ruling interest but includes a concern for unity, harmony and balance in a society based on property, equal opportunity, élite rule and gradual change. Margaret Thatcher gave major prominence to the neo-liberal strand in Conservatism, which stressed the primacy of markets in economics. Major returned to the rhetoric of 'one nation' Conservatism but contained the practice of Thatcherism. Labour began as a socialist party dedicated to the replacement of capitalism by a collectively owned economy, but in government translated this into nationalisation, a policy of doubtful success. In opposition during the 1980s it gradually shed its socialist clothes and donned those of the free market and restricted public spending: in effect a compromise with Thatcherism. Liberal Democrats inherited the 'new liberal ideas', of the early 20th century to which they added an initial disposition to work with the Labour Party in office, something which faded after the invasion of Iraq in 2003.

Discussion points

■ To what extent was Margaret Thatcher a Conservative?

■ Did John Major contribute anything distinctive to Conservative thinking?

■ Did Labour sell out its principles during the 1980s?

■ Is there room for a distinctive third set of political ideas in Britain, and do the Lib-Dems offer them?

Further reading

Andrew Heywood's *Political Ideologies* (1998) is a valuable source, as is the similar book by Ian Adams (1998). The Giddens book, *The Third Way*, has been criticised as too vague, but it is chock full of interesting ideas and more than repays a careful reading. Michael Foley's *Ideas that Shape Politics* (1994) is a useful collection of essays. I am grateful to Richard Kelly, Andrew Russell and John Callaghan for their talks at a student conference at Salford University, 24 March 2006.

References

Adams, I. (1998) *Ideology and Politics in Britain Today* (Manchester University Press).

Ashbee, E. and Ashford, N. (1999) *US Politics Today* (Manchester University Press).

Beer, S.H. (1982) *Britain Against Itself* (Faber).

Crewe, I. and King, A. (1995) *SDP: The Birth, Life and Death of the Social Democratic Party* (Oxford University Press).

Crosland, C.A.R. (1956) *The Future of Socialism* (Jonathan Cape).

Driver, S. and Mantell, L. (1998) *New Labour: Politics after Thatcherism* (Pluto Press).

Field, F. (1995) *Making Welfare Work* (Institute of Community Studies).

Fielding, S. (2003) *The Labour Party* (Palgrave).

Foley, M. (1994) *Ideas that Shape Politics* (Manchester University Press).

Foote, G. (1997) *The Labour Party's Political Thought* (Manchester University Press).

Giddens, A. (1998) *The Third Way: The Renewal of Social Democracy* (Polity Press).

Gould, B. (1989) *A Future for Socialism* (Jonathan Cape).

Gould, P. (1998) *The Unfinished Revolution* (Little, Brown).

Hailsham, Lord (1959) *The Conservative Case* (Penguin).

Heywood, A. (1998) *Political Ideologies*, 2nd edn (Macmillan).

Howell, D. (1980) *British Social Democracy* (Croom Helm).

Hutton, W. (1998) *The Stakeholding Society* (Polity Press).

Kelly, R. (1999) 'The Third Way', *Politics Review*, September.

Kelly, R. (1999) *British Political Parties Today* (Manchester University Press).

Marshall, P. and Laws, D. (2004) *The Orange Book: Reclaiming Liberalism* (Profile Books).

Norton, P. and Aughey, A. (1981) *Conservatives and Conservatism* (Temple Smith).

Policy Exchange (2005) *The Case for Change* (Policy Exchange).

Russell, A. (2004) *Neither Left nor Right – the Liberal Democrats and the Electorate* (Manchester University Press).

Smith, C. (1998) *Creative Britain* (Faber and Faber).

Tressell, R. (1965) *The Ragged Trousered Philanthropists* (Panther; first published 1914).

Tucker, K. (1998) *Anthony Giddens and Modern Social Theory* (Sage).

Whiteley, P. and Seyd, P. (1992) *Labour's Grass Roots: the Politics of Party Membership* (Clarendon).

Useful websites

Centre for Policy Studies: www.cps.org.uk/
Conservative Party: www.conservatives.com/
Institute of Economic Affairs: www.iea.org.uk/
Institute of Public Policy Research: www.ippr.org.uk
Labour Party: www.labour.org.uk/
Liberal Democrats: www.libdems.org.uk/

CHAPTER 7

Political ideas: themes and fringes

Bill Jones

Learning objectives

- To explain and put into context the themes of:
  - feminism;
  - national identity;
  - environmentalism.
- To identify, analyse and elucidate the political fringe on the far left and far right.
- To explain the intellectual source of ideas characterising the political fringe.

Introduction

The first three chapters in this section looked at ideology, political concepts and party political ideas. This fourth chapter addresses three major themes – **feminism**, **national identity** and **environmentalism** – followed by the rarefied world of the political fringe. There are represented by a colourful assemblage of small parties that are not always easy to identify; they may be seen selling their newspapers on the street or taking part in street demonstrations or even contesting national elections. However, their intellectual roots are often connected to major philosophical themes and are therefore of interest. Besides, the Labour Party was just such a fringe party at the turn of the century before the changing social reality enabled it to become a party of government within half a century.

■ Gender issues

Any woman whose IQ hovers above her body temperature must be a feminist.

Rita Mae Brown, author

In 1980, a United Nations report stated:

While women represent 50 per cent of the world's population, they perform nearly two-thirds of all working hours, receive one-tenth of world income and own less than 1 per cent of world property.

Despite the existence of a worldwide feminist movement, the position of women has improved very slightly, if at all, since the dawn of feminism in the late eighteenth century. The rights of women were implicit in the recognition of the rights of 'men', but thinkers such as Locke did not include women in their scheme of things. Rousseau did, however, and in 1792 Mary Wollstonecraft's *A Vindication of the Rights of Women* (see Wollstonecraft, 1967) articulated their rights explicitly (see biography) just as the French Revolution was asserting the rights of oppressed people everywhere. Whether women were 'oppressed' or not was a moot point. Most men assumed that women existed to perform domestic roles: producing and rearing children and caring for their husbands as well as doing all the household chores. Probably most women would have agreed, had they ever been thought themselves important enough to be consulted. They had no possibility of pursuing careers, voting or participating in public life. Their consolation was the power they exercised through this domestic role, influencing their menfolk, maybe even dominating them, behind the scenes.

But the legal position of women at this time was dire: they had no right to divorce (unlike their husbands); they had no right to marital property; and their husbands could beat them quite legally – even rape them should they wish. Moreover, men regularly used prostitutes while preaching fidelity for their wives and divorcing them when this failed, on their side, to be upheld. In 'exchange' women were praised for their femininity and sensitivity and were idealised by the notion of romantic love. An unequal relationship indeed.

BIOGRAPHY

Mary Wollstonecraft (1757–97)

Mary Wollstonecraft was an Anglo-Irish writer and is often cited as the first modern feminist. At the age of 28 she wrote a semi-autobiographical novel, *Maria*. She moved to London to become the 'first of a new genus' of women, a full-time professional writer and editor specialising in women and children. She was closely associated with the group of radical reforming writers called the English Jacobins, where she met her future husband, the philosopher William Godwin. In her book *A Vindication of the Rights of Women* (1792) she argued for equal rights for women in society, especially regarding educational opportunities. Her daughter with Godwin was Mary Shelley, the author of *Frankenstein*.

Emergent socialist ideas supported the position of women. Friedrich Engels argued in his book *The Origin of the Family, Private Property, and the State* (1884) that the pre-historical position of women had been usurped by men so that property now was passed on through the male line instead of the female because men wished to pass on property to their sons. The exploitative relationship between the propertied class and the proletariat was mirrored within the family by the relationship between men and women. A socialist revolution would sweep away private property and remove the economic basis of the exploitative monogamous marriage.

During the nineteenth century the women's movement, such as it was, concentrated on gaining the vote, the belief being that, once this citadel had fallen, the other injustices regarding the imbalance of political and legal rights compared with men would soon be remedied.

To an extent these early feminists were operating with the grain of history, as the franchise for men was being progressively extended at this time. Nevertheless, it took a bitter and militant struggle for the 'suffragettes', led by Emmeline and Christabel Pankhurst, to win through: in 1918 women received the vote, but only if they fulfilled certain educational and property qualifications and were, bizarrely it now seems, over the age of 30. They finally achieved equal political rights in 1928, but this did not automatically transform their position, or make any difference at all in the short and medium term. The women's movement subsided for a number of decades, but the impact of another world war, where women once again played leading roles on the home front, advanced their claims for better treatment. Their purpose was to put an end to the discrimination in a male-dominated world resulting from the widespread male belief that women should look after the home and leave the important jobs to men. Simone de Beauvoir's *The Second Sex* (1952) attacked the asymmetry whereby men were defined as free independent beings and women merely in terms of their relationships with men.

But the so-called 'second wave' of feminism began with Betty Friedan's *The Feminine Mystique* (1963). This major work rejected the myth that women were different and were happy being the domestic adjuncts of their men. Having nominally equal rights did not deliver real equality in a world controlled by men and discriminating against women. In the late 1960s and 1970s, the work of Germaine Greer (*The Female Eunuch*, 1971) and Kate Millett

BIOGRAPHY

Germaine Greer (1939–)

Australian feminist, author and journalist. Educated at Melbourne and Cambridge Universities. Lectured at Warwick University but best known for her book *The Female Eunuch* (1971), which attacked the institution of marriage as a form of slavery and the way women's sexuality was misrepresented and denied by males. She modified her militant position in later life but is still an active advocate for women's rights.

(*Sexual Politics*, 1969) moved the focus of debate from the wider world of career and public life to the micro-worlds that we all inhabit. Greer developed some of the ideas of Herbert Marcuse (1964, 1969a, 1969b), who argued that Western society was sexually repressed. She suggested that women had absorbed the male idea of their sexuality as soft and yielding – a kind of sex image stereotype – while their true and possibly quite different nature was not allowed to be expressed and fulfilled. Concomitant with this went an assertion of lesbianism as a socially demonised activity. Instead of their living out expected roles, Greer was insisting that people could be true to themselves, being 'male' or 'female' according to their own natures. Millett's emphasis was on how women are brainwashed into accepting a given image of themselves regarding their role and even their appearance. This image, according to her, was a reflection of 'patriarchy': constructed by men with their interests in mind. What was attributed to gender roles was in fact no more than a socially constructed role that women were induced to accept from birth via a battery of socialising agencies, including family, tradition, law, the media and popular culture. Women were forced to accept a narrow, constricting role of being gentle, caring mother figures whose job was to tend their men. Alternatively, they were seen as whores and temptresses, equally subservient but this time more dangerous. Millett also directed attention at the family and home, pointing out that here was the most important arena in which the male controlled the key sexual relationship, dominating the female; it followed from this, in that key feminist phrase, that 'the personal is the political'.

BOX 7.1	IDEAS AND PERSPECTIVES

Sexual inequality at work

According to LSE research reports in February 2000 and January 2001, a woman earns on average £250,000 less than a man during a lifetime. This is partly because women workers tend to be concentrated in low-paid jobs but also because they are paid less than men for doing the same work. Women working full time earn 84 per cent of male earnings for the same work, while part-timers receive only 58 per cent. Moreover, the Equal Opportunities Commission reports that women are routinely denied access to bonus payments and pension schemes.

In the 1970s it was observed that liberal feminists, who believed that reform and a high degree of equality were possible in society as it is, coexisted with socialist feminists, who believed that the main inequality was still between classes and not the sexes. They believed that major changes to the economy and society were necessary before women could be truly free. A third group soon emerged: the radical feminists. For them the problem lies not in society or the economy but in human nature, more precisely, male human nature. The problem with women, in other words, is men. In *The Dialectic of Sex* (1980, originally published 1971), Shulamith Firestone perceived a fundamental oppression of women by men as a result of their biological role. Sexual domination therefore both precedes and exceeds economic exploitation. What she advocates is a 'sexual revolution much larger than – inclusive of – a socialist one' to 'eradicate the tapeworm of exploitation'. She argues for a restructuring of society through science, whereby children would be produced artificially and looked after communally so that women's physical and psychological burdens would be removed and they would be free for the first time in history.

Susan Brownmiller – *Against our Will* (1975) – shifts the focus to the violence that men use to threaten women; the fear of rape is used to maintain male dominance, and rapists act for all men in demonstrating the consequences of non-compliance. Other feminist writers, such as Andrea Dworkin and Dale Spender – often called 'supremacists' – assert female moral superiority and argue that the world would be better if women were in control. Often this type of feminist will be separatist in relation to men; their lesbianism consequently has a political quality to it. For them men are not necessary for women, and women who live with men are 'man identified' instead of being 'woman identified'.

It is often said that since the 1970s the women's movement has lost momentum. Certainly the tone has become milder; Greer (1985) and Friedan (1982) have both disappointed radicals by writing approvingly of domesticity and childrearing. The New Right in the USA and UK, moreover, have reinforced 'traditional values' of women's roles and the desirability of marriage (and by implication the subversive effects of one-parent families) to hold society together. In their book *Contemporary Feminist Politics* (1993), Lovenduski and Randall applaud the progress made by the women's movement in permeating institutions and professions and in disseminating feminist values so effectively that they have become widely accepted as orthodoxies. However, they lament the failure to replace activists when they bow out of activity, and the internecine squabbling and fragmentation that have weakened the movement. A report covered by *The Observer* (7 November 1999) questioned whether women have made much progress at all. The American Psychological Association's study concluded that 'even though the fight for equal rights widened opportunities for many, it failed to give women control over their lives'. Experts cited in the article suggested the same could be said of the UK too; two-thirds of the 1300 receiving electroconvulsive therapy each week for depressive illnesses are women. The strong showing of women candidates in the 1997 general election – women MPs virtually doubled from sixty-two to 120, most of them Labour – cheered campaigners for more female representation and those who defended the special Labour measures to favour women candidates in winnable seats. However, some feminists have criticised 'Blair's babes', as they have been dubbed, as performing a decorative but non-feminist role in the governing party. Comparisons are made on the Labour side with the fiercely effective Barbara Castle and on the Conservative side with the legendary Thatcher. Boxes 7.2–7.4 provide chapter and verse on employment and political life in the UK showing that, whilst much has been achieved in the

BOX 7.2   FACT

Women in public and political life

Although women make up 46 per cent of the labour market, they are under-represented in many jobs and positions with power or influence:

- Only 18 per cent of MPs are women.
- 24 per cent of UK MEPs are women.

Members of Parliament 2004 (UK)

Political party	Women		Men	
	Number of MPs	% of party	Number of MPs	% of party
Conservative	14	9	149	91
Labour	94	23	313	77
Liberal Democrat	6	11	49	89
Other parties[a]	5	15	29	85
All parties	119	18	540	82

[a] Includes Speaker and deputies.
Source: House of Commons (2004)

Members of the European Parliament 2004 (UK)

Political party	Women		Men	
	Number of MEPs	% of party	Number of MEPs	% of party
Conservative	2	7	26	93
Labour	7	37	12	63
Liberal Democrat	6	50	6	50
Other parties and independents	4	21	15	79
All parties	19	24	59	76

Source: European Parliament website.

BOX 7.3   FACT

Women and men in Great Britain

Employment
- 46 per cent of people in the labour market are women.
- In the 16–64 age group, two-thirds of women and over three-quarters of men are in employment.
- Nearly half of women (44 per cent) and about one in ten men who work are part-time.

Parents and carers
- Of mothers of under-fives, 52 per cent were in employment, and two-thirds of those working as employees were part-time.
- Since there are almost 4.7 million under-eights in England and just over a million places with child-minders in full day care or in out-of-school clubs, there are four children for each place in these types of provision.

Pay and income
- Average hourly earnings for women working full-time are 18 per cent lower than for men working full-time, and for women working part-time hourly earnings are 40 per cent lower.

BOX 7.4　FACT

Women's representation in the public and voluntary sectors

Women make up:

- 35% of public appointments
- 17.5% of local authority chief executives
- 0.8% of senior ranks in the armed forces
- 10.2% of senior police officers
- 25.5% of Civil Service top management
- 45.2% of chief executives of voluntary organisations
- 8.8% of top judges (high court judge and above)

- 31.8% of secondary school head teachers
- 28.6% of FE college principals
- 11.1% of university vice chancellors
- 28.1% of health service chief executives
- 22.4% of trade union general secretaries or equivalent
- 33.3% of heads of selected professional bodies

Source: Equal Opportunities Commission (2006), p. 9

---

recent past, women are still at a definite disadvantage compared to men.

As if this was not enough to worry about, an article (criticised by several feminist writers) by Professor Alison Wolf, of Kings College London, in a March 2006 edition of *Prospect* magazine, maintained that new attitudes in the workplace are in effect 'killing feminism': 'In the past, women of all classes shared lives centred on explicitly female concerns. Now it makes little sense to discuss women in general. The statistics are clear: among young, educated, full-time professionals, being female is no longer a drag on earnings or progress.' Wolf goes on to argue that total commitment to career diverts the crucial resource of female talent away from the caring professions like teaching, prevents them from volunteering and thus minimises 'female altruism', and dissuades many women from having children.

Box 7.5 provides a useful summary guide of feminist ideas together with their authors.

■ National identity: the English/ British sense of who they are

All countries have some sense of identity – where they have come from, who they are, what they stand for – and, just like individuals, most have some problems in finding satisfactory answers. The USA, for example, comprising a multitude of different elements, experiences a fragile sense of unity and coherence which constantly has to be reinforced by overt – and what to Europeans may seem like manic – statements of patriotism. It also has problems with its attitude to the rest of the world: is it concerned to help alleviate suffering and keep order? Or is it merely concerned to enjoy its comfortable materialism and ignore those parts of the world – like those who diagnose global warming – that interfere with such enjoyment? France too has been undergoing an identity crisis recently, with its famed sense of equality, dating back to the 1789 revolution, being questioned especially by Muslim immigrant groups which declare they are not in any real sense equal when they suffer from racism and widespread unemployment. The British also are undergoing problems in deciding who they are, what they are for and to whom they belong.

Andrew Gamble, in his *Between Europe and America* (2003), addresses this topic and analyses the way in which this sense of identity has changed over the years. First there was the growth of empire (see also *Empire*, by Niall Ferguson, 2003) moving on from the establishment of the United Kingdom by the 1800 Act of Union with Ireland. Then, through the expansion of trade and the Royal Navy, a huge empire was established comprising a quarter of the world's population, living on a quarter of its land mass. For a while, the country dominated the oceans and occupied a position which has been called 'hegemonic'. 'Britain' or 'Great Britain' ('Greater England' would have been more accurate, since 'Britain' and 'England' were often used interchangeably) became

BOX 7.5   IDEAS AND PERSPECTIVES

Feminist debates

This is a schematic summary of the main strands of feminist thought. It is important to understand that these strands are not rigidly separate, that some writers could be entered in more than one category, and that in recent years there has been a significant convergence of apparently competing approaches.

Type of feminism	Key concepts	Goals	Key writers
Liberal	Rights, equality	The same rights and opportunities as for men, with a focus on the public sphere	*Classic:* Mary Wollstonecraft John Stuart Mill *Recent:* Betty Friedan Naomi Wolf Natasha Walter
Radical	Patriarchy, 'the personal is political', sisterhood	Radical transformation of all spheres of life to liberate women from male power. Replace or displace men as the measure of human worth	Kate Millett Andrea Dworkin Catherine MacKinnon Germaine Greer
Socialist and Marxist	Class, capitalism, exploitation	An economically just society in which all women and men can fulfil their potential	*Classic:* William Thompson Friedrich Engels Alexandra Kollontai Sylvia Pankhurst *Recent:* Michelle Barrett Juliet Mitchell Sheila Rowbotham Lynne Segal Anne Phillips
Black	Interactive and multiple oppressions, solidarity, black	An end to the interconnecting oppressions of gender, 'race' and class	*Classic:* Maria Stewart Julia Cooper *Recent:* Patricia Hill Collins bell hooks Angela Davis Heidi Mirza
Postmodern	Fragmentation, discourse, deconstruction, differences	Overcoming binary oppositions. Free-floating, fluid gender identities. However, the idea of a final goal is rejected in principle	Judith Butler Julia Kristeva Joan Scott Denise Riley Michelle Barrett

Source: Valerie Bryson (2003) 'Feminist debates, ideology: feminism', *Politics Review*, Vol. 12, No. 4, April 2003. Reproduced with permission from Philip Allan Updates

the world's policeman, exporting ideas of free trade and, later on, liberal democracy with sovereign parliaments.

The empire created an extensive ruling élite and a world-view which also embodied a degree of smug superiority that often irritated the rest of the world.

But the massive losses of the First World War sapped the nation's power and, even though the postwar settlement expanded the empire, it had lost its stability. The Second World War involved the sacrifice of much of the wealth which the empire represented and by 1945 it was living on borrowed

English football fans display their support for the national team
Source: Neil Tingle / Action Plus

time. The refusal of the US to support Britain's involvement in the attempt to regain the Suez Canal in 1956 was the signal for the further winding up of the imperial dream which independence to India in 1947 had initiated. Those schoolchildren who had felt a thrill of pride in seeing the 1950s map of the world coloured with so much red had soon to adjust to a much more humble role.

Along with imperial decline came its economic concomitant: a slow sinking of Britain from 'workshop of the world' to 'sick man of Europe'. During the seventies the sour mood of the times infected a workforce which became increasingly uncooperative and demanding of higher wages just when the country could no longer afford them. The result was a major upsetting of the postwar settlement whereby agreed increased taxes funded a welfare state and included trade unions as a valued partner of government. Margaret Thatcher set about enthroning the role of markets, removing the inefficient nationalised industries, curbing the over-powerful unions and rolling back the role of the state. But the effects of this harsh medicine on Scotland and Wales gave

added power to the arguments for independence in these countries. When Tony Blair was elected in 1997 the stage was set for the partial dismantling of the constitution, posing a number of questions about the concept of Britain. 'England' is no longer synonymous with 'Britain' once new identities were assumed by the nations of the Celtic fringe, each with their separate assemblies. Irate right-wing commentators like Peter Hitchens, Simon Heffer and Roger Scruton poured their angry scorn on this apparent dismantling of the United Kingdom.

At the same time there is an internal questioning of identity caused by the inflow of immigrants, initially from the empire and Commonwealth after the war, and latterly by economic and political refugees from poorer and strife-torn countries during the latter part of the century. This growing band of ethnic minorities has changed the nature of British cities and arguably made the country a 'multicultural' society. But there are evident strains, sometimes violent, between immigrants and their British neighbours; many resist this loss of their old identity and argue that such people are at heart 'foreigners'. Lord

Norman Tebbit attracted some obloquy and some support for, in effect, demanding that, when cricket teams arrived from their home countries, Commonwealth immigrants should support the English side. Immigrants and their descendants now tend to assume a dual identity of 'black British' or 'British Asian'.

Yet another thread in this complex reworking of identities is the European Union. At the 'Congress of Europe' in May 1948 Winston Churchill made the chairman's address, including the words: 'I hope to see a Europe where men and women of every country will think of being European and wherever they go in this wide domain will truly feel, "I am at home".' The truth is that neither he nor Ernest Bevin, Labour Foreign Secretary from 1945 to 1951, actually believed all the warm words they said about a united Europe. Like US diplomats, they recognised a degree of unity as necessary to resist the Soviet threat and were not opposed to a closer coming together should the nations concerned wish it; the problem was that Britain, when it came down to it, did not.

Bevin had explained in 1946 that Britain saw herself as a 'great power', adding that 'the very fact we have fought so hard for liberty, and paid such a high price, warrants our retaining that position' (Gamble, 2003, p. 189). So Europe was seen as something separate from Britain, which still sat at the 'big boys' table. When the European Iron and Steel Community was established in 1950 – the organisational template, as it turned out, for the later European Community – Britain loftily stood aside, refusing to allow any mere Europeans to decide how these nationalised concerns should be run. The same thing happened with the developments up to 1957 when the Treaty of Rome established the new experiment in supra-nationalism.

Britain initially was not interested but then the devastating American rebuff of Suez, plus the signs that British capitalism was unable to keep pace with the new dynamic customs union based in Brussels, brought about a dramatic change of emphasis and potential allegiance. We applied in 1959 and received another rebuff, this time courtesy of General De Gaulle who repeated the trick in 1967. Running behind the bus trying to catch it and then being thrown off when we did was not the best early experience to have of this economically integrated Europe. We finally made it in 1972 when the General had left the stage and a staunchly Europhile Ted Heath was able to manufacture a majority Commons vote for entry.

But dissent was by no means stilled. At first it was the Labour left which cavilled at this 'capitalist club' but under Thatcher it was the right-wing Conservatives who gave full expression to an anti-European position. They could not begin to accept that the British identity, forged by a thousand years of history, a worldwide empire and heroic struggles against tyranny, could be meekly subsumed into what Margaret Thatcher liked to call 'The Belgian Empire'. Against what proved to be her better judgement she acceded to measures of greater integration but then, after leaving office, became an avid and bitter cheerleader for the Eurosceptic cause.

The dilemma for Britain's changing sense of identity now emerged starkly during the eighties and nineties. The Tory right preferred America to Europe: the American attitude to economics, welfare and, indeed, the management of world order. When Labour entered government many felt this identification would swing back towards our partners in Europe. Certainly Blair subscribed to the Social Chapter upon which Conservative sceptics had poured so much vitriol and joined in the EU (as it was called after Maastricht in 1992) summits, but his desire for Britain to join the common currency, the euro, was prevented by his Chancellor Gordon Brown to whom Blair had conceded virtual control of the economy. So entry into the EU's inner counsels was prevented; EU opponents were pleased and hoped Labour would maintain the pro-American bias favoured by many Conservatives. Brown, in any case, is a warm admirer of the American economic model and has tried hard to keep employment 'flexible', unlike many EU countries where pro-worker employment laws hold down productivity. But the biggest shifting of Gamble's 'four spheres' occurred after the 9/11 attack on the World Trade Center in New York (see Figure 7.1).

At this point, when the world stood back in horror, Blair was quick to offer his 'shoulder to shoulder' support for the USA. Other EU partners expressed outrage but none could match the fervour of Blair's support. Later Blair sent in troops to Afghanistan and then, much more controversially, to Iraq. British public opinion was similar to that of most EU countries, even those who supported George W. Bush – very sympathetic to the USA in the wake of the 9/11 attack but two-thirds of voters were not prepared to envisage an invasion against Iraq, however dreadful its ruler might be. Bush's apparent disregard for multilateral solutions and the gung-ho remarks of his Defence Secretary Donald Rumsfeld alienated much of European and British opinion. Blair refused to be drawn towards the EU consensus and remained

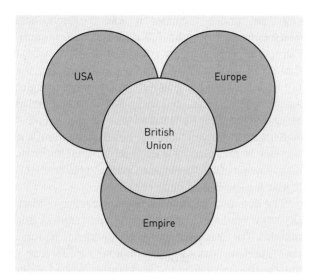

Figure 7.1 The Four Circles of England: in his *Between Europe and America* (2003), Andrew Gamble (pp. 30–4) quotes Churchill's view that Britain lay at the touching point of three circles – Empire, Europe and America. Gamble argues that since devolution, a fourth, that of the 'British Union', should be added

true to his earlier position, matching Bush's rhetoric with his own. But Blair did have an idea of the role his country should perform; as he said in January 2003: 'We can help to be a bridge between the US and Europe.' The problems associated with such a route to a new identity are threefold. Firstly, Blair has shown he is biased quite heavily towards the US, philosophically in terms of economic systems and politically in terms of its world role as a hyper-power. Secondly, Europe's two biggest and leading countries, France and Germany, both leaders and voters, are not at all as enamoured of the US as Tony Blair. Thirdly, on the major issues like Iraq, British public opinion is closer to America's European critics than to Blair's enthusiastic and uncritical support.

■ Green thinking

The ecological perspective rejects philosophies of the right, left and centre as more similar than dissimilar. Sir Jonathon Porritt (now a senior environment adviser to the Blair government) characterises them collectively as '**industrialism**': this 'super-ideology . . . conditioned to thrive on the ruthless exploitation of both people and planet, is itself the greatest threat we face' (Porritt, 1984). Conservat-

ives, socialists and centre politicians argue about rival economic approaches – individualism versus collectivism and how the cake of national income should be sliced up and distributed – but they all agree that the size of the cake should be increased through vigorous economic growth. This is the central proposition that the Greens most emphatically reject. 'Industrialism', they say, is predicated on the continuous expansion of the goods and services and on the promotion of even more consumption through advertising and the discovery of an increasing range of 'needs'. It creates great inequalities whereby a rich and envied minority set the pace in lavish and unnecessary consumption while a substantial number – in many countries a majority – are either unemployed or live in relative, perhaps dire poverty. The Conservatives have presided over an increase in income differentials but have offered economic growth as a panacea: more for the rich and more for the poor. Porritt observes:

If the system works, i.e. we achieve full employment, we basically destroy the planet; if it doesn't, i.e. we end up with mass unemployment, we destroy the lives of millions of people . . . From an industrial point of view it is rational to . . . promote wasteful consumption, to discount social costs, to destroy the environment. From the Green point of view it is totally irrational, simply because we hold true to the most important political reality of all: that all wealth ultimately derives from the finite resources of our planet.

Porritt (1984), pp. 46–7

The Green view goes on to adduce a number of basic principles:

1. *A world approach*: All human activity should reflect appreciation of the world's finite resources and easily damaged ecology.

2. *Respect the rights of our descendants*: Our children have the right to inherit a beautiful and bountiful planet rather than an exhausted and polluted one.

3. *Sufficiency*: We should be satisfied with 'enough' rather than constantly seeking 'more'.

4. *A conserver economy*: We must conserve what we have rather than squander it through pursuit of high-growth strategies.

5. *Care and share*: Given that resources are limited, we must shift our energies to sharing what

we have and looking after all sections of society properly.

6. *Self-reliance*: We should learn to provide for ourselves rather than surrendering responsibility to specialised agencies.

7. *Decentralise and democratise*: We must form smaller units of production, encourage cooperative enterprises and give people local power over their own affairs. At the same time, international integration must move forward rapidly.

Porritt maintains that this amounts to a wholly alternative view of rationality and mankind's existence. He contrasts the two world-views of industrialism and ecology in Table 7.1.

Inevitably, the other major parties have done all they can to climb aboard the Green bandwagon, cloaking their policies in light green clothes and shamelessly stealing the rhetoric of the environmentalists.

As it currently stands, the Greens' political programme is unlikely to fall within the 'art of the possible' (see below). It has established some support in Stroud and among students, and in 1994 it gained four council seats, but its best parliamentary performance was in 1989, when it won 6.1 per cent of the vote in Lambeth, Vauxhall. In May 2003 Greens won seven seats in the Scottish Parliament. In 2005 the Greens fielded 202 candidates but not one got elected. Hardly a launching pad for power, but as Malcolm Muggeridge once pointed out, 'utopias flourish in chaos', and if global warming continues unchecked accompanied by more environmental chaos, it may well be the Greens who inherit politically what is left of the Earth, if it is not already too late by then.

Table 7.1 Two worlds: industrialism versus ecology

Industrialism	Ecology
The environment	
Domination over nature	Harmony with nature
Environment managed as a resource	Resources regarded as strictly finite
High energy, high consumption	Low energy, low consumption
Nuclear power	Renewable sources of energy
Values	
An ethos of aggressive individualism	Cooperatively based communitarian society with emphasis on personal autonomy
Pursuit of material goods	Move towards spiritual, non-material values
Rationality and packaged knowledge	Intuition and understanding
Patriarchal values, hierarchical structure	Post-patriarchal feminist values, non-hierarchical structure
Unquestioning acceptance of technology	Discriminating use and development of science and technology
The economy	
Economic growth and demand stimulation	Sustainability, quality of life and simplicity
Production for exchange and profit	Production for use
High income differentials	Low income differentials
A free-market economy	Local production for local need
Ever-expanding world trade	Self-reliance
Employment as a means to an end	Work as an end in itself
Capital-intensive production	Labour-intensive production
Political organisation	
Centralisation, economies of scale	Decentralisation, human scale
Representative democracy	Direct democracy, participative involvement
Sovereignty of nation-state	Internationalism and global solidarity
Institutionalised violence	Non-violence

Source: Adapted from Porritt (1984) *Seeing Green*, pp. 216–17.

Giddens on the German Greens

The importance of ecological politics goes far beyond whatever influence green social movements might muster, or the proportion of the vote green parties might achieve. In concrete politics the influence of ecological groups has already been considerable, especially in Germany – it isn't surprising that the notion of 'subpolitics' originated there. In their work *The German Left*, Andrei Markowitz and Philip Gorski observe 'throughout the 1980s the greens developed into the German left's socializing agent in the sense that all its new ideas, political innovations, strategic formulations, lifestyle, originated from the greens and their milieu. Chancellor Willy Brandt was fond of saying the greens were the "lost children of the SPD".'

Giddens (1998), p. 54

BOX 7.6   IDEAS AND PERSPECTIVES

Global warming

Of all the many dangers facing the world's environment, it has been the problem of global warming that has most exercised environmentalists and governments in recent years.

The scientific argument on 'greenhouse' gases

It is an obvious fact that the earth receives its warmth from the sun. However, certain gases within the earth's atmosphere have been crucial in helping retain the sun's heat over the billions of years life has been evolving. Some of the sun's heat is reflected back into space but the retention of a portion of this heat, absorbed by the gases, has enabled the earth to achieve a temperature ideal for supporting life. Indeed, without such gases the average temperature of the world would have been −15°C instead of +18°C.

The first person to make the link between climate and greenhouse gases was the Swedish scientist Svante Arrhenius in 1898. He calculated that a doubling of CO_2 would increase world temperatures by 5–6°C. Other scientists observed that volcanic eruptions of sulphur dioxide into the atmosphere, which reflects sunlight, causes a degree of cooling. Some have attributed global warming to the lack of volcanic activity in the twentieth century. In 1988 the UN established the Intergovernmental Panel on Climate Change. The IPCC's latest estimate is of a warming of between 1.4 and 5.8°C by 2100 depending on what is done to curb gas emissions (IPCC, 2001). Other studies suggest even higher rates of warming.

Consequences of global warming

The earth's temperature has provided the conditions in which humans have evolved and flourished, but rapidly rising temperatures would cause deforestation, the loss of fishing stocks, the collapse of many crops, outbreaks of many more destructive tropical storms, the melting of vast permafrosted areas (which would also release massive new stored reserves of CO_2) and the gradual melting of the ice-caps, causing catastrophic rises in sea level amounting to over 200 feet.

The developing world

The surging economies of China and India – often using CO_2-rich emitting energy production methods – hugely increase the threats, but it is hard for the developed world to insist that poorer countries forego the benefits and comforts which the West has enjoyed for many years. Awareness of the dangers grew throughout the latter half of the twentieth century, and in 1997 an agreement was reached at Kyoto whereby signatories agreed to reduce emissions to 5 per cent below the 1990 levels by 2010; in practice this means a reduction of 29 per cent in all greenhouse gases. Developing countries were excluded from this requirement, but the biggest problem lay with the reluctance of the USA to ratify the agreement.

With only 5 per cent of the world's population, the world's biggest economy emits a quarter of the world's CO_2. Energy lobbies in the USA vigorously disputed the thesis that the planet's climate is heating up.

George W. Bush, originally an oil man and advised by many more, refused to accept the Kyoto Protocol. One of his advisers, Myron Ebell, attacked the statement of David King, Britain's Chief Scientific Officer, that global warming was more of a threat to the future of the world than terrorism, on the grounds that King did not have the scientific expertise. He also claimed the whole global warming story was a scare tactic created by Europe to enable their ailing economies to compete more effectively against the USA. Scepticism about global warming remains despite the fact that 99 per cent of scientists in this area of study insist it is a fact. Some people argue that climate has always varied, with the Thames regularly freezing over in the Middle Ages, and Ice Ages occurring not infrequently. Scientists riposte that of the warmest 20 years ever experienced, 16 have happened during the last quarter-century. Temperature increases of that kind are unprecedented and are conclusive evidence that we do have an acute problem which could conceivably lead to the ending of all human life.

The United Kingdom

The UK was an enthusiastic signatory of Kyoto and at first made good progress towards the agreed goal, assisted by a switch of power stations from coal to gas. The 2005 Labour manifesto set a target of 20 per cent, well above the required Kyoto level, but as the deadline has approached performance has declined. On 28 March 2006, Margaret Beckett, the then environment secretary, announced that reductions were likely to be in the range 15–18 per cent instead, blaming increased economic growth and the rise in oil prices which had caused many power stations to return to coal use.

■ The political fringe

The political fringe is the name given to those small factions and groups that often do their political work outside the conference halls of the main parties rather than within them. Those who belong are often determined ideologues, given to regular argument in groups prone to splits and factions. They do have some intrinsic interest, however, as microcosms of political ideas and conflicts. It must also be remembered that in the early part of this century the Labour Party was just such a small faction, snapping around the heels of the Liberal Party. Yet within a couple of decades it was actually in power and destined to be there – with a huge majority – as the new millennium started.

Left and right extremes

We recognise only two classes in society . . . Our problems are the result of a rotten capitalist system.

Arthur Scargill, Socialist Labour Party

But what I am saying is that the prospect of the collapse of everything that is opposed to us is greater than at any time in 20th century Britain.

John Tyndall, British National Party

Far left

Marx, Lenin and Stalin

Most far left groups owe their intellectual debts to Karl Marx. He argued that under a capitalist economy rich property owners would so drive down wages in pursuit of profits and a competitive edge that a vast army of impoverished workers would eventually rise up and sweep away the whole corrupt system. Once private property had been abolished, working people would begin to live new and better lives in an economy in which people would work willingly for each other and not reluctantly for an employer. It did not quite work out that way.

After the Marxist takeover of power in Russia in 1917, a period of great hardship and economic instability followed. Lenin established a political system based on centralised control supported by a network of secret police. He believed in the need for a 'vanguard party' of professional revolutionaries to lead the masses – who were deluded by agencies of capitalism into a 'false consciousness' – when the time came. There had to be rigid discipline and acceptance of the vanguard party's 'dictatorship of the proletariat' while it implemented socialism. Communists claimed that this was the transitional stage the USSR had achieved by the early 1920s, when Lenin died.

BIOGRAPHY

Joseph Stalin (1879–1953)

Soviet dictator. Trained as a priest before becoming a revolutionary in Georgia, Russia. Was secretary to Lenin's Communist Party and after his death deviously manipulated his enemies out of power while placing his own supporters in key positions. Became unchallenged dictator in 1930s and tried to neutralise Hitler by doing a deal with him. Hitler broke the agreement and attacked the USSR in 1941. After initial reverses the Soviets fought back under Stalin's leadership and defeated Hitler. Despite his brutal behaviour Stalin won friends on the left in Western countries, who persisted in believing his propaganda and seeing him as a force for progress.

BIOGRAPHY

Leon Trotsky (1879–1940)

Leon Trotsky was a Russian Jewish revolutionary politician born in the Ukraine. He was arrested for being a Marxist at the age of 19 but escaped from Siberia in 1902. After teaming up with Lenin, he became president of the first soviet in St Petersburg after the abortive 1905 revolution. He escaped to the West but returned to Russia in March 1917 to assist Lenin in organising the Bolshevik Revolution in November of the same year. He conducted peace negotiations with the Germans and led the Red Army of five million men in the ensuing civil war. An inspiring and charismatic leader as well as brilliant intellectually, Trotsky should have succeeded Lenin in 1924, but his theories of permanent world revolution were less well suited to the times than Stalin's pragmatic 'socialism in one country'. Moreover, Stalin was too devious and ruthless for him and he was eventually exiled in 1929, being assassinated in Mexico with an ice pick in 1940 by Ramon del Rio, an agent of Moscow. His ideas live on, but mostly on the radical intellectual fringe in developed countries.

Trotsky – advocate of 'worldwide revolution' – was Lenin's heir apparent, but the dogged, apparently un-intellectual Joseph Stalin, Secretary of the Party, was cleverer than his brilliant colleague. He urged 'socialism in one country' rather than working for an unlikely international conflagration; he out-manoeuvred his rivals and plotted ruthlessly, succeeding in presenting Trotsky as a traitor to the revolution. Stalin eventually drove Trotsky into exile in Mexico, where his agents succeeded in assassinating him in 1940 (see biography).

Stalin, by then, had become a brutal dictator, both paranoid and obsessed with power, claiming to be implementing **communism** but in reality imposing industrialisation, collective farming and his own tyrannical rule on a reluctant and starving peasantry. Anyone less than obsequiously worshipful of their leader was imprisoned, exiled or shot. Overseas communist parties were employed essentially to assist the development of the 'home of socialism', and any deviation from the party line was punished by expulsion or worse.

This is the legacy inherited by extreme left-wing parties in Britain. The Communist Party of Great Britain (CPGB) was founded in 1920 and became the willing tool of Moscow's message in this country, interpreting all the shifts in the official line and condemning anyone perceived as an enemy of the USSR. Members managed to survive the astonishing *volte-face* when Stalin ceased to oppose Hitler as first priority and signed a deal with him in 1939 to partition Poland. Once Hitler had invaded Soviet Russia in 1941, British communists breathed a sigh of relief; they were at last able to luxuriate in a vast amphitheatre of approving views as the whole country applauded the heroic Soviet effort. After the war, the party won two seats – Mile End and West Fife – but Stalin's expansion into Eastern Europe, his blockade of Berlin in 1948 and the crushing (after his death) of the Hungarian rising in 1956 by the Soviet military machine, not to mention Khrushchev's denunciation of Stalin in his secret speech to the 20th Party Congress, substantially disillusioned communists and Moscow 'fellow travellers' alike. The Cold War effectively ruined the chances of communist parties achieving power anywhere in Europe, and they began to wither and atrophy.

In the 1970s and 1980s opposition to communism in Eastern Europe intensified, and the accession of the liberal Mikhail Gorbachev to power in Moscow was the signal for bloodless revolutions throughout the former communist bloc, with only China, Cuba, Vietnam and Laos being spared. The CPGB split into a hard-line pro-Moscow rump and a liberal 'Euro-communist' wing, with the latter seizing control. It tried to transform itself into 'an open, democratic party of the new pluralistic and radical left'. In 1991 it ceased to be the CPGB and renamed itself the Democratic Left, though with little public support. Some of its former supporters, however, stuck with the party paper, *The Morning Star*, and founded the Communist Party of Britain – to little political effect: it has never fought a parliamentary election.

Trotskyism

A number of Trotskyite bodies sprang up during and after Trotsky's lifetime, calling for worldwide revolution. Ted Grant, a South African, was involved with some of them, such as the Militant Labour League, in the 1930s. With Peter Taafe, Grant set up the *Militant* newspaper and adopted the tactic of 'entryism', the idea being to infiltrate members of a 'Militant Tendency' (notice only a 'tendency' and not a separate party, which would have breached Labour rules) into the decaying structure of the 1960s Labour Party. The idea then was to seize leadership at the grass-roots level and, in theory, the country once the time for revolution arrived. The Tendency virtually controlled Liverpool City Council in the 1980s, and two members, Dave Nellist and Terry Fields, were elected MPs, plus Pat Wall for Bradford in 1987 (died 1990). They advocated a number of radical measures, including nationalisation of the top 200 companies, extension of state control over the whole economy, workers' control in state-owned industries, nationalisation of the media, a slashing of defence spending, withdrawal from the EC and abolition of the House of Lords. In 1992, the Tendency expelled its guru Ted Grant, ending its policy of entryism; the movement gave way to Militant Labour, still attempting to influence the Labour Party, but most of the prominent members had faded away and the MPs not only lost their seats but were first expelled from the party. However, Militant MPs, while exercising little influence during their time in the Commons, did impress with their dedication, hard work and refusal to accept more salary for themselves than a skilled worker.

The Workers' Revolutionary Party

Another Trotskyist thread into the colourful tapestry of the far left was provided by 'The Club', a grouping, led by Gerry Healy, which left the Revolutionary Socialist Party in 1947 to infiltrate the Labour Party. Healy was soon expelled from Labour for his Trotskyite views and put his energies into a new party to express and promote the views of his hero. The idea, as with all such parties, is to build up battle-hardened cadres to seize power when capitalism collapses, as it must, in its view. Its newspaper, *Newsline*, was rumoured in the seventies to be funded by Libya's Colonel Qadhafi. Membership was never high and suffered from Healy's imperious and eccentric leadership style, which led to the WRP actually splitting into two versions in the eighties and to his finally being deposed shortly afterwards. Celebrity members such as Vanessa Redgrave and her brother Corin, who stood as candidates in 1974 and 1979, gave the party a high media profile. The WRP still exists, led by Sheila Torrence, and still publishes *Newsline*.

The Socialist Workers' Party

Tony Cliff, who founded the Socialist Workers' Party, was also expelled from Labour for being a Trotskyite. His party has concentrated on international revolution, and international links are stressed. Paul Foot (1938–2004), nephew of Michael and a national columnist, was a high-profile and persuasive member. The SWP printed a newspaper, *The Socialist Worker*, touted by young converts in many university cities. It was also behind the Anti-Nazi League, set up to fight the growth of European Nazism in the seventies and then relaunched in 1992 when Nazism revived in a number of countries, including Austria. These initiatives won an influx of new members; since that heyday it has shrunk substantially though it has been active in fighting its causes and supporting Respect (see below) in local elections.

The Socialist Labour Party

This was formed in 1996 by miners' leader Arthur Scargill following his failure to prevent the rewriting of Clause Four at Labour's conference in 1995. 'We recognise only two classes in society, both of which are recognised by their relationship to the means of production', he explained; 'Our problems are the result of a rotten capitalist system.' Accordingly, his

Socialist Worker

www.socialistworker.co.uk

80p | No 1995 | 8 April 2006

THE DAY TO BURY BLAIR

MAY 4

SR

THE SOCIALIST REVIEW

MAGAZINE WITH SOCIALIST WORKER THIS WEEK

● **Strike to save our pensions**
● **Vote Respect in the local elections**

TONY BLAIR hopes he can ride out the storms of protest over the murderous war in Iraq. He hopes he can brush aside the resistance to the government's plunder of workers' pensions and the plans to make us all work longer.

He hopes he can insert private companies at the very centre of the NHS and schools before he leaves 10 Downing Street.

But on Thursday 4 May we can all do something to bring Blair down sooner rather than later. In the local elections we can campaign and vote for Respect.

If Respect councillors sweep into town halls it will be one of the most powerful weapons to pitch Blair out of office.

And trade union activists are pushing for 4 May to be part of a two-day strike that would

repeat and extend the electrifying success of the 28 March strike over pensions.

We cannot afford to let Blair survive a day longer. Victories for Respect and massive strikes over pensions can make 4 May a day from which he never recovers.

Pensions action >>page 2
Respect election campaign >>page 5

US lied to cover-up massacres in Iraq

THE US has been caught trying to lay the blame for a massacre of Iraqi civilians on the resistance. The revelations come as reports of two new atrocities have surfaced.

The US claimed that one soldier and 15 Iraqi civilians—including seven women and three children—were killed by an insurgent attack on the town of Haditha in November.

But an investigation by Time magazine exposed the story as a lie. Time discovered that US troops went on the rampage through the town in revenge for the death of a Marine earlier that day.

Soldiers then tried to cover up the murders by claiming the civilians were killed by an insurgent bomb.

The revelation comes after the killing of 37 worshipers on

26 March during a US raid on a Shia Muslim mosque in eastern Baghdad.

The US claimed the men were killed after they fired on troops. But locals say that the men were executed by an Iraqi death squad under the control of a US officer.

The attack on the mosque came the day after Iraqi police published an official report on a massacre in the village of Abu Sifa, 37 miles north of Baghdad.

In that attack, which took place on 15 March, 11 civilians were killed, including four children and a six month old baby.

The report states, "US forces gathered the family in one room and executed 11 people, including five children, four women and two men, then they bombed the house, burned three vehicles and killed their animals."

A bad day out for Condi and Jack >>page 6

Egypt's year of resistance
Pages 8&9
Anne Alexander speaks to three women who took up arms against imperialism in 1956

A dirty little secret exposed
Page 3
Simon Basketter reveals the blacklists of union militants held by construction bosses

France at the crossroads
Pages 4&16
François Chesnais, Jim Wolfreys, Danièle Obono, Pierre Khalfa and Basile Pot report on days of hope in France

Beckett: a lust for despair?
Page 13
Sinead Kennedy looks at the life and work of the radical Irish playwright

9 771475 970006 14>

Trotskyist left urges voters to dump Blair
Source: Courtesy of *The Socialist Worker*

party favours common ownership of the economy, full employment, a four-day week, a ban on non-essential overtime, retirement at 56, restoration of union rights, abolition of the monarchy, House of Lords and public schools, and withdrawal from the EU. Only 500 attended the launch in May 1996. Scargill fought Hartlepool against Peter Mandelson in 1997 and 2001 but polled negligibly.

The Socialist Alliance

This was a novel 'umbrella' organisation of left-wing parties that fought the 2001 general election. It was chaired by Dave Nellist, the former Militant MP, and its manifesto was both a scathing critique of New Labour as no better than Thatcherism and a hard-won (far left groups find it hard to agree) common agenda for an 'alternative to the global, unregulated free market'. However, the results did not augur too well for future growth and success. Of the six candidates who stood, four garnered less than 1 per cent,

one received 1.3 per cent and the final one 2.4 per cent.

Respect: The Unity Coalition

This body was set up in 2004 as a result of collaboration between George Galloway, the SWP and members of the Muslim Association of Britain to campaign principally against the ongoing war in Iraq. Galloway was formerly the talented but maverick MP for a Glasgow constituency, expelled from Labour in 2004 for calling on British troops to disobey orders. He fought a clever, though much criticised, campaign in Hackney and Bethnal Green against the sitting MP, Oona King, and won a sensational victory. Apart from its anti-war stance, Respect offers a left-wing socialist prospectus including the end of privatisation and 'the bringing back into democratic public ownership of the other public services'.

John Callaghan, the authority on the far left, judges that 'far left politics is dying in its Leninist form and

---

BOX 7.7 IDEAS AND PERSPECTIVES

The strange case of *Living Marxism*

This magazine, a descendant of the CPGB's *Marxism Today*, morphed into the more modern-sounding *LM* in the late 1990s when it published an article accusing ITN of fabricating the discovery of an apparently emaciated Muslim in a detention camp which in reality was a haven for such refugees. The magazine was sued, lost the action and was forced to close. But it is the provenance of the magazine and the movement it subsequently set in train which are so interesting for students of the far left. The story is traced to 1974 when a Trotskyist faction split from the International Socialists (now the Socialist Workers' Party) – which, in the words of David Pallister and colleages (*The Guardian*, 8 July 2000), 'used to spend most of its time in textual agonizing over the third volume of *Das Kapital*' – to form the Revolutionary Communist Group.

The RCG saw its role as training a 'vanguard elite to storm the citadels of capitalism'. However, Trotskyist groupings are notoriously both fickle and factional, and in 1976 one of the group's thinkers, David Yaffe, led out a like-minded section (broadly in favour of collaborating with certain other far left groups) called the Revolutionary Communist Tendency, later Party, or RCP. *Living Marxism* was its mouthpiece and, as such, it attracted notice for its intellectual energy and creativity. New RCP members were often recruited in 'up-market' places like Oxbridge and Covent Garden and after a period of 'political education' were encouraged to enter the professions, often those associated with the media or academe, and then donate a proportion of their salaries to the party.

In the wake of the Cold War's demise came a change of direction: the RCP was disbanded and *Living Marxism* became *LM*, the *raison d'être* for which was held to be 'freedom' – freedom to challenge, to offend, to say what one wanted. Under the influence of two thinkers, Frank Furedi (Professor of Sociology at the University of Kent) and former social worker Claire Fox, *LM* waged war on what was held to be government-manufactured panics over issues like GM foods, child rearing, AIDS as a heterosexual disease and much else besides.

'The spirit of LM', in Furedi's words, 'is to go against the grain: to oppose all censorship, bans and regulations and codes of conduct; to stand up for social and scientific experimentation; to insist that we have the right to live as autonomous adults who take responsibility for our own affairs.'

The mission of the 'LM Group' was alleged by some to be a permeation of the opinion-forming professions; Fox's Institute of Ideas and LM magazine were two facilitating agencies to these ends, organising seminars and conferences, involving 'Establishment' bodies like the Institute for Contemporary Arts and intellectuals like Blake Morrison, Lisa Jardine and Linda Grant.

This philosophy of 'ban nothing, question everything', unsurprisingly, found supporters on the libertarian right. Pallister *et al.* suggest that the grouping of right-wing **think tanks** and research institutes in the US known as the 'Freedom Network' offered a source of like-minded ideas, support and, indeed, quite possibly finance. So, we see a slightly weird evolution here of an extreme left faction morphing into new forms, imploding and then becoming a broader cultural movement which joined hands with groups that are sufficiently far to the right to make poor old Leon Trotsky revolve in his grave (see also Box 4.3 on Libertarianism for links with the far right, in Chapter 4).

has moved into Green and anti-globalisation movements and has involved former militants from Muslim communities' (e-mail to author, 8 April 2006). But he makes a shrewd point when he points out that far left politics often act as an apprenticeship for future mainstream politicians, citing Alan Milburn and Stephen Byers (former Trotskyists) and John Reid (former member of the CPGB).

Far right

Fascism

This set of ideas, developed by Benito Mussolini in the 1920s and supplemented by Adolf Hitler in the 1930s, was founded on xenophobic nationalism and total submission to the state. Democracy was scorned as the language of weakness and mediocrity; a one-party totalitarian state led by a charismatic leader was the preferred alternative. The leader and his team were seen as the result of an evolving process whereby the best people and ideas won through. It followed that the same thing happened when nations fought; war was the means whereby nations grew and developed. Hitler added a racial twist: the Aryans were the founding race of Europe, a race of conquerors, and the Germans their finest exemplars; all other races were inferior; the Jews in particular were lower than vermin and should therefore be destroyed. In the stressful inter-war years, racked by economic depression and unemployment, these unwholesome ideas seemed attractive and full of hope to many who faced despair as their only alter-

BIOGRAPHY

Adolf Hitler (1889–1945)

German dictator. Was originally an Austrian who tried to make a living as an artist. Fought in the First World War and set up the racist, expansionist Nazi movement in the 1920s. Came to power in the early 1930s and set about dominating Europe via threats, invasions and finally all-out war. In 1942 he dominated the continent but his decision to invade Russia and to declare war on the USA eventually proved his downfall. Still retains his admirers on the political fringe.

native. It is emotionally satisfying perhaps to blame one's troubles on a single group in society, especially one that is quite easily recognisable physically and very successful economically and culturally. It has also to be said that such ideas flourished in the fertile soil of a German culture sympathetic to antisemitism.

In Britain, Sir Oswald Mosley founded a party that evolved into the British Union of Fascists, offering himself as the strong charismatic national leader who would end the party bickering and lead the country into new successes. Mosley proposed that employers and workers should combine in the national interest and work in harmony; strikes and lock-outs should be banned; all major elements in the productive process should work together to plan the economy (corporatism). Moreover, he argued that the British Empire would provide all the things the country needed, and imports that could be made in Britain would be banned. Parliament and the old parties would be reformed and MPs would be elected according to occupational groups. Once elected, Parliament would pass on power to the leader to introduce the 'corporate state'. Parties and Parliament would be ended; everyone and everything would be 'subordinated to the national purpose'. Mosley's antisemitism was disguised in Britain, but his coded references to 'alien influences' were clear enough to most Britons; he favoured sending all the Jews in the world to a barren reservation. When it was revealed that Hitler's remedy to his self-invented 'Jewish problem' had been genocide of the most horrifying kind, a revulsion set in against fascist ideas. But they have proved unnervingly resilient and still appear in the present time in a different form.

The National Front and the BNP

In 1967 the National Front (NF) was formed. Its central message was a racist one, warning against dilution of the British race via intermarriage with other races of different colour which it believed would produce an inferior breed of Briton. Repatriation of black Britons was the answer offered. At the level of theory, however, the Jews were offered as the main threats, being characterised as an international conspiracy to subvert Western economies and introduce communism before setting up a world government based in Israel. This side of the NF and its utter contempt for democracy was disguised in public expressions, but it exercised considerable appeal to young men with a taste for violence and racial hatred. It later changed its name to the National Democrats. In 1983 the 'New' NF – later the British National Party – was born; this is dedicated to infiltration and is more secretive, having many contacts with neo-Nazi groups abroad and many terrorist groups too. Football supporters are often infiltrated by NF members, and in 1994 a friendly football match between Ireland and England was abandoned following thuggish violence instigated by the NF. A related body called Combat 18 (the number in the name relates to the order in the alphabet of Hitler's initials: AH) openly supports Nazi ideas and embraces violence as a political method.

The BNP at the 1997 general election

As previously, the general election of May 1997 saw the usual multicoloured rainbow of fringe joke candidates. But for the far left and far right as well as the pranksters the result was widespread loss of deposits; voters may flirt with the fringe from time to time, but when the election arrives they revert, perhaps fortunately, to 'sensible' voting. In May 2002, the BNP won three council seats in Burnley – the biggest electoral victory for the far right in two decades. The party's new leader, Nick Griffin, with his articulate style and Cambridge education (see quotation from *The Observer* below), gave the party a credibility with arguments that exploited the feelings of poor indigenous voters that somehow immigrants were not only changing the nature of their localities but also receiving favoured treatment. This was argued with particular success in respect of asylum seekers, an issue much loved by the tabloids. These developments worried the mainstream parties, which were keen to nip this electoral upturn in the bud.

The BNP has deliberately become increasingly sophisticated in the last few years to ensure ballot box success. . . . The irony is that it's New Labour who have shown us how to do it; we learnt from them that a party could change without losing its support base. New Labour dropped Old Labour in much the same way as we've moved on from the so-called 'skin head' era. We realized that the type of recruit we needed in the modern world was completely different to the sort we needed when we were engaging in street level activities.

Kevin Scott, North-East Director BNP, quoted in
The Observer, 20 April 2003

The same issue of *The Observer* also published the facts that:

■ Thirteen of the BNP's twenty-eight regional directors or branch organisers in 2002 had criminal records for offences that included assault, theft, fraud, racist abuse and possession of drugs and weapons.

■ Two thousand racial attacks were recorded by the Home Office up to 2003 after the dispersal programme for asylum seekers began in 2001.

■ In 2003, 221 seats were targeted by the BNP, including councils in Lincolnshire, Cumbria,

Surrey, Hampshire, Somerset, Wiltshire, Devon and Cornwall. In the event, on 1 May 2003 the party won thirteen seats nationwide, including eight in Burnley; however, Nick Griffin lost his fight for a seat, and his party won no seats in Sunderland despite fielding twenty-five candidates.

■ In 2004 a BBC undercover reporter recorded a speech in Keighley by Nick Griffin in which he said: 'These 18, 19 and 25 year old Asian Muslims are seducing and raping white girls in this town right now.' He continued: 'It's part of their plan for conquering countries. They will expand into the rest of the UK as the last whites try and find their way to the sea. Vote BNP so the British people really realize the evil of what these people have done to our country.' This speech, and a similar one by a former Leeds City Council candidate, both faced charges of behaviour likely to incite racial hatred in January 2006, but both defendants were sensationally acquitted when the cases came to court in 2005.

BNP leader Nick Griffin celebrates his court acquittal
Source: Gareth Copley / PA / Empics

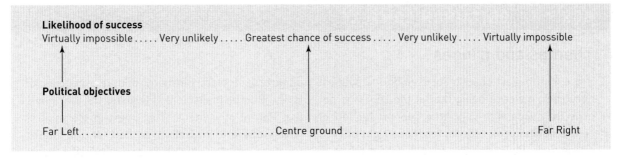

Figure 7.2 The art of the possible

The art of the possible

Politicians on the fringe have made a conscious or unconscious decision regarding the 'art of the possible', Bismarck's acute definition of politics. As Figure 7.2 illustrates, political objectives on the extremes have little chance of success; the best chances exist in the political centre. It is the big mainstream parties that tend to set the agenda and to go on to achieve items upon it. Changing Labour's Clause Four on common ownership was held to be beyond the art of the possible for a long time after Gaitskell's attempt failed in the late 1950s. Later, Callaghan referred to the issue as 'theological', but Blair decided that such a change was necessary to convince the public that Labour was no longer dangerously radical. His brilliant campaign in 1994 to change the clause to some extent redefined the art of the possible (Figure 7.2) in the Labour Party. Items on the far left or right are either unattainable or achievable only if circumstances change radically and, usually, rapidly.

Parties on the fringe have two possible strategies to pursue. First, they can eschew any real chance of winning power and seek merely to change the hearts and minds of citizens to provide the context in which radical change can occur. Early socialists effectively performed this role until the creed became a credible alternative in the mid-twentieth century. Even so, it took over 100 years for socialism to win an electoral victory in Britain, so activists of this type have to be genuinely dedicated to change in the future; few are so patient. Alternatively, the less patient can seek to short-circuit the normal process of propagandising and winning over opinions by manipulating the democratic process. The really extreme activists on the right and left seek to set a revolutionary set of events in train and to seize power rather as the Bolsheviks did in Russia in 1917. As people usually need a substantial period to change their minds completely, this strategy usually requires the use of force, with all its attendant unpredictability and dangers. The early British communists and the Militants sought to reach the same objective through 'entryism': to drive their Trojan horse into a big party, Labour, and to win power through subterfuge. Seemingly underhand, this is not too disreputable a strategy given that the right-wing Conservatives led by Thatcher in the 1970s managed to achieve something similar by using the democratic machinery and then steering the party in a radical direction. Left-wing Labour tried a similar exercise in the early 1980s but was rebuffed so sharply by the electorate in 1983 that it left the way open for the maestros of the centre ground: New Labour. So the radical socialist journalist Paul Foot sought to pursue the 'long haul' route of gradually changing social attitudes through education and exhortation. His uncle, Michael, also a fiery left-winger in his youth, decided to compromise a little and became a mainstream politician in the 1970s with a seat in the Cabinet and later a period as party leader. Time alone will tell how successful the agitators of the present will prove in the future, though those who articulate a 'green' perspective have seen their ideas move rapidly from the extreme left to somewhere much closer to the centre ground in a matter of only two to three decades. Moreover, the local and devolved assembly elections on 1 May 2003 saw one in eight voters casting their vote for parties on the political fringe, provoking the thought that maybe some of those groups on the fringe are destined in the near future to join the mainstream.

BOX 7.8	BRITAIN IN CONTEXT

Themes and fringes

Box 6.4 in the last chapter focused on the political spectrum, my case being that in the USA it is not especially wide with very little support for left of centre positions or, indeed, for those right of centre as well. However, this should not be taken to imply that there are no groups occupying positions substantially to the left and right. Far from it.

The Socialist Party of America was born at the turn of the nineteenth century. Its leader, Eugene Debs, not only went to jail for his beliefs but stood for President on more than one occasion, yet never quite managed to poll a million votes. He was succeeded by Norman Thomas, a graduate of Princeton and a lay minister who also stood for the highest office but did no better than Debs in the end.

During the thirties Roosevelt's New Deal, with its extensive government intervention in the economy, was implicitly socialist, but after the Second World War the backlash began with any left-wing idea being associated with communism and 'un-American' activities. The resultant McCarthyite witch-hunts of the fifties further weakened the left, but the socialist tradition survives in the form of The Socialist Party of the USA – not a major force, with affiliates in only eighteen states. The Communist Party of the USA is even smaller and more ineffective. But there is, at the present time, the Progressive Coalition of House of Representatives members, numbering about sixty, who subscribe to a socialistic set of ideas. However, the only real force on the left is the Democratic Party, and this tends to deter those tending to the left from switching support to a small party with no chance of achieving power. Almost certainly, however, the groups on the far right are more powerful than those on the left.

One variety of socialism, the National Socialist Movement (NSM), is in fact on the far right, being admirers of Nazi Germany and the policies of Hitler. But the main blanket term for the far right is the 'Patriot Movement'. This takes in the militias which operate in well over half of the states together with the rifle clubs and survivalist clubs. These groups, many of them steeped in ultra-nationalism and anti-semitism, were influential in motivating John McVeigh, the Oklahoma Bomber. The worrying aspect of such right-wing groupings is that they reject the *legitimacy* of government, its right to issue laws and levy taxes. Similarly, groups representing the Afro-American minority in the 1960s and 1970s, like the Black Panthers and the Weathermen, refused to accept government authority and were prepared to use violence as a method.

Another characteristic of US society not reflected to the same degree in the UK is the 'culture wars' within it. Here we see groups who believe that a changing society which includes a large number of single-parent families, a variety of races and people of contrasting sexual preferences requires a more liberal and flexible set of values, especially towards sexuality and abortion. Other groups, however, often motivated by religious convictions, hotly resist such a move and are determined, for example, to reverse the Supreme Court ruling which makes abortion legal.

Often supported by their churches, a large section of American society feel that family values are under severe attack and need to be defended against the compromised attitudes of current urban life, reinforced by the media and popular music. Almost 40 per cent of Americans regularly attend church and, under George W. Bush, such leanings have acquired political significance. In Britain only about 5 per cent of people attend church and religion generally has scant influence.

Chapter summary

Feminism is concerned with the unequal position of women in society and falls into liberal, socialist and radical categories. Nationalism emerged in the nineteenth century and, while it is now contested by internationalism, still retains much of its destructive force. Green thinking applies environmentalism to politics, calling for a revolutionary change in the way developed societies live. Far left fringe groups tend to draw on the ideas of Marx and Trotsky; their relevance has declined since the anti-communist revolutions, but many followers still keep up the struggle. Far right groups tend to be neo-fascist and racialist; their support is small but their influence subversive.

Discussion points

■ Has feminism achieved any major victories, and if so what are they?

■ What problems are there in defining the British identity?

■ Is nationalism more dangerous than terrorism?

■ What chance is there of the Greens ever winning power in the UK?

■ Why do you think people join fringe political groups?

Further reading

Lovenduski and Randall (1993) is a thorough review of feminism in Britain; the political ideas books by Adams (1993) and Heywood (1992) have good sections on nationalism; and Dobson (1990) and Porritt (1984) are good on ecology. An excellent study of totalitarianism is Arendt (1951). On fascism, also recommended is Cheles *et al.* (1991); Thurlow (1986) is a history of British fascism to the present day.

References

Adams, I. (1993) *Political Ideology Today* (Manchester University Press).

Adams, I. (1998) *Ideology and Politics in Britain Today* (Manchester University Press).

Arendt, H. (1951) *The Origins of Totalitarianism* (Allen and Unwin).

Bentley, R., Dorey, P. and Roberts, D. (2003) *British Politics Update 1999–2002* (Causeway Press).

Brownmiller, S. (1975) *Against our Will: Men, Women and Rape* (Simon and Schuster).

Bryson, V. (2003) 'Feminist debates, ideology: feminism', *Politics Review*, Vol. 12, No. 4, April 2003.

Callaghan, J. (1987) *The Far Left in British Politics* (Blackwell).

Cheles, L., Ferguson, M. and Wright, P. (1991) *Neo-Fascism in Europe* (Longman).

de Beauvoir, S. (1968) *The Second Sex* (Bantam; first published 1952).

Dobson, A. (1990) *Green Political Thought* (Unwin Hyman).

Dowds, M. and Young, J. (1996) *13th British Social Attitudes Survey* (SPCR).

Equal Opportunities Commission (2006) *Sex and Power: Who Runs Britain? 2006* (Equal Opportunities Commission).

Ferguson, N. (2003) *Empire* (BBC).

Firestone, S. (1980) *The Dialectic of Sex* (Women's Press).

Friedan, B. (1963) *The Feminine Mystique* (Norton).

Friedan, B. (1982) *The Second Stage* (Norton).

Gamble, A. (2003) *Between Europe and America* (Palgrave).

Giddens, A. (1998) *The Third Way* (Polity Press).

Greer, G. (1971) *The Female Eunuch* (Granada).

Greer, G. (1985) *Sex and Destiny* (Harper and Row).

Heywood, A. (1992) *Political Ideologies* (Macmillan).

House of Commons (200) *Weekly Information Bulletin*, 18 December 2004 (HMSO).

Lovenduski, J. and Norris, P. (2003) 'Westminster women: the politics of presence', *Political Studies*, Vol. 51, No. 1, March.

Lovenduski, J. and Randall, V. (1993) *Contemporary Feminist Politics* (Oxford University Press).

Marcuse, H. (1964) *One Dimensional Man* (Beacon).

Marcuse, H. (1969a) *An Essay on Liberation* (Penguin).

Marcuse, H. (1969b) *Eros and Civilisation* (Sphere).

Millett, K. (1969) *Sexual Politics* (Granada).

Nozick, R. (1974) *Anarchy, State and Utopia* (Blackwell).

Paglia, C. (2006) *Break, Blow, Burn* (Vintage).

Porritt, J. (1984) *Seeing Green* (Blackwell).

Reid, J.R. (2004) *The United States of Europe* (Penguin).

Thurlow, R. (1986) *Fascism in Britain* (Blackwell).

Wolf, A. (2006) 'Working girls', *Prospect*, April.

Wollstonecraft, M.A. (1967) *A Vindication of the Rights of Women* (Norton; originally published 1792).

Useful websites

Anti-Nazi League: www.anl.org.uk/campaigns.html

Green Party: www.greenparty.org.uk

National Democrats:
www.netlink.co.uk/users/natdems/

Searchlight Magazine:
www.searchlightmagazine.com/default.asp

Socialist Alliance: www.socialistalliance.net

Socialist Workers' Party: www.swp.org.uk

Workers' Revolutionary Party: www.wrp.org.uk

Who's steering this ship? Power in British politics

Michael Moran

Who has power in British politics? The question is quite simply the most important we can ask about our system of government, because all our important judgements about governing the UK turn on how it is answered. To take only the most obvious: to claim that Britain is a functioning democracy is to make an assertion about the location of power, and about how that power is used: it is to say that in the last analysis power lies with the people at large, and that government is conducted in the interests of the people at large.

Not everyone agrees with that judgement, of course. In very broad terms, there are three competing accounts of where power lies in British politics.

The democratic politics account

This might be dubbed the 'official' version. It is the face British government presents to the world, and it is the version most leading politicians offer. This asserts that, while there are often blemishes in British democracy, in the end power does lie with the people. That power is exercised most clearly, according to this account, through the ballot box, especially in the UK-wide general elections which every four or five years decide who is to control the Westminster-based government. Nor is democracy just a matter of periodic elections. These elections take place in a wider political system where freedom of expression and of political organisation are part of the normal order of things. Once elected, governments are subject to constant criticism and scrutiny: from party opponents; from a free and inquiring mass media; and from a huge range of organised groups in the wider society. Not every decision made is shaped by democracy, but such is the power of the institutions and culture of democratic politics that most decisions in government are shaped by democratic forces, and serve democratic interests. The great intellectual inspiration for modern theories of democratic government is, paradoxically, a study by a Frenchman of the United States. The great French journalist and sociologist Alexis de Tocqueville (1805–59) published his study of *Democracy in America* in two parts in 1835 and 1840, and his account anticipates much of the modern culture and social structure of democratic politics generally.

The élitist account

When democratic political forces first began to demand reform of traditionally hierarchical systems of government in the late nineteenth and early twentieth centuries, a highly influential response came from two of the founders of modern social science, Vilfredo Pareto (1848–1923) and Gaetano Mosca (1858–1941). They founded modern *élitism*. It asserts that democratic rule is impossible, that the practices of democracy are just rituals designed to manipulate the masses, and that rule by some tiny minority – an *élite* – is always inevitable. Those who argue that some élite runs Britain are therefore part of a long tradition of social analysis. But the identified élite often differs greatly according to the observer. A very common argument, heard increasingly as the central 'core executive' in Britain has become more organised, is that the ruling élite controls Britain from a base in Whitehall. Some identify the Prime Minister, with the enormous amount of patronage attached to office, as the key figure in this élite. Some identify the élite with the very top of the Civil Service, who are often credited with obstructing and undermining the efforts of democratically elected governments. A generation ago it was common to identify the ruling élite with an 'establishment' – a unified small group, located in London, joined by common social and institutional links, often sharing a common education in a few exclusive public schools and leading universities.

The ruling class account

The ruling class account is a form of élitism, but it identifies a very particular kind of ruling élite. Its intellectual inspiration comes from the great German sociologist and political activist, Karl Marx (1818–83). Marx argued that political power was shaped by economic power; that any economic system was controlled by those who owned the means of production; and that in a capitalist society this meant those who controlled economic and financial resources. Nobody contests that Britain is a capitalist economy. It follows that Britain cannot be a democracy – government must be controlled by the ruling class of capitalists that owns the means of production. Since the British economy is dominated by a fairly small number of giant corporations, many of them foreign owned and controlled, it follows that real power in

Britain lies in corporate boardrooms – often foreign corporate boardrooms. Democratic political struggles either are irrelevant, or are at best the means by which competing factions within the ruling class struggle for control over government.

Assessing the competing versions

It might be thought fairly straightforward to settle the competing claims of these accounts by systematic inquiry. But the arguments have a perennial flavour, in part because the contending parties cannot agree how to settle the issues. They cannot agree because they usually have different views of what 'power' means. (The most famous exposition of these different meanings is in Steven Lukes, *Power: a Radical View*, 2nd edn, Basingstoke: Palgrave Macmillan, 2004.) Those who hold to the 'democratic' account tend to see power as reflected in the range of decisions taken by government, and track power by studying individual decisions; élitists tend to see power as inherently involving covert manipulation and are unimpressed by evidence from everyday decisions of government; and those who defend the ruling class account see power as something inseparable from structures, notably economic structures, and ground their account in the structures of economic life, and of economic inequality.

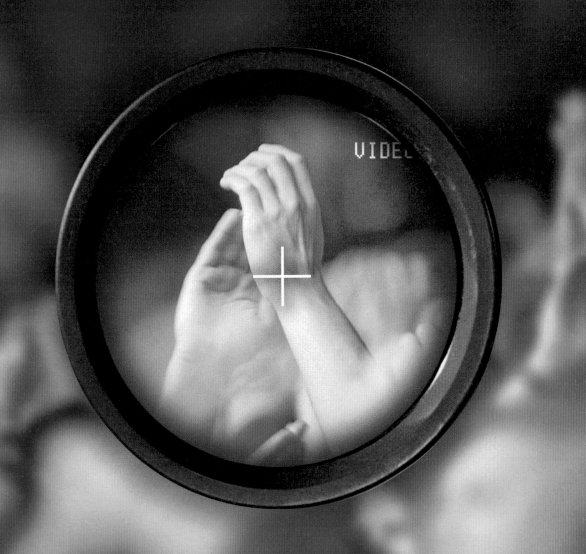

POLITICS UK

PART 3
THE REPRESENTATIVE PROCESS

VIDEO

POLITICS UK

CHAPTER 8

Elections

Dennis Kavanagh

Learning objectives

- To understand the purpose of elections.
- To evaluate the electoral system and its strengths and shortcomings.
- To study changes in campaigns.

Introduction

This chapter begins by discussing the framework in which elections are held. It then considers who is entitled to vote, the rules of the electoral system, the nomination of candidates, expenditure and the role of election campaigns.

Tony Blair tries to bridge the 'trust gap' in the run-up to the 2005 general election
Source: Copyright © Chris Riddell. From *The Observer*, 20 February 2005. Reproduced with permission from Guardian Newspapers Limited

■ Why elections?

Competitive elections to choose governments lie at the heart of the democratic process; a crucial difference between democratic and non-democratic states is to be found in whether or not they hold competitive elections. The best indicator of competition is the existence of a number of political parties at elections. In addition to choice there must also be widespread electoral participation. In Britain, the entire adult population has the right to vote at least once every five years for candidates of different parties in the House of Commons.

Elections in Britain matter for other reasons. They are the most widespread form of political participation; at general elections since 1945, an average of nearly 75 per cent of adults on the **electoral register** turn out to vote, although in recent elections there has been a sharp fall in turnout (Table 8.1). Second, these votes determine

Table 8.1 General election turnouts, 1945–2005

Date	%	Date	%
1945	73.3	October 1974	72.8
1950	84.0	1979	76.0
1951	82.5	1983	72.7
1955	76.8	1987	75.4
1959	78.7	1992	77.8
1964	77.1	1997	71.3
1966	75.8	2001	59.4
1970	72.0	2005	61.2
February 1974	78.1		

Table 8.2 Extension of the suffrage

Date	Adult population with the vote (%)
1832	5
1867	13
1884	25
1919	75
1928	99
1969	99

the composition of the House of Commons and therefore which party forms the government. Third, elections are a peaceful way of resolving questions that in some other countries are settled by force, above all the question 'who is to rule?' They are also important in giving legitimacy to government and therefore oblige the public to obey the laws passed by Parliament. Voting in general elections is how we decide who is to govern us.

■ What are elections?

Elections are a mechanism of social choice, a device by which people choose representatives to hold office and carry out particular functions. In a direct democracy, usually in small societies, people may do the tasks themselves or take turns (rotation) to carry them out. In large-scale societies, however, the election of representatives is necessary.

Election is not the only method by which rulers are chosen. Leaders may emerge, for example, through heredity (e.g. monarchy) or force (e.g. the military), or fraud. Indeed, appointments in many walks of life are made without elections: in the Civil Service and in many professions appointment is on merit (demonstrated, for example, by passing competitive examinations, serving an apprenticeship or gaining a degree, diploma or other mark of competence). But today competitive elections are widely regarded as the symbol of legitimate and representative democracy.

In Britain, competitive elections were well established in the eighteenth and nineteenth centuries, even though the vote was confined to a small number

of males. The **suffrage**, or right to vote, was steadily broadened during the nineteenth century. Britain effectively had mass suffrage by 1928, when the vote was extended to virtually all men and women over the age of 21 (see Table 8.2).

General elections for the House of Commons are called under either of two circumstances: when the parliament has run its full five years (until 1911 the permissible life span of a parliament was seven years) or when it is dissolved by the monarch on the advice of the Prime Minister of the day. In the exceptional conditions of war, the elections due to be held by 1916 and by 1940 were delayed until the cessation of hostilities in 1918 and 1945, respectively. The USA has calendar elections prescribed by the constitution; even in wartime elections for the Congress and presidency went ahead.

Purpose of elections

What are elections for? As a first answer, most people would probably reply along the lines of: 'To express the democratic will of the electorate.' That answer, however, simply raises more questions. Are national elections about choosing effective executives or selecting competent legislatures? Should they provide each voter with a local MP, or each party with its fair share of MPs? In an ideal society one might like an election system which achieved both objectives. However, except in very rare circumstances, that is impossible. We have to decide priorities and strike compromises.

Peter Kellner, 'Never mind the ballots', *The Observer*, 24 March 1996. © Guardian Newspapers Limited, reprinted with permission

Some commentators have argued that the advent of opinion polls and the power to time economic booms for the run-up to an election give the

BOX 8.1	IDEAS AND PERSPECTIVES

Opinion polls

Opinion polls are increasingly used to report on the state of public opinion. These are surveys of the views of a sample of between 1000 and 2000 voters drawn randomly from the electorate. Sampling is done by either quota or probability methods. A quota sample is obtained by allowing the interviewer to find respondents who together match the known age, sex, class and other characteristics of the population. A probability sample is drawn by choosing every nth name on the electoral register. Today most polls rely on quotas. At elections the polls attract an enormous amount of attention for their prediction of which party will win. They claim to be able to predict parties' share of the votes to within 3 per cent in 95 per cent of cases.

The 1992 general election was the most exhaustively polled ever, and the newspapers and television broadcasts often led with the latest results of the opinion poll. The polls do have a good record of predicting winners, although they came unstuck in the 'upset' elections of 1970, February 1974 and 1992. In the 1992 election the eve-of-poll predictions by the main polling organisations overestimated Labour's final share of the vote by 4 per cent, underestimated the Conservatives' by 4 per cent, and overestimated that of the Alliance by 1 per cent. The average forecast of the four major polls published on polling day was for a Labour lead of 0.9 per cent. In the event the Conservatives won by 7.6 per cent – an 8.5 per cent error, the largest ever. After 1992, the idea took hold that a number of Conservatives were more reluctant than supporters of other parties to admit their allegiance. Some pollsters therefore 'adjusted' their figures for voting intentions to allow for a so-called 'spiral of silence'.

In recent years the pollsters have made changes to their methods. Only MORI continues with face-to-face interviews, although it does some telephone polling. Apart from YouGov, which makes use of an Internet panel, all others rely on the telephone. They also weigh their results for the likelihood of voting and the panel's representativeness for age, gender, class, car ownership, newspaper reading and other variables.

Pollsters were quick to claim that the 1997 and 2001 elections were a vindication of their craft. All the polls correctly predicted a Labour victory, and a big one at that, and most came within a 3 per cent margin of error in their forecasts for each party's share of the vote. Yet self-congratulations were overdone. In 1997, there was a 12 per cent range in the polling organisations' final figures for Labour's lead, and four out of five overstated Labour's share of the vote and its lead. Ivor Crewe (1997) points out that the mean error of 2.0 per cent in the final polls was the third largest since 1945. Had the election been close, the polls could have just as easily got it wrong again. In 2001, most again made a substantial overstatement of Labour's actual lead. In 2005 all put Labour ahead by between 3 and 6 per cent, well within the margin of error:

Final opinion polls, 2005

	Labour (%)	Conservative (%)	Lib Dem (%)
NOP	36	33	23
MORI	38	33	23
YouGov	37	32	24
ICM	38	32	22
Populus	38	32	21
Actual result	36	33	23

It is unfortunate that so much concentration is devoted to polls for election forecasting. However, they still remain the best guide to the state of public opinion and are quite superior to hunch, canvass returns, activists' perceptions of mood at public meetings, and the views of the media. Polls also contain much useful information about voters' perceptions of leaders, party images and policy preferences and, over time, they can register shifts in public opinion.

Michael Howard tries to woo voters of middle England in the 2005 election campaign
Source: Copyright © Chris Riddell. From *The Observer*, 6 March 2005. Reproduced with permission from Guardian Newpapers Limited

incumbent too great an advantage (Hailsham, 1979). But John Major's victory in the 1992 general election turned some of the conventional wisdom on its head. John Major had delayed calling an election until late in the parliament – hoping that signs of economic recovery would be more visible and that the opinion polls would move decisively in his favour. Neither had occurred when he had to call the election for April 1992. It is likely that the polls underestimated the Conservative share of the vote – and that the party was leading before and during the campaign – but Major was not to know that. The poor performance in the opinion polls increased the politicians' scepticism about their forecasting ability (see Box 8.1).

If it is defeated on a major issue or loses a vote of censure in the Commons, the government is expected to resign and recommend a dissolution. To date, the only postwar case of a forced dissolution was in 1979, when the Labour government lost a vote of confidence following the failure of its Scottish and Welsh devolution plans to be carried by the necessary majorities in **referendums** in those two nations. This was unusual and arose because the government was in a minority in the Commons.

The other opportunity that British voters have for a nationwide election of representatives is for members of the European Parliament every five years. A significant feature is that the **turnout**, usually around a third of the electorate (less than a quarter in 1999), has until 2004 regularly been the lowest or second lowest in any EU member state (see Table 8.3).

One might also note the introduction of referendums on constitutional issues – over British membership of the European Community in 1975, in Scotland and Wales over devolution in 1979 and again in 1997 over new devolution proposals. Supporters of a referendum claim that when there

Tony Blair and Gordon Brown present a united front on the campaign trail, despite their well documented difficulties
Source: Copyright © Peter Nicholls / Pool / Reuters / Corbis

is a single issue, particularly one that raises constitutional questions and on which the parties are broadly agreed (so reducing the role of a general election in providing a choice for voters), a referendum is appropriate.

■ Who votes?

To be entitled to vote a person must have his or her name on the electoral register of the constituency in which he or she resides. The register is a list compiled each year by the local registration officer. For inclusion on the register the person must be resident in the constituency on the given date, be over 18 years of age and be a British citizen, or a citizen of a Commonwealth country and resident in Britain. Persons lacking a fixed address cannot be registered.

One apparent anomaly is that citizens of the Irish Republic are also entitled to vote if they have had three months' continuous residence in the United Kingdom before the qualifying dates. EU citizens can vote in local and European Parliament elections. Peers and aliens are not allowed to vote, and traditionally inmates of mental homes were not either. However, in the 2000 Representation of the People Act the 200,000 voluntary patients in mental hospitals were given the vote for the first time, although patients with criminal records are still unable to vote. Homeless people will be allowed on to the electoral register if they provide a 'declaration of locality'.

It remains true that the great majority of people confine their political activity to voting at elections, particularly general elections. But now a growing number of people pass up even that opportunity; in May 1997 turnout was 71.4 per cent, the lowest general election figure since 1935. This was in spite of

Table 8.3 Turnout in elections for European Parliament, 1999 and 2004

Country	Turnout (%) 1999	2004
Belgium	91.0	90.8
Luxembourg	87.3	89.0
Italy	70.8	73.1
Greece	75.3	63.2
Ireland	50.2	58.8
Denmark	50.5	47.9
Spain	63.0	45.1
Germany	45.2	43.0
France	46.8	42.8
Austria	49.4	42.4
Finland	31.4	39.4
The Netherlands	30.0	39.3
United Kingdom	24.0	38.8
Portugal	40.0	38.6
Sweden	38.8	37.8

fine weather on polling day, an increase in the number of parties and candidates, an up-to-date register and the opportunity to end eighteen years of one-party rule. The Blair landslide was supported by only 30.9 per cent of the eligible electorate, only just ahead of the number of non-voters. The trend was confirmed with the 24 per cent turnout in the European elections in May 1999 and a record low poll of 19.6 per cent in a by-election at Leeds Central in the same month. Leeds was a safe Labour seat, and elections for the European Parliament did not stimulate much interest.

There was even greater concern when the turnout fell even further, to 59.4 per cent, at the 2001 general election, the lowest turnout since 1918. Was it the nature of the campaign, the perceived lack of significant differences between the political parties (interestingly, many attributed the increase in turnout in the 2004 European election to the intervention of UKIP, which promised a clear choice from other parties), the predictability of the result (turnout dropped most in safe Labour seats), or the media presentation of the election as boring? Or was it part of a wider alienation from the political process?

In spite of calls from the media and the politicians to vote and making the vote easier (by postal ballots), and the prospect of a closer election result, 2005 was no better. The turnout of only 61.2 per cent was in spite of 12 per cent of votes being cast by post. It fell most sharply in safe Labour seats, leading commentators and Labour critics of Blair to claim that this reflected disillusion among the party's heartlands.

Concern about turnout has been expressed on the following grounds:

1. Low turnout weakens the legitimacy of the government (and the opposition for that matter) and the validity of its electoral mandate. Labour's 36 per cent share of the vote in 2005 amounted to just 22 per cent of the total electorate. Fewer people have a stake in the election outcome or feel committed to it.

2. The smaller the turnout the greater the political impact of the strongly committed, including the politically extreme, who are likely to turn out. Commentators and political leaders seized on the relatively low turnout (for France) in the first stage of the presidential election in April 2002, in which Le Pen, the National Front candidate, finished second. They urged people to vote in the British local elections in May for any political party in order to suppress the vote for the National Front.

3. Differential levels of election participation between groups may result in the political élites being more responsive to the groups that are more active, that is, the concerns of older compared with younger voters, middle-class compared with working-class, and well-educated compared with less well-educated count for more.

On the other hand, some commentators take a more relaxed view about declining turnout. They suggest:

1. Low turnout may be a sign of a contented electorate. Interestingly, the only area that had an increase in general election turnout in 2001 was Northern Ireland. Public opinion was more polarised over the Good Friday Peace Agreement. Some would argue therefore that a higher turnout is a sign of a discontented electorate.

2. Disengagement from the party and the electoral process is not necessarily bad if people are

involved in the political process in other ways. There is no sign of a decline in activity in interest groups or interest in political issues.

Voting apathy appears to be part of a broader problem, including a decline in party membership in Britain as well as in other Western states. Participation has long been related to socio-economic factors such as social class, education and age, with the middle class, the well educated and the middle aged having above-average rates of participation. It is higher among those who have more of an interest in politics, identification with a party and a sense of political efficacy, or a belief that one can influence a political system. It is also related to campaign factors such as the competitiveness of the general election and the constituency, and political stimuli such as being canvassed or receiving leaflets from the candidates. But one would expect trends in social class and education to have increased voting. The expectation of a close contest on divisive or exciting issues is likely to increase the sense that an election matters. But these cannot be guaranteed. Since October 1974, only the 1992 election was expected to be close.

What else might be done to reverse the decline in electoral participation? Reformers advocate such devices as holding elections on a Sunday or a public holiday, installing ballot boxes in shopping precincts, making greater use of postal ballots, or introducing **proportional representation** (PR) for Westminster and local elections, so that fewer people will feel that their votes are 'wasted'. Political leaders have often justified their rule on the good democratic grounds that they have a mandate expressed in an election. Low turnouts undermine the validity of the claim.

■ Constituency boundaries

The division of the country into constituencies is in the hands of permanent electoral Boundary Commissions. Each of the four nations has a separate commission and each has the task of establishing an approximately equal size of constituency electorate. The commissions periodically (between ten and fifteen years) review and make recommendations about the size of the constituency electorates. They arrive at a notional **electoral quota** for each nation by dividing the total electorate by the available number of seats.

Notwithstanding the commissions' efforts, once allowances are made for such features as respecting the existing boundaries of counties and London boroughs, sparsely populated constituencies and the sense of 'community' in an existing seat, there are still inequalities in the size of the constituency electorates. Recent boundary reviews have had to take account of the more rapid growth of electorates in the south of Britain and the suburbs compared with the north and the cities, and to award more seats to the former. However, Scotland and Wales have long been given more seats in the House of Commons than the size of their populations strictly justifies, because both were guaranteed a minimum number of seats by the 1944 Redistribution of Seats Act. In 2001 the combined 'bonus' was nineteen seats and was a substantial help to Labour which in the 1997 and 2001 elections won thirty-four of the forty Welsh seats and fifty-six of the seventy-two Scottish seats.

Although the number of seats in Scotland (which now had its own Parliament) was cut from 72 to 59 in 2005, it is unrealistic for Conservatives to expect much from the new boundaries in the next review. First, the new boundaries will be drawn up on the basis of the 2001 electorates and will already be nearly ten years out of date for a 2009/10 general election. Second, the 40 seats in Wales have an average electorate of only 56,000 and in Scotland of 67,000 compared to England's 70,000. These inequalities hand a marked advantage to Labour. And the commissions do not take account of the differences in turnout between seats.

■ The electoral system

An **electoral system** is a set of rules governing the conduct of elections. Electoral systems aim to produce a legislature that is broadly representative of the political wishes of the voters, to produce a government that is representative of the majority of voters and to produce strong and stable government. These aims are not necessarily compatible with one another. A key feature prescribes how popular votes are translated into seats in the legislature. There are, broadly speaking, two types of electoral system. Proportional systems attempt to establish a close relationship between the distributions of votes between parties and the allocation of seats in the legislature. How close depends on the type of system used. Proportional systems may be subdivided

How proportional systems work

There are different systems of PR, none of which achieves perfect proportionality. Recent changes have resulted in different parts of the UK having different systems. No longer is the dominant system the single-member simple-plurality one, which now applies only to elections to the House of Commons and local government elections in England and Wales.

The additional member system (AMS) as used in Germany elects two types of MP. A proportion is elected in single-member constituencies on a plurality basis, as in Britain. Others are elected by a second vote from party lists, which are produced regionally. This allocation is used to achieve some proportionality between the totals of votes and MPs, although the degree depends on the balance struck between the two types of MP. This is the system used to elect members of the Scottish Parliament, Welsh Assembly and Greater London Assembly (GLA).

The single transferable vote (STV), not a strictly PR system, is used in Ireland for large constituencies with several members. Each elector ranks the candidates in order of preference 1, 2, 3, etc. A quota is calculated from the formula *number of votes* divided by *number of seats plus one*. Surplus votes for a candidate who has achieved the quota are transferred to other candidates according to the voters' second and lower preferences. Votes for candidates at the bottom are also redistributed as they are eliminated. This process continues until all the requisite number of candidates with votes above the quota are elected. The system is used to elect MPs in Northern Ireland, and for local government elections in Scotland and Northern Ireland, and will be used for the new Northern Ireland Assembly.

The Regional Party List systems are also applied to large constituencies. The party machine decides the order of candidates and there is no direct link between member and constituency. List systems are widely used in Europe and operate in large constituencies. Under the closed party list system the party decides the ranking order of the candidates; voters choose a party list and have no choice of candidate. This is used in British elections for the European Parliament. A number of other countries, including Denmark and Italy, allow a wider choice of candidate, and the voter may choose candidates from more than one party list.

In the Supplementary Vote system each elector has two votes and ranks candidates in order of preference. If one candidate fails to win 50 per cent of first preference votes, all but the top two candidates are eliminated and the second preference votes for the eliminated candidates are distributed among the remaining two candidates. The winner is the candidate with the most votes.

into party list and transferable vote systems (see Box 8.2). Setting a relatively high threshold (e.g. 5 per cent of votes in Germany) for a party to gain a seat can limit the number of parties represented. A low one (e.g. 0.67 per cent in the Netherlands) encourages fragmentation. In **first-past-the-post** (FPTP) systems, the candidate who achieves a **plurality** of votes wins the seat. Proportional systems have been found largely in Western European states, and first-past-the-post systems are found in Anglo-American societies (the UK, Canada and the USA). It was perhaps significant that the new

democracies in Central and Eastern Europe have all adopted PR systems.

The two systems also broadly correspond to multi-party versus predominantly two-party systems, respectively. But this list of countries has changed somewhat. In a referendum in 1993 Italians voted by a large majority to abandon PR and adopt a largely first-past-the-post system, tempered by proportionality, and New Zealanders by a large majority voted for the German additional member system. Desire for a change to the electoral rules is often a symptom of broader dissatisfaction with the political system.

The Italians have become disillusioned with their political system – its weak coalitions, the lack of effective choice at elections (which means that the same parties and personalities are almost always in government), the lack of political responsibility and the corruption – and regard the PR electoral system as a major cause of the weaknesses. But when the 1995 New Zealand election failed to produce a party with a majority and increased the power of small parties, it prompted demands for the abandonment of PR. These have subsided after a Labour government, elected in 1999 and re-elected twice since, has shown that the new system can provide stability.

The different types of electoral system do seem to reflect national outlooks about government and politics. Proportional systems are often adopted in divided societies – to provide a form of reassurance to minorities and emphasise the importance of the legislature being broadly representative of society. Plurality systems are defended on the grounds that they help to provide a more stable government and, where there is one party in government, allow the voters to hold the government responsible for its record at the next election. Their disproportionality also means that a party often has a majority of seats for a minority of the vote. In October 1974, Labour won a bare majority of seats with only 39.2 per cent of the vote; in 1983, the Conservatives amassed 61 per cent of seats for 42 per cent of the vote; and in 1997 and 2001, Labour was a beneficiary by a virtually similar margin. In 2005 Labour gained 55 per cent of seats for only 36 per cent of the vote, the lowest ever vote share for single-party majority government.

Until recently the British public and much of the élite assumed that the electoral system was satisfactory. Undoubtedly it enjoyed the virtues of familiarity and clarity; in postwar general elections, only in February 1974 has one party failed to gain an overall majority of seats. This assumption also accompanied the belief that the British system of government was superior to that of many Western European states. For the first half of the twentieth century, Britain was an economic and industrial power of the first rank. Its record in resisting Hitler, avoiding political extremism (of both the left- and right-wing varieties) and maintaining political stability was superior to that of many Western European states, which had various forms of proportional representation. General elections were occasions when voters chose a party to form a government. The system had the advantage of allowing the voter to hold

the government accountable at the next election, something not possible with a coalition. Of course all this depended on there being two dominant political parties, so that the voter was given an effective choice between alternative teams bidding to form a government. Above all, however, the two main parties were reluctant to introduce PR, even for direct elections to the European Parliament – which are not about choosing a government – because they would both lose seats.

In the 1990s, however, that complacency and, for Labour, political calculation changed. Demands for reform or 'modernisation' of the constitution grew, and this included the electoral system.

Northern Ireland illustrates the shortcomings of the British electoral system when it operates in a bitterly divided society. The use of the first-past-the-post system meant that, as long as religion dictated voting, the Catholics were in a permanent minority, and this was hardly calculated to build consent. Elections in Northern Ireland for its three seats to the European Parliament were using PR before its introduction to the rest of Britain in 1999.

Criticisms of Britain's first-past-the-post system include:

1. The system does not invariably produce secure majorities for one party. In at least three of the last nine general elections (1964, February 1974 and October 1974) the winning party did not have a majority sufficient to last for a full parliament. Many commentators felt that in the era of three-party politics in the 1980s the chances of an indecisive outcome were greatly increased.

2. Because some three-quarters of seats are safe for the incumbent party, many voters for losing candidates are denied an effective choice in most seats. It produces a House of Commons and a government that do not fairly represent the party support across the nation.

3. As the Liberal and Social Democratic Alliance parties gained significant voting support (over 25 per cent) in the 1980s, so the disproportional effects of the electoral system became more glaring. It can be argued that when the Liberals were gaining less than 10 per cent of the vote this disproportionality was not too objectionable; but when a party gains a quarter of the vote and gets only 3.5 per cent of the seats (as in 1983 and 1987) the distortion is less acceptable. It is worth noting that the British system does not

Table 8.4 Third-party seats in House of Commons

Date	Number of seats	Date	Number of seats
1945	34	October 1974	39
1950	11	1979	27
1951	9	1983	44
1955	8	1987	44
1959	7	1992	44
1964	9	1997	75
1966	14	2001	80
1970	12	2005	92
February 1974	37		

discriminate against all minor political parties. Where a party can consolidate its votes in a region then it can collect a proportional number of seats. However, the system does penalise those parties that spread their votes widely, like the Liberals and now Liberal Democrats.

4. In spite of the electoral system the third party, the Liberal Democrats, have made progress. But another indicator of the decline of the Labour–Conservative dominance is the rise of 'other' parties (Table 8.4). The present figure of 92 non-Conservative, non-Labour MPs, covering Liberal Democrats, nationalists, independents, Respect, and parties in Northern Ireland, would have sufficed to produce a hung Parliament in most postwar general elections. In other words, the electoral system has not prevented the fragmentation of the party system (see Chapters 10 and 12).

5. As the two main parties became more regionally based between the north and south and between urban and suburban/rural areas in the 1980s, so they became less national in their representation. Until 1992 the south of Britain and the Midlands cumulatively became more Conservative, while the north and Scotland became more solidly Labour. Only in 1997 and 2001 did a good number of Labour MPs sit for the affluent and growing population in the southeast of Britain. Conservatives are hardly represented in the major cities and have no representation at all in Liverpool, Manchester, Glasgow, Bradford, Stoke, Newcastle upon Tyne, Leicester, etc.

There is now a massive bias in the electoral system against the Conservative Party. In 1992, the party had a majority of 7.6 per cent of the popular vote over Labour but an overall majority of only twenty-one seats. In 2001, Labour had a lead of 9.3 per cent in the vote over the Conservatives but an overall majority in the House of Commons of 167 seats. The system so operates to the advantage of Labour that if at the next election the two main parties had similar shares of the vote it would have 111 more seats than the Conservatives, and the latter would need to lead Labour by 6.4 per cent of the vote to have the same number of seats. Notwithstanding the best efforts of the Boundary Commissions, Labour has massive advantages because firstly, the average electorate in seats won by Labour is smaller than that in seats won by the Conservatives, and secondly Labour's vote is more 'efficiently' distributed because it wins many seats with small majorities and the Conservatives win many with large majorities.

One may point to shortcomings in most schemes of proportional representation and the coalitions that usually ensue. For example, it is difficult for voters to assign responsibility to any one party for a government's record before or after an election if there are coalition or minority governments. If a coalition government is formed then its programme is very likely to be a result of post-election bargaining between the party leaders. Under the present British system disillusioned voters can turn a government out, but under PR some members of the ousted coalition would probably be members of the new one. Critics also argue that, apart from in wartime – when the overriding goal is national survival – coalitions are likely to be unstable and lack coherence.

It is also likely that if a party list system is used (as in a number of Western European states) and the party headquarters draws up the list of candidates in multi-member seats, then the direct link between an MP and his or her constituents will be weakened. Another form of PR – the additional member system in Germany – also retains the link between constituency and MP. Finally, if a party is short of a working majority by a few seats in the House of Commons, the bargaining power of a small party will be greatly increased. In Germany, the small Free Democrat party was, until 1998, an almost perpetual partner in coalition governments with Christian Democrats or Social Democrats. Critics may ask: is it fair that a small and unrepresentative party should wield such influence?

Prospects for electoral reform

The public does not regard proportional representation as an important issue, certainly in comparison with the attention given by political scientists, commentators and politicians. In the 1990s, however, there was growing interest in electoral reform. In the past, supporters of reform complained about the way in which the present system discriminated against the Liberals. The significant new factor was that many Labour politicians came to support reform. Having by 1987 lost three successive elections to the Conservatives, who were able to gain landslide victories with only 42 per cent of the vote, and aware that a large number of Labour voters were virtually unrepresented in the south of England, some Labour leaders had second thoughts. The occasional spell of Labour government seemed to be a poor return from the first-past-the-post system. Charter 88, a cross-party group but drawn mainly from the Liberal and Labour parties, advocated constitutional reform, including proportional representation.

A potentially decisive step for Labour was when Neil Kinnock agreed to set up a working party under Professor Raymond Plant to look at the electoral systems for a reformed second chamber and regional assemblies. Neil Kinnock agreed to the appointment of a committee as a way of promoting discussion, educating the public and party, and also avoiding a party split on the issue before the 1992 general election. Supporters of reform felt vindicated by the 1992 result. With the Conservatives again winning a majority of seats on 42 per cent of the vote, Labour support for reform would, it was argued, improve relations with the Liberal Democrats and mobilise the anti-Conservative vote. It also fitted in with Labour's programme of constitutional reform.

In 1993, the Plant Committee made a majority recommendation for a switch to the supplementary vote, only a minimal change from the present system. John Smith rejected it, but agreed that a referendum could be held on the issue in the next parliament, and Tony Blair endorsed the position. In 1997, in advance of the general election, a joint Lab–Lib commission agreed to support a referendum on retaining the present system or switching to a form of PR. In October 1997, Lord (Roy) Jenkins, a good friend of Blair, was appointed to chair an Independent Commission on the Voting System. Its terms of reference required it to balance the following objectives:

■ proportionality;

■ stable government;

■ preserving the link between an MP and the constituency.

Jenkins reported in October 1998 and advocated a system of AVPLUS. This is a mixed form of the alternative vote, which would be used to elect 80–85 per cent of MPs, and a top-up of 15–20 per cent of additional members distributed between the parties to achieve greater proportionality. Under the alternative vote system (used in the Australian lower house) voters rank candidates in order of preference; the candidate with the fewest first preferences is eliminated and the second preferences are counted instead; the process continues until one candidate has a clear majority. Voters would cast two ballots, one for 530–560 constituency MPs, the other for a 'top-up' of 100 or so MPs. All constituency MPs would require the support of at least 50 per cent of those voting. The top-up MPs would be chosen from an open list, so that the elector could vote for a party or a candidate on that list. The country would be divided into eighty top-up areas, and MPs would be allocated so that the House of Commons would have a more proportional membership than had been achieved under the constituency ballot.

BIOGRAPHY

Lord Jenkins (1920–2003)

Labour Chancellor of the Exchequer (1966–70), Home Secretary (1974–6) and President of the European Commission (1976–81). On his return from Brussels in 1981 was one of the four co-founders of the Social Democratic Party, largely drawn from centre-right Labour MPs. Elected as MP and became leader of the party until 1983. He and the party advocated sweeping constitutional reform (much of which has been enacted by Tony Blair), including proportional representation. He was close to Blair and shared his aspiration to recreate the Progressive force represented by the Liberals and the infant Labour party before 1914. Blair invited him to head a Royal Commission on electoral systems; it advocated a form of PR in 1998. No action has been taken on the report.

The debate on the Jenkins report in the House of Commons revealed predictable Conservative opposition and Liberal Democrat support, Labour unease and the lack of enthusiasm on the part of the Home Secretary Jack Straw over the proposals. Some part of the reluctance is explained by the fact that as many as 100 Labour MPs would not have been elected in the 1997 or 2001 general elections had the system been in operation. The referendum on the Jenkins report (promised in Labour's 1997 election manifesto) has never taken place and the report is as good as dead. For the present, given continued Conservative opposition and the massive advantage that Labour gains from the present system, the prospect of reform is virtually nil.

In the meantime, the Labour government has taken significant steps in the direction of PR. For the European elections it introduced a regional party list. For the Scottish and Welsh elections nearly 60 per cent of constituency members are elected under FPTP and over 40 per cent are top-up members, drawn from a party list. In the 1999 and 2004 elections to the Scottish Parliament a large minority of Labour voters used their second vote to elect 'other' candidates, including Greens and independents, and in Wales to elect nationalists.

Critics of PR have seized on the outcomes of PR elections for the European Parliament, the Scottish Parliament and the Welsh Assembly. They have not boosted turnout and have produced in Scotland a coalition executive and in Wales a coalition at first and then a minority executive. Critics also pointed to the bargaining between the Scottish Labour Party and the Scottish Liberal Democrats to show that PR produces political uncertainty and bargaining between the parties over posts and policies. However, such criticisms do not impress advocates of PR because it usually leads to coalition and bargaining between parties. A different electoral system often produces a different style of politics and a different system of government.

It would be understandable if the Conservatives now favoured PR, not least to gain seats in Scotland and Wales. But no PR system that takes account of a voter's second as well as their first preference is likely to help the party to achieve at least proportionality as long as to date most Liberal Democrats and Labour voters prefer to vote for each other as their second choice to keep the Conservative candidate out. As noted earlier, the Conservatives also suffer because of how their vote is spread over the country.

Different PR electoral systems will have different outcomes. A form of the additional member system (in which half of MPs are elected in constituencies under the first-past-the-post system and half are chosen from a regional list to bring each party's share of seats into line with the share of votes in the region) would have produced a much more proportional outcome in 1997, and a minority government. The single transferable vote would not have achieved proportionality, because Labour would have benefited from Liberal Democrat second preferences and probably gained an overall majority.

Unless and until the Labour Party comes out for proportional representation, electoral reform is unlikely to be a major political issue. Supporters of change face formidable opposition in the party, notably from John Prescott and Jack Straw, and the many Labour MPs who would lose their seats. It is also reported that Blair was not impressed with the lack of authority shown by leaders of coalition governments in the EU during the Kosovo conflict and the bargaining between Labour and Liberal Democrat leaders in the new Scottish Parliament. But if there were a series of deadlocked parliaments and it seemed that minority governments were here to stay, then a coalition – which would involve at least two parties – might seem the only way of ensuring stable government. In that case PR would be a logical development. The introduction of coalitions and/or a proportional representation system would be likely to alter radically the conduct of British government and politics.

A change in the voting system may lead to more coalitions (as it has in the Scottish Parliament), more bargaining between parties and a less adversarial system. Critics warn of the potentially disproportionate power of a small party whose support may enable a large party to form a government with a majority. In Germany, Free Democrats, who have usually been supported by less than 10 per cent of the vote, have often been in government. But the same criticism can be made of a minority in a government party that has a small overall majority; it can effectively veto measures that it dislikes. This was the fate of Jim Callaghan's minority Labour government in the late 1970s and, at times, of John Major's 1992 government. Critics also object that under some PR systems many of Thatcher's radical (and subsequently applauded) reforms would not have been carried out.

At present, British elections are fought under a maze of different systems (see Box 8.2). The Northern

Ireland Assembly is elected by STV; the European elections have regional party lists; elections to the Scottish Parliament and Welsh Assembly have a proportion of seats decided by simple plurality and a proportion by an additional member system (AMS); Westminster still has simple-plurality single-member FPTP. One can justify the variety on the grounds that each of these elections is for a distinctive purpose and therefore they may have different electoral systems.

The prospects for PR certainly took a large step forward at the end of the 1990s, but its achievement is still distant at Westminster. What is needed is for more Labour or Conservative MPs to be persuaded that it is in their party's long-term interest. At present, Labour is helped enormously by the present system. If a referendum were to give a negative verdict, the prospects would be set back for a generation or so.

■ The electoral process

Nomination

For election to the House of Commons it is virtually necessary to be nominated as a candidate by a *major* political party. Each constituency party nominates a candidate and, if approved by the party headquarters, he or she becomes the constituency's prospective parliamentary candidate. Each major party maintains a list of approved candidates from which local parties may select. If a candidate is not already on the party list, then he or she has to be approved by party headquarters.

This power has been important in the Labour Party. In the 1950s, the party's National Executive Committee (NEC) turned down a number of left-wing nominations by constituencies. In the early 1980s, the NEC came under left-wing control and this power was not exercised. Indeed, reforms at this time (see below) gave more power to constituency activists, who were usually more left-wing than MPs. But under Neil Kinnock the NEC, as part of its drive against Militant, became more interventionist in candidate selection at by-elections and this has continued since. In the 1992 parliament it insisted, against some constituency opposition, on a number of all-women shortlists in safe Labour seats as part of the campaign to boost the number of women MPs. For a time these arrangements were ruled illegal

and abandoned, although not before a large number of women had been adopted.

In the absence of such a firm steer – although there has been exhortation – from the party HQs, the Conservative and Liberal Democrat parties still have an overwhelmingly male list of MPs. In 2002 Conservative Central Office presented local parties with shortlists containing ethnic minority and female candidates. But this and other initiatives have not had much effect in changing the parties in Parliament. The proportion of female candidates in the 2005 general election varied between 19 per cent (Conservative) and 26 per cent (Labour), but the proportions of women MPs were 9 and 28 per cent respectively. What is crucial is to be adopted for a relatively safe seat. The new Conservative leader David Cameron has declared that recruiting more women MPs is a top priority for the party; he wants it to resemble the population more closely. He plans to compile a list of 140 'approved' candidates, of whom half will be women, and constituencies will have to select candidates from it.

To be nominated, a parliamentary candidate must be eligible to vote, be nominated by ten local voters and pay a deposit of £500 to the returning officer, which is forfeited if he or she fails to gain 5 per cent of the vote. In the past, few people participated in the selection process; the numbers ranged from a few dozen in some Labour general management committees to a few hundred in some Conservative associations. The introduction of a system of allowing all members to vote in the selection of candidates has made the process more open.

For many years renomination was assured for virtually all MPs. In the late 1970s, however, Labour left-wingers, as part of their campaign to extend democracy in the party, changed the party rules so that all Labour MPs were subject to mandatory reselection in the lifetime of a parliament. This was widely regarded as a device to make MPs more beholden to leftist activists in the constituencies than to the party whips in Westminster. By 1990, mandatory reselection was effectively overturned when the party conference agreed that contests would take place only if a ballot of local members demanded one. Under Blair, the party headquarters have often 'parachuted' loyal candidates into safe seats and, as an inducement, offered peerages to retiring MPs.

Conservative activists have usually been a force for loyalty to the existing leader. Sir Anthony Meyer, who challenged Margaret Thatcher for the party leadership in 1989, was shortly afterwards deselected by his Clwyd North West association, and supporters of Michael Heseltine's challenge to her in 1990 also came under pressure. In 1996, the anti-Major MP Sir George Gardiner encountered strong opposition in his local Reigate party and was eventually deselected in January 1997. With a notable display of central power on the eve of the 2005 general election, the Tory leader Michael Howard refused to accept Howard Flight, MP for Arundel and South Downs, for claiming that the party planned bigger spending cuts than had been announced. The local association acquiesced.

Money and elections

British constituency elections are cheap in comparison with those in many other Western states, largely because expenditure by local candidates is strictly limited. Each candidate is required to appoint an election agent, who is responsible for seeing that the limits on expenses are not exceeded. The legal limits are usually raised before each election in line with inflation. The maximum permitted in constituencies is around £30,000 for the year to polling day. For all parties the victors were more likely to spend near to the maximum permitted. The bulk of this spending goes on printing a candidate's election leaflets and addresses. Local candidates also have free postage for their election leaflets and free hire of school halls for meetings. The limit on spending means that local candidates can legally do little or no opinion polling, telephone canvassing or media advertising.

In contrast, until 2001, there was no legal limit on the spending by national party organisations and no legal obligation on them to publish their election budgets. Most national spending goes on advertising, opinion polling, the party leader's tours and meetings, and grants to constituency parties. Increasingly, political parties have been caught in an expenditure 'arms race', particularly on advertising. In 1997, the Conservatives paid over £13 million to the M and C Saatchi agency and Labour over £7 million to the BMP agency. Labour was also helped by the large press advertising campaigns run by public sector trade unions appealing for support for the public services. Under new rules, the 2005 election was the most expensive ever, with Labour for the first time narrowly outspending the Conservatives. The Electoral Commission reported that for the year before polling day Labour spent £17.9 million, the Conservatives £17.8 million and the Liberal Democrats £4.3

million. With a further sum of around £10 million spent in the constituencies, the total spend probably exceeded £50 million.

Heavy spending has been making the parties dependent on business or wealthy individuals and has led to inevitable suspicions that cash is traded, however indirectly, for influence. Financing political parties has long been a problem in the developed democracies. It costs some £30 million per year to run the Conservative Party and not much less to run Labour. The chief concern is that certain groups may buy influence and have their interests advantaged at the expense of others.

As Garner and Kelly indicate (1998, pp. 201–17), there are three reasons why election finance has become such a critical issue:

1. The electorate has ceased to feel so closely identified with the parties (see Chapter 9) and less likely to want to join and pay subscriptions. Membership of both major parties has shrunk from over a million each in the 1950s to around a third of a million in the 1990s and less today.

2. The greater role of public relations, not to mention all the various high-tech equipment required to communicate with the public, has added huge additional expenditure costs.

3. In recent years parties have been forced to campaign almost non-stop for the plethora of elections from local to European and referendums.

Conservatives used to derive most of their funding from business, and in the 1990s there were a number of scandals. Labour used to receive most of its funds from the unions and similarly left itself open to the accusation that it exchanged influence for party funds. It faced its own allegations of sleaze in October 1997 when Bernie Ecclestone, the millionaire owner of Formula One racing, seemed to influence the exemption of his sport from the ban on tobacco advertising that Labour had promised in its manifesto. When it transpired that the diminutive tycoon had donated £1 million to Labour, the critical voices became strident and the donation was eventually handed back. Both parties have handed out political honours, including peerages, to rich donors, thus further lowering the status of democratic politics.

Funding remedies

The Houghton Report in 1976 suggested state funding of parties, but no action was taken on it before

Neill Committee proposals on election spending

1. Donations over £5,000 nationally and £1,000 locally to be publicly declared. The figure includes payments in kind. Foreign donations banned. Company shareholders to be balloted over corporate donations. End to 'blind trusts', or arrangements for providing funding by donors who are not known to the beneficiaries.
2. Tax relief for donations up to £500. Policy Development Fund to be provided with funds up to £1 million for policy work. Increase in money for opposition parties.
3. Limit general election spending to £20 million.
4. Provision for unregistered third parties to spend up to £25,000 and for those who are registered to spend up to £1 million in general election campaigns.
5. Electoral Commission to oversee the implementation of the votes. In the interest of greater transparency, parties required to submit audited accounts to the Committee on Standards in Public Life.

Source: Committee on Standards in Public Life (1998)

Labour fell from power in 1979. A Hansard Society report in 1981 suggested 'matching funding' for funds raised by the parties. The Commons Home Affairs Select Committee reported in 1994 but could not agree; the Conservative majority favoured the *status quo*, while the Labour minority wanted state funding. The Conservatives argued that state funding in a democracy is harmful in that it substitutes a government input for what should be a voluntary one drawing on all sections of democratic society. During the long period of Conservative government, the issue of state funding effectively died.

In October 1997, Lord Neill announced that his Committee on Standards in Public Life would look into the vexed area of party finance. His report a year later proposed to ban foreign donations and cap campaign budgets at £20 million (see Box 8.3). The Political Parties, Elections and Referendum Act (2000) implemented many of Neill's recommendations: ban foreign donations; force parties to reveal the name of donors above £5,000; limit general election spending to £20 million per party (both main parties spent over £25 million in 1997); and impose controls over spending on referendum campaigns. There was, however, no tax relief for small donations. An Electoral Commission was also set up with responsibility for registering political parties and checking on their finances. One important difference between election campaigns in Britain and the USA is that British parties are precluded from purchasing time on the broadcasting media, although they can buy advertising in the press. In the USA, there is

little doubt that television advertising has made elections very expensive and heightened the importance of personalities and the wealth of candidates.

In spite of the limits on the parties' election expenditure and the greater transparency, party finance has become a major issue again and the issue of state funding has returned. Indeed, large donations from business have attracted greater public attention because of the Labour government's legislation, which has made them public. Lord Hamlyn, the publisher, and Lord Sainsbury of Turville, a government minister, each contributed £2 million to Labour before the 2001 general election. Blair's first Lord Chancellor, Lord Irvine, held fund-raising dinners for Labour-supporting lawyers, an activity hardly befitting someone who had a key role in making top judicial appointments. There was further criticism over revelations that the Hinduja brothers contributed to financing the Millennium Dome, on the alleged grounds that they hoped this would ease their applications for British citizenship. As Labour reduced its dependence on the trade unions for funding so it has become more reliant on business. This in turn has triggered accusations of sleaze and improper influence.

For the Conservatives, Lord Ashcroft, the party treasurer until 2001, was an expatriate millionaire who contributed £1 million annually and acted as guarantor for the party's deficits. Stuart Wheeler, the chairman of IG Index, contributed £5 million before the general election. But it was the revelation in 2006 that both Labour and Conservative had taken large undeclared loans before the 2005 election that has placed reform on the agenda. The resulting rows have increased the interest of the Labour Party in state funding once again. Blair quickly set up an inquiry under Lord Phillips, a retired senior civil servant, to review party finance. In a historic move for the Conservatives, David Cameron has provided a formula for state funding and a £50,000 cap on individual donations.

It is worth noting that there is some state funding already in the form of the so-called Short Money, the £3 million per annum that is given to the opposition parties to help with policy making and communications. During general elections there is free time in the form of election broadcasts and free delivery of mail.

Politics has become more expensive at a time when party membership is declining. It is no longer possible for political parties to be self-financing. In the 1951 general election, Labour spent £80,000 centrally, the Conservatives £112,000. In 2005, both parties spent just over £17 million on the campaign. The arguments for state funding include:

1. It will reduce dependence on large donors, who may wish to use the donation to exercise improper influence.

2. The money will be guaranteed, so the parties can plan a programme of work.

3. Parties are essential to the democratic process. They are therefore providing a 'public good', just like defence or clean air. As such they should be financed out of taxation.

4. Many other European states provide public funds for the parties.

Against this, critics argue:

1. Political parties are voluntary bodies, and state financing will remove the incentive for them to recruit members and encourage participation.

2. In Germany and the United States, to take two examples, state funding has not removed sleaze and large business donations. Some rich people give or lend money in the reasonable expectation that they will be given honours.

Other possibilities include tax relief for contributions, as was recommended by the Neill Committee, or the state matching the funds raised by political parties. But in a free society there are problems about limiting what people can spend their own money on.

Another difficulty is that if the state provides money, it might also choose to specify what the money is spent on and what is forbidden.

Campaigns

There has long been a ritual element to British general election campaigns. This is particularly so at the constituency level, with candidates and helpers pursuing their time-worn techniques of canvassing, addressing meetings and delivering election leaflets to electors' homes. At the national level, the party leaders continue to address public meetings in the major cities, attend morning press conferences and prepare for national election broadcasts. Elections today are effectively fought on a national scale through the mass media, particularly television. The activities of the party leaders – visiting party committee rooms, factories and old people's homes, speaking at evening rallies and making statements at morning press conferences – are conducted with an eye to gaining such coverage. If activities are not covered by peak time television, they are largely wasted as a means of communicating with the public. One of the most famous images of the 1979 general election was Margaret Thatcher on a Norfolk farm, cuddling a newborn calf. This had little to do with discussion of political issues, but the bonus for the Conservatives was that photographs of the event were carried prominently in almost every national newspaper and on television.

There has been some Americanisation of campaigning in Britain: local face-to-face meetings have declined in importance, while the national parties employ their own opinion pollsters and advertising agencies and make use of computers, direct mail and other modern devices to 'market' themselves, rebut the claims of opponents, and appeal to target voters in key seats. The parties always send their strategists to the United States to learn lessons in 'high tech' methods from the latest Presidential campaign (Kavanagh, 1995). Various labels have been used to describe these developments – the permanent campaign, or scientific electioneering (see Box 8.4).

In the constituencies, parties have borrowed from commercial companies to identify and 'target' key voters – usually defined as those who have not firmly decided how to vote but may vote for the party. Campaigners use databases to study the social characteristics of postcode areas. They can identify, for example, doctors, families with young children,

---

BOX 8.4   EXAMPLE

New-style campaigning

Election campaigns have been made-for-television events since the 1960s. But in the degree of choreography, the amount of effort expended on controlling every aspect of the experience, 2005 set a new standard.

Made-for-television events sometimes became so distanced from the real world as to seem unreal. The phenomenon arguably reached its apogee a week ago. At the Business Design Centre in Islington, where Blair and Gordon Brown arrived to unveil a poster on economic policy . . .

There was no visible backdrop and nobody present except the PM, the Chancellor, journalists, and a ready supply of invited young activists; there were no windows, and no member of the public could have seen the poster. Blair spoke for under a minute, took no questions, and left. The event would have appeared no different to TV viewers had it been pre-recorded at Labour headquarters.

Source: Patrick Barnham *et al.*, 'Stage-managed rings of confidence', *The Guardian*, 5 May 2005.
© Guardian Newspapers Limited, reprinted with permission

---

the elderly, young singles, etc., and tailor campaign messages (direct mail, personal visits and phone calls) to particular groups.

There has been much talk that the use of e-mail is transforming campaigns. Party headquarters use it to communicate with candidates and interest groups for contacting members. But it is still of limited use because of the lack of known addresses and, compared to the United States, few follow the campaign on the Internet. Voters still overwhelmingly rely on television for information. In 2005 NOP found that 72 per cent got a lot or some information about the election from television compared with 8 per cent who mentioned the Internet. But parties do use the Internet for internal communications. Two other developments are worth noting. Some constituencies used the Internet for organising vote swaps between Labour and Lib-Dem supporters. An increasing number of MPs now have their own websites.

It is difficult to prove that election campaigns make much difference to the final result. One party's good campaign in a constituency may fail to show a marked improvement because the opposition parties have also made strenuous efforts in the seat. There is some evidence that an active new MP, perhaps using local radio and television over the lifetime of a parliament, can gain up to 700 'personal' votes at the following general election. For many voters, however, the choice of whom to support on polling day is a product of a lifetime of influences rather than the four weeks of an election campaign.

In 1987, many observers were critical of the Conservatives' campaign but on polling day they had preserved the eleven-point lead over Labour that they enjoyed at the outset of the campaign. Compared with the disaster of 1983, Labour's campaign was admired for its smooth organisation and professionalism. But for all this, and Neil Kinnock's campaigning superiority to Michael Foot, Labour added just 3 per cent to its 1983 record low vote. In 1992 once more, commentators and, according to the polls, voters judged that Labour and Neil Kinnock had campaigned better than the Conservatives and John Major. Even Conservative supporters were critical of their party's campaign. Yet Labour added only 3.6 per cent to its 1987 vote. Packaging and presentation can only do so much.

In 1997, there was widespread admiration for the smoothness of the Labour campaign. Commentators talked about a 'Mandelson effect', named after the party's campaign director, Peter Mandelson. Its disciplined media operation, unit for rapid rebuttal (of opposition attacks), concentration of resources on its key 100 constituencies (those Conservative seats needed to be won for a Labour majority) and advertising all outscored the Conservative Party. And throughout the five-week campaign, the Conservatives were dogged by events – internal divisions over Europe, and damage from sleaze and sex scandals. Yet it is chastening to remember that the average Labour lead in the opinion polls actually fell from 22 per cent in the first week to 13 per cent on polling day, and that Labour's share of the vote in its target seats rose by fractionally less than it did in the non-targeted areas.

In view of the sharp fall in turnout in the last three general elections, some commentators and campaigners wonder whether the more scientific campaigning and undue concentration on a narrow group of seats and target voters is alienating potential voters.

Referendums

Referendums have, quite suddenly, become an accepted part of the political scene. For a long time British politicians would have nothing to do with them. After all, referendums were difficult to square with the sovereignty of Parliament, disciplined and programmatic political parties, and ideas of strong government. All of these features were part of a 'top-down' view of government. When Harold Wilson called the first nationwide British referendum in 1975 to decide on Britain's continuing membership of the European Community, the decision was controversial. Wilson had earlier opposed the idea, and Roy Jenkins resigned as deputy leader of the party in protest at the change of policy. Wilson claimed that it was a unique constitutional occasion, but most people knew that he called a referendum because his party was bitterly divided over British membership and, once the precedent has been set, others would follow.

Since then, and particularly since the election of a Labour government in 1997, referendums have proliferated; indeed, in 1999 some commentators wondered whether they might be inducing voter fatigue. They have been held in September 1997 in Scotland and Wales to approve the devolution plans, in May 1998 in London over an elected mayor, and in September 1998 over the Good Friday Agreement in Northern Ireland. In addition, Labour has promised to call a referendum before Britain joins the single European currency or signs up to a European constitution. The 1997 promise to hold one on the reform of the electoral system seems to have been forgotten.

Why have referendums flourished recently? First, politicians will not have missed the fact that a large majority of voters say in polls that they like referendums if the issue is sufficiently important. Second, the authority of elected politicians has declined along with their reputations, and this device invokes the authority of the people in a very direct way. Both sides of a major issue can favour a referendum

– as over the single currency issue – when both feel they could win the resultant vote. In the 1997 general election, the late Sir James Goldsmith fielded candidates under the banner of the Referendum Party, which sought a ballot on Britain's future relations with the EU. Third, they can be useful when there is a difficult problem on which delay is thought advisable, such as devolution; and technically referendums are only advisory, not binding (although it is hard to believe that a government would totally ignore an emphatic result). Fourth, they can be a useful uniting factor when a party cannot agree, as over membership of the EEC for Labour in 1975; in effect the party says to the country: 'We cannot decide, so why don't you?' John Major's Conservative Party was divided over British membership of the single European currency, and this was a factor that led it to embrace a referendum. Similarly, Labour is divided over electoral reform – one group favours no change and another supports proportional representation; the referendum, it is fondly hoped, will square the circle, although it may merely make matters more complex as most voters are baffled by the respective arguments for and against. This also raises the question of whether referendums are a cop-out for politicians, a way of evading their responsibilities. Critics ask: how can voters decide on the arcane arguments over the single currency? Will the debate be dominated by those who simplify and employ emotive slogans? Don't politicians get elected to make such decisions and use their judgement on behalf of the country? Referendums obviously provide an additional and more specific form of feedback to that of elections. Some link the device to greater use of opinion polls, focus groups, talk shows and phone-ins to claim that the era of representative democracy is passing.

What most of the referendums, achieved and planned, have in common is that they deal with constitutional questions. It is now probable that any constitutional change will be preceded by approval in a referendum. So far politicians have resisted calling them on other issues, for example capital punishment, or recent incursions on civil liberties under the threat of terrorism. But a referendum now appears to be part of the constitutional framework. There is a need to develop clear rules, and these have emerged under the Electoral Commission. For example, there will be a ceiling on spending during a referendum, which could have an impact on business support for a 'yes' vote in a ballot on Britain joining a single currency.

BOX 8.5   BRITAIN IN CONTEXT

American influence on election campaigning

We often talk of globalisation, or an associated term Americanisation, as a key trend in politics, economy and culture. Some would claim that there is a growing Americanisation of campaigning, i.e. election techniques developed in the US are increasingly being borrowed by other countries. The USA has many elections and this has encouraged the growth of a huge army of campaign professionals – fund-raisers, consultants, opinion pollsters and media advisers. The US is at the cutting edge of technology when it comes to marketing, opinion research and use of computers.

Features associated with US campaigns include the following:

- Targeting of voters by detailed research
- The permanent campaign, covering press launches, party conferences, personal appearances, etc.
- Personalism, or the emphasis on the party leader
- Message discipline
- Attack or negative campaigning
- Greater use of professionals in communications
- Intense focus on setting the agenda for the media.

All of these features have been noted in campaigns in many countries. It is no surprise therefore that many parties send their campaign strategists to the US to study the latest techniques and that US campaign experts are exporting their skills to other countries. Many parties in the newly democratic states in Central and Eastern Europe as well as parties in Latin America employed US campaign consultants. In Britain key parts of the modernisation of Labour's campaign have been borrowed from Clinton's success in the 1992 Presidential election, and in 2005 the party's pollster was Mark Penn, formerly a pollster for Clinton. At one time under Margaret Thatcher, the Conservatives employed Ronald Reagan's pollster Dick Wirthlin. Dick Morris, at one time a consultant to Clinton, was the strategist for UKIP in the 2004 European elections.

But the distinctive features of each political system – the nature of the parties, the culture, the political institution and the election rules – modify the impact of the US practices. For example, many broadcasting media in Western Europe do not allow the party or candidate to buy advertising time, a crucial difference from the US; perhaps no European country has elections for such a highly personalised office as the US Presidency; and a number of Western European states (Britain, Germany and Sweden, for example) have stronger parties (more programmatic and disciplined) than the US.

Source: Swanson and Mancini (eds) (1996)

Chapter summary

The British electoral system has for a long time been admired for its simplicity and its effects in producing stable government. It has been questioned in recent years, and reform is now on the agenda. Reform has been stimulated by changes in the party system, changes made in the electoral arrangements for Scotland, Wales, London and the European Parliament, membership of the European Union and calculation of political advantage. Campaigns have also changed because of new technology, public relations and the concentration on 'targeting' key voters and key constituencies. But less is decided by elections than politicians claim, largely because of the limits on the autonomy of the British government and decisions made or shaped by non-elected bodies.

Discussion points

There are a number of questions to ask about the working of the electoral system under the role of elections in Britain today:

■ *Campaign funding*: How might party funding be improved? What might be the consequence for parties and campaigns of an effective limit on national spending or state provision of funding?

■ *Electoral reform*: What are the main obstacles to electoral reform of Westminster elections?

■ *Scottish devolution*: What consequences has the creation of a Scottish Parliament had on the electoral system and style of campaigning?

■ *The importance of elections*: 'Elections have their limitations in deciding public policy'. Discuss.

Further reading

On the working of the British electoral system, see Curtice and Steed (2002), Curtice, Fisher and Steed (2005) and Johnston *et al.* (2001).

References

Barkham, P., Burkeman, O., Meek, J. and Vul, Ed (2005) 'Stage-managed rings of confidence', *The Guardian*, 5 May 2005.

Butler, D. (1963) *The British Electoral System since 1918*, 2nd edn (Oxford University Press).

Butler, D. and Kavanagh, D. (2002) *The British General Election of 2001* (Palgrave).

Committee on Standards in Public Life (1998) *The Funding of Political Parties in the United Kingdom*, October 1998.

Crewe, I. (1997) 'The opinion polls: confidence restored?', *Parliamentary Affairs*, Vol. 50, No. 4, pp. 569–85.

Curtice, J. and Steed, M. (2002) 'The results analysed', in D. Butler and D. Kavanagh, *The British General Election of 2001* (Palgrave).

Curtice, J., Fisher, S. and Steed, M. (2005) 'Appendix 2: The results analysed', in D. Kavanagh and D. Butler, *The British General Election of 2005* (Palgrave).

Denver, D. (2002) *Elections and Voters in Britain* (Palgrave).

Electoral Commission (2003) *The Shape of Elections to Come* (Electoral Commission).

Farrell, D. (2001) *Electoral Systems: A Comparative Introduction* (Palgrave).

Fisher. J. (2002) 'Campaign finance: elections under new rules', *Parliamentary Affairs*.

Garner, R. and Kelly, R. (1998) *British Political Parties Today* (Manchester University Press).

Hailsham, Lord (1979) *Dilemma of Democracy* (Collins).

Johnston, R.J., Pattie, C.J., Dorling, D.F.L. and Rossiter, D.J. (2001) *From Votes to Seats: The Operation of the UK Electoral System since 1945* (Manchester University Press).

Kavanagh, D. (1995) *Election Campaigning: The New Marketing of Politics* (Blackwell).

Kavanagh, D. and Butler, D. (2005) *The British General Election of 2005* (Palgrave).

Kellner, P. (1996) 'Never mind the ballots', *The Observer*, 24 March 1996.

Norris, P. (ed.) (2005) *Britain Votes: 2005* (Oxford University Press).

Reeve, A. and Ware, A. (1991) *Electoral Systems: A Comparative and Theoretical Introduction* (Routledge).

Sarlvik, B. and Crewe, I. (1983) *Decade of Dealignment* (Cambridge University Press).

Swanson, D. and Mancini, P. (eds) (1996) *Politics, Media and Democracy* (Praeger).

CHAPTER 9

Voting behaviour

Dennis Kavanagh

Learning objectives

- To explain how voters are influenced.

- To understand electoral changes and the impact on them of social and political factors.

- To analyse and explain the outcome of the 2005 general election.

Introduction

This chapter discusses the factors that shape voting behaviour, particularly those that have produced changes in party support in recent years. It also assesses the likely impact of these changes on the working of the political system. Finally, it analyses the significance of the 2005 general election.

■ Explanations of voting behaviour

For the first half of the postwar period (1945–70) it was comparatively easy to provide broad explanations of voting behaviour in Britain. Three guidelines simplified analysis. The first was that people were regarded as being either middle or working class on the basis of their occupations. Although there were divisions within these classes, notably between the skilled and unskilled working class, there was a strong correlation between class and vote: the majority of the working class voted Labour, and most of the middle class voted Tory. Second, an average of about 90 per cent of voters supported either Labour or Conservative in general elections. Finally, most voters (over 80 per cent) were partisans or **identifiers** with one or other of the above parties. Surveys indicated that for most people party allegiance hardened over time so that they were unlikely to turn to a new party. Identifiers were and are also more likely than other voters to agree with their party's policies and leaders.

During the 1960s, it was generally believed by psephologists that most British people usually voted according to traditional associations of class and party. By the 1980s, however, such loyalties had waned, allowing issues to become more important. In an era of '**partisan dealignment**' (Sarlvik and Crewe, 1983), fewer people voted blindly for the party of their parents or workmates but listened to what the parties had to say on issues and reacted accordingly – sometimes in a volatile fashion. Sarlvik and Crewe distinguish between 'salience', the extent to which people are aware of an issue, and 'party preferred' in terms of policies on that issue. They believe the Conservative emphasis on taxes, law and order and trade union reform helped to win the 1979 election for them.

In 1987 and 1992, however, Labour led the Conservatives on three of the most salient issues –

BIOGRAPHY

Ivor Crewe (1945–)

Political scientist. Educated at Manchester Grammar School and Lancaster. Professor of Government at Essex University until made Vice Chancellor in 1995. One of the first to note Labour's loss of support among working-class voters and Mrs Thatcher's failure, in spite of landslide election victories, to gain popular acceptance of her values. Recognised as a leading student of elections.

unemployment, health and education – yet easily lost both elections. Surveys showed that voters expected a Labour government to increase taxes but most were prepared to pay higher taxes to fund extra spending on public services.

Perhaps they were. But, crucially, a post-election Gallup poll found that 30 per cent said they would be better off and 48 per cent worse off under Labour's tax and budget proposals. Despite their identification of key issues and their preferences for Labour prescriptions, some voters chose to vote for the party that they thought would deliver the highest degree of personal prosperity. This behaviour calls into question (a) the value of survey responses on issue questions and/or (b) the significance of **issue voting** – at least on this type of question.

A problem with research on issue voting is that one can never prove whether it is the party loyalty or vote that influences the issue preference, or vice versa (which is necessary for issue voting). And such questions are tied up with the broader image of the perceived 'competence' or trustworthiness of the party and the party leader (where Conservatives under Thatcher outscored Labour). At present political scientists are more impressed with the 'competence' and 'trust' factors as influences on the voter.

For most of the postwar period, therefore, social class and partisanship (and, as noted earlier, the electoral system) interacted to buttress the Labour/Conservative party system. There were relatively small margins of change in the parties' share of the vote from one general election to another. Between 1950 and 1970, for example, the Conservative share of the vote ranged from 49.7 per cent (1959) to 41.9 per cent (1945) and Labour's from 48.8 per cent (1951) to 43.8 per cent (1959). Stability was the order of the day, and it was difficult to envisage a change in the party system.

The above description always needed some qualification, not least because between a quarter and a third of the working class usually voted Conservative. Without this so-called '**deviant vote**' there would not have been a competitive two-party system, and the Conservatives would hardly have been the 'normal' party of government in the twentieth century. Paradoxically, it is the lack of class voting that has provided Britain with a competitive two-party system in the past. Another qualification is that class distribution was gradually changing as the proportion of the workforce engaged in manufacturing fell and the proportion employed in service and white collar occupations grew. This trend has accelerated in the past two decades (Table 9.1).

For the past thirty years the old two-party, two-class model has explained a diminishing part of British election behaviour. First, consider partisanship: between 1964 and 2005 the proportion of the electorate identifying 'very strongly' with a political party has fallen from 44 per cent in 1964 to just 8 per cent in 2005. As an increasing number of voters have become less tied to parties, so more are potentially 'up for grabs' at elections, or do not bother to vote.

Second, consider social class. The relationship between class and voting was fairly strong until the mid-1970s. In general elections between 1970 and 1992, Labour's normal two-thirds share of the working-class vote fell to less than a half (and as low as 37 per cent in 1983). Over the same period the Conservatives' normal four-fifths share of the middle-class vote fell to just over half (and is now less than 40 per cent). Within the middle class, Labour and Liberal support has been stronger among the public sector, particularly among the teaching, nursing and local government professions. Quite separate from these trends has been the shift in the

Table 9.1 Decline of class voting, 1992–2005 (MORI)

	AB	C1	C2	DE
Conservative				
1992	56	52	39	32
1997	41	37	27	21
2001	39	36	29	24
2005	37	37	33	25
Change 1992–2005	**−19**	**−15**	**−6**	**−6**
Labour				
1992	19	25	40	49
1997	31	37	50	59
2001	30	38	49	55
2005	28	32	40	48
Change 1992–2005	**+11**	**+7**	**0**	**−1**
Liberal Democrat				
1992	22	19	17	16
1997	22	18	16	13
2001	25	20	15	13
2005	29	23	19	18
Change 1992–2005	**+7**	**+4**	**+2**	**+2**

Source: J. Curtice (2005) 'Historic triumph or rebuff?', *Politics Review*, Vol. 15, No. 1, September. Reproduced with permission from Philip Allan Updates

balance between the classes in the electorate. From a rough 40–60 split between the middle class and working class, the distribution today is the reverse, as a result of changing patterns of employment. In other words, Labour was gaining a diminishing share of a smaller working-class constituency.

BIOGRAPHY

David Butler (1924–)

Founding British psephologist. At Oxford he made election systems his subject of study. Moved on to electoral behaviour and became the recognised expert on elections in the 1970s and 1980s. The Nuffield studies of general elections since 1945, authored by David Butler and Dennis Kavanagh, have become the recognised authoritative accounts and analyses of those events.

Moreover, social changes, promoted to some degree by Thatcher reforms, have weakened the old class bases of the party system. Since 1979 the proportion of council-rented properties has fallen from 45 per cent to 25 per cent of the housing stock, and privately-owned homes have risen from a half to nearly 70 per cent. As a proportion of the workforce trade unionists fell from 53 per cent in 1979 to around a third today. Although many people are now in 'mixed' social class groups, e.g. working-class homeowners, Britain is increasingly becoming a middle-class society. Realising this, Tony Blair has assiduously and successfully courted the middle class. This has coincided with a decline in the number of voters thinking that Labour is looking after the interests of the working class and an increase in those thinking that it protects the interests of the middle class.

Finally, consider the level of support for the two main parties. The Labour and Conservative parties' combined share of 90 per cent of the vote in general elections between 1945 and 1970 has fallen to around 75 per cent in the elections since then and to less than 70 per cent in 2005. Fluidity has replaced electoral stability, and three-party competition (four in Scotland and Wales) and less class-based voting has replaced the two-party, two-class model. As the moorings of class and partisanship have declined, so election campaigns and the build-up to them (and the personalities, issues and events associated with them) may have more influence.

To restate: British voting behaviour has become less predictable and volatile for the following reasons:

1. *Partisanship*: Strong identifiers with parties have declined.

2. *Social class*: Class loyalties have weakened and the working class is diminishing in size.

3. *Social changes*: Housing and occupational patterns have changed, so that Britain is more property-owning and middle-class.

4. *Level of support for the two parties*: This fell from 90 per cent in the 1945–1970 period to 69 per cent in 2005.

5. *Decline in turnout* (see Chapter 8).

It is against this background that we should take account of recent general election results. For the first time ever, Labour now gains nearly as much middle-class support as the Conservatives, and in 1997 nearly two million 1992 Conservatives switched to Labour.

■ Party support

Conservative

The Conservatives were clearly the dominant party in Britain in the twentieth century. Indeed, some would argue that Britain has had a dominant-party system rather than a two-party one (King, 1993). Before the 1997 general election they were in office, alone or in coalition, for over two-thirds of the century and two-thirds of the period since 1945. Indeed, over the century the only four occasions in which the non-Conservative parties have had clear parliamentary majorities have been the 1906–10 Liberal government, the 1945–50 Labour government, the 1966–70 Labour government and the 1997 Labour government. Some part of the Conservative dominance in Parliament has been due to the effects of the first-past-the-post electoral system and the divided opposition. In 1979, 1983 and 1987, for example, 42 per cent of the vote was enough to produce Conservative majorities, including landslides in the House of Commons in 1983 and 1987 as the Alliance or Liberal and the Labour and other parties divided the non-Conservative vote between them (Tables 9.2 and 9.3). The Conservatives have also been the historical beneficiary of Labour's internal divisions, and until 1997 they enjoyed strong support from the press and such powerful groups as the City, business and the farming sector. Labour supporters felt particularly sensitive about the partisanship of the tabloids in 1992, and Neil Kinnock blamed Labour's defeat on their 'bias'. In 1992, many Labour and working-class voters, because they read a tabloid (the *Express*, *Mail* or *Sun*), were exposed to what were then pro-Conservative papers.

Yet in the 1980s (as in the 1950s) the Conservative Party also identified itself firmly with economic prosperity. Margaret Thatcher's party managed to fashion a coalition of voters, including a large minority of the working class that had an interest in the

Table 9.2 How Great Britain voted (%), 1983–2005

	May 2005	May 2001	April 1997	June 1992	June 1987	1983
Conservative	32.4	31.7	30.7	41.9	42.2	42.3
Labour	35.2	40.7	43.2	34.4	30.8	27.6
Alliance/ Lib-Dem	22.0	18.3	16.8	17.8	22.6	25.4
Others	11.0	9.3	9.3	5.8	3.4	4.7

Table 9.3 Government parliamentary majorities, 1945–2005

Year	Overall majority
1945	Labour 147
1950	Labour 6
1951	Conservative 16
1955	Conservative 59
1959	Conservative 99
1964	Labour 5
1966	Labour 97
1970	Conservative 31
1974 (February)	none
1974 (October)	Labour 4
1979	Conservative 44
1983	Conservative 144
1987	Conservative 102
1992	Conservative 21
1997	Labour 179
2001	Labour 167
2005	Labour 66

continuation of Conservative rule. Those who lived in the affluent south and suburbs were often home-owners and share-owners (who expanded from 7 per cent in 1979 to over 20 per cent by 1990), and most of those in work did well in the 1980s. In spite of the return of high levels of unemployment, the longest economic recession for over fifty years, the collapse of business confidence and a sharp decline in house prices, particularly in the Tory heartland of the southeast, the Conservatives still managed to outscore Labour when voters were asked to rate the parties' competence on economic management. This appears to have been a crucial influence on the vote in 1992. In view of the modest Conservative economic record, however, it was more of a rejection of Labour. Whether in prosperity or in recession, most voters were not willing to trust the party. As Ivor Crewe asked: given the Conservative disadvantages, the key question about 1992 was 'why did Labour lose yet again?'. In September 1992, however, the Conservatives lost their reputation for economic competence following the collapse of Britain's membership of the ERM and subsequent tax rises. They have never recovered. Sleaze and divisions over Europe were fatal to the party in 1997. Even though the economy was recovering, the party was not given credit.

In the 1997 election the Conservative party lost a quarter of its 1992 vote, and its number of MPs was reduced to its lowest since 1906. The 13 per cent gap by which it trailed Labour in vote share was comparable with its 15 per cent lead over Labour in the 1983 general election. Scotland and Wales, with a total of 112 seats, became Conservative-free nations. The setback was remarkable for a party that has been the normal party of government and long admired for its tactical flexibility and the prowess of its election machine. In fact, neither of these qualities has been much in evidence since 1992. The party's bitter divisions over Europe and the loss of membership and declining level of activity at grass-roots level proved fatal. Electorally and organisationally the Conservative Party was in a state of crisis at the end of the twentieth century. The party's long period (sixteen years) in government fuelled a powerful mood among voters for change – for less sleaze, a more united government, more spending on public services and a change of government.

The party entered the 2001 general election with a new leader, William Hague, and ruled out membership of the single European currency for the present and next parliaments. But for all the changes in the party structure and Hague's early efforts to make the party more inclusive, the Conservatives were still damaged by:

1. Negative memories of the last years of the Thatcher and Major governments, not least the internal divisions, economic recession and sleaze.

2. The willingness of many voters to give Labour more time to improve public services.

3. The lack of press support, which had been so important under Mrs Thatcher in the 1980s and for John Major in 1992.

Labour enjoyed huge opinion poll leads and there were widespread expectations of another landslide victory. Conservatives promised to match Labour's proposals to increase spending on health and education as well as make a modest income tax reduction. The latter was greeted with widespread scepticism.

How could a government increase spending and cut taxes at the same time? In spite of voters placing public services at the top of their concerns, the Conservatives decided that they could not compete with Labour. Instead, they concentrated on their 'best' issues: Europe, tax, crime and asylum. But, apart from crime, these were not salient to voters. Hague seemed to be concentrating on his core vote rather than reaching out to others.

What is striking is just how little progress the Conservatives have made in the two general elections since the 1997 disaster. In 2001 the party made a net gain of one seat and in 2005 it gained 33 seats but increased its vote share by less than 1 per cent. It made little progress outside the southeast, and much of the north as well as Scotland and Wales remained a virtual no-go zone. The 2005 election result was a particular disappointment because there was so much dissatisfaction with the Labour record and loss of trust in Blair. The Conservatives still trailed Labour on economic competence, leadership and running the public services. The Conservatives' best issues were crime, tax and immigration/asylum but the last two did not rank highly as concerns, at least when it came to voting.

What was depressing for Conservative 'modernisers' was the party's image – how people perceived it. A Populus survey during the election campaign revealed that it was seen as sectional, divided, extreme, lacking strong leaders and not having its heart in the right place. Another poll found that once a relatively popular policy was identified as a Conservative one, support for the policy immediately fell away (Kavanagh and Butler, 2005, pp. 188–9).

Labour

As partisanship and class weakened in the 1970s and 1980s, so Labour's long-term future as a party of government became less secure. Its share of the vote did not reach 40 per cent in any general election between 1970 and 1992. Its 1983 share of 27.6 per cent was its lowest since 1918 (when Labour was still a new party and fighting its first nationwide election). In 1987 and 1992, the party made a modest recovery, but only to 34.4 per cent, over 7 per cent behind the Conservative vote. This was close to the party's 'normal' or expected vote. Increasingly, it seemed that Labour would require a remarkable combination of favourable circumstances to win outright victory at a general election.

Optimists could claim that Labour lost general elections because of the special circumstances associated with each election. It did badly in 1979 largely because of the public's hostile reaction to the trade unions and Labour government after the 'winter of discontent'. Before the 1983 election, there were bitter internal party rows over policies and changes

in the party's constitution, the breakaway of the Social Democrats, the weakness of Michael Foot as Labour leader and the bitter policy divisions. The 1987 election was held against a background of rising living standards; the platform of low inflation and falling unemployment would have made any government unbeatable.

However, it is difficult to find a convincing excuse for 1992. Given the mismanagement of the economy, a Tory campaign that was widely regarded as lacklustre and a government that had been in office for thirteen years, the odds were against the Conservatives. Clearly, more fundamental forces were at work, making the party into an electoral minority. Some political scientists asked whether 1992 was, or the following election would be, 'Labour's last chance' (Heath *et al.*, 1994). The forces are worthy of note. They were:

1. *Demographic*: The faster growth of population in the south compared with the north, the spread of home ownership and decline of council tenancy, contraction of the public sector (through privatisation) and heavy manufacturing jobs and growth of employment in service industries, and the fall in membership of unions: all have weakened the traditional social sources of support for Labour. The old working class – members of trade unions, engaged in heavy industrial work, renting property from a council and employed in the public sector – is a steadily diminishing electoral minority.

2. *Attitudinal*: Post-election research conducted for the party among wavering Conservatives showed the lack of enthusiasm for voting Labour. These target voters wanted to 'get on' or to consolidate the material gains they had made during the Thatcher years. Although they liked Labour's social policies, they regarded the party as a threat to their hopes of material advancement; the party was associated with 'equalising down' and 'holding back'. When he became Labour leader in 1994, Tony Blair was determined to win these people over to the party. The party had little future as – just or even mainly – a party of the working class but had to appeal to the middle class also.

Labour had changed greatly since 1992 and was able to profit from the mood for change. Under Tony Blair it made a hard-headed analysis of what had gone wrong in 1992 and what was required to win the next election. It abandoned its tax-and-spend image, distanced itself from the trade unions, and dismissed policies on defence and crime it had espoused in the 1980s, all in an effort to reassure 'middle England', particularly the middle class and the southeast. The party had to attract traditional non-Labour voters. It accepted much of the Thatcherite agenda – privatisation, existing income tax rates for the next parliament, aggregate public spending figures for the next two years, trade union reforms and a 'wait and see' attitude to British membership of the EU single currency. It embraced the latest techniques in electioneering and in Blair had a leader who made a point of being seen to lead his party, and to lead it in a new direction.

The scale of change in 1997 exceeded previous election landslides. Labour's majority of 179 dwarfed the Liberal one of 130 in 1906, Labour's 146 in 1945 and the Conservative's 142 in 1983. Labour's number of MPs (419) was greater than in 1945 (393). The 10 per cent swing from Conservative to Labour was the largest in any general election since 1945. The party's impressive gains across the country and among all groups in 1997 were held in 2001. If, historically, Conservative success among the majority working class was important in breaking the class–party link and explaining its success, now it was Labour's success in the majority middle class that was significant. In 1992, it trailed the Conservatives by 32 per cent in the middle class; in 2001, it was almost level (Table 9.1).

Third-party voting

The growth of a third force vote – or decline of aggregate support for the two main parties – may have different meanings. In four elections (1983–92) less than 75 per cent of votes were for Labour or Conservative. In the House of Commons, however, nearly 95 per cent of seats were Labour or Conservative. The disproportional effects of the first-past-the-post electoral system 'wasted' much Alliance and Liberal Democratic electoral support. But that picture has changed as of 2005. Tactical voting and concentration of campaign resources helped the Liberal Democrats to gain more seats in the 1997, 2001 and 2005 elections, the number of MPs who are neither Labour nor Conservative has now reached one in seven MPs, and the Labour–Conservative share of seats has fallen to 86 per cent.

In the House of Commons the third force has become particularly heterogeneous, covering nine parties. Apart from the Liberal Democrats it also includes Welsh and Scottish nationalists, the various Northern Ireland parties, Respect and an independent. Much of the popular support to date for 'other' parties outside Northern Ireland has not been translated into a sufficient number of seats to threaten the two main parties. In the 1974 elections the growth in Liberal support (to 19 per cent of the vote in the February election) and the rise of the nationalists in Scotland (to 30 per cent of the Scottish vote in October 1974) represented a potential threat. But these advances were not sustained, and both parties lost seats and votes in 1979. The most formidable threat yet to the dominance of the Labour–Conservative party system developed in 1981. Following the breakaway of a number of leading right-wingers from Labour to form the Social Democratic Party, its alliance with the Liberals enabled the new force to gain greatly from the unpopularity of the two major parties. Between March 1981 and March 1982, the Alliance was regularly first or second in the opinion polls and had a remarkable string of by-election successes. It failed to maintain its support and was disappointed in the 1983 election with its 25 per cent share of the vote and twenty-one seats.

In 2005 the Liberal Democrats won their third highest share of the vote since 1929 and their largest number of seats since 1923. But there were also more 'other' party votes (7.9 per cent) than in any general election since 1918. For example, the Greens gained their highest average vote, 3.4 per cent, where they stood, and did well in seats with university-educated voters; the anti-immigrant BNP did even better, gaining 4.3 per cent where they stood. The first-past-the-post system is less of a protection for the two main parties than it used to be, although it still provides more protection than a more proportional system would. The rejection of the two main parties is even greater if we take account of European elections (in 2004 the combined Labour and Conservative share did not reach 50 per cent) and elections for the devolved legislatures in Scotland and Wales. The fragmentation of political choice, emerging from the growth of minor parties, the impact of PR in non-Westminster elections, and the different party line-ups in different parts of the United Kingdom, mean that British general elections now give less of a national verdict.

Trends in party support

Elections in Britain were pretty competitive over the 1945–79 period, as the Labour and Conservative

Table 9.4 Calculation of the normal vote, 1974–92 (%), and comparisons with 1997–2005

	Conservative	Labour	Liberal	Other
Mean, 1945–70	45.2	46.1	7.1	1.6
Mean, February 1974–92	40.7	34.4	19.5	5.5
Mean, 1997–2005	31.6	39.8	19.0	10.0

parties were evenly matched in total votes and time in office. But since 1979, as in the interwar years, we may say that electoral competition has been imbalanced, with the Conservatives clearly the dominant party for the first half of the period and Labour in the second half. For most of the time parties have won elections with impressive majorities of seats.

Table 9.4 provides a computation of each main party's normal vote, or the share it should gain in normal circumstances. It is derived from each party's average vote share over the 1974–92 general elections. Special factors – e.g. a dynamic leader (Thatcher or Blair), the Falklands War (for the 1983 election) or the winter of discontent (for the 1979 election), or an outstanding or a disastrous economic record in government – can produce a variation in the figure. It is seen that the Conservatives had a substantial advantage over Labour. Yet speculation about Conservative **hegemony** was rudely disrupted only six months after its 1992 election triumph; following the exit from the ERM, no government has ever fallen so low in public esteem since opinion polling began over fifty years ago. ERM failure, tax increases, party divisions and sleaze provided the circumstances that massively reduced the normal vote for the Conservatives. Election results and opinion polls suggest a normal vote of some 32–33 per cent as of 2005.

■ **The 2001 general election**

The key questions for the 2001 election were:

1. Would Labour manage to hold much of its new support gained in 1997 and achieve Blair's ambition to win a second full term of office for the first time in Labour's history?

2. Could the Conservatives recover from the 1997 disaster and at least significantly reduce Labour's lead in seats and votes?

3. Could the breakthrough of nationalist parties in Scotland and Wales in the 1999 devolution elections be sustained?

The answers proved to be, respectively, yes, no, no.

Not all general elections are of equal significance when viewed in the long term. Some American political scientists (e.g. Key, 1955) have distinguished between elections that are:

■ *Maintaining*, in which voters reassert party loyalties and vote along traditional social lines. We would expect the outcomes to resemble the 'normal' pattern of voting as in Table 9.4.

■ *Deviating*, in which the traditional minority party wins, but the change proves to be short-lived.

■ *Critical*, in which new issues and events trigger a **realignment** in the shape of new bases of support for a political party, or the rise of a new party or a new balance between the political parties. Such a change (or changes) lasts for a number of elections.

The 1945 general election was clearly critical in the sense that, for the first time, Labour gained a clear majority of seats and was at last competitive with the Conservative Party. The four elections between 1979 and 1992 might also be considered a critical era, because the Conservatives moved into an average 10 per cent lead over Labour in the share of the popular vote. Labour's large lead in the 1997 election was clearly a break with what had occurred before. Other symptoms of significant change included Labour's substantial increase in support in the southeast and among the middle class (Norris, 1997). It is because these trends were confirmed in 2001 that we may consider the election or, better still, 1997 and 2001 together, to be critical.

The following features suggest that the 2001 general election might be regarded as 'more of the same':

■ Labour gained another landslide majority (167), and the Conservatives suffered another heavy defeat.

■ There was only a small swing (1.8 per cent) to the Conservative Party, and it made a net gain of only one seat.

■ Labour's overall majority over the other parties was cut by twelve and by only seven over the Conservatives.

■ A mere twenty-one out of 641 seats in mainland Britain changed hands. The Liberal Democrats gained six seats and Labour lost six.

■ In Northern Ireland, however, seven of the eighteen seats changed hands.

■ The 2005 general election

The main UK parties had reasons to be both pleased and disappointed with the outcome of the 2005 general election. Labour achieved a historic third victory in succession; the Conservatives could point to a net gain of 33 seats; and the Liberal Democrats had the largest number of seats for a third party since the 1920s. But Labour could also reflect that it lost 6 per cent of its 2001 vote and was forming a government with the lowest vote share ever; the Conservatives that they added only 0.5 per cent to their vote, made no progress in the north and the major cities, and now faced a challenge from the Liberal Democrats in attracting disillusioned Labour voters. Liberal Democrats wondered if they should have done better when faced with two unpopular parties and the advantages of 'one-off' issues like Iraq and tuition fees. But, as reported in Chapter 12, the minor parties continued to do well in 2005.

The pro-Labour impact of the working of the electoral system has been discussed in Chapter 8. For at least the past three decades two political nations have been emerging – a Labour north, Scotland and Wales, and a Conservative southeast and the shires and suburbs of England. However, Labour now has a more national presence because of its gains in the south. Because its support is drawn across social classes and regions it is now a catch-all party (Table 9.5). In contrast, the only groups in which the Conservatives have a clear lead over Labour have been the over-65s and home owners.

Although the Conservatives were probably more successful in getting supporters to vote on polling day than Labour, they are so far behind Labour that getting their voters out is not enough; the party needs to attract support from non-Conservatives and again it failed to do so. Labour ran far ahead on leadership, most of the key issues and party identification. Its challenge in the future is to mobilise its maximum vote (Kavanagh and Butler, 2005). The Liberal Democrats did well in seats with a large number of student or Muslim voters and gained from tactical voting.

Table 9.5 New Labour's support in middle Britain

	2005 vote		
	Conservative	Labour	Lib-Dem
All Great Britain voters	33	38	22
Men	33	38	23
Women	32	38	24
AB (middle class)	37	32	24
C1 (lower middle class)	34	35	24
C2 (skilled workers)	32	43	18
DE (unskilled workers)	28	45	19
65+	42	35	18
Home owners with mortgage	30	39	23
Home owners without mortgage	43	30	20
Council tenants	16	56	19

Source: ICM.

It may be too much of a cliché to refer to the convergence in policy between Labour and Conservative as consensus. But it appears that in large part the policy battles of the 1980s have been settled, for the present at least. Tony Blair had moved Labour to the new centre – largely Conservative-defined – ground. Labour has substantially accepted the principles of a market economy, low levels of direct taxation and flexible labour markets, all historic breaches with the party's traditions. The large number of 1992 Tories who switched to Labour in 1997 and have remained – although with some losses in 2005 – has been as much a reflection of disillusion with the former as a feeling of security with the latter.

But since 1997 the Conservatives have also gradually had to adapt to a Labour agenda. Before the 2001 general election they had accepted devolution, the minimum wage, independence of the Bank of England, the ending of hereditary peers in the House of Lords, the Social Chapter of the European Union, and prioritising more spending on public services over tax cuts. In the 2005 election the party offered very modest tax cuts and agreed to match Labour's planned spending on health and education. Since the general election the new leader, David Cameron, appears to be moving the party even closer to Tony Blair's ground (see Chapter 32). Blair might argue that he has won the battle of the middle ground and forced the Conservatives to accept his settlement.

Tony Blair takes advantage of a very modern innovation to get in front of a camera once again . . .
Source: Getty Images

Modern election campaigns have reached a new level of professionalism – spin doctoring and media management to shape public opinion, targeting of floating voters and key constituencies via computerised data banks, direct mail and telephone canvassing, and disciplined adherence by party spokespersons to messages or themes of the day. Much of this professionalism was more evident on the Labour than on the Conservative side. The controlled communications strategies of the main parties make the campaign less enticing, and the new technologies have lessened the personal contact between candidates and voters. Indeed, the number of voters who had been canvassed or received leaflets is substantially down on old-style elections. The 'targeting' by the parties on particular voters in particular seats, with the result that the parties bypass large parts of the country where the seat is 'safe' for a party, may be an additional factor contributing to the long-term decline in turnout.

The low turnout in general elections has caused much concern. The turnouts of around 60 per cent in 2001 and 2005 mean that the government has been returned by less than a quarter of the total electorate. Possible explanations are discussed in Chapter 8, but at some point support may sink so low that doubts may arise about the legitimacy of the government; after all, the legitimising function of elections has rested in large part on the expectation of high participation.

The Conservatives are still largely a party of the southeast and the shires and suburbs of England. However, Labour now has a more national presence because of its gains in the south. In social classes and regions it is now a catch-all party (see above).

General elections produce different patterns of voting from European (which the Conservatives won in 1999) and the post-devolution elections, in which nationalist support surged. In these 'second-order' elections, voters often take the opportunity to vote against the government of the day.

Despite the political damage inflicted on Tony Blair by the Iraq War, it did not appear to have a significant effect on voting behaviour in the 2005 election
Source: Copyright © Chris Riddell. From *The Observer*, 8 May 2005. Reproduced with permission from Guardian Newspapers Limited

■ The Liberal Democrat dilemma

Until the 1987 general election there was talk of realignment (or change) in the British party system, largely based on the rise of the Alliance, a centre grouping of Social Democrats and Liberals. It then seemed possible that the Alliance might overtake Labour as the second largest party, perhaps replacing that party or establishing itself as one of three major national parties. Labour held on and the Alliance faded. The successor Liberal Democrat Party was formed in 1988 and has never approached the voting strength of the earlier Alliance, although it has been more successful in gaining seats. As noted later in Chapter 12, the transformation of Labour under Tony Blair has squeezed the centre ground for the Liberal Democrats and the two parties cooperated before and after 1997.

Over time, however, the Lib Dems became disappointed with the results of this cooperation, and in 2001 Charles Kennedy abandoned it. After the 2001 election, Liberal Democrats talked about outflanking the Conservative Party, or gaining support from disillusioned Conservatives. But in the second half of the Parliament on many issues they moved to the left of Labour, favouring for example direct election for much of the House of Lords, entry to the European currency and a higher rate of income tax to fund more spending on services. And the party's opposition to the Iraq war and to increased tuition fees for higher education appealed to disillusioned Labour voters. In the past, the party has generally profited from positioning itself in the 'political middle', and gaining from both Conservative and Labour. But a YouGov survey in 2005 showed that as many Liberal Democrat as Labour

BOX 9.1   BRITAIN IN CONTEXT

Parties and finance

Britain is unusual among Western democracies in not providing direct state assistance to the parties or even tax credits for contributions or providing funds which match those raised by the parties/candidates (as in the US). There is of course indirect help for elections in the form of broadcasts.

But parties complain that elections are becoming more expensive (because of larger staffs, techno-logy and the increase in the number of elections and referendums) at a time when their memberships are declining. Their reliance on large donations from wealthy individuals or groups (e.g. trade unions) has led to allegations of money for influence or peerages in Britain. But there are similar problems in many other countries, even those which have state finance. The British parties now seem to be

turning to the idea of state finance. David Cameron has proposed that the taxpayer match the funds raised by parties up to a limit, that funds be related to a party's share of the vote at the previous election – arrangements similar to those in many other countries – and that there be tighter limits on the size of contributions (£50,000) and on campaign spending, though few states impose limits on the size of contributions and where they do the limits are often evaded.

Critics object that state funding will weaken incent-ives for people to join parties, that party leaders will be less beholden to members, that it will be difficult for new parties to compete fairly, and that other bodies (e.g. Political Action Committees in the US) can still spend money.

---

supporters placed themselves on the centre left of the political spectrum and shared many similar policy preferences. An election-day poll for Sky Television found that as many as one in four Liberal Democrat voters would have voted Labour 'but for the Iraq war'.

If there were to be a series of deadlocked parliaments and coalition or minority governments ensued, and there was continued large support

for a third party, pressure would almost certainly increase for a new set of rules of the electoral game. There is little historical evidence about how voters might react to such political and constitu-tional uncertainties. But the devolution elections in Scotland and Wales show that PR and multi-party politics provide voters with the opportunity to vote tactically – possibly against the party they most dislike.

Chapter summary

For much of the postwar period voting was fairly predictable. The dominance of the Conservatives in the 1980s produced new interpretations. There seemed to be a move to one-party government and for Labour to long-term decline. This has been replaced by speculation about Labour's long-term dominance and Conservative decline. The shift in voting behaviour has coincided with changes in the party system and perhaps in the political system.

Discussion points

■ Compare the impact of issues in recent general elections.

■ What is the significance of party leaders in election campaigning?

■ Are class factors still important in shaping voting behaviour?

Further reading

On the 2005 general election see Kavanagh and Butler (2005), Norris (2005), Bartle and King (2005), and Curtice (2005).

References

Bartle, J. and King, A. (eds) (2005) *Britain at the Polls 2005* (CQ Press).

Butler, D. and Kavanagh, D. (2002) *The British General Election of 2001* (Palgrave).

Butler, D. and Stokes, D. (1970, 1974) *Political Change in Britain* (Macmillan).

Curtice, J. (1997) 'Anatomy of a landslide', *Politics Review*, Vol. 7, No. 1.

Curtice, J. (2001) 'Repeat or revolution?', *Politics Review*, September, Vol. 11, No. 1.

Curtice, J. (2005) 'Historic triumph or rebuff?', *Politics Review*, September, Vol. 15, No. 1.

Heath, A., Jowell, R. and Curtice, J. (1994) *Labour's Last Chance?* (Dartmouth).

Kavanagh, D. and Butler, D. (2005) *The British General Election of 2005* (Palgrave).

Key, V.O. (1955) 'A theory of critical election', *Journal of Politics*, Vol. 17, No. 1, pp. 3–18.

King, A. (ed.) (1993) *Britain at the Polls 1992* (Chatham House).

Norris, P. (1997) *Electoral Change since 1945* (Blackwell).

Norris, P. (2002) *Britain Votes 2001* (Oxford University Press).

Norris, P. (ed.) (2005) *Britain Votes 2005* (Oxford University Press).

Norris, P., Curtice, J., Sanders, D., Scammell, M. and Semetko, H. (1999) *On Message* (Sage).

Sarlvik, B. and Crewe, I. (1983) *Decade of Dealignment* (Cambridge University Press).

Useful websites

http://www.psr.keele.ac.uk/area/uk/geol.htm
http://www.election.demon.co.uk
http://www.news.bbc.co.uk

CHAPTER 10

The mass media and political communication

Bill Jones

Learning objectives

- To explain the workings of the media: press and broadcasting.

- To encourage an understanding of how the media interact and influence voting, elections and the rest of the political system.

- To discuss how the pluralist and Marxist dominance theories help to explain how the media operate and influence society.

Introduction

Without newspapers, radio and pre-eminently television, the present political system could not work. The media are so all-pervasive that we are often unaware of the addictive hold they exert over our attentions and the messages they implant in our consciousness on a whole range of matters, including politics. This chapter assesses the impact of the mass media upon the workings of our political system, and some different theories about how they operate in practice.

■ The mass media

At the end of the pulsating European Cup Final in May 1999, the cameras roamed around the stadium, alighting briefly on delirious Manchester United fans waving scarves and chanting ecstatically. Then they moved to the other side of the stadium, where the Bayern Munich fans stood dejectedly, heads bowed in defeat, some in tears. Then these fans suddenly saw their images on the big screen and, forgetting their misery, erupted into delight. They had realised that their images were being broadcast to millions of people, and instantly glee exceeded gloom. This episode helps to illustrate the point made by Canadian writer, Marshall McLuhan, that the principal means of communication in modern society, television, has become more important than the messages it carries – to some extent 'the medium' has become 'the message'. The impact of the mass **media** on society has been so recent and so profound that it is difficult as yet for us to gauge its impact with any precision. But it is important to try, especially in relation to politics, and perhaps some cautious conclusions can thereby be drawn.

The term 'mass media' embraces books, pamphlets and film but is usually understood to refer to newspapers, radio and television. This is not to say that films, theatre, art and books are not important – Queen Elizabeth I (1533–1603), for example, believed that Shakespeare's *Richard II* foreshadowed plots against her, and Stendhal wrote that 'Politics in a literary work are a pistol shot in the middle of a concert, a crude affair though impossible to ignore.' However, perhaps the influence of literature is usually less instant and more long-term. Since the 1950s, television has eclipsed newspapers and radio as the key medium. Surveys indicate that three-quarters of people identify television as the most important single source of information about politics. On average British people now watch over twenty hours of television per week, and given that 20 per cent of television output covers news and current affairs, a fair political content is being imbibed. Indeed, the audience for the evening news bulletins regularly exceeds 20 million. Surveys also regularly show that over 70 per cent of viewers trust television news as fair and accurate, while only one-third trust newspapers.

Television is now such a dominant medium that it is easy to forget that its provenance has been so recent. During the seventeenth and early eighteenth centuries, political communication was mainly verbal: between members of the relatively small political élite; within a broader public at election times; within political groups such as the seventeenth-century Diggers and Levellers; and occasionally from the pulpit. Given their expense and scarcity at the time, books, pamphlets and **broadsheets** had a limited, although important, role to play; at the end of the eighteenth century pamphlets were very important in disseminating radical ideas.

The agricultural and industrial revolutions in the eighteenth century revolutionised work and settlement patterns. Agricultural villages gave way to vast conglomerations of urban industrial workers, who proved responsive to the libertarian and democratic values propagated by the American and French political revolutions. Orator Henry Hunt was able to address meetings of up to 100,000 people (the famous Peterloo meeting has been estimated at 150,000), which he did apparently through the power of his own lungs. (However, the fact is that such speakers had 'shouters' at various points in the vast audiences who turned to shout the speech in a series of relayed messages.) Later in the nineteenth century the Chartists and the Anti-Corn Law League employed teams of speakers supplementing their efforts with pamphlets – which could now be disseminated via the postal system.

By the end of the nineteenth century, newspaper editorials and articles had become increasingly important: *The Times* and weekly journals for the political élite, and the popular press – the *Mail, Mirror* and *Express* – for the newly enfranchised masses. **Press barons** such as Northcliffe, Rothermere and Beaverbrook became major national political figures, wooed and feared by politicians for the power that the press had delivered to them within a democratic political system (see also towards the end of the chapter on newspaper ownership). Britain currently has nine Sunday and ten daily newspapers; some three-quarters of the adult population read one. The **tabloid** *Daily Mirror* and the *Sun* had November 2005 circulations of 2.1 million and nearly 3.2 million, respectively (Table 10.1). There is a smaller but slowly growing aggregate circulation for the 'qualities' such as *The Guardian, The Times, The Independent* and the *Daily Telegraph*. The tabloids have a predominantly working-class circulation, the 'qualities' a more middle-class and well-educated readership. The *Daily Express* and the *Daily Mail* are more up-market tabloids and have a socially more representative readership. However, readerships are usually much greater than sales; for example, the *Sun* claims 8.5 million readers, among them more ABC1 readers than read *The Times* each day. In recent years *The Independent, The Times* and other more up-market titles have reduced the size of their publications to equate with the tabloids. *The Guardian* and *The Observer*, however, have chosen the midway 'Berliner' format; the *Daily Telegraph*, with its traditionally minded readership of nearly a million, has decided not to change. In most cases size reduction seems to have produced increased sales and helped push up sales of the 'quality' titles, while the tabloids (or 'redtops' as they are sometimes called) have generally suffered falling sales, though the *Daily Mail*, with sales of 2.3 million daily, now outsells the *Mirror*: see Table 10.1.

By tradition the British press has been pro-Conservative. In 1945, the 6.7 million readers of Conservative-supporting papers outnumbered the 4.4 million who read Labour papers. During the 1970s, the tabloid *Sun* increased the imbalance to the right, and by the 1992 election the Labour-supporting press numbered only *The Guardian* and the *Daily Mirror*, with the vast majority of dailies and Sundays supporting the government party: 9.7 million to 3.3 million. However, Major's administration witnessed an astonishing shift of allegiance. It had been anticipated by press irritation with Thatcher's imperi-

Table 10.1 Circulation of national UK newspapers, November 2005 (millions)

Dailies

Tabloids

Sun	3.2
Daily Mirror/Daily Record	2.1
Daily Star	0.8
Daily Record	0.4

Mid-market tabloids

Daily Mail	2.3
Daily Express	0.8

National 'quality' press

Daily Telegraph	0.9
The Times	0.7
Financial Times	0.4
The Herald	0.4
The Guardian	0.4
The Independent	0.3
The Scotsman	0.065
Overall total of average daily circulations	**12.765**

Sundays

News of the World	3.7
Mail on Sunday	2.3
Sunday Times	1.4
Sunday Mirror	1.4
The People	0.9
Sunday Express	0.9
Sunday Telegraph	0.7
Sunday Mail	0.5
The Observer	0.4
Star	0.4
Independent on Sunday	0.2
The Business	0.2
Scotland on Sunday	0.083
Sunday Herald	0.061
Overall total of average Sunday circulations	**13.144**

Source: Wring and Deacon (2005)

ous style, continued with the criticism that Major received for being allegedly weak as a leader and insufficiently robust in relation to European issues, and intensified after the disastrous Black Wednesday,

Table 10.2 Readership allegiances (%) of national daily newspapers, 2005 and (in brackets) 2001

	Labour	Con.	Lib Dem	Swing[a]
Guardian	43 (52)	7 (6)	41 (34)	8 (LD)
Independent	34 (38)	13 (12)	44 (44)	2 (LD)
Times	27 (28)	38 (40)	28 (26)	1.5 (LD)
Telegraph	13 (16)	65 (64)	17 (14)	2 (C)
Financial Times	29 (30)	47 (48)	21 (21)	–
Daily Express	28 (33)	48 (43)	18 (19)	5 (C)
Daily Mail	22 (24)	57 (55)	14 (17)	2 (C)
Sun	45 (52)	33 (29)	12 (11)	5.5 (C)
Mirror	67 (71)	11 (11)	17 (13)	4 (LD)
Star	54 (56)	21 (21)	15 (17)	1 (C)
Election result	36 (42)	33 (33)	23 (19)	3.1 (C)

[a] Percentage swings from Labour to (C) Conservatives, or (LD) Liberal Democrats.
Source: Wring and Deacon (2005)

16 September 1992, when Britain was forced out of the exchange rate mechanism. Stalwart Tory press supporters such as the *Mail*, *Times* and *Telegraph* aimed their critical shafts at the government and did not desist even after July 1995 when Major challenged his opponents to stand against him as party leader and won a none-too-convincing victory. In addition to these factors Labour had become **New Labour**, led by the charismatic Tony Blair and shorn of its unpopular policies on unions, taxes and high spending. As the election was announced the *Sun* caused a sensation by emphatically backing Blair. Its Murdoch-owned stable-mate, the Sunday *News of the World*, followed suit later in the campaign. It should be noted that by this time a large proportion of the reading public had decided to change sides, and it could be argued that editors were merely making a commercial judgement in changing sides too (see Tables 10.2 and 10.3 showing circulations and allegiances in the 2001 and 2005 general elections).

Table 10.3 Declarations of national newspapers, 2001 and 2005

	2001		2005	
	Allegiance	Circulation (m)	Allegiance	Circulation (m)
Daily press				
Guardian	Labour	0.40	Labour	0.34
Independent	Anti-Conservative	0.23	Lib Dem	0.23
Times	Labour	0.71	Labour	0.65
Telegraph	Conservative	1.02	Conservative	0.87
Financial Times	Labour	0.49	Labour	0.38
Daily Express	Labour	0.96	Conservative	0.87
Daily Mail	Anti-Labour	2.40	Conservative	2.30
Sun	Labour	3.45	Labour	3.26
Mirror	Labour	2.79	Labour	2.29
Star	Labour	0.60	No Preference	0.85
Sunday press				
Observer	Labour	0.45	Labour	0.42
Independent on Sunday	Anti-Labour landslide	0.25	Lib Dem	0.18
Sunday Times	Labour	1.37	Conservative	1.35
Sunday Telegraph	Conservative	0.79	Conservative	0.65
Mail on Sunday	Conservative	2.33	Anti-Labour	2.37
Sunday Express	Labour	0.90	Conservative	0.84
Sunday Mirror	Labour	1.87	Labour	1.53
News of the World	Labour	3.90	Labour	3.64
People	Labour	1.37	Labour	0.94
Star on Sunday	n/a	n/a	No preference	0.46

Source: Wring and Deacon (2005)

As in 1992, the *Financial Times* also backed Labour, and the *Express*, then owned by Labour peer Lord Hollick, swung leftwards from its usual true blue course before tacking back to the right under current owner and sometime Labour donor, Richard Desmond. No such doubts for the *Mail*, however, or the *Telegraph*, despite its determined scepticism over Europe. *The Times* refused to back any party in 1997 but urged its readers to vote for the Eurosceptic cause. Forced by its owner, Murdoch, to support the man he thought would be Prime Minister, the *Sun* found it difficult to avoid snarling over Blair's commitments to 'getting closer to the EU and giving more recognition to trade unions'. Moreover, the *Sun* ran more stories in favour of the Conservatives than Labour during the campaign, according to researchers at Loughborough University (Norris in King, 1997, p. 119). And in October 1999 it found itself praising the much derided Conservative leader William Hague for promising to resist British entry into the single currency. Finally, a change of course to the right was predicted when David Yelland stood down as editor in January 2003, making way for Rebekah Wade, formerly of the *News of the World* and allegedly a former Conservative supporter. Some claimed the *Sun*'s political editor, Trevor Kavanagh, had never shared Murdoch's enthusiasm for Tony Blair, and the paper often carried bitter criticism of the Labour leader. After David Cameron became leader of the Conservatives, Murdoch let it be known that a shift of his papers back to the Tories was a possibility.

BIOGRAPHY

Rupert Murdoch (1931–)

Australian media magnate. Educated at Oxford, where briefly a Marxist. Learned newspaper business in Australia but soon acquired papers in Britain, most famously the *Sun*, the *News of the World*, *The Times* and the *Sunday Times*. His company News International also owns Sky TV, and he owns broadcasting outlets all over the world, including China. Blair and Murdoch seem to get on well and he regularly calls to see the man he helped to elect in 1997. Even during the war in Iraq the *Sun* remained solidly behind Blair.

■ The tabloids

Many dismiss the tabloids as light on news and seriousness. It is true that the 'redtops' have changed the angle of their coverage in recent years, but the reason has been connected with the general decline in newspaper readership in the Western world.

Sunday paper sales declined from 17 million to 15 million in the period 1990–8, while dailies declined from 15 million to 13 million. Tabloids, less likely to attract loyal readerships, have tried every possible trick to win readers, from 'bimbos to bingo'. Marketing expert Winston Fletcher, writing in *The Guardian* (30 January 1998), pinpointed the formula, deplored by liberal opinion and politicians alike, that won readers: 'Publishers and editors know what is selling their newspapers with greater precision than ever before. And the figures show it is scandals, misfortunes and disasters.' In other words, 'sleaze sells'. Given the razor-sharp competition for audience share, it is surely regrettable but not so surprising that tabloids seize on scandalous stories like hungry dogs on bones. John Major's travails with sleaze stories have been well documented and helped to bring the Conservatives' eighteen years in power to an end in 1997. But Labour has been by no means immune either to sleaze or to the intrusive style of tabloid reporting which politicians and liberal-inclined opinion deplores but eagerly consumes. The foremost victim in recent years was David Blunkett, the remarkable blind Home Secretary who fell in love with a right-wing publisher, Kimberley Quinn, and who then discovered every detail of his relationship being read by the nation over its cornflakes for a number of weeks until evidence of undue favour having been shown to his mistress caused his downfall. After a period of purdah he was brought back into the Cabinet in 2005 only to perish by tabloid once again when his business activities appeared to be in breach of the ministerial code. It is not strictly true to attribute this form of persecution to the tabloids alone; while they often start the process, the quality press watch closely and join in the feeding frenzy as soon as they think it suitable and advantageous to sales.

But there is more to tabloids than lightweight stories; they sell by the million, and even if a vote is bought through blackening a politician's name, it counts as much as any other on election day. Media experts working for parties read the tabloids very carefully and react accordingly. In elections going back to the 1980s a close correlation was noted between issues run by the Conservatives and lead stories in the tabloids; it was known that certain tabloid editors had close links with Conservative Central Office. Tony Blair has long been convinced of the political importance of the tabloids. In 1997, he even wrote a piece pandering to their Euroscepticism explaining why he had a 'love' for the pound. On May Day 2001, the *Sun* championed the case of a Norfolk farmer who had been imprisoned for shooting an intruder in his house. To counter it Blair personally wrote a 975-word rebuttal during a weekend at Chequers. The *Sun* concluded from this evidence of Blair's respect for the tabloids that he was 'rattled'.

Alastair Campbell was chosen by Blair as his Press Secretary because of his intimate knowledge of the tabloids. They may not devote much space to serious politics but, as all votes count the same, they were targeted by New Labour as key opinion formers. Since Campbell left Number 10 in 2003 this view might have changed somewhat since sales have slumped by 20 per cent from 1990 to 1998, reducing the potency of this media sector for politicians.

■ Broadcasting

Adolf Hitler was the first politician to exploit fully the potential of radio for overtly propaganda purposes; Franklin Roosevelt with his fireside chats and Stanley Baldwin with his similar, relaxed, confidential style introduced the medium more gently, respectively, to US and British political cultures. Some politicians such as Neville Chamberlain were quite skilled at addressing cinema audiences via Pathé News films, but others such as the fascist leader Oswald Mosley – a fiery platform speaker – proved surprisingly wooden and ineffective. During the war, radio became the major and much-used medium for political opinion – Churchill's broadcasts were as crucial as many squadrons of aircraft – and news, while film drama was used extensively to reinforce values such as patriotism and resistance.

It was in 1952, however, that the television revolution began in earnest with Richard Nixon's embattled 'Checkers' broadcast, made to clear his name of financial wrongdoing. Offering himself as a hard-working honest person of humble origins, he finished his talk by telling viewers how his daughter had received a puppy as a present: he did not care what 'they say about it, we're gonna keep it!' (see

quotation below). This blatant appeal to sentiment proved spectacularly successful and confirmed Nixon's vice-presidential place on the Eisenhower ticket. Later on, television ironically contributed to Nixon's undoing through the famous televised debates with Kennedy during the 1960 presidential election contest. Despite an assured verbal performance – those listening on the radio thought he had bested Kennedy – Nixon, the favourite, looked shifty with his five o'clock shadow and crumpled appearance. Kennedy's good looks and strong profile gave him the clear edge. Politicians the world over looked, listened and learned that how you appear on television counts for as much as what you say (see below on 'Television and the image').

Richard Nixon – the 'Checkers' speech

I should say this: Pat doesn't have a mink coat, but she does have a respectable Republican cloth coat. One other thing I should probably tell you, because if I don't they'll be saying this about me too. We did get something, a gift, after the election . . . a little cocker spaniel in a crate all the way from Texas . . . And our little girl, Trisha, the six-year-old, named it Checkers. And you know, the kids love that dog, and I just want to say this right now, that regardless of what they say about it, we're gonna keep it!

Richard Nixon, US Vice-President, in the 'Checkers speech', after he had been accused of using campaign funds for his personal gain, 1952 (cited in Green, 1982)

What they say about the papers

The gallery where the reporters sit has become the fourth estate of the realm.

Lord Macaulay, 1828

The business of the New York journalist is to destroy the truth . . . We are the tools and vassals of rich men behind the scenes . . . We are intellectual prostitutes.

John Swinton, US journalist, 1880

As a journalist who became a politician . . . I formed rather a different view about the relations between government and the press. What shocked me when I was in government was the easy way in which information was leaked.

Norman Fowler, *Memoirs*, 1991

I am absolved of responsibility. We journalists don't have to step on roaches. All we have to do is turn on the light and watch the critters scuttle.

P.J. O'Rourke on the duties of journalists in relation to politics, *Parliament of Whores*, 1992, p. xix

The British Broadcasting Corporation (BBC) was established as a public corporation in 1926, a monopoly that was defended on the grounds that it provided a public service. At first, under the influence of John (later Lord) Reith it struck a high moral and 'socially responsible' note with a stated mission to 'inform, educate and entertain' (in that order of priority). The BBC set an example and a standard that influenced emergent broadcasting systems all over the world. Commercial television (ITV) broke the BBC monopoly and began broadcasting in 1955; commercial radio began in 1973. The BBC was granted a second television channel (BBC2) in 1964; a second ITV channel (Channel 4) began broadcasting in 1982, and Channel 5 in 1997. In February 1989, Rupert Murdoch's Sky Television began broadcasting using satellite technology. After a quiet start the new technology took hold and was operating at a profit by 1993. Many of the channels offer old films and popular programme repeats from the USA, but Sky News has established itself in the eyes of the public and politicians as a respectable and competent 24-hour news channel which stands comparison with the BBC's equivalent rolling service.

Although the Prime Minister appoints the chairman of the BBC and its board of governors, and the government of the day reviews and renews the BBC's charter, its governors are supposed to act in an independent fashion. The creation of the independent television network under the IBA in 1954 ended the BBC's monopoly in television broadcasting. Independent Television's chairman, like the BBC's, is appointed by the government. However, since ITV is financed out of advertising revenues it enjoys more financial independence from the government. On Wednesday 15 January 2003, Culture Secretary Tessa Jowell announced a major review of the BBC's remit in the light of the renewal of the corporation's charter in 2006. Much to the dismay of supporters of the BBC, it put the future of the licence fee back on the agenda. Many concerns had been voiced about the power of the corporation under its then Director General Greg Dyke, especially his forays into commercial fields, where existing companies cried foul regarding such taxpayer-funded competition.

BIOGRAPHY

Greg Dyke (1947–)

Source: Copyright © David Bebber / Reuters / Corbis

Director General of the BBC. Educated at Hayes Grammar School and York University, where he studied politics. Began life as a journalist and then moved to London Weekend Television as editor in chief in 1983, whence he held several top jobs at Television South and Pearson Television before becoming deputy DG of the BBC in 2000, shortly before moving up to the top post. Faced opposition from Rupert Murdoch and William Hague as a result of his £50,000 donation to the Labour Party before the 1997 election before being appointed. However, he was widely seen as the most innovative and energetic candidate to run the world's largest and most prestigious broadcasting organisation with a £2 billion per annum budget and 23,000 employees. In February 2004 he was forced to resign from the BBC after the Hutton report criticised the reporting and editing of stories in the aftermath of Andrew Gilligan's accusatory broadcast of 29 May 2003 which itself helped precipitate the suicide of MOD scientist, Dr David Kelly.

■ Media organisations and the political process

Television has influenced the form of political communication

Broadcasting – especially television – has had a transforming impact on political processes. Two minutes of exposure on peak-time television enables politicians to reach more people than they could meet in a lifetime of canvassing, handshaking or addressing public meetings. Alternatively, speaking on BBC Radio 4's early morning *Today* programme gains access to a largely up-market audience of over one million opinion formers and decision makers (Margaret Thatcher always listened to it and once rang in, unsolicited, to comment). In consequence, broadcasting organisations have become potent players in the political game: the regularity and nature of access to television and radio has become a key political issue; interviewers such as John Humphrys, John Snow and Jeremy Paxman have become important – and controversial – national figures; and investigative current affairs programmes – especially during the Thatcher years – have been the source of bitter political controversy.

A veteran US broadcaster's views on television news

For all those who either cannot or will not read, television lifts the floor of knowledge and understanding of the world around them. But for the others, through its limited exploration of the difficult issues, it lowers the ceiling of knowledge. The sheer volume of television news is ridiculously small. The number of words spoken in a half-hour broadcast barely equals the number of words on two-thirds of a standard newspaper page. That is not enough to cover the whole day's major events. Compression of facts, foreshortened arguments, the elimination of extenuating explanation – all are dictated by TV's restrictive time frame and all distort, to some degree, the news on television. The TV correspondent as well as his or her subjects is a victim of this compression. With inadequate time to present a coherent report, the correspondent seeks to craft a final summary sentence that might make some sense of the preceding gibberish. This is hard to do without coming to a single point of view – and a one

line editorial is born. The greatest victim in all this is our political process and in my view this is one of the greatest blots on the recent record of television news. **Soundbite** journalism simply isn't good enough to serve the people in our national elections. Studies have shown that in 1988 the average block of uninterrupted speech by a presidential candidate on the news networks was 9.8 seconds. The networks faithfully promised to do better in 1992. The average soundbite that year was 8.2 seconds. The networks promised to do better in 1996. Further, figures compiled by Harvard researcher Dr Kiku Adatto showed that in 1988 there was not a single instance in which a candidate was given as much as one minute of uninterrupted time on an evening's broadcast.

Compare these figures with those of the newscasts in 1968. Then the average soundbite was 42.3 seconds . . . and 21 per cent of soundbites by presidential candidates ran at least a minute.

In the nineteenth century, it was commonplace for political meetings to entail formal addresses from great orators, such as Gladstone or Lloyd George, lasting an hour or more. Television has transformed this process. To command attention in our living rooms politicians have to be relaxed, friendly, confidential – they have to talk to us as individuals rather than as members of a crowd. Long speeches are out. On television, orators are obsolete. Political messages have to be compressed into spaces of two to three minutes – often less. Slogans and key phrases have become so important that speech writers are employed to think them up. The playwright Ronald Millar was thus employed and helped to produce Margaret Thatcher's memorable 'The lady's not for turning' speech at the 1981 Conservative Party Conference.

Television and the image

Since the arrival of television, appearances have been crucial. Bruce (1992) quotes a study that suggested 'the impact we make on others depends on . . . how we look and behave – 55 per cent; how we speak – 38 per cent and what we say only 7 per cent. Content and form must therefore synchronise for, if they don't, form will usually dominate or undermine content' (p. 41). So we saw Harold Wilson smoking a pipe to pre-empt what his adviser Marcia Williams felt was an overly aggressive habit of shaking his fist to emphasise a point. Margaret Thatcher was the first leading politician to take image building totally professionally under the tutelage of her media guru, Gordon Reece. Peter Mandelson, Labour's premier spin doctor of the 1980s and 1990s, commented that by the mid-1980s 'every part of her had been transformed: her hair, her teeth, her nose I suspect, her eyebrows. Not a part of Mrs Thatcher was left unaltered.' Every politician now has a career reason to be vain; Granada Television's *World in Action* in 1989 wickedly caught David Owen personally adding the final touch to his coiffure from his own can of hair-spray just before going on air. Performing badly on television can have penalties inevitably; when Michael Howard refused to answer a question from Paxman fourteen times when Home Secretary he appeared shifty and evasive. George Galloway, moreover, appearing in the *Big Brother* reality show in 2006 did nothing to advance his political career or ideas – becoming a laughing stock instead. Just looking foolish too does not help, like the time Neil Kinnock, in front of serried ranks of cameras, tripped and fell into shallow waves on the beach at a Blackpool conference, or John Redwood's lips were caught in an agonised attempt to mime the words to the Welsh national anthem when Secretary of State for that country.

Some politicians are arguably barred from the highest office on account of their looks. Some say Kinnock's red hair (when he had any) and abundant freckles turned people off. The late Robin Cook's red hair and 'gnome-like' appearance were said by some experts to have disqualified him from the Labour Party's leadership despite his brilliant forensic skills and ranking as the foremost parliamentarian of his day. American political scientists also conjecture that, were he living today, Lincoln would never have been President with his jutting jaw and sunken eyes; similarly, Herbert Hoover's obesity would have meant failure as early as the nomination stage. The perfect candidate was held by some to be Gary Hart, candidate for the presidency in 1988: very good-looking, charismatic, a good speaker, overloaded with charm and extremely intelligent. It was his excessive liking for pretty young women, and then being found out, that proved his undoing with an American public that can insist on unreasonably high moral standards in its presidential hopefuls – although the success of the far from perfect Bill Clinton in 1992 and 1996, not to mention his survival of an impeachment process over his affair with Monica Lewinsky, suggests

that that nation has become a shade more realistic and more tolerant.

Broadcasters have usurped the role of certain political institutions

Local party organisation is less important now that television can gain access to people's homes so easily and effectively. However, the message is a more centralised national one, concentrating on the party leadership rather than local issues and local people. The phenomenon of the SDP has shown that a national party can now be created through media coverage without any substantial branch network. But it has also revealed how quickly such parties can decline once media interest wanes. (However, local members *are* important; the work of Seyd and Whiteley (1992) has proved that high local party membership and activity rates still have a positive effect on voting behaviour and correlate positively with higher poll results.)

The House of Commons has lost some of its informing and educative function to the media. Ministers often prefer to give statements to the media rather than to Parliament – often on College Green just outside the House – and television interviewers gain much more exclusive access to ministers than the House of Commons can ever hope for. Even public discussion and debate are now purveyed via radio and television programmes such as the BBC's *Today*, *Newsnight* and *Question Time*. Some hoped that televising the House of Commons would win back some of these lost functions, but others worried that the 'cure' would have damaging side-effects on the seriousness and efficacy of parliamentary procedures. Few consider these fears to have been justified after a decade and a half of televised proceedings.

The appointment of party leaders

In 1951, Attlee was asked by a Pathé News reporter how the general election campaign was going. 'Very well', he replied. When it became obvious that the Prime Minister was not prepared to elaborate, the interviewer asked him whether he wished to say anything else. 'No' was the blunt reply. Such behaviour did not survive the 1960s. Sir Alec Douglas-Home's lack of televisual skills was believed to have helped Labour to win the 1964 general election: he was smartly replaced by Edward Heath – himself not much better as it turned out, despite his relative youth. The success of Wilson and to a lesser extent

Callaghan as television communicators made media skills an essential element of any aspiring premier's *curriculum vitae*. This is what made the choice of Michael Foot as Labour's leader in 1981 such a mistake. A powerful public speaker, Foot was ill at ease on television, tending to address the camera like a public meeting and to give long rambling replies. Worse, he tended to appear with ill-chosen clothes and on one occasion with spectacles held together with sticking plaster. These shortcomings may seem trivial but they are important on television; research shows that viewers make up their minds about people on television within seconds. And, as we saw above, manner and appearance are crucial in determining whether the reaction is positive or negative. It could be argued that Neil Kinnock was elected substantially as the televisual antidote to Foot; he was a substantial improvement but still tended to give over-elaborate answers.

Personnel

Unsurprisingly, the media and politics have become more closely interrelated, with media professionals such as David Steel, Tony Benn, Bryan Gould, Austin Mitchell and Peter Mandelson going into politics, and Robert Kilroy-Silk, Brian Walden and Matthew Parris moving out of politics and into the media. The apotheosis of this tendency was represented by former US President Ronald Reagan, who used his actor's ability to speak lines to the camera to compensate, arguably, for other political inadequacies. His astonishing political success, and that of Arnold Schwarzenegger, is testimony to the prime importance of media skills in the current age. The US chat-show host Jay Leno wittily, and cynically, summed up the appeal of television for politicians as 'show business for ugly people'. Professional help has become commonplace, with many ambitious politicians attending television training courses.

Spin doctors

These fearsome-sounding new actors on the political stage focus their energies on ensuring that the media give the desired interpretation of events or statements. Their provenance is usually thought to have been during the eighties when the *New York Times* used the term in an October 1984 article to describe smartly dressed men and women who moved among crowds at political events and sought to explain what their political boss had *really* meant

to say. Since then the popular idea is of somewhat shadowy figures moving around and choreographing press conferences or on the phone to television executives cajoling and bullying to get their way. Kenneth Baker, when chairman of the Conservative Party and therefore a *de facto* senior 'spinner', pulled off one of the great coups of the art in 1991 over the local government elections when – in public fury over the poll tax – Labour won 500 seats and the Conservatives lost 900. However, Baker had assiduously targeted the two 'flagship' boroughs of Wandsworth and Westminster – both setting very low poll tax – and when their majorities actually increased a wholly false impression of victory was conveyed to the press and reflected therein (although having a sympathetic press must have helped).

One of the most controversial aspects of 'spinning' has been the tendency for media advisers to advance the careers of their bosses while undermining those of colleagues perceived as rivals or enemies. Charlie Whelan, for long Gordon Brown's adviser, was often accused of such behaviour, the explanation for which is threefold: that politics is a highly competitive activity in which success or defeat over an issue can determine a career; the media are crucial for the delivery of political messages, thus placing the 'spinner' at the centre of the action; and political advisers are dependent for their jobs on their political masters and the progress of their careers. Roy Hattersley offered a different slant on such briefings on the *World at One* programme on 7 January 2005 when he attributed 'briefing wars' to some extent to the fact that issues were not being properly discussed and resolved in Cabinet under Blair, with the consequence that ministers sought to fight their battles outside the Cabinet in this less formal and undesirable fashion.

The Labour Party, Tony Blair and 'spin'

For a generation . . . New Labour and spin doctors have been inseparable.

Editorial in *The Guardian*, 17 January 2003

One student of the media quoted a senior Labour spin doctor as saying: 'Communications is not an afterthought to our policy. It's central to the whole mission of New Labour' (Barnett and Gaber, 2001, p. 116). So it is hardly surprising that Labour has been demonised as the party that invests too much in presentation, in 'spin'. Roy Greenslade, writing in *The Guardian* on 6 June 2002, argues that it all began in response to the way Neil Kinnock was treated by the right-wing press during the eighties. He was given no 'honeymoon' when elected in 1983, but from the start was attacked as a 'windbag', weak and incompetent. The *Sun*, *Mail* and *Express* pulled no punches and built up their coverage – much of it based on no evidence – throughout the decade. Leading up to the 1992 election, the *Sun*, whose Kinnock-demonising potential was augmented when editor Kelvin McKenzie appointed Richard Littlejohn as a columnist, went to town two days before polling day, devoting nine pages to its 'Nightmare on Kinnock Street' feature. One page featured a 'leading psychic' who informed readers he had been in touch with historical figures on the topic of the election protagonists. Major, it seemed, was picked by Queen Victoria but Kinnock was the choice of Joseph Stalin. On election day itself the *Sun* pictured Kinnock's head in a light bulb with the caption 'If Kinnock wins today will the last person to leave the country please turn out the light.' Given this series of visceral and coordinated attacks, it is understandable that Peter Mandelson, then Labour Director of Communications, should decide on a defensive policy of confronting the right-wing press, of harrying, challenging and demanding retractions. Alastair Campbell, then political editor of the Labour *Daily Mirror*, was also energised in resisting the campaign and these two became recognised as leading the party's media fightback. Given their energy, determination and skill, the right-wing media soon found they were being matched. Some suggest that the word 'spin', with its overtones of deceit, was used by the right-wing press in an attempt to dismiss Labour's efforts, but the term soon became all too synonymous with the New Labour approach. Tony Blair, schooled in the dog days of Labour's years in opposition, needed no encouragement to focus on presentation. He became expert at inserting soundbites into his weekly jousts with John Major at Question Time, at photo-shoots, and in the whole gamut of media manipulation employed to such good effect by Bill Clinton in the USA at that time. Under Mandelson and Campbell, Labour's period in opposition from 1992 to 1997, combined with Major's failing performance, became a one-way street of media dominance. The 1997 election victory was a foregone conclusion but few, including Blair, had expected such a huge majority. Right-wing control of the media had induced a deep sense of insecurity in Labour which did not disperse once the levers of power were in Labour hands.

BIOGRAPHY

Alastair Campbell (1957–)

Tony Blair's press secretary. Educated at Cambridge; had a career in tabloid journalism before joining Blair's personal staff. Often referred to as the 'real Deputy Prime Minister', he had constant access to his boss, and his words were held to carry the authority of the PM. He was well known to journalists and he used charm and threats to get his own way. Some Labour voices always believed him too powerful, but his appearance before a Commons Select Committee revealed that he can defend himself with gusto and effectiveness. In 2003 he was incensed when accused via a BBC interview of 'sexing up' the intelligence dossier used to justify the decision to go to war in Iraq. He was exonerated eventually but the ensuing media furore – during which he was accused of vindictiveness against the BBC – proved to be his swansong as he stepped down in the autumn of that year, still defiant and largely contemptuous of the nation's media.

Mr Campbell lives and breathes for Tony Blair. He is the tough aggressive half of Tony Blair, the side of Tony Blair you never see in public. He writes most of what Tony Blair says. He writes almost everything that appears under Tony Blair's name. So sometimes, when Mr Blair is answering questions in the Commons, I like to watch Mr Campbell as he sits above his boss in the gallery. You sense his face is reflecting what the Prime Minister is thinking but cannot possibly reveal to MPs. When he comes up with a good line, and the loyal sycophants behind him applaud, Mr Campbell beams happily. Sometimes he rolls his head in pleasure at his own jokes. When Mr Blair is worsted, as happens quite a lot these days, Mr Campbell has two expressions. One is merely glum; the other a contemptuous grimace, which implies only a moron could imagine that Mr Hague had scored any kind of point.

Source: Simon Hoggart, 'Commons Sketch: no joke for No. 10 when Hague gag hits the target', *The Guardian*, 11 November 1999. © Guardian Newspapers Limited 1999, reproduced with permission

It soon became evident to commentators (e.g. Franklin, 1999) that the iron discipline regarding the media which had helped Labour win power was being retained in office, often involving the same people and the same ruthless focus on presentation. After a while Labour became associated, in a pejorative sense, with the word 'spin'. Evidence that some claims of increased expenditure on health and education involved double counting of sums already announced reinforced the impression that the word of New Labour could not be wholly trusted. The editorial in *The Observer* of 19 May 2002 commented that 'Health Secretary Alan Milburn and Chancellor Gordon Brown have only themselves to blame if they are criticized for these unnecessary exaggerations.' It soon became so much of an embarrassment that by the spring of 2002 Mandelson and Campbell sought to remove the slur by relaxing lobby rules and making its workings more transparent, and making Blair more available to both the media and Parliament with in-depth *Newsnight* interviews with Jeremy Paxman. This did not deter former deputy leader Roy Hattersley from declaring that 'Campbell is a liability and must go.' In reality the coordination of communications was extended across the whole gamut of government.

Veteran spin doctor Bernard Ingham was not fooled; he did not believe spin had been banished. 'Spin is still everywhere', he wrote in the *Sunday Times* of 16 March 2003, 'and because of spin, Blair has forfeited the trust of the nation and . . . parliament.' Opinion polls gauging public trust in Blair certainly reinforced such a judgement, and some even attributed the shockingly low turnout in the 2001 election to a collapse of voter belief in what the government was saying. Ingham claimed that New Labour, once in power after 1997, had quickly culled the ranks of the Government Information Service (GIS) of anyone not sympathetic to the government and had effectively 'hijacked the GIS for party political ends.' Out of 44 top posts in the GIS, 25 had left within a year of Blair entering Downing Street. Ingham estimated that up to half of the 81 'special advisers' appointed by Labour were involved with the media. In January 2003 even Speaker of the Commons Michael Martin joined predecessor Betty Boothroyd's August 1998 call for the harnessing of 'party apparatchiks' by describing spin doctors as 'an absolute nuisance' whom he urged ministers to 'do away with'. And with the spin came paranoia: just like the Conservatives, Labour aimed some of its bile against the *Today* programme on Radio 4,

blaming John Humphrys for grilling ministers with what it felt was excessive zeal.

Spin came back to bite Blair again over the Iraq War in 2003 when it was alleged that the dossier prepared by government based on intelligence reports had been the product of spin doctor embellishments. Official reports by Lords Hutton and Butler cleared Blair and his office of impropriety but, for many, evidence submitted to the inquiries proved the charge fairly convincingly. Campbell stepped down from leading Blair's media operation in September 2003 but he returned to assist during the 2005 election. Mandelson, after being forced to resign a second time in 2001, departed to become an EU Commissioner in 2004, but it was an open secret that he was still available to advise his old friend via the phone. Evidence of how controversial Labour communications management had become was the establishment in January 2003 of an independent review to be chaired by Bob Phillis (see Box 10.1).

It would be foolish to accuse New Labour of inventing spin; even before the advent of mass media, governments sought to offer the best possible interpretations of their actions. Yet, for all its expertise, Blair's operation has lacked subtlety. Campbell acquired too high a profile as the demonic spinner and even featured as the subject of a televised profile. Blair too once asked in a leaked 2000 memo for 'more eye-catching initiatives' to combat Conservative policy statements. If 'Iraq' is to be inscribed on Tony Blair's political tombstone, as seems likely, then the word 'spin' will be right alongside it.

The televising of Parliament

When the proposal that the proceedings of Parliament be televised was first formally proposed in 1966, it was heavily defeated. While other legislative chambers, including the House of Lords, introduced the cameras with no discernible ill effects, the House of Commons resolutely refused, chiefly on the grounds that such an intrusion would rob the House of its distinctive intimate atmosphere: its 'mystique'. By the late 1970s, however, the majorities in favour of exclusion were wafer thin and the case would have been lost in the 1980s but for the stance of Margaret Thatcher. In November 1985, it was rumoured that she had changed her mind, but at the last minute she decided to vote true to form and a number of Conservative MPs – known for their loyalty (or obsequiousness, depending on your viewpoint)

BOX 10.1   IDEAS AND PERSPECTIVES

The Phillis Report

Set up in January 2003 to review Whitehall communications, the Phillis Report came out a year later, making the following major recommendations.

1. *A strong central communications structure*: The appointment was urged of a permanent secretary for government communications to work alongside the Director of Communications in order to build a 'new and authoritative communications service within government'. In July 2004 Howell James was appointed to such a post to provide 'strategy and coordination and effectiveness across Whitehall'.
2. *Disband the Government Information and Communications Service (GICS)*: Weaknesses had been found in the existing service which made it 'no longer fit for purpose'.
3. *Greater emphasis on regional communication*: People want information which is more relevant to them and so more communicating is necessary at the local and regional levels.
4. *Recruitment and training* to raise professional standards and maintain Civil Service impartiality.
5. *Clearer definitions of boundaries* between special advisers and the Civil Service.
6. *Effective implementation of the Freedom of Information Act 2000*: A culture of secrecy persists in Whitehall.
7. *New briefing of media policy*: All major briefings to be on the record, live on television and radio with full transcripts available promptly online.
8. *Reappraisal of relationship between politicians and the media*: Need to consider how trust in legitimate government can be restored.

– about to vote for the televising of the House instead rushed to join their leader in the 'No' lobby.

Even after the vote in favour of a limited experiment the introduction of the cameras was substantially delayed, and the Select Committee on Procedure introduced severe restrictions on what the cameras could show: for example, only the head and shoulders of speakers could be featured, reaction shots of previous speakers were not allowed, and in the event of a disturbance the cameras were to focus immediately on the dignified person of the Speaker. Finally, however, on 21 November 1989 the House appeared on television, debating the Queen's Speech. Margaret Thatcher reflected on the experience as follows:

I was really glad when it was over because it is ordeal enough when you are speaking in the Commons or for Question Time without television, but when you have got television there, if you are not careful, you freeze – you just do . . . It is going to be a different House of Commons, but that is that.

The Times, 24 November 1989

In January 1990 the broadcasting restrictions were relaxed: reaction shots of an MP clearly being referred to were allowed, together with 'medium-range' shots of the chamber some four rows behind the MP speaking or from the benches opposite. By the summer of 1990, it was obvious even to critical MPs that civilisation as we know it had not come to an end. On 19 July, the Commons voted 131–32 to make televising of the chamber permanent. David Amess MP opined that the cameras had managed to 'trivialise our proceedings and we have spoilt that very special atmosphere we had here'. His was a lone voice, although in December 1993 Michael Portillo surprisingly joined him, regretting his own original vote in favour. However, one unforeseen consequence of the cameras has been the reduction of members in the chamber. Now it is possible for MPs to sit in their offices and do their constituency business while keeping abreast of proceedings on their office televisions.

Television has transformed the electoral process

Since the 1950s, television has become the most important media element in general elections. Unlike in the USA, political advertising is not allowed on British television, but party political broadcasts are allocated on the basis of party voting strength. These have become important during elections and increasingly sophisticated, and some – like the famous Hugh Hudson-produced party political broadcast on Neil Kinnock in 1987 – can have a substantial impact on voter perceptions. More important, however, is the extensive news and current affairs coverage, and here US practice is increasingly being followed:

1. Professional media managers – such as Labour's Peter Mandelson – have become increasingly important. Brendan Bruce, Conservative Director of Communications 1989–91, comments: 'The survival of entire governments and companies now depends on the effectiveness of these advisers yet few outside the inner circles of power even know these mercenaries exist or what their true functions are' (Bruce, 1992, p. 128). The Conservatives employ professional public relations agencies, the most famous of which was Saatchi and Saatchi. Labour could not afford such expensive help in the 1980s, so a group of volunteers from the advertising world was set up known as the 'Shadow Communications Agency'. Later Labour did employ a specialist PR company and Philip Gould, a former advertising executive, became one of Blair's closest advisers. It is also possibly the case that Conservative media managers have not been quite as able as Labour's, though their recruitment of Lynton Crosby for the 2005 election was perhaps an exception. The Conservatives lost, of course, but Crosby's focus on winnable seats was shrewd and paid some kind of dividend with a small overall increase in the party's vote.

2. Political meetings have declined. Political leaders now follow their US counterparts in planning their activities in the light of likely media coverage. The hustings – open meetings in which debates and heckling occur – have given way to stage-managed rallies to which only party members have access. Entries, exits and ecstatic applause are all meticulously planned with the all-ticket audience as willing and vocal accomplices. Critics argue that this development has helped to reduce the amount of free public debate during elections and has shifted the emphasis from key issues to marketing hype. Defenders of the media answer that its discussion programmes provide plenty of debate; during the seventies and eighties Granada TV ran a television version of the hustings – *The Granada 500* – whereby a representative 500 people from the northwest regularly questioned panels of politicians and experts on the important issues. Moreover BBC's *Question Time* attracts good audiences and provides a national forum for debate involving the public, politicians and other well-known personalities.

3. Given television's requirements for short, easily packaged messages, political leaders insert pithy, memorable passages into their daily election utterances – the so-called soundbite – in the knowledge that this is what television wants and will show in their news broadcasts and summaries throughout the day (see quote from Walter Cronkite above).

4. Party Political Broadcasts (PPBs) comprise slots allocated to the parties either on the basis of their voting performance at the previous election or on the number of candidates they are fielding. The first was made by Lord Samuel for the Liberals in 1951 but they were seldom skilfully made until 1987 when Hugh Hudson made a film of Neil Kinnock which was widely praised and impressively raised his personal ratings. In 1992 a similar PPB appeared about John Major's life but it lacked the same impact. In 1997 Major vetoed a PPB which represented Blair as a Faust-like figure, prepared to sell his principles for electoral victory. In recent years PPBs have declined further in importance. During the 1980s they averaged nine minutes in length but by 2005 this figure had come down to a mere two and a half minutes.

The media and pressure groups

Just as individual politicians influence the media and seek their platforms to convey their messages, so do pressure groups as they seek to influence government policy. Pressure group campaigners such as Peter Tatchell of Outrage! and Tony Juniper of Friends of the Earth are expert in knowing about and massaging the form in which the press and television like to receive stories. Because it has been so successful, much pressure group activity now revolves around using the media. Anti-blood-sports campaigners use yellow smoke when trying to disrupt hunting events as they know television responds well to it. Greenpeace campaigners occupied a French ship in the Pacific during the nuclear tests in 1995 and kept in touch with the world's press right up to the moment when they were forcibly ejected and were able to adopt 'martyrs' clothes' on behalf of their organisation. A similar approach was used by Greenpeace during the 1995 campaign to prevent Shell's oil platform, *Brent Spar*, from being disposed of by sinking it in the ocean. On a more limited but no less effective level, the Snowdrop campaign to achieve a total ban on handguns following the Dunblane massacre of schoolchildren by a crazed gunman in 1996 was able to win the nation's attention through a huge petition and high-profile appearances by its leaders at the 1996 Labour Party conference and on countless news bulletins on both television and radio. These examples merely underline the axiom that to a large extent in modern, developed societies, politics – at all levels – is conducted via the media.

The mass media and voting behaviour

Jay Blumler *et al.* wrote in 1978 that 'modern election campaigns have to a considerable extent become fully and truly television campaigns.' But what impact do the mass media have on the way in which citizens cast their votes? Does the form that different media give to political messages make any major difference? Substantial research on this topic has been undertaken, although with little definite outcome. One school of thought favours the view that the media do very little to influence voting directly but merely reinforce existing preferences.

Blumler and McQuail (1967) argued that people do not blandly receive and react to political media messages but apply a filter effect. Denver (1992, p. 99) summarises this effect under the headings of selective exposure, perception and retention.

1. *Selective exposure*: Many people avoid politics altogether when on television or in the press, while those who are interested favour those newspapers or television programmes that support rather than challenge their views.

2. *Selective perception*: The views and values that people have serve to 'edit' incoming information so that they tend to accept what they want to believe and ignore what they do not.

3. *Selective retention*: The same editing process is applied to what people choose to remember of what they have read or viewed.

This mechanism is most likely to be at work when people read newspapers. Most people read a newspaper that coincides with their own political allegiances. Harrop's studies produce the verdict that newspapers exert 'at most a small direct influence on changes in voting behaviour among their readers' (quoted in Negrine, 1995, p. 208 – see Table 10.4 later in this chapter for differences between press and television influences).

Election results in 1983 and 1987 have given support to the reinforcement-via-filter-effect argument. In a thorough empirical study of these elections, Newton (1992) found a result that was 'statistically and substantively significant'. The impact seemed to vary from election to election and to be greatest when the result was closest. It would also seem that the Labour press was more important for the Labour vote than the Conservative press for the Conservative vote (Newton, 1992, p. 68). Both these media-dominated election campaigns, moreover, had little apparent impact on the result. Over 80 per cent questioned in one poll claimed they had voted in accordance with preferences established before the campaign began, and the parties' eventual share of the vote accorded quite closely with pre-campaign poll ratings. In 1983, the Conservatives kicked off with a 15.8 per cent lead over Labour and finished with a 15.2 per cent advantage. Some weeks before the election in 1987 the average of five major polls gave Conservatives 42 per cent, Labour 30.5 per cent and the Alliance 25.5 per cent; the final figures were 43, 32 and 23 per cent, respectively – and this despite a Labour television campaign that was widely described as brilliant and admired even by opponents. Perhaps people had 'turned off' in the face of excessive media coverage? Certainly, viewing figures declined and polls reflected a big majority who felt coverage had been either 'too much' or 'far too much'.

However, the filter-reinforcement thesis seems to accord too minor a role to such an all-pervasive element. It does not seem to make 'common' sense. In an age when party preferences have weakened and people are voting much more instrumentally, according to issues (as we saw in Chapter 9), then surely the more objective television coverage has a role to play in switching votes? Is it reasonable to suppose the filter effect negates all information that challenges or conflicts with established positions? If so, then why do parties persist in spending large sums on party political broadcasts? Some empirical data support a direct-influence thesis, especially in respect of television:

1. Professor Ivor Crewe maintains that during election campaigns up to 30 per cent of voters switch

their votes, so despite the surface calm in 1983 and 1987 there was considerable 'churning' beneath the surface. These two elections may have been unusual in any case: the before and after campaign variations were much larger in 1979, 1974 and 1970 although not in the landslide 1997 election.

2. Many studies reveal that the four weeks of an election campaign provide too short a time over which to judge the impact of the media. Major shifts in voting preference take place between elections, and it is quite possible that media coverage plays a significant role.

3. Following the Hugh Hudson-produced party political broadcast in 1987, Neil Kinnock's personal rating leapt sixteen points in polls taken shortly afterwards. It could also be that without their professional television campaign Labour might have fared much worse.

4. In the wake of the 1992 victory, the former Conservative Party treasurer, Lord McAlpine, congratulated the tabloid press for effectively winning the election. The *Sun* responded with the headline (12 April) 'It's the Sun wot won it'. Neil Kinnock agreed. In November 1995, Martin Linton of *The Guardian* reported on a twelve-month study which supported the view that the *Sun* and other tabloids had made a crucial difference to the election result. Labour's *post mortem* inquiry calculated that 400,000 votes were swung by the tabloids in the crucial last week of the campaign; MORI's research, based on 22,000 voters, reinforced this claim and the proposition that the tabloids could have made the difference between who won and who lost.

Assessing the effect of the media

Judging the effect of the media on voting behaviour is very difficult, because it is so hard to disentangle it from a myriad of factors such as family, work, region and class that play a determining role. However, it seems fair to say that:

1. *The media do reinforce political attitudes*: This is important when the degree of commitment to a party can prove crucial when events between elections, as they always do, put loyalties to the test.

2. *The media help to set the agenda of debate*: During election campaigns party press conferences

attempt to achieve this, but the media do not always conform, and between elections the media, especially the print media, play a much more important agenda-setting role.

3. *It is clear that media reportage has some direct impact* on persuading voters to change sides, but research has not yet made clear whether this effect is major or marginal.

The 2005 general election campaign

As in 2001 the Conservatives were the first out of the trap with a succession of populist themes like dirty hospitals and discipline in schools. Their slogan 'Are you thinking what we're thinking?' was cleverly pitched to appeal both to former Conservatives and to those irritated by Labour's alleged political correctness. As the campaign progressed the Conservatives focused more on immigration, the issue on which polls showed them to be favoured more than any other issue. But some evidence emerged that the public was reacting negatively to this concentration of attention. In South Dorset, where Labour held on with a wafer-thin majority, the Tory candidate played the immigration card but saw his opponent's majority increase. Michael Howard was the focus of much electioneering but his personal image was so compromised by his time in previous Tory governments that his attractive wife, Sandra, was made his constant companion.

Labour suffered to some extent from a lack of Gordon Brown in the early stages of the campaign – upset that Alan Milburn had been given his job of election manager, so it was said. Another disadvantage was the party's campaign slogan – 'Forward not Back' – surely a candidate for the most vacuous slogan ever coined? After a lacklustre beginning, Brown joined the fray and Labour picked up, influenced possibly by Brown's higher trust rating and by a positive public reaction to both men working together. Towards the end of the campaign, revelations that Lord Goldsmith, the Attorney-General, had changed his mind over the legality of the Iraq War in the run-up to the invasion caused extreme discomfort for Blair, but the Conservatives were hampered from exploiting this by their own support for the conflict. Blair decided to confront his critics on the war head-on in a number of public meetings. This approach – the so-called 'Masochism Strategy' – had the advantage of displaying courage under fire but the degree of success it achieved was arguably negative.

Alan Milburn came out of semi-retirement to manage the election campaign, but was much criticised for his efforts
Source: Copyright © Toby Melville / Reuters / Corbis

The Liberal Democrats did benefit from their anti-war stance, and the laid-back style of Charles Kennedy suited those who had tired of the noisy two-party debate. Unfortunately for Kennedy, such a laid-back style did not prove suitable for the post-election period when he was criticised for lack of dynamism and ideas (he resigned several months later through an admitted drink problem).

An American view on election coverage

'Then there was the astonishing performance of a man called Jeremy Paxman. Americans are used to outsize television personalities . . . but this coiffed, smug pompous jerk? He seemed to ask no questions that demanded an answer; he insulted with a form of adjacent arrogance; he interrupted any response he didn't want . . .'

Andrew Sullivan, *Sunday Times*, 8 May 2005

Focus groups

Much has been written about New Labour and focus groups, and a great deal of it has been uncomplimentary. They have been cited as evidence of Labour's concern with the superficial, with adapting policy on the basis of marketing expediency and not principle – in other words, as the thin end of the wedge that Old Labour critics argue has robbed the party of its moral purpose and integrity. This point of view is hotly refuted by the chief enthusiast for the technique in the Blairite party: Philip Gould, former advertising expert, who has written a fascinating book on the evolution of the 'new' party and its march to power (Gould, 1999). In the following extract he explains the technique and his own reasons for having faith in it:

I nearly always conduct focus groups in unassuming front rooms in Watford, or Edgware or Milton Keynes or Huddersfield, in a typical family room stacked with the normal knick-knacks and photos. The eight or so members of the group will have been recruited by a research company according to a formal specification: who they voted for in the last election, their age, their occupation . . . I do not just sit there and listen. I challenge, I argue back, I force them to confront issues. I confront issues myself. I like to use the group to develop and test ideas.

I nearly always learn something new and surprising. People do not think in predictable ways or conform to conventional prejudice. In a group it is possible to test out the strength and depth of feeling around an issue, which can be more difficult, although not impossible with a conventional poll.

I do not see focus groups and market research as campaigning tools; increasingly I see them as an important part of the democratic process: part of a necessary dialogue between politicians and the people, part of a new approach to politics.

Gould (1999), pp. 327–8

On 22 April 2003, *The Guardian* reported how the Department of Education's use of focus groups had effectively torpedoed government plans for a graduate tax at that time: they had revealed that middle-class voters 'could not stomach the prospect of paying back more than the cost of their university course after they graduate through the tax system'.

The permanent campaign

In 2000, Ornstein and Mann edited a book entitled *The Permanent Campaign, and its Future*. The

BOX 10.2 **EXAMPLE**

Cheriegate – Jonathan Freedland's rules for surviving the media

In November–December 2002, Cherie Blair was revealed to have taken advice from an aide's boyfriend, one Peter Foster, who turned out to be a convicted conman. In the ensuing row, exposed by the *Daily Mail* and which rumbled on for weeks, Cherie was much traduced, and in December she made an emotional public statement in an attempt to clear up the matter. *The Guardian*'s Jonathan Freedland, in the wake of the speech (11 December 2002), offered ten rules for surviving the media in such situations. They included the following:

1. *It's never the crime, it's always the cover-up*: This is a lesson exemplified by Presidents Nixon and Clinton, but it is still ignored; it was by Cherie Blair, who initially seemed economical with the truth, thus egging on her pursuers.
2. *Get all the facts out in one go*: The media love to let such facts seep into the public domain, each one offered as a sensational revelation.
3. *Context and timing is all*: Blair got away with the Bernie Ecclestone affair in 1997 because it fell in the 'honeymoon' period. By 2002, the public mood was more cynical and less easy to reassure that all was well.
4. *Hypocrisy is always a killer*: Major was damaged by 'back to basics' as the revelations of Conservatives' peccadilloes seemed to attach a big label of 'hypocrite' to the whole party.
5. *Scandals are not legal, they're political*: Cherie tended to offer a legal defence initially, while the political problem required the more emotional statement she made later.
6. *Guilt by association may not be fair, but it's real*: People are judged by their friends to a large extent; a Prime Minister's wife has to realise this.
7. *When all else fails make a personal statement*: Cherie did this brilliantly on 10 December.

BOX 10.3 **IDEAS AND PERSPECTIVES**

John Lloyd's critique of the media, and a journalist's response

In his book *What the Media are Doing to Our Politics* (Lloyd, 2004), journalist John Lloyd diagnoses a parlous condition in the strained dealings between media and politics in Britain, not to mention other Western liberal democracies. He sees the relationship as one which has evolved from a fractious symbiosis to a damaging struggle for power in which the media have:

Claimed the right to judge and condemn; more, they have decided – without being clear about the decision – that politics is a dirty game, played by devious people who tell an essentially false narrative about the world and thus deceive the British people. This has not been the only, but it has been the increasingly dominant narrative which the media have constructed about politics over the past decade or so and, though it has suffered some knocks, remains dominant.

Lloyd (2004), p. 35

Certainly politicians presaged Lloyd's claims in the form of Charles Clarke's broadside in *The Times* of 12 June 2002 in which he accused 'the hypocritical media of bringing democratic politics into disrepute'. Geoff Mulgan, one of Blair's closest advisers, added his view in May 2004 that government was losing its legitimacy through the media's 'systematic failure to report the truth'. More support for Lloyd's thesis perhaps is evident in the aggressive interviewing techniques – which seem to assume ulterior dark or hidden motives – that have placed politicians on the defensive since about the mid-sixties, and also, more arguably, in the assumptions underlying the BBC's stigmatising of the government over the Gilligan interview in May 2003 which set in train the events leading to the death of Dr David Kelly and the ensuing Hutton and Butler reports. In his Reuters lecture in October 2005, Lloyd discerned a 'parallel universe' which his colleagues inhabited and described but which bore little relation to the real world in which the real actors – politicians, corporate executives, trade union leaders, bishops, NGO heads – live and seek to do their jobs. But do these negative assumptions constitute a correct view or are these actors justified in complaining that what the media report is 'deeply inadequate'?

Various journalist reviewers of Lloyd's book were not impressed, but on 10 October 2005, *The Guardian* asked a number of these 'actors' to give their own views. Most felt the charges were justified. Tony Wright MP, academic and chair of the Public Administration Select Committee, felt the media should accept that they too had played a role in 'the collapse of trust in politics and politicians' which newspapers enjoy trumpeting in their pages, because they have helped to '. . . nourish a culture of contempt, engulfing the whole of public life.' Michael Bichard, one-time Permanent Secretary in the Civil Service and currently Rector of the University of the Arts, supported Lloyd's argument:

There is much evidence – especially in the press – of lazy, complacent and arrogant practice and the consequence of this is the parallel universe to which Lloyd refers.

Richard Eyre, the stage and screen director, observed:

Journalists often regard Daniel Ellsberg's maxim – 'all leaders lie and it's our duty to expose their lies' – as a vindication of, at least, deviousness and, at worst, blackmail, while blinding themselves to the fact zealous exposure of lies isn't always the same thing as revelation of the truth. And the motives of individual journalists are at least as venal and self-interested as those who they are indicting . . .

Anthony Sampson, who reviewed all these responses to Lloyd's critique, concluded:

Most respondents think [that Lloyd is right], and there can be no doubt about the genuine anguish of many distinguished people who feel aggrieved or simply resigned to the misrepresentations of the press.

So is the press malign and determined to distort perceptions of those in power? David Leigh, also of *The Guardian*, writing 'from the front line', as it were, contributes a powerful defence of the toiling hack. From his own experience he argues: '. . . when a journalist asks members of British institutions uncomfortable questions about what is going on, they respond with more or less polished evasions or with downright lies. They employ expensive PR teams to paint pictures that drift artistically away from reality. They try to intimidate with their lawyers. They conceal what they can and what they can't conceal, they distort.' He argues that all people in power are prone to this tendency: dictatorships try to suppress all dissent but democracies are not saved by elections every five years but by 'free speech coupled with a network of civic agencies which are truculent and unfettered. It's important that the various media behave as counter-vailing powers in a democracy; in fact it's absolutely necessary.' He goes on to say, even more controversially, that: '. . . In a society like ours, those who have to fight their way to the top of the political heap often have unusual psychologies. Like police officers, or gynaecologists, some of them are quite deranged.' Leigh concludes that on balance journalists do a necessary job pretty well but their performance is marred and debased by the fact that there is 'a race to the bottom in a declining market' and that it is true that 'some newspaper owners and newspaper people are venal, vain, cynical, sycophantic, low minded, partisan, unscrupulous or vindictive.' However, he excludes his own newspaper from such criticism: *The Guardian* he describes as 'trying hard to raise standards'. In *The Times* a few weeks earlier (8 December 2004), Simon Jenkins anticipated much of Leigh's case, writing that 'The British press is the most reptilian in the world', adding that 'it needs to be', given the weakness of Parliament in calling Blair to account and the way his government used spin to obfuscate every move it made.

Both sides of the argument can be supported and justified, it would seem, but for us humble voters, the best advice is perhaps to be aware of the tendencies on both sides and to refine our own 'falsification detectors' when either listening to politicians' claims and appeals or reading journalists' accounts and analyses of what they have said.

provenance of the phrase lay in 1982 with Sidney Blumenthal, who used it to describe the emergent style of media coverage in the USA. Assiduous USA watchers in New Labour's élite seem to have absorbed the new approach and made it their own: 'a nonstop process of seeking to manipulate sources of public approval to engage in the act of governing itself' (Hugh Heclo in Ornstein and Mann, 2000, p. 219). In other words, government and campaigning have become indistinguishable. The tendency now is for parties in government to view each day as something to be 'won' or 'lost'. Campbell is said to have constructed a 'grid' highlighting government announcements and connecting them to other political happenings. Certainly, Blair's government seemed to follow mantras like that of Heclo above as evidenced by Jo Moore, the media adviser to Stephen Byers, who with breathtaking cynicism e-mailed colleagues just after the planes hit the World Trade Center on 11 September 2001 that this was now a 'good day to bury bad news'.

■ The political impact of the media: the process

Given the ubiquity of media influence, Seymour-Ure is more than justified in judging that 'the mass media are so deeply embedded in the [political] system that without them political activity in its contemporary form could hardly carry on at all' (Seymour-Ure, 1974, p. 62; see also Table 10.4). He directs attention to the factors that determine the political effects of media messages and that will naturally have a bearing upon the way in which politicians attempt to manipulate them.

The *timing* of a news item 'can make all the difference to its significance' (p. 28). For example, Sir Alan Walters, Margaret Thatcher's part-time economic adviser, wrote an article in 1988 in which he described the European monetary system that Chancellor Nigel Lawson wanted Britain to join as 'half-baked'. Had it appeared immediately it might have caused some temporary embarrassment, but

Reporters stand by during a typical media frenzy
Source: Rex Features / Nils Jorgensen

Table 10.4 The press, television and political influence

Television	Press
Balanced	Partisan
Trusted	Not trusted
Mass audience	Segmented audience
'Passive' audience politically	'Active' audience
Most important source of information	Secondary source

Source: Lecture by David Denver, September 1996

coming out as it did eighteen months later, in the middle of a highly publicised row over this very issue between Margaret Thatcher and her Chancellor, it contributed importantly to Nigel Lawson's eventual resignation on 26 October 1989.

The *frequency* with which items are featured in the mass media will influence their impact. The unfolding nature of the Westland revelations (when Michael Heseltine resigned over a dispute involving Westland Engineering), for example, kept Margaret Thatcher's political style on top of the political agenda for several damaging weeks in January and February 1986.

The *intensity* with which media messages are communicated is also a key element. The Westland crisis was so damaging to Margaret Thatcher because every daily and Sunday newspaper – serious and tabloid – and every radio and television news editor found these crises irresistible. The Lawson resignation story made the front page for over a week, while two successive Brian Walden interviews with Margaret Thatcher and Lawson (29 October and 5 November 1990, respectively) were themselves widely reported news events.

■ The mass media and the theory of pluralist democracy

If the mass media have such a transforming impact on politics, then how have they affected the fabric of British democracy? It all depends on what we mean by democracy. The popular and indeed 'official' view is that our elected legislature exerts watchdog control over the executive and allows a large degree of citizen participation in the process of government. This pluralist system provides a free market of ideas and a shifting, open competition for power between political parties, pressure groups and various other groups in society. Supporters of the present system claim that not only is it how the system ought to work (a normative theory of government) but it is, to a large extent, also descriptive: this is how it works in practice.

According to this view, the media play a vital political role:

1. They report and represent popular views to those invested with decision-making powers.

2. They inform society about the actions of government, educating voters in the issues of the day. The range of newspapers available provides a variety of interpretations and advice.

3. They act as a watchdog of the public interest, defending the ordinary person against a possibly over-mighty government through their powers of exposure, investigation and interrogation. To fulfil this neutral, disinterested role it follows that the media need to be given extensive freedom to question and publish.

This pluralist view of the media's role, once again both normative and descriptive, has been criticised under the following points.

Ownership and control influence media messages

Excluding the BBC, the media organisations are substantially part of the business world and embrace profit making as a central objective. This argument has more force since, following Murdoch's smashing of the trade union stranglehold over the press through his 'Wapping' revolution, newspapers now make substantial profits. This fact alone severely prejudices media claims to objectivity in reporting the news and reflecting popular feeling. In recent years ownership has concentrated markedly. About 80 per cent of newspaper circulation is in the hands of four conglomerates: Associated Newspapers, owned by the Rothermere family and controlling the *Daily Mail* and the *Mail on Sunday*; the Mirror Newspaper Group, owning the *Mirror*, *Sunday Mirror* and *Sunday People*; United Newspapers, owning the *Express*, the *Sunday Express*, the *Star* and the *Standard*; and News International, owning *The Times*, *Sunday Times*, *News of the World* and the *Sun*. These latter-day press barons and media groups also own rafts of the regional press and have strong television interests: Murdoch, for example, owns Sky Television. Conrad Black's Hollinger International ceased to own the *Daily Telegraph* and *Sunday Telegraph* in 2005 following a 2004 court case; the titles were purchased by the financier Barclay Brothers.

Newspaper and television ownership is closely interlinked and has become part of vast conglomerates with worldwide interests. Does it seem likely that such organisations will fairly represent and give a fair hearing to political viewpoints hostile to the capitalist system of which they are such an important part?

True, Maxwell's newspapers supported the Labour Party, but they did not exhibit anything that could be called a coherent socialist ideology. Maxwell was certainly interested in dictating editorial policy, using his papers as a personal memo pad for projecting messages to world leaders (there is little or no evidence that anyone ever listened). Murdoch's newspapers used to support the Tories loudly, although disenchantment with Major's leadership led to a cooling off from about 1994 onwards, until the general election in 1997 precipitated a 'conversion' to Blair's campaign. In the case of *The Observer* and *The Guardian*, it can be argued that ownership is separate from control. However, Tiny Rowland when he owned the former used it shamelessly to advance his feud with Mohamed Al Fayed. Murdoch too exerts strong personal editorial control, usually in support of his business interests; he decided to drop the BBC from his far eastern satellite broadcasting operation, for example, because the Chinese government objected to the criticism of human rights suppression that the BBC included in its reports. On balance press barons have less power and influence than is often thought. Beaverbrook, for example, pursued a number of policy objectives through his papers, none of which were achieved.

Nor is the press especially accountable: the Press Council used to be a powerful and respected watchdog on newspaper editors, but in recent years it has meekly acquiesced in the concentration of ownership on the grounds that the danger of monopoly control is less unacceptable than the bankruptcy of familiar national titles. Moreover, since the *Sun* has regularly flouted its rulings, the council has lost even more respect and has been unable, for example, to prevent the private lives of public figures being invaded by tabloid journalists to an alarming degree.

Television evinces a much clearer distinction between ownership and control and fits more easily into the pluralist model. The BBC, of course, is government-owned, and in theory at least its board

BIOGRAPHY

Sir Christopher Meyer, Chairman of the Press Complaints Commission (1944–)

Oxbridge-educated Meyer is a career diplomat who stepped in to take over the PCC chair when Lord Wakeham became enmired in the 2002 Enron scandal. He served in Moscow, Brussels, Bonn and Washington and is fluent in all the relevant languages. In the 1980s, he was the chief Foreign Office spokesman under Geoffrey Howe and then took over as chief press officer. It is said that Meyer was pivotal in building a good relationship between Blair and Bush in the wake of the latter's controversial election – though much of this could be explained by good personal chemistry. In 2005 he published memoirs entitled *DC Confidential* which distributed insights into the way in which Blair operated (not good on detail), Prescott (poor on expressing himself), Jack Straw ('more to be liked than admired') and sundry other ministers whom he described as 'pygmies'. Apart from these personal swipes, however, there was little of substance in the book and Meyer survived calls for him to resign his PCC post.

of governors exercises independent control. Independent television is privately owned, and this ownership is becoming more concentrated, but the Independent Broadcasting Authority (IBA) uses its considerable legal powers under the 1981 Broadcasting Act to ensure 'balance' and 'due accuracy and impartiality' on sensitive political issues. This is not to say that television can be acquitted of the charge of bias – as we shall see below – but merely that television controllers are forbidden by law to display open partisanship and that those people who own their companies cannot insist on particular editorial lines.

News values are at odds with the requirements of a pluralist system

In order to create profits media organisations compete for their audiences, with the consequent pursuit of the lowest common denominator in public taste. In the case of the tabloids this means the relegation of hard news to inside pages and the promotion to the front page of trivial stories such as sex scandals, royal family gossip and the comings and goings of soap opera stars. The same tendency has been apparent on television, with the reduction of current affairs programmes, their demotion from peak viewing times and the dilution of news programmes with more 'human interest' stories. As a result of this tendency it can be argued that the media's educative role in a pluralist democracy is being diminished. Some would go further, however, and maintain that the dominant news values adopted by the media are in any case inappropriate for this role. The experience of successful newspapers has helped to create a set of criteria for judging newsworthiness that news editors in all branches of the media automatically accept and apply more or less intuitively. The themes to which the public are believed to respond include:

1. *Personalities*: People quickly become bored with statistics and carefully marshalled arguments and relate to stories that involve disagreement, personality conflicts or interesting personal details. Westland and the Nigel Lawson resignation demonstrated this tendency in action when the clashes between Thatcher and her Cabinet colleagues were given prominence over the important European questions that underlay them.

2. *Revelations*: Journalist Nicholas Tomalin once defined news as the making public of something that someone wished to keep secret. Leaked documents, financial malpractice and sexual peccadilloes, e.g. the revelation that John Major had a four-year affair with Edwina Currie, are assiduously reported and eagerly read.

3. *Disasters*: The public has both a natural and a somewhat morbid interest in such matters.

4. *Visual back-up*: Stories that can be supported by good photographs (or film footage on TV) will often take precedence over those that cannot be so supported.

It is commonly believed that newspapers which ignore these ground rules will fail commercially and that current affairs television which tries too hard to be serious will be largely ignored and described, fatally, as 'boring'. There is much evidence to suggest that these news values are based on fact: that, perhaps to our shame, these are the themes to which we most readily respond. However, it does mean that the vast media industry is engaged in providing a distorted view of the world via its concentration on limited and relatively unimportant aspects of social reality.

Dumbing down television

Steven Barrett and Emily Seymour's [study shows] that in the drama and current affairs departments television has become immeasurably more foolish. By comparing the time given to serious subjects in 1978 and 1998, they find that foreign coverage has all but disappeared from ITV and is increasingly confined to BBC2. There is less peak-time current affairs on ITV than ever before and on all channels crime documentaries are what the controllers want. (Crime is cheap. The police provide free help if you show them as the thin blue line fighting monstrous evil.)

Nick Cohen, *The Observer*, 24 October 1999.
© Guardian Newspapers Limited, reprinted with permission

The lobby system favours the government of the day

The pluralist model requires that the media report news in a truthful and neutral way. We have already seen that ownership heavily influences the partisanship of the press, but other critics argue that the lobby system of political reporting introduces a distortion of a different kind. Some 150 political journalists at Westminster are known collectively as 'the lobby'. In effect, they belong to a club with strict rules whereby they receive special briefings from government spokesmen in exchange for keeping quiet about their sources. Supporters claim that this is an important means of obtaining information that the public would not otherwise receive, but critics disagree. Anthony Howard, the veteran political commentator, has written that lobby correspondents, rather like prostitutes, become 'clients' or otherwise 'instruments for a politician's gratification' (Hennessy, 1985, p. 9). The charge is that journalists become lazy, uncritical and incurious, preferring to derive their copy from bland government briefings – often delivered at dictation speed. Peter Hennessy believes that this system 'comes nowhere near to providing the daily intelligence system a mature democracy has the right to expect . . . as it enables Downing Street to dominate the agenda of mainstream political discussion week by week' (1985, pp. 10–11). *The*

BOX 10.4	IDEAS AND PERSPECTIVES

Bias, broadcasting and the political parties

Harold Wilson was notoriously paranoid about the media and believed that not only the press but also the BBC was 'ineradicably' biased against him, full of 'card carrying Tories', in the words of Michael Cockerell. Perhaps it is being in government that explains it, as in the 1980s it was Margaret Thatcher and her 'enforcer' Norman Tebbit who seemed paranoid. He launched ferocious attacks on the corporation, calling it 'the insufferable, smug, sanctimonious, naive, guilt-ridden, wet, pink, orthodoxy of that sunset home of that third rate decade, the sixties'. Conservatives complained bitterly again when their campaign, supported by the *Sun*, in favour of stopping Greg Dyke being made Director General of the BBC failed in 1999; they claimed it was a disgrace that the job had gone to a man who had donated £50,000 to the Labour Party before the 1997 election.

Answering questions in the House can be stressful amid all the noise, but ultimately the barbs can be ignored and the questions avoided easily. But on radio or television well-briefed interviewers can put politicians on the spot. This is why ministers have complained so vehemently. Jonathan Aitken (then Chief Secretary to the Treasury) in March 1995 won ecstatic applause from Conservatives when he delivered a speech cleared by No. 10 attacking the 'Blair Broadcasting Corporation'. In the firing line on this occasion were *Today* presenter John Humphrys (who had given him a bad time on the *Today* programme) and *Newsnight*'s Jeremy Paxman (the *bête noire* of all ministers), accused of 'ego trip interviewing'. Unfortunately for the interviewers the Director General of the BBC, John Birt, had earlier made a speech in Dublin criticising 'sneering and overbearing' interviewers, although he took the trouble to write to both men denying he was attacking them (although it is hard to think to whom else he could have been referring). Cockerell explains that Humphrys is not a 'politically motivated questioner; his aim is to strip away the public relations gloss and to use his own sharp teeth to counter pre-rehearsed soundbites'. He continues, 'Aitken was really objecting to the BBC doing its job: it is one that the politicians of both parties have wanted to do since the earliest days' (*The Guardian*, 28 May 1996).

This probably gets to the heart of the perennial conflict between politicians and the media. Politicians in power ideally would like to control the media – Mrs Thatcher once said she did not like short interviews but would like instead to have four hours of airtime on her own – and resent the criticism that they receive from journalists and interviewers. In a pluralist democracy it is indeed the job of the media to make government more accountable to the public, and perhaps it is when politicians do not like it that the media are doing their jobs most effectively. However, Labour government ministers would have been unlikely to have accepted this point in March 2003. *The Observer* on 30 March reported a row between the government and the BBC over the reporting of the Iraq war. It seemed that John Reid, the party chairman, had accused the corporation of 'acting like the friend of Baghdad'. Andrew Marr, political editor of the BBC, rejected this view, adding that 'the government is angry that they can control where reporters go but what they cannot control is what they see'. Jack Straw, the Foreign Secretary, wondered whether it would have been possible to evacuate Dunkirk under the scrutiny of 24-hour rolling news, which he said 'changes the reality of warfare. It compresses timescales'.

Guardian and *The Independent* were so opposed to the system that for a while they withdrew from it. However, the lobby system, in the face of such sustained criticism, has been weakened if not virtually dismantled in recent years. Alastair Campbell agreed to be named as the premier's 'spokesman', and Blair has agreed to televised press conferences.

Television companies are vulnerable to political pressure

Ever since the broadcasting media became an integral part of the political process during the 1950s, governments of all complexions have had uneasy relationships with the BBC, an organisation with a worldwide reputation for excellence and for accurate, objective current affairs coverage. Margaret Thatcher, however, took government hostility to new lengths; indeed, 'abhorrence of the BBC appeared for a while to be a litmus test for the Conservativeness of MPs' (Negrine, 1995, p. 125). Governments seek to influence the BBC in three major ways. First, they have the power of appointment to the corporation's board of governors. The post of chairman is especially important; Marmaduke Hussey's appointment in 1986 was believed to be a response to perceived left-wing tendencies (according to one report, he was ordered by Norman Tebbit's office to 'get in there and sort it out – in days and not months'). Second, governments can threaten to alter the licence system (although former Home Secretary Willie Whitelaw knew of no occasion when this threat had been used): Margaret Thatcher was known to favour the introduction of advertising to finance the BBC, but the Peacock Commission on the financing of television refused to endorse this approach. Third, government's attempt to exert pressure in relation to particular programmes – often citing security reasons. The range of disputes between the Thatcher governments and the BBC is unparalleled in recent history. In part this was a consequence of a dominant, long-established and relatively unchallenged Prime Minister as well as Thatcher's determination to challenge the old consensus – she long suspected that it resided tenaciously within the top echelons of the BBC. During the Falklands War, some Conservative MPs actually accused BBC reports of being 'treasonable' because they questioned government accounts of the progress of the war. On such occasions, they claimed, the media should support the national effort. In 1986, a monitoring unit was set up in Conservative Central Office, and in the summer a highly critical report on the BBC's coverage of the US bombing of Libya was submitted together with a fusillade of accusations from party chairman Norman Tebbit. The BBC rejected the accusations and complained of 'political intimidation' in the run-up to a general election. The pressure almost certainly had some effect on the BBC's subsequent news and current affairs presentation – supporting those who claim that the pluralist analysis of the media's role is inappropriate.

Television news coverage tends to reinforce the *status quo*

The argument here is that television news cannot accurately reflect events in the real world because it is, to use Richard Hoggart's phrase, 'artificially shaped' (Glasgow University Media Group, 1976, p. ix). ITN's editor, David Nicholas, says that '90 per cent of the time we are trying to tell people what we think they will want to know' (Tyne Tees TV, April 1986). It is what he and his colleagues think people want to know that attracts the fire of media critics. Faced with an infinitely multifaceted social reality, television news editors apply the selectivity of news values, serving up reports under severe time constraints in a particular abbreviated form. According to this critical line of argument, television news reports can never be objective but are merely versions of reality constructed by news staff.

Furthermore, reports will be formulated within the context of thousands of assumptions regarding how news personnel think the public already perceive the world. Inevitably they will refer to widely shared consensus values and perceptions and will reflect these in their reports, thus reinforcing them and marginalising minority or radical alternatives. So television, for example, tends to present the parliamentary system as the only legitimate means of reaching decisions and tends to present society as basically unified without fundamental class conflicts and cleavages. Because alternative analyses are squeezed out and made to seem odd or alien, television – so it is argued – tends to reinforce *status quo* values and institutions and hence protect the interests of those groups in society that are powerful or dominant. The Greens offer an interesting case study in that for many years they fell outside the consensus. Towards the end of the 1980s, however, it suddenly became apparent even to the main party leaders that the Green arguments had earned a place for themselves within rather than outside the mainstream of political culture.

The Glasgow University Media Group took this argument further. On the basis of their extensive programme analyses they suggest that television coverage of economic news tends to place the 'blame for society's industrial and economic problems at the door of the workforce. This is done in the face of contradictory evidence, which when it appears is either ignored [or] smothered' (1976, pp. 267–8). Reports on industrial relations were 'clearly skewed against the interests of the working class and organised labour . . . in favour of the managers of industry'. The Glasgow research provoked a storm of criticism. David Nicholas dismissed it as a set of conclusions supported by selective evidence (Tyne Tees TV, April 1986). In 1985, an academic counterblast was provided by Martin Harrison (1985), who criticised the slender basis of the Glasgow research and adduced new evidence that contradicted its conclusions.

Marxist theories of class dominance

The Glasgow research is often cited in support of more general theories on how the media reinforce, protect and advance dominant class interests in society. Variations on the theme were produced by Gramsci, in the 1930s by the Frankfurt School of social theorists and in the 1970s by the sociocultural approach of Professor Stuart Hall (for detailed analysis see McQuail, 1983, pp. 57–70; Watts, 1997), but the essence of their case is summed up in Marx's proposition that 'the ideas of the ruling class are in every epoch the ruling ideas'. He argued that those people who own and control the economic means of production – the ruling class – will seek to persuade everyone else that preserving *status quo* values and institutions is in the interests of society as a whole.

The means employed are infinitely subtle and indirect, via religious ideas, support for the institution of the family, the monarchy and much else. Inevitably the role of the mass media, according to this analysis, is crucial. Marxists totally reject the pluralist model of the media as independent and neutral, as the servant rather than the master of society. They see the media merely as the instrument of class domination, owned by the ruling class and carrying their messages into every home in the land. It is in moments of crisis, Marxists would claim, that the fundamental bias of state institutions is made clear. In 1926, during the General Strike,

Lord Reith, the first Director General of the BBC, provided some evidence for this view when he confided to his diary, 'they want us to be able to say they did not commandeer us, but they know they can trust us not to be really impartial'. Marxists believe that the media obscure the fact of economic exploitation by ignoring radical critiques and disseminating entertainments and new interpretations that subtly reinforce the *status quo* and help to sustain a 'false consciousness' of the world based on ruling-class values. For Marxists, therefore, the media provide a crucial role in persuading the working classes to accept their servitude and to support the system that causes it. Table 10.5 usefully contrasts the pluralist with the class dominance model.

Which of the two models better describes the role of the media in British society? From the discussion so far, the pluralist model would appear inadequate in a number of respects. Its ability to act as a fair and accurate channel of communication between government and society is distorted by the political bias of the press, the lobby system, news values and the tendency of television to reflect consensual values. Moreover, the media are far from being truly independent: the press is largely owned by capitalist enterprises, and television is vulnerable to government pressure of various kinds. Does this mean that the dominance model is closer to the truth? Not really.

While the dominance model quite accurately describes a number of media systems operating under oppressive regimes, it greatly exaggerates government control of the media in Britain.

Table 10.5 Dominance and pluralism models compared

	Dominance	Pluralism
Societal source	Ruling class or dominant élite	Competing political social, cultural interests and groups
Media	Under concentrated ownership and of uniform type	Many and independent of each other
Production	Standardised, routinised, controlled	Creative, free, original
Content and world view	Selective and coherent, decided from 'above'	Diverse and competing views responsive to audience demand
Audience	Dependent, passive, organised on large scale	Fragmented, selective, reactive and active
Effects	Strong and confirmative of established social order	Numerous, without consistency or predictability of direction, but often 'no effect'

Source: D. McQuail (1983) *Mass Communication Theory*, p. 68. Copyright © 1983 Sage Publications Ltd, reprinted by permission

1. As David Nicholas observes (Tyne Tees TV, April 1986), 'trying to manipulate the news is as natural an instinct to a politician as breathing oxygen', but because politicians try does not mean that they always succeed. People who work in the media jealously guard their freedom and vigorously resist government interference. The *This Week* 'Death on the Rock' programme on the SAS killings in Gibraltar was after all shown in 1988 despite Sir Geoffrey Howe's attempts to pressure the IBA. And Lord Windlesham's subsequent inquiry further embarrassed the government by completely exonerating the Thames TV programme.

2. The media may tend to reflect consensual views, but this does not prevent radical messages regularly breaking into the news – sometimes because they accord with news values themselves. Television also features drama productions that challenge and criticise the *status quo*: for example, at the humorous level in the form of *Bremner, Bird and Fortune* and *In the Thick of It* and at the serious level in the form of the BBC's regular *Panorama* critical reports. Even soap operas such as *EastEnders* often challenge and criticise the *status quo*.

3. Programmes such as *Rough Justice* and *First Tuesday* in the past have shown that persistent and highly professional research can shame a reluctant establishment into action to reverse injustices – as in the case of the Guildford Four, released in 1989 after fifteen years of wrongful imprisonment. Consumer programmes such as the daily Radio 4 series *You and Yours* do champion the individual, as do regular newspaper campaigns.

4. News values do not invariably serve ruling-class interests, otherwise governments would not try so hard to manipulate them. Margaret Thatcher, for example, cannot have welcomed the explosion of critical publicity that surrounded Westland, her July 1989 reshuffle or the Lawson resignation. And even the most serious of the quality newspapers will join the feeding frenzy of a scandal like the one which submerged David Blunkett in 2004, once they deem the appropriate point has been reached.

Each model, then, contains elements of the truth, but neither comes near the whole truth. Which is the nearer? The reader must decide; but despite all its inadequacies and distortions the pluralist model probably offers the better framework for understanding how the mass media interact with the British political system. Table 10.6 reveals the complexity of the argument: some elements fit neatly into a supporting role, while others do not.

Table 10.6 Summary table to show 'democrativeness' of media elements

Democratic criteria	Media and democrative tendency[c,d,e]				
	Broadsheets	**Tabloids**	**Radio**	**BBC**	**Commercial TV**
Easily accessible (for target audience)	+	+	+	+	+
Varied and plentiful	+	+	+	+	+
Concentration of ownership	–	–	–	+	–
Reliable factually	+	–	+	+	+
High-value political content	+	–	0	–	+
Accountability 1[a]	+	–	+	–	+
Accountability 2[b]	–	–	–	–	–
Low bias	0	–	+	+	+

[a] Accountability 1 = tendency for the media element to facilitate democracy.
[b] Accountability 2 = degree of accountability of medium to public.
[c] + = high tendency to encourage democracy.
[d] – = low tendency to encourage democracy.
[e] 0 = neutral effect (i.e. '0' is given for BBC radio as most of its five channels are music-based, and '0' for the bias of broadsheets as they tend to take give space to alternative opinions to their editorials).
Source: B. Jones (2000) 'Media and Government' in R. Pyper and L. Robins (eds) *United Kindom Governance*. Reprinted by permission of Palgrave Macmillan

■ Language and politics

All this modern emphasis on technology can obscure the fact that in politics language is still of crucial importance. Taking the example of Northern Ireland, we have seen how the precise meaning of words has provided a passionate bone of contention. When the IRA announced its ceasefire in 1994, its opponents insisted it should be a 'permanent' one. However, the paramilitary organisation did not wish to abandon its ability to use the threat of violence as a negotiating counter and refused to comply, insisting that its term 'complete' ceasefire was as good as the British government needed or would in any case get. Gerry Adams, president of the political wing of the IRA, Sinn Fein, had a similar problem over his attitude towards bombings. His close contact with the bombers made it impossible for him to condemn the bombing of Manchester in June 1996, so he used other less committing words like 'regret' or 'unfortunate'. Another aspect is tone of voice, which can bestow whole varieties of meaning to a statement or a speech. Sir Patrick Mayhew, for example, John Major's Northern Ireland Secretary, specialised in being 'calm'. After the reopening of violence in the summer of 1996 he had much need for this, enunciating his words slowly and with great care as if attempting to soothe the wounded feelings of the antagonists and reassure the rest of the country that, contrary to appearances, everything was all right. A more absurd example is Margaret Thatcher's opposition to the wording on a proposed AIDS prevention poster; according to *The Guardian* (18 July 1996), she felt that the clearly worded warnings about anal sex were too shocking to be used.

Another example of language being of crucial importance occurred in November 1996, when whip David Willetts was accused of interfering with the deliberations of the Commons Standards and Privileges Committee regarding the investigation of Neil Hamilton's alleged receipt of cash for parliamentary activities on behalf of Mohamed Al Fayed. According to Willetts' own notes of his meeting with the chairman of the committee, Sir Geoffrey Johnson-Smith, he 'wants' advice. On the face of it, this seemed as if the government was interfering with the quasi-judicial procedures of the House. In explanation to the committee, the whip said that he meant the word in the biblical sense of 'needs'. Most commentators were unimpressed. Writing in *The Observer*, 24 October 1999, Andrew Marr noted the increase in vituperation characterising British politics: *The*

Times running a cartoon on 'The Lying King'; the *Daily Telegraph* reporting 'The New Labour Lie Machine' and Blair's 'repulsive political calculus'. On the other hand, 'Labour attack dogs snarl at Hague – the cruel rejoicing at Thatcher's alleged "Wee Willie" remark, the jeering about his looks and voice. Galloping abuse inflation is everywhere . . . You would think from the violence of the language that our society was undergoing a nervous breakdown.' Marr concludes that journalists are 'using abuse too casually to secure our meal tickets in a difficult market'.

I went to the CBI conference in Birmingham to hear the Prime Minister speak, and there on a giant TV screen . . . was our very own Big Brother. This Big Brother smiles a lot in a self deprecating kind of way. He uses 'um' and 'well' as a rhetorical device, to convince us he's not reading out a prepared text, but needs to pause to work out exactly what he means. There is a prepared text of course but he adds to it phrases such as 'I really think' and 'you know I really have to tell you' and 'in my view'. This is the new oratory. The old politicians told us they were right, and that there was no room for doubt, the new politician is not telling us truths, but selling us himself . . . His message is that you should take him on trust; you should believe him because you love him.

Simon Hoggart, 'Commons Sketch: Blair lays on the therapy for the terracotta army', *The Guardian*, 3 November 1999. © Guardian Newspapers Limited, reprinted with permission

■ The media and politics: future developments

The structure of television underwent an upheaval in the early 1990s at the hands of the 'deregulators' led by Thatcher. She had dearly wished to end the licence fee that funds the BBC, but the lukewarm response of the Peacock Commission set up to look at this problem headed off this possibility for the time being at least (until 2007). In October 1991, franchises were sold off for independent television regions. Critics complain that these new developments will dilute still further the standards in broadcasting established by the BBC's famous former head, the high-minded Lord Reith. The inception of satellite broadcasting in 1982 via the Murdoch-owned

Sky Television opened up the possibility of a very large number of channels, all aimed at the same markets and all tending to move the locus of their messages downmarket. Sky News, a 24-hour news service, has allayed some fears by developing, after a shaky start, into a competent and well-respected service. With over 130 satellite channels in Europe and cable companies making a huge investment in access for their service, the expansion of choice is set to be exponential over the next decade or more. The inception of digital television, which entails the conversion of the broadcast signal into a computerised message, will revolutionise a sector virtually in permanent revolution anyway. This system requires the use of a set-top decoder but can receive signals from satellite or terrestrial stations. Some critics fear that Rupert Murdoch will be able to control access to this new technology by being the first in the field to provide the decoders – the argument being that consumers will happily buy one but not any more, so that the company in first will effectively be the gatekeeper. Media companies hope that Murdoch will be forced by government regulation to make his technology available to other broadcasters, but the Australian multimillionaire is as much interested in power as in money and is unlikely to relinquish his option for more of both easily, if at all.

Some critics claim that the new profusion of television channels will mark the end of quality. They point to the USA, where there is a very wide diversity yet – apart from a few areas of excellence – an unremitting mediocrity, and predict that the UK will go the same way.

The future of the BBC

In January 2003, Culture Secretary Tessa Jowell announced a review, to begin in the autumn, into the funding of the BBC to be undertaken by Ofcom, the new media regulator headed by Lord Currie. It was reckoned at the time that this report would help to set the framework for the renewal of the BBC's charter in 2006. A few days later, she warned that the corporation will be expected to justify its licence fee, adding that it did not have *carte blanche* to do anything it liked. Possibly this comment was a response to Rupert Murdoch's complaint in November 2002 that the 'BBC gets anything it wants'. The media tycoon had been unhappy that the publicly funded BBC was entering into areas of the market – 24-hour news, childrens' programmes – with an unfair advantage over the rest of the industry.

Meanwhile, the press faces an immediate threat from the electronic flank. Xerox announced in October 1999 that it had signed a deal to produce electronic paper on an industrial scale. As Andrew Marr wrote wonderingly in *The Observer* (17 October 1999), 'It can be "bound" and loaded with a "wand", bringing whole books on to it at incredible speed. You can carry it in your pocket, and fold it, treat it as a newspaper or magazine updated every few minutes – so abolishing the daily deadline and the entire traditional process'. However, seven years on, such revolutionary developments have not entered the mainstream, and newspapers still look like newspapers – even if a number have shrunk to a 'compact' size.

For politics, the technology with the most potential might well prove to be the Internet, for which one needs only a telephone line, a modem, some software and a computer. Currently, nearly a billion are logged on worldwide, but the service is expanding rapidly and has all kinds of implications:

1. *Information*: It is now possible to download immense amounts of up-to-date information about political issues via the Net.

2. *E-mail*: It is possible to communicate with politicians and the politically active all over the world, extending enormously the scope of political action.

3. *Interactive democracy*: By being hooked up to the Net, it might be possible for politicians or government in democracies to seek endorsement for policies directly from the people. This would have all kinds of drawbacks, e.g. it could slow down the political process even more than at present in developed countries; it could give a platform to unsavoury messages like racism and power-seeking ideologues; it might enthrone the majority with a power it chooses to abuse. But these opportunities exist, and it is virtually certain that they will be experimented with if not adopted in the near future.

4. *Blogs*: It is now possible for anyone to set up their own website and issue opinions and information to the world on a regular basis. In the year 2005 it was calculated that 80,000 weblogs (blogs) were created and their rate of increase has now become exponential. Many younger people now use such sources as a matter of course, and some – like the US Drudge Report – break new stories or influence election campaigns.

Fareed Zakaria offers this insight into the implications of the revolution currently taking place (see also Box 10.5):

Today's information revolution has produced thousands of outlets for news that make central control impossible and dissent easy. The Internet has taken this process another huge step forward, being a system where, in the columnist Thomas Friedman's words, 'Everyone is connected but no one is in control.'

Zakaria (2004)

BOX 10.5 BRITAIN IN CONTEXT

The media

The nature of the media in any country is usually a reflection of its political character. Democracies believe in freedom of speech and hence in open media, though politicians in democracies seek constantly to manipulate the media to their own advantage. In authoritarian systems the media are usually heavily controlled in terms of what newspapers can print or broadcasters can say on air.

The media in the UK play a similar role to those in the USA. The major difference is that in the latter, candidates can buy airtime to show their own political ads and to issue 'attack ads' to weaken opposing candidates. As such ads are very expensive, this gives an advantage to campaigns which are well funded. Indeed, many candidates in the US and incumbent legislators, governors and so forth, spend much of their energies raising campaign cash. The phenomenon of 'spin doctors' was more or less invented in the US where sculpting messages or media images for mass consumption has been something of a growth industry; they have since been disseminated worldwide to wherever democratic elections are regularly held. Much campaign output is either 'semi-mediated' like the presidential debates or 'mediated' in news broadcasts, but in the latter case candidates and their aides have become clever in gaining favourable media attention.

Many media critics claim that in the US the media favour the right in that they reflect and reinforce attitudes wholly accepting of the *status quo*. They point to Fox News, owned by Rupert Murdoch, which arguably leans towards a Bush interpretation of issues and news stories. As in the UK debate, others deny such bias and argue the media are essentially free. But this argument attains a worldwide dimension when ownership of the media is examined. Huge media conglomerates like Murdoch's News Corporation or Berlusconi's Mediaset control media in other countries and there is concern that some political control is thereby connected. Murdoch, for example, broadcasts satellite television into China and has agreed to some censorship controls demanded by the government of that country.

China has also sought to censor one of the fastest growing media forms: communication via the Internet. Here it is the search engine company, Google, which has attracted criticism for agreeing to controls over its activities in China. But such control cannot stop the burgeoning spread of such communication, especially the 'blogosphere'. Blogs are online logs or diaries which are essentially forms of personal websites. They can be purely individual and carry all kinds of information from the person concerned – for example, 'I got up this morning and worked in the garden for two hours', about a business venture, about musical enthusiasms, about political issues, or, like the most successful and much visited ones, about celebrity gossip.

Writing in *The Guardian* on 9 February 2006, Charles Arthur reported that the blogosphere was 60 times its size of three years earlier and was doubling in size every 5 months; 75,000 are created every day and over 13 million were still active three months after their creation. Quite where this explosion of Internet communication will lead is unclear. It could prove to be a force for subversion – chipping away at the base of the *status quo* in a number of countries. Or it could be the object of government censorship in some countries, with governments hunting down these individuals hunched in front of their flickering screens. Or it could be neither and merely take its place as yet another logical element of globalisation.

5. *Mobile phones*: Virtually everyone now owns a mobile phone and this fact, together with the onrush of technology, has produced the transmission of more and more different types of information via their tiny screens. Some political parties have issued text messages to phone owners, but in 2006 more possibilities were opened up by the mobile provider which announced the results of an experiment whereby television had been broadcast direct to mobile phone subscribers. Despite the smallness of the screens, the trial was declared successful with thousands of mobile owners watching several hours of television a week – though most of it at home rather than on the move. Inevitably news and political content will in future be imbibed via this unlikely route and will become yet another facet of the political media.

Chapter summary

The spoken voice was the main form of political communication until the spread of newspapers in the nineteenth century. Broadcasting introduced a revolution into the way politics is conducted as its spread is instant and its influence so great. New political actors have emerged specialising in the media, and politicians have learned to master their techniques. Press news values tend to influence television also, but the latter is more vulnerable to political pressure than the already politicised press. Class dominance theories suggest that the media are no more than an instrument of the ruling class, but there is reason to believe that they exercise considerable independence and are not incompatible with democracy.

Discussion points

■ Should British political parties be allowed to buy political advertising on television?

■ Has televising Parliament enhanced or detracted from the efficacy of Parliament?

■ Does television substantially affect voting behaviour?

■ Do the media reinforce the political *status quo* or challenge it?

■ Should interviewers risk appearing rude when confronting politicians?

■ How important have blogs become in disseminating news and comment?

Further reading

A useful but now dated study of the media and British politics is Watts (1997). Also useful is Negrine (1995). Budge *et al.* (2007) provide two excellent chapters (13 and 14) on the media and democracy; this topic is also dealt with by Jones (1993). The two most readable studies of leadership, the media and politics are both by Michael Cockerell (Cockerell, 1988; Cockerell *et al.*, 1984). Bruce (1992) is excellent on the behaviour of politicians in relation to the media. Blumler and Gurevitch (1995) is an essay on the crisis of communication for citizenship and as such is an interesting source of ideas. See Jones (1993) on the television interview. The most brilliant and funny book about the press is Chippendale and Orrie's history of the *Sun* (1992).

References

Barnett, S. and Gaber, I. (2001) *Westminster Tales: The 21st Century Crisis in Political Journalism* (London Continuum).

Bilton, A., Bennett, K., Jones, P., Skinner, D., Stanworth, M. and Webster, A. (1996) *Introductory Sociology*, 3rd edn (Macmillan).

Blumler, J.G. and Gurevitch, M. (1995) *The Crisis of Public Communication* (Routledge).

Blumler, J.G. and McQuail, D. (1967) *Television in Politics* (Faber and Faber).

Blumler, J.G., Gurevitch, M. and Ives, J. (1978) *The Challenge of Election Broadcasting* (Leeds University Press).

Bruce, B. (1992) *Images of Power* (Kogan Page).

Budge, I., Crewe, I., McKay, D. and Newton, K. (2007) *The New British Politics* (Longman).

Chippendale, P. and Orrie, C. (1992) *Stick it Up Your Punter* (Mandarin).

Cockerell, M. (1988) *Live from Number Ten* (Faber and Faber).

Cockerell, M., Walker, D. and Hennessy, P. (1984) *Sources Close to the Prime Minister* (Macmillan).

Cohen, N. (1999) *The Observer*, 24 October 1999.

Cronkite, W. (1997) *A Reporter's Life* (Knopf).

Denver, D. (1992) *Elections and Voting Behaviour*, 2nd edn (Harvester Wheatsheaf).

Donovan, P. (1998) *All Our Todays: Forty Years of the Today Programme* (Arrow).

Franklin, B. (1999) *Tough on Sound-bites, Tough on the Causes of Sound-bites: New Labour News Management* (Catalyst Pamphlet).

Geddes, A. and Tonge, J. (1997) *Labour's Landslide* (Manchester University Press).

Glasgow University Media Group (1976) *Bad News* (Routledge and Kegan Paul).

Gould, P. (1999) *The Unfinished Revolution* (Abacus).

Green, J. (1982) *Book of Political Quotes* (Angus and Robertson).

Harrison, M. (1985) *TV News: Whose Bias* (Hermitage, Policy Journals).

Hennessy, P. (1985) *What the Papers Never Said* (Political Education Press).

Hoggart, S. (1999a) 'Commons Sketch: Blair lays on the therapy for the terracotta army', *The Guardian*, 3 November 1999.

Hoggart, S. (1999b) 'Commons Sketch: no joke for No. 10 when Hague gag hits the target', *The Guardian*, 11 November 1999.

Ingham, B. (2003) 'The wages of spin', *Sunday Times*, 16 March (adapted from *The Wages of Spin*, John Murray, 2003).

Jones, B. (1993) '"The pitiless probing eye": politicians and the broadcast political interview', *Parliamentary Affairs*, January.

Jones, B. (2000) 'Media and government', in R. Pyper and L. Robins (eds), *Governance in the United Kingdom* (Macmillan).

King, A. (ed.) (1997) *New Labour Triumphs: Britain at the Polls* (Chatham House).

Lloyd, J. (2004) *What the Media are Doing to Our Politics* (Constable).

Marr, A. (1999) 'And the news is . . . electric', *The Observer*, 17 October.

McQuail, D. (1983) *Mass Communication Theory: An Introduction* (Sage).

Negrine, R. (1995) *Politics and the Mass Media*, 2nd edn (Routledge).

Newton, K. (1992) 'Do voters believe everything they read in the papers?', in I. Crewe, P. Norris, D. Denver and D. Broughton (eds), *British Elections and Parties Yearbook* (Harvester Wheatsheaf).

Ornstein, N. and Mann, T. (2000) *The Permanent Campaign, and its Future* (AET).

O'Rourke, P.J. (1992) *Parliament of Whores* (Picador).

Sevaldsen, J. and Vardmand, O. (1993) *Contemporary British Society*, 4th edn (Academic Press).

Seyd, P. and Whiteley, P. (1992) *Labour's Grass Roots* (Clarendon Press).

Seymore-Ure, C. (1974) *The Political Impact of the Mass Media* (Constable).

Watts, D. (1997) *Political Communication Today* (Manchester University Press).

Whale, J. (1977) *The Politics of the Media* (Fontana).

Wring, D. and Deacon, D. (2005) 'The election unspun' in A. Geddes and J. Tonge, *Britain Decides* (Palgrave).

Zakaria, F. (2004) *The Future of Freedom* (Norton).

Useful websites

UK Media Internet Directory: Newspapers: www.mcc.ac.uk/jcridlan.htm
Daily Telegraph: www.telegraph.co.uk
The Independent: www.independent.co.uk
The Times: www.the-times.co.uk
The Guardian: www.guardian.co.uk
The Economist: www.economist.co.uk
BBC Television: www.bbc.co.uk
BBC charter review: www.bbc.charterreview.org.uk
ITN: www.itn.co.uk
CNN: www.cnn.com

Blog sites
http://skipper59.blogspot.com/ (run by the author of this chapter)
http://5thnovember.blogspot.com/
http://normblog.typepad.com/
http://samizdata.net/blog/
http://chickyog.blogspot.com/
http://oliverkamm.typepad.com/

CHAPTER 11

Pressure groups

Bill Jones

Learning objectives

- To explain that formal democratic government structures conceal the myriad hidden contacts between government and organised interests.

- To analyse and explain the way in which groups are organised and operate.

- To introduce some familiarity with theories regarding this area of government–public interaction.

- To provide some specific examples of pressure group activity.

Introduction

The Norwegian political scientist Stein Rokkan, writing about his country's system, said 'the crucial decisions on economic policy are rarely taken in the parties or in Parliament.' He judged 'the central area' to be 'the bargaining table' where the government authorities meet directly with trade union and other group leaders. 'These yearly rounds of negotiations mean more in the lives of rank and file citizens than formal elections.'

British politics is not as consensually well organised or cooperative as the Norwegian model, but there is a central core of similarity in respect of pressure group influence. Accordingly, this chapter examines the way in which organised groups play their part in the government of the country. Democratic government predicates government by the people, and politicians often claim to be speaking on behalf of public opinion. But how do rulers learn about what people want? Elections provide a significant but infrequent opportunity for people to participate in politics. These are held every four years or so, but pressure groups provide continuous opportunities for such involvement and communication.

Tony Blair faced a threat to his public sector pay policy from the stubborn refusal of the firefighters' union to reach a settlement
Source: Copyright © Chris Riddell. From *The Observer*, 17 November 2002. Reproduced with permission from Guardian Newspapers Limited

■ Definitions

Interest or **pressure groups** are formed by people to protect or advance a shared interest. Like political parties, groups may be mass campaigning bodies, but whereas parties have policies for many issues and, usually, wish to form a government, groups are essentially sectional and wish to influence government only on specific policies.

The term 'pressure group' is relatively recent, but organised groups tried to influence government long before the modern age of representative democracy. The Society for Effecting the Abolition of the Slave Trade was founded in 1787 and under the leadership of William Wilberforce and Thomas Clarkson succeeded in abolishing the slave trade in 1807. In 1839, the Anti-Corn Law League was established, providing a model for how a pressure group can influence government. It successfully mobilised popular and élite opinion against legislation that benefited landowners at the expense of the rest of society and in 1846 achieved its objective after converting the Prime Minister of the day, Sir Robert Peel, to its cause. It proved wrong the cynical dictum that the interests of the rich and powerful will invariably triumph over those of the poor and weak and strengthened the supporters of Britain's at that time nascent representative democracy. In the twentieth century, the scope of government has grown immensely and impinges on the lives of many different groups. After 1945, the development of the mixed economy and the welfare state drew even more people into the orbit of governmental activity. Groups developed to defend and promote interests likely to be affected by particular government policies. For its own part, government came to see pressure groups as valuable sources of information and potential support. The variety of modern pressure groups therefore reflects the infinite diversity of interests in society. A distinction is usually drawn between the following:

1. **Sectional** or **interest groups**, most of which are motivated by the particular economic interests of their members. Classic examples of these are trade unions, professional bodies (e.g. the British Medical Association) and employers' organisations.

2. **Cause** or **promotion groups**, which exist to promote an idea not directly related to the personal interests of its members. Wilberforce's

was such a group, and in modern times the Campaign for Nuclear Disarmament (CND), the Child Poverty Action Group (CPAG) and the Society for the Protection of the Unborn Child (SPUC) can be identified. Of the environmental groups, the Ramblers' Association, Greenpeace and Friends of the Earth are perhaps the best examples.

Other species of pressure group include:

■ *Peak associations*: These are umbrella organisations that represent broad bands of similar groups such as employers (the Confederation of British Industry, CBI) and workers (the Trades Union Congress, TUC).

■ *'Fire brigade' groups*: So called because they form in reaction to a specific problem and disband if and when it has been solved. They are often 'single-issue' groups; the Anti-Corn Law League could, at a pinch, be regarded as one such, and the contemporary coalition of environmental groups supporting the Road Traffic Reduction Campaign (see Box 11.1) is another.

■ *Episodic groups*: These are usually non-political but occasionally throw themselves into campaigning when their interests are affected: for example, sports clubs campaigning for more school playing fields.

Membership of sectional groups is limited to those who are part of the specific interest group, for example coal miners or doctors. In contrast, support for a cause such as nuclear disarmament or anti-smoking can potentially embrace all adults. However, the two types of group are not mutually exclusive. Some trade unions take a stand on political causes, for example (in the past) on apartheid in South Africa, or on poverty, sexual equality or foreign policy (e.g. Bill Morris's advice to Tony Blair in September 2002 to resist American plans to invade Iraq). Some members of cause groups may have a material interest in promoting the cause, for example teachers in the Campaign for the Advancement for State Education or teacher members of the Politics Association, which campaigns for improved political literacy. It should be noted that pressure groups regularly seek to influence each other to maximise impact and often find themselves in direct conflict over certain issues, for example, and most obviously, 'Forest' which defends the rights of smokers and 'Ash', the anti-smoking body.

BOX 11.1 EXAMPLE

The Road Traffic Reduction Campaign

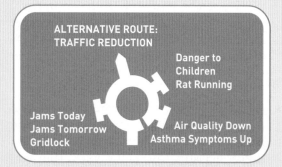

ALTERNATIVE ROUTE:
TRAFFIC REDUCTION

Danger to
Children
Rat Running

Jams Today
Jams Tomorrow
Gridlock

Air Quality Down
Asthma Symptoms Up

This campaign is a collaborative venture by groups perceiving a shared interest in reducing traffic congestion. If the campaign proves successful, it could be regarded as a 'fire brigade' grouping. Members of the Campaign Steering Group include Friends of the Earth, the National Asthma Campaign, the Civic Trust, the cycling group Sustrans and the Green Party, among many others.

In June 1999, they circulated an 'update' article to supporters that recorded their activities and noted their successes. Glenda Jackson, the transport minister, was congratulated for saying (7 May 1999) 'We will set national traffic reduction targets before the end of this parliament' and Michael Meacher, environment minister, for saying that 'overall traffic reduction remains a commitment'. Such plaudits are disingenuous in that their main purpose is to repeat stated commitments important to the movement so that the politicians involved will find it more difficult to ignore or disown them. On the reverse side of the article, transcripts of the ministerial statements are revealed to be the result of clever and sharp questioning at public meetings by campaign members. Indeed, a cynical reader of these transcripts might conclude that the commitments were extracted from somewhat reluctant politicians. Whatever the truth about the politicians' commitment, the result is effective pressure group action. Campaign supporters were enjoined to undertake actions such as writing to congratulate the ministers on their statements, to ask Labour groups on local councils to pass supporting resolutions, and to ask councillors to propose similar motions for the council to send.

Source: From the Road Traffic Reduction Campaign. Reproduced with permission from the Friends of the Earth

■ Civil society and groups

Civil society has a long provenance in political thought, being related to the seventeenth-century notion of a 'state of nature', which humans in theory inhabited before entering the protective confines of the state (see Chapter 4). The idea of such an independent social entity enabled the likes of Hobbes and Locke to argue that citizens had the right to overthrow a corrupt or failing government. Civil society was held to be the not overtly political relationships in society: those of family, business, church and, especially according to the modern sense of the term, voluntary organisations. These relationships help people to live together, cooperating, compromising; accepting both leadership and responsibility; providing the very basis of democratic activity; and training members in the art of democratic politics. Some commentators have argued that, while citizen protest led to the overthrow of communist govern-

ments, the absence of a strong or 'thick' civil society in Eastern European countries has hindered their transition from totalitarian to democratic society. The ability to form organisations independent of the state is one of the hallmarks and, indeed, preconditions of a democratic society. A study by Ashford and Timms (1992) revealed substantial membership of groups in the UK, including 16 per cent in church or religious organisations, 14 per cent in trade unions, 17 per cent in sporting organisations and 5 per cent in environmental or ecological groups.

An interesting change in the attitudes of the public has occurred over recent decades in most developed Western societies: people increasingly prefer to invest energy in groups – cause, single-issue, protective – rather than in political parties. Indeed, membership of political parties or groups mustered only 4.9 per cent in the Ashford and Timms' survey cited above. The increased membership of 'new social movements', especially those concerned with environmental concerns, has provided an inverse mirror of faith in the political system. An opinion poll taken in 1981 in eleven Western European countries and repeated in 1991 registered a fall in confidence in government competence in six countries, no change in four and an increase in only one: Denmark (Nye, 1997). The same survey, however, perhaps explaining the appeal of the new social movements, revealed a 90 per cent endorsement of 'a democratic form of government' and of the suggestion that 'we should look for ways to develop democracy further'. Ulrick Beck writes of the emergence of 'sub politics': popular movements such as Greenpeace and Oxfam, as well as single-issue ones, that have gravitated downwards away from the legislature (Beck, 1992).

'Bowling alone'

One American student of civil society, Robert Putnam (1995), offers a depressing analysis in his essay 'Bowling alone'. He points out that despite rising levels of education – usually associated with increased participation – involvement with voluntary bodies was in decline: parent–teacher association membership had fallen from 12 million in 1982 to 5 million in 1995. Unions, churches and many other bodies reported similar declines. Moreover, people were less likely to socialise – the percentage who socialised with neighbours on more than one occasion during the year dropped from 72 per cent in 1974 to 61 per cent in 1993. The title of his book derived from the statistic that while the numbers involved in bowling between 1980 and 1993 increased by 10 per cent, the number playing in league teams plummeted by 40 per cent. Americans were 'bowling alone'. Putnam saw this as merely one symptom of 'disengagement': fading away of groups; the decline of solidarity and trust; and a detachment from the political process evidenced in falling turnouts at elections. Some bodies have huge memberships but, as Putnam shows in the USA, these are often 'passive memberships' where someone pays an annual subscription but attends no meetings. If Britain is anything like America – and it often mimics trends a few years removed – a slow decline in pressure group activity and a 'thinning' of civic society would seem to be a worrying possibility.

Research by Peter Hall (1999) has suggested that Britain has a much healthier pattern of voluntary group membership than the USA, but a report by the Institute of Education in February 2003 suggested worrying similarities with our transatlantic cousins. The study was based on three birth cohorts – 1946, 1958 and 1970. The first group produced a figure of 60 per cent membership of voluntary groups, the second only 15 per cent and those born in 1970 a mere 8 per cent.

However, more reassuringly, the 'Citizen Audit' programme at Sheffield University seemed to bear out Hall's findings. This report suggests that, despite the low turnout in the 2001 general election, the 'British public is politically engaged'. Its findings, based on interviews with 13,000 people, found that three-quarters had engaged in one or more political activities, more particularly:

■ 29 million had given money to a 'citizens' organisation;

■ 14 million had raised money for such an organisation;

■ 22 million had signed a petition;

■ 18 million had boycotted certain products in their shopping;

■ 17 million had bought certain goods for political reasons;

■ 2.5 million had taken part in a public demonstration.

Quite why a 'politically engaged' public should do all these things and yet not bother to vote in such massive numbers in 2001 is still unclear.

We were somewhat slow in understanding that these groups were tending to acquire authority. We underestimated the extent of these changes – we failed to engage in a serious dialogue with these new groups . . . simply put, the institutions of global society are being reinvented as technology redefines relationships between individuals and organisations.

World Chairman of Shell following its climbdown over the disposal of the *Brent Spar* oil platform in the face of widespread protest led by Greenpeace

---

■ Pressure groups and government

The relationship between interest groups and government is not always or even usually **adversarial**. Groups may be useful to government. Ministers and civil servants often lack the information or expertise necessary to make wise policies, or indeed the authority to ensure that they are implemented effectively. They frequently turn to the relevant representative organisations to find out defects in an existing line of policy and seek suggestions as to how things might be improved. They sound out groups' leaders about probable resistance to a new line of policy. Moreover, an interest group's support, or at least acceptance, for a policy can help to 'legitimise' it and thus maximise its chances of successful implementation. If bodies involved in a new law refuse to cooperate and organise against it – as in the case of the poll tax in 1990 – a law can become unenforceable. The accession to power of Labour in May 1997 raised the spectre of union influence once again dominating policy, as in the 1970s. Blair has been emphatic that unions, like any other group seeking influence, will receive 'fairness but no favours'. Indeed, Blair has often seemed more concerned to woo business groups than the electorally unpopular unions, so much so that Wyn Grant, an authority on pressure groups, has judged Blair's Labour government more pro-business than any other of which he can think.

In the several stages of the policy process, groups have opportunities to play an important role (see Chapter 24):

1. At the initial stage they may put an issue on the policy agenda (e.g. environmental groups promoted awareness of the dangers to the ozone layer caused by many products and have forced government to act).

2. When governments issue Green Papers (setting out policy options for discussion) and White Papers (proposals for legislation), groups may **lobby** back-benchers or civil servants.

3. In Parliament, groups may influence the final form of legislation. As we can see from Figure 11.1, groups are involved at virtually every stage of the policy process.

Insider–outsider groups

Groups are usually most concerned to gain access to ministers and civil servants – the key policy makers. Pressure group techniques are usually a means to that end. When government departments are formulating policies there are certain groups they consult.

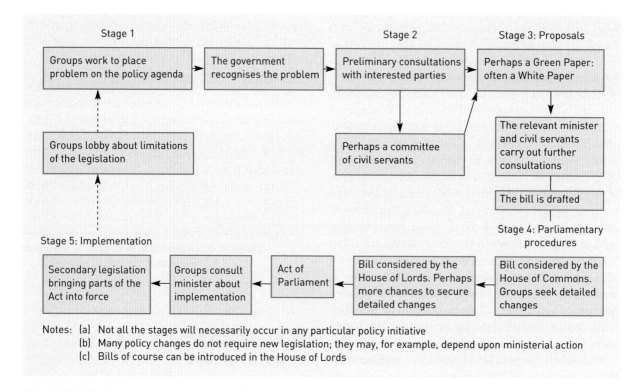

Notes: (a) Not all the stages will necessarily occur in any particular policy initiative
(b) Many policy changes do not require new legislation; they may, for example, depend upon ministerial action
(c) Bills of course can be introduced in the House of Lords

Figure 11.1 Pressure groups and the policy process
Source: From W. Grant (1998) 'Pressure groups and the policy process', *Social Studies Review*, Vol. 3, No. 5. Reproduced with permission from the California Council for Social Studies

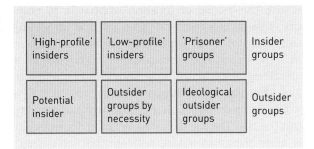

| 'High-profile' insiders | 'Low-profile' insiders | 'Prisoner' groups | Insider groups |
| Potential insider | Outsider groups by necessity | Ideological outsider groups | Outsider groups |

Figure 11.2 Grant's typology of pressure groups
Source: From W. Grant (1985) 'Insider and outsider pressure groups', *Social Studies Review*, Vol. 1, No. 1. Reproduced with permission from the California Council for Social Studies

The Ministry of Agriculture, Fisheries and Food, when it existed under that name, was in continuous and close contact with the National Farmers' Union. Indeed, in 1989, in the wake of the salmonella food-poisoning scandal, it was alleged by some that the ministry neglected the interests of consumers compared with those of the producers. Wyn Grant (1985) has described groups that are regularly consulted as 'insider groups'; in the study of pressure groups this has become possibly the most important distinction.

On the other hand, the Campaign for Nuclear Disarmament, for example, mounts public campaigns largely because it has no access to Whitehall; in Grant's language it is an 'outsider group'. Not only does it lack specialist knowledge on foreign policy or defence systems, but the policies it advocates are flatly opposed to those followed by every postwar British government. Grant's classification of groups is summarised in Figure 11.2.

To gain access to the inner sanctums of decision making, groups usually have to demonstrate that they possess at least some of the following features:

1. *Authority*, which may be demonstrated in the group's ability to organise virtually all its potential members. The National Union of Mineworkers spoke for nearly 100 per cent of miners for many years, but its authority was weakened not just by the fall-off in membership after the disastrous 1983–4 miners' strike but also by the formation in 1985 of the breakaway Union of Democratic Miners. Similarly, the authority of the teachers' unions has been weakened because of the divisions between so many different groups. Overwhelming support by members for their group

leadership's policies is another guarantor of authority.

2. *Information*: Groups such as the British Medical Association and the Howard League for Penal Reform command an audience among decision makers because of their expertise and information.

3. *The compatibility of a group's objectives with those of the government*: For example, trade unions traditionally received a more friendly hearing when pressing for favourable trade union legislation or state intervention in industry from a Labour than from a Conservative government. The TUC always received short shrift from Margaret Thatcher, who made no effort to disguise her hostility or even contempt. But even when likely to receive a friendly hearing, groups seeking access to the policy process are not advised to put forward demands that the government regards as unreasonable.

4. *Compatibility of group objectives with public sympathies*: A group out of sympathy with public views – for example, advocating the housing of convicted paedophiles in residential areas – is unlikely to gain inner access to decision making.

5. *Reliable track record for sensible advice in the past and the ability, through knowledge of Whitehall, to fit in with its procedures and confidential ethos*. Most insider groups, like the BMA, CBI and NFU, fit this profile.

6. *Possession of powerful sanctions*: Some groups of workers are able to disrupt society through the withdrawal of their services. The bargaining power of coal miners, for example, was very strong in the mid-1970s, when Middle East oil was in short supply and expensive, but much weaker a decade later, when cheaper oil was more available as a source of energy. The ability of electricians to inflict injury on society was greater even than the miners', but after the privatisation of electricity their ability to 'close down' the nation was fragmented.

But becoming and remaining an insider group requires the acceptance of constraints. Group leaders, for example, should respect confidences, be willing to compromise, back up demands with evidence and avoid threats (Grant, 1989, 1990). Grant accepts that this typology is not quite as clear-cut as it at first seems. For example, some groups can be insider and outsider at the same time, e.g. Greenpeace. Also, insider groups, in the present day, are not invariably more influential than outsider ones: groups connected with the fuel crisis of 2000 brought the country to a standstill within days.

Being on the inside is still thought by many to be better than on the outside, though this does amount to a kind of Faustian pact that groups sign with government. If government fails to deliver the influence that group leaders expect, they can find themselves in trouble with their membership. Alternatively, they can become so closely associated with a particular government policy that they can lose credibility if that policy fails (but see below for Grant's recent thinking on the evolution of group relations with government).

Pressure group methods can be seen on a continuum running from peaceful methods to violent ones (see Figure 11.3). Anyone working for a pressure group, especially if it is a local one focusing on, say, a planning issue, will find themselves working hard at routine chores such as stuffing envelopes, ringing up supporters, delivering publicity and collecting signatures on petitions. However, other groups use different techniques. Trade unions use or threaten

to use the 'denial of function' approach; in practice, this means going on strike, a kind of holding to ransom of those who benefit from their labour. In some cases, however, such methods encounter moral restraints; for example, should nurses refuse to look after patients in support of a pay dispute? Few would find this easy. Other groups are concerned to test the law. The Ramblers' Association, for example, is quite happy to ignore notices from landowners denying them access if the notices are not legal; in such circumstances, its members are happy to assert their legal rights and to clear any obstructions that may have been put in place. However, they stop short of actually breaking the law. Other groups are prepared to go even further. Some anarchist groups deliberately break the law as part of a strategy of undermining law and order and existing civil society; others do so to attract the publicity of a court case and possibly a 'martyred' period in jail for an activist.

Such groups and sentiments are still rare. Most groups concentrate their efforts at the peaceful end of the spectrum, but a change in the political culture is discernible over the last decade.

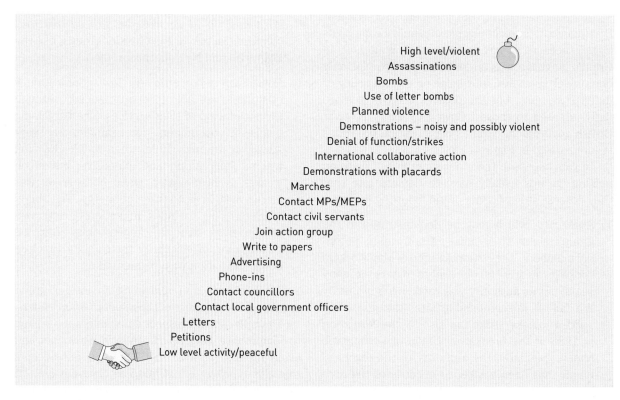

High level/violent
Assassinations
Bombs
Use of letter bombs
Planned violence
Demonstrations – noisy and possibly violent
Denial of function/strikes
International collaborative action
Demonstrations with placards
Marches
Contact MPs/MEPs
Contact civil servants
Join action group
Write to papers
Advertising
Phone-ins
Contact councillors
Contact local government officers
Letters
Petitions
Low level activity/peaceful

Figure 11.3 Pressure group methods continuum

The growth (and increasing respectability) of direct action

Some groups either are so passionate or have become so impatient with the slow-moving wheels of government that they have deliberately used high-profile and illegal tactics. Brian Cass, the chief executive of Huntingdon Life Sciences, which conducts experiments on animals, was once beaten by animal rights activists wielding baseball bats and in April 2003 won a court injunction to prevent protesters from approaching within 50 yards of employees' homes. However, the best known of such extremists have probably been the protesters against the Newbury bypass and later the new runway at Manchester Airport. These protesters have broken new ground in pressure group techniques by using their own bodies as shields. They have, for example, sought to implant themselves in places that would halt further work on the project concerned. These have included the building of tree houses, which security guards have been obliged to scale in order to winkle out the intrepid protesters, and the building of a network of tunnels within which some protesters have padlocked themselves to blocks of concrete. Some of the right-wing newspapers began by demonising these as dirty illegal protests, but the young people involved often turned out to be the children of middle-class professionals, articulate and attractive people not at all like the right-wing stereotype of scruffy Marxist ideologues. In consequence, the protesters were often not criticised but lauded and turned into minor folk heroes. Daniel Hooper, who under his activist name of 'Swampy' featured in many protests, became a frequent guest on chat shows and was even, for a while, given his own newspaper column.

One of the key reasons why such methods did not occasion the opprobrium usual for the excesses of youth was that the causes involved were often supported by middle-class people. The comfortable denizens of Wilmslow and surrounding areas were hotly opposed to the runway project and, while they might baulk at some of the methods used, were certainly willing to offer moral support to the mud-covered martyrs. Perhaps the endorsement of 'respectable' middle-class opinion is crucial in terms of how the media cover such stories. The Greenham Common women – often muddy, strident, badly dressed and with crew-cut hair – who camped outside US cruise missile bases in the UK during the 1980s were generally given negative coverage, especially by the right-wing press. Environmental protests, however, were in a different category, as were those against the export of live animals (see Box 11.2). *The Observer* (6 June 1999) featured comments by six women supporting Genetix Snowball 'leading the fight against GM crops'. The six women were all middle-class, educated and committed to the cause. 'Do I look like an anarchist weirdo?' asked one. Another said 'Direct action is about ordinary people doing something, a problem for everybody to be involved in. If the government isn't going to get involved, then it's up to us. For me that's imperative.' Yet another pointed out: 'We may be a little dull. I don't have dreadlocks. I go climbing and walking around the Peak District. An awful lot of people think they are powerless. When you do something you realise the power you have.' Perhaps this new militancy is part of a growing awareness of political power among ordinary citizens. It also suggests that a sea-change has occurred regarding citizens' view of themselves (see Box 11.8 below).

When he [Bertrand Russell, venerable philosopher and CND stalwart] attempted, Luther like, to hammer a petition to the very door of the Ministry it opened before him, only to reveal an official armed with a polite attitude and some Sellotape. The police watched with scarcely veiled amusement.

Jonathan Green, *All Dressed Up: The Sixties and the Counter Culture*, 1999

Terror tactics

The use of terroristic methods in Western societies has usually been strongly opposed by the general public, but they have been used, and not just by extremist political groups like the Baader-Meinhof group in Germany. In the USA, anti-abortion campaigners have shot doctors who undertake abortion work, and closer to home the Animal Liberation Front has regularly held hostile and sometimes violent demonstrations outside laboratories conducting experiments on animals (see Box 11.3). In some cases the group has also planted bombs.

On 18 June 1999, the group Reclaim the Streets and an alliance of environmental groups took over the City of London in an action that involved violence. In an article in *The Observer* (31 October 1999) entitled 'The New Revolutionaries', anti-GM campaigner Jo Hamilton is quoted as saying: 'What

BOX 11.2 EXAMPLE

Export of live animals, 1997, Brightlingsea

Once the ferries banned the export of animals, exporters had to find alternative ports. Brightlingsea in Essex could only be accessed via a three-mile road through residential housing, and the movement of animal-laden lorries was therefore highly visible and vulnerable to protesters who lined the road. The prime targets for such protests were lorries containing calves destined to become veal on continental tables. Bull calves are much less valuable to farmers than milk-producing heifers and so are exported to Europe at one week old to be turned into veal. This is a heartless process entailing the enclosing of the calf in a solid-sided crate with a slatted floor. They are locked into this darkened space, unable to turn around, and kept for six months until ready for slaughter. The calf is kept without straw and fed on a liquid diet designed to produce the distinctive white-coloured meat. In January 1995, the animal welfare group CIWF issued a video of how calves were treated *en route* to their destinations and it attracted much publicity, putting the treatment of animals on the political agenda. The campaign was not presented as a vegetarian one – 'You don't have to stop eating meat to care – ban live exports' – and this attracted a broad base of public support. Respectable middle-class people who had never demonstrated before were seen lining the road to Brightlingsea, on one occasion blocking the road with sand. Such activities have lent illegal tactics some new 'respectability', but it all depends on the issue concerned. After all, according to McLeod's survey (1998), over 70 per cent of British people currently care for a pet, and this contact clearly encourages sympathy with the plight of agricultural animals, which are often treated abominably by 'factory' farming techniques.

Source: Adapted from Simpson (1999)

BOX 11.3 EXAMPLE

The case of Darley Oaks Farm and Gladys Hammond

In October 2004, thieves stole the body of Gladys Hammond, mother-in-law to Christopher Hall, owner of a farm in Staffordshire which bred guinea pigs for scientific experimentation. In 2005 four activists were charged with conspiracy to backmail. The leader of the group was revealed as Jon Ablewhite, a clergyman's son, who had led a six-year campaign against the farm. He was a charismatic character, six feet plus, according to a fellow activist: motivated and organised – 'amicable and educated, just the type you need'. When the farm eventually stopped breeding guinea pigs he was ecstatic, saying: 'Factory farming is on the same moral level as the Holocaust because of the systematic abuse and killing of these animals. Don't forget that Goebbels learned from factory farmers and used their methods to execute the Jews.' Mrs Hammond's remains were recovered in 2006 and reburied on 31 May.

Jon Ablewhite, accused of desecration of Gladys Hammond's grave
Source: Chris Radburn / PA / Empics

some people would consider "criminal" action is appropriate in some cases, including criminal damage. You have to look at the action in a broader perspective. It is not a black and white area. I think there is real violence when there is enough food to eat but people are starving because of the economic system.'

Such sentiments reveal that some groups begin with limited aims focusing on one policy area, then widen their focus to take in wider targets for change. Another activist for RTS is quoted as saying: 'We tried all the tree hugging at the Newbury bypass. It did get some great publicity, but the road still got built. We lost. There are a lot of us who now

recognise we can't pick individual battles; we have to take on the whole system.' The article also pointed out that some protest action has become international with coordination made easier through the Internet. At this point pressure groups are beginning to leave the world of merely influencing policy and are joining that of political parties.

A curious example of a pressure group which was undermined by members prepared to use extremist methods is Fathers 4 Justice. This was formed in December 2002 by marketing executive Matt O'Connor who had suffered from legal decisions denying him access to his children after divorce. His idea was to use high profile but basically amusing

BOX 11.4   IDEAS AND PERSPECTIVES

Violence as a political weapon

Writing in *The Guardian* on 14 November 2005, columnist Gary Younge discussed the riots devastating French suburbs and considered the efficacy of violent means to achieve political ends. He quoted African-American abolitionist Frederick Douglass's aphorism that 'Power concedes nothing without a demand. It never did and it never will.' He pointed out that the mostly unemployed ethnic minorities, living in run-down estates and suffering racial discrimination, had nothing to lose, but their actions immediately won concessions and government actions designed to alleviate their problems: better employment possibilities, tax breaks for companies in sink estates, lump sums for the jobless who return to work, extra teachers and 10,000 scholarships to encourage brighter pupils to stay on at school. Younge comments that 'none of this would have happened without the riots.' Any amount of peaceful measures would have attracted feeling attention but it was the damage to property and the threat to life which galvanised the French government. He goes on to say that 'When all non-violent, democratic means of achieving a just end are unavailable, redundant or exhausted, rioting is justifiable', but he goes on to add: 'Rioting should be neither celebrated nor fetishised, because it is a sign not of strength but of weakness. Like a strike, it is often the last and most desperate weapon available to those with the least power.' He warns that rioting easily becomes an end in itself and something which can polarise, divide and set loose murder and mayhem in society. He issues something like a partial endorsement of violence as a political weapon, urging that it be used with restraint and economy. Yet, critics might suggest to him, such methods are effective only because they threaten such irrational and cataclysmic spirals into chaos. The problem is that using the threat of chaos to win concessions is perilously close to unleashing the real thing.

Also addressing this topic, Professor Timothy Garton Ash, writing in *The Guardian* on 2 March 2006, perceived the emergence of a 'group veto' by groups who say:

We feel so strongly about this that we are going to do everything we can to stop it. We recognize no moral limits. The end justifies the means. Continue on this path and you must fear for your life . . .

If the intimidators succeed, then the lesson for any group that strongly believes in anything is: shout more loudly, be more extreme, threaten violence, and you will get your way.

Inch by inch, paragraph by paragraph, we are becoming less free.

He concludes that any point of view which does not threaten harm should be tolerated – even right-wing historian David Irving's Holocaust denials – but that any person or group which urges 'kill the Jews!' or 'kill the Muslims!' should be 'met with the full rigour of the law'.

stunts to win public attention: 'ordinary dads doing extraordinary things'. So 200 members dressed up as Santa and raided the Lord Chancellor's Department. In November 2003 David Chick caused gridlock when he dressed as Spiderman and climbed a crane on Tower Bridge. Several other stunts took place involving men dressed as superheroes, but tactics were ratcheted up in May 2004 when members bombed Blair with condoms filled with purple flour. Finally, the organisation overstretched itself when on 18 January 2006 it transpired that a group connected with Fathers 4 Justice had planned to kidnap Tony Blair's five-year-old son Leo. The idea, it seemed, was to hold him for a while and then set him free unharmed, but Matt O'Connor was dismayed: 'We do peaceful direct action with a dash of humour. We're in the business of uniting dads with their kids, not separating them.' He indicated that his group would cease to function.

Aiming for the power points

Pressure groups seek to influence the political system at the most accessible and cost-effective 'power points'. The obvious target areas include:

1. *The public at large*: Groups seek to raise money, train staff, attract and mobilise membership, to assist in group activities and to apply pressure on their behalf.

2. *Other pressure group members*: Groups with similar objectives will often duplicate membership, e.g. Friends of the Earth members may also join Greenpeace. Moreover, such groups can combine forces over particular campaigns such as the traffic reduction one (see Box 11.1) or the Countryside Alliance, which coordinated a heterogeneous collection of groups against Labour's threatened ban on fox hunting (see Box 11.9 below).

3. *Political parties*: Groups will seek to influence the party that seems most sympathetic to its views. Inevitably trade unions – the historical crucible of the labour movement – look to Labour, and business groups tend to concentrate on the Conservatives (see below). Constitutional reform groups such as Charter88 initially looked to the Liberal Democrats but, as such support was already solid, it embarked on a successful campaign to convert the Labour Party. Interestingly, the Campaign for Nuclear Disarmament achieved a similar conversion back in the 1960s

and in the early 1980s but never achieved its objective, as Labour decided to abandon such a policy during the later part of the decade.

4. *Parliament*: Especially the House of Commons, but in recent years increasingly the House of Lords. The Commons is more attractive to groups as this is where the important debates on legislation occur. As Box 11.1 shows, groups often draft amendments for friendly MPs – often asked to hold voluntary office – to submit in Parliament. MPs are also sought – and this may be their most important function for some groups – for their ability to provide access to even more important people, such as the increasingly important Select Committees and (especially) regular meetings with ministers and civil servants (see Box 11.1 again). This ability to provide access – sometimes at a price – has been at the centre of the rows over sleaze that dogged Major's government and has also affected Blair's administration. The academic Study of Parliament Group surveyed a number of groups, discovering that over three-quarters were in regular contact with MPs; some 60 per cent said the same of members of the Lords.

5. *Ministers and civil servants*: Clearly, ministers and their civil servants are natural targets for groups. Regular access provides 'insider' status and potentially composition of the policy-making 'triangle' also comprising ministers and civil servants (see Chapter 24). Baggott's research shows that 12 per cent of insider groups will see Cabinet ministers weekly, 45 per cent monthly; the figures for junior ministers were 14 and 67 per cent, respectively; for senior civil servants 25 and 49 per cent; for junior civil servants 55 and 76 per cent.

Groups anxiously seek membership of key bodies, which include:

■ Over 300 executive bodies with 4,000 members with the power to disburse financial resources.

■ Nearly 1,000 advisory committees with some 10,000 members.

■ Committees of inquiry into a myriad of topics (Labour, especially, have favoured such task forces since coming to power).

■ *Royal Commissions*: Not favoured by Conservative governments after 1979 but re-embraced by Blair's Labour government.

■ *Pre-legislative consultation*: It is established government practice that all interested parties should be asked to consult and give their views on proposed new legislation. For example, changes affecting universities are circulated not just to them but to groups with a strong interest in such education such as the Association of University Teachers. It was alleged that the Conservative governments after 1979 went through the motions of consulting but often allowed only a very short time and then ignored the advice anyway.

6. European Union (EU): Pressure group activity is like a river in that it seeks out naturally where to flow. Since power has shifted to Brussels so groups have automatically shifted their focus too. In the early days, when there was no elected European Parliament, their activities helped to reduce the '**democratic deficit**' (Greenwood, 1997, p. 1), but since the Single European Act in 1986 groups have played an increasingly important role as the competence of EU institutions has expanded to include the environment and technology. The Maastricht Treaty of 1992 also extended EU powers into health and consumer protection. The Commission has calculated that there are 3,000 interest groups in Brussels, including more than 500 Europe-wide federations and employing 10,000 personnel (Greenwood, 1997, p. 3). In addition there are over 3,000 lobbyists, a huge increase in just a few years. These lobbyists and groups – especially the business ones – invest the substantial resources needed to set up shop in the heart of Belgium because they feel the stakes are so high. The EU can make decisions that deeply affect, among others, the work and profits of fishermen, farmers and the tobacco industry, as well as the conditions of employment of trade unionists. Greenwood discerns five areas of EU activity that attract group pressure:

■ *Regulation*: Much of the EU's output of directives comprises rules governing the way the consumer is served. Indeed, in some sectors the bulk of new regulatory activities now takes place not in Whitehall but in Brussels.

■ *Promotion*: For example, the development of key technologies to support export drives.

■ *Integration*: Such as the measures to advance free and fair competition in the Single Market.

■ *Funding*: Such as the Structural Funds to reduce regional imbalances or funds for research activities.

■ *Enablement*: Such as measures to support environmental improvement.

Baggott (1995, pp. 209–10) provides some examples of successful lobbying, including Friends of the Earth's pressure on the EU to hold the UK to water quality directives and the success of motorcyclists and manufacturers in persuading the European Parliament to reject a Commission ban on high-performance motorcycles. He also points out that groups have altered their focus as the powers of the institutions have evolved. The SEA and Maastricht Treaty expanded the power of the European Parliament and made it possible for it to amend legislation; pressure groups directed their attentions accordingly. But the major source of group interest remains the Commission, a relatively small number of officials who can be influenced via the usual processes of presentations, briefing documents, networks, lunches and so forth. Some directorates are more receptive than others, but on the whole the institutions of the EU expect to be lobbied and welcome such attentions on the grounds that people wishing to influence measures usually represent those who will be affected by them and hence are likely to make useful inputs. The cross-sectoral federations are often consulted as they are thought to be broadly representative: for example, UNICE (Union of Industrial Confederations of Europe), the highly influential EUROCHAMBRES (the association of European Chambers of Commerce), and ETUC (European Trade Union Confederation).

7. *The media*: The director of the charity Child Poverty Action once said that 'coverage by the media is our main strategy' (Kingdom, 1999, p. 512). Such a statement could equally be made by virtually all pressure groups outside those few insider groups at the epicentre of government policy and decision making. Unless influence is virtually automatic, any group must maximise its ability to mobilise the public to indicate its authority, its power and potential sanction; influencing the public can be achieved only via the media. Therefore ensuring that group activities catch the eye of the media is the number one priority. Unsurprisingly, Baggott's findings revealed that 74 per cent of outsider groups contacted the media weekly and 84 per cent did so monthly.

Interestingly, the percentages for the insider groups were even higher at 86 and 94 per cent, respectively, suggesting that media coverage serves important interest reinforcement functions even for those with a direct line to the government's policy-making process.

8. *Informal contacts*: So far the contacts mentioned have been ones that are in the public domain; it is quite possible that most would have a written minute of proceedings. However, the world does not function just on the basis of formal, minuted meetings. Britain is a relatively small island with a ruling élite drawn substantially from the 7 per cent of the population who are educated in public schools. It might be claimed that such a critique is a little old-fashioned but many argue that the deep connections of class, blood, marriage, shared education and leisure pursuits link decision makers in the country in a way that makes them truly, in the words of John Scott (1991), a 'ruling class'. It might also be claimed that the above analysis relates more to the Conservative political élite than to the more widely drawn and variegated New Labour equivalent. But arguably political decision-making is only one aspect of power in society – economic and cultural decisions can be very important for millions of people. Glinga (1986) describes the manifold ways in which the upper-class British mix at their public schools, carrying the badge of their accent with them as an asset into the outside world, where they continue to enact school-like rituals in gentlemen's clubs such as the Athenaeum, Brooks's, White's and the Army and Navy. There they can exchange views and influence friends in the very highest of places. Jeremy Paxman points out (Paxman, 1991) that when Sir Robin Butler was made Cabinet Secretary he was at once proposed for membership of the exclusive Athenaeum, Brooks's and the Oxford and Cambridge clubs. It was almost as if the 'Establishment' had made the appropriate room at their top table for the new recruit. In addition, when not in their clubs they can meet in other élite leisure places such as the opera at Covent Garden, Glyndebourne and Henley. This form of the 'Establishment' still exists and still exerts much influence; arguably the tendency for even New Labour to be agnostic over the social provenance of its élite members helps extend its influence. It is impossible to reckon the influence of such informal contacts, but some, especially

BIOGRAPHY

Sir Robin Butler (1938–)

Former Secretary to the Cabinet. Educated at Oxford, from where he joined the Treasury. Worked in private offices of Wilson and Heath before rising to Permanent Secretary in the Treasury and then Secretary to the Cabinet 1988–97. Perhaps appropriately for Britain's top civil servant, Butler seemed to epitomise many of the ideals of the British ruling élite: he was the well-rounded man (he was also a rugby blue); he was apparently modest, articulate and effortlessly able while at the same time being 'infinitely extendable': able to cope with any crisis or any demands on his time or intellect. In 2005 he issued his report into the intelligence on which the decision to go to war in Iraq was based, a report which contained a degree of criticism rare for such a senior member of the Establishment, though his solution was scarcely revolutionary: a return to traditional Cabinet government where papers are tabled and discussed with minutes taken and circulated.

the Marxists, claim that this is how the really big decisions are always made: in private and in secret between fellow members of the closely interlinked networks of the ruling élite. What follows in public is merely the democratic window dressing for self-interested fixing.

Factors determining effectiveness

Baggott (1988) points out that the effectiveness of pressure groups is also a function of organisational factors. They need:

- a coherent organisational structure;
- high-quality and efficient staff (these days they recruit direct from the best universities);
- adequate financial resources;
- good leadership;
- clear strategy.

Economic interest groups are usually well financed, but cause groups can often command significant

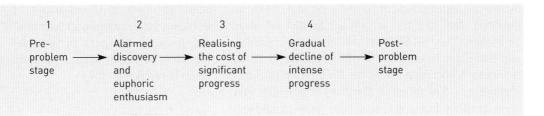

1	2	3	4	
Pre-problem stage	→ Alarmed discovery and euphoric enthusiasm	→ Realising the cost of significant progress	→ Gradual decline of intense progress	→ Post-problem stage

Figure 11.4 The issue attention cycle
Source: From A. McCulloch (1998) 'Politics and the environment', *Talking Politics*, Autumn 1998. Reproduced with permission from The Politics Association

annual income also. For example, Help the Aged raised over £50 million in 1996, the Salvation Army £70 million, cancer charities nearly £250 million and overseas charities over £300 million. In addition, cause groups can compensate for shoestring resources by attracting high-quality committed leadership; for example, in the recent past, Jonathon Porritt (Friends of the Earth), Frank Field (CPAG), Mike Daube (ASH) and perhaps the most effective popular campaigner of them all, Des Wilson of Shelter and many other causes.

Good organisation is also of key importance, and the best pressure groups are as efficiently organised as any business, with high-class staff recruited from the best universities.

Issue attention cycle

The American political scientist Anthony Downs has suggested that the media and the public's receptivity to pressure group messages is another potent factor influencing effectiveness. He pointed out that the new cause groups must run the gauntlet of the 'issue attention' cycle (see Figure 11.4). The pre-problem stage is followed by alarmed discovery, coupled with the feeling that something could and should be done. When it becomes clear, as it usually does, that progress will not be easy, interest declines and this is when the pressure group faces its toughest tests. This has certainly been true of environmental, nuclear disarmament and AIDS campaigns, but all three of these reveal that with new discoveries and fresh events the issue attention cycle can be rerun – possibly frequently over time.

Economic interest groups

The policies of the government in such areas as interest and exchange rates, taxation, spending, trading policy and industrial relations are important in providing the context for the economy. Two of the most powerful interest groups that try to influence these policies are business and trade unions.

Business

Business is naturally deeply affected by government economic policies, and it is understandable that its representatives will seek to exert influence. Many firms depend on government handouts, subsidies and orders and will seek to influence the awarding of contracts. This is particularly true of shipbuilding, highway construction, building construction (the sale of houses is heavily dependent on the interest rate) and defence. But others will certainly be interested in policy matters such as interest rates, taxation levels and so forth.

Globalised business and pressure

In one sense any sizeable business organisation acts like a pressure group. Multinational companies – many with turnovers larger than those of small countries – make their own regular and usually confidential representations to government. When conditions for trading appear more favourable in another country, they pack up and move their whole operation, often within months. The threat to do this and deny employment is a potent weapon which such large companies use to barter advantages from governments.

Strength in unity

Particular industries often form federations, such as the Society of Motor Manufacturers or the Engineering Employers' Federation, and seek strength in unity. The Confederation of British Industry (CBI) was formed in 1965 and since that date has acted as an overall 'peak' organisation to provide a forum for discussion – it holds an annual conference – and to represent the views of members to government.

It has a membership of 15,000, employs several hundred staff and has an annual budget of some £5 million. The CBI is dominated by big companies, and this helps to explain the 1971 breakaway Small Business Association (later the Federation of Small Businesses). For much of Margaret Thatcher's first term of office her policies of high interest and exchange rates damaged manufacturing industry, and the CBI criticised her for it. It blamed the government for not spending enough on infrastructure; it complained that the high exchange rate made exporting difficult and that high interest rates were discouraging investment. On one famous occasion, the then Director General of the CBI, Sir Terence Beckett, called for a 'bare-knuckle' fight to make Margaret Thatcher change her deflationary policies, but his violent rhetoric abated after a stormy confrontation with that formidable lady Prime Minister. In recent years, the CBI has been more supportive of the Conservative government line: John Banham, one of Sir Terence's successors, lined up against the European Social Charter in November 1989, for example, but disagreed over the European Monetary System, which the CBI believed Britain could and should join. Under Tony Blair's business-friendly Labour administration the CBI under Adair Turner was generally supportive of government policy, whilst his highly extrovert, near demagogic successor, Digby Jones, was more critical of government. It is expected that Richard Lambert, appointed to the post in March 2006 and a more cerebral insider (as a Labour-supporting former editor of the *Financial Times*), will be more measured and possibly more effective.

The Institute of Directors is a more right-wing and political campaigning body. It opposed prices and incomes restraints, which the CBI was prepared to support in the 1970s, and it vigorously supported the Conservative government's policies of privatisation, cutting public spending and encouraging free-market economics. The institute also welcomed Conservative measures to lower direct taxation, reform the trade unions and limit minimum wage regulations, and ideally it would like such policies to go further. Other organisations, such as Aims of Industry, are used as means of raising support and indirectly revenue for the Conservative Party. Although no business group has a formal association with the Conservative Party, a number of major firms do make financial contributions. Many businesses utilise the informal contacts mentioned above, especially when the Conservatives are in power, as this tends to open up the channels of communication between government and business. These may take the form of whispers in the ears of government ministers at dinner parties, in gentlemen's clubs and elsewhere (see p. 257).

Trade unions

Trade unions perform two distinct roles. The first is political. Since they helped to form the Labour Party in 1900 they have played, and still play, a decisive role in the internal politics of that party. Trade unions are overtly involved in party politics more deeply than any other interest group.

The second role of individual trade unions is industrial bargaining, to represent the interests of their members on pay and working conditions in negotiations with employers. Three-quarters of all unions are affiliated to the Trades Union Congress (TUC), which speaks for the trade union movement as a whole. In the past this function has involved unions directly in the political life of the country.

Various attempts were made by Labour and Conservative governments to win the agreement of unions to pay policies that would keep inflation in check and the cost of British exports competitive in overseas markets. By the late 1960s, Harold Wilson had become so exasperated with striking trade unions that he proposed measures to curb their tendency to strike and cripple the economy. However, his White Paper *In Place of Strife* was attacked by the unions, and James Callaghan led a successful revolt against it in the Cabinet, destroying the authority of Wilson's government. Ted Heath's administration after 1970 worked hard to solve the problem of union disruption and eventually tried a statutory (i.e. passing new laws) approach, but this foundered hopelessly and resulted in an election in 1974, which he lost. Labour back in power tried to stem the rocketing inflation by engineering a 'Social Contract' with the unions whereby they agreed to restrain wage demands in exchange for favourable policies on pensions, low pay and industrial legislation. This succeeded to an extent and for a while the UK had a pay regime that was almost Scandinavian in its harmony between business and workers, but in 1978 Callaghan's call for a 5 per cent limit was rejected by the unions, and his government descended into the ignominy of the 'winter of discontent' (January–February 1979) with, infamously, bodies left unburied and operating theatres without electricity.

BOX 11.5 **IDEAS AND PERSPECTIVES**

Trade unions and Labour

Ever since February 1900, when the Labour Representation Committee, the embryo of the party, was formed, trade unions have played a key role and are the category of pressure group most closely involved in mainstream politics. Tony Blair famously sought to weaken the link between party and unions, but the many connections still amount to a virtual umbilical cord.

- *Affiliation*: Half of all trade unions are affiliated to the party including the majority of the big unions: Amicus, CWU, TGWU and USDAW. Other unions can have more complex relationships with the party: Unison has a general political fund as well as an affiliated one. Others, like the PCS and NUT, have never been affiliated. The RMT was disaffiliated in 2004 for allowing branches to support other political parties, though it contested this decision. The FBU disaffiliated itself with a view to supporting other left-wing parties; the GMB avoided such action but managed to grumble loudly. With union membership in decline (see Box 11.6), unions wish to conserve the diminishing funding raised for their own purposes.

- *Money link*: A union's political fund receives money from members along with their subscriptions unless they specifically 'contract out'. Unions, if affiliated, decide how much to give to Labour from their funds. One calculation in 2005 was that contributions collected in this fashion and donated to Labour amounted to £24 million between 2002 and 2005, comprising half of the funding the party needs annually. As Labour often runs a deficit, this funding is crucial, so unions have tried to influence the party over issues like Iraq and public service reform by threatening to withdraw funding.

- *Membership*: Each union decides how many members it wishes to say pay the political levy. Those union members who pay the levy can join the party at a reduced rate.

- *Representation*: Union 'block votes' – leaders casting votes on behalf of affiliated members – used to dominate conference voting decisions, but the proportion allowed to count by the block votes was reduced to only 50 per cent in 1996, and the party's stated aim is to achieve 'one member, one vote' eventually. Unions can no longer use block votes to select candidates in local constituencies, and in the electoral college that elects the leader unions have lost the 40 per cent they were allowed in 1981 and now count for 33 per cent. However, they still elect twelve of the twenty-nine seats of the party's ruling committee, the National Executive. So whilst diminished, unions still exercise considerable influence. As this connection was attacked by the Conservatives and was seen as a vote loser, Blair has been careful to stress the distance between party and unions.

- *Volunteers*: These provide the foot soldiers of the Labour Party; nearly three-quarters of trade unionists are party members and over half voted Labour at the last two elections.

- *Problems in Blair's second and third terms*: Blair's predilection for 'modernising' public services by involving private companies in their operations won him few friends in the unions, especially the new breed of leaders he now faced, who had not experienced the dog years of Labour's opposition to Thatcher. He found hostile motions being passed at the party conferences and outright opposition when he sided with George W. Bush over military action against Iraq in 2003. By 2005 the unions were also expressing acute concerns over pensions, as many companies revealed deficits in their pension funds and declared that previous levels of pension payments could no longer be sustained.

Subsequently, Margaret Thatcher introduced a series of laws that emasculated union power: five Employment Acts and the 1984 Trade Union Act. These made unions liable for the actions of their members and rendered their funds liable to seizure by the courts, as the miners found to their disadvantage in 1984 when their lack of a strike ballot made them liable to sequestration of assets. Their bitter strike slowly ran out of steam and they suffered a humiliating defeat, which set the tone for

BIOGRAPHY

John Monks (1945–)

Former General Secretary TUC, 1993–2003. Educated at Manchester University. Lifelong union official and made it to top TUC job when Norman Willis resigned in 1992. Moderate and conciliatory but – a sign of how the unions were moving against Blair – was moved to criticise the exclusion of unions from policy making under Blair. He sided with the Fire Brigades Union in autumn 2002 when it went on strike in support of a 40 per cent pay demand. He stood down in 2003 and was succeeded by Brendan Barber.

union dealings with government for the rest of the decade. Days lost through strikes fell to an all-time low, and a kind of industrial peace held sway, although at the cost of much bitterness. Margaret Thatcher refused to consult with the unions, and their occasional meetings proved to be cold and wholly unproductive. Unemployment helped to reduce the size of union membership by three million (a quarter) from 1979 to 1989. The growth of part-time work, mostly by women, did not help to swell membership much either, as such workers are notoriously difficult to organise. To minimise the impact of recession and shrinkage some unions decided to merge, such as Unison, the 1.3-million member public service organisation.

Margaret Thatcher, then, destroyed the power of the unions and John Major was the beneficiary, not to mention the leader of the incoming government, Tony Blair. In the run-up to the 1997 election the TUC sought to fashion an appropriate new role in relation to the government, which it expected to be a Labour one. Denying there had been any deal with Labour, John Monks said on 26 February 1997: 'We know there will be no special tickets to influence based on history or sentiment.'

At the 1997 TUC Conference, Prime Minister Blair lectured the unions on their need to 'modernise': his favourite mantra. In 1999, he sought to charm them with a piece of doggerel verse. However, Blair has been careful not to encourage any thinking that the historical closeness of unions to Labour entitled them to any special treatment: 'fairness not favours' were the bluntly ungenerous terms to which he adhered. Some of his advisers were known to take seriously the possibility of severing the umbilical link with the unions. Blair showed every sign of wishing to maintain unions in the weakened state in which Thatcher had delivered them: reduced membership, limited ability to wage industrial conflict plus lowered morale and expectations after the trauma of the miners' strike. Despite some bitter conflicts like the firemen's strike in 2002, Blair has enjoyed relative freedom from industrial conflict, and while they have not enjoyed their diminished status, union leaders have had to accept that most working people are much less militant now than during the seventies and eighties. The corollary of this has also been the substantially diminished power that unions have had to accept within the labour movement generally.

By September 1999, however, Will Hutton in *The Observer* (13 September 1999) was discerning a 'reinvention' of the unions after the debilitating experiences under the previous government and

BOX 11.6 | FACT

Union membership

- The TUC has seventy-six member unions, representing 7.62 million members in 1992 – a figure which dropped to 6.49 million by 2004.
- Unison is the biggest affiliated union, with 1.3 million members, although the merger between Amicus, GMB and TGWU by 2007 promises to form an organisation with 2.6 million members.
- 38 per cent of employees in their 40s are union members, but only 19 per cent of 19-year-olds.
- Women in full-time jobs are more likely to be union members than men in full-time jobs.
- 60 per cent of workers in the public sector are unionised, while only 20 per cent of private sector workers are members.

noted the increase in membership. He reported on a survey which revealed that workers had never felt more insecure – more work for the same pay, less regular employment, greater threat of redundancy, collapse of trust at work – and were more likely to seek the 'support, security and protection' of union membership. Modern companies often have to face the imperatives of shareholder demands for high share prices, ironically such shareholders often being the pension funds that were set up to look after the interests of the very workers whose livelihood they were threatening. Hutton saw the seeds of future problems for the Labour government in the renewed solidarity of the union movement. Monks himself expressed anger at being frozen out of industrial policy making, saying he was 'very disappointed with the government's rejection of a European-style social dialogue – the idea of people working together under ministers to draw up strategies for the economy and the labour market. The European social model makes economic sense, and is crucial for the survival and prosperity of trade unions' (*The Guardian*, 12 September 1999).

However, at the conference on 13 September 1999 Monks looked forward to a continuing growth of membership by over a million in five years, brought about by the climate created by the Employment Relations Act, which obliged employers to recognise unions for negotiation purposes provided that a majority of members' votes are in favour. 'The industrial pendulum is definitely starting to swing back', said GMB leader John Edmonds. 'During the Thatcher era we would be lucky to get more than two or three recognition deals a year. But the employers are beginning to see the benefits to be gained from working with unions rather than opposing them.' Arthur Scargill gave the sort of speech at the conference that used to bring delegates to their feet: 'Fighting for our members will bring people back. They see no prospect of the trade union movement taking up the cudgels on their behalf.' One and a half decades after the abortive miners' strike, the reaction to the veteran unreconstructed socialist was muted indeed.

After the 2001 election victory, a new militancy seemed to emerge in the union movement with more outspoken leaders not prepared to keep quiet (see Box 11.7). As the 2002 TUC Conference approached, a raft of issues divided unions from government: the firefighters' demands for a 40 per cent wage increase in the face of only a 4 per cent offer; the collapse of several pension schemes in private companies, leading unions to demand compulsory employer contributions; desire for clarity over joining the euro; demand for more legal rights for unionists, who work within the most restrictive legislative framework in Europe; and, finally, demands that Blair oppose US President George W. Bush's plans to invade Iraq.

It has also to be remembered in addition that it was not only the unions that were shaken up by the Conservative years. Local government, traditionally a strong pressure group on Whitehall, was seriously weakened during the years after 1979 and its policy-making role in housing and education reduced. Some of the professions lost a number of their privileges

BOX 11.7 IDEAS AND PERSPECTIVES

The 'Awkward Squad'

Tony Blair was fortunate to inherit a labour movement tamed by eighteen years of Conservative government. The early years were relatively smooth, with Sir Ken Jackson of Amicus being his most effective ally. However, as Blair's policies failed to satisfy union leaders, especially those, like PFI, involving cooperation with the private sector, a number of left-wing leaders came to the fore: Dave Prentis at Unison, Mick Rix at ASLEF, Billy Hayes at the Communication Workers Union (CWU), Bob Crow at the RMT (Rail, Maritime and Transport), Mark Sewotka at the PCS (Public and Communication Services), and Derek Simpson, who defeated Jackson for the leadership of Amicus. Several of these new leaders are concerned to 'reclaim' Labour from New Labour, arguing that the latter has no roots in the party and that constituency parties are so inactive that they are ripe for a takeover campaign. Other leaders favoured diverting political funds to more radical parties like the Scottish Socialist Party, Respect or the Greens. Despite the publicity given to these more bellicose leaders, they had scarcely lived up to dire expectations by the autumn of 2006.

and were exposed to market forces. Solicitors lost their monopoly on conveyancing, opticians on the sale of spectacles, and university lecturers their guaranteed tenure.

Tripartism

This was the name given to Harold Macmillan's strategy of institutionalising contact between unions, employers and government in the form of the 1961 National Economic Development Council (NEDC). It was hoped this approach – similar to those used in Germany and Nordic countries – would improve Britain's notoriously volatile industrial relations. Critics accused such developments as unwelcome examples of **corporatism**.

Thatcher and tripartism

Tripartite forms of policy making and the 'Social Contract' between government and the unions in the seventies were not successful in the long term. Neither the TUC nor the CBI has sufficient control over its members to make their deals stick. Incomes policies broke down after two or three years. Moreover, after 1979 Margaret Thatcher set her face against such tripartism and relied more on market forces. Before 1979, governments usually tried to pursue consensus policies, and their policies (e.g. on regional aid, incomes and price controls) required consultation with the producer groups. After 1979, Margaret Thatcher's determination to break with the consensus and her pursuit of different economic policies shut the groups (particularly the unions) out of the decision-making process. From 1990, John Major showed more willingness to meet union leaders, but there were no signs of any return to the pre-Thatcher consensual approach and in April 1993 Major abolished the NEDC.

Blair and the unions

Under Tony Blair there has been closer consultation between unions and government, but Monks has still complained at being frozen out of key discussions. In March 2002, he described Blair as 'bloody stupid' in supporting the right-wing Italian leader Berlusconi's hostile line on workers' rights. Monks was highly regarded by Downing Street, especially as he spent 80 per cent of his lobbying behind the scenes and only 20 per cent disagreeing in public – unlike John Edmonds of the GMB, who reflects the reverse proportions. Monks was particularly upset when Blair used a local government conference in February 2002 to condemn union 'wreckers' of his

public service reforms. George Monbiot saw the emergent opposition to Blair within the unions as 'not only about the poorer conditions of the workforce, but also the quality and scope of the public services. They see part-privatisation as symptomatic of the corporate takeover of Britain, the government's capitulation to big business, in turn, as symptomatic of its willingness to side with power against the powerless' (George Monbiot, on the day Tony Blair addressed the TUC, 10 September 2002). Meanwhile the bigger unions were gathering together to maximise their influence. In September 2005 Derek Simpson, General Secretary of Amicus, announced the formation of a new 'super-union' embodying his own with the GMB and TGWU: 2.6 million members in all. Simpson was unapologetic about the power this new grouping would wield and said he hoped Blair would have departed by the time the union came into being in January 2007.

Trade Union and Labour Party Liaison Organisation (TULO) and the Warwick Agreement, 2004

This forum exists to discuss policy issues of mutual concern. It comprises the general secretaries of the affiliated unions plus the Prime Minister, the deputy Prime Minister, the Chair of the Labour Party and other party officials. Regional and devolved national equivalents mirror the national committee. At the National Policy Forum in July 2004 in Warwick a series of agreements were achieved which succeeded in mending some of the fences between the unions and a Labour government contemplating a third term. The agreement covered improved working conditions including the guarantee of four weeks paid holiday, exclusive of bank holidays; protection of pension funds in company transfer or mergers; a series of guarantees for workers in public services; and a similar package for those in manufacturing, including extending the restrictions on sacking striking workers from eight to twelve weeks. 'Warwick changed the mood', one senior official was quoted (John Kampfner, 2 September 2004); 'we now have to see if these pledges are acted on.' Blair's strategy was to make limited concessions on employment rights while not budging on his public services reform agenda or on collective employment rights. However, critics of the deal lamented it had not touched on repeal of anti-union legislation, putting an end to the much-hated Private Finance Initiative and introducing more progressive taxation. Relations between Blair and the newly radicalised trade union leaders were far from warm: the umbilical link between Labour and unions had stretched almost to breaking point by the time of the 2005 election.

The growth of professional lobbying

One of the striking features of recent years has been the rapid growth of professional lobbying companies. These offer to influence policy and effect high-level contacts in exchange for large amounts of money. Often, the lobbyists are selling the excellent contacts they have made during a previous career in Parliament or the Civil Service. In this respect, Britain has once again moved towards the American model; on Capitol Hill, this kind of activity has been an accepted part of political life for decades.

In Britain, over sixty lobbying organisations have been set up, ranging from the small Political Planning Services to the large (now defunct) Ian Greer Associates. Most major public relations companies have lobbying operations, either in house or via an established lobbying company. Over thirty Conservative MPs worked for lobbyists before the Nolan Report; consultancies could pay anything up to and beyond £10,000 per year.

There has been pressure for the regulation of such agencies (in Washington, they have to be registered), but one brave voice dared to suggest that the lobbyist emperors have no clothes. Charles Clarke, former right-hand man to Neil Kinnock, set up his own company (before becoming an MP and then cabinet minister in Blair's government), Quality Public Affairs, offering an alternative and much cheaper service. In *The Guardian* on 30 September 1993, he claimed that lobbying government is a gigantic con-trick trading on the mystique of Parliament:

I am telling them that, if they spend £5,000 with me, they can save double the money within a year, once they get to know what to do . . . Thousands of pounds are spent by firms getting information that they could easily get for themselves.

Westminster lobbyists can charge clients around £30,000 a year for a 'full service', including lobbying ministers, civil servants and MPs to push their case.

New Labour and lobbying

Labour has not been immune from the obloquy attracted by professional lobbyists. Derek Draper,

formerly an aide to Peter Mandelson, joined the staff of a lobbying company after the election and freely boasted of his ability to provide clients with access to the very top echelons of New Labour. Moreover, an embarrassing episode occurred soon after the establishment of the devolved Scottish executive when *The Observer* newspaper sent journalists to pose as American businessmen seeking access to the new centre of power in Edinburgh. The firm, Beattie Media (BMR), had employed John McConnell, former secretary to the Scottish Labour Party, in expectation that he would win a safe seat in the new assembly and possibly be given office. McConnell was duly given office, and BMR arranged for an employee who used to be his secretary to join him in his new capacity. Also working for the company was the son of John Reid, the Scottish Secretary. Writing in *The Guardian* (30 September 1999), former firebrand, Jimmy Reid, identified other sons of prominent Scottish politicians with links to the lobbying firm. He commented that 'The grave danger is that Scotland's new parliament will be drowned in a sea of cynicism even before it gets off the ground.'

Moreover, New Labour attracted criticism at the Bournemouth conference in 1999, when businessmen were offered dinners with ministers and possibly even the Prime Minister at £350 per head. Many can recall Labour's ridicule of the Conservative's Premier Club, which had sought to do something similar in the mid-1990s.

Lord Nolan and the removal of sleaze

Sleaze is not an invention of New Labour by any means and its roots go back at least a decade and a half. On 15 January 1990, the Granada TV programme *World in Action* broadcast its report on MPs and outside interests. It quoted Richard Alexander MP, who had placed an advertisement in the House of Commons magazine as follows: 'Hard working backbench Tory MP of ten years standing seeks consultancy in order to widen his range of activities.' The programme was only one of several investigations at that time and later of how MPs used 'consultancy', often for commercial interests; in effect they were paid to apply pressure through their network of contacts in Parliament and Whitehall. In 1994, the *Sunday Times* approached two MPs, under the guise of being a commercial interest, and asked them to place questions on its behalf in exchange for money. In the ensuing media row the newspaper was criticised by many Conservative MPs for its underhand tactics, but the two MPs concerned, Graham Riddick and David Tredinnick, were the object of much more widespread and impassioned obloquy. A commission on 'standards in public life' – 'sleaze' according to the popular media – was set up by John Major under the judge Lord Nolan. This reported in the autumn of 1995 and was debated in November. Nolan suggested curbs on the economic activity of MPs and urged that they be obliged to reveal the extent of their earnings. On 6 November, Nolan's proposals were agreed and a new system was introduced whereby MPs are:

■ obliged to disclose earnings, according to income bands;

■ forbidden from tabling questions and amendments on behalf of outside interests;

■ restricted in what they can say in the chamber on behalf of such interests;

■ obliged to register all details of contracts with a new and powerful Parliamentary Commissioner (since March 1996).

Edward Heath and David Mellor, both MPs enriched by considerable outside work, declared only that work which was directly attributable to their position as MPs and controversially excluded large amounts of income earned through other activities.

However, the subject of sleaze was not excluded from the news even after Nolan, much as Major would have appreciated this. *The Guardian* newspaper ran a story accusing a junior trade minister, Neil Hamilton, of accepting money when a backbench MP in exchange for asking questions and being in the employ of the well-known lobbying company Ian Greer Associates, the then agent of the owner of Harrods, Mr Mohamed Al Fayed. Al Fayed was running a campaign to prevent the tycoon Tiny Rowlands from regaining control of the store, and he also desperately wanted to win British citizenship. Hamilton declared that he would sue (as he had successfully and sensationally against the BBC when *Panorama* had accused him of fascist tendencies).

However, in October 1996, in a major climbdown, he announced the withdrawal of his action on grounds of finance. *The Guardian* responded by calling him a 'liar and a cheat' on its front page. The story continued when the subject was referred to the Standards and Privileges Committee. Hamilton was trounced in the general election by the anti-corruption independent candidate Martin Bell. The memory of Conservative sleaze did not go away but

Labour too came in for criticism. On 24 May 2005 *The Guardian* reported that a number of former ministers – Helen Liddell, Alan Milburn and Lewis Moonie – had joined lobbying firms, thus exploiting contacts and knowledge they had made when employed as ministers. These posts were not opposed by the watchdog Advisory Committee on Business Appointments, despite the fact that one of the firms – Sovereign Strategy – had donated a large sum to the Labour Party and that it was not a member of the Association of Professional Political Consultants, a body which forbids employment or pay to any MP, peer or MEP. This was but one of the sleaze stories which made Labour into a classic case of 'the biter bit'.

Pressure groups and democracy

Do pressure groups contribute towards a healthier democracy? As in the debate over the media in Chapter 10, it depends on what is meant by 'democracy'. The commonly accepted version of British representative or pluralist democracy accords the media a respected if not vital role. According to this view:

1. Pressure groups provide an essential freedom for citizens, especially minorities, to organise with like-minded individuals so that their views can be heard by others and taken into account by government.

2. They help to disperse power downwards from the central institutions and provide important checks against possibly over-powerful legislatures and executives.

3. They provide functional representation according to occupation and belief.

4. They allow for continuity of representation between elections, thus enhancing the degree of participation in the democratic system.

5. They provide a 'safety valve', an outlet for the pent-up energies of those who carry grievances or feel hard done by.

6. They apply scrutiny to government activity, publicising poor practice and maladministration.

However, some claim that groups operate in a way that harms democracy. They claim the following:

1. The freedom to organise and influence is exploited by the rich and powerful groups in

society; the poor and weak often have to rely on poorly financed cause groups and charitable bodies.

2. Much influence is applied informally and secretly behind the closed doors of ministerial meetings, joint civil service advisory committees or informal meetings in London clubs. This mode of operating suits the powerful insider groups, while the weaker groups are left outside and have to resort to ineffective means such as 'knocking on the door' through merely influencing public opinion.

3. By enmeshing pressure groups into government policy-making processes, a kind of 'corporatism' (see below) has been established that 'fixes' decisions with ministers and civil servants before Parliament has had a chance to make an input on behalf of the electorate as a whole.

4. Pressure groups are often not representative of their members and in many cases do not have democratic appointment procedures for senior staff.

5. Pressure groups are essentially sectional – they apply influence from a partial point of view rather than in the interests of the country as a whole. This tendency has led some political scientists to claim that in the 1970s Britain became harder to govern (King, 1975b), exacerbating conflict and slowing down important decision-making processes.

■ Theoretical perspectives

Pluralism

This approach is both descriptive in that it claims to tell us how things are and normative in that it believes this is generally a good way for things to be. The importance of pressure group activity was first recognised by commentators in this country in the 1950s, taking their lead (as so often before and since) from an American scholar, on this occasion Robert Dahl, who believed that major decisions were taken in an American democracy – where power was widely dispersed and shared – through negotiation between competing groups. In 1957, British journalist Paul Johnson said pretty much the same thing about his own country, adding 'Cabinet ministers are little more than the chairmen of arbi-

tration committees'. Samuel Beer, with his concept of 'new group politics', supported this view, believing the wartime controls, in which groups voluntarily aided the government in getting things done, to have survived the peace with the 'main substance' of political activity taking place between the 'public bureaucrats' of the government and the 'private bureaucrats . . . of the great pressure groups'.

However, this pluralist approach was soon much criticised for claiming that power was equally dispersed and that access to government was open. Critics maintained that rich business interests would always exercise disproportionate influence and win better access. Writing two decades later, pluralists such as Robert Dahl and Charles Lindblom adjusted their earlier theories to create a 'neo-pluralism'. This embodied a stronger role for government in relation to groups and a more explicit recognition of the disproportionate power of some groups.

Policy networks

This theory was constructed by political scientists Richardson and Jordan, with considerable help from Rhodes. It suggested that groups and other sources of advice were crucial to the formation of policy. They saw departments constructing 'policy communities' with stable membership of just a few insider groups; policy would flow from this community in consultation with ministers and officials. A looser collection of groups was discerned in 'issue networks'. These comprised a shifting membership of groups and experts who were only occasionally consulted and were – to use American parlance – 'outside the loop' (see also Chapter 24).

Corporatism

Corporatism – sometimes prefixed by 'neo-' or 'meso-' (Smith, 1993, Chapter 2) – was in some ways a development of **pluralism** in that it perceived a contract of sorts taking place between the most powerful groups in the country, rather as Beer saw happening in the war, whereby the government exchanged influence with the groups for their agreement to lead their members along government-approved policy lines: for example, the attempts by governments to achieve agreement on a prices and incomes policy in the late 1960s and early 1970s. In the Scandinavian countries and Germany, something very like this contract had already become a regular part of the political process.

BOX 11.8 IDEAS AND PERSPECTIVES

The importance of citizen campaigning

Des Wilson was probably the best-known popular campaigner in the country – during the 1960s and 1970s – before he became a 'poacher turned gamekeeper' and joined the public relations staff of British Airports Authority. On a Tyne Tees TV programme in 1986 he explained his own philosophy on citizen campaigning and suggested ten guidelines for people wishing to become involved in such campaigns.

It is very important to remember that the very existence of campaigners, the fact that people are standing up and saying 'No, we don't want this, this is what we want instead', is terribly important because it makes it impossible for the political system to claim that there is no alternative to what they are suggesting.

Citizen organisations are about imposing citizen priorities on a system which we have set up which doesn't always act as well for us as it should. The more we can impose human values by maintaining surveillance, getting involved in organisations, being prepared to stand up and be counted, the better. Even if we are beaten the important thing is that the case has been made, the voice has been heard, a different set of priorities has been set on the table.

Our movement is, if you like, the real opposition to the political system because I believe all the political parties are actually one political system which runs this country. If we are not satisfied, it's no use just switching our vote around and it's no use complaining 'They're all the same, those politicians'. We can create our own effective opposition through our own lives by standing up and making demands on our own behalf.

Guidelines for campaigners

1. *Identify objectives*: Always be absolutely clear on what you are seeking to do. It is fatal to become side-tracked and waste energy on peripheral issues.
2. *Learn the decision-making process*: Find out how decisions are made and who makes them.
3. *Formulate a strategy*: Try to identify those tactics that will best advance your cause and draw up a plan of campaign.
4. *Research*: Always be well briefed and work out alternative proposals to the last detail.
5. *Mobilise support*: Widespread support means more political clout and more activists to whom tasks can be delegated.
6. *Use the media*: The media are run by ordinary people who have papers or news bulletins to fill. They need good copy. It helps to develop an awareness of what makes a good story and how it can be presented attractively.
7. *Attitude*: Try to be positive, but also maintain a sense of perspective. Decision makers will be less likely to respond to an excessively strident or narrow approach.
8. *Be professional*: Even amateurs can acquire professional research media and presentational skills.
9. *Confidence*: There is no need to be apologetic about exercising a democratic right.
10. *Perseverance*: Campaigning on local issues is hard work: this should not be underestimated. Few campaigns achieve their objectives immediately. Rebuffs and reverses must be expected and the necessary resilience developed for what might prove to be a long campaign.

Source: Jones (1986)

Pahl and Winkler (1974) argued that the British government through **tripartism** was exercising 'corporatism' in that it aimed to 'direct and control predominantly private-owned business according to four principles: unity, order, nationalism and success'. Corporatism, in one sense, was a means of bridging the gap between a capitalist economy and the socialist notions of planning and democratic consultation. To some extent this altered analysis matched the transition in Britain from a governing Conservative Party, whose ethos was against intervention, to a Labour one, whose ethos was in favour.

The drift towards something called corporatism was perceived at the time and criticised by left-wingers such as Tony Benn and centrists such as David Owen.

The Marxist analysis of pressure groups

Marxists would argue that the greater role accorded to the state in corporatism is only an approximation of the real control exercised by business through the state; as Marx said, 'the state is nothing but an executive committee for the bourgeoisie'. The whole idea of pluralist democracy, therefore, is merely part of the democratic window dressing that the ruling economic group uses to disguise what is in reality its hegemonic control. Naturally, according to this view, the most potent pressure groups will be the ones representing business, while trade unions, for the most part, will be given a marginal role and will in any case act as 'duped' agents of the capitalist system, labouring under the 'false consciousness' that they are not being exploited. Marxists would also argue that most members of élite decision-making groups implicitly accept the dominant values whereby inequality and exploitation are perpetuated. In consequence, most pressure group activity will be concerned with the detailed management of inequality rather than the processes of or progress towards genuine democracy.

New Right

According to the New Right analysis, shared by Margaret Thatcher, pressure groups do not enhance democracy as they are primarily interested in their own concerns and not those of wider society. They represent only a section of society, usually the producers, and leave large groups, such as the consumers, unrepresented. Also according to this view, pressure groups 'short-circuit' the proper working of the system by promiscuously influencing the legislature and the executive so that the former cannot properly represent the interests of all and the latter cannot implement what has been decided (see Baggott, 1995, pp. 47–53).

Are pressure groups becoming less effective?

The decline of tripartism has led some commentators to answer the question in the affirmative. Certainly trade unions have been virtually excluded from important policy-making processes, and almost certainly other pressure groups will have been cold-shouldered by ministers and Whitehall. Margaret Thatcher asserted a powerfully self-confident message: she did not need advice. After many years in office, this message and *modus operandi* spread downwards to ministers and outwards through the civil service network. Baggott (1995, pp. 46–53) shows how both the authoritarian conservative and free-market liberal elements in New Right or Thatcherite thinking (see Chapter 6) were hostile to pressure group activity. According to this view, even quite small groups were able to hoodwink or blackmail Labour into acceding to their demands. In consequence, Thatcher and her ministers broke with the tradition of seeking consent for new policies and preferred to impose their views in defiance of outraged group opinion. They did this, as appropriate, through vigorous industrial conflict (miners' strike), providing very short consultation periods – on average only thirty-nine days (Baggott, 1995, p. 126) – or, more generally, just by ignoring certain groups altogether such as the TUC and more or less dismantling the network of consultations constructed during the neo-corporatist 1970s. Baggott's survey of pressure groups in 1992 revealed that 38 per cent felt the atmosphere had improved for them, but 58 per cent believed it had not changed. As Baggott recognises, this pre-election period was slightly untypical as the government was reaching out to all sections to maximise support in a tight contest.

But what of the pressure groups that are in sympathy: intellectual think-tanks such as the Institute for Economic Affairs, business groups such as the Institute of Directors or media barons? There is much evidence that their advice was well received, at least during the Thatcher years, and it follows that their 'pull' in the highest quarters was enhanced rather than diminished during the 1990s. Think-tanks in fact offer another aspect of pressure group activity. Their influence has declined since Thatcher, but the Institute for Public Policy Research (IPPR) has become something of a source of high-level research and policy ideas for New Labour (see also Chapter 24). It also needs to be remembered that pressure group activity at the popular level grew apace during the 1970s and 1980s. In Chapter 5, this feature was noted as a major new element in the pattern of participation in British politics. Inglehart (1977) has sought to explain this as a feature of affluent societies, where people are less concerned with economic questions and more with quality of life. Other explanations can be found in the decline of class as the basis of party political activity in Britain. As support for the two big class-based parties has diminished, so cause-based pressure group activity has won popular support. As Moran (1985) notes:

Once established class and party identification weakens, citizens are free to enter politics in an almost infinite variety of social roles. If we are no longer 'working class' we can define our social identity and political demands in numerous ways: so groups emerge catering for nuclear pacifists, radical feminists, homosexuals, real ale drinkers, single parents and any combination of these.

Some of the upsurge in pressure group activity has been in direct response to the policies of Thatcherism and its style of exclusion – CND provides the best example here – but much of it has been in support of cross-party issues, particularly those relating to the environment. A letter to Greenpeace members in November 1989, perhaps marking its graduation from 'outsider' to 'insider' status, reports on activities during the year and comments on the organisation's increased effectiveness:

This has been the fastest growing year in Greenpeace history . . . We have emerged as a respected, radical voice, authoritative as well as provocative. We have, after all, been proved right on issue after issue. It is a long time since we could be dismissed as a bunch of fanciful troublemakers.

Pressure group activity is more widespread and more intense. Much of this is 'outsider' activity, attempting to raise public consciousness, but environmental groups have shown that, with the occasional help of events such as the Chernobyl explosion, decision makers can be influenced and, in the case of the protests against the Newbury bypass and the export of veal calves, activists have brought their subjects into the forefront of national consciousness.

While the power of some of the most important groups such as trade unions has fallen in recent years, pressure groups remain one of the most important means by which citizens can take part in politics. However, it remains a fact that Tony Blair's government, while unusually sensitive to the Countryside Alliance's demands and activities, was unmoved by the million plus who demonstrated in London against the decision to join Bush in invading Iraq. Part of the price he has paid, however, includes the collapse of trust in his leadership and the extreme difficulty he

faces, at the time of writing, in piloting his reform agenda for the public services through Parliament.

In this chapter, we have given special attention to unions and business because they have been at the centre of policy processes in Britain in recent decades. But it is important to realise that the range of groups is much wider than the two sides of industry. There has also been a renaissance in grassroots popular movements, especially those concerned with the environment. Important groups can be found in the professions (medicine, law), among the churches and in the wide spectrum of organisations – sporting, charity, artistic – in the community. Virtually everyone is a member of a group that tries to exercise influence on policy because virtually everybody is a member of some organisation or other; and sooner or later every organisation, even the most unworldly, tries to influence an item of public policy. It is to be hoped that the apathy evidenced by the turnout in the 2005 general election does not spread into the area of pressure group activity too (see above on 'civil society').

From the politics of production to the politics of consumption

At a conference at Salford University in March 2002, Professor Wyn Grant explained the evolution of pressure groups since the end of the Second World War. He perceived four phases:

1. *1945–60, establishment politics*: This occurred in response to the vast Keynesian extension of government intervention in the economy and the life of the country via the welfare state. Groups representing staff in these new public sector activities negotiated closely with governments of both colours and established rules as well as conventions of behaviour.

2. *1960–1979, tripartism*: Emergence of a new generation of cause groups. Government consultation with business and unions became formalised into tripartism, but cause groups were beginning to change with an explosion of membership for environmental groups.

3. *1979–1997, tripartite and professional groups downgraded*: Mrs Thatcher felt that she did not need advice from groups and resisted the close contact they demanded. She also saw herself on a mission to dismantle the privilege and unfair practices that characterised many professions and their representative bodies. Insider groups

still operated, but they were even less visible and were often disappointed.

4. *1997–, third way?* Tony Blair started by appearing willing to consult widely, although with definite care in respect of the unions. However, the rise of well-organised popular movements like the fuel protesters in September 2000, the Countryside Alliance and the Anti-War Movement in March 2003 revealed that 'outsider' groups were usurping the previously dominant role of insider groups: the former can now fill the streets and affect policy through delay or even effect reformulation. Grant assesses the Blair government as the most pro-business government (accepting of the disciplines of globalisation) since the war – more so even than Thatcher. He also suggests that a major shift has taken place from the 'politics of production' to the 'politics of collective consumption'. The former involved struggles over the 'fruits of the production process' via élite bargaining, tending to use 'corporatism' to affect sectional issues. The latter, by contrast, uses the Internet to organise dispersed support, tends to concentrate on 'public goods' and core social values (e.g. GM crops), and tends to be very media-driven (e.g. the fuel crisis of September 2000).

The Blair government and pressure groups

In its White Paper *Modernising Government* in March 1999, the government spoke of involving those people who deliver in 'the front line'. Certainly it has improved the opportunities for commenting on Green Papers. Labour has a different set of emphases from the Conservative governments, and it was inevitable that it should give something to its own 'insiders', the unions – the minimum wage, assistance to the poor, union recognition, the

The hunting fraternity lamented the ban on their pastime, but did their best to get round its provisions
Source: Copyright © Chris Riddell. From *The Observer* 21 November 2004. Reproduced with permission from Guardian Newspapers Limited

European Working Time Directive – but it has been careful to keep a prudent distance from allies who have proved a liability in the past. However, some groups, according to Baggott (interview with author, 1999) have complained that they have been overlooked by ministers just as they were when the Conservatives were in power. And Labour has shown itself vulnerable to those with muscle: in the autumn of 1997, it gave a crucial exemption to Bernie Ecclestone's Formula One racing business regarding the ban on tobacco advertising; it has slowly retreated from its 'green' position on the car and listened to the importunate voices of the car lobby. In 2001, Blair showed himself open to influence by the Indian steel magnate Laksmi Mittal, who enlisted the British Prime Minister in his bid to buy a Romanian steel business following a big contribution to Labour Party funds.

The government has also shown that it can be influenced by the massed ranks of big pressure groups, for example the marches of the Countryside Alliance. In September 1999, it advanced noisily on the Bournemouth conference centre where Blair was making his speech to the party faithful. In the wake of the much publicised march he diluted his earlier pledge, given during a summer interview, to ban fox hunting and opined that there might not be time to include it in the current parliamentary session. Critics accused him of 'running scared' (see Box 11.9).

BOX 11.9 EXAMPLE

Banning fox hunting

In his 1997 manifesto, Tony Blair promised to ban fox hunting, and the Commons voted to do so in November 1997 by 411 votes to 151. However, the House of Lords rejected the bill and shortly afterwards the Countryside Alliance and its allies mobilised an impressive campaign involving a mass march to London. In July 1999, Blair revived the question by reasserting on television that a ban would indeed be passed. Lord Burns, former Treasury head, submitted a report in June 2000 which concluded that fox hunting 'seriously compromises the welfare of the fox'. Home Secretary Jack Straw then drew up a bill with three options: the *status quo*, a ban or a form of licensed hunting activity. The political problem for Blair was that his back-benchers saw the issue more as a 'class' issue in which ending the pastime of the horse-riding middle classes was seen to strengthen their left-wing *bona fides*. However, the advantages of a ban began to look less attractive once the pressure groups involved mounted a mass opposition, which also persuaded sceptical middle-class voters that maybe hunting was something which should be allowed after all.

In December of the same year, the Commons voted for a ban 373–158, but the Lords went for the *status quo* and the bill failed for lack of time in the Lords Committee stage. In June 2001, a commitment to a ban was repeated in Labour's manifesto; in March 2002, the Lords voted for the middle way 'licensed option'. Opponents of the legislation used clever public relations stunts, including a horse and dogs parade outside Parliament in May 2002. In July four Labour MPs, including the agriculture minister Elliot Morley, had their constituency offices attacked by balaclava-helmeted militants. The same group, the Real Countryside Alliance, disowned by the original body, defaced many public signs and buildings as part of its campaign in the north of England. Then in September 2002 an unusual approach was taken by the rural affairs minister Alun Michael. He invited a number of the protagonists in the debate to air their views over three days under his chairmanship. The first day looked at the utility of hunting as a way of controlling the number of foxes. The result seemed to indicate that hunting contributed only minimally to any curb on the fox population and that foxes were not major predators of newborn lambs during the lambing season. After three days of this innovative form of consultation, Michael announced that a bill would be drawn up shortly. It would bring fox hunting within the ambit of animal welfare legislation, which bans unnecessary cruelty. It was intended that local tribunals would decide where hunting performed a useful purpose to farmers or the landscape, outweighing suffering caused to animals. Michael commented: 'There is an increasing recognition that animal welfare and the eradication of cruelty are important considerations against which any activity has to be judged. . . . There is an increasing intellectual common ground and that is important'.

On Sunday 22 September 2002, a huge demonstration was mounted by the Countryside Alliance in London. Called the Liberty and Livelihood March, it involved over 400,000 marchers: the biggest demonstration ever in the British capital, although it must be pointed out that while it was the catalyst, fox hunting was only one of the many rural issues publicised by means of the march. However, as the former Conservative media director pointed out to Tony Blair in *The Guardian* (24 September), 'I don't think any political leader would ignore something like this. It's absolutely unprecedented . . . You'd ignore that kind of public outpouring at your peril.' Certainly the government retreated from the outright ban for which many of its supporters craved, and the resultant Hunting Bill sought to allow hunting to proceed on a licensed basis. In the summer of 2003 Labour's Commons majority, on a free vote, overturned the government's preferred option of regulating fox hunting, and banned it completely. However, on 21 October the Lords rejected the ban and reinstated the regulated proposal. The legislative part of the saga was ended in November 2004 when Speaker Martin invoked the Parliament Act – used for only the fourth time since 1949 when it was passed – meaning that the ban on fox hunting came into force in February 2005. Pressure groups representing rural interests indulged in last-minute demonstrations and were galvanised to work against a Labour victory in the May election, but the political facts were that public opinion was generally in favour of a ban, so were a massive majority of Labour MPs, and Blair won a comfortable victory in May 2005. Since then the issue has subsided somewhat, though it seems some local hunts insist on riding out and stretching the law to its absolute limits, if not beyond on some occasions. Writing in *The Observer* on 26 February 2006, Nick Cohen argued that: 'The anti-hunting law that aroused so much passion is now producing contempt and indifference. Only one hunt has closed and hunters behave as if the 700 hours of parliamentary debate that preceded the ban was so much wasted breath. . . . The difficulty was always that the anti-hunters weren't trying to protect foxes, but punish a particular kind of hunter: the Tory toff with red coat and redder face. . . . Today a farmer can still shoot or snare a fox, but if he goes after it with more than two dogs, the police will arrest him. That's the theory. In practice, the police have arrested hardly anyone.'

BOX 11.10 BRITAIN IN CONTEXT

Pressure/interest groups

Most political systems contain concentrations of power which can exert some control over the system as a whole or over specific policies. This is true for democracies and autocracies alike, though the respective roles played by groups in both types of government differ greatly.

'Lobbies', as interest groups are called in the US – the most important of which are based in K St, Washington DC – have a particularly high profile for a number of reasons. Firstly, the three separate institutions of government – legislature, executive, judiciary – invite access in Washington and in their state-level equivalents, not to mention the primaries and related campaigns which groups can

influence through financial contributions. Secondly, lobbyists are accepted as legitimate players in the political system, advancing views in a free society. Thirdly, interests surrounding presidents have tended to occupy favoured places in the White House. Thus civil rights bodies flourished and advanced their causes when Kennedy and Johnson were in office; while oil interests, especially the Halliburton company, have won contracts and powerful executive offices for former employees under the present incumbent.

The downside of all this activity is the constant suspicion that wealthy interests are winning favours in exchange for cash payments – either direct to politicians or indirectly via election campaign funds. Currently Jack Abramoff, a colourful and hugely influential Washington lobbyist, is on trial effectively for bribing powerful politicians to make decisions in the interests of his clients. Court cases are rare but serve to confirm the 'tip of the iceberg' suspicion that this has become almost an accepted part of the way in which American politics works.

Because US politics, not unlike those of the UK, are so open, the accusation of *'corporatism'* – when state and interest groups combine to dominate decision-making – is seldom made. Countries regarded as much more corporatist are usually found in Europe, examples being Austria, Denmark, Germany, Finland and Ireland.

At the other end of the political scale autocratic governments do not usually allow formal access to groups. Less well developed countries, especially those in Africa, face the constant danger that the military – often the most powerful group in the country – will step in to take over, or at least do the bidding of a dictator who does not have national interests closest to his heart. But even a regime like that of the Chinese will consult widely with its doctors before changing its medical arrangements or with its businessmen and women before joining international trade organisations. Dictators should beware: if the needs of their people are constantly and flagrantly ignored, history suggests they will invariably rise up and cast off the shackles. Countless examples can be cited from Latin America, Africa and in the 1980s Eastern Europe where, for example, the Romanian leader Ceauşescu was overthrown and summarily executed.

In recent years the advance of globalisation has seen the emergence of hundreds of NGOs or 'non-government organisations' that may be associated with global bodies like the United Nations or the World Bank, with charities like Oxfam and Médecins sans Frontières, or with environmental issues like Greenpeace.

Chapter summary

Pressure groups seek to influence policy and not control it. 'Insider' groups, which have won acceptance by government, have traditionally had a privileged position compared with 'outsider' groups on the periphery, which tend to use high-profile techniques that serve to disguise their lack of real influence. Business groups seek to influence through the CBI and other channels, while trade unions have lost much power since 1979. Theoretical approaches include pluralism, corporatism and Marxism. The professional lobbying of Parliament and government has raised questions of democracy and legality, which the Nolan Committee was set up to address. On balance, pressure group influence has probably waned since 1979 but some groups, concerned with environmental and animal issues, have increased their influence and membership. Perhaps a shift has occurred in the way pressure groups interact with government, with widely popular movements now placing government under a kind of intense pressure it is loath to ignore.

Discussion points

■ Why do pressure groups emerge?

■ Why does government seek out groups and try to gain their cooperation?

■ Describe an example of pressure group activity from the recent past and consider what it tells you about the way groups operate.

■ Why do New Right thinkers dislike the influence of pressure groups?

Further reading

For the student the books and articles by Grant (1985, 1988, 1989, 2000) are the clearest and most useful, but Baggott (1995) is one of the most comprehensive current accounts and is very accessible. Smith (1993) is a study of some of the more theoretical aspects of the topic. On trade unions, see McIlroy (1995), Taylor (1993) and, on the impact of the Thatcher years, Marsh (1993). Baggott (1995) is good on European groups (pp. 206–19), and Greenwood (1997) offers a comprehensive study. Of the big textbooks, Kingdom (1999) provides excellent coverage (pp. 507–36), as does Coxall and Robins (1998) (pp. 167–86).

References

Ashbee, E. (2000) 'Bowling alone', *Politics Review*, September.

Ashford, N. and Timms, D. (1992) *What Europe Thinks: A Study of Western European Values* (Dartmouth).

Baggott, R. (1988) 'Pressure groups', *Talking Politics*, Autumn.

Baggott, R. (1992) 'The measurement of change in pressure group politics', *Talking Politics*, Vol. 5, No. 1.

Baggott, R. (1995) *Pressure Groups Today* (Manchester University Press).

Beck, U. (1992) *The Risk Society* (Sage).

Casey, T. (2002) 'Devolution and social capital in the British regions', *Regional and Federal Studies*, 12.3.

Coxall, B. and Robins, L. (1998) *Contemporary British Politics* (Macmillan).

Giddens, A. (1998) *The Third Way* (Polity Press).

Glinga, W. (1986) *Legacy of Empire* (Manchester University Press).

Grant, W. (1985, 1990) 'Insider and outsider pressure groups', *Social Studies Review*, September 1985 and January 1990.

Grant, W. (1988) 'Pressure groups and their policy process', *Social Studies Review*.

Grant, W. (1989) *Pressure Groups, Politics and Democracy in Britain* (Phillip Allan).

Grant, W. (2000) *Pressure Groups and Politics* (Macmillan).

Greenwood, J. (1997) *Representing Interests in the European Union* (Macmillan).

Hall, P. (1999) 'Social capital in Britain', *British Journal of Political Science*, 29.3, pp. 417–61.

HMSO, *Modernising Government*, March 1999, Cmnd 4310.

Inglehart, R. (1977) *The Silent Revolution: Changing Values and Political Styles among Western Publics* (Princeton University Press).

Jones, B. (1986) *Is Democracy Working?* (Tyne Tees Television).

King, A. (1975a) 'Overload: problems of governing in the 1970s', *Political Studies*, June.

King, A. (1975b) *Why Is Britain Becoming Harder to Govern?* (BBC Books).

Kingdom, J. (1999) *Government and Politics in Britain* (Polity Press).

Marsh, D. (1993) *The New Politics of British Trade Unionism* (Macmillan).

McCulloch, A. (1988) 'Politics and the environment', *Talking Politics*, Autumn.

McIlroy, J. (1995) *Trade Unions in Britain Today*, 2nd edn (Manchester University Press).

McLeod, R. (1998) 'Calf exports at Brightlingsea', *Parliamentary Affairs*, Vol. 51, No. 3.

Moran, M. (1985) 'The changing world of British pressure groups', *Teaching Politics*, September.

Nye, J. (1997) 'In government we don't trust', *Foreign Policy*, Autumn.

Pahl, R. and Winkler, J. (1974) 'The coming corporatism', *New Society*, 10 October.

Paxman, J. (1991) *Friends in High Places* (Penguin).

Political Studies Association News, Vol. 13, No. 5, March 2003.

Putnam, R.D. (1995) 'Bowling alone', *Journal of Democracy*, January.

Reeves, R. (1999) 'Inside the violent world of the global protestors', *The Observer*, 31 October.

Scott, J. (1991) *Who Rules Britain?* (Polity Press).

Simpson, D. (1999) *Pressure Groups* (Hodder & Stoughton).

Smith, M. (1993) *Pressure Power and Policy* (Harvester Wheatsheaf).

Taylor, R. (1993) *The Trade Union Question in British Politics* (Blackwell).

Useful websites

Directory of 120 NGO websites: www.oneworld.org/cgi-bin/babel/frame.pl

Amnesty International: www.amnesty.org

Countryside Alliance: www.countryside-alliance.org/index.html

Friends of the Earth: www.foe.co.uk

Greenpeace: www.greenpeace.org.uk

Outrage!: www.outrage.org.uk

Trades Union Congress: www.tuc.org.uk

Blog: http://skipper59.blogspot.com/

CHAPTER 12
Political parties

Dennis Kavanagh

- To understand the changing functions of political parties.
- To examine the internal organisation of the major parties.
- To explain the important characteristics of the party system.
- To examine the patterns of leadership in the major parties and organisations.

Introduction

I n the British political system parties have long been important. They involve and educate their members, who also provide the key personnel for democratic control of central and local government. The majority party in the Commons, providing it can maintain cohesion and discipline, has virtually unrestricted influence over the legislative system and command of the executive machine. Parties are the crucial link between voters and Parliament. Doubts, however, have been raised about whether parties are performing this last function as effectively as they once did.

■ The role of political parties

While pressure groups are concerned to influence specific policies, political parties set themselves more ambitious objectives. They aim to initiate rather than merely influence policy, address the whole range of government policies and seek to win control of the representative institutions. They do not wish to influence the government so much as to become the government. According to the dominant pluralist theory of democracy, however, political parties perform other vital functions:

1. *Reconciling conflicting interests*: Political parties represent coalitions of different groups in society. They provide a means whereby the conflicting elements of similar interests are reconciled, harmonised and then fed into the political system. At general elections people vote for the party rather than the candidate.

2. *Participation*: As permanent bodies, parties provide opportunities for citizens to participate in politics, e.g. in choosing candidates for local and parliamentary elections, in campaigning during elections, and in influencing policy at party conferences.

3. *Recruitment*: Parties are the principal means whereby democratic leaders are recruited and trained for service in local councils, Parliament, ministerial and Cabinet office.

4. *Democratic control*: It is the democratically elected members of political parties who as ministers are placed in charge of the day-to-day running of the vast government apparatus – employing millions of people and spending in total over £500 billion per annum.

5. *Choice*: By presenting programmes and taking stands on issues, parties allow voters to choose between rival policy packages.

6. *Representation*: According to the strictly constitutional interpretation, elected candidates represent territorial constituencies – but they also serve to represent a range of socio-economic groups in the national legislature.

7. *Communication*: Parties provide sounding boards for governments and channels of communication between them and society, e.g. when MPs return to their constituencies at weekends to hold surgeries and attend functions.

8. *Accountability*: At election times, the party (or parties) forming the government is held accountable for what it has done during its period of office.

Parties, or groups of like-minded MPs, have existed in the House of Commons for centuries. But they emerged in their recognisably modern form of being disciplined, policy-oriented, possessing a formal organisation in the country and appealing to a large electorate after the second Reform Act (1867). Indeed, the growth of a large electorate required the parties to develop constituency associations in the country. At that time, the two main parties were the Conservatives and Liberals. But with the presence of about eighty Irish Nationalists between 1880 and 1918 and then some thirty Labour MPs between 1906 and 1918, Britain had a multi-party system in the early years of this century. After 1918, the Irish Nationalists withdrew from the British Parliament and the Liberals went into decline. The new post-1918 party system pitted the rising Labour Party against the established power of the Conservatives and Liberals, although the latter still gained substantial support until 1929. The interwar years saw a period of Conservative dominance of government. Between 1945 and 1992, the Labour and Conservative parties together always gained over 90 per cent of the seats in elections to the House of Commons

Table 12.1 General election results: seats and vote share, 1945–2005

Election	Conservative		Labour		Liberal parties		Others	
	Seats	Vote (%)	Seats	Vote (%)	Seats	Vote (%)	Seats	Vote (%)
1945	213	39.8	393	47.8	12	9.0	22	3.4
1950	298	43.5	315	46.1	9	9.1	3	0.7
1951	321	48.0	295	48.8	6	2.5	3	0.7
1955	344	49.7	277	46.4	6	2.7	3	1.2
1959	365	49.4	258	43.8	6	5.9	1	0.9
1964	304	43.4	317	44.1	9	11.2	0	1.3
1966	253	41.9	363	47.9	12	8.5	3	1.7
1970	330	46.4	287	43.0	6	7.5	7	3.1
1974 (February)	297	37.9	301	37.1	14	19.3	23[a]	5.7
1974 (October)	277	35.8	319	39.2	13	18.3	26	6.7
1979	339	43.9	269	36.9	11	13.8	16	5.4
1983	397	42.4	209	27.6	23[b]	25.4	21	4.6
1987	375	42.3	229	30.8	22[b]	22.6	24	4.3
1992	336	41.9	271	34.4	20	17.8	24	5.8
1997	165	30.7	418	43.2	46	16.8	30	9.3
2001	166	31.7	412	40.7	52	18.3	29	9.3
2005	198	32.4	356	35.2	62	22	30	10.4

[a] Northern Irish MPs are counted as 'others' from 1974.
[b] In 1983 and 1987, Liberal figures cover the results for the SDP/Liberal Alliance.

(Table 12.1), but the Conservatives were the dominant party.

Although the two-party system is based on a selective reading of British party history in the twentieth century, it has been central to perceptions of the British political system. The expectation of one-party majority government lies at the heart of ideas that British government is strong and that the majority party in the House of Commons can virtually guarantee the passage of its legislation through Parliament. The two-party system similarly is alleged to provide a coherent choice at election time, structure debate and determine the conduct of business in the House of Commons. Finally, the two-party system has shaped the idea that Britain has responsible government. Because the parties are programmatic, offering **manifestos** at election time, voters are able to deliver a **mandate** for the winning party. In turn, the electorate is able to hold the government accountable at the subsequent election. Some, such as Patrick Dunleavy, have challenged commentators to explain what they mean by the two-party system, other than the fact that the two main parties are

greatly helped by the electoral system. After all, they do not gain even 70 per cent, let alone 80 or 90 per cent of the vote at general elections between them, and when a PR system allows voters an effective choice, as in elections for the London Assembly, Scottish Parliament or European Parliament, voters are even more willing to support other parties.

■ The Conservative Party

The Conservative Party is noted for its pragmatism and opportunism, qualities that have helped it to survive and thrive (see Chapter 6). The party was in office alone or in coalition for two-thirds of the twentieth century, making the latter a *Conservative century* (Seldon and Ball, 1994). The party suffered a shattering defeat in the 1945 election, the year of a Labour landslide. The electorate was clearly in favour of the full employment and welfare policies that Labour promised, as well as greater conciliation of trade unions, and it probably supported an

Big donors to Conservative and Labour parties raise suspicion that they are 'buying influence'
Source: Copyright © Chris Riddell. From *The Observer*, 7 January 2001. Reproduced with permission of Guardian Newspapers Limited

extension of public ownership in the basic industries. The Conservative Party promised to go some way in accepting these, except for public ownership. But the electorate voted for the Labour Party, which believed in them more fully and was not associated with the mass unemployment of the 1930s.

After 1945, the Conservative Party faced a problem similar to that of the Labour Party in the 1980s. Should it carry on clinging to the policies that the electorate had repudiated, or should it come to terms with the changed circumstances? Key figures favoured the latter course. R.A. Butler and Harold Macmillan played an important role in redefining Conservative policies, accepting many of the main planks of the Labour government's programme. Between 1951 and 1964, the Conservative governments largely accepted the greater role of the trade unions and the mixed economy (although in 1953 the government reversed the nationalisation of iron and steel), acquiesced in and continued the passage of many countries from colonial status to independ-

ence, protected the welfare state and maintained a high level of public spending. Much of the above was a social democratic package, and many commentators believed that it prevailed regardless of whether Labour or the Conservatives were in office. There is some dispute about the accuracy of referring to the continuity as a postwar consensus (Kavanagh, 1990; Marsh *et al.*, 1999).

Conservative leaders until Margaret Thatcher were careful to position themselves on the party's centre-left. They believed, first, that maintaining the postwar consensus was the only way to run the country. In other words, one had to maintain full employment, consult with the main economic interests and intervene in the economy (in the interests of maintaining high levels of employment, helping exports and assisting the more depressed regions). Second, they accepted that such policies were necessary to win that crucial portion of working-class support on which Conservative electoral success depended.

Yet there have been tensions in the Conservative Party. Historians often distinguish two strands: Tory or 'One Nation' Conservatism, which accepted the above policies; and the neo-liberal strand, which upholds the role of the free market and is sceptical about the benefits of much government activity (see Chapters 4 and 6).

Until recently, the authority of the Conservative Party leader has not been subject to the formal checks and balances of the Labour equivalent. However, this did not mean that the party leader had a completely free hand. He or she had to keep the leadership team reasonably united and also maintain the morale of the party. When choosing the Cabinet or Shadow Cabinet, a leader has to make sure that people are drawn from different wings of the party. Margaret Thatcher, for example, gave office to many leading 'wets', people who, particularly in her first government, had doubts about her economic policies. In addition, the party leader may have to compromise over policy. Margaret Thatcher was unable to get the public spending cuts that she wished in her first Cabinet and was not able to move as far as she wished in matters such as the introduction of more market-oriented welfare reforms, in part because many Conservatives had doubts about such measures. She was forced, reluctantly on her part, to take Britain into the exchange rate mechanism (ERM) in October 1990 under pressure from her Chancellor (John Major) and Foreign Secretary (Douglas Hurd). She had already lost two previous holders of these posts (Nigel Lawson and Sir Geoffrey Howe) in part over her resistance to this step and was not strong enough to sustain her veto.

Until 1965, the leader '**emerged**' when the party was in office (which was usually the case), and the monarch invited a prominent Conservative minister to form a government after consulting senior party figures. In 1965, the party adopted a system under which MPs elected the leader: Ted Heath in the same year was the first leader to be so chosen. However, there was no provision for making the leader submit to a contest. In 1975 a new provision was introduced, the annual re-election of the leader, principally to ensure that an unpopular leader like Heath could be disposed of efficiently.

It was under these revised rules that, in February 1975, Margaret Thatcher stood against Heath and was rewarded – quite unexpectedly at the time – by a narrow majority in the first ballot. By the time heavyweights such as Willie Whitelaw joined in the second ballot it was too late and she had increased her momentum to romp home. For fifteen years the mechanism lay unused until Sir Anthony Meyer chose to challenge Thatcher in December 1989 – some said as a 'stalking horse' candidate to be followed by a heavyweight – but was easily defeated. The outcome was to be very different when Margaret Thatcher was challenged again in November 1990 and she was far weaker. Her deputy, Geoffrey Howe, had resigned on 1 November and had made a devastating speech on 13 November, which served to encourage Michael Heseltine to make his leadership move. Thatcher's campaign was handled badly, and on the first ballot she fell just four votes short of the required number to be 15 per cent in front of her nearest challenger. When she realised that she had lost the support of Cabinet colleagues, she resigned, and in the subsequent ballot of MPs John Major, seen as Thatcher's choice, won easily.

Conservative decline

The decline of the Conservative Party since 1992 has been remarkable. When John Major led the party to victory in 1992, in spite of an economic recession and the strong mood for change, commentators wrote of Britain having a one-party system. In general elections the party regularly gained around 60 per cent of the Lab/Con vote and attracted voters across social classes. It outscored Labour as the party of economic competence and best able to defend the national interest. It also, effectively, won the battle of political ideas, with Labour largely accepting its policies on industrial relations, privatisation, education standards and income tax and on encouraging a more market-oriented economy.

John Major had a troubled tenure as party leader. The personal benefits of the party's unexpected general election victory in 1992 soon disappeared. His nominal majority in the Commons of 21 was soon reduced because of dissent in his party. The turning point in his and his government's fortunes was Britain's humiliating withdrawal from the ERM in September 1992. This was followed by a striking slump in the polls in the standing of himself and his party, and by-election and local government election disasters. The party's growing divisions over Europe, already apparent under Thatcher, worsened. His authority was regularly flouted by party rebels, concentrated mainly on the Eurosceptic and right wing of the party: the government only just managed to carry the ratification of the Maastricht Bill through the Commons. The party critics looked to Margaret

Thatcher for implicit support, and each year there was talk of the right wing putting up a leadership challenger to John Major. The provision for the annual election of the leader was now a source of instability. Finally, in an unprecedented move in June 1995, Major challenged his critics to 'put up or shut up' and resigned the party leadership in order to fight to be re-elected and see off his critics. The Secretary of State for Wales, John Redwood, also on the party's right wing, resigned from the Cabinet and challenged Major.

Major's victory by 218 to 89 votes did little to secure his authority or reunite the party. Eurosceptics, aided by traditionally pro-Conservative newspapers, continued to undermine Major. His defenders claim that his small majority prevented him from striking out in a radical direction. His Citizen's Charter was designed to improve the quality and responsiveness of public services to citizens, but it did not capture the public imagination. The big deficit in public finances limited scope for tax cuts. But it is worth noting that the government pressed on with privatisations – of coal, nuclear power and the railways. Major's battered administration finally came to an end when Labour overwhelmed it with a landslide majority of 179 in 1997. He immediately announced his resignation, and the fight for succession was joined.

However, the party had forfeited its reputation for economic competence after the ERM exit and for governing effectively because of internal divisions. For two decades it has hardly had a political presence in the great cities outside London and only a handful of parliamentary seats in Scotland and Wales. On virtually every test of public opinion until 2006, the party barely rose above a 33 per cent share of the vote (see Chapter 9). The habit of dissent has been growing in the party for at least two decades, and both Thatcher (eventually) and Major, Hague and Duncan Smith were undermined by the decline in loyalty or deference to the leader; indeed the latter was sacked by MPs after two years in the post. MPs who had been fired from ministerial posts or passed over for promotion were more willing to defy the party whips. An indicator of poor morale is that so many leading Conservative MPs refused to serve on the front bench of Hague or Duncan Smith. Internal democracy (in the form of annual elections for the party leader) in a divided party only added to the problems of party management. The best guarantee of Conservative Party unity has been a leadership that is strong and consistent and

looks like delivering election victory. The last is something that since 1992 no leader, until perhaps David Cameron, has offered.

In the EU the pace of greater political and economic integration quickened and steps such as the extension of majority voting, the social chapter, the single currency and a general shift towards greater integration concerned many in the Conservative Party. The party membership and MPs, the public and sections of the press were all becoming more Eurosceptic. The party was notably divided on Europe, but it also suffered from a culture of disloyalty, as rebels eagerly sought access to the airwaves so that they could broadcast their dissent or made their support conditional on concessions from the whips. A less deferential party conference applauded Eurosceptics and other Conservative critics of Major's government. Philip Norton (2006, p. 47) has written that the party's problem is not one of *the leader* but of *leadership*, that is, *MPs not allowing the leader to lead*. John Major confided privately that some of his MPs had a death wish. A new generation of Conservative MPs, some of whom looked to Mrs Thatcher for a lead, regarded the developing EU as a threat to the independence of the British state and to the market economy. MPs in the 1997 and 2001 Parliaments were increasingly Eurosceptic, as is the public. But it does not help the party at general elections. William Hague and Iain Duncan Smith, both sceptics, struggled to head off demands that the party campaign to pull out of the EU.

The impact of Hague

Following the 1997 election defeat and John Major's speedy announcement of his intention to resign, it was clear that any successor would face a formidable challenge, not least in reforming the party and in transforming its image. William Hague, after flirting with support for Michael Howard, eventually beat Kenneth Clarke for the prize. He inherited a party in a sorry state. Membership had sunk to below 200,000, the average age was well over 60, few members were in employment and only a small proportion were politically active, often merely selling raffle tickets. But constituency associations still controlled the selection of Conservative candidates; they had backed dissidents under John Major and refused to adopt women and ethnic candidates in winnable seats.

In reforming the party, William Hague looked to what Blair had done to Labour. He wanted to offer members the opportunity to shape policy. Policy votes at Conservative conferences were rare and had no authority, and members had only an indirect and advisory role in the election of the party leader. In *The Fresh Future* package of party reforms, Hague embraced Labour's **one member, one vote (OMOV)** culture by creating a central register of members. He had to overcome the fury of many MPs at the prospect of losing their sole right to choose the leader. The result of the membership ballot on *The Fresh Future* was announced at a special convention in March 1998. Only one-third of the ballots were returned, but 96 per cent of those approved the proposals. The spirit of the reforms bore similarities to what Kinnock and Blair had done to Labour. They included:

■ The creation of a board responsible for a single party outside Westminster. The board oversees a new Ethics and Integrity Committee, which has powers to suspend any member who is judged to have brought the party into disrepute.

■ The selection of parliamentary candidates is to be made by all constituency association members.

■ The creation of a new policy forum to discuss policy.

■ The creation of a new national party convention.

■ Revised rules for challenging a Conservative leader. The process begins with a motion of no confidence, which is activated at the request of at least 15 per cent of MPs. If the motion is defeated, there will not be another one for a further 12 months. But if it is carried, the leader will resign and take no further part in the process. In the event of only two candidates emerging, there will be a postal ballot of individual members of at least three months' standing. If more than two candidates emerge, MPs will hold a series of ballots, eliminating one candidate at a time until two candidates emerge and then the membership will vote. In other words, it is a two-stage process: MPs decide the short list; the membership chooses the leader.

Critics doubt that these reforms have produced an effective democratisation of the party. The forum and the convention are only advisory, and a Tory leader can call ballots of members to outflank critics and claim a mandate. It is also harder to challenge a leader, because the trigger to activate the no-confidence election has risen from 10 to 15 per cent.

Like Blair, a Conservative leader may use the ballots to provide a plebiscitary leadership. And, in practice, the MPs may not short-list an MP who is a favourite of the mass members, or list one who lacks broad support among MPs, as happened with Duncan Smith (see below).

As leader, Hague rejected Britain's membership of the single currency for at least two parliaments and resisted further integration into the EU. The party abandoned John Major's (and Blair's) 'wait and see' line on the single currency and is now more fully Eurosceptic. Given the views of most of the party's MPs and the mood of the grass roots, it was difficult for William Hague to hold John Major's old line. Yet he still met opposition from heavyweight figures such as Kenneth Clarke and Michael Heseltine.

In his first two years as leader, Hague sought to show that it was a more inclusive party – he took a liberal line on gender and race. In the tradition of the Conservative scepticism of change, he opposed many of Blair's constitutional reforms – until they were accomplished. Some of his circle called this a 'reach-out' operation, trying to attract back people who had deserted in 1997. But when the party sought to reassure voters that the public services would be safe under their stewardship, it was not believed. As the party failed to progress in the polls, Hague feared that his leadership was at risk and concentrated on appealing to his party's core vote – activists who were most exercised about Europe, immigration and tax.

The chief Conservative problem on policy was that Labour under Blair now espoused its ideas of privatisation, free markets, a flexible labour force and low income tax. Like most opposition leaders, Hague waited for the Labour government to make mistakes, and/or for public opinion to turn against it. Apart from the fuel protests in 2000 and Labour's brief downturn in the polls, he waited in vain. The Conservative party was simply distrusted by many on the key issue of improving public services.

William Hague resigned on 8 June 2001, hours after the general election result was known. The election showed that the Conservative Party had made up no ground since 1997. On virtually all the key image questions of leadership, party unity, governing competence and policy, it was further behind (Butler and Kavanagh, 2002). The choice of his successor would say much about the future direction of the Conservative Party. The 'old guard' of Kenneth Clarke, Michael Heseltine, Edward Heath and Chris

Patten claimed that Hague's strategy had been a disaster and that by concentrating on a core vote right-wing strategy, which appealed to *Daily Mail* and *Daily Telegraph* readers, he had alienated the broad mass of voters that the party needed to attract. They also claimed that his concentration on Europe and saving the pound had made the party seem obsessive about the issue, one that was a bore to most voters. The party had to change and show that it had changed. It had to do what Tony Blair had done for Labour.

The impact of Duncan Smith

In the election to succeed Hague, Michael Portillo was the early favourite. Traditionally associated with the Right, he had changed in recent years, admitted a homosexual past and now expressed support for more socially liberal policies. He wanted the party to be more inclusive and to begin a major policy review.

The first ballot was a surprise because Michael Portillo, although a clear leader, did not do as well as

BIOGRAPHY

George Osborne (1971–)

Osborne and David Cameron are at the forefront of the project to modernise the Conservative Party. Because of the project and their youth and ability they are sometimes referred to as the Blair and Brown of the Conservative Party. Like Cameron, Blair and Brown, Osborne is very much a professional politician, getting on to the ladder very young. Soon after university he joined the Conservative Research Department and then served as a special adviser to a Cabinet minister and for a few months in Number 10 under John Major in 1997. He served as Political Secretary to the new party leader William Hague between 1997 and 2001, and gained a reputation for preparing Hague for Prime Minister's Questions. By the time he was elected as MP for Tatton in 2001 he had already been at the centre and apex of his party. He acted as Cameron's campaign manager in the 2005 leadership contest and the successful Cameron appointed him shadow Chancellor of the Exchequer.

expected. The second ballot was another surprise. Compared with the first ballot, Portillo (52 votes) gained hardly any votes but the Eurosceptic Iain Duncan Smith (53 votes) gained eleven and the pro-European Ken Clarke (59 votes) twenty. By one vote, Duncan Smith beat Portillo and would be the candidate of the Eurosceptics as well as the Right. Clarke's substantial vote showed that many MPs put their Euroscepticism to one side because they thought he was more popular with the electorate. Opinion polls suggested that Clarke was more popular with voters but opponents feared he would split the party. Duncan Smith represented the views of the grass roots but his views, particularly his hostility to Europe (he was a famous rebel over the passage of the Maastricht Treaty), seemed to offer a replay of the failed Hague leadership. In the event, he won decisively by a 3 to 2 margin. The question remained: if the members chose a leader who reflected their views, how could the party get a leader to appeal to target voters, who often had very different views?

The early stages of Duncan Smith's leadership seemed to confirm the fears of his critics. Many senior figures from William Hague's front bench all decided not to serve and this underscored his lack of support among MPs. Duncan Smith gave key jobs to a number of right-wingers and recalled as Shadow Chancellor Michael Howard, who had been John Major's Home Secretary. Michael Howard placed investment in public services ahead of tax cuts, the first time in memory that a Conservative Party had made this choice. For long, the party has been seen as unsympathetic to public services, and Labour portrayed the party as having a secret agenda of encouraging privatisation. In the past, Conservatives had been able to offset this disadvantage with a reputation of better economic competence. This was no longer the case. Although he was seen as something of a Europhobe, as leader he placed the issue on the back burner.

IDS's support of the 2003 Iraq war meant he was unable to exploit, as the Liberal Democrats did, the massive public opposition to the war, or the intelligence row over Iraq's supposed weapons of mass destruction which led to the death of Dr David Kelly and the Hutton Inquiry. The policy documents produced during his leadership – focusing on decentralisation, consumer choice and more competition – were well received in the party and the press for the most part. But what was lacking was any enthusiasm for the leader, who was thought to be uninspiring and responsible for the fact that the

Conservative 2005 general election pledges to deal with practical problems

Lower taxes, cleaner hospitals, more police, controlled immigration, school discipline.

To the above ten words, Michael Howard added one other word, '**accountability**', designed to break through voters' mistrust of all politicians.

party had not won a single by-election since being in opposition and had 'flatlined' in the polls at a little over 30 per cent.

Following a party Conference, dominated by plotting against the leader, media coverage concentrated on the party's disarray. Finally, on 28 October 2003, Sir Michael Spicer, Chairman of the 1922 Committee, revealed that at least 15 per cent or 25 MPs had called for a vote of confidence in the leader, so triggering a vote. IDS eloquently warned of the damage the MPs were doing to the party by so often challenging the leader. But it was of no avail. He was defeated, though by the respectable margin of 90 to 75. A problem was that, under the selection rules introduced during Hague's reign, only one-third of the parliamentary party had voted for Duncan Smith back in 2001 and he never really won the confidence of the party where it matters most: in the legislature.

The impact of Michael Howard

In getting rid of Duncan Smith most MPs were determined not to allow the party membership to choose his successor – as the Hague rules required. They did not think there was time for a prolonged leadership election with a general election probably due in 18 months, and they did not want to risk the members choosing the 'wrong man' again. They rallied behind one candidate, Michael Howard, and he was made leader in a virtual 'coronation'.

Under Howard the party was certainly more united, with less plotting against the leader. And he did well at PMQs against Blair. However, he had some drawbacks as a leader. He was old enough at 63 not to be a long-term prospect as PM, maybe a 'caretaker' at best; he also reminded some voters of the dog days of Thatcherism as the minister in charge of the hated poll tax; he had also been an exceedingly unpopular Home Secretary and had come last in the leadership poll of 1997. On all leadership

ratings he trailed Blair, in spite of the distrust of the latter. When YouGov asked voters a 'forced question' to choose between a government led by Blair or Howard, Blair led on polling day by 19 per cent.

Like Duncan Smith, Howard decided to play down his opposition to more EU integration and entry to the single currency. Opposition was popular with the largely Conservative readership of the *Telegraph* and *Daily Mail* but it was too redolent of the failed 2001 campaign and made the party seem obsessive. For the same reasons – although he faced criticisms from the Tory press and his MPs – Howard decided to offer only a modest and gradual cut in income tax. Surveys showed that this was not a priority for voters and the party had to protect itself against predictable Labour charges of 'cuts' to public services. Indeed, aware of its poor standing on the public services, it pledged to match Labour's planned spending on health and education. It promised to cut out 'waste' in the public sector and get better value from the government's big increase in spending. Howard carried on with most of Duncan Smith's policies and offered a series of pragmatic policies under the banner 'Timetable for Action' (see Box 12.1). But he failed to change voters' unflattering perceptions of the party and Labour still led on most of the issues that concerned voters. Howard gained seats at the 2005 general election but added only 0.5 per cent to the party's share of the vote.

Conference

The role of conference is formally advisory. It has been an annual rallying of the faithful and a public relations exercise in which the leader receives a standing ovation (a regulation ten minutes for Margaret Thatcher in the 1980s); an impression of euphoric unity is assiduously cultivated for public consumption. As a policy-making body the conference has traditionally been dismissed – Balfour said

BIOGRAPHY

David Cameron (1966–)

The arrival of David Cameron as leader gave the
Tories a much-needed injection of vigour and –
initially, at least – popularity
Source: PA Wire/Empics

Elected as Conservative Party leader in 2005, in
succession to Michael Howard. Educated at
Eton and Oxford, where he studied Philosophy,
Politics and Economics. Member of the party's
Research Department and then a special
adviser to the Chancellor, Norman Lamont, and
then to Michael Howard when the party was last
in government. Became MP in 2001, member
of Shadow Cabinet in 2004. Was elected party
leader on a platform of 'changing' the Conservative Party and moving it to the centre ground.
Seen as a younger Conservative Tony Blair.

1992, John Major's government, already unpopular
because of the ERM exit, faced a Eurosceptic
onslaught from delegates. The 2005 Conference
took on a new role as the five candidates in the election to succeed Michael Howard had the chance
to address members and be covered on television.
The speech by David Davis, the front-runner in that
he had the declared support of more MPs than
anybody else, was judged to be a disappointment
and planted doubts that he could project himself on
the national stage. The youthful David Cameron, an
outsider, won plaudits for his speech, made without
notes. The momentum he gained soon made him
the favourite and he went on to win the leadership decisively. One may now make a serious case –
contrary to caricature and formal party statements
– that the Labour Party Conference may be more
successfully 'managed' by the leaders than is the
Conservative gathering.

One of the main aims of conference is to send party
workers home buoyed up with new enthusiasms for
their constituency tasks: recruiting members, attending committees, organising social and fund-raising
events, leafleting, exploiting issues at the local level
and, most important of all, seeking victory in local
and national elections. Studies suggest that the
membership is predominantly elderly, 'de-energised'
and inactive. Party workers may well have been
discouraged by the steady reduction in the role
of local government, which means that they have
fewer opportunities to hold positions of local political responsibility, participate in politics or enjoy
patronage. The disastrous local election results in
the 1990s mean that there are few Conservative
councillors on the ground in the major cities –
Manchester, Liverpool, Newcastle, Sheffield and
Leeds – where the party has been overtaken by the
Liberal Democrats as the rival to Labour.

Local associations retain the important power
of selecting candidates for general elections. They
have steadily resisted leadership appeals to secure
more women and ethnic minority candidates. In
2006 David Cameron is taking more radical steps to
press the associations to draw up more socially representative short-lists for selecting candidates, with
the objective of recruiting more women as MPs.

The central organisation of the party receives
about one-tenth of its funding via a quota system
levied on local constituency organisations, with the
balance provided by individual and company donations. The party has consistently opposed the idea
of state financing of political parties. But it has

he would rather take advice from his valet. Richard
Kelly (1989), however, has argued that the consensual conference culture masks an important form
of communication: that of 'mood'. Party leaders, he
maintains, listen to (or decode) the messages that
underlie the polite contributions from grass-roots
members and act, or even legislate, accordingly.
It was pressure from the conference floor in 1987
that persuaded Margaret Thatcher and Nicholas
Ridley to introduce the poll tax in one step, rather
than phasing it in – with politically disastrous
consequences. Margaret Thatcher confused the
enthusiasm of the activists with that of voters. In

experienced severe financial pressures for several years – a consequence of the unwillingness of firms and companies to contribute in the recession in the 1990s, Labour's attractiveness (as a government) to business, and declining membership. Outside general elections, it has had to reduce its staff and virtually dismantle its regional support staff. Increasingly, in recent years it has relied on wealthy supporters providing loans on favourable and on commercial rates, and the former do not have to be declared. The party was unable to exploit Labour's embarrassment over revelations in 2006 about its undeclared loans because it also relied on them so heavily.

■ The Labour Party

Labour's organisation differs from that of the Conservative Party in several respects:

1. Unlike the Conservative Party, which developed from within Parliament, Labour developed as a grass-roots popular movement outside the legislature. In 1900 the trade unions, cooperative and socialist societies formed the Labour Representation Committee (LRC) to represent the interests of trade unions and assist the entry of working men into Parliament. In 1906, the LRC changed its name to the Labour Party.

2. The Conservatives have been in power – either alone or as the dominant coalition partner – for two-thirds of the years since 1918, Labour for less than a third.

3. Conservatives have traditionally been the party of the *status quo*, Labour the party dedicated to social and economic reform.

4. Labour was originally a federation rather than a unified party like the Conservatives, comprising trade unions and intellectual socialist societies, each with its own self-governing mechanisms. Despite the formation of a single party in 1918, a similar federalism still underlies Labour Party structure.

Power and leadership in the Labour Party

The contrasting '**top-down**' and '**bottom-up**' provenance of the two big parties explains why the Conservative Party in the country had until 1998

been organisationally separate and subservient to the parliamentary party, while for Labour the situation is – at least in theory – reversed. This proviso is important, because the relationship between the parliamentary Labour Party (PLP) and the other party organs is complex and has changed over time. The 1918 constitution aimed to provide a happy marriage between the different elements of Labour's coalition: the trade unions, socialist societies, local constituency parties, party officials and Labour MPs. Institutionally the marriage – which has not been an easy one – expressed itself in the form of the PLP, the National Executive Committee (NEC), constituency parties and the annual Conference. The absence of trade unions from this list is misleading because in practice they play a leading role, although one that is being reduced (for more on this see Chapter 11).

Unlike the Conservatives, who have emphasised loyalty, hierarchy and strong leadership – although with less effectiveness in the last decade – Labour's ethos was founded in democracy, egalitarianism and collective decision-making (Minkin, 1980). The German sociologist Robert Michels propounded his 'iron law of oligarchy' theory arguing that mass organisations can never be run democratically. This was reinforced by Robert McKenzie (1963) in a classic study of Britain's political parties in which he claimed that, appearances notwithstanding, both major parties reflected similar concentrations of power and authority in the parliamentary leadership, with the external party organisations playing a merely supportive role. Ramsay MacDonald, the first Labour Prime Minister (1924), accepted all the conventions with respect to the office of the Prime Minister and of cabinet government and undermined the notion that conference constitutes the 'parliament' of the Labour movement, at least when the party is in government. And in 1960 the party leader Hugh Gaitskell refused to accept a conference resolution embracing unilateralism and succeeded in reversing it in the following year. Moreover, Harold Wilson as Prime Minister ignored a series of conference decisions in the late 1960s and survived, while James Callaghan did much the same when Prime Minister in the 1970s.

To dismiss Labour's intra-party democracy as unimportant would be foolish, however. Minkin (1980) points out that while Harold Wilson, as Prime Minister from 1964, was defying conference resolutions and pursuing foreign, economic and industrial policies deeply offensive to the party's left wing, he was also losing the loyalty and hence control of crucial elements in the party. Gradually the constituency parties, the NEC and the trade unions turned against him.

In opposition after 1970, conference shifted sharply to the left and by 1974 most constituency parties and the NEC were also firmly in the left-wing camp. The result was that the Labour governments of Wilson and Callaghan (1974–9) were 'obviously at odds with the party machine . . . it was as if there were two Labour parties, one with the voice of the NEC and the conference and the other with that of the parliamentary leadership' (Butler and Kavanagh, 1980). Disillusion with government policies caused an exodus of party supporters, leaving 'shell' constituency parties vulnerable to takeovers by far-left activists, especially members of the Militant Tendency. During the 1970s, constituency management committees (GMCs) in many parts of the country were taken over by the Left; as these controlled the selection of candidates it was not surprising that the trend gave rise to an increasing number of left-wing candidates.

The limits of the 'iron law' became apparent when Labour again became the opposition party in 1979. The parliamentary leadership was much weaker and in no position to resist the pressures from a more left-wing conference and NEC. The new party policies represented a sharp break with those of the Callaghan government. Labour was now pledged to come out of the European Community (this time without holding a referendum), and adopted a unilateralist defence policy, sweeping measures of public ownership and redistribution, and the repeal of many Tory measures, notably those affecting the trade unions. Moreover, the Left embarked on a series of reforms designed to prevent the 'iron law' from recurring.

Internal party divisions reached a new degree of bitterness in 1979 in the wake of the so-called 'winter of discontent', when the collapse of Labour's incomes policy produced industrial paralysis and defeat in the general election. On the eve of the election, Callaghan vetoed measures that the Left wished to include in the party's election manifesto – including the abolition of the House of Lords. He thus alienated the Left still further and set the battle lines for a fratricidal fight over the reform of the party's constitution.

The party's left wing pressed for radical changes in the rules of the party; in particular, they wished to introduce greater 'democracy' into the party. The

Left insisted that the party leader be elected by the members and not by MPs alone. In 1981, the Wembley conference agreed to set up an **electoral college** in which the trade unions would have 40 per cent of the vote, constituency parties 30 per cent and MPs 30 per cent. A second aim was for **mandatory reselection** of MPs within the lifetime of a parliament (to enable right-wing MPs to be deselected by left-wing local activists). They succeeded in this, but they failed in their third goal, which was to give control of the party's manifesto to the National Executive Committee. The central thrust of all these reforms was to increase the power of the extra-parliamentary elements of the party, particularly the activists (who were rarely representative of the views of ordinary party voters), over MPs. Mandatory reselection was a factor that persuaded some threatened MPs to 'jump' into the SDP in 1981 and 1982, for the reselections favoured the Left.

Yet, if the Left managed to overturn the constitution, help to drive some disillusioned right-wing MPs to the SDP and force the party to adopt a series of left-wing policies in the 1983 election, its victories were short-lived. The disastrous 1983 general election result, when the party scored its lowest share of the vote in over fifty years and was nearly overtaken by the Alliance parties, forced a rethink. Neil Kinnock gradually managed to impose his authority on the party machine, particularly the NEC. This continued after the 1987 election defeat. The Militant leaders were expelled from the party; left-wing MPs were marginalised or moved to the centre; more central control was exercised over constituency parties and over the selection of candidates at by-elections; the party's aims and principles were restated in a less left-wing form; and socialism was all but abandoned. In the 1992 election Neil Kinnock and his office effectively took key decisions. When he resigned the leadership in 1992, he left a more centrally controlled party machine to John Smith.

The 'modernisation' of Labour

The Kinnock 'project' of the modernisation of the party was designed to make Labour electable again. The so-called modernisers were convinced that the party, because of the damage caused by left-wing activists, had lost touch with the concerns of many ordinary Labour voters. The 1981 changes had been a party revolution; now there would be a counterrevolution. After the 1987 election defeat, Neil Kinnock launched an ambitious policy review. The consequence was a shift to the political centre and the acceptance of a number of Thatcherite policies (see Chapter 6). Kinnock was also concerned to strengthen the authority of the leader over the party organisation. The system of one member, one vote (OMOV) was eventually extended to the election of parliamentary candidates and members of the NEC; the leader's office became more influential, under Peter Mandelson; and a shadow communications agency drawn from experts in media and communications played an important role in preparing the party's election strategy.

The project may have resulted in a more leader-dominated and policy-centrist Labour Party by 1992. But it did not deliver victory in the general election, as the party slumped to a fourth successive, and unexpected, defeat. After the election, party leaders were convinced that it was their spending and taxation proposals, as well as Kinnock's leadership, that had held them back from victory. Survey evidence suggested that the electorate still did not trust Labour, particularly when it came to managing the economy. John Smith succeeded Neil Kinnock as leader in 1992 and backed off many of its taxing and spending proposals; it had been scarred by the strong Conservative attack on it in the 1992 election as the party of high taxes. John Smith had not been

BIOGRAPHY

Peter Mandelson (1953–)

One of the original Labour modernisers. Director of Campaigns and Communications (1985–90) under Neil Kinnock. Introduced modern communication methods and sought to reassure the middle classes that Labour was not loony left. MP for Hartlepool in 1992, very close to Tony Blair. Made Secretary of State for Trade and Industry in 1998 but resigned when it was revealed that he had taken a large loan to help with a house purchase and not disclosed this to his Permanent Secretary. Recalled to the Cabinet as Secretary for Northern Ireland in 1999 but had to resign in January 2001 over alleged intervention for speedy processing of a passport application by a Hinduja brother. Resigned seat in 2004 to become European Commissioner.

a prominent supporter of Neil Kinnock's party reforms, but in spite of opposition from prominent trade unions, he staked his authority on OMOV, which was carried narrowly at the party conference in 1993. Trade unions' influence in the electoral college for electing the party leader was diluted, as all three elements – trade unions, PLP and constituency parties – had equal shares of one-third of the vote. Although the union **block vote** (winner takes all) was abolished and replaced by individual voting, the party has not, strictly speaking, moved to OMOV. Some trade union members can vote in two or all three sections. The unions' share of the vote at annual Conference was reduced to 50 per cent when the party membership reached 300,000.

Following John Smith's sudden death from a heart attack in May 1994, Tony Blair, a figure from the party's centre-right, was easily elected leader; he was helped by the decision of Gordon Brown not to run. Blair resumed the Kinnock project with a vengeance. A symbol of his determination to reform the party was his decision to rewrite Clause Four of the party's constitution, committing the party to widespread public ownership. This was the ideological statement that Labour was a socialist party. In office, however, the party had rarely taken the clause seriously. When it had taken services and industries into public ownership it had done so largely for pragmatic rather than ideological reasons. At a time when state ownership was becoming widely discredited in the West and even abandoned in Eastern Europe, Blair calculated that it was a liability. Labour should mean what it said and say what it meant. The new clause, carried by a two-thirds majority at a special conference in April 1995, claims that Labour works for a dynamic economy, a just society, an open democracy and a healthy environment.

The party continued to accept many of the Thatcher and Major governments' policies. Labour also redefined its electoral market, realising that it had to reach beyond the working class and trade unions, both now diminishing minorities. Blair wished to appeal to 'all the people', not least middle-class voters. Not surprisingly, these policies and theories were leading to further marginalisation of the Left, and there were complaints that the Blair leadership was highly centralised. Labour has become what Otto Kirchheimer called a catch-all political party seeking votes, not primarily from the working class and trade unionists, but across the social spectrum and ditching ideology (see Chapter 6). Traditional

BOX 12.2	DEBATE

'Old' Labour versus 'New' Labour

Old Labour

- Appeal to working class.
- Importance of public ownership of 'commanding heights' of economy (Clause Four).
- Sweeping redistribution from middle to working class via taxation and public spending.
- Key role of trade unions in party and economy.
- Limits on parliamentary leadership from party institutions.
- Campaign through party activists.
- Slight interest in constitutional reforms.

New Labour

- Appeal to all voters.
- Rely on markets for economic growth as much as possible. Ditch Clause Four.
- Redistribution via economic growth and incentives to enter workforce.
- No privileges for unions. Importance of good relations with business.
- Trust the leadership.
- Campaign through modern communications and public relations.
- Constitutional reform to provide 'modernised' government and decentralisation – although not in party management.

divisions between the left and the right have been transmuted into divisions between Old and New Labour, with Roy Hattersley of the old right and Tony Benn of the old left associated with the former (see Box 12.2).

Traditional notions of democracy in the party have been redefined. The policy role of conference has been modified, as the new, more easily influenced (by the leadership), Policy Forum and its policy commissions make a more important contribution. Conference is 'managed' to be more supportive of the leadership, so reinforcing the image of Labour as a responsible party of government with strong leaders. The last three party leaders improved their public standing by challenging conference: e.g. Kinnock's attack on Militant in 1986, Smith's stand on OMOV in 1993 and Blair on Clause Four in 1995. Blair has increasingly relied on ballots of ordinary members to outflank the delegates and activists, who could be unrepresentative of Labour voters. The use of ballots among many party members for the Clause Four vote, annual elections for the NEC and parliamentary candidates has till recently helped the leadership and weakened dissenters. Persistent electoral defeats and hunger for office led to a weakening of the 'old' mechanisms of intra-party democracy, a rallying behind the leader and a

stifling of internal debate – which, Blair argued, can easily be portrayed by opponents as disunity.

Blair's attempt to rebuild and broaden electoral support among new groups also had consequences for traditional supporters. Business was actively courted; business leaders were recruited to give advice on policy and join project teams; corporations received addresses by Blair and Brown and were successfully solicited for funds. Key business figures such as Lords Sainsbury, Haskins, Simon and (Gus) MacDonald held offices in the new Labour government. This was a signal that the trade unions no longer had a special relationship with the party. Before the 1997 election, some modernisers even talked of breaking the link. Between 1986 and 1996, trade union contributions fell from three-quarters to a half as a proportion of party funds. The party established a high-value donor unit for donations of £50,000 or more. The £1 million contribution from the Formula One entrepreneur Bernie Ecclestone proved embarrassing when it was revealed after the 1997 election that his races would be exempt from the ban on tobacco advertising. Inevitably, there were accusations of cash for influence. Embarrassment has increased in subsequent years because of undeclared loans from millionaires and links to peerages (see below, 'New Labour in government').

Having left the Cabinet to spend 'more time with his family', Alan Milburn rejoined his 'political family' in September 2004, to find them at war
Source: Copyright © Chris Riddell. From *The Observer*, 12 September 2004. Reproduced with permission of Guardian Newspapers Limited

Finally, discipline and self-discipline were tightened. A code of discipline was imposed on the members of the NEC under which they have to clear requests for media interviews with the party's press office. A similar code provides for sanctions to be used against party members who engage 'in a sustained course of conduct prejudicial to the party'. Control was also tightened over the selection of parliamentary candidates, and the leadership intervened heavily over elections to the NEC, selection of the party candidate for the London mayoral election and the election of Alun Michael as First Minister in Wales. The OMOV system was rejected and the discredited electoral college system revised – as a device to deny Ken Livingstone the nomination as Labour candidate for London's mayor. Key policy decisions were shaped less by the views of party activists and more by private opinion polling and focus groups conducted by the political strategist Philip Gould. The target voters interviewed were overwhelmingly weak Conservatives or weak Labour

and usually reinforced a centrist political message. Internal party democracy was downgraded as the party was led increasingly in a 'top-down' way by ministers and officials and regarded as a campaign support for the government.

Many factors have contributed to the transformation to what Blair calls New Labour. The four successive crushing election defeats showed the extent to which Britain had changed, socially and culturally. Labour had to take account of these changes if it was to be a credible party of government. The party also had to come to terms with the fact that many of the Conservative policies it had opposed were popular or now too firmly entrenched to be repealed. This included the privatisation measures, changes in industrial relations, Britain's membership of the European Union and cuts in marginal rates of direct taxation. Academic studies and doorstep feedback showed that the party also had to remove the many 'negatives' in its image, which proved an easy target for Conservative propaganda and hostile tabloids, and alienated potential supporters. Many defectors from Labour associated the party with 'holding back' people who wanted to better themselves and their families. Labour appeared to want to penalise or begrudge success. Blair succeeded brilliantly in changing the party's image. Above all, a growing awareness of the interdependence of national economies and the need for economic policies to take account of the likely constraints of financial markets showed that socialism in one nation was no longer practical politics (Shaw, 1996; Ludlam and Smith, 2001). One should also note that most electorally successful social democratic parties across Europe, aware of global economic competition and voter resistance to higher taxes, have also moved in a broadly new Labour direction.

New Labour in government

It is often the case that the vitality of a party machine declines when a party is in government for a long time. Ministers have departments to run and the responsibilities of government to discharge, and they usually see more of their civil servants than of party officials and party workers. Indeed, as many advisers move into government, so the organisation becomes de-energised. The danger is of a breach opening between the party and the country, and the party and government, as happened under the previous governments of Wilson and Callaghan. Blair's reforms of conference and the NEC – allied to the activities of the alleged 'control freaks' of party headquarters – were designed to head off such opposition.

Labour, pressed for funds, has emulated the Conservative Party in seeking large donations from wealthy individuals or companies. Some trade unions, disenchanted with the party's private finance plans for public services, have cut back on their affiliation fees. Individual membership is falling, and companies are becoming more nervous because a sceptical media is quick to see contributions to the party as an attempt to buy access and influence. In 2002, substantial donations were reported from Mittal and Paul Drayson, and one of £100,000 from the press and pornography proprietor Richard Desmond. All coincided with ministers making decisions favourable to the operations of these contributors, although there was no proof of any wrongdoing. Labour's legislation, which requires the reporting of donations over £5,000, has given an opportunity for the media and the opposition to exploit these cases. As a result, many Labour ministers and officials have long made the case for state funding of political parties, but Blair has been reluctant to do this without agreement from other parties. The revelation in 2006 that before the general election of 2005 the party had received undeclared loans at commercial rates of interest to the value of £13.9 million has transformed the debate. The party Treasurer and key figures were kept in the dark and, given the correlation between generous donors and lenders and the award of knighthoods and peerages, the subject of party funding became closely associated in some minds with sleaze. It may have the side-effect of advancing the case for state funding. (See also Box 12.4.)

The National Executive Committee (NEC) has lost influence since the late 1980s. Under the new *Partnership in Power* arrangements, approved by conference in 1997, MPs were excluded from standing in the NEC's constituency and trade union sections; they now have their own section. The NEC now meets every two months instead of monthly. Conference has become increasingly stage-managed for the benefit of television. It has also lost influence on policy to the new policy commissions. Reports on policies are considered by a Policy Forum and the NEC, which makes amendments, and the reports are then discussed at conference. The process is then repeated before there is final approval at conference. The Joint Policy Committee, chaired by the party leader, makes the key policy decisions. Conference can at times be unpredictable; in 2000, angered by a 75p increase in the old-age pension, it voted to restore the link between increases in pensions and average earnings, and later voted against government policies on foundation hospitals and the private finance initiative. Activists are also angry that the policy-making machinery was not used for controversial policies on Iraq, top-up fees, foundation hospitals and ID cards.

In the 1997 Parliament Labour MPs were ultra-loyal and their 'soft' questions for Blair at PMQs prompted much derisive comment, although there were rebellions over benefit cuts for single mothers and the disabled and the asylum bill. But until the Iraq war the large majority meant that the whips had little trouble. This has changed. According to Philip Cowley, the 2001 Parliament turned out to be the most rebellious on the government side in modern times. A total of 139 Labour MPs voted against the Iraq war and defections meant that the government only narrowed passed its bill on tuition fees. The narrower Labour majority in the 2005 Parliament has not reduced the tendency to rebel; indeed it has spread beyond what the whips usually dismiss as 'the usual suspects' (who include the growing number of ministers sacked by Blair), notably over ID cards, anti-terrorism laws and the schools bill in March 2006. The last was carried only because of support from the Conservatives, as 52 Labour MPs voted against and 25 abstained.

The 2001 and 2005 general elections, with their sharp fall in turnout in Labour strongholds, reflected some disillusion that in his pursuit of middle-England votes, Blair was losing support among Labour's traditional supporters. Indeed, the party has held its share of the middle-class vote in the election and lost its share of working-class support. In the Labour heartlands of Sheffield (until 2001) and Liverpool, Liberal Democrats actually ran the local councils. Activists object that Blair has too cosy a relationship with big business, is too supportive of President Bush and has been too close to right-wing European leaders like Berlusconi (Italy), and complain about the market-oriented reforms in health and education. Party membership and activity have also fallen substantially.

■ Other parties

We all 'know' that the main party battle is between Conservative and Labour, but since 1970 there has been a steady growth in electoral support for 'other' parties. Only the disproportional effects of the Westminster electoral system have prevented the votes of the 'other' parties being reflected in a large number of seats. In five general elections (1983–2001), those parties have gained an average of some 25 per cent of the vote and around forty seats (as opposed to the 160–170 they would have got under a pure proportional system). In 2005 the figures reached new highs of over 30 per cent and over 80 seats. But this third force of parties in the Commons is diverse, including Liberal Democrats, Welsh and Scottish Nationalists, Respect, and four different parties in Northern Ireland as well as an independent.

From the Liberals to the Liberal Democrats

The main third party after 1918 was the Liberal Party. It had been one of the two parties of government between 1867 and 1918, but it declined steadily during the interwar years and attracted only minuscule support for much of the postwar period. Perhaps it was doomed to decline once the Labour Party developed and appealed to the mass of newly enfranchised workers. But before 1914 it was the party of constitutional reform, decentralisation and devolution (e.g. giving Home Rule to Ireland) and the welfare state, all with the help of the infant Labour Party. However, Britain's two-party system, supported by the electoral system, seemed to have no space for the Liberals.

But the party steadily improved its level of support and gained 19 per cent of the poll in February 1974. However, the first-past-the-post electoral system remained a barrier and prevented it from receiving a proportional share of seats in the House of Commons. Its most distinctive policies in recent years have been political decentralisation and constitutional reform (more open government, proportional representation and a Bill of Rights; see also Chapter 8).

An opportunity for a realignment of the party system came in 1981, when Labour right-wingers broke away to form the Social Democratic Party. In 1983, its twenty-nine MPs (all but one of whom came from Labour) formed a partnership with the Liberals. The two parties had a common programme, a joint leader (SDP leader Roy Jenkins was Prime Minister designate of a hypothetical government) and an electoral pact, and fought under the label of the Alliance. As noted in Chapter 9, the Alliance gained 25.4 per cent of the vote in 1983 but only 3.5 per cent of the seats, and in 1987 the two parties gained 22.6 per cent of the vote but even fewer seats. In 1988, the Liberals and a majority of the SDP merged in a Social Liberal Democratic Party, soon to become known as the Liberal Democrats.

In June 1990, the SDP gave up the unequal struggle and formally wound itself up. SDP members could comfort themselves with the notion that their party had forced Labour to abandon its left-wing adventures and adopt a programme more in keeping with the expectations of the ordinary voter. By 1997, Blair's Labour Party had a programme very close in essentials to that offered by the SDP throughout its nine-year history.

New Labour quickly moved to the central ground and cut into Liberal territory. Paddy Ashdown repositioned his party from being even-handed between the Conservative and Labour parties and took a pro-Labour stance. The two parties took broadly similar positions on Europe, devolution, constitutional reform and education and training. Before 1997 the Blair leadership realised that Liberal support would be crucial if Labour had only a narrow majority or no majority at all, and the leadership wished to free itself from dependence on left-wing Labour MPs.

There was overt cooperation between the parties, for example in developing a programme of constitutional reform that the parties would try to achieve in a new parliament and in the Scottish Constitutional Convention, and in their joint agreement to stand down candidates in Tatton in the general election so that Martin Bell could run as an 'anti-sleaze' candidate. More secretly, there were also negotiations between Blair and Ashdown and their respective teams over cooperation in the forthcoming election campaign and the referendum on devolution in Scotland. The two leaders even discussed coalition, with Liberal Democrats taking seats in a Blair Cabinet. Labour's huge majority in the general election put paid to the last scheme. However, Blair established a Joint Cabinet Committee, containing members of both parties, to consider constitutional matters, and in 1999 its remit was extended to cover other issues.

Blair had often spoken about his wish to recreate the pre-1914 progressive alliance of Liberals and the infant Labour Party, regarding it as a means of achieving centre-left domination of politics in the twenty-first century, just as the Conservatives had done in the twentieth century. The 1997 general election provided mixed fortunes for the Liberal Democrats. A mix of factors, including targeting and tactical anti-Conservative voting, meant that although its vote share fell, the party doubled its number of seats. Unfortunately, a breakthrough in seats (forty-six) was set alongside Labour's 179-seat majority in the new parliament. In 2001, its fifty-two seats were set against Labour's 163-seat majority.

The election of Charles Kennedy as leader in 1999 gave the party the opportunity to review the benefits from cooperation with Labour. Some Liberal Democrats reflected that Blair, in not taking electoral reform forward, had deceived them. In the 2001 Parliament there was much less convergence. Liberal Democrats were opposed to the government's initiatives on tuition fees, ID cards, terrorist legislation, House of Lords reform, taxation and, above all, the war in Iraq. As of 2005 the party was positioning itself less in the middle and more to the left of Labour.

The election of David Cameron as Conservative leader and positive media coverage of his early leadership brought the doubts about Kennedy of some leading Liberal Democrats to a head. They reflected that, given the unpopularity of the two main parties, the party should have done better in 2005. They also complained of Kennedy's lack of energy (sometimes code for charges that he had a drink problem) and failure to give positive leadership. Early in 2006 he stepped down and Menzies Campbell, the foreign affairs spokesman, was elected leader. It is therefore likely that at the next general election each of the three main parties will line up with new leaders from 2005.

The minor parties

The British Green Party began life in 1973 as an environmental pressure group. In 1985, the party changed its name from the Ecology Party to the Green Party and thus came into line with environmental parties internationally. During the 1980s, Green support in Western Europe grew apace: candidates were elected to eleven national parliaments around the world. In Britain, however, in 1983, 108 candidates mustered barely 1 per cent of the votes (55,000). But after the decline of the Alliance the Greens captured the 'protest' vote, taking an astonishing 15 per cent of the vote in the 1989 elections to the European Parliament, overtaking the Liberals. A sign of the fragility of this support was shown in 1992, when the party gained an average of 1.3 per cent where a Green candidate stood, worse than in 1987.

However, some recovery has come with the introduction of PR for non-Westminster elections. Two MEPs were elected in 1999, as well as one member of the Scottish Parliament and three Greater London councillors. In the 2001 and 2005 general elections the Greens managed to save deposits (a minimum 5 per cent of the vote) in ten seats, appealing in particular to well-educated young professionals.

The United Kingdom Independence Party (UKIP), founded in 1993 to campaign for British withdrawal from the EU, has also gained from electoral reform. In 1997, it had been overtaken by the lavishly funded Referendum Party, which called for a referendum on Britain joining the single currency. With the death of its founder and main financial backer, Sir James Goldsmith, the Referendum Party was wound up and left the field to the UKIP, which gained three seats in the European elections. Its breakthrough

Following the resignation of Charles Kennedy, Sir Menzies Campbell was elected leader of the Liberal Democrats in January 2006, continuing the political merry-go-round
Source: Rex Features

came in the 2004 European election, when it collected 16 per cent of the vote and returned twelve MEPs, but it did poorly in the 2005 general election.

On the far right, the British National Party (BNP) is both anti-immigrant and anti-EU. In the 2001 election it saved its deposit in five seats, but in the 2002 local elections, perhaps in the wake of the success of Le Pen in the French presidential election, as well as public concern over asylum seekers, it gained seats in Burnley, Bradford and Oldham. It made further progress in 2005, saving its deposit in ten seats, which were predominantly in deprived areas with a significant proportion of ethnic minorities.

In 2003 George Galloway, MP for Glasgow Central, was expelled from the Labour party on account of his stance on the war in Iraq. He formed a new left-wing party, Respect, with its main focus on opposition to the war in Iraq. In the general election Galloway captured the Bethnal Green seat from Labour.

Nationalist parties

The presence of nationalist parties in Scotland, Wales and Northern Ireland makes the pattern of party competition different from that in England. Party politics in Northern Ireland is different again, in part because of the dominance of issues regarding the border, religious rivalries between Protestants and Catholics and disagreement among Unionists over whether to work with the executive. The two main Unionist parties are the Ulster Unionist Party (UUP), and the Democratic Unionist Party (DUP) led by Dr Ian Paisley. The latter opposed power sharing with the Catholic community in any Northern Ireland legislature and the Anglo-Irish agreement (1985), which gave the Irish government a voice in Northern Ireland's affairs. Attempts to establish a sustained multi-party regime, as envisaged in the Good Friday Agreement of 1998, have not yet succeeded, foundering over the question of the decommissioning of weapons. In the 2005 general election the DUP emerged as the clear voice of Unionism as the Ulster Unionist Party were reduced to just one seat. Sinn Fein, the parliamentary wing of the IRA, has also emerged as the dominant voice of the Irish nationalists at the expense of the more moderate Social Democratic and Labour Party.

In Scotland and Wales, nationalist parties want independence (see Chapter 9) for their nations and regard devolution as a staging post on the way. They had seven MPs in the 1992 parliament and ten in 1997, six for the Scottish Nationalist Party (SNP) and four for Plaid Cymru. The Scottish Nationalists cooperated with Labour and the Liberal Democrats in the 1997 referendum to set up a parliament that had tax-raising powers. This was easily carried. In the elections for the Scottish parliament in 1999, thanks to PR, the SNP became the official opposition, with 29 per cent of the vote and a quarter of the MPs, but it polled only 20 per cent in the 2001 general election. Scottish voters clearly appreciate that the decisions of the Edinburgh parliament now matter more to them than those of Westminster. In Wales, also, the nationalists represented by Plaid Cymru enjoyed an upsurge of support for the first devolved Assembly election. The party gained nearly a third of the vote, hurting Labour in its heartlands, and became the official opposition. In the Westminster election it fell back, like the SNP, although its 14.3 per cent share of the vote was an advance on 1997 and the highest ever. In the 2005 elections support for both nationalist parties declined, the SNP to its lowest vote share since 1987 while Plaid Cymru lost nearly 2 per cent of its 2001 vote.

In Northern Ireland, the mainland parties do not run candidates, and in Scotland and Wales the Conservative Party has been virtually extinguished in Westminster elections. In Scotland and Wales the introduction of devolved elections, with PR (which of course lowers the barriers to entry), has created a more favourable environment for the nationalist parties. Clearly, many voters are prepared to vote differently for Westminster and in the devolved elections.

The decline of the two-party system, apparent in the mid-1970s, shows no sign of being reversed; rather, the opposite. Not since the 1920s has the party system been so pluralistic, and outside England the Labour/Conservative choice has been replaced by a variety of alternatives for voters (see also Chapter 9).

■ The effect of parties

Some commentators have seen the failures of many postwar governments, notably in the economic sphere, as signs of weak government and therefore of parties. According to Professor Richard Rose, in *Do Parties Make a Difference?* (1984), British parties are ill-equipped to direct government. Rose points in particular to the failure of pre-1979 governments to improve macro-economic conditions (such as inflation, unemployment, economic growth and balance of payments) to show that parties do not make much difference in reversing the trend.

Against this, some argue that the parties in government may have too much power. The relative ease with which they get their legislation through Parliament, for example, in the absence of formal checks and balances, and the extension of non-elected quangos, have prompted concern. Critics advocate the introduction of a proportional electoral system, partly on the grounds of fairness (since to have a majority of seats in the Commons, governments would also need the support of a majority, or near majority, of the voters), and more decentralisation.

In the fields of industrial relations, abandonment of formal incomes policy and tripartite style of decision making, privatisation of state industries and services, the Thatcher record shows that parties can make a difference, particularly when they have a determined leader who has a political strategy and are in office for a lengthy period. Conservatives had the opportunity to make their policy changes in the 1980s well-nigh irreversible. Labour, under the impact of four successive general election defeats, gradually accepted many of the policies they had once opposed, e.g. council house sales, membership of the European Community/Union, trade union reforms, privatisation, making low inflation the priority of economic policy, and lower rates of marginal income tax.

Having read the political runes of the 1980s, Labour policy converged so closely with that of the Conservatives that it was difficult for voters to distinguish between them. They seem to have decided in 1997 that the Conservatives were too tired and incompetent as well as arguably dishonest, and that it was safe to vote for 'new' Labour under Blair. In government, Blair has sought to combine economic efficiency with social justice, what he calls a Third Way that regards the traditional right versus left and capitalism versus socialism as outdated (see Box 12.3). Now the Conservatives have had to come

BOX 12.3   IDEAS AND PERSPECTIVES

The 'Third Way'

Tony Blair realised that his New Labour project needed a philosophical basis, just as Mrs Thatcher could point to neo-liberalism and its defence of the free market. Socialism, in the sense of state ownership and direction of the economy, had clearly failed, and reform of Clause Four of the party constitution acknowledged this. How could he move on to new ground, recognising the limits of both free market and the state?

Blair and President Clinton promoted the Third Way, a pragmatic borrowing of what they considered to be the best of left and right ideologies (and the most electorally popular!). The advisers and intellectual supporters of both men met periodically for seminars. Blair has also sought to interest centre-left parties in Europe in the ideas. Third Way advocates start from the basis that rapid social and international changes have made much of the old left and right ideas redundant (Giddens, 1998). Among the key features of the Third Way are the following:

■ Limits on the state have increased because of international forces (globalisation) and social complexity.
■ The role of the state should be as a facilitator and regulator, rather than as a deliverer of services. Making the market work more efficiently and improving education and training will help economic efficiency. Unlike Thatcher, Blair believes in an active role for the state, in providing education and training, infrastructure and regulation. It also helps to provide social justice.
■ Citizenship involves responsibilities as well as rights. Parents have to be responsible for children, curbs should be imposed on antisocial neighbours, and welfare reform must emphasise that there is no unlimited right to benefit and must link benefits to training and incentives to work.
■ There should be greater cooperation between individual states to tackle global problems.

Critics dismiss much of the Third Way as vague rhetoric or unprincipled pragmatism. After all, British politicians have usually pursued a middle path when it comes to fighting election campaigns (see also Chapter 6).

to terms with a long period of Labour hegemony. They now accept Labour's constitutional changes, independence of the Bank of England, the minimum wage and the Social Chapter; they support Blair's plans to extend consumer choice in public services; and in the 2005 general election they were committed to accepting Labour's plans for increasing spending on health and education for the coming Parliament.

Of course, during elections and at party conferences the leaders concentrate on the differences between the parties and exaggerate the difference they would make if they were in government. Voters today seem less impressed by the distinctive policy positions parties take and are more interested in the parties' competence or reliability. For example, surveys show that most do not believe promises of realistic tax cuts by any party, fearing that spending on public services will be cut or that other taxes (e.g. council tax) will go up. Voters appear broadly agreed on policy goals – safer streets, control of immigration, better hospital treatment, and so on – and more interested in better delivery of policies.

■ Problems for parties

Britain is widely regarded as the home of strong parties. They have a reputation for being disciplined and programmatic and for providing a clear choice for voters at elections and stable one-party government. Yet there are signs that parties are in trouble. Symptoms, which are found in many other countries, include the following:

1. *Declining popular attachment*: Surveys over the years show that the proportion of voters who identify very strongly with the Labour and Conservative parties has fallen, from over two-fifths in 1964 to less than a fifth today, with the

big decline occurring in the mid-1970s. Surveys show that very few members are willing to canvass by telephone for the party they support or stop strangers in the street and discuss their party's strengths.

2. *Falling membership*: Party membership has declined in Britain, as it has in a number of other Western states. The Labour Party had a million individual members in the 1950s, but this had fallen to just over 250,000 in 1992, recovering to nearly 400,000 in 1997, and falling again to 201,000 by the end of 2004. From the 1950s to the 1990s, Conservative Party membership fell from a claimed 2.8 million to some 300,000; its membership is relatively elderly. Only some 2 per cent of adults are actually party members, lower than in many other Western states.

3. *People have other, non-political interests*: Competition for the time and interest of voters has developed from television, various leisure activities and interest groups. If voters are becoming more instrumental in their outlooks, they may find it more profitable to advance their specific concerns through participation in local protest bodies. The decline in party membership has not been matched with a decline in membership of many cause groups or a fall in reported interest in public affairs. It seems to reflect a turning away from parties and the electoral process (see Chapter 9).

4. *Interest groups are reluctant to associate closely with a political party*: The trade union connection with Labour has not inspired others to follow, and group spokespersons are increasingly likely to seek direct access to ministers rather than to operate through a political party. Parties lack effective control over the mass media. The last national newspaper to be connected to a political party was the *Daily Herald*, and this ceased publication long ago. There is no popular market for a party political newspaper, and newspapers are less enthusiastic in their support for a party at election time – a reflection of voters' turning away from parties. *The Economist* observed in 1999 that 'belonging to a political party is more like being a supporter of some charity: you may pay a membership fee, but will not necessarily attend meetings or help to turn out the vote at election time'.

5. *Parties are turning elsewhere for relevant skills*: They court think-tanks for ideas rather than their own research departments (e.g. Labour

---

BOX 12.4 BRITAIN IN CONTEXT

Party systems and alternation in government

Britain is one of the few democracies in which general elections can and do result in a complete alternation of the party in government. Elections may result in (a) complete alternation, (b) partial alternation, or (c) no or minor alternation. The extent depends on the nature of the party system, including the number of effective parties, the ideological distance between them, and the 'gap' in electoral strength between the first and second parties.

The US, New Zealand and Britain are regarded as two-party systems (but see the qualification for Britain, above) and the choice for control of the executive is between single parties. In Sweden and Norway the alternation has been between dominant Social Democrat and Labour parties, respectively, and centre-right coalitions; in these countries *the alternation is wholesale*.

In Germany, where the Greens or the FDP is often a junior member of a coalition government, *the change is only partial*. The same was true in Italy between 1946 and 1994 where the dominant Christian Democrats were always in a coalition government, and always as the largest party.

In countries like Switzerland, India and Japan, for much of the past fifty years a dominant party or coalition has usually been in government; here *the alternation is negligible*.

The above differences are crucial in helping elections to directly designate the government and to hold it accountable at the next general election.

Source: P. Mair (1996) 'Party systems and structures of competition', in L. Le Duc, R. Niemi and P. Norris (eds) *Comparing Democracies*. Reprinted by permission of Sage Publications Ltd

draws on the Institute of Public Policy Research and on the think-tank Demos, and the Conservatives turn to Policy Exchange and the Centre for Policy Studies) and look to opinion pollsters, advertising agencies and communication specialists for help with election campaigning. In government, Labour has established several working parties and policy review bodies, and has given leaders from business and commerce a leading role. In government, Blair has appointed as advisers and ministers (in the Lords) people with little or no background in the Labour Party.

Chapter summary

The strength and competitiveness of the party system has suffered because of the weakness of Labour after 1979 and of Conservatives since 1997. Under Blair, the Labour Party has effectively abandoned socialism and in many ways is more leader-driven and disciplined than the Conservative Party. It remains to be seen whether Labour's landslide victories in 1997 and 2001 and its third win in 2005 have enabled it to become the 'dominant' ruler and shape the agenda as Thatcher did.

Discussion points

■ Compare the nature and effects of the recent changes in the Conservative and Labour annual conferences; does either have any real impact on policy formulation?

■ To what extent does the Conservative party leader dominate his or her party organisation more than the Labour leader does his or hers?

■ Consider the arguments for and against state funding of political parties.

■ Do we still have a two-party system?

Further reading

On party structure and internal politics, McKenzie (1963) is still a classic, although dated. Garner and Kelly (1998) and Norton (2006) consider more recent developments in the two main parties. See also Kelly (1999, pp. 233–43) for the impact of parties. The work of Seyd and Whiteley (1995, 2004) is essential for an understanding of party memberships.

References

Ball, S. and Seldon, A. (2005) *Recovering Power* (Palgrave).

Butler, D. and Kavanagh, D. (1980) *The British General Election of 1979* (Macmillan).

Butler, D. and Kavanagh, D. (2002) *The British General Election of 2001* (Palgrave).

Callaghan, J. (1987) *The Far Left in English Politics* (Blackwell).

Crewe, I. and King, A. (1995) *SDP: The Birth, Life and Death of the Social Democratic Party* (Oxford University Press).

Garner, R. and Kelly, R. (1998) *British Political Parties Today*, 2nd edn (Manchester University Press).

Giddens, A. (1998) *The Third Way* (Polity Press).

Jenkins, S. (1996) *Accountable to None* (Penguin).

Kavanagh, D. (1990) *Thatcherism and British Politics*, 2nd edn (Oxford University Press).

Kavanagh, D. (2002) 'The paradoxes of British political parties', in C. Hay (ed.), *British Politics Today* (Polity Press).

Kavanagh, D. and Butler, D. (2005) *The British General Election of 2005* (Palgrave).

Kelly, R. (1989) *Conservative Party Conferences* (Manchester University Press).

Kelly, R. (1999) 'Power in the Conservative Party: the Hague effect', *Politics Review*, February, pp. 28–30.

Kelly, R. (2001) 'Farewell conference, hello forum', *Politics Review*, February.

Ludlam, S. and Smith, M. (2001) *New Labour in Government* (Palgrave).

Mair, P. (1996) 'Party systems and structures of competition', in L. Le Duc, R. Niemi and P. Norris (eds), *Comparing Democracies* (Sage).

▶

Marsh, D. *et al.* (1999) *Postwar British Politics in Perspective* (Polity Press).

McKenzie, R.T. (1963) *British Political Parties* (Heinemann).

Minkin, L. (1980) *The Labour Party Conference* (Manchester University Press).

Minkin, L. (1992) *The Contentious Alliance* (Edinburgh University Press).

Norton, P. (2006) 'The Conservative Party: the politics of panic', in J. Bartle and A. King (eds), *Britain at the Polls 2005* (CQ Press).

Rose, R. (1984) *Do Parties Make a Difference?*, 2nd edn (Macmillan).

Seldon, A. and Ball, C. (eds) (1994) *Conservative Century: The Conservative Party since 1900* (Oxford University Press).

Seyd, P. (1987) *The Rise and Fall of the Labour Left* (Macmillan).

Seyd, P. and Whiteley, P. (1995) 'Labour and Conservative Party members compared', *Politics Review*, February.

Seyd, P. and Whiteley, P. (2004) 'British party members: an overview', *Party Politics*, Vol. 10, No. 4, pp. 355–66.

Shaw, E. (1996) *The Labour Party since 1945* (Blackwell).

Stark, L. (1996) *Choosing a Party Leader* (Macmillan).

Useful websites

http://www.conservatives.com
http://www.labour.org.uk
http://libdems.org.uk
http://green party.org.uk
www.plaidcymru.org
www.snp.org

CHAPTER 13

Pathways into politics

Michael Moran

Learning objectives

- To understand the connection between the idea of democracy and **political participation** and recruitment in Britain.

- To understand why some people participate in politics and others do not.

- To understand why some people are recruited into positions of political leadership and some are not.

- To understand how participation and political recruitment have been changing in Britain.

Introduction

he great American President Abraham Lincoln (1809–65 and President 1861–5 during the American Civil War) offered what has probably come to be understood as the best-known definition of **democracy**: 'Government of the people, by the people, for the people'. But what does government by the people involve? The great traditions of republican government that helped to inspire American democracy originated in the city republics of ancient Greece – in communities where it was possible to gather all citizens together into a single forum to make important decisions. That is plainly not possible in a political system like the United Kingdom, governing as it does over 60 million people. Yet popular participation is central to democracy: that is signalled both in the Greek root of the word and in our everyday understanding as epitomised by Lincoln's definition. What sort of participation exists, and what sort is possible in a system claiming, as does the United Kingdom, to be democratic? That is the central question answered in this chapter. We look at three issues in particular: what patterns of popular participation exist; who is recruited into political leadership, and how; and what changes are taking place in patterns of participation and recruitment. These issues do not provide the full picture of participation, but seeking answers to them will illustrate two of its most important features: on the one hand, what opportunities exist for normal citizens, as distinct from professional politicians, to take part in political life; and on the other, who gets recruited into the very top levels of elected office, in the House of Commons and thus into government.

■ Democracy and participation

Democratic politics in Britain involves a complex mixture of direct and indirect participation: citizens can intervene directly in politics, or they can be represented indirectly by others whom they select.

The single most striking feature of direct participation is its rarity: in particular, only a tiny minority of the population are involved to a high degree in *conventional* political participation. (The importance of italicising this word to our understanding of the changing nature of participation will become clear by the end of the chapter; but for the moment we focus on this world of conventional participation.) Table 13.1 draws on the most authoritative study of conventional political participation to illustrate the point. The table shows popular participation to have two important features. First, the most common forms of participation are infrequent and/or sporadic: they take the form of voting in elections or signing petitions. Second, participation that takes a significant commitment of time and effort – for example canvassing in an election campaign – draws in only a tiny minority. The evidence in this table is now quite old; the original survey material was gathered in the 1980s. But the passage of time

has actually made the evidence more pointed, for over the last couple of decades these forms of participation – voting, canvassing for a candidate – have actually declined further.

Even these low figures overstate the extent of people's willingness to participate in politics. They report what a representative sample of the population claimed to do and, since participation is widely thought to be a good thing, there is evidence that people overstate what they do: for instance, the **turnout** in local elections and in elections for the European Parliament has never been anywhere near the numbers suggested by these figures, and in the most recent European elections in 2004 only just over 38 per cent of the electorate voted. (For the significance of recent turnout in UK parliamentary elections, see the section on the participation crisis near the end of the chapter.)

On this evidence the British are not political animals; only a minority, the **active minority**, give a substantial part of their lives over to political participation. Who are these people, and how do they differ from the majority of citizens? Some of the correlates of high participation are unsurprising: education, income and occupation are all implicated. The patterns of inequality in the distribution of

Table 13.1 Percentage of population who have engaged in different forms of participation

	'Yes'/at least once (%)			'Yes'/at least once (%)
Voting in elections			*Contacting*	
Local	68.8		Member of Parliament	9.7
General	82.5		Civil servant	7.3
European	47.3		Councillor	20.7
			Town hall	17.4
Party campaigning			Media	3.8
Fund raising	5.2			
Canvassing	3.5		*Protesting*	
Clerical work	3.5		Attended protest meeting	14.6
Attending rally	8.6		Organised petition	8.0
			Signed petition	63.3
Group activity			Blocked traffic	1.1
Informal group	13.8		Protest march	5.2
Organised group	11.2		Political strike	6.5
Issue in group	4.7		Political boycott	4.3
			Physical force	0.2

Source: G. Parry, *et al.* (1992) *Political Participation and Democracy in Britain*, p. 44. Reproduced with permission from Cambridge University Press

---

BOX 13.1 IDEAS AND PERSPECTIVES

Apathy and British politics

Who cares about politics? The popular view is that it is dull, politicians are all the same and nothing changes. The preoccupation now is the pursuit of personal happiness – how much money you can earn and how well your personal life is going are Britons' main concern. To attend a political meeting or worry about politics is for anoraks and sad people with no other interests. Hence the fall in voter turnouts for last Thursday's European elections.

Yet politics represents the best of what it can mean to be a citizen. To gain power and to use it in the public interest are at the heart of democracy. The right to vote was hard won, and the wide agreement that politics and public affairs are increasingly dull, even purposeless, is to devalue our society. We are more than pleasure seekers.

It will be objected that the European elections, to a distant and controversial European Parliament, are scarcely a litmus test, but, if so, why was the turnout so much higher five years ago? Why are local election turnouts falling? Why are all branches of the media less and less confident that political coverage and analysis of public policy is what their audiences want?

Source: From an editorial in *The Guardian*, 17 June 1999. © Guardian Newspapers Limited, reprinted with permission

---

resources outlined in Chapter 3 are partly reproduced in patterns of participation: those who participate most tend to have higher than average levels of education and higher than average income and are disproportionately from professional occupations. But the words 'tend to' and 'partly' are very important here; the study of participation in Britain by Parry and his colleagues cited above showed that there is no simple connection between wealth, education and participation (Parry *et al.*, 1992). At every level of British society, even among those groups most disposed to take an active part in politics, only a minority do so. More university professors than university porters take part in politics, but even among university professors politics is still a minority taste. Parry and his colleagues found that over half the population took part in only one activity, voting, which of course happens infrequently. By contrast, they identified a core of 'complete activists', who make up only 1.5 per cent of the population (just over 600,000). This is an absolutely large number of people. They are a minority, vital for the health of democracy, for whom politics is a consuming passion – the political system's equivalent of obsessive stamp collectors or snooker fanatics. But participation in snooker, billiards and pool is actually much commoner than political participation: about 20 per cent of men and 4 per cent of women report that they play. Viewed thus, politics counts as a small minority sport. Even opera – usually classed as a typical pursuit of the rich – is more popular among unskilled manual workers than is politics: 1 per cent of unskilled manual workers report that they attend opera. All these figures put into context the significance of participation in politics, and they are particularly worth bearing in mind when we consider how well politicians can claim to represent the popular will.

■ Democracy and non-participation

The politically active citizen is in a small minority, and that fact is a problem in achieving government 'by the people'. It is, however, a problem that may be soluble, because the overwhelming majority of the people participate sporadically, and through elections help to select some of the representatives who ensure indirect participation. But for the effectiveness of democracy an even more troubling feature is that part of the population – a minority – take no part in politics at all. It is not easy to get a clear picture of those who are completely excluded – or who exclude themselves – from all political participation, since one of the main means of studying who takes part in politics is the mass survey – and those who avoid politics are precisely those who are often difficult to contact by surveys.

Some of the totally inactive present a problem for any theory of democracy that demands the active involvement of all citizens, but their inactivity need not itself be taken as a sign that the British system is malfunctioning. There is a minority in the population – found in all classes – who are so obsessed with some other pursuit, be it train spotting or opera, that they have neither the desire nor the time to commit to politics in any form. They may be seen as the mirror image of the minority so obsessed by politics that they can commit to nothing else. Societies need these

A politically apathetic nation? A million indignant protestors take to the streets of London to protest against the Iraq war
Source: Philip Langeskov

obsessives, otherwise train spotting, opera and demo-cracy would die out. This random distribution of obsessives thus produces considerable social benefits.

Much more serious than the minority who rationally exclude themselves from all political par-ticipation are those who are excluded – particularly because the politically excluded also disproportion-ately suffer social, economic and cultural exclusion. We can begin to see why the problem is serious by considering some of the more obvious sources of exclusion. Consider the commonest form of conven-tional participation, voting. To vote, one must first be on an electoral register. An absolutely large num-ber of adults are excluded by virtue of committal to institutions, notably prisons and mental hospitals. Britain has one of the largest prison populations in Europe: for some years now it has consistently exceeded 70,000. Most prisoners have been legally debarred from voting. While recent court judge-ments may reverse this formal state of affairs, the practical effect of legal changes is unlikely to be great. This is because prisoners face considerable obstacles to participating in political life. The social mix of the prison population is not a cross-section of the population: prisons form a concentration of the poor, the least well educated (including the illiterate), the unskilled, those unable to get any sort of job, and those with mental and physical health problems. In the prison population, we see the most extreme and most visible (because confined in a state institution) bit of the iceberg of the politic-ally excluded. Outside prison, another substantial excluded group until recently were the homeless. Voting requires registration, and to register required a fixed abode. The very nature of homelessness makes an accurate estimate of the numbers difficult. However, in a national survey in the mid-1990s, 6 per cent of all households reported some experi-ence of homelessness in the preceding decade. In other words, being homeless is not a great rarity. The social profile of the homeless is also, unsurpris-ingly, distinctive: for instance, 30 per cent of lone parents with dependent children have reported some experience of homelessness. The requirement that a fixed abode is needed to register was relaxed in the Political Parties, Elections and Referendums Act of 2000. Nevertheless, given their condition of life it is unlikely that many of the homeless do actually register. Overall, Weir and Beetham have estimated that somewhere between 2 million and 3.5 million people are disenfranchised at any one time (Weir and Beetham, 1999, p. 41).

All this adds up to a pattern that is problematic for democracy: exclusion from labour and housing markets goes with political exclusion. Exclusion from the system could lead to a build-up of frustration at not being heard, something to which some comment-ators attributed disturbances which have occurred periodically in some cities since the early 1980s. Beyond these visibly excluded groups is a less easily measurable world of political exclusion, but the weight of circumstantial evidence overwhelmingly points to the conclusion that those who take no part in politics are usually the poorest of the poor. Whether some other mechanisms of democratic politics can remedy these exclusionary features is considered later in this chapter.

■ Democracy and political recruitment

Political participation as an active citizen is one thing; being recruited into a full-time political posi-tion is another. But **political recruitment** of the latter kind is central to the workings of democracy in Britain for a reason we have already encountered: the scale and complexity of governing the United Kingdom means that, inevitably, there has to be some political specialisation; a minority has to make a career out of political leadership. That is the essence of representative democracy. How well the mechanisms of political recruitment function is therefore a critical matter as far as the evaluation of British democracy is concerned.

Getting citizens to participate voluntarily in politics is, as we have seen, a difficult business. But in the case of recruitment to full-time elected office, 'many are called but few are chosen' – there are far more aspirants than there are places. The most important gateway into this kind of political leader-ship is via a seat in the House of Commons, and the only realistic way into the House of Commons is through competing as the candidate of a leading political party. Competition for party nomination is intense. If we focus on the very top of the political tree – the leading positions in Cabinet, for instance – we find that, by the time people get there, a drastic process of selection has taken place.

How does this drastic selection process work? We will find that three features are important: politics at the top is now a full-time occupation; the selection process is brutal and gets more brutal the closer the top is reached; and right at the top, luck – good and bad – is very important.

The first of these features actually highlights the single most important fact about elected political leadership in Britain: it is a full-time profession, demanding total dedication. It is extremely difficult to combine with a serious, long-term commitment to any other job. That is a great change from a generation ago, when politics could be combined with another occupation. This is one of the keys to understanding the recruitment process. It is helpful to think of the road to the top as a bit like a long march by an army of hopefuls several thousand strong. They start out in their twenties wanting to reach the very top. By the time this young army reaches middle age all but the handful in or around the Cabinet have dropped out, exhausted or destroyed by the journey. The Labour Party leader (1963–76) and Prime Minister Harold Wilson was famously photographed as a child outside the door of No. 10 Downing Street; numberless others have been so photographed without coming near to entering through that door as Prime Ministers. They dropped out somewhere on the long march. Like an army losing soldiers, the process of elimination is governed by a number of features, ranging from the initial suitability of those who joined the march in the first place, to sheer luck. Broadly speaking, in the early stages of the march those who fall out are marked by consistent features; as the march reaches its close, luck starts to play an increasingly important part.

The best way to appreciate this is to start with those who have made a successful start on the long march – who have actually managed to become full-timers by virtue of being elected as Members of Parliament. This is the point at which most of those on the march to political leadership drop out, and for an obvious reason: there are only 646 seats in the House of Commons, and at any one election, because most incumbents are reselected, only a small number are actually available to new aspirants. With a few exceptions, election to the House of Commons has been the prime condition for achieving high political office in the United Kingdom. (The new devolved Parliament in Scotland and Assembly in Wales now offer an alternative route to governmental office.) But narrow though the passage is through which those on the long march to political leadership have to pass, it is narrower even than the figures for the size of the House of Commons would suggest. The chances of reaching and staying on the **front bench** are maximised by securing, at an early age, a safe

parliamentary seat – and the number of these is, naturally, considerably smaller than the total of parliamentary seats.

The 'gateway' into a seat in the House of Commons is very important to political recruitment, then, for a number of reasons. For all the evidence of the marginal role of the Commons itself to the making of policy, a seat in the House is virtually a condition of enjoying a career at the very top of national politics. The narrowness of the gateway makes this the key point at which most abandon the march to the top. Elections are dominated by parties. Only three members of the current House of Commons could be considered political independents. Even one of these, George Galloway, was elected on an anti-Iraq war ticket for his Respect Party, though that party is essentially a Galloway vehicle. Thus, any realistic chance of entering the House of Commons depends on securing a party nomination. In the two leading parties, even nominations for hopeless seats are strongly contested, partly because contesting a hopeless seat is now a more or less compulsory apprenticeship for someone who aspires to nomination to a safe seat. Doing the rounds of local parties to secure nominations is the point at which some of the brutal realities begin further to weed out all but those most intensely committed. Although politics has become increasingly professionalised, it lacks many of the traditional features of a middle-class profession: hours of work are highly unsociable and difficult to reconcile either with family life or with most second occupations; it is a highly precarious source of income; and, while the national parties do try to exert some influence over candidate selection, the final say is still lodged with activists in individual constituency parties.

This last fact helps to explain some of the broad social characteristics of MPs as reflected in Table 13.2. Although some social skills – the ability to 'work a room', talking quickly and superficially to complete strangers – are important to potential MPs, most selection processes in constituencies put a high premium on speaking skills fostered by high levels of formal education and the practice of professions such as the law. Parliamentary politics is still a highly 'oral' occupation, and the ability to speak well in public is a highly valued skill. Those who make the selection at constituency level are able to make choices that reflect their preferences, both open and unacknowledged. These preferences go some way towards explaining the make-up of the House of Commons. As Table 13.3 shows, the

Table 13.2 Selected characteristics of Labour and Conservative Members of Parliament, 2005 general election (% of total for each party)

	Labour Party	Conservative Party
University education	64	81
Professional or business occupation	47	76
Manual worker	12	1

Source: Calculated from Criddle (2006), pp. 164–5

Table 13.3 Women's share of seats in a selection of popularly elected chambers*

	Women's share (%)
Sweden	45.3
Norway	38.2
Finland	37.5
Denmark	36.9
Netherlands	36.7
New Zealand	28.3
Austria	33.9
Germany	32.8
Iceland	30.2
UK (House of Commons)	19.7

* The figures are for popularly elected lower houses. Most are for elections during 2002–4; the UK figure is for the House of Commons elected in 2005.
Source: Adapted from the Inter-Parliamentary Union website (www.ipu.org/wmn-e/classif.htm). Reproduced with permission

representation of women in Parliament is low by international standards. Some of this is due to the fact that local selection committees often do not wish to select women as candidates – a prejudice that was both more open and more extensive in the past but which continues to influence the make-up of Parliament. Some is due to the sheer difficulty of combining a Parliamentary career with the demands of homemaking and parenthood that even now still fall disproportionately on women (Norris and Lovenduski, 1995). Likewise, open or unrecognised prejudice against some ethnic minorities, notably Afro-Caribbeans, helps to explain why the proportions of those in Parliament are well below the proportions in the wider population.

Once through the very narrow passage of a safe parliamentary seat – especially if it is acquired while someone is still in their thirties – the path to the top becomes considerably easier. The odds on reaching the front bench, especially in government, are not long. A government needs to fill over 100 ministerial offices. At any one time, a proportion of the parliamentary party will be ruled out – by manifest incompetence, some serious problem in private life, age (it is increasingly rare for someone to be given office for the first time once they have passed 50) or the fact that they have fallen foul of the leadership. The simple staying power guaranteed by a safe seat thus gives the ambitious an advantage. Beyond that, the pathway to the top starts to depend on a large number of difficult-to-control circumstances. Connections and patrons help, especially in getting a foot on the lower rungs of the ladder. Luck (being available when some accident, scandal or resignation causes a vacancy) plays a part. For instance, John Major (Conservative leader and Prime Minister, 1990–7) had his route to the top cleared by a succession of events in which he had no direct role: two important Cabinet resignations and then Mrs Thatcher's defeat in a leadership election within the Conservative Party. Finally, physical and mental robustness are very important. At the top political life is extraordinarily stressful. The successful need a physical constitution able to cope with long, odd hours, little leisure or exercise and the temptation to over-indulge in rich food and drink. It helps to be clever to survive at the top, but it is essential to be physically strong; any physical weakness will soon show itself, and any serious ill health is a virtually certain bar to office. At the very top, Prime Ministers tend to be highly robust: every postwar Prime Minister has survived into advanced old age bar Major and Blair, who of course have yet to live that long. It is also essential in British government to have a particularly robust mental make-up: a large ego and enormous self-confidence. Political life is so intensely adversarial that anyone near the top will be subject to constant criticism and hard questioning. A tendency to self-doubt, or an inability to shrug off personal attacks, is almost as fatal to success as physical ill health. Getting to the very top – to be Prime Minister or Leader of the Opposition – is then heavily influenced by chance. Political life is full of ex-future Prime Ministers who looked certainties for the top job but who never made it; by contrast, it would have been impossible to predict the identity of the last six leaders of the Conservative

Prime Ministers in waiting? Eton College has provided 18 Prime Ministers, the last in 1963; but is this bastion of Old England about to provide another? And, if so, what does it tell us about modern British society?
Source: © Tim Graham / Corbis

Party (Thatcher, Major, Hague, Duncan Smith, Howard, Cameron) even a year before they took office. Indeed the Conservatives' latest leader, David Cameron, came unexpectedly up on the rails only a few short months before his victory in December 2005.

The importance of single-minded ambition in reaching the top is well illustrated by two figures who will dominate electoral politics until at least the next general election: David Cameron, the new Leader of the Conservative Party selected in December 2005; and Gordon Brown, Chancellor

---

BOX 13.2 IDEAS AND PERSPECTIVES

How to get to the top in British politics

- Be born a male
- Be born white and English
- Go to university
- Start early: enter Parliament by the age of 35
- Get a safe seat
- Acquire a powerful patron, preferably in the Cabinet

- Never suffer serious illness – if you must, conceal it
- Have a large ego – never experience self-doubt
- Spend every waking hour on politics and your career
- Above all, be lucky.

David Cameron (1966–)

David Cameron was elected leader of the Conservative Party in December 2005, defeating the one-time hot favourite David Davis. For over forty years the Conservative Party has generally preferred to choose leaders from comparatively modest social backgrounds. Cameron superficially represents a return to an older tradition: educated at the most élitist of all public schools, Eton, and at Oxford University. But in fact he is the very pattern of a modern politician. He has done little in his adult life other than full-time politics. He won the leadership because, unlike his rival, he showed immense talent in exploiting the tools of modern politics, notably communication via the mass media. This talent enabled to him to emerge within a few weeks from the position of outsider in the Conservative leadership contest to that of hot favourite – a position confirmed by his victory in the December 2005 election among Conservative Party members. The importance of presentation skills is emphasised by the fact that Cameron has no experience of government office, nor much even of public life (he only became an MP in 2001). Contrast his predecessor Michael Howard who had a long political career, including holding major public offices such as Home Secretary, before becoming leader.

since 1997 and virtually a certainty to succeed Tony Blair as Prime Minister before the next general election. Superficially they look dissimilar: Cameron is a quintessential product of the socially exclusive south of England upper class, educated at Eton College and Oxford; Brown is the state-educated son of a church minister, educated at a Scottish state school and Edinburgh University. Actually they are very alike in their dedication to their political career: in their adult lives they have been virtually nothing but full-time politicians. The jobs they held before entering Parliament (both, as it happens, at one time working for TV companies) were just preparations for the life of full-time politics. Both entered Parlia-

ment early (Brown at 32, Cameron at 35) for safe seats, thus insulating themselves from the ups and downs of the electoral fortunes of their parties. Both live for politics and their career. And both are hugely skilled at the techniques of modern politics, notably at the rapid assimilation of information and its conversion into attractively packaged statements and soundbites suitable for the modern mass media, especially television.

■ Changing patterns of participation and recruitment

The preceding sections are designed to give a couple of 'snapshots' of pathways into politics: the pathways by which citizens who are not committed to a political career nevertheless participate in political life; and the pathways by which those with aspirations to full-time elected office make their way to the pinnacle. But as important as any snapshot is some sense of how things are changing over time. The evidence is that changes, both as regards participation and as regards political recruitment, are having contradictory effects – in some ways opening up new pathways to politics, while closing others off.

What features are weakening and what strengthening democratic participation?

Factors making democratic participation weaker

Some state policies have raised the barriers to participation. An obvious example is the aftermath of the **community charge**. In the late 1980s and early 1990s, large-scale popular resistance to the community charge (the 'poll tax', designed to replace rates on domestic property) was accompanied by widespread evasion – one of the commonest means of which was simply not to be recorded on the electoral register. Even after the repeal of the community charge, this has probably produced a permanently disenfranchised minority. The very fact that many of those who fail to register are engaged in hiding themselves from the state makes estimation of the numbers difficult, but there are almost certainly at least one million potential voters excluded in this way.

The decline of trade unionism, especially among manual workers, has also made participation more problematic for manual workers. Total membership of trade unions has fallen sharply in recent years. Moreover, this fall has been disproportionately concentrated in unions in heavy industries employing, predominantly, male manual workers. Active participation in unions was always confined to a small minority, but the decline of male manual worker trade unionism has significant implications for working-class political participation. For the participating minority, union activity was an exceptionally important channel not only in industrial relations but, through the unions' close connections with the Labour Party, in wider political life. The internal political life of unions was also a means by which groups of workers with little formal education acquired the skills that allow most effective participation – skills in public speaking, in running meetings and in organising groups. The decline of male manual worker trade unionism is probably the single most damaging social change as far as democratic participation in Britain is concerned.

Factors making democratic participation stronger

Although some public policies have made participation weaker, some have made it easier. The proliferation of candidates from minority parties at general elections is in part the result of a decline in the historic cost of running candidates. A parliamentary candidate in a general election must deposit £500 (refundable only if at least 5 per cent of the vote

---

BOX 13.3 IDEAS AND PERSPECTIVES

Referendums

A referendum is a vote allowing choice on a particular issue, as distinct from an election, which is a vote allowing choice between candidates. Traditional constitutional conventions were hostile to the referendum mechanism, and it was first used as a means of expressing popular views on a single important issue only in the 1970s; before that it had been used to decide comparatively minor issues like pub licensing laws in some localities. In 1975, a referendum was held to affirm approval or disapproval of the terms of our membership of the Common Market, which had been renegotiated by a new Labour government. At the time it was commonly argued that the referendum breached important constitutional conventions, such as that collective responsibility for major decisions should lie with a Cabinet answerable to the House of Commons. But the referendum proved its worth by settling a huge, and hugely divisive, political issue: after the 'yes' vote in 1975 Britain's continuing membership of the Common Market ceased to be a significant line of political division.

Since then, the referendum has become established as a major means of making decisions on historic political issues. In 1979, proposals to introduce devolved government in Wales and Scotland fell through failure to secure required majorities in referendums in the two countries. In 1997, by contrast, votes favouring the principle of devolution in the two countries led to major devolution Acts being passed in the following year. And in 1998, referendums in both Northern Ireland and the Republic of Ireland produced large majorities in favour of the Good Friday Agreement, the agreement by which the peace settlement in Northern Ireland is popularly known.

These examples also illustrate the ambiguous meaning of the referendum in modern Britain. It is now undoubtedly established as a means of expressing popular will – and thus of popular participation at historic moments. But as the most recent cases show, the people at large have typically been allowed to have a say only at the end of bargaining, as in the case of the Good Friday Agreement, when all kinds of alternatives that might have been popularly preferred have been closed off by the political élite. There has always been an argument about how far a referendum allows serious popular choice and how far it is just a means of giving a popular rubber stamp, or legitimacy, to policies worked out by the governing élite. And that uncertainty continues to surround the referendum in Britain.

is received). The original amount was set in 1918, at £150: had that amount been increased in line with inflation the required deposit would now be in excess of £3,000. Yet another policy change which has widened opportunities to participate is described in detail in Box 13.3: the referendum, once of no importance in British political life, is becoming increasingly common and increasingly important.

An even more significant factor encouraging participation is the accumulation of the '**social capital**' on which much democratic participation draws. 'Social capital' refers, in this connection, to the existence of a well-developed network of associations that underpin democratic politics. As the decline of manual worker trade unions shows, associations are critical to fostering participation in political systems – like that of the United Kingdom – where size and scale rule out much direct participation in decision making. The evidence both that associational life is becoming healthier and that associations are encompassing groups formerly excluded from participation is therefore important evidence in assessing the health of British democracy.

What is the evidence that these 'beneficial' changes are taking place? One striking sign is summarised in Table 13.4. This compares two surveys of associational life in Britain's second city, Birmingham. Two features of this table are noteworthy: the much larger number of associations when the 1990s are compared with the 1960s; and the striking rise in the number of religious groups. In part the latter change is connected to immigration to Birmingham, but the experience of immigration is common to most of the large cities of the United Kingdom, so we can be pretty sure that we are picking up a national trend here. The connection between the renewal of 'social capital' and immigration also highlights another feature central to democratic participation: many of these groups cater precisely for those, like recent immigrants, who would otherwise find participation in conventional politics difficult. In other words, they are a powerful means of countering political exclusion.

The groups that are counted in estimates of 'social capital' more often than not have little to do with political participation directly – religious groups are a good example. But just as trade unions were historically 'schools' where members could learn the skills of organisation and participation, so the same can be said of religious denominations. More directly, we know that organised denominations

Table 13.4 Comparison of number of voluntary associations in Birmingham in 1970 and 1998

Type of association	Number in 1970	Number in 1998
Sports	2,144	1,192
Social welfare	666	1,319
Cultural	388	507
Trade associations	176	71
Professional	165	112
Social	142	398
Churches	138	848
Forces	122	114
Youth	76	268
Technical and scientific	76	41
Educational	66	475
Trade unions	55	52
Health	50	309
Not classified	–	75
Total	**4,264**	**5,781**

Source: From W. Maloney *et al.* (2000) 'Social capital and urban governance: adding a more contextualized "top-down" perspective', *Political Studies*, 48:4, pp. 802–20. Reproduced with permission of Blackwell Publishing Ltd

have historically been important means of political mobilisation: famously, the origins of the Labour Party owed more to Methodism than to Marxism. And the same pattern seems to be repeating itself with the newer groups: the study of Birmingham by Maloney and his colleagues referred to in Table 13.4 showed that many of the new groups created since the 1960s are deeply involved in consultations over public policy, especially in the sphere of community relations.

The renewal of social capital has also brought into being other kinds of association that are mobilising the previously excluded. One of the most graphic examples is provided by the case of the sick – traditionally, a weak group often very difficult to organise for the purposes of participation in politics. The very group who might be thought to have the greatest interest in shaping health policy was the most likely to be excluded from it. However, Wood has shown that there has been a mushrooming of patient organisations: he paints a picture where numerous groups of patients, especially those suffering from long-term illnesses, are organising to an increasing extent; 88 per cent of the patient groups he identified had been formed since 1960 (Wood, 2000).

What explains this apparent transformation of the landscape of participation? Three forces are important:

1. Long-term social changes have altered both the capacities and the outlook of the whole population. For instance, the long-term rise in the formal educational attainments of the population may be important, since the likelihood of participation rises with education: in the mid-1960s only about 5 per cent of 18-year-olds were in higher education; now the figure is above 40 per cent, and the official medium-term target is 50 per cent. Culturally, there has been an explosive growth in interest in the natural world and protecting the environment. As Table 13.5 shows, this has been reflected in a huge growth in membership of environment-related organisations. Of course, few people join organisations such as the Royal Society for the Protection of Birds to campaign politically; but the growing resources of these organisations are used to *represent* the concerns of members – thus contributing to the second (indirect) form of representation.

2. Advances in techniques of political organisation and in technology are making it easier to form and maintain groups. Pioneers in effective group organisation can be imitated very quickly: many of the campaigning groups of the 1990s – for instance, groups campaigning for the environment or for the disabled – are copying and adapting successful tactics, such as public demonstrations, developed in the 1960s and 1970s. Sometimes the transmission process is international: witness the success of the international environmental organisation Greenpeace, which did not even exist in the UK in the early 1970s. Meanwhile,

the development of cheap desktop computing power makes the organisation of groups much easier than in the past: databases, mailing lists, and targeted mail shots to raise support and money are all now within the reach of even relatively small, impoverished organisations. Growing popular access to the Internet will make the electronic organisation of political movements even easier in the future.

3. These electronic and social developments have given a considerable spur to the growth of **political entrepreneurship**. Political life, like economic life, is a kind of marketplace; and just as successful business entrepreneurs live by spotting and filling a gap for economic goods and services, the same can happen in political life. Entrepreneurs 'spot' groups that do not, or cannot, participate in political life and either organise them to participate or organise a group to lobby on their behalf. Political entrepreneurship is a very important development, since it is a key means by which the voice of the previously excluded, or the silent, can be heard in politics.

Changing patterns of recruitment

If we compare the present with a generation ago, two features dominate the pattern of change in political recruitment:

1. There has been a considerable narrowing of the social range in recruitment. A generation ago, two social groups now little represented in Parliament made up a sizeable proportion of the benches on both the Conservative and the Labour sides: on the former, a considerable group with established upper-class connections; on the latter, a considerable group who had spent part of their adult life as manual workers. The 'shorthand' signs of this were, on the one side, education at the most exclusive public school, Eton, and on the other occupation before entering Parliament. The 2005 general election saw only seventeen Etonians (fifteen of whom were Conservatives) returned to Parliament. While this was actually a small advance on the 2001 total (of fourteen), the Etonian contingent is in long-term decline. Although the percentage of Labour MPs who were once manual workers also showed a slight advance over 2001 (from 10 per cent to 12 per cent), this group too is in long-term decline (Butler and Kavanagh, 2002, pp. 202–4 and

Table 13.5 The rise of the environmental movement: membership of selected groups (United Kingdom, thousands)

	1971	2004
National Trust	278	3,400
Royal Society for the Protection of Birds	98	1,010
Ramblers' Association	22	143

Source: For 1971, Office for National Statistics (1999), Table 11.4; for 2004, annual reports of the organisations

Criddle 2006 allow comparison of figures). Although strenuous efforts have been made in both leading parties in recent decades to 'democratise' their back benches, the effect, curiously, has been to mould MPs into something like a single prototype regardless of party. The typical MP, almost regardless of party, is now a middle-class professional.

2. This narrowing of the social range of political leaders is connected to a second development: the rise of the professional politician. The demands of most professional occupations – in business or elsewhere – are now so great that it is virtually impossible to make a long-term success while committed to politics. Even if an individual does not set out to be exclusively committed to one or the other, fairly early in a career a decision has to be made to concentrate either on politics or on a chosen profession. The demands of politics – especially parliamentary politics – now virtually rule out combining an active role in Parliament with a serious profession. Politics at this level is increasingly a full-time job, especially for the most ambitious MPs.

The decline of the working-class MP has been hastened by other social forces. It partly reflects the declining influence of manual worker trade unionism in the Labour Party, because these unions were powerful patrons of manual workers. It partly reflects social change: although manual workers are in decline in Parliament, many of those with middle-class professional characteristics are 'meritocrats' from working-class families educated to university level. But the change is also due in part to the rise of politics as a full-time professional career. Professionalism makes early commitment to parliamentary ambitions even more important than in the past. The manual worker who made a mark in unions and then entered Parliament in fairly advanced middle age is much rarer than in the past.

A crisis of participation – or a crisis of conventional participation?

Democracy, however we define it, depends on extensive popular participation in important parts of political life. Yet there is a great deal of evidence

---

BOX 13.4 BRITAIN IN CONTEXT

Political participation in comparative context

This chapter makes abundantly clear that many forms of participation have declined in Britain in recent decades. But are the British unique in this respect? By some comparative measures participation is indeed low. Thus turnout in elections for local government and for the European Parliament are particularly low in Britain. But in the case of the former, at least, this is probably a perfectly rational response by voters, for British local authorities are especially powerless in comparison to most of their European neighbours. The British participation tradition is also especially restricted: compare the UK historically with the United States, where a wide range of local offices have been open to electoral choice and where the second Chamber – the Senate – has been popularly elected for nearly a century. (Contrast the case of the House of Lords.) As we have seen already in the chapter, this restricted participation tradition is changing: there is an increasingly wide range of opportunities to

vote either for candidates for office, or in referendums governing policy choice. Many of the most important signs of 'participation decline' are common across the world of economically advanced democracies: for instance, the political party with a mass membership is losing its hold virtually everywhere, as a means of getting people either to vote or to become active in politics more generally. Most of the forces making for changes in participation in Britain are also common to other advanced industrial societies: for instance, the way innovative electronic technologies are spurring new forms of participation. Indeed, one of the marked features of many of the new groups who are drawing people into active politics is that they are linked in international networks: consider the examples of Amnesty International and Greenpeace International, both of which are virtually global movements. British political participation can thus no longer be considered simply a 'British affair'.

that participation in many important political activities is falling. This was dramatised by the historically low turnout in the general election of 2001, and by the barely marginal recovery in the election of 2005, but there is other important evidence. One of the most important signs is the declining willingness of citizens to join, and take an active part in, political parties: parties now have about three million fewer members than in the early 1950s. (The figures are approximate because until recently total membership figures were approximations.) Yet parties are the main institutions by which political competition is organised in Britain, and governments are overwhelmingly dominated by parties: that is why we routinely speak of the 'Labour' or the 'Conservative' government. Sharp falls in participation thus seem to suggest a wider crisis of democracy.

However, a more optimistic view would argue that we are just seeing a perfectly rational shift by citizens away from ineffective and often boring forms of participation – such as the tedium of local political party life – to more focused and effective participation: for instance, in special interest groups and in campaigning movements like those for the protection of the environment. We saw earlier (Table 13.5) that the membership of environmental groups has grown hugely in recent years. Of course, most people join the Royal Society for the Protection of Birds (the largest environmental organisation in Western Europe) because they are interested in nature, not because they are interested in politics. But in the heyday of political parties, members also joined parties for social reasons. The fall in the membership of the Conservative and Labour parties is partly because leisure possibilities are now richer and more interesting. In many parts of Britain in the 1950s life was so dull that the most exciting thing to do was to go to the local Conservative dinner dance.

When we join environmental groups we may not be consciously acting politically, but our action, and our subscription fee, help to make stronger an organisation that does campaign over a whole range of important political issues. The significance of the figures for environmental groups is that they may be part of a wider pattern of change in the nature of participation in Britain: a shift from what we have been calling 'conventional' to more unconventional kinds of participation. These patterns are detectable in the very latest surveys of the nature of participation (see, for example, Pattie *et al.*, 2003, 2004). Based on national surveys Pattie and his colleagues unearthed a whole world of participation beyond the conventional range of parties and elections. To take a single example, over 30 per cent of those surveyed claimed to have boycotted purchase of some product within the preceding twelve months – in other words, tried to put pressure on a business to change its practices by using their power as consumers. Well-known campaigns of this kind have, for example, targeted producers of baby food on the grounds that their marketing practices in the developing world were injurious to the health of mothers and children, and targeted oil companies on the grounds that their production practices were environmentally damaging. We do not instinctively think of a visit to the supermarket or the petrol pump as involving a political action, but it is not hard to see that this kind of unconventional participation can be very significant indeed.

That there is a crisis of 'conventional' participation is thus pretty well established, and it is very worrying for those who control the best established institutions of conventional participation – which means those who lead the major political parties and fight parliamentary elections. But the rise of other modes of less conventional participation means that we should be cautious about concluding that there is a general crisis of participation, or that democracy is endangered by the decline of conventional participation. Democracy requires effective participation by the people; it is not obvious that direct action like boycotting products is less effective participation than being a rank and file member of a political party.

Chapter summary

What does evidence about political participation tell us about the health of British democracy? The evidence does not all point in the same direction: the pessimist would see the glass as half empty, the optimist as half full. The pessimist would see that mass popular participation in British politics is limited, mostly, to occasional voting in a general election; and there is some evidence that the appeal of this is declining. Only a small proportion of the population takes a sustained part in politics, and some forms of established participation – such as activism in a political party – are in steep decline. Sustained and high-level political activity has always been a bit like any other obsessive hobby, such as train spotting or an enthusiasm for opera: confined to a tiny minority. But whereas the disappearance of the train spotter or the opera buff would be a matter of regret, it would not fundamentally damage British democracy. The disappearance of the political activist, by contrast, would be very bad news for democratic politics in Britain. The optimist, on the other hand, would point out that, while the proportion of the total population participating in politics is small, the absolute numbers are still very large. What is more, many unconventional forms of activism, for example in various loosely organised political networks, have grown greatly in recent years. And in the new devolved institutions such as those in Scotland and Wales the opportunities to participate, by voting, have actually increased.

Discussion points

■ Can you think of any reforms that might make participation in politics more widespread?

■ What are the advantages, and what are the disadvantages, of the rise of the professional politician?

■ Is direct popular participation needed for effective democracy?

■ You are increasingly concerned about the environment and want to make government policy 'greener'. You do not have much spare time and can afford to take an active part in only one organisation. Discuss the pros and cons of what would be your most effective choice: joining a political party or joining an environmental pressure group.

Further reading

Parry *et al.* (1992) is the most authoritative study of popular participation in Britain. Pattie *et al.* (2004) paint a very different, more contemporary picture, while the article by the same authors (2003) gives a good thumbnail sketch of their core argument. Weir and Beetham (1999) is an attempt to sum up the present state of democracy; Norris and Lovenduski (1995) examine paths to the top in Britain.

Acknowledgement

Note: I am grateful to Byron Criddle of the University of Aberdeen for kindly allowing me a sight of the proof copy of his chapter on 'MPs and candidates' in Butler and Kavanagh (2006) – the latest in his invaluable snapshots of candidate and MP selection at successive general elections. Figures for the 2005 general election have been calculated from his chapter.

References

Butler, D. and Kavanagh, D. (2002) *The British General Election of 2001* (Palgrave).

Criddle, B. (2006) 'MPs and candidates', in D. Butler and D. Kavanagh, *The British General Election of 2005* (Palgrave).

Maloney, W., Smith, G. and Stoker, G. (2000) 'Social capital and urban governance: adding a more contextualised "top down" perspective', *Political Studies*, Vol. 48, No. 4, pp. 802–20.

Norris, P. and Lovenduski, J. (1995) *Political Recruitment: Gender, Race and Class in the British Parliament* (Cambridge University Press).

Office for National Statistics (1998) *Social Trends 28* (Stationery Office).

Office for National Statistics (1999) *Social Trends 29* (Stationery Office).

Parry, G., Moyser, G. and Day, N. (1992) *Political Participation and Democracy in Britain* (Cambridge University Press).

Pattie, C., Seyd, P. and Whiteley, P. (2003) 'Citizenship and civic engagement: attitudes and behaviour in Britain', *Political Studies*, Vol. 51, No. 3, pp. 433–68.

Pattie, C., Seyd, P. and Whiteley, P. (2004) *Citizenship in Britain: Values, Participation and Democracy* (Cambridge University Press).

Weir, S. and Beetham, D. (1999) *Political Power and Democratic Control in Britain* (Routledge).

Wood, B. (2000) *Patient Power? Patients' Associations and Health Care in Britain and America* (Open University Press).

Useful websites

An invaluable source of information about the rules governing participation, and of policy changes designed to encourage participation, is the website of the Electoral Commission, an official body established in 2000: www.electoral-commission.gov.uk. The web pages of two of the new elected bodies created by the devolution reforms are also very informative, providing lots of primary material that would be very useful for projects or dissertations: the Welsh Assembly at www.wales.gov.uk and the Scottish Parliament at www.scottish.parliament.uk. Some of the most important work on participation in recent years is at the time of writing being carried out via a research programme funded by the UK Economic and Social Research Council. To see the projects and researchers visit www.essex.ac.uk/democracy. The information in the chapter on the proportions of women members of legislatures in different countries is taken from the website of the international parliamentary union, a fund of information about all kinds of democratic participation: www.ipu.org. All the campaigning groups that, as the chapter shows, have become important to participation in recent years have websites. For a typical example, see www.greenpeace.org.

CHAPTER 14

Devolution

Bill Jones

Learning objectives

- To place devolution in the context of 'core–periphery' theory.

- To explain the background of nationalism within the different elements of the UK.

- To analyse the movements towards decentralised assemblies in the UK.

- To cover the story of New Labour's creation of the new assemblies and executives in Edinburgh and Cardiff.

- To analyse some of the problems and changes that devolution has caused.

Introduction

At the end of the nineteenth century, Britain lay at the centre of an empire upon which, famously, 'the sun never set'. After two debilitating world wars, the ability of the UK to maintain its empire disappeared – it melted away in a series of independence negotiations during the three postwar decades. The rump of the original United Kingdom remained but faced further threats to its integrity from the northern tip of its former possession, Ireland, together with the Celtic fringes of Scotland and Wales. Tony Blair's Labour government succeeded in devolving the over-centralised British state where his 1974–9 predecessor had failed so disastrously. However, in solving one major problem Blair has discovered that he has created the possibilities for several more.

Tony Blair won't stop interfering with the leaderships of his devolved assemblies
Source: Copyright © Chris Riddell. From *The Observer*, 12 March 2000. Reproduced with permission from Guardian Newspapers Limited

■ Core–periphery theory

One of the more interesting ways of looking at devolution is the 'core–periphery' analysis that informs the writings of Michael Hechter (1975) and the late Jim Bulpitt (1983). These political scientists attempted to explain the pattern of political relationships between the centre of the UK political system – London – and the outer areas such as Scotland, Ireland and Wales using an 'internal colonialism' and a 'territorial politics' perspective, respectively.

Four geographical zones were discerned by Hechter: a core in the southeast; an 'outer core' comprising the Midlands, East Anglia and Wessex; an inner periphery made up by the southwest, the north and Wales; and an outer periphery – Scotland and Ireland. Steed (1986) argues that the Civil War was a triumph of the 'inner core' over the 'outer periphery'. Hechter argues that the process of state building in the UK was similar to the process of imperialism used against other states to achieve dominance. He perceives four stages in the process:

1. There are advanced and less advanced groups within the state, reflecting the spatially uneven wave of modernisation over state territory.

2. The more advanced core area seeks to reinforce its position through entrenching the power relationships between itself and the periphery.

3. The consequence of this is the political and cultural domination as well as economic exploitation of the periphery by the core.

4. Such relationships are counterproductive, as the periphery sustains its character and eventually reacts against core dominance.

Bulpitt saw the dichotomy between the core and periphery as synonymous with 'court and country'. Initially, the royal court was the centre of the core but later, when power moved away from the monarch, the core became the Cabinet. Later still it became a 'political-administrative community' of senior ministers and top civil servants. From this point of view, the periphery was the rest of the country. Bulpitt also saw a key distinction between high and low politics. 'High politics' comprised the major matters of state: foreign policy; managing the currency and the economy; internal security. 'Low politics' was what was left for the periphery. Inevitably, high politics was conducted from the core centre, while low politics was entrusted to 'local élite collaborators'. In this way, so the theory goes, the periphery won itself a substantial measure of autonomy.

Such theorising is a stimulant to understanding the process of devolution, especially the phenomenon of Celtic nationalism as an expression of the periphery's surviving identity and rejection of the core. But to gain a more practical understanding, some recent history needs to be surveyed, especially the provenance of nationalism (see also Chapter 7).

■ Nationalism

Nationalism in the Celtic fringe has had long histories reaching back to the time when there were separate Welsh, Scottish and Irish parliaments in the fourteenth, seventeenth and eighteenth centuries, respectively. Throughout their subsequent subservience to England, fierce national identities were preserved. Ireland received its independence in 1920 apart from the six counties in the north, which was given a devolved parliament it had not requested. Plaid Cymru (PC) in Wales and the Scottish National Party (SNP) were established during the interwar years, although neither polled over 1 per cent in the 1945 election.

However, a subsequent growing feeling that the identities of their countries were being submerged and their economic interests ignored enabled the nationalist parties to gather some popular support. In 1966, the first Plaid Cymru MP was elected; a year later the SNP won the Hamilton by-election, and perhaps it was this event which finally nudged the big parties to take some notice. In 1968 Edward Heath, at the Conservative Party conference in Scotland, set up a committee to look at the possibility of an elected assembly. Labour, then in government, chose the same year to set up a Royal Commission on the constitution under Lord Kilbrandon:

To examine the present functions of the central legislature and government in relation to the several countries, nations and regions of the United Kingdom.

The aim of the government, and possibly the opposition too, was to satisfy the Scottish and Welsh thirst for running their own shows without giving away the ultimate control exercised by Parliament in London. The Kilbrandon Commission did not really achieve this objective, as it could not agree on the most desirable form of legislative 'devolution'.

However, the idea of devolution had been implanted, and both main parties hurried to pronounce it a 'good thing' before the 1974 elections. The SNP had worked hard to stake a claim for 'Scottish oil' and was rewarded with 22 per cent of Scottish votes. Labour, dependent on Scottish and Welsh seats for its wafer-thin majority, was keen to keep potential nationalist voters happy. Its White Paper in 1974 offered Scotland 'substantial powers over the crucial areas of decision-making'. In the October election the SNP seized one-third of the votes, suggesting that even a slight swing to

The Welsh electorate narrowly vote for devolution
Source: Copyright © Chris Riddell. From *The Observer*, 21 September 1997. Reproduced with permission from Guardian Newspapers Limited

them would rake in the seats Labour needed in Westminster. Labour was thus locked into its devolution strategy by urgent political necessity. But the issue was highly contentious, and the bill languished in committee stage until two separate bills were substituted and passed in 1978. But Labour had many opponents in its own ranks, enough of whom supported the crucial condition that 40 per cent of the Scottish and Welsh electorates had to support devolution in a referendum for the related legislation to go through. Labour had to force its measures through using the guillotine in the Commons to circumvent the extensive filibustering used by opponents. In the event, the referendums were held in March 1979 and did not achieve the requisite levels. In Wales the result was a swingeing four to one defeat for devolution, and in Scotland only 33 per cent of the electorate were for, with 31 per

cent against. The SNP actually went on to precipitate Labour's eighteen-year absence from power by failing to offer support over a crucial vote of confidence in the Callaghan government. Once in power, Margaret Thatcher reversed the acts in June 1979 and, in accord with the Conservative opposition to devolution, chose to ignore the issue completely. However, it did not go away: in many ways it festered and grew acute, each country in its separate way, during the Conservative governments of 1979–97.

■ Labour and devolution

Labour, meanwhile, was powerfully influenced by arguments in favour of devolution. Firstly, they seemed to chime in with Labour's democratic tradition – though the left, wedded to central control and uniform national standards, favoured the *status quo*. Secondly, the constitutional pressure group, Charter88, expressing much of the nation's progressive intellectual opinion, had succeeded in winning over the party to the majority of its objectives by the middle of the nineties, having already won over the Liberal Democrats some time before. Thirdly, Scotland and Wales were strongholds of Labour sympathy and electoral support, both of which grew significantly in response to the harsh economic policies of Thatcher's administrations. Fourthly, and most importantly, Labour was worried that the nationalist challenge in Scotland and Wales might eclipse its own role as principal opposition party. John Smith became a firm advocate of devolution by the middle of the decade but when he died Tony Blair was not thought to be as enthusiastic a bearer of the flag. However, Smith's chief lieutenants – Brown, Cook, Dewar and Robertson – were insistent that devolution had become a foundation plank of the party's programme. Blair appointed Lord Irvine to fulfil Smith's legacy as chairman of a secret committee in 1995 (Seldon, 2005, pp. 205–6). Blair's biographer Anthony Seldon notes that Blair's sole major intervention was to weigh in on the side of a referendum and that in the case of Scotland a question be added on tax-raising powers. For Wales, it seems, Blair was 'adamant' that the Assembly should not be a full legislative one. Irvine went on in government to chair the Cabinet committees on constitutional reform and drove through these issues with great commitment and speed. Blair was keen to 'get it through as soon as possible, so that it did not block anything' (*ibid.*, p. 207). With the exception of Ireland, a country in thrall to its violent history and misgovernment, devolution proceeded with relative ease at the outset of the Blair era.

■ Ireland

Ireland was joined to the UK in 1801 by an Act of Union, partly to pre-empt any possible alliance with the forces of the then enemy, France. Throughout the century the connection was troublesome and, after conceding Catholic Emancipation in 1828, the Westminster Parliament had to contend with a noisy, disaffected band of Irish nationalists on its benches. For the last decade of the century and the first two decades of the next, nationalists dominated the 103 Irish seats. Gladstone had decided in 1885

that **Home Rule** was the only solution, a policy that split his party and let in the Conservative and Unionist Party under Salisbury for a long period in office. In 1907, Sinn Fein was founded to advance the cause so nearly won under Gladstone. But the armed militancy of the Protestants in the northern counties of Ulster, supported by the Conservatives, raised the prospect of civil war. The upshot of the increasingly bloody conflict was the formation of the Irish Free State in 1921, which delivered independence to Ireland with the exception of six counties in the north, which were to be administered via a devolved parliament at Stormont. However, the Protestants were unwilling to allow the substantial Catholic minority (then around a third, now closer to 40 per cent) in the province to exercise any significant power; they used a variety of dubious political devices to achieve this, resulting in 'the Troubles' in the late 1960s, which continue to the present day.

The attitude of governments of both major parties has been to introduce a form of devolution that gives both the divided communities a decent share of the power to decide local issues. Several attempts to introduce 'power sharing' after 1972 failed. In 1999, a patient process started by John Major and then Tony Blair (not to exclude his two Northern Ireland ministers, Mo Mowlam and Peter Mandelson) came to a conclusion that offered the best chance of a solution to date. However, attempts to set up a power-sharing executive failed, and the Good Friday Agreement of 1998 awaited the requirement of the Unionists that the IRA begin to 'decommission' their weapons (disarm). The new executive did manage to get established in December 1999, but David Trimble, the First Minister, pledged to resign if the IRA had failed to begin the process of decommissioning by February 2000. When this failed to happen, Northern Ireland Secretary Peter Mandelson suspended the process of devolution and resumed direct rule (see Chapter 30). Eventually, the assembly-controlled executive in Northern Ireland began to operate with Martin McGuinness, widely assumed to have been a senior IRA officer, as minister of education. The peace held for a while but by 2002 was perhaps more nominal than real. In October, a scandal broke involving the discovery of a Sinn Fein spy ring in the Northern Ireland Office, and David Trimble took his Ulster Unionist party out of the power-sharing executive. Another attempt to break the impasse failed in April 2003 when Tony Blair was not prepared to accept the form of words used by Sinn Fein to renounce nationalist paramilitary activities. Elections scheduled for the end of

May were further postponed until the autumn of 2003 when Sinn Fein and Paisley's DUP greatly improved their positions, thus making cooperation between the warring tribes even more difficult. In April 2006 Blair met up with Ahern to give the main parties involved until the autumn to find some kind of settlement to their differences. (See Chapter 30 for full coverage of Northern Ireland.)

■ Scotland

Union with Scotland occurred in 1707, but it was more by agreement than by conquest, and Scotland retained strong elements of its identity including its own judiciary, Church and educational system. Government of Scotland was essentially a local affair, mostly via boards based in Edinburgh with a provenance that predated the Union. By the end of the nineteenth century a feeling had developed, nourished by an awareness that the scope of government had expanded rapidly, that the Scots should have a minister in the London 'core' to look after their interests. Prime Minister Salisbury wrote of the new office of Secretary for Scotland as a post that had been formed to 'redress the wounded dignities of the Scotch people – or a section of them who think that not enough is made of Scotland' (Mitchell, 1999, p. 113). The post became Secretary of State for Scotland in 1926. The scope of government grew exponentially during the next century, and in consequence Scotland enjoyed substantial 'administrative devolution' issuing from Edinburgh rather than London. However, such recognition of Scottish distinctiveness was insufficient to assuage the demands of the Scottish Nationalist Party (SNP), especially when the cabinet minister in charge of Scotland was from a party that, after 1959, polled a minority of the votes at general elections. Under Thatcher, the Conservatives' performance at elections was 31 per cent in 1979 to Labour's 42 per cent, 28 to 35 in 1983, 24 to 42 in 1987 and 25 to 39 in 1992. Given the distortions caused by the first-past-the-post electoral system, the distribution of seats was even more skewed against the party in power in London: 22 to 44 in 1979; 21 to 41 in 1983; 10 to 50 in 1987; and 11 to 49 in 1992. The Secretary of State for Scotland was therefore in an invidious position: in charge of a country where less than a third of voters had supported his own party. There can be little doubt that the right-wing policies of Thatcherism helped accelerate the mood in Scotland in favour of greater autonomy.

In addition, the Scottish Grand Committee, a House of Commons device set up to deal with Scottish legislative matters, had a role to play. Second and third readings of bills and the report stages of non-controversial bills were held in this forum, often meeting in Scotland. Since 1981, when the committee was set up, it has comprised Scottish MPs. During the Conservative years it therefore reflected an opposition majority. This led Michael Forsyth, then Scottish Secretary, to point out in 1995 that Westminster had an 'absolute veto' over Scottish business and the committee was not a 'Scottish Parliament' (Bogdanor, 1997, p. 26). This kind of rebuff only fuelled the Scottish sense of injury, something that happened many times during the 1980s. The poll tax, for example, was actually introduced first in Scotland and provoked resentment equal to that later experienced and better publicised south of the border. Nationalism benefited from the unpopular period of Thatcher's followed by Major's rule, and the SNP's share of the vote grew from 12 per cent in 1983 to 22 per cent in 1992. However, the SNP refused to join in the deliberations of the Scottish Constitutional Convention, set up in March 1989 following a report from the Campaign for a Scottish Parliament. The SNP decided that a gathering which would not discuss political independence was not for nationalists; the Conservatives, who opposed the very idea of devolution, also refused to participate. Mrs Thatcher always insisted that the Scots were well looked after because, as she (correctly) believed, they received proportionately more government spending *per capita* than those living in England.

Labour and Lib-Dem politicians therefore held sway, although they were augmented by the Scottish TUC and CBI as well as the churches. The final report, *Scotland's Parliament, Scotland's Right*, was published in November 1995. This envisaged a parliament elected by a German-style proportional representation system in which voters would have two votes: one for a conventionally elected constituency member and one for a 'top-up' list of members.

Of 129 MSPs, seventy-three would be elected from Westminster constituencies by the first-past-the-post system; the remaining fifty-six would be elected in groups of seven from the eight Euro-constituencies on a list basis to ensure that the final result in terms of seats was more or less congruent with the distribution of votes between the parties.

Parliaments would be for a fixed term and would have the power to vary income tax by plus or minus 3p as well as spending a block grant allocation from Westminster. The Scottish Parliament would have the power to legislate on home policies such as education, health, planning, environment, industry, housing, local government, arts and media, heritage and sport. Westminster would retain control over defence and foreign affairs, the constitution of the UK, some health issues including abortion, transport and safety, immigration, nationality, social security and the economy. In the 1997 general election, Labour polled 45.6 per cent of votes and took fifty-six seats; the Conservatives polled a mere 17.5 per cent and took not one.

Scottish Labour members were angry just before the election when Tony Blair stepped in to announce the referendum, which would ask two crucial questions – did Scotland want:

1   a parliament?

2   a parliament with some tax-altering powers?

Blair was concerned that, just before a general election, voters might respond to the Conservative claim that there was no evidence the Scottish people really wanted such changes, especially what it had cleverly dubbed the 'tartan tax'. Even ruffled Scottish Labour MPs agreed subsequently, however, that it was a wise precaution. The result in the event on 11 September 1997 (see Table 14.1) reinforced Labour's policy convincingly, with three-quarters supporting the parliament proposal and two-thirds the tax-varying powers.

Elections to the Scottish Parliament in Holyrood Palace, Edinburgh, took place on 6 May 1999. The results are shown in Table 14.2, which also indicates how well the parties did in the two sections of the

Table 14.1 The 1997 Scottish referendum results

	% of votes cast	% of electorate
Q1. Support a Scottish parliament?		
Yes	74.3	44.7
No	25.7	15.5
Q2. Support tax-varying powers?		
Yes	63.5	38.1
No	36.5	21.9
Turnout		60.2

Table 14.2 Votes and seats in the Scottish Parliament elections, 6 May 1999

Party	% votes (1st vote:2nd vote)	Seats
Conservatives	15.6:15.4	18 (0 directly elected, 18 top-up)
Labour	39:34	56 (53 direct, 3 top-up)
Lib-Dems	14.2:12.5	17 (12 direct, 5 top-up)
SNP	28.7:27	35 (7 direct, 28 top-up)
Others		3 (Green, Scottish Socialist Party, Independent)

poll. Labour managed to accumulate fifty-six MSPs, nine short of a majority (feminists celebrated the fact that half were women). Conservatives managed eighteen seats (three women) on only 16 per cent of the vote – evidence that the new PR system benefited them considerably. Lib-Dems mustered seventeen seats (two women) on 14 per cent. Finally, the SNP won an impressive thirty-five seats (fifteen of whom were women).

Everyone expected that the election would create the need for a coalition unless Labour decided to govern as a minority administration. This option was unattractive to Donald Dewar, the Scottish Labour leader, as he faced a group of MSPs – including John McAllion, MSP for Dundee East – in his own party who were opposed to parts of its programme. Consequently, he negotiated an alliance with the Liberal Democrats. However, there was a catch. The Lib-Dems, the Tories and the SNP had made election pledges to abolish in Scotland the £1,000 per year tuition fee that university students all over the UK had had to pay since the Blair government introduced it shortly after coming to power in order to finance future expansion. To effect the alliance, the Lib-Dems' leader, Jim Wallace, insisted that his pledge be redeemed. After a great deal of haggling the alliance was forged (or perhaps 'fudged'?) after an uneasy compromise whereby an independent commission of inquiry into the student fee problem was accepted for the time being. The result of the negotiations was a twenty-four-page coalition agreement between Labour and the Lib-Dems. On 17 May 1999, 'First Minister' Donald Dewar posed with his eleven Cabinet colleagues together with eleven junior ministers. Wallace was given the deputy's role and another colleague a Cabinet post plus two junior appointments. Moreover, Lord Steel, former

BIOGRAPHY

Alex Salmond (1954–)

Leader of the Scottish Nationalist Party. Educated at Linlithgow Academy and St Andrews University and worked as an economist before becoming MP for Banff and Buchan from 1987. Led the SNP with some flair, 1990–2000, regarding the Scottish Parliament as a 'halfway house' to independence. He was criticised for poor tactics during elections for the Scottish Parliament in May 1999. Resigned as leader, being succeeded by John Swinney who proved unable to halt the party's decline. Salmon was re-elected as leader of his party in September 2004.

Lib-Dem leader, was elected Presiding Officer of the new parliament.

Back down south in Westminster, John Reid was appointed Secretary of State for Scotland; his role was destined to be reduced dramatically after 1 July, when the new executive formally took charge of domestic matters north of the border. He was succeeded by Helen Liddell when Reid replaced Mandelson in the Northern Ireland Office. Some voices argue for a 'devolution' minister in the Cabinet to sweep up all the residual jobs of the Secretaries for Scotland, Wales and Northern Ireland, and something like this happened in mid-June 2003, when Lord Falconer was made Secretary of State for Constitutional Affairs with some collective residual responsibilities of the Secretaries of State for the devolved countries. However, vestigial ministries persisted; there was criticism at the subsuming of the posts, especially as there would be only part-time representation in the Commons via 'spokesmen': Peter Hain (Leader of the House and former Welsh Secretary, for Wales) and Alistair Darling (Transport Secretary and spokesman for Scotland). Critics focused on the bungled nature of the reform whereby the Scottish Office first took down the plate outside its door and then put it back up later in the same day. On 16 June the new law-making agenda for the Scottish Parliament – the first since 1707 – was announced by Donald Dewar in a low-key equivalent of the Queen's speech. The programme included some important proposals, such as the

abolition of the feudal rights of landlords and the giving of tenants on Highland estates the right to buy the land they worked. Otherwise it lacked anything major or even controversial: improvements in education; ethical standards for local government; the creation of national parks in Scotland (which, surprisingly, had none); and a transport bill allowing tolls on motorists using motorways or entering towns or cities. Compared with Westminster's annual programme of some twenty bills, eight seemed a relatively light load. *The Economist* (18 June 1999) concluded that Dewar was 'not at all anxious to stir up nationalist passions. He is keen that the Parliament should settle down and become preoccupied with routine political work which results in achievement.' Dewar sadly died in 2000 and was replaced by Henry McLeish, who was forced to resign after a scandal involving income from his office space. He was replaced by former finance minister Jack McConnell.

In the June 2001 general election the SNP won 20 per cent of the vote (two points down on 1997) and five seats (one down on 1997). This result was a setback for the nationalists, representing an eight-point reduction on their 1999 assembly elections performance. However, the party decided to accentuate rather than dilute its message and proposed that an independent Scotland would pay its own way via taxes raised in Scotland and take up its own place within the EU.

In July 2002 *The Economist*'s columnist 'Bagehot' assessed the work of the first Scottish Parliament. He judged the coalition between the Lib-Dems and Labour to have been uneasy and unstable. Labour's partners had forced more money for students, who do not have to pay tuition fees in Scottish universities; in addition, they had insisted that elderly Scots be provided with free home care, in contrast to their English equivalents. But there had been some controversial issues: the spiralling cost of the new parliament building (see Box 14.1); MSPs' generous gift to themselves of a 13.5 per cent pay increase; teachers being given a 21.5 per cent increase along with a reduced 35-hour week; and parents no longer being legally able to smack children under three. In addition, Section 28 of the Local Government Act, which forbade the 'promotion of homosexuality' in schools – a sensitive issue north of the border – was abolished. Money has been forthcoming so far for much of what the Parliament has wanted largely because, thanks to the Barnett formula (see later in this chapter), Scotland receives

BOX 14.1 FACT

Holyrood, seat of the Scottish Parliament

Holyrood, seat of the Scottish Parliament, cost ten times the original estimate, a worthwhile investment?
Source: PA Wire / Empics

The project to build a new site for the Parliament proved to be highly contentious. The architect, the acclaimed Eric Miralles, developed a design that was based on flower paintings by Charles Rennie Mackintosh and was intended to appear to be 'growing out of the land'. The building was constructed from a mixture of steel, oak and granite and has been praised as one of the world's most remarkable new buildings. The problems were mostly about the cost. Initial estimates were an acceptable £40 million but by 2001 this had risen to £195 million. Eventually the best estimate of the overall cost was placed at a massive and much criticised £431 million. The building opened for business on 8 September 2004, but on its first day suffered the embarrassment of the microphones failing to work. In early March a 3.6-metre oak beam fell into the debating chamber, while in the same week a puddle formed on the floor of the Lord Rogers-designed dockside Welsh assembly building in Cardiff.

Table 14.3 Results of Scottish Parliament elections, 1 May 2003

Party	Seats (direct:top-up)	% change in vote since 1999
Conservatives	3:15	0.1
Greens	0:7	3.3
Labour	46:4	−4.3
Lib-Dems	13:4	−0.6
Scottish Socialists	0:6	5.7
SNP	9:18	−6.4
Other	2:2	3.2
Turnout	49.2%	−8.8

23 per cent more public spending per head than England. Bagehot concluded that Scotland's politics resemble those of 'old style municipal socialism' run by 'parochial pragmatists'.

On 1 May 2003, the second elections for the Scottish Parliament took place (Table 14.3). They left Labour still in control, courtesy of the Lib-Dems again, but with a substantially reduced cushion of safety. Its loss of six seats and the disappointing turnout (well down at 49.4 per cent), plus the significant votes for minority parties, especially the Scottish Socialist Party under a jubilant Tommy Sheridan, made it a sobering night for the ruling coalition in Scotland. The Greens were also delighted to make seven gains, and Scottish pensioners saw one of their activists elected for the first time. The Conservatives confounded the pundits and defended their total number of seats successfully. The most disappointed party of the night was the SNP, whose holding was slashed by eight seats including some of their most able candidates. SNP leader John Swinney came in for immediate criticism. Conservatives were pleased to have avoided losses predicted by some: 'We are on our way back' said leader David McLetchie. John Harper of the Greens said after the results 'we now have six-party government in Holyrood'. First Minister Jack McConnell ruefully commented after the vote which saw his party lose six seats: 'Low turnout, protest votes, votes for minority parties sent a signal to all politicians that the people of Scotland are impatient for change.' However, his colleagues were less than enthusiastic about the changes demanded by their coalition partner the Lib-Dems. Jim Wallace, their leader, sought

more power in Cabinet plus PR for local government elections.

After decades of struggle, the fight for a devolved parliament has been won, but what political significance does the Scottish experience indicate?

■ It seemed to validate the 'core–periphery' theory to the extent that the periphery had asserted itself loudly and often enough for action to be taken. It signalled the end of the Union as we knew it and the inception of a new kind of politics.

■ Part of this new politics was the use of PR and the appearance of a coalition government in the UK for the first time, formally, since the Second World War.

■ The experience has probably made voting reform less likely to take place as it seems to have strengthened its opponents in the governing party: some were aghast that the automatic majority they had long enjoyed in the country had been sacrificed on the altar of a political experiment; others were irritated that the Lib-Dems had been able to cause so much trouble in negotiating their deal with Labour.

■ The existence of a First Minister and a surviving 'Spokesman of State' for Scotland – doubled up in the form of the Secretary of State for Transport (see above) – has created a potential clash of responsibilities and some resentment.

■ The lack of tax-raising powers may inhibit the ability of the new set-up to do its job properly. As *The Economist* (6 November 1999) noted: 'In effect this new arrangement gives Scotland the ability to call the tune without giving it the wherewithal to pay the piper.'

■ The establishment of a new power centre in Scotland is bound to precipitate political conflict between London and Edinburgh and give reason for the SNP to claim that the only logical progression from the present is political independence and an end to the Union. Moreover, the SNP is now the official opposition in Scotland, and in democracies it normally follows that oppositions eventually get to exercise power. What would the SNP do if it were to win such power? Would it really go ahead and introduce an independent Scotland?

■ So far there seems to be no solution to the West Lothian problem (see Box 14.2).

BOX 14.2 IDEAS AND PERSPECTIVES

The West Lothian question

In the 1970s, MP Tam Dalyell asked whether it is possible to devolve powers to just one area of a country that otherwise remains a unitary state. He pointed out that after devolution Westminster MPs would no longer be able to vote on issues such as education in West Lothian, while Scottish MPs would be able to do so in West Bromwich. This would give Scottish MPs an unfair advantage and enable a Labour government dependent on Scottish MPs – as in 1964 and 1974 – for its majority to legislate in England and Wales. It has been argued that the existence of Ulster MPs between 1921 and 1972 did not cause any insuperable problems, but against this it has been pointed out that only twelve MPs were involved.

William Hague, the Conservative leader, caused a storm in July 1999 when he suggested that Scottish and Welsh MPs should be banned from voting on purely English matters at Westminster. In justification, he claimed that 'English consciousness' – evidenced by the St George flags and painted faces at World Cup matches the previous year – must have a 'legitimate outlet'. However, his use of the terms the 'time bomb of English national feeling' and 'the drums of English nationalism', not to mention the slogan 'English votes on English laws', opened him to the accusation that he was attempting to fan nationalist flames for political advantage. John Reid, Donald Dewar's successor in the Cabinet, accused his solution to the West Lothian question of 'feeding the very resentment he claims he wants to avoid'. Another problem that the Hague solution would cause is the fact that it would alter the majority available to the government. Suppose Scottish MPs represented the government's majority; then withholding their votes on English matters would render the government impotent. Furthermore, if Scottish MPs cannot vote on English matters, then they would have no say in the fortunes of a neighbour whose progress is integrally linked to their own. The problem has existed since Gladstone (Bogdanor, 1997, pp. 33–7) and would indeed appear to be, as Michael Forsyth called it, 'The Bermuda Triangle of devolution' (Bogdanor, 1997, p. 38).

■ The existence of the Scottish Parliament raises the question of whether the proportionately greater numbers of MPs – seventy-two – than England should be reduced. John Reid, the replacement Scottish Secretary, admitted the anomaly on 1 July and recognised the need for constitutional change in the light of the functions that MPs have surrendered to MSPs. Any such reduced figure – fifty-nine seats was the provisional recommendation by the Scottish Boundary Commission on 7 February 2002 – would threaten the ability of Labour to command majorities in the Commons. Both Wilson and Callaghan depended for their majorities on their Welsh and Scottish MPs, as they had no majority in England. By the 2005 election the number of Scottish seats had been duly reduced to fifty-nine.

■ One of the positive aspects of Scottish devolution has been the fillip it has given to democratic innovation. The scholar David Arter has written of one innovation associated with the Scottish Parliament – its attempt to forge a new relationship with voters. He has analysed (Arter, 2005) how the parliament has established peripatetic committees which travel around and 'engage in rigorous consultation in the deliberations of proposed legislation'.

■ There are a number of potential friction points between the two parliaments. For example, Scotland can decide on its own priorities when it comes to spending its £22 billion budget, but will this be possible if they are politically different from Whitehall or the government in power?

■ When John Reid, a Scottish MP, was made Secretary of State for Health when Alan Milburn left to spend more time with his family, his appointment was criticised by some in that he had no jurisdiction over devolved health matters in Scotland and was effectively a minister for English health.

■ Wales

Most students of Celtic nationalism agree that a qualitative difference exists between the Welsh and Scottish varieties. Scotland has retained a fair amount of identity through its legal and educational system, not to mention its own Church. It has also tended to emphasise economic aspects of its resentment against England: 'It's our oil', for example. Support for devolution was accordingly higher in Scotland, as in the referendum result of September 1997. The cultural aspect of the movement seems not to be decisive; less than 2 per cent speak Gaelic. Welsh nationalism, on the other hand, has a long history of resentment against English cultural colonialism; Lloyd George smarted under the restrictions on speaking Welsh in school as a boy. Indeed, the modern rise of nationalism in the country dates back to a broadcast made by the founder of Plaid Cymru (Party of Wales), Saunders Lewis, in 1962. He argued forcefully that the language had to be defended militantly, and that this was more important than self-government itself. The Welsh Language Society was founded as a result of the broadcast, and in 1966 the language was given official status; in the same year, Gwynfor Evans was elected as the first Welsh Nationalist Member of Parliament at a by-election in Carmarthen. The Free Wales Army was a tiny militant expression of the movement, but the Sons of Glyndwr caused more of an impact through their policy of burning down holiday homes in Wales, insisting that they raised the cost of housing for Welsh people. Another colourful aspect of the cultural divide between Wales and England is the rugby matches between the two countries, where pride and passion combine, for the Welsh, to make them the major sporting events of any year (disappointing ones for the last two decades – but joyful in 2005 when Wales beat the old enemy to win the Six Nations Championship).

In spite of all this, support for an assembly has been markedly weaker in Wales than in Scotland. The referendum in 1979 saw 79.8 per cent of Welsh people voting against devolution and only 20.2 per cent in favour. During the 1980s, however, this trend was reversed and support for the measure grew. All the Conservative Secretaries of State for Wales (a post invented in 1965) were MPs for English constituencies (apart from Nicholas Edwards, 1979–87, who was the member for Pembroke). Further, it was widely believed in Wales that the Conservatives, beaten electorally, had set up quangos, often headed

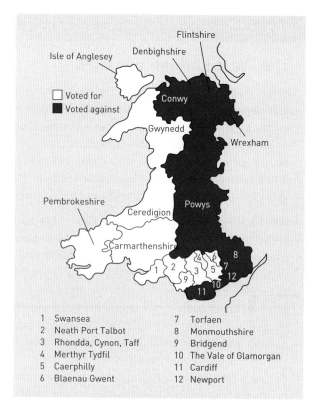

Figure 14.1 Support for Welsh devolution
Source: From *The Daily Telegraph*, 20 September 1997.
© Copyright of Telegraph Group Limited 1997, reproduced with permission

by ex-Conservative politicians, to administer directly issues once the preserve of elected Welsh local government. But when it came to the referendum in Wales in September 1997, support for devolution was still half-hearted. Only 50.12 per cent of the electorate voted in the first place; those in favour represented only 50.3 per cent to 49.7 per cent opposed: the thinnest of margins. The map in Figure 14.1 shows how support for devolution was strongest in the north and west with a broad eastern corridor adjoining England expressing opposition.

Between the referendum in 1997 and the elections for the Assembly in 1999 an instructive passage of politics occurred. It had been assumed by everyone that the First Minister of Wales would be the Welsh Labour leader, Ron Davies. However, he resigned after a bizarre sequence of events in which he had allegedly been mugged by a man whom he had befriended on Clapham Common, a well known gay pick-up area. The whole country, especially the tabloid element of the press, was intrigued by this strange occurrence, and many jokes were cracked at Davies's expense, but it ultimately succeeded in

Table 14.4 The Michael effect? (Welsh Assembly elections, 1999, %)

Party	First vote	Change since 1997	Second vote	Change since 1997
Labour	37.6	−17.1	35.4	−19.3
Plaid Cymru	28.4	18.5	30.5	20.6
Conservatives	15.9	−3.7	16.5	−3.1
Liberal Democrats	13.4	1.0	12.6	0.2
Other	4.7	1.3	5.1	1.7

Source: John Curtice, CREST

ending the political career of the architect of Welsh devolution. Ever aware of the political costs of a gay politician in a country better known for its macho feats on the rugby field, No. 10 was content to see Davies consigned to relative political oblivion as a mere member of the Assembly. When it came to his successor, however, No. 10 did not want the popular but allegedly 'off-message' Rhodri Morgan as replacement for Davies and worked hard – and some said using shameful 'old Labour' manipulations – to achieve the election of safe Blairite Alun Michael, the existing Secretary of State for Wales, as the Welsh leader and thus First Minister. Come 6 May 1999, Welsh voters delivered an unpleasant surprise to London's Labour élite.

First, the turnout indicated anything but a ringing endorsement of the new arrangements: only a quarter of the electorate bothered to vote. Even worse, the small turnout did no damage to the party that argues for complete independence; Plaid Cymru had a fabulous result, winning seats in the traditional Labour heartlands of Islwyn, Llanelli and the Rhondda. As Tables 14.4 and 14.5 show, Labour lost heavily compared with the 1997 election. The story was no better in the more English southeast of the country, where disaffected farmers helped to force Labour to give way in Monmouth to the Conservatives. Ironically, Labour's poor showing entitled it to one top-up seat in the Mid and West Wales area, and this was the 'backdoor' through

which the little-lauded Welsh Labour leader, Alun Michael, crept into the Assembly.

Initially, it seemed that Mr Michael was exploring the possibilities of coalition with the Lib-Dems but eventually Labour, so used to ruling the roost in Wales, decided to govern as a minority party. This was not as risky a path as it might at first seem, as both Plaid Cymru and the Lib-Dems had a vested interest in making a success of the little-supported new assembly. Rhodri Morgan, Michael's leadership rival, was given responsibility for economic development and Europe – something likely to keep him both happy and quiet. Michael's predecessor Ron Davies was bitterly disappointed to be excluded from the Cabinet but was given the chairmanship of the economic development committee. However, he lost even this consolation prize when revelations that he was receiving therapy for obsessive 'risk taking' led, sadly, to his resignation. A further scandal in March 2003 led to his virtual retirement from politics.

The Welsh Assembly, in line, perhaps, with the markedly lower level of enthusiasm for devolution in Wales, has fewer powers than the Scottish Parliament. In theory at least, it takes over responsibility for a 2005–6, £12.6 billion annual budget and the functions of the old Welsh Office, including education, health, local government, housing, planning, agriculture, environment, industry and training, culture and sport. But its responsibilities will not extend, for example, to teacher training policies; nor is it able to pass primary legislation or raise taxes. It can, though, introduce or amend statutory instruments, the important regulations that amplify the often outline 'delegated' legislation from Westminster. As *The Economist* noted on 3 July 1999, the Welsh Secretary had to approve 500 such instruments a year in the past; in future, the Assembly may want to amend or reject these as well as pass its own. There remains a vestigial Welsh Secretary in the Cabinet (Peter Hain) as there is for Scotland (Alistair

Table 14.5 Welsh Assembly seats, 6 May 1999

Party	Seats (direct:top-up)
Labour	28:1
Plaid Cymru	17:8
Conservatives	9:1
Liberal Democrats	6:3

Table 14.6 Results of Welsh Assembly elections, 1 May 2003

Party	Seats (direct:top-up)	% change in vote since 1999
Conservatives	1:10	2.7
Plaid Cymru	5:7	−10.8
Labour	30:0	1.2
Lib-Dems	3:3	0.2
Other	1	6.7
Turnout	38.2%	−8.2

Darling). Most experts agree that the exact division of powers between Cardiff and London is unclear. 'Whereas the Westminster Parliament remains theoretically sovereign, the Assembly derives its powers from the Government of Wales Act. So it will need to demonstrate, for each decision it takes, that it is acting within its powers' (*The Economist*, 3 July 1999; for a full discussion of how the Assembly works in practice see Pilkington, 2002, Chapter 7).

After Labour's losses in the English local elections, it took some pleasure in its 2003 success (see Table 14.6) in recovering ground lost to Plaid Cymru in 1999 – regaining the Rhondda, Islwyn and Llanelli were especially celebrated – and taking half the available seats, making an alliance with the Lib-Dems unnecessary. It was a 'manageable' majority in the words of Rhodri Morgan, the Welsh Labour leader, 'enough to govern, that's for sure'. Peter Hain, Secretary of State for Wales, said: 'Plaid Cymru's fantasy of an independent Wales has been buried for ever . . . this is the best result for Labour in the elections anywhere in Britain.' Again the turnout was shockingly low, slumping to 38.16 per cent: a fall of 8.12 per cent. As in Scotland, the nationalists were the biggest losers – they lost five seats – prompting the question of whether their message is any longer all that relevant to Celtic voters. Daffydd Wigley, the Manchester University educated leader of the party since 1991, resigned in 2000 and the former MP, Ieuan Wyn Jones, took over. However, the party's failure to gain or maintain any electoral momentum in the Assembly elections led to the replacement leader being heavily criticised by party newspapers to the extent that Daffydd Iwan, the former folk-singing president of the nationalists, sought to defuse tensions in mid-September 2005.

The balance of power between centre and periphery is currently being worked out, especially via the new 'subject committees'. These contain the cabinet minister plus members from all parties and meet once a fortnight in the company of civil servants. In theory these committees are only advisory, but their frequency and influential membership give them a potential substantially beyond that role. Welsh devolution hit a major crisis in February 2000 that challenged Blair's much criticised placeman, Alun Michael. Wales qualified for so-called Objective One category funds from the EU, but the grants could only be made in the event of matching funding from the UK Treasury (given that Wales cannot raise any taxation itself). Michael claimed that he was confident of raising the cash, but Plaid Cymru demanded a guarantee on pain of a no-confidence vote. Given that Labour had only twenty-eight Assembly members and the Conservatives and Liberal Democrats were supporting Plaid, the answer was a foregone conclusion. Michael pre-empted the vote by resigning, and the Labour group was able to elect its populist favourite Rhodri Morgan instead as acting First Secretary. With the well-known, independently minded Morgan in control, the opposition parties were less likely to create problems; they agreed to accept his new position and he was elected unopposed on 15 February. Surprisingly, given his earlier opposition, Tony Blair changed his tune on the man on whom he had used every trick to keep out of power; now it seemed that Rhodri was not a problem. As a result of the crisis, Welsh Labour got the man it had always wanted and the future of devolution was restored. Whether Blair's was a genuine change of heart or the best spin No. 10 could put on a situation it could not change is anyone's guess.

The Constitution Unit's review of the Welsh Assembly concluded that it was still finding its way, still writing its rule book. In terms of making a difference, Pilkington (2002) identifies four areas:

1. European Objective One funding was at the centre of the row leading to Alun Michael's downfall.

2. Free eye tests were allowed following back-bench pressure – something that has to be paid for in England.

3. Judicial review decided that the Assembly could impose different settlements regarding performance-related pay for teachers to that obtaining in England.

4. Welsh agriculture consistently won attention in BSE and foot-and-mouth related matters as a result of Assembly pressure.

Pilkington concludes that such matters demonstrate the need for a clearer division of powers between the Assembly's executive and legislative functions, and the possibility of primary legislative powers for Wales.

The Welsh experience of devolution offers the following political features:

■ While the opposition parties are keen to make life difficult for Labour, its minority administration was sustained to some extent by the reluctance of the opposition to undermine the viability of the Assembly in its early stages.

■ The Welsh Assembly was already, in the autumn of 1999, pressing for more powers to place it on a par with the Scottish Parliament.

■ Tony Blair made much of how devolution would entail decentralisation, or giving away of power from Whitehall: an answer to critics who accuse his style of being obsessively centralised. However, Westminster still retains much power over Welsh affairs, and the centre displayed a somewhat undemocratic concern to choreograph the selection of people it liked in local leadership roles and to block those it did not like.

■ Such interference can backfire badly, as the elections to the Assembly revealed, with Labour strongholds being stormed successfully by the nationalists. Nationalist sentiment is very sensitive to such attempts and, as in the case of Ireland, full-scale revolt can be the consequence.

■ Mere legal powers cannot determine how power relationships work out in practice; witness the possibility that the subject committees are forging a unique new legislative/executive role for themselves.

■ Welsh opinion was not best pleased when Blair sought to rationalise the reduced duties of the Secretary of State for Wales by subsuming them into the job description of the Leader of the House, Peter Hain.

■ Devolution differences summarised

Between Welsh Assembly and Scottish Parliament

While the voting arrangements are the same for both, the Scottish Parliament is clearly more powerful than the Welsh Assembly. The Scottish Parliament can discuss legislation through three stages and then pass it before it receives the Royal Assent. The Welsh Assembly, in contrast, has no such legislative competence. Nor can the Welsh influence taxation, unlike the Scots who can vary it by up to 3 pence in the pound.

Between the devolved assemblies and Westminster

Both the Scottish Parliament and the Welsh Assembly represent substantial departures from the Westminster way of proceeding:

1. The elections are fixed-term, meaning First Ministers, apart from in exceptional circumstances, are bound by set dates and cannot manipulate the economy, taxes and the media for partisan ends like the London-based Prime Minister.

2. Business is not conducted in the archaic manner of the Commons and Lords, with antique forms of address and ancient costumes for officials. Voting is via electronic means and not the Commons' endless meandering through the lobbies.

3. The proportional voting system, in which each voter casts two votes, has not produced majorities as with first-past-the-post and arguably produces more accurate reflections of society, with a variety of smaller groups being represented in Scotland.

4. The dominant Westminster pattern of 'government and opposition' has been broken, with coalitions governing in both Scotland and Wales; this has created a more cooperative political culture, compared to the adversarial one of the Commons.

5. There is more transparency in the assemblies, with the Cabinet minutes published almost immediately on the Web rather than after the 30-year time delay insisted upon for their London equivalent.

■ How much difference has devolution made?

This is a complex question and it may be a little early to make judgements but some tentative observations can be offered:

■ For *Scotland*, where the Parliament had passed some sixty bills into law by the end of 2004, the major differences include free personal care for elderly people, the abolition of fox hunting without any of the extended problems experienced in Westminster, the smoking ban in March 2006, and the abolition of tuition fees for university students. Some suggest Scotland is 'ahead' of England in introducing new measures, but the truth could be that it is easier to pass certain controversial items in the devolved assemblies than in Westminster.

■ For *Wales*, with the weaker Assembly, the list is less impressive but includes the abolition of medical prescription charges for the over-50s and under-25s, free school milk for under-7s, free bus passes for pensioners, and six weeks' free home care for the elderly upon leaving hospital.

■ The *Northern Ireland* Executive has been suspended for long periods but has still managed one or two changes like the abolition of the 11-plus exams, free fares for elderly people and the abolition of league tables for schools.

National identity

In addition, devolution has produced some things that are much less easy to measure. Certainly Scotland and Wales have developed a new political culture based on their elected assemblies and a new kind of identity is emerging, looking less to London but more to Cardiff, Edinburgh and Brussels. Northern Ireland's identity has not been obviously affected by its assembly but with so little opportunity to put down roots, this is not altogether surprising. Certainly the strength of nationalism in both Scotland and Wales seems to have declined somewhat as a result of devolution, but there is always the chance of the SNP or Plaid Cymru doing well enough in elections to form the government of their respective country and that is a scenario for which no one can prescribe or offer answers at the present time.

■ Devolution and the EU

Devolution has complicated further the UK's relations with the EU; a number of new potential points of conflict have emerged. For example, Scotland provides over half of the UK's fishing industry, but it will be the UK government that leads negotiations in Europe. However, this is not to say that a Scottish minister might not be briefed on the fishing issue and be a key player in the UK negotiating team in Brussels; similar things happen with the German *Länder* in some cases.

It remains the case that London will still decide on the boundaries of the poorer areas that qualify for EU assistance. However, devolved parliaments and executives will have the duty of implementing the mandatory EU directives. There is no doubt that the relations of devolved assemblies to the EU will be asymmetrical. Scotland is some way ahead of Wales and Northern Ireland in relating to the EU institutions. Through the Scottish Office, it has been active in relation to the EU for many years and on a much more intensive basis than Cardiff or Belfast. It is, for example, possible for Scotland to be represented directly in certain meetings where Wales is not.

This imbalance is likely to continue with Scotland setting up a permanent office in Brussels in July 1999. In the case of Northern Ireland, there is an assembly but, at the time of writing, still no functioning executive. Some observers have noted that the collaboration necessary for the working of certain assistance schemes funded by Brussels has facilitated cooperation between the two estranged communities in the province. The development of the EU's regional policy may encourage English regions to seek assemblies in order to lobby more effectively for Structural Funds and other EU assistance.

The Economist on 6 November 1999 explained the wider significance of the EU for the nationalist movements. To the 'sneer' that small nations such as Scotland (5 million) and Wales (3 million) cannot cast themselves adrift in a 'lonely world', it points out that the nationalists 'do not plan to be alone: they want Scotland to become a full member of the EU in its own right . . . Without the EU there would be gaping holes in the nationalist case. How would an independent Scotland defend itself? What currency would it use? . . . The EU promises access to the world's richest market, a common money and eventually a common defence and foreign policy.'

The SNP has proposed a Scottish European Joint Assembly comprising MSPs and Scottish MEPs to coordinate Scottish dealings with the EU. 'In time', says *The Economist*, 'the nationalists hope people in Scotland and Wales will see their relationship with Brussels as more important than that with Westminster.' A survey published in the same issue

Table 14.7 Influence

Q. In twenty years' time, which of these bodies, if any, do you expect to have most influence over your life and the lives of your children? (%)

	Britain	England	Scotland	Wales
My local council	13	14	5	7
Scottish Parliament/ Welsh Assembly/my regional assembly	13	9	46	26
Westminster Parliament	22	23	8	25
European Parliament/ European Union	44	46	31	37
Don't know	8	8	10	6

Source: From *The Economist*, 6 November 1999. Copyright © The Economist Newspaper Limited 1999. All rights reserved. Reproduced with permission

Table 14.8 Regional identification

Q. Which two or three of these, if any, would you say you most identify with? (%)

	Britain	England	Scotland	Wales
This local community	41	42	39	32
This region	50	49	62	50
England/Scotland/Wales	45	41	72	81
Britain	40	43	18	27
Europe	16	17	11	16
Commonwealth	9	10	5	3
The global community	8	9	5	2
Don't know	2	2	1	0

Source: From *The Economist*, 6 November 1999. Copyright © The Economist Newspaper Limited 1999. All rights reserved. Reproduced with permission

tended to support this idea, revealing that, in twenty years' time, over a third of people living in these countries expected Brussels to 'have the most influence' over their lives and the lives of their children (see Tables 14.7 and 14.8).

However, another aspect of the opinion poll should be noted. When asked which would be the most reliable ally in a crisis, only 16 per cent said Europe and nearly 60 per cent said the USA.

■ England and its regions

Regional assemblies

One result of UK membership of the EU has been the creation by John Major's government in 1994 of regional assemblies in nine areas of the UK: Greater London, South East, South West, East Midlands, West Midlands, Northwest, Northeast, Yorkshire & Humberside and East of England. These regions provide the constituencies for Euro-elections, fit into the EU regional structure and, in addition, have relatively unsung and unnoticed regional assemblies. They are not elected but are appointed by county and borough councils and have no real powers but act in an advisory capacity with varying degrees of success. It is this 'democratic deficit' which advocates of regional devolution seek to address.

City regions idea

This idea grew out of the one region of the nine listed above – Greater London – which has an elected assembly as well as an elected mayor. Enthusiasts for devolution see the cities as the 'drivers' of change and development and think this model is more attractive than the elected regional council one (see below). However, Professor Robert Hazell (see Box 14.5 below) perceives no appetite for the disturbances of another episode of constitutional reform in general and very little enthusiasm for elected mayors-cum-city government in particular.

English nationalism

English people often claim that they have an immunity to anything as vulgar as mere patriotism. However, the evidence from history and other sources suggests that a fervent nationalism is lurking just beneath the surface in England. It may not be overtly stated, but witness the mobilisation by Churchill of a sense of Englishness during the Second World War and the passionate national pride – sometimes an ugly manifestation – that English football can elicit on the international stage. England is, perhaps paradoxically, the odd one out in this discussion about nationalism. This is because England has been so central to the emergence of the 'United Kingdom'. It was England which expanded to absorb its Celtic fringe by the end of the seventeenth century when the great enterprise of empire was already underway. During the next two centuries the empire grew apace, exporting artifacts by the shipload but also the ideas of free trade and liberal democracy. Andrew Gamble (2003) argues that while Wales, Scotland and, for a time, Ireland were involved in the imperial venture, it was 'England which was inevitably at the heart of the state, its dominance reflected in many ways, not least in the common use of the term "England" as the shorthand term for the state.' This derived from a reading of British history which emphasised the 'uniqueness of England, and sees Britain, for the most part a vehicle for England. It is an idea of "England" as an entity greater than itself, a world island.' Gamble sees a new form of politics post-devolution in which the English are still coming to terms with their new separateness rather than as part of the 'state and empire which they took the lead in creating.'

It seems English nationalism is most likely to express itself if people think the country is not receiving a fair deal. There are three possible ways in which devolution could prompt such an expression, the first being the differing slices of public expenditure received by England compared with the Celtic nations.

Table 14.9 Regional GDP *per capita*, 2002

Region	GDP (£) *per capita*
London	26,000
Southeast	17,000
Scotland	15,840
East of England	15,400
Southwest	15,180
West Midlands	14,690
East Midlands	14,450
Northwest	14,440
Yorkshire & Humberside	14,409
Northern Ireland	12,950
Northeast	12,700
Wales	12,600

Source: Office of Deputy Prime Minister

Scotland, Wales and Northern Ireland all receive more government spending *per capita* than England, and devolution has directed more attention to this imbalance. The original formula for setting the block grants was devised by Joel (now Lord) Barnett when Chief Secretary to the Treasury in the late 1970s. This formula was based on calculations that all three were, on balance, places of greater need than England and consequently were allocated more spending per head in them than in England. Since then, their economic performance has improved so much that Scotland's GDP per head is almost up to the English level, as Table 14.9 shows. The figure for Wales, however, at the foot of the table explains why some Welsh MPs, especially the nationalists, call for a review of the Barnett formula in Wales's favour.

The Barnett formula

Because the Celtic fringe tended to be poorer than the regions of England, the then Chief Secretary to the Treasury, Joel Barnett, formulated a formula which gave more spending to Wales and Scotland (see Table 14.10). Barnett had based the formula on

Table 14.10 Government block grants, 2005–6 (£ billion)

Scottish Office	22.9
Welsh Office	12.6
Northern Ireland Office	10.1

population and not real need and assumed it would last no longer than twelve months. In reality it has survived for some four decades. Barnett himself confesses to mixed feelings:

It is an embarrassment to have my name attached to so unfair a system, especially as when I introduced it, it was only going to last for a year . . . Income per head in the northwest and northeast is now much lower than in Scotland yet under the formula Scotland gets around £1,000 a head or more in public spending than the average in England . . . Now the present government won't change it for fear of upsetting the Scots.

Manchester Evening News, 6 February 2004

In November 2001 Barnett actually called for the formula to be scrapped.

According to one calculation, Scotland receives 23 per cent more per head than England, and Wales receives 16 per cent more per head. Because of its special political problems, Northern Ireland receives a massive 30 per cent more than English taxpayers (see Figure 14.2). Should the level of expenditure be reduced to that of England, Scotland would lose a massive £1 billion plus. Even its ability to levy an additional 3p in the pound income tax would bring in only £450 million. So far the English regions have been relatively silent about the differential, with the exception of Sir George Russell, Chairman of the Northern Development Company, who in 1999 complained that 'The Barnett formula is no longer necessary or just.'

Second, England might argue in time that it needs its own parliament to match the political representation of the Celtic fringe. This solution seems logical and would set up the conditions for the federal structure the Lib-Dems favour. However, the major flaw in the scheme is that England, with

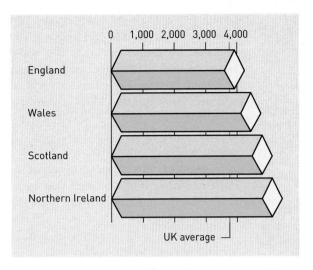

Figure 14.2 The English disadvantage
Source: From *The Guardian*, 7 November 1999. © Guardian Newspapers Limited 1999, reproduced with permission

80 per cent of the population and vastly superior economic strength, would dominate any such federation to an excessive degree (see Box 14.5).

Third, there is the famous West Lothian question, which queries why Scottish and Welsh MPs should vote on English matters when the reverse was not possible through devolution of powers. William Hague, the Conservative leader, opened a potential Pandora's box in July 1999 when he suggested that Scottish and Welsh MPs should be prevented from voting on Westminster issues pertaining to England alone (see Box 14.2 on the West Lothian question, and Box 14.3).

The regions of England

The Kilbrandon Commission suggested that the regions of England should have elected councils to provide more democratic accountability for those

---

BOX 14.3 **FACT**

Powers devolved to Edinburgh
- Home affairs and the judiciary
- Health
- Housing, local government
- Farming and fishing
- Education
- Social services
- Implementing European directives

Powers retained by London
- Employment law
- Economic and monetary policy, taxation
- Social security benefits and pensions
- Passports, immigration
- Negotiating with European Union
- Foreign affairs

Source: The Guardian, 20 July 1999

administrative functions already devolved. The suggestion was lost in the chaotic end to the 1970s devolution episode but arose again in the wake of the more successful experience under Blair's government. Labour promised to consider regional government in an *ad hoc* manner: 'Each area would be treated individually, with no single model imposed from the centre' (Bogdanor, 1997, p. 122). However, survey evidence suggested a mixed set of attitudes to regional government. A report in *The Economist* in March 1999 revealed that large percentages of residents in England were unaware of the region in which they lived. Moreover, similar majorities believed that such assemblies would result in more bureaucracy in the region.

However, with the devolution genie let out of the bottle, the idea of regionalism seemed to acquire some new life. The establishment of regional development agencies (RDAs) on 1 April 1999 was presented as a forerunner of a new kind of regional government involving elected assemblies. They have an important role in drawing up the regional development strategies for each region and engage in close consultation with relevant government offices in the regions. The hope behind the RDAs was that they would help to reduce the imbalance between the regions (see Table 14.9). Greater London and the southeast are rich by any standards, yet Cornwall and South Yorkshire compare with the poorest regions in the EU such as rural Spain and Greece. The RDAs are run by twelve member boards drawn from business rather than local councils and employ staffs some 100 strong. They share a budget from the Treasury with matching amounts to be raised from the private sector. They spend it on urban regeneration and setting up business parks. In 2001 they had £1 billion to spend, but Gordon Brown decided to increase this by half as much again in the run-up to proposals to introduce elected regional assemblies. This development was foreshadowed by the establishment of eight appointed regional chambers comprising councillors, churchmen and business people.

White Paper on Regional Government, 10 May 2002

This region has a semi-colonial relationship with England. It wasn't just the Scots and Irish who were conquered, it was also the North-East.

John Tomaney, lecturer at Newcastle University and supporter of the Northeast Constitutional Convention

Last year Scotland was able to spend £2.56 per capita on tourism compared to Northumbria Tourist Board's 8p. And for every £100 spent on health services in the North-East, Scotland can spend £126.

The Journal, regional newspaper in the northeast, 1999

Many North-Eastern politicians argue that until the region gets its own assembly and first minister – to match Scotland's – its voice will be drowned out in Westminster and Brussels.

The Economist, 27 March 1999

While Tony Blair has never been overly enthusiastic about regional devolution, his deputy John Prescott was. It was he who presented a White Paper setting out the government's promise of a 'new constitutional settlement' in May 2002 in Newcastle. The approach, though, was not to be a national one; it would be step by step and depend on the support for the move within the region itself. It was expected that at least one referendum would be held – in the northeast – before the next election. Regional assemblies would be able to levy a 'precept' on local council taxes to fund their activities. Powers of the assemblies would resemble those of the Greater London Authority, the most important being transport, planning and economic development (see Box 14.4). However, unlike the GLA they would have no responsibility for the fire service or police.

England now includes virtually the only regions within the European Union which do not have the choice of some form of democratic regional governance.

White Paper on Regional Government, 2002

To critics who say that this idea is no more than an extra layer of bureaucracy, the government could retort that the White Paper envisaged the removal of one tier of local government, at either the district or county level. While the new assemblies would be mandatory, where there was public support for them a referendum would be held to test the water. Surveys suggested that support for the idea of regionalism was growing, if slowly, especially in the northeast. *The Economist* (11 May 2002) reported a poll that revealed substantial support for regional assemblies, rising from 49 per cent in the southeast to over 70 per cent in the northwest and east. On 16 June 2003, Prescott announced plans to hold referendums in the northwest, the northeast, and Yorkshire and Humberside in October 2004.

BOX 14.4 **FACT**

Proposed powers of regional assemblies

- *Economic development*: Oversight of regional development agency within their region.
- *Planning*: Ensuring that large new developments blend in with those that already exist or are planned in the future.
- *Housing*: Oversight of the funding for social housing.
- *Transport*: Alleviating congestion and assisting public transport.
- *Health*: Strategies for the long-term health of people in the region.
- *Culture and tourism*: Funding and coordination.
- *Skills and employment*: Coordination with Skills and Learning Councils to raise the skill levels of the workforce.
- *Waste*: Catalysing recycling and establishing targets for the proper management of waste throughout the region.

Critics pointed to the possible discontinuity of a reform based on the whim of regional electorates and the weakness of assemblies compared with their Scottish and Welsh equivalents. Even business interests worry that the assemblies would over-politicise the work of the regional development agencies. However, the new thrust of constitutional reform seemed to have the Chancellor and the Deputy Prime Minister on board and, in name at least, the Prime Minister himself. However, as *The Economist* pointed out, the ultimate worry is that the assemblies might not have the clout or the resources to do a great deal, thus 'making it easier for a future government to abolish them' (11 May 2002) (see also Box 14.5).

The referendum in the northeast, November 2004

The referendum in the northeast, intended as the trailblazer for Prescott's plans for elected regional government in 2006–7, occurred in November 2004. Prescott had anticipated the vote with a statement that £7m had been set aside for referendums in the three northern regions in 2004. Along with a cast of supporting celebrities (though Blair kept carefully away), he worked tirelessly, campaigning in the region most likely to support his pet scheme. *The Guardian* reported the campaign to be 'on a knife edge' (15 October) but its correspondent was mistaken. On the day Prescott took 'a geordie kicking' according to the *Sunday Times* (7 November),

the electorate rejected regional government in the northeast by 696,519 votes to 197,310. This was a humiliating result for the Deputy Prime Minister, who quickly announced the abandonment of plans for the other referendums. In the Commons on 8 November, he tried to salvage something from the whopping 78–22 per cent defeat by praising the 48 per cent turnout and suggesting that, as with devolution to Wales and Scotland, the idea would gestate and eventually come to fruition. This is not, perhaps, such a fanciful idea; *The Guardian* had pointed out on 6 November that in 1979 Wales rejected the notion of devolution by four to one, yet a quarter of a century later there was an assembly 'well embedded in Welsh life. It is hard now to imagine Wales without it'. Some critics argued that the northeast rejected the idea because of its expense – calculated to be £30m per year – and the paucity of real power for the assembly would have made it an expensive talking shop.

So voters seem to have baulked at any transition of devolution downwards to the regional level – something which Gamble's study in 2003 rather assumed they would. But his general definition of the 'English question' remains relevant:

Should the English now accept that Britain is plural rather than singular, composed of several nations rather than one, and that its political institutions should be federal rather than unitary, based on a new partnership between the British nations of Wales, Scotland and

BOX 14.5 IDEAS AND PERSPECTIVES

English devolution: a sceptic's view

Writing in *The Guardian* on 29 March 2006, Professor Robert Hazell examined the issues involved in devolving political power within England.

Regional government

Hazell agrees that this solution could bring government closer to the people and amplify the regional voice in comparison with the elected assemblies. However, the crushing defeat of the Prescott-led northeast referendum in 2004 'has raised the bar' (see text).

'City regions'

This suggestion is based on the example of London which is governed via an elected council and, of course, an elected mayor. However, such an innovation would require yet another 'round of local government reorganisation, for which there is no public appetite'. He concludes that 'elected mayors have had their moment, with only 11 towns and no large cities opting for a mayor in local referendums since 2001.' Hazell comments, however, that the incremental growth of *administrative regionalism* (e.g. police and fire services have recently been added to regional functions) will mean the question will inevitably come around again in the future. He suggests the model offered might be given strengthened powers and functions to become more credible.

English Parliament

Hazell argues that an English Parliament would set up 'in effect . . . a federation of the historic nations of the UK', but that such a creation would not work because 'England would be too dominant with 85 per cent of the population.' He points out, moreover, that only the Conservatives briefly took this idea seriously and that public support has never risen above 19 per cent.

English votes on English laws

Another suggestion, and one which would assuage English militants while solving the West Lothian question (see Box 14.2). However, Hazell points out that 'there is no such thing as an "English law"'; each time the Speaker judged what should be 'English only', the decision 'would be heavily contested'. It would also lead to two classes of MP – those who could vote on English matters and those who could not – and effectively invent 'a parliament within a parliament, with an English parliament operating within the shell of Westminster.'

Conclusion

Hazell concludes that the above solutions are 'feasible', 'but unlikely to happen'. He suggests two more acceptable measures would be further reductions in the numbers of Welsh and Scottish MPs and the introduction of PR which would reduce Labour's exaggerated representation in the Celtic nations.

Source: Robert Hazell, 'The English question', *The Guardian*, 29 March 2006

those others from Northern Ireland to Gibraltar and the Falklands, who still define themselves as British? Or should the English gradually disengage from Britain and Britishness altogether, ultimately becoming an independent nation-state once again and recovering a separate sense of Englishness? Should they celebrate the new multicultural and multiethnic character which has become characteristic of the whole of Britain or should they reject it, trying to preserve as far as they can an ethnic and cultural homogeneity, based on whiteness and Protestantism?

Gamble (2003), p. 160

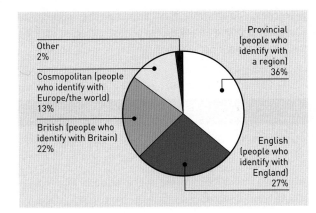

Figure 14.3 England's new tribes
Source: 'How devolution is changing our identity' in *The Guardian*, 29 March 2002. Opinion Research Services for the BBC. © Guardian Newspapers Limited 2002, reproduced with permission

Citizenship

Figure 14.3 reveals the clash of loyalties that characterise people living in the UK. It would seem that the notion of 'Britishness' is fading, to be replaced by one of 'Englishness' focusing on the regions. Peter Hetherington in *The Guardian* sees it as a reaction to the perception that Blair's government has 'pulled more power to the south and to the centre, disadvantaging the less favoured regions in the north'. The change of identity therefore has 'devolved' from the nation to the region. Figure 14.3 reveals four distinct groups, with 36 per cent relating to region, town or community rather than to country (27 per cent). Only 22 per cent identify with 'Britain' and 13 per cent with 'Europe/the world'. However, Madeleine Bunting, writing in *The Guardian* on 14 March 2005, questions the shrinking of the English identity and sees it re-emerging in defensive response to a perception that Blair is 'anti-English', but concludes that 'Englishness remains elusive' in a world where identity is increasingly fragmented.

■ Devolution has changed the nature of British government

After six years of devolved assemblies it is now possible to discern the beginnings of far-reaching changes to UK government. First, it can be argued that the Celts have done pretty well out of the deal.

Elderly Scots receive free personal care, unlike their English equivalents; students study free of tuition fees and receive grants. Meanwhile Welsh under-twenty-fives receive free prescriptions and dental treatment; their pensioners get free bus travel. These are just a few of the benefits devolution has transferred to Scotland and Wales; the Scots have not even had to utilise their ability to raise another 3p in the pound income tax – it's all been courtesy of the obsolete Barnett formula. So we now have two classes of voter in the UK – English and Celtic – regarding welfare entitlement. We also have two types of MP: those who represent Celtic constituencies yet can vote on English matters, and their English equivalents who have no reciprocal jurisdiction. Moreover, Labour's relatively narrow victory over Foundation Hospitals on 8 July 2003 was made possible only by the votes of Scottish and Welsh MPs who had no control over the devolved health authorities of their own countries. In addition to all the bounty from the British Treasury, which is denied the English regions, Celtic politicians have, in relation to their smaller populations, dominated UK government: three Welsh Cabinet ministers and four Scots. Perhaps these anomalies and inequities will remain and become yet more elements of the UK's arcane pattern of government, inherited from centuries of piecemeal change. Or they may begin to penetrate English consciousness and lead to demands for a resolution in that country's favour. But one thing is now beyond doubt: the process of devolution, which was entered into by Labour with naive hope rather than meticulous planning, and with a less than wholly enthusiastic leader, is slowly producing its own distinctive political systems in Scotland, Wales and Northern Ireland and transforming the once unitary nature of the British state. To date the fading of the nationalist vote at the 2003 elections suggests that the political purpose of the policy – to assuage and vitiate the nationalists' challenge – has succeeded, but should such a party ever gain control of one of the Celtic assemblies, the UK would be waters both fraught and unknown.

Finally, this chapter ends with a quotation from *The Guardian*, 11 March 2006:

Devolved government has bedded down. Critics have mostly been silenced, if not converted. In Wales – which voted for an Assembly in 1997 by a hairsbreadth – there is support for a parliament with stronger powers. In Scotland most people think devolution is working. Voters have wholly reasonable doubts about the quality of politicians putting themselves forward and election turnout is much too low. But as a study funded by the Economic and Social Research Council concluded

yesterday, devolution has allowed the people of Scotland, England and Wales to choose different policies for different nations, which is what it is meant to do.

BOX 14.6   BRITAIN IN CONTEXT

Sub-national government

Most countries of any size divide their territory into regions or localities to assist efficient government. It follows that central government in a nation's capital cannot be aware of the finer points of conditions on the ground miles away. The United Kingdom has never pursued any coherent policy on devolving power from the centre until Blair took control in 1997. The United Kingdom was once four separate countries which, as we have seen, merged into one via three stages: in the years 1536, 1707 and 1800. Each union was subtly different and each destined to be modified in administrative and finally legislative terms under New Labour. The Liberal Democrats are the only enthusiasts for a British federal arrangement but the dominance of England compared with the Celtic countries would cause severe problems for such a structure. Other countries outside the UK, have followed different paths.

The United States enjoyed the advantage of inventing its own constitution and its own kind of sub-national government. Already made up of 13 states in 1776, it opted for a federal structure with each constituent state having certain rights and powers protected from the overarching government based in Washington. This means there are 50 separate centres of political authority in the US, each with their own character, history and jealously guarded traditions of independence and their own patterns of local government. The House of Representatives represents voters in constituencies all over the US while the Senate represents the states comprising two representatives from each. Other nations – especially the larger ones – have similar arrangements.

Australia originally comprised colonies of transported convicts that went on to form the basis of the 'Commonwealth' of six states formed in 1901.

Later two more territories were added. Again a Senate contains representatives from each state. Switzerland, after a period of civil war, enacted a new constitution in 1848 which established a unified federal state with 22 constituent 'cantons', each with defined degrees of independence. South Africa too is a federation with nine provinces, each sending 10 representatives to the Senate in the legislative capital of Capetown.

In 1988 the European Union established a Committee of the Regions which is only consultative but underlines the emergence of the regions as participants within the 'multi-level' character of EU governance. Britain, with its devolved assemblies but lack of proper English regions, struggles to fit in easily. Other EU members on the other hand have better patterns of devolved power. Germany is another federal system with 16 Länder (or states), each with their own constitution, legislature and governments. France's system of sub-national government owes something to the Revolution of 1789, something to Napoleon's centralised style of rule and something to the 1958 constitution of the 5th Republic. Devolved government in France is via the 96 departments (plus 10 overseas departments) each with an officer of central government, a 'prefect' – usually a product of the élite Ecole Nationale d'Administration (ENA) – exercising substantial executive powers, though moderated under the 5th Republic by a degree of democratic control.

As well as devolving substantial power from the centre, France has more small locally-elected local councils than any EU partner country. Indeed the UK has the largest average population in its elected local authorities at over 100,000; Ireland is not far behind with 40,000, Finland has 10,000 and France the smallest of them all with only 1,500.

Chapter summary

Core–periphery theory provides a framework that offers an explanation of Westminster's dealings with the Celtic fringe and the English regions. The establishment of regional assemblies has a provenance in the original autonomy of Ireland, Scotland and Wales and the surviving sense of identity that flourishes in these countries. Nationalist movements persuaded the Labour Party – in the 1970s unsuccessfully and in the 1990s successfully – to establish such assemblies and to devolve substantial power from Westminster. In Scotland, Labour formed a coalition government with the Lib-Dems, while in Wales it decided to govern from a minority position. A number of intractable political problems have resulted from the process, including the London Labour leadership's lack of enthusiasm for some of the things done in Labour's name by the new administrations. Two persistent problems yet to be solved are the so-called West Lothian question and the possibility that devolution will prove to be merely a stepping stone for the nationalists to achieve their aims and break up the Union. Devolution to English regions remains a possibility but one that is remote after the failure of northeasterners to be moved by the idea in a referendum on 5 November 2004.

Discussion points

■ To what extent was there independence in Ireland, Scotland and Wales before their union with England?

■ What differences are there between the nationalism of each country?

■ Why do you think support for devolution is greater in Scotland than in Wales?

■ Why do critics of Blair claim that devolution has demonstrated his 'control freak' tendencies?

■ What problems have been thrown up by the devolution policies?

Further reading

Bogdanor (1997, 1999) provides a thorough discussion of the political issues surrounding the topic, especially the West Lothian question. Bulpitt (1983) is best on the territorial dimension, but also very clear and useful is Coxall and Robins (1998, Chapter 18). An excellent chapter on 'Devolved systems of governance' can be found in Michael Moran's *Politics and Governance in the UK* (2005). Also useful is the book by Colin Pilkington: *Devolution in Britain Today* (2002).

The Economist provides a rich source of data and comment on the topic throughout the crucial years 1997–9.

References

Arter, D. (2005) 'Scottish Committee activity outside Edinburgh', paper delivered to American Political Science Association.

Bogdanor, V. (1997) *Power and the People* (Gollancz).

Bogdanor, V. (1999) *Devolution in the United Kingdom* (Oxford University Press).

Bradbury, J. (1999) 'Labour's bloody nose: the first Welsh general election', *Politics Review*, November.

Bulpitt, J. (1983) *Territory and Power in the United Kingdom* (Manchester University Press).

Coxall, B. and Robins, L. (1998) *Contemporary British Politics* (Macmillan).

Economist (1999) 'Towards a federal Britain', 27 March, pp. 25–9.

Gamble, A. (2003) *Between Europe and America: the Future of British Politics* (Palgrave).

Hazell, R. (2006) 'The English Question', *The Guardian*, 29 March 2006.

Hechter, M. (1975) *Internal Colonialism* (Routledge).

Kay, A. (2000) 'Evaluating devolution in Wales', *Political Studies*, Vol. 51, No. 1, March.

Kumar, K. (2003) *The Making of English National Identity* (Cambridge University Press).

Marr, A. (2000) *The Day Britain Died* (Profile Books).

Mitchell, J. (1999) 'Devolution', in B. Jones (ed.), *Political Issues in Britain Today* (Manchester University Press).

Moran, M. (2005) *Politics and Governance in the UK* (Palgrave).

Nairn, T. (2000) *After Britain: New Labour and the Return of Scotland* (Granta).

Pilkington, C. (2002) *Devolution in Britain Today* (Manchester University Press).

Seldon, A. (2005) *Blair* (Free Press).

Steed, M. (1986) 'The core–periphery dimension in British politics', *Political Geography Quarterly*, October.

Useful websites

Northern Ireland Assembly: www.ni-assembly.gov.uk

Scottish Parliament: www.scottish.parliament.uk

Welsh Assembly: www.wales.gov.uk

Regional Coordination Unit: www.rcu.gov.uk

White Paper on Regional Government: www.regions.odpm.gov.uk/governance/whitepaper/index.htm

Scottish Affairs Select Committee: www.parliament.uk/commons/selcom/scothome.htm

And another thing . . .

Voting with our feet: the turnout 'problem' in Britain

David Denver

The big problem we have here is that we do look as though we are running into a kind of turnout time bomb crisis in elections.

Professor Patrick Dunleavy giving oral evidence to the House of Commons Select Committee on Public Administration, 15 March 2000

Just provide the voters with a closely fought election at which a great deal is at stake and, make no mistake, they will again turn out in their droves.

Professor Anthong King, Daily Telegraph, 17 May 2001

Trends in turnout

When Prime Minister Tony Blair called a general election in 2001, at the end of his government's first term, it was widely anticipated that there would be a second Labour landslide – and that is what duly transpired. What few anticipated was that the main talking point of the election results would be the dramatic slump in turnout, to 59.4 per cent across the UK – by far the lowest turnout in any general election since the war. The election outcome, according to Pippa Norris (2001), was an 'apathetic landslide'.

Subsequently, there was much hand-wringing about poor turnout on the part of the chattering classes (with the Electoral Commission to the fore) and there were numerous reports, conferences and investigations into what could be done about it. Various experiments using different methods of voting – including allowing only postal voting – were tried out at local and European Parliament elections. Nonetheless in the 2005 general election turnout remained relatively low.

To put the 2001 and 2005 figures into perspective, Figure 1 shows the trend in turnout at UK general elections since 1950. The first two elections in the series (1950 and 1951) had very high turnouts (higher, indeed, than in any election since 1910). After that, the next eleven elections (1955–92) showed no real trend, although there was a notable low point in 1970, which was the first election after the voting age was reduced from 21 to 18. Turnout fell quite sharply in 1997 but then plummeted in 2001 before recovering slightly in 2005. Clearly, then, there is something to be explained. Why has turnout been so low in the last three elections?

Explaining turnout trends

It does not appear to be the case that recent poor turnouts are simply a reflection of more general apathy about politics. British Election Study (BES) surveys in the 1970s found that, on average, 63 per cent of respondents said that they had 'a great deal' or 'some' interest in politics. In 1997, 2001 and 2005 the comparable figures were 69 per cent, 71 per cent and 72 per cent. Similarly, at the 1964 and 1966 elections an average of 71 per cent said that they cared 'a great deal' who won. For the last three elections the figures were 76 per cent, 70 per cent and 72 per cent. Other evidence confirms that British electors are still as satisfied and engaged with the political

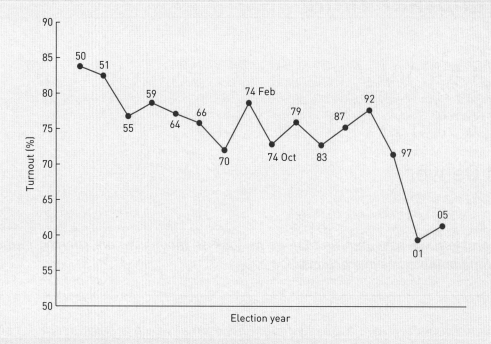

Figure 1 Turnout in UK general elections, 1950–2005
Sources: Rallings and Thrasher (2000, 2005); Electoral Commission (2001)

system as they ever were (Clarke *et al.*, 2004, Chapter 9). We must look elsewhere for explanations.

There is a large literature suggesting that propensity to vote varies across different social groups. The resources that underpin political participation (knowledge, skills, time), it is suggested, are unevenly distributed across groups. In addition, levels of involvement in community networks vary across different groups. As Table 1 shows, there are clear social differences in turnout in Britain. Unlike in many other countries, there is no significant difference between men and women in this respect, but turnout tends to be higher among those who are married, have white-collar occupations, are owner-occupiers, are better educated and better off, and have lived in their neighbourhood longer. Turnout also increases very steadily with age, with the youngest age group having a particularly poor voting rate.

There is nothing new about these sorts of patterns – they are regularly found in election surveys and are reflected in constituency figures. In broad terms turnout tends to be higher in more affluent suburbs, small towns and rural areas and lower in more deprived inner cities. However, this approach to turnout cannot explain the recent decline in participation. Indeed, given that over the past twenty years Britain has become more middle-class, many more people have become owner-occupiers, many

more have gone to university and the proportion of older people has increased significantly, we would expect turnout to have risen rather than declined!

A second approach to explaining turnout variations derives from rational choice theory and directs attention to the costs and benefits of voting. In this view, voters act instrumentally. Turnout will be higher when there are more incentives to vote and costs are kept at a minimum. When the incentives are less strong and/or costs are higher, turnout will be lower. A simple application of rational choice theory would suggest that electors would be more inclined to go to the polls in places where the contest is likely to be close than in places that are rock-solid for one party or another. This is, indeed, what happens in British elections. Table 2 shows that when constituencies are categorised on the basis of the winning party's majority in 2001, turnout in 2005 was highest in the 'super-marginal' category (majority up to 5 per cent) and clearly lowest in safe seats (majority greater than 20 per cent). This might also be due to the campaigning strategies of the parties. Increasingly from the 1990s onwards, the parties have virtually ignored seats that they consider safe or as hopeless prospects and have concentrated campaign resources into 'target' (marginal) seats. Since strong constituency campaigning increases turnout (see Denver *et al.*, 2004) it is little wonder

Table 1 Turnout of social groups in 2005

	%		%
Sex		*Housing*	
Men	61	Owner-occupiers	69
Women	62	Renters	44
Marital status		*Residence in neighbourhood*	
Married	69	Less than ten years	58
Living with partner	46	Ten or more years	73
Separated/divorced	53	*Highest educational qualification*	
Widowed	75	None	57
Single/never married	48	CSE (or equivalent)	56
Occupation		A-level (or equivalent)	61
Professional and managerial	73	Degree	74
Other non-manual	62	*Income*	
Manual	54	Lowest third	56
		Middle third	63
Age		Top third	67
18–24	34		
25–34	43		
35–44	58		
45–54	63		
55–64	73		
65+	76		

Source: BES 2005 cross-section survey. The original data have been weighted to reflect the actual turnout in the election

Table 2 Mean turnout by marginality of constituencies, 2005

	Super-marginal	Marginal	Comfortable	Safe
Mean % turnout	66.9	65.2	64.3	57.6
No. of cases	(50)	(75)	(178)	(322)

that turnout in safe seats is lower (and has declined more rapidly since 1992) than in marginal seats.

Applying the same sort of reasoning to overall general election turnouts would suggest that electors have more incentive to turn out if they think that an election is likely to be close, rather than a foregone conclusion, and if they believe that the winning party will bring in policies that are significantly different from those that the losing party would have pursued. Here, the evidence is

encouraging. The trend in turnout from 1964 to 1997 matches well with trends in the proportions of people seeing a good deal of difference between the parties and the expected closeness of the election in question (Heath and Taylor, 1999). Extending this analysis, in 2001 the proportion seeing a great difference between the Conservative and Labour parties fell to its lowest ever level (18 per cent) and a second Labour landslide was expected – hence a very low turnout. In 2005, a closer result was predicted and that probably explains the slight recovery in turnout.

Nonetheless, this is far from the whole story. For many citizens voting is not a matter of calculating costs and benefits but can be described as 'expressive' or 'normative'. 'Expressive' voters are frequently expressing their long-term commitment to, or support for, a party – their party identification. The more strongly someone identifies with a party,

Table 3 Turnout by strength of party identification, 1992–2005

	Very strong (%)	Fairly strong (%)	Not very strong (%)	No party identification (%)
Voted 1992	92	90	80	58
Voted 1997	89	87	73	51
Voted 2001	81	72	50	28
Voted 2005	82	73	59	36

Source: BES surveys

the more likely they are to vote. This is not difficult to understand; people who are strong party supporters are more likely to want to demonstrate their support by going out to vote for their party than those who are less strongly committed. The figures in Table 3 show that this happens consistently. Moreover, the decline in turnout over the period is steepest among non-identifiers and slightest among 'very strong' identifiers. The problem is that there are now fewer strong identifiers than there used to be. Between 1992 and 2005 very strong party identifiers declined from 19 per cent to 10 per cent of the electorate, while the proportion feeling no attachment at all to a party rose from 6 to 12 per cent. So the highest turnout group has been decreasing in size and the lowest turnout group increasing. We have here a major source of turnout decline.

'Normative' voters go to the polls because they see it as part of a citizen's duty. Even in 2005 large majorities of BES respondents agreed that it is every citizen's duty to vote (78 per cent) and that non-voting is a serious neglect of duty (70 per cent). When the figures are broken down by age, however (see Table 4), a striking pattern emerges. Younger people are much less likely to think of voting as being a duty than older people. Although similar data from before 2001 are not available for comparison, detailed analysis suggests that this is not something that

younger people will grow out of, as it were (Clarke *et al.*, 2006). Rather, it is suggested, the 'Thatcher' and 'Blair' generations are significantly less 'civic minded' than their elders and this will continue to have a depressing effect on turnout for a long time.

To sum up, declining turnout in the UK has little to do with changes in the social structure. The causes are mainly political – the campaigning strategies of the parties, the fact that the voters can see less difference between the parties than they used to and have become less strongly committed party supporters, and the fact that some recent elections have been seen as foregone conclusions. In addition, there has been a marked decline in a sense of civic duty among voters aged under 40.

What can be done to improve turnout?

The short answer is 'not much'. In their attempts to improve matters the authorities have concentrated on trying to reduce the 'costs' of voting. In fact, almost all the various experiments – voting by Internet and telephone, polling booths in supermarkets and the like – have been a waste of time. This is not surprising since for most people the costs involved in voting are trivial in any event. The exception is distributing ballot papers to voters and requiring them to be returned in the post. In the short term, at least, this appears to boost turnout a little. Widespread postal voting raises other difficulties, however, in that it allows greater opportunities for fraud and corruption in elections.

At root the problem is a political one. Anthony King (quoted above) is quite right but for a variety of reasons there appears to be less 'at stake' in elections than there used to be. In particular, the parties now crowd the 'centre-ground' of politics. As illustrated by New Labour after 1997 and the

Table 4 Voting as duty by age group (2005)

	Age group						
	18-24	25-34	35-44	45-54	55-64	65+	All
Agree voting is duty (%)	61	66	73	76	89	93	78
Agree non-voting is serious neglect of duty (%)	50	54	65	67	80	90	70

Source: BES survey 2005

Conservatives after the election of David Cameron as leader in late 2005, this is a deliberate strategy. It makes good political sense to move to the centre since that is where most voters are, but it does little to enthuse core supporters and contributes to the declining strength of party identification. In addition, the parties are unlikely to reverse their highly targeted constituency campaigning.

It would help, of course, if a greater sense of civic-mindedness could somehow be inculcated in younger voters. Anyone who knows how to do this successfully would probably be in line for a Nobel prize. Whatever prescriptions are offered or adopted, significantly increasing the proportion thinking that it is their duty to vote would be a long haul.

References

Clarke, H.D., Sanders, D., Stewart, M.C. and Whiteley, P. (2004) *Political Choice in Britain* (Oxford University Press).

Clarke, H., Sanders, D., Stewart, M. and Whiteley, P. (2006) 'Taking the bloom off New Labour's rose: party choice and voter turnout in Britain, 2005', *Journal of Elections, Public Opinion and Parties*, Vol. 16.

Denver, D., Hands, G. and MacAllister, I. (2004) 'The electoral impact of constituency campaigning in Britain, 1992–2001', *Political Studies*, Vol. 52, No. 4, pp. 289–306.

Electoral Commission (2001) *Election 2001: The Official Results* (Politico's).

Heath, A. and Taylor, B. (1999) 'New sources of abstention?', in G. Evans and P. Norris (eds), *Critical Elections* (Sage), pp. 164–80.

Norris, P. (2001) 'Apathetic landslide', in P. Norris (ed.), *Britain Votes 2001* (Oxford University Press).

Rallings, C. and Thrasher, M. (2000) *British Electoral Facts 1832–1999* (Ashgate).

Rallings, C. and Thrasher, M. (2005) *Election 2005: The Official Results* (LGC Elections Centre).

POLITICS UK

PART 4
THE LEGISLATIVE
PROCESS

Introduction

Bill Jones

So far this book has addressed the non-institutional elements of British politics; the remainder of the volume deals with the institutional aspects together with specific policy areas. Institutions can often seem confusing to students, who tend to study them individually and find it difficult to grasp how they relate to and inter-act with each other. Accordingly, this short section gives two contrasting overviews of how the system works.

■ Two overviews of the British political system

The functions of government

It is helpful to contrast the British political system with that of the USA. It is well known that the eighteenth-century framers of the US constitution wrote into their 1787 document a strict separation of powers. The legislature (Congress) and the exec-utive (the Presidency) were to be elected separately for terms of differing length, with the **judiciary** (the Supreme Court) appointed by the President for life. In diagrammatic form, the functions can be repres-ented by three separate and independent circles (see Figure 1).

The purpose of this arrangement was to disperse power to institutions that would check each other and ensure that no branch of government became over-mighty. In Britain, however, there never was such a separation. The three functions overlap signi-ficantly. To change or re-elect a government there is only one election and that is to the legislative chamber, the House of Commons. After the election, the majority party in that chamber invariably forms

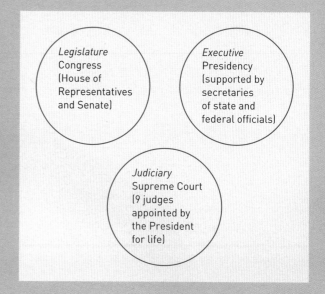

Figure 1 Functions of government: USA

the executive. The crucial overlap between the leg-islative and executive spheres therefore comprises Prime Minister, Cabinet and the other seventy or so junior ministers. Until 2006, the judiciary was similarly appointed by the executive: not by the Prime Min-ister but by the Lord Chancellor, the government's chief law officer, who sat in the Cabinet and presided over the House of Lords (see Figure 2).

The US constitution ensures that the President cannot be overthrown by Congress – except through impeachment – but looser party discipline means that the President cannot regularly command congressional support for his policies; indeed, like Presidents Bush, for a while, and Clinton, his party may be in the minority in Congress. The British Prime Minister, in contrast, has more power: provided that the support of the majority party is sustained, he or she leads both the executive and

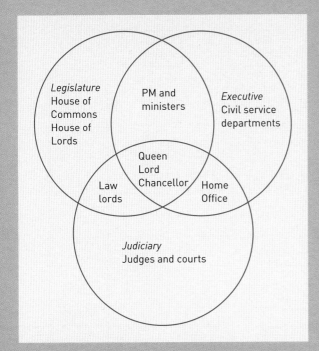

Figure 2 Functions of government: UK

legislative arms of government. However, loss of significant party support can bring down the British Prime Minister, as it did Chamberlain in May 1940 and Thatcher in 1990. This possibility clearly acts as a constraint upon potential prime ministerial action, but the fact is that parties in government very rarely even threaten to unseat their leaders, because they fear the electoral con-sequences of apparent disunity.

The executive's power is further reinforced by the doctrine of parliamentary sovereignty, which enables it to overrule any law – constitutional or otherwise – with a simple majority vote; and considerable residual powers of the monarch via the royal prerogative. The power of the House of Lords of legislative delay only (other than for bills originating

in the Lords), and local government's essentially subservient relationship to Westminster, complete the picture of an unusually powerful executive arm of government for a representative democracy.

Representative and responsible government

Represented in a different way, the British political system can be seen as a circuit of representation and responsibility. Parliament represents the electorate but is also responsible to it via elections. In their turn, ministers represent majority opinion in the legislature (although they are appointed by the Prime Minister, not elected) and are responsible to it for their actions in leading the executive. Civil servants are not representatives but as part of the executive are controlled by ministers and are responsible to them. Figure 3 illustrates the relationship.

This, of course, is a very simplistic view, but it does express the underlying theory of how British government should work. The reality of how the system operates is infinitely more complex, as Figure 4 – itself highly simplified – seeks to illustrate. Earlier chapters have explained how the different elements of British government operate in practice:

1. Parliament provides the forum, the 'playing field' on which the ordered competition of democratic government is publicly conducted.

2. Political parties dominate the system, organising the electorate, taking over Parliament and providing the ministers who run the Civil Service.

3. The Prime Minister as leader of the majority party can exercise considerable personal power and in recent years has become more akin to a presidential figure.

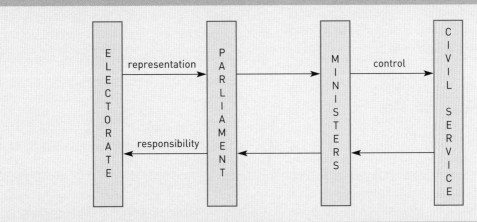

Figure 3 Representative and responsible government

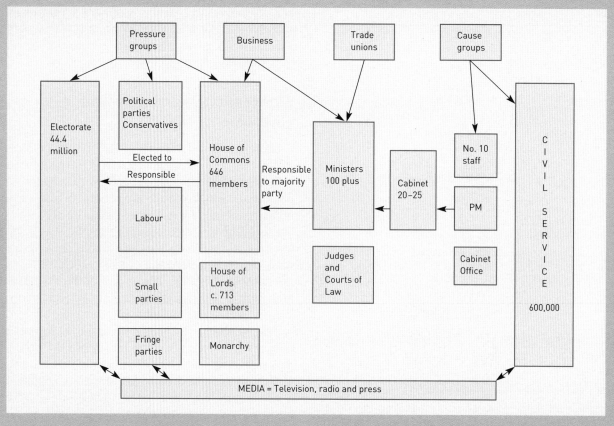

Figure 4 Elements of UK central government

4. The judiciary performs the important task of interpreting legislation and calling ministers and officials to account if they act without statutory authority.

5. Civil servants serve ministers, but their permanence and their professionalism, their vested interests in searching for consensus and defending departmental interests raise suspicions that they occasionally or even regularly outflank their ministerial masters.

6. Pressure groups infiltrate the whole gamut of government institutions, the most powerful bypassing Parliament and choosing to deal direct with ministers and civil servants. (See Chapter 11.)

7. The media have increasingly usurped the role of Parliament in informing the public and providing a forum for public debate. Television is a potent new influence, the impact of which is still to be fully felt. (See Chapter 10.)

Does the reality invalidate the theory? It all depends upon how drastically we believe Figure 4 distorts Figure 3. Indeed, Marxists would declare both to be irrelevant in that business pressure groups call the shots that matter, operating behind the scenes and within the supportive context of a system in which all the major actors subscribe to their values. Former cabinet minister Tony Benn would argue that the executive has become so dominant at the expense of the legislature that the PM's power can be compared with that of a medieval monarch. As we have seen, Britain's constitutional arrangements have always allowed great potential power – potential that strong Prime Ministers like Margaret Thatcher have been keen and able to realise when given the time. But I would maintain, and cite in support the analyses offered by the authors of this book, that the essential features of the democratic system portrayed in Figure 3 just about survive in that:

 party-dominated governments are removable;

 Parliament still applies watchdog controls (and just occasionally reminds the executive by biting);

 the electorate has a choice between parties;

 civil servants ordinarily seek to obey their political masters;

 pressure groups influence but do not dictate.

Part 4 explains how the legislative system works; Part 5 explains the executive process; and Part 6 looks at a number of policy areas.

CHAPTER 15

The changing constitution

Philip Norton

Learning objectives

- To identify the sources and key components of the British constitution.

- To analyse the nature of the debate about the British constitution.

- To consider the major changes and modifications made to the constitution in recent years.

- To detail the arguments for and against some of the major changes that have taken place or are proposed to the constitution, including electoral reform.

- To address the problems faced by political parties as a consequence of constitutional change.

Introduction

In the quarter-century following the Second World War, the constitution rarely figured in political debate. It was seen as the preserve more of lawyers than of politicians. In the last three decades of the century, it became a subject of political controversy. Demands for reform of the constitution grew. Many of those demands were met by the Labour government elected in May 1997, with major changes being made to the constitutional framework of the country. Some critics demand further change. The changes that have taken place have created problems for the three main political parties.

■ The constitution

What, then, is a **constitution**? What is it for? What is distinctive about the British constitution? Where does it come from? What are the essential constituents of the 'traditional' constitution? What challenges has it faced in recent years? What changes have been made to it? What are the problems posed to the political parties by such changes? And what is the nature of the debate taking place about further constitutional change?

Definition and sources

What is a constitution? A constitution can be defined as the system of laws, customs and **conventions** that defines the composition and powers of organs of the state (such as government, Parliament and the courts) and regulates the relations of the various state organs to one another and of those state organs to the private citizen.

What are constitutions for? Constitutions vary in terms of their purpose. A constitution may be constructed in such a way as to embody and protect fundamental principles (such as individual liberty), principles that should be beyond the reach of the transient wish of the people. This is referred to as **negative constitutionalism** (see Ivison, 1999). The constitution of the United States, for example, falls into this category. A constitution may be constructed in order to ensure that the wishes of the people are paramount. This is referred to as **positive constitutionalism**. Here, there are few if any restraints on the people's elected representatives. The UK leans towards a qualified form of positive constitutionalism.

What form do constitutions take? Most, but not all, are drawn up in a single, codified document.

Some are short, others remarkably long. Some embody provisions that exhort citizens to act in a certain way ('It shall be the duty of every citizen . . .'); others confine themselves to stipulating the formal structures and powers of state bodies. Processes of interpretation and amendment vary. Most, but not all, have entrenched provisions: i.e. they can only be amended by an extraordinary process beyond that normally employed for amending the law.

The British constitution differs from most in that it is not drawn up in a single codified document. As such, it is often described as an 'unwritten' constitution. However, much of the constitution does exist in 'written' form. Many Acts of Parliament – such as the European Communities Act 1972, providing the legal basis for British membership of the European Community, and the Constitutional Reform Act 2005, creating a Supreme Court – are clearly measures of constitutional law. Those Acts constitute formal, written – and binding – documents. To describe the constitution as unwritten is thus misleading. Rather, what Britain has is a part-written, uncodified constitution.

Even in countries with a formal, written document, 'the constitution' constitutes more than the simple words of the document. Those words have to be interpreted. Practices develop, and laws are passed, that help to give meaning to those words. To understand the contemporary constitution of the United States, for example, one has to look beyond the document to interpretations of that document by the courts in the USA, principally the US Supreme Court, and to various acts of Congress and to practices developed over the past 200 years. The constitutions of most countries thus have what may be termed a primary source (the written document) and secondary sources (judicial interpretation, legislative acts,

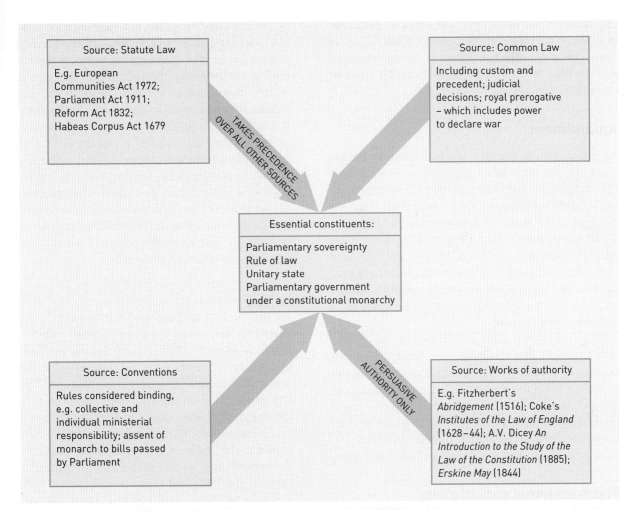

Figure 15.1 The traditional constitution: sources and constituents
Source: From P. Norton (1986) 'The constitution in flux', *Social Studies Review*, Vol. 2, No. 1. Reproduced with permission from the California Council for Social Studies

established practice). The UK, without a written document, lacks the equivalent primary source. Instead, the constitution derives from sources that elsewhere would constitute secondary sources of the constitution. The principal sources of what may be termed the 'traditional' constitution – that which was in place for most of the twentieth century and which has its roots in the Glorious Revolution of 1688–9 – are four in number (see Figure 15.1). They are:

1. *statute law*, comprising Acts of Parliament and subordinate legislation made under the authority of the parent Act;

2. *common law*, comprising legal principles developed and applied by the courts, and encompassing the prerogative powers of the crown and the law and practice of Parliament;

3. *conventions*, constituting rules of behaviour that are considered binding by and upon those who operate the constitution but that are not enforced by the courts or by the presiding officers in the Houses of Parliament;

4. *works of authority*, comprising various written works – often but not always accorded authority by reason of their age – that provide guidance and interpretation on uncertain aspects of the constitution. Such works have persuasive authority only.

Statute law is the pre-eminent of the four sources and occupies such a position because of the doctrine of **parliamentary sovereignty**. Under this judicially self-imposed concept, the courts recognise only the authority of Parliament (formally the Queen-in-Parliament) to make law, with no body other than

Parliament itself having the authority to set aside that law. The courts cannot strike down a law as being contrary to the provisions of the constitution. Statute law, then, is supreme and can be used to override common law.

Amendment

No extraordinary features are laid down in Parliament for the passage or amendment of measures of constitutional law. Although bills of constitutional significance usually have their committee stage on the floor of the House of Commons, rather than in a standing committee (see Chapter 17), there is no formal requirement for this to happen. All bills have to go through the same stages in both Houses of Parliament and are subject to simple majority voting. As such, the traditional constitution is, formally, a **flexible constitution**.

However, as we shall see, there are two recent developments that challenge this flexibility: membership of the European Community/Union and the incorporation of the European Convention on Human Rights into British law. The devolution of powers to elected assemblies in different parts of the United Kingdom may also be argued to limit, in effect, the capacity of Parliament to pass any legislation it wishes.

The traditional constitution: essential constituents

The traditional constitution existed for most of the twentieth century. It had four principal features. Although, as we shall see, these features have been challenged by changes in recent years, each nonetheless remains formally in place:

1. *Parliamentary sovereignty* has been described as the cornerstone of the British constitution. As we have seen, it stipulates that the outputs of Parliament are binding and cannot be set aside by any body other than Parliament itself. The doctrine was confirmed by the Glorious Revolution of 1688 and 1689, when the common lawyers combined with Parliament against the King. Since the Settlement of 1689 established that the King was bound by the law of Parliament, it followed that his courts were also so bound.

2. *The rule of law* was identified by nineteenth-century constitutional lawyer A.V. Dicey as one of the twin pillars of the constitution and is generally accepted as one of the essential features

of a free society. However, it is logically subordinate to the first pillar – parliamentary sovereignty – since Parliament could pass a measure undermining or destroying the rule of law. It is also a matter of dispute as to what the term encompasses. In terms of the law passed by Parliament, it is essentially a procedural doctrine. Laws must be interpreted and applied by an impartial and independent **judiciary**; those charged under the law are entitled to a fair trial; and no one can be imprisoned other than through the due process of law. However, there is some dispute as to how far the doctrine extends beyond this, not least in defining the extent of the power of the state to regulate the affairs of citizens.

3. *A unitary state* is one in which formal power resides exclusively in the national authority, with no entrenched and autonomous powers being vested in any other body. In federal systems, power is shared between national and regional or state governments, each enjoying an autonomous existence and exercising powers granted by the constitution. In the UK, state power resides centrally, with the Queen-in-Parliament being omnicompetent. Parliament can create and confer certain powers on other bodies – such as assemblies and even parliaments in different parts of the UK – but those bodies remain subordinate to Parliament and can be restricted, even abolished, by it.

4. *A parliamentary government under a **constitutional monarchy*** refers to the form of government established by, and developed since, the Glorious Revolution. That revolution established the supremacy of Parliament over the King. The greater acceptance of democratic principles in the nineteenth and twentieth centuries has resulted in the enlargement of the franchise and a pre-eminent role in the triumvirate of Queen-in-Parliament (monarch, Commons, Lords) for the elected chamber, the House of Commons. 'Parliament' thus means predominantly – although not exclusively – the House of Commons, while 'parliamentary government' refers not to government by Parliament but to government through Parliament. Ministers are legally answerable to the crown but politically answerable to Parliament, that political relationship being governed by the conventions of collective and individual **ministerial responsibility**. A government is returned in a general election

and between elections depends on the confidence of a majority of Members of Parliament both for the passage of its measures and for its continuance in office.

Three of these four features (parliamentary sovereignty, unitary state, parliamentary government) facilitated the emergence of strong, or potentially strong, government, a government secure in its majority in the House of Commons being able to enact measures that were then binding on society and that could not be set aside by any body other than Parliament itself. There were no other forms of government below the national enjoying autonomous powers (the consequence of a unitary state); no other actors at national level were able to countermand the elected House of Commons, be it the crown or the House of Lords (the consequence of the growth of parliamentary government under a constitutional monarchy) or the courts (the consequence of the doctrine of parliamentary sovereignty). The United Kingdom thus enjoyed a centralised system of government.

That system of government, made possible by the essential features of the constitution, was variously described as the Westminster system of government. At the heart of the system was the Cabinet, sustained by a party majority in the House of Commons. Each party fought a general election on the basis of a party manifesto and, if elected to office, it proceeded to implement the promises made in the manifesto. Parliament provided the legitimacy for the government and its measures, subjecting those measures to debate and scrutiny before giving its approval to them. *Party* ensured that the government almost always got its way, but the *party system* ensured that the government faced the critical scrutiny of the party in opposition.

The traditional constitution can, as we have seen, be traced back to the Glorious Revolution of the seventeenth century, but it emerged more fully in

Twenty-first century or not, debates cannot ensue in the House of Commons chamber unless the Mace is properly in position
Source: PA Wire / Empics

the nineteenth century with the widening of the franchise. It emerged in the form we have just described – the Westminster system – essentially in the period from 1867, with the passage of the second Reform Act (necessitating the growth of organised parties), and 1911, when the Parliament Act (restricting by statute the powers of the House of Lords) was passed. From 1911 onwards, power in the UK resided in the party that held a majority of seats in the House of Commons. In so far as the party in government expressed the will of the people and it achieved the measures it wanted, then the UK acquired, in effect, a limited form of positive constitutionalism.

■ Challenges to the traditional constitution

The traditional constitution was in place from 1911 to 1972. Although it was variously criticised in the years between the two world wars, especially in the depression of the 1930s, it went largely unchallenged in the years immediately after the Second World War. The nation's political institutions continued to function during the war, and the country emerged victorious from the conflict. In the 1950s, the nation enjoyed relative economic prosperity. There appeared little reason to question the nation's constitutional arrangements. That changed once the country began to experience economic recession and more marked political conflicts. The constitution came in for questioning. If the political system was not delivering what was expected of it, was there not then a case for changing the system itself? The issue of constitutional reform began to creep onto the political agenda.

Since 1970, the traditional constitution has faced two major challenges. Both have had significant consequences for the nation's constitutional arrangements. The first was membership of the European Community (now the European Union). The second was the constitutional changes introduced by the Labour government elected in May 1997.

Membership of the European Community/Union

A judicial dimension

The United Kingdom became a member of the European Community (EC) on 1 January 1973. The Treaty of Accession was signed in 1972 and the legal basis for membership provided by the European Communities Act 1972. The motivation for joining the Community was essentially economic and political. However, membership had significant constitutional consequences, primarily because it:

■ Gave the force of law not only to existing but also to all future EC law. As soon as regulations are made by the institutions of the EC, they have binding applicability in the UK. The assent of Parliament is not required. That assent has, in effect, been given in advance under the provisions of the 1972 Act. Parliament has some discretion as to the form in which EC directives are to be implemented, but the discretion refers only to the form and not to the principle.

■ Gave EC law precedence over UK law. In the event of a conflict between EC law and UK law, the European law takes precedence. The full effect of this was only realised with some important court cases in the 1990s (Fitzpatrick, 1999). In the *Factortame* case of 1990–1, the European Court of Justice held that the courts in the UK could suspend the provisions of an Act of Parliament, where it appeared to breach EC law, until a final determination was made. In the case of *Ex Parte EOC*, in 1994, the House of Lords struck down provisions of the 1978 Employment Protection (Consolidation) Act as incompatible with EC law (Maxwell, 1999).

■ Gave the power to determine disputes to the courts. Where there is a dispute over European law, the matter is resolved by the courts. Questions of law have to be decided by the European Court of Justice (ECJ). Where a question of European law reaches the highest domestic court of appeal, the House of Lords, it has to be referred to the ECJ for a definitive ruling; lower courts may ask the ECJ for a ruling on the meaning of treaty provisions. All courts in the UK are required to take judicial notice of decisions of the ECJ.

The effect of these changes has been to challenge the doctrine of parliamentary sovereignty. The decisions of Parliament can, in certain circumstances (where they conflict with EC law), be set aside by a body or bodies other than Parliament itself – namely, the courts. In sectors that now fall within the competence of the European Union, it can be argued that the UK now has something akin to a written constitution – that is, the treaties of the European Union.

The doctrine of parliamentary sovereignty remains formally in place because Parliament retains the power to repeal the European Communities Act. The ECJ is able to exercise the power it does because an Act of Parliament says that it can. However, the effect of repealing the 1972 Act would be to take the UK out of the European Union. (This in itself would be a breach of treaty provisions, under which membership is in perpetuity.) The claim that Parliament retains the power to repeal the 1972 Act appears to be accepted by most constitutional lawyers, although some now question this, and the longer the Act remains in force the more the doctrine of parliamentary sovereignty will be challenged and may eventually fade away.

A political dimension

As a consequence of membership, the constitution thus acquired a new judicial dimension, one that challenged the doctrine of parliamentary sovereignty. At the same time, it also acquired a new political dimension, one that challenged the decision-making capacity of British government. Under the terms of entry, policy-making power in various sectors of public policy passed to the institutions of the European Community. Subsequent treaties have served both to extend the range of sectors falling within the competence of the EC and to strengthen the decision-making capacity of the European institutions.

The Single European Act, which came into force in 1987, produced a significant shift in the power relationship between the institutions of the Community and the institutions of the member states, strengthening EC institutions, especially through the extension of qualified majority voting (QMV) in the Council of Ministers. The Act also brought about a shift in the power relationships within the institutions of the Community, strengthening the European Parliament through the extension of the cooperation procedure, a procedure that provides a greater role for the Parliament in Community law making. Further shifts in both levels of power relationship were embodied in the Treaty on European Union (the Maastricht Treaty), which took effect in November 1993. This established a European Union with three pillars (the European Community, common foreign and security policy, justice and home affairs), extended the sectors of public policy falling within the competence of the European Community and established a new co-decision procedure for making law in certain areas, a procedure that strengthened

again the position of the European Parliament. It now became a partner, with the Council of Ministers, in law making. A further strengthening of the position of the EC, now the European Union, took place with the implementation in 1999 of the Amsterdam Treaty. This extended the range of subjects falling within the competence of the EU and widened the range of issues subject to the co-decision procedure. The Nice Treaty, which took effect in 2003, introduced reforms to the Council and Commission in preparation for the enlargement of the EU that took place in 2004. With enlargement, the UK became but one of twenty-five members. The Convention on the Future of Europe developed further proposals for major reforms, including the introduction of a constitution for the EU. Though the constitution fell foul of 'no' votes in referendums in France and Holland, a number of member states pressed for further institutional change.

As a result of membership of the European Community, the British government is thus constrained in what it can do. Where matters have to be decided by the Council of Ministers, the UK minister may be outvoted by the ministers of the other member states. A decision may thus be taken that is then enforced within the UK, even if it does not have the support of the British government and Parliament. (Under the Luxembourg Compromise, agreed in 1966, a government may veto a proposal if it conflicts with the nation's vital national interests. Some governments, including the British and French, have argued that the compromise can still be used, but it has not been cited since the Single European Act was agreed, and various authorities question whether it could now be invoked.) If the government takes an action that appears to conflict with EC law, it can be challenged in the courts and then required to bring itself into line with EC law. An Act of Parliament, as we have seen, does not take precedence over European law. Membership of the European Community – now the European Union – has thus added a new element to the constitution, one that does not fit easily with the existing features of that constitution.

Constitutional reform under the Blair government

Background to reform

The 1970s and 1980s witnessed growing demands for reform of the existing constitution. The system of government no longer appeared to perform as well as it had in the past. The country experienced economic difficulties (inflation, rising unemployment), industrial disputes, civil unrest in Northern Ireland and some social unrest at home (riots in cities such as Bristol and Liverpool). There were problems with the political process. Turnout declined in general elections. The proportion of electors voting for either of the two major parties fell. Two general elections took place in one year (1974), with no decisive outcome. A Labour government elected with less than 40 per cent of the vote in October 1974 was able to implement a series of radical measures.

Critics of the constitution argued the case for change. Some politicians and lawyers argued the case for an entrenched Bill of Rights – putting rights beyond the reach of simple majorities in the two Houses of Parliament. The case for a Bill of Rights was put by Lord Hailsham in a 1976 lecture, subsequently published in pamphlet form under the title *Elective Dictatorship*. Some politicians wanted a new electoral system, one that produced a closer relationship between the proportion of votes won nationally and the proportion of seats won in the House of Commons. The case for a new electoral system was made in an influential set of essays, edited by Professor S.E. Finer in 1975. Finer argued that electoral reform would help to put an end to the harmful consequences of partisanship, not least the policy discontinuity that results when one party replaces another in government.

There were also calls for power to be devolved to elected assemblies in different parts of the United Kingdom and for the use of referendums. Both changes, it was argued, would push decision making down from a centralised government to the people. The Labour government elected in 1974 sought, unsuccessfully, to pass measures providing for elected assemblies in Scotland and Wales. The government did make provision for the first UK-wide referendum, held in 1975 on the issue of Britain's continued membership of the European Community.

The demands for change were fairly disparate and in most cases tied to no obvious intellectually coherent approach to constitutional change. However, as the 1980s progressed, various coherent approaches developed (Norton, 1982, 1993). These are listed in Box 15.1. Each approach had its advocates, although the high Tory and Marxist approaches were essentially overshadowed by the others. The corporatist, or group, approach was

more to the fore in the 1970s, when a Labour government brought representatives of trade unions and business into discussions on economic policy. It retained some advocates in the 1980s. The socialist approach, pursued by politicians such as former Labour cabinet minister Tony Benn, had a notable influence in the Labour Party in the early 1980s, the Labour manifesto in the 1983 general election adopting an essentially socialist stance. The New Right approach found some influential supporters in the Conservative Party, notably cabinet minister Sir Keith Joseph; it also influenced the Prime Minister, Margaret Thatcher.

However, the two most prominent approaches were the liberal and the traditionalist. The liberal approach was pursued by the Liberal Party and then by its successor party, the Liberal Democrats. It also attracted support from a much wider political spectrum, including some Labour supporters and even some ex-Marxists. In 1988, a constitutional reform movement, Charter88, was formed (the year of formation was deliberate, being the tercentenary year of the Glorious Revolution) to bring together all those who supported a new constitutional settlement.

The liberal approach made much of the running in political debate. However, the traditional approach was the more influential by virtue of the fact that it was the approach adopted by the Conservative government. Although Prime Minister Margaret Thatcher supported reducing the public sector, she nonetheless maintained a basic traditionalist approach to the constitution. Her successor, John Major, was a particularly vocal advocate of the traditional approach. Although the period of Conservative government from 1979 to 1997 saw some important constitutional changes – such as a constriction of the role of local government and the negotiation of new European treaties (the Single European Act and the Maastricht Treaty) – there was no principled embrace of radical constitutional change. The stance of government was to support the existing constitutional framework.

As the 1990s progressed, the debate about constitutional change largely polarised around these two approaches. The collapse of communism, the move from Labour to New Labour in Britain and the demise of Margaret Thatcher as leader of the Conservative Party served to diminish the impact of several of the other approaches. As the liberal approach gained ground, so supporters of the traditional approach began to put their heads above the parapet in support of their position.

BOX 15.1 IDEAS AND PERSPECTIVES

Approaches to constitutional change

High Tory

This approach contends that the constitution has evolved organically and that change, artificial change, is neither necessary nor desirable. In its pure form, it is opposed not only to major reforms – such as electoral reform, a Bill of Rights and an elected second chamber – but also to modifications to existing arrangements, such as the introduction of departmental select committees in the House of Commons. Its stance on any proposed reform is thus predictable: it is against it. The approach has been embraced over the years by a number of Conservative MPs.

Socialist

This approach favours reform, but a particular type of reform. It seeks strong government, but a party-dominated strong government, with adherence to the principle of intra-party democracy and the concept of the mandate. It wants to shift power from the existing 'top-down' form of control (government to people) to a 'bottom-up' form (people to government), with party acting as the channel for the exercise of that control. It favours sweeping away the monarchy and the House of Lords and the use of more elective processes, both for public offices and within the Labour Party. It is wary of, or opposed to, reforms that might prevent the return of a socialist government and the implementation of a socialist programme. It is thus sceptical of or opposed to electoral reform (potential for coalition government), a Bill of Rights (constraining government autonomy, giving power to judges) and membership of the European Union (constraining influence, sometimes viewed as a capitalists' club). For government to carry through socialist policies, it has to be free of constitutional constraints that favour or are dominated by its opponents. The most powerful advocate of this approach has been former Labour cabinet minister Tony Benn.

Marxist

This approach sees the restructuring of the political system as largely irrelevant, certainly in the long run, serving merely to delay the collapse of capitalist society. Government, any government, is forced to act in the interests of finance capital. Changes to the constitutional arrangements may serve to protect those interests in the short term but will not stave off collapse in the long term. Whatever the structures, government will be constrained by external élites, and those élites will themselves be forced to follow rather than determine events. The clash between the imperatives of capitalism and decreasing profit rates in the meso-economy determines what capitalists do. Constitutional reform, in consequence, is not advocated but rather taken as demonstrating tensions within the international capitalist economy. This approach has essentially been a 'pure' one, with some Marxists pursuing variations of it and some taking a more direct interest in constitutional change.

Corporatist

The corporatist, or group, approach seeks the greater incorporation of groups into the process of policy making in order to achieve a more consensual approach to public policy. The interdependence of government and interest groups – especially sectional interest groups – is such that it should be recognised and accommodated. A more integrated process can facilitate a more stable economic system. Supporters of this approach have looked to other countries, such as Germany, as examples of what can be achieved. This approach thus favours the representation of labour and business on executive and advisory bodies and, in its pure form, the creation of a functionalist second chamber. It was an approach that attracted support, especially in the 1970s, being pursued in a mild form by the Labour government from 1974 to 1979 and also being embraced, after 1972, by Conservative Prime Minister Edward Heath.

New Right

This approach is motivated by the economic philosophy of the free market. State intervention in economic affairs is viewed as illegitimate and dangerous, distorting the natural forces of the market and denying the consumer the freedom to choose. The state should therefore withdraw from economic activity. This viewpoint entails a contraction of the public sector, with state-owned industries being returned to the private sector. If institutions need reforming in order to facilitate the free market, then so be it: under this approach, no institution is deemed sacrosanct. Frank Vipert, the former deputy director of the free-market think-tank the Institute of Economic Affairs, has advocated a 'free market written constitution'. It is an approach associated with several politicians on the right wing of the Conservative Party, such as John Redwood.

Liberal

Like the New Right approach, this is a radical approach to constitutional change. It derives from traditional liberal theory and emphasises the centrality of the individual, limited government, the neutrality of the state in resolving conflict and consensual decision making. It views the individual as increasingly isolated in decision making, being elbowed aside by powerful interests and divorced from a governmental process that is centralised and distorted by partisan preferences. Against an increasingly over-mighty state, the individual has no means of protection. Hence, it is argued, the need for radical constitutional change. The liberal approach favours a new, written constitution, embodying the various reforms advocated by Charter88, including a Bill of Rights, a system of proportional representation for elections, an elected second chamber, and a reformed judiciary and House of Commons. In its pure form, it supports federalism rather than devolution. Such a new constitutional settlement, it is argued, will serve to shift power from government to the individual. The only reform about which it is ambivalent is the use of referendums, some adherents to this approach seeing the referendum as a device for oppression by the majority. It is an approach pursued by Liberal Democrats, such as Shirley Williams, and by some Labour politicians.

Traditional

This is a very British approach and derives from a perception of the 'traditional' system as fundamentally sound, offering a balanced system of government. It draws on Tory theory in its emphasis on the need for strong government and on Whig theory in stressing the importance of Parliament as the agent for setting the limits within which government may act. These emphases coalesce in the Westminster model of government, a model that is part descriptive (what is) and part prescriptive (what should be). Government, in this model, must be able to formulate a coherent programme of public policy – the initiative rests with government – with Parliament, as the deliberative body of the nation, subjecting the actions and the programme of government to rigorous scrutiny and providing the limits within which government may govern. This approach recognises the importance of the House of Commons as the elected chamber and the fact that the citizen has neither the time nor the inclination to engage in continuous political debate. There is thus a certain deference, but a contingent deference, to the deliberative wisdom of Parliament. The fact that the Westminster model is prescriptive means that traditionalists – unlike high Tories – will entertain change if it is designed to move present arrangements towards the realisation of that model. They also recognise with Edmund Burke that 'a state without the means of some change is without the means of its conservation' and are therefore prepared to consider change in order to maintain and strengthen the existing constitutional framework. Over the years, therefore, traditionalists have supported a range of incremental reforms, such as the introduction of departmental select committees in the House of Commons, but have opposed radical reforms – such as electoral reform – which threaten the existing framework. There is a wariness about membership of the European Union, with involvement accepted as long as it does not pose a major threat to the existing domestic arrangements for decision making. It is an approach pursued by many mainstream Conservative politicians and by some Labour MPs.

Supporters of the liberal approach argued that a new constitution was needed in order to push power down to the individual. Power was too heavily concentrated in public bodies and in special interests. Decentralising power would limit the over-mighty state and also be more efficient, ensuring that power was exercised at a more appropriate level, one more closely related to those affected by the decisions being taken. Supporters of the traditional approach countered by arguing that the traditional constitution had attributes that, in combination, made the existing arrangements preferable to anything else on offer. The attributes were those of coherence, accountability, responsiveness, flexibility and effectiveness. The system of government, it was argued, was coherent: the different parts of the system were integrated, one party being elected to office to implement a programme of public policy placed before electors. The system was accountable: electors knew who to hold to account – the party in government – if they disapproved of public policy; if they disapproved, they could sweep the party from office. The system was responsive: knowing that it could be swept from office at the next election, a government paid attention to the wishes of electors. Ministers could not ignore the wishes of voters and assume they could stay in office next time around as a result of post-election bargaining (a feature of some systems of government). The system was flexible: it could respond quickly in times of crisis, with measures being passed quickly with all-party agreement. The system was also effective: government could govern and could usually be assured of parliamentary approval of measures promised in the party's election manifesto. Government could deliver on what in effect was a contract with the electors: in return for their support, it implemented its promised package of measures.

The clash between the two approaches thus reflected different views of what the constitution was for. The liberal approach, in essence, embraced negative constitutionalism. The constitution was for constraining government. The traditional approach embraced a qualified form of positive constitutionalism. The Westminster system enabled the will of the people to be paramount, albeit tempered by parliamentary deliberation. The qualification is an important one.

Reform under a Labour government

In the 1970s, Labour politicians tended to adopt an essentially traditionalist stance. There was an attempt to devolve powers to elected assemblies in Scotland and Wales and the use of a national referendum, but these were not seen as part of some coherent scheme of constitutional reform. The referendum in particular was seen as an exercise in political expediency. In the early 1980s, the influence of left-wing activists pushed the party towards a more socialist approach to the constitution. Under the leadership of Neil Kinnock, the party was weaned off this approach. It began to look more in the direction of the liberal approach. The longer the party was denied office, the more major constitutional reform began to look attractive to the party. It was already committed to devolution. In its socialist phase, it had adopted a policy of abolishing the House of Lords. It moved away from that to committing itself to removing hereditary peers from the House and introducing a more democratic second chamber. Having previously opposed electoral reform, some leading Labour MPs began to see merit in introducing proportional representation for parliamentary elections. John Smith, leader from 1992 to 1994, committed a future Labour government to a referendum on the issue of electoral reform. The party also began to move cautiously towards embodying rights in statutory form: in 1992 it favoured a charter of rights. It also committed itself to strengthening local government.

The move towards a liberal approach was apparent in the Labour manifesto in the 1992 and 1997 general elections. In both elections, the Conservatives embraced the traditional approach and the Liberal Democrats the liberal approach. Table 15.1 shows the stance taken by each of the parties on constitutional issues in their 1997 election manifestos. The constitution was one subject on which it was generally acknowledged that there was a clear difference in policy between the parties.

Looking in greater detail at the Labour Party's proposals in the 1997 manifesto, the party advocated:

■ devolving power to Scotland and Wales;

■ removing hereditary peers from the House of Lords;

■ incorporating the European Convention on Human Rights into British law;

■ appointing an independent commission to recommend a proportional alternative to the existing electoral system;

■ holding a referendum on the voting system;

Table 15.1 Stance of parties on constitutional issues, 1997 general election

Party	Voting system	House of Lords	Devolution	Regional/local government	Protection of rights	House of Commons
Liberal Democrat	Introduce PR at local, national, European levels	Reform: have a predominantly elected chamber	Home Rule with elected Scottish and Welsh parliaments	Regional assemblies in England; strategic authority for London	Bill of Rights preceded by incorporation of ECHR	Fixed-term parliaments; reduce number of MPs to 200
Conservative	Against PR	No mention, but against wholesale reform	Committed to Union; sees Home Rule and devolution as leading to break-up of UK	Against regional assemblies	Against a Bill of Rights	Two-year rolling parliamentary programme
Labour	Referendum on electoral reform	Remove hereditary peers	Elected Scottish and Welsh assemblies preceded by referendums	New Greater London Authority; elected mayors	Incorporation of ECHR	Select committee on modernisation of the House

- introducing a system of proportional representation for the election of UK members of the European Parliament;

- legislating for an elected mayor and strategic authority for London;

- legislating to give people in the English regions power to decide by referendum, on a region by region basis, whether they wanted elected regional government;

- introducing a Freedom of Information Bill;

- holding a referendum if the government recommended joining a single European currency;

- setting up a parliamentary committee to recommend proposals to modernise the House of Commons.

Following its election to office in 1997, the new Labour government moved to implement its manifesto promises. In the first session (that is, the first year) of the new parliament, the government achieved passage of legislation providing for referendums in Scotland and Wales. In these referendums, electors in Scotland voted by a large majority for an elected parliament with legislative and some tax-varying powers. Voters in Wales voted narrowly for an elected assembly to determine spending in the Principality of Wales (see Table 15.2). The government then introduced measures to provide for an elected parliament in Scotland and an elected

Table 15.2 Referendum results in Scotland and Wales, 1997

Scotland		
	A Scottish Parliament	Tax-varying powers
Agree	1,775,045 (74.3%)	1,512,889 (63.5%)
Disagree	614,400 (25.7%)	870,263 (36.5%)
Turnout: 60.4%		

Wales	
	A Welsh Assembly
Yes	559,419 (50.3%)
No	552,698 (49.7%)
Turnout: 50%	

assembly in Wales. Elections to the new bodies were held on 6 May 1999, and Scotland and Wales acquired new forms of government. The government also introduced legislation providing for a new 108-member assembly in Northern Ireland with a power-sharing executive. This, along with other unique constitutional arrangements – including a North/South Ministerial Council and a Council of the Isles – had been approved by electors in Northern Ireland in a referendum in May 1998.

In the first session, the government also achieved passage of the Human Rights Act, providing for the incorporation of the European Convention on Human

Rights into British law – thus further reinforcing the new judicial dimension of the British constitution – as well as a bill providing for a referendum in London on whether or not the city should have an elected mayor and authority. The referendum in London, in May 1998, produced a large majority in favour of the proposal: 1,230,715 (72 per cent) voted 'yes' and 478,413 (28 per cent) voted 'no'. The turnout, though, was low: only 34.1 per cent of eligible electors bothered to vote. The House of Commons appointed a Select Committee on Modernisation. Within a year of its creation, it had issued seven reports, including one proposing various changes to the way legislation was considered in Parliament. The government also introduced a bill providing for a closed member list system for the election of British Members of the European Parliament (MEPs). The House of Lords objected to the provision for closed lists (electors voting for a list of party candidates, with no provision to indicate preferences among the party nominees) and pushed for an open list system, allowing electors the option to indicate preferences. The government resisted the Lords and eventually the Bill had to be passed, in the subsequent session of Parliament, under the provisions of the Parliament Act.

At the end of 1997, the government appointed a Commission on the Voting System to make a recommendation on a proportional alternative to the existing electoral system. The commission was asked to report within a year. The five-member body, chaired by Liberal Democrat peer Lord Jenkins of Hillhead, reported in October 1998. It considered a range of options but recommended the introduction of an electoral system known as the Alternative Vote Plus ('AV Plus'). Under this system, constituency MPs would be elected by the alternative vote but with top-up MPs, constituting between 15 and 20 per cent of the total number of members, being elected on an area-wide basis (such as a county) to ensure some element of proportionality.

In the second session of Parliament, the government achieved passage of the House of Lords Act. Taking effect in November 1999, the Act removed most hereditary peers from membership of the House of Lords. At the same time as introducing the House of Lords Bill, the government established a Royal Commission on the Reform of the House of Lords, under a former Conservative minister, Lord Wakeham, to make recommendations for a reformed second chamber once the hereditary peers had gone. The commission was asked to report within a year and did so. It recommended that a proportion of the membership of the second chamber be elected by popular vote.

Lord Jenkins presided over the 1998 report, which urged voting reform – these recommendations are yet to be taken up
Source: Empics Sports Photo Agency

The government also achieved passage of three other measures of constitutional significance during the parliament. The Greater London Authority Act brought into being an elected mayor and a strategic authority for the metropolis. The Freedom of Information Act opened up official documents, with certain exceptions, to public scrutiny. The Political Parties, Elections and Referendums Act created a new Electoral Commission, stipulated new rules governing donations to political parties and introduced provisions to cover the holding of referendums. Given that referendums had been promised on various issues, the measure was designed to ensure some consistency in the rules governing their conduct.

After a reforming first Parliament, constitutional change appeared to take a back seat to other measures introduced by the Blair government. However, a further major change was enacted at the end of the second Parliament, one not envisaged in the party's manifesto. The Constitutional Reform Act 2005 linked the position of Lord Chancellor (a Cabinet minister at the head of the judiciary) to that of Secretary of State for Constitutional Affairs and provided that the holder need not be a lawyer or a peer. It also transferred the judicial powers of the Lord Chancellor (a political appointee) to the Lord Chief Justice (a senior judge) and created a new supreme court. Instead of the highest court of appeal being law lords sitting in a judicial committee of the House of Lords, it was now to be an independent body sitting separately from a legislative chamber. The court did not come into immediate being. It was anticipated that it would start sitting in 2009 once a building was ready for it.

In less than a decade, the Labour government of Tony Blair thus saw through major changes to the country's constitution. These changes variously modified, reinforced or challenged the established tenets of the traditional constitution. Each tenet was affected in some way by the changes shown in Table 15.3.

Parliamentary sovereignty, already challenged by British membership of the European Community, was further challenged by the incorporation of the European Convention on Human Rights. This gave the courts an added role, in effect as protectors of the provisions of the convention. If a provision of UK law was found by the courts to conflict with the provisions of the ECHR, a court could issue a declaration of incompatibility. It was then up to Parliament to act on the basis of the court's judgement. The

Table 15.3 Changes to the established tenets of the traditional constitution

Tenets	Affected by
Parliamentary sovereignty	Incorporation of ECHR Ratification of Amsterdam and Nice Treaties
Rule of law	Incorporation of ECHR Creation of a supreme court
Unitary state	Creation of Scottish Parliament, Welsh Assembly and Northern Ireland Assembly
Parliamentary government under a constitutional monarchy	Use of referendums Proposed new voting system Removal of hereditary peers from the House of Lords Freedom of Information Act Modernisation of the House of Commons

ratification of the Amsterdam Treaty further strengthened the European Union by extending the area of its policy competence, thus putting various areas of public policy beyond the simple decision-making capacity of national government and Parliament. The Nice Treaty limited existing member states by creating a new system of weighted voting for when new members joined.

The rule of law was strengthened by the incorporation of the European Convention on Human Rights. The effect of incorporation could be seen as providing a little more balance between the twin pillars of the constitution identified by Dicey (parliamentary sovereignty and the rule of law). The courts could now protect the rule of law against Parliament in a way that was not previously possible. The transfer of powers from the Lord Chancellor to the Lord Chief Justice, and the provision for a new supreme court, was also designed to demonstrate judicial independence.

The unitary state was challenged by the creation of elected assemblies in Scotland, Wales and Northern Ireland. In Scotland, the new Parliament was given power to legislate on any matter not reserved to the UK Parliament. It was also given power to vary the standard rate of taxation by 3p in the pound. The UK Parliament was expected not to legislate on matters that fell within the competence of the Scottish Parliament. The powers previously exercised by the Welsh Office were devolved to a Welsh Assembly. Legislative and administrative powers were also provided for a new Northern Ireland Assembly.

The devolution of such powers raised questions as to the extent to which Parliament should intervene in matters that were exclusive to a part of the UK other than England. As such, devolution may be seen to limit, in effect, the flexibility of the traditional constitution. As we shall see (Chapter 23), devolution also serves to reinforce the judicial dimension to the constitution, giving the courts a role akin to constitutional courts in determining the legal competence of the new assemblies.

The creation of these new assemblies also challenged some of the basic tenets of a parliamentary government under a constitutional monarchy. Decision-making power was being hived off to bodies other than the British Cabinet. Some decision-making competences had passed to the institutions of the European Union, others to elected bodies in different parts of the United Kingdom. The coherence inherent in central parliamentary government was being challenged. Parliamentary government was also challenged by the use of referendums. Referendums provide for electors, rather than Parliament, to determine the outcome of particular issues. Opponents of a new electoral system also argued that, if the proposals for electoral reform were implemented, the capacity of the political system to produce accountable government would be undermined. The removal of most hereditary peers proved controversial – not least, and not surprisingly, in the House of Lords – although the full consequences for parliamentary government were not apparent: in the event, it proved to be a more independent House, willing to challenge the House of Commons. The reforms proposed by the Select Committee on Modernisation of the House of Commons served, albeit marginally, to strengthen the House.

The collective effect of these changes has been to modify, rather than destroy, the traditional constitution. Formally, each of the elements of the constitution remains in place:

1. The doctrine of parliamentary sovereignty may be challenged by incorporation of the ECHR, but formally Parliament is not bound by the rulings of the courts. The courts may issue declarations of incompatibility, but it is then up to Parliament to act on them. Parliament retains the formal power not to take any action (even if the reality is that it will act on them).

2. The minister responsible for introducing the Human Rights Act – the Lord Chancellor, Lord Irvine – conceded that the Human Rights Act 'may be described as a form of higher law' but stressed that the Act decrees that the validity of any measure passed by Parliament is unaffected by any incompatibility with the ECHR. 'In this way, the Act unequivocally preserves Parliament's ability to pass Bills that are or may be in conflict with the convention' (House of Lords *Hansard*, written answer, 30 July 2002).

3. Devolution may challenge the concept of a unitary state, but ultimate power still resides with the centre. Devolved powers – indeed, devolved assemblies – may be abolished by Parliament. The Westminster Parliament can still legislate for the whole of the UK, even in areas formally devolved. (Indeed, it variously does legislate for Scotland in devolved areas, albeit at the invitation of the Scottish Parliament.)

4. Formally, referendums are advisory only. Although it would be perverse for Parliament, having authorised a referendum, to ignore the outcome, it nonetheless has the power to do so.

5. The creation of a supreme court entails moving law lords out of the House of Lords but confers no new powers to strike down Acts of Parliament.

6. Although a new electoral system may destroy the accountability inherent in the present system, no new electoral system has been introduced for elections to Parliament. Instead, new systems have been employed for other assemblies.

Although the practical effect of some of the changes may be to challenge and, in the long run, undermine the provisions of the traditional constitution, the basic provisions remain formally in place. The fact that they have been modified or are under challenge means that we may be moving away from the traditional constitution but, as yet, no new constitution has been put in its place. The traditional approach to the constitution has lost out since 1997, but none of the other approaches can claim to have triumphed.

■ Parties and the constitution

In the wake of the general election of 1997, the stance of the parties on constitutional issues was clear. The Labour Party had been returned to power with a mandate to enact various measures of constitutional reform. The party's election manifesto was frequently quoted during debate on those measures, not least during debate on its House of Lords Bill. The Conservative Party remained committed to the traditional approach to the constitution. It had proposed no major constitutional reform in its election manifesto and was able to take a principled stand in opposition to various of the measures brought forward by the Labour government. However, the measures brought forward by the government created problems for both major parties and, to a lesser extent, for the Liberal Democrats.

The Labour Party

For the Labour Party, there were two problems. One was practical: that was, trying to implement all that it had promised in its election manifesto. A three-figure parliamentary majority in the period from 1997 to 2005 was not sufficient to stave off problems. The narrowness of the vote in the referendum in Wales in 1997 appeared to deter ministers from moving quickly to legislate for referendums in the English regions. When, in 2002, Deputy Prime Minister John Prescott published a White Paper on regional government, the proposals were cautious, providing for regional referendums on a rolling basis. It was recognised that not all regions would necessarily vote for a regional assembly. Initially, referendums in three regions were planned, but this was then reduced to one. When, in the first regional referendum, in the northeast in 2004, there was a decisive 78 per cent 'no' vote, the policy was effectively put on hold. The proposal for a referendum on a new electoral system encountered opposition. The report of the Commission on the Voting System in 1998 attracted a vigorous response from both Labour and Conservative opponents of change – one report suggested that at least 100 Labour MPs, including some members of the Cabinet, were opposed to electoral reform – and this appeared to influence the government. No referendum was held during the parliament and none was promised in the party's 2001 and 2005 election manifestos. The House of Lords Bill encountered stiff opposition in the House of Lords and the government was unable (and in this case largely unwilling) to mobilise a Commons majority to carry through further change. The Freedom of Information Bill ran into opposition from within the ranks of the government itself, various senior ministers – including Home Secretary Jack Straw – not favouring a radical measure. When

the Bill was published in 1999, it was attacked by proponents of open government for not going far enough.

The constitution thus did not change in quite the way that the party had intended. This practical problem also exacerbated the second problem. The party was unable to articulate an intellectually coherent approach to constitutional change. It had moved away from both the socialist approach and the traditional approach and some way towards the liberal approach. However, it only partially embraced the liberal agenda. It was wary of a new system for elections to the House of Commons and appeared to have dropped the idea by the time of the 2001 election. The government hesitated to pursue regional assemblies in England. It set up a Royal Commission to consider reform of the House of Lords but was reluctant to embrace demands for an elected second chamber. When in February 2003 several options for reform were debated in both Houses, senior ministers, including the Prime Minister, voted against having a partially or wholly elected upper house. They were opposed to any change that might challenge the primacy of the House of Commons, in which they had a parliamentary majority. In respect of both devolution and the incorporation of the European Convention on Human Rights, the government ensured that the doctrine of parliamentary sovereignty remained in place.

Although the Labour government was able to say what it was against, it was not able to articulate what it was for, at least not in terms of the future shape of the British constitution. What was its approach to the constitution? What did it think the constitution was for? What sort of constitution did it wish to see in place in five or ten years? When these questions were put to ministers, they normally avoided answering them. The Prime Minister, Tony Blair, avoided making speeches on the subject (Theakston, 2005, p. 33). However, in a debate on the constitution in the House of Lords in December 2002, the Lord Chancellor, Lord Irvine, did concede that the government did not have an overarching approach, arguing instead that the government proceeded 'by way of pragmatism based on principle'. The three principles he identified were:

- ■ *To remain a parliamentary democracy, with the Westminster parliament supreme and within that the Commons the dominant chamber.*
- ■ *To increase public engagement with democracy, 'developing a maturer democracy with different*

centres of power, where individuals enjoy greater rights and where the government is carried out close to the people'.

■ *'To devise a solution to each problem on its own terms'.*

House of Lords Hansard, 18 December 2002, Vol. 642, col. 692; www.publications.parliament.uk/pa/ld200203/ldhansrd/vo021218/text/21218-05.htm

The problem with these 'principles' is that they are not obviously compatible with one another: the first two are in conflict as to where power should reside – should it be in Westminster or in other centres of power?– and the third is a let-out clause, enabling policy to be made up as one goes along.

The government thus lay open to the accusation that it had no clear philosophical approach, nothing that would render its approach predictable or provide it with a reference point in the event of things going wrong. Opponents were thus able to claim that it has been marching down the path – or rather down several paths – of constitutional reform without having a comprehensive map and without any very clear idea of where it is heading.

The Conservative Party

The Conservative Party encountered a problem, although one that was essentially in the future. In the short term, it was able to adopt a consistent and coherent position. It supported the traditional approach to the constitution. It was therefore opposed to any changes that threatened the essential elements of the Westminster system of government. It was especially vehement in its opposition to proposals for electoral reform, mounting a notable campaign against the recommendations of the Commission on the Voting System in 1998. It published a defence of the existing electoral system at the same time as the commission report was launched. It opposed devolution, fearing that it would threaten the unity of the United Kingdom. It opposed the House of Lords Bill, not least on the grounds that the government had not said what the second stage of reform would be.

The party encountered some practical problems. It took time to organise itself as an opposition, having difficulties marshalling its forces to scrutinise effectively the government's proposals for referendums. The Conservative leader in the Lords, Lord Cranborne, negotiated a private deal with the government to retain some hereditary peers in the second chamber: he was sacked by the party leader, William Hague, for having negotiated behind his back. There were also some Conservative MPs who inclined towards a more liberal approach to the constitution, favouring an elected second chamber and an English Parliament. Some, especially after the party's third consecutive election defeat in 2005, favoured electoral reform.

However, the most important problem facing the party was long-term rather than short-term. How was a future Conservative government to respond to the constitutional changes made under the Labour government? The constitution would no longer be the traditional constitution the party had been defending up to 1997. Should a future Conservative government go for the reactionary, conservative or radical option (Norton, 2005)? That is, should it seek to overturn the various reforms made by the Labour government, in effect reverting to the *status quo ante* (the reactionary option)? Should it seek to conserve the constitution as it stood at the time the Conservatives regained power (the conservative option)? Or should it attempt to come up with a new approach to constitutional change (the radical option)?

The Conservative leader, William Hague, recognised the conundrum facing the party and, in a speech in London in February 1998, challenged the party to address the issue. 'What happens to the defenders of the *status quo*', he asked, 'when the *status quo* itself disappears?' The party could not simply shrug its shoulders, he said, and accept whatever arrangements it inherited. Nor could the party reverse every one of Labour's constitutional changes. The clock could not be put back. 'Devolution or the politicisation of the judiciary are not changes that can easily be undone. Attempting to return the constitution to its *status quo ante* would be a futile task.' The party, he declared, would need to adopt its own programme of constitutional reform. He accepted that devolution was a fact and he committed the party to fighting for seats and working in the new assemblies. He outlined some of the issues, such as the relationship between Parliament and the judiciary and between Parliament and government, that the party would have to address. He later appointed commissions to address various aspects of constitutional change – on reform of the House of Lords, on a single currency and on strengthening Parliament. In 1999, he spoke of the need to address the 'English question' in Parliament: how should legislation relating exclusively to England be dealt with by a Parliament made up of members from all parts of the United Kingdom? He sought to make some of the running in considering constitutional change. In so doing, he explicitly acknowledged the basic problem facing the party. As he pithily put it: 'you can't unscramble an omelette'. A new – radical – approach had to be taken.

In 2005, the new party leader, David Cameron, appointed a Democracy Taskforce to consider how democracy could be strengthened. However, the chair of the Taskforce, former cabinet minister Kenneth Clarke, admitted that it was unlikely that the members would reach agreement on all issues of constitutional reform. Although successive party leaders have occasionally come out with proposals for specific change – such as favouring a predominantly elected second chamber, part of the liberal rather than the traditional agenda – none has produced a clear, intellectually coherent approach. The party, in this respect, appears to be emulating its opponents.

Liberal Democrats

The Liberal Democrats could claim to be in the strongest position on issues of constitutional change. They embraced the liberal approach to constitutional change. They therefore had a clear agenda. They were able to evaluate the government's reform proposals against that agenda. Given that the government fell short of pursuing a wholly liberal agenda, they were able to push for those measures that the government had not embraced. Their stance was thus principled and consistent.

In so far as they encountered problems, they were practical problems. Because they favoured the reform measures espoused by the Labour government, they accepted an invitation to participate in a Cabinet committee comprising ministers and leading Liberal Democrats to discuss constitutional change. There was close, private contact between the Prime Minister, Tony Blair, and the leader of the Liberal Democrats, Paddy Ashdown. The party thus had some input into deliberations on the future of the constitution. This cooperation engendered some debate within the party as to how far it might be taken. It also threw up problems for the party in terms of how far the government was prepared to go. Was the party sacrificing its principles for the sake of some peripheral involvement in government, receiving very little in return? It was widely reported that one condition of Liberal Democrat agreement to cooperate was a government commitment to

a referendum on electoral reform. However, the failure of the government to act on this promise following publication of the report of the Commission on the Voting System – chaired by a leading Liberal Democrat – resulted in no notable action on the part of the party leader. Ashdown's successor, Charles Kennedy, elected in 1999, appeared less keen on maintaining close links with the government. The Cabinet committee remained formally in existence in the 2001 Parliament, but did not meet, and in 2005 was wound up. The party could claim that various reforms had been achieved, but it had carried little weight in pressing government to achieve some of its key goals. The bottle of constitutional reform may be half full but it was also half empty.

■ The continuing debate

The constitution remains an issue of debate. It does so at two levels. One is at the wider level of the very nature of the constitution itself. What shape should the British constitution take? How plausible are the various approaches to constitutional change? The Liberal Democrats, along with various commentators, advocate the liberal approach. The other parties have yet to articulate what sort of constitution they want to see in the future. The Conservatives have favoured the traditional approach but have yet to articulate how they propose to respond in government to the constitutional framework they inherit from the Labour government. They continue to defend certain features of the traditional model, such as the existing electoral system, but not others, the party leadership having made a case for a predominantly elected second chamber. The Labour Party wants to move away from the traditional model but not to the extent that it prevents a Labour government from governing.

The other level is specific to various measures of constitutional change. Some changes have been made to the constitution. Other changes are advocated, not least – although not exclusively – by advocates of the liberal approach. Electoral reform remains an issue on the political agenda. Supporters of change want to see the introduction of a system of proportional representation for parliamentary elections. Opponents advance the case for the existing first-past-the-post method of election (see Box 15.2). The use of referendums, and the promise of their use on particular issues, has spurred calls for their more regular use. Opponents are wary of

BOX 15.2 DEBATE

Electoral reform (proportional representation)

The case for

- Every vote would count, producing seats in proportion to votes.
- It would get rid of the phenomenon of the 'wasted vote'.
- It would be fairer to third parties, ensuring that they got seats in proportion to their percentage of the poll.
- On existing voting patterns, it would usually result in no one party having an overall majority – thus encouraging a coalition and moderate policies.
- A coalition enjoying majority support is more likely to ensure continuity of policy than changes in government under the existing first-past-the-post system.
- A coalition enjoying majority support enjoys a greater popular legitimacy than a single-party government elected by a minority of voters.
- Coalitions resulting from election by proportional representation can prove stable and effective.
- There is popular support for change.

The case against

- Very few systems are exactly proportional. Little case to change to a relatively more proportional system than the existing system unless other advantages are clear.
- A system of proportional representation would give an unfair advantage to small parties, which would be likely to hold the balance of power.
- The government is most likely to be chosen as a result of bargaining by parties after a general election and not as a deliberate choice of the electors.
- It would be difficult to ensure accountability to electors in the event of a multi-party coalition being formed.
- Coalitions cobbled together after an election – and for which not one elector has definitively voted – lack the legitimacy of clear electoral approval.
- There is no link between electoral systems and economic performance.
- Coalitions resulting from election under a system of proportional representation can lead to uncertainty and a change of coalition partners – as happened in West Germany in 1982 and Ireland in 1994.
- Bargaining between parties can produce instability, but coalitions can also prove difficult for the electorate to get rid of.
- There is popular support for the consequences of the existing electoral system – notably a single party being returned to govern the country.
- 'Proportional representation' is a generic term for a large number of electoral systems: there is no agreement on what precise system should replace the existing one.

any further use; some are opposed to referendums on principle (see Box 15.3). The role of the second chamber also generates considerable debate. Should there be a second chamber of Parliament? Most of those engaged in constitutional debate support the case for a second chamber but do not agree on the form it should take. Should it be wholly or partly elected? Or should it be an appointed House? (See Chapter 18.) The election of a Labour government under Tony Blair, committed to various measures of constitutional reform, did not put an end to debate

about the future of the British constitution. If anything, it gave it new impetus, leaving the issue of the constitution very much on the political agenda.

The relationship between the debate about the constitution and about particular measures of constitutional reform throws up a vital question. Should specific reforms derive from a clear view of what the constitution, as a constitution, should look like in five or ten years? Or should the shape of the constitution be determined by specific changes made on the basis of their individual merits?

Referendums

The case for

- A referendum is an educational tool – it informs citizens about the issue.
- Holding a referendum encourages people to be more involved in political activity.
- A referendum helps to resolve major issues – it gives a chance for the voters to decide.
- The final outcome of a referendum is more likely to enjoy public support than if the decision is taken solely by Parliament – it is difficult to challenge a decision if all voters have a chance to take part.
- The use of referendums increases support for the political system – voters know they are being consulted on the big issues. Even if they don't take part, they know they have an opportunity to do so.

The case against

- Referendums are blunt weapons that usually allow only a simple answer to a very general question. They do not permit explanations of why voters want something done or the particular way in which they want it done.
- Referendums undermine the position of Parliament as the deliberative body of the nation.
- There is no obvious limit on when referendums should be held – if one is conceded on the issue of Europe, why not also have referendums on capital punishment, immigration and trade union reform? With no obvious limit, there is the potential for 'government by referendum'.
- Referendums can be used as majoritarian weapons – being used by the majority to restrict minorities.
- There is the difficulty of ensuring a balanced debate – one side may (indeed, is likely to) have more money and resources.
- There is the difficulty of formulating, and agreeing, a clear and objective question.
- Research shows that turnout in referendums tends to be lower than that in elections for parliamentary and other public elections. In the UK, for example, there have been low turnouts in Wales (1997) and London (1998).
- Referendums are expensive to hold and are often expensive ways of not deciding issues – if government does not like the result it calls another referendum (as has happened in both Denmark and Ireland over ratification of European treaties).

A distinctive constitution

The United Kingdom is distinctive for having an uncodified constitution. The laws, rules and customs determining how it is to be governed are not drawn up in a single document. This is a distinction it shares with only two other countries: Israel and New Zealand. Other states have drawn up codified documents as a consequence of being newly formed or having to start afresh, having broken away from a colonising power or having been defeated in battle. Britain has not suffered a distinctive constitutional break since the seventeenth century. An attempt to impose a codified, or 'written', constitution during the period of the Protectorate was abandoned with the restoration of the monarchy in 1660. When

James II fled the country in 1688, he was deemed to have abdicated and those responsible for inviting his daughter and son-in-law, Mary and William of Orange, to assume the throne were keen to stress continuity in the nation's constitutional arrangements. The nation's constitutional foundations thus pre-date the creation, starting with the USA in the eighteenth century, of formal codified constitutions.

There are other distinctive features of the nation's constitutional arrangements. Many countries have entrenched constitutions: that is, they are amendable only through some extraordinary process, such as a two-thirds majority in the legislature and/or approval by the people in a referendum. In the UK, laws that change the nature of the constitution – such as the Human Rights Act 1998 – go through the same process as those that determine that it is an offence to leave the scene of an accident.

In terms of the basic structure of government, the UK is also distinctive, but not unique, in having a particular form of parliamentary government. Some systems are presidential, where the head of government and the legislature are elected separately and where neither depends on the other for continuation in office. In a parliamentary system, the head of government and other ministers derive their positions through election to the legislature – they are not elected separately – and they depend for their continuation in office on the confidence of the legislature. There are two basic types of parliamentary government: the Westminster par-liamentary system and the continental. The West-minster model stresses single-party government, elected normally through a first-past-the-post electoral system, with two major parties competing for the all-or-nothing spoils of electoral victory. The continental parliamentary system places stress on consensus politics, with coalition government derived from elections under electoral systems of proportional representation. The Westminster model has been exported to many Commonwealth countries, though a number have departed from it; New Zealand, for example, has adopted a system of proportional representation. There are also various hybrid presidential–parliamentary systems, where the president is directly elected but a government, under a prime minister, is formed through elections to the legislature. France has a hybrid system; hybrid systems have been adopted widely in the new democracies of central and eastern Europe.

Chapter summary

The British constitution remains distinctive for not being codified in a single document. It is drawn from several sources and retains the main components that it has developed over three centuries. Although little debated in the years between 1945 and 1970, it has been the subject of dispute – and of change – in the years since. Proponents of reform have argued that existing constitutional arrangements have not proved adequate to meet the political and economic challenges faced by the United Kingdom. They have pressed for reform, and various approaches to change have developed. Debate has polarised around two approaches: the liberal, favouring a new constitutional settlement for the United Kingdom; and the traditional, favouring a retention of the principal components of the existing constitution.

The constitution has undergone significant change as a result of British membership of the EC/EU and the return of a Labour government in May 1997. The judicial dimension of the constitution has been strengthened as a result of the incorporation of the European Convention on Human Rights into British law; by the devolving of powers to elected bodies in different parts of the UK, the courts acting in effect as constitutional courts for the devolved bodies; and by the creation of a supreme court. New European treaties have resulted in more policy-making power passing upwards to the institutions of the European Union. Devolution has seen some powers pass downwards to a Parliament in Scotland and an Assembly in Wales. The consequence of these changes has been to change the contours of the 'traditional', or Westminster, model of government, although not destroying the model altogether.

The constitution remains a subject of political controversy, posing problems for each of the main political parties. The Labour government has pursued a reform agenda but has done so on a pragmatic basis, embracing no particular approach to change. It has, in effect, fallen somewhere between the liberal and traditional approaches. For the Conservative Party, there is the challenge of determining how a future Conservative government will respond to the new constitutional arrangements. For the Liberal Democrats, there is the dilemma of determining how far to go along with a government that supports some of its goals but is unwilling to embrace a new constitutional settlement for the United Kingdom.

The British constitution has changed significantly in recent years and continues to be the subject of demands for further change, but its future shape remains unclear.

Discussion points

■ How does the constitution of the United Kingdom differ from that of other countries? What does it have in common with them?

■ Which approach to constitutional change do you find most persuasive, and why?

■ How convincing are the principal arguments against holding referendums?

■ Is electoral reform desirable?

■ What are the main obstacles to achieving major constitutional change in the United Kingdom?

Further reading

For a valuable overview of constitutional change in the twentieth century, see the contributions to Bogdanor (2003). For the principal features of the contemporary constitution, see, for example, Alder (2005).

For the early seminal works favouring reform, see Finer (1975) and Hailsham (1976). For leading critiques of the traditional constitution in the 1990s see especially Marr (1995), Hutton (1995) and Barnett (1997). A Conservative view of the constitution is to be found in Patten (1995), Lansley and Wilson (1997) and Norton (2005).

Recent works addressing constitutional change under the Labour government include Hazell (1999), Blackburn and Plant (1999), King (2001), Morrison (2001), Richards and Smith (2001), Forman (2002), Oliver (2003), Marquand (2004) and Johnson (2004). Of these, the King volume is a short one, offering a summary and analysis of the changes that have been introduced. Morrison offers a detailed review, richly illustrated by interviews. Oliver offers a developed overview. Marquand and Johnson offer critical reflective analyses. The journal *Parliamentary Affairs* carried an annual review of constitutional developments, the most recent (and last in the series) being Kelly, Gay and White (2004). (There will be a future annual review in a volume edited by Michael Rush and Philip Giddings and published by Palgrave Macmillan; see Norton 2006.) The

Fourth Report from the House of Lords Constitution Committee (2002), Session 2001–2002, entitled *Changing the Constitution: The Process of Constitutional Change*, provides a useful overview of the way in which constitutional change takes place in the United Kingdom.

There are various useful publications that address specific issues. Most of these are identified in subsequent chapters (monarchy, Chapter 16; House of Commons, Chapter 17; House of Lords, Chapter 18; the judiciary, Chapter 23). Chapter 23 also addresses issues arising from membership of the European Union, the incorporation of the European Convention on Human Rights, devolution and the Constitutional Reform Act. On electoral reform, see Dunleavy *et al.* (1997), the Independent Commission on the Voting System (1998), the Independent Commission to Review Britain's Experience of PR Voting Systems (2004), the Electoral Reform Society (2005) and – for the case against – Norton (1998).

References

Alder, J. (2005) *Constitutional and Administrative Law*, 5th edn (Palgrave Macmillan).

Barnett, A. (1997) *This Time: Our Constitutional Revolution* (Vintage).

Barnett, A., Ellis, C. and Hirst, P. (eds) (1993) *Debating the Constitution* (Polity Press).

Benn, T. (1993) *Common Sense* (Hutchinson).

Blackburn, R. and Plant, R. (eds) (1999) *Constitutional Reform: The Labour Government's Constitutional Reform Agenda* (Longman).

Bogdanor, V. (ed.) (2003) *The British Constitution in the Twentieth Century* (Oxford University Press/British Academy).

Brazier, R. (1994) *Constitutional Practice*, 2nd edn (Oxford University Press).

Constitution Committee, House of Lords (2002) *Changing the Constitution: The Process of Constitutional Change*, Fourth Report, Session 2001–2002, HL Paper 69 (HMSO).

Dunleavy, P., Margetts, H., O'Duffy, B. and Weir, S. (1997) *Making Votes Count* (Democratic Audit, University of Essex).

Electoral Reform Society (2005) *The UK General Election of 5 May 2005: Report and Analysis* (Electoral Reform Society).

Finer, S.E. (ed.) (1975) *Adversary Politics and Electoral Reform* (Wigram).

Fitzpatrick, B. (1999) 'A dualist House of Lords in a sea of monist community law', in B. Dickson and P. Carmichael (eds), *The House of Lords: Its Parliamentary and Judicial Roles* (Hart Publishing).

Foley, M. (1999), *The Politics of the British Constitution* (Manchester University Press).

Forman, N. (2002) *Constitutional Change in the UK* (Routledge).

Hailsham, Lord (1976) *Elective Dictatorship* (BBC).

Hazell, R. (ed.) (1999) *Constitutional Futures* (Oxford University Press).

Hutton, W. (1995) *The State We're In* (Jonathan Cape).

Independent Commission on the Voting System (1998) *Report of the Independent Commission on the Voting System*, Cm 4090–1 (Stationery Office).

Independent Commission to Review Britain's Experience of PR Voting Systems (2004) *Final Report of the Independent Commission to Review Britain's Experience of PR Voting Systems* (Constitution Unit).

Institute for Public Policy Research (1992) *A New Constitution for the United Kingdom* (Mansell).

Ivison, D. (1999) 'Pluralism and the Hobbesian logic of negative constitutionalism', *Political Studies*, Vol. 47, No. 1.

Johnson, N. (2004) *Reshaping the British Constitution* (Palgrave Macmillan).

Kelly, R., Gay, O. and White, I. (2004) 'The Constitution: into the sidings', *Parliamentary Affairs*, Vol. 58, No. 2.

King, A. (2001) *Does the United Kingdom Still Have a Constitution?* (Sweet & Maxwell).

Labour Party (1997) *New Labour: Because Britain Deserves Better* (Labour Party).

Lansley, A. and Wilson, R. (1997) *Conservatives and the Constitution* (Conservative 2000 Foundation).

Marquand, D. (2004) *The Decline of the Public: The Hollowing Out of Citizenship* (Polity Press).

Marr, A. (1995) *Ruling Britannia* (Michael Joseph).

Maxwell, P. (1999) 'The House of Lords as a constitutional court – the implications of Ex Parte EOC', in B. Dickson and P. Carmichael (eds), *The House of Lords: Its Parliamentary and Judicial Roles* (Hart Publishing).

Morrison, J. (2001) *Reforming Britain: New Labour, New Constitution?* (Reuters/Pearson Education).

Norton, P. (1982) *The Constitution in Flux* (Blackwell).

Norton, P. (1986) 'The constitution in flux', *Social Studies Review*, Vol. 2, No. 1.

Norton, P. (1993) 'The constitution: approaches to reform', *Politics Review*, Vol. 3, No. 1.

Norton, P. (1998) *Power to the People* (Conservative Policy Forum).

Norton, P. (2005) 'The Constitution', in K. Hickson (ed.), *The Political Thought of the Conservative Party Since 1945* (Palgrave Macmillan).

Norton, P. (2006) 'The Constitution in 2005', in M. Rush and P. Giddings (eds), *The Palgrave Review of British Politics* (Palgrave Macmillan).

Oliver, D. (2003) *Constitutional Reform in the UK* (Oxford University Press).

Patten, J. (1995) *Things to Come* (Sinclair-Stevenson).

Richard, Lord and Welfare, D. (1999) *Unfinished Business: Reforming the House of Lords* (Vintage).

Richards, D. and Smith, M.J. (2001) 'The Constitution and reforming the state', in S. Ludlow and M.J. Smith (eds), *New Labour in Government* (Macmillan).

Royal Commission on the Reform of the House of Lords (2000) *A House for the Future*, Cm 4534.

Theakston, K. (2005) 'Prime Ministers and the Constitution: Attlee to Blair', *Parliamentary Affairs*, Vol. 58, No. 1.

Tyrie, A. (1998) *Reforming the Lords: A Conservative Approach* (Conservative Policy Forum).

Useful websites

Organisations with an interest in constitutional change

Campaign for the English Regions: www.cfer.org.uk (last updated 2003)

Charter88:   www.charter88.org.uk

Constitution Unit: www.ucl.ac.uk/constitution-unit

Electoral Reform Society: www.electoral-reform.org.uk

Campaign for Freedom of Information:
www.cfoi.org.uk
Make Votes Count:
www.makevotescount.org.uk/news/html

Reports

Constitution Committee of the House of Lords:
Fourth Report, Session 2001–2002, *Changing the Constitution: The Process of Constitutional Change*:   www.parliament.the-stationery-office.co.uk/pa/ld200102/ldselect/ldconst/69/6901.htm
Electoral Reform Society, *The UK General Election of 5 May 2005: Report and Analysis*:
www.electoral-reform.org.uk/publications/briefings/gefinal2005.pdf
Independent Commission on the Voting System (the Jenkins Commission):
www.archive.official-documents.co.uk/document/cm40/4090/4090.htm
Independent Commission to Review Britain's Experience of PR Voting Systems:

www.ucl.ac.uk/constitution-unit/reports/elections.htm#108
Royal Commission on the Reform of the House of Lords (the Wakeham Commission):
www.archive.official-documents.co.uk/document/cm45/4534/4534.htm

Government departments with responsibility for constitutional issues

Department for Constitutional Affairs:
www.dca.gov.uk
Office of the Deputy Prime Minister:
www.odpm.gov.uk
Home Office: www.homeoffice.gov.uk

Other official bodies

The Electoral Commission:
www.electoralcommission.org.uk

European bodies

European Convention on Human Rights:
www.echr.coe.int

CHAPTER 16

The crown

Philip Norton

Learning objectives

- To identify the place of the monarchy in British constitutional history.

- To detail the political significance of 'the crown'.

- To outline the roles that citizens expect the monarch to fulfil and the extent to which they are carried out.

- To outline criticisms made of the monarchy – and the royal family – in recent years.

- To look at proposals for change.

Introduction

I t is an extraordinary fact, often overlooked, that Britain's representative democracy evolved over a thousand years out of an all-encompassing monarchy underpinned by the religious notion of the divine right of kings. The monarchical shell remains intact, but the inner workings have been taken over by party political leaders and civil servants. The shell itself has been the subject of critical comment, especially in recent years. This chapter analyses the emergence of the modern monarchy and considers its still important functions together with the arguments of the critics.

■ The monarchy

The crown is the symbol of all executive authority. It is conferred on the monarch. The monarchy is the oldest secular institution in England and dates back at least to the ninth century. In Anglo-Saxon and Norman times, the formal power that the crown conferred – executive, legislative and judicial – was exercised personally by the monarch. The King had a court to advise him and, as the task of government became more demanding, so the various functions were exercised on the King's behalf by other bodies. Those bodies now exercise powers independent of the control of the monarch, but they remain formally the instruments of the crown. The courts are Her Majesty's courts and the government is Her Majesty's government. Parliament is summoned and prorogued by royal decree. Civil servants are crown appointees. Many powers – prerogative powers – are still exercised in the name of the crown, including the power to declare war. The monarch exercises few powers personally, but those powers remain important. However, the importance of the monarchy in the twenty-first century derives more from what it stands for than from what it does.

The monarchy has been eclipsed as a major political institution not only by the sheer demands of governing a growing kingdom but also by changes in the popular perception of what form of government is legitimate. The policy-making power exercised by a hereditary monarch has given way to the exercise of power by institutions deemed more representative. However, the monarchy has retained a claim to be a representative institution in one particular definition of the term. It is this claim that largely defines the activities of the monarch today.

The monarchy predates by several centuries the emergence of the concept of representation. The term 'representation' entered the English language through French derivatives of the Latin *repraesentare* and did not assume a political meaning until the sixteenth century. It permits at least four separate usages (see Birch, 1964; Pitkin, 1967):

1. It may denote acting on behalf of some individual or group, seeking to defend and promote the interests of the person or persons 'represented'.

2. It may denote persons or assemblies that have been freely elected. Although it is not always the case that persons so elected will act to defend and pursue the interests of electors, they will normally be expected to do so.

3. It may be used to signify a person or persons typical of a particular class or group of persons. It is in this sense that it is used when opinion pollsters identify a representative sample.

4. It may be used in a symbolic sense. Thus, individuals or objects may 'stand for' something: for example, a flag symbolising the unity of the nation.

The belief that free election was a prerequisite for someone to claim to act on behalf of others grew in the nineteenth century. Before then, the concept of 'virtual representation' held great sway. This concept was well expressed by Edmund Burke. It was a form of representation, he wrote, 'in which there is a communion of interests, and a sympathy in feelings and desires, between those who act in the name of any description of people, and the people in whose name they act, though the trustees are not actually chosen by them'. It was a concept challenged by the perception that the claim to speak on behalf of a particular body of individuals could not be sustained unless those individuals had signified their agreement, and the way to signify that agreement was through the ballot box. This challenge proved increasingly successful, with the extension of the franchise and, to ensure elections free of coercion,

Royal ceremonial is symbolic of continuity with the past and of national unity
Source: Copyright © Pool / Tim Graham Picture Library / Corbis

changes in the method of election (the introduction of secret ballots, for example). By the end of the 1880s, the majority of working men had the vote. By Acts of 1918 and 1928, the vote was given to women.

The extension of the franchise in the nineteenth and early twentieth centuries meant that the House of Commons could claim to be a representative institution under the first and second definitions of the term. The unelected House of Lords could not make such a claim. The result, as we shall see (Chapter 17), was a significant shift in the relationship between the two Houses. However, it was not only the unelected upper house that could not make such a claim. Nor could the unelected monarch. Nor could the monarch make a claim to be representative of the nation under the third definition. The claim of the monarch to be 'representative' derives solely from the fourth definition. The monarch stands as a symbol. The strength of the monarch as symbol has been earned at the expense of exercising political powers. To symbolise the unity of the nation, the monarch has had to stand apart from the partisan fray. The monarch has also had to stand aloof from any public controversy. When controversy has struck – as during the abdication crisis in 1936 and during periods of marital rift between members of the royal family in the 1990s – it has undermined support for the institution of monarchy and called into question its very purpose.

■ Development of the monarchy

The present monarch, despite some breaks in the direct line of succession, can trace her descent from King Egbert, who united England under his rule in AD 829. Only once has the continuity of the monarchy been broken, from 1642, when Charles I was deposed (and later executed) until the Restoration in 1660, when his son Charles II was put on the throne, restoring the line of succession. The principle of heredity has been preserved since at least the eleventh century. The succession is now governed by statute and common law, the throne descending to the eldest son or, in the absence of a son, the eldest daughter. If the monarch is under eighteen years of age, a regent is appointed.

Although all power was initially exercised by the monarch, it was never an absolute power. In the coronation oath, the King promised to 'forbid all rapine and injustice to men of all conditions', and he was expected to consult with the leading men of his realm, both clerical and lay, in order to discover and declare the law and before the levying of any extraordinary measures of taxation. Such an expectation was to find documented expression in Magna Carta, to which King John affixed his seal in 1215 and which is now recognised as a document of critical constitutional significance. At the time, it was seen by the barons as an expression of existing rights, not a novel departure from them.

The expectation that the King would consult with the leading men of the realm gradually expanded to encompass knights and burgesses, summoned to assent on behalf of local communities to the raising of more money to meet the King's growing expenses. From the summoning of these local dignitaries to court there developed a Parliament – the term was first used in the thirteenth century – and the emergence of two separate houses, the Lords and the Commons.

The relationship of crown and Parliament was, for several centuries, one of struggle. Although formally the King's Parliament, the King depended on the institution for the grant of supply (money) and increasingly for assent to new laws. Parliament made the grant of supply dependent on the King granting a redress of grievances. Tudor monarchs turned to Parliament for support and usually got it; but the effect of their actions was to acknowledge the growing importance of the body. Stuart kings were less appreciative. James I and his successor, Charles I, upheld the doctrine of the **divine right** of kings: that is, that the position and powers of the King are given by God, and the position and privileges of Parliament therefore derive from the King's grace. Charles' pursuit of the doctrine led to an attempt to rule without the assent of Parliament and ultimately to civil war and the beheading of the King in 1649. The period of republican government that followed was a failure and consequently short-lived. The monarchy was restored in 1660, only to produce another clash a few years later.

James II adhered to the divine right of kings and to the Roman Catholic faith. Both produced a clash with Parliament, and James attempted to rule by **royal prerogative** alone. A second civil war was averted when James fled the country following the arrival of William of Orange (James's Protestant son-in-law), who had been invited by leading politicians and churchmen. At the invitation of a new Parliament, William and his wife Mary (James's daughter) jointly assumed the throne. However, the offer of the crown had been conditional on their acceptance of the Declaration of Right – embodied in statute as the 1689 Bill of Rights – which declared the suspending of laws and the levying of taxation without the approval of Parliament to be illegal. As the historian G.M. Trevelyan observed, James II had forced the country to choose between royal absolutism and parliamentary government (Trevelyan, 1938, p. 245). It chose parliamentary government.

The dependence of the monarch on Parliament was thus established, and the years since have witnessed the gradual withdrawal of the sovereign from the personal exercise of executive authority. Increasingly, the monarch became dependent on ministers, both for the exercise of executive duties and in order to manage parliamentary business. This dependence was all the greater when Queen Anne died in 1714 without an heir (all her children having died) and yet another monarch was imported from the continent – this time George, Elector of Hanover. George I of Britain was not especially interested in politics and in any case did not speak English, so the task of chairing the Cabinet, traditionally the King's job, fell to the First Lord of the Treasury. Under Robert Walpole, this role was assiduously developed and Walpole became the most important of the King's ministers: he became 'prime minister'. Anne's dying without an heir and George's poor language skills facilitated the emergence of an office that is now at the heart of British politics.

George III succeeded in winning back some of the monarchy's power later in the eighteenth century. It was still the King, after all, who appointed ministers, and by skilfully using his patronage he could influence who sat in the House of Commons. This power, though, was undermined early in the nineteenth century. In 1832, the Great Reform Act introduced a uniform electoral system, and subsequent reform acts further extended the franchise. The age of a representative democracy, displacing the concept of virtual representation, had arrived. The effect was to marginalise the monarch as a political actor. To win votes in Parliament, parties quickly organised themselves into coherent and highly structured movements, and the leader of the majority party following a general election became Prime Minister. The choice of Prime Minister and government – what Bagehot referred to as 'the elective function' – remained formally in the hands of the monarch, but in practice the selection came to be made on a regular basis by the electorate.

Queen Victoria was the last monarch seriously to consider vetoing legislation (the last monarch actually to do so was Queen Anne, who withheld Royal Assent from the Scottish Militia Bill in 1707). The year 1834 was the last occasion that a ministry fell for want of the sovereign's confidence; thereafter, it was the confidence of the House of Commons that counted. Victoria was also the last monarch to exercise a personal preference in the choice of Prime Minister (later monarchs, where a choice existed, acted under advice) and the last to be instrumental in pushing successfully for the enactment of particular legislative measures (Hardie, 1970, p. 67). By the end of her reign, it was clear that the monarch, whatever the formal powers vested by the constitution, was constrained politically by a representative assembly elected by the adult male population, the government being formed largely by members drawn from that assembly. Victoria could no longer exercise the choices she had been able to do when she first ascended the throne.

The monarch by the beginning of the twentieth century sat largely on the sidelines of the political system, unable to control Parliament, unable to exercise a real choice in the appointment of ministers, unable to exercise a choice in appointing judges. The extensive power once exercised by the King had now passed largely to the voters and to politicians. The elective power was exercised by voters on election day: between elections it was the Prime Minister who exercised many of the powers formally vested in the monarch. By controlling government appointments, the Prime Minister was able to dominate the executive side of government. And as long as he could command majority support in Parliament, he was able to dominate the legislative side of government. Power thus shifted from an unelected monarch to what one writer later dubbed an 'elected monarch' (Benemy, 1965) – the occupant not of Buckingham Palace but of 10 Downing Street.

The shift to a position detached from regular partisan involvement, and above the actual exercise of executive power, was confirmed under Victoria's successors. 'Since 1901 the trend towards a real political neutrality, not merely a matter of appearances, has been steady, reign by reign' (Hardie, 1970, p. 188). The transition has been facilitated by no great constitutional act. Several statutes have impinged on the prerogative power, but many of the legal powers remain. There is nothing in law that prevents the monarch from vetoing a bill or from exercising personal choice in the invitation to form a government. The monarch is instead bound by conventions of the constitution (see Chapter 15). Thus, it is a convention that the monarch gives her assent to bills passed by Parliament and that she summons the leader of the largest party following a general election to form a government. Such conventions mean that the actions of the monarch are predictable – no personal choice is involved – and they have helped to ease the passage of the monarch from one important constitutional position to another.

These changes have meant that we can distinguish now between 'the crown' and 'the monarch'. The former denotes the executive authority that formally rests with the monarch but is in practice exercised in the name of the monarch, and the latter is the individual who is head of state and performs particular functions. The separation of the two is significant constitutionally and has major political consequences.

■ Political significance of the crown

The transfer of power from monarch to a political executive meant that it became possible to distinguish between head of state and head of government. It also ensured that great political power rested with ministers. Prerogative powers, as we have seen, remain important. They are powers that have always resided in the crown and that have not been displaced by statute. Many such powers remain in existence, though just how many is not clear. There is no definitive list, though a parliamentary committee in 2004 published a list supplied by the government, listing what it considered to be the main prerogatives. They include the summoning, prorogation and dissolution of Parliament; the appointment and deployment of armed forces; declarations of war; the giving of royal assent to Bills; the negotiation and ratification of treaties; the appointment of ministers, civil servants, senior figures in the church (the monarch is supreme governor of the Church of England) and in the judiciary; and the recognition of foreign states.

These powers are exercised now in the name of the crown and, as prerogative powers, are not formally subject to parliamentary approval. In the United States, the power to declare war is conferred by the constitution on Congress. In the United Kingdom, as the foregoing list shows, the power to declare war falls within the royal prerogative. So too does the ratification of treaties. Although it would be an unwise government that embarked on war without parliamentary support, it is the Cabinet that can decide to commit the country to war and do so without reference to Parliament. The action is taken formally in the name of the crown, but the political reality is that it is the decision of Her Majesty's ministers gathered in the Cabinet.

The monarch is thus the person in whom the crown vests, but the powers inherent in the crown are exercised for her by her ministers. In most cases, those powers are exercised directly by ministers. In other words, the monarch does not even announce the decisions taken by ministers in her name. In 1939, the announcement that Britain was at war with Germany was made not by the King, George VI, but by the Prime Minister, Neville Chamberlain. The decision to send a task force to repel the Argentine invasion of the Falkland Islands in 1982 was taken by Margaret Thatcher and the Cabinet. The Chief of Naval Staff told her that a force could retake the islands. 'All he needed was my authority to begin to assemble it. I gave it to him . . . We reserved for Cabinet the decision as to whether and when the task force should sail' (Thatcher, 1993, p. 179). Announcements about the conflict were subsequently made from Downing Street or the Ministry of Defence. In 2003, decisions about joining with the USA in an attack on Iraq were taken by the Prime Minister, Tony Blair. Media attention focused on 10 Downing Street, not Buckingham Palace. Treaties negotiated with other countries are signed by ministers. The Treaty of Accession to the European Community (now the European Union) was signed in 1972, not by the Queen but by the Prime Minister, Edward Heath. The monarch is the supreme governor of the Church of England and, as such, is responsible for choosing archbishops and bishops. In practice, the task is undertaken in 10 Downing Street. In July 2002, the new Archbishop of Canterbury was named as Dr Rowan Williams. The decision to appoint him was made by the Prime Minister, Tony Blair, and the announcement of the appointment was made from Downing Street. Peers are created by the monarch but, in practice, the decision is taken by the Prime Minister and, again, announcements are usually made from Downing Street. Other honours, with certain limited exceptions, are also decided by or require the ultimate approval of the Prime Minister.

As we have noted already, the appointment of ministers, as well as the Civil Service, also falls under the prerogative. The Prime Minister thus decides who will be ministers – and who will not – and can determine who will occupy the senior positions in the Civil Service. He or she can also determine, within a five-year statutory limit, when Parliament shall be dissolved.

The prerogative is frequently exercised through rules, known as Orders in Council, that by virtue of their nature require no parliamentary authorisation. (Some Orders, though, are also made under statutory authorisation.) Orders in Council allow government to act quickly. Thus, for example, an Order in Council in 1982 allowed the requisitioning of ships for use in the campaign to retake the Falkland Islands. Not only are prerogative powers exercised without the need for Parliament's approval, they are in many cases also protected from judicial scrutiny. The courts have held that many of the powers exercised under the royal prerogative are not open to judicial review.

Although the monarch will normally be kept informed of decisions made in her name, and she sees copies of state papers, she is not a part of the decision making that is involved. Nonetheless, the fiction is maintained that the decisions are hers. Peter Hennessy records that it was explained to him why the Table Office of the House of Commons would not accept parliamentary questions dealing with honours: 'It's the Palace', he was told (Hennessy, 2000, p. 75). In other words, it was a matter for the Queen.

The maintenance of the royal prerogative thus puts power in the hands of the government. The government has, in effect, acquired tremendous powers, which it can exercise unilaterally. Parliament can question ministers about some aspects of the exercise of powers under the royal prerogative and could ultimately remove a government from office if dissatisfied with its conduct. However, so long as a government enjoys an overall majority in the House of Commons, it is unlikely to be much troubled about its capacity to exercise its powers. Parliament could curtail the prerogative powers by statute but in so doing it would, in effect, be curtailing the powers of government. Consequently, ministers are not too keen to support such curtailment. In October 2005, former cabinet minister Clare Short introduced a Private Member's Bill to provide for parliamentary authorisation for the deployment of British forces abroad. The Leader of the House, Geoff Hoon, made sure that the Bill made no further progress.

One of those least likely to support curtailment of prerogative powers is the Prime Minister (see Blackburn, 1999, pp. 149–51). He or she is the monarch's first – or prime – minister and therefore exercises the principal powers that are still exercisable under the royal prerogative. Although the monarch now acts in a symbolic capacity, the country still has a form of medieval monarch – the Prime Minister. The monarch reigns, the Prime Minister rules. The Prime Minister enjoys the powers that he does because of the confluence of two things: a majority in the House of Commons and the royal prerogative.

■ The contemporary role of the monarchy

Given that the powers of the crown have almost wholly passed to the government, what then is the role of the monarch? Most people still believe that the monarchy has an important role to play in the future of Britain. In a MORI poll in January 2002, 80 per cent of those questioned said that the monarchy was important to Britain, as against 18 per cent who said that it was not.

What, then, is the monarch's contemporary role? Two primary tasks can be identified. One is essentially a representative task: that is, symbolising the unity and traditional standards of the nation. The second is to fulfil certain political functions. The weakness of the monarch in being able to exercise independent decisions in the latter task underpins the strength of the monarchy in fulfilling the former. If the monarch were to engage in partisan activity, it would undermine her claim to symbolise the unity of the nation.

Symbolic role

The functions fulfilled by the monarch under the first heading are several. A majority of respondents in a poll in the late 1980s considered six functions to be 'very' or 'quite' important. As we shall see, the extent to which these functions are actually fulfilled by members of the royal family has become a matter of considerable debate. Two functions – preserving the class system and distracting people from problems affecting the country – were considered by most respondents as 'not very' or 'not at all' important.

Representing the UK at home and abroad

As a symbolic function, representing the country at home and abroad is a task normally ascribed to any head of state. Because no partisan connotations attach to her activities, the sovereign is able to engage the public commitment of citizens in a way that politicians cannot. When the President of the United States travels within the USA or goes abroad he does so both as head of state and as head of government; as head of government, he is a practising politician. When the Queen attends the Commonwealth Prime Ministers' conference, she does so as symbolic head of the Commonwealth. The British government is represented by the Prime Minister, who is then able to engage in friendly, or not so friendly, discussions with fellow heads of government. The Queen stays above the fray. Similarly, at home, when opening a hospital or attending a major public event, the Queen is able to stand as a symbol of the nation. Invitations to the Prime Minister or leader of an opposition party to perform such tasks run the risk of attracting partisan objection.

At least two practical benefits are believed to derive from this non-partisan role, one political, the other economic. Like many of her predecessors, the Queen has amassed considerable experience by virtue of her monarchical longevity. According to one of her Prime Ministers, Edward Heath: 'The Queen is undoubtedly one of the best-informed people in the world' (Heath, 1998, p. 318). In 2002, she celebrated her fiftieth year on the throne. During her half-century on the throne, she had been served by ten Prime Ministers. Prime Minister Tony Blair was born the year after she ascended to the throne. Her experience, coupled with her neutrality, has meant that she has been able to offer Prime Ministers detached and informed observations. (The Prime Minister has an audience with the Queen each week.) As an informed figure who offers no challenge to their position, she also offers an informed ear to an embattled premier. 'After 50 years on the throne, the Queen harbours a greater store of political knowledge and wisdom than any prime minister whose length of career is at the mercy of fickle voters' (Hamilton, 2002, p. 17). The value of the Queen's role to premiers has been variously attested by successive occupants of Downing Street (see Shawcross, 2002). These have included Labour Prime Ministers

Harold Wilson and James Callaghan, who were especially warm in their praise, as well as the present occupant of the office. Tony Blair said at the time of the Queen's golden wedding anniversary that he enjoyed his weekly audience with the Queen, not simply because of her experience but because she was an 'extraordinarily shrewd and perceptive observer of the world. Her advice is worth having' (*The Times*, 21 November 1997).

The political benefit has also been seen in the international arena. By virtue of her experience and neutral position, the Queen enjoys the respect of international leaders, not least those gathered in the Commonwealth. During the 1980s, when relations between the British government led by Margaret Thatcher and a number of Commonwealth governments were sometimes acrimonious (on the issue of sanctions against South Africa, for example), she reputedly used her influence with Commonwealth leaders 'to ensure that they took account of Britain's difficulties' (Ziegler, 1996). There were fears that, without her emollient influence, the Commonwealth would have broken up or that Britain would have been expelled from it.

In terms of economic benefit, some observers claim – although a number of critics dispute it – that the Queen and leading members of the royal family (such as the Prince of Wales) are good for British trade. At home, royal palaces are major tourist attractions, though critics point out that Versailles – the royal palace in republican France – gets more visitors than Buckingham Palace. The symbolism, the history and the pageantry that surround the monarchy serve to make the Queen and her immediate family a potent source of media and public interest abroad. Royal (although not formal state) visits are often geared to export promotions, although critics claim that the visits do not have the impact claimed or are not followed up adequately by the exporters themselves. Such visits, though, normally draw crowds that would not be attracted by a visiting politician or industrialist. In 2001, the use of a member of the royal family to boost exports was put on a more formal footing when Prince Andrew, the Duke of York, was appointed as a special representative for international trade and development, working in support of British Trade International, a government body that encourages foreign investment and supports UK companies that trade overseas. Shortly after his appointment, he opened the Great Expectations exhibition of British design in New York as well as visiting Bulgaria and the Gulf states.

Setting standards of citizenship and family life

For most of the present Queen's reign, this has been seen as an important task. The Queen has been expected to lead by example in maintaining standards of citizenship and family life. As head of state and secular head of the established Church, she is expected to be above criticism. She applies herself assiduously to her duties; even her most ardent critics concede that she is diligent (Wilson, 1989, p. 190). In April 1947, at the age of 21, while still Princess Elizabeth, she said in a broadcast to the Commonwealth: 'I declare before you that my whole life, be it long or short, shall be devoted to your service.' She reiterated her vow in a speech to both Houses of Parliament in 2002. She and members of the royal family undertake a wide range of public duties each year. In 2001, for example, the Queen fulfilled 2,200 official engagements. The Queen lends her name to charities and voluntary organisations. Other members of her family involve themselves in charitable activities. The Prince of Wales established the Prince's Youth Business Trust, which has been responsible for funding the launch of 30,000 small businesses. The work of the Princess Royal (Princess Anne) as president of the Save the Children Fund helped to raise its international profile. Indeed, the name of a member of the royal family usually adorns the headed notepaper of every leading charity.

Up to and including the 1980s, the Queen was held to epitomise not only standards of good citizenship, applying herself selflessly to her public duties, but also family life in a way that others could both empathise with and hope to emulate. (Queen Elizabeth the Queen Mother – widow of George VI – was popularly portrayed as 'the nation's grandmother'.) Significantly, during the national miners' strike in 1984, the wives of striking miners petitioned the Queen for help. However, the extent to which the Queen fulfils this role has been the subject of much publicised debate since the late 1980s. The problem lay not so much with the Queen personally but with members of her family. By 1992, the Queen was head of a family that had not sustained one successful lasting marriage. The Prince of Wales, as well as the Princess, admitted adultery. The Duchess of York was pictured cavorting topless with her 'financial adviser' while her daughters were present. By the end of the decade, the divorced heir to the throne was attending public engagements with his companion, Camilla Parker-Bowles. In a MORI poll in January 2002, respondents were divided as to whether or not members of the royal family had 'high moral standards': 48 per cent thought that they did, and 44 per cent thought that they did not.

The claim to maintain high standards was also eroded by the collapse of a trial in 2002 involving the butler to Diana, Princess of Wales. The butler, Paul Burrell, was charged with stealing many items belonging to his late employer. The trial collapsed after it emerged that the Queen recalled a conversation with Burrell in which he said that he was storing items for safe keeping. This brought the Queen into controversy, but the consequences were greatest for the Prince of Wales after allegations were made about the running of his household, including the claim that staff were allowed to keep or sell gifts given to the Prince of Wales. There were also allegations of a cover-up involving claims of male rape made against a member of his staff. The media interest led to an inquiry by Sir Michael Peat, the Prince's new secretary, and by a leading lawyer. Publication of their report in March 2003 was more critical than many observers expected. It identified flaws in the way the Prince's affairs had been conducted. The Prince's principal aide and confidant resigned. Following the collapse of the Burrell trial, a YouGov poll (17 November 2002) found that 17 per cent of respondents thought that 'recent revelations' had damaged the royal family 'a great deal' and 41 per cent 'a fair amount'. Following publication of the report in March 2003, there was a marked increase in the number of people believing that Prince Charles should not succeed to the throne. In April 2002, 58 per cent of respondents thought he should succeed; following publication of the report, it was 42 per cent.

Uniting people despite differences

The monarch symbolises the unity of the nation. The Queen is head of state. Various public functions are carried out in the name of the crown, notably public prosecutions, and as the person in whom the crown vests the monarch's name attaches to the various organs of the state: the government, courts and armed services. The crown, in effect, substitutes for the concept of the state (a concept not well understood or utilised in Britain), and the monarch serves as the personification of the crown. Nowhere is the extent of this personification better demonstrated than on British postage stamps. These are unique:

British stamps alone carry the monarch's head with no mention of the name of the nation. The monarch provides a clear, living focal point for the expression of national unity, national pride and, if necessary, national grief.

This role is facilitated by the monarch largely transcending political activity. Citizens' loyalties can flow to the crown without being hindered by political considerations. The Queen's role as head of the Commonwealth may also have helped to create a 'colour-blind' monarchy, in which the welfare of everyone, regardless of race, is taken seriously. At different points this century, members of the royal family have also shown concern for the economically underprivileged and those who have lost their livelihoods – ranging from the 'something must be done' remark in the 1930s of the then Prince of Wales (later Edward VIII) about unemployment while visiting Wales to the work of the present Prince of Wales to help disadvantaged youths.

This unifying role has also acquired a new significance as a consequence of devolution. The crown remains the one unifying feature of the United Kingdom. The UK traditionally comprises one constitutional people under one crown and Parliament. The position of the UK Parliament is circumscribed by virtue of devolving powers to elected assemblies in different parts of the UK. The royal family anticipated the consequences of devolution by seeking funding for an enhancement of the royal offices and residence in Scotland. The Queen opened the Scottish Parliament as well as the National Assembly for Wales. In the event of conflict between a devolved government and the UK government, the Queen constitutes the one person to whom members of both governments owe an allegiance.

The extent to which this unifying feature remains significant was exemplified by the funeral of Queen Elizabeth the Queen Mother, who died in 2002 at the age of 101. The number of people queuing up to pay their respects as the Queen Mother's coffin lay in Westminster Hall, as well as those lining the route for the funeral, far exceeded expectations. When questioned as to why they were queuing for hours to pay their respects, some people responded by saying that it was because it enabled them to express their sense of identity as being British. The Queen Mother's funeral and the Queen's Golden Jubilee celebrations (see Box 16.1) acted as a focal point for the expression of national identity, of bringing people together – a million people lined the Mall in London for the Queen's Golden Jubilee celebrations

BOX 16.1 IDEAS AND PERSPECTIVES

Golden Jubilee year, 2002

The Queen celebrated fifty years on the throne in 2002. Two major events affecting the royal family dominated the year. The first was the death of Queen Elizabeth the Queen Mother at the age of 101. The second was the celebration of the Queen's half-century on the throne. Both attracted crowds on a scale that far exceeded most expectations. The press was downplaying popular interest in the Queen Mother's funeral in the immediate wake of her death. Many in the media anticipated that the Golden Jubilee celebrations would fail to ignite popular interest. They were proved wrong.

The Queen Mother died at the Royal Lodge in Windsor Great Park on 31 March. Her body was transported to one of the chapels of St James' Palace in London. It was later moved from the chapel to lie in state at Westminster Hall. The journey to Westminster Hall was a short one of half a mile. Approximately 400,000 people lined the route for that journey. Over the next few days, more than 200,000 filed passed the coffin in Westminster Hall in order to pay their respects. It had been anticipated that probably no more than 70,000 would do so (if that), and in anticipation Westminster Hall was only to be open for certain hours each day. In the event, the hall stayed open almost round the clock as people queued for hours – some suffering from hypothermia during the cold nights – in order to walk past the coffin. The doors of the hall were only finally closed at 6.00 am on the morning of the funeral. The funeral took place at Westminster Abbey on 9 April. Parliamentarians gathered in Westminster Hall for the departure of the coffin. Members of the royal family walked behind it for the short journey to the abbey. After the service, the coffin was carried by hearse to its final resting place at Windsor. It is estimated that one million people lined the route, 400,000 of them in central London and the rest on the route to Windsor.

The numbers turning out to watch, and the number filing past the coffin, were not the only indication of how people reacted to the Queen Mother's death. An estimated 300 million viewers worldwide watched the funeral on television. Perhaps as tellingly, the National Grid recorded a significant drop in demand of 2,400 megawatts during the hour before the two-minute silence at 11.30 am. This was more than the fall recorded during the solar eclipse in 1999. It compares with a drop of 2,700 megawatts (the highest fall of all) during the three-minute silence in memory of those killed in the attacks in New York and Washington on 11 September 2001.

The popular reaction to the death of the Queen Mother took the mass media by surprise. The scale of the reaction resulted in a marked increase in coverage. It also appeared to galvanise the media to give greater attention to the celebrations of the Queen's Golden Jubilee. The Queen undertook a jubilee tour of the United Kingdom. It began on 1 May. On that day, about 6,000 anti-globalisation protesters descended on London. While they were protesting, the Queen visited Exeter in Devon: 30,000 people turned out to welcome her. During her tour, between May and August, she visited seventy cities and towns in England, Scotland, Wales and Northern Ireland, usually attracting large and enthusiastic crowds. The Jubilee culminated in a weekend of celebrations, including classical music and pop concerts in the grounds of Buckingham Palace. The pop concert, on 3 June, was followed by a massive firework display involving 2.5 tonnes of fireworks and attracted a television audience worldwide that was put at 200 million. An estimated one million people lined the Mall for the event, the area from Buckingham Palace to Admiralty Arch thronging with flag-waving celebrants. A similar number were in central London the following day when the Queen attended a service of thanksgiving in St Paul's Cathedral followed by a Golden Jubilee Festival in the Mall. And, over a six-month period, there were 28 million hits on the Golden Jubilee website.

Why did so many people turn out for, or watch on television, the Queen Mother's funeral and the Queen's Golden Jubilee celebrations? There are several possible explanations.

Personal respect for the Queen Mother and the Queen
The Queen Mother was often portrayed as the nation's 'favourite grandmother'. She was a strong, charismatic woman, driven by a sense of public duty. She refused to leave the country during the war. She took an interest in all the organisations of which she was a patron, in many cases visiting regularly. She continued to fulfil public engagements long after she turned 100. It has been argued that the crowds loved her largely because she loved the crowds. Her daughter, the Queen, inherited her sense of public duty. At 76, the Queen was the oldest monarch to celebrate a Golden Jubilee. The death of her mother so soon after the death of her sister (Princess Margaret) and the dignified way she coped with the funeral are argued by some to have increased public sympathy and support for her, encouraging people who might not otherwise have done so to turn out for the jubilee celebrations.

Respect for the institution of monarchy
It is difficult to separate the individual from the institution. The Queen Mother had become Queen Consort in 1936. She was the last Empress of India. Queen Elizabeth, as Queen Regnant, is head of state and the embodiment of the attributes that many look for in a monarch. Turning out for both the Queen Mother's funeral and the Queen's jubilee celebrations was seen by some as representing respect for the institution and the fact that both Queen Elizabeth the Queen Mother and Queen Elizabeth II were part of the nation's history. A MORI poll for the ITV programme *Tonight with Trevor MacDonald* in May found that 41 per cent of those questioned 'felt that the monarchy has strengthened following the deaths of Princess Margaret [the Queen's sister] and the Queen Mother'.

Expressing a sense of identity
The Queen is the one unifying element of the British constitution. Though some decision-making powers have been devolved to elected bodies in different parts of the United Kingdom, the Queen remains the

sovereign of all the people or peoples of the United Kingdom. The Queen Mother's funeral and the Golden Jubilee celebrations provided occasions for people to come together at a time when fragmentary pressures were at work. The World Cup in 2002 allowed English supporters to support the England team and Scottish supporters the Scottish team. The Golden Jubilee brought everyone together. *The Times* (10 April 2002, special supplement) quoted one 54-year-old woman from Enfield who had turned out for the Queen Mother's funeral: 'We have to be here. We are Londoners and we are British'.

Media manipulation

Critics argue that much of the popular celebration was contrived by the media and by the royal family. The broadcast media gave the funeral and the jubilee celebrations blanket live coverage. The Director General of the BBC, Greg Dyke, was quoted as saying that the BBC had saved both itself and the monarchy. The Queen made a dignified broadcast, and the Prince of Wales a very personal one, following the death of the Queen Mother. Various members of the royal family, including the Duke of York and the Princess Royal, spent time meeting people who were queuing to pay their respects in Westminster Hall. The concerts at Buckingham Palace were carefully organised to ensure that people were chosen by ballot, not by social position. The firework display was a massive popular entertainment.

These explanations are not mutually exclusive nor are they necessarily exhaustive. There is relatively little hard data available yet to prove which is the most plausible. The least plausible is the last, in that it appears that the media were following rather than leading public opinion. In 2000, the BBC decided not to broadcast the birthday parade to celebrate the Queen Mother's 100th birthday. A MORI poll for the *Daily Mail* found that 56 per cent thought the decision was wrong; only 34 per cent thought it was right. A memo was also circulated in the BBC ahead of the jubilee celebrations indicating that the coverage should be more critical. The people lining the streets when the Queen Mother's coffin was moved to Westminster Hall alerted the media to the fact that they might have misjudged the popular mood and they responded accordingly. The BBC coverage of the funeral was judged by 64 per cent of respondents in one poll to be 'about right'.

The strength of the attachment to the monarchy is also reflected in one finding of a poll, carried out by Mediaedge:CIA for the *Daily Telegraph*. It found that 40 per cent of those questioned would alter their viewing habits and follow coverage of the Jubilee, compared with only 25 per cent who gave the same response for the World Cup.

---

in June 2002 – in a way that no other national figure or institution could do.

However, the extent to which this role is fulfilled effectively does not go unquestioned. Critics, as we shall see, claim that the royal family occupies a socially privileged position that symbolises not so much unity as the social divisions of the nation. Although the royal household is known for having gays in its employ, critics have drawn attention to the dearth of employees in the royal household drawn from ethnic minorities. In 1997, for example, there was not one black employee among 850 staff at Buckingham Palace. Nor were there any on the staff of the Prince of Wales. Staff employed in the royal household are poorly paid. There have been

attempts since to widen recruitment, but pay and conditions remain relatively poor.

Allegiance of the armed forces

The armed services are in the service of the crown. Loyalty is owed to the monarch, not least by virtue of the oath taken by all members of the armed forces. It is also encouraged by the close links maintained by the royal family with the various services. Members of the royal family have variously served in (usually) the Royal Navy or the Army. Most hold ceremonial ranks, such as colonel-in-chief of a particular regiment. Prince Andrew was a serving naval officer and a helicopter pilot during the 1982

The Queen's interest in military matters extends, on this occasion, to overseeing her grandson as he finds a royal role for the twenty-first century
Source: Empics / Associated Press

Falklands War. The Queen takes a particular interest in military matters, including awards for service. 'With the outbreak of the troubles in Ulster in the late 1960s she was a moving force in getting a medal created for services there, and she reads personally all the citations for gallantry there – as she had always done for medals of any sort' (Lacey, 1977, p. 222). Such a relationship helps to emphasise the apolitical role of the military and provides a barrier should the military, or more probably sections of it, seek to overthrow or threaten the elected government. (In the 1970s, there were rumours – retailed in the press and on a number of television programmes – that a number of retired officers favoured a coup to topple the Labour government returned in 1974.) In the event of an attempted military coup, the prevailing view – although not universally shared – is that the monarch would serve as the most effective

bulwark to its realisation, the Queen being in a position to exercise the same role as that of King Juan Carlos of Spain in 1981, when he forestalled a right-wing military takeover by making a public appeal to the loyalty of his army commanders.

Maintaining continuity of British traditions

The monarch symbolises continuity in affairs of state. Many of the duties traditionally performed by her have symbolic relevance: for example, the state opening of Parliament and – important in the context of the previous point – the annual ceremony of Trooping the Colour. Other traditions serve a psychological function, helping to maintain a sense of belonging to the nation, and a social function. The awarding of honours and royal garden parties are viewed by critics as socially élitist but by supporters as helping to break down social barriers, rewarding those – regardless of class – who have contributed significantly to the community. Hierarchy of awards, on this argument, is deemed less important than the effect on the recipients. The award of an MBE (Member of the Order of the British Empire) to a local charity worker may mean far more to the recipient, who may never have expected it, than the award of a knighthood to a senior civil servant, who may regard such an award as a natural reward for services rendered. Investiture is often as important as the actual award. 'To some it is a rather tiresome ordeal but to most a moving and memorable occasion. A fire brigade officer, who was presented with the British Empire Medal, spoke for many when he said: "I thought it would be just another ceremony. But now that I've been, it's something I'll remember for the rest of my days"' (Hibbert, 1979, p. 205). Each year 30,000 people are invited to royal garden parties. Few decline the invitation. During the Queen's reign, more than one million people have attended the garden parties.

Again, this function does not go unchallenged. The award of honours, for example, is seen as preserving the existing social order, the type of honour still being determined by rank and position. It is also seen as a patronage tool in the hands of the Prime Minister, given that only a few honours (Knight of the Garter, the Order of Merit and medals of the Royal Victorian Order) are decided personally by the Queen. However, both Buckingham Palace and Downing Street have sought to make some changes while preserving continuity. Successive Prime Ministers have tried to make the honours system more inclusive – in recent years, for example, knighthoods have been conferred on head teachers – and the monarchy has sought to be more open.

Preserving a Christian morality

The Queen is supreme governor of the Church of England, and the links between the monarch and the church are close and visible. The monarch is required by the Act of Settlement of 1701 to 'joyn in communion with the Church of England as by law established'. After the monarch, the most significant participant in a coronation ceremony is the Archbishop of Canterbury, who both crowns and anoints the new sovereign. Bishops are, as we have seen, formally appointed by the crown. National celebrations led by the Queen will usually entail a religious service, more often than not held in Westminster Abbey or St Paul's Cathedral. The Queen is known to take seriously her religious duties and is looked to, largely by way of example, as a symbol of a basically Christian morality.

Preserving what are deemed to be high standards of Christian morality has been important since the nineteenth century, although not necessarily much before that: earlier monarchs were keener to protect the Church of England than they were to practise its morality. The attempts to preserve that morality in the twentieth century have resulted in some notable sacrifices. Edward VIII was forced to abdicate in 1936 because of his insistence on marrying a twice-married and twice-divorced woman. In 1955, the Queen's sister, Princess Margaret, decided not to marry Group Captain Peter Townsend because he was divorced. She announced that 'mindful of the Church's teaching that Christian marriage is indissoluble, and conscious of my duty to the Commonwealth, I have resolved to put these considerations before others.' However, two decades later, with attitudes having changed, the Princess herself was divorced. Her divorce was followed by that of Princess Anne and Captain Mark Phillips and later by that of the Duke and Duchess of York and the Prince and Princess of Wales. Following the death of Diana, Princess of Wales, the Prince of Wales began to be seen in public with his companion, Camilla Parker-Bowles. Although attitudes towards divorce have changed, divorces and separations in the royal family – and the heir to the throne admitting to adultery – have nonetheless raised questions about the royal family's capacity to maintain a Christian morality. The capacity to do so has also been challenged explicitly by the heir to the throne, Prince Charles, who has said that he would wish to be 'a Defender of Faiths, not the Faith'.

The stance of the Prince of Wales also reflects criticism by those who do not think that the royal family *should* preserve a morality that is explicitly or wholly Christian. Critics see such a link as unacceptable in a society that has several non-Christian religions. The connection between the crown and the Christian religion may act against the crown being a unifying feature of the United Kingdom. The problem was exemplified in August 2002, when a Muslim traffic warden objected to the badge worn by police officers and traffic wardens. The badge comprised a crown with a cross, symbol of the Christian faith, on top of it.

Those who think the royal family should preserve a strict Christian morality appear to be declining in number. This was reflected at the start of the twenty-first century in popular attitudes towards the relationship of Prince Charles and Camilla Parker-Bowles. Mrs Parker-Bowles was divorced and her former husband was still living. She and Prince Charles engaged in an affair while both were still married. In a YouGov poll in August 2002, when asked what they believed should happen at the end of the Queen's reign, a majority of respondents – 52 per cent – said that Prince Charles should become King and be allowed to marry Mrs Parker-Bowles. No less than 60 per cent would approve of the Archbishop of Canterbury allowing them to have a Church of England wedding (*Evening Standard*, 15 August 2002). In the event, they married in a civil ceremony in April 2005.

Exercise of formal powers

Underpinning the monarch's capacity to fulfil a unifying role, and indeed underpinning the other functions deemed important, is the fact that she stands above and beyond the arena of partisan debate. This also affects significantly the monarch's other primary task: that of fulfilling her formal duties as head of state. Major powers still remain formally with the monarch. Most prerogative powers, as we have seen, are now exercised by ministers on behalf of the crown. A number of other powers, which cannot be exercised by ministers, are as far as possible governed by convention. By convention, as we have seen, the monarch assents to all legislation passed by the two Houses of Parliament; by convention, she calls the leader of the party with an overall majority in the House of Commons to form a government. Where there is no clear convention governing what to do, the Queen acts in accordance with precedent (where one exists) and, where a choice is involved, acts on advice. By thus avoiding any personal choice – and being seen not to exercise any personal choice – the monarch is able to remain 'above politics'. Hence the characterisation of the monarch as enjoying strength through weakness. The denial of personal discretion in the exercise of inherently political powers strengthens the capacity of the monarch to fulfil a representative – that is, symbolic – role.

However, could it not be argued that the exercise of such powers is, by virtue of the absence of personal choice, a waste of time and something of which the monarch should be shorn? Why not, for example, vest the power of dissolution in the Speaker of the House of Commons, or simply – as suggested by Blackburn (1999) – codify existing practice in a way that requires no involvement by the monarch? There are two principal reasons why the powers remain vested in the sovereign.

First, the combination of the symbolic role and the powers vested in the crown enables the monarch to stand as a constitutional safeguard. A similar role is ascribed to the House of Lords, but that – as we shall see (Chapter 18) – is principally in a situation where the government seeks to extend its own life without recourse to an election. What if the government sought to dispense with Parliament? To return to an earlier example, what if there was an attempted military coup? The House of Lords could not act effectively to prevent it. It is doubtful whether a Speaker vested with formal powers could do much to prevent it. The monarch could. As head of state and as commander-in-chief of the armed forces, the monarch could deny both legitimacy and support to the insurgents. This may or may not be sufficient ultimately to prevent a coup, but the monarch is at least in a stronger position than other bodies to prevent it succeeding. Thus, ironically, the unelected monarch – successor to earlier monarchs who tried to dispense with Parliament – serves as an ultimate protector of the political institutions that have displaced the monarchy as the governing authority (see Bogdanor, 1995).

Second, retention of the prerogative powers serves as a reminder to ministers and other servants of the crown that they owe a responsibility to a higher authority than a transient politician. Ministers are Her Majesty's ministers; the Prime Minister is invited by the sovereign to form an administration. The responsibility may, on the face of it, appear purely formal. However, although the monarch is precluded from calling the Prime Minister (or any minister) to account publicly, she is able to require a private explanation. In *The English Constitution*, Walter Bagehot offered his classic definition of the monarch's power as being 'the right to be consulted, the right to encourage, the right to warn'. The Queen is known to be an assiduous reader of her official papers and is known often to question the Prime Minister closely and, on other occasions, the relevant departmental ministers. Harold Wilson recorded that in his early days as Prime Minister he was caught on the hop as a result of the Queen having read Cabinet papers that he had not yet got round to reading. 'Very interesting, this idea of a new town in the Bletchley area', commented the Queen. It was the first Wilson knew of the idea. More significantly, there are occasions when the Queen is believed to have made her displeasure known. In 1986, for example, it was reported – although not confirmed – that the Queen was distressed at the strain that the Prime Minister, Margaret Thatcher, was placing on the Commonwealth as a result of her refusal to endorse sanctions against South Africa (see Pimlott, 1996; Ziegler, 1996); she was also reported to have expressed her displeasure in 1983 following the US invasion of Grenada, a Commonwealth country (Cannon and Griffiths, 1988, p. 620). Indeed, relations between the Queen and her first female Prime Minister were claimed to be strained (see Hamilton, 2002), although Mrs Thatcher said that her relationship with the Queen was correct. The Queen is also believed to have signalled her displeasure when Prime Minister Tony Blair failed to include her in the itinerary of a visit to the UK by US President Bill Clinton (Pierce, 1999). Nonetheless, former Prime Ministers have variously attested to the fact that the Queen is a considerable help rather than a hindrance, offering a private and experienced audience. She also serves as a reminder of their responsibility to some other authority than political party. She also stands as the ultimate deterrent. Although her actions are governed predominantly by convention, she still has the legal right to exercise them. When the government of John Major sought a vote of confidence from the House of Commons on 23 July 1993 (following the loss of an important vote the previous evening), the Prime Minister made it clear that in the event of the government losing the vote, the consequence would be a general election. (By convention, a government losing a vote of confidence either resigns or requests a dissolution.) However, the government took the precaution of checking in advance that the Queen would agree to a dissolution.

■ Criticisms of the monarchy

Various functions are thus fulfilled by the monarch and other members of the royal family. There has tended to be a high level of support for the monarchy and popular satisfaction with the way those functions are carried out. The level of satisfaction was notable during the Queen's Golden Jubilee in 2002. However, a high level of support for the institution of monarchy has not been a constant in British political history. It dropped during the reign of Queen Victoria when she withdrew from public activity following the death of Prince Albert. It dropped again in the 1930s as a result of the abdication crisis, which divided the nation. It increased significantly during the Second World War because of the conduct of the royal family and remained high in post-war decades. It dipped again in the 1990s: 1992 was described by the Queen as her *annus horribilis* (horrible year). The monarchy was no longer the revered institution of preceding decades, and its future became an issue of topical debate. Even at times of high popular support, it has never been free of criticism. In recent years, the criticisms have been fuelled by the activities of various members of the royal family, the Prince of Wales coming in for especial criticism in 2002 and 2003.

Four principal criticisms can be identified: that an unelected monarch has the power to exercise certain political powers; that, by virtue of being neither elected nor socially typical, the monarchy is unrepresentative; that maintaining the royal family costs too much; and that the institution of monarchy is now unnecessary. The last three criticisms have become more pronounced in recent years.

Potential for political involvement

The actions of the sovereign as head of state are governed predominantly by convention. However, not all actions she may be called on to take are covered by convention. This is most notably the case in respect of the power to appoint a Prime Minister and to dissolve Parliament. Usually, there is no problem. As long as one party is returned with an overall majority, the leader of that party will be summoned to Buckingham Palace (or, if already Prime Minister, will remain in office). But what if there is a 'hung' parliament, with no one party enjoying an overall majority, and the leader of the third-largest party makes it clear that his or her party will be prepared to sustain the second largest party in office, but not the party with the largest number of seats? Whom should the Queen summon? Following the February 1974 general election, Edward Heath resigned as Prime Minister after his party lost its majority and he failed to negotiate a deal with the Liberal parliamentary party. The Queen then summoned Labour leader Harold Wilson. Labour constituted the largest party in the House of Commons, but it was more than 30 seats short of an overall majority. What if, instead of attempting to form a minority government, Wilson asked immediately for another general election? What should the Queen have done? Her advisers deliberated in case it happened, but in the event Wilson formed a government before seeking an election later in the year (see Hennessy, 2000, Chapter 3). There is no clear convention to govern the Queen's response in such circumstances, and the opinions of constitutional experts as to what she should do are divided. Similarly, what if the Prime Minister was isolated in Cabinet and requested a dissolution, a majority of the Cabinet making it clear that it was opposed to such a move, would the Queen be obliged to grant her Prime Minister's request?

These are instances of problems that admit of no clear solution, and they pose a threat to the value that currently derives from the sovereign being, and being seen to be, above politics. She is dependent on circumstances and the goodwill of politicians in order to avoid such a difficult situation arising. When the Queen was drawn into partisan controversy in 1957 and 1963 in the choice of a Conservative Prime Minister, the obvious embarrassment to the monarchy spurred the party to change its method of selecting the leader. There remains the danger that circumstances may conspire again to make involvement in real – as opposed to formal – decision making unavoidable.

Given this potential, some critics contend that the powers vested in the monarch should be transferred elsewhere. Various left-of-centre bodies have advocated that some or all of the powers be transferred to the Speaker of the House of Commons. The proposal was advanced in 1996, in a Fabian Society pamphlet, by Labour parliamentary candidate Paul Richards, and again in 1998 by the authors of a pamphlet published by the left-wing think-tank Demos (Hames and Leonard, 1998). Defenders of the existing arrangements contend that the retention of prerogative powers by the crown has created no major problems to date – one constitutional historian, Peter Hennessy, in a 1994 lecture, recorded only five 'real or near real contingencies' since 1949 when the monarch's reserve powers were relevant (Marr, 1995, p. 234; see also Bogdanor, 1995) – and it serves as a valuable constitutional long-stop. Giving certain powers to the Speaker of the Commons would be to give them to a member of an institution that may need to be constrained and would probably make the election of the Speaker a much more politicised activity. Furthermore, the Speaker or other such figure would be likely to lack the capacity to engage the loyalty of the armed forces to the same extent as the monarch.

Unrepresentative

The monarchy cannot make a claim to be representative in the second meaning of the term (freely elected). Critics also point out that it cannot make a claim to be representative in the third meaning (socially typical). The monarchy is a hereditary institution, based on the principle of primogeniture: that is, the crown passes to the eldest son. By the nature of the position, it is of necessity socially atypical. Critics contend that social hierarchy is reinforced by virtue of the monarch's personal wealth. The Queen is believed to be among the world's richest women and may possibly be the richest. Many of the functions patronised by the Queen and members of the royal family, from formal functions to sporting events, are also criticised for being socially élitist. Those who surround the royal family in official positions (the Lord Chamberlain, ladies-in-waiting and other senior members of the royal household), and those with whom members of the royal family choose to surround themselves in positions of friendship, are also notably if not exclusively drawn from a social élite. In the 1950s, Lord Altrincham criticised the Queen's entourage for constituting 'a tight little enclave of British "ladies and gentlemen"' (Altrincham et al., 1958, p. 115). Various changes were made in the wake of such criticism – the royal family became more publicly visible, the presentation of débutantes to the monarch at society balls was abolished – but royalty remains largely detached from the rest of society. The closed nature of the royal entourage was attacked in the 1990s by the Princess of Wales, who had difficulty adapting to what she saw as the insular and stuffy nature of the royal court. Even at Buckingham Palace garden parties, members of the royal family, having mixed with those attending, then take tea in a tent reserved for them and leading dignitaries. Focus groups, commissioned by Buckingham Palace in 1997, concluded that the royal family was out of touch because of their traditions and upbringing as well as remote because of 'the many physical and invisible barriers thought to have been constructed around them' (quoted in Jones, 1998). It was widely reported in 2002 that the most trusted aide to the Prince of Wales even squeezed his toothpaste onto his toothbrush for him. In a MORI poll in 2002, 68 per cent of those questioned thought that the royal family was 'out of touch with ordinary people'; only 28 per cent thought that it was not.

Pressures continue for the institution to be more open in terms of the social background of the Queen's entourage and, indeed, in terms of the activities and background of members of the royal family itself. The public reaction to the death, in a car crash in 1997, of Diana, Princess of Wales – popular not least because of her public empathy with the frail and the suffering – and the findings from the focus groups (commissioned in the wake of the Princess's death) are believed to have been influential in persuading the Queen to spend more time visiting people in their homes and exploring how people live (for example, by travelling on the underground and by visiting a supermarket). Defenders of the royal family argue that it is, by definition, impossible for members of the family to be socially typical – since they would cease to be the royal family – and that to be too close to everyday activity would rob the institution of monarchy of its aura and charm.

Overly expensive

The cost of the monarchy has been the subject of criticism for several years. This criticism became pronounced in the 1990s. Much but not all the costs of the monarchy have traditionally been met from the civil list. The civil list constitutes a sum paid regularly by the state to the monarch to cover the cost of staff, upkeep of royal residences, holding official functions, and of public duties undertaken by other members of the royal family. (The Prince of Wales is not included: as Duke of Cornwall his income derives from revenue-generating estates owned by the Duchy of Cornwall.) Other costs of monarchy – such as travel and the upkeep of royal castles – are met by government departments through grants-in-aid from Parliament. In 1990, to avoid an annual public row over the figure, agreement was reached between the government and the Queen that the civil list should be set at £7.9 million a year for ten years. When the other costs of the monarchy – maintaining castles and the like – are added to this figure, the annual public expenditure on the monarchy was estimated in 1991 to exceed £57 million.

In the 1970s and 1980s, accusations were variously heard that the expenditure was not justified, in part because some members of the royal family did very little to justify the sums given to them and in part because the Queen was independently wealthy, having a private fortune on which she paid no tax. (When income tax was introduced in the nineteenth century, Queen Victoria voluntarily paid

tax. In the twentieth century, the voluntary commitment was whittled down and had disappeared by the time the Queen ascended the throne in 1952.) These criticisms found various manifestations. In 1988, 40 per cent of respondents to a Gallup poll expressed the view that the monarchy 'cost too much'. In a MORI poll in 1990, three out of every four people questioned believed that the Queen should pay income tax; half of those questioned thought the royal family was receiving too much money from the taxpayer. Certain members of the royal family became targets of particular criticism.

These criticisms became much louder in 1991 and 1992. They were fuelled by a number of unrelated developments. The most notable were the separation of the Duke and Duchess of York and – in December 1992 – of the Prince and Princess of Wales, following newspaper stories about their private lives. The result was that members of the royal family became central figures of controversy and gossip. In November 1992, fire destroyed St George's Hall of Windsor Castle, and the government announced that it would meet the cost of repairs, estimated at more than £50 million. Public reaction to the announcement was strongly negative. At a time of recession, public money was to be spent restoring a royal castle, while the Queen continued to pay no income tax and some members of the royal family pursued other than restrained lifestyles at public expense. A Harris poll found three out of every four respondents believing that ways should be found to cut the cost of the royal family.

Six days after the fire at Windsor Castle, the Prime Minister informed the House of Commons that the Queen had initiated discussions 'some months ago' on changing her tax-free status and on removing all members of the royal family from the civil list other than herself, the Duke of Edinburgh and the Queen Mother. The Queen herself would meet the expenditure of other members of the royal family. (This amounts to just over £1.2 million a year.) The Queen announced the following year that Buckingham Palace was to be opened to the public, with money raised from entrance fees being used to pay the cost of repairs to Windsor Castle. These announcements served to meet much of the criticism, but the controversy undermined the prestige of the royal family. Critics continued to point out that most of the costs of the monarchy remained unchanged, funded by public money, and drew attention to the fact that the Queen was using novel devices of taking money from the public (entrance fees to the Palace) in order to fund Windsor Castle repairs rather than drawing on her own private wealth.

Controversy was again stirred in January 1997 when Defence Secretary Michael Portillo announced plans for a new royal yacht, to replace *Britannia*, at a cost of £60 million. Public reaction was largely unfavourable, and Buckingham Palace let it be known that the government had not consulted members of the royal family before making the announcement. The plan to build a replacement yacht was cancelled a few months later by the new Labour government.

Supporters of the monarchy point out that savings have been made in recent years. The decommissioning of the royal yacht has saved £12 million a year. The royal family has made economies in travelling. By 2004–5, Head of State Expenditure was £36.7 million, a massive reduction in the costs compared with ten years previously. The cost of the contemporary monarchy, it is argued, is modest, amounting to the equivalent cost of a loaf of bread for every citizen. Defenders contend that the country obtains good value for money from the royal family, the costs of monarchy being offset by income from crown lands (land formerly owned by the crown but given to the state in return for the civil list), which in 2003–4 amounted to £177 million, and by income from tourism and trade generated by the presence and activities of the Queen and members of her family. They also point out that much if not most of the money spent on maintaining castles and other parts of the national heritage would still have to be spent (rather like Versailles in France) even if there was no royal family. When such money is taken out of the equation, the public activities of the Queen and leading royals such as the Princess Royal are deemed to represent good value for public money. The cost of the monarchy in the United Kingdom, for example, is less than the cost of maintaining the presidency in Italy. However, despite the various savings made, people in the UK are split as to whether monarchy offers value for money. In a MORI survey in 2002, 45 per cent of respondents thought that it did offer value for money, as against 48 per cent who thought that it did not. In the same poll, 55 per cent thought that members of the royal family could be described as 'extravagant'.

Unnecessary

Those who criticise the monarchy on grounds of its unrepresentative nature and its cost are not necessarily opposed to the institution itself. A more open and less costly monarchy – based on the Scandinavian model, with the monarch mixing more freely with citizens and without excessive trappings – would be acceptable to many. However, some take the opposite view. They see the monarchy as an unnecessary institution; the cost and social élitism of the monarchy are seen as merely illustrative of the nature of the institution. Advocates of this view have included Tom Nairn in *The Enchanted Glass: Britain and its Monarchy*, Edgar Wilson in *The Myth of the British Monarchy*, Jonathan Freedland in *Bring Home the Revolution*, the contributors to Cyril Meadows, *Ending the Royal Farce*, and *The Economist* magazine. Wilson contends that the various arguments advanced in favour of the monarchy – its popularity, impartiality, productivity, capacity to unite, capacity to protect democratic institutions of state, and ability to generate trade – are all myths, generated in order to justify the existing order. To him and similar critics, the monarchy forms part of a conservative establishment that has little rationale in a democratic society. They would prefer to see the monarchy abolished. 'The constitutional case for abolishing the Monarchy is based mainly on the facts that it is arbitrary, unrepresentative, unaccountable, partial, socially divisive, and exercises a pernicious influence and privileged prerogative powers' (Wilson, 1989, p. 178). *The Economist* has taken a similar line, albeit expressed in less strident terms and acknowledging that, if popular opinion wants to keep a monarchy, then it should stay. The monarchy, it declared, 'is the antithesis of much of what we stand for: democracy, liberty, reward for achievement rather than inheritance.' Its symbolism was harmful: 'the hereditary principle, deference, *folies de grandeur*'. It was 'an idea whose time has passed' (*The Economist*, 22 October 1994). Necessary functions of state carried out by the monarch could be equally well fulfilled, so critics contend, by an elected president. Most countries in the world have a head of state not chosen on the basis of heredity. So why not Britain?

Supporters of the institution of monarchy argue that, despite recent criticisms, the Queen continues to do a good job – a view that, according to opinion polls, enjoys majority support – and that the monarchy is distinctive by virtue of the functions it is able to fulfil. In a MORI poll in May 2002, 82 per cent of respondents were satisfied with the way the Queen was doing her job. It is considered doubtful that an appointed or elected head of state would be able to carry out to the same extent the symbolic role, representing the unity of the nation. For a head of state not involved in the partisan operation of government, it is this role (representative in the fourth sense of the term) that is more important than that of being an elected leader. Indeed, election could jeopardise the head of state's claim to be representative in the first sense of the term (acting on behalf of a particular body or group). The monarch has a duty to represent all subjects; an elected head of state may have a bias, subconscious or otherwise, in favour of those who vote for him or her, or in favour of those – presumably politicians – who were responsible for arranging the nomination. The Queen enjoys a stature not likely to be matched by an elected figurehead in engaging the loyalty of the armed forces; and by virtue of her longevity and experience can assist successive Prime Ministers in a way not possible by a person appointed or elected for a fixed term. Hence, by virtue of these assets particular to the Queen, the monarch is deemed unique and not capable of emulation by an elected president. Although these assets may have been partially tarnished in recent years, it is argued that they remain of value to the nation.

■ Proposals for change

The monarchy has never been wholly free of critics. In the 1970s and 1980s, those critics were relatively few in number. In the early 1990s, they became far more numerous and more vocal. There were various calls for changes to be made in the institution of the monarchy and in the conduct of members of the royal family. Those most responsible for this situation arising were members of the royal family themselves. The marital splits, the antics of various royals, the public perception of some members of the royal family as 'hangers-on' (enjoying the trappings of privilege but fulfilling few public duties) and the failure of the Queen to fund the restoration of Windsor Castle herself contributed to a popular mood less supportive of the monarchy than before. This critical mood was tempered at the start of the new century.

Although the public standing of the monarchy improved in 2002, with three-quarters of those questioned in a MORI poll saying they would be celebrating the Queen's Golden Jubilee, calls for change continued to be made. These were fuelled by the public controversy surrounding the running of the Prince of Wales's household. Various options were discussed. These can be grouped under four heads: abolition, reform, leave alone and strengthen.

Abolition

The troubles encountered by the royal family in the late 1980s and early 1990s appeared to influence attitudes toward the monarchy itself. As we have seen, the Queen described 1992 as her *annus horribilis* – her horrible year. That was reflected in popular attitudes towards the monarchy. Until the middle of 1992, fewer than 15 per cent of people questioned in various polls wanted to see the monarchy abolished. A Gallup poll in May 1992 found 13 per cent of respondents giving such a response. By the end of the year, the figure had increased to 24 per cent. As we have seen, those favouring abolition gained the support of a leading magazine, *The Economist*, in 1994.

Not only was there an increase in the percentage of the population expressing support for the abolition of the monarchy; there was also an increasing agnosticism among a wider public. In 1987, 73 per cent of respondents in a MORI poll thought that Britain would be worse off if the monarchy were abolished. In December 1992, the figure was 37 per cent; 42 per cent thought it would make no difference. The same poll found, for the first time, more people saying that they did not think that the monarchy would still exist in fifty years' time than saying it would: 42 per cent thought it would not against 36 per cent saying it would.

However, those who argue the case for the retention of the monarchy appear still to have a considerable edge over those demanding abolition. The early 1990s represented the low point in terms of popular disaffection with royalty. The number of those thinking that Britain would be worse off if the monarchy were to be abolished has increased since 1992, although it is still not back to the level of the 1980s. (In June 2000, 50 per cent thought that Britain would be worse off; 37 per cent said it would make no difference and 10 per cent said better off.) Support for abolition of the monarchy has varied but usually no more than one in five express support for a republic (Table 16.1). Those who do favour abolition are more likely to be found among the left-leaning members of the professional classes than the lower middle or working class: 'abolition of the monarchy is much more a demand of liberal intellectuals . . . than of the traditional working class left' (Mortimore, 2002, p. 3). Although the proportion

Table 16.1 Attitudes towards the monarchy

Q. If there were a referendum on the issue, would you favour Britain becoming a republic or remaining a monarchy? (%)

	April 1993	Dec 1994	Sept 1997	August 1998	Feb 2002	Apr/May 2004[a]	Apr 2005
Republic	18	20	18	16	19	20	22
Monarchy	69	71	73	75	71	71	65
Don't know/other	14	9	9	9	10	10	13

[a] Question differs slightly for the 2004 survey.

Sources: From MORI, *British Public Opinion*, 25(1), Spring 2002 and www.mori.com. Copyright © Ipsos MORI, reproduced with permission

dipped in April 2005 (around the time of the marriage of Prince Charles), usually about seven out of ten people questioned favour retaining the monarchy (Table 16.1). In a MORI poll in 2002, the proportion thinking the monarchy would still exist in fifty years' time stood at 44 per cent, 8 per cent more than had given a similar answer in 1992.

Reform

Recent years have seen a growing body of support for some change in the nature of the monarchy and especially in the royal family. Some proposals for reform are radical. The authors of the Demos pamphlet, *Modernising the Monarchy*, argue the case not only for transferring the monarch's prerogative powers to the Speaker of the House of Commons but also for holding a referendum to confirm a monarch shortly after succeeding to the throne (Hames and Leonard, 1998). There are some survey data to suggest that more people support the first of these proposals than oppose it. In a MORI poll in August 1998, 49 per cent thought that the powers should be removed, against 45 per cent who thought they should be retained.

There is also a desire for more general change in the way the monarch, and other members of the royal family, conduct themselves. This desire has been tapped by opinion polls as well as by the focus groups commissioned by Buckingham Palace. The public preference is for a more open and less ostentatious monarchy, with the Queen spending more time meeting members of the public, and with other members of the royal family, especially the 'minor royals', taking up paid employment (as some have) and blending into the community. A Granada TV deliberative poll in 1996, which involved interviewing people before and after discussing the subject with experts, found that the biggest percentage of affirmative responses was for the statement that 'members of the royal family should mix more with ordinary people'. The percentage agreeing was initially 66 per cent and, after discussion, it increased to 75 per cent. In a MORI poll in January 2002, 54 per cent of those questioned agreed with the statement that 'the monarchy should be modernised to reflect changes in public life'. Only 28 per cent felt that 'the monarch's role should remain broadly unchanged'.

There is also some support for a change in the order of succession. A small number of people favour the Queen abdicating in favour of Prince Charles, but the number is declining: it reached a peak at 47 per cent in a 1990 MORI poll but was down to 28 per cent in August 1998. A slightly larger percentage support 'skipping a generation' and allowing Prince William, Prince Charles's elder son, to succeed to the throne in place of his father. In a MORI poll in September 1997, in the wake of the death of Diana, Princess of Wales, 54 per cent supported such a move: by November 1998, the percentage giving the same response was 34 per cent. The proportion increased markedly in March 2003 following the publication of the critical report on the way Prince Charles's household was run. By 2005, opinion was evenly divided. A MORI poll in April 2005 found that 43 per cent favoured such a move against 40 per cent opposed. However, the option of skipping a generation would require a change in the law. A decision by the Queen, or by Prince Charles upon or at the time of his succession to the throne, to abdicate is not one that can be taken unilaterally. Under the Act of Succession, Prince Charles will become King automatically on the death of his mother. There is no formal power to abdicate. That would require – as it did in 1936 – an Act of Parliament.

Another change that has variously been discussed, but which has less immediate relevance, is that of allowing the eldest child to succeed, regardless of gender. (Given that Prince Charles is the eldest child of the sovereign and his eldest child is a male, it will be at least two generations before any change becomes relevant.) In 1996, it emerged that the senior members of the royal family, apparently prompted by Prince Charles, had formed a small group (the 'Way Ahead Group' composed of senior royals and Buckingham Palace officials) to meet twice a year to consider various changes to existing arrangements. One proposal considered by the group was to allow the eldest child to succeed to the throne; another was to end the ban on anyone who marries a Roman Catholic succeeding to the throne.

The measures taken by the Queen in recent years – notably the decision to pay income tax, to limit the civil list and to spend more time meeting ordinary members of the public – appear to enjoy popular support. The deliberations of the Way Ahead Group were designed also to bring the institution up to date and enhance such support. The financial accounts (once highly secret) are now published, the jubilee celebrations in 2002 were carefully planned, and junior royals have a somewhat lower public profile than before as well as receiving no support from public funds. In 2002, the Queen became the first member of the royal family to receive a gold disc from the recording industry: 100,000 copies of the CD of the *Party at the Palace*, produced by EMI, were sold within a week of release.

Leave alone

The monarchy as it stands has some ardent admirers. Conservative MPs have generally moved quickly to defend the monarchy from criticism. When a Fabian Society pamphlet, *Long to Reign Over Us?*, was published in August 1996 (Richards, 1996) advocating a referendum on the monarchy, a Conservative cabinet minister, Michael Portillo, immediately portrayed it as an attack on the institution of monarchy. 'New Labour should be warned that they meddle with the monarchy at the nation's peril', he declared. After 1997, some of the attempts by Prime Minister Tony Blair to encourage change also encountered criticism. In 1999, the leading historian, Lord Blake, declared: 'Reform has gone far enough . . . The monarchy is one of the fixed points of the British constitutional firmament. It cannot be subjected to constant change' (Pierce, 1999).

Although this stance attracts support, it tends to be outweighed by those favouring some reform (a fact acknowledged in effect by the royal family in the creation of the Way Ahead Group). As we have seen, most people questioned in the MORI poll in January 2002 favoured some change; only 28 per cent wanted to leave the monarchy broadly unchanged. Those favouring modest reform appear to be in a majority among voters. It is also the stance favoured by the Labour government of Tony Blair. 'Palace officials have been told clearly by Downing Street that there is strong political pressure for a much leaner monarchy' (Pierce, 1999). Although some of the proposals emanating from Downing Street, such as reducing the ceremony of the state opening of Parliament, have been resisted by Buckingham Palace (see Pierce, 1999), the need for reform has generally been accepted by the royal family.

Strengthen

The final option is that of strengthening the role and powers of the monarchy. A Gallup poll in 1996 for the *Sunday Telegraph* tapped a body of support for giving the Queen a greater role. This was especially marked among working-class respondents and among the 16- to 34-year-old age groups: 57 per cent of working-class respondents thought that the Queen should be given 'a more substantial role in government'; and 54 per cent of respondents aged 16 to 34 also thought that she should have a more substantial role (Elliott and McCartney, 1996). The nature of the role was not specified. As we have seen, the potential for the Queen to be drawn into decision making exists, and that potential may increase as a consequence of recent constitutional changes. The exercise of some of these powers may not prove unpopular to a section of the population. It was notable in the 1996 poll that many respondents regarded the Queen as having superior skills to those of the then Prime Minister, John Major: 46 per cent thought that the Queen would make a 'better Prime Minister than John Major'; 39 per cent thought that she would make a better Prime Minister than Tony Blair; and 47 per cent of working-class respondents thought that she would run the country 'more wisely than politicians'.

There is thus some body of support for the Queen exercising more power in the political affairs of the nation. However, that view is not widely held among politicians, nor – as far as one can surmise – among members of the royal family. As we have seen, the strength of the monarchy rests largely on the fact that it is detached from the partisan fray and is not involved in having to exercise independent judgement. Having to make independent decisions would be popular with some but, and this is the crucial point in this context, not with all people. Those adversely affected by a decision would be unlikely to keep their feelings to themselves. The monarchy would be drawn into the maelstrom of political controversy, thus ridding it of its capacity to fulfil the principal functions ascribed to it.

■ Conclusion

The monarch fulfils a number of functions as head of state. Some of those functions are not peculiar to the monarch as head of state: they are functions that are typically carried out by a head of state. Supporters of the monarchy argue that a number of functions are particularly suited to the monarch and, in combination, could not be fulfilled by an elected or appointed head of state. The monarchy was under strain in the early 1990s as a result of various disconnected events, and its public standing declined markedly. The nature of the monarchy was further called into question following the death of the popular Diana, Princess of Wales, in August 1997. The Queen and other members of the royal family have responded to criticism by implementing changes in structures and activities designed to create a more open and responsive monarchy. The actions of the Queen and her family appeared to bear fruit, especially in the celebration of the Queen's Golden Jubilee in 2002. There is no strong desire to get rid of the monarchy. However, there is scepticism about the future of the monarchy. Although most people (82 per cent in a 2002 MORI poll) think that the monarchy will still exist in ten years' time and, as we have seen, 44 per cent of respondents think that it will exist in fifty years' time, only 26 per cent think it will exist in 100 years' time. However, if it is abolished, that may not be an end of a public role for members of the royal family. In the 1996 Gallup poll that found some support for strengthening the monarchy, 37 per cent said they would vote for the Queen if she led a political party. A MORI poll in December of the same year offered thirteen candidates for an elected president. As *The Economist* noted (11 January 1997), 'The clear winner, ahead of politicians and businessmen, was the queen's own daughter, Princess Anne. And therein lies a lesson for any budding constitutional reformer.'

BOX 16.2 BRITAIN IN CONTEXT

Presidents and monarchs

The United Kingdom is not unusual in having a monarchy. There are basically two types of head of state: presidents and hereditary rulers. Presidents are typically elected, though their role in government may vary. Some combine executive powers as head of government with formal ceremonial power as head of state; the President of the USA combines both. Some are predominantly ceremonial, that is, serving as head of state but not head of government; the President of Ireland is an example of this type. The same distinction can be drawn in terms of hereditary rulers. Some are both head of government and head of state. The number is now small, concentrated especially in the Middle and Far East, as powerful rulers over time have been overthrown, removed by popular vote or reduced to playing a largely ceremonial role. (In some countries, such as Nepal, the monarchy has, under great pressure, conceded power.) More than two-thirds of hereditary rulers have a predominantly or wholly ceremonial role, exercising few or no independent political powers. Most hereditary rulers take the title of king or queen, but some have the title of emir, grand duke, prince, sheik, or sultan; they are generally subsumed under the generic title of monarchs.

Monarchies account for less than one-quarter of the nations that now exist. There is a notable concentration of ceremonial monarchies in Western Europe – Belgium, Denmark, the Netherlands, Norway, Spain, Sweden and the United Kingdom are monarchies; Luxembourg is a Grand Duchy and Monaco a principality. The number of countries with a monarch exceeds the number of monarchs, as some monarchs reign over more than one country: the Queen of Denmark, for example, is also Queen of Greenland. None, though, can match the British monarch, who is Queen of fifteen Commonwealth countries and of a number of non-sovereign territories such as Bermuda, Gibraltar, the British Virgin Islands and the Falkland Islands.

Chapter summary

The monarchy remains an important institution in British political life. The monarch's transition from directing the affairs of state to a neutral non-executive role – with executive powers now exercised by ministers in the name of the monarch – has been a gradual and not always smooth one, but a move necessary to justify the monarch's continuing existence.

Transcending partisan activity is a necessary condition for fulfilling the monarch's symbolic ('standing for') role and hence a necessary condition for the strength and continuity of the monarchy. The dedication of the present monarch has served to sustain popular support for the institution. That support dropped in the 1990s, criticism of the activities of members of the royal family rubbing off on the institution of monarchy itself. Popular support for the institution remains and received a particular boost in the Golden Jubilee year of 2002. However, most people when questioned want to see some change, favouring the monarchy and royal family being more open and approachable.

Discussion points

- What is the point in having a monarchy?

- Does the royal family represent value for money?

- What are the most important roles fulfilled by the Queen in contemporary society?

- What public role, if any, should be played by members of the royal family, other than the Queen?

- Should the monarchy be left alone, reformed or abolished?

Further reading

There are few substantial analyses of the role of the crown in political activity. The most recent scholarly analysis – that by Bogdanor (1995) – seeks to transcend recent controversy. The book provides a good historical perspective on the role of the monarchy as well as offering a defence of the institution. Hardie (1970) provides a useful guide to the transition from political involvement to neutrality; Hibbert (1979) also offers a useful overview. Lacey (1977, Golden Jubilee edition 2002) and Pimlott (1996, Golden Jubilee edition 2002) have produced useful and readable biographies of the Queen. Recent books about the monarchy include Douglas-Home (2000) and Shawcross (2002). Strober and Strober (2002) offer quotations from people who have been close to the Queen during her fifty-year reign.

In terms of the debate about the future of the monarchy, the most recent reform tracts are those by Barnett (1994), Richards (1996) and Hames and Leonard (1998). The principal works arguing for abolition are Nairn (1988), Wilson (1989), Freedland (1999) and Meadows (2003). The issue of *The Economist*, 22 October 1994, advocating abolition, also provides a substantial critique. On the case for monarchy, see Gattey (2002).

In terms of the controversies of the early 1990s, the book that sparked media interest in the state of the Prince of Wales's marriage was Morton (1992), followed later by a revised edition (Morton, 1997). The biography of Prince Charles by Jonathan Dimbleby (1994) also contributed to the public debate. On the work undertaken by Prince Charles, see Morton (1998).

References

Altrincham, Lord, *et al.* (1958) *Is the Monarchy Perfect?* (John Calder).

Barnett, A. (ed.) (1994) *Power and the Throne: The Monarchy Debate* (Vintage).

Benemy, F.W.G. (1965) *The Elected Monarch* (Harrap).

Birch, A.H. (1964) *Representative and Responsible Government* (Allen & Unwin).

Blackburn, R. (1992) 'The future of the British monarchy', in R. Blackburn (ed.), *Constitutional Studies* (Mansell).

Blackburn, R. (1999) 'Monarchy and the royal prerogative', in R. Blackburn and R. Plant (eds), *Constitutional Reform* (Longman).

Bogdanor, V. (1995) *The Monarchy and the Constitution* (Oxford University Press).

Cannon, J. and Griffiths, R. (1988) *The Oxford Illustrated History of the British Monarchy* (Oxford University Press).

Dimbleby, J. (1994) *The Prince of Wales. A Biography* (Little, Brown).

Douglas-Home, C. (2000) *Dignified and Efficient: The British Monarchy in the Twentieth Century* (Claridge Press).

Elliott, V. and McCartney, J. (1996) 'Queen should have real power, say Britain's youth', *Sunday Telegraph*, 21 April.

Freedland, J. (1999) *Bring Home the Revolution* (Fourth Estate).

Gattey, C.N. (2002) *Crowning Glory: The Merits of Monarchy* (Shepheard Walwyn).

Hames, T. and Leonard, M. (1998) *Modernising the Monarchy* (Demos).

Hamilton, A. (2002) 'Ten out of ten, Ma'am', *London Diplomat*, May/June.

Hardie, F. (1970) *The Political Influences of the British Monarchy 1868–1952* (Batsford).

Heath, E. (1998) *The Course of My Life: My Autobiography* (Hodder & Stoughton).

Hennessy, P. (2000) *The Prime Minister: The Office and its Holders since 1945* (Allen Lane/Penguin Press).

Hibbert, C. (1979) *The Court of St James* (Weidenfeld & Nicolson).

Jones, M. (1998) 'Queen to appoint royal spin doctor to boost ratings', *Sunday Times*, 22 February.

Lacey, R. (1977) *Majesty* (Hutchinson).

Lacey, R. (2002) *Royal: Her Majesty Queen Elizabeth II*, The Jubilee Edition (TimeWarner).

Marr, A. (1995) *Ruling Britannica* (Michael Joseph).

Meadows, C. (ed.) (2003) *Ending the Royal Farce* (Republic).

Mortimore, R. (2002) 'The monarchy and the jubilee', *MORI: British Public Opinion Newsletter*, Spring, Vol. XXV, No. 1.

Morton, A. (1992) *Diana: Her True Story* (Michael O'Mara Books).

Morton, A. (1997) *Diana, Her True Story – In Her Own Words* (Michael O'Mara Books).

Morton, J. (1998) *Prince Charles: Breaking the Cycle* (Ebury Press).

Nairn, T. (1988) *The Enchanted Glass: Britain and its Monarchy* (Century Hutchinson Radius).

Pierce, A. (1999) 'Spin meister of royal reform trips up', *The Times*, 4 September.

Pimlott, B. (1996) *The Queen* (HarperCollins).

Pimlott, B. (2002) *The Queen: Elizabeth II and the Monarchy*, Golden Jubilee edition (HarperCollins).

Pitkin, H.G. (1967) *The Concept of Representation* (University of California Press).

Richards, P. (1996) *Long to Reign Over Us?* (Fabian Society).

Shawcross, W. (2002) *Queen and Country* (BBC).

Strober, D. and Strober, G. (2002) *The Monarchy: An Oral History of Elizabeth II* (Hutchinson).

Thatcher, M. (1993) *The Downing Street Years* (HarperCollins).

Trevelyan, G.M. (1938) *The English Revolution 1688–9* (Thornton Butterworth).

Wilson, E. (1989) *The Myth of the British Monarchy* (Journeyman/Republic).

Ziegler, P. (1996) 'A monarch at the centre of politics', *Daily Telegraph*, 4 October.

Useful websites

Official royal websites
Royal family: www.royal.gov.uk
Online monthly magazine of the above:
    www.royalinsight.gov.uk
Prince of Wales: www.princeofwales.gov.uk
Prince Michael: www.princemichael.org.uk
Crown Estate: www.crownestate.co.uk

Organisations favouring reform
Republic: www.republic.org.uk
Centre for Citizenship: www.centreforcitizenship.org

Organisation supporting the monarchy
Constitutional Monarchy Association:
    www.monarchy.net

Survey data on attitudes towards the Royal Family
MORI: www.mori.com/polls/indroyal.shtml

CHAPTER 17

The House of Commons

Philip Norton

Learning objectives

- To explain the importance of the House of Commons in terms of its history and its functions.

- To identify and assess the means available to Members of Parliament to fulfil those functions.

- To describe and analyse pressures on the House and proposals for reform.

- To identify different approaches to parliamentary power.

Introduction

The House of Commons has evolved over seven centuries. At various times, it has played a powerful role in the affairs of the nation. Its most consistent activity has been to check the executive power. Its power has been limited by royal patronage and, more recently, by the growth of parties. It nonetheless remains an important part of the political process. It constitutes the only nationally elected body. It has to give its assent to measures of public policy. Ministers appear before it to justify their actions. It remains an arena for national debate and the clash of competing party views. It provides an important institutional constraint on the actions of government. However, its capacity to fulfil its functions has been the subject of debate. Criticism has led to various demands for change.

■ Origins of Parliament

Parliament has its origins in the thirteenth century. It was derived not from first principles or some grand design but from the King's need to raise more money. Its subsequent development may be ascribed to the actions and philosophies of different monarchs, the ambitions and attitudes of its members, external political pressures and prevailing assumptions as to the most appropriate form of government. Its functions and political significance have been moulded, though not in any consistent manner, over several hundred years.

Despite the rich and varied history of the institution, two broad generalisations are possible. The first concerns Parliament's position in relation to the executive. Parliament is not, and never has been on any continuous basis, a part of that executive. Although the Glorious Revolution of 1688 confirmed the form of government as that of 'parliamentary government', the phrase, as we have seen already (Chapter 15), means government through Parliament, not government by Parliament. There have been periods when Parliament has been an important actor in the making of public policy, not least for a period in the nineteenth century, but its essential and historically established position has been that of a reactive, or policy-influencing, assembly (Box 17.1; see Mezey, 1979; Norton, 1993); that is, public policy is formulated by the executive and then presented to Parliament for discussion and approval. Parliament has the power to amend or reject the policy placed before it, but it has not the capacity to substitute on any regular basis a policy of its own. Parliament has looked to the executive to take the initiative in the formulation of public policy, and it continues to do so.

The second generalisation concerns the various tasks, or functions, fulfilled by Parliament. Parliament is a multifunctional body. Not only does it serve as

BOX 17.1 IDEAS AND PERSPECTIVES

Types of legislature

- *Policy-making legislatures*: These are legislatures that not only can modify or reject measures brought forward by the executive but also can formulate and substitute policy of their own (e.g. the US Congress).
- *Policy-influencing legislatures*: These are legislatures that can modify and sometimes reject measures brought forward by the executive but lack the capacity to formulate and substitute policy of their own (e.g. UK Parliament, German Bundestag).
- *Legislatures with little or no policy effect*: These are legislatures that can neither modify nor reject measures brought forward by the executive, nor formulate and substitute policies of their own. They typically meet for only a short period each year to give formal approval to whatever is placed before them (e.g. former legislatures of Eastern European communist states, such as East Germany).

a reactive body in the making of public policy, it also carries out several other tasks. Its principal tasks were established within the first two centuries of its development. In the fourteenth century, the King accepted that taxes should not be levied without the assent of Parliament. The giving of such assent was variously withheld until the King responded to petitions requesting a redress of grievances. At the same time, Parliament began to take an interest in how money was spent and began to look at the actions of public servants. It became, in a rather haphazard way, a body for the critical scrutiny of government.

■ The development of Parliament

Knights and burgesses were summoned in the thirteenth century in order to give assent to the King's decision to raise extra taxes. They joined the King's court, comprising the leading churchmen and barons of the realm. In the fourteenth century, the summoning of knights and burgesses became a regular feature of those occasions when the King summoned a 'parliament'. At various times during the century, the knights and burgesses sat separately from the churchmen and barons, so there developed two chambers – the Commons and the Lords.

The House of Commons became more significant in subsequent centuries. It was an important political actor during the Tudor reigns of the sixteenth century and a powerful opponent of the Stuart monarchs, who asserted the divine right of kings to rule in the seventeenth. Clashes occurred between Parliament and Charles I – leading to the beheading of the King and a short-lived period of republican government under Oliver Cromwell – and, later, between Parliament and James II. The fleeing of James II in 1688 allowed leading parliamentarians to offer the throne to James's daughter and son-in-law (Mary and William) on Parliament's terms, and the supremacy of Parliament was established. Henceforth, the King could not legislate – or suspend laws – without the assent of Parliament.

Parliament nonetheless continued to look to the executive power – initially the King, and later the King's ministers assembled in Cabinet – to take the initiative in formulating measures of public policy. When measures were laid before Parliament, assent was normally forthcoming. In the eighteenth century, royal influence was employed, either directly or through the aristocratic patrons of 'rotten boroughs', to ensure the return of a House favourable to the ministry. This influence was broken in the nineteenth century. The 1832 Reform Act enlarged the electorate by 49 per cent and abolished many, although not all, rotten boroughs. The effect of the measure was to loosen the grip of the aristocracy on the House of Commons and to loosen the grip of the monarch on the choice of government. The last time a government fell for want of the monarch's confidence was in 1834. MPs entered a period when they were relatively independent in their behaviour, being prepared on occasion to oust ministers and sometimes governments (as in 1852, 1855, 1856 and 1866) and to amend and variously reject legislation. Except for the years from 1841 to 1846, party ties were extremely loose.

This so-called **golden age** was to prove short-lived. At that time, there was little public business to transact and what there was of it was reasonably easy to comprehend. Members were not tied overly to party and could make a judgement on the business before them. The consequence of the 1867 Reform Act, enlarging the electorate by 88 per cent, and of later Acts reducing corrupt practices, was to create an electorate too large, and too protected by the law, to be 'bought' by individual candidates. Extensive organisation was necessary to reach the new voters, and organised political parties soon came to dominate elections. For a winning party to govern effectively, its members in the House of Commons needed to be united, and by the end of the century cohesive party voting was a feature of parliamentary life. Party influence thus succeeded royal patronage in ensuring the assent of MPs for measures brought forward by ministers of the crown.

The effect on Parliament of the rise of a mass electorate was profound. Governments came to be chosen by the electorate, not – as had occasionally happened in preceding years – by the House of Commons. Popular demands of government engendered not only more measures of public policy, but more extensive and complex measures. By the turn of the century, Parliament lacked the political will and the institutional resources necessary to subject increasingly detailed government bills to sustained and effective scrutiny. Albeit in a somewhat different form to earlier centuries, executive dominance had returned.

For the House of Commons, though, the developments of the nineteenth century served to confirm it as the pre-eminent component of the Crown-in-

Parliament. The Glorious Revolution had established Parliament's supremacy over the King. The rise of the democratic principle in the nineteenth century established the supremacy of the elected House over the unelected. The House of Commons was clearly a representative chamber in that it was freely elected and in that its members were returned to defend and pursue the interests of electors (see Chapter 16). The House of Lords could claim to be representative in neither sense. The subordinate position of the House of Lords was confirmed by statute in the Parliament Act of 1911.

The position so established in the nineteenth century continued into the twentieth. The House of Commons remained – and remains – the dominant chamber in a Parliament dominated by party, with the initiative for measures of public policy resting with the Cabinet and with a party majority in the House ensuring the passage of those measures.

That sets the historical context. What, then, is the contemporary position of the House of Commons? What are the essential characteristics of the House – its members and its procedures? What functions does it fulfil? What tools does it have at its disposal to fulfil them? And to what extent have developments in recent years strengthened or weakened its capacity to carry out those functions?

■ The House of Commons

The House of Commons now has 646 members. The number has varied, ranging in the twentieth century from a high of 707 (1918–22) to a low of 615 (1922–45). The number was reduced in 1922 because of the loss of (most) Irish seats; it has varied in post-war years and from 1945 to 1974 stood at 630; because of the increase in the size of the population, it was increased in 1974 to 635, in 1983 to 650, in 1992 to 651 and in 1997 to 659. In 2001, there was the first reduction since 1922: the number of seats in Scotland went down from 72 to 59 to take account of the fact that Scotland had its own parliament.

Elections

The maximum life of a parliament is five years. Between 1715 and 1911, it was seven years. Members (MPs) are returned for single-member constituencies. These have been the norm since the Reform Act of 1885, although twelve double-member constituencies survived until the general election of 1950. The method of election employed is the 'first-past-the-post' system, with the candidate receiving the largest number of votes being declared the winner. This again has been the norm since 1885, although

---

BOX 17.2   IDEAS AND PERSPECTIVES

The atmosphere of the House

By the standards of the Palace of Westminster, the House of Commons (Figure 17.1) is not a particularly ornate chamber. Relatively new compared with the rest of the Palace – rebuilt after being destroyed on 10 May 1941 by enemy bombing – it has a fairly functional feel to it. When it was rebuilt, there was a change in the style but not in the size. This meant that it was too small to accommodate every member. This has proved to be beneficial on two counts. First, on the rare occasions that the House is full, it conveys a sense of theatre: some members sit on the steps in the aisles, some crowd around the Speaker's chair, some stand in packed ranks at the bar of the House. Tension rises as the Prime Minister, or another senior minister, closes for the government and the Speaker rises to put the question. Members then troop into the voting lobbies either side of the chamber. If the outcome of the vote is uncertain, the tension is close to unbearable. After ten to fifteen minutes – sometimes longer – the tellers return and those representing the winning side line up on the right at the table, facing the Speaker. Once those on the winning side realise they have won, a massive cheer goes up. The most dramatic vote of recent history was on 28 March 1979, when the Labour government lost a vote of confidence by one vote. There have been dramatic votes in the twenty-first century when the Labour government has come close to defeat, as on the second reading of the Education Bill in 2003 – even the government whips were not sure who had won

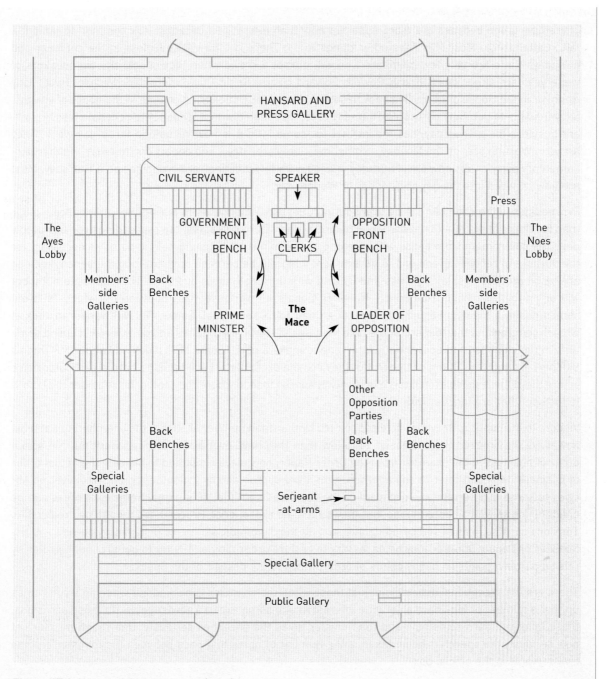

Figure 17.1 House of Commons seating plan

– or the one occasion when it was defeated: in November 2005 on a provision to allow 90-day detention without trial.

The second reason why the small chamber is better than a larger one is simply because such dramatic occasions are rare. Most of the time the chamber is notable for the rows of empty green benches as a handful of MPs sit around listening – or half-listening, or whispering to a neighbour – as one of their number delivers a speech from notes, sometimes quite copious notes. The chamber looks cavernous on such occasions. With a much larger chamber, the sheer emptiness of the place would be overwhelming.

▶

The empty green benches are more apparent now than in previous decades. It is common to lament a fall in attendance. Most MPs have other things to do. There is little vital business in the chamber and nowadays there are very few members who will attract a crowd when they speak: the big speakers of yesteryear are either dead (Enoch Powell, Edward Heath, Robin Cook), departed (Michael Foot, Tony Benn) or in the House of Lords (Michael Heseltine, Margaret Thatcher). A change in the hours of sittings, allowing MPs to get away early on a Thursday evening, coupled with a tendency to schedule less important business for a Thursday, has meant that for some MPs it is now virtually a three-day week. They arrive in Westminster on the Monday – sometimes late in the day – and depart on Thursday. Neither parliamentary party meets now on a Thursday; indeed, very few meetings are organised on a Thursday. Most are now crowded into the day on Tuesday or Wednesday.

Proceedings in the chamber can be lively during Question Time, but even during that attendance – other than for Prime Minister's Questions – can be pretty poor. During debates, the proceedings can be notably dull. The government front bench will have one or two ministers listening, taking notes as necessary for the purpose of replying at the end. A government whip will be perched further along the bench, keeping an eye on proceedings, taking notes and liaising with the Chair about business. Their opposite numbers will be on the Opposition front bench. Notes or signals will variously pass between the whips, followed sometimes by a meeting behind the Speaker's Chair to fix some deal. Some MPs will wander in, look at what is going on and then depart. Some take their seats, stay a few minutes and go. A few will spend some time in the chamber and occasionally intervene to make a point. Some MPs (such as Labour MP Dennis Skinner) are regulars in the chamber, but they are the exceptions. Each tends to have a particular place where they like to sit, so even if there is plenty of space close to where they enter the chamber they move to the spot they are familiar with.

Visitors to the public gallery may be disappointed by the small number of MPs in the chamber, but at least nowadays the proceedings are easier to follow than they have ever been. One can work out the actual order of business in the chamber from the Order Paper, nowadays simplified to indicate the actual order of business. MPs still refer to one another in the third person and by constituency, but whenever an MP rises to speak or intervene the occupant of the Chair calls out the MP's name. Some exchanges can be enlightening as well as entertaining, but they tend to be exceptional. Proceedings tend to be predictable. Tensions can rise in an ill-tempered debate, and all the diplomatic skills – or disciplinary powers – of the Speaker or Deputy Speaker may be necessary to restore order. Some MPs try to get around the rules by raising partisan points on bogus points of order, much to the despair of the Speaker.

There are the exceptional debates, not just those when the chamber is packed but when an issue comes up that a number of MPs have a genuine interest in and some expert knowledge of. On those occasions, those listening learn something and the minister takes the speeches seriously. One rough measure of how seriously the speech is being taken is the number of notes that pass between the minister and the civil servants in the official box.

For members of the public, proceedings are not only easier to follow than before but they are also now permitted to take notes. One inconvenience, however, is that they now sit behind a screen to watch MPs at work. The screen was installed for reasons of security – not so much to protect ordinary MPs but rather the Prime Minister and members of the Cabinet – and serves as a reminder of the difficult times in which public figures have to operate.

not until the general election of 1950 (with the abolition of university seats, for some of which a system of proportional representation was used) did it become universal. All seats nowadays are contested by two or more candidates. Again, this is a relatively recent development. In elections before 1945 a significant fraction of members – an average of 13 per cent – were returned unopposed. As late as the 1951 election, four Ulster Unionist MPs were returned in uncontested elections.

Each constituency comprises a defined geographical area, and the MP is returned to represent all citizens living within that area. (University seats were exceptional: the constituencies comprised graduates of the universities, regardless of where they were living.) Constituency boundaries are at present drawn up and revised regularly by independent Boundary Commissions (one covering each country – England, Scotland, Wales and Northern Ireland); each commission is chaired formally by the Speaker of the House of Commons, although the essential work of leadership is undertaken by a deputy, who is a judge. Under existing legislation, boundary reviews are required every eight to twelve years. The commissions are enjoined to produce constituencies within each country of roughly equal size (in terms of the number of electors), although as far as possible retaining existing county and natural boundaries. Under the Political Parties, Elections and Referendums Act 2000, the Boundary Commissions will in due course be absorbed by the Electoral Commission. The Electoral Commission, created by the 2000 Act, reports on elections and referendums, oversees the registration of, and donations to, political parties, and seeks to raise public awareness of elections.

Members

Although the House may constitute a representative assembly in that it is freely elected and MPs are returned to defend and pursue the interests of constituents, it is not a representative assembly in being typical of the socio-economic population that elects it. The members returned to the House are generally male, middle-class and white. These characteristics have been marked throughout the twentieth century. The House has tended to become even more middle-class in the years since 1945. Before 1945, and especially in the early years of the century, the Conservative ranks contained a significant number of upper-class and upper middle-class men of private means, while the parliamentary Labour Party (the PLP) was notable for the number of MPs from manual working-class backgrounds: they constituted a little over half of the PLP from 1922 to 1935 and before that had been in an overwhelming majority (Rush, 1979, pp. 69–123). Since 1945, the number of business people on the Conservative benches has increased, as has the number of graduates, often journalists or teachers, on the Labour benches.

Table 17.1 University-educated MPs, 2005 (%)

Party	University (all)	Oxford and Cambridge
Labour	64	16
Conservative	81	43
Liberal Democrat	79	31

Source: B. Criddle (2005) 'MPs and candidates', in D. Kavanagh and D. Butler (eds), *The British General Election of 2005*. Reproduced with permission of Palgrave Macmillan

The shift in the background of Conservative MPs since 1945 is reflected in education as well as occupation. In 1945, just over 83 per cent of Conservative MPs had been educated at public schools – 27 per cent at Eton. Almost two-thirds – 65 per cent – had been to university, with half having gone to Oxford or Cambridge. Sixty years later – in the parliament elected in 2005 – 60 per cent were public school educated, with just under 8 per cent having been at Eton; 81 per cent had been at university, the proportion having gone to Oxford or Cambridge comprising 43 per cent (see Table 17.1). The party has witnessed, particularly in the general elections in and since 1979, a growing number of newly elected candidates who have gone to state schools and then gone on to Oxbridge or some other university. The underlying trend continues to be for the proportion of university-educated MPs to be greater among the new intake of MPs than among the parliamentary party as a whole, and for a university education to be more prevalent among MPs than among unsuccessful candidates. The trend also continues of new MPs being less likely to have attended Eton than Conservative MPs as a whole. In the 2005 general election, 'the new Conservative intake was less elitist with fewer than half from private schools and fewer with the elitist pedigree of "public school and Oxbridge" – only 22 per cent of newcomers compared to 35 per cent in the entire Parliamentary Party' (Criddle, 2005, pp. 165–6). The members of the parliamentary party are not socially typical, but they are somewhat more middle-class than the members elected in the years before 1979.

On the Labour side, the notable change in educational background has been the rise in the number of graduates. In 1945, just over one-third of Labour MPs (34 per cent) had been to university. By 1970, just over half of the PLP were university graduates. In the parliaments of Labour governments from 1997 onwards, approximately two out of every three

Labour MPs had been to university, though the figure dipped slightly in 2005. In 1997 the figure was 66 per cent, in 2001 it was 67 per cent and in 2005 it was 64 per cent (Table 17.1). Most of these were graduates of universities other than Oxford and Cambridge. The percentage of Oxbridge-educated Labour MPs has shown little change – the percentage educated at Oxbridge in 2005 (16 per cent) was almost identical to that of 1945.

These figures reflect the growing middle-class nature of the PLP. The percentage of manual workers in the party declined in each successive parliament until 1974, increased in 1979 and 1983, but then dropped back in subsequent elections. Only 17 per cent of new Labour MPs in 1992 were drawn from manual backgrounds. It declined further in subsequent elections, reaching its lowest percentage ever – 10 per cent – in 2005; only two of the new intake in 2005 came from a manual background. 'Labour MPs', as Byron Criddle noted in his analysis of the 2005 Parliament, 'were increasingly drawn from the ranks of professional politicians, who dominated the new intake and who had come to rival the weight of the teaching profession' (Criddle, 2005, p. 166).

Indeed, there is something of a convergence between members on both sides in terms of education and background. Of new MPs elected to the House of Commons, the vast majority – on both sides of the House – are university-educated, and a large proportion are drawn not only from some middle-class occupation but from an occupation that is in the domain of politics or communication. Teachers, journalists and political staffers have been notable among the new intake of Labour MPs in and since 1997; just over 20 per cent of Labour MPs returned in 2005 had been academics or teachers. Business and the professions continue to dominate on the Conservative benches, though 17 per cent of the Tory MPs elected in 2005 had been political organisers, publishers or journalists.

This convergence also reflects the growth of the 'career politician' – the individual who lives for politics, who seeks entry to the House of Commons as early as possible and who seeks to stay in the House for as long as possible, ideally holding government office along the way (King, 1981; Riddell, 1993). Career politicians are contrasted with old-style MPs, who used to make a mark in other fields before becoming involved in politics and who could – and variously did – leave the House of Commons to pursue some other interest (for example, heading a major company or the family firm). The old-style

members may have been ambitious in terms of government office, but they recognised that there was more to life than politics. For career politicians, politics is their life. The career politician has always existed in British politics, but their numbers have grown in recent years. They often (though not in all cases) hold a job in an area related to politics before seeking election. The consequence of the growth of the career politician is something we shall consider later.

Where there is a difference between the two sides is in terms of council experience and in terms of gender. Labour MPs are more likely to have served as local councillors. Of the new MPs elected in 1997, almost two-thirds of Labour MPs had served as councillors, compared with one-quarter of Conservative MPs. The new but relatively small Labour intake of 2001 also included a number of long-standing councillors, especially in safe Labour seats (Criddle, 2002, p. 192). There are also many more women sitting on the Labour benches than on the Conservative (and Liberal Democrat) benches.

Women became eligible to sit in the House only in 1918. The number elected since then has been small. Between 1918 and 1974, the total number of women elected to the House was only 112 (including Countess Markievicz, the first woman elected but who, as a Sinn Fein candidate, did not take her seat). In the 1983 general election, twenty-three women were elected to the House; in 1987 the figure was forty-one and in 1992 it was sixty, still less than 10 per cent of the membership. The Labour Party in 1993 adopted a policy of all-women short lists in a number of constituencies in order to boost the number of female Labour MPs. Although the policy was struck down by an employment tribunal in 1996 (see Chapter 23) on the grounds that it breached sex discrimination legislation, this did not affect seats where female candidates had already been selected. As a result, a record number of female Labour MPs were elected in 1997: no less than 101, sixty-four of them elected for the first time. Labour replaced all-women short lists with 50–50 short lists (half of the candidates female, the other half male) but this failed to push up the number of women candidates. In the 2001 election, the number of women MPs dropped to 118. However, more were adopted for safe seats in the subsequent Parliament and in 2005 the number increased to an all-time high of 128, just under 20 per cent of the total.

The number of women MPs on the Labour benches is more marked than on the benches of

Table 17.2 Women elected to Parliament, 2005

Party	Number of women MPs (2001 figure in parentheses)	
Labour	98	(95)
Conservative	17	(14)
Liberal Democrat	10	(5)
SNP	0	(1)
United Ulster Unionists	1	(1)
Democratic Unionists	1	(1)
Sinn Fein	1	(1)
Other	0	(0)
Total	128	118

Source: From B. Criddle (2005) 'MPs and candidates', in D. Kavanagh and D. Butler (eds) *The British General Election of 2005*, p. 159. Reproduced with permission of Palgrave Macmillan

other parties. Although Conservative leaders have encouraged local parties to adopt female candidates, very few have done so. The result has been a notable disparity between the parties (see Table 17.2). In 2005, seventeen women were elected as Conservative MPs, three more than in 1997; although a record number, it still represented less than 9 per cent of the parliamentary party. The Liberal Democrats have also had problems in getting more women elected; in 2005 they managed to double – from five to ten – the number of female MPs; again, an all-time high but one that represented only 16 per cent of Liberal Democrat MPs. The percentage of women MPs in the House of Commons in recent parliaments remains low compared to some other countries – especially the Nordic countries – but it is now above the average for national parliaments. Data compiled by the Inter-Parliamentary Union show that in 2005 the UK ranked fifty-first out of 187 national parliaments in terms of the proportion of women members.

The number of non-white MPs remains very small. For most of the twentieth century there were none at all. The first non-white MP was elected in 1892: Dadabhai Naoroji, an Indian, was elected as Liberal MP for Finsbury Central. Another Indian was elected as a Conservative three years later. A third sat from 1922 to 1929. There was then a fifty-eight-year gap. In 1987, four non-white MPs were elected. In 1992 the number increased to six (five Labour and one Conservative) and in 1997 to nine (all Labour), including the first Muslim MP and two Sikhs. In 2001, the figure reached twelve, again all sitting on

the Labour benches (although the Conservatives did have one MP who was Anglo-Indian). In 2005, the number increased to fifteen, with thirteen on the Labour benches (four of them Muslims) and the Conservatives now having two MPs from ethnic backgrounds – one black and one Asian. The fifteen represent 2.3 per cent of MPs – another all-time high – but still less than half of what would correspond to the proportion in the population.

One reason for the persistence of white, male MPs is the length of time that MPs typically serve in the House. Some MPs sit for thirty or forty years. The Father of the House of Commons (the longest continuously serving MP), Labour MP Alan Williams, was first elected in 1964. Another MP, Conservative Sir Peter Tapsell, was elected in 1959 but has not had continuous service, losing his seat in 1964 and being returned for another in 1966. Seven MPs – including well-known figures such as Kenneth Clarke, John Prescott and Dennis Skinner – have served continuously since 1970. A typical member sits for about twenty years. Given the growth in the number of career politicians, it is unlikely that this figure will decrease; if anything, the reverse. Even if parties are keen to replace existing MPs with candidates from a wider range of backgrounds, the opportunity to replace them does not necessarily come up very quickly. The length of service of legislators is a particular feature of the British House of Commons: MPs tend to serve as members longer than legislators in other comparable legislatures (see Table 17.3). Even in the 1997 general election,

Table 17.3 Average length of legislative service, 1994

Country	Average length of service (years)
Canada	6.5
France	7
Denmark	7.8
Germany	8.2
Israel	11
USA (Senate)	11.1
USA (House)	12.2
New Zealand	13.1
Japan	15
United Kingdom	20

Source: A. Somit and A. Roemmele (1995) 'The victorious legislative incumbent as a threat to democracy', *Legislative Studies Newsletter*, Vol. 18, No. 2, July. Reproduced by permission of A. Somit

which – as a result of a massive swing to the Labour party – brought in a record number of new MPs (no fewer than 253), more than 60 per cent of MPs had served in the previous parliament. More than thirty MPs had first been elected to parliament in 1970 or earlier. However, the figures suggest that even when the opportunity exists to select a new candidate, local parties tend to select candidates in the same mould as their predecessors.

Members are paid an annual salary, but until 1912 they received no payment at all. Since then, they have been paid, but on a relatively modest basis. In 1954, for example, the salary was £1,250 and in 1964 it was increased to £3,250. In January 1996, an MP's salary was £34,086, fairly modest by international comparison – legislators in Italy, the USA, France and Germany were all paid considerably more (more than twice as much in Italy and the USA) – and by comparison with higher levels of management in the UK. (Ministers receive higher salaries.) In July 1996, MPs voted to increase their salaries by 26 per cent, to £43,000. The increase was controversial, and unpopular, but it still left MPs lagging behind the salaries of members of other comparable legislatures. The salary has increased since and, in April 2005, it was set at £59,095.

Since the 1960s, parliamentary facilities have also improved. In the mid-1960s, an MP was guaranteed only a locker in which to keep papers and received no allowance, whether for hiring a secretary or even to cover the cost of telephone calls. If an MP was lucky enough to have an office, it was usually shared with several other MPs. A secretary had to be paid out of the MP's own pocket. A secretarial allowance was introduced in 1969. This allowance evolved into an office cost allowance, allowing an MP to hire one and sometimes two secretaries and in most cases a research assistant (more often than not, part-time). In 1999, the office cost allowance stood at £50,264. In 2001, the House agreed to a new system. Each MP can claim a Staff Cost Allowance, enabling them to employ up to the equivalent of three full-time staff, but with the staff paid centrally by the House authorities and on agreed rates with standard contracts. For 2005/6, the Staff Cost Allowance was a maximum of £84,081. Each MP can also claim a further £20,000 towards incidental expenses. Other costs, such as IT and training, are now met from central funds. MPs can also claim travel expenses and, for those living outside London (and thus having to maintain two homes), an Additional Costs Allowance up to £21,634. MPs with inner London constituencies receive a London supplement of £2,613.

The physical space available to MPs has also increased. Buildings close to the Palace of Westminster – including the former Scotland Yard buildings in Derby Gate, known as the Norman Shaw Buildings – were acquired for parliamentary use. More recently, buildings in Parliament Street – between Whitehall and Parliament Square – were taken over and redeveloped, retaining the exterior but with a modern and integrated complex of offices inside. They have the address of 1 Parliament Street. To these have been added a major purpose-built parliamentary building, known as Portcullis House, in Bridge Street, just across the road from Big Ben. With the completion of Portcullis House, which includes rooms for committee meetings as well as suites of offices for MPs, each MP now has an office.

Sittings of the House

The House to which Members are returned meets annually, each parliamentary session running usually now from November to November. There is a long summer adjournment, but the session is not prorogued (formally closed) until shortly after the House returns in the autumn; that allows the House to meet and deal with bills which have not completed their passage. The effect of prorogation is to kill off unfinished public business; any bills that have not received the Royal Assent fall, though there is now provision for some bills to be carried over from one session to another.

The House usually sits for more than 150 days a year, a not unusual number compared with some other legislatures, such as those of the USA, Canada and France, although considerably more than most other legislatures. What makes it distinctive is the number of hours for which it sits: it sits for more than 1,200 hours a year. The figures for the 2001–5 parliament are given in Table 17.4. In previous parliaments, the sittings were sometimes longer, averaging nearly 1,500 hours in non-election sessions in the 1987–92 parliament. Other elected chambers are not able to compete with these figures.

Until 1999, the House sat at 2.30 p.m. on the first four days of the week and at 9.30 a.m. on Fridays. On the first four days, it usually rose by 10.30 p.m. In an experiment started in 1999, it started meeting at 11.30 a.m. on Thursdays (rising earlier in the evening, usually by 7.00 or 8.00 p.m.). In 2002, the House agreed to meet at 11.30 a.m. on Tuesdays

Table 17.4 The House of Commons: length of sittings, 2001–5

Session	Number of sitting days	Number of hours sat	Average length of sitting day
2001–2[a]	201	1,297	7 hours 40 minutes
2002–3	162	1,287	7 hours 57 minutes
2003–4	157	1,215	7 hours 44 minutes
2004–5[b]	65	535	8 hours 14 minutes

[a] Long session following a spring general election.
[b] Short session, because of the calling of a general election.
Source: From the *House of Commons Sessional Information Digests, 2001–5*. © Parliamentary Copyright 2005. Parliamentary copyright material is reproduced with the permission of the Controller of Her Majesty's Stationery Office (HMSO) on behalf of Parliament

and Wednesdays as well, with the House rising by 7.00 p.m. (by 6.00 p.m. on Thursdays). The new sitting times took effect in 2003. However, they did not prove popular with all MPs (especially with MPs living long distances from London) and in 2005 the House voted to revert to a 2.30 p.m. start on a Tuesday, though agreeing to sit at 10.30 a.m. on a Thursday. The House thus has an uneven pattern of sitting times: 2.30 p.m. on Monday and Tuesday, 11.30 a.m. on Wednesday, 10.30 a.m. on Thursday, and (if sitting) 9.30 a.m. on Friday. Sittings may, in certain circumstances, be extended in order to transact particular business. Late or all-night sittings variously take place to get through the remaining stages of a bill. (If the House has an all-night sitting and is still sitting when the new day's sitting is scheduled to commence, then the business for that next day falls.) Late-night sittings became rare in the 1992–7 parliament but were employed again following the return of a Labour government in 1997 in order to get some of its major legislation through. On Fridays, when **private members' bills** are normally discussed, the House rises at 3.00 p.m. To give MPs more time to be in their constituencies, the House does not sit every Friday: ten Fridays each session are designated as non-sitting Fridays.

As a result of a change agreed by the House in 1999, there is also a 'parallel chamber', or 'main committee', allowing MPs to meet and discuss issues separate from the main chamber (see Box 17.3). This allows for non-contentious issues to be debated. Meetings are held in the Grand Committee Room, just off Westminster Hall, and are known formally as meetings in Westminster Hall. The topics covered on Tuesdays and Wednesdays each week are proposed by private Members; the Thursday sitting is given over to a debate on a subject of general interest or a select committee report. All MPs can attend – as in the main chamber – although in practice few do so.

Function

The principal function of the House is often seen as involvement in law making. It is, after all, classified as a legislature and the name means carrier, or giver, of law. In practice, as we have seen, the House essentially responds to the measures that the government brings forward. Furthermore, much of the time of the House is given over to business that has nothing directly to do with legislation. Question Time is now an established feature of the House. It is not part of the legislative process. When the House debates the economy or the government's industrial policy, those debates again are not part of the formal legislative process. The House has an important role to play in the legislative process, but it is clearly not its only role.

The principal functions of the House can be grouped under four headings: those of legitimisation, recruitment, scrutiny and influence, and expression. Several other functions can be identified (see Norton, 2005) but these can largely be subsumed under these four broad headings.

Legitimisation

The primary purpose for which the representatives of the counties and boroughs (the communes) were first summoned was to assent to the King's demand for additional taxes. Subsequently, their assent also came to be necessary for legislation. The House has thus been, since its inception, a legitimising body.

The House fulfils the task of 'manifest legitimisation', that is, the overt, conscious giving of assent. In the UK the function has two elements: the giving of

BOX 17.3   IDEAS AND PERSPECTIVES

Meetings in Westminster Hall

In December 1999, the House of Commons introduced a new form of meeting – meetings in Westminster Hall. These enable MPs to meet separately from the main chamber, and the gathering is sometimes described as a parallel chamber. (The parallel chamber is modelled on Australian experience.) Meetings in Westminster Hall are open to all MPs. They can come in as they can in the main chamber. The principal differences between the main chamber and the room used for the parallel chamber are of size and structure. The room used – the Grand Committee Room, located just off the cavernous Westminster Hall – is much smaller than the chamber of the House of Commons. (For part of 2006 another room was used while the Grand Committee Room was redeveloped.) It also differs in structure. MPs sit at desks arranged in a semicircle around a raised dais. The desks are fixed and have desktop microphones. Meetings are presided over by a Deputy Speaker or one of the MPs on the Chairmen's Panel (senior MPs who are drawn on in order to chair standing committees) and are usually used for discussing non-contentious business. Votes cannot be held. Meetings now take place from 9.30 a.m. to 2.00 p.m. on Tuesdays, from 9.30 to 11.30 a.m. and from 2.30 to 5.00 p.m. on Wednesdays, and from 2.30 to 5.30 p.m. on Thursdays. On Tuesdays and Wednesdays, there are short debates on topics raised by individual members. Thus, for example, on Tuesday 15 November 2005, four of the five debates were on constituency-related issues, such as the performance of the West Mercia constabulary and transport in Pudsey. The following day, topics included a tunnel for the A3 at Hindhead and the NHS in Oxfordshire. Thursday sittings are given over to debates on general topics (such as eGovernment) or select committee reports. Thus, on Thursday 17 November 2005, the report of the Home Affairs Committee on the Rehabilitation of Offenders was considered. Attendance at meetings is low – usually a handful of MPs – not dissimilar to the chamber itself when private members' motions are taken.

The creation of the parallel chamber was controversial. Supporters see it as a way of allowing issues, for which there would otherwise be no time in the chamber, to be discussed. Most Conservative MPs voted against setting it up because they feared it would serve to distract attention from the chamber and absorb MPs' energies on minor issues. In the event, meetings of the new body have proved low-key, attracting virtually no media attention (the inaugural meeting was effectively ignored) and very little attention on the part of MPs. The chamber was initially employed on an experimental basis, but MPs subsequently voted to make it permanent. It was not seen as damaging to the main chamber and back-benchers have found it useful as a means of raising issues that they might not have the opportunity to raise in the main chamber. Each debate brings an issue to the attention of government, with a junior minister replying. The proceedings are published in *Hansard*.

assent to bills and to requests for supply (money) and the giving of assent to the government itself. The government depends on the confidence of the House of Commons for its continuance in office. If the House withdraws its confidence, then by convention the government resigns or requests a dissolution of Parliament.

The House proceeds on the basis of motions laid before it: for example, to give a bill a second reading or to express confidence in the government. By approving such motions, the House gives its formal – manifest – assent. Members may vote on motions. The Speaker of the House asks those supporting the motion to say 'aye', those opposing to say 'no'. If no dissenting voices are heard, the Speaker declares that 'the ayes have it'. If some MPs shout 'no' and persist then members divide (that is, vote). A simple majority is all that is necessary. (This is subject to two basic requirements: that at least forty MPs – a quorum – are shown by the division to be present and that, in voting on a closure motion, at least 100 MPs have voted in favour.) Members vote by trooping through two lobbies, known as the division lobbies (an 'aye' lobby and a 'no' lobby), where they are counted and their names recorded. The result of the vote is then announced in the chamber.

It is this accepted need for the House to confer legitimacy through giving its assent that constitutes the basic power of the House in relation to government. Initially, the knights and burgesses summoned to the King's court were expected to give assent. Gradually, members began to realise that, as a body, they could deny assent to supply and later to legislation. This formed the basis on which they could ensure the effective fulfilment of other functions. It remains the basis of the power of the House of Commons. Without the assent of the House, no measure can become an Act of Parliament. The contemporary point of contention is the extent to which the House is prepared to use its power to deny assent. Critics contend that the effect of the growth of party and hence party cohesion has largely nullified the willingness of the House to employ it.

The House also fulfils what Robert Packenham has termed the function of 'latent legitimisation'. According to Packenham, this derives from the fact that 'simply by meeting regularly and uninterruptedly, the legislature produces, among the relevant populace and élites, a wider and deeper sense of the government's moral right to rule than would otherwise have obtained' (Packenham, in Norton, 1990, p. 87). However, it can be argued that such activity is necessary but not sufficient to generate such an underlying sense of legitimacy. Latent legitimacy can be said to derive from the House fulfilling the other functions expected of it (Norton, 2005, p. 10). Given that Parliament not only sits regularly but has fulfilled a range of tasks expected of it for a considerable period of time, it is arguably a much stronger agent of latent legitimisation than many other legislatures. It would seem plausible to hypothesise that the function is weaker in a political system in which the legislature is a recent and conscious creation of resuscitation by the prevailing regime and fails to carry out tasks expected of it by the people.

Recruitment

Ministers are normally drawn from, and remain within, Parliament. The situation is governed solely by convention. There is no legal requirement that a minister has to be an MP or peer.

The practice of appointing ministers from those who sit in Parliament derives from expediency. Historically, it was to the King's benefit to have his ministers in Parliament, where they could influence, lead and marshal support for the crown. It was to the benefit of Parliament to have ministers who could answer for their conduct. An attempt was made early in the eighteenth century to prevent ministers

from sitting in Parliament, but the legislation was superseded by another law allowing the practice to continue (Norton, 2005, p. 43).

The convention that ministers be drawn from and remain within Parliament – predominantly now, by convention, the House of Commons – is a strong one inasmuch as all ministers are currently MPs or peers. It is extremely rare for a minister to be appointed who does not sit in either House and even rarer for that person to remain outside Parliament while in office: the person is either elevated to the peerage (nowadays the most used route) or found a safe seat to contest in a by-election. On occasion, one of the Scottish law officers – the Solicitor General for Scotland – was appointed from the ranks of Scottish lawyers and remained outside Parliament, but that was the exception that proves the rule. The post ceased to be part of the UK government following devolution.

The relationship between the House and ministers is governed by convention. Under the convention of individual ministerial responsibility, ministers are answerable to the House for their own conduct and that of their particular departments. Under the convention of collective ministerial responsibility, the Cabinet is responsible to the House for government policy as a whole. It is this latter convention that requires a request for a dissolution of Parliament or the resignation of the government in the event of the House passing a **motion of no confidence** in the government.

The fact that ministers remain in Parliament clearly has a number of advantages to government. Things have not changed that much from earlier centuries in that ministers can use their positions to lead and marshal their supporters. Ministers themselves add notably to the voting strength of the government, the so-called 'payroll vote' in the House. Just over eighty ministers serve in the Commons and just over twenty in the Lords. With ministers' unpaid helpers – parliamentary private secretaries – added to the number, the payroll vote usually comprises a third or more of the MPs sat on the government side of the House. The government thus has a sizeable guaranteed vote to begin with. Party loyalty – and ambition for office – usually ensures that the votes of **back-benchers** follow those of ministers.

The convention that ministers be drawn from the ranks of parliamentarians has certain advantages for Parliament. It ensures that members are close to ministers, both formally and informally. Ministers can be questioned on the floor of the House; members can waylay them in the corridors and the division lobbies for private conversations. The fact that ministers remain as members of the House means that they retain some affinity with other members. MPs elevated to ministerial office retain their constituency duties.

Above all, though, the convention renders the House of Commons powerful as a recruiting agent. The route to ministerial office is through Parliament. In some other systems, the legislature is but one route to the top. In the USA, for example, there are multiple routes: cabinet ministers – and presidents – can be drawn from the ranks of business executives, academics, state governors, army officers and lawyers. The US Congress enjoys no monopoly on recruitment to executive office. In the UK, Parliament does have such a monopoly. Parliament is the exclusive route for those intending to reach the top of the political ladder. Those aspiring to ministerial office thus have to seek election to the House of Commons (or hope – often in vain – for a peerage) and have to make their mark in the House. The House also serves as an important testing ground for potential ministers and, indeed, for those on the ministerial ladder (see Norton, 2005, pp. 50–2). A poor performance at the despatch box can harm a minister's chances of further promotion. A consistently poor performance can result in the minister losing office. Conversely, a bravura performance at the despatch box may save a minister who is under pressure to go. For ambitious politicians, the chamber matters.

Scrutiny and influence

Scrutiny and influence are essentially conjoined functions. The House subjects both the measures and the actions of government to scrutiny. It does so through various means: debate, questioning and committee deliberations. If it does not like what is before it, it can influence the bill or the policy under consideration. It may influence solely by the force of argument. It may influence by threatening to deny assent (that is, by threatening to defeat the government). Ultimately, it may actually refuse its assent, denying the government a majority in the division lobbies.

These two functions are central to the activity of the House and absorb most of its time. Government business enjoys precedence on most days. The House spends most of its time discussing legislation and the policy and actions of ministers. Although the dominance of *party* has ensured that normally the government is assured a majority in divisions, the party *system* helps to ensure that government is subject to critical scrutiny from opposition parties in the House. The procedures of the House are premised on the existence of two principal parties, with each having the opportunity to be heard. Membership of all committees of the House replicates party strength on the floor of the House, thus ensuring that the opposition has an opportunity to offer critical comments and to force government to respond at all stages of the parliamentary process.

Furthermore, scrutiny and influence may also take place outside, or despite, the context of party. MPs sit for particular constituencies. Although elected on a party label, they are nonetheless expected to ensure that government policy does not damage constituency interests. They may also be influenced by moral and religious views that ensure they pay careful attention to bills and government policies that run counter to their personal convictions. They may also listen to bodies outside Parliament – charities, consumer groups, professional organisations, companies – that have a particular interest in, or knowledge of, the subject under debate.

However, the extent to which the House actually fulfils these functions is a matter of dispute. Critics contend that the government stranglehold, via its party majority, ensures that the House is denied the means for sustained and effective scrutiny, and that, inasmuch as it may exert some limited scrutiny, that scrutiny is not matched by the capacity to influence government. MPs may consider and find fault with a particular measure but not then prove willing to use their power to amend or reject it.

Expression

The House serves not one but several expressive functions. Members serve to express the particular views and demands of constituents. An individual constituent or a group of constituents may be affected adversely by some particular policy or by the actions of some public officials. Constituents may feel that a particular policy is bad for the constituency or for the country. Contacting the local MP will usually result in the MP passing on the views to the relevant minister and may even result in the member raising the issue on the floor of the House. The pursuit of such cases by MPs ensures that they are heard and their points considered by ministers.

MPs also express the views of different groups in society as a whole. A range of issues that do not fall within the ambit of party politics are taken up and pursued by private members. MPs may express the views of organised interests, such as particular industries or occupations. They may express the views of different sectors of society, such as students or the elderly. Many will give voice to the concerns of particular charitable, religious or moral groups. For example, some MPs press for reform of the laws governing abortion, some want to liberalise the laws concerning homosexuality, and some want to strengthen the laws on road safety. These issues can be pursued by MPs through a number of parliamentary procedures (see Cowley, 1998). In some cases, members table amendments to government bills. Another route is through the use of private members' bills. Although the more contentious the issue, the less likely the bill is to be passed, the debate on the bill serves an important function: it allows the different views to be expressed in an authoritative public forum, heard by the relevant minister and open to coverage by the mass media.

MPs, then, serve to express the views of constituents and different groups to the House and to government. MPs may also serve to express the views of the House and of government to constituents and organised groups. The House may reach a decision on a particular topic. Members may then fulfil an important role in explaining why that decision was taken. Members individually may explain decisions to constituents. **Select committees** of the House may, in effect, explain particular policies through their reports, which are read not just by government but also by groups with a particular interest in the committee's area of inquiry. The House thus has a tremendous potential to serve several expressive functions. The extent to which it does so is a matter of considerable debate. MPs have limited time and resources to pursue all the matters brought to their attention. The attention given to their activities by the media and by government may be slight. Many groups may bypass Parliament in order to express their views directly to ministers. Furthermore, it is argued, the views expressed by MPs on behalf of others are drowned out by the noise of party battle. By limiting the resources of the House and by keeping information to itself, the government has limited the capacity of the House to arm itself with the knowledge necessary to raise support for public policies.

These are the most important functions that may be ascribed to the House. The list is not an exhaustive one. Other tasks are carried out by the House. These include, for example, a disciplinary role (punishing breaches of privilege and contempt) and a small quasi-judicial role, primarily in dealing with **private legislation** (legislation affecting private interests, not to be confused with private members' legislation). Other functions often ascribed to the House can, as we have explained, be subsumed under the four main headings we have provided. However, two other functions, identified by Walter Bagehot in *The English Constitution* in 1867, have been lost by the House. One, the 'elective' function – that is, choosing the government – was held only briefly during the nineteenth century. Before then it was a function exercised by the monarch. Since then, it has passed largely, although not quite exclusively, to the electorate. The electorate chooses a government on a regular basis at general elections. The House retains the power to turn a government out through passing a motion of no confidence; but it is not a power it has exercised regularly – in the past century, it was used only in 1924 and 1979, opposition parties combining to turn out a minority government.

The other function is that of 'legislation'. Initially, the need for the House to give its assent was transformed by members into the power to initiate measures, first through the presentation of petitions to the crown and later through the introduction of bills. This power was important in the nineteenth century, when the House could be described as sharing the legislative power with government. Even so, its exercise was limited. Most legislation introduced into the House was private legislation. Since then, **public legislation** has expanded as parties have become more powerful. Parties have ensured that the power to formulate – to 'make' – legislation rests with government, with the House then giving its assent. In so far as the House has retained a residual legislative power, it is exercised through the medium of private members' legislation. However, even that legislative power can be described now as one shared with government. Since 1959, no private member's bill that has been the subject of a vote at second reading (the debate on principle) has made it to the statute book without government providing time for it.

■ Scrutiny and influence

The functions that the House retains can be described as modest but appropriate to a reactive legislature. They have developed over time. But how well are they currently carried out? The principal functions of the House in relation to the executive are those of scrutiny and influence. The means available to the House to fulfil those functions are also at the disposal of members for expressing the views of their constituents and of wider interests. They can be grouped under two headings: legislation and executive actions.

Legislation

For Parliament, the legislative process constitutes the consideration of a bill once it has been formally introduced. In recent years, some bills have been published in draft form and considered by a committee prior to formal introduction (Kennon, 2004; Hansard Society, 2004; Constitution Committee, 2004; Norton, 2005, pp. 75–7). From 1997–8 to 2003–4, twenty-nine bills were subject to such pre-legislative scrutiny. Such scrutiny enables members to examine and comment before the government has decided on the final wording, and hence may be more willing to make changes before it commits itself to the measure. Bills subject to pre-legislative scrutiny have been variously amended as a result of recommendations by the committees considering them (Norton, 2005, p. 77). The committees engaging in such scrutiny have normally been departmental **select committees**.

When a bill is formally introduced into Parliament, it has to go through a well-established process involving debate and consideration in committee. About 30–40 per cent of the time of the House is taken up with debate on bills. In the 2003–4 session – the last full-length session of the 2001–5 Parliament – it was just over 38 per cent (see Table 17.5). The bulk of this time is given over to government bills. (Private members' legislation usually occupies just under, or occasionally just over, 5 per cent of time on the floor of the House.) Every bill has to go through three 'readings' plus a committee and (usually) a report stage. The stages are shown in Table 17.6.

The first reading marks the formal introduction. No debate takes place. Indeed, at this stage there is not even a printed bill. All that is read out is the bill's title. Following first reading, the bill is printed. The second reading comprises a debate on the principle of the measure. Most government bills will be allocated a half or a full day's debate for second reading. Major bills, especially of constitutional significance, may be given two or more days for debate.

Table 17.5 Time spent on the floor of the House, 2003–4

Business	%
Addresses, including debate on Queen's Speech	3.1
Government bills	
Second reading	12.0
Committee of the whole House	1.4
Report	10.8
Third reading	1.9
Lords amendments	4.6
Allocation of time orders	1.4
Private members' bills (including ten-minute rule bills)	6.3
Private business	0.0
Government motions	
EC documents	0.4
General	2.5
Opposition motions	11.4
Adjournment	
Government debates	8.3
Last day before recess	1.2
Daily half-hour debates (at end of business)	6.6
Estimates	1.0
Money resolutions	0.3
Ways and Means resolutions (including Budget debate)	2.3
Statutory instruments	1.2
Question Time	10.9
Statements (including private notice questions and business statements)	9.4
Miscellaneous	1.3
Daily prayers	1.1
Total	**99.4**[a]

[a] Below 100 per cent because of rounding.
Source: Calculated based on data from the *House of Commons Sessional Information Digests, 2003–4*. © Parliamentary Copyright 2004. Parliamentary copyright material is reproduced with the permission of the Controller of Her Majesty's Stationery Office (HMSO) on behalf of Parliament

In the 1997–2001 Parliament, for example, the bills providing for devolution to Scotland and Wales, for an elected Greater London Authority, and for removal of most hereditary peers from membership of the House of Lords were each accorded a two-day debate.

Table 17.6 Legislative stages

Stage	Where taken	Comments
First reading	On the floor of the House	Formal introduction: no debate
Second reading	On the floor of the House[a]	Debate on the principle
[Money resolution	On the floor of the House	Commons only]
Committee	In standing committee in the Commons unless House votes otherwise (certain bills taken on the floor of the House); usually on the floor of the House in the Lords	Considered clause by clause; amendments may be made
Report[b]	On the floor of the House	Bill reported back to House; amendments may be made
Third reading	On the floor of the House	Final approval: no amendments possible in the Commons
Lords (or Commons) amendments	On the floor of the House	Consideration of amendments made by other House

[a] In the Commons, non-contentious bills may be referred to a committee.
[b] If a bill is taken in committee of the whole House in the Commons and no amendments are made, there is no report stage.

The debate itself follows a standard pattern: the minister responsible for the bill opens the debate, explaining the provisions of the bill and justifying its introduction. The relevant shadow minister then makes a speech from the opposition front bench, outlining the stance of the opposition on the bill. After these two front-bench speeches, most members present tend to leave the chamber, usually leaving a small number of MPs to listen to the remaining speeches. Back-benchers from both sides of the House are then called alternately, plus usually a member from one or more of the minor parties, and the debate is then wound up with speeches from the opposition and government front benches. (The House tends to fill up again for the winding-up speeches.) If the bill is contested, the House then divides. Debates, though not always predictable in content, are generally so in outcome: only three times in the past 100 years has the government lost a vote on second reading (in 1924, 1977 and 1986). Speeches on occasion may influence some votes, even whole debates, but they are exceptional. A government sometimes loses the argument but not usually the vote.

Once approved in principle, the bill is then sent to committee for detailed scrutiny. Some bills, because of their constitutional significance or because of the need for a speedy passage, will have their committee stage on the floor of the House. In most sessions the number is very small. The majority of bills, though, are sent to a **standing committee**, the standard practice since 1907. The name 'standing committee' is a misnomer: there is nothing permanent, or 'standing', about the committees, other than their names. The membership of each committee is appointed afresh for each bill. The committees are identified by letters of the alphabet: standing committee A, standing committee B, and so on. One committee (standing committee C) normally deals with private members' legislation. Once standing committee A has completed consideration of a bill, a new standing committee A – that is, with a different membership – is appointed to consider another bill. Because of the number of bills introduced each session, it is common for ten standing committees to be appointed; some may deal with four or five bills in a session. Each committee comprises between sixteen and fifty members. For most bills, the number appointed will usually be at the lower end of the range (sixteen to twenty members), although a larger number is appointed for big bills such as the annual finance bill. The membership reflects proportionately the party strength in the House as a whole. The purpose of the committee is to render a bill 'more generally acceptable' through scrutinising it and, if necessary, amending it. (It cannot reject it or make any amendment that runs counter to the principle of the bill that has been approved by the House on second reading.) The committee considers only the bill that is before it. Unlike a select committee, it is not empowered to receive evidence, so any outside body seeking to inform and influence it in its deliberations has to write to individual members. Each bill is considered clause by clause, the committee discussing and deciding on any amendments tabled to a clause before approving (or rejecting) the motion 'that the clause stand part of the bill'.

Each committee resembles the House in miniature, with a minister and a **whip** appointed on the government side, and the minister's opposite number and a whip serving on the opposition side. Both sides face one another, and the whips operate to marshal their members. Although cross-voting by government back-benchers can result in some defeats for the government, such occurrences are rare. The government is able to call on its supporters, who constitute not only a majority but also often a fairly silent majority on the committee. In order not to delay proceedings, government back-benchers are encouraged to keep as quiet as possible. In consequence, service on standing committees is often not popular, government back-benchers treating it as a chore and using the opportunity to read and sometimes write replies to correspondence.

After the committee stage, a bill returns to the House for the report stage. This provides an opportunity for the House to decide whether it wishes to make any further amendments and is often used by the government to introduce amendments promised during committee stage, as well as any last-minute (sometimes numerous) amendments of its own. There is, though, no report stage if a bill has been taken for its committee stage on the floor of the House and been passed without amendment.

There then follows the bill's third reading, when the House gives its final approval to the measure. Such debates are often short. If the bill is not contentious, there may be no debate at all. On completion of its third reading, the bill then goes to the House of Lords and, if the Upper House makes any amendments, the bill then returns to the Commons for it to consider the amendments. In most cases, the amendments are accepted. If not, the House of Lords usually gives way. Once both Houses have approved the bill, it then goes to the Queen for the Royal Assent. Once that assent is given, then that, as far as Parliament is concerned, concludes the legislative process.

The process is fairly well established but much criticised. The committee stage in particular was seen as partisan and unproductive (see Brazier, 2004), opposition MPs prolonging debate on early contentious clauses and the government then introducing a timetable, or guillotine, motion to impose time

limits for consideration of the remaining provisions. Guillotine motions had been variously employed since 1887 but their increased use in the last quarter of the twentieth century attracted frequent condemnation. Because of the criticism, the two principal parties agreed in 1994 to a voluntary timetabling of bills. This meant that each bill was subject to an agreed timetable, thus avoiding the need for a guillotine to be introduced. However, this agreement was not sustained in the new parliament returned in May 1997 and the Labour government variously resorted to the use of the guillotine, or what were termed programme motions, to get measures through. In 2000–1, new standing orders were introduced for programming motions, and programming is now a common and much disputed feature of business. Programme motions differ from the previous use of the guillotine in that they are introduced and agreed by the House following the second readings of bills. Most government bills are now subject to such motions. The most stringent part of programming tends to be for consideration of Lords amendments, where it is not uncommon for a programme motion to stipulate that debate on the amendments, however many or important they are, is limited to one hour.

Bills thus follow a fairly predictable route. There are some variations: some non-contentious bills, for example, can be sent to a second reading committee, thus avoiding taking up valuable debating time on the floor of the House. There is also provision for bills to be considered at committee stage by a special standing committee, the committee being empowered to take evidence from witnesses. This power, though, has been used only sparingly (see Norton, 2004, p. 11). Private members' bills are also treated differently, primarily in terms of timetabling. They have to go through all the stages listed, but time for their consideration on the floor of the House is extremely limited. Each session a ballot is held and the names of twenty private members are drawn. They are then entitled to introduce bills during the Fridays allocated to such bills, but only about the top half-dozen are likely to achieve full debates.

Bills constitute primary legislation. They often contain powers for regulations to be made under their authority once enacted. These regulations – known as delegated legislation and usually taking the form of what are termed statutory instruments – may be made subject to parliamentary approval. (Under the affirmative resolution procedure, the regulation must be approved by Parliament in order to come into force; under the negative resolution procedure, it comes into force unless Parliament disapproves it.) Some regulations, though, only have to be laid before the House and others do not even have to be laid.

Given the growth of delegated legislation in post-war years – sometimes more than 1,500 statutory instruments are introduced in a session – the House has sought to undertake scrutiny of it (Norton, 2005, pp. 91–3). Detailed, and essentially technical, scrutiny is undertaken by a Select Committee on Statutory Instruments. However, there is no requirement that the government has to wait for the committee to report on a regulation before bringing it before the House for approval, and on occasion – although not frequently – the government will seek approval before a regulation has been considered by the committee. Time for debate is also extremely limited, and much delegated legislation is hived off for discussion in a standing committee on delegated legislation. There is also a separate committee and procedure for dealing with regulatory reform orders, enabling primary legislation imposing a regulatory burden to be changed by order. There are also separate committees and procedures for dealing with draft European legislation: it is considered by a European Scrutiny Committee and, if recommended for debate, is discussed normally by one of three European standing committees.

Executive actions

Various means are employed to scrutinise and to influence the actions of government. These same means can be and usually are employed by MPs to express the views of constituents and different interests in society. The means essentially are those available on the floor of the House (debates and Question Time), those available on the committee corridor (select committees) and those available off the floor of the House (early day motions, correspondence, the parliamentary commissioner for administration, party committees and all-party groups). Some individually are of limited use. It is their use in combination that can be effective in influencing government.

Debates and Question Time

Most of the time of the House is taken up debating or questioning the actions of government. *Debates* take different forms. They can be on a substantive motion (for example, congratulating or condemning the policy of the government on a particular issue) or, in order to allow wide-ranging discussion (especially on a topic on which the government may have no fixed position), on an adjournment motion ('That this House do now adjourn'). For example, prior to the Gulf War at the beginning of 1991, the situation in the Persian Gulf was debated on an adjournment motion. After military action had begun, the House debated a substantive motion approving the action. Adjournment debates under this heading can be described as full-scale adjournment debates. They are distinct from the half-hour adjournment debates that take place at the end of every sitting of the House. These half-hour debates take the form of a back-bencher raising a particular issue and the relevant minister then responding. After exactly half an hour, the debate concludes and the House adjourns.

Debates are initiated by different bodies in the House. Most motions introduced by government are to approve legislation. However, the government occasionally initiates debates on particular policies. These can range from major issues of public policy, such as war in Iraq in 2003 to debate on essentially parliamentary matters, such as select committee nominations and the installation of the security screen in the public gallery. More frequently, debates are introduced by opposition parties. Twenty days each year are designated as opposition days. On seventeen of these twenty days, the motion (or motions – a day's debate can be split into two) is chosen by the Leader of the Opposition. On the remaining three days, the topic is chosen by the leader of the third-largest party in the House (the Liberal Democrats). One or two additional days are usually found for other parties. There are also three estimates days each session, the choice of estimate for debate being made by a select committee of the House: the Liaison Committee, comprising the MPs who chair other select committees. Private members are also responsible for initiating the topics in the daily half-hour adjournment debates: on four days a week, members are selected by ballot, and on one the Speaker chooses the member. These back-benchers' occasions provide opportunities to raise essentially non-partisan issues, especially those of concern to constituents. Although such debates are poorly attended, they allow members to put an issue on the public record and elicit a response from government.

The half-hour adjournment debates involve a back-bencher raising an issue, sometimes one or two other back-benchers making quick contributions, and then a response from a minister. Full-scale

A full House of Commons generates an atmosphere that can be gladiatorial at times
Source: PA / Empics

half-day or full-day debates initiated by government or opposition resemble instead the practice adopted in second reading debates. There are speeches from the two front benches, followed by back-bench speeches alternating between the two sides of the House, followed by winding-up speeches from the front benches and then, if necessary, a vote. The term 'debate' is itself a misnomer. Members rarely debate but rather deliver prepared speeches, which often fail to take up the points made by preceding speakers. Members wishing to take part usually inform the Speaker in advance and can usually obtain some indication from the Speaker if and when they are likely to be called. There is a tendency for members not to stay for the whole debate after they have spoken. Members, especially back-benchers, frequently address a very small audience – sometimes no more than half a dozen MPs. There is a prevailing view in the House that attendance

has dropped over recent years. MPs now have offices they can spend time in. There are competing demands on their time, and as the outcome of most votes is predictable – and members know perfectly well how they intend to vote – there appears little incentive to spend time in the chamber. Major set-piece debates – as on a motion of confidence – and a debate in which the outcome is uncertain can still attract a crowded chamber, some members having to sit on the floor or stand at the bar of the House in order to listen to the proceedings. Occasionally a particularly good speaker, such as former Conservative leader William Hague, may attract members into the chamber. Such occasions are exceptional. On most days, MPs addressing the House do so to rows of empty green benches.

Debates take place on motions. However, there is one form of business taken on the floor of the House that departs from the rule requiring a motion to be before the House. That is *Question Time*. This takes place on four days of the week – Monday to Thursday – when the House is sitting. It is the first substantive order of business once the House sits: it commences once prayers and some minor business – announcements from the Speaker, certain non-debatable motions concerning private legislation – are completed. It concludes exactly one hour after the House has commenced sitting.

Question Time itself is of relatively recent origin (see Franklin and Norton, 1993). The first recorded instance of a question being asked was in the House of Lords in 1721, and the first printed notice of questions to ministers was issued in 1835. The institution of a dedicated slot for Prime Minister's Questions is of even more recent origin, dating from July 1961. From 1961 to 1997, the Prime Minister answered questions for fifteen minutes on two days of the week (Tuesday and Thursday). In May 1997, the new Labour Prime Minister, Tony Blair, changed the procedure, answering questions for thirty minutes once a week on a Wednesday.

The practice of asking questions is popular with MPs, and the demand to ask questions exceeds the time available. Members are thus restricted in the number they can put on the order paper: no more than one to any one department on any day and no more than two in total on the day. (It is thus possible to have a question to the department answering before Prime Minister's Questions and one to the Prime Minister). Questions can be tabled up to three days in advance (five for those to the secretaries of state for Northern Ireland, Scotland and Wales) and are selected by a random computer shuffle. Questions must be precisely that – statements and expressions of opinion are inadmissible – and each must be on a matter for which the minister has responsibility. There is also an extensive list of topics (including arms sales, budgetary forecasts and purchasing contracts) on which government will not answer questions.

Ministers answer questions on a rota basis, most ministries coming up on the rota every four weeks. Some of the smaller ministries have slots for the last twenty minutes of Question Time. All questions tabled by members used to be printed on the order paper, a practice that was costly and largely pointless. The number tabled often ran into three figures, but the number of questions actually answered in the time available was usually fewer than twenty. Following changes approved by the House in 1990, only the top twenty-five – fewer if the department is

not taking up the whole of Question Time – are now printed.

The MP with the first question rises and says 'Question Number One, Mr Speaker' and then sits down. The minister rises and replies to the question. The MP is then called to put a follow-up – or 'supplementary' – question, to which the minister responds. Another member may then be permitted by the Speaker to put another supplementary. If an opposition **front-bencher** rises, he or she has priority. During Prime Minister's Question Time, the Leader of the Opposition is frequently at the despatch box and is permitted up to six interventions (and the leader of the Liberal Democrats three). The Speaker decides when to move on to the next question.

During an average session, about 2,000 to 3,000 questions will receive an oral answer. In the 2003–4 session, for example, the number was 2,206 (out of 3,687 that were published on the order paper). With supplementaries included, the figure is nearer 6,000: in 2003–4 it was 5,844.

Question Time is not the only opportunity afforded to MPs to put questions to ministers. Members can also table questions for written answer. These provide an opportunity to elicit more detailed answers than can be obtained through an oral question and are particularly useful for obtaining data from departments. The questions, along with ministers' answers, are published in *Hansard*, the official record of parliamentary proceedings. There is no limit on the number of written questions that an MP can table. The average MP tables just over 100 a session. Exceptionally, some Members table in excess of 1,000: in 2001–2, for example, Tory MP John Bercow tabled 4,206. The number tabled each year has risen over the decades (see Franklin and Norton, 1993, p. 27). By the 1990s, some sessions saw more than 40,000 questions being tabled and that figure has since been exceeded. In the 2003–4 session, the number was 54,875.

Question Time itself remains an important opportunity for back-benchers to raise issues of concern to constituents and to question ministers on differing aspects of their policies and intentions. However, it has become increasingly adversarial in nature, with opposition front-benchers participating regularly – a practice that has developed over the past thirty years – and with questions and supplementaries often being partisan in content. Some members view the proceedings, especially Prime Minister's Question Time, as a farce. However, it remains an occasion for keeping ministers on their toes (figuratively as well as literally), and it ensures that a whole range of issues is brought to the attention of ministers. It also ensures that much material is put on the public record that would not otherwise be available.

Select committees

The House has made greater use in recent years of select committees, appointed not to consider the particular details of bills (the task of standing committees) but to consider particular subjects assigned by the House. Historically, they are well-established features of parliamentary scrutiny. They were frequently used in Tudor and Stuart parliaments. Their use declined in the latter half of the nineteenth century, the government – with its party majority – not looking too favourably on bodies that could subject it to critical scrutiny. For most of the twentieth century, the use of such committees was very limited. The position changed in the 1960s and, more dramatically, in the 1970s.

The House has a number of long-standing select committees concerned with its privileges and internal arrangements. However, for the first half of the twentieth century, the House had only two major select committees for investigating the policy or actions of government: the Public Accounts Committee (PAC) and the Estimates Committee. Founded in 1861, the PAC remains in existence and is the doyen of investigative select committees. It undertakes *post hoc* (i.e. after the event) scrutiny of public expenditure, checking to ensure that it has been properly incurred for the purpose for which it was voted. The Estimates Committee was first appointed in 1912 for the purpose of examining ways in which policies could be carried out cost-effectively. In abeyance from 1914 to 1921 and again during the Second World War, it fulfilled a useful but limited role. It was abolished in 1971 and replaced by an Expenditure Committee with wider terms of reference.

The PAC and Estimates Committees were supplemented in the 1940s by a Select Committee on Statutory Instruments and in the 1950s by one on nationalised industries. There was a more deliberate and extensive use of select committees in the latter half of the 1960s, when the Labour Leader of the House, Richard Crossman, introduced several reforms to try to increase the efficiency and influence of the House. A number of select committees were established, some to cover particular policy sectors (such as science and technology) and others

particular government departments (such as education). One was also appointed to cover the newly created Parliamentary Commissioner for Administration (PCA), better known as the ombudsman. However, the experience of the committees did not meet the expectations of their supporters. They suffered from limited resources, limited attention (from back-benchers, government and the media), limited powers (they could only send for 'persons, papers and records' and make recommendations), the absence of any effective linkage between their activities and the floor of the House, and the lack of a coherent approach to, and coverage of, government policy. Some did not survive for very long. The result was a patchwork quilt of committees, with limited coverage of public policy.

Recognition of these problems led to the appointment in 1976 of a Procedure Select Committee, which reported in 1978. It recommended the appointment of a series of select committees, covering all the main departments of state, with wide terms of reference and with power to appoint specialist advisers as the committees deemed appropriate. It also recommended that committee members be selected independently of the whips, the task to be undertaken by the Select Committee of Selection, the body formally responsible for nominating members. At the beginning of the new parliament in 1979, the Conservative Leader of the House, Norman St John-Stevas, brought forward motions to give effect to the Procedure Committee recommendations. By a vote of 248 to 12, the House approved the creation of the new committees. Initially, twelve were appointed, soon joined by committees covering Scottish and Welsh affairs. In the light of their appointment, various other committees were wound up. The PAC and the Committee on the Parliamentary Commissioner were retained. In 1980, a Liaison Select Committee, comprising predominantly select committee chairmen, was appointed to coordinate the work of the committees.

The fourteen new committees began work effectively in 1980. Their number has fluctuated since, usually reflecting changes in departmental structure. Committees were also added to cover sectors or departments not previously covered, notably science and technology and, in 1994, Northern Ireland. In the parliament returned in 1997, sixteen departmental select committees were appointed. The number increased in the following parliament after changes in the structure of departments and by the end of the parliament eighteen were in existence:

Second Report
from the

Foreign Affairs Committee

Session 1998-99

Sierra Leone

Response of the Secretary of State for
Foreign and Commonwealth Affairs

Presented to Parliament
by the Secretary of State for Foreign and Commonwealth Affairs
by Command of Her Majesty
April 1999

Source: From the Foreign and Commonwealth Office
(http://www.fco.gov.uk/Files/kfile/FACresponse029899,0.pdf)

they were reappointed in the 2005 parliament. There is also what is known as the Quadripartite Select Committee, drawing four members from each of four departmental select committees (defence, foreign affairs, international development, and trade and industry) in order to examine strategic export controls. There are also several non-departmental select committees. These comprise principally 'domestic' committees – such as the Committee on Standards and Privileges and the Finance and Services Committee – but they also include investigative committees such as the PAC, Environmental Audit, Public Administration, European Scrutiny and Statutory Instruments Committees.

The eighteen departmental select committees appointed in 2005 are listed in Table 17.7. Each committee is established 'to examine the expenditure, administration and policy' of the department or departments it covers and of associated public bodies. As can be seen from the table, just over half have eleven members each; those covering the most important political subjects have fourteen. The Northern Ireland Affairs Committee is exceptional with thirteen members. (It was given thirteen mem-

bers at a time when the norm was eleven, in order to allow for MPs from Northern Ireland constituencies to be appointed.) The chairmanships of the committees are shared between the parties – usually in rough proportion to party strength in the House – although committee members are responsible for electing one of their own number from the relevant party to the chair. This power vested in committee members has variously resulted in the election of independent-minded chairmen, such as Nicholas Winterton (Conservative chairman of the Health Committee, 1991–2), Frank Field (Labour chairman of the Social Security Committee, 1990–7), Chris Mullin (Labour chairman of the Home Affairs Committee, 1997–9 and 2001–3) and Gwyneth Dunwoody (Labour chairman of the Transport Sub-Committee 1997–2002, Transport Committee since 2002).

Each committee has control of its own agenda and decides what to investigate. Unlike standing committees, they have power to take evidence, and much of their time is spent questioning witnesses. Each committee normally meets once a week when the House is sitting in order to hold a public, evidence-taking session. Unlike standing committees, the committees

Table 17.7 Departmental select committees, 2005

Committee (number of members in parentheses)	Chairman
Constitutional Affairs (11)	Rt Hon. Alan Beith (Lib Dem)
Culture, Media and Sport (11)	John Whittingdale (Con)
Defence (14)	Rt Hon. James Arbuthnot (Con)
Education and Skills (11)	Barry Sheerman (Lab)
Environment, Food and Rural Affairs (14)	Rt Hon. Michael Jack (Con)
Foreign Affairs (14)	Mike Gapes (Lab)
Health (11)	Rt Hon. Kevin Barron (Lab)
Home Affairs (14)	Rt Hon. John Denham (Lab)
International Development (11)	Malcolm Bruce (Lib Dem)
Northern Ireland Affairs (13)	Sir Patrick Cormack (Con)
Office of the Deputy Prime Minister (11)	Dr Phyllis Starkey (Lab)
Science and Technology (11)	Phil Willis (Lib Dem)
Scottish Affairs (11)	Mohammad Sarwar (Lab)
Trade and Industry (14)	Peter Luff (Con)
Transport (11)	Gwyneth Dunwoody (Lab)
Treasury (14)	Rt Hon. John McFall (Lab)
Welsh Affairs (11)	Dr Hywel Francis (Lab)
Work and Pensions (11)	Terry Rooney (Lab)

are not arranged in adversarial format, government supporters facing opposition MPs, but instead sit in a horseshoe shape, MPs sitting around the horseshoe – not necessarily grouped according to party – with the witness or witnesses seated in the gap of the horseshoe. Each session will normally last between one and two hours.

Committee practices vary. Some hold long-term inquiries, some go for short-term inquiries, and some adopt a mixture of the two approaches. Some will also summon senior ministers for a single session just to review present policy and not as part of a continuing inquiry. The Chancellor of the Exchequer, for example, appears each year before the Treasury Committee for a wide-ranging session on economic policy. Although committees cannot force ministers to attend, the attendance of the appropriate minister is normally easily arranged. So, too, is the attendance of civil servants, although they cannot divulge information on advice offered to ministers or express opinions on policy: that is left to ministers. Attendance by ministers and civil servants before committees is regular and frequent, although most witnesses called by committees represent outside bodies. In investigating a particular subject, a committee will call as witnesses representatives of bodies working in the area or with a particular expertise or interest in it. Figure 17.2 shows but part of the agenda of select committee meetings and witnesses in a typical week.

Tuesday 6 December 2005

CULTURE, MEDIA AND SPORT

Subject: Analogue Switch-Off

Witnesses: Clive Jones, Chief Executive, ITV News and Regions, and Christy Swords, Director of Regulatory Affairs for ITV plc and Managing Director of ITV London, ITV; Andy Duncan, Chief Executive and David Scott, Consultant, Channel 4; Iona Jones, Chief Executive and Arshad Rasul, Director of Engineering and Technology, S4C; Jane Lighting, Chief Executive, Grant Murray, Director of Finance (also member of Board of Digital UK) and Sue Robertson, Director of Corporate Affairs, Five

WELSH AFFAIRS

Subject: Proposed Changes to the Police Forces in Wales

Witnesses: The Chief Constables of Wales; representatives from the Welsh Police Authorities

TRADE AND INDUSTRY

Subject: Progress on the WTO negotiations leading up to the Hong Kong Ministerial meeting

Witnesses: Christian Aid, Oxfam and the World Development Movement; Ian Pearson MP, Minister of State for Trade, Department for Trade and Industry

HEALTH

Subject: Public Expenditure

Witness: Rt Hon Patricia Hewitt MP, Secretary of State for Health

CONSTITUTIONAL AFFAIRS

Subject: Compensation culture

Witnesses: Rt Hon Lord Phillips of Worth Matravers, Lord Chief Justice; Council of Circuit Judges and Association of District Judges

OFFICE OF THE DEPUTY PRIME MINISTER: HOUSING, PLANNING, LOCAL GOVERNMENT AND THE REGIONS

Subject: Affordability and the Supply of Housing

Witnesses: Northern Way, West Midlands Regional Assembly; London Borough of Barking & Dagenham; Campaign to Protect Rural England (CPRE)

Figure 17.2 Meetings of select committees

At the conclusion of an inquiry, a committee draws up a report. The report is normally drafted by the committee clerk – a full-time officer of the House – under the guidance of the chairman. (Though some committees are chaired by women, both Houses retain the formal title of chairman.) It is then discussed in private session by the committee. Amendments are variously made, although it is relatively rare for committees to divide along party lines. Once agreed, the report is published. The committees are prolific in their output. From their creation in 1979 through to the summer recess in 2004, they published a total of 1,932 reports. Among the subjects being examined in 2006 were HIV/AIDS and the provision of anti-retrovirals, smoking in public places, terrorism detention powers, globalisation, the role of the IMF, piracy on the high seas, organised crime in Northern Ireland, and the efficiency savings programme in Jobcentre Plus. Most reports embody recommendations for government action. Some of the recommendations are accepted. Others become subject to the 'delayed drop' effect: the government rejects or ignores a report but several years later, without necessarily acknowledging the work of the committee, implements some of the recommendations. Overall, only a minority of the recommendations emanating from committees will be accepted and acted on by government. A more common response is to note a recommendation or to say that it is under review. A select committee has no formal powers to force the government to take any action on a report. All that the government is committed to do is to issue a written response to each report within two months of the report being published. The two-month target is not always met.

The departmental select committees, like the House itself, are multifunctional. They serve several purposes. They have added considerably to the store of knowledge of the House. They provide an important means for specialisation by members. They serve an important expressive function. By calling witnesses from outside groups, they allow those groups to get their views on the public record. The evidence from witnesses is published. Reports are now not only published in paper form but also made available on the Internet (www.parliament.uk, see under 'committees'). More time is now devoted to committee reports as a result of various Thursdays being devoted to debating them in Westminster Hall. The committees may take up the cases espoused by some of the groups, ensuring that the issue is brought onto the political agenda. The reports from the committees are read and digested by the groups, thus providing the committees with the potential to serve as important agents for mobilising support. Above all, though, the committees serve as important means for scrutinising and influencing government, especially the former. Ministers and civil servants know they may be called before committees to account for their actions. Committee sessions allow MPs to put questions to ministers in greater detail than is possible on the floor of the House. They give MPs the only opportunity they have to ask questions of officials. Not only will poor performances be noted – not least by the media – but also poor answers may attract critical comment in the committee's report. No minister or official wishes to be seen squirming in the face of difficult questions.

Select committees have thus developed as a major feature of parliamentary activity, with most MPs viewing that activity in a positive light. Their purview now even encompasses the Prime Minister. Prior to 2002, Prime Minister Tony Blair had refused requests to appear before the Public Administration Select Committee, citing the fact that his predecessors had not appeared before select committees. In 2002, he reversed his stance and agreed to appear before the Liaison Committee to answer questions. His first appearance, for two and a half hours, took place on 16 July. He now appears before the committee twice a year.

Despite these various strengths and advances, limitations remain. The membership is largely determined through the party whips. The committees have limited powers and limited resources. They have the time and resources to investigate only a small number of issues. The number of reports they issue exceeds the time available on the floor of the House or in Westminster Hall to debate them. Most reports will not be mentioned on the floor of the House or even read by most MPs. Government is committed to providing a written response to committee reports but under no obligation to take action on the recommendations made in those reports. And although ministers and officials appear before committees, they do not necessarily reveal as much as the committees would like. Although the committees constitute a major step forward for the House of Commons, many MPs would like to see them strengthened.

Early day motions

Of the other devices available to members, early day motions (EDMs) are increasingly popular, although of limited impact. A member may table a motion for debate 'on an early day'. In practice, there is invariably no time to debate such motions. However, they are printed and other MPs can add their names to them. Consequently, they are used as a form of parliamentary notice board. If a motion attracts a large number of signatures, it may induce the government to take some action or at least to pause, or it may seriously embarrass the government. This happens occasionally. In 2002, an EDM calling for the second chamber to be substantially elected attracted the signatures of more than 300 MPs and helped to undermine the Labour government's proposals to have only 20 per cent of the members elected. An EDM in 2002–3 expressing concern over possible military action against Iraq attracted the signatures of more than 150 Labour MPs, seen as a signal that the government might run into substantial opposition on its own side if it were precipitate in agreeing to use force to topple the Iraqi regime; the government subsequently suffered the largest rebellious vote by back-benchers in the postwar era. Such occasions, though, are rare. EDMs are more often used for fulfilling a limited expressive function, allowing members to make clear their views on a range of issues, often reflecting representations made to them by people and groups outside the House. Examples of such EDMs are illustrated in Figure 17.3. The range of topics is extremely broad and the number of motions tabled an increasingly large one, exacerbated by motions unrelated to public policy, for example, congratulating particular sporting teams or individuals on their achievements.

In the 1970s and 1980s, about 300–400 EDMs were tabled each year. In the 1990s, the number each year exceeded 1,000. In the 1992–7 parliament, a total of 7,831 were tabled – an average of just over 1,500 a session. The number dipped in the 1997–2001 parliament, when 3,613, an average of just over 900 a year, were submitted, but increased to a record level in the 2001–5 parliament when MPs put in a total of 6,767 – an average of 1,691 a session. Between the start of the 2005 parliament and the Christmas recess – covering five sitting months – no fewer than 1,417 EDMs and amendments were tabled. Of those, only two – one on Lupus Awareness Month and the other on Carers' Week – each attracted more than 300 signatures. The consequence of excessive use of EDMs is that their value as a means of indicating strength of opinion on an issue of political significance is devalued. Their utility, which was always limited, is thus marginal, although not non-existent.

Each is studied by the relevant government department and they still give MPs the opportunity to put issues of concern on the public record.

Correspondence

The means so far considered have been public means by which MPs can scrutinise government and make representations to it. However, a number of private means exist, two official and two unofficial. One official means is through corresponding with ministers. Since the 1950s, the flow of letters to MPs from constituents and a range of organisations (companies, charities and the like) has grown enormously. The flow increased significantly in the 1960s and increased dramatically in subsequent decades. In the late 1960s a typical MP would receive something in the region of 2,000 to 3,000 items of mail every year. In 2003, no fewer than 10 million items of mail were delivered to the House of Commons: an average of 15,000 items per MP (Norton, 2005, p. 182). The usual method for an MP to pursue a matter raised by a constituent is by writing to the relevant minister, usually forwarding the letter from the constituent. At least 10,000 to 15,000 letters a month are written by MPs to ministers.

For an MP, writing to a minister is one of the most cost-effective ways of pursuing constituency casework (see Norton and Wood, 1993, Chapter 3). A letter invites a considered, often detailed response, usually free of the party pressures that prevail in the chamber; by being a private communication, it avoids putting a minister publicly on the defensive. Ministers are thus more likely to respond sympathetically in the use of their discretion than is the case if faced with demands on the floor of the House. Furthermore, there is no limit on the number of letters an MP can write, and those letters can usually be dictated at a time of the member's choosing. Letters from MPs to ministers are accorded priority in a department – each is circulated in a special yellow folder – and have to be replied to by a minister. If a letter fails to obtain the desired response, the member has the option of then taking the matter further, either by seeing the minister or by raising the matter publicly on the floor of the House.

Correspondence is a valuable and efficient means of ensuring that a matter is considered by a minister. A great many letters on a particular problem can alert a minister to the scale of that problem and produce action. Letter writing is also a valuable means of fulfilling an expressive function. Most constituents

EDM 1300

TERMINATOR TECHNOLOGY   19.12.2005

George, Andrew   10 signatures

That this House notes the recent efforts to commercialise Terminator Technology, a genetic use restriction technology, which is designed to prevent through genetic modification farm-saved seeds from germinating; further notes the recent granting of a Terminator patent in Europe; is concerned that this technology will force farmers to purchase new seed each season, thus increasing corporate control of the food supply and threatening the food security of people in developing countries; is not convinced that this technology will prevent GM contamination of non-GM crops, food and feed supplies; is further concerned that this technology may present a threat, especially to farmers' and indigenous peoples' livelihoods, health and biodiversity; and urges the UK Government to follow the precautionary principle and therefore continue to defend, in upcoming meetings of the United Nations Convention on Biological Diversity and elsewhere in 2006, the existing decision that products incorporating Genetic Use Restriction Technologies should not be approved for field testing and commercialisation.

EDM 1291

HEALTH SERVICES IN HUDDERSFIELD AND CALDERDALE   19.12.2005

Sheerman, Barry   6 signatures

That this House notes the consultation on health services in Calderdale and Huddersfield being conducted by Calderdale and Huddersfield NHS Trust and the Huddersfield and South Huddersfield Primary Care Trusts; calls upon the trusts to ensure the provision of full maternity services, with midwives backed up by physicians in Huddersfield; urges the trusts to reconsider plans to transfer maternity, obstetrics and paediatric services to Calderdale Royal Hospital; and calls on them to prioritise the health and wellbeing of mothers and children by ensuring they have access to full specialist maternity services in Huddersfield.

EDM 1293

ZIMBABWEAN ASYLUM SEEKERS AND THE RIGHT TO WORK   19.12.2005

Hoey, Kate   21 signatures

That this House accepts that Zimbabweans refused asylum in the UK cannot be returned to Zimbabwe because of conditions prevailing in that country; is concerned that their ineligibility for state benefits renders many destitute; and calls on the Home Secretary to grant them the right to work so they can support themselves financially and make a contribution to society during their time in the UK while developing their professional and technical skills in order to contribute to the rebuilding of Zimbabwe once political change renders it safe for them to return.

Figure 17.3 Examples of early day motions to show how MPs use this device to draw attention to particular issues

who write do so to express a particular viewpoint or in order to obtain an authoritative explanation of why some action was or was not taken; only a minority write to try to have a particular decision changed. Writing to the MP is a long-established, and now much used, means for citizens to have some input into the political process. Nonetheless, correspond-ing with ministers has a number of limitations (see Norton, 2005, Chapter 9). MPs are not always well versed in the subjects raised with them by consti-tuents. Some lack sufficient interest, or knowledge of the political system, to pursue cases effectively. Increasingly, they have difficulty finding the time to deal with all the matters raised by them.

Parliamentary commissioner for administration

Since the late 1960s, MPs have had another option at their disposal in pursuing particular issues raised by constituents. The Parliamentary Commissioner for Administration – or ombudsman – was established under an Act of 1967 to investigate cases of maladministration within government. The term 'maladministration' essentially covers any error in the way a matter is handled by a public servant: it does not extend to cover the merits of policies. The ombudsman considers only complaints referred by MPs: a citizen cannot complain directly. The Commissioner enjoys some protection in office in that he or she can only be removed by an address by both Houses of Parliament to the crown. (The first female ombudsman – Ann Abraham – was appointed in 2002.) She has a relatively modest staff of just over fifty. She can summon papers and take evidence under oath. When an inquiry is completed, she sends a copy to the MP who referred the case as well as to the relevant department. Her recommendations are normally acted on. However, she labours under a number of limitations: she has a limited remit, limited resources and limited access to certain files – she has no formal powers to see Cabinet papers. Perhaps most notably, she has no powers of enforcement. If she reports that officials have acted improperly or unjustly in the exercise of their administrative duties, it is then up to government to decide what action to take in response; if it fails to act, the only remaining means available to achieve action is through parliamentary pressure.

The number of cases referred to the ombudsman has increased over the years. Most complaints are deemed not to fall within her remit. At the start of 2003–4, the ombudsman's office was dealing with 2,319 cases. Many are not taken forward – 810 in 2002–4 – and in other cases inquiries are undertaken to see whether the body that is the subject of the complaint wishes to take action that meets with the approval of the complainant. This frequently happens. In 2003–4, for example, 919 complaints were resolved in this way, with the ombudsman completing only 148 statutory investigations. Although the relevant departments usually act on the ombudsman's recommendations, the government has since 2002 twice rejected recommendations that certain factual information should be released under the Code of Practice on Access to Government Information, in 2005 rejecting the findings in a case where some applicants to a scheme to compensate people interned by the Japanese in the Second World War were excluded because they or their parents were not born in the United Kingdom, and in 2006 rejecting the findings in a case on the handling of pension schemes.

The ombudsman reports to the Public Administration Committee in the Commons which can then pursue any matters that have not been resolved satisfactorily. In December 2005, for example, it held a hearing on the report concerning the treatment of those interned by the Japanese who were denied compensation. In appearing before the committee, the relevant minister announced that the issue was being urgently reviewed.

The Commissioner thus serves a useful service to MPs – and their constituents – but constitutes something of a limited last resort and one that has no direct powers of enforcement. MPs prefer to keep casework in their own hands and pursue it with government directly. For most members, the preferred device for pursuing a matter with a minister remains that of direct correspondence.

Party committees

An important unofficial means of scrutinising and influencing government is that of party committees. These are unofficial in that they are committees of the parliamentary parties and not officially constituted committees of the House.

Each parliamentary party has some form of organisation, usually with weekly meetings of the parliamentary party. The two largest parties – Conservative and Labour – have traditionally had a sufficient number of members to sustain a series of committees. Conservative backbench committees were first established in the 1920s and established a reputation for being politically powerful (Norton, 1979, 1994). The committees had elected officers and usually met weekly to discuss forthcoming business and topics of interest, often with invited speakers. Any Tory MP could attend and if a controversial issue attracted a large audience, it signalled to the whips that there was a problem. However, the early 1990s witnessed a decline in attendance at meetings – members had many competing demands on their time – and the massive decline in the number of Conservative MPs in the 1997 general election meant that the party had insufficient numbers to maintain the committees on the scale of previous decades. As a result, the number of committees was scaled down and in 2003 a new practice instituted, with four omnibus committees sharing the same time slot and meeting on a rota basis.

Labour backbench committees traditionally lacked the clout of Conservative committees, but in the 1992–7 parliament the standing orders of the Parliamentary Labour Party (PLP) were changed in order to enhance the consultative status of the committees. Since 1997, Labour ministers have consulted with back-bench committees, some achieving a reputation for being assiduous in doing so. The committees also serve another purpose: they allow MPs to specialise in a particular subject. They enable an MP, through serving as officer of a committee, to achieve some status in the parliamentary party. This is often especially helpful to new members, giving them their first opportunity to make a mark in parliamentary life. It may also serve as way of getting noticed for the purpose of being promoted to ministerial office. However, despite their attraction to MPs and their influence within party ranks, the committees have to compete for the attention of members – there are many other demands on members' time.

All-party groups

All-party groups, like party committees, are not formally constituted committees of the House. They are formed on a cross-party basis, with officerships being shared among members of different parties. They have proved particularly popular in recent decades. In 1988 there were 103 all-party subject groups. By 2004, the number had grown to 303. (There are also 116 country groups, each bringing together MPs – and peers – with a special interest in the country concerned.) Some of the groups, known as all-party parliamentary groups, are confined to a parliamentary voting membership; some – known as associate parliamentary groups – include non-parliamentarians. The subjects covered by these groups are diverse, including, for example, AIDS, alcohol abuse, boxing, compassion in dying, electoral reform, gas safety, girl guiding, hill farming, Irish in Britain, roma affairs, and tourism. Some exist in name only. Others are active in discussing and promoting a particular cause, some pressing the government for action. Among the more influential are the disability group, the long-established parliamentary and scientific committee, and the football group, which has been active in influencing policy on such issues as safety in sports grounds (see Norton, 1993,

p. 64). The breast cancer group has been especially active in raising parliamentary awareness of the condition. Many of the all-party groups have links with relevant outside bodies – about two-thirds receive support, usually administrative, from interest groups (Norton, 2005, p. 128) – and can act as useful means of access to the political process for such groups. Like party committees, all-party groups have to compete with the other demands made on MPs' time.

In combination, then, a variety of means are available to MPs to scrutinise and influence government and through which they can serve to make known the views of citizens. The means vary in effectiveness and viewed in isolation may appear of little use. However, they are not mutually exclusive, and MPs will often use several of them in order to pursue a particular issue. An MP may write privately to a minister and, if not satisfied with the response, may table a question or seek a half-hour adjournment debate. In order to give prominence to an issue, a member may table an EDM, speak in debate and bombard the minister with a series of written questions. The most effective MPs are those who know how to use these means in combination and – on occasion – which ones to avoid.

■ Members under pressure

MPs are called on to carry out the tasks of the House. As we have seen, the resources available to them to carry out those tasks have increased in recent years. MPs have more resources than before. They have a better salary than before, and they have office and support facilities far in excess of those available to their predecessors. However, the demands on the typical MP have increased massively in recent decades, on a scale that far surpasses the increase in the resources available to deal with them. The increase in demands on MPs' time can be ascribed to four sources: public business, organised interests, constituents and MPs themselves.

Public business

The volume of business has increased in recent decades. This is particularly pronounced in terms of legislation. The number of bills introduced by the government is nowadays not much greater than it was in earlier decades. What has increased is the volume. Bills are much longer than they used to be. They are also more complex. Before 1950, no more than 1,000 pages of public Acts were passed each year. Before 1980, no more than 2,000 pages were passed each year. Since 1980, the figure has usually been in excess of 2,500 pages and on occasion has surpassed 3,000 pages. Since 2000, some bills, such as the Enterprise Bill in 2002, have been so big that they have had to be published in two parts. This increased volume places a significant strain on parliamentary resources. Most bills go to standing committees. The longer and more complex the bill, the more time it needs in committee. The Education Reform Bill in 1987–8 received more parliamentary time (200 hours) than any other postwar measure. Given that several standing committees will normally be in existence at the same time – bills frequently go for committee consideration at the same time in the session – there is a tremendous strain on the finite resources of MPs, in terms of both their number and the time they have at their disposal.

In addition to the greater volume of public legislation, there is also the burden of other business. This includes, for example, having to scrutinise EU legislation, a task that falls principally on the European Scrutiny Committee (which considers all EU documents submitted to the House) and three European standing committees, responsible for discussing documents that the House considers worthy of further consideration. It also includes the work of the select committees. As can be calculated from Table 17.7, the departmental select committees take up the time of 218 MPs. Committee work, which often requires reading a substantial amount of paperwork submitted by witnesses and outside bodies, can be time-consuming. Some of the material can be detailed and complex. All this work – in terms of both the European committees and the departmental select committees – represents a relatively recent increase in the workload of MPs; there were no European committees prior to the 1970s and, as we have seen, only a few investigative select committees. Then there are the other select committees, both investigative and domestic. Some MPs can be appointed to serve on three or four separate committees.

Organised interests

MPs have always been subject to lobbying by outside groups – groups wanting members to push for a particular outcome in terms of public policy.

However, that lobbying has become pronounced in recent decades (Norton, 2005, Chapter 10). Since 1979, organised interests – firms, charities, consumer groups, professional bodies, pressure groups – appear to have 'discovered' Parliament. Government appeared to adopt more of an arm's-length relationship with outside bodies. The departmental select committees came into being and provided particular targets for organised interests. The 1970s had also seen something of a growth in the voting independence of MPs. As a consequence of these several developments, the House of Commons looked far more attractive than ever before to organised interests wanting to influence public policy (Rush, 1990; Norton, 1999a). One survey of organised interests found that three-quarters had 'regular or frequent contact with one or more Members of Parliament' (Rush, 1990, p. 280). Of the groups that had such contact, more than 80 per cent had asked MPs to table parliamentary questions, and almost 80 per cent had asked MPs to arrange meetings at the House of Commons. Over half had asked MPs to table amendments to bills and to table a motion. It is common to hear MPs in debates refer to material they have received from interest groups (see Norton, 2005, p. 201). This contact between organised interests and MPs has a number of beneficial consequences. Among other things, Members are provided with advice and information that can prove useful in questioning government and in raising new issues. However, it also has some negative consequences. One is the demand on MPs' time. One survey of 248 MPs in 1992 found that on average an MP spent over three and a half hours a week meeting group representatives (Norris, 1997, pp. 36–7). Further time is taken up by acting on the requests of such groups and by reading and, if necessary, responding to the mass of material that is mailed by the groups. MPs now have difficulty coping with the sheer volume of lobbying material that is sent to them.

Constituents

Organised interests have been responsible for a marked increase in the mailbag of MPs. So too have constituents. We have touched already on the volume of mail received in the House of Commons in the twenty-first century. For the MP, constituency work takes priority and can occupy a large portion of the day in dictating replies to constituents' letters. It can also occupy most of every weekend, through both appearances at constituency functions and holding constituency surgeries – publicly advertised meetings at which constituents can see the MP in private to discuss particular concerns.

When an MP receives a letter from a constituent that raises a particular grievance (failure to receive a particular state benefit, for example) or issue of public policy, the MP will normally pursue the matter with the government through writing to the relevant minister. Ministers answer in the region of 250,000 letters a year, mostly from MPs.

The burden of constituency demands continues to increase, and MPs have difficulty finding the time to cope with constituency demands and the demands of public business (see Norton and Wood, 1993; Norton, 2005, pp. 189–91). By 1996 it was estimated that MPs devoted almost 40 per cent of their time to constituency business (Power, 1996, p. 14). The problem is particularly acute for MPs with constituencies close to Westminster: constituents expect them to find the time to be at constituency events, even when the House is sitting. The burden has also increased as constituents – as well as pressure groups – have made increasing use of e-mail. In 2002, the Information Committee of the Commons reported that 10–20 per cent of an MP's correspondence might be received electronically, a figure which it noted was set to climb. E-mail is quick as well as cheap – unlike letters, no stamps are required.

MPs themselves

MPs are also responsible for adding to their own burden and to that of the resources of the House. As we have seen, recent years have seen the growth of the career politician. There is a greater body of members who are keen to be re-elected and to achieve office. They are keen to be noticed in the House. Achieving a high profile in the House helps them to be noticed locally. This may help, albeit at the margins, with re-election (see Norton and Wood, 1993) and, indeed, may help with reselection by the local party. It is also considered necessary for the purposes of promotion, given the growing number of career politicians and hence the more competitive parliamentary environment. The tendency of the career politician is to table as many questions as is permissible: research assistants will variously be asked to come up with suitable drafts (see Franklin and Norton, 1993). The career politician will try to intervene as often as possible in the chamber and will table early day motions to raise issues. There is

also likely to be an allied tendency to attract media attention, not least with frequent press releases. All this adds to the burden of the MP as well as that of the MP's staff and the employees of the House.

All these pressures add up to create a particular burden for MPs. Surveys by the senior salaries review body have shown that, over the decades, the amount of time devoted to parliamentary duties has increased. One study in the 1990s suggested that MPs typically work in excess of a seventy-hour week. It is difficult for MPs to keep pace with all the demands made of them. Their resources have improved in recent years, and they have been aided considerably by new technology, but the resources have not kept pace with the demands made of members. For many MPs, it is a case of running in order to stand still. For others, it is a case of slipping backwards. There is a particularly important conflict between trying to find time for constituency work and finding time for dealing with public business in the House (Norton and Wood, 1993; Norton, 2005, pp. 189–91). So long as constituency work takes priority, then the time needed for public business is under particular pressure.

■ The House under pressure

The fact that MPs work hard for their constituents is frequently acknowledged by constituents. In the 1991 MORI state of the nation poll, 43 per cent of those questioned said they were satisfied with the job their local MP was doing for the constituency, against 23 per cent who said they were not satisfied. The figure remained virtually unchanged in later state of the nation polls in 1995 and 2001 (Norton, 2005, p. 192). The view held by citizens about the House of Commons appears more ambivalent, certainly more volatile, than the views they hold of the local MP. Over the period for which views about the local MP stayed the same, attitudes towards Parliament showed a marked shift. In the 1991 MORI poll, 59 per cent of those questioned thought that Parliament worked well or fairly well. In 1995, that figure was down to 37 per cent (see Table 17.8). The number saying it worked fairly or very badly increased from 16 to 38 per cent. As can be seen from Table 17.8, the figures have improved since but show no clear upward trend. In 1998, just over 50 per cent thought that it worked well. In 2001, with a somewhat differently worded question, the figure

Table 17.8 Views on the efficacy of Parliament overall: how well or badly do you think Parliament works?

	1973 (%)	1991 (%)	January 1995 (%)	April–May 1995 (%)	1998 (%)	2001[a] (%)
Very well	12	5	2	4	4	4
Fairly well	42	54	35	39	49	41
Neither well nor badly	n/a	21	20	22	19	16
Fairly badly	34	12	25	19	17	19
Very badly	5	4	13	11	4	11
Don't know	5	4	5	6	7	9

[a] The question asked 'how satisfied are you with the way the Westminster Parliament works?' Very satisfied, fairly satisfied, neither satisfied nor dissatisfied, fairly dissatisfied, very dissatisfied, don't know
Source: MORI, *British Public Opinion*, Vol. 21, No. 6, August 1998; and www.mori.com. Copyright © Ipsos MORI, reproduced with permission

was 45 per cent. While it can be argued that these figures do not reveal a crisis in attitudes towards Parliament, neither do they represent an overwhelming vote of confidence. Even when Parliament achieves its best ratings, this entails only five or six out of every ten citizens saying that it works well. Fewer than one in twenty say that it works very well.

What, then, might explain why attitudes towards Parliament are not more positive? The House of Commons has seen major changes in recent decades. Some of these changes, such as the creation of the departmental select committees, have reinforced the capacity of the House to fulfil a number of its functions. However, other changes – internal as well as external to the House – have served to challenge its public standing and its capacity to fulfil the tasks expected of it. These can be summarised under the headings of sleaze, partisanship, executive dominance and the creation of other policy-making bodies.

Sleaze

Throughout the twentieth century, there were various scandals involving politicians accepting illicit payments in return for some political favour. In the 1970s and 1980s, there was criticism of MPs for accepting payment to act as advisers to lobbying firms or hiring themselves out as consultants. One book, published in 1991, was entitled *MPs for Hire* (Hollingsworth, 1991). At the time it was published, 384 MPs held 522 directorships and 452 consultancies. In 1994, the issue hit the headlines when a journalist, posing as a businessman, offered twenty MPs £1,000 each to table parliamentary questions. Two Conservative MPs did not immediately say no

to the offer. The story attracted extensive media coverage. The two MPs were briefly suspended from the service of the House. The story was further fuelled later in the year when *The Guardian* claimed that two ministers had, when back-benchers, accepted money to table questions; one, Tim Smith, then promptly resigned as a minister and the other, Neil Hamilton, was eventually forced to leave office. The furore generated by the stories led the Prime Minister, John Major, to establish the Committee on Standards in Public Life, under a judge, Lord Nolan. In 1995, the House accepted the recommendations of the committee about payment from outside sources, though not without opposition from some Conservative Members. MPs went further than the committee recommended in deciding to ban any paid advocacy by MPs: members cannot advocate a particular cause in Parliament in return for payment. Members also have to disclose income received from outside bodies that is paid to them because they are MPs (for example, income as a result of working as a barrister or dentist does not have to be disclosed, but money from a company for advice on how to present a case to government does). The House also approved the recommendation to establish a code of conduct and appoint a Parliamentary Commissioner for Standards to ensure that the rules are followed. The code was subsequently drawn up and agreed. It is accompanied by a guide to the rules of the House relating to members' conduct.

The effect of the 'cash for questions' scandal was reflected in opinion polls. In a 1985 MORI poll, 46 per cent thought that 'most' MPs made a lot of money by using public office improperly. In 1994, the figure was 64 per cent, and 77 per cent agreed with the statement that 'most MPs care more about special interests than they care about people like you'. A Gallup poll found that the overwhelming majority of those questioned thought that it was wrong to accept payment for tabling parliamentary questions, to accept free holidays and to take payment for advice about parliamentary matters. Almost half thought that it was wrong to accept a free lunch at a restaurant or to accept bottles of wine or whisky at Christmas. Although there is now a code of conduct and a Parliamentary Commissioner for Standards who oversees and advises on the new rules, there appears to remain a clash between what citizens expect their MPs to do and what MPs are allowed to do under the rules of the House. MPs can still receive payment for giving advice on parliamentary matters and can receive hospitality, so long as the payment and the gifts are declared in the register of MPs' interests. There is also a clash in terms of how the rules should be enforced. Parliament relies on the Parliamentary Commissioner. In the 2000 state of the nation poll, only 7 per cent of those questioned thought that the existing system should be left as it is. Most respondents wanted either the existing system tightened up (21 per cent) or the rules to be made law, enforceable in the civil courts (34 per cent) or the criminal courts (29 per cent). A report prepared for an international body, the Council of Europe, and published in 2001 also recommended that the UK Parliament tighten its procedures (Doig, 2002, pp. 398–9). Continuing allegations of breaches of the rules after the return of a new government in 1997 did nothing to help Parliament's reputation (see Doig, 2001, 2002). The zeal with which the Parliamentary Commissioner, Elizabeth Filkin, pursued some complaints upset some parliamentarians. The failure of the House authorities to appoint Mrs Filkin to a second term in 2002 further fuelled criticism of the way that the House regulated itself. Mrs Filkin accused some MPs and ministers of applying 'quite remarkable' pressure on her.

Partisanship

The clash between the parties is a characteristic of British political life. It is a long-standing feature of the House of Commons. There is a perception that, in recent years, it has become more intense. This is reflected, for example, in the nature of Prime Minister's Question Time, where the desire for partisan point-scoring has largely squeezed out genuine attempts to elicit information (see Franklin and

Norton, 1993). However, perhaps most importantly of all, partisanship is now more publicly visible. The introduction of the television cameras to the Commons means that, in a single news broadcast covering the House, more people will see the House in that single broadcast than could ever have sat in the public gallery of the House. Although there is general support for broadcasting proceedings among public and politicians, the focus on the chamber has tended to encourage a negative perception. A 1996 MORI poll revealed a very clear perception of politicians engaged in negative point-scoring (Table 17.9). As the author of a 1999 Hansard Society study of the broadcasting of Parliament noted, 'The overwhelming perception of parliamentarians as point-scoring, unoriginal and dogmatically partisan can not be blamed entirely on negative reporting by journalists. If one purpose of broadcasting Parliament was to allow people to judge it for themselves, the low esteem MPs are held in by the public has not been elevated by ten years of live exposure' (Coleman, 1999, p. 21). When people see the House on television, they see either a largely empty chamber – MPs are busy doing things elsewhere – or a body of baying MPs, busy shouting at one another and cheering their own side. That is particularly noticeable at Prime Minister's Question Time. One Gallup poll in 1993 found that 82 per cent of those questioned agreed that what took place 'sounds like feeding time at the zoo'. As Peter Riddell noted of Prime Minister's Question Time, 'no other aspect of parliamentary life generates more public complaints' (*The Times*, 4 April 1994). For MPs who want to win the next election, supporting their own side in the chamber takes precedence over maintaining public trust in the institution (see Norton, 1997, p. 365). Given that the television coverage focuses on the chamber and not on the committee work of the House, then the enduring perception that viewers have is of a House of noisy, point-scoring MPs, contributing little new to political debate.

Executive dominance

There has been a perception of a growth in executive dominance in the UK (see Allen, 2001). The effect of this, it is argued, is a greater marginalisation of Parliament. Party dominates the House, and this stranglehold has been exacerbated as more and more power has been concentrated in Downing Street. This perception of executive dominance was marked when Margaret Thatcher occupied Downing

Table 17.9 Perceptions of MPs

Response	%
Q. When you hear politicians from different parties on radio and television, do you have the impression that they are mainly concerned with reaching agreement or are they mainly concerned with scoring points off each other?	
Reaching agreement	3
Scoring points	93
Don't know	4
Q. When you hear politicians on television or radio, do you feel that they fairly often break new ground, or do you almost always feel you've heard it all before?	
New ground	4
Heard it before	92
Don't know	4
Q. When you hear politicians on television or radio, do you feel that they are usually saying what they believe to be true, or are they usually merely spouting the party line?	
Truthful	6
Party line	88
Don't know	6

Source: From S. Coleman (1999) *Electronic Media, Parliament and the Media*, p. 20. Reproduced with permission from the Hansard Society

Street and was revived under the premiership of Tony Blair. The extent to which Parliament is marginalised has been the subject of academic debate, but the perception of a peripheral legislature resonates with the public. The MORI state of the nation polls in the 1990s and in 2000 found a growing body of respondents who believed that Parliament did not have sufficient control over what the government does (Table 17.10). By the mid-1990s, a majority of respondents – 52 per cent – agreed with the statement that Parliament does not have sufficient control over what the government does. Only 18 per cent disagreed. This perception appears to have been reinforced under the Labour government of Tony Blair. As can be seen from Table 17.10, by 2000 the biggest change was in the percentage of respondents who agreed 'strongly' with the statement.

The popular perception of Labour MPs slavishly voting as they are told was encapsulated by a *Guardian* cartoon showing a Labour MP holding an electronic voting device displaying two options: 'Agree with Tony [Blair]' and 'Strongly Agree with Tony'. As research by Philip Cowley (2002, 2005) has shown, this perception is overstated. The Blair government has faced unprecedented rebelliousness by its back-benchers. The two most notable occasions took place in 2003, when 122 Labour MPs voted against government policy on Iraq, the biggest

rebellion on foreign policy faced by any Labour government, and in 2005 when the government suffered its first defeat at the hands of MPs, Labour MPs voting with opposition parties to vote down a government proposal to allow detention without charge for ninety days. Labour MPs have been willing to vote against the government to a degree not popularly recognised. However, the perception of executive dominance persists – the Prime Minister governing with little regard to Parliament – and it remains the case that the government will almost always get its way in a parliamentary vote. The defeat in 2005 was the first in more than 2,000 votes to take place in the Commons since the Labour government was returned in 1997. There remains a popular view of a House of Commons that is not calling government to account. The House is weak in the face of a strong executive.

Creation of other policy-making bodies

The capacity of the House to fulfil its functions is undermined not only by executive domination of the House but also by the creation of other policy-making bodies. Even if MPs had the political will to determine outcomes, their capacity to do so is now limited by the seepage of policy-making powers to other bodies. There are three principal bodies or rather three collections of bodies involved: the

Table 17.10 Perceptions of parliamentary control over government: Parliament does not have sufficient control over what the government does

	1991 (%)	1995 (%)	2000 (%)
Strongly agree	10	13	21
Tend to agree	40	39	32
Neither agree nor disagree	19	21	20
Tend to disagree	20	15	8
Strongly disagree	3	3	4
No opinion	9	9	15

Sources: MORI state of the nation poll 1995, ICM Research state of the nation poll 2000. Copyright © Ipsos MORI, reproduced with permission

institutions of the EU, the courts and the devolved assemblies.

The effect of membership of the European Union has been touched on already in Chapter 15. We shall return to its legal implications in Chapter 23. Membership has served to transfer policy competences in various sectors to the institutions of the European Union: they have increased in number with subsequent treaty amendments. Parliament has no formal role in the law-making process of the EU. It seeks to influence the British minister prior to the meeting of the relevant Council of Ministers, but – if qualified majority voting (QMV) is employed – the minister may be outvoted. There is nothing that Parliament can do to prevent regulations having binding effect in the UK or to prevent the intention of directives from being achieved.

The courts have acquired new powers as a result of British membership of the EU as well now as a consequence of the incorporation of the European Convention on Human Rights (ECHR) into British law and as a consequence of devolution. The effect of these we shall explore in greater depth in Chapter 23. Various disputed issues of public policy are now resolved by the courts, which have the power to suspend or set aside British law if it conflicts with EU law. The courts are responsible for interpreting the provisions of the ECHR. The courts are also responsible for determining the legal limits established by the Acts creating elected bodies in Scotland, Wales and Northern Ireland. The capacity of the House of Commons to intervene or to overrule the courts is now effectively limited.

The devolution of powers to elected assemblies in different parts of the United Kingdom also limits the decision-making capacity of Parliament. Parliament is not expected to legislate on matters devolved to the Scottish Parliament (see Chapter 15). The

Scottish Parliament has been given power to legislate in areas not reserved under the Scotland Act and has also been given power to amend primary legislation passed by Parliament. The scope of decision making by Parliament is thus constricted.

■ Pressure for change

These variables combine to produce a House of Commons that is under pressure to restore public confidence and to fulfil effectively the functions ascribed to it. There are various calls for reform of the House in order to address both problems. However, not all MPs and commentators accept that there is a significant problem. Not all those demanding reform are agreed on the scale of the problem, and they come up with very different proposals for reform. There are, put simply, three principal approaches to reform. Each derives from a particular perception of the role of the House of Commons in the political system. They can be related very roughly to the three types of legislature identified at the beginning of the chapter.

1. *Radical*: The radical approach wants to see Parliament as a policy-making legislature. Parliament is seen as weak in relation to the executive – and is seen to be getting weaker. Reform of the House of Commons within the present constitutional and political framework is deemed inadequate to the task. Without radical constitutional reform, the House of Commons will remain party-dominated and under the thumb of the executive. To achieve a policy-making legislature, the radical approach not only supports reform within the institution but also wants major reform of the constitution

in order to change fundamentally the relationship between Parliament and government. Such change would include a new electoral system as well as an elected second chamber. As such, this radical approach can be seen to fit very much within the liberal approach to the constitution (see Chapter 15). The most extreme form of this view advocates a separation of powers, with the executive elected separately from the House of Commons. Only with radical reform, it is argued, can high levels of public trust in Parliament be achieved.

2. *Reform*: This approach wants to strengthen the House of Commons as a policy-influencing body, the onus for policy-'making' resting with government but with the House of Commons having the opportunity to consider policy proposals in detail and to influence their content. As such, it falls very much within the traditional approach to constitutional change (see Chapter 15), although it is not exclusive to it. Traditionalists, for example, can find common cause with adherents to the socialist approach in respect of some reforms. Even adherents of the liberal approach will support reform, although arguing that it does not go far enough. (For traditionalists, reform is both necessary and sufficient. For liberals, it is necessary but not sufficient.) Reformers favour structural and procedural changes within the House. They want to strengthen committees – standing committees as well as select committees – with standing committees being reformed as part of a series of reforms to the legislative process. They also favour an increase in resources to enable MPs to cope with the demands made of them as well as to tempt a wider range of people to enter Parliament. The sorts of reforms that are advocated are listed in Table 17.11. Reformers claim that opinion poll data show that there is a need for reform but that there is no clear case for more radical surgery. More people think that Parliament works well than think that it does not. The figures are a cause for concern, and informed reform, not a cause for panic.

3. *Leave alone*: This approach, as the name suggests, opposes change. It is the stance of a High Tory (see Chapter 15) although it is not exclusive to the High Tory approach. Some Labour MPs have opposed reform, wanting to retain the chamber as the central debating forum. Those who support this stance stress the importance of the chamber as the place where the great issues of the day are debated. Committees and greater specialisation detract from the fulfilment of this historical role, allowing MPs to get bogged down in the detail rather than the principle of what is proposed by government. Providing MPs with offices takes them away from the chamber. Although not quite envisaging a House with little or no policy effect, advocates of this approach see the role of the House as one of supporting government. They emphasise that there is no great public demand for change. Most people think that Parliament works fairly or very well.

For radicals, the contemporary emphasis on constitutional reform gives them hope that their stance may be vindicated. The creation of new elected

Table 17.11 Reform of the House of Commons: proposals to strengthen the House

- Make pre-legislative scrutiny the norm by publishing all bills, before their introduction into Parliament, in draft form and allowing select committees to study them

- Require each bill at some stage during its passage to be subject to examination by an evidence-taking committee

- Provide for most bills to be subject to post-legislative scrutiny, to determine whether they have fulfilled their purpose

- Give departmental select committees an annual research budget (Banham, 1994, p. 50, suggested £2 million a year for each committee)

- Provide more extensive resources to each MP to communicate quickly and effectively with the outside world, including the constituency and the institutions of the EU

- Create new procedures for examining delegated legislation and give the House the power to amend statutory instruments

- Give select committees, and the Speaker, powers to summon ministers

- Reduce the number of MPs, creating a smaller and more professional House

assemblies in Scotland and Wales – both elected for fixed terms – will, they hope, act as a spur to radical change in England. Scotland and Wales not only have new elected assemblies, they also have a new electoral system. With the use also of different electoral systems for the Greater London Assembly and the European Parliament, the UK Parliament remains the only legislative body elected by the first-past-the-post system. Those who adopt this radical stance view electoral reform as a crucial mechanism for revitalising the House of Commons.

For reformers, reform constitutes a practical as well as a desirable option. They point to what has happened in recent years as well as to various reform tracts identifying the case for further change. The introduction of the departmental select committees in 1979 showed what could be achieved in strengthening Parliament as a policy-influencing legislature. Some reforms have been carried out since 1997 as a consequence of reports issued by the Select Committee on Modernisation of the House of Commons (see Brazier *et al.*, 2005). These have included the creation of the 'parallel chamber' in Westminster Hall, as well as some changes in the legislative process, including allowing some bills to carry over from one session to another and the use of pre-legislative scrutiny. More modest changes have included the introduction of payment for those who chair both select and standing committees.

Reformers want to see more significant changes, and recent years have seen the publication of various reform tracts, including the reports of the Conservative Party's Commission to Strengthen Parliament (the Norton Report) 2000, the Hansard Society's Commissions on Parliamentary Scrutiny (the Newton Report) 2001 and on the Communication of Parliamentary Democracy (the Puttnam Report) 2005, as well as reports from the Modernisation Committee in the Commons and the Constitution Committee in the House of Lords. The Constitution Committee's report, *Parliament and the Legislative Process* (2004), advocated not only reform of the legislative process, but also more extensive pre-legislative and post-legislative scrutiny. As a result of its recommendations, the government asked the Law Commission – which advises on legal reform – to come up with proposals for implementing the recommendation for post-legislative scrutiny.

Those who want to leave the House of Commons alone take heart from the fact that they are likely to succeed, not least by default (see Norton, 1999b). Many ministers are not too keen on any significant reform that will strengthen the capacity of Parliament to criticise government or prevent it having its way. They want Parliament to expedite government business, not have it delayed. Robin Cook, when Leader of the House (2001–3), had difficulty carrying his colleagues with him in pursuing a reform agenda. The whips have proved reluctant to see change and in 2002 were accused of encouraging Labour MPs not to agree to all the recommendations of the Modernisation Committee. Also, MPs – once a parliament is under way – become too tied up with the day-to-day demands of constituency work and public business to stand back and address the issue of parliamentary reform. The 'leave alone' tendency may not be strong in its advocacy but can be quite powerful in achieving the outcome it wants.

Parliamentary reform came onto the parliamentary agenda in and after 2000, with reformers gaining some ground. However, the problem in achieving reform is the classic one. Most MPs are elected to support the party in government. At the same time, they are members of a body that is supposed to subject to critical scrutiny the very government they are elected to support. Are they going to vote to strengthen the House of Commons if the effect is to limit the very government they were elected to support? The options are not necessarily mutually exclusive – reformers argue that good government needs an effective Parliament – but perceptions are all-important. If ministers think a strengthened Parliament is a threat, will they not be inclined to call on their parliamentary majority to oppose it? In those circumstances, back-benchers may have to choose between party and Parliament.

■ Explaining Parliamentary power

As is apparent from the figures in Tables 17.8 and 17.10, as well as the demands for reform made by observers and many politicians, there is a widespread perception that Parliament is not doing as good a job as it should be doing. The House of Commons is seen as weak in the face of executive dominance. Yet Parliament has survived for several centuries; it is at the heart of our political system. Just how powerful is it? On the face of it, not very, yet much depends on how power is defined. There are different approaches. The three principal approaches derive from explaining the capacity to affect outcomes in terms of observable decision making (the pluralist approach), non-decision making (deriving from élite theory) and institutional constraints (Norton, 2005).

Decision making

This approach focuses on how issues are resolved once they are on the political agenda. Once a government brings forward a proposal, what difference does Parliament make to it? Does the measure emerge in the form in which the government introduced it or at least in the form it wants it? From this perspective, Parliament exercises some power, but it is limited. Parliament has the coercive capacity to say 'no' to government. Legislation is dependent on the assent of Parliament. If MPs vote down a bill, then it cannot proceed. However, as we have seen, the use of this coercive capacity is rare. MPs also have a persuasive capacity: that is, they may induce government not to proceed with a measure (or to change it) even though it has the option of proceeding. Ministers may be persuaded by the force of argument, by a desire to maintain goodwill on the part of their own supporters, by the desire to avoid embarrassing publicity (the public appearance of a divided party), or by the threat of defeat. Even with large majorities in the 1997 and 2001 parliaments, Labour ministers occasionally made concessions to their own back-benchers. Thus, for example, Jack Straw as Home Secretary made changes to the Criminal Justice (Terrorism and Conspiracy) Bill as well as to the Immigration and Asylum Bill in order to assuage the criticisms of Labour MPs (Cowley, 2002, pp. 32, 52–4). When one Labour MP opposed to provisions for incapacity benefit embodied in a welfare bill went to see the then Social Security Secretary, Alistair Darling, he was asked 'What's your price?' (Cowley, 2002, p. 47). This persuasive capacity became more pronounced in the 2005 parliament, when – with a reduced overall majority – the threat of defeat became more potent.

MPs thus have the capacity to affect the outcome of measures, but that capacity is extremely limited. Most bills will clear the Commons in the form they were introduced or at least in the form preferred by government. Amendments made in response to back-bench pressure – or from members of other parties – are few and far between. Concessions are occasionally offered in order to ensure that enough MPs are prepared to vote for the bill. Ministers generally opt for the minimum they can get away with in terms of concessions; in the 1997–2001 parlia-

ment, for example, negotiations 'rarely yielded anything that discontented backbenchers wanted' (Cowley, 2002, p. 180). The House of Commons *can* make a difference and occasionally the difference is significant and high-profile, but on the whole it is usually at the margins. From this perspective, Parliament is not a particularly powerful body and certainly not as powerful as many would wish it to be.

Non-decision making

Non-decision making is the capacity to keep certain things off the political agenda. The pluralist, or decision-making, approach is concerned with outcomes once an issue is on the agenda. The élitist, or non-decision making approach, focuses on how issues get on to the agenda in the first place. Non-decision making is when an issue is kept off the agenda. In élite theory, there is a body that acts as a gatekeeper, ensuring that certain fundamental matters never become the subject of political debate. Parliament is not seen as part of such an élite, but the concept of non-decision making is relevant in so far as it relates to anticipated reaction. An issue may be kept off the political agenda because those responsible for agenda setting realise that it would encounter significant and possible fatal opposition. There may be occasions, therefore, when the government decides not to bring forward a bill because it does not believe it could get it through Parliament. On occasion, the adverse reaction may be so obvious that ministers do not even need to discuss it. As a consequence, there are obvious problems in detecting instances of non-decision making. There have been cases, though, where a government has been known not to proceed with a measure because of anticipated reaction. When Prime Minister, Margaret Thatcher once said that she had not been as radical in economic policy as she would have liked because she would not have been able to get the approval of Parliament. That may have been a *post hoc* rationalisation for not being more radical rather than the actual reason, but it points to the potential power of Parliament. In 2004, the government decided not to proceed with a bill to remove the remaining hereditary peers from the House of Lords because it feared that Labour MPs, supported by others, might vote to amend the bill in a way unacceptable to ministers.

Anticipation of how MPs may behave thus has some influence on government. It is a feature not confined to the UK. As Cox and Morgenstern (2002,

p. 446) have observed, 'the venerable "rule of anti-cipated reactions" makes even primarily reactive legislatures . . . relevant.' If government becomes too extreme, then Parliament may act to constrain it. Knowing that, government avoids the extremes. As such, Parliament is powerful, though the number of occasions when ministers have actually contem-plated introducing a measure but then decided not to because of anticipated parliamentary reaction is likely to be very small. Given the problems of identifying non-decision making, that can only be surmised, but the existence of overall majorities for government and the willingness of MPs to vote loyally with their party make it plausible.

Institutional constraints

The institutional approach is not so much concerned with the substance of a measure but rather with the institutional structures and norms that determine how an issue is resolved. Here the concern is not with how MPs behave – whether they vote for a bill or not – but with the rules (and the acceptance of those rules) that determine how a bill becomes law. However large the government's parliamentary majority, it cannot simply get all the measures it wants passed by Parliament within a matter of days or weeks. Each bill, as we have seen, has to go through a set procedure. There are several stages each bill has to go through and there are gaps between each stage. As we have seen, there is lim-ited parliamentary time available. The finite number of MPs available to serve on standing committees may be seen as a problem for Parliament but it also limits the number of bills that can be considered at the same time. Government thus has to consider which bills it wishes to introduce each year. There is not sufficient parliamentary time to deal with all the bills it would like to introduce and only a minority of bills put forward by departments are accepted for introduction in a particular session. Even then, there is the problem of miscalculation and a bill may not get through in the time available. A bill is more likely to fail because of misjudgements about timing

(or the calling of a general election, prematurely bringing a Parliament to an end) than it is because MPs have voted it down.

From this institutional perspective, Parliament is a notably powerful body. For bills to become law and be enforced by the courts, they have to be assented to by Parliament. There is no alternative process. The parliamentary *process* is thus crucial and that process is governed by a large body of often com-plex rules. The book embodying all the rules and precedents, known as *Erskine May* (the name of the clerk who first produced it in the nineteenth century), runs to more than 1,000 pages. Though the House of Commons is master of its procedure, and the govern-ment could use its majority to change the rules (and sometimes does), it cannot embark on wholesale change. Ministers are not procedural experts – they rely on the clerks, who are politically neutral – and the House proceeds on the basis of a common accept-ance of the rules. There is a general acceptance that government is entitled to get its business done and the opposition is entitled to be heard.

Parliament thus functions on the basis of a con-sensus on the rules. If government tried to manip-ulate the rules excessively in its favour, opposition parties may refuse to continue playing by those rules. There is thus what has been termed an 'equi-librium of legitimacy' (Norton, 2001a, p. 28), each side accepting the legitimacy of the other in what it seeks to do. That acceptance allows the process to function effectively. It is an acceptance that under-pins the institutional power of Parliament. It is an acceptance that shapes ministers' behaviour. Bills have to be drawn up in a particular form for intro-duction to Parliament. Ministers are not only drawn from Parliament – and remain constituency MPs – they also have to appear in Parliament to justify their measures and their policies and to answer MPs' ques-tions. There is no legal requirement for ministers to turn up at Question Time to answer questions, but the accepted rules of procedure ensure that they do. Whether they like it or not, Parliament shapes what they do. As an *institution*, Parliament is a powerful body.

BOX 17.4 BRITAIN IN CONTEXT

Ancient and large, but not unusual

The Westminster Parliament is distinctive because of its longevity. It is one of the oldest parliaments in the world. However, in terms of its place in the political system – especially in its relationship to the executive – it is not unusual. Of the types of legislature identified in Box 17.1, it is the first – that of *policy-making legislatures* – that is notable for not being a crowded category. Of national legislatures, only the US Congress has occupied the category for any continuous period of time. It is joined by the state legislatures of the USA and a few legislatures of more recent creation.

The category of *policy-influencing legislatures* is the crowded category and encompasses most legislatures in western Europe and the Commonwealth. It has also been swelled by the changes in the legislatures of the new democracies of southern, central and eastern Europe: previously they occupied the third category, that of *legislatures with little or no policy effect*, but – with democratisation – they have now moved up to occupy the second or even (sometimes briefly) the first category. The third category is now largely confined to dictatorships and one-party states, where legislatures exist for the purpose of giving assent to whatever is placed before them.

Within the category of policy-influencing legislatures, the UK Parliament is not ranked in the top reaches of the category; that is, there are other legislatures that utilise more extensively the capacity to amend or reject measures brought forward by the executive. The Italian parliament and the Scandinavian legislatures are among the strongest legislatures in the category. Westminster, and other Westminster-style legislatures, has less impact on public policy by virtue of the fact that it exists in a Cabinet-centred, two-party system, where the parties compete for the all-or-nothing spoils of electoral victory under a first-past-the-post electoral system. Continental parliamentary systems, utilising different electoral systems, place more stress on coalitions, with parliaments operating through committees on a more consensual basis.

The UK Parliament, however, is not seen as the weakest legislature in the category of policy-influencing legislatures. In western Europe, the weakest in this category are the French and Irish parliaments.

The categories identified in Box 17.1 cover legislatures in relation to public policy. Most legislatures fulfil a range of other functions. The UK Parliament is distinctive, but not unique, for the emphasis that its members give to constituency work. In common with other parliamentary – as opposed to presidential – systems, it serves as the route for advancement to executive office. It shares many of its functions with other policy-influencing legislatures. As with many other legislatures, it is under threat from the expansion of executive power. Where it is distinctive is in terms of its size. Both the House of Commons (646 members) and the House of Lords (just over 700 members) are, in comparative terms, large legislative bodies. (The US Congress, for example, has a total of 535 members; some legislatures in small states have fewer than 100 members.) The membership of both renders the UK Parliament the largest legislature in the democratic world. Both chambers, in terms of sitting hours, are also among the busiest legislative chambers in the world.

Chapter summary

Parliament is an institution at the heart of the British political system. The principal role of the House of Commons is one of scrutinising government. Various means are available to MPs to undertake this role. Those means have been strengthened in recent years but have made only a modest contribution to improved scrutiny. Members and the House have been subject to pressures that have made it difficult for MPs to fulfil their jobs effectively. Some politicians see no need for change. Others advocate reform of the House, some through radical constitutional change, others through reform from within the institution. Inertia may prevent reform being achieved, but the issue is on the political agenda.

Discussion points

- What are the most important functions of the House of Commons?

- What purpose is served by select committees? Should they be strengthened?

- Should, and can, the House of Commons improve its scrutiny of government legislation?

- Is the increase in the constituency work of MPs a good or a bad thing?

- Will reforming the practices and procedures make any difference to public perceptions of the House of Commons?

- Should MPs be paid more?

- What would *you* do with the House of Commons – and why?

Further reading

The most recent texts on Parliament, useful for the student, are Riddell (2000), Rogers and Walters (2006), Rush (2005) and Norton (2005). Riddell analyses the pressures faced by Parliament. Rogers and Walters offer a good overview of Parliament, especially its procedures. Rush and Norton are designed for student use, the latter analysing Parliament from different theoretical perspectives as well examining the relationship of Parliament to the citizen as well as to government. There is also a wide range of essays, by practitioners and academics, on different aspects of Parliament in Baldwin (2005).

The socio-economic background of MPs is covered by Rush (2001) and the behaviour of MPs in recent parliaments by Cowley (2002, 2005). The largely neglected relationship of Parliament to pressure groups is the subject of Rush (1990). Parliamentary questions are considered extensively in Franklin and Norton (1993) and briefly in Giddings and Irwin (2005). The Procedure Committee of the House of Commons has also published a number of reports on parliamentary questions: the most recent (HC 622) was published in 2002. MPs' constituency service is covered in Norton and Wood (1993), Power (1998) and Chapter 9 of Norton (2005). Parliamentary scrutiny of executive agencies is the subject of Giddings (1995). The relationship of Parliament to the law is discussed in Oliver and Drewry (1998). The relationship of Parliament to the European Union is covered comprehensively in Giddings and Drewry (2004). Many of these books are the products of research by study groups of the Study of Parliament Group (SPG), a body that draws together academics and clerks of Parliament. A reflective set of essays, by members of the SPG, on parliamentary change and the issues facing Parliament in the twenty-first century is to be found in Giddings (2005). The relationships of Parliament to the European Union, government, pressure groups and citizens are put in comparative context in Norton (1996), Norton (1998), Norton (1999a) and Norton (2002) respectively.

A critique of Parliament's scrutiny of the executive is to be found in Weir and Beetham (1999). On reform of the House of Commons, see the Commission to Strengthen Parliament (2000), Norton (2001b), the Hansard Society Commission on Parliamentary Scrutiny (2001), the report of the Constitution Committee of the House of Lords (2004) and Brazier (2004). It is also worth looking at reports of the Modernisation Committee

▶

of the House of Commons. (Committee reports can be found on the Parliament website.) On the consequences of attempts at modernisation, see Brazier *et al.* (2005).

References

Allen, G. (2001) *The Last Prime Minister* (Graham Allen).

Baldwin, N.D.J. (ed.) (2005) *Parliament in the 21st Century* (Politico's).

Banham, J. (1994) *The Anatomy of Change* (Weidenfeld & Nicolson).

Brand, J. (1992) *British Parliamentary Parties* (Oxford University Press).

Brazier, A. (2004) 'Standing Committees: imperfect scrutiny', in A. Brazier (ed.), *Parliament, Politics and Law Making* (Hansard Society).

Brazier, A., Flinders, M. and McHugh, D. (2005) *New Politics, New Parliament?* (Hansard Society).

Coleman, S. (1999) *Electronic Media, Parliament and the Media* (Hansard Society).

Commission to Strengthen Parliament (2000) *Strengthening Parliament* (Conservative Party).

Constitution Committee, House of Lords (2004) *Parliament and the Legislative Process*, 14th Report, Session 2003–4, HL Paper 173-I (The Stationery Office).

Cowley, P. (ed.) (1998) *Conscience and Parliament* (Cass).

Cowley, P. (2002) *Revolts and Rebellions* (Politico's).

Cowley, P. (2005) *The Rebels* (Politico's).

Cowley, P. and Norton, P. (1996) *Blair's Bastards* (Centre for Legislative Studies).

Cox, G.W. and Morgenstern, S. (2002) 'Epilogue: Latin America's assemblies and proactive presidents', in S. Morgenstern and B. Nacif (eds), *Legislative Politics in Latin America* (Cambridge University Press).

Criddle, B. (1992) 'MPs and candidates', in D. Butler and D. Kavanagh (eds), *The British General Election of 1992* (Macmillan).

Criddle, B. (1997) 'MPs and candidates', in D. Butler and D. Kavanagh (eds), *The British General Election of 1997* (Macmillan).

Criddle, B. (2002) 'MPs and candidates', in D. Butler and D. Kavanagh (eds), *The British General Election of 2001* (Macmillan).

Criddle, B. (2005) 'MPs and candidates', in D. Kavanagh and D. Butler (eds), *The British General Election of 2005* (Palgrave Macmillan).

Doig, A. (2001) 'Sleaze: picking up the threads or "back to basics" scandals?', *Parliamentary Affairs*, Vol. 54, No. 2.

Doig, A. (2002) 'Sleaze fatigue in "the house of ill-repute"', *Parliamentary Affairs*, Vol. 55, No. 2.

Drewry, G. (ed.) (1989) *The New Select Committees*, revised edn (Oxford University Press).

Franklin, M. and Norton, P. (eds) (1993) *Parliamentary Questions* (Oxford University Press).

Giddings, P. (ed.) (1995) *Parliamentary Accountability* (Macmillan).

Giddings, P. (ed.) (2005) *The Future of Parliament* (Palgrave Macmillan).

Giddings, P. and Drewry, G. (eds) (2004) *Britain in the European Union* (Palgrave).

Giddings, P. and Irwin, H. (2005) 'Objects and questions', in P. Giddings (ed.), *The Future of Parliament* (Palgrave Macmillan).

Griffith, J.A.G. and Ryle, M. (1989) *Parliament* (Sweet & Maxwell).

Hansard Society (1993) *Making the Law: Report of the Commission on the Legislative Process* (Hansard Society).

Hansard Society (2004) *Issues in Law-Making 5. Pre-Legislative Scrutiny* (Hansard Society).

Hansard Society Commission on the Communication of Parliamentary Democracy, *Members Only?* (Hansard Society).

Hansard Society Commission on Strengthening Parliament (2001) *The Challenge for Parliament: Making Government Accountable* (Vacher Dod Publishing).

Hollingsworth, M. (1991) *MPs for Hire* (Bloomsbury).

Kennon, A. (2004) 'Pre-legislative scrutiny of draft bills', *Public Law*, Autumn, pp. 477–94.

King, A. (1981) 'The rise of the career politician in Britain – and its consequences', *British Journal of Political Science*, Vol. 11.

Mezey, M. (1979) *Comparative Legislatures* (Duke University Press).

Norris, P. (1997) 'The puzzle of constituency service', *The Journal of Legislative Studies*, Vol. 3, No. 2.

Norton, P. (1979) 'The organization of parliamentary parties', in S.A. Walkland (ed.), *The House of Commons in the Twentieth Century* (Oxford University Press).

Norton, P. (ed.) (1990) *Legislatures* (Oxford University Press).

Norton, P. (1993) *Does Parliament Matter?* (Harvester Wheatsheaf).

Norton, P. (1994) 'The parliamentary party and party committees', in A. Seldon and S. Ball (eds), *Conservative Century: The Conservative Party since 1900* (Oxford University Press).

Norton, P. (ed) (1996) *National Parliaments and the European Union* (Cass).

Norton, P. (1997) 'The United Kingdom: restoring confidence?', *Parliamentary Affairs*, Vol. 50, No. 3.

Norton, P. (ed) (1998) *Parliaments and Governments in Western Europe* (Cass).

Norton, P. (1999a) 'The United Kingdom: parliament under pressure', in P. Norton (ed.), *Parliaments and Pressure Groups in Western Europe* (Cass).

Norton, P. (1999b) 'The House of Commons: the half empty bottle of reform', in B. Jones (ed.), *Political Issues in Britain Today*, 5th edn (Manchester University Press).

Norton, P. (2001a) 'Playing by the rules: the constraining hand of parliamentary procedure', *The Journal of Legislative Studies*, Vol. 7.

Norton, P. (2001b) 'Parliament', in A. Seldon (ed.), *The Blair Effect* (Little, Brown).

Norton, P. (ed) (2002) *Parliaments and Citizens in Western Europe* (Cass).

Norton, P. (2004) 'Parliament and legislative scrutiny: an overview of issues in the legislative process', in A. Brazier (ed.), *Parliament, Politics and Law Making* (Hansard Society).

Norton, P. (2005) *Parliament in British Politics* (Palgrave Macmillan).

Norton, P. and Wood, D. (1993) *Back from Westminster* (University Press of Kentucky).

Oliver, D. and Drewry, G. (eds) (1998) *The Law and Parliament* (Butterworth).

Power, G. (1996) *Reinventing Westminster* (Charter88).

Power, G. (1998) *Representing the People: MPs and their Constituents* (Fabian Society).

Riddell, P. (1993) *Honest Opportunism* (Hamish Hamilton).

Riddell, P. (2000) *Parliament Under Blair* (Politico's).

Rogers, R. and Walters, R. (2006) *How Parliament Works*, 6th edn (Longman).

Rush, M. (ed.) (1979) 'Members of Parliament', in S.A. Walkland (ed), *The House of Commons in the Twentieth Century* (Oxford University Press).

Rush, M. (1990) *Pressure Politics* (Oxford University Press).

Rush, M. (2001) *The Role of the Member of Parliament Since 1868* (Oxford University Press).

Rush, M. (2005) *How Parliament Works* (Manchester University Press).

Select Committee on Procedure (1990) *The Working of the Select Committee System*, Session 1989–90, HC 19 (HMSO).

Somit, A. and Roemmele, A. (1995) 'The victorious legislative incumbent as a threat to democracy: a nine nation study', *American Political Science Association: Legislative Studies Section Newsletter*, Vol. 18, No. 2, July.

Weir, S. and Beetham, D. (1999) *Political Power and Democratic Control in Britain* (Routledge).

Useful websites

Parliamentary websites

Parliament: www.parliament.uk

House of Commons: www.parliament.uk/about_commons/about_commons.cfm

House of Commons select committees: www.parliament.uk/commons/selcom/cmsel.htm

Modernisation Committee of the House of Commons: www.parliament.uk/parliamentary_committees/select_committee_on_the_modernisation_of_the_house_of_commons.cfm

Procedure Committee of the House of Commons: www.parliament.uk/parliamentary_committees/procedure_committee.cfm

Parliamentary Education Unit Home Page: www.explore.parliament.uk

House of Commons Factsheets: www.parliament.uk/parliamentary_publications_and_archives/factsheets.cfm

Directories of MPs: www.parliament.uk/directories/directories.cfm

House of Commons weekly information bulletin: www.publications.parliament.uk/pa/cm/cmwib/ahead.htm

Other related websites

BBC A–Z of Parliament: www.news.bbc.co.yk/1/hi/uk_politics/a-z_of_parliament/default.htm

Commission to Strengthen Parliament (the Norton Report): www.conservatives.com/pdf/norton.pdf

Hansard Society for Parliamentary Government: www.hansard-society.org.uk

CHAPTER 18

The House of Lords

Philip Norton

Learning objectives

- To describe the nature, development and role of the House of Lords.

- To identify the extent and consequences of fundamental changes made to the House in recent years.

- To assess proposals for further change to the second chamber.

Introduction

The House of Lords serves as the second chamber in a **bicameral legislature**. The bicameral system that the United Kingdom now enjoys has been described as one of asymmetrical bicameralism. That is, there are two chambers, but one is politically inferior to the other. The role of the second chamber in relation to the first moved in the twentieth century from being co-equal to subordinate. As a subordinate chamber, it has carried out tasks that have been recognised as useful to the political system, but it has never fully escaped criticism for the nature of its composition. It was variously reformed at different times in the twentieth century, the most dramatic change coming at the end of the century. Debate continues as to what form the second chamber should take in the twenty-first century.

The House of Lords is remarkable for its longevity. What makes this longevity all the more remarkable are two features peculiar to the House. The first is that it has never been an elected chamber. The second is that, until 1999, the membership of the House was based principally on the hereditary principle. The bulk of the membership comprised **hereditary peers**. Only at the end of the twentieth century were most of the hereditary peers removed. The removal of the hereditary peers was not accompanied by a move to an elected second chamber. Whether the United Kingdom is to have an elected or unelected second chamber remains a matter of dispute. It perhaps says something for the work of the House of Lords that the contemporary debate revolves around what form the second chamber should take rather than whether or not the United Kingdom should have a second chamber.

What, then, is the history of the House of Lords? How has it changed over the past century? What tasks does it currently fulfil? And what shape is it likely to take in the future?

■ History

The House of Lords is generally viewed by historians as having its origins in the Anglo-Saxon *Witenagemot* and more especially its Norman successor, the *Curia Regis* (Court of the King). Two features of the King's *Curia* of the twelfth and thirteenth centuries were to remain central characteristics of the House of Lords. One was the basic composition, comprising the **lords spiritual** and the **lords temporal**. At the time of the Magna Carta, the *Curia* comprised the leading prelates of the kingdom (archbishops, bishops and abbots) and the earls and chief barons. The main change, historically, was to be the shift in balance between the two: the churchmen – the lords spiritual – moved from being a dominant to being a small part of the House. The other significant feature was the basis on which members were summoned. The King's tenants-in-chief attended court because of their position. Various minor barons were summoned because the King wished them to attend. 'From the

beginning the will of the king was an element in determining its make up' (White, 1908, p. 299). If a baron regularly received a summons to court, the presumption grew that the summons would be issued to his heir. A body thus developed that peers attended on the basis of a strictly hereditary dignity without reference to tenure. The result was to be a House of Lords based on the principle of heredity, with writs of summons being personal to the recipients. Members were not summoned to speak on behalf of some other individuals or bodies. Any notion of representativeness was squeezed out. Even the lords spiritual – who served by reason of their position in the established Church – were summoned to take part in a personal capacity.

The lack of any representative capacity led to the House occupying a position of political – and later legal – inferiority to the House of Commons. As early as the fifteenth century, the privilege of initiating measures of taxation was conceded to the Lower House. The most significant shift, though, took place in the nineteenth century. As we have seen

The statue of Richard the Lionheart stands outside the entrance to the House of Lords
Source: one-image photography / Alamy

(Chapter 17), the effect of the Reform Acts was to consign the Lords to a recognisably subordinate role to that of the Commons, although not until the passage of the Parliament Act of 1911 was that role confirmed by statute. Under the terms of the Act, the House could delay a non-money bill for no more than two sessions, and money bills (those dealing exclusively with money, and so certified by the Speaker) were to become law one month after leaving the Commons whether approved by the House of Lords or not. Bills to prolong the life of a parliament, along with delegated legislation and provisional order bills, were excluded from the provisions of the Act. The two-session veto over non-money bills was reduced to one session by the Parliament Act of 1949.

The subordinate position of the House of Lords to the House of Commons was thus established. However, the House remained a subject of political controversy. The hereditary principle was attacked by those who saw no reason for membership of the second chamber to be determined by accident of privileged birth. It was attacked as well because the

bulk of the membership tended to favour the Conservative cause. Ever since the eighteenth century, when William Pitt the Younger created peers on an unprecedented scale, the Conservatives enjoyed a political ascendancy (if not always an absolute majority) in the House. In other words, occupying a subordinate position did not render the House acceptable: the composition of the House, however much it was subordinated to the Commons, was unacceptable. There were some attempts in the period of Conservative government from 1951 to 1964 to render it more acceptable, not by removing hereditary peers or destroying the Conservative predominance but rather by supplementing the existing membership with a new type of membership. The Life Peerages Act 1958 made provision for people to be made members for life of the House of Lords, their titles – and their entitlement to a seat in the House of Lords – to cease upon their death. This was designed to strengthen the House by allowing people who objected to the hereditary principle to become members. Following the 1958 Act, few hereditary peerages were created. None was created under Labour governments, and only one Conservative Prime Minister, Margaret Thatcher, nominated any (and then only three – Harold Macmillan, who became the Earl of Stockton; George Thomas, former Speaker of the House of Commons; and William Whitelaw, her Deputy Prime Minister). The 1963 Peerages Act made provision for hereditary peers who wished to do so to disclaim their titles. Prior to 1999, these were the most important measures to affect the membership of the House. Although both measures – and especially the 1958 Act – had significant consequences, pressure continued for more radical reform. In 1999, acting on a commitment embodied in the Labour manifesto in the 1997 general election, the Labour government achieved passage of the House of Lords Act. This removed from membership of the House all but ninety-two of the hereditary members. The effect was to transform the House from one composed predominantly of hereditary peers to one composed overwhelmingly of **life peers**. However, the removal of the hereditary peers was seen as but one stage in a process of reform. The House of Lords created by their removal was deemed to be an interim House, to remain in place while proposals for a second stage of reform were considered. The issue of what should constitute the second stage of reform has proved highly contentious.

■ Membership and attendance

Until the passage of the House of Lords Act, which removed most hereditary peers from membership, the House of Lords had more than 1,000 members, making it the largest regularly sitting legislative chamber in the world. Its size was hardly surprising given the number of peers created over the centuries by each succeeding monarch, although the largest increase was in the twentieth century. In 1906, the House had a membership of 602. In January 1999, it had 1,296. Of those, 759 were hereditary peers. (The figure includes one prince and three dukes of the blood royal.) The remaining members comprised 485 life peers, twenty-six peers created under the Appellate Jurisdiction Act 1876 (the law lords, appointed to carry out the judicial business of the House) and twenty-six lords spiritual (the two archbishops and twenty-four senior bishops of the Church of England). With the removal of all but ninety-two of the hereditary peers, the House remains a relatively large one. In the immediate wake of the removal of the hereditary peers, the House had 666 members. With new creations and deaths, the figure has fluctuated since. In December 2005, there were 721 members. (The figure excludes twelve members on leave of absence.) The figure increased further in 2006 as a result of new creations.

The membership of the House has thus been affected dramatically by the 1958 Life Peerages Act and the 1999 House of Lords Act. In many respects, the former made possible the latter, creating a new pool of members who could serve once hereditary peers were removed. Indeed, the creation of life peerages under the 1958 Act had a dramatic effect on the House in terms both of composition and activity. The impact of the 1999 Act will be considered in greater detail later.

■ Composition

In terms of composition, the 1958 Act made possible a substantial increase in the number of Labour members. Previously, Labour members had been in a notable minority. In 1924, when Labour first formed a minority government, the party had only one supporter in the Upper House. The position changed only gradually. In 1945, there were eighteen Labour peers. Forty-four Labour peers were created in the period of Labour government from 1945 to 1951, but their successors did not always support the Labour Party. By 1999, there were only seventeen hereditary peers sitting on the Labour benches. Life peerages enabled Labour's ranks to be swelled over time. Prominent Labour supporters who objected to hereditary peerages were prepared to accept life peerages, so various former ministers, ex-MPs, trade union leaders and other public figures were elevated to the House of Lords. At the beginning of 1999, there were more than 150 life peers sitting on the Labour benches. Apart from former ministers and MPs, they included figures such as the broadcaster Melvyn Bragg, film producer David Puttnam, crime writer Ruth Rendell, and TV presenter and doctor Robert Winston. Further creations helped bring the number above 200 and by December 2005 there were 210 Labour peers as against 207 Conservatives.

The creation of life peers from 1958 onwards served to lessen the party imbalance in the House. In 1945, Conservative peers accounted for 50.4 per

Table 18.1 Composition of the House of Lords, December 2005

Grouping	Number of peers	
	All peers	Life peers
Conservative	207	158
Labour	210	206
Liberal Democrat	74	69
Cross-bench	193	161
Archbishops/bishops	26	0
Other	11	9
Total	721	603

Source: House of Lords (2006) *House of Lords Annual Report and Accounts 2005–2006*. © Parliamentary Copyright 2006. Parliamentary copyright material is reproduced with the permission of the Controller of Her Majesty's Stationery Office (HMSO) on behalf of Parliament

cent of the membership. In 1998, the figure was 38.4 per cent (Baldwin, 1999). Before 1999, the second-largest category in the House comprised those peers who choose to sit independently of party ranks and occupy the cross-benches in the House. At the beginning of 1999 – that is, in the pre-reform House – the state of the parties was Conservative 473, Labour 168, Liberal Democrats 67 and cross-benchers 322. This left in excess of 250 other peers who did not align themselves with any of these groupings. The effect of the removal of most hereditary peers in 1999 was to create greater equality between the two main parties, leaving the balance of power being held by the cross-benchers and the Liberal Democrats. The composition of the House, as at 1 December 2005, is given in Table 18.1.

The creation of life peers drawn from modest backgrounds has also served to affect the social profile of the membership. Hereditary peers were typically drawn from the cream of upper-class society. Life peers were drawn from a more diverse social background. However, even with the influx of life peers, the membership remained, and remains, socially atypical. Life peerages are normally conferred on those who have achieved some particular distinction in society, be it social, cultural, sporting, economic or political. By the time the recipients have achieved such a distinction, they are, by definition, atypical. There was therefore little chance of the House becoming socially typical. Members of the House are drawn notably from backgrounds in the law, the Civil Service and the teaching profession, these

three categories accounting for nearly 40 per cent of the membership (Criddle *et al.*, 2005, pp. 34–5). The next largest category – accounting for just nearly 5 per cent of the membership – is that of trade union officials. The House is also atypical in terms of age and gender. It is rare for people to be made life peers while in their twenties or thirties. The mean age of the membership is 67. The youngest peer to be created was television mogul Lord Alli (born 1964), who was elevated to the peerage in 1998 at the age of 34. The hereditary peerage produced some young peers, succeeding their fathers at an early age, but they were small in number and largely disappeared as a result of the House of Lords Act. One who remains as an elected hereditary, Lord Freyberg (born 1970), entered the House at the age of 23. Women, who were first admitted to the House under the provisions of the 1958 Life Peerages Act, also constitute a minority of the membership, but a growing one. In 1990, there were eighty women in the House, constituting 7 per cent of the membership. The removal of a large number of – overwhelmingly male – hereditary peers and the creation of more women life peers has meant that the number, and proportion, of women peers has increased notably. At the beginning of December 2005, there were 135 women peers, constituting 19 per cent of the membership. Of these, 131 held life peerages. Recent years have seen several black and Asian peers created, although they constitute a small proportion of the total. Lord Alli and former cabinet minister Lord Smith of Finsbury are the only openly gay peers to sit in the House.

There has been another consequence of life peerages in terms of the membership of the House. It has brought into the House a body of individuals who are frequently expert in a particular area or have experience in a particular field. This claim is not exclusive to life peers – some hereditary peers are notable for their expertise or experience in particular fields – but it is associated predominantly with them. This has led to claims that when the House debates a subject, however arcane it may be, there is usually one or more experts in the House to discuss it (Baldwin, 1985). Thus, for example, in the field of higher education, the House has among its members a number of university chancellors, masters of university colleges, former vice-chancellors, an array of professors, former secretaries of state for education, and peers who chair bodies in higher education (such as the funding council). When, in November 2005, the House held a short debate on the impact of bureaucracy on universities, the

The Chamber of the House of Lords
Source: Rolf Richardson / Alamy

debate was initiated by a university professor and those taking part comprised members who had served as secretary of state for education, director of the London School of Economics, minister of higher education, pro-vice-chancellor of Oxford University, and the chairman of the higher education funding council for England (and of the national committee of inquiry into higher education); of the three front-bench speakers, two, including the minister, had been university dons. (One-third of the speakers in the debate were women.) This claim to expertise in many fields is often contrasted with membership of the House of Commons, where the career politician (see Chapter 17) – expert in the practice of politics – dominates. The body of expertise and experience serves, as we shall see, to bolster the capacity of the House to fulfil a number of its functions.

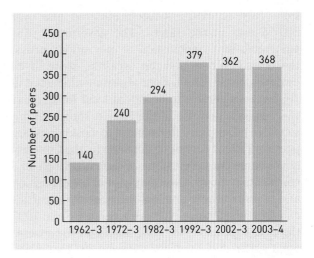

Figure 18.1 Average daily attendance in the chamber, 1962–2004

Source: House of Lords (2006) *House of Lords Annual Report and Accounts 2005–2006.* © Parliamentary copyright 2006. Parliamentary copyright material is reproduced with the permission of the Controller of Her Majesty's Stationery Office (HMSO) on behalf of Parliament

■ Activity

The creation of life peers also had a dramatic effect on the activity of the House. In the 1950s, the House met at a leisurely pace and was poorly attended. Peers have never been paid a salary and many members, like the minor barons in the thirteenth century, found attending to be a chore, sometimes an expensive one: the practice, as in the thirteenth century, was to stay away. The House rarely met for more than three days a week, and each sitting was usually no more than three or four hours in length. For most of the decade, the average daily attendance did not reach three figures. Little interest was shown in its activities by most of its own members; not surprisingly, little interest was shown by those outside the House.

This was to change significantly in each succeeding decade (see Figure 18.1). Life peers were disproportionately active. Although they constituted a minority of the House, they came to constitute a majority of the most active members of the House. The effect of the increasing numbers of life peers was apparent in the attendance of members (see Figure 18.1). Peers attended in ever greater numbers and the House sat for longer. Late-night sittings, virtually unknown in the 1950s and for much of the 1960s, have been regular features since the 1970s. In the 1980s and 1990s, the average daily sitting was six or seven hours. By the end of the 1980s, more than 800 peers – two-thirds of the membership – attended one or more sittings each year and, of

those, more than 500 contributed to debate. By the time of the House of Lords Act in 1999, the House was boasting a better attendance in the chamber than the House of Commons. The effect of the 1999 Act was to result in a House in which the active members dominated. Although the membership halved in 1999, the daily attendance hardly changed (Figure 18.1). Whereas the average daily attendance figure for 1992–3 constitutes just under one-third of the membership, that for the post-reform 2003–4 session constitutes more than half. In the 2003–4 session, 50 per cent of the members attended 65 per cent or more of the sittings – a remarkable achievement given that many members had full-time posts outside the House, attending in order to give the benefit of their expertise.

One other consequence of the more active House was that the number of votes increased. They were few and far between in the 1950s, about ten to twenty a year. By the 1980s and 1990s, the figure was usually closer to 200. The political composition of the House meant that a Labour government was vulnerable to defeat. In the period of Labour government from 1974 to 1979, the government suffered 362 defeats at the hands of the House of Lords. However, Conservative governments were not immune. The preponderance of Conservative peers did not always translate into a majority for a Conservative government. In the period of Conservative government from 1979 to 1997, ministers suffered just over 250 defeats in the House. The government was vulnerable to a combination of opposition parties, the cross-benchers and, on occasion, some of its own supporters. The Labour government elected in 1997 was vulnerable to defeat, at least for the first two sessions, because of the large number of Conservative peers. Since the removal of most hereditary peers in 1999, it cannot be defeated by the Conservatives alone but is vulnerable to defeat because of a combination of opposition parties or of the opposition and cross-benchers or of all the opposition parties and a preponderance of cross-benchers. From 1997 through to the end of the 2004–5 session, the government suffered 353 defeats; of these, 283 took place in the post-1999 reformed House. A future Conservative government will be as vulnerable to the combination of forces as the Labour government; as such, both parties now enjoy equality in the House.

The House also became more visible to the outside world. In 1985, television cameras were allowed to broadcast proceedings. There was a four-year gap before the televising of Commons proceedings began: in those four years, the House of Lords enjoyed exclusive television coverage. In the 1990s, the House was also ahead of the House of Commons in appointing an information officer and seeking to ensure better public understanding of its role and activities. The Information Office of the House has been highly active in disseminating information about the work of the House, generating booklets and information packs for which the House of Commons has no equivalent.

■ Procedures

The House differs significantly from the Commons not only in its size, composition and remuneration (peers can claim allowances to cover travel, accommodation, subsistence and some secretarial support, but they still receive no salary) but also in its procedures. The presiding officer of the House, who sits on the Woolsack, has no powers to call peers to speak or to enforce order. The maintenance of the rules of order is the responsibility of the House itself, although peers usually look to the Leader of the House to give a lead. Peers wishing to speak in a set-piece debate, such as a second reading debate, submit their names in advance (they can now do so electronically), and a list of speakers is circulated shortly prior to the debate. Peers then rise to speak in the order on the list. At other times, as in Question Time, if two peers rise at the same time, one is expected to give way. (If neither does so, other peers make clear their preference as to who should speak by shouting out the name of the person they wish to hear.) If a speaker strays from what is permissible, other peers shout 'Order'. If a speaker goes on for too long, it is always open to another peer to rise and call attention to the fact (a task normally undertaken by the government whip on duty) or, in extreme cases, to move the motion 'That the noble peer be no longer heard', but this is a device rarely employed. The Lords remains a more chamber-oriented institution than the Commons, although – as we shall see – it is making more use of committees than before. Although the House votes more frequently than it used to, the number of divisions in the Lords is fewer than in the Commons. (There will usually be about three times as many votes each year in the Commons as in the Lords.) This in part reflects the recognition by peers of the political predominance of the elected chamber. Peers are often reluctant to press issues to a vote and rarely do so on the principle of a measure. By virtue of an agreement reached between the two party leaders in the Lords in 1945, the House does not divide on the second reading of any bill promised in the government's election manifesto and, by extension now, any bill appearing in the government's programme for the session. This is known as the Salisbury convention, named after the Conservative leader in the Lords who enunciated it.

There are also two other features where it differs from the Commons and which enhance its capacity to affect the outcome of legislation. First, the House discusses all amendments tabled to bills. In the Commons, the chair selects only a limited number for debate. Second, there are no timetable (guillotine) motions. Debate continues so long as peers wish to speak. There are also considerable opportunities for peers to raise issues in the House. Some debates are time-limited (although not the committee and report stages of bills) and a fifteen-minute time limit operates for back-bench speeches in set-piece debates. Peers may be asked to keep their speeches even shorter if a great many of them sign up to speak in a time-limited debate. Time limits force peers to think about what they want to say and to ensure that they focus on the main points. The results tend to be a series of short, informed and often highly educative speeches.

■ Functions

The debate about reform of the House of Lords has focused largely, though not wholly, on its composition. The functions of the House – the tasks that it carries out – have not generated as much controversy. There has been a wide body of agreement that the functions it fulfilled in the twentieth century, and continues to fulfil in the twenty-first, are appropriate to a second chamber. As we shall see, this view is not necessarily held by all those expressing views on the House of Lords. Nonetheless, the view has tended to predominate among those engaged in the debate, including the government of the day. The functions are broadly similar to those of the Commons but not as extensive. The extent to which they differ derives from the fact that politically the House is no longer co-equal with the Commons.

Legitimisation

The House fulfils the functions of both manifest and latent legitimisation, but on a modest scale. It is called upon to give the seal of approval to bills, but if it fails to give that approval, it can be overridden later by the House of Commons under the provisions of the Parliament Acts. Only in very rare circumstances – as in the case of a bill to lengthen the life of a parliament, secondary legislation or (somewhat more significantly) bills originating in the Lords – is its veto absolute. By virtue of being one of the two chambers of Parliament and by fulfilling the functions it does effectively, the House may have a limited claim to fulfilling a function of latent legitimisation. It is a long-established part of the nation's constitutional arrangements. However, such a claim is offset by the House having no claim to being a representative assembly – neither speaking for particular bodies in society nor being socially typical – and by its limited legislative authority. A claim to traditional authority has been superseded by a claim to specialised knowledge, the House being able to draw on experience and expertise in considering the measures before it, but that 'technocratic' legitimacy is not on a par with the legitimacy of the elected chamber.

Recruitment

The House provides some of the personnel of government. As we have seen (Chapter 17), ministers are drawn from Parliament and, by convention, predominantly now from the elected House.

The Prime Minister appoints a number of ministers from the Upper House primarily for political and managerial reasons. Although the government is normally assured of getting its bills through the House, it is not necessarily guaranteed getting them through in the form it wants them. It is therefore prudent to have ministers in the Lords in order to explain bills and to marshal support. In addition, the House provides a pool from which the Prime Minister can draw in order to supplement ministers drawn from the Commons. The advantage offered by peers is that, with no constituency responsibilities, they are able to devote more time to ministerial duties than is the case with ministers who have constituency duties to attend to. It also has the advantage of widening the pool of talent available to the Prime Minister. Someone from outside Parliament can be elevated to the peerage at the same time as being appointed to government office. Four people who had no parliamentary experience were brought into government through this route by Tony Blair in the first two years of his premiership: Charles Falconer (Lord Falconer of Thoroton), a lawyer, appointed in 1997 as Solicitor General; David Simon (Lord Simon of Highbury), a former chairman of British Petroleum, appointed in 1997 as Competition Minister; David Sainsbury (Lord Sainsbury of Turville), chairman and chief executive of supermarket giant Sainsbury, appointed in 1998 as Minister for Science; and Gus MacDonald (Lord MacDonald of Tradeston), a Scottish television executive, appointed in 1998 as a junior minister in the Scottish Office. Later appointments included Sally Morgan (Baroness Morgan of Huyton), the Prime Minister's political secretary, created a peer in 2001 and appointed as a Cabinet Office minister, and Andrew Adonis, a former member of the Number Ten policy unit, created a peer in 2005 and appointed as a junior education minister.

Ministerial appointments in the Lords have also enabled women politicians to be promoted. Three women have served as Leaders of the House of Lords (Baroness Young 1981–2, Baroness Jay 1998–2001, and Baroness Amos since 2003). Of the ministers in the Lords at the beginning of 2006, 35 per cent were women, compared to 28 per cent in the Commons. Two of the ministers – Baroness Amos and Home Office minister, Baroness Scotland – are black.

However, the number of ministers appointed in the Lords is relatively small. At least two peers have traditionally served in the Cabinet (Lord Chancellor and Leader of the House) but usually no more than four. Four is a rarity and two, until 2005, the norm. Under the Constitutional Reform Act 2005, the Lord Chancellor need no longer be a peer, so if an MP is appointed to the post only one peer will automatically serve in the Cabinet. Up to fifteen other ministers are drawn from the Lords, supplemented by eight whips (including the Chief Whip). The number of ministers does not match the number of ministries, with the result that the whips have to take on responsibility for answering for particular departments – another difference from the House of Commons, where the whips have no responsibility for appearing at the despatch box. A frequent speaker at the despatch box is the government deputy chief whip, who often represents one or more senior departments without a junior minister. Even with a small number of posts to be filled, governments have on occasion had difficulty in finding suitable peers for ministerial office. It used to be the case that Conservative governments had sometimes to draw on young hereditary peers. Labour governments were limited by the relatively small number of Labour peers. The creation of life peerages in recent years, quantitatively and qualitatively, has widened the pool of talent. Both sides have tended to use the Whips' Office as a training ground for substantive ministerial office.

Scrutiny and influence

It is in its remaining functions that the House of Lords is significant. The House performs an important role as an agent of scrutiny and influence. The House does not undertake the task of scrutiny on behalf of constituents, as peers have none. Rather, the House undertakes a more general task of scrutiny. Three features of the House render it particularly suitable for the detailed scrutiny of legislation. First, as an unelected House, it cannot claim the legitimacy to reject the principle of measures agreed by the elected House. Thus, basically by default, it focuses on the detail rather than the principle. Second, as we have noted already, its membership includes people who have distinguished themselves in particular fields – such as the sciences, the law, education, business, industrial relations – who can look at relevant legislation from the perspective of practitioners in the field rather than from the perspective of elected party politicians. And, third, the House has the time to debate non-money bills in more detail than is usually possible in the Commons – as we have seen, there is no provision for a guillo-

tine, and all amendments are discussed. The House thus serves as an important revising chamber, trying to ensure that a bill is well drafted and internally coherent. In order to improve the bill, it will often make amendments, most of which will be accepted by the Commons. In terms of legislative scrutiny, the House has thus developed a role that is viewed as complementary to, rather than one competing with (or identical to), that of the Commons.

The value of the House as a revising chamber is shown by the number of amendments it makes to legislation. Most of these are moved by the government itself, but a significant proportion of these are amendments promised by government in response to comments made by back-bench members. The number of amendments made in the Lords far exceeds the number made in the Commons. Each session, the House will typically agree 2,000 to 3,000 amendments to bills. (In 1999–2000, the number was 4,761, an all-time record.) In the 2003–4 session, of 9,602 amendments that were tabled, 3,344 were agreed (see House of Lords Information Office, 2005). Of these, all bar 164 were agreed to without a vote.

Even these figures do not do justice to the scrutiny undertaken by the Lords. The scrutiny is frequently constructive and is acknowledged as such by the government. Thus, for example, during the 1998–9 session, 108 non-government amendments were moved to the Access to Justice Bill. Of these, seventy-one received a ministerial response that was positive. The responses were important not only for their number but also for their range: they included promising to consider points raised in debate (twenty-eight occasions), accepting the principle of an amendment (twenty-one occasions) and promising to draw a point to the attention of those responsible for drafting the bill (three occasions) (Norton, 1999). Ten amendments were accepted as they stood. The constructive work undertaken by the House was conceded by the Lord Chancellor, Lord Irvine of Lairg, at the conclusion of the bill's passage through the House. The importance of these figures lay not only in the number of constructive responses from government but also in the fact that it is difficult to envisage scrutiny in the House of Commons producing such a response.

This role in scrutinising legislation – in so far as it constitutes a 'second look' at legislation – is of special importance given that it has been characterised as one of the two core functions of the House (Norton, 1999), meaning that it is a function that is particular to the House as the second chamber. It is not a function that the House of Commons can carry out, since it is difficult if not impossible for it to act as a revising chamber for its own measures; that has been likened to asking the same doctor for a second opinion. The role of the House as a revising chamber is thus offered as being central to the case for retaining a second chamber. It is also the role that occupies the most time in the House: usually about 50 to 60 per cent is devoted to considering legislation.

The House also scrutinises, and on occasion influences, government policy. Peers can debate policy in a less partisan atmosphere than the Commons and are not subject to the constituency and party influences that dominate in the elected House. They are therefore in a position to debate issues of public policy that may not be at the heart of the partisan battle and which, consequently, receive little attention in the Commons. Given their backgrounds, peers are also often – although not always – able to debate public policy from the perspective of those engaged in the subject. The House is able to debate science policy, for example, or medical ethics with considerable authority. The Lords contains several distinguished scientists and members with expertise in medicine and ethics. We have mentioned already the number of peers who can speak with authority on higher education; although the House of Commons contains some former university lecturers, it does not have members with the same experience and status in education as those in the Upper House.

Expression

The House, like the Commons, also fulfils a number of expressive functions. It can bring issues onto the political agenda in a way not always possible in the Commons. MPs are wary of raising issues that may not be popular with constituents and that have little salience in terms of party politics. Peers are answerable to no one but themselves. They can raise whatever issues they feel need raising. The House may thus debate issues of concern to particular groups in society that MPs are not willing to address. Formally, it is not a function the House is expected to fulfil. Indeed, according to *Erskine May*, the parliamentary 'bible' on procedure, Lords may indicate that an outside body agrees with the substance of their views, but they should avoid creating an impression that they are speaking as representatives of outside bodies. Thus, not only is the House not a representative assembly, it should avoid giving the impression of being one! In practice, peers take up

issues that concern them, often alerted to the issue by outside bodies. Peers are frequently lobbied by outside organisations. One extensive survey in the 1990s found that half of the groups surveyed were in touch with peers at least once a month, and almost one in five were in contact on a weekly basis (Baggott, 1995, pp. 93, 164). Each peer receives on average in excess of 3,000 items of mail each year, most of it from outside organisations. Some groups write to ask peers to move amendments to bills, some merely keep members informed of what is happening with the organisation, and some are keen that peers raise issues with government, if necessary on the floor of the House. Some peers are particularly active in raising the concerns of particular groups, such as farmers, the disabled, the terminally ill, or the people of Zimbabwe, or pursuing very particular issues, such as railways, the effects of smoking or the upkeep of war graves.

The House also has the potential, only marginally realised, to express views to citizens and influence their stance on public policy. The function is limited by the absence of any democratic legitimacy, the capacity to influence deriving from the longevity of the House and its place as one of the two chambers of Parliament, as well as from the authority of the individual peers who may be involved. However, the scope for fulfilling this function is somewhat greater than in the House of Commons, simply because more time is available for it in the House of Lords. Between 20 and 30 per cent of the time of the House is given over each session to debates on motions tabled by peers: about 20 per cent of time is given over to general debates, and between 4 and 10 per cent of the time is given over to 'unstarred questions', in effect short debates on specific topics.

Other functions

To these functions may be added a number of others, some of which are peculiar to the Upper House. Foremost among these historically has been the judicial function. The House presently constitutes the highest court of appeal within the United Kingdom. Although formally a function residing in the House as a whole, in practice it is carried out by a judicial committee comprising the twelve **law lords** and peers who have held high judicial office. Between five and ten will normally sit to hear a case. Hearings take place in a committee room, although the decision is delivered in the chamber at a time separate from the normal sittings of the House: the only peers present are usually the law lords, and the senior law lord presides. By convention, other peers do not take part in judicial proceedings. One peer early in the twentieth century did try to participate but was ignored by the members of the committee. The law lords, though members of the House, avoid speaking on any matters that may be deemed partisan or involve measures on which they may later have to adjudicate in a judicial capacity. They also normally abstain from voting, though on occasion a law lord has voted on an issue that has been the subject of a free vote. However, this long-standing judicial function will cease to reside in the House in 2009, when a new supreme court, created under the Constitutional Reform Act 2005, will come into being (see Chapter 23) and the function will transfer to the new court.

Like the Commons, the House also retains a small legislative role, primarily in the form of private members' legislation. Peers can introduce private members' bills, and a small number achieve passage, but it is small – even compared with the number of such bills promoted by MPs. The introduction of such bills by peers is more important in fulfilling an expressive function – allowing views on the subject to be aired – than in fulfilling a legislative role. Time is found to debate each private member's bill and, by convention, the government – even if opposed to the measure – does not divide against it. In the 1995–6 session, for example, a Sexual Orientation Discrimination Bill was introduced, which, even though it stood little chance of passage (there was no time in the Commons), got the issue of discrimination against homosexuals discussed. In 1999, a former Conservative Leader of the House, Lord Cranborne, introduced a Parliamentary Government Bill, designed to call attention to the need to strengthen parliamentary control of the executive. The debate on second reading was replied to by the Lord Chancellor. The time given to private members' legislation is important but not extensive: it occupies usually less than 3 per cent of the time of the House.

The House is also ascribed a distinct role, that of a constitutional safeguard. This is reflected in the provisions of the Parliament Acts. The House, as we have noted, retains a veto over bills to extend the life of a parliament. It is considered a potential brake on a government that seeks to act in a dictatorial or generally unacceptable manner: hence it may use its limited power to amend or, more significantly, to delay a bill. In practice, though, the power is a limited one, as well as one not expected to require action by the House on any regular basis. The House lacks a legitimate elected base of its own that would allow it to act, on a substantial and sustained basis, contrary to the wishes of an elected government. Even so, it constitutes the other core function of the House in that it is a function that the House alone, as the second chamber, can fulfil: the House of Commons cannot act as a constitutional check upon itself.

In combination, these various functions render the House a useful body – especially as a revising chamber and for raising and debating issues on which peers are well informed – but one that is clearly subordinate to the elected chamber. The fact that the House is not elected explains its limited functions; it is also the reason why it is considered particularly suited to fulfil the functions it does retain.

■ Scrutiny and influence

The means available to the House to fulfil the tasks of scrutiny and influence can be considered, as with the Commons, under two heads: legislation and executive actions. The means available to the House are also those available to fulfil its expressive functions.

Legislation

As we have seen, 50 to 60 per cent of the time of the House is given over to legislation. Bills in the Lords have to go through stages analogous to those in the House of Commons. There are, though, differences in procedure. First readings are normally taken formally, but there have been rare occasions when they have been debated: on four occasions (in 1888, 1933, 1943 and 1969) first readings were actually opposed. Second readings, as in the Commons, constitute debates on the principle of the measure. However, votes on second reading are exceptionally rare. Because of the Salisbury convention, the House does not vote on the second reading of government bills. A vote may take place if, as exceptionally happens, a free vote is permitted. This happened in 1990 on the War Crimes Bill and in 1999 on the Sexual Offences (Amendment) Bill to lower the age of consent for homosexual acts to 16. Both bills had been passed by large majorities in the House of Commons but both were rejected, on free votes, in the House of Lords. Both occasions were exceptional.

The main work of the House takes place at committee and report stages. For some bills, the committee stage is actually dispensed with. After second reading, a motion may be moved 'That this Bill be not committed' and, if agreed to, the bill then awaits third reading. This procedure is usually employed for supply and money bills when there is no desire to present amendments. For those bills that do receive a committee stage, it is usually taken on the floor of the House. All amendments tabled are debated. The less crowded timetable of the House allows such a procedure. It has the advantage of allowing all peers with an interest or expertise in a measure to take part and ensures consideration of any amendments they believe to be relevant. There is thus the potential for a more thorough consideration than is possible in the Commons. The emphasis is on ensuring that the bill is well drafted and coherent.

Since 1968, the House has been able to refer bills for committee consideration in the equivalent of standing committees, known as public bill committees, although it rarely does so. More recently, the House has experimented with sending a bill to a special procedure public bill committee, which is empowered to take oral and written evidence. Of longer standing is the power to refer a bill, or indeed any proposal, to a select committee for detailed investigation. It is a power that has been utilised when it has been considered necessary or desirable to examine witnesses and evidence from outside bodies. Between 1972 and 1991, seven bills were sent to select committees. All bar one of the bills were private members' bills. More recently, select committees have been appointed to consider a major government bill (the Constitutional Reform Bill) and a Private Member's Bill (the Assisted Dying for the Terminally Ill). For bills that are not considered highly partisan, it may also now be sent for its committee stage to a grand committee.

The grand committee is, in effect, something of a parallel chamber. It comprises all members of the House and can meet while the House is in session. In practice, attendance is relatively small – comprising those with a particular interest in the measure – permitting sessions to be held in the Moses Room, an ornate committee room just off the Peers' Lobby. The use of grand committees has become more pronounced in recent years, providing in effect considerable extra time to the House for the detailed consideration of bills. In the 2003–4 session, for example, there were grand committee sittings on sixty-three days, totalling 225 hours; in 2004–5,

there were sittings on fifty-eight days, totalling 210 hours (House of Lords, 2005, p. 10). Votes cannot take place in grand committee, so amendments can only be accepted if no member objects. (If objection is made, the matter has to be held over to report stage.) Of 3,247 amendments moved in grand committee in 2003–4, 817 were accepted.

Report and third reading provide further opportunities for consideration. Report may be used by government to bring forward amendments promised at committee stage and also to offer new amendments of its own. It is also an opportunity for members to return to issues that received an inadequate response by government at committee stage (although amendments rejected by the House at committee stage cannot again be considered). It is also possible for amendments to be made at third reading, and this opportunity is variously employed. The motion for third reading is put formally and agreed to and then amendments are taken. Once they have been dealt with, the motion 'That the Bill do now pass' is put. The result is that some bills, especially large or contentious bills, can and do receive a considerable amount of attention at different stages in the House of Lords.

Executive actions

As in the House of Commons, various means are available for scrutinising the actions of the executive. The principal means available on the floor of the House are those of debate and questions. Off the floor of the House, there are select committees and, at the unofficial level, party meetings.

Debates

Debates, as in the Commons, take place on motions. These may express a particular view, or they may take the form of either 'take note' motions or motions calling for papers. 'Take note' motions are employed in order to allow the House to debate reports from select committees or to discuss topics on which the government wishes to hear peers' views: ministers use 'take note' motions rather than motions calling for papers because with the latter they are responsible for supplying the papers being called for. Motions calling for papers are used by back-benchers to call attention to a particular issue; at the end of the debate it is customary to withdraw the motion, the purpose for which it was tabled – to ensure a debate – having been achieved.

All peers who wish to speak in debate do so, and there is a greater likelihood than in the Commons that the proceedings will constitute what they purport to be: that is, debates. Party ties are less rigid than in the Commons, though nonetheless still strong (see Norton, 2003), and peers frequently pay attention to what is being said. Although the order in which peers speak is determined beforehand, it is common practice for a peer who is speaking to give way to interventions. Within the context of the chamber, the chances of a speech having an impact on the thought and even the votes of others are considerably greater than in the more predictable Lower House. Indeed, it is not unknown for peers when, uncertain as to how to vote, to ask 'what does X think about it?'.

One day each week is given over to two general debates. (The debate day used to be Wednesday but in 2005 the House agreed to change it to Thursday.) Once a month, the debates are determined by ballot. Peers wishing to have debates submit motions which then appear on the order paper and two are drawn at random by the clerk on a set day. The topics on the remaining debate days are allocated to each of the parties in turn and to the cross-benchers. The two debates last up to a total of five hours. The balloted debates are automatically each of two and a half hours in length. On the party days, the time, within the five-hour maximum, is varied depending on the number of speakers. These general debates are occasions for issues to be raised by back-benchers rather than front-benchers. The purpose of each short debate is to allow peers to discuss a particular topic rather than to come to a conclusion about it. Topics discussed tend to be non-partisan, and the range is broad. On 11 January 2006, for example, Lord Clarke of Hampstead moved a motion to call attention to the case for a government policy towards the Royal Mail which best reflected the national interest, and Baroness Gibson of Market Rasen moved a motion to call attention to the impact of the National Offender Management Service on the Criminal Justice System. Both motions provided the opportunity for interested peers to offer their views and for ministers to explain the government's position and to reveal what proposals were under consideration by the relevant department. The time devoted to each debate is divided equally among the number of back-bench speakers (the opener and the minister replying have fixed time limits) and, in the event of many peers wishing to speak, the time available to each may be as little as four or five minutes.

Questions

Questions in the Lords are of two types: starred and unstarred. Starred questions are non-debatable questions, and unstarred questions are questions on which a short debate may take place. (Lords may also table questions for written answer, and nowadays they do so in increasing numbers.) Starred questions are taken in Question Time at the start of each sitting: the House sits at 2.30 p.m. on Monday and Tuesday, 3.00 p.m. on Wednesday and 11.00 a.m. on Thursday. (If sitting on a Friday, it sits at 11.00 a.m. but no questions are taken.) Question Time lasts for up to a maximum of thirty minutes and no more than four questions may be taken. Questions are similar to those tabled for oral answer in the Commons, although – unlike in the Commons – they are addressed to Her Majesty's Government and not to a particular minister (see Figure 18.2). Also, there is no departmental rota: the questions may be to different departments. A question to an environment minister, for example, may be followed by one to a defence minister. A peer rises to ask the question appearing in his or her name on the order paper, the relevant minister (or whip) replies for the government, and then supplementary questions – confined to the subject of the original question – follow. This procedure, assuming the maximum number of questions is tabled (it usually is), allows for seven to eight minutes for supplementary questions to each question, the peer who tabled the motion by tradition being allowed to ask the first supplementary. Hence, although Question Time is shorter than in the Commons, the concentration on a particular question is much greater and allows for more probing.

At the end of the day's sitting, or during what is termed the 'dinner hour' (when the House breaks in mid-evening from the main business), there is also usually an unstarred question: that is, one that may be debated (as, for example, Figure 18.2). If taken during the dinner hour, debate lasts for a maximum of sixty minutes. If taken as the last business of the day, it lasts for a maximum of ninety minutes. Peers who wish to speak do so – signing up in advance – and the appropriate minister replies to the debate. The advantages of such unstarred questions are similar to those of the half-hour adjournment debates in the Commons, except that in this case there is a much greater opportunity for other members to participate. For example, when Baroness Rawlings on 8 July 2002 asked what action the government was taking in response to the international

NOTICES AND ORDERS OF THE DAY

*Items marked † are new or have been altered. Items marked ‡ are
expected to be taken during the dinner adjournment.*

TUESDAY 9TH MAY

At half-past two o'clock

*The Lord Moran – To ask Her Majesty's Government whether they will take steps to ensure that the British organ building industry is permanently exempted from the provisions of European Directives 2002 95/EC and 2002 96/EC which after 1st July may make it illegal to build in the European Union new musical instruments containing both lead and electric parts.

*The Baroness Scott of Needham Market – To ask Her Majesty's Government what are the parameters of the second Barker Review of the planning system.

*The Lady Saltoun of Abernethy – To ask Her Majesty's Government what discussions they have had with the government of the United States about the possibility of military action against Iran.

†*The Lord Wallace of Saltaire – To ask Her Majesty's Government what steps they are taking, in cooperation with other governments, to ensure that financial assistance to the Palestinian administration continues.

Company Law Reform Bill [HL] – Report [The Lord Sainsbury of Turville]

‡The Baroness Miller of Chilthorne Domer – To ask Her Majesty's Government what progress they have made in implementing the Water Framework Directive.

In the Moses Room
At 3.30 pm

Health Bill – Further consideration in Grand Committee [The Lord Warner] [*16th Report from the Delegated Powers Committee*]

Figure 18.2 House of Lords order paper: in the House of Lords, questions are addressed to Her Majesty's Government and not to a particular minister

development annual report, she was followed by no fewer than twelve speakers before the minister replied. As it was taken during the dinner hour, the debate lasted for only one hour, a limit that imposed a tight discipline on those taking part.

Committees

Although the House remains a chamber-oriented institution, it has made greater use in recent years of committees. Apart from a number of established committees dealing, for example, with privilege and the judicial function of the House, it has variously made use of *ad hoc* select committees. Some *ad hoc* committees have been appointed to consider the desirability of certain legislative measures. A number have been appointed to consider issues of public policy. (Some are also appointed to deal with essentially internal matters, such as the speakership of the House.) The House has also made use of its power to create sessional select committees, i.e. committees appointed regularly from session to session rather than for the purpose of one particular inquiry. The House has three established committees with

reputations as high-powered bodies. They have been joined by two more, plus a joint committee.

The most prominent of the established committees is the *European Union Committee* (known, until 1999, as the European Communities Committee). Established in 1974, it undertakes scrutiny of draft European legislation, seeking to identify those proposals that raise important questions of principle or policy and which deserve consideration by the House. All documents are sifted by the chairman of the committee – who also holds the formal and salaried position of deputy chairman of committees – with those deemed potentially important being sent to a subcommittee. The committee works through seven subcommittees (see Table 18.2), each subcommittee comprising two or more members of the main committee and several co-opted members. In total, the subcommittees draw on the services of seventy to eighty peers. Each subcommittee covers a particular area. Subcommittee E, for example, deals with law and institutions. Members are appointed on the basis of their particular expertise. Subcommittee E includes some eminent lawyers – it is by convention chaired by a law lord – as well as

Table 18.2 Committees in the House of Lords, 2006

Name of Committee	Chairman
Constitution	Lord Holme of Cheltenham (Lib Dem)
Delegated Powers and Regulatory Reform	Lord Dahrendorf (Cross-bencher)
Economic Affairs	Rt Hon. Lord Wakeham (Con)
European Union Committee	Lord Grenfell (Other)
Sub-committees:	
A. Economic and financial affairs, and international trade	Rt Hon. Lord Radice (Lab)
B. Internal market	Lord Wolmer of Leeds (Lab)
C. Foreign affairs, defence and development policy	Lord Bowness (Con)
D. Environment and agriculture	Rt. Hon. Lord Renton of Mount Harry (Con)
E. Law and institutions	Rt Hon. Lord Brown of Eaton-under-Heywood (Law Lord)
F. Home affairs	Lord Wright of Richmond (Cross-bencher)
G. Social policy and consumer affairs	Baroness Thomas of Walliswood (Lib-Dem)
Merits of Statutory Instruments	Lord Filkin (Lab)
Science and Technology	Lord Broers (Cross-bencher)
[Joint Committee on Human Rights	Andrew Dismore MP (Lab)]

members who have experience of government. A subcommittee, having had documents referred to it, can decide that the document requires no further consideration, or can call in evidence from government departments and outside bodies. If it decides that a document requires further consideration, then it is held 'under scrutiny' – that is, subject to the scrutiny reserve. The government cannot, except in exceptional circumstances, agree to a proposal in the Council of Ministers if it is still under scrutiny by Parliament.

Written evidence to a subcommittee may be supplemented by oral evidence and, on occasion (though not often), a minister may be invited to give evidence in person. The subcommittees prepare reports for the House (in total, about twenty to thirty a year), including recommendations as to whether the documents should be debated by the House. (About 2 per cent of the time of the House is taken up debating EC documents, usually on 'take note' motions.) The EU Committee has built up an impressive reputation as a thorough and informed body, issuing reports that are more extensive than its counterpart in the Commons, and which are considered authoritative both within Whitehall and in the institutions of the EU. The House, like the chambers of other national legislatures, has no

formal role in the European legislative process (see Norton, 1996) and so has no power, other than that of persuasion, to affect outcomes. The significance of the reports, therefore, has tended to lie in informing debate rather than in changing particular decisions (Norton, 2005, p. 153).

The *Select Committee on Science and Technology* was appointed in 1979 following the demise of the equivalent committee in the Commons. (The Commons committee has since been re-created.) The remit of the committee – 'to consider science and technology' – is wide, and its inquiries have covered a broad range. The committee is essentially non-partisan in approach and benefits from a number of peers with an expertise in the subject. The chairman, Lord Broers, is President of the Royal Academy of Engineers – his predecessor was a former rector of the Imperial College of Science, Technology and Medicine – and its membership includes dons and practitioners in fields such as obstetrics, palliative medicine, fertility and science research. For its inquiry into pandemic influenza in 2005 it co-opted Lord May, the President of the Royal Academy (a former chief scientific adviser to the government), and Lord Soulsby of Swaffham Prior, President of the Royal Institute of Public Health (and previously a professor of parasitology). It issues several reports each year. Since the beginning of 2004, it has reported on radioactive waste management, renewable energy practicalities, science and treaties, the scientific aspects of ageing, energy efficiency, and pandemic influenza. The committee has raised issues that otherwise might have been neglected by government – and certainly not considered in any depth by the Commons – and various of its reports have proved influential (see Grantham, 1993; Hayter, 1992).

The *Delegated Powers and Regulatory Reform Committee*, previously known as the Delegated Powers and Deregulation Committee, looks at whether powers of delegated legislation in a bill are appropriate and makes recommendations to the House accordingly (see Himsworth, 1995). It also reports on documents under the Regulatory Reform Act 2001, which allows regulations in primary legislation to be removed by secondary legislation. The committee has established itself as a powerful and informed committee, its recommendations being taken seriously by the House and by government. None of its recommendations have been rejected by the government. At report stage of the Access to Justice Bill in February 1999, for example, the government moved thirty-four amendments to give effect to the recommendations of the committee.

These committees have been supplemented by two more. The *Constitution Committee* was established in 2001 to report on the constitutional implications of public bills and to keep the operation of the constitution under review. In its first four years, it issued more than thirty reports, mostly on legislation, but also issued major reports on the process of constitutional change, devolution, inter-institutional relations in the UK, the regulatory state, and Parliament and the legislative process. For its inquiry into devolution, it took evidence in Edinburgh, Cardiff and Belfast as well as in Westminster. When the evidence taken by the committee was published, ahead of its report on the subject, it ran to more than 400 pages. The *Economic Affairs Committee* was also appointed in 2001. The committee undertook a major two-year inquiry into the global economy, taking evidence from a wide range of witnesses, including, for example, the chairman of the major multinational company Unilever. It subsequently appointed a subcommittee to examine the annual finance bill.

As a consequence of the passage of the Human Rights Act 1998, the two Houses have also created a *Joint Committee on Human Rights*. The committee is chaired by an MP, but it follows Lords procedures. It has six members drawn from each House. It considers matters relating to human rights and has functions relating to remedial orders (bringing UK law into line with the European Convention on Human Rights) under the 1998 Act. Its main task is reporting to the House on bills that have implications for human rights. It was particularly influential, for example, in reporting on the Anti-Terrorism, Crime and Security Bill in 2001. In the light of the committee's report, and pressure from members in both chambers, the government agreed to make changes to the bill.

These permanent committees are variously supplemented by *ad hoc* committees, appointed to consider particular issues. Committees reporting in the twenty-first century have covered the monetary policy committee of the Bank of England (reported in 2001), stem cell research (2002), the crash of Chinook helicopter ZD576 (2002), animals in scientific procedures (2002), religious offences (2003), the Constitutional Reform Bill (2004) and the Assisted Dying for the Terminally Ill Bill (2005). Most of these attracted considerable media attention. The report on the Chinook helicopter crash was debated in both Houses. In 2005 the House appointed a BBC Charter Review committee.

The use of committees thus constitutes a modest but valuable supplement to the work undertaken on the floor of the House. They allow the House to specialise to some degree and to draw on the expertise of its membership, an expertise that cannot be matched by the elected House of Commons. They also fulfil an important expressive function. The committees take evidence from interested bodies – the submission of written evidence is extensive – thus allowing groups an opportunity to get their views on the public record. Given the expertise of the committees, reports are treated as weighty documents by interested groups; consequently, the committees enjoy some capacity to raise support for particular measures of public policy. Committees also have the capacity to elicit a government response at the despatch box as well as in writing. The government provides a written response to each committee report – agreeing in 2005 to do so within two months, bringing it into line with the Commons – but if the committee recommends that a report be debated in the House, then time is found to debate it. The House has agreed that such debates should be in prime time, but this is not always possible to achieve.

Party meetings

The parties in the Lords are organised, with their own leaders and whips. Even the cross-benchers, allied to no party, have their own elected leader (known as the convenor) and circulate a weekly document detailing the business for the week ahead. (They even have their own website: www. crossbenchpeers.org.uk.) However, neither the Conservative nor the Labour Party in the Lords has a committee structure. Instead, peers are able to attend the Commons back-bench committees or policy group meetings, and a number do so. Any attempt at influence through the party structure in the Lords, therefore, takes the form of talking to the whips or of raising the issue at the weekly party meeting.

Party meetings, as well as those of cross-bench peers, are held each week. (The meeting day has changed in recent years, following changes to the arrangement of business in the House.) Such meetings are useful for discussing future business as well as for hearing from invited speakers. For example, in meetings of the Association of Conservative Peers (ACP) – the Lords equivalent to the 1922 Committee – the business usually comprises a short talk by a member of the executive of the 1922 Committee about developments in the Commons, the Chief Whip announcing the business for the following week, and a discussion on a particular issue or a talk from a front-bencher or expert on a particular subject. When a major bill is coming before the House, the relevant member of the Shadow Cabinet (or, if in government, minister) may be invited to attend, along with a junior spokesperson, to brief peers on the bill. Sometimes party meetings have the characteristics of a specialist committee, since often peers with an expertise in the topic will attend and question the speaker. For a minister or shadow minister, or even an expert speaker, the occasion may be a testing one, having to justify a measure or proposal before an often well-informed audience.

Party meetings are useful as two-way channels of communication between leaders and led in the Lords and, in a wider context, between a party's supporters in the Lords and the leadership of the whole party. Given the problems of ensuring structured and regular contact between whips and their party's peers, the party meetings provide a useful means of gauging the mood of the regular attenders. They are also useful ways of enhancing communication with the Commons, former MPs often being active in the membership. In 2006, both the main party groups were chaired by ex-MPs.

■ Reform: stage one

Demands for reform of the House of Lords were a feature of both the late nineteenth century and the twentieth. As the democratic principle became more widely accepted in the nineteenth century, so calls for the reform of the unelected, Conservative-dominated House of Lords became more strident. Conservative obstruction of Liberal bills in the 1880s led the Liberal Lord Morley to demand that the Upper House 'mend or end', an approach adopted as Liberal policy in 1891. In 1894, the Liberal conference voted in favour of abolishing the Lords' power of veto. When the Lords rejected the Budget of the Liberal government in 1909, the government introduced the Parliament Bill. Passed in 1911, the preamble envisaged an elected House. An inter-party conference in 1918 proposed a scheme for phasing out the hereditary peers, but no time was found to implement the proposals. A 1948 party leaders' conference agreed that heredity alone should not be the basis for membership. Again, no action was taken. In 1969, the Parliament (No. 2) Bill, introduced by the Labour government led by Harold Wilson, sought to phase out the hereditary element. The bill foundered in the House of Commons after encountering opposition from Conservative MPs, led by Enoch Powell, who felt it went too far, and from Labour MPs, led by Michael Foot, who believed it did not go far enough. The willingness of the House of Lords to defeat the Labour government in the period from 1974 to 1979 reinforced Labour antagonism. In 1983, the Labour Party manifesto committed the party to abolition of the Upper House. Under Neil Kinnock (leader 1983–92) this stance was softened. In its election manifesto in 1992, the party advocated instead an elected second chamber. This was later amended under Tony Blair's leadership to a two-stage reform: first, the elimination of the hereditary element; and, second and in a later Parliament, the introduction of a new reformed second chamber. The Liberal Democrats favoured a reformed second chamber – a senate – as part of a wider package of constitutional reform. Charter 88, the constitutional reform movement created in 1988 (see Chapter 15), included reform of the Upper House 'to establish a democratic, non-hereditary second chamber' as a fundamental part of its reform programme.

The Labour manifesto in the 1997 general election included the commitment to reform in two stages. 'The House of Lords', it declared, 'must be reformed. As an initial, self-contained reform, not dependent on further reform in the future, the rights of hereditary peers to sit and vote in the House of Lords will be ended by statute.' That, it said, would be the first step in a process of reform 'to make the House of Lords more democratic and representative'. A committee of both Houses of Parliament would be appointed to undertake a wide-ranging review of possible further change and to bring forward proposals for reform.

The Labour victory in the 1997 general election provided a parliamentary majority to give effect to the manifesto commitment. However, anticipating problems in the House of Lords, the government delayed bringing in a bill to remove hereditary peers until the second session of the parliament. The bill, introduced in January 1999, had one principal clause, Clause 1, which ended membership of the House of Lords on the basis of a hereditary peerage. It was passed by the House of Commons by a large majority. In the House of Lords, peers adhered to the Salisbury convention and did not vote on second reading. However, they subjected it to prolonged debate at committee and report stage. In the Lords, an amendment was introduced – and accepted by the government – providing that ninety-two hereditary peers should remain members of the interim House. The ninety-two would comprise seventy-five chosen by hereditary peers on a party basis (the number to be divided according to party strength among hereditary peers), fifteen to be chosen by all members of the House for the purpose of being available to serve the House, for example as Deputy Speakers, and the Earl Marshal and the Lord Great Chamberlain, in order to fulfil particular functions associated with their offices. The government had indicated in advance that it would accept the amendment, on condition that the Lords did not frustrate passage of the bill. Although the House made various other amendments to the bill, against the government's wishes, the bill made it eventually to the statute book. All bar the ninety-two hereditary peers exempted by the Act ceased to be members at the end of the session. When the House met for the state opening of Parliament on 17 November 1999, it was thus a very different House from that which had sat only the week before. It was still a House of Lords, but instead of a House with a membership based predominantly on the heredity principle, it was now primarily an appointed House, the bulk of the members being there by virtue of life peerages.

■ Reform: stage two

After the return of the Labour government in 1997, opponents criticised ministers for not having announced what form stage two of Lords reform would take. The government responded by appointing a Royal Commission on Reform of the House of Lords to consider reform in the light of other constitutional developments while having regard to the need to maintain the Commons as the pre-eminent chamber. The Commission, chaired by a Conservative peer, Lord Wakeham (a former Leader of both the House of Commons and the House of Lords), was appointed at the beginning of 1999 and was required to report by the end of the year. It held a number of public meetings in different parts of the country and completed its report by the end of 1999: it was published in January 2000.

In its report, *A House for the Future* (Cmd 4534), the Royal Commission recommended a House of 550 members, with a minority being elected. It identified three options for the size of the elected element:

1. *Option A*: sixty-five elected members, the 'election' taking place on the basis of votes cast regionally in a general election.

2. *Option B*: eighty-seven elected members, directly elected at the same time as elections to the European Parliament.

3. *Option C*: 195 elected members, elected by proportional representation at the same time as European Parliament elections.

Under options B and C, a third of the members would be elected at each European Parliament election. A majority of the members of the Commission favoured option B. It was proposed that the regional members – whatever their number and method of selection – should serve for the equivalent of three electoral cycles and that the appointed members should serve for fixed terms of fifteen years. Under the proposals, existing life peers would remain members of the House.

The Commission's report was extensive, but the reaction to it focused on its recommendations for

Blair gives scant regard to the Wakeham report on reforming the Lords
Source: Copyright © Chris Riddell. From *The Observer*, 23 January 2000. Reprinted with permission from Guardian Newspapers Limited

election. Supporters of an appointed second chamber felt that it went too far. Supporters of an elected second chamber argued that it did not go far enough. Many critics of the report felt that at least 50 per cent of the members should be elected. The report did not get a particularly good press.

Although not well received by the press, the Commission's report was received sympathetically by the government. Following its 1997 manifesto commitment, it sought to set up a joint committee of both Houses, but the parties could not agree on what the committee should do. The Labour manifesto in the 2001 general election committed the government to completing reform of the House of Lords: 'We have given our support to the report and conclusions to the report of the Wakeham Commission, and will seek to implement them in the most effective way possible.' In November 2001, the government published a White Paper, *Completing the Reform*, proposing that 20 per cent of the members be elected. It invited comments, and the reaction it got

was largely unfavourable. In a debate in the House of Commons, many Labour MPs argued that the White Paper did not go far enough. Both the Conservative and Labour parties supported a predominantly elected second chamber. The Public Administration Committee in the Commons issued a report, *The Second Chamber: Continuing the Reform*, arguing that, on the basis of the evidence it had taken, the 'centre of gravity' among those it had consulted was for a House with 60 per cent of the membership elected. An early day motion favouring a predominantly elected second chamber attracted the signatures of more than 300 MPs.

Recognising that its proposals were not attracting sufficient support in order to proceed, the government decided to hand over responsibility to Parliament itself. It recommended, and both Houses agreed to, the appointment of a joint committee. The committee comprised twelve members from each House and, under its terms of reference, was to consider issues relating to House of Lords reform and to present options to both Houses. After meeting twice, the committee issued a short report explaining how it intended to proceed. It indicated that it would proceed in two stages. The first would involve looking at all the existing evidence and outlining options for the role and composition of the second chamber. The second would involve seeing whether the opinions expressed by both Houses on the options could be brought closer to one another, if not actually reconciled. The committee would then address more detailed matters, along with any outstanding issues concerning the functioning of Parliament and any constitutional settlement that might be necessary in determining the relations of the two Houses. 'The Committee believes that such a settlement would need to be robust, practical and command broad support in Parliament and beyond if it is to have any chance to endure.'

The committee completed the first stage of its work at the end of 2002, when it published a report addressing functions and composition. It argued that the existing functions of the House were appropriate. On composition, it listed seven options – ranging from an all-appointed to an all-elected House – and recommended that each House debate the options and then vote on each one. Both Houses debated the joint committee's report in January 2003. Opinion in the Commons was divided among the several options. Opinion in the Lords was strongly in favour of an all-appointed House. On 4 February, both Houses voted on the options. MPs voted down the all-appointed option but then proceeded to vote down all the remaining options favouring partial or total election (see Maclean *et al.*, 2003; Norton, 2004). (An amendment favouring unicameralism was also put and defeated.) Peers voted by a three-to-one majority in favour of the all-appointed option and, by a similar margin, against all the remaining options. Of the options, that of an all-appointed chamber was the only one to be carried by either House. The outcome of the votes in the Commons was unexpected – commentators had expected a majority in favour of one of the options supporting election (the vote on 80 per cent of members being elected was lost by three votes) – and it was widely assumed in the light of the votes that there was little chance of proceeding with moves towards a second stage of reform involving election (see Norton, 2004, pp. 195–7).

Instead, the government decided to introduce a bill to remove the remaining hereditary peers from the House of Lords, establish a statutory appointments commission and provide that peers could be expelled if convicted of an offence subject to a certain term of imprisonment. However, the government abandoned the idea when it failed to craft an amendment-proof bill: it feared that MPs might try to amend it by introducing provisions for election. Some parliamentarians sought to keep the issue on the political agenda. The debate divided between those who were interested in reforming the powers of the Upper House and those who wanted to change its composition.

Labour peers in the Lords established a working party to review the powers, procedures and conventions of the House. Its report, published in 2004, favoured a new Parliament Act, embodying a time limit for bills in the Lords (and for bills starting life in the Lords to be brought within the scope of the Act), as well as a codification of conventions (Labour Peers Group, 2004). The recommendations received a mixed response from peers, but in replying the Lord Chancellor, Lord Falconer, indicated sympathy with the argument for putting a time limit on bills in the Lords.

The debate then switched to those who favoured a reform of the composition of the House. In 2005, five prominent MPs – including former Conservative Chancellor Ken Clarke and former Labour Foreign Secretary Robin Cook – published a reform tract, *Reforming the House of Lords*, in which they argued the case for a 350-member second chamber, with 70 per cent elected, the elected members serving for the equivalent of three parliaments and with one-third of the membership being renewed at each general election (Clarke *et al.*, 2005). Led by Liberal Democrat Paul Tyler, they introduced a private member's bill, the Second Chamber of Parliament Bill, designed to give effect to their recommendations. The bill made no progress.

Labour's 2005 election manifesto showed that the government was drawn more to a reform of powers than a major change in composition. Declaring that a reformed Upper House 'must be effective, legitimate and more representative without challenging the primacy of the House of Commons', it said that, following a review by a committee of both Houses, 'we will seek agreement on codifying the key conventions of the Lords, and developing alternative forms of scrutiny that complement rather than replicate those of the Commons; the review should also explore how the upper chamber might offer a better route for public engagement in scrutiny and policy making.' It also committed the party to legislate to place 'reasonable limits on the time bills spend in the second chamber – no longer than 60 sitting days for most bills.' The paragraph dealing with composition was short: 'As part of the process of modernisation, we will remove the remaining hereditary peers and allow a free vote on the composition of the House.'

In the new 2005 parliament, supporters of an elected House followed their practice of previous sessions of tabling an early day motion (EDM). Conservative MP David Curry tabled a motion favouring a 'predominantly elected chamber'. By September, it had attracted eighty-one signatures, though predominantly of Labour, Liberal Democrat and Nationalist MPs. For the government, however, the issue was not a priority. The Queen's Speech in 2005 promised only that the government 'would bring forward proposals to continue the reform of the House of Lords.' By the beginning of 2006, there had been no progress on appointing a joint committee.

Various participants in the debate on the future of the House noted that the House of Lords that followed the Parliament Act of 1911 had been intended as an interim House until legislation could be passed to provide for a more democratic chamber. That interim House lasted for nearly ninety years. Some wondered whether the interim House that existed following the passage of the House of Lords Act might not now last a similar period of time.

■ The future of the second chamber?

The question of what to do with the House of Lords has thus been a notable item on the political agenda. Given that the removal of hereditary peers from membership of the House was intended as the first stage in a two-stage process, the future shape of the House remains a matter of debate. What are the options?

In the period leading up to the reform of the House in 1999, four approaches to reform were identified (Norton, 1982, pp. 119–29). These were known as the four Rs – retain, reform, replace or remove altogether. With some adaptation, they remain the four approaches following the passage of the House of Lords Act.

Retain

This approach favours retaining the House as a non-elected chamber. It argues that the interim House, comprising predominantly life peers, is preferable to an elected or part-elected chamber. The House, it is argued, does a good job. It complements the elected House in that it carries out tasks that are qualitatively different from those of the House of Commons. It is able to do so because its members offer particular expertise. By retaining a House of life peers, one not only creates a body of knowledge and experience, one also creates a body with some degree of independence. The cross-benchers in the House hold the balance of power and are able to judge matters with some degree of detachment. If the House were to be elected, it would have the same claim to democratic legitimacy as the Commons and would either be the same as the Commons – thus constituting a rubber-stamping body and achieving nothing – or, if elected by a different method or at different times, have the potential to clash with the Commons and create stalemate in the political system. Election would challenge, not enhance, the basic accountability of the political system. Who would electors hold accountable if two elected chambers failed to reach agreement?

This approach was taken by some of those giving evidence to the Royal Commission on Reform of the House of Lords. They included this writer (Norton, 1999). Another prominent supporter was a former Chancellor of the Exchequer, Foreign Secretary and Deputy Prime Minister, Geoffrey Howe (Lord Howe of Aberavon). Having initially reluctantly conceded that there could be an elected element, he changed his mind and wrote in support of the stance taken by this writer (see Howe, 1999). In 2002, a campaign to argue the case against an elected second chamber was formed within Parliament. Led by an MP (Sir Patrick Cormack, Conservative MP for Staffordshire South) and a peer (this writer), it attracted a growing body of cross-party support in both Houses (Norton, 2004). Whips in the Commons observed a shift of opinion in favour of appointment. In the Lords debate in January 2003, the Lord Chancellor came out in favour of a wholly appointed chamber. Shortly afterwards, in Prime Minister's Question Time, Prime Minister Tony Blair did the same.

Reform

This approach, advocated by the Royal Commission, favours some modification to the interim House, although retaining what are seen as the essential strengths of the existing House. It acknowledges the value of having a membership that is expert and one that has a degree of independence from government.

At the same time, it argues that a wholly appointed chamber lacks democratic legitimacy. Therefore it favours a mix of appointed and elected members. The advantages of such a system were touched on in the government's 1998 White Paper, *Modernising Parliament* (pp. 49–50): 'It would combine some of the most valued features of the present House of Lords with a democratic basis suitable for a modern legislative chamber.' The extent of the mix of nominated and elected members is a matter of some debate. Some would like to see a small proportion of members elected. The Royal Commission, as we have seen, put forward three options. The government, in its 2001 White Paper, recommended that 20 per cent of the membership be elected. Some reformers favour an indirect form of election, members serving by virtue of election by an electoral college comprising, say, members of local authorities or other assemblies.

Replace

This approach favours doing away with the House of Lords and replacing it with a new second chamber. Some wish to replace it with a wholly elected house. Election, it is contended, would give the House a legitimacy that a nominated chamber, or even a part-elected chamber, lacks (see Box 18.1). That greater legitimacy would allow the House to serve as a more effective check on government, knowing that it was not open to accusations of being undemocratic. It would have the teeth that the House of Lords lacks. Government can ignore the House of Lords: it could not ignore an elected second chamber. If members were elected on a national and regional basis, this – it is argued – would allow the different parts of the United Kingdom (Scotland, Wales, Northern Ireland and the English regions) to have a more distinct voice in the political process. As we have seen, this stance is taken by a number of organisations, including the Liberal Democrats and Charter88. Both favour an elected senate. It is also the stance taken by a former Labour Leader of the House of Lords, Lord Richard (see Richard and Welfare, 1999) and, as we have seen, by some senior MPs (Clarke *et al.*, 2005).

Others who favour doing away with the House of Lords want to replace it not with an elected chamber but with a chamber composed of representatives of different organised interests – a **functional chamber**. This, it is claimed, would ensure that the different groups in society – trade unions, charities, industry,

---

BOX 18.1   DEBATE

An elected second chamber

The case for
- Democratic – allows voters to choose members of the chamber.
- Provides a limit on the powers of the first chamber.
- Provides an additional limit on the powers of government.
- Gives citizens an additional channel for seeking a redress of grievance or a change of public policy.
- Can be used to provide for representation of the different parts of the United Kingdom.
- Confers popular legitimacy on the chamber.

The case against
- Rids the second chamber of the expertise and the experience provided by life peers.
- Undermines accountability – who should electors hold accountable if the second chamber disagrees with the first?
- Superfluous if dominated by the same party that has a majority in the first chamber.
- Objectionable if it runs into frequent conflict with the popularly elected first chamber.
- Will not be socially representative – election tends to favour white, middle-aged and male candidates – and would thus, in any event, simply replicate the House of Commons.
- May prevent the elected government from being able to implement its manifesto commitments.
- Legitimacy of the political process will be threatened if conflict between the two chambers produces stalemate or unpopular compromise policies.

consumer bodies – had a direct input into the political process instead of having to lobby MPs and peers in the hope of getting a hearing. The problem with this proposal is that it would prove difficult to agree on which groups should enjoy representation in the House. Defenders of the existing House point out that there is extensive *de facto* functional representation in any event, with leading figures in a great many groups having been ennobled.

There is also a third variation. Anthony Barnett and Peter Carty of the think-tank Demos have made the case for a second chamber chosen in part by lot (see also Barnett, 1997). In evidence to the Royal Commission in 1999, they argued that people chosen randomly would be able to bring an independent view. 'We want "People's Peers" but they must come from the people and not be chosen from above, by an official body. It is possible to have a strong non-partisan element in the Second Chamber, and for this to be and to be seen to be democratic and lively.' The principle of public participation, they argued, should be extended to the national legislature.

Remove altogether

Under this approach, the House of Lords would be abolished and not replaced at all. Instead, the UK would have a **unicameral legislature**, the legislative burden being shouldered by a reformed House of Commons. Supporters of this approach argue that there is no case for an unelected second chamber, since it has no legitimacy to challenge an elected chamber, and that there is no case for an elected second chamber, since this would result in either imitation or conflict. Parliament should therefore constitute a single chamber, like legislatures in Scandinavia and New Zealand. The House of Commons should be reformed in order that it may fulfil all the functions currently carried out by the two chambers.

Opponents of this approach argue that a single chamber would not be able to carry the burden, not least given the volume of public business in a country with a population of 60 million, many times larger than New Zealand and the Scandinavian countries with unicameral legislatures. Furthermore, they contend, the House of Commons could not fulfil the task of a constitutional safeguard, since it would essentially be acting as a safeguard against itself. Nor would it be an appropriate body to undertake a second look at legislation, since it would not be able to bring to bear a different point of view and

different experience from that brought to bear the first time around.

Although abolition has on occasion attracted some support – including, as we have seen, at one point from the Labour Party – it is not an approach that has made much of the running in recent debate. It did, though, attract 172 votes when MPs voted on it in February 2003.

Polls reveal that opinion on the Lords is mixed. Supporters of change cite opinion polls showing that most respondents generally favour the reform or replace options, though with no clear majority for either. In a MORI poll in 1998, 24 per cent of respondents wanted to replace the House with a new second chamber elected by the public; 23 per cent wanted to replace it with a part-elected, part-nominated chamber; 20 per cent wanted to leave the House as it was (with the passage of the 1999 Act their preferred option fell by the way); 13 per cent favoured removing hereditary peers and having new peers nominated by government; and only 12 per cent favoured abolition. In a December 2001 ICM/Democratic Audit poll, 27 per cent favoured a wholly elected House, 27 per cent a House with most members elected, 14 per cent a House with a minority of members elected and 9 per cent a wholly appointed House. (Abolition was not offered as an option.) Almost a quarter of the respondents gave a 'don't know' response.

Supporters of an appointed chamber cite polls which show that people view the work of the House of Lords in a positive light and do not regard reform as a priority for government. An ICM poll for the think-tank *Politeia* in March 2005 found that 72 per cent of respondents thought that the House of Lords did a very or fairly good job; only 23 per cent thought that it did a fairly bad or very bad job. A similarly large majority – 71 per cent – thought that the House provided an effective check on the power of the government. Almost two-thirds – 63 per cent – believed that the powers of the Lords should not be reduced. Though there may be support for change, it appears not to be very deep: 59 per cent of those questioned agreed that reform of the Lords was not a priority for the next five years.

The debate continues. The options in terms of the contemporary debate are those of retain, reform, replace or remove altogether. Each, as we have seen, has its proponents. The arguments for and against an elected chamber are considered in Box 18.1. The battle to determine the future shape of the second chamber has not yet been won.

BOX 18.2 IDEAS AND PERSPECTIVES

The atmosphere in the House

The House of Lords is stunning in its grandeur. For some, it is awe-inspiring; for others, it is suffocating. The House combines crown, Church and a chamber of the legislature. The magnificent throne dominates the chamber. On entering the chamber, a peer bows to the cloth of estate – just above the throne – as a mark of respect. (Unlike the Commons, there is no bowing when leaving the chamber.) Look up and you see the magnificent stained glass windows. Look down and you see the red benches of a debating chamber. The House combines symbolism with the efficiency of a working body. From the bar of the House you see the throne: lower your eye-line and you see the laptop computer on the table of the House. The clerks sit in their wigs and gowns, using the laptop as well as controlling the button for resetting the digital clocks in the chamber.

On Mondays to Thursdays, the benches are usually packed for the start of business. The combination of increasing attendance and a relatively small chamber means that peers often have to get in early to get their preferred spot on the benches. (Unlike the Commons, one cannot reserve a seat in advance.) The Lord Speaker's procession mirrors that of the Speaker of the House of Commons in its pomp and dignity. Peers bow as the mace passes. Once the Lord Speaker has taken her place on the Woolsack, prayers are said. Once these are over, members of the public are admitted to the gallery and other peers come into the chamber. At the start of Question Time, the Clerk of the Parliaments, sitting bewigged at the table, rises and announces the name of the peer who has the first question on the Order Paper. The peer rises and declares, 'I beg leave to ask the question standing in my name on the Order Paper'. The answering minister rises to the despatch box and reads out a prepared response. The peer rises to put a supplementary, followed later by others. If two peers rise at the same time, one is expected to give way; otherwise, as a self-regulating chamber, it is members who decide – usually by calling out the name of the peer they wish to hear, or else by shouting 'this side', indicating that the last supplementary was put by someone on the other side of the House. If neither gives way, the Leader of the House usually intervenes, but the Leader can be overruled by the House. Normally, good manners prevail.

Peers take a lively interest in questions. There are approximately seven or eight minutes available for each question. If time on a question goes beyond that, peers shout 'next question'. Ministers need to be well briefed. It is usually obvious when ministers are out of their depth or have been caught out. Question Time can be educational. The topics are diverse and usually there is knowledge on the part of questioners and ministers. If a minister runs into trouble, the fact that the chamber is packed adds to the tension. Question Time can also be funny. When a minister, questioned about the use of mobile 'phones on aeroplanes, faced a supplementary about the perils of mobile telephones 'on *terra firma*', he did not hear the full supplementary and had to ask a colleague. Realising he had taken some time to return to the despatch box, he rose and said: 'I am sorry My Lords, I thought *terra firma* might be some obscure airline!' On another occasion, a question about the safety of a female chimpanzee that had been mistreated received a very detailed answer, which included the facts – as I recall – that the chimp was now in a sanctuary with other chimps, that the group was led by a male of a certain age and that the chimp was enjoying herself. Whereupon the redoubtable Baroness Trumpington got to her feet and declared: 'My Lords, she is better off than I am!'

The House of Lords is a remarkably egalitarian institution: members are peers in the true sense. The atmosphere of the House can be tense, sometimes exciting – the results of votes are sometimes uncertain – and occasionally a little rough. Maiden speeches, given priority in debates and heard in respectful silence (peers cannot enter or leave the chamber while they are taking place), can be nerve-wracking, even for the most experienced of public speakers. Most of the time the House has the feel of what it is: a working body, engaged in debate and legislative scrutiny. The emphasis is on constructive debate and revision. Partisan shouting matches are rare. At times, especially at the committee stage of bills, attendance can be small, the main debate taking place between the two front benches, but the effect of the

▶

probing from the opposition benches ensures that ministers have to offer informed responses. Notes frequently pass from civil servants in the officials' box to the minister at the despatch box. The quality of ministers can be very good. Ministers who are well regarded and who take the House seriously can rely on the occasional indulgence of the House if they make a slip. The responsibilities of some ministers mean that they spend a great deal of time in the chamber. In the 2005–6 session, the home office minister, Baroness Scotland, was regularly at the despatch box, taking bills through the House, as was the constitutional affairs minister, Baroness Ashton of Upholland. In 2004, Baroness Scotland was voted peer of the year by the Political Studies Association, and in the 2005 *House Magazine* Parliamentary Awards ceremony, Baroness Ashton was voted minister of the year.

The only way to appreciate the atmosphere, and the productive nature of the House, is to be there. One certainly cannot glean it from television – the House is squeezed out by the Commons – or from the official report. *Hansard* is good at tidying up speeches, correcting grammar and titles. The tidying up can also have the effect of sanitising proceedings. During the passage of the Access to Justice Bill, Conservative Baroness Wilcox – a champion of consumers – moved an amendment dealing with consumer affairs. The Lord Chancellor, to the delight – and obvious surprise – of Lady Wilcox, promptly accepted the import of the amendment. Lady Wilcox rose and exclaimed 'Gosh. Thanks'. This appeared in *Hansard* as 'I thank the noble and learned Lord. He has pleased me very much today'! When the House collapses in laughter – as it did after the minister's *terra firma* remark or Baroness Trumpington's intervention – this either appears in *Hansard* as 'Noble Lords: Oh!' or else is ignored. No, one definitely has to be there to appreciate the atmosphere.

BOX 18.3 BRITAIN IN CONTEXT

A distinctive second chamber

The House of Lords is distinctive as a second chamber because of its existence as a second chamber, its membership and its size.

It is distinctive, but far from unique, in existing as a second chamber; that is, as part of a bicameral legislature. Almost two-thirds of countries have uni-cameral legislatures (Massicotte, 2001). Bicameral legislatures are, however, common in Western countries, especially larger ones, and in federal systems.

It is distinctive, but again not unique, in that its members are appointed rather than elected. (It was unique in the period up to 1999, when most of its members served in the House by virtue of having inherited their seats; no other major national legislature had a chamber based on the hereditary principle.) Of the sixty-six second chambers that exist, seventeen use appointment as the predominant method of selection: the most prominent in the Western world are the UK and Canada. Of the remaining countries with second chambers, twenty-seven employ direct election as the predominant method of selection;

the rest employ indirect election or some other method of selection (Russell, 2000, pp. 29–32).

The House of Lords is unusual in that it has no fixed membership – the membership varies as some members die and others are appointed at different times. Members are also exceptional in terms of their tenure. Though it is common for members of second chambers to serve longer terms than members of the first chamber, no other chamber is based predominantly on life membership. In the House of Lords, all members serve for life other than the Lords Spiritual, who cease to be members when they retire as Archbishops or Bishops. The House is remarkable also in terms of its size. Whereas it is common for second chambers to have a smaller membership than the first, the House of Lords is larger than the first and, indeed, has a claim to be the largest second chamber in the democratic world; the House of Commons has a claim to be the largest first chamber. Together, they form the largest legislature in the democratic world.

Chapter summary

The House of Lords serves as a notable body of scrutiny – both of legislation and of public policy – and as a body for giving expression to views that otherwise would not be put on the public record. As such, it adds value to the political process. The fact that it is not elected means that it has limited significance as a body for legitimising government and measures of public policy and as a body through which politicians are recruited to ministerial office. The fact that it is not elected also makes it a target of continuing demands for reform.

The question of what to do with the House of Lords has been a matter of debate for more than a century. The election of a Labour government in 1997, committed to reform of the House, brought it to the forefront of debate. The removal in 1999 of most hereditary peers from membership fundamentally changed the composition of the House. It became a chamber composed overwhelmingly of life peers. For some, that was a perfectly acceptable chamber. For others, it was not. The House of Lords serves not only as a forum to discuss political issues. It is itself a political issue. That is likely to remain the case.

Discussion points

■ What are the principal functions of the House of Lords? Are they appropriate functions for a second chamber of Parliament?

■ Does the House of Lords do a better job than the House of Commons in scrutinising government legislation? If so, why?

■ Should the institutions of the European Union pay attention to reports from the House of Lords?

■ Was the government right to get rid of most hereditary peers from the House of Lords? Should it have got rid of *all* of them?

■ What would *you* do with the House of Lords – and why?

Further reading

Crewe (2005) constitutes a fascinating anthropological study and the only recent book-length study devoted to the House of Lords. On the work of the contemporary House, see also Part IV of Blackburn and Kennon (2003), Chapter 6 of Baldwin (2005), Norton (2005) *passim*, Shell (2005) and material produced by the Information Office of the Lords, especially *The Work of the House of Lords* (2005) (also available online: see below). On peers' voting behaviour, see Norton (2003). On the House prior to the reform of 1999 see Shell and Beamish (1993) and Dickson and Carmichael (1999), the latter providing useful material on the House in both its political and judicial roles. Shell also provides a useful chapter on questions in the Lords in Franklin and Norton (1993) and, more generally on the role of the House, in Patterson and Mughan (1999).

On Lords reform, see Kent (1998), Tyrie (1998), Richard and Welfare (1999), Norton (1999), the Report of the Royal Commission on the Reform of the House of Lords, *A House for the Future* (2000), the Government White Paper, *The House of Lords: Completing the Reform* (2001), the report from the Public Administration Select Committee, *The Second Chamber: Continuing the Reform* (2002), Norton (2004), Shell (2004), and Clarke *et al.* (2005). Morrison (2001), Chapter 5, offers an overview enriched by extensive interviews. Useful comparative information is to be found in Russell (2000). There is also valuable material on the websites of the Royal Commission and Parliament. Through the Parliament website, one can also read debates in the two Houses on the House of Lords Bill (1999), on the Government's White Paper (2001), debated in both Houses in January 2002, and on the report of the Joint Committee on Lords reform, debated on 21/22 January 2003 in the Lords and on 21 January in the House of Commons.

▶

References

Baggott, R. (1995) *Pressure Groups Today* (Manchester University Press).

Baldwin, N.D.J. (1985) 'The House of Lords: behavioural changes', in P. Norton (ed.), *Parliament in the 1980s* (Blackwell).

Baldwin, N.D.J. (1999) 'The membership and work of the House of Lords', in B. Dickson and P. Carmichael (eds), *The House of Lords: Its Parliamentary and Judicial Roles* (Hart Publishing).

Baldwin, N.D.J. (ed.) (2005) *Parliament in the 21st Century* (Politico's).

Barnett, A. (1997) *This Time: Our Constitutional Revolution* (Vintage).

Blackburn, R. and Kennon, A. (2003) *Griffith and Ryle on Parliament: Functions, Practice and Procedures*, 2nd edn (Sweet & Maxwell).

Clarke, K., Cook, R., Tyler, P., Wright, T. and Young, G. (2005) *Reforming the House of Lords* (The Constitution Unit).

Constitution Unit (1996) *Reform of the House of Lords* (The Constitution Unit).

Constitutional Commission (1999) *The Report of the Constitutional Commission on Options for a New Second Chamber* (Constitutional Commission).

Crewe, E. (2005) *Lords of Parliament* (Manchester University Press).

Criddle, B., Childs, S. and Norton, P. (2005) 'The make-up of Parliament', in P. Giddings (ed.), *The Future of Parliament* (Palgrave Macmillan).

Dickson, B. and Carmichael, P. (eds) (1999) *The House of Lords: Its Parliamentary and Judicial Roles* (Hart Publishing).

Drewry, G. and Brock, J. (1993) 'Government legislation: an overview', in D. Shell and D. Beamish (eds), *The House of Lords at Work* (Oxford University Press).

Franklin, M. and Norton, P. (eds) (1993) *Parliamentary Questions* (Oxford University Press).

Grantham, C. (1993) 'Select committees', in D. Shell and D. Beamish (eds), *The House of Lords at Work* (Oxford University Press).

Hayter, P.D.G. (1992) 'The parliamentary monitoring of science and technology', *Government and Opposition*, Vol. 26.

Himsworth, C.M.G. (1995) 'The Delegated Powers Scrutiny Committee', *Public Law*, Spring.

House of Lords: Completing the Reform (2001) Cmd 5291 (The Stationery Office).

House of Lords (2005) *House of Lords: Annual Report 2004–05* (The Stationery Office).

House of Lords (2006) *House of Lords Annual Report and Accounts 2005–06*. (The Stationery Office).

House of Lords Information Office (2005) *The Work of the House of Lords* (House of Lords).

Howe of Aberavon, Lord (1999) 'This House is built on solid ground', *The Times*, 2 August.

Kent, N. (1998) *Enhancing Our Democracy* (Tory Reform Group).

Labour Peers Group (2004) *Reform of the Powers, Procedures and Conventions of the House of Lords* (Labour Peers Group, 2004).

Maclean, I., Spirling, A. and Russell, M. (2003) 'None of the above: the UK House of Commons vote reforming the House of Lords, February 2003', *Political Quarterly*, Vol. 74.

Massicotte, L. (2001), 'Legislative unicameralism: a global survey and a few case studies', *The Journal of Legislative Studies*, Vol. 7, No. 1, pp. 151–70.

Modernising Parliament: Reforming the House of Lords (1999) Cm 4183 (The Stationery Office).

Morrison, J. (2001) *Reforming Britain: New Labour, New Constitution?* (Reuters/Pearson Education).

Norton, P. (1982) *The Constitution in Flux* (Basil Blackwell).

Norton, P. (1993) *Does Parliament Matter?* (Harvester Wheatsheaf).

Norton, P. (ed.) (1996) *National Parliaments and the European Union* (Cass).

Norton, P. (1999) 'Adding value to the political system', submission to the Royal Commission on the House of Lords.

Norton, P. (2003) 'Cohesion without voting: party voting in the House of Lords', *The Journal of Legislative Studies*, Vol. 9.

Norton, P. (2004) 'Reforming the House of Lords: a view from the parapets', *Representation*, Vol. 40.

Norton, P. (2005) *Parliament in British Politics* (Palgrave Macmillan).

Patterson, S.C. and Mughan, A. (eds) (1999) *Senates: Bicameralism in the Contemporary World* (Ohio State University Press).

Public Administration Select Committee (2002) *The Second Chamber: Continuing the Reform*, Fifth Report, Session 2001–2002, HC 494-I (The Stationery Office).

Richard, Lord and Welfare, D. (1999) *Unfinished Business: Reforming the House of Lords* (Vintage).

Royal Commission on the Reform of the House of Lords (2000) *A House for the Future*, Cm 4534 (The Stationery Office).

Rush, M. (ed.) (1990) *Parliament and Pressure Politics* (Clarendon Press).

Russell, M. (2000) *Reforming the House of Lords: Lessons from Overseas* (Oxford University Press).

Shell, D. (1983) 'The House of Lords', in D. Judge (ed.), *The Politics of Parliamentary Reform* (Heinemann).

Shell, D. (1992) *The House of Lords*, 2nd edn (Harvester Wheatsheaf).

Shell, D. (2004) 'The future of the Second Chamber', *Parliamentary Affairs*, Vol. 57.

Shell, D. (2005) 'The House of Lords: a chamber of scrutiny', in P. Giddings (ed.), *The Future of Parliament* (Palgrave Macmillan).

Shell, D. and Beamish, D. (eds) (1993) *The House of Lords at Work* (Oxford University Press).

Tyrie, A. (1998) *Reforming the Lords: A Conservative Approach* (Conservative Policy Forum).

White, A.B. (1908) *The Making of the English Constitution 1449–1485* (G.P. Putnam).

Useful websites

Parliamentary websites

Parliament: www.parliament.uk

House of Lords:
    www.parliament.uk/about_lords/about_lords.cfm

Guide to what the House of Lords does:
    www.parliament.uk/about_lords/
    what_the-lords_do.cfm

The Work of the House of Lords:
    www.parliament.uk/documents/upload/
    HoLwork.pdf

House of Lords Select Committees:
    www.parliament.uk/parliamentary_committees/
    parliamentary_committees26.cfm

Government Whips' Office: www.lordswhips.org.uk
    (provides details on future business, including
    speakers)

Parliamentary debates (*Hansard*):
    House of Commons:
    www.parliament.uk.hansard/hansard2.cfm
    House of Lords:
    www.parliament.uk/hansard/hansard.cfm

Cross-bench peers: www.crossbenchpeers.org.uk

Reform

Report of the Royal Commission on the Reform of the House of Lords (Wakeham Commission):
    www.archive.official-documents.co.uk/
    document/cm45/4534/contents.htm

Government 1999 White Paper on Lords Reform:
    www.archive.official-documents.co.uk/
    document/cm41/4183/4183.htm

Public Administration Committee of the House of Commons (Report *The Second Chamber: Completing the Reform*):   www.publications.
    parliament.uk/pa/cm200102/cmselect/cmpubadm/
    794/79402.htm

Joint Select Committee on House of Lords Reform:
    www.parliament.uk/parliamentary_committees/
    joint_committee_on_house_of_lords_reform.cfm

Charter88:   www.charter88.org.uk

And another thing . . .

The Premier League: ranking Tony Blair

Kevin Theakston

At Mount Rushmore in South Dakota the faces of four of the greatest American presidents (George Washington, Thomas Jefferson, Abraham Lincoln and Theodore Roosevelt) are carved into the face of a mountain. Who would we put among the granite heroes in a British version of Mount Rushmore? It is unlikely that the sculptors would be carving Tony Blair into the monument. In the political science equivalent of the Mount Rushmore memorial, a poll of academic experts in British politics and modern British history reveals that Blair still has some way to go until he can be regarded as one of the greatest British prime ministers (Theakston and Gill, 2006). The survey, carried out in the autumn of 2004, asked respondents to indicate on a score of 0 to 10 how successful or unsuccessful they considered each prime minister to have been. A total of 139 university academics replied, and the results put Blair in sixth place in the league table of twentieth-century premiers (Table 1).

Blair has some claims to a place in the record books. Aged only 43 when he first entered Number 10, he was the youngest twentieth-century prime minister and the seventh-youngest prime minister ever. (William Pitt's record of becoming prime minister aged 24 in 1783 is unlikely ever to be beaten!) Also, he had the ability and the luck to get to the top of the 'slippery poll' pretty quickly – after only fourteen years as an MP. Only John Major, who had been an MP for eleven years before becoming prime minister, had less experience in Parliament among twentieth-century premiers. Compare that with Churchill's forty years as an MP, Attlee's twenty-three years, Callaghan's thirty-one years and Thatcher's twenty years before they got the top job. Blair was unusual too in having no previous ministerial experience before taking on the job of

Table 1 Ranking twentieth century Prime Ministers

Ranking	Prime Minister	Mean score
1	Clement Attlee (Lab. 1945–51)	8.34
2	Winston Churchill (Con. 1940–5, 51–5)	7.88
3	David Lloyd George (Lib. 1916–22)	7.33
4	Margaret Thatcher (Con. 1979–90)	7.14
5	Harold Macmillan (Con. 1957–63)	6.49
6	Tony Blair (Lab. 1997–)	6.30
7	Herbert Asquith (Lib. 1908–16)	6.19
8	Stanley Baldwin (Con. 1923–4, 24–9, 35–7)	6.18
9	Harold Wilson (Lab. 1964–70, 74–6)	5.93
10	Lord Salisbury (Con. 1895–1902)	5.75
11	Henry Campbell-Bannerman (Lib. 1906–8)	5.01
12	James Callaghan (Lab. 1976–9)	4.75
13	Edward Heath (Con. 1970–4)	4.36
14	Ramsay MacDonald (Lab. 1924, 29–31, 31–5)	3.73
15	John Major (Con. 1990–7)	3.67
16	Andrew Bonar Law (Con. 1922–3)	3.50
17	Neville Chamberlain (Con. 1937–40)	3.43
18	Arthur Balfour (Con. 1902–5)	3.42
19	Alec Douglas-Home (Con. 1963–4)	3.33
20	Anthony Eden (Con. 1955–7)	2.53

Source: From MORI and the University of Leeds. Copyright © Ipsos MORI, reproduced with permission

prime minister (of the other twentieth-century prime ministers only Ramsay MacDonald, like Blair, had come straight in at the top and had not served a Cabinet or government apprenticeship). He won three elections in a row (two with landslide majorities, albeit on only 43 per cent of the vote), something no other Labour premier has done. And he is the longest-serving Labour prime minister we have had, outstripping both Attlee and Harold Wilson in that category.

Because Blair was still in post at the time of the survey, his rating should perhaps be considered as a provisional one. Future political scientists and historians may rate him higher up the league table – or, of course, in a lower position. There have been many surveys, going back to the 1940s, of American academics, producing league tables of the 'best' and 'worst' US presidents, and while the 'greats' and the 'duds' are usually the same in the different studies, in the middle places some of the rankings and evaluations do seem to vary over time. We do not know where Tony Blair or John Major will be placed in the 'league table' in 30 years' time.

Rating or ranking exercises like these can be something of a game for political junkies. Can the performance of political leaders, their successes and failures, what they got right and their mistakes, be boiled down to a simple score out of ten? No two prime ministers are ever dealt the same hand, and we need to take account of the historical and political contexts they faced, the situations they inherited, the problems they had to deal with, and so on, before we can properly say how well they performed. But the league table does prompt us to ponder what the important factors are making for effective or successful leadership in government by prime ministers.

Harold Wilson always used to say that the ability to sleep soundly and a sense of history were the main essentials of a successful prime minister. Edward Heath thought that the ability to keep your head in a crisis was the key quality. Political scientist Simon James says that successful prime ministers need 'the combined skills of prophet, conciliator, tactician and sheepdog' (James, 1999, p. 90). Historian Robert Blake's checklist of prime-ministerial qualities included courage, tenacity, determination, firm nerves, clarity of mind, a thick skin and the absence of an original mind (Blake, 1975, pp. 19–22).

The American academic, Fred Greenstein, has looked at the qualities and skills affecting the performance of US presidents (Greenstein, 2001).

Making allowances for the differences between the two political systems, his six-point model provides some good questions to ask when we try to assess the effectiveness of British prime ministers.

■ How good are they as *communicators*? How well do they perform in Parliament, on the public platform and on television, 'selling' themselves and their policies? Harold Wilson and Tony Blair, with his thespian skills, stand out as the two best performers among recent prime ministers under this heading. John Major, Alec Douglas-Home, Ted Heath and the clam-like Clement Attlee were all poor communicators and paid a price for handling the media badly.

■ How well do they *organise Number 10 and the government*? The issue here is less about the size of the prime minister's staff (which Blair has built up) and more about being open to competing ideas and constructive dissent, and avoiding 'groupthink' (where both Thatcher and Blair suffered from the creation of a 'bunker mentality' in Number 10). Some prime ministers (Wilson and Heath) have tinkered endlessly with the machinery of government – usually fruitlessly. Attlee created hundreds of Cabinet committees but Thatcher and Blair preferred to govern through smaller informal groups and so-called 'bilaterals' (the Butler inquiry exposing the drawbacks of Blair's approach). And another problem is that prime ministers rarely have much interest in or experience of managing institutions, people and systems to produce results.

■ How good are their *political skills*? Some prime ministers (Macmillan, Wilson, Callaghan) have, in different ways, been very accomplished political operators – cunning, guileful, sometimes even Machiavellian. John Major's people-skills in terms of negotiation, conciliation and networking should not be underestimated. But Heath was, curiously, much better at administration and government than at politics (often being rude and high-handed with his back-benchers, for instance). And Thatcher's hectoring and bullying style was ultimately counter-productive and alienated her ministers and MPs.

■ Do they have a strong *policy vision*? Thatcher provided a radical vision and a driving sense of mission. But many prime ministers have themselves actually had few clear long-term policy goals and little in the way of a sense of direction.

That may not matter if – as under Attlee – the Cabinet and the party have a sense of purpose and remain united. Pragmatists – even opportunists – have been much more common in Number 10 than vision-driven politicians.

■ What is their *cognitive style*? How do they process advice and information? Churchill was impulsive, imaginative and fertile in ideas whereas Heath was cool, rational and problem-solving. Wilson liked hopping from issue to issue; Callaghan preferred to deal with one problem at a time (and was overwhelmed when they all crowded in together during the 'Winter of Discontent'). Major made decisions by listing the pros and cons in two columns on a sheet of paper – not the approach of someone with a clear agenda of his own. Thatcher had 'instant certainty' and an immense command of detail, and she liked to test ministers and policies through a pretty brutal process of argument. Blair is more interested in the 'big picture' and in 'presentation' than in policy details.

■ Do they possess *emotional intelligence*? It was said that American president Franklin Roosevelt had the ideal combination – a 'second-class intellect' but a 'first-class temperament'. How far can leaders manage their emotions and cope with the stress of the top job? Attlee was patient, stable, self-controlled and self-effacing, but underneath his impenetrable shyness had plenty of intellectual self-confidence and the necessary toughness. Churchill experienced major mood-swings and was prone to depression. Eden was highly-strung, thin-skinned, volatile, petulant, a great fusser, and easily upset and annoyed – he cracked up with a combination of illness and the strain of the Suez crisis. Major was the perhaps the nicest person among the last three prime ministers but wanted to be liked too much and lacked the inner toughness to provide steely leadership when his government ran into difficulties.

None of our recent prime ministers has had all the required skills and qualities highlighted in this model, and it is unlikely that all of them will ever be concentrated in one person. But the model does provide a way of understanding the strengths and weaknesses of past prime ministers – and maybe a checklist we should bear in mind when selecting future party leaders and evaluating potential prime ministers.

Reviewing the records of twentieth-century prime ministers in the league table above, we can say that all successful PMs need to be able to point to major policy achievements at home. Historians single out the Attlee government's welfare state reforms and the creation of the National Health Service as the key twentieth-century domestic policy achievements. As important, Attlee shaped the framework of politics and the political agenda for a whole generation, until the 1970s. Margaret Thatcher was the other great 'political weather-maker' of the twentieth-century premiers. She had a massive and transforming impact on the economy, on British society, on the political landscape, and on the terms of political argument. Even into his third term, Blair still needs to do something significant in terms of historical achievement to measure up against them. Labour's successful economic policy has borne the imprint of Gordon Brown, not the prime minister. Blair's repeated stress on 'delivery' and on public service reform cannot disguise a sense of prime ministerial frustration at what has been achieved so far and of promise unfulfilled. On Europe, he has arguably missed his moment.

It is also clear that prime ministers need to be able to demonstrate a basic 'governing competence'. Can they keep the government afloat, maintain a sense of direction, and survive the day-to-day pressure of 'events, dear boy, events', as Harold Macmillan once put it? Jim Callaghan was actually a better prime minister than he was often given credit for in this sense, playing the part of the 'calm pilot in the storms' during the troubled 1970s. John Major's inability or unwillingness to exert himself led to charges of weakness, dithering, and letting circumstances and the push and pull of the Tory factions determine issues. Blair's record here is mixed. There has been since 1997 too much emphasis on short-term media management, 'spin' and fighting for tomorrow's headlines. He has kept switching priorities rather than pushing through strategy to a conclusion (few people in Number 10 – including Blair – have any experience of managing anything). His centralising and presidential, but dangerously informal, style of government has come in for criticism – from within his own party and from outside inquiries like the Butler Committee.

Wars and international crises can make and unmake premierships. Churchill and Lloyd George are the two great war-winners of twentieth-century prime ministers. Victory in the Falklands boosted Mrs Thatcher's popularity with the electorate. But

Asquith and Chamberlain were destroyed as prime ministers by their failures of leadership during the First World War and the struggle against Hitler, respectively. And Eden's premiership and his reputation were both sunk by the Suez crisis. Iraq is unlikely to secure Blair's place in history, at least in a positive sense.

A final point is that prime ministers have to know when to go – when their time is up. The only other prime minister in the last 100 years who won three elections in a row – Margaret Thatcher – went on to be overthrown by her own Cabinet. Only two twentieth-century prime ministers retired at a time of their own choosing: Harold Wilson (in 1976) and Stanley Baldwin (in 1937). Some were evicted by the electorate (including Major, Callaghan, Attlee and Heath). Illness removed others (such as Macmillan and, at the age of 81, Churchill). But some were dragged out kicking and screaming, as it were (in different ways: Thatcher, Chamberlain, Asquith, Lloyd George). Blair has said that he will not seek a fourth term of office, but how long into his third term he stays is uncertain and the management of the 'handover' is proving tricky. Since the 2005 election Blair has seemed a prime-minister-in-a-hurry, sensing that he has only a relatively short time left to make a lasting mark and obsessed by his 'legacy'.

References

Blake, R. (1975) *The Office of Prime Minister* (Oxford University Press).

Greenstein, F. (2001) *The Presidential Difference: Leadership Style from FDR to Clinton (with a new afterword on George W. Bush)* (Princeton University Press).

James, S. (1999) *British Cabinet Government*, 2nd edn (Routledge).

Theakston, K. and Gill, M. (2006) 'Rating 20th-century British prime ministers', *British Journal of Politics and International Relations*, Vol. 8, pp. 193–213.

PART 5
THE EXECUTIVE PROCESS

CHAPTER 19

The Cabinet and the Prime Minister

Dennis Kavanagh

Learning objectives

- To provide a full analysis of the role of Prime Minister.

- To assess the importance of Tony Blair's premiership.

- To examine the role of cabinet ministers.

- To evaluate the possibilities for reform at the centre of British government.

Introduction

This chapter examines the work of the Prime Minister and Cabinet and the emergence of a core executive. It examines the roles and powers of the Prime Minister and the structure of the office, and assesses the impact of recent holders of the office. It discusses the factors that influence the Cabinet's size and composition, then analyses the structure of the Cabinet and its committees and evaluates proposals for improving the coordination of policies. The final section reviews some criticisms of the system and suggestions that have been made for reform.

■ The Prime Minister's roles and powers

There is no constitutional definition of a Prime Minister's role. The first statutory reference to the office of the Prime Minister was as recent as 1937. Much of the job is actually what he or she chooses to do. Once allowance is made for variations of circumstances and personality, it is difficult to generalise about the office. Personality alone does not explain Tony Blair's dominance or John Major's weaknesses. For much of the first two terms of his premiership, Blair had a huge majority in Parliament, record high popularity with the public, the most united and faction-free Labour Party in memory and no opposition worth speaking of. Contrast any of those features with John Major's beleaguered position between 1992 and 1997.

The powers of the Prime Minister are subject to constraints. The right to time a general election is obviously a political advantage. But if the premier gets it wrong, in the sense of losing – as in 1970, February 1974 and 1979 – he usually pays a heavy personal price. The power to hire and fire ministers is also subject to limits, not least the ability to make enemies among those dismissed or passed over. By 1990, Mrs Thatcher had sacked scores of Conservative ministers: they were not disposed to be charitable to her in the leadership contest. The same has happened to Blair, as the sacked Frank Dobson, Michael Meacher, Glenda Jackson and resigner Clare Short regularly oppose his policies.

We often classify Prime Ministers as 'strong' or 'weak'. Strong leaders, however, usually fall spectacularly, following a reaction to their record of disturbing interests and offending people. When the Conservative Party withdrew from Lloyd George's coalition in 1922, he resigned immediately and was never a serious force again. Margaret Thatcher was humiliated when nearly 40 per cent of Conservative MPs refused to vote for her in the leadership election in 1990. In each case it was the failure to retain the support of fellow-MPs, rather than that of the electorate, that proved decisive. The general election defeats of 'lesser' Prime Ministers such as Callaghan, Heath and Major, or the retirements of Wilson and Eden, are less traumatic. The British system, with the high place it has accorded to Cabinet and the party in Parliament, has not been kind to strong Prime Ministers, even though it is the latter who leave their mark on history.

Ever since Walter Bagehot's *English Constitution* (1865), comparisons have been drawn between the US presidential and British **Cabinet** systems. Contemporary British politics is allegedly becoming 'Americanised' and the Prime Minister likened to the President. In fact, the analogy is not useful because of significant constitutional and political differences between the two countries. A Prime Minister may wish for the direct popular mandate that a President has, but Presidents Clinton or Bush could only envy Blair's huge parliamentary majority.

There is an ebb and flow in the analysis and perceptions of the premiership. For most of the time a Prime Minister is seen as dominant because the Cabinet is weak, and *vice versa*. Power is seen in zero-sum terms. When Mrs Thatcher fell and was replaced by the more collegial John Major, the Cabinet was temporarily restored as a body of influence. After the exit from the ERM in September 1992, Major's fear of divisions and 'leaks' made him reluctant to trust his Cabinet. Under Blair it has remained marginal.

If an old school of analysis gives pride of place to Cabinet, a new one claims that resources are dispersed between several actors and agencies. Martin

A strong leader or a weak leader?
Source: Empics Sports Photo Agency

Smith (1999) argues that the debate about the relative power of the Prime Minister and the Cabinet is too narrow. There are other institutions and actors who count in what political scientists now call the **core executive**, and actors wield power by building coalitions among different power holders, including the Treasury, the Cabinet Office, and the relevant department. Prime Minister and ministers can check each other, and the exercise of power over time requires them to bargain and cooperate (Figure 19.1). A minister pushing a policy requires a Prime Minister's support, not least in Cabinet and in battles with the Treasury. Deals between a Prime Minister and a Cabinet minister are quite difficult for other ministers to overturn. But a Prime Minister also has to beware of pushing a minister so far that he resigns (Sir Geoffrey Howe's resignation proved fatal for Mrs Thatcher), and he also has to recognise the resources that reside in departments. Departments have the budgets, staff, expertise and

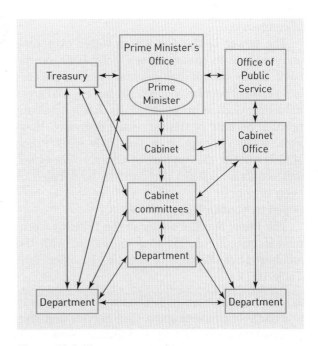

Figure 19.1 The core executive

Even strong Prime Ministers face constraints from powerful colleagues
Source: Copyright © Chris Riddell. From *The Observer*, 18 February 2001. Reproduced with permission from Guardian Newspapers Limited

policy networks, and the Secretary of State has statutory powers. Number 10 can look threadbare in comparison.

The power of the key actors varies over time and depends on circumstances. Tony Blair, on the back of his outstanding general election success and personal popularity, obviously has enjoyed great influence. Gordon Brown, similarly, has a dominant position because of the successful economy. However, a more unpopular or politically weak Prime Minister needs the support of Cabinet colleagues, and economic policies perceived to have failed or been unpopular can weaken a Chancellor, as happened to Norman Lamont (1990–3).

The Prime Minister's roles in the British governmental system coincide to some extent with the administrative divisions of the No. 10 office (see Table 19.1):

1. *Head of the executive*: The Prime Minister is in charge of overseeing the Civil Service and government agencies, and is ultimately answerable for all its decisions.

2. *Head of government policy*: Although most policy is produced through the departments and the party's own policy-making apparatus, the Prime Minister has a key influence over the party's election manifesto and the annual Queen's Speech outlining government legislation for the coming year, and more generally can choose which policies he or she wishes to highlight or play down. Prime Ministers traditionally are particularly influential in economic and foreign policy decisions.

3. *Party leader*: The Prime Minister not only is in organisational charge of the party as well as the government but also is the figure personifying that party to the public at large.

4. *Head appointing officer*: For posts throughout the political and administrative executive branch, as well as the various appointing powers in the Church and academia exercised on behalf of the monarch.

5. *Party leader in Parliament*: The Prime Minister is the principal figure in the House of Commons,

Table 19.1 The Prime Minister's roles

Function	Supporting office
Head of the executive	Cabinet secretariat Private Office
Head of government policy	Policy Unit Press Office (communication)
Party leader	Political secretary (party outside Parliament) Parliamentary private secretary
Head appointing officer	Appointments secretary (crown appointments) Cabinet Secretary (senior civil service) Principal private secretary (ministers)
Leader of party in Parliament	Parliamentary private secretary Private secretary – parliamentary affairs
Senior British representative overseas	Cabinet Secretary (Commonwealth) Principal private secretary Private secretary – foreign affairs Cabinet secretariat – EU affairs
Government communicator	Press Office

above all in weekly Question Time, when the Prime Minister's performance can affect party morale and public perception, particularly since the televising of the Commons in 1989.

6. *Senior UK representative overseas*: Since the 1970s, Prime Ministers have been involved in increasing amounts of travel and meetings with foreign heads of government. There are several regular engagements per year (the G8, UN and up to four European Councils) and several less frequent regular events such as the biannual Commonwealth Heads of Government Meeting as well as other less structured summits, most frequently with Ireland and the USA.

7. *Government communicator*: Prime Ministers have many opportunities to defend, represent and perhaps personify the work of the government (Foley, 2001).

■ The Prime Minister's offices

Number 10

Number 10 Downing Street, despite its modest outside appearance, is in fact a fair-sized office block in which over 200 people, including secretaries and security staff, work. The divide between 'political'

and 'official' is a good way of analysing the Prime Minister's different staff, although the distinction has been blurred somewhat under Blair. Political Number 10 comprises the Policy Unit and the Political Office. The Policy Unit was created in 1974 as a more personal resource for the Prime Minister. Harold Wilson felt that, lacking a department or a team of personal advisers, he needed help to take a strategic and more political view of where the government as a whole was going. The Policy Unit before Blair consisted of no more than eight appointees, a mix of secondees from the Civil Service and from party politics or business who are classified as temporary civil servants for their stay in the unit. Different Prime Ministers have used the Policy Unit to a greater or lesser extent. Blair has considerably strengthened his unit: in his first term it had thirteen members and was well placed to convey his views to departments and his reaction to papers from them. It was merged with the Private Office between 2001 and 2005 but has now been recreated as a separate body dealing with Blair's policy priorities.

The Political Office deals with communication between the Prime Minister and the party organisation, both at the centre with party professionals and in dealing with correspondence and events of a party political nature. It is paid for out of party rather than public funds. The Prime Minister, like other ministers, has one or two parliamentary private secretaries (PPS) – MPs whose job it is to keep the Prime Minister in contact with back-bench opinion at Westminster.

The official institutions of No. 10 are older than the political ones. The core of Downing Street is the Private Office, headed by the Principal Private Secretary. This consists of civil servants usually in their forties, often the most impressive high fliers of their generation, on three-year loan from their departments. Because of the day-to-day contact with the Prime Minister, the job of Principal Private Secretary is the third most influential in the Civil Service, after the Cabinet Secretary and Permanent Secretary to the Treasury. There are in addition private secretaries for parliamentary affairs, home affairs, economic affairs, and three or more for foreign affairs. Within their remit, they handle all official papers destined for the Prime Minister from other government departments, foreign governments and others having official business. Private secretaries quickly learn how to regulate the flow of papers to the Prime Minister, and the best can second-guess with great accuracy what interests the Prime Minister and what he or she will decide. Also in the private office is Blair's chief of staff, Jonathan Powell, who has remained with him in that post since January 1995.

The Press Office regulates the Prime Minister's relations with journalists, including the broadcast media, and covers a range of concerns from issuing government statements to arranging interview appointments. In view of the growing media demands on the Prime Minister and a leadership's concern to 'manage' the media, the post is more important than ever. The job is a Civil Service post, usually filled from the professional press officers of the government information service, although different Prime Ministers and press secretaries have taken different approaches to the obvious political aspects of press relations. Some press secretaries have been drawn not from the Civil Service but from journalism (Joe Haines (1969–70 and 1974–6) under Harold Wilson, and Alastair Campbell (1997–2003) under Tony Blair). Bernard Ingham (1979–90), a civil servant, became heavily – too heavily in the eyes of some – politically identified with Thatcher. Campbell also helped with speech writing, as did Haines, and media strategy. Interestingly, both were tabloid journalists before moving to No. 10. Campbell is also credited with strong influence on Blair over political tactics. Blair has also established a strategic communications unit to coordinate communications across departments and whole policy and presentation.

The Appointments Office deals with the various Church of England, university and a whole range of other appointments outside politics for which the Prime Minister is responsible.

When Tony Blair formed his new government in June 2001, he quickly consolidated some of the changes in his first term and created further institutions to improve the delivery of the government's policies. The fact that he made so many new changes reflected his dissatisfaction with how the government machine had worked in his first term. The main changes from his first term were:

1. Combining the Private Office and Policy Unit to form a **Policy Directorate**. This took further the idea of civil servants and special advisers working side by side. In 2005 they were demerged, to recreate the original two bodies.

2. Creating a Forward Strategy Unit under Geoff Mulgan, to do some so-called 'blue skies' thinking up to ten years ahead.

3. Establishing a Delivery Unit under Michael Barber, formerly special adviser to David Blunkett on education. Its task is to collect the data (e.g. pupil truancy or hospital waiting lists) to ensure that progress is being made on meeting the government's targets for improvements in key public services.

4. Creating an Office of Public Service Reform, charged with taking forward the reforms of the Civil Service so that departments will be better equipped to deliver reforms in public services.

5. Creating a new communications and strategy unit from the Press Office, Strategic Communications Unit and Research and Information Unit.

6. Creating a new post of Director of Government Relations, liaising between the centre and administrations in Scotland, Wales and Northern Ireland.

To all intents and purposes, Blair has formed a Prime Minister's Department. Some units and most of the staff are based in the Cabinet Office, simply because they cannot be accommodated in Downing Street. Blair does not call it a Prime Minister's Department, because that would raise so many constitutional objections, including questions about the role of the Cabinet, Secretaries of State and Cabinet Secretary, and about conventions of collective and ministerial responsibility.

Prime Ministers' styles

Prime Ministers naturally make their own personal contributions to the office, and all have demonstrated different approaches to policy, politics and relations with the Cabinet. Obviously each occupant is different, but the most important influences on the role and style of particular Prime Ministers are contingent on factors subject to limited or no control from Downing Street. To an extent, the fluctuations in party support in interim elections (by-elections, European and local), in polls and approval ratings for the Prime Minister also create conditions for weak or strong prime ministerial leadership. The state of the economy and a 'feel-good' mood among voters are key variable factors: if favourable, the Prime Minister's position will be enhanced. As a general election draws near, the Cabinet and party usually rally to the Prime Minister, in the realisation that they will prosper or falter depending on how united they are behind the leadership. Prime Ministers are constrained in their influence by other political factors – the extent of willing support that can be gathered from the Cabinet, the Ministers may choose how to allocate their time and energy between the different duties outlined in Table 19.1. John Major's lack of a parliamentary majority for much of the 1992 parliament meant that he devoted much time, along with his Chief Whip and Leader of the House of Commons, to managing parliamentary business. Margaret Thatcher and Tony Blair until recently were backed by large majorities and had no such worries. Tony Blair has taken his role as the communicator for the government, particularly the ideas of New Labour and the Third Way, very seriously. This includes making speeches and writing for the press. Prime Ministers may also choose which policy areas to concentrate on. Mrs Thatcher was famous for intervening across the board. But foreign affairs, notably Europe, and the economy are so central to the standing of the government as a whole that all Prime Ministers have to take a close interest in them. He or she regularly answers for the government at Question Time in the House of Commons, in media interviews and in summits with leaders of other states. Mrs Thatcher was something of a warrior in her attack on institutions, some of which, like the BBC, Foreign Office, universities and the Church of England, she identified with consensus politics. Tony Blair shows a similar impatience to her in his attitude to many institutions and practices. Unlike her, however, he has been more successful in reaching out across the political divide – the so-called 'big tent' strategy. He has given key jobs to Conservatives: Lord Wakeham chaired the Royal Commission on the House of Lords; Chris Patten chaired a commission into policing in Northern Ireland, and Michael Heseltine was on a committee overseeing the work of the Millennium Dome; and Lord Jenkins chaired the commission on electoral reform. Blair also invited the Liberal Democrats to join a Cabinet committee.

Margaret Thatcher as Prime Minister

Margaret Thatcher proved to be the most dominant peacetime Prime Minister in the last century. She broke with many policies pursued by her Conservative predecessors and is credited with substantially changing the agenda of British politics. Many of the policies are associated with her personally, including trade union reform, income tax cuts, privatisation and a reduced role for local government. She was forceful in Cabinet and in Parliament and willing to be seen as a figure apart from Cabinet, which did not score high on collegiality. She kept a close rein on her Chancellors and her Foreign Secretaries and, as a result, had troubled relationships with some of them. By the end, her hostile attitude to the European Community (as it then was called) lost her the support of a number of her senior ministers. Mrs Thatcher is an outstanding example of somebody who regarded herself as a conviction rather than a consensus politician. She must be regarded as a successful Prime Minister, in terms of winning three successive general elections and introducing lasting radical policies, many of which have been accepted by her successors, including Tony Blair.

The reasons why Margaret Thatcher became more dominant provide important insights into the source of prime ministerial power. They include:

1. Her successful use of Cabinet reshuffles – or the power to hire and fire. She had originally appointed her supporters to the key economic departments in 1979. During 1981, she gradually dismissed a number of dissenters from her Cabinet, and appointed newcomers such as Cecil Parkinson, Norman Tebbit, Leon Brittan, Tom King, Lord Young and Nigel Lawson, who were more supportive of her policies and owed their promotion to her.

2. She gained from policy successes, particularly the downturn in inflation in 1982 then, decisively,

the recapture of the Falklands, the steady rise in the living standards of those in work, the curbing of the unions, and, of course, from general election victories in 1983 and 1987.

3. She bypassed the Cabinet on occasions, relying heavily on her Policy Unit and making decisions in Cabinet committees, in bilateral meetings between herself and her advisers and the departmental minister or in high-powered interdepartmental task forces of able civil servants reporting direct to No. 10. Peter Hennessy described a typical example of this way of working:

    Mrs Thatcher will ask a particular Cabinet colleague to prepare a paper on a particular issue just for her, not for the Cabinet or her Cabinet Committee. The Minister is summoned to Number Ten with his back-up team. He sits across the table from Mrs Thatcher and her team which can be a blend of people from the Downing Street Private Office, the Policy Unit, the Cabinet Office and one or two personal advisers. She then, in the words of one Minister, proceeds to 'act as a judge and jury to her own cause'.

    Hennessy (1986), p. 289

4. She also interfered energetically in departments, seeking outside advice via seminars, trusted individuals and think-tanks, following up initiatives and taking a close interest in the promotion of senior civil servants.

But the above 'strengths' or assets were not permanent. By 1990 she had lost the confidence of many of her Cabinet; the government was unpopular, notably over the unpopular poll tax and rising inflation; she paid a price for her treatment of Cabinet colleagues as many of them felt little sense of ownership of some policies, and there was resentment of the influences exercised by Bernard Ingham and her foreign affairs adviser, Charles Powell.

John Major as Prime Minister

John Major's premiership was marked by his collegial approach to Cabinet, autonomy for most Secretaries of State in managing their departments, and a low-key approach to national leadership. Major was most definitely a 'stabiliser', without an overriding political project (save perhaps his consensus-seeking desire for 'a country at ease with itself') rather than a 'mobiliser' like Thatcher, who sought radical changes. As Prime Minister, Major appeared to feel constrained by:

■ the circumstances of his succession (Margaret Thatcher and her supporters felt that she had been stabbed in the back when she stepped down from the leadership; she soon became a menacing presence for John Major and in the first two years he was careful to seek her support);

■ his lack of his own electoral mandate until 1992;

■ his willingness to defer to more senior and experienced colleagues.

The Major years saw distinct periods in which prime ministerial power, relations with Cabinet colleagues and perceived policy success shifted. The first was from November 1990 to the summer of 1992. Major inherited the office after a particularly brutal demonstration of the limits of his power, with a deeply divided Cabinet and party. His Cabinet became a forum for more general discussion than had taken place since 1979 and there were few divisions. Major held the party together, made necessary policy changes (abandoning the poll tax), won a close general election against the odds and expectations, and proved an asset to the government in public opinion terms. His reassuring national leadership, particularly during the Gulf War, suited the mood better than Thatcher's triumphalism.

The second phase lasted from autumn 1992 until the 1997 general election. Growing turmoil over Europe, plus the humiliation of 'Black Wednesday', the day when Britain withdrew from the exchange rate mechanism, and increasing taxes in spite of an election pledge to cut them, all gravely weakened the Prime Minister's position. The initial general election majority of twenty-one had dwindled to single figures by 1994, inhibiting freedom of manoeuvre. Existing Cabinet divisions over Europe, particularly the stance about Britain's membership of the single currency, proved difficult to manage; some ministers, notably John Redwood and Michael Portillo, engaged in more or less open acts of defiance that would have resulted in dismissal during the 1980s. As the popularity of the government fell to record depths, Major's power to enforce collective discipline declined. Characteristics acclaimed as Major virtues in the first phase were widely criticised as weaknesses in the second. Major was unable to articulate a strong sense of where the government was going, and policy appeared to be a mix of scrapings of the barrel of Thatcherism (rail privatisation) with attempts to return to basic values in education and public order. He lost much of his ability to speak for the nation, being treated by some of the media as a target for ridicule. Progress in Northern Ireland was the principal prime ministerial achievement in this difficult period. The line of 'wait and see', or what Major called 'negotiate and decide', on whether Britain would join the single currency just about held among cabinet ministers until the general election. His successor as party leader, William Hague, quickly abandoned it.

Tony Blair as Prime Minister

Tony Blair has shown himself to be a dominant Prime Minister. His style of leadership in government closely resembles that of his leadership of the party in opposition. His reforms of the party, particularly of conference and NEC, were designed to make them more supportive of the leadership and limit scope for dissent. In opposition, he recruited a large team of aides to support him in the leader's office, and he relied on these and key figures such as Gordon Brown rather than the Shadow Cabinet. He attached importance to good communications and took seriously his role as the spokesperson for his New Labour project and key themes. To guard

against the media portraying the party as divided, untrustworthy and extreme, he emphasised the need for self-discipline, and his press secretary, Alastair Campbell, took central control of party communications. He also noted how John Major had been weakened by the media coverage of attacks on him made by his Conservative critics. Being seen to be in charge was an important means of actually being in charge for Blair.

In No. 10, Blair has strengthened the Prime Minister's office to a greater degree than any of his predecessors. It is no exaggeration to say that by 2001 he had produced more changes than over the previous fifty years combined. He has made his mark by boosting the size of his political staff in No. 10, creating new units, adding political appointments to many units, and substantially increasing the number of aides with communication skills. The informality of Blair's discussions with aides on the sofa in his office and without officials being present has been called a 'denocracy'. The resulting lack of consultation with ministers, and lack of papers and minutes, have disturbed some observers and led, they claim, to poor decision making. Lord Butler of Brockwell, a former Cabinet Secretary, reported in 2004 on the

BIOGRAPHY

Tony Blair's apprenticeship (1953–)

Tony Blair was born in Edinburgh. He attended an Edinburgh public school, Fettes, then read law at Oxford and qualified as a barrister. Blair entered Parliament in 1983, in an election Labour decisively lost on its most left-wing manifesto for over fifty years. When Neil Kinnock resigned the party leadership after the 1992 general election, some Labour modernisers regretted the opportunity to skip a generation and elect a younger leader like Blair or Gordon Brown. Under John Smith, Tony Blair became shadow Home Secretary where he showed his determination to stamp out the widespread perception that Labour was 'soft' on crime and sympathetic to criminals.

When Smith died in 1994, Blair was easily elected as leader; his close friend and rival Gordon Brown, the Shadow Chancellor, had been regarded as the more likely figure but decided not to enter the contest now that Blair had overtaken him. As leader, he continued Neil Kinnock's reforms of the party but further repositioned Labour in an effort to try to steal strong Conservative issues of law and order, low taxes, plus higher standards and traditional forms of education. Rather like Thatcher, Blair has been determined to create a new Labour Party, moving it to a so-called middle ground and broadening its appeal to the middle class. Blair survived all criticisms to deliver the promised prize on 1 May 1997: a huge majority of 179 over a still-divided Conservative Party. In 2001 he led the party to another landslide victory, the first time that Labour has won two successive full terms, and again in 2005. In power Blair is intent on making the present century one dominated by the centre-left instead of the centre-right, which dominated the last one. But his second and third terms have been controversial, because of the war in Iraq and his public service reforms.

| BOX 19.1 | IDEAS AND PERSPECTIVES |

Key features of new-style Prime Ministers

- Appearing live in the television age
- Spending less time in the House of Commons
- Regarding lengthy Cabinet meetings as often unproductive
- Working with concentric circles of confidants and advisers
- Blurring the distinction between the traditional advisory role of the civil servant and that of political adviser
- Increasing the political staff of No. 10 and making some of them into temporary civil servants who may act 'in a political context'.

Source: Adapted from Rose (2001)

quality of the intelligence before the war in Iraq, noted the absence of minutes for many meetings and complained that the Blair approach suffered from 'a lack of reasoned deliberation' and 'too much central control'.

Blair illustrates a number of features of the premiership today (Box 19.1). Many forces are tending to pull the Prime Minister away from or even elevate him above his senior colleagues. The growth of summits, including the regular G8, European Union and Commonwealth sessions, as well as unscheduled events like 11 September 2001 and the wars in Kosovo and Iraq, make huge inroads on a Prime Minister's time. The paradox is that Britain has lost an empire and has less influence in international affairs but the Prime Minister is busier than ever on the international stage.

Not surprisingly, the PM spends less time in the House of Commons. Research by Patrick Dunleavy and his colleagues at the London School of Economics shows that there has been a steady decline in the number of Commons statements and participation in debates by Prime Ministers over the twentieth century. As Prime Minister, Blair has voted in only 5 per cent of House of Commons divisions, and the reduction of Prime Minister's Questions to one weekly slot reduces the opportunities for MPs to have a word with him or for him to 'sense' the atmosphere in the Commons. This is part of a bigger picture, as MPs and ministers regard a slot on the *Today* programme as more important than a speech in the House of Commons and as most MPs have finished their week in Westminster by Thursday afternoon.

The mass media increasingly focus on the party leaders, particularly at election and party conference time. Blair, more than any other recent Prime Minister, has been the communicator in chief for the government. Even before Blair's arrival, Professor

Michael Foley had noted 'the rise of the British Presidency' (Foley, 1993); as in the United States, British political leaders not only try to manage the media but also try to bypass it by going 'direct' to voters, appearing on 'chat' shows and writing newspaper articles. Over the first two years, it has been calculated that Blair signed more than 150 newspaper articles on issues of the day. In addition, he does regular question and answer sessions with the public, some of which have been televised. More than any other, his is the communicating premiership.

The key figure in the Cabinet, after Blair, is Gordon Brown, the Chancellor; the two were the key architects of the New Labour project. Brown has been given a good deal of leeway to influence much of the domestic agenda, shape the spending of departments, particularly in welfare, to appoint his own special advisers (even when this caused tensions with No. 10), and effectively to operate what at times has appeared to be a dual premiership. Commentators have claimed that it is Brown who will decide whether his 'five conditions' for British entry into the single currency are satisfied (see Chapter 32). But the bad personal relations between the two men and their 'tribes' and Brown's claims that Blair has broken 'promises' to hand over to him were destabilising for the government's second term.

Blair's Cabinet meets on average for less than an hour each week, and therefore there is little time for discussion. Instead, he prefers to work with small groups of staff who are informed on the issue at hand and with aides in No. 10 whose judgement he trusts. His particular interests are in the European Union, Northern Ireland (these have become virtually prime ministerial issues), welfare, education and, increasingly, health and transport. He also regards himself as the custodian of the New Labour strategy. His

BOX 19.2 IDEAS AND PERSPECTIVES

Should Prime Ministers have their own department?

It is sometimes argued that a Prime Minister should have a department of his or her own, structured along the lines of those available for some foreign political leaders. Such a scheme was considered in 1977 (under Callaghan) and 1982 (under Thatcher), and some of Blair's aides flirted with the idea in opposition in 1996. The Prime Minister needs greater resources because of the growing demands on his time, particularly from the media and foreign affairs, and to enable him to represent the government to the world outside Westminster and to lend strategic direction and cohesion to the government. Such a department could emerge from combining the different units already in No. 10. In some ways the Cabinet Office performs some of the functions usually associated with a Prime Minister's department.

The disadvantages would be in fitting such a department into the hierarchy of Cabinet: could the junior aides of the Prime Minister issue orders to Cabinet ministers or to permanent secretaries? Would it cut the Prime Minister off and act as a buffer between him or her and the rest of the government? Might it encourage the Prime Minister to develop a different political agenda from that of particular Cabinet ministers? If so, might it be simpler to reshuffle the ministers?

Tony Blair, while rejecting the idea of a Prime Minister's department, has greatly strengthened the resources in No. 10, first in 1997–9 and again in 2001. The changes mentioned earlier are designed to link policy with presentation and achieve more integration between the Private Office and the Policy Unit, and to improve delivery. He has also strengthened the Cabinet Office and created units to assist 'joined-up' policy, making departments cooperate where their policies impact on a problem area or group of people.

opening words on entering Downing Street as Prime Minister, 'We were elected as New Labour and we will govern as New Labour', were a warning to MPs and cabinet ministers to follow his line.

For much of his premiership, Blair has been helped by his remarkable popularity with voters, a large Commons majority and a weak opposition. His style and methods involve a relative downgrading of both Cabinet and Parliament. Peter Hennessy, a Whitehall watcher, dubs it 'a command premiership' and warns of the dangers of over-centralisation and political isolation because of Blair's undue reliance on his own staff and possible isolation from his party. Others argue that a stronger Prime Minister, giving direction to departments and communicating with the public, are essential for an effective twenty-first century premiership (Box 19.2).

Indeed, since the aftermath of the Iraq war many political commentators focus on the decline of Blair's standing with colleagues, his party and the public. He has lost key ministers, divided the party on Iraq and public service reforms, notably on health and education, and seen his poll ratings tumble. In 2004 it was reported that he was on the point of resigning and declared that he would stand down before the next-but-one general election. He was persuaded by campaign strategists to share public platforms with

Gordon Brown during the 2005 general election as a means of holding on to Labour support. His reputation has also been damaged by the revelations in 2006 about the party's undeclared loans for the 2005 election.

Over time, the British Prime Minister has probably become stronger in Whitehall and Westminster. But one can also argue that a British Prime Minister has become weaker on the wider stage than his predecessors of forty or fifty years ago, simply because of the relative decline of the British state. Since 1945, Britain's loss of empire and decline in its relative international standing, the government's diminished control over the economy and utilities (in the wake of privatisation), and the 'hollowing out' of the state because of the loss of power to the EU, Scottish Parliament, Bank of England Monetary Committee and other agencies, have reduced the writ of the Prime Minister.

Possible reforms

Two reforms have been suggested as ways of improving the operation of the office of Prime Minister:

1. A Prime Minister's department (Box 19.2): This would involve a larger executive office than

No. 10, on the lines of the Chancellor in Germany and the Taoiseach in Ireland.

2. A regularised and powerful Deputy Prime Minister, with his or her own department. Such an office was created in May 2002. The title has traditionally been used for buying off a dangerous political rival with a title (Howe, 1989–90), or appointing a senior figure to coordinate other cabinet ministers and adjudicate in disputes (Whitelaw, 1983–8) – or indeed both (Heseltine, 1995–7). Under Blair, John Prescott chairs a large number of cabinet committees and deputises on less significant foreign trips. Prime Ministers have often felt the need for a 'fixer' or 'troubleshooter' who would sort out problems with colleagues. It

has rarely worked out, and any Prime Minister will be wary of creating a powerful rival.

■ Cabinet

The Prime Minister chairs the Cabinet, selects its members and recommends their appointment to the monarch. Most members are Secretaries of State by title. The Secretary of the Cabinet is responsible for the preparation of records of its discussions and decisions; the latter become conclusions of Cabinet. The modern Cabinet evolved from the Privy Council in the sixteenth century, a small group of advisers

---

BOX 19.3 FACT

Dimensions of prime ministerial power

Prime Minister and government: the power of appointment

Sources
1. Appoints all ministers and subsequently promotes, demotes, dismisses.
2. Decides who does what in Cabinet.
3. Appoints chairmen of Cabinet committees (now increasingly important).
4. Approves choice of ministers' parliamentary private secretaries.
5. Other patronage powers, e.g. chairmen of commissions, knighthoods, peerages and sundry other awards.
6. Dismissal or resignation of unhappy colleagues may create powerful enemies who, on the back benches, are free from the constraints of collective responsibility (e.g. Howe and Heseltine under Thatcher).

Constraints
1. Seniority and political weight of colleagues demands their inclusion and sometimes in particular posts.
2. Availability for office – experience, talent, willingness to serve.
3. Need for balance: ideological, left + right; regional; occupational; Lords.
4. Debts to loyal supporters.
5. Shadow Cabinet expectations.

Prime Minister and Cabinet direction

Sources
1. Summons meetings.
2. Determines agenda.
3. Sums up 'mood' of meeting.
4. Approves minutes.
5. Spokesman for Cabinet to outside world and Parliament.
6. Existence of inner Cabinet (intimate advisers).

Constraints
1. Needs Cabinet approval for controversial measures.
2. Determination of groups of ministers to press a case or oppose a particular policy.
3. Power of vested departmental interests backed up by senior civil servants.
4. Convention dictates that certain items will appear regularly on Cabinet agenda.

Prime Minister and Parliament

Sources
1. Commands a majority in House (usually).
2. Spokesman for government.
3. Weekly Question Time provides platform upon which PM can usually excel.

Constraints
1. Activities of opposition.
2. Parliamentary party meetings.
3. Question Time: not always a happy experience.

Prime Minister and party

Sources
1. 'Brand image' of party, especially at election time: PM's 'style' is that of the party.
2. Control over appointments.
3. Natural loyalty of party members to their leader and their government.
4. Threat of dissolution (seldom a credible threat, though).
5. Fear of party members that opposition will exploit public disagreements.

Constraints
1. Danger of election defeat: can lead to loss of party leadership.
2. Existence of ambitious alternative leaders.
3. Need to command support of parliamentary party, particularly when majority is thin or non-existent.
4. For Labour premiers, some constraints from party outside Parliament, e.g. National Executive Committee and party conference.

Prime Minister and administration

Sources
1. Appoints permanent secretaries.
2. Cabinet Office: acts for PM to some extent.
3. High-powered policy unit in No. 10.
4. Traditional loyalty of civil servants to political masters.
5. Is not constrained by departmental responsibilities.

Constraints
1. Sheer volume of work: limit to the amount a PM can read.
2. Power of departmental interests – 'departmentalism'.
3. Treasury: exerts financial constraints over whole of government.

Prime Minister and the country

Sources
1. The most prestigious and publicly visible politician in the country.
2. Access to instant media coverage for whatever purpose.
3. Access to top decision makers in all walks of public life.
4. Ability to mount high-prestige meetings with foreign leaders, trips abroad, etc.

Constraints
1. Those vested interests represented by powerful pressure groups.
2. The public's potential for boredom with the same leader.
3. The tendency of the public to blame the PM for failure beyond the control of No. 10.
4. Failure of the economy.
5. Growing media exposure of 'spin' and 'sleaze', often connected to No. 10.

to the monarch. Over time, the Cabinet became responsible to Parliament and then to the electorate as the government needed to have the confidence of the Parliament and then of the electorate at large.

Functions of Cabinet

The Cabinet as such has no legal powers; powers are vested in the Secretaries of State. But because it has **collective responsibility** to Parliament, all its members are bound to support Cabinet decisions. If they cannot do so they are expected to resign. In addition:

■ It plans the business of Parliament, usually a week or so in advance, making decisions about timetabling of legislation and choosing major government speakers.

■ It provides political leadership for the party, in Parliament and in the country.

■ It arbitrates in cases of disputes between departments, for example in the case of departments failing to agree their spending totals with the Treasury or battles between ministers over 'turf'. Sometimes the arbitration is done by the Prime Minister or by a troubleshooter he has appointed.

■ Although it does not actually decide many policies, it is the arena in which most important decisions are registered. Often the Cabinet is receiving reports or ratifying recommendations from committees. In the case of the annual Budget, Cabinet ministers merely hear the

Chancellor of the Exchequer's main recommendations shortly before his statement to the House of Commons.

It is important to emphasise, however, that these functions are shared with the core executive (see Figure 19.1) and particularly the Prime Minister and staff close to him or her. The Cabinet meets weekly on Thursday mornings for an hour or so and (under Blair) less frequently during holiday periods, unless in emergencies when summoned by the Prime Minister. A good part of its business is fairly predictable. Regular items include reviews of foreign affairs, European Union affairs, home affairs and a parliamentary business report from the Leader of the House of Commons. In addition, issues that are politically sensitive or highly topical are usually considered. Blair has added an item on 'current events', which deals with announcements and events and the 'line' to be taken with the media for the following week.

In chairing the Cabinet, the Prime Minister may wish to promote a particular line, but more often he or she wants to establish how much agreement there is about a proposed course of action. At the end of the discussion the Prime Minister sums up the mood of the meeting. Once the summary is written in the minutes it becomes a decision of the Cabinet. Votes are rarely taken; they advertise divisions, may fail to reflect the different political weight and experience of ministers and detract from Cabinet's role as a deliberative body. But the Prime Minister is very aware of the balance of opinion within Cabinet when summing up and reaching his or her own decision.

This last point is important and means that a Prime Minister may decide not to refer an issue to Cabinet because it is too controversial or he or she will not get the desired outcome. Mrs Thatcher for years refused to allow full Cabinet discussion about British membership of the ERM; she was opposed, but knew that the majority was in favour. John Major also kept issues from Cabinet because of fears of mischievous 'leaks'. For much of the time Cabinet is simply not equipped to decide or to challenge a decision already agreed by a Prime Minister and a departmental minister or a Chancellor and a minister. But Cabinet still usually discusses the public spending priorities of the government and the contents of the Queen's Speech. Ministers can also become more involved when there are political cabinets and civil servants leave the Cabinet Room. It is plausible to argue that the Cabinet meetings are now more important for team building, increasing the sense of shared ownership of the government programme among ministers and underpinning a sense of collective responsibility, rather than for deciding policies. Following the Butler Report's criticism in 2004 of his neglect of Cabinet (see above, under 'Tony Blair as Prime Minister') Blair has allowed more Cabinet discussion of issues.

Size

Peacetime Cabinets in the twentieth century varied in size between sixteen (Bonar Law in 1922) and twenty-four (Wilson in 1964). The average size of Cabinets in the twentieth century was twenty. The wartime Cabinets of Lloyd George and Winston Churchill have been much praised, and both contained fewer than ten members. Thatcher, Major and Blair experimented with small war Cabinets for the short Falklands, Gulf and Kosovo campaigns respectively. However, it is important to note that in war very different considerations operate from peacetime politics.

Decisions about Cabinet size and composition have to balance the needs of decision making and deliberation against those of inclusiveness. Cabinet has to be small enough to allow ministers the opportunities to discuss, deliberate and coordinate major policies, yet it must also be large enough to include heads of major departments and accommodate different political views in the party. Lobbies for different interests, e.g. education or health, expect to have 'their' minister represented in Cabinet. A larger Cabinet increases a Prime Minister's patronage.

Cabinet is almost too large to be a useful decision-making or deliberative group. Outside Scotland and Wales, many question the right of these two nations still to have ministers in Cabinet now that they have their own First Ministers in Edinburgh and Cardiff.

Cabinet committees

The system of **Cabinet committees** is a practical response to the increasing workload of Cabinet. As part of the Cabinet system the committees' deliberations are bound by secrecy and they are served by the Cabinet secretariat. There are various types of Cabinet committee. Standing committees are permanent for the duration of the Prime Minister's term in office, while miscellaneous or *ad hoc* committees are set up to deal with particular issues. A third category is official committees, which consist only of civil servants.

A number of critics have seen the development of the committee system as a means for the Prime Minister to bypass the full Cabinet and expand his or her own power. The Prime Minister decides to set up committees and appoint their members, chairmen and terms of reference. *Ad hoc* committees increase the scope for prime ministerial influence, since the PM has more discretion to define their terms of reference than those of the standing committees, such as defence and foreign affairs. Supporters of the system observe that it is the only way a modern Cabinet can cope with the increased volume of work and is a sign of the Cabinet's adaptability. Ministers can appeal against a committee's conclusion to the full Cabinet, but only with the approval of the committee chairman.

Thatcher was more reluctant than her predecessors to set up Cabinet committees. She preferred to hold 'bilateral' meetings with the minister and officials in a department or 'working parties' to tackle a problem. Under Major, the Cabinet and Cabinet committee system reverted to the normal pattern after the battering of the Thatcher years. Major was exceedingly keen to bind his ministers into decisions and to ensure that the widest group of relevant ministers was party to key decisions. The only occasion on which big decisions were taken on core government policy outside the Cabinet and committee system was on leaving the ERM on 16 September 1992, but even then Major took care to consult in an *ad hoc* way all his most senior ministers – Norman Lamont, Kenneth Clarke, Douglas Hurd and Michael

Heseltine. Blair also likes to make policy in bilaterals with his Cabinet ministers.

But as ministers and the Prime Minister are required to be away from London – on EU business, for example – so Cabinet committees are more difficult to arrange. The result is that more business is done by correspondence between ministers and copied to the Prime Minister. As noted, Tony Blair works more informally with working groups and has regular stocktaking sessions with individual Cabinet ministers who are responsible for education, health, transport and tackling crime to monitor progress on delivering the government's policy commitments.

The Cabinet Office

Until 1916, there were no formal procedures for keeping minutes of Cabinet meetings or records of decisions. In that year, however, Lloyd George set up the Cabinet Office or secretariat. Today it is at the heart of the government machine. Its main tasks in relation to Cabinet and the committees are to prepare the agenda of the Cabinet by circulating relevant papers to ministers beforehand; to record Cabinet proceedings and decisions; and to follow up and coordinate the decisions by informing the departments of decisions and checking that appropriate action has been taken.

The Cabinet Office has also come to play an important coordinating role in a number of areas. Its European Secretariat coordinates departmental views and formulates Britain's negotiating position with EU member states. Blair is particularly concerned to promote what he calls 'joined-up' government and policies that require the cooperation of departments and the contribution of people and skills from outside the Civil Service. He has set up several new units, including the Social Exclusion Unit and the Strategy Unit; both are designed to combat departmentalism and promote wider objectives of the government, and are based in the Cabinet Office.

The Cabinet Secretary traditionally worked closely with the Prime Minister over security matters involving MI5 and MI6, and, as head of the home Civil Service, issues affecting the conduct of the Civil Service and ministers. For example, Sir Richard Wilson, Cabinet Secretary until 2002, interviewed Ron Davies about the circumstances that led to his resignation as Secretary of State for Wales in 1998. He also advised the Prime Minister on the events leading to Peter Mandelson's resignation in February

2002 over the Hinduja affair and the breakdown of relations between Stephen Byers and the department's head of media relations, Martin Sixsmith, in 2002. The present Cabinet Secretary Gus O'Donnell adjudicated in 2006 on whether Tessa Jowell had broken the ministerial code in her association with her husband's financial dealings. As well as being a troubleshooter, he also works closely with the Prime Minister on key projects.

There was a change in the Cabinet Secretary's remit when Andrew Turnbull succeeded Wilson in 2002. The growing importance after 9/11 of terrorism, security and intelligence led to these issues being handled separately. The removal of these tasks allowed Turnbull to concentrate on improving the delivery of improved public services – Blair's priority.

Coordination and joining-up

Some observers have suggested that British government resembles a medieval system in which the departments operate as relatively independent fiefdoms. Bruce Headey (1974) interviewed a number of former and present Cabinet ministers and found that most of them regarded themselves primarily as representatives or spokesmen for the department *vis-à-vis* Parliament, the Cabinet and the public. Others emphasised the internal aspect of their work, managing and organising the department. Only one in six regarded themselves as initiators of policies, in the sense of defining the department's policy options. Ministers were, rather, *ambassadors* for their departments. The departmental pressures on many ministers tended to limit their opportunities to contribute to the formation of government policy making in general. Thus Headey argued that Britain had departmental rather than **Cabinet government**.

A later study (Smith *et al.*, 2000) of ministers qualifies part of Headey's picture. It stresses that all the roles (policy initiator, manager and ambassador) are part of a minister's job and mutually reenforcing. The policy role of a minister now looms larger. Some ministers, like Kenneth Baker at Education under Thatcher, Michael Howard at the Home Office under Major, and David Blunkett at Education and Gordon Brown at the Treasury under Blair, have certainly changed the policies and standing of their departments.

There are many forces making for a departmental model of government. Departments have many resources, not least in terms of staff, established

Appointed Cabinet Secretary in June 2005, Sir Gus O'Donnell is the highest-ranking civil servant in the British Civil Service
Source: PA Wire / Empics

policy lines or views, budgets and regular contact with pressure groups. Moreover, the minister knows he or she gains political credit by battling success-fully to maintain their department's resources and protecting its autonomy. Select committees, which scrutinise the work of government, are organised on departmental lines. The convention of ministerial responsibility also leads to the expectation that the minister will be answerable for the work of their departments. In other words, the culture of politics and of Whitehall is heavily geared towards depart-mentalism. If departments cooperate or 'join up' pol-icy, there are costs in terms of the time spent in coordinating and no certainty about who will get the credit if the policy is a success.

The need for coordination has increased in recent years. The growing role of the EU, the effects of devolution to Scotland and Wales – and the opportunities to develop different policies in these jurisdictions – the privatisation of formerly state-owned enterprises, and the creation of Next Steps agencies have all removed levers for coordination from the central government. Yet there has been a growing awareness of the problems that fall between departments or of problems that are not the respons-ibility of a department. Social exclusion, for example, covering homelessness, drug dependency, poor edu-cation and unemployment, is a many-sided problem and requires the cooperation of multiple agencies. There is also awareness that the side-effects, how-ever unintended, of a policy to tackle one problem may create new difficulties elsewhere. Excluding unruly pupils from school, for example, may improve the learning opportunities for the remaining pupils but at the cost of adding to the crime and delinquency rates when the excluded pupils are on the streets.

How, therefore, is government policy coordinated? How do ministers have a sense of strategy, a sense of where, collectively, they are going? Techniques include:

1. Treasury control of public spending and the annual spending reviews provide the opportun-ity to review priorities, although coordination is a

secondary aim. Gordon Brown has strengthened this control by awarding shared budgets to inter-departmental projects.

2. Informal consultations between senior officials of departments as well as formal meetings.

3. The Cabinet Office, which services the Cabinet and its committees, prepares and circulates papers and follows up Cabinet decisions.

4. The system of Cabinet committees itself.

5. The Prime Minister, and No. 10 office, can take an overview across all government policy. Blair has also set up various units, so-called 'tsars' (e.g. for drugs and women) and task forces to promote coordination.

But Cabinet cannot do much. Cabinet ministers suffer from sheer overload of work, which results in them lacking sufficient time to read and digest papers on many matters outside their departmental responsibilities. The Cabinet is not particularly good at coordinating policy (see above). In part this is a consequence of so much of ministers' time being spent on running and representing their own departments. A number of ex-ministers have remarked on how rare it was for them to comment on other issues before the Cabinet. Many illustrations of these pressures are to be found in the published diaries of Richard Crossman and Barbara Castle: ministers, for example, arrived at Cabinet having only glanced at papers that did not concern their own departments. The Central Policy Review Staff was established in 1970 with a remit to provide ministers with briefs that did not reflect a departmental view. It failed, and Mrs Thatcher abolished it in 1983.

Reforms affecting Cabinet

Among reforms of the Cabinet that have been canvassed in recent years are the following:

1. A body that can help the Cabinet to deal with strategy. This may include the recreation of something along the lines of the Central Policy Review Staff, which existed between 1970 and 1983.

2. A Prime Minister's department, although this might well involve a downgrading of Cabinet (see above). In fact, Blair has moved in this direction.

3. More political aides or advisers for ministers. Blair's government had doubled the number under John Major to seventy-eight by 2000. It is often argued that this system should be extended and strengthened, as in France and the USA. This is urged on the grounds of strengthening ministerial influence in the department rather than enhancing the collective role of the Cabinet.

4. A reduction in the power of the Prime Minister, so developing what Tony Benn, in 1979, called a constitutional premiership. Benn objected to the scale of the Prime Minister's patronage as well as other fixed powers. He advocated the election of cabinet ministers and allocation of their duties by Labour MPs and the confirmation of public appointments by Parliament. Another possibility is to recognise the greater power of the Prime Minister and No. 10, and to make his aides more directly accountable to Parliament, by, for example, appearing before select committees. Blair has now agreed to appear twice a year before the Commons Liaison Committee.

■ Ministers

Appointments

If the size of the Cabinet has hardly grown in the twentieth century, that of the government certainly has. The major increase since 1900 has been in government appointments outside the Cabinet – non-Cabinet ministers of state, junior ministers and parliamentary private secretaries (PPSs) in the House of Commons. In 1900, forty-two MPs were involved in government; today, the number is well over 100, nearly a third of MPs on the government side. Although the PPSs are unpaid they are still bound by the doctrine of collective responsibility.

The increase in patronage is obviously an advantage for Prime Ministers. They can use it to reward or punish colleagues and perhaps to promote policies. However, it is a power that is exercised subject to several administrative and political limitations. Ministers must sit in Parliament, and most of them must be members of the House of Commons. A few cabinet ministers have been appointed shortly after their election to the House of Commons. The trade union leader Ernest Bevin, at the Ministry of Labour in 1940, was a success, but another trade unionist, Frank Cousins, Minister of Technology (1964–7), and a businessman, John Davies, at Trade and Industry (1970–4), were less effective. A Cabinet must also contain at least two peers, the Lord Chancellor and the Leader of the House of Lords. The parliamentary background increases the likelihood that ministers will be skilled in debate and able to handle parliamentary questions competently. Blair has given peerages to a number of businessmen and then given them ministerial posts, e.g. Lords Sainsbury, Simon, (Gus) MacDonald and (Andrew) Adonis. He did the same for his lawyer friend Lord Falconer, now Lord Chancellor. Elevating lay people to the peerage and then giving them office is a way of utilising extra-parliamentary talent, but it can cause resentments in the government's parliamentary party.

A second limitation is that appointments also need to take account of a person's political skill and administrative competence. In any Cabinet there are at least half a dozen ministers whose seniority and reputation are such that it is unthinkable to exclude them. Increasingly, the Leader of the Opposition uses his Shadow Cabinet to enable his shadow ministers to gain expertise in posts they will take over in government. Tony Blair appointed virtually all his Shadow Cabinet to the same posts in government.

The qualifications appropriate for particular posts are not always obvious – witness the apparently haphazard movement of ministers between departments. Kenneth Clarke moved from Health (1988) to Education (1990) to the Home Office (1992) and to the Treasury (1993), and John Reid has been equally peripatetic under Blair. On the other hand, appointments as legal officers (Lord Chancellor, Attorney General and Solicitor General) must be made from lawyers in the party. Nigel Lawson (Thatcher's Chancellor of the Exchequer for the six years before he resigned in October 1989) took a degree in politics, philosophy and economics and was a financial journalist before he went into politics. The Secretaries of State for Scotland and Wales are expected to sit for Scottish and Welsh seats, respectively, and if possible be nationals of the country concerned.

In general, however, ministers are expected to have skills in managing Parliament and conducting meetings, reading papers quickly, making decisions, and defending them convincingly in public. If we exclude as effectively 'ineligible' for office MPs who are very young or inexperienced, too old, or suffering from political or personal deficiencies, the Prime Minister may actually be giving government appointments to about half of the 'eligible' MPs in his party.

Prime Ministers usually make some appointments to reward loyalty and limit dissent or outright opposition. Thatcher pointedly excluded Heath from her Cabinet in 1979, and Heath excluded Enoch Powell in 1970. Both were powerful figures but had been at odds with so many aspects of the party's policies and with the party leader personally that their presence would have made the Cabinet a divisive body. The Cabinets of Wilson in 1964 and Thatcher in 1979 contained majorities who had almost certainly voted against them at the first stage of the leadership elections in 1963 and 1975, respectively, but both had to take account of administrative talent and political weight. Tony Benn was a prominent left-wing dissenter from the Labour leadership in the 1970s, but Wilson and Callaghan thought it safer to keep him in the Cabinet rather than act as a focus for opposition on the back benches. In November 1990, Major gave the difficult job of Environment Secretary to the man who had precipitated Thatcher's downfall, Michael Heseltine. The appointment recognised Heseltine's strength in the party but promised to keep him absorbed with fulfilling his claims over reforming the poll tax. Similar calculations prompted Major's promotion of Heseltine to Deputy Prime Minister in 1995.

A final constraint is that Prime Ministers usually want their Cabinets to be representative of the main elements in the party. This has been particularly the case with the Labour Party, which has had well-defined left- and right-wing factions. Major felt bound to include in his Cabinet opponents of his European policy, including Michael Howard, Peter Lilley, Michael Portillo and, until 1995, John Redwood. Under Blair, left–right divisions have declined and the differences between Old and New Labour have not developed into factions, although the left-wing Campaign group of MPs have firmly opposed the Iraq war and the market orientation of his public service reforms.

There is no adequate preparation for being a Cabinet minister. The third and fourth constraints mentioned above remind us that Cabinet is a political body and that the Prime Minister is a party politician. The British tradition has been to rely on a form of on-the-job learning in which ministers, like civil servants, pick up the skills as they settle into the job. Four background features that most ministers have and that probably shape the way they work are:

1. *Lengthy tenure in the House of Commons*: Since 1945, the average length of time spent in the House of Commons, prior to becoming a Cabinet minister, has been fourteen years, a sufficient period of time to acquire parliamentary skills.

2. *Experience on the ladder of promotion, or ministerial hierarchy, which most politicians ascend*: In an ideal world they would start off as parliamentary private secretaries and move through the ranks of junior minister, minister outside the Cabinet and then through some of the Cabinet positions, ending with the most senior ones like Chancellor of the Exchequer or Foreign Secretary and then perhaps Prime Minister.

3. *Party standing*: A politician with a strong party following also has claims. Excluded from Cabinet and the restraints of collective responsibility, he or she may provide a focus for criticism of the Prime Minister.

4. *Preparation in opposition*: In 1955, Labour leader Clement Attlee formalised the party's arrangements of a Shadow Cabinet in opposition, in which a front-bench spokesman 'shadows' a cabinet minister. Both Heath and Thatcher used the opportunity of making appointments in opposition in order to prepare for office. For example, all but two of Heath's appointments in the consultative committee (the Conservative front-bench team in opposition) in 1969 went to similar Cabinet postings.

Not all departments or ministers are of equal importance to a Prime Minister. Obviously, his most frequent contacts are with the next-door neighbour in 11 Downing Street, the Chancellor of the Exchequer, the Leader of the House of Commons (on parliamentary business) and the Foreign Secretary. A Prime Minister regularly holds meetings with holders of these two or three senior posts, not least because he often has to answer or discuss topics in these areas at international meetings. Because of Blair's policy priorities, or the pressure of events, he has also spent a great deal of time with ministers for Northern Ireland, education, health, and law and order.

A Prime Minister is not well placed to shape policy in more than a handful of departments at any one time. He can certainly veto a line of policy, but he lacks the resources available to a department to initiate policies. He therefore depends on the minister and the departmental officials. If the minister fails, the Prime Minister may install a replacement. But there are always political costs in sacking a minister. On the other side, a department will profit from the goodwill of the Prime Minister for help in gaining time for legislation and extra funding, or protection against Treasury demands for cuts. Hence the regular contacts between the No. 10 Private Office and Policy Unit and officials and advisers in a department. Ministers and Prime Ministers each have resources and need each other if policy is to be successful. This is one of the reasons why some researchers on the core executive talk less about the Prime Minister's power and more about interdependence between key actors.

Ministerial and collective responsibility

According to the doctrine of ministerial responsibility, each minister is responsible to Parliament for his or her own personal conduct, the general conduct of his or her department, and the policy-related actions or omissions of his or her civil servants. The most important consequence of the convention is that the minister is answerable to Parliament for the work of his or her department. Another interpretation is that Parliament can actually force the resignation of a minister who has been thought to be negligent. The outstanding resignation on grounds of policy in recent years was that of the Foreign Secretary, Lord Carrington (and two other ministers), in April 1982, following the widespread criticism of his department's failure to anticipate Argentina's capture of the Falklands.

However, there are two difficulties in the way of the Commons forcing the dismissal of a minister. One is that MPs in the majority party can usually be counted on to support a minister under pressure. In addition, the Cabinet is also responsible for policy, and a Prime Minister knows that a minister's resignation often reflects badly on the work of the government. Collective responsibility may therefore weaken a minister's individual responsibility (for further discussion, see Chapter 20). This surely was a reason that produced pressure on Norman Lamont to resign from the Treasury in September 1992. He had frequently defended Britain's membership of the ERM, excluded the possibility of withdrawal and claimed that it was the basis of Britain's anti-inflationary strategy. The forced departure from the ERM was, by any standards, a failure of policy. The same is true of the failed poll tax, which cost huge sums of money. In the seven years it took to devise, implement and repeal the tax, there were eight ministers for local government. But nobody resigned. One can point to similar failures under Blair, starting with the Millennium Dome and including the Child Support Agency and transport, and a similar lack of resignations. Indeed, resignations on the grounds of policy failure are now so rare that the notion of resignation as part of the responsibility convention has virtually disappeared. Ministers are more likely to resign following a press campaign about their private behaviour.

According to the convention of collective responsibility, Cabinet ministers assume responsibility for all Cabinet decisions, and a minister who refuses to accept, or opposes, a decision is expected to resign. The convention of collective responsibility now extends to incorporate all junior government ministers, including even the unpaid and unofficial parliamentary secretaries. The doctrine is supported by the secrecy of the Cabinet proceedings: the refusal to make public the differences of opinion that precede or follow a Cabinet decision assists the presentation of a united front to Parliament and the country. Another aspect of the convention is that the government is expected to resign or seek to dissolve Parliament if it is defeated on a vote of confidence in the House of Commons. In other words, the Cabinet is collectively responsible for policy to the Commons.

In recent years, however, both aspects of the convention have come under pressure. The 1974–9 Labour government relaxed the principle of collective responsibility over the referendum on Britain's membership of the EEC in 1975 and the vote on the European Assembly Elections Bill in 1977. On both issues the Cabinet was divided. The myth of Cabinet unity has also been exploded by the increase in the leaks to the news media of Cabinet discussions in recent years. But a Prime Minister, by refusing to act collegially, can also strain collective responsibility. Mrs Thatcher used up much goodwill among colleagues and probably paid a price in the bitter resignations of such major figures as Michael Heseltine, Nigel Lawson and Sir Geoffrey Howe.

■ Conclusion

Dissatisfaction with the structure and performance of Cabinet government is hardly surprising in view of the criticisms of Britain's economic performance in the postwar period. Among criticisms that have been advanced are the following:

1. Ministers are too frequently generalists and appointed to posts for reasons that may have little to do with their presumed policy expertise.

In cases of routine policy making – with ministers lacking the time and often the experience to become versed in the detail – it is perhaps not surprising that civil servants may often shape policy, and the principle of ministerial responsibility may provide a shield behind which the Civil Service dominates the policy process.

2. The frequent turnover of ministers, who last an average of just over two years in post, shows a rate of change exceeding that in most other Western states. Such turnover means that at any one time a number of ministers are actually learning their jobs. Under Harold Wilson (1964–70) the average ministerial tenure was less than two years. In his 1966–70 government only three ministers as well as Wilson himself held the same office for the duration of the government, and in the lifetime of Thatcher's 1979–83 government only six ministers held the same office. Within fourteen months over 2004–5 Blair had four different Secretaries of State of Work and Pensions. It is difficult to think of any other organisation that has such a rapid turnover of its senior management. On the other hand, it is often claimed that if a minister spends too long in a department he or she may 'go native' and perhaps become too closely identified with its interests. The case for introducing a new minister is that he or she is likely to provide a stimulus to the policy routine. But many reshuffles of ministers are made for reasons that have little to do with policy and more to do with public opinion or party management.

3. Ministers are often so overloaded with work that the functions of oversight and discussion are neglected. In his revealing book *Inside the Treasury* (1982), the former Labour minister Joel Barnett commented on how 'the system' can defeat ministers:

The sheer volume of decisions, many of them extremely complex, means that by the time even a fairly modest analysis of a problem is done, and the various options considered, you find yourself coming up against time constraints. Consequently ministers often find themselves making hasty decisions, either late at night or at an odd moment during a day full of meetings.

Barnett (1982), p. 20

4. Decisions are taken for short-term political gain, as instanced in Barnett's book as well as in

ministers' diaries. As Home Secretary, Kenneth Baker's Dangerous Dogs Act (1991) was rushed through Parliament and was certainly shaped by tabloid press pressure. More telling, perhaps, was the leak of a memo in 2000 from Tony Blair, appealing to his aides for an 'eye-catching initiative' with which he could be personally associated.

BOX 19.4   BRITAIN IN CONTEXT

Leadership

At many international gatherings of democratic leaders a British Prime Minister may feel that he holds a relatively strong office. In the European Union, most other leaders lead coalition governments and have to keep leaders of member parties on side or the coalition collapses. At times Tony Blair has complained as other EU leaders have delayed taking decisions until they had the agreement of other parties in their governments. And even 'strong' leaders like the US or French Presidents may have to share power with a legislature controlled by the opposition party or, in the case of France, a Prime Minister from the opposition ('cohabitation'). The British Prime Minister's position – one-party government and a majority in the Commons – is more straightforward. But the Presidents have an independent base of power because they are directly elected, whereas the Prime Minister depends on the support of his or her party. They also have a more secure tenure because they are elected for a fixed term of four years (USA) or seven years (France), for example.

As a postscript, it is instructive to compare the 'route to the top' for British Prime Ministers and the Presidents of the USA and France:

	Britain	USA	France
Media visibility	high	high	high
Route to top	Parliament	Governor	Civil Service
Election	party	popular	popular
Term	insecure	4 years	7 years
Checks	few, informal	Supreme Court, Congress	'Cohabitation'
Domestic policy	high	medium	high
Foreign policy	via EU	high	via EU

Source: R. Rose and T.J. Pitcher (2001) *The Prime Minister in a Shrinking World*, p. 242. Reproduced with permission of Polity Press Ltd

---

Chapter summary

The Prime Minister is the most powerful figure in British government, but his or her power is not fixed: it depends in part on the personality and style of the incumbent and the strength of the Cabinet he or she faces. Cabinet itself has undergone major changes in the last twenty-five years and is now substantially run by a series of committees, which do the detailed work. The heart of British government, the Prime Minister, Cabinet and departments, is under closer scrutiny now than possibly ever before. Tony Blair has proved to be an innovator: in strengthening the staff at his disposal, reinforcing No. 10's control over communications and expecting the Cabinet Office to promote Whitehall's awareness of its need to deliver the government's overall objectives.

Discussion points

- Is the Prime Minister (still) too powerful?

- What if anything does Cabinet government mean today?

- How has Blair centralised power around the Cabinet Office and No. 10?

- Should there be a Prime Minister's department?

Further reading

On Cabinet history Mackintosh (1962) is still the best guide. Hennessy (1986) and James (1999) provide a lively analysis of more recent developments. Donoughue (1987), Barnett (1982), Lawson (1992), Thatcher (1993) and Howe (1994) are perceptive insider accounts. On the core executive see Smith (1999). On how Prime Ministers, including Blair, and their staff operate see Kavanagh and Seldon (1999) and Seldon (2005), and on the limits on the Prime Minister see Rose (2001).

References

Barnett, J. (1982) *Inside the Treasury* (Deutsch).

Burch, M. and Holliday, I. (1996) *The British Cabinet System* (Prentice Hall).

Clark, A. (1993) *Diaries* (Weidenfeld & Nicolson).

Donoughue, B. (1987) *Prime Minister* (Cape).

Foley, M. (1993) *The Rise of the British Presidency* (Manchester University Press).

Foley, M. (2001) *The British Presidency* (Manchester University Press).

Garnett, M. (2005) 'Still first among equals?', *Politics Review*, April.

Headey, B. (1974) *British Cabinet Ministers* (Allen & Unwin).

Hennessy, P. (1986) *Cabinet* (Blackwell).

Hennessy, P. (2000) *The Prime Minister: The Office and its Holders since 1945* (Penguin).

Howe, G. (1994) *Conflict of Loyalty* (Macmillan).

James, S. (1999) *British Cabinet Government*, 2nd edn (Routledge).

Kavanagh, D. (2000) 'Inside No. 10', *Talking Politics*.

Kavanagh, D. and Seldon, A. (1999) *The Powers behind the Prime Minister* (HarperCollins).

King, A. (ed.) (1985) *The British Prime Minister*, 2nd edn (Macmillan).

Lawson, N. (1992) *The View from Number 11* (Jonathan Cape).

Mackintosh, J. (1962) *The British Cabinet* (Stevens).

Rentoul, J. (2001) *Tony Blair* (Little, Brown).

Rose, R. and Pitcher, T.J. (2001) *The Prime Minister in a Shrinking World* (Polity Press).

Seldon, A. (ed.) (2001) *The Blair Effect* (Little, Brown).

Seldon, A. (2005) *Blair* (Little, Brown).

Smith, M. (1999) *The Core Executive in Britain* (Palgrave).

Smith, M., Richards, D. and Marsh, D. (2000) *The Changing Role of Central Government Departments* (Palgrave).

Thatcher, M. (1993) *Thatcher: The Downing Street Years* (HarperCollins).

Useful websites

http://www.cabinet-office.gov.uk/
http://www.od.pm.gov.uk
http://www.number-10.gov.uk

CHAPTER 20

Ministers, departments and civil servants

Philip Norton

Learning objectives

- To promote an understanding of the place and significance of government departments in British government.

- To identify the role and political impact of ministers in policy making.

- To assess the relationship between ministers and civil servants.

- To summarise and assess competing models of policy making.

Introduction

Departments form the building blocks of British government. Each is headed by a minister, who has responsibility for government policy in the sector covered by the department. Each is staffed by a body of professional civil servants, responsible for advising the minister on policy and for ensuring that policy is implemented. The capacity for ministers to determine policy has been increasingly constrained by external pressures, but ministers remain significant players in policy making.

■ Ministers

Ministers stand at the heart of British government. In legal terms, they are the most powerful figures in government. When an Act of Parliament confers powers on government to do something, it does not say 'The Prime Minister may by order . . . [do this or that]'; nor does it say 'The Cabinet may by order . . .'. What it says is 'The Secretary of State may by order . . .'. In other words, legal powers are vested in senior ministers, not in the Prime Minister or Cabinet. Senior ministers are those appointed to head government departments. Their formal designation is Ministers of the Crown. Most will be given the title of Secretary of State (Secretary of State for Education, Foreign Secretary, Secretary of State for Home Affairs – popularly known as the Home Secretary – and so on). Originally, there was only one Secretary of State to assist the King. The post was subsequently divided, but the fiction was maintained that there was only one Secretary of State, and that fiction is maintained to the present day. That is why Acts of Parliament still stipulate that 'The Secretary of State may by order . . .' or 'The Secretary of State shall by order . . .'. There is no reference to 'The Secretary of State for Education' or 'The Foreign Secretary' but simply 'The Secretary of State'.

Each Minister of the Crown heads a government department. Each has a number of other ministers, known as junior ministers, to assist in fulfilling the responsibilities of the office. Each senior minister has one or more political advisers. Each has a body of civil servants – permanent, non-political professionals – to advise on policy and to ensure the implementation of policy once it is agreed on. The number of civil servants in each department will normally run into thousands.

Each Minister of the Crown is thus vested with important legal powers. Each has a department to assist in carrying out the policy or decisions that he or she has made. Each is thus, in formal terms, an important political figure, vital to the continuation of government in the United Kingdom. However, in the view of many commentators, the legal position does not match the political reality. Although legal power may be vested in senior ministers, the real power, it is argued, is exercised elsewhere. The capacity to determine policy has, on this argument, passed to other political actors, not least the European Union, the Prime Minister and civil servants. One argument is that senior ministers are now not principals in terms of policy making but rather agents, be it of the Prime Minister, of the civil servants in their department or of the European Union.

What, then, is the structure and operation of government departments? What are the powers of a senior minister? What are the limitations? To what extent is a senior minister able to deploy the powers of the office to achieve desired outcomes? And what is the best model that helps us to understand the position of senior ministers in British government? Are they agents of other actors in the political system? Or are they powerful independent figures?

■ Departments

Each Minister of the Crown heads a **department**. The structure is essentially hierarchical. Figure 20.1 shows, in basic outline, a typical department. The actual structure of a department is more complex. Figure 20.2 shows the actual organisational structure of a particular department, the Department for Constitutional Affairs, in 2006. The structure differs from department to department. Some have far more extensive and complex structures than the Lord Chancellor's Department. Within each department,

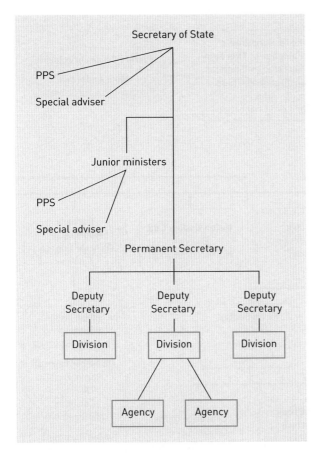

Figure 20.1 Structure of a government department

the senior minister has a range of individuals to assist in formulating public policy. They can be grouped under two headings: the political and the official. The political appointees comprise the junior ministers, parliamentary private secretaries and special advisers. The officials comprise the civil servants in the department, headed by the Permanent Secretary, and those employed in agencies that fall within the remit of the department.

Political appointees

Junior ministers

There are three ranks of junior minister: ministers of state, parliamentary under-secretaries of state and parliamentary secretaries. (Because the acronym for the parliamentary under-secretaries of state is PUSS, they are known in Whitehall as 'pussies'.) They are appointed to assist the senior minister in carrying out the minister's responsibilities. They will normally be allocated particular tasks. Thus, for instance, one of the junior ministers in the Department of Trade

and Industry is Minister for Science. In the Department for Culture, Media and Sports, one of the junior ministers is designated as Minister for Sport. In the Department of Health, one of the ministers is Minister for Public Health.

Junior ministers are appointed by the Prime Minister, although sometimes after consultation with the minister heading the department. Their authority derives from the senior minister. It is the senior minister who decides what responsibilities they shall have and, in effect, how powerful they shall be in the department. They act on behalf of the senior minister. They have no formal line control over civil servants. A junior minister, for example, cannot overrule the Civil Service head of the department, the Permanent Secretary. A dispute between a junior minister and the Permanent Secretary would have to be resolved by the senior minister.

The number of junior ministers has grown over the past half-century. In the years after the Second World War, it was usual for a senior minister to be assisted by a single junior minister, normally a parliamentary secretary. The Foreign Secretary had two under-secretaries, as did the Scottish Secretary, but they were unusual. The number of junior ministers was thus similar to that of cabinet ministers. Since then, the number of junior ministers has tripled. By the beginning of 2006, there were 22 cabinet ministers and 67 junior ministers (as well as 23 whips). It is not unusual for a department to have four or five junior ministers; at one point in the late 1990s, one department had eight.

Serving as a junior minister is usually a prerequisite for serving as a senior minister. It is rare for an MP to be appointed to the Cabinet straight from the back benches. An ambitious back-bencher will normally hope to be appointed as a parliamentary under-secretary of state and then as a minister of state before being considered for appointment to the Cabinet. Not all aspiring politicians make it beyond the ranks of junior minister. Some are dismissed after two or three years; some serve for several years without making it to the Cabinet. Tony Blair variously reshuffled and dismissed junior ministers following the 2001 and 2005 general elections. At least two of the junior ministers dismissed in 2005 had served in government since 1997.

The sheer number of junior ministers has been a cause of some controversy. Although their number helps to spread the workload within a department, some observers and former ministers have argued that there are too many of them. The increase in

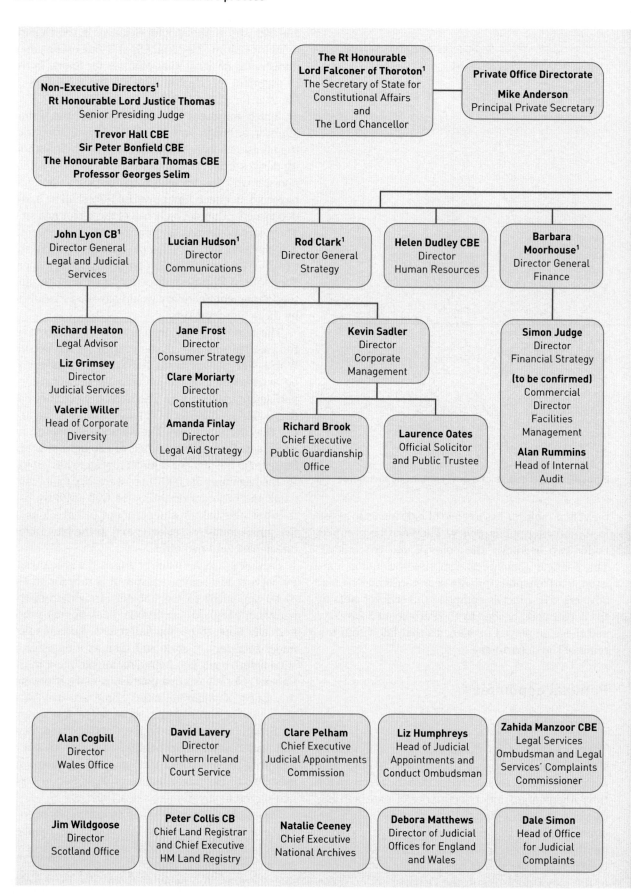

Figure 20.2 Structure of the Department of Constitutional Affairs ([1]Ministerial Executive Board Member(s)
Source: From the Department of Constitutional Affairs website (www.dca.gov.uk/dept/orgchart/orgchart-print.pdf)

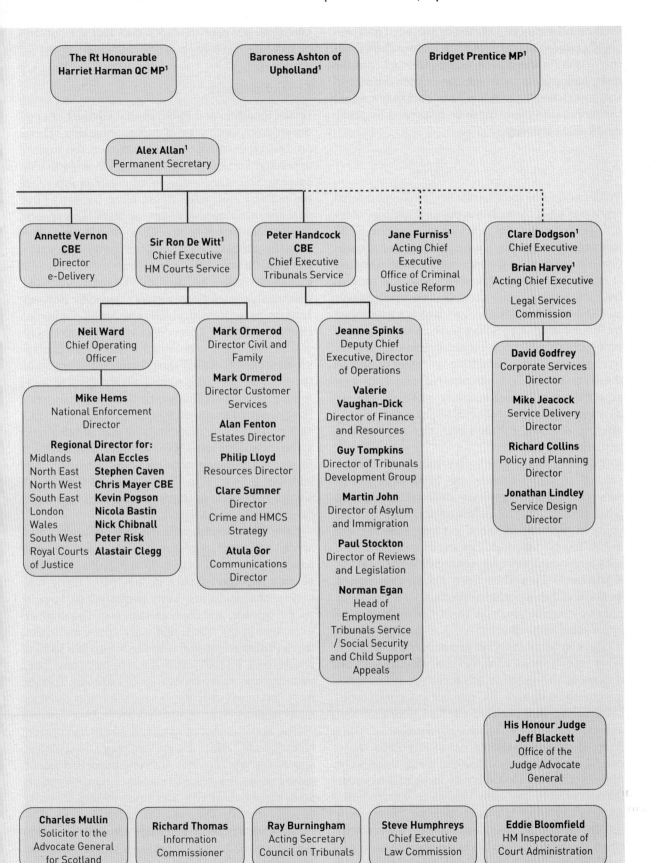

The Rt Honourable
Harriet Harman QC MP[1]

Baroness Ashton of
Upholland[1]

Bridget Prentice MP[1]

Alex Allan[1]
Permanent Secretary

Annette Vernon
CBE
Director
e-Delivery

Sir Ron De Witt[1]
Chief Executive
HM Courts Service

Peter Handcock
CBE
Chief Executive
Tribunals Service

Jane Furniss[1]
Acting Chief
Executive
Office of Criminal
Justice Reform

Clare Dodgson[1]
Chief Executive

Brian Harvey[1]
Acting Chief Executive

Legal Services
Commission

Neil Ward
Chief Operating
Officer

Mike Hems
National Enforcement
Director

Regional Director for:
Midlands   Alan Eccles
North East   Stephen Caven
North West   Chris Mayer CBE
South East   Kevin Pogson
London   Nicola Bastin
Wales   Nick Chibnall
South West   Peter Risk
Royal Courts Alastair Clegg
of Justice

Mark Ormerod
Director Civil and
Family

Mark Ormerod
Director Customer
Services

Alan Fenton
Estates Director

Philip Lloyd
Resources Director

Clare Sumner
Director
Crime and HMCS
Strategy

Atula Gor
Communications
Director

Jeanne Spinks
Deputy Chief
Executive, Director
of Operations

Valerie
Vaughan-Dick
Director of Finance
and Resources

Guy Tompkins
Director of Tribunals
Development Group

Martin John
Director of Asylum
and Immigration

Paul Stockton
Director of Reviews
and Legislation

Norman Egan
Head of
Employment
Tribunals Service
/ Social Security
and Child Support
Appeals

David Godfrey
Corporate Services
Director

Mike Jeacock
Service Delivery
Director

Richard Collins
Policy and Planning
Director

Jonathan Lindley
Service Design
Director

His Honour Judge
Jeff Blackett
Office of the
Judge Advocate
General

Charles Mullin
Solicitor to the
Advocate General
for Scotland

Richard Thomas
Information
Commissioner

Ray Burningham
Acting Secretary
Council on Tribunals

Steve Humphreys
Chief Executive
Law Commission

Eddie Bloomfield
HM Inspectorate of
Court Administration

their number may be justified by the need for managerial efficiency (i.e. spreading the workload), but the reason for the growth may be the fact that the more junior posts there are the greater the size of the government's payroll vote in Parliament – and the more posts there are to be dispensed by prime ministerial patronage.

Parliamentary private secretaries

Traditionally, one route to reaching junior ministerial office has been through serving as a parliamentary private secretary (PPS). (The other principal route has been through serving as an officer of a backbench committee.) A parliamentary private secretary is appointed to assist a minister. The post is unpaid, the holder is not officially a member of the government and the tasks undertaken are largely determined by the minister. A PPS may serve as the minister's principal link with back-benchers, listening to what has been said and transmitting the views of MPs to the minister. The PPS will also normally help with arranging friendly parliamentary questions and act as a message carrier between the minister and the officials' box in the House of Commons during a parliamentary debate.

The PPS is selected by the minister, although subject to confirmation by the Prime Minister. In some cases, ministers will use their PPSs as trusted advisers. They may also arrange for them to have desks in their departments and may include them in the regular meetings (known as 'prayers') held with junior ministers and senior civil servants in the department. They thus learn how a department works, and if they perform especially well the senior minister may recommend them for promotion to junior ministerial office.

The number of PPSs has grown over the decades. Whereas only senior ministers used to appoint PPSs, it is now the practice for ministers of state to appoint them as well. The number has grown especially in the past decade, a record number being appointed under the Labour government of Tony Blair. There are now in excess of fifty PPSs (fifty-one at the beginning of 2006; in 2002, there were fifty-seven). Such numbers may be helpful to junior ministers. They are also helpful to government. Although PPSs are not paid, they are nonetheless usually treated as being part of the government when it comes to votes in the House of Commons. A PPS who votes against the government is liable to be dismissed. The result is, in effect, to increase by almost 50 per cent the block vote that the government whips can rely on in a parliamentary vote.

Special advisers

Unlike ministers and PPSs, special advisers are not drawn from the ranks of parliamentarians. There are two types of special adviser. One is the expert, appointed because of an expertise in a particular subject. The other – the more common type – is the political, appointed to act as an adviser to the minister on a range of issues, to assist with speech writing and to act as a political link between the minister and the party and with other bodies outside the department. They are typically young, bright graduates who are politically ambitious. (One of the special advisers to Conservative Chancellor Norman Lamont from 1992 to 1993 was David Cameron, elected in 2005 as Conservative leader.) Their loyalty is to the minister, who is responsible for appointing them and to whom their fortunes are linked: if the minister goes, the special adviser goes as well. A minister may, and frequently does, invite the special adviser to stay with them if they are moved to another post. Sometimes an incoming minister may invite the special adviser to the previous incumbent to stay on. However, the link is normally with one minister. It is thus in the interests of the special adviser to be loyal to the minister and to work hard to ensure the minister's success.

Like junior ministers and PPSs, the number of special advisers has grown in recent years. Special advisers have their origins in the 1960s, but they became important figures in the 1970s: then, only very senior ministers were permitted to have a special adviser, and no more than one. The number expanded in the 1980s and early 1990s and there was a further expansion with the return of a Labour government in 1997, with some departments permitted to have more than two special advisers. Though most continued with one or two, some appointed as many as four.

The appointment of special advisers has proved controversial. Some critics are wary of political appointees who are not answerable to Parliament having such a role close to ministers. Some see them as being too powerful and undermining the role of civil servants. 'They seem to have taken over the Prime Minister's office and largely run the Treasury' (Denman, 2002, p. 254). Supporters point out that special advisers are actually of value to civil servants in that they can absorb political work that civil servants should not be asked to do (such as liaising with party bodies and replying to correspondence that has a partisan flavour). However, if they encroach on functions assigned to civil servants, or seek to give orders to civil servants, then problems may arise and, as we shall see, in recent years have arisen.

The officials

The bulk of the people working in government departments are **civil servants**. Since 1996, the most senior posts – just over 3,300 – have been brought together to form the 'Senior Civil Service'. A new pay and performance management system was introduced in April 2002, with new salary bands introduced on the basis of recommendations from the Senior Salary Review Body. After 1 April 2005, the salary range for Permanent Secretaries was £130,350 to £264,250 and for Pay Band 3, occupied by those immediately below Permanent Secretaries, it was £93,139 to £198,197. Pay is performance related.

Permanent Secretary

The Permanent Secretary is the permanent head of a department. He (very rarely she) will usually have spent his entire career in the Civil Service, rising up the ranks in the service before being appointed Permanent Secretary in a department. Formally, the Permanent Secretary has line control within a department. That is, all communication between civil servants and a senior minister is formally channelled through the Permanent Secretary. In practice, that is now administratively impossible. Instead, submissions will normally go straight to the minister, and the minister may call in the relevant civil servants to discuss particular issues for which they have responsibility. Nonetheless, submissions will be copied to the Permanent Secretary, and the Permanent Secretary will normally sit in on all discussions concerning important policy and administrative matters.

The Permanent Secretary is answerable to the minister for what goes on in the department. However, there is one exception. The Permanent Secretary is the accounting officer for the department. That means that responsibility for ensuring that money is spent for the purposes for which it has been voted by Parliament rests with the Permanent Secretary. The Permanent Secretary is answerable for the accounts, and if those accounts are the subject of an investigation and report by the National

Cambridge-educated Sir Kevin Tebbit is the Permanent Secretary at the Ministry of Defence
Source: Empics Sports Photo Agency

Audit Office, then it is the Permanent Secretary who appears before the Public Accounts Committee of the House of Commons to answer questions raised by the report.

The Permanent Secretary is, in effect, the chief executive of the department, but training for the role has usually been acquired over twenty or thirty years in the Civil Service. One study of 111 permanent secretaries in four periods between 1945 and 1993 found that all bar three were men (Theakston, 1995, pp. 36–43). They were usually educated at public school or grammar school before going on to Oxford or Cambridge University. Most went straight from university into the Civil Service and spent twenty-five years in Whitehall before taking up their present positions. Most had also served in more than one department, a feature especially of the latter half of the century. They were also predominantly 'generalists' – with degrees in classics or the arts

Sir Richard (now Lord) Wilson, the self-effacing, urbane mandarin who served as Cabinet Secretary, 1998–2002
Source: Empics Sports Photo Agency

– rather than specialists in law or economics; occasionally, a Permanent Secretary would be appointed who had some specialist knowledge of the subject covered by the department, but such figures were – and remain – rare. Just as ministers are normally generalists rather than specialists in a subject, so too are the civil servants who run the department. Their specialist knowledge is of how the machinery of government operates.

Senior civil servants

A similar pattern is to be found for those below the rank of Permanent Secretary. The typical senior civil servant is a white male; recent years have seen an increase in the number of women entering the Senior Civil Service, though more than two-thirds of posts are held by men. In April 2005, 29 per cent of senior civil servants were women, up from 18 per cent in 1999; 2.8 per cent were drawn from ethnic minorities.

Recent years have, however, seen major changes in terms of both roles and structures. A more open structure has been introduced, with greater emphasis on bringing in people with outside experience. Civil servants are increasingly being recruited by open competition. This is especially the case with the chief executives of government agencies, although it extends to other senior posts. Of the most senior posts in the Civil Service, about 30 per cent are open to external candidates.

The Civil Service has a less rigid hierarchy than it had in the 1970s and 1980s. There is less rigidity in terms of the positions held by senior civil servants (titles are now likely to be more managerial, such as director, than bureaucratic, such as assistant secretary) and responsibility for pay and recruitment is no longer centralised but instead delegated to individual departments. Each department also has responsibility for training, although courses have been provided centrally. These used to be provided by the Civil Service College. The college was incorporated by the incoming 1997 Labour Government in a Centre for Policy and Management Studies (the CPMS). The CPMS was itself incorporated in the National School of Government, established in June 2005 to help public sector organisations build capacity in good governance. The School links with academic bodies to provide training in management. It offers senior manager workshops for senior civil servants as well as programmes in, for example, people management, leadership, financial management and policy delivery.

Most civil servants work in agencies. These agencies, such as the Benefits Agency, began to be created in 1988 following publication of a report, *Improving Management in Government: the Next Steps*, by Sir Robin Ibbs. Most executive responsibilities of government have been hived off to such agencies, and today just over 73 per cent of civil servants are employed in 'Next Steps' agencies. (Of 523,000 full-time equivalent permanent posts in the Civil Service in 2004, 381,000 were in executive agencies or bodies such as the Inland Revenue.) The intention behind the agencies has been to separate the service-delivery responsibilities of government from policy making. Those senior civil servants responsible for policy advice to ministers remain at the heart of government departments.

Two features of the Civil Service over the past two decades are of particular relevance in studying government departments. The first is the greater emphasis on managerial and business skills. This emphasis developed under the Conservative governments of Margaret Thatcher and John Major. It has been continued under the Labour government of Tony Blair. There is demand on the part of the government for the Civil Service to have much clearer goals and to operate in terms of performance indicators and to deliver on targets that are set for it. Prime Minister Tony Blair has been particularly keen to shake up Whitehall and to ensure that civil servants are capable of delivering on the goals set by government. The various changes that have been introduced over the past twenty years have been brought together under the umbrella term 'new public management' (NPM). This is considered in greater depth in Chapter 21. There has also been the introduction of 'prior options' testing to ensure that the services provided are necessary and best carried out by public bodies. The result has been the privatisation of various agencies. This, along with other changes (including the earlier privatisation of bodies in the public sector), has served to reduce the size of the Civil Service. In 1976, there were just over 750,000 civil servants; by 2004, there were just over half-a-million, though the figure was below half-a-million from the mid-1990s to the beginning of the twenty-first century.

The second change is less often commented on but is more central to explaining the relationship between ministers and civil servants: that is, the less rigid structure within the 'core' of each department. The old hierarchical structure, policed and protected by senior civil servants who had been in place for years, has given way to a more flexible arrangement, not just in terms of formal structure but also in terms of the contact that ministers have with civil servants. Permanent Secretaries tend no longer to be the gatekeepers of what advice is or is not sent to a minister. The change in the structure of the Civil Service not only has made departments more open in terms of the people recruited to serve in senior posts but also has coincided with changes introduced by ministers. In recent years, ministers have been more prone to move away from a culture of paperwork – making decisions based on papers placed before them by officials – and towards a more open and interactive culture, calling in civil servants to discuss with them the proposals embodied in their papers.

Senior ministers thus head departments that have a more managerial and business-oriented ethos than before. Those departments, although they have shrunk in staff terms over recent years, can still be significant employers. The three largest are the Ministry of Defence (39,240 civil servants in 2004, excluding executive agencies), the Department of Work and Pensions (19,300) and the Home Office

(18,780). However, the policy-making side of each department is relatively small. Those employed in the top echelons of the Civil Service – the old Principal grade and above – comprise no more than 20,000 people. At the very top are the 3,300 forming the Senior Civil Service. These are the people – overwhelmingly white, male and non-science graduates – who advise ministers.

■ Ministerial power

It has been argued that ministerial power – the power to determine particular outcomes – derives from several variables (Figure 20.3). One is specific to the office: the legal, departmental and political powers of the office deriving from the convention of individual ministerial responsibility. Two others are specific to the individual: the purpose of the incumbent in taking office, and the skills of the incumbent. And there are three that are essentially external to the office: the power situation, the climate of expectation and international developments.

The office

Ministers are powerful by virtue of the constitutional convention of individual ministerial responsibility (see Norton, 1997b). The doctrine confers important legal, departmental and even parliamentary powers.

The legal dimension is central. We have touched on this at the beginning of this chapter. No statutory powers are vested in the Prime Minister or Cabinet. As Nevil Johnson has written, 'the enduring effect of the doctrine of ministerial responsibility has been

The office
Legal, departmental and political powers

The individual in the office
Purpose in taking office
Skills of the incumbent

External environment
The power situation
Climate of expectation
International developments

Figure 20.3 The components of ministerial power
Source: Adapted from Norton (1997a) 'Leaders or led? Senior ministers in British government', *Talking Politics*, Vol. 10, No. 2, pp. 78–85. Reproduced with permission of The Politics Association

over the past century or so that the powers have been vested in ministers and on a relentlessly increasing scale' (Johnson, 1980, p. 84). Postwar years have seen a substantial increase in the volume of legislation passed by Parliament. Bills are not more numerous, but they are longer and more complex. It is common for bills to confer powers on ministers and to do so in broad terms.

The doctrine confers important departmental powers in that it asserts ministerial line control. The focus of much of the writing on the doctrine has often been the culpability of ministers for the actions of their civil servants, but more importantly and more pervasively the doctrine establishes that civil servants are answerable to the minister and to no one else. Civil servants answer to the minister formally through the Permanent Secretary. The creation of the Next Steps agencies has not destroyed this basic relationship. Agency heads have some degree of autonomy, but the agencies remain within government, under a sponsoring department, and the agency chief is responsible – answerable – to the minister in that department.

The doctrine may also be deemed important in that the minister is answerable to Parliament for the department. That may appear a limitation – in that the minister is the subject of parliamentary questioning and attack – but it is also a power in that the minister alone is answerable to Parliament. Civil servants are not answerable to Parliament. They cannot appear at the despatch box. They may be summoned before a select committee, but they have no independent voice before that committee.

Parliamentary powers also derive from being Her Majesty's ministers. Since the crown alone can request money, money resolutions have to be moved by a minister. Parliamentary rules also provide that certain other motions, such as the motion to suspend the seven or ten o'clock rule – allowing debate to continue beyond the set time for the conclusion of business – can be moved only by ministers. Parliamentary business proceeds on the basis of an agenda set largely by government, and that business largely entails bills and motions brought forward by government. That business is normally departmental business: bills are brought forward by individual departments and steered through Parliament by the ministers of that department. Ministers generally have a far greater opportunity to speak than is the case with other parliamentarians.

Ministers, then, enjoy considerable formal powers. They also enjoy some public visibility – itself a potential source of power – deriving from their position in government. A senior minister will have a greater chance of persuading a newspaper editor to come to dinner than will a member of the Opposition front bench or a humble back-bencher. A minister will be able to attract publicity by virtue of exercising the power of the office or by announcing an intention to exercise that power. Even if no formal power to act exists, a minister may attract publicity by making a statement or letting the press know informally what is planned. Departments have press officers, but ministers may also use their special advisers to brief journalists. Press officers are civil servants. Special advisers, as we have seen, are political appointees.

Senior ministers also have some power by virtue of their political position. That is, they will be drawn (by convention) from one of the two Houses of Parliament. Unlike ministers in some other countries, they retain their seats in the legislature. More importantly, though also subject to much greater variability, they may also enjoy a power base in Parliament. They may seek to build that power base, for instance through regular contact with back-benchers. Under the Labour government of Tony Blair, the Chancellor of the Exchequer, Gordon Brown, has acquired a reputation for assiduously courting back-benchers and newly appointed ministers. Such a power base may give them leverage in relation to other ministers and to their departments. It may also make it very difficult for a Prime Minister to sack them.

The individual in the office

There are two dimensions to the individual in the office: purpose and skills. A minister may have important powers as a minister, but knowing that fact tells us little about how and why the power is exercised. For that, we have to turn to the person in the office. Ministers become ministers for a variety of reasons. Some simply want to be ministers. Some want to achieve particular policy outcomes. Some want to be Prime Minister. What they want will determine how they act.

Consequently, how ministers act varies considerably. As one former cabinet minister recorded in her memoirs, 'there are as many ministerial styles as there are ministers' (Shephard, 2000, p. 105). However, it is possible to identify different types of minister. One study has identified five types of senior minister – team player, commander, ideologue, manager and

Figure 20.4 Types of senior minister

agent (Figure 20.4) (Norton, 2000). The types relate to different locations of decision-making power. With commanders, ideologues and managers, power-making power is retained in the office but exercised in different ways. With team players and agents, policy is 'made' elsewhere, either because ministers cannot prevent it or because they prefer to abdicate power to these locations.

Team player

A team player is someone who believes in collective decision making and wants to be part of that team. This correlates more or less precisely with the concept of Cabinet government. Proposals may be put by a minister to Cabinet, but it is the Cabinet that deliberates and decides on the policy. In practice, the Cabinet has difficulty in fulfilling this role because of lack of time. It is also constrained from fulfilling this role by the fact that few ministers want to be team players. There is very little evidence to suggest that many senior ministers see themselves primarily as 'team players'.

Commander

Commanders are those who have very clear ideas of what they want to achieve, and those ideas derive from their own personal preferences and goals. (Preferences should be taken to include ambition.) These may derive from their own past experiences in business or government, or simply from their personal reflections. When they accept a particular office, they usually have some idea of what they want to achieve. Individuals may not be consistent commanders throughout their ministerial career. They may have a very clear idea of what they want to achieve in one or more particular office but not in another. For example, one politician who held five

Cabinet posts during the Thatcher and Major premierships had a clear idea of what he wanted to achieve in three of them (one was the post he had always wanted); in another he had a general idea (even though it was a post he had not wanted) and in the other – a rather senior post – he had no clear perception of what he wanted to achieve. Rather, he assumed one of the other roles: that of 'manager'. There are normally commanders in each era of government. There are commanders in the Labour government of Tony Blair, foremost among them being Chancellor of the Exchequer Gordon Brown. Others who have served in Labour Cabinets have included David Blunkett, Robin Cook and Clare Short.

Ideologue

An ideologue is someone who is driven by a clear, consistent philosophy. Thus, whatever office they occupy, the policies they pursue will derive from that philosophy. There were some ideologues – pursuing a neo-liberal philosophy – in the period of Conservative government from 1979 to 1997. These included Sir Keith Joseph, Nicholas Ridley and John Redwood. However, they were not as numerous as is often supposed. This, in part, reflects the fact that Prime Ministers have rarely appointed ministers on purely ideological grounds. Prime Minister Margaret Thatcher largely left junior ministerial appointments to others, thus restricting her choice when it came to choosing cabinet ministers. Some ministers who may appear to be ideologues are not; rather, their views in particular sectors coincide with those of a particular ideological strand. One minister who held office under Margaret Thatcher conceded that in one particular post he had what he described as 'Thatcherite priorities'; but when he occupied another more senior post later, he was certainly not seen as a Thatcherite but rather viewed by Thatcherites as having 'gone native'. There are few obvious ideologues in the Cabinet under Tony Blair.

Manager

Here the minister takes the decisions but is not driven by any particular ideology or personal worldview. Instead, the approach is pragmatic, sometimes Oakeshottian: that is, helping to keep the ship of state afloat and operating efficiently. Ministers may anticipate issues; more frequently they respond to them. They do not necessarily take the departmental line but decide it for themselves. When several competing demands are made of them, they act as brokers, listening and weighing the evidence and then taking a view. A good example of a manager during the period of Conservative government in the 1990s was Foreign Secretary Douglas Hurd. There have been a number of managers under Tony Blair, including, in the 2005 Cabinet, Environment Secretary Margaret Beckett and Health Secretary Patricia Hewitt.

Agent

Here the minister essentially acts on behalf of another body. There are two principal types of agent: those of the Prime Minister and those of the Civil Service.

1. *Prime Ministerial*: Here the minister is appointed to ensure that the wishes of the Prime Minister are carried out. (This is distinct from an ideologue, who may share the Prime Minister's ideology but is an enthusiast for the ideology and will give that preference over the Prime Minister's wishes.) Occasionally, a Prime Minister may decide, in effect, to be their own Foreign Secretary or Chancellor of the Exchequer, although that depends on the willingness of the minister in question to comply: Margaret Thatcher had an easier time influencing economic policy with Sir Geoffrey Howe as Chancellor than she did when that office was held by Nigel Lawson. During the Thatcher era, there were various media reports that some ministers were put in at middle-ranking level to act as the Prime Minister's eyes and ears in a department. Several members of the Cabinet under Tony Blair have variously been described as 'Blairites', essentially there to deliver the vision of the Prime Minister.

2. *Civil Service*: Here the minister essentially adopts the departmental brief and does what the officials in the department want the minister to do. Ministers may adopt this role because they want a quiet life – some actually move up the 'greasy pole' of government despite being remarkably lazy – or because they do not have the personal will or intellect to resist the persuasive briefings of officials. Civil servants can be remarkably persuasive, and indeed devious (papers put in late, or among a mass of papers in the red box), and one or two departments, such as the Foreign Office, do have reputations for pursuing a particular departmental 'ideology'. On some issues, ministers don't take a stand, and,

as Gerald Kaufman recounts in *How To Be a Minister*, will read out their departmental brief in Cabinet committee (Kaufman, 1997).

Ministers, then, have important powers and some of them want to exercise those powers. However, whether they do so successfully depends on their skills and the political environment they occupy.

Skills

In a study of prime ministerial power, published in *Teaching Politics* in 1987, it was argued that the essential skills needed by a Prime Minister, in addition to those of selection, were those of leadership, anticipation and reaction, and that a number of strategic options were available to them to achieve the desired outcome (Norton, 1987, pp. 325–45). The strategic options were those of command, persuasion, manipulation, and hiding. These skills and options also apply to senior ministers:

1. *Command*: Ministers may have a clear intellectual view of what they want to achieve, but actually taking decisions to ensure that view is realised may be difficult. One cabinet minister in the early 1980s, Sir Keith Joseph, was notorious for having difficulty making decisions to achieve his ideological goals. Conversely, some ministers have no difficulty making decisions: examples in the 2005 Cabinet included Defence Secretary John Reid and Trade and Industry Secretary Alan Johnson.

2. *Persuade*: Some ministers may know what they want to achieve and take a clear view. However, they need on occasion to be able to carry colleagues and others – MPs, outside organised interests, the public – with them. There are different devices that ministers may employ to bring the different actors onside: meetings with the relevant back-bench committee, for example; a 'dear colleague' letter to the party's MPs; a press conference; private briefings for journalists; and 'keeping No. 10 briefed' ('No. 10' meaning principally the Prime Minister but also, on occasion, other actors in Downing Street, such as the head of the No. 10 Policy Unit or the relevant person in the unit). Some ministers will also spend time meeting affected bodies, for example by making an effort to attend their annual conferences and accepting invitations to speak. Some ministers in the Blair government have

reputations for being persuaders, being willing to see MPs privately to discuss their concerns and if necessary agree compromises. They included, in the 2005 Cabinet, Foreign Secretary Jack Straw and Transport Secretary Alistair Darling.

3. *Manipulate*: The Prime Minister is sometimes devious, and the same applies to senior ministers. On occasion, one may have to play off one body against another. Manipulation may entail 'kite flying' in the media, feeding a misleading story that can be denied and then using it as leverage to achieve a particular outcome. Manipulation may be met by manipulation. When a story leaked in December 1996 that the Prime Minister, John Major, was thinking of abandoning the government's 'negotiate and decide' policy on a single European currency, Deputy Prime Minister Michael Heseltine said publicly that there had been no change in government policy, and at the despatch box in the afternoon John Major was forced to acknowledge that this was the case, thus forcing him to stick with the policy he had apparently been hoping to abandon.

4. *Hide*: Ministers need to know when to avoid a particular problem. Sometimes it is better to keep one's head below the parapet rather than risk putting it above the parapet and getting shot at by the media and disgruntled MPs. One of the values of having junior ministers is that they can be put up to take the flak. For example, when the Child Support Agency (CSA) attracted enormous criticism in the first half of the 1990s, it was the relevant junior minister, rather than the Secretary of State, who appeared principally before the cameras to justify the government's position. When senior ministers decided on the evening of 'Black Wednesday' in September 1992 to suspend British membership of the European exchange-rate mechanism (ERM), they avoided giving television interviews and instead put up the party chairman – who was not even a minister – to respond.

These are strategic options. However, there are two other skills that ministers need in order to achieve their goals: they need to be good time managers, and they need to understand how the system – and their particular department – works.

1. *Effective time management*: The work of a senior minister is extraordinarily time-consuming. One Scottish Secretary was told by his private office that on average 1,000 items passed through the office every week, of which he saw 700 – in other words, 100 items a day (Lang, 2002, p. 65). Dealing with such items is in addition to a range of meetings, preparation for speeches and being in the House. For ministers, it is therefore essential to organise their time effectively. Some former cabinet ministers have admitted that they had difficulty prioritising their activities and saying 'no' to various activities. Some expressed admiration for their colleagues who managed to organise their time and stay on top of their departments. One minister was described as 'superbly professional. Those who worked with him . . . say that he was ruthless in doing only what he considered essential' (Shephard, 2000, p. 118). One means of relieving some of the pressure is by delegation. Some ministers are good at delegating and making use of junior ministers. One Conservative cabinet minister in the Thatcher government, for example, gave his junior ministers particular responsibilities and then had them draw up a work programme for the next two years, and every three months he had a meeting with each minister to discuss progress. Others are less well organised, and some have difficulty delegating tasks effectively.

2. *Understanding the system*: Ministers need to know how the process works. 'The nature of a department and the tools at its disposal to achieve change are important factors in the exercise of power. Understanding them is necessary to achieve change, and to respond to pressure, whether of politics, circumstance or crisis' (Shephard, 2000, pp. 114–15). Very occasionally, some ministers are appointed without any prior experience of Parliament, but the experience has rarely been a happy one, those involved displaying a lack of sensitivity to the needs of a department and of the parliamentary environment. One way to understand the system is by study. Prior to the 1997 general election, seminars were organised for shadow ministers on the workings of government. Another way – the more frequently used – is by ministerial apprenticeship. Holding junior ministerial office is useful as a way of seeing how the system works from the inside. One of the points made by one former minister was that in order to be effective in achieving your goals as a senior minister it helped, first, to have been a junior minister in the department that one was

appointed to head; and, second, to have served in the Whips' Office. As a junior minister, one gets to know how the particular department works (departments differ enormously), and as a whip one gets to know how to handle MPs and to anticipate what is likely to cause trouble in the House. Understanding of a department may also derive from longevity in the office, but that is something largely beyond the control of the incumbent.

Without some (ideally, all) of these skills, a minister – however intelligent and self-driven – is not likely to succeed and may find their ministerial career stunted or destroyed altogether. Within a few months of the appointment of the new Labour government in May 1997, there were reports that some members of the Cabinet would not last beyond the autumn: the one most frequently mentioned was Gavin Strang, largely because he was indecisive and was poor at the despatch box; in other words, he was poor at command and persuasion. He was dismissed in 1998. Another, frequently reported as being outmanoeuvred in Cabinet committee by Home Secretary Jack Straw, was the Chancellor of the Duchy of Lancaster, Dr David Clark (Morrison, 2001, pp. 307–9). He too was dismissed in 1998. Culture, Media and Sport Secretary Dr Chris Smith also attracted criticism for his handling of his department: he was dropped following the general election in 2001.

External environment

Ministers may also find that their capacity to achieve desired outcomes is enhanced by the environment external to their department. This environment includes the power situation, the climate of expectations and international developments:

1. *Power situation*: The power situation overlaps with the powers and constraints of the office but provides a dynamic element. Power relationships are not static. And what the 'power situation' refers to is the relationship between different bodies in the immediate political environment. In terms of ministers, this covers especially Downing Street, Cabinet, Parliament, the Civil Service and the media.

   A previously popular Prime Minister may lose support among the parliamentary party or the public and start to seek support from particular ministers, doing so through being more supportive of their policies. A minister may find it easier to push a policy through as the authority of a Prime Minister wanes. There may be a shift in the power situation as a result of a Cabinet reshuffle. A minister may find that colleagues opposed to a particular policy have been moved or sacked. Elections of officers of back-bench party committees may result in opponents of a minister's policy being replaced by supporters. Changes of ownership of particular newspapers may result in greater media support for a policy. Changes may occur that make the power situation unfavourable, but at times it may be highly favourable to a particular minister and the policies of that minister. Martin Smith sums up the difficulties faced by Prime Minister John Major compared with Margaret Thatcher not in terms of weak and strong personality but in terms of a changed power situation: 'Major had no majority in parliament, the government was divided, and the popular perception was that his government lacked economic competence – circumstances created Major's indecisiveness; it was not indecisiveness that led to the Conservative defeat' (quoted in Morrison, 2001, p. 279).

2. *Climate of expectation*: The expectations of citizens are clearly important and change over time. The Conservative Party was the beneficiary of a particular climate of expectation in 1979 and the victim of a very different climate in 1997. The popular mood may initially be hostile to a particular proposal and then, perhaps induced by particular events, swing in support of it. Particular ministers may benefit from a particular climate of expectation, a popular mood favouring what they want to achieve. That mood can be a political resource for the minister, making it difficult for the Cabinet to resist a proposal for which there is clearly overwhelming popular support.

3. *International developments*: What happens elsewhere in the world may limit ministers in terms of what they wish to achieve but on occasion may also make it possible for ministers to achieve what they want. A natural disaster or civil war may strengthen the position of a minister who wishes to increase foreign aid or to intervene militarily in a conflict. A shift in power or in policy in another state may facilitate a minister achieving a particular outcome. A change of government in another EU country may enable a minister to get a particular proposal adopted by the EU Council of Ministers.

Two conclusions can be drawn from the foregoing analysis. The first is that senior ministers have the potential to be significant figures in determining public policy. The second is that ministerial power is variable, not constant. It can be subject to a wide range of constraints. Let us consider in a little greater depth the constraints.

Constraints

Ministers labour under a number of constraints. The most important are constitutional, legal and managerial. Constitutionally, they are constrained by the doctrine of collective ministerial responsibility. Major decisions have to percolate up for Cabinet approval, which means, in practice, Cabinet committee; and approval may not always be forthcoming. The constitutional power exercised by the Prime Minister to hire, fire and shuffle ministers may also be a powerful constraint on ministerial policies, and it may be exercised in order to reflect the Prime Minister's policy preferences.

At the individual level, there are two important constitutional constraints. One is the convention of individual ministerial responsibility. The other is the ministerial code. The convention of individual ministerial responsibility is one that, as we have seen, ensures that statutory powers are vested in ministers and that they have line control within their departments; it is also one that renders ministers answerable for what takes place within their departments. This is often assumed to mean that, in the event of an error within a department, the minister resigns. Although ministers may be deemed culpable for what goes on in their departments, this has rarely meant having to resign if mistakes are made. Ministers have variously resigned because of personal scandal, such as David Blunkett in 2004, or disagreement with government policy, such as Robin Cook in 2003, but very rarely because of a mistake made within their department (see Norton, 1997b; see also Woodhouse, 1994). A distinction is frequently drawn between policy and operation: if the policy is right but is not carried out, then those public officials who have failed to carry it out are the ones who are disciplined. However, the dividing line is not always clear. The creation of executive agencies has created officials more clearly identifiable as being responsible for delivering policies, but there have been various clashes between ministers and officials over responsibility for determining action by the agencies. Conservative Home Secretary Michael Howard dismissed the head of the Prison Service, Derek Lewis, in 1995 over prison escapes, but was accused by the Opposition of being responsible for a failure of policy. This reflects the weakness as well as the strength of the convention: ministers may not necessarily resign but they have to answer for what happens in their department. Even if the minister does not resign, the minister's career may be adversely affected.

Ministers are also constrained by the ministerial code. This is a code of conduct drawn up by the Prime Minister. The first modern version was drawn up by Clement Attlee in 1945 and was variously revised by his successors. It was formally a secret document until John Major agreed to its declassification in 1992. The code stipulates how ministers should conduct themselves in their dealings with others, including the Civil Service and Parliament, and how they should conduct their personal life in order to avoid conflicts of interest. The code shapes ministers' behaviour and breaches may be punished by the Prime Minister. It was a failure to comply with one of the recommendations of the code that led to David Blunkett's second resignation from the Cabinet in 2005. Following accusations that the Prime Minister was both prosecutor and jury in respect of the code, Tony Blair in 2006 announced that he was appointing the Comptroller and Auditor General, Sir John Bourn, to advise him on complaints about ministerial conduct.

Legal constraints exist in that ministers may be limited by the powers conferred on them by Parliament. They have increasingly to be sensitive to the risk of acting *ultra vires* (beyond powers). A greater degree of judicial activism in recent decades may be the product of a change of judicial culture (or of those who are affected by government being more prepared to seek judicial review) or a change in the nature of government; but whichever it is, the courts are now more willing than previously to review the legality of ministerial actions.

The courts, as we shall see in Chapter 23, are also more active as a consequence of various constitutional changes. Ministers are constrained by the conditions of membership of the European Union, by the incorporation of the European Convention on Human Rights (ECHR) into British law, and by the devolution of powers to elected assemblies in different parts of the United Kingdom. In policy areas that fall within the competence of the EU, ministers can no longer exercise power unilaterally but rather form part of a collective decision-making body (the Council of Ministers) in which they may be overruled. As their responsibilities have increased as a consequence of the UK's membership of the EU, so their capacity to affect outcomes has decreased. Ministers are constrained by the provisions of the ECHR and in introducing bills now have to confirm that they comply with the provisions of the ECHR. Devolution has moved certain policy areas to the competence of elected assemblies, especially the Scottish Parliament, and a UK minister may have difficulty moving ahead with a policy without the support of the executives in Scotland and Wales.

Ministers are also subject to what may be termed managerial constraints. Ministers have a mass of responsibilities and duties: they are departmental ministers; they are members of the Cabinet; they are members of the appropriate EU Council of Ministers; they are party and political figures (invited to attend and address a mass of meetings); they are ministers answerable to Parliament; they are (except for those ministers who are peers) constituency MPs; and they are party MPs who have to attend Parliament to vote for their party. Ministers have difficulty managing their time. Their evenings are taken up reading and signing the papers that are crammed into their ministerial red boxes. Their days may be full of meetings with officials and representatives of outside bodies, leaving little time for sustained reflection. Time spent travelling between meetings is variously spent dictating constituency correspondence into a dictaphone.

Ministers are also public and political figures, driven increasingly by the demands of a 24-hour news service. The media demand instant comments, and there are now the means for immediate communication. Ministers – and those wanting to interview them – are rarely without their mobile telephones and pagers.

The consequence of these demands is that ministers are frequently in a reactive, rather than a proactive, mode, having to rush to deal with problems and queries placed before them – on a relentless scale – and with little time to stand back and to think through what they want to achieve and whether they are on the path to achieving it.

■ Explaining ministerial power

Ministers are powerful figures in government. At the same time, they are subject to remarkable constraints. How, then, can one make sense of their role in British government? Various models have been created to help us to understand the role of ministers in policy making. Let us assess three that provide very different perspectives: the principal–agent model, the power-dependency model and the baronial model.

Principal–agent model

This stipulates that ministers are essentially the agents of a principal. Thus, although some ministers may be commanders, ideologues or managers, most fall under the category, identified earlier, of agents. One school of thought contends that the UK has **prime ministerial government**, and thus that ministers are agents of the Prime Minister. Another school of thought advances the proposition that the UK has Civil Service government, and thus that ministers are agents of civil servants.

The prime ministerial government school of thought argues that the powers of the Prime Minister are such that the Prime Minister is in a position to determine public policy. He or she makes policy preferences through the choice of senior ministers. If the Prime Minister wishes to achieve a particular policy outcome, he can effectively require a senior minister to agree to that policy. A minister failing to comply with prime ministerial wishes may cease to be a minister. Furthermore, the Prime Minister can ensure particular outcomes through control of the Cabinet agenda and through chairing the Cabinet. Blair in particular has been accused of marginalising his Cabinet in order to ensure he gets his way (see Kavanagh and Seldon, 1999; Foster, 2005). The Prime Minister can keep a tight rein on ministers through monitoring their speeches and through requiring the text of speeches to be cleared by Downing Street. Government policy, it is argued, is increasingly being made in Downing Street and not in the individual government departments.

The Civil Service school of thought argues that it is the Civil Service that determines policy outcomes. Working through departments, civil servants can help to shape, even determine, the minister's agenda. 'In practice', according to Weir and Beetham (1999, p. 167), 'ministers rely almost wholly on their departments, senior bureaucrats and private offices, and the resources and advice they can provide.' Civil servants have an advantage over ministers in terms of their numbers, permanence, expertise and cohesion. There is one senior minister heading a department. The number of senior civil servants in the department may run into three figures. A minister, even with the help of a number of junior ministers, cannot keep track of everything that is going on in a department. A senior minister will, on average, serve in one ministerial post for two years. (In the decades before the Second World War, the average was four years.) Civil servants will be in place in the department before a minister arrives and will usually still be in place once a minister has departed. A new minister provides civil servants with an opportunity to fight anew battles that may previously have been lost. Furthermore, that permanence also allows civil servants to build up a body of administrative expertise that is denied to a transient minister. Civil servants may be in a position to know what is achievable, and what is not, in a way that ministers cannot. Civil servants, it is argued, are also more politically and socially cohesive than ministers: politically cohesive in that they imbue a particular Civil Service and departmental ethos, and their approach is shaped by that ethos; and socially cohesive in that they tend to be drawn from the same or similar social backgrounds and to be members of the same London clubs. Ministers, on the other hand, imbue no particular ethos and are drawn from somewhat disparate backgrounds. They do not tend to mix socially together in the way that senior civil servants do.

Civil servants are in a position to influence, even control, the flow of information to a minister. A minister may not always receive every piece of information relevant to a particular proposal. The minister's diary may be filled with meetings that are largely inconsequential or so numerous as to squeeze out time to do other things (see Shephard, 2000, p. 119). The minister's red boxes may be filled with a mass of papers, the more important tucked away at the bottom. Officials may put up position papers, outlining various options, but omitting others or skewing the material in support of each in such a way that only one option appears to be viable. Indeed, ministers may have little chance to think and write anything of their own. One cabinet minister, deciding that he wanted to jot down some thoughts of his own, looked for some clean paper and found that there was none in his office. He asked his private secretary for some.

He went out and came back after a pause, holding in front of him like a dead rat, one single sheet of plain white paper, which he solemnly laid on the desk. After an apprehensive glance at me he left and I suddenly realised how civil servants controlled their masters: always keep them supplied with an endless supply of neatly prepared memoranda. Never give them time to think for themselves. Above all, never give them paper with nothing on it.

Lang (2002), p. 65

Civil servants also monitor ministers' calls and may seek to limit formal contact between one minister and another and, indeed, between ministers and people outside the department. One minister encountered opposition when she decided to hold a series of breakfasts for businesswomen: 'The roof fell in. There was strong Treasury resistance – "But why, Minister?" – and a total inability to provide a tablecloth or anything to eat or drink, much less to get anyone else to do so' (Shephard, 2000, p. 112). If a minister takes a view contrary to that adopted by civil servants in the department, the civil servants may ask civil servants in other departments to brief their ministers to take a contrary line when the matter comes before Cabinet committee. There is also extensive contact between officials in the UK government and in the EU Commission. Ministers, with little time to prepare for meetings, often have to be briefed on the plane to Brussels. On this line of argument, ministers have little scope to think about policy goals and to consider information and advice other than that placed before them by their officials. Sometimes the limitations are purely those of time. In other cases, they may be intellectual, ministers not having the mental capacity to challenge what has been laid before them. As one Chief Secretary to the Treasury once recorded, on complex issues ministers not directly involved in an issue would read the briefs, prepared by civil servants, the night before or as the argument proceeded. 'More often that not . . . they would follow the line of the brief' (Barnett, 1982, p. 41). The dependence on the papers prepared by officials can occur at the highest levels. The Cabinet Office prepares a brief for the Prime Minister for Cabinet meetings indicating, on the basis of papers circulated and knowledge of those involved, the line the PM may wish to take ('Subject to discussion, the Prime Minister might wish to conclude . . .'). This is a form of prompt to the PM, who may or may not choose to utilise it. However, one senior civil servant records the occasion when Prime Minister Harold Wilson had to leave during a discussion and handed over to his deputy, Edward Short:

Short was a Bear of Little Brain and would have been as capable of understanding, let alone summarising, the previous discussion as he would have been at delivering a lecture on quantum mechanics. He presided wordlessly over the discussion for a further five minutes, then spoke. 'I find we have agreed as follows' – and read out the draft conclusions penned before the discussion had begun . . . Not without a modest satisfaction, the Secretariat recorded the conclusions read out by the Deputy Prime Minister.

Denman (2002), p. 169

This view of the power of the Civil Service over ministers has been voiced by former ministers – among them Tony Benn – and was famously encapsulated in a popular television series, *Yes Minister*, in the 1980s. The Permanent Secretary, Sir Humphrey Appleby, and other civil servants were able to out-manoeuvre the minister, Jim Hacker, in a way that finds resonance in the memoirs of some ministers.

However, both schools of thought have been challenged. The prime ministerial government model overlooks, according to critics, the limited time, resources and interest of the Prime Minister. The Prime Minister occupies a particular policy space – that of high policy (dealing with the economic welfare and security of the nation) – and has limited time to interfere in middle-level policy generated by ministers (see Norton, 1997a, 2000). Furthermore, despite an extension of policy resources in Downing Street under Tony Blair, the resources available to a Prime Minister in Downing Street are limited. A senior minister has more advisers than the Prime Minister has in the minister's sector of public policy. Even though material must be cleared through Downing Street, some ministers are slow in submitting texts of speeches; some may never even reach Downing Street. Ministers may brief the press, or even give interviews, without clearance from No. 10 (see Short, 2004, p. 177). Prime Ministers rarely have a grasp of, or a deep interest in, every sector of public policy. Instead, they leave it to ministers to get on with their jobs, frequently free of interference from Downing Street. Indeed, one of the most remarkable findings of recent research into senior ministers was that it is very rare for a Prime Minister, when appointing someone to Cabinet office, to tell the minister what is expected of them (Norton, 2000). Nigel Lawson recalls that when he accepted the post of Chancellor of the Exchequer, he was offered only one piece of advice by the Prime Minister: 'That was to get my hair cut' (Lawson, 1992, p. 249). The advice offered to John Major when he was appointed Foreign Secretary was also brief and unrelated to specific policy: 'You had better hang on to your seatbelt' (Seldon, 1997, p. 87).

The Civil Service school of thought is challenged by the claim that civil servants are not as proactive and as cohesive as proponents of this thesis suggest. The demands made of civil servants are such that they too have little time for sustained thought and reflection. Although research suggests that civil servants in some departments imbue a particular departmental ethos, most civil servants seek to carry out the wishes of their ministers, regardless of their own views or prior departmental preferences. Indeed, recent research points to the extent to which civil servants are loyal to their ministers (Norton, 2000). Far from seeking to impede them, they work hard to carry out their wishes. One Conservative minister, Cecil Parkinson, recorded in his memoirs that civil servants were 'very stimulating to work with, very loyal and incredibly hard working' (Parkinson, 1992, p. 154). Another, Norman Tebbit, recorded that he found he had 'the benefit of officials of the highest integrity and ability. Once I had laid down policy they were tireless in finding ways to deliver what I wanted' (Tebbit, 1989, p. 231). Ministers are also now more likely to call civil servants in to quiz them about the papers they have submitted. Ministers themselves may also discuss matters privately, free from Civil Service involvement. Some of these meetings are bilateral rather than multilateral. One minister, interviewed by this author, recalled with wry amusement how his civil servants tried to limit his contacts with other ministers, largely oblivious to the fact that once he was in his minister's room in the Commons he could quite easily pop to see other ministers, in adjoining offices, to have a quiet chat.

Civil Service cohesion, and the ethos attached to the service and to particular departments, is also being eroded by the people from outside the Civil Service being brought in to senior posts and also by the greater emphasis being placed on managerial skills. Civil servants are being trained to deliver certain specified goals. A perceived failure to deliver under the Labour government of Tony Blair has resulted in pressure being put on senior civil servants to improve their performance in meeting the government's targets (see Gray and Jenkins, 2005). As civil servants are under greater pressure to deliver what ministers expect of them, so ministers are also bringing in more political appointees in order to provide advice and to handle their relations with the media (see Foster, 2005, pp. 207–22). That greater dependence on special advisers has been marked in recent years, generating public controversy and creating a grey area between civil servants and special advisers. Relations became especially strained in 2001–2 in the Transport Department between civil servants and the minister's special adviser, Jo Moore. Relationships broke down in the department, leading to the resignation of not only the special adviser but also the minister, Stephen Byers. Under the Blair government, his chief of staff (Jonathan Powell) and communications secretary (Alastair Campbell), both special advisers, were given executive powers, allowing them to give instructions to civil servants, a position that led to criticism and claims of a politicisation of the Civil Service. There has also been a tendency to seek advice from a range of bodies outside government – think-tanks, advisory committees and task groups. In many cases, civil servants are not seen as being in the decision-making loop.

A seminal work on cabinet ministers by Bruce Headey, published in 1974, found that civil servants looked to ministers for leadership. They preferred ministers who could take decisions and fight (and win) departmental battles (Headey, 1974, pp. 140–53). That appears to remain the case. As one former Permanent Secretary put it in a lecture in 1995, 'To some it might seem like heaven on earth to have a Minister who has no ideas and is endlessly open to the suggestions or recommendations of officials. But that is not the case. Officials need ministers with ideas . . . Officials need stimulus; need leadership; and, on occasion, conflict' (Holland, 1995, p. 43). This suggests that civil servants are more likely to welcome an effective commander, ideologue or manager as their minister than an agent or team player.

Power-dependency model

This model has been developed by R.A.W. Rhodes (1981, 1997). Although used to cover particularly, but not exclusively, centre–local relations, it is relevant for a study of the relationship between ministers and other actors in the political system. It is based on several propositions. One of the principal propositions is that any organisation is dependent upon other organisations for resources. Thus, the Prime Minister is dependent on the resources available in government departments; he does not have all the resources he needs in Downing Street. Ministers are dependent on their departments: they need civil servants to provide advice and to carry out their decisions. Civil servants need ministers to deliver resources through fighting battles with the Treasury and in Cabinet. Far from being in conflict with one another, the relationship may be closer to a partnership (Weir and Beetham, 1999, pp. 172–5). A second proposition is that in order to achieve their goals, organisations have to exchange resources. In other words, no body can operate as an exclusive and effective body. Actors within the political system need others in the system to help them to achieve their goals. There is a dependence on others (see Norton, 2003). That means that alliances have to be created. The model recognises that there may be a body or group of bodies that dominate in the relationship but that the relationship may change as actors fight for position.

The relevance for understanding the role of senior ministers is that it stands as something of a corrective to the principal–agent model. Although there may be times when the Prime Minister or civil servants are to the fore in determining policy outcomes, ministers are not relegated to some supporting role. They need the Prime Minister and civil servants, but conversely the Prime Minister and civil servants need them: they are an important resource, and they cannot necessarily be taken for granted. A Prime Minister may thus need to build support in Cabinet to get a controversial measure approved: the support of senior ministers thus constitutes a vital, indeed a necessary, resource. It may be necessary, but it may not be sufficient. Statutory powers, as we have seen, are vested in senior ministers. The Prime Minister, and Cabinet, thus need to ensure that the relevant minister is willing to exercise those powers. Others may thus depend on the resources at the disposal of ministers. At the same time, ministers themselves are dependent on the resources of others. They need the political support of the Prime Minister. They need their civil servants to carry out their wishes. They also need different bodies outside government to accept and to help to implement their policies. The Lord Chancellor, for example, may need to mobilise the support of the Bar in order to achieve reform of the legal system.

The power-dependency model thus suggests a more complex and less hierarchical political process than that advanced by the principal–agent model. Although the Prime Minister may predominate, it is not to the extent that we can claim the existence of prime ministerial government. Ministers are more important players in the process than the principal–agent model suggests. Although important, ministers themselves are not dominant either. They too depend on others in the political process. The process of policy making is thus an essentially crowded and interactive one.

The power-dependency model has been variously criticised (see Rhodes, 1997, p. 37). In terms of understanding the place of senior ministers in government, it does not necessarily help to explain who is predominant at any one time. Extensive empirical research would be necessary to do that. It also runs foul of objections from advocates of the principal–agent model. They contend that senior ministers may be resources that a Prime Minister needs, but they are subordinate resources that can be drawn on by the Prime Minister without the need for persuasion. The power-dependency model does not help to explain cases where the Prime Minister has achieved a particular outcome by adopting a confrontational stance rather than an alliance-building one. As various cabinet ministers noted, Margaret Thatcher as Prime Minister was not noted for seeking to build alliances in Cabinet. Similarly, Tony Blair has been criticised for distancing himself from the Civil Service and others, substituting detachment and prime ministerial instructions for mutual dependence (Norton, 2003, pp. 543–59). It also does not help to explain those cases where ministers can, and do, ignore civil service advice and act unilaterally and, on occasion, go beyond the bounds of normal ministerial powers. In the words of one former civil servant, 'We have to recognise that the assumption that the civil service is there to keep the government within the bounds of constitutional propriety is so threadbare it would be unwise to rely on it' (Jenkins, 2004, p. 807).

Baronial model

This model has been developed by this writer. It posits that ministers are like medieval barons in that they preside over their own, sometimes vast, policy territory. Within that territory they are largely supreme. We have identified the formal and informal underpinnings of this supremacy. Ministers head their respective departments. They have the constitutional authority and the legal power to take decisions. No one else enjoys that power. Junior ministers have no formal power and can act only on the authority of the senior minister. Once the minister has taken a 'view' – that is, made a decision – the civil servants in the department implement it. The ministers have their own policy space, their own castles – even some of the architecture of departments (such as the Ministry of Defence and the Ministry of Health, both in Whitehall) reinforces that perception – and their own courtiers. Indeed, recent years have seen a growth in the coterie of courtiers appointed by some senior ministers, some – such as the Chancellor of the Exchequer, Gordon Brown – being seen almost as having an alternative court to that of the Prime Minister (see Naughtie, 2001, pp. 124–5). The minister's baronial position is also protected to some degree by what is termed a 'silo mentality' in the Civil Service (Page, 2005): officials want to protect their particular departmental turf and will support the minister in seeking to protect or extend the responsibilities, and budget, of the department. The ministers fight – or form alliances – with other barons in order to get what they want. They resent interference in their territory by other barons and will fight to defend it.

The analogy is not altogether accurate in that the barons have no responsibility for raising taxes. (The exception is the Chancellor of the Exchequer, who has become more powerful than the original holders of the ancient office.) The Prime Minister also has greater power than a medieval monarch to dispense with the services of the barons, although the differences are not as great as may be supposed: a Prime Minister has difficulty dispensing with the services of powerful barons. He has his court and they have theirs. Despite the absence of a precise fit, the model has utility for understanding the nature and fluidity of power relationships within government. It has found resonance in various works on the Blair premiership, as in Francis Beckett and David Hencke's *The Blairs and their Court* (2004). Far from Cabinet being a homogeneous body of prime ministerial agents, it is a heterogeneous gathering and includes usually some powerful individuals.

Furthermore, reinforcing the baronial model is the approach taken by ministers to their jobs. Although Prime Ministers can use ministerial appointments as a way of changing or confirming their own policy preferences, they rarely choose a Cabinet of similar ministerial types. A Cabinet typically contains a mix of commanders, managers and ideologues, with the interests of the individual ministers around the table, and their particular departmental territories, taking precedence over any concept of altruistic collective decision-making.

This provides a new perspective on the relationship between senior ministers and the Prime Minister. Rather than being able to give directions, as in a principal–agent relationship, a Prime Minister has to be prepared to bargain with the more powerful barons in his government. He may be able to control some of the weaker members of the Cabinet, but others may be too powerful to be subject to prime ministerial direction. Reducing the power of the Cabinet may not necessarily have diminished the position of individual ministers, with whom the Prime Minister has to deal directly. At a minimum, ministers have an important gatekeeping role. To follow the analogy, they can close their departmental drawbridges and deny the Prime Minister entry to their policy domain. If the Prime Minister wants a particular policy implemented, the relevant minister has the formal power to say no, and a strong-minded commander or ideologue, even a determined manager, may have the political will to exercise that power.

A Prime Minister has limited scope to act unilaterally. He has no departmental responsibilities. Furthermore, the Prime Minister has limited resources to ensure that ministers act in accordance with his wishes. His own court, as we have noted, is a relatively small one. Attempts by Prime Minister Tony Blair to strengthen the coordination and oversight of Downing Street are testimony to this limited capacity. The more cunning of senior ministers can frequently circumvent attempts to limit what they say and do. Speeches may be sent late to Downing Street. Back-benchers or the media may be mobilised in support of a particular policy. Outside bodies may come to the defence of a minister they believe to be sympathetic to their cause.

The senior barons are thus able to plough their own furrows, making their own speeches, leaking – through their courtiers – their own side of a particular argument and their own perception of what has taken place in Cabinet or Cabinet committee. They can and do form alliances to achieve the approval of measures subject to Cabinet – which usually means Cabinet committee – approval (middle-level policy) and may operate unilaterally in laying orders that they are empowered by statute to make (low-level policy). Sometimes Prime Ministers – especially at times when their political authority is weakened – are in a constricted position, having to remind their ministers not to leak details of what has taken place and not to speak to the press without clearance.

Ministers develop their own ways of preserving their territorial integrity. Some adopt an isolationist stance, others a confrontational stance (see Norton, 2000). The stances taken reflect both the variety of approaches taken by ministers and the fact that they cannot be characterised as agents. They are barons, and in order to get their way they sometimes have to fight other barons as well as the monarch.

Characterising senior ministers as barons is also appropriate in that, like medieval barons, they are powerful but not all-powerful. They are constrained by other powerful actors, including the monarch (Prime Minister) and other barons (senior ministers), and by a recognition that they have to abide by laws and conventions. Indeed, as we have seen, they are increasingly constrained as the political environment has become more crowded, with groups coming into existence and making more demands of them – groups that they may need to cooperate with in implementing policy – and with more actors with the power to take decisions of their own. Ministers may thus find their time consumed by fighting battles with other political actors, be it bodies within the European Union or within the UK. Consequently, to provide a dynamic of the present state of senior ministers in British government, one can offer a model of barons operating within a shrinking kingdom (Norton, 2000).

This model is compatible with the power-dependency model, but it provides a greater emphasis on the role of ministers and encompasses the different strategies adopted by ministers, including fighting battles as well as alliance building. It is geared more directly than the power-dependency model to senior ministers. However, it has been criticised on the grounds that the fit with medieval barons is far from perfect – that the power and activity of the barons bears little relevance to senior ministers today. It can also be challenged on the grounds that it underestimates the power of the Prime Minister. As someone close to Tony Blair said while Labour was still in Opposition: 'You may see a change from a feudal system of barons to a more Napoleonic system' (Hennessy, 2000, p. 478; Naughtie, 2001, p. 96). Napoleon, though, needed his generals and his form of rule was, and is, difficult to sustain.

The model also has the same drawback as the other models in that they are models rather than theories. However, it stands as a useful counterpoint to the principal–agent model. It provides a new perspective on the role of senior ministers, emphasising the role played in government by ministers as ministers, rather than seeing them solely as a collective body, subsumed under the heading of government or Cabinet. This model suggests that senior ministers are more important figures in British government than is generally realised.

BOX 20.1 BRITAIN IN CONTEXT

Bureaucrats and politicians

The distinction between ministers and civil servants – that is, elected politicians and full-time officials – is not distinctive to the UK. What is notable is the extent to which the integrity of the Civil Service is maintained. Despite accusations of a creeping politicisation of the Civil Service, the extent to which the Civil Service in the UK is a body of permanent public servants, there to serve the government whichever party is in power, is remarkable in comparative context. The distinction is one that has been exported to many Commonwealth countries, though not necessarily maintained to the same degree as in the UK.

In some countries, the senior administrative posts in government are essentially patronage posts. In the USA, not only are cabinet ministers, and their juniors, appointed by the President, but so too are the administrative posts below them; the President has more than 2,000 administrative posts in his gift. In some countries, such as France, the distinction is not always a clear one to draw, with senior civil servants sometimes being appointed to senior ministerial posts, including that of Prime Minister.

The relationship between the head of government and cabinet ministers also differs, especially depending on the type of government that exists. In presidential systems, Cabinet members are usually dependent solely on the patronage of the President. They typically enjoy no separate political legitimacy of their own, since – under the separation of powers – they are not members of the legislature. In parliamentary systems, Cabinet members may be drawn from and remain within the legislature; in some, they may be drawn from, but are precluded from remaining in, the legislature. The principal difference between the two systems, though, is that a President cannot usually be brought down by the legislature. In a parliamentary system, the head of government is dependent on the confidence of the legislature. That dependence may sometimes give other members of the leader's party a significant political clout, especially if they have a following of their own in the legislature. Relationships between the Prime Minister and Cabinet may thus be more complex, potentially rendering the Prime Minister vulnerable to a Cabinet coup or challenge by a senior member.

Chapter summary

Ministers of the Crown head government departments. Those departments are extensive and complex bodies. Ministers enjoy substantial formal as well as political powers. The extent to which they are able to utilise those powers will depend upon the purpose and skill of the individual minister as well as the power situation, the climate of expectation and international developments. Ministers face considerable constraints, especially in recent years as the domain in which they operate has been constricted.

Ministers operate in a complex political environment. Different models seek to locate the place of ministers in that environment. The principal–agent model contends that ministers are agents of the Prime Minister or of civil servants. The power-dependency model posits an environment in which ministers have to negotiate with other actors in order to achieve desired outcomes. The baronial model posits that ministers have their own policy territory, castles and courtiers and fight or build alliances in order to get their way. The last two models suggest that ministers enjoy a greater role in policy making than is generally realised in the literature on British politics.

Discussion points

■ Is there an ideal type of senior minister?

■ Why are departments the basic building blocks of British government?

■ What should be the relationship between a minister and civil servants?

■ What is the relationship between ministers and civil servants?

■ Which model best explains the position of senior ministers in British government?

Further reading

There are many books of memoirs by former ministers. Especially good in providing insights into the role of the minister are Lawson (1992), Hurd (2003) and Cook (2003). Short (2004) also has some useful sections; Shephard (2000) provides a succinct, and very readable, commentary in her section on 'Ministers and Mandarins'. Kaufman (1997) provides a humorous but pertinent guide as to how to be a good minister. However, very few academic works have appeared that look conceptually at the role of ministers. Rose (1987) provides a functional analysis, and Brazier (1997) offers a more formal analysis. A broader analysis, encompassing the dynamics of ministerial office, is provided by Norton (2000). Junior ministers are covered by Theakston (1987). The relation of ministers to Parliament is dealt with by Woodhouse (1994, 2002). Political, and judicial, accountability is also covered by Flinders (2001).

There are various works on departments and, more especially, civil servants. A massive work, looking at departments and the civil servants that work in them, is that of Hennessy (2001). More recent works include Theakston (1995, 1999), Barberis (1997), Richards (1997), Rhodes (2001), Gray and Jenkins (2005) and, for a useful historical overview, Bogdanor (2003); see also Chapter 15 of Foster (2005). Lipsey (2000) provides a useful analysis of relationships in the Treasury. Jenkins (2004) offers a useful and brief overview from the perspective of a former civil servant. Denman (2002) offers a wonderfully readable and insightful view from the perspective of a senior civil servant. Stanley (2004) offers the civil servant equivalent to Kaufman's book: Chapter 1 covers working with ministers. For more material, see Chapter 21 of the present volume.

References

Barberis, P. (ed.) (1997) *The Civil Service in an Era of Change* (Dartmouth).

Barnett, J. (1982) *Inside the Treasury* (André Deutsch).

Beckett, F. and Hencke, D. (2004) *The Blairs and their Court* (Aurum Press).

Bogdanor, V. (2003) 'The Civil Service', in V. Bogdanor (ed.), *The British Constitution in the Twentieth Century* (The British Academy/Oxford University Press).

Brazier, R. (1997) *Ministers of the Crown* (Clarendon Press).

Cook, R. (2003) *Point of Departure* (Simon & Schuster).

Denman, R. (2002) *The Mandarin's Tale* (Politico's).

Flinders, M. (2001) *The Politics of Accountability and the Modern State* (Ashgate).

Foster, C. (2005) *British Government in Crisis* (Hart Publishing).

Gray, A. and Jenkins, B. (2005) 'Government and administration: public service and public servants', *Parliamentary Affairs*, Vol. 58.

Headey, B. (1974) *British Cabinet Ministers* (George Allen & Unwin).

Hennessy, P. (2000) *The Prime Minister: The Office and its Holders since 1945* (Allen Lane/Penguin Press).

Hennessy, P. (2001) *Whitehall*, revised edn. (Pimlico).

Holland, Sir G. (1995) 'Alas! Sir Humphrey, I knew him well', *RSA Journal*, November.

Hurd, D. (2003) *Memoirs* (Little, Brown).

Jenkins, K. (2004) 'Parliament, government and the Civil Service', *Parliamentary Affairs*, Vol. 57.

Johnson, N. (1980) *In Search of the Constitution* (Methuen).

Kaufman, G. (1997) *How to be a Minister* (Faber and Faber).

Kavanagh, D. and Seldon, A. (1999) *The Powers Behind the Prime Minister* (HarperCollins).

▶

Lang, I. (2002) *Blue Remembered Years* (Politico's).

Lawson, N. (1992) *The View from No. 11* (Bantam Press).

Lipsey, D. (2000) *The Secret Treasury* (Viking).

Morrison, J. (2001) *Reforming Britain: New Labour, New Constitution?* (Reuters/Pearson Education).

Naughtie, J. (2001) *The Rivals* (Fourth Estate).

Norton, P. (1987) 'Prime ministerial power: a framework for analysis', *Teaching Politics*, Vol. 16, No. 3, pp. 325–45.

Norton, P. (1997a) 'Leaders or led? Senior ministers in British government', *Talking Politics*, Vol. 10, No. 2, pp. 78–85.

Norton, P. (1997b) 'Political leadership', in L. Robins and B. Jones (eds), *Half a Century in British Politics* (Manchester University Press).

Norton, P. (2000) 'Barons in a shrinking kingdom? Senior ministers in British government', in R.A.W. Rhodes (ed.), *Transforming British Government*, Vol. 2 (Macmillan).

Norton, P. (2003) 'Governing alone', *Parliamentary Affairs*, Vol. 56.

Page, E.C. (2005) 'Joined-up government and the Civil Service', in V. Bogdanor (ed.), *Joined-Up Government* (The British Academy).

Parkinson, C. (1992) *Right at the Centre* (Weidenfeld & Nicolson).

Pyper, R. (1995) *The British Civil Service* (Prentice Hall/Harvester Wheatsheaf).

Rhodes, R.A.W. (1981) *Control and Power in Centre–Local Government Relationships* (Gower).

Rhodes, R.A.W. (1997) *Understanding Governance* (Open University Press).

Rhodes, R.A.W. (2001) 'The Civil Service', in A. Seldon (ed.), *The Blair Effect* (Little, Brown).

Richards, D. (1997) *The Civil Service under the Conservatives, 1979–1997* (Academy Press).

Rose, R. (1987) *Ministers and Ministries* (Clarendon Press).

Seldon, A. (1997) *Major: a Political Life* (Weidenfeld & Nicolson).

Shephard, G. (2000) *Shephard's Watch* (Politico's).

Short, C. (2004) *An Honourable Deception?* (The Free Press).

Stanley, M. (2004) *Politico's Guide to How to be a Civil Servant* (Politico's).

Tebbit, N. (1989) *Upwardly Mobile* (Futura).

Theakston, K. (1987) *Junior Ministers* (Blackwell).

Theakston, K. (1995) *The Civil Service since 1945* (Blackwell).

Theakston, K. (1999) *Leadership in Whitehall* (Macmillan).

Weir, S. and Beetham, D. (1999) *Political Power and Democratic Control in Britain* (Routledge).

Woodhouse, D. (1994) *Ministers and Parliament* (Clarendon Press).

Woodhouse, D. (2002) 'The reconstruction of constitutional accountability', *Public Law*, Spring.

Useful websites

Ministers

List of government ministers:
www.number10.gov.uk/output/Page2988.asp

Ministerial responsibilities: www.cabinet-office.gov.uk/central/index/lmr.htm

Machinery of Government Secretariat:
www.cabinet-office.gov.uk/central/index/mog.htm

Ministerial Code: www.cabinet-office.gov.uk/central/2001/mcode/contents.htm

Civil Service

Civil Service: www.civil-service.gov.uk

First Division Association of Civil Servants:
www.fda.org.uk

Cabinet Office: www.cabinet-office.gov.uk/cservice
www.cabinet-office.gov.uk/guidance

Reform of the Civil Service:
www.civil-service.gov.uk/reform

National School of Government:
www.nationalschool.gov.uk/index.asp

Related websites

Public Administration Committee of the House of Commons:
www.parliament.uk/parliamentary_committees/public_administration_select_committee.cfm

Guide to being a civil servant: www.civilservant.org.uk

CHAPTER 21

Civil Service management and policy

Robert Pyper

- To encourage an understanding of the link between politics and issues of public service management.

- To establish the scale and nature of the reforms that have taken place and continue to be rolled out within the organisation responsible for managing central government services.

- To address key questions concerning the extent to which the Civil Service has been fundamentally changed by managerial reforms and the degree to which service delivery has been improved.

Introduction

The Civil Service stands at the core of the UK's political system. It is a vital connection between people and government. As we saw in the previous chapter, it provides ministers with expert advice on how to give life to the political programmes on which they were elected. Charged with the ultimate responsibility for the efficient and effective delivery of government policies, it is required to manage the full range of central state services in a manner which meets the needs of two very different 'client' groups: public service users and government ministers. This chapter focuses on the major changes introduced in order to modernise and improve the management of central government services, and the key questions these raise about the future purpose and direction of the Civil Service.

'Why don't you reform the Civil Service?' she suggested. She makes it sound like one simple little task instead of a lifetime of dedicated carnage. Which reforms in particular did she have in mind, I wondered? Anyway, any real reform of the Civil Service is impossible, as I explained to her.

'Suppose I thought up fifty terrific reforms. Who will have to implement them?'

She saw the point at once. 'The Civil Service', we said in unison, and she nodded sympathetically. But Annie doesn't give up easily.

'All right' she suggested, not fifty reforms. Just one'.

'One?'

'If you achieve one *important reform of the Civil Service – that would be something'.*

Something? It would get into the Guinness Book of Records.

Jonathan Lynn and Antony Jay, *Yes Minister. The Diaries of a Cabinet Minister* by the Rt Hon James Hacker MP. BBC, 1983

■ History

For most of its history the British Civil Service seemed to epitomise all that was traditional and unchanging in our system of government and politics. In spite of numerous attempts to reform and modernise it, as it entered the last quarter of the twentieth century, the key features of the Whitehall machine were broadly similar to those which had been put in place over 100 years earlier. Naturally, certain aspects of the organisation had changed over this period, and although critics tended to focus on the more backward-looking features of the administrative structure, the standard of public service provided remained relatively high. Nonetheless, the dominant image of the Civil Service was of a bastion of tradition, with a built-in capacity to resist basic change. Then, in the course of a relatively short period, virtually everything changed. The size, shape, structure and even the purpose of the Civil Service came under close scrutiny and yielded to the forces of modernisation. As rolling programmes of reform swept through Whitehall the sustained pace and radical nature of the changes could not fail to attract serious academic and political scrutiny.

This chapter offers an overview and analysis of the main changes introduced in the Civil Service during this period of reform, together with some perspectives on the future direction of the state's administrative arm.

■ Inside the Civil Service

Structures: the lasting significance of Next Steps

The basic structure of the Civil Service today was shaped by the advent of executive agencies through the **Next Steps** initiative. Although this started in 1988, and had run its course by the end of the first term of the Blair government, its impact was, and remains, of great importance. The overall effect of

At the front line: Gus O'Donnell, the new Head of the Civil Service, meets the staff
Source: PA Wire / Empics

the process of 'agencification' was to supplement the traditional departmental mode of organisation with one based on the idea that certain key departmental functions could be carried out by 'satellites' of the Whitehall departments. For example, the full range of social security benefits would be delivered to the public through an executive agency of the Department of Social Security rather than by the traditional branch offices of the Department itself. Other agencies might focus on the provision of in-house services, such as information technology or property management. The whole point of this structural reorganisation was to improve service delivery while modernising the management of the Civil Service itself.

The principle of decentralising executive, managerial and service delivery functions within a framework of continuing policy control from the centre had become increasingly attractive to some senior figures in the Thatcher government during the 1980s. This was not a particularly novel concept – indeed, one element of the Civil Service reforms which had been inspired in an earlier generation

by the Fulton report of 1968 was the 'hiving-off' of certain functions into executive agencies. The Defence Procurement Executive emerged from the Ministry of Defence, the Property Services Agency from the Department of the Environment, and the Manpower Services Commission from the Department of Employment. Headed by chairmen who were appointed by the Secretaries of State in the parent departments, these agencies were given responsibility for delivering specified services to the armed forces (in the case of the DPE), government departments generally (in the case of the PSA) and the unemployed (in the case of the MSC). With substantial responsibility for their own budgets, and significant operational freedom, the agencies nonetheless remained constitutionally accountable to ministers. Although these bodies were in many respects the forerunners of the executive agencies spawned by the Next Steps programme from the late 1980s onwards, at the time they appeared more like *ad hoc* experiments with decentralisation in an era otherwise dominated by the concept of 'giant' government departments.

However, in the late 1980s, the agency concept was revived and radically expanded to the point where it became the keystone of Civil Service reform. At its launch in 1988, the Next Steps programme advanced the concept of decentralisation and set in motion the process which came to be known as the agencification of the Civil Service. To a considerable extent, Next Steps resulted from the perceived limitations of the first waves of Thatcherite reform in central government. The programme of efficiency scrutinies coordinated by Margaret Thatcher's special adviser Derek Rayner, and the resulting **Financial Management Initiative**, brought significant managerial changes in their wake, but they ultimately failed to transform the prevailing management culture of the Civil Service to the satisfaction of the Prime Minister.

Rayner's successor as Head of the Downing Street Efficiency Unit, Robin Ibbs, produced a report which reviewed the Civil Service managerial changes which had already been introduced, identified the obstacles to further change and made recommendations about the next steps to be taken (Efficiency Unit, 1988). The implicit conclusion of the Ibbs, or Next Steps, Report was that the managerial reforms introduced since 1979 had failed to transform and modernise the Civil Service. The document argued that the most significant obstacles in the way of fundamental managerial change could be overcome only if the entire structure of the Civil Service was overhauled, facilitating the creation of new executive agencies, headed by Chief Executives with significant managerial freedoms and operating at arm's length from the core parent departments, to which they would be, nonetheless, ultimately accountable. Since the report's authors estimated that 95 per cent of the Civil Service dealt with the executive

functions of policy implementation and service delivery, it was clear that the creation of agencies to carry out this work would amount to a fundamental structural reform of the central government machine.

The Thatcher government formally accepted and launched the Next Steps programme in February 1988, and this quickly became accepted as the most significant Civil Service reform since the implementation of the Northcote–Trevelyan Report in the late nineteenth century (for details, see Greer, 1994; Pyper, 1995; James, 2003). Every government department was obliged to conduct ongoing analyses of their detailed activities and programmes. 'Prior options' were examined, including the possibility of privatising the activity or leaving it within the traditional departmental framework. However, if a department concluded that an activity or service might be run without ministerial control on a day-to-day basis, might be a suitable case for managerial innovation and might be large enough to justify significant organisational change, the Next Steps option became distinctly feasible. Following successful consultations between the parent department, the agency-candidate, the Next Steps Unit in the Cabinet Office and the Treasury, a framework document would be produced as a prelude to the creation of an executive agency. The framework document would set out information about the agency's policy objectives, performance targets, relationship with the parent department and pay and personnel issues.

Within a decade of the publication of the Next Steps Report, UK central government had been fundamentally restructured to the point where over 76 per cent of the Civil Service was in executive agencies, of which 138 were Next Steps agencies. Box 21.1 and Table 21.1 provide details of the scale

BOX 21.1 FACT

The scale of Next Steps

By spring 2002 (formal end of initiative):
127 executive agencies employing 277,000 civil servants

Plus:
Executive units of Customs and Excise, Inland Revenue and the Immigration and Nationality Directorate of the Home Office (total of 95,000 civil servants)

Total of 372,000 civil servants in agencies working on 'Next Steps' lines (78 per cent of all civil servants)

Source: Office of Public Services Reform (2002)

Table 21.1 Next Steps executive agencies at end of initiative (2002)

Parent department	Agencies
Attorney General	Treasury Solicitor's Department
Cabinet Office	Government Car and Dispatch Agency; Central Office of Information
Department for Culture, Media and Sport	Royal Parks Agency
Department for Environment, Food and Rural Affairs	Central Science Laboratory; Centre for Environment, Fisheries and Aquaculture Science; Pesticides Safety Directorate; Rural Payments Agency; Veterinary Laboratories Agency; Veterinary Medicines Directorate
Department of Health	Medical Devices Agency; Medicines Control Agency; NHS Estates; NHS Pensions Agency; NHS Purchasing and Supply Agency
Department of Trade and Industry	Companies House; Employment Tribunals Service; Insolvency Service; National Weights and Measures Laboratory; Patent Office; Radiocommunications Agency; Small Business Service
Department for Transport, Local Government and the Regions	Driver and Vehicle Licensing Agency; Driving Standards Agency; Fire Service College; Highways Agency; Maritime and Coastguard Agency; Planning Inspectorate; Ordnance Survey; Queen Elizabeth II Conference Centre; The Rent Service; Vehicle Certification Agency; Vehicle Inspectorate
Department for Work and Pensions	Appeals Service Agency; Benefits Agency (closed March 2002); Child Support Agency; Employment Service (closed March 2002). New from April 2002: Jobcentre Plus; The Pension Service
Food Standards Agency	Meat Hygiene Service
Forestry Commission	Forest Enterprise; Forest Research
Foreign Office	Wilton Park
Treasury	Debt Management Office; Royal Mint; National Savings; Office for National Statistics
Home Office	Forensic Science Service; HM Prison Service; United Kingdom Passport Agency
Inland Revenue	Valuation Office
Lord Chancellor's Dept	Court Service; Public Guardianship Office; HM Land Registry; Public Record Office
Ministry of Defence	Armed Forces Personnel Administration; Army Base Repair Organisation; Army Personnel Centre; Army Training and Recruiting Agency; British Forces Post Office; Defence Analytical Services Agency; Defence Aviation Repair Agency; Defence Bills Agency; Defence Communications Services Agency; Defence Dental Agency; Defence Estates; Defence Geographic and Imagery Intelligence Agency; Defence Housing Executive; Defence Intelligence and Security Centre; Defence Medical Training Organisation; Defence Procurement Agency; Defence Science and Technology Agency; Defence Secondary Care Agency; Defence Storage and Distribution Agency; Defence Transport and Movements; Defence Vetting Agency; Disposal Sales Agency; Duke of York's Royal Military School; Medical Supplies Agency; Meteorological Office; MoD Police; Naval Manning Agency; Naval Recruiting and Training Agency; Pay and Personnel Agency; Queen Victoria School; RAF Personnel Management Agency; RAF Training Group Defence Agency; Service Children's Education; UK Hydrographic Office; War Pensions Agency; Warship Support Agency
Northern Ireland Office	Compensation Agency; Forensic Science Agency; Northern Ireland Prison Service
Northern Ireland Executive	Business Development Agency; Construction Service; Driver and Vehicle Licensing; Driver and Vehicle Testing Agency; Environment and Heritage Service; Forest Service; Government Purchasing Agency; Health Estates; Industrial Research and Technology Unit; Land Registers of Northern Ireland; Northern Ireland Child Support Agency; Northern Ireland Statistics and Research; Ordnance Survey of Northern Ireland; Planning Service; Public Record Office of Northern Ireland; Rate Collection Agency; Rivers Agency; Roads Service; Social Security Agency (Northern Ireland); Valuation and Lands Agency; Water Service
Scottish Executive	Communities Scotland; Fisheries Research Services; HM Inspectorate of Education; Historic Scotland; National Archives of Scotland; Scottish Agricultural Science Agency; Scottish Court Service; Scottish Fisheries Protection Agency; Scottish Public Pensions Agency; Scottish Prison Service; Student Awards Agency for Scotland; Registers of Scotland
Welsh Assembly	Cadw: Welsh Historic Monuments; Welsh European Funding Office

Source: Office of Public Services Reform (2002) *Better Government Services. Executive Agencies in the 21st Century.* © Crown Copyright 2002. Crown copyright material is reproduced with the permission of the Controller of Her Majesty's Stationery Office (HMSO)

of Next Steps and the agencies associated with particular parent departments.

The agencies were headed by Chief Executives, predominately recruited via open competition, and a significant proportion of these appointments (34 per cent by the late 1990s) went to external candidates (Next Steps Team, 1998, pp. 68–9). This new breed of Civil Service managers was employed on renewable, fixed-term contracts, with salaries linked to performance. The Next Steps approach to recruitment and pay was to become increasingly common at the top levels of the Civil Service.

All of the Next Steps **executive agencies** were subjected to periodic reviews, during which all future options, including **privatisation** (which would also have been considered as a possible outcome for the service at the stage when the agency was first established), were considered. As a result of this process, some agencies (including HMSO and the Recruitment and Assessment Services Agency) were moved into the private sector, while some others were redesignated, merged, returned to their parent department, had their functions contracted out or were abolished, as set out in the examples in Table 21.2.

Next Steps served as a catalyst for broad-ranging managerial and structural change within the Civil Service. Pay, recruitment and promotion 'flexibilities' were developed around the Next Steps agency model, and subtle alterations were gradually made to established parliamentary procedures in order to facilitate the accountability of the Chief Executives.

At its heart, Next Steps was an attempt to bring about improvements to the management and delivery of services by means of structural change and the application of new managerial methods. However, there was a distinct failure to think through the implications of this reform for accountability, and some serious problems resulted, as we shall see. Still, it seems clear that the creation of a plethora of executive agencies under the Next Steps initiative had important implications for the accountability of civil servants.

When introducing Next Steps, the Thatcher government had declared that this would have no implications for accountability. The officials working in executive agencies would be subject to scrutiny by select committees and the Parliamentary Ombudsman in the same way as other civil servants. As in the past, this would be deemed to be indirect accountability in the sense that the officials would merely be helping their ministers to be properly accountable to Parliament. However, in practice, ministers were gradually forced to move away from this position and tolerate the increased accountability of civil servants to Parliament, even if this was achieved without formal recognition of a constitutional change. The first move came when the early agencies were established, and it was decided that Parliamentary Questions relating to matters of agency management or administration would be answered, not as in the past by means of ministerial replies published in *Hansard*, but by letters from agency Chief Executives to the MPs who had asked the questions. MPs were clearly dissatisfied with this arrangement and their protests led to a decision that all replies by Chief Executives would be placed in the library of the House of Commons. Continued

Table 21.2 Former Next Steps agencies – some examples

Reason for abolition	Agency
Privatisation	DVOIT, National Engineering Laboratory, HMSO, Paymaster, Building Research Establishment, Laboratory of the Government Chemist, Transport Research Laboratory, National Resources Institute, Chessington Computer Centre, Occupational and Health Service Agency, Recruitment and Assessment Services Agency
Contracted out	Accounts Services Agency, National Physical Laboratory, Teachers' Pensions Agency
Subject to mergers	Warren Spring Laboratory, Central Science Laboratory, Chemical and Biological Defence Establishment, Defence Operational Analysis Centre, Defence Research Agency, Coastguard, Marine Safety Agency
Subject to demerger	Defence Accounts Agency
Functions abolished	Resettlement Agency
Change of status	Historic Royal Palaces (became a non-departmental public body)
Returned to a department	Security Facilities Executive Agency

Source: Next Steps Team (1998) *Next Steps Briefing Note*, September 1998, pp. 64–5. © Crown Copyright 1998. Crown copyright material is reproduced with the permission of the Controller of Her Majesty's Stationery Office (HMSO)

concern on the part of MPs, who argued that even this arrangement was an inadequate substitute for the old system, led to a final concession by the government which allowed for the publication of all Chief Executives' replies in *Hansard*. This was a clear break with the precedent that only government ministers could formally answer Parliamentary Questions in the official record of proceedings, and an implicit recognition of direct Civil Service accountability to Parliament.

Recurring crises surrounding the work of some agencies, including the Child Support Agency and the Prison Service Agency, indicated that serious flaws remained in the system of accountability, but these cases should not be allowed to detract from the fact that Next Steps, taken as a whole, brought about increased 'visibility' of senior civil servants and helped to change at least some elements of the system of official accountability.

The executive agency concept was designed to emphasise the supposedly clear distinction between the policy-making and policy-execution functions of government. At the heart of Next Steps there was an underlying assumption that there exists a reasonably clear divide between matters of policy, which are largely the preserve of ministers, and matters of administration and management, which lie in the domain of the Civil Service. However, in the real world matters are not always as clear and simple as this. Although the work of most agencies ran relatively smoothly, in two high-profile cases these supposedly clear distinctions between matters of policy and management eventually broke down and were shown to be severely problematic in terms of accountability. In both the Child Support Agency and the Prison Service Agency the Chief Executives struggled, and ultimately failed, to maintain the distinction between matters of policy and matters of management.

The first Chief Executive of the CSA, Ros Hepplewhite, pursued the logic of Next Steps to its conclusion as she attempted to differentiate between her responsibility to account for the management and operation of the agency, and the accountability of ministers for the policy and legal framework within which the agency operated. However, the CSA faced fundamental problems. This agency had been created solely and specifically to implement a particular policy, framed under the Child Support Act, but this policy and the Act were seriously flawed. The policy failings of ministers then became translated into the managerial failings of the agency,

as it generated massive backlogs of work, repeatedly missed its performance targets and produced huge numbers of 'customer' complaints. Finally, as it became clear that the CSA had failed to meet even its revised targets and news broke that a team of management consultants was being sent in to review the agency, Hepplewhite resigned in 1994. This case provided a clear demonstration of the close interaction between matters of policy and management, and the serious consequences which can arise, in this instance for a senior civil servant, when this is not fully recognised by ministers.

Similar themes could be seen in the case of the Prison Service Agency, where running disputes broke out between the minister at the parent department (Michael Howard, the Home Secretary) and the agency Chief Executive (Derek Lewis, Director General of the Prison Service). Howard blamed Lewis for overall management failings which led to a series of high-profile escapes by prisoners from top security establishments, while Lewis attributed at least some of the managerial problems to ministerial policy and interference. In the end, Lewis was dismissed by his ministerial superior, although he successfully challenged this in court and won substantial compensation.

Despite the problems posed by these cases, Next Steps continued to attract broad, cross-party approval. This effectively guaranteed the programme's long-term significance. The Labour Party's attitude towards executive agencies remained supportive. When they came, criticisms tended to focus on the scandals associated with the Prison Service Agency and the Child Support Agency (see Box 21.2), during which attacks would be based on the issues of ministerial conduct or lack of accountability, while the general principles and impact of Next Steps would be praised. Before the 1997 general election, Tony Blair's senior policy advisers on the Civil Service admitted that executive agencies '. . . have improved the delivery of government services through better management and delegation' (Mandelson and Liddle, 1996, p. 251). On its election in 1997, the Labour government recognised the accountability problems posed by the child support and prisons cases. The Child Support Agency was subjected to much closer ministerial oversight through a review process which also saw the establishment in 1999 of the CSA Standards Committee to provide the Chief Executive with an independent commentary on the quality of decision making and service delivery within the agency. However,

| BOX 21.2 | EXAMPLE |

Child Support Agency – a troubled history

- Child Support Agency established 1993
- Chief Executive Ros Hepplewhite apologises for low service standards and missed targets (£112m shortfall), July 1994
- Hepplewhite resigns, September 1994
- Further evidence of case errors (reaching 86 per cent) in final years of Conservative government
- New Labour government (1997) planned simplification of CSA operations, established CSA Standards Committee to support Chief Executive, purchased £456m computer system to improve service
- Computer system plagued by problems, resulting in massive caseload backlogs (increasing by 30,000 per month) by March 2003. This prompts further reform and simplification of the child maintenance scheme
- Chief Executive Doug Smith resigns, March 2005
- Research for Department of Work and Pensions reveals CSA staff grievances about lack of training, computer problems. Morale very low and most staff want to leave the agency
- Prime Minister Blair says CSA is 'not suited' to its task, November 2005. Agency running costs now £4m per year higher than figure it recovers from parents. Payment arrears £3.3 billion, case backlog 300,000
- Further reforms being seriously considered in Whitehall, January 2006, including using private debt collectors to deal with payment arrears and giving the Revenue and Customs Agency responsibility for regular child support payments. Under this plan, the CSA would have a more limited role as the assessor of cases

repeated attempts to modernise the computer system on which the day-to-day work of the CSA depended met with failure, customer complaints multiplied, and staff morale plummeted. In November 2005 Tony Blair publicly questioned the CSA's suitability for its key tasks, and a further series of reforms were under consideration in January 2006, including giving private firms powers to collect debts on behalf of the agency and assigning responsibility for collecting regular payments to the new HM Revenue and Customs Agency (the merged Inland Revenue and Customs and Excise). Meanwhile the accountability arrangements for the Prison Service were changed, with ministers assuming full responsibility for accounting to Parliament for this sensitive area of public policy and management.

Overall, under New Labour, Next Steps rolled on into its final stages. A natural end to the process of agency creation was reached, and the impact of Next Steps was there for all to see in virtually every part of the Civil Service. A major official review of the history, development and future of the executive agency scheme was published in the summer of 2002 (Office of Public Services Reform, 2002). This con-

cluded that the agency model had been a success, while noting the need for agencies to continually evolve in order to meet the challenge of improved delivery of public services.

Size and location

Recurring themes in the development of the Civil Service have been concerns with the size, scale and geographical location of the organisation. As successive governments face budgetary constraints and attempt to meet the challenges of modernisation and increased efficiency in the delivery of public services, critical eyes turn in the direction of the Civil Service. In modern times, the Thatcher government launched various plans to cut the size of government departments, and disperse Civil Service work away from the costly heartlands of London and the southeast of England, with only limited success in the long term. Some in the Conservative administrations of the 1980s and early 1990s came to accept that significant net cuts in Civil Service numbers were likely to have a serious impact on the government's ability to deliver its programmes, and the best they could hope for was to control the growth in staff.

The Blair government's clearest and most serious attempt to cut the size of the Civil Service and relocate at least a proportion of its activities started in 2004, with the publication of Sir Michael Lyons' Independent Review of Public Sector Location, and Sir Peter Gershon's Independent Review of Public Sector Efficiency (as the names suggest, these reviews extended beyond the Civil Service, but each had a particular focus on central government departments and agencies). Lyons identified 20,000 jobs to be relocated from London and the southeast, and the government adopted a plan to implement a dispersal scheme (Lyons, 2004). Gershon had been commissioned by the Prime Minister and the Chancellor of the Exchequer to find ways to release resources to 'front line services', in line with the priorities of the government's successive Public Spending Reviews (Gershon, 2004, pp. 5, 47–57). As one analyst noted, Gershon's recommendations were 'essentially cost-containment measures or economies rather than efficiencies' (O'Toole, 2004, p. 8). In particular, this produced a proposal for a gross reduction of over 84,000 Civil Service posts, broken down into specific job cut targets for each department and its associated agencies to meet by 2007–8 (see Gershon, 2004, Appendix C). This programme would be implemented through continuing dialogues between the departments and the Treasury, focusing on the opportunities to make efficiency savings in 'back office' functions (including finance, IT, legal services and human resource services). In the wake of Gershon's publication, the opposition parties launched their own plans for cutting the size of the Civil Service, seeking to outbid the government on the scale of the job cuts, while claiming that their plans would create more efficient delivery of public services.

The overall impact of Gershon will take some time to assess. The initial reaction of the Civil Service trade unions was one of anger, and a series of one-day strikes was called in protest against the proposed job cuts which the unions argued would damage public services, especially in the area of benefits delivery. Other analyses were less certain about the significance of Gershon, however. For example, a *Guardian* editorial, published just after the Chancellor of the Exchequer had commended Gershon to the Commons, noted that the gross reduction in posts (over 84,000) became 70,000 once staff redeployments had taken place, and,

even then, this would not necessarily bring about a significant reduction in the overall size of the Civil Service (from over 500,000 to around 480,000 by 2008) because 'the 70,000 figure . . . could be notional numbers of posts foregone or rendered unnecessary by greater efficiency or slower spending growth in the future: not real jobs as such, but posts that would have been created in other circumstances had the status quo remained in force' (*Guardian*, 2004). Similarly, Hencke (2005) saw Gershon as partly a 'smoke and mirrors' exercise, with job creation in other public services significantly outnumbering the proposed loss of posts in central government. Nonetheless, this critic did acknowledge that particular departments, especially the Ministry of Defence, the Department for Work and Pensions, and the merged Inland Revenue and Customs & Excise, would carry the burden of most of the proposed job cuts.

People

Two important human resource management agendas which have been developed under the auspices of the broad Civil Service modernisation programme are the drive for greater diversity among staff, and the framework for introducing professional skills across all areas of central government. In each case, there is a fairly ambitious strategy to introduce cultural changes in the Civil Service, and although it will take some time to properly assess the outcomes, the basic elements of these agendas can be set out at this stage.

As an element of the Blair government's modernisation programme, the diversity agenda for the Civil Service was designed to accelerate the progress being made towards more proportional representation (particularly at senior levels) of women, people with disabilities, and people from ethnic minority communities. Much attention was given to the fact that under 18 per cent of the Senior Civil Service was female in 1998, but the proportions of disabled staff and people from ethnic minority backgrounds were much smaller. The 'Modernising Government' White Paper (Prime Minister, 1999) set diversity targets for the period through until 2005, at which point a new '10-point plan' for delivering a more diverse Civil Service was published (Cabinet Office, 2005). This plan contained specific targets for the composition of the Senior Civil Service, which are to be achieved by 2008:

In the run-up to the 2005 election many eyes were on potential cuts in the Civil Service
Source: Copyright © Steve Bell. From *The Guardian*, 18 January 2005. Reproduced with permission

■ 37 per cent to be women (from 29.1 per cent in April 2005)

■ 4 per cent to be from ethnic minorities (2.8 per cent in April 2005)

■ 3.2 per cent to be disabled staff (2.9 per cent in April 2005)

Progress towards these targets, and the broader aim of diversifying the Civil Service beyond the senior levels (women have long been a majority of the total Civil Service workforce, but the percentages of ethnic minority and disabled staff remain in single figures) was to be monitored for the Civil Service Management Board by a 'Diversity Champion' (Bill Jeffrey) and 'Chief Diversity Adviser' (Waqar Azmi). They would identify emerging diversity policy issues for the Civil Service as a whole, share best practice

across departments through a benchmarking exercise, give support to departments as they develop and implement their own diversity policies, promote key diversity networks and a partnership schemes, and link with the Equality Coordination Unit in the Department of Trade and Industry (which coordinates legislation, policy, and public sector targets) and the Women and Equality Unit in the Cabinet Office.

The Professional Skills for Government (PSG) agenda, launched in October 2004, was the latest in a long line of initiatives designed to end the traditional Civil Service distinction between 'generalist administrators' and 'specialists' such as accountants, scientists, lawyers and other professionals (see, for example, Mottram, 2005). The aim was to 'professionalise' all aspects of work at the senior and middle management levels of the Civil Service by creating three broad career groupings:

■ Operational delivery – officials involved in managing and delivering services, mainly to the public

■ Policy delivery – staff dealing with the formulation, development and evaluation of policy

■ Corporate services delivery – civil servants primarily providing support services including HR, finance, IT, procurement and marketing to government departments and agencies.

The Professional Skills for Government agenda requires civil servants to possess specific skills and expertise in order to gain entry to, and progress within, the key middle and senior management grades. Thus, 'leadership skills' would have to be demonstrated by those in or entering the Senior Civil Service; 'core skills' of analysis and use of evidence, financial and people management, and programme and project management would be required for the middle management grades (additional skills in communications, marketing and strategy would be needed from Senior Civil Servants); 'professional expertise' would be expanded in all staff groupings via continual professional development (CPD) schemes; and 'experience' of other career groupings would be expected from officials reaching the more senior levels.

A key role in the implementation of the PSG agenda was assigned to the new National School of Government, launched in June 2005. This was the latest, and arguably the most focused version of the former Civil Service College (later part of the Centre for Management and Policy Studies, itself succeeded by the NSG), and it was designed to address a range of management training and education needs through its own in-house activities and by working with external partners. As with the diversity and PSG agendas, however, the overall impact of the National School would take some time to assess.

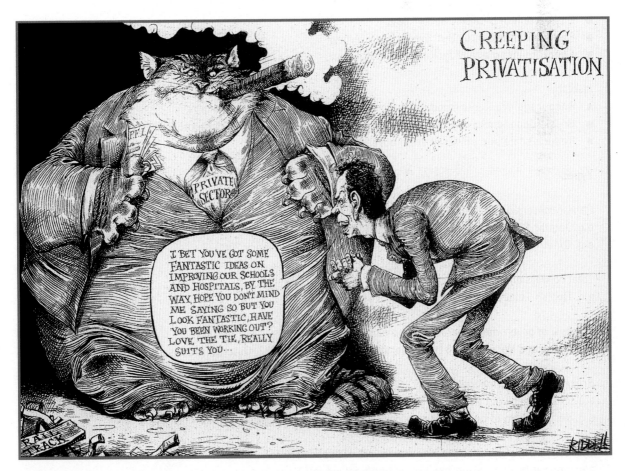

Blair looks to the private sector to reform public service institutions
Source: Copyright © Chris Riddell. From *The Observer*, 24 January 2001. Reproduced with permission from Guardian Newspapers Limited

■ The public–private mix

Privatisation

The policy of privatisation affected public services at all levels of the system of government. In local authorities, the National Health Service, central government and the parts of the system which did not fall neatly into one or other of these spheres (in the world of quangos, for example), assets and services moved from the public to the private sector throughout the 1980s and 1990s. In this chapter, our concern is with the Civil Service, and therefore with central government, although we should note that the themes and issues associated with privatisation cut across governmental sectors.

Box 21.3 sets out the main reasons for, and the most significant forms of, privatisation.

BOX 21.3 **IDEAS AND PERSPECTIVES**

Rationale for, and types of, privatisation

Rationale

Efficiency
- State control/public ownership equated with inefficiency and lack of competitiveness

Control of public expenditure
- Ease problem of public sector pay
- Reduce Public Sector Borrowing Requirement
- Generate income (and facilitate tax cuts)

Ideology
- Encourage economic freedom and market forces
- Break 'dependency-culture' and create 'property and share-owning democracy'
- Reduce scale and power of state bureaucracy

Types

Partial conversion to a limited company
e.g. Jaguar Cars element of British Leyland 1984
e.g. QinetiQ element of Defence Evaluation and Research Agency 2000–2

Total conversion to a limited company
e.g. British Telecom 1984; British Gas 1986

Disposal of government shares in a company
e.g. Cable and Wireless 1981–5; Amersham International 1982; QinetiQ (proposed) 2006

Breaking of state monopoly
e.g. 1983 Energy Act permitted private generation of electricity
e.g. deregulation of bus routes

Injection of private provision within framework of public service
e.g. competitive tendering/market testing/best value
e.g. Private Finance Initiative

Put simply, there are three broad reasons for the emergence of privatisation. In government from 1979, the Thatcherite Conservatives equated state control and public ownership with fat, flabby and inefficient organisations, over-dependent on subsidy, unaware of their true cost and unable to meet the demands of their customers. Allied to this view was the attraction of easing the strain on the Public Sector Borrowing Requirement by transferring large numbers of workers from the public to the private sector, reducing Treasury lending and providing a flow of funds into the Exchequer through the sale of assets. Finally, there was an ideological imperative, which became increasingly significant as time passed. Privatisation fitted neatly into the Thatcherite crusade to encourage economic 'freedom', create a 'property and share owning democracy' and cut the state machine down to size. The Labour government after 1997 showed a willingness to retain privatisation as an option, largely for pragmatic rather than ideological reasons. Substantial share flotations and the introduction of private ownership were not to be discarded as options, although it was not until 2006 that the Blair administration looked set to complete its first full flotation of a public sector entity, the defence equipment body QinetiQ (see Box 21.4). However, Labour tended to place more emphasis on the creation of public–private 'partnerships' through devices such as **Better Quality Services** and the Private Finance Initiative, as discussed below. A more partial and selective use of the privatisation option became the order of the day.

This serves to illustrate the point that, over the years, the policy of privatisation has taken different shapes and forms, including the total or partial conversion of a public corporation or nationalised industry into a limited company, government disposal of all or some of the shares it holds in specific bodies, or breaking the monopoly held by a state concern. A further dimension of privatisation, which continued to find favour with the post-1997 Labour governments, involves injecting elements of private provision into public services. Although competitive tendering or market testing in public bodies does not necessarily amount to 'privatisation', it can lead to the introduction of private sector managerial methods and practices or to the provision of a service by a private company for a fixed term. Similarly, the Private Finance Initiative involves the transfer of capital assets such as hospital or prison buildings to the private sector, while the state remains in control of the service. As these forms of privatisation, or partial privatisation, have had a particular impact on the Civil Service, we will examine them more closely below. Before doing so, however, it is worth noting some of the particular accountability challenges posed by privatisation, and outlining the methods used in order to address these.

When plans were announced to transfer major public utilities to the private sector, serious questions were raised about the possible dilution of public accountability which might result. Partly in an effort to address this issue, at the point of privatisation, regulatory agencies were set up to issue licences to the commercial participants in the developing markets (or 'quasi-markets' where privatisation had not brought immediate competition), negotiate and then enforce the pricing formulae, obtain and publish information helpful to the service users, and oversee the systems for resolving consumer complaints. These regulatory agencies were non-ministerial government departments, headed by directors general. Modelled to a considerable extent on the existing Office of Fair Trading, the Offices of Telecommunications

BOX 21.4 EXAMPLE

QinetiQ: New Labour's first full privatisation?

- Defence Evaluation and Research Agency (DERA) split in 2001, with sensitive work assigned to Defence Science and Technical Laboratory and rest to QinetiQ, which would make military software, gadgets for MI5 and MI6, banking security systems
- In 2002 the MoD sold 31 per cent of QinetiQ to Carlyle Group for £42m.
- In January 2006 MoD announces sale of its majority shareholding (while retaining 'special share') in QinetiQ in a £1.1 billion flotation.
- National Audit Office launches immediate investigation into proposed sale, raising concerns about value for money, terms of 2002 sale, windfall profits for Carlyle directors, depletion of MoD research

(OFTEL), Gas Supply (OFGAS), Electricity Regulation (OFFER) and Water Services (OFWAT) were established. In 2000 OFGAS and OFFER were merged into a single energy regulator, OFGEM. Each utility privatisation brought in its wake a new regulator, with broadly similar powers.

In some spheres, a complex array of regulators emerged. For example, following rail privatisation regulatory functions were dispersed among the following:

■ *Ministers*: set the regulatory framework.

■ *Rail Regulator*: issues licences to train operating companies and enforces licence conditions relating to safety.

■ *Chief Inspector of Railways*: leads the Rail Inspectorate, which is part of the Health and Safety Executive. Approves and monitors safety systems.

■ *Strategic Rail Authority*: sets and monitors service standards for the twenty-five train operating companies.

■ *Railtrack*: owned and managed track, stations, tunnels, level crossings, viaducts and bridges. Set and policed safety standards until stripped of this role following the Paddingdon rail disaster in October 1999. Railtrack was placed in administration in October 2001 and ceased trading in December 2002 when it was taken over by Network Rail, a not-for-profit company set up by the government.

In broad terms, privatisation was accompanied by the retention of a form of public accountability, and the emergence of a new set of scrutineers. The focus of accountability had shifted away from Parliament, and the records of the regulators were variable (influenced by such factors as the approach of the Director General, the scale of the utility being regulated, and the prevailing style of the utility's board of directors). While in some spheres the existence of these dedicated and specialised agencies successfully addressed most of the concerns about the impact of privatisation on public accountability, serious problems arose in others. In the rail utility, for example, generally poor service standards and the serious train crashes at Southall in 1997, Paddington in 1999, Hatfield in 2002 and Potters Bar in 2002 raised serious doubts about the effectiveness of the regulatory regime.

During the 1980s, **compulsory competitive tendering** (CCT) swept through local government

and the National Health Service. Under this programme, specified activities such as catering, cleaning and refuse collection were compulsorily put out to tender, with the contract for providing the service being awarded to the most competitive bid. As a result, in some cases the service was contracted out, with private companies winning the contracts.

The Civil Service was affected by these developments only marginally. Central government services and functions were not subject to compulsory competitive tendering. As a result of the essentially voluntary nature of the process, only a relatively small number of quite low-grade manual and clerical tasks were exposed to competitive tendering. However, in 1991 the Competing for Quality White Paper announced the expansion of CCT throughout the public sector, including the Civil Service where the process was to be styled '**market testing**'. The new wave of competition was to involve professional, 'white collar' activities including accountancy, information and legal services, as well as the more traditional targets for tendering. The Conservative government argued that even where services ultimately remained 'in house', with the existing Civil Service providers, the tendering process would have the effect of sharpening up management and enhancing efficiency. The results were mixed. The government's deadlines and targets for market testing in the Civil Service were repeatedly revised and shifted, debates raged about the cost of the process and the extent of the savings generated (see Pyper, 1995, pp. 64–70). By 1996 the government was citing savings of £720 million per year, with staff cuts of around 30,000. Where in-house bids were allowed, and went forward, they succeeded in winning about 75 per cent of the contracts, but there were no in-house bids in half of the contracts put out to tender. The Civil Service trade unions and the opposition parties attacked the market testing process on the grounds that it spawned its own bureaucracy, cost millions of pounds in management consultancy fees, led to job cuts and adversely affected morale. In addition, it infringed upon the managerial freedom of agency chief executives, raised important questions about service standards, security and confidentiality (especially in relation to the contracting-out of IT services) and threatened the principle of public service provision in some spheres.

The Labour Party's opposition to the dogmatic elements of market testing led to a new approach following the 1997 election. The new government's stated objective was to ensure that all departments reviewed the full range of their services and functions over a five-year period starting in 1999. Within the broad framework of its **Public–Private Partnerships** policy, the aim would be to identify the 'best supplier' of each service and function, while improving quality and value for money across government. Under this Better Quality Services (BQS) initiative, departments were required to have plans in place for the programme of reviews by October 1999.

The focus of BQS was on end results and service standards while securing the best quality and value for money for the taxpayer. The 'best supplier' of a service was identified through considering the possibility of competition, but in a major change from the market testing programme, there was no compulsion to set up a tendering process. If internal restructuring or managerial 'reprocessing' resulted in quality improvements, no competition was necessary. However, these internal reviews had to be 'robust', and were subject to oversight by the Cabinet Office, the Treasury and a key Cabinet Committee (PSX).

Following the 2001 general election, BQS was subsumed within the government's 'second phase of public sector reform', styled as 'the focus on delivery'. Spearheaded by the Office of Public Service Reform and the Prime Minister's Delivery Unit, this was designed to identify and overcome the problems and blockages affecting improved delivery of public services while addressing four principles of public sector reform:

■ adherence to a national framework of standards and accountability;

■ devolution of more local power to 'the frontline' service providers;

■ more flexible working to keep pace with constant change;

■ more choice for customers and the opportunity to have an alternative provider if service is poor.

By the time of the third Blair administration, from 2005, overt references to Better Quality Services had ceased and this initiative was no longer coordinated from the centre, although it continued to be used as a management tool by departments and agencies, as they judged appropriate.

The Private Finance Initiative

Put simply, PFI is a way of getting public buildings built or refurbished without recording capital spending in the national accounts. It was dreamt up by John Major as yet another wheeze for a public unwilling to face the true cost of the public services it says it wants. PFI is what poor people used to call the 'never-never': you get something bright and shiny now but end up paying a lot more than its present cost over the long run.

Walker (1999)

Needless to say, David Walker's sceptical view of the Private Finance Initiative was not shared by the Conservative government ministers who introduced the scheme in 1992, nor by the members of the Labour government who retained and developed it within the context of their Public–Private Partnerships policy. For government departments, and public authorities more generally, the attraction of the PFI lies in the avoidance of major capital investment and the resulting opportunity to keep public expenditure under control. Private sector expertise can be exploited, while maintenance costs for the facility are transferred. Effectively, this means that governments purchase maintained highways instead of building roads, buy custodial or healthcare services instead of building prisons and hospitals, and pay for managed IT services instead of buying computers and software. At the end of the contract, which may be in thirty years' time, the facility will be handed back to the public sector body which issued the contract. Private sector contractors provide the initial capital, as well as assuming the risks associated with construction, in return for operating licences for the resulting facility, which enable them to recoup their costs.

Although the PFI started slowly, failed to have the expected impact on the Conservative government's public expenditure plans, and became associated with high tendering costs and bureaucratic bidding procedures (Terry, 1996), it developed in significance as time passed. It underpinned major projects, including the Channel Tunnel, the high-speed rail link to the Tunnel, toll bridges including the Skye road bridge, prisons, hospitals and a range of other facilities. Although the Labour government immediately ended the requirement that all public sector capital projects should be tested for PFI potential, ministers remained fully committed to a revised and refocused version of the initiative. During the first two years of the Labour government, some £4.7 billion worth of PFI deals were signed (making a total of £13 billion since the launch of PFI) and another £11 billion worth were put in place for the period 1999–2002. Within the National

---

BOX 21.5   **EXAMPLE**

PFI in practice – Docklands Light Railway Extension

A joint-venture PFI project between: the former Department of the Environment, Transport and the Regions and City Greenwich Lewisham (CGL) Rail Link plc.

The project: A 24.5-year concession (from September 1996) to design, build, finance and maintain a 4.2 km extension to the DLR. The line runs under the Thames and adds new stations south of the river to create direct access between the City and Docklands, and SE London and Kent. Opened to passengers in 2000.

Cost: £200 million.

Private sector funding: £165 million raised through bond issue.

Public sector funding: £35 million in contributions from central government, Deptford City Challenge, London Boroughs of Lewisham and Greenwich.

CGL Rail opportunities and risks: Company receives fees for use of the Extension. Risks include franchising; cost and time overruns; levels of passenger usage; construction; installation of automatic train control system; integrating the Extension with the existing rail system.

Source: HM Treasury

Health Service alone, PFI deals would underpin the building of thirteen new hospitals.

In practice, PFI projects tend to take two forms:

1 *Financially free-standing projects*: Here, the private sector supplier designs, builds, finances and then operates the asset. Costs are recovered through charges on the users of the facility. Examples are the Second Severn Bridge and the Dartford River Crossing.

2 *Joint ventures*: In these, the costs of the project are not met fully through charges, but are partly subsidised from public funds because there are wider social benefits involved, such as reduced congestion or local economic regeneration. Examples are business park developments, city centre regeneration schemes, Manchester's Metrolink and the Docklands Light Railway Extension (see Box 21.5).

Labour attempted to address the managerial problems surrounding the PFI by accepting the recommendations of a report by Sir Malcolm Bates, Chairman of Pearl, and setting up a Taskforce based in the Treasury and headed by Adrian Montague, a former city banker. In July 1999 the government responded to a second Bates report by announcing that the Taskforce would be replaced in 2000 by Partnerships UK, a permanent body which would improve the central coordination of the initiative by acting as the overall project manager for PFI deals. There would also be a much greater standardisation of the bidding and contractual process. Formed as a plc, the new body would symbolise the public–private partnership ethos. The private sector would take a majority share in Partnerships UK, which would provide public sector organisations with expert advice on PFI matters. It was hoped that this would prevent any repetition of the disastrous problems associated with the large PFI computer contracts, epitomised by the Passport Agency's misconceived deal with the electronics corporation Siemens, which produced massive backlogs in the passport application system in 1999. However, continuing problems with the IT systems of the Child Support Agency (see above) seemed to indicate that flaws in computer contracts were endemic. Companies considering bidding for PFI deals would also be able to use Partnerships UK on a voluntary basis. Although it would not function as a bank, the new body would provide development funds to get PFI deals off the ground, perhaps by bundling together a number of projects which, individually, would be too small to attract private sector bidders.

Clearly committed to the long-term development of the PFI, the Labour government's confidence in its management of this controversial scheme was emphasised in September 1999, when ministers welcomed a new independent inquiry into the entire initiative, to be conducted by the Institute for Public Policy Research (Atkinson, 1999). The final report (Institute for Public Policy Research, 2001) struck a pragmatic note by emphasising the need to avoid dogmatic views for or against PFI and Public–Private Partnerships generally. However, the mixed record of PFIs in areas such as health and education was identified, and caution was urged with regard to the government's planned PPPs in the London Underground and the National Air Traffic Control System. Despite this, and in the face of strong opposition from, for example, Ken Livingstone, the Mayor of London, the government pushed on.

Some observers were even more sceptical than the IPPR. Sir Peter Kemp (1999), the former senior Treasury and Cabinet Office civil servant, thought the case for some types of Public–Private Partnership was 'pretty thin' and raised serious questions about the 'hidden spending' and unconventional 'value for money' studies surrounding PFI projects. Certainly, there is a high long-term price to pay in return for quick access to nice, shiny, new assets. A new infirmary in Edinburgh would have cost £180 million if paid for from taxation or government borrowing. A PFI deal allowed a private consortium to design, own and service the hospital, and then rent it to the public for £30 million a year over thirty years – a total cost of £900 million (Cohen, 1999). As the Blair administration moved into its third term, however, there was no slackening in enthusiasm for PFI within the government. Annual reports were published by the Advisory Council of Partnerships UK, and made available through the Treasury website. These charted the development and expansion of the PFI projects, and the changing rules and regulations surrounding the contracting process. PFI had become a firmly established weapon in the Treasury's armoury.

■ The delivery agenda

Importance of 'customer service'

Dismissed by many observers as a gimmick when it appeared as John Major's 'big idea' in 1991, the Citizen's Charter established itself and was then refashioned as Service First by the Blair government in June 1998. By 2006 the government was apparently satisfied that the Charter programme had entrenched 'consumerism' and respect for the 'customer' in the delivery of public services, and Service First was deemed to be completed.

When it was launched, the Citizen's Charter was partly designed to differentiate John Major's civil and public service policy from that of his predecessor Margaret Thatcher, and partly to counter the opposition parties' interest in citizens' rights and constitutional change. It encompassed a range of linked initiatives including the Charter Mark scheme (which rewards organisations deemed to have delivered improved quality services) and extended beyond the Civil Service, into the public service at large. The basic objectives were to improve the quality of public services and make service providers more answerable to those variously described as 'citizens', 'clients', 'consumers' and 'customers'. Under the Citizen's Charter umbrella, 'mini-Charters' were published in increasing numbers, covering the full range of public service users, including those seeking employment, Benefits Agency customers, NHS patients, rail passengers, taxpayers, parents of school children, students in higher education and people using the courts. Many of the 'mini-Charters' would be published in varied forms for England, Scotland, Wales and Northern Ireland. The Charter's attempts to bring about improvements in the management and delivery of services, while enhancing the means for redressing consumers' grievances, would have a particular significance in many of the executive agencies responsible for delivering services directly to the public.

Although a government review in 1996 praised the Charter's achievements (Prime Minister, 1996), some observers saw **Charterism** as a triumph of style over substance, pointing to the initiative's limited definition of citizenship, the fact that service standards are set by the service providers themselves and are not legally enforceable, the failure to create genuinely new mechanisms of accountability and redress, and the elements of farce such as the abortive telephone helpline Charterline and the widely mocked Cones Hotline (see Falconer and Ross, 1999, for a summary of the main political and academic arguments surrounding the Charter). The opposition parties supported the idea of improved answerability and better service delivery and Labour even argued that Major had 'stolen' the Charter concept from the customer contract initiatives within some Labour-controlled local authorities. However, questions were raised about the extent to which the Charter's objectives could be achieved without extra funding.

Committed to 'relaunch and refocus' the Citizen's Charter, the Blair government announced its intention to replace the 'top-down' system it had inherited from the Conservatives with a 'bottom-up' approach. In simple terms, this means the existing Charters were seen as having been the property of the service providers, drawn up with little or no consultation with those who use the services. New charters would be drawn up in consultation with the public and the vague statements and easily achievable targets of old would be replaced with clear information about the 'outcomes' service users should expect, together with meaningful indicators of service quality (Cabinet Office, 1998). Under the Service First programme, new principles of public service delivery were published, building upon the existing charter principles (see Box 21.6). All exist-ing Charters were reviewed, and replaced with new versions. A new audit team continually monitored the quality of Charters, while the Charter Mark scheme became more rigorous. One indication of progress on this front came when the Passport Agency, which had held a Charter Mark since 1992, was stripped of the award in the summer of 1999 following weeks of chaos in its operations and a backlog of around 500,000 passport applications. Although some organisations had voluntarily given up their Charter Marks in the past, or failed to have them renewed after the initial three-year period, this was the first instance of award-stripping.

Although successive official reports indicated that government departments and agencies had made good progress in relation to the six standards of public service (see, for example, Modernising Public

---

BOX 21.6　FACT

The principles and standards of public service

Service First: principles
These built upon and expanded existing Charter principles:

- Set standards of service
- Be open and provide full information
- Consult and involve
- Encourage access and the promotion of choice
- Treat all fairly
- Put things right when they go wrong
- Use resources effectively
- Innovate and improve
- Work with other providers.

The six Whitehall standards
In servicing the public, every central government department and agency aims to:

1. Answer letters quickly and clearly. Each department and agency sets a target for answering letters and publishes its performance against this target.
2. See people within ten minutes of any appointments they have made.
3. Provide clear and straightforward information about services and at least one number for telephone enquiries.
4. Consult users regularly about the services provided, and report on the results.
5. Have at least one complaints procedure for the services provided, and send out information about the procedure on request.
6. Do everything that is reasonably possible to make services available to all, including people with special needs.

Source: Cabinet Office

BOX 21.7 FACT

Tony Blair's changing agendas for the Civil Service: seven challenges and seven keys

The PM's seven challenges for the Civil Service: 1998
1. Implement constitutional reform in a way that preserves a unified Civil Service, ensures close working between UK government and the devolved administrations.
2. Staff in all departments to integrate the EU dimension into policy making.
3. Public services to be improved, more innovative and responsive to users, and delivered in an efficient and joined-up way.
4. Create a more innovative and less risk-averse culture in the Civil Service.
5. Improve collaborative working across organisational boundaries.
6. Manage the Civil Service so as to equip it to meet these challenges.
7. Think ahead strategically to future priorities.

The PM's seven keys to transformation of the Civil Service: 2004
1. A smaller, strategic centre.
2. A Civil Service with professional and specialist skills.
3. A Civil Service open to the public, private and voluntary sectors and encouraging interchange among them.
4. A Civil Service with more rapid promotion and an end to tenure for senior posts.
5. A Civil Service equipped to lead, with proven leadership in management and project delivery.
6. A more strategic and innovative approach to policy.
7. Organising government around problems, not problems around government.

Sources: Cabinet Office and 10 Downing Street

Services Group, 2001), questions remained about the extent to which Service First represented a genuine development and improvement of the old Citizen's Charter. The Blair government eventually wound up Service First (arguing that its principles had become entrenched in the delivery of public services), while retaining the Charter Mark scheme as a mechanism for recognising high standards of service provision.

Modernising government, reforming public services and improving delivery

The Blair government made it clear from the outset that the Civil Service would be required to play a major part in the implementation of Labour's programme, while continuing the process of managerial change which had transformed the machinery of government. The Prime Minister issued the Civil Service with seven 'challenges' (see Box 21.7) and then, with his senior colleagues, he set about drafting a framework for future governance, which would give civil servants the chance substantially to meet these challenges.

The result, which emerged in March 1999, drew together many of the managerial and service delivery themes which had been developing piecemeal during the life of the Blair administration, and indeed before. In several respects, however, the ***Modernising Government*** White Paper (Prime Minister, 1999; for a summary, see Box 21.8) was a typical Blair product, with its short phraseology gleaned from the world of image makers and PR consultants. Not all of the snappy concepts seemed full of meaning (even the 'central objective' was rather opaque). The document's desire to be 'modern' in every way could seem a little bit forced at times. One observer commented wryly:

One of the best pictures is of community policing . . . and shows a boy with extended tongue in a pushchair, with the attractive teletubby Tinky Winky looking over his left shoulder. It would be difficult to get more modern than that.

Chapman (1999), p. 9

BOX 21.8 FACT

Modernising Government: 1999 White Paper sets agenda for reforms of Blair governments

Central objective
'Better government to make life better for people'

Aims
- Ensure that policy making is more 'joined up' and strategic.
- Focus on public service users, not providers.
- Deliver high quality and efficient public services.

New reforms
- 'Government direct': public services available twenty-four hours a day, seven days a week, where there is a demand.
- 'Joined-up government': coordination of public services and more strategic policy making.
- Removal of unnecessary regulation: requirements that departments avoid imposing new regulatory burdens and submit those deemed necessary to Regulatory Impact Assessments.
- Information-age government: target for all dealings with government to be deliverable electronically by 2008.
- 'Learning labs': to encourage new ways of front-line working and suspend rules that stifle innovation.
- Incentives: for public service staff – including financial rewards for those who identify savings or service improvements.
- New focus on delivery within Whitehall: permanent secretaries to pursue delivery of key government targets, recruit more 'outsiders', promote able young staff.

Key commitments

Forward-looking policy making
- Identify and spread best practice via new centre for management and policy studies (which will incorporate the Civil Service College).
- Joint training of ministers and civil servants.
- Peer review of departments.

Responsive public services
- Remove obstacles to joined-up working through local partnerships, one-stop shops and other means.
- Involve and meet the needs of different groups in society.

Quality public services
- Review all government department services and activities over five years to identify best suppliers.
- Set new targets for all public bodies with focus on real improvements in quality and effectiveness.
- Monitor performance closely to strike balance between intervention when things go wrong and allowing successful organisations freedom for management.

Information-age government
- An IT strategy for government to coordinate development of digital signatures, smartcards, websites and call centres.
- Benchmark progress against targets for electronic services.

Public service
- To be valued, not denigrated.
- Modernise the Civil Service (including revision of performance management arrangements; tackle under-representation of women, ethnic minorities and people with disabilities; build capacity for innovation).
- Establish a public sector employment forum to bring together and develop key players across the public sector.

An administrative apparatus was speedily constructed around the Modernising Government programme. Within the Cabinet Office the Modernising Public Services Group was created and charged with responsibility for implementing the White Paper's reforms. This group worked with the Modernising Government Project Board (containing both external and Civil Service members) to draw up an Action Plan. The early priorities were categorised as 'responsiveness', 'effectiveness and efficiency', 'joined-up government' and 'quality'.

Following its victory in the 2001 general election, the Labour government adopted a new focus on public service delivery and the reform of public services, to be spearheaded by the Delivery Unit in Number 10 Downing Street, and the Office of Public Services Reform in the Cabinet Office. By the time of the third Blair administration, following the 2005 general election, in the wake of yet another restructuring exercise, the work of the OPSR was reallocated as part of the wider work programme of the Cabinet Office. By this stage, the imperative of 'joined-up government' had resulted in a proliferation of 'cross-cutting units' at the heart of Whitehall. One example of this was the Office of the e-Envoy (1998–2004) which was charged with coordinating the move to 'information-age government' across the whole span of government. In 2004, the e-Envoy's functions were taken over within an expanded e-Government Unit in the Cabinet Office. The challenges associated with 'joined-up government' in an era of increasingly complex administrative structures and sub-structures were acute (see, for example, Page, 2005). In this context, the Modernising Government programme effectively came to be divided up into a series of key components which were to be taken forward by units and sections within the Cabinet Office.

Among the initiatives which pre-dated the White Paper but were given renewed emphasis under the Modernising Government umbrella were benchmarking, Public Service Agreements and the People's Panel.

Benchmarking is the practice of comparing the management processes and procedures in different organisations, with the aim of transferring the best practices from one to the other. This can be done within the public sector, for example by using value-for-money audits as mechanisms for transferring good financial management practices. However, the Blair government has placed increasing emphasis on benchmarking against the private sector by using the 'Business Excellence' model.

Public Service Agreements are really forms of performance indicators. The PSAs are designed to set out in detail what people can expect in return for public expenditure on services. Here, the purpose is to clearly shift the focus to the quality of service outputs generated.

The People's Panel was a 5,000-strong, nationally representative group, set up to tell the government 'what people really think' about public services and the efforts being taken to modernise and improve them. Members of the public were randomly selected for the panel, and its sub-groupings, and it was used between 1998 and 2002 as the basis for successive waves of research designed to generate representative views about attitudes to public services in general, the work of specific providers, and levels of service provision. This was a very typical New Labour product in the sense that it was essentially a larger and more sophisticated version of the type of focus group the party uses to test policies. The results of the continuing People's Panel surveys and interviews were fed into the Modernising Government/focus on delivery/reforming public services agenda. The Cabinet Office announced the end of the People's Panel in January 2002, claiming that there was now less need for a centrally based body of this kind since departments and agencies had developed their own customer consultation initiatives.

By the autumn of 2005 an additional drive to enhance towards modernisation and improved delivery was under way in the form of a rolling programme of 'capability reviews' of government departments. Led by the Cabinet Office, but with inputs from the National Audit Office and the Audit Commission, these were designed to identify scope for improvements across Whitehall.

Modernisation, reform and improved delivery of public services is clearly a continuous and long-term project which will be subject to constant fine-tuning. At the time of the publication of the *Modernising Government* White Paper, Richard Chapman (1999, p. 8), the senior academic analyst of the British Civil Service, had no doubts about its potential impact:

. . . in ten or twenty years' time, the influence and significance of this White Paper is quite likely to be comparable to that of the Next Steps Report.

However, only two years after its launch the Modernising Government initiative effectively evolved into a component of the 'focus on delivery' and 'reforming public services'. In this light, it became increasingly difficult to be specific about the precise impact of each element of the reform agenda on the culture and management of the Civil Service. By the time of the third Blair administration, the Modernising Government programme was said to be 'complete', although this seemed to mean in practice that the modernisation initiatives were being taken forward by a range of other bodies and units, including the Prime Minister's Delivery Unit, the Strategy Unit, and various elements of the Cabinet Office.

■ Conclusion: twenty-first century challenges

The fictional minister Jim Hacker and his permanent secretary Sir Humphrey Appleby would recognise a great deal about the Civil Service of the twenty-first century, but they would probably be astonished at the sheer scale of the changes which have taken place in this organisation over a relatively short period of time. They would certainly find it extremely difficult to come to terms with the continuous, on-going nature of managerial reform in the modern Civil Service. While there is general agreement about the volume of change, analysts and observers are divided on the question of its impact. For some, the managerial and structural changes in the Civil Service have failed to alter the fundamental character of a backward-looking institution. John Garrett (1999), formerly Labour spokesman on the Civil Service, was sceptical about his party's attempts at reform, largely because he believed the top Whitehall posts were likely to remain in the hands of traditionalists:

New Labour's white paper promises 'joined-up government', 'joined-up policy-making', 'joined-up working' and 'joined-up public service delivery'. It proposes to open up the 'senior' Civil Service of 3,000 top jobs to women, ethnic minorities and people with disabilities. But, crucially, it intends to keep a fast-stream programme for generalist mandarins headed for the top jobs. Sir Humphrey has secured the future for his clones.

An academic critic, Colin Talbot, argues that there is enough evidence of persistent poor performance by the Civil Service in the management of public services and the discharge of its policy functions to show that the impact of reform and modernisation to date has been, at best, limited. His prescription for change involves effective abolition of the existing Civil Service, with the creation of a small, expert government policy service, and a national public service (extending beyond the current Civil Service, into all areas of public administration and management) focused on delivery (Talbot, 2005).

Others have taken the view that the overall impact of managerial change has been very significant. For some, the effect has been negative, on the whole. According to this perspective, the Next Steps programme together with the process of contracting-out key functions have led to the effective 'Balkanisation' of the Civil Service. Breaking the service up into increasingly independent components, it is argued, has diluted the cohesiveness, character and ethical base of Civil Service work (see, for example, Chapman, 1997). The long-term impact of devolution on the concept of a unified, British Civil Service remains to be seen, but even in its early phase of development, it was clear that this constitutional reform had created new tensions which would have to be managed properly if

BIOGRAPHY

Sir Gus O'Donnell (1953–)

Cabinet Secretary and Head of the Home Civil Service from September 2005. Educated at Warwick and Oxford, lectured in Economics at Glasgow University before joining Treasury in 1979. Seconded to Washington in early 1980s, then worked with Chancellors of the Exchequer Nigel Lawson and John Major. Press Secretary to Prime Minister Major, 1990–4. Between 1994 and 1997 he was Deputy Director at the Treasury, then UK representative on the IMF and the World Bank while based at the British Embassy in Washington. Returned to the Treasury in 1997, taking charge of macro-economic policy and international finance and becoming head of the Government Economics Service. Permanent Secretary at the Treasury, 2002–5. Succeeded Sir Andrew Turnbull as Cabinet Secretary and Head of the Home Civil Service.

cohesiveness was to be retained (see Pyper, 1999; Parry, 2001).

Other observers are more relaxed (see, for example, Hennessy, 1993; Butler, 1993) and locate the recent reforms within the evolutionary tradition of a service which has always been prepared to adapt to change. The former Head of the Civil Service, Sir Richard Wilson, although a traditionalist in many respects, was keen to embrace change, while emphasising that this need not be at the expense of 'our core values' (Wilson, 1999). In a speech at the Centre for Policy and Management Studies shortly before he retired, Sir Richard looked back on his four-year tenure (1998–2002) as a time of 'fundamental change' during which various strands of modernisation ('the growing recognition of the needs of the customer', 'continuous search for efficiency', 'improved policy making', 'opening up the service to talent' and 'radically improving our management') had been taken forward (Wilson, 2002). His examples tended to be linked to developments which had been set in motion before he took over at the top of the Civil Service, and this perhaps

undermined his argument about the 'fundamental' nature of the changes which took place between 1998 and 2002. Indeed, in the period leading up to the announcement of Sir Richard's successor, there was considerable speculation about Tony Blair's desire to see the appointment of a more radical moderniser, perhaps in the mould of a chief executive with a clear focus on matters associated with service delivery distinct from the Cabinet Secretary function. In the event, however, with the appointment of Sir Andrew Turnbull, the posts of Cabinet Secretary and Head of the Home Civil Service remained combined. On Turnbull's retirement in 2005, the combined posts were retained when Sir Gus O'Donnell was appointed (see biography). Turnbull believed the major achievements of his tenure were the stronger emphasis given to the provision of services and the increased importance attached to leadership skills within the Civil Service (Turnbull, 2005). The early pronouncements of the new Head of the Civil Service suggested that he recognised the continuing importance of that traditional challenge for occupants of his post: striking the right balance between maintaining the 'historic values' of the Civil Service, while equipping it with the 'dynamism' required to meet the challenges of modern government (O'Donnell, 2006).

The debates about the Civil Service's future shape and direction will continue during the vital period ahead, as this cornerstone of the UK political system adapts to meet the challenges posed by successive waves of reform.

BIOGRAPHY

Professor Peter Hennessy (1950–)

Constitutional authority. Educated at Cambridge. Journalist on *The Times*, *Financial Times* and *The Economist* before becoming academic at Queen Mary College, London. His *Never Again* (1992) was an award-winning study of Britain during the Attlee government's term of office, while *Whitehall* (1989) and *The Prime Minister: The Office and Its Holders Since 1945* (2001) provided authoritative coverage of the official and political core of UK government.

BOX 21.9 BRITAIN IN CONTEXT

Benchmarks for comparing the Civil Service in the UK with others

- *Constitutional setting*: liberal democratic, ideological purity not important, non-partisan ethos.
- *Nature of senior posts*: 'permanent, career, civil service'. Compare with the USA where senior civil service posts are filled by political appointees in a 'spoils system'.
- *Educational background and training*: despite numerous attempts to change, the British Civil Service remains largely composed of people with 'liberal arts' backgrounds supplemented by a relatively small amount of 'professional' training. Compare with the European (especially French) tradition of intensive and highly specialised training for future civil servants in the '*Grandes Ecoles*'.
- *Scope of bureaucracy*: in the UK, the Civil Service encompasses only those working for central and devolved government departments and

agencies. In other systems (especially in Europe) all elements of the state machine (including local government, health service, central government and some industries) form part of the civil service.
- *Engagement with 'New Public Management'*: in the UK, the USA, Canada, Australia and New Zealand, civil servants over the past twenty years have been obliged to engage with this in more detailed and comprehensive fashion than their counterparts in Europe.
- *Culture*: a clear contrast between the prevailing European civil service culture with a strong basis in constitutional law (work focuses on drafting laws and implementing legal codes) and the much more policy-orientated Anglo-American civil service cultures.

Chapter summary

This chapter has set out the major reforms which have changed the management and shape of the Civil Service. We have discussed the impact of structural changes, the debates about the size and location of the Civil Service, current human resource management issues, the increased emphasis given to public–private partnerships in schemes such as the Private Finance Initiative, attempts to address the needs of service users through a range of devices and initiatives, and the implications of the all-embracing modernisation agenda, with its focus on delivery and ongoing reforming of public services. Key issues and debates have been explored as a means of enhancing understanding of the Civil Service as a central component of the government system.

Discussion points

- What was the objective behind the creation of executive agencies, and to what extent was this achieved?
- What part should the private sector play in the provision of public services?
- Have the programmes designed to improve the quality of services delivered to the public been successful?
- To what extent have the initiatives within the Modernising Government programme, the focus on delivery and public services reform helped to create better public services?
- Has the Civil Service been changed for the better as a result of the managerial reforms of recent years?
- How significant have the Civil Service reforms of the Blair government been?

Further reading

There is now a considerable literature on the Civil Service and public sector management. Accounts of the development of the modern Civil Service and some of the major reforms can be found in Theakston (1995) and Pyper (1995). Some of the key documents, commentaries and analysis are contained in the excellent books by Barberis (1996, 1997). The new public management initiatives, which have underpinned most of the recent changes in the Civil Service, are given good coverage in Horton and Farnham (1999) and Massey and Pyper (2005). Students wishing to keep up to date with the ever-increasing pace of change in the Civil Service must be prepared to look beyond books, however. A range of journals and periodicals provide regular articles and features on the themes discussed in this chapter. These include *New Statesman, Parliamentary Affairs, Public Money and Management, Public Administration, Policy and Politics, Public Policy and Administration, Politics Review* and *Talking Politics*.

References

Atkinson, M. (1999) 'Inquiry to look at PFI', *The Guardian*, 20 September.

Barberis, P. (1996) *The Whitehall Reader. The UK's Administrative Machine in Action* (Open University Press).

Barberis, P. (1997) *The Civil Service in an Era of Change* (Dartmouth).

Butcher, T. (1998) 'The Blair government and the civil service', *Teaching Public Administration*, Vol. 18, No. 1.

Butler, Sir R. (1993) 'The evolution of the civil service – a progress report', *Public Administration*, Vol. 71, No. 3.

Cabinet Office (1998) *Service First: The New Charter Programme* (Cabinet Office).

Cabinet Office (2005) *Delivering a Diverse Civil Service. A 10-Point Plan* (Cabinet Office).

Chapman, R.A. (1997) 'The end of the civil service', in P. Barberis (ed.), *The Civil Service in an Era of Change* (Dartmouth).

Chapman, R.A. (1999) 'The importance of "Modernising Government" ', *Teaching Public Administration*, Vol. 19, No. 1.

Cohen, N. (1999) 'How Britain mortgaged the future', *New Statesman*, 18 October.

Efficiency Unit (1988) *Improving Management in Government: the Next Steps* (HMSO).

Efficiency Unit (1991) *Making the Most of Next Steps: the Management of Ministers' Departments and Their Executive Agencies* (HMSO).

Falconer, P.K. and Ross, K. (1999) 'Citizen's Charters and public service provision: lesson from the UK experience', *International Review of Administrative Sciences*, Vol. 65.

Garrett, J. (1999) 'Not in front of the servants', *New Statesman*, 4 October.

Gershon, Sir P. (2004) *Releasing Resources to the Front Line. Independent Review of Public Sector Efficiency* (Stationery Office).

Greer, P. (1994) *Transforming Central Government: the Next Steps Initiative* (Open University Press).

The Guardian (2004) 'Wither Whitehall', Editorial, 14 July.

Hencke, D. (2005) 'Axing Whitehall jobs is smoke and mirrors', *The Guardian*, 10 January.

Hennessy, P. (1993) 'Questions of ethics for government', *FDA News*, Vol. 13, No. 1.

Horton, S. and Farnham, D. (eds) (1999) *Public Management in Britain* (Macmillan).

Institute for Public Policy Research (2001) *Building Better Partnerships. The Final Report from the Commission on Public Private Partnerships* (Central Books).

James, O. (2003) *The Executive Agency Revolution in Whitehall. Public Interest Versus Bureau-Shaping Perspectives* (Palgrave Macmillan).

Kemp, Sir P. (1999) 'Please stop fiddling the books', *New Statesman*, 18 October.

Lyons, Sir M. (2004) *Well Placed to Deliver? Shaping the Pattern of Government Service. Independent Review of Public Sector Relocation* (Stationery Office).

Mandelson, P. and Liddle, R. (1996) *The Blair Revolution. Can New Labour Deliver?* (Faber and Faber).

Massey, A. and Pyper, R. (2005) *New Public Management and Modernisation in Britain* (Palgrave Macmillan).

▶

Modernising Public Services Group (2001) *The Six Service Standards for Central Government. Performance of the Main Central Government Departments and Agencies, 1 April 2000 to 31 March 2001* (Cabinet Office).

Mottram, R. (2005) 'Professional skills for government: death of the generalist', *Public Management and Policy Association Review*, Number 30, August.

Next Steps Team (1998) *Next Steps Briefing Note September 1998* (Cabinet Office).

O'Donnell, Sir G. (2006) 'The modern Civil Service. The fusion of historic values with 21st century dynamism', speech, *Guardian* Public Services Summit, St Albans, 27 January 2006.

Office of Public Services Reform (2002) *Better Government Services. Executive Agencies in the 21st Century* (Stationery Office).

Osborne, D. and Gaebler, T. (1992) *Reinventing Government. How the Entrepreneurial Spirit is Transforming the Public Sector* (Plume).

O'Toole, B.J. (2004) 'The challenge of change in the civil service: 2004 in retrospect', *Public Policy and Administration*, Volume 19, Number 4, Winter.

Page, E.C. (2005) 'Joined-up government and the Civil Service', in V. Bogdanor (ed.) *Joined-Up Government* (Oxford University Press).

Parry, R. (2001) 'Devolution, integration and modernisation in the United Kingdom Civil Service', *Public Policy and Administration*, Volume 16, Number 3, Autumn.

Prime Minister (1996) *The Citizen's Charter – Five Years On*, Command Paper 3370 Session 1995–6.

Prime Minister (1999) *Modernising Government*, Command Paper 4310 Session 1998–9.

Pyper, R. (1995) *The British Civil Service* (Prentice-Hall/Harvester Wheatsheaf).

Pyper, R. (1999) 'The civil service: a neglected dimension of devolution', *Public Money and Management*, Vol. 19, No. 2.

Talbot, C. (2005) 'The future of the Civil Service – a growing debate', *Public Management and Policy Association Review*, Number 31, November.

Terry, F. (1996) 'The Private Finance Initiative – overdue reform or policy breakthrough?', *Public Policy and Management*, Vol. 16, No. 1.

Theakston, K. (1995) *The Civil Service Since 1945* (Blackwell).

Turnbull, Sir A. (2005) *Farewell Letter to All Civil Servants* 26 July.

Walker, D. (1999) 'Malignant growth', *The Guardian*, 5 July.

Wilson, Sir R. (1999) 'The civil service in the new millennium', unpublished lecture, May.

Wilson, Sir R. (2002) 'Portrait of a profession revisited', speech, Centre for Management and Policy Studies, 26 March 2002, www.cabinet-office.gov.uk.

Useful websites

Cabinet Office gateway to all aspects of Civil Service management: www.cabinet-office.gov.uk

Delivery and reform issues in the Civil Service: www.civil-service.gov.uk/reform

Child Support Agency: www.csa.gov.uk

The Treasury site, with access to information on PFI and PPPs: www.hm-treasury.gov.uk

The National School of Government site: www.nationalschool.gov.uk

The energy regulator: www.ofgem.gov.uk

The telecommunications regulator: www.oftel.gov.uk

The water services regulator: www.ofwat.gov.uk

General gateway to all government departments and agencies: www.ukonline.gov.uk

CHAPTER 22

Local government

Colin Copus

Learning objectives

- To consider the implications of the dual role of local councils in acting as politically representative institutions and as the providers of important public services.

- To explore whether widespread public apathy about local government undermines local democracy in Britain.

- To consider the impact on local government of the introduction of political executives: directly elected mayors and indirectly elected leaders and their cabinets.

- To examine whether local councils should have more freedom from central control.

- To examine whether councillors represent the community or their party.

- To explore the relationship between British local government and the European Union's policy-making network.

In the nineteenth century cities built fine town halls to display their success and dynamism
Source: Copyright © Tim Hawkins; Eye Ubiquitous / Corbis

Introduction

There are around 22,000 councillors in Britain of whom (at the beginning of 2006) 8,181 were Conservative, 6,514 were Labour, and 4,754 were Liberal Democrat. In addition, the Scottish National Party had 186 elected councillors, Plaid Cymru had 182, and there were some 2,206 who were independent of political parties, or who stood for election for a non-party organisation such as a residents' association or a community group. In Northern Ireland, which uses the Single Transferable Vote system, we find a broader range of political representation and the representation of different shades of unionist and nationalist opinion. The seats held by the various parties in Northern Ireland after the 2005 elections were Democratic Unionist Party 182, Sinn Fein 126, Ulster Unionist Party 115, Social Democratic and Labour Party 101, Alliance Party 30, and others 28.

Local councils are political and democratically elected bodies and this chapter will explore the tensions that exist between local government as a politically representative set of institutions and a local authority as a body that manages and administers the provision of a complex range of local services. It will, however, focus more closely on the political role of the local council, as, in discussions about the financing, organisational administration of large public bureaucracies, management of public services and arguments about the amount of control central government should have over councils, it is easy to forget that they are elected bodies with their own policy agenda and their own special relationship with local voters. The politics of local government often become submerged under discussions about running schools, providing social care, lighting, repairing and sweeping the streets and the emptying of dustbins. All of which, of course, are vital public services, but if all 22,000 councillors across Britain disappeared tomorrow, then these services would still continue to be provided. So, this chapter will deliberately concentrate on the politics of local government and the vital role councillors play as elected representatives and governors, rather than the role they often find themselves playing – that of an elected service manager!

The chapter will explore the long-term relationship between local government and local politics. In the first section it will examine the development and structure of British local government; in the second it will explore the relationships between local and central government; the third will consider the growth, impact and role of party politics at the local level; and the fourth section will examine the changes made to the way in which political decisions are made by the Local Government Act 2000, which introduced directly elected mayors and executive council leaders into local government. This section will also look at other key aspects of what has been known as the 'modernising agenda' for local government; the fifth section will consider the policy environment of local government; and the final section will look at the government's apparently ill-fated proposals for elected regional assemblies in England and the more successful devolution to Scotland and Wales. It will also look at the relationship between local government and the European Union.

■ Background

British local government has always been subordinate to central control. Unlike many of its continental counterparts, British local government remains constitutionally unprotected from the political ideologies, policies, priorities and, indeed, caprice of central government. The shape, size, structure, functions,

powers, duties and very existence of local councils rest in the hands of central government to decide and the courts to interpret. Indeed, central government could abolish all local government and replace it with a system of central administration by the simple process of passing an Act of Parliament to that effect. Such a Bill for the Abolition of Local Government would simply have to pass the same

Parliamentary procedures as any other Bill on any other subject – it would not have to navigate some special constitutional procedure. Moreover, British councils can do only that which the law grants them permission or powers to do; any action not sanctioned by law is *ultra vires* (beyond the powers) and liable to be quashed or rendered null and void by the courts.

The constitutionally subordinate role of local government to the centre at Westminster and Whitehall has led many to regard the work of local councils as no more than an administrative process – devoid of its own political life. Indeed, as Gyford (1976, p. 11) points out, some maintain that it is management and administration that solves local problems, not the making of what are political, and party political, choices about the allocation of scarce resources. Moreover, central government concerns (justified or otherwise) about the efficiency of local government service provision and about variations in service standards within and across councils and across the country, coupled with central government regulation of local authorities and large-scale public apathy when it comes to local elections, raise questions about the continued existence of, or need for, independent local government (Byrne, 1983, p. 24).

To the litany of criticism that has often been heaped upon local government can be added time-consuming and opaque decision-making structures; the supposedly poor calibre of many local councillors; party politics, leading to unnecessary conflict and confrontation; large and remote units of local government distant from many of the communities represented and served; the tension between political and community representation and notions of technical efficiency of service administration (the technocrat–democrat argument); and the constraints on local action and decision-making arising from wider economic and social factors (Stanyer, 1976; Dearlove, 1979; Elcock, 1982; Hampton, 1987; Wolman and Goldsmith, 1992). Despite questions as to its value and relevance, local government and, indeed, local democracy and autonomy hold an important position in the political structure and processes of British governance. Indeed, local self-government and the existence of democratically elected councils provide an all too vital safeguard against an over-powerful central government and also ensure that political space and positions exist for those that do not share the political affiliation of the government of the day. While the British government is always assured of its own way, the usual practice in policy-making has been for some degree of negotiation, compromise and bargaining to occur between central government and the localities. Local government and locally elected councillors are seen as vital for any democratic country.

Local government, and the decisions made by councils and councillors, comes with a legitimacy that flows from the consequences of the electoral process. Local elections produce a layer of political representatives able to claim a mandate from local citizens for the decisions they make and the policies they pursue. Moreover, those councillors operate in a greater proximity to the citizen than does the Member of Parliament and the government. While the local electoral mandate theory has been criticised by comparison with its national counterpart, councillors acting as duly elected representatives of the people provide an important legitimacy to the activities of local government (Wolman and Goldsmith, 1992). It is the people's vote that prevents local government from being wholly an administrative arm of central government. But it is a vote that turnout in local elections indicates the public are less and less willing to grant.

Yet, despite present-day local government being based on notions of representative democracy and one person one vote, this was not always the case. The development of the local franchise was originally concerned to ensure that the electorate, and the candidates from whom they could select, fulfilled some property qualification (Keith-Lucas, 1952). Councillors during the Victorian period were often seen less as local politicians and more as keepers of the public purse (councillors today still have a fiduciary as well as a political relationship to the voter). Indeed, the development of local government has been described as less a search for representative democracy and more the development of a form of ratepayer democracy (Young, 1989, p. 6). But today, councillors hold office as a consequence of the public vote, and the vast majority of councillors are affiliated to one of the national parties and often see their role not only as a local representative but also from a wider party political viewpoint (HMSO, 1986b; Young and Davis, 1990; Copus, 2004).

■ British local government: from confusion to cohesion

The uniformity displayed by the current map of local government structure is a recent phenomenon. Indeed, it is the myth of the importance of uniformity that enabled the demands of service management and administration to sideline political representation as the driving force for local self-government. British local government has gone through a process of evolution interspersed with periodic revolution; growing from the naturally formed communities of Anglo-Saxon times, local government took on a shape, size and structure that reflected its roots in very local communities. Parishes, boroughs and counties developed over time, sharing the provision of services and local administrative matters with an often confusing mix of other statutory, non-statutory and private providers, alongside magistrates and sheriffs and other local offices appointed by the monarch.

As new problems and issues of government arose, dealing with the impact of an increasingly complex world became the local responsibility of a range of local bodies and appointed boards. Parishes, boroughs and counties overlapped in area and responsibilities with a host of boards and commissions such as those for improvement, street paving, drainage, public health and, of course, the Poor Law Guardians. The evolutionary development of local government saw administration and local decision-making shared between single- and multi-purpose bodies, formed variously by statute, appointment, self-selection or election. The structures and arrangements for managing local affairs prior to 1835 would be barely recognisable when compared to today's local councils.

It was the reforming zeal and legislative whirlwind of activity during the Victorian period that began to give some national coherence to the shape and responsibilities of local government while continuing to deal, in an *ad hoc* fashion, with many of the problems generated by, and for, the developing capitalist system. Commencing with the 1835 Municipal Corporations Act, described by Wilson and Game (2002) as the 'foundation of our present day local government', and up to the 1899 reform of London government, the Victorians gave a basis to local government of popular – although not universal – election, financial responsibility and uniformity of purpose, shape and process. By the turn of the century, local authorities looked and felt like the 'governments' of their localities but were ironically being increasingly controlled by the centre. The structure of counties, districts, non-county boroughs and all-purpose county boroughs, with parishes as a fourth sub-tier, promoted some uniformity. But it left unanswered the question of how many layers (or tiers) of local government there should be to meet the often conflicting requirements of political representation and effective and efficient service provision.

The legislatively enforced uniformity of local government continued throughout the twentieth century, as did the preoccupation of central governments, of all political colours, with the regulation of local activity and the diminution of local autonomy. It was in the period after the Second World War, when policy makers were grappling with rapidly changing demographic, political, social and technological developments, and a rapidly expanding welfare state, that the demands of efficient service administration and responsive, democratic local government needed to be reconciled (Young and Rao, 1997). Yet, reconciling political representation with service provision proved a difficult task as one facet of local government could easily sideline the other. Technocratic and democratic needs are driven by different factors, with technocracy requiring bigger and bigger units of local government, and local democracy requiring smaller and more cohesive communities. Throughout the twentieth century, the technocracy of service provision, management and administration won a series of important battles over the needs of local democracy as a politically representative process. These victories become very apparent when looking at the shape, size and structure of local government.

The Herbert Commission Report on London Government (Cmnd 1164) resulted in the replacement in 1965 of the London County Council (created in 1889) as the strategic authority by the geographically larger Greater London Council. In addition, thirty-two London boroughs and the City of London Corporation had responsibility for the provision of day-to-day services (replacing the twenty-eight boroughs introduced in 1899) (see Pimlott and Rao, 2002; Travers, 2004). As with other reorganisations, size mattered, and as a consequence local cohesion and community representation lost out. In 1966, the Labour government set up a Royal Commission on Local Government in England, with separate inquiries into the future of local government in Wales and Scotland. The Report of the Royal Commission (Cmnd 4040), while accepting the importance of democratic local government, expressed the belief that it was then too numerous and fragmented, but it was equally unable to agree unanimously a blueprint for change. The majority report suggested a unitary solution with fifty-eight authorities outside London responsible for all local government services. However, a minority report argued for a two-tier division of function and structure based on city regions and 'shire' and 'district' councils. The Labour government accepted the majority report, but its Conservative successor elected in 1970, and

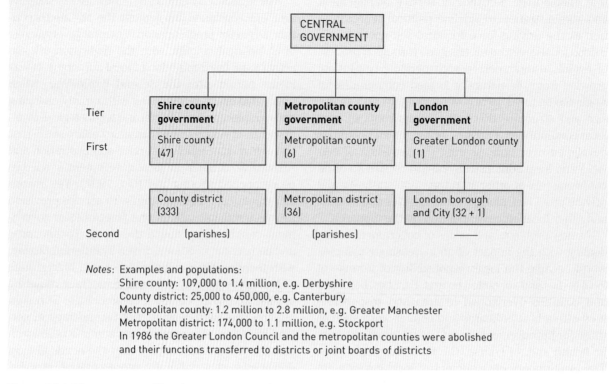

Figure 22.1 The structure of local government in England and Wales after 1974
Source: Adapted from Gray (1979)

mindful of its strengths in the shires, introduced a new two-tier structure through the 1972 Local Government Act.

As a consequence, on 1 April 1974 the map of local government changed dramatically (Figure 22.1). The systems of local government for the big cities and counties were the inverse of each other. In the major conurbations, six metropolitan counties were created alongside thirty-six metropolitan districts. The metropolitan counties were major strategic authorities, while the metropolitan districts had responsibility for the large-spending services such as education, social services and housing.

In the shires the situation was almost reversed: the counties – forty-seven of them – were the education and social service authorities as well as having a wider strategic remit. The districts were responsible for housing, with leisure as the other major spending service, alongside planning and waste-removal functions. In England and Wales, the number of counties was reduced from fifty-eight to forty-seven and the districts from 1,249 to 333. As a result of the Wheatley Commission (Cmnd 4159, HMSO, 1969), local government in Scotland was also reorganised on a two-tier basis with nine large regional councils

and fifty-three districts, alongside three island authorities. Thus, in 1974 British local government became less local and more subject to division of function between increasingly large and remote units.

The political debate behind the 1974 reorganisation is often overshadowed, and indeed obscured, by the technocratic versus democratic arguments of large efficient local government against small responsive self-governing communities. In the 1960s and 1970s, the Labour and Conservative parties saw the structure of local government, the allocation of services between tiers and the drawing of authority boundaries as important political considerations: not a new phenomenon but one shared by Victorian Conservative and Liberal governments. Labour's support for a unitary solution – still current Labour Party policy – saw large, urban-centred councils running all services, and because of the party's urban base, these would be mainly Labour-controlled.

Conservative support for the two-tier approach and the 1970 government's allocation of services between the tiers equally displayed its party political preoccupations. Shire counties received the more powerful and expensive services, as by and large these counties would be Conservative-dominated. The metropolitan districts were given similar functional responsibilities, which would enable Conservatives in some of the more affluent metropolitan areas to control significant local services. Thus, for the Labour and Conservative parties, the importance of the structure of local government rested not only on the technocratic against democratic arguments but also on the realities of political control and power.

The political considerations concerning local government were at the fore in most of the reorganisations that occurred in the 1980s and 1990s, instigated again by a Conservative government. The metropolitan counties, and particularly the Greater London Council, led from 1981 by Ken Livingstone, had become troublesome for the Thatcher government. The Conservatives' 1983 manifesto had pledged to abolish these authorities, and after the publication of a White Paper, *Streamlining the Cities* (Cmnd 9063, HMSO, 1983), this was duly accomplished in 1986. The responsibilities of the GLC and six metropolitan counties were transferred to the boroughs below them, or to a series of joint boards. While the Conservative government argued that the metropolitan counties had outlived their usefulness and were large, remote, unresponsive, bureaucratic and expensive, they had, at a stroke, removed from the local and national scene a source of acute political embarrassment and opposition.

The reorganisations of the 1990s display similar political and party political undercurrents as well as an interesting shift by the Conservatives towards favouring a unitary system of local government. In 1992, John Major's Conservative government established a Local Government Commission, chaired by Sir John Banham (former Director of Audit at the Audit Commission and Director General of the Confederation of British Industry), to review the structure of local government. Government guidance to the commission favoured the unitary system and stressed the importance of local government efficiency, accountability, responsiveness and localness, criteria that display the contradictions inherent in the technocratic–democratic arguments that had been played out since 1945 (Young and Rao, 1997).

Yet the commission rejected the production of a national blueprint for local government structure and instead recommended the creation of all-purpose, single-tier **unitary authorities** in some areas and the retention of the two-tier system or a modified version of it in other areas. The commission justified its recommendations, which often conflicted with the favoured approach of the government, on the basis of cost, community identity and local geography, and the degree of local support for change. The Secretary of State's replacement of Sir John Banham as chairman of the Commission with Sir David Cooksey, again from the Audit Commission, resulted in the formation of a few more unitary authorities than otherwise would have been the case, but no new nationwide reorganisation resulted.

In the meantime, much animosity had been generated between the counties fighting for survival and the districts campaigning to enlarge their area, population, power and political influence at the expense of the counties. The only area of local government to benefit from the antagonism caused by the review was the parishes, which found themselves courted by counties and districts alike. Parishes were often promised enlarged responsibilities and consultative opportunities and lauded as an essential element of the local representative processes. With the end of the local government review came the end of such blandishments. However, the animosity between districts and counties generated by the review process in many cases remains today; county and district relationships can often be tense even if they are controlled by the same party.

Local government in Scotland and Wales fared differently from that in England. The local government reviews of the 1990s led to the imposition of a unitary system across both. The 1992 Local Government Act abolished the county and district councils in Wales and the regional and district councils in Scotland, replacing them with twenty-two unitaries in Wales and thirty-two in Scotland. By contrast, in England the last unitary authorities to come into existence in 1998 left a system consisting of unitary authorities in some areas and a two-tier system of counties and districts in others, alongside the London boroughs.

Local government in Northern Ireland had been reorganised earlier than the introduction of unitary councils to Scotland and Wales. The Local Government Act (Northern Ireland) 1972 created twenty-six district councils, which replaced the system of counties, county borough councils and urban and rural districts that had been created across the whole of Ireland by the Local Government (Ireland) Act 1898. Yet, as a result of the community strife that existed at the time of the 1972 Act and in an effort to ensure equality between communities, certain key services were not given to local government to provide. Ironically, democratically elected local councils were not trusted to be democratic in the treatment of various communities and in the provision of certain services. The district councils were not given powers over education, housing or road building and these responsibilities went to special, appointed boards; neither are the district councils planning authorities, having merely the right to be consulted about planning applications. They do, however, provide leisure and community services and distribute grants to a range of bodies, as well as having responsibility for other local government services. Yet, these councils are also expected to act as the place in which the various currents of political opinion existing in Northern Ireland could find some democratic platform, and as representative institutions they may well have provided a better forum for political deliberation than many councils on the mainland.

The final twentieth-century reorganisation of UK local government came with the Blair government's Greater London Authority Act 1999, which set up the new Greater London Authority, consisting of the London Assembly and the directly elected mayor of London. The Assembly has twenty-five elected members, fourteen of whom are members elected from constituencies formed from the London boroughs and elected by the first-past-the-post system; eleven are members from across London, with no specific constituencies, elected from a party (or independent) list. The London mayor is elected by the supplementary vote system. The current incumbent, Ken Livingstone (also the last leader of the GLC), is serving his second consecutive term, having been first elected as an Independent candidate in May 2000, and re-elected as a Labour candidate in 2004. Unlike all other local authorities in Great Britain, the GLA is more about political representation than service delivery, while it does have a strategic role in relation to London government.

Thus, at the end of the twentieth century and at the beginning of the twenty-first, there exists a patchwork of local authorities (see Figure 22.2) – unitary and two-tier – to mirror the more fragmented patchwork existing at the end of the nineteenth century. But, at the beginning of the twenty-first century,

---

BOX 22.1 | **IDEAS AND PERSPECTIVES**

The future of Northern Ireland local government: the review of public administration

As a result of a review of public administration in Northern Ireland, set up by the Northern Ireland Executive, some major changes are planned for the way in which local government operates. The main points of the proposals are:

■ The 26 districts are to be merged into seven large councils.
■ Each council is to have a maximum of 50 councillors.
■ Elections to the new councils will be held in 2008 and the councils will officially be launched in 2009.
■ Councils are to become planning authorities.
■ Members of the Northern Ireland Assembly will not be able to serve as councillors while they are Assembly Members.
■ Four health boards are to be replaced by a Strategic Health and Social Services Board.
■ Five education boards are to be replaced by a new Education Authority (social services and education, then, will not go to local government).

While ministers have lauded these proposals as leading to improvements in services and lowering of costs, we can see that as in English local government, the needs of technocracy (service administration and management) have once again defeated the needs of democracy (community and political representation, and community cohesion and engagement). The result of the review process is bigger and more remote local government. In addition, the reduction in the number of councillors from around 580, at the moment, to 350 means less publicly legitimised space for democratic debate and representation; having fewer councillors damages the fabric and process of local democracy, but certainly fits in with a managerial rather than a political vision of local government.

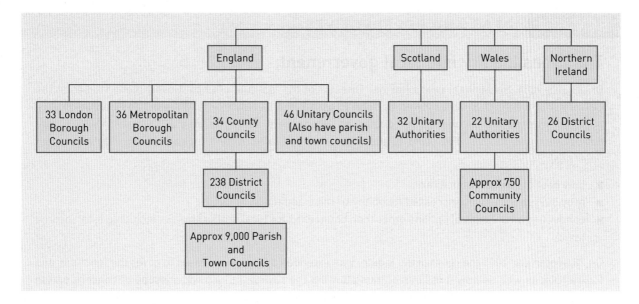

Figure 22.2 The structure of local government in England, Scotland, Wales and Northern Ireland

local government is larger, and more remote and distant from the communities it serves. As Stewart reminds us:

After re-organisation [1974] the average population of shire districts was over ten times the average of the lower tier in Europe. Many district councils appeared artificial, bringing together in a single authority, towns that in most countries in Europe would be authorities in their own right.

Stewart (2003), p. 181

There appears, however, to be a slowly emerging reaction to the overly large size of councils in this country. Indeed, David Miliband, the minister for Communities and Local Government, commented at the New Local Government Network (a local government think-tank) annual conference on 18 January 2006 that:

. . . it is also the case that despite the sterling work of the nearly 9,000 parish councils in England the lowest principal tier of local government in England is ten times the size of the lowest tier in other countries, covering about 150,000 people, compared to around 50,000 in the US, 30,000 in Sweden and 20,000 in Australia. In France, there are 36,000 communes for a population roughly 10% bigger than ours. In Germany there are 15,000 Municipalities for a population a third bigger, compared to England's 350 local councils.

So people want more power. But government can seem remote. These factors come together to create a power gap. It is a gap which is out of sync with modern needs, and it needs to be closed.

While this does not necessarily represent a sea-change in government attitude about council size, it is fascinating for a government minister to be raising questions around what, until very recently, appeared to be a resolved issue. Moreover, the 'bigger is better' lobby still have powerful advocates and allies among government, other political parties, and within local government itself; but the debate has, at least, been reopened.

■ Intergovernmental relations: general competence or general dogsbody?

The chapter has already set out British local government's subordinate role to central government. Such an arrangement is not the only relationship between national and sub-national governments, and this section will consider, in the light of the Blair government's modernising agenda for local government, how the centre and the localities could interact on a more equal footing.

The British unitary state and unwritten constitution, resting on the doctrine of Parliamentary supremacy, ensure that the party with a majority in Parliament is able to legislate as it thinks fit,

BOX 22.2   IDEAS AND PERSPECTIVES

The Lyons Inquiry into local government

On 20 July 2004, Sir Michael Lyons (former Director of the Institute of Local Government Studies at the University of Birmingham) was asked by John Prescott, the Deputy Prime Minister, and Gordon Brown, the Chancellor of the Exchequer, to conduct an independent inquiry to look at the way in which local government was funded. The remit of the inquiry was to explore, and make recommendations about (*inter alia*):

- how best to reform council tax;
- providing councils with increased flexibility to raise additional funding;
- conducting an analysis of options other than council tax for local authorities . . . including local income tax. . . .

On 20 September 2005 the remit of the inquiry was extended by the government to cover the functions and future role, as well as how it is funded, thus allowing the review a much wider scope of concern and to engage in a wide debate with communities and business about what local government should be doing and how.

In December 2005 a consultation paper and interim report was published by the Lyons Inquiry which called for a wide and coherent debate about the role and functions of local government that would consider its strategic role: devolution and decentralisation of powers and responsibilities, the relationship between central and local government, and, of course, local government funding. The inquiry will produce a final report in late 2006.

Currently local authorities, on average, receive 75 per cent of their income from central government, relying on the council tax for, on average, 25 per cent of their income (these are average figures across the country, and all councils do generate some income for themselves through a wide range of fees and charges they can levy for certain activities).

unhindered by any mechanisms for constitutional restraint. While the courts may interpret government legislation, they cannot hold it unconstitutional and unenforceable, effectively striking legislation down as the US Supreme Court may do. Thus, intergovernmental relations in Britain are conducted in an environment where political control of the machinery of central government allows national political concerns and policy to supersede local discretion.

Despite the supremacy of Parliament, much of the relationship between national and sub-national governments is conducted within a framework where bargaining between institutions is the norm. However, this bargaining occurs in an unbalanced context, with central government ultimately assured of its own way. Local authorities are able to redress some of that imbalance by challenge and seeking compromise (Rhodes *et al.*, 1983). However, local authorities have no general competence to act for the citizens of their

area. Thus they are not representative bodies that are able to govern their locality but may act only where Parliament has granted 'positive authority for their actions in a specific law' (Hampton, 1987).

General competence, on the other hand, would see councils able to govern their localities within a broad framework of powers set out by Parliament. It would not necessarily mean that councils could take whatever action they wished, rather that they would not require specific legislative authority for each action and would be less constrained by the courts than at present. Much of the debate concerning general competence centres on the powers, roles and responsibilities of local government and how the discretion to act at the local level is defined and codified in relation to central government.

Should local councils be subordinate to central control and regulation? Should they be able to act only in cases where Parliament gives express authority?

Or should local councils be granted a power of general competence to govern their own localities as they think fit and in accordance with the wishes of their electorate? Councils are elected bodies, comprising the local political representatives of the citizenry, and councillors hold office by virtue of the public vote, so should they not have the powers to act accordingly? Moreover, councils and councillors are closer to the people they represent than central government, MPs and civil servants. The issues they deal with often have a more immediate and greater specific impact on the day-to-day well-being of local citizens than the activities of central government. In addition, strong and independent local councils can act as a counterbalance to the political power of central government and are a means by which local voices can be heard at the heart of government. With this in mind, the question of general competence for local government becomes one of balancing the political power of the centre and the localities.

While Prime Minister Blair's modernising agenda for local government does not envisage a general competence for British local government like that possessed by most other European countries (Wilson and Game, 2002), Section 1 of the Local Government Act 2000 gives councils a duty to promote the social, economic and environmental well-being of local communities (for a detailed exploration of how sub-national governments can affect the welfare or well-being of citizens, see Wolman and Goldsmith, 1992). As Wilson and Game (2002) point out, Section 1 of the Act enables local government to become involved in areas such as tackling social exclusion, reducing health inequalities, promoting neighbourhood renewal and improving local environmental quality. There is, however, still some reticence in local government about experimenting with the well-being aspects of the Act. Such reticence, which results from centuries of central control and court intervention, has produced a culture of subservience and conservatism that will need some time to dissipate, despite the years that have elapsed since the passing of the Act. While the new duty is clearly not a power of general competence, it represents a nudge in that direction, providing local government with an opportunity to act in a far more flexible and legally certain environment than has hitherto been the case.

The Blair government's modernising agenda for local government is clearly displayed in a number of publications: *Renewing Democracy: Rebuilding Communities* (Labour Party, 1995); the 1997 and 2001 Labour Party election manifestos; and the Green and White Papers *Local Democracy and Community Leadership* (DETR, 1998a), *Modern Local Government: In Touch with the People* (DETR, 1998b), *Local Leadership: Local Choice* (DETR, 1999a), *Strong Local Leadership: Quality Public Services* (DTLR, 2001) and *Vibrant Local Leadership* (ODPM, 2005). While these documents can be seen as a blueprint for local government in the twenty-first century, they do not seek in any way to address the balance between the sovereign and supreme centre by giving local government the power of general competence. Rather, discussions about neighbourhood government and citizen participation have been seen by some as devolving power from elected councils to smaller communities, whilst leaving central control untouched. Local government in Britain will always be subordinate to central government unless Britain moves to a written constitution that codifies and legally enshrines the relationship between elements of the state (for an example of such a written constitution, which suggests a power of general competence of local government, see IPPR, 1991). Such a move from any British government is, for the foreseeable future, a flight of fantasy. Yet, a continued debate about the relationship between central and local government, and indeed between central and local government and the citizens they seek to serve, govern and represent, would be beneficial to the health of British democracy.

The modernising agenda is also concerned with the way in which councils conduct their affairs and make political decisions and this is considered in the section entitled 'Creating a new form and approach to local politics'. But, first, we need to consider what constitutes local politics in local government.

■ Local government and local politics

Despite folklore to the contrary, local government and local and national politics have had a long and intertwined association, an association stretching back much further than the 1974 local government reorganisation, often wrongly identified as the point when national politics invaded local council chambers. Indeed, prior to the 1835 Municipal Corporations Act, local government was already politicised, controlled for the most part by what Fraser (1979) described as self-perpetuating Tory–Anglican élites. Moreover, the first municipal elections after the 1835 Act were essentially party battles between the holders of, and contenders for, local political power. Even in the towns that did not immediately incorporate after the 1835 Act, the campaign for new municipal status often divided along party lines. Similar party battles occurred throughout the nineteenth century over the reform, and control, of London government (Young, 1975).

Gyford (1985) summarised the long-term process of the party politicisation of local government, identifying five distinct stages: Diversity (1835–65), Crystallisation (1865–1905), Realignment (1905–45), Nationalisation (1945–74) and Reappraisal (1974 onwards). The stages chart the gradual solidification of the party system in local government and indicate that while party politics has had a constant presence in the campaigns for control of local councils and in the conduct of council business, the context and texture of party activity have changed.

Local politics has moved from a time when candidates and councillors often disguised their national party allegiances (see also Grant, 1973; Clements, 1969) to today, where something like 80 per cent of all councils have been categorised as 'politicised'. Indeed, political party involvement in local government has been described as almost 'universal' (HMSO, 1986b; see also Wilson and Game, 2002, pp. 276–80).

As representative bodies, with the ability to distribute scarce local resources and decide broad policy approaches to important local services, councils are inherently political bodies. It is therefore no surprise that members and supporters of national political parties have had an interest in securing representation on and control of councils. Hennock (1973), Jones (1969) and Lee (1963) indicate not only the long association between local government and political parties but also the different texture that party politics has taken and the varied relationships that have existed within and between parties.

Bulpitt (1967) has summarised these differences into a typology of local party systems as either negative or positive, the main distinction between the systems being the degree to which councillors act as coherent political groupings to accept responsibility for the control of council policy and the settling of patronage issues. What has varied over time and place is the nature of the relationship between the parties and the degree to which councillors

sharing the same political allegiance cohere as distinct party groups. It is the rigidity with which party groups cohere to provide a council with a governing administration, or an opposition bloc, that distinguishes the conduct of party politics in council chambers from its more fluid predecessors (Young and Davis, 1990).

Today the overwhelming majority of council elections are contested by members of national political parties, and most local elections have the flavour of a series of mini general elections (Newton, 1976). That is, local elections reflect voters' national preoccupations rather than local concerns; thus local elections often turn on the national fortunes of the main political parties. Indeed, a casual glance at the election-night programmes will give you constant analysis by the experts of what this, or that, result means for the government, or for the recovery of the Conservative Party, or for the fortunes of the new Leader of the Liberal Democrats, and far less about what the results in South Lakeland or Vale of White Horse means for local citizens and for the way in which those councils had hitherto been run.

However, conflicting views exist as to the balance of local and national influences at local elections, with some evidence suggesting that local issues are important when voters cast a local ballot (HMSO, 1986a; Green, 1972). Indeed, as turnout declines, it is more likely that the voter going to the polls is more concerned about local issues and the running of the council than national party fortunes, and recent local election results as a consequence are less reliable tools from which to try to extrapolate national election results.

Cross-national comparisons of local turnout are problematic because of elements of compulsory voting for nations at the top of the table and different structures and tiers of sub-national government. However, Britain can take little comfort, with local turnout bumping along at around 40 per cent. Indeed, in some by-elections turnout has fallen to single figures. Poor turnout raises serious questions about the democratic legitimacy of local government and the ability of councillors to claim an electoral mandate for their policies.

While Table 22.1 shows that Britain lags behind the rest of Europe when it comes to turnout at local elections, the 2005 local elections saw average turnout reach around 60 per cent. These elections, however, were held on the same day as the general election and also would have seen turnout benefit from experiments in some areas with increased use

Table 22.1 Average turnout in sub-national elections in EU countries

EU country	Mean (%)
Luxembourg	93
Italy	85
Belgium	80
Denmark	80
Germany	72
France	68
Spain	64
Ireland	62
Portugal	60
Netherlands	54
Great Britain	40

Source: C. Rallings and M. Thrasher (1997) *Local Elections in Britain*. Reproduced with permission of Routledge

of postal voting (see Local Government Elections Centre at www.research.plymouth.ac.uk/elections). The reader should compare the 2005 figure for local voting – boosted as it was by the general election – with the results of the 2006 local elections (as well as past figures) to get a clearer indication of how local turnout is affected by concurrent local and national elections.

Poor turnout no doubt damages local accountability and legitimacy. But, added to this is the party group system and the way in which groups organise to conduct their business and the business of the council, alongside the loyalty and discipline they expect of and by and large receive from councillors, that have the potential to further damage local accountability and representation (Copus, 1998, 1999a, 1999b). The party group system sees councillors bound to the decisions of their groups, taken in private and closed meetings, and expected to publicly support, or at least acquiesce in, the outcomes of those meetings.

Loyalty to the party group is expected of the councillor, almost irrespective of how he or she may have spoken or voted in the group meeting. Once the group has made a decision, the councillor must adhere to it in public, whatever he or she thinks and irrespective of any articulated community opinion existing in his or her ward. While most party groups show some flexibility when it comes to councillors acting against their own group when strong opinions

are expressed by local communities, the issue generating those opinions must usually be purely local in nature. That is, they must be located in the councillor's electoral area and have little or no link to any wider policy concern. Such isolated issues do arise, but they are a rarity.

The organisation and activity of party groups varies depending on the party concerned, but each of the three main national and two nationalist parties produces model standing orders for their council party groups. Standing orders are open to interpretation by individual groups, such interpretations depending on the personnel of the group, the nature of the relationship between the groups and the political composition of the council. Indeed, patterns of party interaction and competition will vary depending on the type of council concerned (Rallings and Thrasher, 1997; Wilson and Game, 2002). Largely, however, groups are well organised and structured, with a range of officers undertaking different tasks and clearly identified expectations of loyalty from their membership. In addition, party groups have a range of disciplinary procedures and sanctions available to use against recalcitrant members. The nature of and willingness to use such disciplinary mechanisms vary across the parties, as does the willingness to take a flexible interpretation of standing orders and allow councillors to act at variance with group decisions.

The result of group discipline and loyalty, which plays itself out differently depending on the political affiliation of the councillor, is that councillors often come to represent their political party – or rather the party group – to the electorate and council. Indeed, the party group is now the most important theatre for the conduct of local representation and for council decision making (Hampton, 1970; Saunders, 1979; Stoker, 1991; Game and Leach, 1995).

The group is the place where important local issues are discussed, party lines agreed and political options considered, and for the majority group in particular it is where council decisions are made. What took place in the public meetings of the council and its committees, prior to the reorganisation of political decision making via the 2000 Act, was the ratification of decisions made in the private party group meeting, a practice not altered by the 2000 Act. The group will take into account a range of views when making its decisions; it is to the source of those views and attempts to influence local government policy making that the chapter now turns.

Ken Livingstone's decision to fight for London mayor makes Labour vulnerable to his criticisms
Source: Copyright © Chris Riddell. From *The Observer*, 30 April 2000. Reproduced with permission Guardian Newspapers Limited

■ Creating a new form and approach to local politics

When elected in 1997, the Blair government was committed to a widespread review of the British constitution; much of the previous Conservative government's policies towards local government were to be scrapped or radically changed. Indeed, when in opposition Labour had recognised the importance to political pluralism of a vibrant, healthy and vigorous local government and local politics. The government's agenda for reform is displayed in a Green Paper, three White Papers, a discussion paper and two Acts of Parliament: *Local Democracy and Community Leadership* (DETR, 1998a), *Modern Local Government: In Touch with the People* (DETR, 1998b), *Local Leadership: Local Choice* (DETR, 1999a), *Strong Local Leadership: Quality Public Services* (DTLR, 2001), *Vibrant Local Leadership* (ODPM, 2005), and the 1999 London and 2000 Local Government Acts. It is appropriate

then to review the main elements of that agenda and to suggest briefly what the modernised local council could look like.

The agenda falls into three main areas:

1. Reorganising political decision-making arrangements.

2. Creating a new ethical framework for local government.

3. Performance improvement through Best Value and the Comprehensive Performance Assessment (CPA).

New political arrangements

It is somewhat ironic that, some five years after the passing of the Local Government Act 2000, many in and around local government are still referring to 'new political management arrangements' to describe the provisions of Part II of the Act, which requires all councils with populations above 85,000 to introduce one of three new-style executive political decision-making arrangements. While those councils had to scrap the committee system of decision-making, councils with populations under 85,000 could keep that system but had to reduce the number of committees they had: what became known as alternative arrangements. When considering which option for decision-making arrangements to introduce, all councils are required under the Act to consult their citizens before coming to a decision and to show how the decision reflected the views of the citizenry. The government published guidance notes to ensure that consultation was fair, balanced and unbiased (DETR, 2000). The three executive options available under the Act are:

1. a directly elected executive mayor and cabinet;

2. a mayor and council manager; and

3. an indirectly elected executive leader and cabinet.

The indirectly elected leader and cabinet option has been the one preferred by the overwhelming majority of councils, which is not surprising as this option represents the least change to existing practices and structures. Here, the council, but in reality the ruling party group, selects one of its members to be the leader of the council. A cabinet of up to nine councillors (plus the leader of the council) is formed, again normally from the majority party group unless the council has no overall control; the leader and cabinet form the council's political executive. The system is not dissimilar to that existing prior to the 2000 Act, when the ruling group would ensure that the council appointed its leader as council leader and went on to elect a number of committee chairs and vice-chairs from among its number. The leader and committee chairs usually acted as an informal cabinet, but one without executive powers, i.e. day-to-day decision-making ability. That is the main difference introduced by the 2000 Act: the leader and cabinet are formally and legally constituted as a political executive with day-to-day decision-making power. The main requirement of the Act is that all councils with populations over 85,000 must formally distinguish between those councillors forming an executive and the rest of the council membership, who are charged with holding the executive to account and scrutinising its activity.

Before moving to one of the options involving a directly elected mayor, a binding referendum must be held, called either by the council or as the result of a petition containing signatures of 5 per cent of the local population (10 per cent in Wales). Much debate has centred on the directly elected mayor, a political office very different from the current ceremonial and largely non-partisan mayor who chairs council meetings. Despite many councillors complaining that the mayoral office would see the concentration of inordinate power in the hands of a single individual, the reality is different from that which is often claimed. The directly elected mayor has broadly similar powers to that of the indirectly elected leader save that the mayor has the right to appoint his or her own cabinet, and that's it! Yet to hear many councillors talk of this new office, one could be forgiven for thinking that these new mayors have the power of life or death. It appears that councillors are happy to be able to appoint the political head of the council – the indirectly elected leader – themselves, but they object most strongly to the voters being able to choose who holds the top political job in the council; it's not the power of the office holder many complain about, simply how the office is obtained!

Under both the mayoral options the mayor would be elected by all the voters of a council area and thus come with a direct electoral mandate far more powerful and legitimate than the indirect one granted to an indirectly elected council leader by fellow councillors. The directly elected mayor is to be elected by the supplementary vote system, where voters place a cross in a first- and second-preference column against their preferred two candidates. After the first count, if no one candidate achieves 50 per cent of the votes cast, all but the top two candidates are eliminated and the second-preference votes redistributed to the remaining candidates if the voter has selected either one of them as a second preference. The system ensures that any victorious candidate secures over 50 per cent of the votes cast. Once elected, the mayor selects a cabinet from among the council members and allocates portfolios.

The mayor becomes a highly visible political head of the council with responsibility for providing political leadership, proposing the policy framework for the council, preparing the council's budget and taking executive decisions. The council would be responsible for scrutinising the work of the mayor and his or her cabinet and proposing amendments to policy and the budget.

The mayor and council manager option would again see a directly elected mayor chosen by all the voters, but here the executive consists of only two people: the mayor and an appointed council manager. Most executive power would rest with the council manager, a paid appointee of the council but under the direction of the mayor. Most policy and budgetary responsibility would rest with the council manager, a kind of super chief executive. It is not an option that councillors in Britain favour, often complaining that their position is already undermined by senior officers. Appointing an officer with legislatively enshrined executive responsibilities would be anathema to many councillors. Only one council, the city of Stoke-on-Trent, from the twelve that have introduced an elected mayor after a successful referendum, had the mayor and manager option on the ballot paper. After defeating the sitting independent mayor in the 2005 elections, the Labour Party in Stoke-on-Trent has announced that it wishes to change back to a council leader system, where the ruling party – not the voters – choose the top council post; a referendum will be needed before this can happen.

However, it is fair to say that giving the public the right to select directly the political head of the council, rather than having the choice made for them by councillors, has failed to ignite a blaze of interest in the mayoral option. So far, only eleven of the thirty referendums held outside London have returned a 'yes' vote. Table 22.2 displays the referendum results so far obtained.

In May and October 2002 the elections for directly elected mayors were held, and Table 22.3 shows the outcomes of these contests. What is clear from the results is that voters in at least half the mayoral contests have taken the opportunity the new arrangements have given them to reject candidates from political parties and often from the party that has long controlled the council.

In any of the above options, those councillors remaining outside the executive are charged with the duty of scrutinising, through a number of overview and scrutiny committees, the activities of the council's executive. These councillors would be expected to put party loyalty to one side and publicly criticise a council executive that may well comprise their own party colleagues, whom they themselves may have voted into executive office. The modernising agenda rests on councillors' willingness to scrutinise an executive in public, but so far it has underestimated the pull of party group loyalty. It is unlikely that the sort of scrutiny envisaged by the government will occur overnight when

councillors are expected to scrutinise the activities of their party colleagues.

The introduction of new political arrangements into councils and a clear distinction between executive and scrutiny members is aimed at overcoming the secretive and opaque nature of much local political decision-making. It aims to make decision-making open and transparent and thereby enhance local accountability, the committee system being seen as responsible for diffusing responsibility and thus making the holding of individuals to account almost impossible. Indeed, even a committee chair could not be said to be responsible for a committee decision.

In May 2005, Mayors Drummond in Hartlepool, Winter in Doncaster and Wolfe in Stoke-on-Trent faced the voters as incumbents to seek re-election after three years in office. Mayor Arkley in North Tyneside had been elected in the first ever mayoral by-election which was held in June 2003, so she faced the voters after only two years in office. The results delivered the re-election of one independent and one Labour incumbent; the defeat of one independent mayor in Stoke-on-Trent, who did not even make it through to the second round; and the defeat of the Conservative mayor in North Tyneside; Labour candidates won the Stoke and North Tyneside battles, bringing Labour's total number of elected mayors to seven (including the Mayor of London). In October 2005, a Conservative mayor was elected in Torbay, to face a Liberal Democrat-controlled council.

Whether the new political arrangements result in more visible and accountable local leadership, as they are intended to, depends largely on how the voters react when casting a vote in a local election. One thing is certain: the electorate have been given an opportunity to locate their vote in a far more sophisticated fashion than was possible in the past and have been given greater control over the council and the individual who holds the top political job. One other thing is also clear, as the referendum results show: voters across the country do not appear all that interested in having that power!

A word about alternative arrangements

The real story of the Local Government Act 2000 is the story of political executives, but as a piece of political expediency to ensure the passage of the bill through the House of Lords, the government was forced to concede the alternative arrangement option. That is, authorities with populations of 85,000 or less could introduce a slimmed-down

Table 22.2 Results in mayoral referendums, 2001–2

Council	Date	Result	For	%	Against	%	Turnout (%)	Type
Berwick-upon-Tweed	7 Jun 2001	No	3,617	26	10,212	74	64	poll with general election
Cheltenham	28 Jun 2001	No	8,083	33	16,602	67	31	all postal
Gloucester	28 Jun 2001	No	7,731	31	16,317	69	31	all postal
Watford	12 Jul 2001	Yes	7,636	52	7,140	48	24.5	all postal
Doncaster	20 Sep 2001	Yes	35,453	65	19,398	35	25	all postal
Kirklees	4 Oct 2001	No	10,169	27	27,977	73	13	normal
Sunderland	11 Oct 2001	No	9,593	43	12,209	57	10	normal
Hartlepool	18 Oct 2001	Yes	10,667	51	10,294	49	31	all postal
LB Lewisham[a]	18 Oct 2001	Yes	16,822	51	15,914	49	18	all postal
North Tyneside	18 Oct 2001	Yes	30,262	58	22,296	42	36	all postal
Middlesbrough	18 Oct 2001	Yes	29,067	84	5,422	16	34	all postal
Sedgefield	18 Oct 2001	No	10,628	47	11,869	53	33.3	all postal
Brighton and Hove	18 Oct 2001	No	22,724	38	37,214	62	32	all postal
Redditch	8 Nov 2001	No	7,250	44	9,198	56	28.3	all postal
Durham	20 Nov 2001	No	8,327	41	11,974	59	28.5	all postal
Harrow	7 Dec 2001	No	17,502	42	23,554	58	26.06	all postal
Plymouth	24 Jan 2002	No	29,553	41	42,811	59	39.78	all postal
Harlow	24 Jan 2002	No	5,296	25	15,490	75	36.38	all postal
LB Newham[a]	31 Jan 2002	Yes	27,163	68.2	12,687	31.8	25.9	all postal
Shepway	31 Jan 2002	No	11,357	44	14,438	56	36.3	all postal
LB Southwark[a]	31 Jan 2002	No	6,054	31.4	13,217	68.6	11.2	normal
West Devon	31 Jan 2002	No	3,555	22.6	12,190	77.4	41.8	all postal
Bedford	21 Feb 2002	Yes	11,316	67.2	5,537	32.8	15.5	normal
LB Hackney[a]	2 May 2002	Yes	24,697	58.94	10,547	41.06	31.85	all postal
Mansfield	2 May 2002	Yes	8,973	54	7,350	44	21.04	normal
Newcastle-under-Lyme	2 May 2002	No	12,912	44	16,468	56	31.5	normal
Oxford	2 May 2002	No	14,692	44	18,686	56	33.8	normal
Stoke-on-Trent	2 May 2002	Yes	28,601	58	20,578	42	27.8	normal
Corby	3 Oct 2002	No	5,351	46	6,239	53.64	30.91	all postal
LB Ealing[a]	12 Dec 2002	No	9,454	44.8	11,655	55.2	9.8	combination postal and ballot
Ceredigion	20 May 2004	No	5,308	27	14,013	73	36	unknown
Torbay	14 July 2004	Yes	18,074	55	14,682	45	32.1	unknown

[a] LB = London Borough
Source: From the New Local Government Network website, nlgn.org.uk, April 2003. Reproduced with permission of the New Local Government Network

committee system instead of a political executive. Government regulations flowing from the 2000 Act set out how alternative arrangements can be configured within council chambers. The full council will set the policy framework and approve the budget and be supported by up to five 'policy committees'. One or more overview and scrutiny committees will hold the policy committees to account and assist them in

Table 22.3 Mayoral election results, May and October 2002

Council	Winning candidate	Political affiliation	Elected on 1st or 2nd count	Electorate	Turnout
May 2002					
Doncaster	Martin Winter	Labour	2nd	216,097	58,487 (27.07%)
Hartlepool	Stuart Drummond	Independent	2nd	67,903	19,544 (28.78%)
LB Lewisham[a]	Steve Bullock	Labour	2nd	179,835	44,518 (24.75%)
Middlesbrough	Ray Mallon	Independent	1st	101,570	41,994 (41.34%)
LB Newham[a]	Robin Wales	Labour	1st	157,505	40,147 (25.49%)
North Tyneside	Chris Morgan	Conservative	2nd	143,804	60,865 (42.32%)
Watford	Dorothy Thornhill	Liberal Democrat	2nd	61,359	22,170 (36.13%)
October 2002					
Bedford	Frank Branston	Independent	2nd	109,318	27,717 (25.35%)
LB Hackney[a]	Jules Pipe	Labour	2nd	130,657	34,415 (26.34%)
Mansfield	Tony Egginton	Independent	2nd	72,242	13,350 (18.48%)
Stoke-on-Trent	Mike Wolfe	Mayor 4 Stoke	2nd	182,967	43,985 (24.04%)

[a] LB = London Borough

Source: From the New Local Government Network website: nlgn.org.uk, October 2003. Reproduced with permission of the New Local Government Network

Former police Superintendent Ray Mallon was elected mayor of Middlesbrough in October 2002
Source: Empics Sports Photo Agency

their work (DETR, 2000, para 9.8). Membership is limited by regulation to fifteen for a committee and ten for a subcommittee (DETR, 2000, para 9.13). At the outset, of the eighty-six councils to which alternative arrangements could apply, fifty-nine chose to go down that route.

A new ethical framework

The Nolan Committee (HMSO, 1997) on standards in public life conducted an investigation into the ethical arrangements and practices of local government. Its report was largely accepted by the government and formed the basis of the proposals contained within *Local Leadership: Local Choice* for developing the ethical framework of local government. The Nolan Committee effectively gave local government a glowing bill of health, but concerns about the probity and conduct of councillors and officers remained. The government was as keen to avoid the appearance of wrongdoing in local government, as much as any wrongdoing itself, and as a result Part III of the Local Government Act 2000 created a new ethical framework within which councils must operate.

The Act introduced a new model code of conduct governing the behaviour of councillors and all elected, co-opted and independent members of local authorities, including parish councils, fire, police and national parks authorities are covered by the code and must sign an agreement to abide by its conditions. All newly elected councillors must sign such an agreement before taking up office. Authorities can choose to add their own local rules to the model code, although most have adopted it without additions. The code covers areas of individual behaviour such as members not abusing their position or not misusing their authority's resources, and there are rules governing disclosure of interest and withdrawal from meetings where councillors may have some personal connections to the matters being considered. Councillors are also required to record in a public register their financial and other interests, such as property they own and business interests.

There are two types of interest councillors may have: *personal* and *prejudicial*. A *personal interest* occurs either:

■ when a councillor has an interest in a matter which might reasonably be regarded as affecting to a greater extent than other council taxpayers, ratepayers or inhabitants of the authority's area, the well-being or financial position of the individual or of any employment or business, any firm in which he or she is a partner, or any company of which he or she is a director; or, any body in which he or she holds more than £5,000 in securities; or

■ where the beneficiary of any decision or act in which the councillor takes part is a spouse, partner, parent, parent-in-law, son, daughter, stepson, step-daughter, child of a partner, brother, sister, grandparent, grandchild, uncle, aunt, nephew, niece, or the spouse or partner of any of the preceding persons; and, a member of a couple who live together.

Where a councillor has a *personal interest* in a matter and goes to a council meeting at which the matter is considered, he or she must disclose it at the beginning of the meeting, or when the interest becomes apparent.

A *prejudicial interest* occurs where a councillor has a personal interest in a matter and when the interest is one which a member of the public would reasonably regard as so significant that it is likely to prejudice the member's judgement of the public interest (see HMSO, 2001).

Under the Act, each council must form a standards committee consisting of at least two members of the council and an independent co-opted member, who is not an elected councillor of the authority. The committee is responsible for ensuring that councillors adhere to the code of conduct, for arranging training for councillors to enable them to meet the new ethical requirements, and for monitoring the general ethical environment of the council.

The Act also created the National Standards Board, appointed by the Secretary of State and responsible for ensuring the probity and ethical conduct of local councillors. Using ethical standards officers (ESOs), the board is able to investigate complaints made by the public about the behaviour of councillors. ESOs have statutory powers to access information and documents pertinent to any investigation being conducted. The ESO will decide as a result of a complaint that either there is no evidence of misconduct, or there is evidence of misconduct but no action need be taken, or matters should be referred to the council's monitoring officer, or the case should be referred to an adjudication panel of the board for a formal hearing. The Adjudication Panel for England is a separate body from the National Standards Board that will hear cases referred to it by ESOs. The panel can make the following adjudications as a result of a hearing: suspension of the councillor, or co-opted member, from the council; partial suspension, i.e. from involvement in a particular committee or function; disqualification from being or becoming a member; or no disciplinary action. A right of appeal to the High Court exists against the decision of the panel. Suspension or partial suspension may be for a maximum of one year and disqualification for a maximum of five years.

Table 22.4 shows the number of allegations made to the Standards Board and the percentage of cases

Table 22.4 Allegations to the National Standards Board

Period	Number of allegations	Cases with no further action (%)
April 2002 – March 2003	2,948	50
April 2003 – March 2004	3,566	60
April 2004 – March 2005	3,752	66

BOX 22.3 EXAMPLE

No more Mayor of London: at least for a month, anyway

The Standards Board has had its high-profile test case. In February 2006, the Mayor of London, Ken Livingstone, was suspended from office for one month (and not even allowed into his office, for that matter!). The suspension was to commence on 1 March 2006 and was ordered by a three-member adjudication panel, which came to its verdict as a result of comments Livingstone was alleged to have made to a Jewish journalist of the *Evening Standard*. Those comments were held by the panel to be 'unnecessarily insensitive' and 'offensive'. The decision to suspend Livingstone has been criticised by the Prime Minister, the Conservative Party mayoral candidate Steven Norris, pop singers and even the public. Livingstone appealed to the High Court and successfully had the decision to suspend him suspended; he is applying for a judicial review and the outcome of this process is still awaited at the time of writing.

The implications and irony of the situation are overwhelming:

■ Three unelected, appointed administrators (the adjudication panel) have attempted to overturn the decision of 685,541 voters who gave Livingstone their first preference vote, and of some 828,300 voters when second preferences are counted.

■ The Prime Minister has leapt to Livingstone's defence; they are not the best of political friends.

■ The decision of the panel reflects the current culture of political correctness and the demand that giving offence to anybody about anything should be avoided at all costs; Livingstone has effectively been hoisted by his own politically correct petard!

in which no further action was taken. That does not mean that in the remainder of cases the allegation was upheld, but rather that some further investigation was required, or an adjudication panel was necessary, before a final outcome was delivered.

Best Value and the Comprehensive Performance Assessment

The Local Government Act 1999 replaces the Compulsory Competitive Tendering (CCT) regime introduced by the 1980 Planning and Land Act and extended by the 1988 Local Government Act. CCT placed a duty on councils to put certain services out to competitive tender in the private sector and for a council's own workforce to bid against private providers to win council contracts. While the Conservative government that introduced CCT argued that it improved the efficiency and effectiveness of service provision, others argued that it was ideologically driven and designed to destroy councils' ability to provide services by biasing the tendering regime in favour of the private sector.

In January 2000, Best Value replaced CCT as the prime mechanism by which councils will ensure the economy, efficiency, effectiveness and responsiveness of service delivery. Based on the mantra of 'challenge, compare, consult, compete', Best Value does not remove the idea of competitive comparisons with the private sector; rather, it removes the compulsory element and the requirement that contracts go to the lowest tender in all but the most exceptional circumstances.

Best Value is a more comprehensive system of service improvement than the CCT regime. It covers all local authority services, with councils expected to review each of their service areas to secure continual improvement to the way they exercise their functions. Indeed, 'authorities will be expected to show that they have considered the underlying rationale for the service(s) under review and the alternative ways in which it might be provided' (DETR, 1999b). Councils will also be required to prepare Best Value performance plans, providing a clear statement about:

■ what services an authority will deliver to local people;

■ how it will deliver them;

■ to what levels services are currently delivered;

- what levels of service the public should expect in the future;

- what action it will take to deliver those standards and over what timescale (DETR, 1999b).

Central to the Best Value regime is public consultation. Indeed, the consultation Green Paper *Improving Local Services through Best Value* (DETR, 1998c) states that:

the local consultation process will be effective only insofar as it secures and sustains a positive response from local people. This will depend in part on local authorities' responsiveness, and the skill and transparency with which the issues are presented.

DETR (1998c)

In addition, local authorities will be expected to set rigorous targets and performance indicators as well as to address a number of nationally inspired performance targets for their services. While the passing of CCT has been little mourned, it is the prescriptive nature of the Best Value legislation, its all-encompassing remit and the plethora of inspections that go with the Best Value regime that have caused local government some concern about the degrees of central control involved. Coupled to this is a deep local government suspicion of the wide powers of intervention that will rest with the Secretary of State when a council is deemed to be 'failing' in its duty to secure Best Value. The intervention the Secretary of State could take may result in the authority concerned losing the ability to provide a service and an outside provider being imposed (DETR, 1999b). However, the government presents these reserve powers as a last resort and has devised protocols for their use. The authority that moves substantially towards achieving Best Value, the modernising council, will have little to fear from central control.

The White Paper, *Strong Local Leadership: Quality Public Services* (DTLR, 2001), set out a new approach to securing performance improvement in local government services by way of a comprehensive performance framework, which built on existing audit, inspections and other assessments. The Audit Commission has since become responsible for what is known as the Comprehensive Performance Assessment (CPA) for each council and, as a result of that assessment, councils were placed into one of the following five categories: excellent, good, fair, weak or poor. The system caused much consternation in local government and even saw the

London Borough of Ealing take the Audit Commission to court over the review process (a case which the Appeal court found in the Audit Commission's favour). The system of assessment has now been changed and councils are given two assessment results: from zero to four stars for performance and a second award for what the Audit Commission calls the 'direction of travel', or how well the council is likely to perform in the future. That direction of travel falls into the following categories: improving strongly, improving well, improving adequately and not improving adequately. In England, in January 2006, some thirty-nine councils had been awarded four stars; sixty-three had three stars; thirty-six had two stars; nine had one star; and one council had been awarded no stars (three councils were still subject to review).

Whether the voting public is aware of the current assessment process, or any process for performance assessment for that matter, and whether the public is aware of the grading of their council, is moot. If the voting public were aware, whether that grading would have an impact on voting behaviour is even more debatable. Yet, the detailed assessment of a council's performance by an outside body can have a tendency to distract that council from its own political priorities and policies, as supported by the electorate at the council election, and direct them into following priorities set by an external, administrative body that is not accountable to local voters. Unless any assessment of council performance is light-touch and does not dominate council attention and resources, then it can have the affect of damaging local democracy. After all – if the voters want to vote for cheap, poor quality services and low council tax, then they have the right to – don't they?

■ Local government: a changing policy environment

While councillors have links to the external environment through their parties and communities, and business, professional and political organisations, the decisions they take rest heavily on the advice they receive from officers employed by the authority. These professionals and managers form an important antenna for councillors on the outside world.

Many alternative sources of information exist for councillors to that received from officers, but, as the paid employees and advisers to the council, senior officers are a potentially powerful influence on councillors' final decisions. Moreover, officers can influence councillors in their private discussions in the party group through the production of council minutes and reports that councillors consider in their group meetings, and, by attendance at those meetings, on request, to answer questions and give advice, which until quite recently was largely accepted. Young and Laffin (1990) indicate that party politics has radically altered the patterns of interaction between officers and councillors and that the task of advising councillors no longer comes with the certainty of officer influence that it once had. The fact remains that for the vast majority of councillors the advice received from officers is among the most important and influential they receive; securing alternative sources of advice and support comes at a premium. Even the new overview and scrutiny committees formed by councils under the 2000 Act have yet to provide councillors with much direct access to sources of information and advice apart from local government officers.

Local government officers coming from a range of professional backgrounds, mainly associated with the specialist services provided by local authorities or from the wider professions such as the law, interact with colleagues whose profession is management. The professional as expert and the professional manager now operate in what is the accepted principle of local government management: the corporate approach. This approach was championed in 1972 by the Bains Report, which challenged the then dominant functional approach to local government organisation and management.

The Bains Report took a managerial perspective towards the role of the officer, but as Stewart (1986, p. 132) reminds us, 'decisions made by a manager can have important and unexpected political consequences'. Indeed, it is senior officers and senior councillors acting as a 'joint élite' (Stoker, 1991) that is at the heart of local government political management. While tensions may exist between the élite of senior councillors and officers, the carving out of spheres of influence enables an uneasy alliance between officers and members to contribute a dynamic tension to the local policy processes. The uneasy but dynamic tension existing between councillors and officers risks disruption by pressure from external sources for the council to respond to particular demands, or to interact with external bodies

David Miliband was appointed to the Cabinet to regenerate local communities in May 2005
Source: PA Wire / Empics

around various local issues and events. External pressure on local authorities comes from the local citizenry, regional institutions of governance and the European Union.

■ The citizenry: consultation and participation

Local government policy-making is not inevitably informed by the citizenry simply because the council is closer to the people it represents than the national Parliament. Local people are able to be part of the process of local decision-making only if two conditions are met: first, the council has a range of mechanisms by which the views of the citizen can be sought; and second, the council, and councillors in particular, are willing to respond positively to the views of the citizen and indeed to change and develop council policy accordingly. Public involvement in local government is not a case of a council convincing the people it has the right answers but of developing those answers to ensure congruence between policy and the views of the citizen. Such a process is set within a representative framework where councillors will assess the outcomes of citizen consultation and participation but be responsible for making the final decisions on important local issues.

The Blair government's modernising agenda for local government recognises the inherent tension between local representative democracy and enhanced citizen participation. The modernising agenda does not set out to replace representative democracy with a participative variant; rather, it seeks to use citizen involvement to inform the outcomes of the representative processes as they link to local policy-making. *Local Democracy and Community Leadership* (DETR, 1998a) exhorts councils to involve the public more in their decision-making processes and urges that such involvement be a regular rather than an episodic feature. The government has set out the virtues of enhanced public involvement thus:

The prize is an ever closer match between the needs and aspirations of communities and the services secured for them by their local authority, better quality services, greater democratic legitimacy for local government and a new brand of involved and responsible citizenship; in short, reinvigorated local democracy. Increasingly, the degree to which an authority is engaged with its stake-holders may become a touchstone for the authority's general effectiveness.

DETR (1998a), p. 16

It is clear that local government officers and councillors are expected to engage far more closely with the communities they serve and represent than has so far been the norm. So how can the public become more closely involved in the activities of the local council aside from standing for election and voting? *Local Democracy and Community Leadership* (DETR, 1998a) provides an answer by setting out a clear expectation that councils will use a number of specific mechanisms for seeking and responding to the views of the citizen. Moreover, it recognises that 'different forms of consultation may be appropriate to the different stages in the development of a policy or a strategy' (DETR, 1998a, p. 16).

Councils are encouraged to use the following methods for citizen involvement:

■ citizen juries

■ focus groups

■ visioning conferences

■ deliberative opinion polls

■ citizens' panels

■ community forums or area-based neighbourhood committees

■ interest and user group forums

■ referendums to test public opinion on specific local issues.

Further to these exhortations, the Local Government Act 1999, which introduced the Best Value regime, places a duty on councils to consult the public on a range of issues connected with service provision, even to the extent of questioning whether certain services should be provided at all. In addition, the Local Government Act 2000 required all councils to consult with the public on the form of political executive to be introduced into council decision making: a leader and cabinet; a directly elected mayor and cabinet; or a mayor and council manager. It also required councils to demonstrate publicly how the results of such consultation display themselves in the final decision made by the council on executive arrangements (Copus, 2000).

While many councils have for some time been using a number of other methods of assessing community opinion, particularly experimenting with various approaches to decentralised decision making, others have done little in the way of encouraging citizen involvement. A lack of engagement between local citizens and local councils has potentially damaging consequences for the future of local democracy. Past government research in 1967 and 1986 revealed a low level of knowledge among the public about local government, the functions it provides and the way it is organised (HMSO, 1967b, 1986a, 1986b). Moreover, these and other studies have indicated that local government holds a low salience for the public; this lack of importance allowed the Conservative governments of the 1980s and 1990s radically to undermine much of the power, functions and activities of local government.

The government has further developed and refined its idea of how councils should be engaging with their communities and how the role of the councillor should continue to meet the dual responsibilities of being involved in governing an area as a whole and representing and championing the communities in the wards or divisions they represent (ODPM, 2005). Indeed, the government sees the councillor as being at the heart of the local neighbourhood, proving political leadership in a very local context. Yet, the government also see a greater role for the citizen working alongside the councillor, particularly through area and neighbourhood forums.

Greater engagement between the citizen and local council and enhanced public involvement in local political decision-making do pose a challenge to long-established views about representative democracy and the balance of input to decision-making between the community and the elected councillor. It is for both citizens and councillors to make local representative democracy develop with a more participative edge and thus improve the health of local democracy.

■ The regional agenda

Regional government has existed in England for some time, with a number of **quangos**, or government offices, or other public organisations, organising and operating on a regional basis and formulating and implementing regional policy and spending taxpayers' money on regional initiatives. What is missing from the equation is any form of democratically controlled regional government (see the North East result, Box 22.4 below).

As part of the package of constitutional reform introduced by the Blair government, eight new English regional development agencies (RDAs) were launched on 1 April 1999, formed by the Regional Development Agencies Act 1998. These agencies were created to ensure that decisions about regeneration and regional policy and priorities were made within the regions concerned and to address economic imbalances between regions. The RDAs cover the following areas: North East, North West, Yorkshire and the Humber, West Midlands, East Midlands, East of England, South West, and South East, with the London RDA, introduced in 2000, to link with the arrival of the London mayor and the Greater London Authority. With the agencies also formed for Scotland, Wales and Northern Ireland, the RDAs covered the whole of the UK.

The RDAs took over responsibility for the urban regeneration work (revival of areas made derelict, usually through industrial failure) of English Partnerships, the Rural Development Commission and the Single Regeneration Budget. Each of the RDAs has an appointed board to manage its affairs consisting of twelve members – four from local authorities in the region.

The main objectives of the RDAs are:

- economic development and social and physical regeneration;
- business support, investment and competitiveness;
- enhancing regional skills;
- promoting employment;
- sustainable development.

The RDAs' brief, set by the government, is to raise the average prosperity of their regions to that of the rest of the European Union. While the RDAs are clearly regional bodies, the focus for much of their work will be to integrate the economic prospects of the English regions with the European Union and its regions. The work of the RDAs is regional, their focus European. The RDAs were given as their first task the production of draft regional economic development strategies for public consultation. These documents set out a five- to ten-year strategic vision for their regions, addressing the needs of wide and often socially, economically and geographically diverse areas and drawing into the planning process a wide range of partnership bodies from the private, public and voluntary sectors.

The introduction of the little-hailed RDAs is a first, not final, step on the road to devolution to the English regions. The RDAs are appointed bodies, not elected chambers, and as such lack the electoral legitimacy of the Scottish Parliament and Welsh Assembly. While some RDAs were shadowed by appointed regional chambers, a clear democratic deficit has opened up at the regional level. The government's White Paper, *Your Region, Your Choice: Revitalising the English Regions* (DTLR, 2002), set out how that democratic deficit would be addressed and considered the role, purpose and focus of any elected regional chamber that may be formed in England.

John Prescott has been widely acknowledged as the government's regional assemblies champion, and the Regional Assemblies Preparations Act 2003 gave the Secretary of State the power to call a referendum on the introduction of an elected regional chamber into any region he chooses, based on the existence of a clear public demand for such a move. Now, coupled to the question asking the public whether they want an elected regional chamber to govern the region, is a clear indication of the Labour government's continued favouring of unitary local government (despite the pronouncement of David Miliband, reported above). At the same time as the regional question, voters are asked to choose not whether they want a unitary system of local government (single-tier) to replace the existing structure, but only which of a number of unitary options they would like to see introduced alongside the chamber. Thus, existing councils would disappear should the referendum say 'yes' to a regional chamber.

The government's unnecessary linking of regional chambers to the introduction of unitary local government has no basis in either theory or the practice of sub-national governments in continental Europe, where local government can and does work within a regional framework with different tiers and types of local councils (depending on the country). Insisting on a unitary system of local government before regional assemblies can be introduced will inevitably lead to even larger and more remote local government. Indeed, local government will become less and less local. Citizens will be faced with regional assemblies covering vast tracts of the country with no small, compact units of local government to ensure that the voice of the community is heard: a recipe for even greater disengagement between citizen and council and a contradiction of the stated intention to bring councils and citizens closer together. Moreover, concern exists within local government as to the responsibilities and duties of any new regional layer of government, elected or otherwise. Will regional chambers draw their powers and responsibilities downwards from central government or upwards from local government?

The Scottish and Welsh dimensions

A vital part of the Blair government's constitutional reform package, and one quickly acted upon after the 1997 election victory, was the introduction of an

---

BOX 22.4 **FACT**

The North East says 'no'

Since the advent of the Regional Assemblies Preparations Act 2003 there has been only one referendum on the introduction of a democratically elected regional chamber. It was held on 4 November 2004 in what is known as the North East region. The question was:

Should there be an elected assembly for the North East region?

Of a possible 1.9 million voters, 197,310 voted 'yes' (22.1%) and 893,829 voted 'No' (77.9%); the vote was conducted on a local authority basis and not one of the twenty-three local authority areas (and two county councils) recorded a majority in favour of a 'yes' vote. It was a decisive rejection of an elected regional chamber.

Triumphant 'no' campaigners claimed that regional government had been stopped. It hasn't; the plethora of regionally organised bodies that govern great chunks of the country and spend vast amounts of public money still remain – what has been stopped is any form of democratically elected regional government to hold those non-elected bodies to account.

elected Scottish Parliament and a Welsh Assembly, the first elections to which were held in May 1999, with the second set of elections held in 2003. The Scottish Parliament and the Welsh Assembly represent a major change in the structure and processes of British government and a transference of political and legislative power from Westminster to alternative parliaments. Although the powers of the 129-seat Scottish and sixty-seat Welsh chambers vary, they represent a model of devolution that some in the English regions wish to emulate and perhaps take further. Local government in Scotland and Wales had already been reorganised on a wholly unitary basis, with thirty-two unitary councils in Scotland and twenty-two in Wales, avoiding the need for the Blair government to reorganise local government while introducing the devolved political arrangements to Scotland and Wales. The two chambers have developed their own unique relationships with their local government and have introduced a distinct Scots and Welsh dimension to local government legislation emanating from the Westminster Parliament; both chambers have responsibility for local government matters.

While, generally, local government in England, Scotland and Wales now has features that distinguish them from each other, the most distinctive change is yet to come. The 2007 local elections in Scotland will be conducted under the Single Transferable Vote system and readers should check those results for the impact they have had on the party composition of Scottish councils. Local government in England and Wales will continue to be elected by first-past-the-post.

What about poor old England?

So, Scotland has its Parliament, Wales and Northern Ireland their Assemblies, but what about the biggest country in the UK, with a population of just over 49 million (2001 census) and which contributes the most, by way of tax, to the UK government? Poor old England is left without a democratically elected chamber to speak up for it. Moreover, legislation regarding English local government is left to the UK Parliament, where, as on all other legislation affecting England alone, Scottish and Welsh MPs can also vote. Ironically, the government's devolution agenda has opened up a gaping democratic deficit of its own creation and left a clear piece missing in the UK constitutional and governing jig-saw; the 'Campaign for an English Parliament' is seeking to fill that gap.

Maybe the solution to the UK's democratic and representative arrangements is not regional government, but an English Parliament, sitting alongside the Scottish, Welsh and Northern Ireland bodies, in a Federal UK – now that would be a constitutional revolution.

■ Local government and the European Union

The relationship between British local government and the EU has come a long way since a 1991 Audit Commission report drew attention to its often 'blinkered' approach to EU matters. Relationships between sub-national government such as British local councils and supra-national bodies such as the EU will always be conducted in a complex environment and through a complex system. John (1996) describes this system as triadic, that is conducted between three groups of actors at each of the three levels of governmental interaction. Indeed, the relationship between the EU and local government is influenced by two major factors: European law and policy; and the relationships between local and national government. Moreover, some local governments see the EU as a way around problematic relationships with national government and economic and political constraints, a situation that applied particularly in the UK throughout the 1980s and early 1990s (John, 1996).

The impact of the EU on local government is less clear than the impact of national government but just as important. The EU affects local councils through a range of policy initiatives and demands: environmental health, consumer protection, public protection and even social and human rights legislation. These all impact on the activities of local government, and many councils have expressed concerns about the level of resources involved.

Even so, many local authorities have recognised the importance of securing funding from the EU and contributing to the EU policy-making process, to the extent that many UK local councils employ specialist staff to deal with European issues and negotiate with the EU (Goldsmith and Sperling, 1997). Indeed, some have formed special committees of the council to deal with European matters and have European liaison officers, often with an economic development specialism, and located within economic development departments (Preston, 1992a, 1992b).

Some councils have established Brussels offices, either individually or as part of a consortium, and, while often small-scale affairs, they can disseminate information and establish links with the EU and other European national and sub-national governments. These offices are able to prepare funding bids, lobby for policy initiatives or changes, work with other bodies attempting to influence the EU, draw the private and voluntary sector closer into the EU policy network and place their local authority at the heart of the EU. John (1994) sees such Brussels offices as a cross-national marketplace to develop partnership funding bids and to indulge in informal lobbying of EU officials – a process in which many British councils lose out compared with their European counterparts, who place far more emphasis on resourcing such offices.

Local government placing itself at the heart of the EU serves three purposes:

1. Authorities can develop a range of funding partnerships with a diverse group of organisations.

2. It fosters inter-municipal learning.

3. It enables regions and councils to learn of, and shape, new EU policy initiatives (Ercole *et al.*, 1997).

Preston (1992b) indicates why local government is anxious to develop good relationships with the EU, highlighting the financial and policy benefits that flow from successful applications for European Social Fund and European Regional Development Fund support. The financial resources available from these programmes have enabled British local councils to pursue expansionist economic development policies in spite of tight controls from central government. Indeed, something like 74 per cent of British councils have applied for EU structural funds (Goldsmith and Sperling, 1997).

Another reason for the popularity of the EU within local government is that element of the Maastricht Treaty concerning subsidiarity. This is popularly taken to mean by local councils that decisions should be decentralised to the lowest appropriate level of government, thus locating functions and powers with sub-national governments. However, John (1996) points out that this is a matter of political interpretation, as the treaty itself refers to relations between member states and the EU, not between states and local government. On the other hand, the Council of European Municipalities and Regions is campaigning for changes to the treaty that will clarify the meaning of subsidiarity in relation to the role of sub-national governments in policy and decision making. The European Charter of local self-government, which the Blair government signed up to immediately after the 1997 election as a sign of commitment to local government, already recognises that many areas of public policy and political affairs are properly administered at the local or regional level.

The EU provides British local government with:

■ access to funding;

■ an opportunity to pursue its own policy agenda despite central government restrictions and direction – indeed, the possibility of a way around the unitary British state;

■ political influence in important EU policy networks, linkages with other European local governments and local government consortiums;

■ opportunities to strengthen its role, functions, powers and responsibilities.

As British local government comes to terms with devolved parliaments and chambers, it may find valuable resources in the EU that will enable it to ward off the possible centralising tendencies of yet more layers of government above local authorities.

BOX 22.5   BRITAIN IN CONTEXT

No right to local self-government?

To see what other countries say about their local government and the nature of the relationship between central and local government, and between central and local government and the citizen, go to www.constitution.org. Here, you can view the written constitutions of countries across the globe; note that after the UK there is the comment 'no constitution' but the site refers to Magna Carta and the Bill of Rights. Yet a random glance at some of the constitutions provides stark evidence of the context within which UK local government sits.

Ireland

Article 28A

■ The State recognises the role of local government in providing a forum for the democratic representation of local communities, in exercising and performing at local level powers and functions conferred by law and in promoting by its initiatives the interests of such communities.

Poland

Article 16

■ The inhabitants of the units of basic territorial division shall form a self-governing community in accordance with law.
■ Local government shall participate in the exercise of public power. The substantial part of public duties which local government is empowered to discharge by statute shall be done in its own name and under its own responsibility.

Croatia

■ Citizens shall be guaranteed the right to local self-government.
■ The right to local self-government shall include the right to decide on needs and interests of local significance, particularly on regional development and town planning, organization of localities and housing, public utilities, child care, social welfare, culture, physical culture, sports and technical culture, and the protection and promotion of the environment.

Germany

Article 28

■ Article 28 (Federal guarantee concerning Laender constitutions, guarantee of self-government for local authorities).
■ The constitutional order in the Laender must conform to the principles of republican, democratic, and social government based on the rule of law, within the meaning of this Basic Law. In each of the Laender, counties and communities, the people must be represented by a body chosen in universal, direct, free, equal and secret elections. In the communities the assembly of

the community may take the place of an elected body.
■ The communities must be guaranteed the right to regulate on their own responsibility all the affairs of the local community within the limits set by law. The associations of communities also have the right of self-government in accordance with the law within the limits of the functions given them by law.

These, and the other constitutions you can access, give to local government in the countries concerned something that is lacking in the UK: the constitutional right for local self-government to exist, in one form or another. Moreover, they provide a clear set of principles on which the relationship between the central government and local sub-national government will be conducted, and on what central government can and cannot do to local government. In Britain, no such restraint exists on what central government can do to the localities, from rearranging responsibilities for certain services, to large-scale reorganisation of the size and shape of councils, to outright abolition of councils, such as in the 1974 reorganisation and the abolition of the metropolitan counties in 1986. Moreover, citizens have no say over the shape, size, responsibilities or powers of councils as for example exists in many US states. In Britain, local government is subservient to central government and the citizen subservient to both, at least in constitutional terms.

Unlike much, though by no means all, local government elsewhere, UK local government is heavily constrained by the law and the doctrine of *ultra vires*, that is, acting beyond powers specifically granted to it by statute. Before a council in Britain can do anything, it must be certain that there is legislation in existence saying it can do what it proposes to do. Other nations approach the power and role of local government differently by granting, often in a written constitution, the power of general competence. General competence means that local government can do whatever it wishes to do for the good of its citizens, so long as any actions are not prohibited by law. Put simply, British local government can do only what the law says it can do; elsewhere local government can do anything so long as the law does not say that it can not.

By looking at the UK it is often easy to conclude that the words 'local government' are a misnomer – local maybe, but government certainly not. Different nations come to different constitutional settlements between the centre and the localities and we have an arrangement that emerged from the histories and traditions of the British Isles; other nations, at various times, have had the opportunity to sit down and devise a system of government and thus have created something different from our own approach to the power of government. Who is to say who has it right? But, there is choice to be made between an all-powerful central government which can control the localities, and powerful councils that can react to the wishes of local citizens – even if they conflict with the government's policies. If your council wanted to double the level of council tax, you might want the government to be able to stop it; or you might want your council to be able to spend as much as it likes on local services, whatever the tax. What do you think?

Chapter summary

The chapter has considered British local government as a politically representative set of arrangements designed to ensure responsiveness to the demands of local citizens. It has also outlined the constitutionally subordinate nature of local government to central control but indicated that this need not be the only constitutional settlement available between the localities and the centre. The chapter has investigated the role of political parties in local government and the wider political process of local democracy as they are enacted through local councils. As well as a political process, it has considered local government as a set of institutional relationships between citizens, the centre and the EU. It has also discussed the main elements of the government's modernising agenda.

The chapter has also emphasised the politically dynamic nature of local government, which exists not only as a means of providing services – important though that may be – but also as a means by which the will of local people can be expressed and realised.

Discussion points

■ Has the British system of local government been over-reformed since the early 1970s?

■ Should local government get bigger or smaller, or stay the same size, and why?

■ Should we have a tiered or unitary structure of local government?

■ Should local government have more or less freedom to do what it wants to?

■ In what ways has the funding of local government proved to be a problem?

■ Given the increasing central control of local government, would it be best to run it from London?

■ In what ways are the new political arrangements for local government, such as elected mayors and cabinets, likely to lead to more citizen interest in local affairs?

■ Should unelected administrators have the power to suspend or remove elected politicians from office (see Box 22.3) or is that the electorate's job? How could the power of the people over their politicians be improved?

Further reading

For a classic but still highly relevant analysis of party politics in local government, there is Bulpitt (1967) *Party Politics in English Local Government*. Copus (2004) *Party Politics and Local*

Government has updated the exploration of local politics, placing it in its contemporary, executive setting. For a deep and rich case study analysis of the politics of particular councils you won't go far wrong with Dearlove (1979) *The Reorganisation of British Local Government: Old Orthodoxies and a Political Perspective*; Lee (1963) *Social Leaders and Public Persons: A Study of County Government in Cheshire since 1888*; and, Newton (1976) *Second City Politics: Democratic Processes and Decision-Making in Birmingham*. To put local government into an up-to-date perspective see Stewart (2003) *Modernising British Local Government: An Assessment of Labour's Reform Programme*; and, any of Stoker's recent works (2000, 2003, etc). For an assessment of how local political leadership in Britain has developed, see Leach and Wilson (2000) *Local Political Leadership*. To put British local government and local politics into a broad international perspective, Berg and Rao (2005) *Transforming Local Political Leadership*, and Denters and Rose (2005), *Comparing Local Governance: Trends and Developments*, provide a country-specific, cross-national comparison.

References

Audit Commission (1991) *A Rough Guide to Europe: Local Authorities and the EC* (HMSO).

Bains, M.A. (1972) *Working Group on Local Authority Management Structures, The New Local Authorities: Management and Structure* (HMSO).

Bulpitt, J.J.G. (1967) *Party Politics in English Local Government* (Longman).

Byrne, T. (1983) *Local Government in Britain* (Pelican).

Clements, R.V. (1969) *Local Notables and the City Council* (Macmillan).

Copus, C. (1998) 'The councillor: representing a locality and the party group', *Local Governance*, Vol. 24, No. 3, Autumn, pp. 215–24.

Copus, C. (1999a) 'The political party group: model standing orders and a disciplined approach to local representation', *Local Government Studies*, Vol. 25, No. 1, Spring, pp. 17–34.

Copus, C. (1999b) 'The councillor and party group loyalty', *Policy and Politics*, Vol. 27, No. 3, July, pp. 309–24.

Copus, C. (2000) 'Consulting the public on new political management arrangements: a review and some observations', *Local Governance*, Vol. 26, No. 3, Autumn, pp. 177–86.

Copus, C. (2004) *Party Politics and Local Government* (Manchester University Press).

Dearlove, J. (1979) *The Reorganisation of British Local Government: Old Orthodoxies and a Political Perspective* (Cambridge University Press).

DETR (1998a) *Local Democracy and Community Leadership*.

DETR (1998b) *Modern Local Government: In Touch with the People*.

DETR (1998c) *Improving Local Services through Best Value*.

DETR (1999a) *Local Leadership: Local Choice*.

DETR (1999b) *Implementing Best Value: A Consultation Paper on Draft Guidance*.

DETR (2000) *New Council Constitutions: Consultation Guidelines for English Local Authorities*, C. Copus, G. Stoker and F. Taylor.

DTLR (2001) *Strong Local Leadership: Quality Public Services*.

DTLR (2002) *Your Region, Your Choice: Revitalising the English Regions*.

Elcock, H. (1982) *Local Government: Politicians, Professionals and the Public in Local Authorities* (Methuen).

Ercole, E., Walters, M. and Goldsmith, M. (1997) 'Cities, networks, EU regions, European offices', in M. Goldsmith and K. Klausen (eds), *European Integration and Local Government* (Edward Elgar), pp. 219–36.

Fraser, D. (1979) *Power and Authority in the Victorian City* (St Martins Press).

Game, C. and Leach, S. (1995) *The Role of Political Parties in Local Democracy*, Commission for Local Democracy, Research Report No. 11 (CLD).

Goldsmith, M. and Sperling, E. (1997) 'Local government and the EU: the British experience', in M. Goldsmith and K. Klausen (eds), *European Integration and Local Government* (Edward Elgar), pp. 95–120.

Grant, W.P. (1973) 'Non-partisanship in British local politics', *Policy and Politics*, Vol. 1, No. 1, pp. 241–54.

Gray, A. (1979) 'Local government in England and Wales', in B. Jones and D. Kavanagh (eds), *British Politics Today* (Manchester University Press).

Green, G. (1972) 'National, city and ward components of local voting', *Policy and Politics*, Vol. 1, No. 1, September, pp. 45–54.

Gyford, J. (1976) *Local Politics in Britain* (Croom Helm), p. 11.

Gyford, J. (1985) 'The politicisation of local government', in M. Loughlin, M. Gelfand and K. Young, *Half a Century of Municipal Decline* (Allen and Unwin), pp. 77–97.

Hampton, W. (1970) *Democracy and Community: A Study of Politics in Sheffield* (Oxford University Press).

Hampton, W. (1987) *Local Government and Urban Politics* (Longman).

Hennock, E.P. (1973) *Fit and Proper Persons: Ideal and Reality in Nineteenth-Century Urban Government* (Edward Arnold).

HMSO (1960) *Royal Commission on Local Government in Greater London, 1957–60* (The Herbert Commission), Cmnd 1164.

HMSO (1967a) *Report of the Royal Commission on Local Government* (Redcliffe-Maud Report), Cmnd 4040.

HMSO (1967b) *Committee on the Management of Local Government*, Research Vol. III, *The Local Government Elector*.

HMSO (1969) *Royal Commission on Local Government in Scotland* (The Wheatley Commission), Cmnd 4159.

HMSO (1983) *Streamlining the Cities*, White Paper, Cmnd 9063.

HMSO (1986a) *Committee of Inquiry into the Conduct of Local Authority Business*, Research Vol. III, *The Local Government Elector*, Cmnd 9800.

HMSO (1986b) *Committee of Inquiry into the Conduct of Local Authority Business*, Research Vol. I, *The Political Organisation of Local Authorities*, Cmnd 9798, pp. 25, 197.

HMSO (1997) *Committee on Standards in Public Life*, Vol. II, *Standards of Conduct in Local Government in England and Wales*, Cmnd 3702 – II.

HMSO (1998) *Modern Local Government: In Touch with the People*, Cmnd 4014.

HMSO (1999) *Local Leadership: Local Choice*, Cmnd 4298.

HMSO (2001) Local Authorities (Model Code of Conduct) (England) Order 2001, Statutory Instrument 2001, No. 3575.

Institute for Public Policy Research (1991) *The Constitution of the United Kingdom*.

John, P. (1994) 'UK sub-national offices in Brussels: diversification or regionalism?', paper presented to the ESRC Research Seminar: British Regionalism and Devolution in a Single Europe, LSE.

John, P. (1996) 'Centralisation, decentralisation and the European Union: the dynamics of triadic relationships', *Public Administration*, Vol. 74, Summer, pp. 293–313.

Jones, G.W. (1969) *Borough Politics: A Study of Wolverhampton Borough Council 1888–1964* (Macmillan).

Keith-Lucas, B. (1952) *The English Local Government Franchise* (Basil Blackwell).

Labour Party (1995) *Renewing Democracy: Rebuilding Communities*.

Lee, J.M. (1963) *Social Leaders and Public Persons: A Study of County Government in Cheshire since 1888* (Clarendon Press).

Newton, K. (1976) *Second City Politics: Democratic Processes and Decision-Making in Birmingham* (Clarendon Press).

Office of the Deputy Prime Minister (2005) *Vibrant Local Leadership*.

Pimlott, B. and Rao, N. (2002) *Governing London* (Oxford University Press).

Preston, J. (1992a) 'Local government and the European Community', in S. George (ed.), *Britain and the European Community: The Politics of Semi-Detachment* (Clarendon Press).

Preston, J. (1992b) 'Local government', in S. Bulmer, S. George and J. Scott (eds), *The United Kingdom and EC Membership Evaluated* (Pinter).

Rallings, C. and Thrasher, M. (1997) *Local Elections in Britain* (Routledge).

(1999) *Regional Development Agencies and Regional Chambers* (Ludgate Public Affairs).

Rhodes, R.A.W., Hardy, B. and Pudney, K. (1983) *Power Dependence, Theories of Central–Local Relations: A Critical Assessment* (University of Essex, Department of Government).

Saunders, P. (1979) *Urban Politics: A Sociological Interpretation* (Hutchinson).

Stanyer, J. (1976) *Understanding Local Government* (Fontana).

Stewart, J. (1986) *The New Management of Local Government* (Allen & Unwin).

Stewart, J. (2003) *Modernising British Local Government: An Assessment of Labour's Reform Programme* (Palgrave).

Stoker, G. (1991) *The Politics of Local Government* (Macmillan).

Travers, T. (2004) *The Politics of London: Governing an Ungovernable City* (Palgrave).

Wilson, D. and Game, C. (2002) *Local Government in the United Kingdom*, 3rd edn (Palgrave Macmillan).

Wolman, H. and Goldsmith, M. (1992) *Urban Politics and Policy: A Comparative Approach* (Blackwell).

Young, K. (1973) 'The politics of London government 1880–1899', *Public Administration*, Vol. 51, No. 1, Spring, pp. 91–108.

Young, K. (1975) *Local Politics and the Rise of Party: The London Municipal Society and the Conservative Intervention in Local Elections 1894–1963* (Leicester University Press).

Young, K. (1989) 'Bright hopes and dark fears: the origins and expectations of the county councils', in K. Young (ed.), *New Directions for County Government* (Association of County Councils), p. 6.

Young, K. and Davis, M. (1990) *The Politics of Local Government Since Widdicombe* (Joseph Rowntree Foundation).

Young, K. and Laffin, M. (1990) *Professionalism in Local Government* (Longman).

Young, K. and Rao, N. (1997) *Local Government Since 1945* (Blackwell).

Useful websites

Office of the Deputy Prime Minister: odpm.gov.uk

Local Government Association: lga.gov.uk

Improvement and Development Agency: idea.gov.uk

Local Government Information Unit: lgiu.gov.uk

New Local Government Network: nlgn.org.uk

National constitutions: www.constitution.org

For a directory of all local council websites, try: tagish.co.uk/tagish/links/localgov.htm

The Labour Party: labour.org.uk

The Conservative Party: conservativeparty.org.uk

The Association of Liberal Democrat Councillors: aldc.org.uk

The Green Party: greenparty.org.uk

Local Government Elections centre: research.plymouth.ac.uk/elections

The National Standards Board: standardsboard.co.uk

The Lyons Inquiry: lyonsinquiry.org.uk

CHAPTER 23

The judiciary

Philip Norton

Learning objectives

- To identify the relationship of the judicial system to other parts of the political process.

- To describe the basic structure of that system, and how it has changed in recent years as a result of a greater willingness of judges to undertake judicial review, and as a consequence of constitutional change.

- To consider demands for change because of perceived weaknesses in the system.

Introduction

Britain does not have a system like the USA, where the Supreme Court acts as ultimate interpreter of the constitution and pronounces upon the constitutionality of federal and state laws together with the actions of public officials. Since 1688, British courts have been bound by the doctrine of parliamentary sovereignty. They have been viewed as subordinate to the Queen-in-Parliament and detached from the political process. However, the received wisdom has not always matched the reality, and recent years have witnessed a growth in judicial activism. British membership of the European Union has added a significant judicial dimension to the constitution. So too has the incorporation of the European Convention on Human Rights (ECHR) into British law and legislation providing for devolution of powers to elected bodies in different parts of the United Kingdom. There is also a significant change being brought about by the Constitutional Reform Act 2005. Under its provisions, a Supreme Court will be created in 2009. The UK will thus have a court that has a physical similarity to, though not the powers of, its US namesake. The courts are now important political actors. Recent years have also seen criticism of the way the courts dispense justice. This chapter explores the nature of the British judicial system and growing concern about its powers and competence.

■ The judicial process

The literature on the judicial process in Britain is extensive. Significantly, most of it is written by legal scholars: few works on the courts or judges come from the pens of political scientists. To those concerned with the study of British politics, and in particular the process of policy making, the judicial process has generally been deemed to be of peripheral interest.

That this perception should exist is not surprising. It derives from two features that are considered to be essential characteristics of the judiciary in Britain. First, in the trinity of the executive, legislature and judiciary, it is a subordinate institution. Public policy is made and ratified elsewhere. The courts exist to interpret (within defined limits) and apply that policy once enacted by the legislature; they have no intrinsic power to strike it down. Second, it is autonomous. The independence of the judiciary is a much vaunted and essential feature of the rule of law, described by the great nineteenth-century constitutional lawyer A.V. Dicey as one of the twin pillars of the British constitution. The other pillar – parliamentary sovereignty – accounts for the first characteristic, the subordination of the judiciary to Parliament. Allied with autonomy has been the notion of political neutrality. Judges seek to interpret the law according to judicial norms that operate independently of partisan or personal preferences.

Given these characteristics – politically neutral courts separate from, and subordinate to, the central agency of law enactment – a clear demarcation has arisen in recent decades, the study of the policy-making process being the preserve of political scientists, that of the judiciary the preserve of legal scholars. Some scholars – such as J.A.G. Griffith, formerly Professor of Law at the University of London – have sought to bridge the gap, but they have been notable for their rarity. Yet in practice the judiciary in Britain has not been as subordinate or as autonomous as the prevailing wisdom assumes. The dividing line between politics and the law is blurred rather than rigid and it is becoming more blurred.

■ A subordinate branch?

Under the doctrine of parliamentary sovereignty, the judiciary lacks the intrinsic power to strike down an Act of Parliament as being contrary to the provisions of the constitution or any other superior body of law. It was not always thus. Prior to the Glorious Revolution of 1688, the supremacy of **statute law** was not clearly established. In *Dr Bonham's Case* in 1610, Chief Justice Coke asserted that 'when an Act of Parliament is against common right and reason, or repugnant, or impossible to be performed, the common law will control it, and adjudge such act to

The Scales of Justice, on top of the Old Bailey building in London, symbolise the machinery of British justice
Source: Ian McKinnell / Alamy

be void.' A few years later, in *Judge* v. *Savadge* (1625), Chief Justice Hobart declared that an Act 'made against natural equity, as to make a man judge in his own case' would be void. Statute law had to compete not only with principles of common law developed by the courts but also with the prerogative power of the King. The courts variously upheld the power of the King to dispense with statutes and to impose taxes without the consent of Parliament.

The Glorious Revolution put an end to this state of affairs. Thereafter, the supremacy of statute law, under the doctrine of parliamentary sovereignty, was established. The doctrine is a judicially self-imposed one. The common lawyers allied themselves with Parliament in its struggle to control the **prerogative** powers of the King and the prerogative courts through which he sometimes exercised them. The supremacy of Parliament was asserted by the Bill of Rights of 1689. 'For the common lawyers, there was a price to pay, and that was the abandonment of the claim that they had sometimes advanced, that Parliament could not legislate in derogation of the principles of the common law' (Munro, 1987, p. 81). Parliamentary sovereignty – a purely legal doctrine asserting the supremacy of statute law – became the central tenet of the constitution (see Chapter 15). However, the subordination of the common law to law passed by Parliament did not – and does not – entail the subordination of the judiciary to the executive. Courts retain the power of interpreting the precise meaning of the law once passed by Parliament and of reviewing the actions of ministers and other public agents to determine whether those actions are *ultra vires*, that is, beyond the powers granted by statute. The courts can quash the actions of ministers that purport to be, but that on the court's interpretation are not, sanctioned by such Acts.

If a government has a particular action struck down as *ultra vires*, it may seek parliamentary approval for a bill that gives statutory force to the action taken; in other words, to give legal force to that which the courts have declared as having – on the basis of existing statutes – no such force. But seeking passage of such a bill is not only time-consuming; it can also prove to be politically contentious and publicly damaging. It conveys the impression that the government, having lost a case, is trying to change the rules of the game. Although it is a path that governments have variously taken, it is one they prefer to – and often do – avoid.

The power of judicial review thus provides the judiciary with a potentially significant role in the policy cycle. It is a potential that for much of the past century has not been realised. However, recent decades have seen an upsurge in judicial activism, judges being far more willing both to review and to quash ministerial actions. The scope for judicial activism has also been enlarged by three other developments: British membership of the European Union, the incorporation of the European Convention on Human Rights (ECHR) into British law and the devolution of powers to elected assemblies in different parts of the UK. Indeed, the first two of these developments have served to undermine the doctrine of parliamentary sovereignty, giving to the courts a new role in the political process. Whether they wanted to or not, the courts now find themselves playing a more central role in the determination of public policy. That role is likely to become more visible as the highest court of appeal ceases to be the House of Lords (in other words, the law lords) and, in 2009, becomes a Supreme Court, housed in its own building in Parliament Square.

■ An autonomous branch?

The judiciary is deemed to be independent of the other two branches of government. Its independence is, in the words of one leading textbook, 'secured by law, by professional and public opinion' (Wade and Bradley, 1993, p. 60). Since the Act of Settlement, senior judges hold office 'during good behaviour' and can be removed by the Queen following an address by both Houses of Parliament (see Jackson and Leopold, 2001, pp. 433–4). (Only one judge has ever been removed by such a process. Jonah Barrington, an Irish judge, was removed in 1830 after it was found that he had misappropriated litigants' money and had ceased to perform his judicial duties.) Judges of inferior courts enjoy a lesser degree of statutory protection. Judges' salaries are a charge upon the consolidated fund: this means that they do not have to be voted upon each year by Parliament. By its own resolution, the House of Commons generally bars any reference made by MPs to matters awaiting or under adjudication in criminal and most civil cases. By convention, a similar prohibition is observed by ministers and civil servants.

For their part, judges by convention refrain from politically partisan activity. Indeed, they have generally refrained from commenting on matters of public policy, doing so not only of their own volition but also for many years by the direction of the Lord Chancellor. The Kilmuir guidelines issued in 1955 enjoined judges to silence, since 'every utterance which he [a judge] makes in public, except in the course of the actual performance of his judicial duties, must necessarily bring him within the focus of criticism.' These guidelines were relaxed in the late 1970s but then effectively reimposed by the Lord Chancellor, Lord Hailsham, in 1980. For judges to interfere in a contentious issue of public policy, one that is not under adjudication, would – it was felt – undermine public confidence in the impartiality of the judiciary. Similarly, for politicians to interfere in a matter before the courts would be seen as a challenge to the rule of law. Hence the perceived self-interests of both in confining themselves to their own spheres of activity.

However, historically the dividing line between judges and politicians – and, to a lesser extent, between judicial and political decision making – is not quite as sharp as these various features would suggest. In terms of personnel, memberships of the executive, legislature and judiciary are not mutually exclusive. Particularly in the higher reaches, there has been some overlap. The most obvious and outstanding example is to be found in the figure of the Lord Chancellor. Prior to the passage of the Constitutional Reform Act 2005, he was head of the judiciary, the presiding officer of the House of Lords, and a member of the Cabinet. The 2005 Act changed this situation, providing for the transfer of his judicial role to the Lord Chief Justice – the transfer took place in 2006 – and enabling someone other than a peer and senior lawyer to hold the post. The post of Lord Chancellor remains, as a conjoined role with that of Secretary of State for Constitutional Affairs, and has responsibility for the management of the courts system.

Other executive office holders with judicial appointments are the Law Officers: the Attorney General and the Solicitor General. They lead for the crown in major court cases as well as serving as legal advisers to the government. Within government, the legal opinion of the Law Officers carries great weight and, by convention, is treated in confidence. In a parliamentary debate in 2005, the government made clear that it had no plans to change the position.

The highest court of appeal in the United Kingdom is, until 2009, the House of Lords. For judicial purposes, this constitutes an appellate committee of the House, comprising the law lords – appointed to the House for the purpose of fulfilling its judicial

functions – and peers who have held high judicial office. (It has been a convention since 1844 that no other peers should take part in the appellate work of the House.) Some Members of Parliament serve or have served as recorders (part-time but salaried judges in the Crown Court) and several sit as local magistrates. Judges in the High Court, Court of Appeal and Court of Session are barred by statute from membership of the Commons, and any MP appointed to a judgeship becomes ineligible to remain in the House. No such prohibition exists in the case of the House of Lords, and a number of members of the House hold judicial posts.

Although those holding political office seek as far as possible to draw a clear dividing line between political and judicial activity, that line cannot always be maintained. At times, they have to take judicial or quasi-judicial decisions. However, they remain members of an executive accountable, unlike judges, to Parliament. This remains the case with the Law Officers. (There are separate law officers for

Lord Irvine of Lairg was Lord Chancellor, 1997–2003; he attracted controversy, especially for his expensive choice of wallpaper for refurbishing his apartment
Source: Copyright © Corbis Sygma

Scotland.) It used to be the case also with the Lord Chancellor and, to some extent, the Home Secretary, who exercised quasi-judicial functions, but the functions involved in both cases have now been transferred to the courts. The Attorney General may intervene to prevent prosecutions being proceeded with if he considers such action to be in the public interest. Under powers introduced in 1989, he may refer to the Appeal Court sentences that appear to the prosecuting authorities to be unduly lenient. He also has responsibility in certain cases for initiating proceedings, for example under the Official Secrets Act, and although he takes decisions in such matters independently of his government colleagues, he remains answerable to Parliament for his decisions. These powers, along with the Attorney's role as legal adviser to the government, can bring the Law Officers into the realms of political controversy. This was the case most notably with the Attorney General's advice to the government in 2003 that it was lawful for it to commit troops to the invasion of Iraq. Some lawyers questioned the legality of the war, and rumours that the Attorney's advice had raised some doubts about the legality led to demands that it be published – the advice is normally confidential – and led eventually to it being put in the public domain.

Judges themselves do not completely stand apart from public controversy. Because they are detached from political life and can consider issues impartially, they are variously invited to chair public inquiries into the causes of particular disasters or scandals and to make recommendations on future action. This practice has been employed for many years. Recent examples have included the inquiries into the collapse of the BCCI bank (Sir Thomas Bingham, 1991), into standards in public life (Lord Nolan, 1995), into the sale of arms-making equipment to Iraq (Sir Richard Scott, 1996), into the police handling of the murder of black teenager Stephen Lawrence (Sir William Macpherson of Cluny, 1999), into the shootings during 'Bloody Sunday' in Northern Ireland (Lord Saville of Newdigate, 2001–), and into the death of Dr David Kelly (Lord Hutton, 2003–4). The inquiries or the reports that they issue are often known by the name of the judge who led the inquiry (the Nolan Committee, the Scott Report, the Hutton Report). The reports are sometimes highly controversial and may lead to criticism of the judge involved (see McEldowney, 1996, p. 138). One irate Conservative MP berated Lord Nolan outside the Palace of Westminster in 1995, and his report was the subject of heated debate in the House of Commons. Sir Richard Scott was heavily criticised by many Conservative MPs and by a former Foreign Secretary, Lord Howe of Aberavon, for the way he conducted his inquiry. Lord Hutton's report, which led to the resignation of the director general of the BBC (Greg Dyke), was largely discredited when a subsequent report (the Butler report) found that there had been significant changes to the government's dossier making the case for war with Iraq.

Judges themselves have also been more willing in recent years to enter public debate of their own volition. The past decade or so has seen a tendency on the part of several judges to justify their actions publicly, and in 1988 Lord Chancellor Mackay allowed some relaxation of the Kilmuir rules in order that judges may give interviews. One judge in particular – Judge Pickles – made use of the opportunity to appear frequently on television. A greater willingness to comment on issues of public policy has also been apparent on the part of the most senior judges. The appointment of Lord Justice Bingham as Master of the Rolls and Lord Justice Taylor as Lord Chief Justice in 1992 heralded a new era of openness. Both proved willing to express views on public policy, both advocating the incorporation of the European Convention on Human Rights into British law. Taylor not only gave press interviews but also used the floor of the House of Lords to criticise government policy. In 1995, he addressed the Leeds Race Issues Advisory Committee on 'Race and Criminal Justice'. He retired in 1996 on health grounds to be succeeded by Bingham. Bingham's successor as Master of the Rolls, Lord Justice Woolf, maintained the practice of giving interviews. One of his first acts was to appear on a Sunday lunchtime current affairs programme. In 2000, Bingham was made the senior Law Lord (see biography) and he was succeeded as Lord Chief Justice by Lord Woolf.

Thus, although the two generalisations that the judiciary constitutes a subordinate and autonomous branch of government – subordinate to the outputs of Parliament (Acts of Parliament) but autonomous in deciding cases – remain broadly correct, both are in need of some qualification. The courts are neither as powerless nor as totally independent as the assertion would imply. For the student of politics, the judiciary is therefore an appropriate subject for study. What, then, is the structure of the judicial system in Britain? Who are the people who occupy it? To what extent has the judiciary become more active in recent years in reviewing the actions of government? What has been the effect of membership

BIOGRAPHY

Lord Bingham, the senior law lord (1933–)

Source: Empics Sports
Photo Agency

Thomas Bingham was born in Surrey and was head boy of Sedbergh School before going on to read history at Balliol College, Oxford, where he graduated with a first. He studied law and came top in his Bar finals in 1959. He joined the liberal legal chambers of Lord Scarman. In 1972, at the age of 38, he became a Queen's Counsel and three years later was appointed a Crown Court Recorder.

Bingham achieved public prominence in 1977 when he was appointed to investigate alleged breaches of sanctions against Rhodesia by UK companies. Three years later, he became a High Court judge and was knighted. He was appointed to the Court of Appeal in 1986. In 1991 he conducted another inquiry, this time into the collapse of the Bank of Credit and Commerce International (BCCI). He attracted criticism for taking evidence in private, though this did not dent his reputation or his advancement. The following year he was appointed Master of the Rolls. He achieved a reputation as a reformer, arguing the case for the incorporation of the European Convention on Human Rights into British law.

On 4 June 1996, he became Lord Chief Justice at the age of 62. His appointment was considered unconventional in that his career was not forged in the criminal courts. He was keen to cut the costs and delays of the legal system and to make courts more accessible. He took part in debates in the House of Lords to raise issues of concern to the judiciary. He took part in the proceedings on the Access to Justice Bill in 1998 and 1999, speaking during the second reading debate, raising 'three matters central to the Bill on which acute concern is felt by my judicial colleagues'.

In 2000, he was appointed as senior law lord, an unexpected change that was interpreted as intended to strengthen the highest domestic court of appeal. Another law lord, by reason of seniority, would otherwise have assumed the position. Bingham favoured the creation of a dedicated Supreme Court, with its own building and infrastructure, and such a court is now provided for under the Constitutional Reform Act 2005.

His wife has been politically active, campaigning for the Liberal Democrats. He likes modern art and brisk walks. In 2003, he was a candidate for the Chancellorship of Oxford University.

of the EC/EU, the incorporation of the ECHR into British law, and of devolution? And what pressure is there for change?

■ The courts

Apart from a number of specialised courts and tribunals, the organisational division of courts is that between **criminal law** and **civil law**. The basic structure of the court system in England and Wales is shown in Figure 23.1. (Scotland and Northern Ireland have different systems.) Minor criminal cases are tried in the magistrates' courts, minor civil cases in county courts. Figure 23.1 also shows the higher courts that try serious cases and the routes through which appeals may be heard. The higher courts – the Crown Court, the High Court and the Court of Appeal – are known collectively, if confusingly, as the Supreme Court. This nomenclature will cease once the new Supreme Court comes into being in 2009. At the head of the system, at least until 2009, stands the House of Lords.

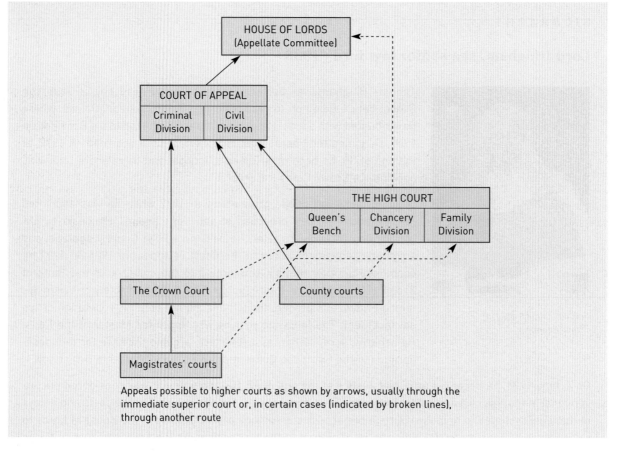

Appeals possible to higher courts as shown by arrows, usually through the immediate superior court or, in certain cases (indicated by broken lines), through another route

Figure 23.1 The court system in England and Wales

Criminal cases

About 98 per cent of criminal cases in England and Wales are tried in magistrates' courts. This constitutes each year almost two million cases. (The number was higher before 1987 but dropped following the introduction of fixed-penalty fines for summary motoring offences.) The courts have power to levy fines, the amount depending on the offence, and to impose prison sentences not exceeding six months. The largest single numbers of cases tried by magistrates' courts are motoring offences. Other offences tried by the courts range from allowing animals to stray onto a highway and tattooing a minor to burglary, assault, causing cruelty to children and wounding. It takes on average between 100 and 130 days from the offence taking place for it to be tried. Once before a court, a majority of minor offences are each disposed of in a matter of minutes; in some cases, in which the defendant has pleaded guilty, in a matter of seconds.

Magistrates themselves are of two types: professional and lay. Professional magistrates are now known, under the provisions of the 1999 Access to Justice Act, as district judges (magistrates' courts); they were previously known as stipendiary magistrates. They are legally qualified and serve on a full-time basis. They sit alone when hearing cases. At 1 January 2005, there were 124 of them. Lay magistrates are part-time and, as the name implies, are not legally qualified, although they do receive some training. Lay magistrates are drawn from the ranks of the public, typically those with the time to devote to such public duty (for example, housewives, local professional and retired people), and they sit as a bench of between two and seven in order to hear cases, advised by a legally qualified clerk. They constitute the largest of the two categories. At the beginning of 2005, there were just over 28,000. Cities and larger towns tend to have district judges (magistrates' courts); the rest of England and Wales relies on lay magistrates.

Until 1986, the decision whether to prosecute – and the prosecution itself – was undertaken by the police. Since 1986, the Crown Prosecution Service (CPS), headed by the Director of Public Prosecutions, has been responsible for the independent review and prosecution of all criminal cases instituted by police forces in England and Wales, with certain specified exceptions. In Scotland, responsibility for prosecution rests with the Crown Office and Procurator Fiscal Service. Members of this service – like the CPS in England and Wales – are lawyers.

Appeals from decisions of magistrates' courts may be taken to the Crown Court or, in matrimonial cases, to the Family Division of the High Court, or – on points of law – to the Queen's Bench Division of the High Court. In practice, appeals are rare: fewer than 1 per cent of those convicted appeal against conviction or sentence. The cost of pursuing an appeal would, in the overwhelming majority of cases, far exceed the fine imposed. The time of the Crown Court is taken up instead with hearing the serious cases – known as indictable offences – which are subject to a jury trial and to penalties beyond those that a magistrates' court can impose. In 2004, just over 79,000 cases went to the Crown Court.

The Crown Court is divided into six court circuits and a total of around 90 courts. The most serious cases will be presided over by a High Court judge, the most senior position within the court; a circuit judge or a recorder will hear other cases. High Court and circuit judges are full-time, salaried judges; recorders are legally qualified but part-time, pursuing their normal legal practice when not engaged on court duties.

Appeals from conviction in a Crown Court may be taken on a point of law to the Queen's Bench Division of the High Court but usually are taken to the Criminal Division of the Court of Appeal. Appeals against conviction are possible on a point of law and on a point of fact, the former as a matter of right and the latter with the leave of the trial judge or the Court of Appeal. Approximately 10 per cent of those convicted in a Crown Court usually appeal. In 2004, for example, the Court of Appeal dealt with 7,591 appeals. The Appeal Court may quash a conviction, uphold it or vary the sentence imposed by the lower courts. Appeals against sentence – as opposed to the conviction itself – are also possible with the leave of the Appeal Court and, as we have already seen, the Attorney General now has the power to refer to the court sentences that appear to be unduly lenient. In cases referred by the Attorney General, the court has the power to increase the length of the sentence imposed by the lower court.

The Court of Appeal consists of judges known as Lords Justices of Appeal and four judges who are members *ex officio* (the Lord Chief Justice, the Master of the Rolls, the President of the Family Division of the High Court and the Vice-Chancellor of the Chancery Division), although the composition varies from the criminal to the civil division. Appeals in criminal cases are usually heard by three judges. Although presided over by the Lord Chief Justice or a Lord Justice, judges of the Queen's Bench may also sit on the court.

From the Court of Appeal, a further appeal is possible to the House of Lords if the court certifies that a point of law of general public importance is involved and it appears to the court, or to the Lords, that the point ought to be considered by the highest domestic court of appeal. For the purposes of such an appeal, the House of Lords – as we have seen – does not comprise all members of the House but rather a judicial committee (the Appellate Committee). The work of the committee is undertaken by the law lords, known as Lords of Appeal in Ordinary (appointed to the Lords in order to carry out this judicial function), and those members of the Lords who have held high judicial office. Between five and eleven will sit to hear a case (in practice, it is usually five and in exceptional cases seven), the hearing taking place in a committee room of the House of Lords but with the judgement itself being delivered in the chamber. Before 1966, the House considered itself bound by precedent (that is, by its own previous decisions); in 1966, the law lords announced that they would no longer consider themselves bound by their previous decisions, being prepared to depart from them when it seemed right to do so.

One other judicial body should also be mentioned. It does not figure in the normal court structure. That is the Judicial Committee of the Privy Council, essentially a product of the country's colonial history. This committee was set up in 1833 to exercise the power of the Privy Council in deciding appeals from colonial, ecclesiastical and admiralty courts. Its composition is more or less the same as the Appellate Committee of the House of Lords. Three to five Lords of Appeal in Ordinary sit, and the committee also includes those who have held high judicial office. Most of its functions have disappeared over time, but it has retained a limited role in considering particular appeals in certain criminal cases from a number of Commonwealth countries and from certain domestic bodies, such as disciplinary committees in the medical, veterinary and other healthcare professions. However, as we shall see, it has assumed a new – though, in the event, short-lived – significance as a consequence of devolution. Legal challenges to the powers exercised by the Scottish Parliament and the Welsh Assembly are heard by the Judicial Committee. These powers, however, will pass to the new Supreme Court in 2009.

Civil cases

In civil proceedings, some minor cases (for example, involving the summary recovery of some debts) are dealt with in magistrates' courts. However, most cases involving small sums of money are heard by county courts; more important cases are heard in the High Court.

County courts are presided over by circuit judges. The High Court is divided into three divisions, dealing with **common law** (the Queen's Bench Division), equity (Chancery Division) and domestic cases (Family Division). The Court comprises the three judges who head each division and just over eighty judges known as puisne (pronounced 'puny') judges. In most cases judges sit alone, although a Divisional Court of two or three may be formed, especially in the Queen's Bench Division, to hear applications for writs of *habeas corpus* and writs requiring a public body to fulfil a particular duty (*mandamus*), to desist from carrying out an action for which it has no legal authority (prohibition) and to quash a decision already taken (*certiorari*). Jury trials are possible in certain cases tried in the Queen's Bench Division (for example, involving malicious prosecution or defamation of character) but are now rare.

Appeals from magistrates' courts and from county courts are heard by Divisional Courts of the High Court: appeals from magistrates' courts on points of law, for example, go to a Divisional Court of the Queen's Bench Division. From the High Court – and certain cases in county courts – appeals are taken to the Civil Division of the Court of Appeal. In the Appeal Court, cases are normally heard by the Master of the Rolls sitting with two Lords Justices of Appeal.

From the Court of Appeal, an appeal may be taken – with the leave of the Court or the House – to the House of Lords. In rare cases, on a point of law of exceptional difficulty calling for a reconsideration of a binding precedent, an appeal may go directly, with the leave of the House, from the High Court to the House of Lords.

Cases brought against ministers or other public bodies for taking actions that are beyond their powers (*ultra vires*) will normally be heard in the Queen's Bench Division of the High Court before being taken – in the event of an appeal – to the Court of Appeal and the House of Lords. Thus, in 1993, when Lord Rees-Mogg brought an action challenging the powers of the government to ratify the Maastricht Treaty (see Box 23.1), the case was heard in the Queen's Bench Division before three Lords Justices.

BOX 23.1   **EXAMPLE**

Challenging the Maastricht Treaty

In the United Kingdom, ratification of a treaty is a prerogative power (see Chapter 15). An Act of Parliament is only necessary where provisions of the treaty are intended to have the force of law in the UK. Thus, the 1972 European Communities Act was not a measure to ratify the treaty of accession to the Community but an Act to give effect to what was described as 'the legal nuts and bolts' necessary for membership.

However, Parliament made a change in 1978 when it passed the European Assembly Elections Act. Section 6 of the Act stipulated that 'No treaty which provides for an increase in the powers of the European Parliament shall be ratified by the United Kingdom unless it has been approved by an Act of Parliament'. In 1991, the Maastricht Treaty, designed to achieve economic and monetary union, increased the powers of the European Parliament. As a result, ratification in the UK required an Act of Parliament. The European Communities (Amendment) Bill was introduced in 1992 and, after a difficult parliamentary passage, received the Royal Assent in July 1993.

Shortly before the bill received the Royal Assent, an opponent of the Treaty, Lord Rees-Mogg (a former editor of *The Times*), launched a legal challenge. He claimed that the government would be in breach of the 1978 Act if it ratified the treaty because Parliament had approved the Treaty but not the protocols attached to it, and the social protocol would increase the power of the European Parliament. He also claimed that the government had no lawful prerogative to ratify the social protocol, because it would alter the Treaty of Rome, which, as a fundamental part of domestic law, required parliamentary approval. And he further claimed that the crown had no lawful prerogative to transfer elements of Britain's foreign and security policy to the European Community, as the fundamental prerogatives of the crown could not be transferred to some other person.

Lord Rees-Mogg claimed that it was the 'most important constitutional issue to be faced by the courts for 300 years'. He was granted leave to seek a review by the High Court. The action of the courts in giving him leave was then challenged in the House of Commons by Labour MP Tony Benn, who claimed that it was a breach of privilege as the bill had not yet been passed by Parliament. The Speaker, Betty Boothroyd, ruled that it was not a breach but, unusually, read a statement giving her reasons for so ruling. The sole basis for her decision, she emphasised, was because the bill had already gone to the House of Lords when Lord Rees-Mogg made his legal challenge. However, she reminded the courts of the Bill of Rights of 1689, stating that the proceedings of Parliament could not be challenged by the courts.

The case of *Regina* v. *Secretary of State for Foreign and Commonwealth Affairs, ex parte Rees-Mogg* was heard in the High Court by a Divisional Court of the Queen's Bench Division comprising Lord Justice Lloyd, Lord Justice Mann and Mr Justice Auld. On 30 July 1993, Lord Justice Lloyd delivered the twenty-two-page judgement of the court. The court, he said, had heard nothing to support or even suggest that by bringing the proceedings the applicant had trespassed on the privileges of Parliament, and while it was an important case it was an exaggeration to describe it as the most important constitutional case for 300 years. On the three arguments advanced by counsel for Lord Rees-Mogg, the court rejected each one. The fact that the protocols were annexed to the treaty did not show that they were not also part of the treaty. The construction of section 2 of the 1993 Act allowed incorporation of the protocols. On the second point, the social protocol was not intended to apply in UK law. The argument that it might have some indirect effect in UK law was too slender a basis on which to hold that Parliament had implicitly excluded or curtailed the crown's prerogative to alter or add to the Treaty of Rome. On the third point, the part of the treaty that established a common foreign and security policy among member states was an inter-governmental agreement that could have no impact on UK domestic law. Title V of the 1993 Act could not be read as a transfer of prerogative powers. It was an exercise of those powers. In the last resort, it would presumably be open to the government to denounce the treaty or fail to comply with its inter-national obligations under Title V. In so far as the point was justiciable, their Lordships ruled that it failed on the merits.

After the judgement was delivered, Lord Rees-Mogg said he would give careful thought as to whether to appeal. However, given that the judgement of the court had been unanimous and had comprehensively rejected the points advanced by counsel for him, the chances of achieving a reversal on appeal appeared slim, and he soon announced that he would not be pursuing the case. Consequently, the government – which had said it would not ratify the Maastricht Treaty until the legal challenge was out of the way – moved promptly and ratified it.

Tribunals

Many if not most citizens are probably affected by decisions taken by public bodies, for example those determining eligibility for particular benefits or compensation for compulsory purchase. The postwar years have seen the growth of administrative law, providing the legal framework within which such decisions are taken and the procedure by which disputes may be resolved.

To avoid disputes over particular administrative decisions being taken to the existing, highly formalised civil courts – overburdening the courts and creating significant financial burdens for those involved – the law provides for a large number of tribunals to resolve such disputes. There are now tribunals covering a wide range of issues, including unfair dismissal, rents, social security benefits, immigration, mental health and compensation for compulsory purchase. Those appearing before tribunals will often have the opportunity to present their own case and to call witnesses and cross-examine the other side. The tribunal itself will normally – although not always – comprise three members, although the composition varies from tribunal to tribunal: some have lay members, others have legally (or otherwise professionally) qualified members; some have part-time members, others have full-time members. Employment tribunals, for example, each comprise an independent chairman and two members drawn from either side of industry.

Tribunals offer the twin advantages of speed and cheapness. As far as possible the formalities of normal courts are avoided. Costs tend to be significant only in the case of an appeal.

The activities of tribunals are normally dull and little noticed. On rare occasions, though, decisions may have political significance. In January 1996, an employment tribunal in Leeds held that the policy of the Labour Party to have women-only short lists for some parliamentary seats breached sex discrimination legislation. Rather than pursue an appeal, which could take up to twenty months to be heard, the party decided not to proceed with such short lists.

The judges

At the apex of the judicial system stands the Lord Chancellor and the Law Officers. As we have seen, these are political appointments and the holders are members of the government. Below them are the professional judges. The most senior are the law lords, the Lords of Appeal in Ordinary, at present twelve in number. They are appointed by the crown on the advice of the Prime Minister, and they must have held high judicial office for at least two years. By virtue of their position they are members of the House of Lords, and they remain members even after ceasing to hold their judicial position. Indeed, they constitute the earliest form of life peers, the first Lord of Appeal in Ordinary being created under the provisions of the Appellate Jurisdiction Act of 1876.

The other most senior judicial appointments – the Lord Chief Justice (head of the Appeal Court in criminal cases), Master of the Rolls (head of the Appeal Court in civil cases), President of the Family Division and the Lords Justices of Appeal – are also made by the crown on the advice of the Prime Minister. In practice, the Prime Minister's scope is restricted. The Lords Justices are drawn from High Court judges or from barristers of at least ten years' standing, although solicitors are now also eligible for consideration. Other judges – High Court judges, circuit judges and recorders – are drawn principally from barristers of at least ten years' standing, although solicitors and circuit court judges may be appointed to the High Court.

The attraction in becoming a judge lies only partially in the salary (see Table 23.1) – the top earners among barristers can achieve annual incomes of several hundred thousand pounds. Rather, the attraction lies in the status that attaches to holding

Table 23.1 Judicial salaries, 2004–5

Position	Annual salary (£) from	
	April 2004	**April 2005**
Lord Chief Justice	205,242	211,399
Master of the Rolls/senior Law Lord	185,705	191,276
Law Lords	179,431	184,814
Lords Justices of Appeal	170,554	175,671
High Court judges	150,878	155,404
Senior Circuit Court judges	122,139	125,803
District judges		

Source: Adapted from the Department of Constitution Affairs website (www.dca.gov.uk/judicial/2004salfr.htm). © Crown Copyright 2005. Crown copyright material is reproduced with the permission of the Controller of Her Majesty's Stationery Office (HMSO)

Table 23.2 Gender of senior judges, October 2004

Position	Male	Female	Total
Lords of Appeal in Ordinary	11	1	12
Lords Justices of Appeal	31	2	33
High Court Judges	94	10	104
Circuit Judges	481	56	537
Total	617	69	686

Source: Adapted from the Department of Constitutional Affairs website (www.dca.gov.uk/judicial/ethmin.htm). © Crown Copyright 2005. Crown copyright material is reproduced with the permission of the Controller of Her Majesty's Stationery Office (HMSO)

a position at the top of one's profession. For many barristers, the ultimate goal is to become Lord Chief Justice, Master of the Rolls or a law lord.

Judges, by the nature of their calling, are expected to be somewhat detached from the rest of society. However, critics – such as J.A.G. Griffith, in *The Politics of the Judiciary* (5th edn, 1997) – contend that this professional distance is exacerbated by social exclusivity, judges being predominantly elderly upper-class males.

Although statutory retirement ages have been introduced, they are generous in relation to the normal retirement age: High Court judges retire at age 75, circuit judges at 72. Less than 8 per cent of judges of the High Court and above are female (see Table 23.2). In 2004, there was only one female law lord – Baroness Hale of Richmond, the first ever female law lord – and two women among thirty-three Lords Justices of Appeal. And as Table 23.2 reveals, of 104 judges of the High Court, only ten were women. The position improves marginally at the level of circuit judges, where just over 10 per cent are female. Those from ethnic minority backgrounds are even scarcer: one High Court judge and six circuit judges.

In their educational backgrounds, judges are also remarkably similar. The majority went to public school (among law lords and Lords Justices, the proportion exceeds 80 per cent) and the vast majority graduated from Oxford and Cambridge Universities; more than 80 per cent of circuit judges did so, and the proportion increases the further one goes up the judicial hierarchy.

Senior judgeships are the almost exclusive preserve of barristers. It is possible – just – for solicitors to become judges. However, few have taken this route: in 1999, two out of ninety-eight High Court judges were drawn from the ranks of solicitors. The

proportion of solicitors is greater among the ranks of circuit judges: just over 13 per cent are solicitors.

Judges thus form a socially and professionally exclusive or near-exclusive body. This exclusivity has been attacked for having unfortunate consequences. One is that judges are out of touch with society itself, not being able to understand the habits and terminology of everyday life, reflecting instead the social mores of thirty or forty years ago. The male-oriented nature of the judiciary has led to claims that judges are insufficiently sensitive in cases involving women, especially rape cases. The background of the judges has also led to allegations of in-built bias – towards the government of the day and towards the Conservative Party. Senior judges, according to Griffith (1997), construe the public interest as favouring law and order and upholding the interests of the state.

Though Griffith's claim about political bias has not been pursued by many other writers, the effect of gender and social exclusivity has been a cause of concern among jurists as well as ministers. Such concern exists at a time when the judiciary has become more active. There has been a greater willingness on the part of judges to review the actions of ministers (Stevens, 2003, pp. 358–9). There has also been increased activity arising from the UK's membership of the European Community/Union. The incorporation of the ECHR into British law and the creation of devolved assemblies have also widened the scope for judicial activity. In combination, these developments have raised the courts in Britain to a new level of political activity – and visibility.

■ Judicial activism

The common law power available to judges to strike down executive actions as being beyond powers granted – *ultra vires* – or as contrary to natural law was not much in evidence in the decades prior to the 1960s. Courts were generally deferential in their stance towards government. This was to change in the period from the mid-1960s onwards. Although the judiciary changed hardly at all in terms of the background of judges – they were usually the same elderly, white, Oxbridge-educated males as before – there was a significant change in attitudes. Apparently worried by the perceived encroachment of government on individual liberties, they proved increasingly willing to use their powers of judicial review.

The Law Lords criticise the Home Secretary's proposed anti-terror legislation
Source: Copyright © Chris Riddell. From *The Observer*, 19 December 2004. Reproduced with permission from Guardian Newspapers Limited

In four cases in the 1960s, the courts adopted an activist line in reviewing the exercise of powers by administrative bodies and, in two instances, of ministers. In *Conway* v. *Rimmer* in 1968, the House of Lords ruled against a claim of the Home Secretary that the production of certain documents would be contrary to the public interest; previously, such a claim would have been treated as definitive. Another case in the same year involved the House of Lords considering why, and not just how, a ministerial decision was made. It was a demonstration, noted Lord Scarman (1974, p. 49), that judges were 'ready to take an activist line'.

This activist line has been maintained and, indeed, become more prominent. Successive governments have found ministerial actions overturned by the courts. There were four celebrated cases in the second half of the 1970s in which the courts found against Labour ministers (Norton, 1982, pp. 138–40), and then several in the 1980s and the 1990s, when they found against Conservative ministers.

Perceptions of greater judicial activism derive not just from the cases that have attracted significant media attention. They also derive from the sheer number of applications for **judicial review** made to the courts (Stevens, 2003, p. 358). At the beginning of the 1980s, there were about 500 applications a year for leave to apply for judicial review. The figure grew throughout the decade, exceeding 1,000 in 1985, 1,500 in 1987 and 2,000 in 1990. In the 1990s, it generally exceeded 3,000 and in 1998 it reached 4,539. The annual figure has since remained in excess of 4,000. In 2004 there were 4,207 applications. 'Judicial review was the boom stock of the 1980s', declared Lord Bingham in 1995. 'Unaffected by recession, the boom has roared on into the 1990s.' The figures show that it roared on into the new century.

Each year, a number of cases have attracted media attention and been politically significant. In 1993, as we have already noted, Lord Rees-Mogg challenged the power of the government to ratify the Maastricht Treaty. His case was rejected by a

Divisional Court of the Queen's Bench Division. The same month – July 1993 – saw the House of Lords find a former Home Secretary, acting in his official ministerial capacity, in contempt of court for failing to comply with a court order in an asylum case. The ruling meant that ministers could not rely on the doctrine of crown immunity to ignore the orders of a court. *The Times* reported (28 July 1993):

Five law lords declared yesterday that ministers cannot put themselves above the law as they found the former home secretary Kenneth Baker guilty of contempt of court in an asylum case. The historic ruling on Crown immunity was described as one of the most important constitutional findings for two hundred years and hailed as establishing a key defence against the possible rise of a ruthless government in the future.

Ironically, the case was largely overshadowed by attention given to the unsuccessful case pursued by Lord Rees-Mogg. Kenneth Baker's successor as Home Secretary, Michael Howard, also variously ran foul of the courts, the Appeal Court holding that he had acted beyond his powers. Indeed, tension between government and the courts increased notably in 1995 and 1996 as several cases went against the Home Secretary (Woodhouse, 1996). In 1995, a criminal injuries compensation scheme he had introduced was declared unlawful by the House of Lords. A delay in referring parole applications by a number of prisoners serving life sentences was held by the High Court to be unreasonable. In July 1996, the court found that he had acted unlawfully in taking into account a public petition and demands from members of the public in increasing the minimum sentence to be served by two minors who had murdered the two-year-old Jamie Bulger. Nor were cases confined to the period of Conservative government. After the return of the Labour government in 1997, Home Secretary Jack Straw (1997–2001) and his successor David Blunkett (2001–4) variously fell foul of the courts. In July 1999, Straw's attempts to retain his power to ban journalists who were investigating miscarriages of justice from interviewing prisoners was declared unlawful by the House of Lords. The same month, the Court of Appeal found against him after he sought to return three asylum seekers to France or Germany. In 2001, an order made by Mr Straw, and approved by Parliament, designating Pakistan as a country that presented no serious risk of persecution was quashed by the Court of Appeal. All these cases, along with several

other high-profile judgements – including a number by European courts – combined to create a new visibility for the judiciary.

The courts, then, are willing to cast a critical eye over decisions of ministers in order to ensure that they comply with the powers granted by statute and are not contrary to natural justice. They are facilitated in this task by the rise in the number of applications made for judicial review and by their power of statutory interpretation. As Drewry (1986, p. 30) has noted:

Although judges must strictly apply Acts of Parliament, the latter are not always models of clarity and consistency . . . This leaves the judges with considerable scope for the exercise of their creative skills in interpreting what an Act really means. Some judges, of which Lord Denning was a particularly notable example, have been active and ingenious in inserting their own policy judgements into the loopholes left in legislation.

Judicial activism is thus well established. The courts have been willing to scrutinise government actions, and on occasion strike them down, on a scale not previously witnessed. Some commentators in the 1990s saw it as a consequence of the Conservative Party being in government for more than a decade. However, the courts have maintained their activism under a Labour government, much to the displeasure of some ministers and resulting, as we shall see, in some high-profile clashes between ministers and the courts.

However, the extent and impact of such activism on the part of judges should not be exaggerated. There are three important caveats that have to be entered. First, statutory interpretation allows judges some but not complete leeway. They follow well-established guidelines. Second, only a minority of applications for judicial review concern government departments: a larger number are for review of actions taken by local authorities. (Government departments are respondents in about 25 per cent of cases and local authorities in 35 per cent.) Third, most applications made for judicial review fail. In an interview in July 1996, Lord Woolf claimed that for every case that the government lost, there were ten more that it won. 'It is becoming more difficult to achieve success in such cases', noted *The Times* (19 July 1993). 'High Court leave for a review is harder to obtain and legal aid is more scarce. Fewer than half of applicants obtain leave to proceed.' Of the 4,207 applications for leave to apply for judicial review in 2004, only just over 27 per cent were allowed. Of the 345 substantive applications disposed of that year, only 45 per cent (156) were allowed.

Even so, activism on the part of the courts constitutes a problem for government. Even though the percentage of applications where leave is given to proceed has declined, the absolute number has increased. And even though government may win most of the cases brought against it, it is the cases that it loses that attract the headlines.

■ Enforcing EU law

The United Kingdom signed the treaty of accession to the European Community in 1972. The European Communities Act passed the same year provided the legal provisions necessary for membership. The UK became a member of the EC on 1 January 1973. The European Communities Act, as we have seen in Chapter 15, created a new judicial dimension to the British constitution.

The 1972 Act gave legal force not only to existing EC law but also to future law. When regulations have been promulgated by the Commission and the Council of Ministers, they take effect within the United Kingdom. Parliamentary assent to the principle is not required. That assent has already been given in advance by virtue of the provisions of the 1972 Act. Parliament may be involved in giving approval to measures to implement directives, but there is no scope to reject the purpose of the directives. And, as we recorded in Chapter 15, under the provisions of the Act, questions of law are to be decided by the European Court of Justice (ECJ), or in accordance with the decisions of that court. All courts in the United Kingdom are required to take judicial notice of decisions made by the ECJ. Cases in the UK that reach the House of Lords are, unless the law lords consider that the law has already been settled by the ECJ, referred to the European Court for a definitive ruling. Requests may also be made by lower courts to the ECJ for a ruling on the meaning and interpretation of European treaties. In the event of a conflict between the provisions of European law and those of an Act of Parliament, the former are to prevail.

The question that has most exercised writers on constitutional law since Britain's accession to the EC has been what British courts should do in the event of the passage of an Act of Parliament that

expressly overrides European law. The question remains a hypothetical one. Although some doubt exists – Lord Denning when Master of the Rolls appeared to imply on occasion that the courts must apply EC law, Acts of Parliament notwithstanding – the generally accepted view among jurists is that courts, by virtue of the doctrine of parliamentary sovereignty, must apply the provisions of the Act of Parliament that expressly overrides European law (see Bradley, 1994, p. 97).

Given the absence of an explicit overriding of European law by statute, the most important question to which the courts have had to address themselves has been how to resolve apparent inconsistencies or conflict between European and domestic (known as municipal) law. During debate on the European Communities Bill in 1972, ministers made clear that the bill essentially provided a rule of construction: that is, that the courts were to construe the provisions of an Act of Parliament, in so far as it was possible to do so, in such a way as to render it consistent with European law. However, what if it is not possible to construe an Act of Parliament in such a way? Where the courts have found UK law to fall foul of European law, the UK government has introduced new legislation to bring domestic law into line with EC requirements. But what about the position prior to the passage of such legislation? Do the courts have power to strike down or suspend Acts of Parliament that appear to breach European law? The presumption until 1990 was that they did not. Two cases – the *Factortame* and *Ex Parte EOC* cases – have shown that presumption to be false. The former case involved a challenge, by the owners of some Spanish trawlers, to the provisions of the 1988 Merchant Shipping Act. The High Court granted interim relief, suspending the relevant parts of the Act. This was then overturned by the House of Lords, which ruled that the courts had no such power. The European Court of Justice, to which the case was then referred, ruled in June 1990 that courts did have the power of injunction and could suspend the application of Acts of Parliament that on their face appeared to breach European law until a final determination was made. The following month, the House of Lords granted orders to the Spanish fishermen preventing the Transport Secretary from withholding or withdrawing their names from the register of British fishing vessels, the orders to remain in place until the ECJ had decided the case. The case had knock-on consequences beyond EU law: having decided that an injunction could be granted against the crown in the field of EU law, the courts subsequently decided that it could then be applied in cases not involving EU law (Jacobs, 1999, p. 242). However, the most dramatic case in terms of EU law was to come in 1994. In *R. v. Secretary of State for Employment, ex parte the Equal Opportunities Commission* – usually referred to as *Ex Parte EOC* – there was a challenge to provisions of the 1978 Employment Protection (Consolidation) Act. The House of Lords held that the provisions of the Act effectively excluded many part-time workers from the right to claim unfair dismissal or redundancy payments and were as such unlawful, being incompatible with EU law (Maxwell, 1999). Although the *Factortame* case attracted considerable publicity, it was the *EOC* case that was the more fundamental in its implications. The courts were invalidating the provisions of an Act of Parliament. Following the case, *The Times* declared 'Britain may now have, for the first time in its history, a constitutional court' (5 March 1994, cited in Maxwell, 1999, p. 197).

The courts have thus assumed a new role in the interpretation of European law, and the court system itself has acquired an additional dimension. The ECJ serves not only to hear cases that emanate from British courts but also to consider cases brought directly by or against the EC Commission and the governments of the member states. Indeed, the ECJ carries a significant workload, so much so that it has to be assisted by another court, the Court of First Instance, and both are under considerable pressure in trying to cope with the number of cases brought before them. In the twenty-first century, the ECJ alone receives 800 to 900 cases a year.

There is thus a significant judicial dimension to British membership of the European Union, involving adjudication by a supranational court, and the greater the integration of member states the greater the significance of the courts in applying European law. Furthermore, under the Maastricht Treaty, which took effect in November 1993, the powers of the ECJ were strengthened, the court being given the power to fine member states that did not fulfil their legal obligations. Although the cases heard by the ECJ may not often appear to be of great significance, collectively they produce a substantial – indeed, massive – body of case law that constitutes an important constraint on the actions of the UK government. Each year, that body of case law grows greater.

Against this new judicial dimension has to be set the fact that the doctrine of parliamentary sovereignty remains formally extant. Parliament retains the power to repeal the 1972 Act. The decisions of the ECJ have force in the United Kingdom inasmuch as Parliament has decreed that they will. When Lord Rees-Mogg sought judicial review of the government's power to ratify the Maastricht Treaty, the Speaker of the House of Commons, Betty Boothroyd, issued a stern warning to the courts, reminding them that under the Bill of Rights of 1689 the proceedings of Parliament could not be challenged by the courts. (Lord Rees-Mogg, whose application was rejected, emphasised that no such challenge was intended.) And it was the British government that instigated the provision in the Maastricht Treaty for the ECJ to fine member states. The number of cases brought in the ECJ against the UK, alleging a failure to fulfil its obligations, is a relatively small one: of 144 cases brought before the ECJ in 2004 only nine were brought against the UK. Even so, the impact of membership of the EC should not be treated lightly. It has introduced a major new judicial dimension to the British constitution. It has profound implications for the role of the courts in influencing public policy in the United Kingdom. That was emphasised by the ruling of the House of Lords in the *Ex Parte EOC* case. The courts now appear to have acquired, in part, a power that they lost in 1689.

■ Enforcing the ECHR

Reinforcing the importance of the courts has been the incorporation of the European Convention on Human Rights into British law. Although not formally vesting the courts with the same powers as are vested by the 1972 European Communities Act, the incorporation nonetheless makes British judges powerful actors in determining public policy.

The European Convention on Human Rights was signed at Rome in 1950 and was ratified by the United Kingdom in March 1951. It came into effect in 1953. It declares the rights that should be protected in each state – such as the right to life, freedom of thought and peaceful assembly – and stipulates procedures by which infringements of those rights can be determined. Alleged breaches of the Convention are investigated by the European Commission on Human Rights and may be referred to the European Court of Human Rights.

The convention is a treaty under international law. This means that its authority derives from the consent of the states that have signed it. It was not incorporated into British law, and not until 1966 were individual citizens allowed to petition the commission. In subsequent decades, a large number of petitions were brought against the British government. Although the British government was not required under British law to comply with the decisions of the court, it did so by virtue of its international obligations and introduced the necessary changes to bring UK law into line with the judgement of the court. By 1995, over 100 cases against the UK government had been judged admissible, and thirty-seven cases had been upheld (see Lester, 1994, pp. 42–6). Some of the decisions have been politically controversial, as in 1994 when the court decided (on a ten–nine vote) that the killing of three IRA suspects in Gibraltar in 1988 by members of the British security forces was a violation of the right to life.

The decisions of the court led to calls from some Conservative MPs for the UK not to renew the right of individuals to petition the commission. Liberal Democrats and many Labour MPs – as well as some Conservatives – wanted to move in the opposite direction and to incorporate the ECHR into British law. Those favouring incorporation argued that it would reduce the cost and delay involved in pursuing a petition to the commission and allow citizens to enforce their rights through British courts. It was also argued that it would raise awareness of human rights. This reasoning led the Labour Party to include a commitment in its 1997 election manifesto to incorporate the ECHR into British law. Following the return of a Labour government in that election, the government published a White Paper, *Rights Brought Home*, and followed it with the introduction of the Human Rights Bill. The bill was enacted in 1998.

The Human Rights Act makes it unlawful for public authorities to act in a way that is incompatible with convention rights. It is thus possible for individuals to invoke their rights in any proceedings brought against them by a public authority or in any proceedings that they may bring against a public authority. 'Courts will, from time to time, be required to determine if primary or secondary legislation is incompatible with Convention rights. They will decide if the acts of public authorities are unlawful through contravention, perhaps even unconscious contravention, of those rights. They may have to award damages as a result' (Irvine of Lairg, 1998, p. 230). Although the courts are not empowered to

set aside Acts of Parliament, they are required to interpret legislation as far as possible in accordance with the convention. The higher courts can issue declarations of incompatibility where UK law is deemed incompatible with the ECHR: it is then up to Parliament to take the necessary action. The Act makes provision for a 'fast-track' procedure for amending law to bring it into line with the ECHR.

The incorporation of the ECHR into British law creates a new role for British judges in determining policy outcomes. In the words of one authority, 'it gives the courts an increased constitutional role, moving them from the margins of the political process to the centre and increasing the underlying tension between the executive and the judiciary' (Woodhouse, 1996, p. 440). Indeed, the scale of the change was such that senior judges had to be trained for the purpose and, in order to give the courts time to prepare, the principal provisions of the Act were not brought into force until October 2000. (One effect, though, was immediate. The provision requiring ministers to certify that a bill complies with the provisions of the ECHR was brought in immediately following enactment.) By the end of 2003, the courts had issued declarations of incompatibility in fifteen cases, though five of these were overturned on appeal (see www.humanrights.gov.uk/decihm.htm). Of the ten not overturned on appeal, one involved a section no longer in force and in another no further prosecutions were brought under the section deemed incompatible. The eight remaining cases resulted in orders or primary legislation to bring the law into line with declarations of the courts. In April 2003, for example, in the case of *Bellinger* v. *Bellinger*, the courts held that section 11(c) of the Matrimonial Causes Act 1973 was incompatible with Articles 8 and 12 of the Convention. This led to Parliament enacting the Gender Recognition Act conferring rights on those who changed gender, including the right to a new birth certificate. Also in April 2003, the courts in *Blood and Tarbuck* v. *Secretary of State for Health* issued a declaration in respect of a provision of the Human Fertilisation and Embryology Act 1990 which prevented the use of a dead husband's sperm to be used by the mother to conceive. A private member's bill was employed, with government assistance, to change the law. However, the most significant case was to come in December 2004, when the House of Lords held that powers in Part 4 of the Anti-Terrorism, Crime and Security Act breached the provisions of the Convention in that they were disproportionate and discriminatory in applying only to foreign nationals. The decision, as we shall see, caused a political storm and contributed to a major clash between executive and judiciary. The government nonetheless introduced a Terrorism Bill with new provisions in place of those embodied in the 2001 Act.

The Act has thus had a major effect on the relationship of Parliament and the executive to the courts. Parliament has, in effect, handed over its traditional power of protecting rights to the courts. Enforcing those rights has brought the courts into conflict with the executive. The position was summarised by Jeffrey Jowell, in writing that the Human Rights Act 'may on the face of it be just another unentrenched statute, but its effect is to alter constitutional expectations by creating the presumption across all official decision-making that rights do and should trump convenience' (Jowell, 2003, p. 597). It is the courts that decide when such trumping should take place.

■ The impact of devolution

The devolution of powers to elected assemblies in different parts of the United Kingdom (see Chapter 15) has also enlarged the scope for judicial activity. The legislation creating elected assemblies in Wales and Scotland stipulates the legal process by which the powers and the exercise of powers by the assemblies can be challenged. It provides a particular role for the Judicial Committee of the Privy Council.

Under the Government of Wales Act, there are complex provisions for determining whether a particular function is exercisable by the Welsh Assembly, whether the Assembly has exceeded its powers, whether it has failed to fulfil its statutory obligations or whether a failure to act puts the Assembly in breach of the ECHR. These are known as 'devolution issues'. A law officer can require a particular devolution issue to be referred to the Judicial Committee of the Privy Council. It is also open to other courts to refer a devolution issue to higher courts for determination. Devolution issues considered by the High Court or the Court of Appeal may be appealed to the Judicial Committee, but only with the leave of the court or the Judicial Committee. If a devolution issue arises in judicial proceedings before the House of Lords, the law lords may refer it to the Judicial Committee unless they consider it more appropriate that they determine the issue. This point may appear a little academic as, in terms of personnel, by referring it to the Judicial Committee they are simply referring it to themselves. If a court finds that the Assembly has exceeded its powers in making subordinate legislation, it can make an order removing or limiting any retrospective effect of the decision, or suspend the effect of the decision for any period and on any conditions to allow the defect to be corrected.

The Scotland Act also provides for a similar process. The Law Officers may refer a devolution issue to the Judicial Committee of the Privy Council. Courts may refer devolution issues to higher courts for determination. Appeals from the High Court or Court of Appeal go to the Judicial Committee. If a court finds that an Act of Parliament or subordinate legislation is *ultra vires*, it can make an order removing or limiting any retrospective effect of that decision for any period and on any conditions to allow the defects to be remedied. In Scotland, as in Wales, a Law Officer can make a pre-enactment reference to the Judicial Committee to determine whether a bill or a provision of a bill is within the competence of the Parliament. In other words, it is not necessary for the measure to be enacted: a Law Officer can seek a determination while the measure is in bill form.

The provisions of both Acts create notable scope for judicial activity. As John McEldowney has noted in respect of Scotland, the Judicial Committee of the Privy Council 'may be regarded as a constitutional court for Scottish matters' (McEldowney, 1998, p. 198). There is scope for the courts to interpret the legislation in a constrictive or an expansive manner. The approach taken by the courts has major implications for both elected bodies. There is also scope for the courts to move away from the intentions of the Westminster Parliament. The longer an Act of constitutional significance survives, the intent of Parliament in passing it gradually loses its significance (Craig and Walters, 1999, p. 289). The policing of the powers of the two elected bodies by the courts has political as well as legal implications. The point has been well put by Craig and Walters. As they note, the Scotland Act, while giving the Scottish Parliament general legislative powers, also limits those powers through a broad list of reservations. 'At the minimum, this means that the Scottish Parliament will have to become accustomed to living with the "judge over its shoulder". Proposed legislation will have to be scrutinised assiduously lest it fall foul of one of the many heads of reserved subject matter . . . The need for constant recourse to lawyers who will, in many instances, indicate that proposed action cannot be taken, is bound to generate frustration and anger in Scotland' (Craig and Walters, 1999, p. 303). As they conclude, 'The courts are inevitably faced with a grave responsibility: the way in which they interpret the SA [Scotland Act] may be a significant factor in deciding whether devolution proves to be the reform which cements the union, or whether it is the first step towards its dissolution' (Craig and Walters, 1999, p. 303).

Although most cases considered by the Judicial Committee derive from its Commonwealth jurisdiction, a number have already come before it under the devolution legislation. In 2001, for example, it dealt with ten appeals in five groups. All of them were brought under the Scotland Act, and all but one group involved claims made in Scottish criminal proceedings that the Lord Advocate [the Scottish equivalent of the Attorney General], as prosecutor, was infringing their human rights. One group related to proceedings arising from a law passed by the Scottish Parliament that prevented the discharge from hospital, where the safety of the public so required, of a patient suffering from a mental disorder even if not detained for medical treatment. Of the ten appeals, five were dismissed and five were allowed.

■ Demands for change

Recent years have seen various calls for change in the judicial process. Some of these have focused on the court's constitutional role in relation to government and the protection of rights. Others have focused on decisions of the courts in domestic criminal and civil cases.

Constraining the executive

In terms of the place of the courts in the nation's constitutional arrangements, there have been various demands to strengthen the powers of the courts, and some of these calls have borne fruit, primarily with the incorporation of the ECHR into British law. Some want to go further. Some want to see a more inclusive document than the ECHR. The ECHR, for example, excludes such things as a right to food or a right of privacy (see Nolan and Sedley, 1997). The

Liberal Democrats, Charter88 and a number of jurists want to see the enactment of a judicially enforceable Bill of Rights. In other words, they want a measure that enjoys some degree of protection from encroachment by Parliament. Formally, as we have seen, Parliament does not have to act on declarations of incompatibility issued by the courts. Under the proposal for an entrenched Bill of Rights, the courts would be able to set aside an Act of Parliament that was in conflict with the ECHR, rather in the same way that the courts have set aside the provisions of an Act deemed to be incompatible with EU law.

The powers acquired by the courts – and the calls for them to be given further powers – have not been universally welcomed (see Box 23.2). Critics view the new role of the courts as a threat to the traditional Westminster constitution (see Chapter 15), introducing into the political process a body of unaccountable and unelected judges who have excessive powers to interpret the provisions of a document drawn in general terms. Instead of public policy being determined by elected politicians – who can be turned out by electors at the next election – it can be decided by unrepresentative judges, who are immune to action by electors. As we have seen, the powerful position of the courts has not commended itself to all ministers. In 2001, Home Secretary David Blunkett attacked the interference by judges in political matters and even raised the possibility of 'suspending' the Human Rights Act (Woodhouse, 2002, p. 261). In December 2004, following the decision of the House of Lords to strike down certain provisions of the Anti-Terrorism, Crime and Security Act, Foreign Secretary Jack Straw said that the law lords were 'simply wrong' to imply that detainees were being held arbitrarily; it was for Parliament and not the courts to decide how best Britain could be defended from terrorism (see Norton, 2006). Following terrorist bombings in London in July 2005, ministers wanted new anti-terrorist legislation but were worried it may fall foul of the courts. In announcing a series of measures to address the terrorist threat, Prime Minister Tony Blair in August 2005 stirred controversy by declaring 'the rules of the game are changing'. He conceded it was likely that the legislation would be tested in the courts. 'Should legal obstacles arise', he said, 'we will legislate further including, if necessary, amending the Human Rights Act in respect of their interpretation of the European Convention on Human Rights and apply it directly in our own law.' In response to a questioner, he declared, 'Let me say this to people

BOX 23.2 DEBATE

More power to judges?

The European Convention on Human Rights has been incorporated into British law. This gives a new role to judges. Some proposals have been put forward to strengthen the courts even further by the enactment of an entrenched Bill of Rights, putting fundamental rights beyond the reach of a simple parliamentary majority. Giving power to judges, through the incorporation of the ECHR and, more so, through an entrenched document, has proved politically contentious. The principal arguments put forward both for and against giving such power to the courts are as follows:

The case for
- A written document, such as the ECHR, clarifies and protects the rights of the individual. Citizens know precisely what their rights are, and those rights are protected by law.
- It puts interpretation in the hands of independent judges. The rights are interpreted and protected by judges, who are independent of the political process.
- It prevents encroachment by politicians in government and Parliament. Politicians will be reluctant to tamper with a document, such as the ECHR, now that it is part of the law. Entrenchment of the measure – that is, imposing extraordinary provisions for its amendment – would put the rights beyond the reach of a simple majority in both Houses of Parliament.
- It prevents encroachment by other public bodies, such as the police. Citizens know their rights in relation to public bodies and are able to seek judicial redress if those rights are infringed.
- It ensures a greater knowledge of rights. It is an educative tool, citizens being much more rights-conscious.
- It bolsters confidence in the political system. By knowing that rights are protected in this way, citizens feel better protected and as such are more supportive of the political system.

The case against
- It confuses rather than clarifies rights. The ECHR, like most Bills of Rights, is necessarily drawn in general terms and citizens therefore have to wait until the courts interpret the vague language in order to know precisely what is and what is not protected.
- It transfers power from an elected to a non-elected body. What are essentially political issues are decided by unelected judges and not by the elected representatives of the people.
- It does not necessarily prevent encroachment by public bodies. Rights are better protected by the political culture of a society than by words written on a document. A written document does not prevent public officials getting around its provision by covert means.
- It creates a false sense of security. There is a danger that people will believe that rights are fully protected when later interpretation by the courts may prove them wrong. Pursuing cases through the courts can be prohibitively expensive; often only big companies and rich individuals can use the courts to protect their interests.
- If a document is entrenched, it embodies rights that are the product of a particular generation. A document that is not entrenched can be modified by a simple majority in both Houses of Parliament. If it is entrenched – as many Bills of Rights are – it embodies the rights of a particular time and makes it difficult to get rid of them after their moral validity has been destroyed, as was the case with slavery in the United States and is still the case in the USA with the right to bear arms. The ECHR is not formally entrenched, but it will be difficult, politically, for Parliament to change it.

very very clearly, this is the beginning of, and there will be lots of battles in the months ahead of this, let's be quite clear because of the way that the law has been interpreted over a long period of time, and I am prepared for those battles in the months ahead. I am absolutely and completely determined to make sure that this happens.'

The Prime Minister's comments were seen as a challenge to the judiciary. Critics of his statement contended that the courts were not the problem: they had simply been applying the law as passed by Parliament. Roger Smith, the Director of the pressure group JUSTICE, argued that, if the Prime Minister wanted to amend the ECHR, success would be unlikely; if he wanted to loosen its provisions, he would get little support. 'Mr Blair may want to amend the domestic implementation of the Convention: it is difficult to see how this might work. Finally, he may just want to intimidate the UK judiciary: that would be unworthy' (*The Times*, 20 September 2005). Portraying the courts as part of the problem, rather than as part of the solution, meant the government was drawing the courts into the political fray, essentially anticipating conflict and doing so at a time of major change in the highest echelon of the judicial system.

Applying the law

The courts have thus proved controversial in terms of their constitutional role. They have also been the subject of debate in terms of their traditional role in interpreting and enforcing the law. The debate has encompassed not only the judges but also the whole process of criminal and civil justice.

In 1999, the usually sure-footed law lords encountered criticism when they had to decide whether the former Chilean head of state, General Augusto Pinochet, who had been detained in the UK, should be extradited from Britain to Spain. The first judgement of the court had to be set aside when one of the law lords hearing the case was revealed to have been a director of a company controlled by a party (Amnesty International) to the case. It was the first time that the law lords had set aside one of their own decisions and ordered a rehearing. Especially embarrassing for the law lords, it was also the first case in which an English court had announced its decision live on television (see Rozenburg, 1999).

Lower courts, including the Court of Appeal, came in for particular criticism in the late 1980s and early 1990s as a result of several cases of miscarriages

of justice (see Mullin, 1996; Walker and Starmer, 1999). In 1989, the 'Guildford Four', convicted in 1975 of bombings in Guildford, were released pending an inquiry into their original conviction; in 1990, the case of the Maguire family, convicted of running an IRA bomb factory, was referred back to the Appeal Court after the Home Secretary received evidence that the convictions could not be upheld; and in 1991, the 'Birmingham Six', convicted of pub bombings in Birmingham in 1974, were released after the Court of Appeal quashed their convictions. The longest-running case was the Bridgewater case, in which several men had been convicted in 1979 of the murder of newspaper boy Carl Bridgewater. The Court of Appeal refused leave to appeal in 1981 and had turned down an appeal in 1987, before the case was again brought back in 1996. The men were released in 1997. In 1998, the Court of Appeal decided to set aside posthumously the conviction of Derek Bentley, hanged in 1953 for murder, after deciding that he had been deprived of a fair trial. Several previous attempts to get the conviction set aside had failed. Various lesser-known cases have also resulted in earlier convictions being overturned. By the end of July 2002, the Court of Appeal had quashed a total of seventy-one convictions referred to it by the Criminal Cases Review Body.

The judges involved in the original cases were variously criticised for being too dependent on the good faith of prosecution witnesses – as was the Court of Appeal. The Appeal Court came in for particular criticism for its apparent reluctance even to consider that there might have been miscarriages of justice. As late as 1988, the court had refused an appeal by the 'Birmingham Six', doing so in terms that suggested that the Home Secretary should not even have referred the case to the court. When lawyers for the 'Birmingham Six' had earlier sought to establish police malpractice by bringing a claim for damages, the then Master of the Rolls, Lord Denning, had caused controversy by suggesting, in effect, that the exposure of injustice in individual cases was less important than preserving a façade of infallibility (Harlow, 1991, p. 98). By the 1990s, that façade had been destroyed. Although the cases were few in number – and only a small fraction of the applications made to the Criminal Cases Review Body result in cases being referred to the Appeal Court – it has been the high-profile cases that have undermined the position of the courts.

Another criticism has been the insensitivity of some judges in particular cases, notably rape cases.

In 1993, for example, the Attorney General referred to the Court of Appeal a lenient sentence handed out by a judge in a case where a teenager had been convicted of the attempted rape of a nine-year-old girl. The judge had said that he received evidence that the girl in the case was 'no angel herself'. The comment attracted widespread and adverse criticism. The Appeal Court, while asserting that the judge had been quoted out of context, nonetheless condemned the sentence as inappropriate and increased it. An earlier case, in which another judge had awarded a young rape victim £500 to go on holiday to help her to forget about her experience, attracted even more condemnation. Such cases highlighted a problem that appears pervasive. A survey published in 1993 revealed that 40 per cent of sentences by circuit courts in rape cases were of four years or less, even though Appeal Court guidelines recommend that five years should be the starting point in contested rape cases. (The maximum sentence possible is life imprisonment.) Lenient sentences in a number of cases involving other offences also fuelled popular misgivings about the capacity of the courts to deliver appropriate sentences.

In 2000, the European Court of Human Rights ruled that the minimum term of imprisonment (or 'tariff') for murder committed by juveniles should be set by the courts and not by the Home Secretary. In effect, the power thus passed to the Lord Chief Justice. It was first used in the case of two young men, Thompson and Venables, who as minors had abducted and killed two-year-old Jamie Bulger. Lord Woolf recommended a reduction in the tariff set by a previous Home Secretary, a reduction that meant that both became eligible for parole immediately. The case had aroused strong feelings, and the Lord Chief Justice's decision was unpopular. Equally unpopular was a subsequent granting by a senior judge of an injunction preventing publication of any information that might lead to the identity or future whereabouts of the two.

The result of such cases may have limited public regard for judges, albeit not on a major scale. In a 2002 MORI poll, the proportion of respondents expressing satisfaction with the way judges did their job was less than for most of the other professions mentioned. Although 60 per cent were satisfied or very satisfied with the way judges did their job – against 15 per cent who were fairly or very dissatisfied – the figure was notably below that for nurses, doctors, dentists, teachers and the police.

Only lawyers, politicians generally, and government ministers received lower satisfaction ratings. Nonetheless, the figures show four times as many people satisfied than dissatisfied, with the percentages showing little change in recent years. Polls also show that, perhaps not surprisingly, most people trust judges to tell the truth.

Other aspects of the criminal justice system have also attracted criticism. The activity and policy of the Crown Prosecution Service have also been particular targets. The CPS has been largely overworked and has had difficulty since its inception in recruiting a sufficient number of well-qualified lawyers to deal with the large number of cases requiring action. In 1999, it was revealed that stress was a particular problem for many CPS lawyers. The CPS has also been criticised for failing to prosecute in several highly publicised cases where it has felt that the chances of obtaining a conviction were not high enough to justify proceeding. Damning reports on the organisation and leadership of the CPS were published in 1998 and 1999. As a response to the latter report, the new Director of Public Prosecutions undertook to reform the service, providing a more organised and transparent system of public prosecutions.

Another problem has been that of access to the system. Pursuing a court case is expensive. In civil cases, there is often little legal aid available. Those with money can hire high-powered lawyers. In cases alleging libel or slander, only those with substantial wealth can usually afford to pursue a case against a well-resourced individual or organisation, such as a national newspaper. Millionaires such as the singer-songwriter Sir Elton John have pursued cases successfully, but for anyone without great financial resources the task is virtually impossible. Cases can also be delayed. Many individuals have neither the time nor the money to pursue matters through the courts. That is likely to be exacerbated with the creation of the Supreme Court. The costs of the new body will be far greater than the existing appellate committee of the House of Lords (which draws on many facilities already provided in the Palace of Westminster); the additional cost will be recouped through increasing the fees charged to litigants.

Implementing change

Various proposals have been advanced for reform of the judiciary and of the system of criminal justice. A number, as we have seen, have been implemented.

There have been moves to create greater openness in the recruitment of senior judges as well as to extend the right to appear before the senior courts. In 1998, new judges were required to reveal whether they were freemasons. (It was feared that membership of a secret society might raise suspicions of a lack of impartiality.) The 1999 Access to Justice Act created a community legal service (CLS) to take responsibility for the provision of legal advice and for legal aid. It also created a criminal defence service, to provide that those charged with criminal offences receive a high-quality legal defence. Legal language has also been simplified: the old terms and Latin phrases have gone. The Crown Prosecution Service is undergoing change. A Commissioner for Judicial Appointments, to oversee judicial appointments, was put in place in 2001. The Constitutional Reform Act 2005 created a Judicial Appointments Commission. There have also been various reforms to criminal law in terms of sentencing and the management of cases in the magistrates' courts. In 2002, the government published a White Paper, *Justice for All*, proposing further changes to the criminal justice system. These included changing the rules as to what evidence may be presented, having judge-only trials in serious and complex fraud cases, removing the double jeopardy rule (preventing someone from being tried twice for the same offence), and creating a Sentencing Guidelines Council to ensure more uniformity in sentencing. Some of these have been implemented, including the ending, in certain exceptional circumstances, of the double jeopardy rule and the creation of a Sentencing Guidelines Council. Attempts to reduce the number of jury trials have variously run foul of opposition in the House of Lords. And, as we have seen, the Lord Chancellor's position as head of the judiciary has been transferred to the Lord Chief Justice and, in 2009, the law lords will transfer from the House of Lords to a dedicated Supreme Court.

The courts are undergoing significant change – the changes of the past decade probably surpassing anything experienced in the previous half-century – but the pressure for reform continues. As the constitution has acquired a new judicial dimension, so the courts have become more visible and embroiled in political controversy. The creation of a Supreme Court will, in the eyes of some, strengthen the position of the judiciary. The government has argued that it will strengthen the independence of the courts (Department for Constitutional Affairs, 2003, p. 4). In 2005, the retiring Lord Chief Justice, Lord Woolf, thought that the creation of the court would be as important as Magna Carta (*Daily Telegraph*, 23 September 2005). Others have taken a more sceptical view, arguing that the detachment of the judges from the House of Lords would deny them an important protective shield and buffer (Norton, 2005, pp. 321–3). The presence of the law lords has enabled peers to understand and appreciate their role, and provide something of a protective shield; the law lords, for their part, have been enabled to understand the nature of the parliamentary system. The Lord Chancellor has also traditionally been in a position to protect the interests of the judicial system within government. The creation of a Supreme Court, and the ending of the traditional role of the Lord Chancellor, may leave senior judges isolated and hence more exposed to attack from senior ministers. The judges have become more important political actors and, as such, more significant targets of political attack.

BOX 23.3 BRITAIN IN CONTEXT

Common Law versus Civil Law

Courts in the UK differ from those in most other countries in that they do not have responsibility for interpreting a codified constitution. Their role has principally been that of engaging in statutory, not constitutional, interpretation; courts in other countries generally engage in both (though not always: there are countries with codified constitutions, such as the Netherlands, which maintain the principle of parliamentary sovereignty). The role of the courts in the UK has changed significantly as a consequence of the UK's membership of the EC/EU and the passage of the Human Rights Act 1998 – the treaties of the EU and the European Convention of Human Rights having the characteristics of higher law documents – but the basic distinction still remains. In so far as the courts are empowered to interpret such documents, they do so under the authority of Parliament and not a written constitution.

They also differ from their continental counterparts in that – along with the USA and most Commonwealth jurisdictions – they are based on the principles of common law rather than civil (or Roman) law. The common law tradition is based on law deriving from particular measures and their interpretation by the courts; much rests on judge-made law. The civil law tradition rests on a particular legal code stipulating the general principles of law that are to apply.

Not all systems follow the British in adopting an adversarial format – a feature of the common law tradition, the case being argued by competing counsel – nor in the presumption of being innocent until proven guilty. Some systems adopt a form of religious or socialist law, in some cases requiring the accused to prove their innocence or simply presuming guilt, with the accused having no real opportunity to put their case.

Though generalisations can be drawn about courts in the United Kingdom, these can only be taken so far. Scotland has its own legal system. Though the Act of Union 1707 resulted in a unitary state, Scotland nonetheless retained its legal system. There is thus one court system, and body of law, for England and Wales and another for Scotland.

However, though there are significant differences between the legal system (or rather systems) in the UK and those in other countries, there are also features that are increasingly common. The effect of international treaties is to create common obligations. Thus, for example, the United Kingdom is a signatory to the European Convention on Human Rights; so too are more than forty other countries. The European Court of Human Rights is ultimately responsible for the interpretation of the Convention. Though the British courts are now empowered to consider Convention rights, their interpretation can be challenged in the European Court in Strasbourg. The UK is one of twenty-five members of the European Union and each is bound by the treaties establishing the European Community and Union. The interpretation of the treaties lies ultimately with the European Court of Justice, which sits in Luxembourg. European countries are witnessing what, in effect, constitutes a common judicialisation of their political systems.

Chapter summary

Although not at the heart of the regular policy-making process in Britain, the courts are nonetheless now significant actors in the political system. Traditionally restricted by the doctrine of parliamentary sovereignty, the courts have made use of their power of judicial review to constrain ministers and other public figures. The passage of two Acts – the European Communities Act in 1972 and the Human Rights Act in 1998 – has created the conditions for judges to determine the outcome of public policy in a way not previously possible. Judges now have powers that effectively undermine the doctrine of parliamentary sovereignty, with the outputs of Parliament not necessarily being immune to challenge in the courts. The passage of the Government of Wales Act 1998 and the Scotland Act 1998 has also enlarged the scope for judicial activity, with potentially significant constitutional and political implications. The Constitutional Reform Act 2005 will also result in a detached Supreme Court, separate from the House of Lords. The greater willingness of, and opportunity for, the courts to concern themselves with the determination of public policy has been welcomed by some jurists and politicians while alarming others, who are fearful that policy-making power may slip from elected politicians to unelected judges. The courts are having to meet the challenge of a new judicial dimension to the British constitution while coping – not always successfully – with the demands of an extensive system of criminal and civil justice.

▶

Discussion points

■ Why should the courts be independent of government?

■ What role is now played by judges as a result of Britain's membership of the European Union?

■ Can, and should, judges be drawn from a wider social background?

■ Is the incorporation of the European Convention on Human Rights into British law a good idea?

■ Will the creation of a Supreme Court strengthen or weaken the position of the senior judiciary?

Further reading

Basic introductions to the legal system can be found in student texts on constitutional and administrative law. Recent examples include Carroll (1998), Jackson and Leopold (2001) and Alder (2005). The most recent and succinct analysis of the changing role of judges in the nation's constitutional arrangements is Stevens (2002); see also Stevens (2003). The classic and controversial critique of the judiciary is that provided by Griffith (1997). Drewry (1991) addresses the question of judicial independence.

On judicial review, see Forsyth (2000). On the impact of membership of the EC/EU on British law, see Fitzpatrick (1999), Maxwell (1999) and Loveland (2003). On the incorporation of the ECHR, see Beatson *et al.* (1998), Lord Irvine of Lairg (1998), Klug (1999), Loveland (1999), Woodhouse (2002) and Klug and O'Brien (2002); for a critical view, see Ewing (2004). The journal *Public Law* regularly carries scholarly legal articles on different implications of the Act. On the debate as to whether Britain needs an entrenched Bill of Rights, see Norton (1982, Chapter 13), Puddephatt (1995), Gearty (1996) and Blackburn (1997). On the implications for the courts of devolution, see especially Craig and Walters (1999). On the case for a Supreme Court, see Bingham (2002), Banner and Deane (2003) and the Department for Constitutional Affairs (2003); for the implications of the creation of the Court, see Le Sueur (2004) for a detailed legal analysis of its role in the United Kingdom and Norton (2005) for a brief consideration of its constitutional implications. On the Constitutional Reform Act, see Windlesham (2005). On the abolition of the role of Lord Chancellor, see Oliver (2004).

References

Alder, J. (2005) *Constitutional and Administrative Law*, 5th edn (Palgrave Macmillan).

Banner, C. and Deane, A. (2003) *Off with their Wigs: Judicial Revolution in Modern Britain* (Imprint Academic).

Beatson, J., Forsyth, C. and Hare, I. (eds) (1998) *Constitutional Reform in the United Kingdom: Practice and Principles* (Hart Publishing).

Bingham, Lord (2002) *A New Supreme Court for the United Kingdom* (The Constitution Unit).

Blackburn, R. (1997) 'A Bill of Rights for the 21st century', in R. Blackburn and J. Busuttil (eds), *Human Rights for the 21st Century* (Pinter).

Bradley, A.W. (1994) 'The sovereignty of Parliament – in perpetuity?', in J. Jowell and D. Oliver (eds), *The Changing Constitution*, 3rd edn (Oxford University Press).

Bradley, A.W. and Ewing, K.D. (1997) *Constitutional and Administrative Law*, 12th edn (Longman).

Carroll, A. (1998) *Constitutional and Administrative Law* (Financial Times/Pitman Publishing).

Craig, P. and Walters, M. (1999) 'The courts, devolution and judicial review', *Public Law*, Summer.

Department for Constitutional Affairs (2003) *Constitutional Reform: A Supreme Court for the United Kingdom*, CP/11/03.

Drewry, G. (1986) 'Judges and politics in Britain', *Social Studies Review*, November.

Drewry, G. (1991) 'Judicial independence in Britain: challenges real and threats imagined', in P. Norton (ed.), *New Directions in British Politics?* (Edward Elgar).

Ewing, K. (2004) 'The futility of the Human Rights Act', *Public Law*, Winter.

Fitzpatrick, B. (1999) 'A dualist House of Lords in a sea of monist Community law', in B. Dickson and P. Carmichael (eds), *The House of Lords: Its Parliamentary and Judicial Roles* (Hart Publishing).

Forsyth, C. (ed.) (2000) *Judicial Review and the Constitution* (Hart Publishing).

Gearty, C.A. (1996) 'An answer to "Legislating liberty: the case for a Bill of Rights" by Andrew Puddephatt', *The Journal of Legislative Studies*, Vol. 2, No. 2.

Griffith, J.A.G. (1997) *The Politics of the Judiciary*, 5th edn (Fontana).

Harlow, C. (1991) 'The legal system', in P. Catterall (ed.), *Contemporary Britain: An Annual Review* (Blackwell).

Home Office (1998) *Rights Brought Home: The Human Rights Bill*, Cm 3782 (Stationery Office).

Irvine of Lairg, Lord (1998) 'The development of human rights in Britain under an incorporated convention on human rights', *Public Law*, Summer.

Jackson, P. and Leopold, P. (2001) *O. Hood Phillips and Jackson, Constitutional and Administrative Law*, 8th edn (Sweet & Maxwell).

Jacobs, F. (1999) 'Public law – the impact of Europe', *Public Law*, Summer.

Jowell, J. (2003) 'Judicial deference: servility, civility or institutional capacity?' *Public Law*, Winter.

Klug, F. (1999) 'The Human Rights Act 1998, *Pepper* v. *Hart* and all that', *Public Law*, Summer.

Klug, F. and O'Brien, C. (2002) 'The first two years of the Human Rights Act', *Public Law*, Winter.

Klug, F. and Starmer, K. (2001) 'Incorporation through the "front door": the first year of the Human Rights Act', *Public Law*, Winter.

Le Sueur, A. (ed.) (2004) *Building the UK's New Supreme Court: National and Comparative Perspectives* (Oxford University Press).

Lester, Lord (1994) 'European human rights and the British constitution', in J. Jowell and D. Oliver (eds), *The Changing Constitution*, 3rd edn (Oxford University Press).

Loveland, I. (1999) 'Incorporating the European Convention on Human Rights into UK law', *Parliamentary Affairs*, Vol. 52, No. 1.

Loveland, I. (2003) 'Britain and Europe', in V. Bogdanor (ed.), *The British Constitution in the Twentieth Century* (British Academy/Oxford University Press).

Maxwell, P. (1999) 'The House of Lords as a constitutional court – the implications of *Ex Parte EOC*', in B. Dickson and P. Carmichael (eds), *The House of Lords: Its Parliamentary and Judicial Roles* (Hart Publishing).

McEldowney, J. (1996) *Public Law* (Sweet & Maxwell).

McEldowney, J. (1998) 'Legal aspects of relations between the United Kingdom and the Scottish Parliament: the evolution of subordinate sovereignty?', in D. Oliver and G. Drewry (eds), *The Law and Parliament* (Butterworth).

Mullin, C. (1996) 'Miscarriages of justice', *The Journal of Legislative Studies*, Vol. 2, No. 2.

Munro, C. (1987) *Studies in Constitutional Law* (Butterworth).

Munro, C. (1992) '*Factortame* and the constitution', *Inter Alia*, Vol. 1, No. 1.

Nolan, Lord and Sedley, Sir S. (1997) *The Making and Remaking of the British Constitution* (Blackstone Press).

Norton, P. (1982) *The Constitution in Flux* (Blackwell).

Norton, P. (2005) 'Parliament and the courts', in N.D.J. Baldwin (ed.), *Parliament in the 21st Century* (Politico's).

Norton, P. (2006) 'The constitution: selective incrementalism', in M. Rush and P. Giddings (eds), *The Palgrave Review of British Politics* (Palgrave Macmillan).

Oliver, D. (2004) 'Constitutionalism and the abolition of the office of the Lord Chancellor', *Parliamentary Affairs*, Vol. 57.

Puddephatt, A. (1995) 'Legislating liberty: the case for a Bill of Rights', *The Journal of Legislative Studies*, Vol. 1, No. 1.

Rozenburg, J. (1999) 'The *Pinochet* case and cameras in court', *Public Law*, Summer.

Scarman, Lord (1974) *English Law – The New Dimensions* (Stevens).

Stevens, R. (2002) *The English Judges* (Hart Publishing).

Stevens, R. (2003) 'Government and the judiciary', in V. Bogdanor (ed.), *The British Constitution in the Twentieth Century* (British Academy/Oxford University Press).

Wade, E.C.S. and Bradley, A.W. (1993) *Constitutional and Administrative Law*, 11th edn, A.W. Bradley and K.D. Ewing (eds) (Longman).

Walker, C. and Starmer, K. (1999) *Miscarriages of Justice* (Blackstone Press).

Windlesham, Lord (2005) 'The Constitutional Reform Act 2005: ministers, judges and constitutional change', *Public Law*, Winter.

▶

Woodhouse, D. (1996) 'Politicians and the judges: a conflict of interest', *Parliamentary Affairs*, Vol. 49, No. 3.

Woodhouse, D. (2002) 'The law and politics: in the shadow of the Human Rights Act', *Parliamentary Affairs*, Vol. 55, No. 2.

Zander, M. (1989) *A Matter of Justice*, revised edn (Oxford University Press).

Useful websites

Judicial process in the UK

Court Service: www.courtservice.gov.uk

Criminal Justice System – England and Wales: www.cjsonline.org/home.html

Department for Constitutional Affairs: www.dca.gov.uk

Judges: www.dca.gov.uk/judicial/judgesfr.htm

Judicial Committee of the Privy Council: www.privy-council.org.uk/output/page1.asp

Judicial work of the House of Lords: www.parliament.uk/judicial_work/judicial_work.cfm

Magistrates' Association: www.magistrates-association.org.uk

Other relevant sites

European Court of Justice (ECJ): www.europa.eu.int/cj/en/index.htm

European Court of Human Rights: www.echr.coe.int

The marriage of true minds?
The Blair–Brown relationship

Andrew Rawnsley

In the early years in government, when some affection still lingered between them, Tony Blair would often describe his relationship with Gordon Brown as 'a marriage'. That it was: the most productive, tempestuous and tortured partnership between two men of power in modern times. When they were working together, they were undefeatable. When they were waging their uncivil wars, it terrified the Cabinet, horrified their party, astounded civil servants, obsessed the media and froze the government.

Their relationship was the foundation of New Labour's greatest successes and the source of its most self-destructive tendencies.

As characters, they presented a contrast. Tony Blair was one of the most instinctive personalities to occupy Number 10. He placed great store on his ability to read other political players and intuit public feeling. He was a leader attuned to moods much more than he was interested in structures. He was an acrobat among politicians rather than a weightlifter. Gordon Brown was a much less emotionally intelligent politician and a man much more engaged with systems. The Chancellor would sweat the midnight oil; the Prime Minister was more likely to fly by the seat of his pants. Brown would obsess over one big project at a time; Blair would spin many plates simultaneously.

Blair was the much more accomplished at the thespian aspects of leadership in a 24/7 media age while the saturnine Brown never looked comfortable with what he would deride as 'touchy-feely stuff'. Blair was a brilliant tactician. Brown was the more efficient and ruthless at framing and executing strategies, an attribute which he frequently used to frustrate his nominally more powerful next-door neighbour.

As an electoral combination, they had a complementary appeal to voters. Blair could reach parts of the electorate, especially Middle England, which Brown found it more difficult to relate to. Brown, as the more palpable product of the Labour tribe, had more touching points with the party's traditional supporters.

Blair secured a larger majority for Labour in 1997 than Brown as leader would have been likely to manage. Brown did not get the leadership three years earlier because of the belief among nearly all of their senior colleagues, supported by the attitudes of newspapers and the findings of focus groups and opinion polls, that Blair had the broader appeal. By 2005, Blair was compelled to cleave to Brown to be sure of re-election. Though he had wanted to win that election by himself, the damage done to his reputation by the Iraq War forced him to bow to the advice of his advisers and bind himself to Brown whom polling evidence suggested was now the more trusted figure of the two.

Blair's ability to capture and shape the public mood allied with Brown's merciless exploitation of the vulnerability of opponents made them one of the most formidable electoral machines ever seen in Britain.

For the purpose of winning office, the pairing was hugely effective. As a means of exercising power, the results were much more mixed.

At the beginning of its life, the government was effectively divided into hemispheres of interests. Brown concentrated on economic and welfare policy while Blair devoted most attention to foreign affairs, Northern Ireland and education. Cabinet ministers would refer to 'Tony's departments' and 'Gordon's departments'.

This dual monarchy was the deal Brown believed he had extracted from Blair when he stood aside from contesting the Labour leadership after the death of John Smith. As Blair came to see how much power and freedom he had ceded to the other man, and particularly when he tried to claw some of it away from the Treasury and back to Number 10, the marriage became progressively more antagonistic.

In the early life of the government, it was heavily spun and largely believed that the relationship was an unusually harmonious one which defied Lloyd George's prediction that there can be 'no friendship at the top'. That fiction was exploded in January 1998 when I first reported in *The Observer* that someone with an extremely good claim to know the mind of the Prime Minister believed the Chancellor suffered from 'psychological flaws'. From that point on, the relationship went through cycles of hostility and cooperation marked by each low point being lower than the previous one.

When the relationship was in a particularly poisonous phase, the rivalry became debilitating to government to the point where it led to paralysis as both men expended precious reserves of time and nervous energy prosecuting the rivalry.

Some of the tensions were the natural products of the different priorities and perspectives of a Prime Minister and a Chancellor. Blair would nearly always want to tax less and spend more than Brown regarded as prudent. When the Chancellor used inflated figures in his first spending review to suggest that he was spending more than he actually was, this device seemed to be designed to bamboozle Blair as much as it was intended to gull the media.

Brown found it harder with each passing year to conceal his anger and bitterness that he was not the Prime Minister, nor could he disguise his impatience that Blair would not retire in the second term to let him have what he saw as his birthright. That corrosive resentment became mutual as Blair began to regret that he had surrendered so much power and independence to Brown.

More than once, Blair seriously considered trying to lever Brown out of the Treasury. More than once when Blair was vulnerable, Brown's allies urged him to launch a coup. Both men drew back from an ultimate combustion for fear that it would result in mutually assured destruction.

Civil servants who were witnesses to some of their confrontations would express their astonishment at the barely concealed disdain Brown would display to Blair's face. In any government, the most crucial relationship is that between Number 10 and the Treasury. Rarely, if ever, has it been as dysfunctional as it was during this period. Information is power in Whitehall. The Treasury made a policy of starving Number 10 of information about its intentions. Before one Budget, Blair was reduced to begging Brown to 'give us a clue' what might be in it. Blair would retaliate by making *ex cathedra* commitments to spending which would infuriate Brown.

Blair devoted an enormous amount of his time to trying to manage Brown and his ambitions. His basic approach was to string the other man along. At least twice Blair indicated dates to Brown when the Chancellor could expect to take over, only then to change his mind, breeding further mistrust between them. Brown likewise expended a lot of his energy trying to undermine any potential Blairite rival for the premiership and to thwart ideas from Number 10 that he disagreed with.

The spillover into policy-making was at its most striking in relation to reform of the public services and became more acute during the second and third terms when their ideas became increasingly divergent. Blair was now convinced that choice and competition were the most effective drivers of higher standards in health and education. The much more statist Brown did not believe that the consumer could be sovereign in public services. As a result of this fundamental philosophical difference, reform was either stymied or it emerged in a muddled, distorted or feeble form.

Each man used the other as the alibi for some of his own failings. Brown would position himself a few degrees to the left of Blair, implying to the Labour Party that the government would be more left-wing if only it weren't for Tony Blair.

The Prime Minister found it convenient to blame Brown for his failure to fulfil two of the big objectives that he had initially regarded as central to his premiership. Blair did not succeed in engineering an alliance with the Liberal Democrats through electoral reform to heal the historic schism of the British progressive parties. He also failed to take Britain into the European single currency. There were several reasons why neither happened, but a common one was the hostility of Brown. Blair could blame the obstructiveness of his Chancellor rather than address himself to how much of the culpability belonged to his own lack of will.

Towards the end it had become an exceptionally loveless marriage, so much so that it blinded the two men to what they still owed to each other.

Among the advantages of their partnership was that they could compensate for the flaws in each other. A serious weakness of early-period Blair was his compulsion to govern by headline, pursuing the 'eye-catching initiatives' he would demand of his staff. This was mitigated by Brown's tendency to think more for the long-term by, for instance, giving operational independence to the Bank of England.

Brown was instinctively cautious. This was balanced by Blair's willingness to take greater risks in pursuit of objectives. It is a notable feature of Blair's premiership that he took his largest gambles – notably in securing the Good Friday Agreement in Northern Ireland, prosecuting the Kosovo War and joining the invasion of Iraq – in arenas where he was largely or wholly free to operate without reference or deference to Brown. On the other side, Blair might well have ruled out raising National Insurance during the 2001 election campaign but for Brown insisting that they keep the option open. That allowed them to use an increase in their second term to bring spending on the NHS up towards the European average.

On the positive side, their partnership fashioned a programme which delivered sustained and stable economic growth along with large increases in investment in public services. Despite some appearances to the contrary, there was a substantial redistribution of resources from the more affluent to the less well-off, engineered by Brown while Blair provided the cover with Middle England. They jointly so changed the terms of political trade that the Conservatives had to start coming to terms with the Blair–Brown settlement just as Labour had previously been forced to come to terms with the Thatcherite legacy.

For all the toxins in the bloodstream of the relationship, it lasted so long that they became the most enduring pairing of Prime Minister and Chancellor since the Napoleonic Wars.

Both men felt thwarted by their long marriage. Tony Blair and Gordon Brown came to believe that they might have been more successful but for the other. The truth is that neither would probably have been as effective without the other.

POLITICS UK

PART 6

THE POLICY PROCESS

CHAPTER 24

The policy-making process

Bill Jones

Learning objectives

- To define policy in government.
- To encourage familiarity with the most popular models of policy making.
- To introduce the notion of policy networks.
- To give some examples of questionable policy making.

Introduction

This chapter examines the anatomy of policy and policy making in central government, focusing on the stages of policy making together with some theories relating to the process before concluding with a look at two case studies where outcome failed to match expectations and one of a policy currently in the making. This chapter delves briefly into the complex area of policy studies, an area that has attracted attention, because it deals with political outcomes and draws together so many elements, embodying so much of the political universe: process, influence, power and pressure as well as the impact of personality. Consequently, policy studies has emerged as a kind of sub-discipline with some claim to be a focus for a social science approach to human interaction involving such subjects as psychology, sociology, economics, history, philosophy and political science. Policy studies was essentially born in the USA, so much of it focuses on American examples and policy environments; but more generally it draws on public policy in Western liberal democracies as a whole. The reference section provides an introduction to some of the voluminous literature in the field.

■ How policy is made

Policy can be defined as a set of ideas and proposals for action culminating in a government decision. To study policy, therefore, is to study how decisions are made. Government decisions can take many forms: Burch (1979, p. 108) distinguishes between two broad kinds, as follows:

1. Rules, regulations and public pronouncements (e.g. Acts of Parliament, Orders in Council, White Papers, ministerial and departmental circulars).

2. Public expenditure and its distribution: the government spends some £400 billion per annum, mostly on public goods and services (e.g. education, hospitals) and transfer payments (e.g. social security payments and unemployment benefit).

Figure 24.1 portrays the government as a system that has as its input political demands together with resources available and its 'output' as the different kinds of government decision. The latter impact on society and influence future 'inputs', so the process is circular and constant. Students of the policy

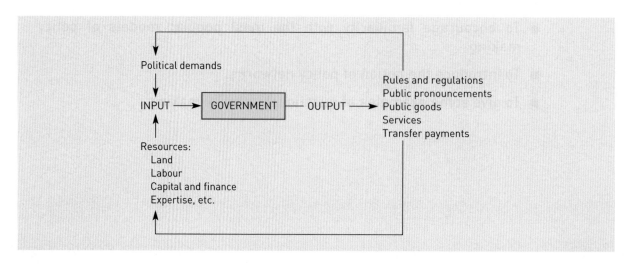

Figure 24.1 The policy process
Source: Burch (1979)

process disagree as to how policy inputs are fed into government and, once 'inside', how they are processed. For a much more complex model-building approach see the work of David Easton, who constructed a more elaborate 'black box' model (Parsons, 1995, p. 23).

Both Burch and Wood (1990) and Jordan and Richardson (1987) review a number of different analyses as 'models': possible or approximate versions of what happens in reality. Eight of these are summarised below. For a fuller account of the available models, see Parsons (1995), John (1998) and Hill (1997).

■ Models of policy making

1. *The conventional model*: This is the 'official' explanation of policy making found in Central Office of Information publications and the utterances of civil servants in public (though seldom in private). This maintains that Parliament represents and interprets the public will through its representatives, who support government ministers, who formulate executive policies, which are thereupon faithfully and impartially implemented by civil servants. The notion that a 'thin red line' of democracy connects voters with civil servants via the nominee of a political party in Parliament strikes many as tenuous but this is the officially sanctioned theory of how policy is made.

2. *The ruling-class model*: This is effectively the Marxist assertion, that those empowered with taking key decisions in the state – civil servants and politicians – subscribe consciously or unconsciously to the values of the dominant economic class, the property-owning upper middle classes. It follows that 'the executive of the modern state is but a committee for managing the common affairs of the whole bourgeoisie' (Marx and Engels, 1848). According to this view, most policy outputs will have the effect of protecting dominant group interests. It also assumes that the superstructure of democracy is all false, hiding the true 'hegemony' of the economic class. Ralph Miliband (1969) provides a good analysis of this approach (though, ironically, two of his sons are now key people in this very system); for a summary of the argument see John (1998), Chapter 5.

The following two models attribute decisive importance to differing elements within the political system.

3. *The pluralist model*: This is often associated with the US political scientist Robert Dahl. It assumes that power is dispersed within society to the various interest groups that constitute it – business, labour, agriculture, and so forth – and that they can 'make themselves heard effectively at some crucial stage in the process of decision' (Jordan and Richardson, 1987, p. 16). According to this view, interest groups interact and negotiate policy with each other in a kind of free market, with government acting as a more or less neutral referee.

4. *Corporatism*: This is associated with the work of Philippe Schmitter and is offered as an alternative to pluralism. This model perceives an alliance between ministers, civil servants and the leaders of pressure groups in which the last are given a central role in the policy-making process in exchange for exerting pressure upon their members to conform with or accept government decisions. In this view, therefore, interest groups become an extension – or even a quasi-form – of government. Corporatism has also been used pejoratively by British politicians of the left (Benn), right (Thatcher) and centre (Owen) to describe the decision-making style of the discredited 1974–9 Labour government.

The next two models ascribe key importance to two specific elements of the system.

5. *The party government model*: The stress here is on political parties and the assertion that they provide the major channel for policy formulation. Some, like Wilensky (1975), regard 'politics' as peripheral to the formation of policy, while others, like, Castles (1989) maintain that the agenda is shaped by the processes of liberal democracy (Parsons, 1995, section 2.11).

6. *The Whitehall model*: This contends that civil servants either initiate major policy or so alter it as it passes through their hands as to make it substantially theirs – thus making them the key influence on policy. Allison (1971) argued that bureaucracies do not meekly do the bidding of elected masters but are fragmented, competing centres of power: in John's words, 'Policy often arrives as the outcome of an uncoordinated fight between government bureaus' (John, 1998,

p. 44). Ministers discuss possible future actions with their very experienced and able advisers. If a trusted senior civil servant advises against a new initiative, this is bound to give the minister pause for more thought and adjustments might be made or the idea might even be dropped completely. Whitehall is not just 'in the loop' of policy making, *it is an essential part* of this loop.

The final two theories concentrate upon the way in which decision makers set about their tasks.

7. *Rational decision making*: This approach assumes that decision makers behave in a logical, sequential fashion. Accordingly, they will identify their objectives, formulate possible strategies, think through their implications and finally choose the course of action that on balance best achieves their objectives. This approach is consistent with the traditional model in that civil servants undertake the analysis and then offer up the options for popularly elected politicians to take the decisions (see Parsons, 1995, section 3.4; John, 1998, Chapter 6).

8. *Incrementalism*: This approach, associated with the hugely influential work of Charles Lindblom, denies that policy makers are so rational and argues that in practice they usually try to cope or 'muddle through'. They tend to start with the *status quo* and make what adjustments they can to manage or at least accommodate new situations. In other words, policy makers do not solve problems but merely adjust to them. The case of privatisation argues against this 'adjusting' approach in that when Nigel Lawson came to consider it in the early 1980s the cupboard, in terms of relevant files and experience, was totally bare. Instead, Conservative ministers had to devise wholly new approaches and, whatever one's views on the outcome, it is perhaps to their credit that – even allowing for a determined Prime Minister and a large majority – they succeeded in a government culture so resistant to radical innovation.

It is clear that most of these models are basically descriptive, while others, like the rational choice and conventional models, are also partially prescriptive – they offer an ideal approach as to how policies should be made – but cannot necessarily tell us how decisions are actually made.

It is also obvious that echoing somewhere within each approach is the ring of truth. It would not be too difficult to find examples in support of any of the above models. The truth is that policy making is such a protean, dense area of activity that it is extremely difficult to generalise and be accurate in all cases. Nevertheless, the search for valid statements is worth the effort, otherwise our political system will remain incomprehensible. We will therefore look at the process in greater detail in a search for some generally true propositions about it.

■ The policy cycle

If they agree on nothing else, policy study scholars seem to agree that policy making can be understood better as a cycle; a problem arrives on the agenda and is processed by the system until an answer is found. Analyses of the cycle can be quite sophisticated. Hogwood and Gunn (1984) discern a number of stages: deciding to decide (issue search and agenda setting); deciding how to decide; issue definition, forecasting; setting objectives and priorities; options analysis; policy implementation, monitoring and control; evaluation and review; and policy maintenance, succession or termination. However, Lindblom disagrees. He argues that 'Deliberate or orderly steps . . . are not an accurate portrayal of how the policy process actually works. Policy-making is, instead, a complexly interactive process without beginning or end' (Lindblom and Woodhouse, 1993, p. 11, quoted in Parsons, 1995, p. 22). However, policy studies can appear overly abstract and removed from reality at times; for the limited purposes of this chapter, three easily understood stages will suffice: initiation, formulation and implementation.

Policy initiation

Agenda setting

Each government decision has a long and complex provenance, but all must start somewhere. It is tempting to think that they originate, eureka-like, in the minds of single individuals, but they are more often the product of debate or a general climate of opinion involving many minds. Policy initiatives, moreover, can originate in all parts of the political system. Setting the political agenda is a curiously elusive process. Items can be deliberately introduced by government, and clearly it has many routes available to it, e.g. Tony Blair in the summer

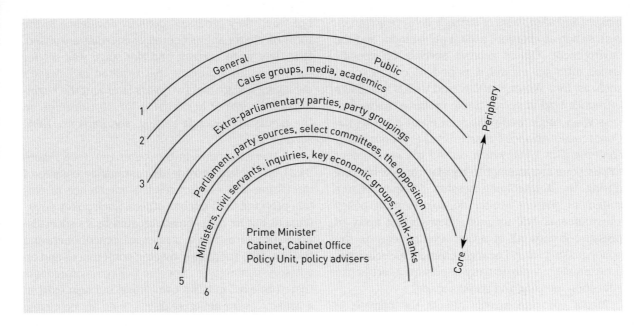

Figure 24.2 Policy initiatives

of 1999 announcing in an interview that fox hunting really *would* be banned; or Blair again, announcing, in the wake of the 'cash for peerages' scandal in March 2006, that greater transparency would be introduced regarding loans to political parties. The media too have enormous power to set the agenda: Michael Buerk's reports from Ethiopia detailing a scale of famine that touched the nation and initiated assistance; Alan Milburn, in an interview on 9 April 2006, refusing to say he would not be a candidate for the leadership when Blair stood down.

Figure 24.2 depicts six groups of possible policy initiators placed on a continuum starting from the periphery and moving in towards the nerve centre of government in No. 10. The figure uses the idea of 'distance from the centre', capturing the truth that the routes into policy making are many and varied (see also Parsons, 1995, section 2.4).

General public

The public's role in policy making is usually limited to (the democratically vital function of) voting for a particular policy package at general elections. They do have other occasional opportunities, however, for example the referendums on the EC and Scottish and Welsh devolution in the 1970s, and pressures can be built up through lobbying MPs, as when, in the mid-1980s, Sir Keith Joseph was forced to withdraw his proposals to charge parents for a

proportion of their children's university tuition fees. Occasionally, events occur that create widespread public concern, and governments often take action in the wake of them. For example, legislation on dogs was enacted after a spate of attacks by dogs on children one summer in the 1980s, and handguns were banned after the Dunblane shootings of March 1996. In many cases – as in the two just cited – such precipitate action, in reaction to the sudden rousing of public opinion, proves to be poorly framed and receives much criticism. In more recent years, public opinion has been roused by the proposed fox hunting ban and the war in Iraq in spring 2003. Both attracted huge demonstrations in London; in the former case they had some observable effect in delaying and altering proposed measures, but in the latter case Tony Blair carried on, convinced that he was right, and ignored the public outcry. However, the repercussions and damage of ignoring public and party opposition may take years to make themselves felt; what is without doubt is that Blair paid a heavy price in political support for ignoring the outcry over Iraq.

Cause groups, media and academic experts

Many cause groups (see also Chapter 11) operate in the 'wilderness' – their values antithetical to government and not listened to – and many also stay there, but some do influence public opinion and decision makers and after years of struggle achieve action on issues such as abortion, capital punishment and the environment. Others achieve success on specific issues after an extended period of campaigning, such as Des Wilson's 1960s and 1970s campaign to reduce lead in petrol. Some groups achieve success via a single well-publicised event such as the Countryside Alliance's march on the Labour Party conference in 1999, which caused the government to postpone any attempt to legislate on fox hunting during the forthcoming session (despite Blair's statement that he would do so). Certain policy 'environments' will include a bewildering array of pressure groups, all of which seek to lean on the policy-making tiller. Local government associations, for example, are particularly important in areas like education, housing and social services.

Media coverage heavily affects the climate in which policy is discussed, and important policy proposals occasionally emerge from television programmes, newspaper editorials, articles in journals and so forth. One editorial on its own would have little effect, but a near consensus in the press might well stimulate action. Occasionally ideas are picked up from individual journalists – Mrs Thatcher used to be advised regularly by right-wing journalists such as Woodrow Wyatt, Paul Johnson and Simon Heffer. Other media figures who used to be consulted regularly on policy matters by Margaret Thatcher included the press magnates Rupert Murdoch and Conrad Black. Murdoch is also rumoured to advise Blair whenever he chooses to visit Downing Street and where, because of his massive media clout, he is assured of a warm welcome. We also know that a wide range of influential people are regularly invited to dine with the Blairs at the PM's official rural retreat, Chequers, and almost certainly dinner-table conversation occasionally results in some kind of action. Lord Levy, a tennis partner of Tony Blair, eventually found himself acting as Blair's emissary to the Middle East and later as a key fund raiser (in March 2006 controversially so, when the 'loans for peerages' row erupted) for the Labour Party.

Occasionally the media provide crucial information. The classic example of this was in 1987, when Nigel Lawson, as Chancellor, denied entry to the ERM by prime ministerial veto, had tried to achieve his object by other means, namely manipulating the value of the pound to shadow that of the deutschmark. When *Financial Times* journalists interviewed Margaret Thatcher, they questioned her about this policy. She denied any knowledge of it but when they produced definitive evidence in the form of charts she accepted, somewhat surprised, that they were correct, and the stage was set for the mammoth argument that resulted in Lawson's damaging resignation two years later and the beginning of the end of her reign in No. 10 (for more on the media and agenda setting, see Parsons, 1995, section 2.3).

All these agencies in the 'outer rim' (see Figure 24.2) interact to provide that intangible climate of discussion that encourages the emergence of certain proposals and inhibits others. Each policy environment has its own climate created by its specialist press, pressure groups, academics, practitioners and the like, who frequently meet in conferences and on advisory committees. Specific policy environments therefore exist in their 'own' world but also exist in a wider, overarching reality – e.g. an economic recession, an overseas war – which sets limits to and influences policy content.

However, an interesting feature of these peripheral bodies is that from time to time they are blessed with favour, their arguments listened to, their proposals adopted, their leaders embraced by government and given advisory or even executive status. It is almost as if, godlike, the government has reached down and plucked them up to place them – albeit temporarily – on high.

BIOGRAPHY

David Hume (1711–73)

Scottish philosopher and historian. Studied in Edinburgh – where his depressive temperament meant it took time for him to settle – but went to live in France, where he wrote his *Treatise on Human Nature* (1739). He questioned the validity of principles, which he described as 'artificial', and challenged the notion of natural law as well as the social contract ideas of Hobbes, Locke and Rousseau. Hume was bitterly disappointed when his opus failed to make much impact, but his *Essays Moral and Political* (1743), produced shortly afterwards, were an instant success and confirmed his reputation as one of the founding, and greatest, British empiricist philosophers of his age.

Lord Anthony Giddens, Blair's sociologist guru on Third Way thinking
Source: Associated Press

Part 2 of this book explained how policy emerged out of an ideological framework and pointed out how academics, philosophers and other thinkers had contributed towards these frameworks. The most obvious influences on the Left would include Karl Marx, R.H. Tawney, Harold Laski, William Beveridge and, incomparably in the economic sphere, J.M. Keynes. Right-wing writers would include figures such as David Hume and Michael Oakeshott and (on economics from the 1970s onwards) the two overseas academics Friedrich Hayek and Milton Friedman. Academics specialising in specific policy areas such as transport, housing, criminology and so forth also regularly come up with proposals, some of which are taken up or drawn upon. John Major welcomed the views of the so-called 'seven wise men' (selected academics) on economic policy. Blair and Brown have established a formal committee called the Monetary Policy Committee comprising academics and financial experts who every month advise the Bank of England on interest rates. On other occasions, academics can suddenly be welcomed

BIOGRAPHY

Michael Oakeshott (1901–90)

Conservative philosopher. Educated at Cambridge, where he taught until 1949. *Experience and its Modes* (1933) was his first notable work. His writings lie within the pragmatic, sceptical traditions of Conservative thinking. He did not believe the purpose of politics was to achieve any particular end; rather, he saw the politicians' role as guiding the ship of state, enabling people to live their lives. He was a professor at the London School of Economics from 1950 to 1969.

in by leading figures in government, as when sociologist Anthony Giddens was used by Blair as a kind of 'guru' regarding the formulation of 'Third way' thinking.

Extra-parliamentary parties and party groupings

Both the Labour and Conservative extra-parliamentary parties find it easier to influence their respective leaders in opposition than in government. As Chapter 14 noted, Labour's system of internal democracy gave a substantial policy-making role to the trade unions, the National Executive Committee and the party conference during the 1930s and up until the 1970s (New Labour somewhat emasculated conference during and since the 1990s). The Conservative Party is far less democratic, but conference can set the mood for policy formulation, the research department can initiate important proposals, and the Advisory Committee on Policy did much to reformulate the main outlines of Conservative policy in the late 1970s.

Party groupings – many of which have contacts with Parliament – can also exert influence. The Fabian Society, founded in 1884, has long acted as a kind of left-wing think-tank (see Box 24.1), and in the 1980s the once left-wing Labour Coordinating Committee was influential in advising Neil Kinnock as he shifted Labour's policies towards the centre. Similarly, the No Turning Back Group in the Conservatives sought to keep the party on the right-wing track indicated by their heroine Margaret Thatcher, both before and after her fall from power, and it took the 'Cameron uprising' in the autumn of 2005 to remove what many perceived as its dead hand. The Institute for Public Policy Research (IPPR) has established itself over the past decade as a kind of Blairite think-tank, constantly on hand to feed in relevant ideas and research findings.

BOX 24.1   IDEAS AND PERSPECTIVES

Think-tanks

In the winter of 1979–80, Margaret Thatcher presided over what looked like a crumbling party and a collapsing economy. Tory grandees talked of dumping the leader. Mandarins, muttering 'I told you so', prepared to welcome the consensual 'Mr Butskell' back from retirement. Mrs Thatcher regained her momentum partly because she discovered 'Thatcherism': a new set of ideas comprising the abolition of supply constraints in the economy, privatising state-owned enterprises and reform of the public sector. They were provided by the intelligentsia of the 'New Right', many of them working through think-tanks (*The Economist*, 18 November 1992).

After the demise of Thatcher in 1990, these American-style independent hot-houses of ideas took something of a back seat. The Centre for Policy Studies (CPS) used to issue a report every fortnight, but with Major in power rather than its original patron, its output slowed to zero. The Adam Smith Institute (ASI), once a pioneer in privatisation ideas, also reduced its output and with Blair in power was reduced to producing a complimentary report on his first 200 days. The Institute for Economic Affairs (IEA) was the oldest right-wing think-tank, but it also curtailed its activities once the Thatcherite glory days had gone. It also has to be said that the disaster of the poll tax, a product of the ASI, contributed to their declining respect. And the splits did not help: Graham Mather left the IEA to form his own European Policy Forum, while David Willetts at the CPS left after criticism to become an MP and director of the Social Market Foundation.

Labour has been relatively light on think-tanks, but the Fabian Society, set up by the Webbs in 1884, has been a valuable and highly influential think-tank for over 100 years. It still exists with an impressive membership from the public and the parliamentary party. It organises seminars and conferences and keeps up a good flow of pamphlets and serious studies, a post-1997 one being the work of a certain Tony Blair. In addition, at the current time there is the Institute for Public Policy Research (IPPR), which has produced a number of New Labour studies. Demos – initially headed by Geoff Mulgan before he became a No. 10 adviser and now led by Tom Bentley – has been especially influential. Catalyst is another of the left-of-centre think-tanks that issues studies on the likes of the media (Franklin, 1998), the government's practice of setting up task forces (Platt, 1998) and the NHS (Rowlands and Pollock, 2004).

Parliament

The role of Parliament in initiating policy can be considered under two headings: party sources and party groups, and non-party sources. In government, parliamentary parties have to work through their backbench committees, although individual MPs seek to use their easy access to ministers to exert influence and press their own solutions. One Conservative MP, David Evans, pulled off the remarkable coup of convincing his Prime Minister that the identity card system introduced by Luton Town Football Club should be compulsorily introduced nationwide. His success was short-lived: the scheme was dropped in January 1990 (though it did not die – see the section on identity cards towards the end of this chapter).

The Opposition is concerned to prepare its policies for when and if it takes over the reins of government. As we saw in Chapter 12, Neil Kinnock wrested future policy making out of the party's NEC with his policy review exercise (1987–9), involving leading members of his front-bench team in the process. However, the Opposition also has to make policy 'on the hoof' in reaction to political events. It is their function and in their interests to oppose, to offer alternatives to government – but this is not easy. Opposition spokesmen lack the detailed information and support enjoyed by government; they need to react to events in a way that is consistent with their other policy positions; they need to provide enough detail to offer a credible alternative, yet avoid 'hostages to fortune' and closing options should they come to power. The Conservatives after 1997 found it hard to perform as an effective opposition, through splits in their ranks and uncertain leadership. Most commentators judged that this was not good for the health of the nation's democracy; the election of the young and dynamic new leader, David Cameron, in December 2005 transformed this situation. Unsurprisingly, he initially poured energy into changing the unpopular image and 'brand' of his party, and his policy statements were little more than statements of intent, designed to drag the party into the middle ground on social justice and the environment. Creating detailed policies, announced Oliver Letwin in April 2006, would take another eighteen months of focused effort. Received wisdom for oppositions is that such exercises are best left until close to the election; an abiding problem for oppositions is that any good ideas they might come up with can be stolen by government and represented as its own.

Party groups (some of which have membership outside Parliament) such as the Bow Group, Monday Club, Tribune and Campaign Group can all have peripheral – but rarely direct – influence on policy making.

The seventeen departmental select committees regularly make reports and recommendations, some of which are adopted. Most experts agree that these committees are more important now that their proceedings can be televised. Most reports represent cross-party consensus on specific issues but others, such as the Social Services Committee, once chaired by the much admired (and briefly a minister) Frank Field, can offer wide-ranging and coherent alternatives to government policy. Individual MPs probably have a better chance of influencing specific, usually very specific, policy areas through the opportunities available to move private members' bills (see Chapter 17).

Failure to utilise the policy-making machinery provided by the governing party can lead to dissent. In May 2003, certain Labour MPs were complaining that the Prime Minister, set on ignoring Parliament, was now introducing policy – especially that relating to foundation hospitals – that had originated wholly in his own office and not at all in the governing party. The same accusation was made by party critics of the 'top-up fees' in higher education in the autumn of 2003. Downing Street adviser Andrew Adonis – appointed and not elected, of course – was said to be the author of a policy which many in the party passionately opposed. After a cliff-hanging process of accommodation by the government of these internal criticisms, the bill eventually became an act on 27 January 2004 by a majority of only five. Adonis was later elevated to the peerage and made schools minister after the 2005 election.

Ministers, departments, official inquiries and 'think-tanks'

Strong-minded ministers will always develop policy ideas of their own either as a reflection of their own convictions or to get noticed and further their ambitions. Michael Heseltine, in the wake of the Toxteth troubles, probably shared both motivations when he submitted a paper to the Cabinet called 'It Took a Riot', proposing a new and un-Thatcherite approach to inner city regeneration: the policy was not accepted by Cabinet but was partially implemented in Merseyside, though not elsewhere. Such major initiatives are not the province of civil servants, but through their day-to-day involvement in running the country they are constantly proposing detailed improvements and adjustments to existing arrangements. Such initiatives are not necessarily the preserve of senior officials: even junior officers can propose changes that can be taken up and implemented.

A Royal Commission can be the precursor to major policy changes (for example, the Redcliffe-Maud Royal Commission on Local Government, 1966–9), but Margaret Thatcher was not well disposed towards such time-consuming, essentially disinterested procedures – she always felt she knew what needed doing – and during the 1980s none was set up. Major, however, set up the Royal Commission on Criminal Justice, and Blair the Royal Commission on the House of Lords in 2000 chaired by Lord Wakeham. He has also initiated scores of task forces and inquiries to prepare the ground for new legislation. Departments, anyway, regularly establish their own inquiries, often employing outside experts, which go on to make important policy recommendations.

Right-wing think-tanks were especially favoured by Margaret Thatcher (see Box 24.1). *The Economist* (6 May 1989) noted how she spurned Oxbridge dons – the traditional source of advice for No. 10 – and suggested that 'the civil service is constitutionally incapable of generating the policy innovation which the prime minister craves'. Instead, as a reforming premier she instinctively listened to the advice of 'people who have been uncorrupted by the old establishment'. Think-tank advice was often channelled to Margaret Thatcher via the No. 10 Policy Unit. Their radical suggestions acted as a sounding board when published and helped to push the climate of debate further to the right. If new ideas are received in a hostile fashion, ministers can easily disavow them. For example, on 8 February 1990, a think-tank suggested that child benefit be abolished: Thatcher told the Commons that her government had no 'immediate' plans to do this. The 'privatisation' of government advice in the form of think-tanks was a striking feature of Margaret Thatcher's impact upon policy making. The Institute for Public Policy Research (IPPR) has established itself over the past decade as a kind of Blairite think-tank, constantly on hand to feed in relevant ideas and research findings (see Box 24.1).

Prime Minister and Cabinet

This is the nerve centre of government, supported by the high-powered network of Cabinet committees, the Cabinet Office, the No. 10 Policy Unit and

policy advisers. After a period of ten years in office, it is likely that any Prime Minister will dominate policy making. Chapter 19 made it clear that while many sought to whisper policy suggestions in her ear, Margaret Thatcher's radical beliefs provided her with an apparently full agenda of her own. The evidence of her extraordinary personal impact on major policy areas is plain to see: privatisation, trade union legislation, the environment, the exchange rate, sanctions against South Africa, the poll tax and Europe – the list could go on. However, she was also unusual in taking a personal interest in less weighty matters such as her (ill-starred) attempt to clean up litter from Britain's streets following a visit to litter-free Israel. Harold Wilson saw himself as a 'deep lying halfback feeding the ball forward to the chaps who score the goals'. Thatcher was not content with this role: she wanted to score the goals as well. Wilson also said that a Prime Minister governs by 'interest and curiosity': Thatcher had insatiable appetites in both respects and an energy that enabled her to feed them to a remarkable degree. Under her, assisted by her own relentless energy and a constitution that delivers so much power to the executive, the office of Prime Minister took on a policy-initiating role comparable, perhaps, with that of the US President. John Major was also exceptionally hardworking, as premiers must be, but he was happy to delegate more than his predecessor and to listen to voices around the Cabinet table, especially that of his powerful deputy, Michael Heseltine. Blair has proved to be a premier more in the Thatcher mould, bypassing Cabinet and making decisions in small groups of close advisers (allegedly sitting on the sofa in Number 10 Downing Street), especially his 'kitchen cabinet', which originally included Alastair Campbell, Jonathan Powell and, more often than not, unelected aides rather than elected politicians (see Chapter 19). Blair has continued the 'presidentialising' tendency in British politics, dominating the spotlight of national attention and conducting a very personal style of government. The decision to back George W. Bush in his assault on Iraq in 2003 was very much the result of Blair's own passionate determination that this policy was the morally correct one. In her evidence to the Foreign Affairs Select Committee on 17 June 2003, Clare Short claimed a 'shocking collapse in proper government procedure' in that all the main decisions were made by Blair and a small unelected entourage of Blair, Alastair Campbell, Lady (Sally) Morgan, Jonathan Powell and adviser David Manning. Throughout the process, Foreign Secretary Jack Straw had been a mere 'cypher'. However, Blair has by no means had an easy ride as Prime Minister as throughout his time in Number 10, he has had to deal with a powerful and by no means ideal colleague, Gordon Brown (see Box 24.2 later in this chapter).

The concept of the core executive

This approach to understanding the nerve centre of British government has come into its own in recent years as it provides a clearer picture of how decision-making occurs while supplying a number of useful correctives to more traditional thinking (for a fuller discussion see Chapter 19). The basic idea of the core executive is that decision-making takes place at the highest level, constituted by a body of leading figures drawn, depending on the issue, from the Prime Minister's Office, the Cabinet and Cabinet Office plus the head officials of the departments concerned with the particular issue. This is a more helpful concept in that it reduces the notion of a simple hierarchy and replaces the idea of a tip to the pyramid with that of a halo or circle of key people. This is also useful in that it avoids the diversion of the difference between the political and administrative, the minister and civil servant. Anyone who has been involved in policy-making will describe how civil servants – in theory policy 'eunuchs' who merely stand by loyally while politicians undertake this democratically driven function – participate in its evolution as centrally as any politician. And the same goes, in recent years, for the top political advisers like Alastair Campbell. It also embraces the idea of a permanent core of central 'players' on the policy-making stage plus a regular cast who visit according to the issue on the agenda. One of the best short accounts of the core executive – Moran (2005), *Politics and Governance in the UK* – elaborates usefully on the modern PM's office:

The details [of the PM's Office] constantly change, partly because prime ministers constantly worry about whether they are being adequately served, and partly because life at the centre has a frenetic, hothouse quality: little empires are constantly being built (and dismantled) as different people struggle for the ear of the prime minister and for their own personal advancement. The atmosphere is rather like that of the court of a monarch, where the skill lies in catching the ear and the eye of the powerful one.

Moran (2005), p. 118

So private secretaries will process the information and paper which goes before the top person; combinations of civil servants and political advisers will feed in policy advice; and the press office will seek to ensure that what disseminates out to the wider political system, and beyond that to voters themselves, is formulated – with great sensitivity and sophistication – in a way which will advance policy objectives and not undermine them.

From this brief and admittedly selective description it is clear that:

■ Policy can be initiated at both the micro and macro levels from within any part of the political system, but the frequency and importance of initiatives grow as one moves from the periphery towards the centre.

■ Even peripheral influences can be swiftly drawn into the centre should the centre wish it.

■ Each policy environment is to some extent a world unto itself with its own distinctive characteristics.

■ The core executive, comprising the system's top decision-makers, will be complicit in formulating high policy and directing it outwards and downwards to the relevant parts of the government machine.

Higher education policy making, for example, will include, just for starters, the Prime Minister, the Cabinet, the No. 10 Policy Unit, plus senior officials from Education (the core executive) assisted by think-tanks, numerous parliamentary and party committees, more middle-ranking officials from the Departments of Education and Employment, the Treasury, the funding councils for the universities, the Committee of Vice-Chancellors and Principals, the Association of University Teachers and other unions, and *The Times Higher Education Supplement*, together with a galaxy of academic experts on any and every aspect of the subject. Downing Street policy – not just the PM but his network of aides and advisers – is now of key importance in this high-profile policy area. It was strongly rumoured that Estelle Morris resigned as Education Secretary partly because she did not agree with the university top-up fees favoured by former Policy Unit head and now education specialist, Andrew Adonis. The same adviser became a hands-on ennobled education minister in 2005 and was rumoured to have drafted the hugely controversial Education White Paper, proposing independence and trust status for successful schools and a slackening of local education authority control.

Policy formulation

Once a policy idea has received political endorsement it is fed into the system for detailed elaboration. This process involves certain key players from the initiation process, principally civil servants, possibly key pressure group leaders and outside experts (who usually are also political sympathisers) and, usually at a later stage, ministers. In the case of a major measure, there is often a learning phase in which civil servants and ministers acquaint themselves with the detail of the measure: this may require close consultation with experts and practitioners in the relevant policy environment. The measure, if it requires legislation, then has to chart a course first through the bureaucracy and then the legislature.

The bureaucratic process

This will entail numerous information-gathering and advisory committee meetings and a sequence of coordinating meetings with other ministries, especially the Treasury if finance is involved. Some of these meetings might be coordinated by the Cabinet Office, and when ministers become involved the measures will be progressed in Cabinet committees and ultimately full Cabinet before being passed on to parliamentary counsel, the expert drafters of parliamentary bills.

The legislative process

As Chapters 17 and 18 explained, this process involves several readings and debates in both chambers. Studies show that most legislation passes through unscathed, but controversial measures will face a number of hazards, which may influence their eventual shape. Opposition MPs and peers may seek to delay and move hostile amendments, but more important are rebellions within the government party: for example, the legislation required to install the community charge, or poll tax, in 1988–9 was amended several times in the face of threatened and actual revolts by Conservative MPs. Determined backbench Labour opposition to the university top-up fees legislation in January 2004 produced a series of amendments to the measure which made the

original proposal almost unrecognisable – though such examples are rare. The task of piloting measures through the legislature falls to ministers, closely advised by senior officials, and this is often when junior ministers can show their mettle and make a case for their advancement.

From this brief description it is clear that four sets of actors dominate the policy formulation process: ministers, civil servants, pressure group leaders and an array of experts appropriate to the subject. Some scholars calculate that the key personnel involved in policy formulation might number no more than 3,500. As in policy initiation, Margaret Thatcher also played an unusually interventionist role in this process. Reportedly she regularly called ministers and civil servants into No. 10 to speed things up, shift developments on to the desired track or discourage those with whom she disagreed. It would seem that Tony Blair is in the same mould and maybe more so, raging in public and private at the inertia of the public sector and the more general 'forces of conservatism' he criticised at the 1999 Bournemouth party conference. Dynamic politicians like Thatcher and Blair become impatient at the slowness with which the wheels of government turn and so seek to catalyse its progress through personal interventions. Since being in power Blair has also appointed a cabinet minister – sometimes called an 'enforcer' – who chases up and progresses issues: the first was Jack Cunningham and the most recent Lord (Gus) MacDonald. Clare Short, who resigned in May 2003 over the role of the UN in reconstructing Iraq, bitterly attacked Blair's centralisation of policy-making in a fashion which was still valid in 2006:

I think what's going on in the second term in this government, power is being increasingly centralised around the prime minister and just a few advisers, ever increasingly few. The Cabinet is now only a 'dignified' part of the constitution. It's gone the way of the Privy Council. Seriously, various policy initiatives are being driven by advisers [in No. 10] who are never scrutinised, never accountable.

Lord Butler of Brockwell, former Cabinet Secretary, was a well-known sceptic of Blair's methods involving political aides and meetings on the Number 10 sofa. His July 2004 *Review of Intelligence on Weapons of Mass Destruction*, arising from the decision to invade Iraq alongside US forces, contained a section on the machinery of government. In it the report cited evidence from two former Cabinet members who 'expressed their concern about the informal nature of much of the Government's decision-making process, and the relative lack of use of established Cabinet Committee machinery' (pp. 146–7). Specifically, the report pointed out that from April 2002 to the outbreak of hostilities, the Defence and Overseas Policy Committee did not meet once, yet there were 'some 25 meetings attended by key Ministers, officials and military officers most closely involved [who] provided the framework of discussion and decision-making within Government.'

Policy implementation

It is easy to assume that once the government has acted on something or legislated on an issue it is more or less closed. Certainly the record of government action reveals any number of measures that have fulfilled their objectives: for example, the Attlee government wished to establish a National Health Service and did so; in the 1980s, Conservative governments wished to sell off houses to council tenants and did so. But there are always problems that impede or sometimes frustrate implementation or that produce undesired side-effects. Between legislation and implementation many factors intervene. Jordan and Richardson (1982, pp. 234–5) quote the conditions that Hood suggests need to be fulfilled to achieve perfect implementation:

1. There must be a unitary administrative system rather like a huge army with a single line of authority. Conflict of authority could weaken control, and all information should be centralised in order to avoid compartmentalism.

2. The norms and rules enforced by the system have to be uniform. Similarly, objectives must be kept uniform if the unitary administrative system is to be really effective.

3. There must be perfect obedience or perfect control.

4. There must be perfect information and perfect communication – as well as perfect coordination.

5. There must be sufficient time for administrative resources to be mobilised.

To fulfil wholly any, let alone all, of these conditions would be rare indeed, so some degree of failure is inevitable with any government programme. Examples are easy to find.

Education

The 1944 Education Act intended that the new grammar, technical and secondary modern schools were to be different but share a 'parity of esteem'. In practice this did not happen: grammar schools became easily the most prestigious and recruited disproportionately from the middle classes. The government could not control parental choice. To remedy this, comprehensive schools were set up in the 1950s and 1960s, but it was the middle-class children who still performed best in examinations. Reformers also neglected one crucial and in retrospect blindingly obvious factor: comprehensive schools recruit from their own hinterlands, so inner-city schools draw children from predominantly working-class areas with a culture tending to produce lower educational standards, while suburban schools are drawn from more middle-class families who place a high value on education and whose children consequently achieve higher standards. The government made policy on the basis of inadequate information and awareness.

The economy

Burch and Wood (1990, pp. 172–3) record how governments have consistently planned on the basis of public expenditure plans that in the event were exceeded: an estimated increase of 12 per cent in 1971 for the year 1975 proved to be 28.6 per cent in practice. The government lacked control over its own spending departments. Following the stock market crash of 1987, Chancellor Nigel Lawson lowered interest rates to 9.5 per cent to avoid the danger of a recession. However, this measure led to an explosion of credit, fuelling an inflationary spending boom that required high interest rates to bring under control. High interest rates in their turn went on to cause economic recession in 1990. The government chose to ignore relevant information offered by advisers in 1988.

Inner-city policy

In the wake of her 1987 election victory, Margaret Thatcher resolved to tackle the problems of the inner cities. In March 1988, the Action for Cities initiative was launched with considerable fanfare. In January 1990, the National Audit Office reported that it had achieved only 'piecemeal success' (*The Guardian*, 25 January 1990); departments had 'made no overall assessment of inner cities' "special requirements"', and there was 'insufficient information to assess the strategic impact of the various programmes and initiatives involved'.

Poll tax

The euphemistically named 'community charge' – known as the poll tax – was the brainchild variously of right-wing think-tanks, Kenneth Baker, William Waldegrave and others (although following its collapse most people were keen to disclaim parentage – political failures, unsurprisingly, are always 'orphans'). The rationale behind it was logical; local taxes – the 'rates' – were based on property but penalised the wealthy, who paid more on big properties. However, over half were either exempted or received rebates yet still enjoyed the benefits of local services; consequently they had no reason to vote for lower rates and were not 'accountable' for them in the opinion of Conservatives like Thatcher, a keen supporter of the scheme. The new tax was to be a flat-rate one and payable by all to some degree, even students and the unemployed. The obvious unfairness of taxing the poor as heavily as the rich was widely recognised, even by Conservative voters. Yet Thatcher's personal support, defiant style and the pusillanimous nature of many MPs and ministers – Michael Portillo informed conference that he was not daunted but 'delighted' to be placed in charge of it – let a clearly flawed law onto the statute book. In March 1990, polls showed a huge majority opposed it and on 7 April a riot erupted in London. When John Major succeeded Thatcher he quickly replaced the measure with one more closely resembling the old property-based rates, and the heat soon left the issue of local government finance (for more on the poll tax, see Chapter 22). Programme failure also often results from the operation of constraints that constantly bear upon policy makers.

Constraints upon policy makers

Financial resources

Policy makers have to operate within available financial resources, which are a function of the nation's economic health at any particular time, and the willingness of key decision makers, especially in the Treasury, to make appropriate provision from funds available to government.

Political support

This is initially necessary to gain endorsement for a policy idea, but support is also necessary throughout the often extended and complex policy-making process. Lack of it, for example, characterised the tortured birth of the poll tax as well as its ignominious demise. Support at the political level is also crucial, but it is highly desirable within the bureaucracy and elsewhere in the policy environment. Resistance to policies can kill them off *en route*, and anticipated resistance is also important; as Jordan and Richardson (1982, p. 238) hypothesise: 'There are probably more policies which are never introduced because of the anticipation of resistance, than policies which have failed because of resistance.' Some departments now seek to gauge levels of popular support through the use of focus groups, a technique borrowed from commercial and political marketing (see Chapter 10).

Competence of key personnel

An able, energetic minister is likely to push policy measures through; a weak minister is not. Civil servants are famously able in Britain, but even they need to work hard to be up to the task of mastering rapidly the detail of new measures; their failure will impede the progress of a measure and limit its efficacy. Tony Blair has created (maybe necessary) waves in the Civil Service by emphasising the primacy of 'delivery'. Civil servants must be able to achieve practical things as well as advise ministers.

Time

New legislative initiatives need to carve space out of a timetable so overcrowded that winners of Private Members' ballots are lobbied by departments themselves to adopt bills awaiting parliamentary consideration. Moreover, the whole system is arguably over-centralised and, some would say, chronically overloaded.

Timing

Measures can fail if timing is not propitious. Just after a general election, for example, is a good time to introduce controversial measures. Margaret Thatcher, it will be recalled, was unable to secure the sale of British Leyland to an American company in the spring of 1986 because she had lost so much support over the Westland episode.

Coordination

Whitehall departments divide up the work of government in a particular way: proposals that fall between ministries are often at a disadvantage, and the job of coordinating diverse departments is not, in the view of critics, managed with particular efficiency. Burch (1979, p. 133) also notes that:

Too often policy making becomes a conflict between departments for a share of the limited resources available. This is . . . especially true of expenditure politics when departments fight for their own corner at the cost of broader policy objectives.

Personality factors

Key decision makers are not as rational as perhaps they ought to be. They might have personal objectives – ambition, desire for image and status,

and rivalries – which lead them to oppose rather than support certain policy objectives. The best recent example of this is the row between Margaret Thatcher and Nigel Lawson in the late 1980s over Britain's proposed entry into the exchange rate mechanism (ERM), which caused policy to drift. Another example is the differing attitude towards entering the single currency, with the Prime Minister enthusiastic and Chancellor Brown very cautious. That disagreement touches on one of the most thorny relationships in modern British politics, that of Gordon Brown and Tony Blair.

Geographical factors

A bias in favour of the southeast is often detectable in government policies – for example, in the granting of defence contracts – partly because decision makers in our centralised system live in the home

---

BOX 24.2	IDEAS AND PERSPECTIVES

The Blair and Brown rivalry

Much has been written in the press on this topic and eagerly read by a public which relishes struggles at the top of the greasy pole of politics. Allegedly it all started with an agreement between the two young stars of the party in the wake of John Smith's death back in 1994. At the Granita restaurant in Islington it was said by 'Brownites' that they agreed Brown would stand aside for Blair but that Blair had promised to stand aside in turn after a certain time had passed. 'Blairites' dispute this story and, in some cases, deny that it matters anyway. No conclusive proof exists either way to verify this story and both protagonists deny any deal was struck. Certainly, there is nothing conclusive written down. But it seems clear that Brown harbours a lifelong ambition to be Prime Minister as well as a burning resentment that Blair has let him down. A book by Robert Peston in early 2005 suggested that Brown was furious at Blair for allegedly betraying a promise to stand aside before the end of 2004.

The rivalry between Labour's two big beasts has dominated New Labour governments, fuelled by erstwhile aides who have briefed the press against the opposing politician, most notably Alastair Campbell for Blair and Charlie Whelan for Brown. When challenged, both men have denied such unseemly sentiments as rivalry or jealousy and both wish to remove suggestions that major decisions are affected by mere personality considerations. However, it does seem as if Brown, while a co-author of the New Labour 'project', is more committed to removing inequality and poverty and prefers more traditional approaches to the public services with less reliance on the private sector. In addition he seems less Europhile and has clearly frustrated Blair's enthusiasm for joining the euro. Some commentators have suggested that while Blair travels the world schmoozing world leaders, Brown has been efficiently directing the domestic agenda.

So dominating has the fraught relationship become that every reshuffle is interpreted in terms of whether Blair's or Brown's supporters have benefited from it. In September 2004 a major move appeared to have been made by Blair when he appointed Alan Milburn to be in charge of the election campaign instead of Brown who had performed this job in 1997 and 2001. In response Brown was said to have sulked and been quiescent during the early, difficult days of the campaign. However, he eventually decided to join the fray and accompanied Blair for much of the latter stages, even making a party political broadcast of them both speaking with fraternal affection to each other. Maybe Brown had realised that there was no purpose in inheriting a party divided by such a feud and weakened by a poor electoral performance.

Both must have appreciated that voters warmed to the idea of them working in harness and campaigning on the strength of the economy. Perhaps out of gratitude or, indeed, necessity, Blair announced during the campaign that Brown would stay on as Chancellor after the election, thus scotching rumours that he would be demoted to somewhere like the Foreign Office. Whether the dour, intellectual Scot will be able to manufacture a political coalition as powerful and lasting as Blair has managed, is something the future will reveal, always assuming Brown's ambitions are realised. There are precedents for premiers denying the crown to apparent successors: Churchill delayed his departure for years to keep Anthony Eden waiting in the fifties; and a few years on Macmillan frustrated the succession claims of R.A. Butler. Moreover there is no constitutional reason why Blair should step aside, and if Brownites try to force Blair out the collateral, divisive damage to the party might keep it out of office for a long time. Finally, at the time of writing, Blair has just survived an attempt to unseat him. Brown denied any involvement in this alleged 'coup' but he was damaged in the fall-out from the political machinations.

counties, partly because the southeast has a more buoyant economy and partly as a result of political factors: this after all is the heartland of the traditional party of government. (For a subtle and controversial analysis of territorial politics in the UK, see Bulpitt (1983).)

International events

The increasing interdependence of the large economies has made events such as the quadrupling of oil prices in the early 1970s major constraints upon policy making. In some cases these constraints are formal, as when the International Monetary Fund attached strict public expenditure conditions to its 1976 loan to Callaghan's Labour government. Political events such as the Falklands War can clearly have an enormous impact upon major policy areas, while the 1989 revolutions in the communist countries changed the whole context within which foreign policy is formulated. The greatest perturbations in the present century were caused initially by the terrorist attacks of 11 September 2001 followed by the successive US-led wars in Afghanistan and Iraq.

The influence of Europe

Treaty obligations and the growing power of Community institutions have imposed increasingly powerful constraints upon the freedom of action that British policy makers have enjoyed (see Chapter 31).

British policy-making is now well embedded into the Brussels machinery with senior civil servants constantly travelling on the shuttle to Brussels, Strasbourg and Luxembourg.

Policy networks

Jordan and Richardson (1987) argued that policy making in Britain is not uniform; every aspect has its own specific characteristics. They lay less stress on manifestos or the activities of Parliament but point to the mass of interconnecting bodies that have an interest in the policy area: the 'policy community'.

To some extent this is a theory about how interest groups interact with government to help formulate policy. Access to the policy community is restricted to actors prepared to play the game: act constitutionally, accept that the government has the last word, keep agreements and make reasonable demands. These rules automatically exclude radical groups with high-profile campaigning styles in most cases, although the accession to power of a radical political message can alter this, as in the case of Thatcherism. To exercise real clout, a group has to become an 'insider' (see Chapter 11). Communities have a core and a periphery – rather like that suggested in Figure 24.2 – with the stable core continuously involved in the policy process and a secondary group, less stable in membership, involved from time to time but lacking the resources to be in the core.

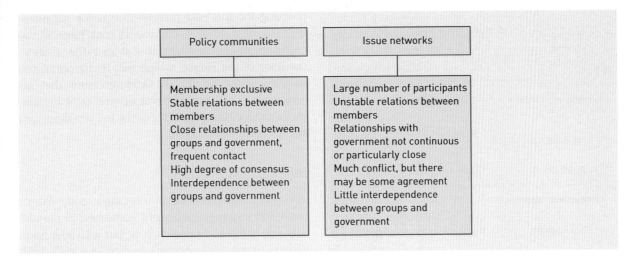

Figure 24.3 Policy networks
Source: Baggott (1995), p. 24

Professor Rod Rhodes developed this idea but saw that often the policy community was not cohesive or sharply defined; he began to discern a more fragmented and more accessible form: a 'policy network' with a very large and constantly changing membership, often with conflicting views. Baggott's diagram (Figure 24.3) shows the contrast between the two ideas with some clarity. Baggott (1995, p. 26) criticises the approach for not explaining the provenance of the networks and over-concentrating on the group–government nexus to the exclusion of the broader political environment.

Comprehensive political marketing

Jennifer Lees-Marchment wrote a book in 2001 which argued that marketing had become so all-pervasive in modern politics that politicians now 'design' policies for the electoral market and then deliver them once in power. She claims parties no longer dispense 'grand ideologies' striving to convert voters to their faiths. Instead they have adjusted to the way we now vote: instrumentally, expecting parties to deliver on promises made in the market-place of election campaigns. She argued that initially Labour was 'product-based' in the early 1980s when it persisted in selling something no one wanted. The result was failure. Then the party tried a 'sales-oriented' approach, improving its campaigning capacity through advertising, direct mailings and so forth. The result was better but still not enough to win. Then, as New Labour, it began to listen to 'market' demands via focus groups and polls, and fashioned

a 'product' the market, i.e. voters, really wanted. The result was the 1997 landslide. The thesis has been criticised as showing politics as devoid of real passion, or any meaning at all; but the analysis is sufficiently acute for much of it to emit the ring of truth.

■ Case studies in policy making

This chapter concludes with an examination of policy formulation and implementation in three case studies: the privatisation of British Telecom (BT) in 1984, the much criticised Millennium Dome project in the run-up to the year 2000, and the ongoing issue of identity cards.

British Telecom privatisation

While Conservative ideology had long argued for minimal state interference, official policy on privatisation was very cautious as late as 1978. 'Denationalisation', reported a Conservative policy study group in that year before the invention of the now familiar term, 'must be pursued cautiously and flexibly, recognizing that major changes may well be out of the question in some industries' (Lee, 1989, p. 139). The 1979 election manifesto had spoken only of selling just under a half share in selected industries. On 21 November 1980, a bill was presented separating the postal from the telephone side of the General Post Office. On 27 July 1981, British

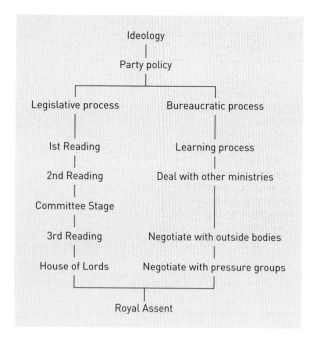

Figure 24.4 Negotiating the policy process
Source: From B. Jones (1986) *Is Democracy Working?*
Reproduced with permission of Tyne Tees TV

Telecom came into being. Shortly afterwards, Sir Geoffrey Howe inaugurated the age of privatisation with the announcement that several industries were being considered for this treatment: the biggest was British Telecom. Figure 24.4 characterises in a very simplified form the policy process that any measure has to negotiate.

Legislative process

When the bill to privatise BT was introduced it faced great opposition. The Post Office Engineering Union (POEU) had sponsored three MPs in the Commons, led by John Golding, who went on to become its general secretary (under its changed name, the National Communications Union). Golding spoke for eleven hours in the committee stage, but it was the general election that caused the bill to lapse in May 1983. Margaret Thatcher was quick to reintroduce an amended form of the bill after the election and, after a speedy progress helped by the guillotine, it became an Act on 12 April 1984.

By common consent, the second bill was a much more workable piece of legislation. In a Tyne Tees TV programme in August 1986, John Golding claimed some of the credit. Having realised that the large Conservative majority would ensure the bill's eventual success, he had decided to cut his losses by

pressing for the best possible terms for his members. Most of the important work took place in the corridors and at the committee stage rather than on the floor of the House, which was thinly populated during the debate stages. Golding claims that his own advice and expertise was often sought by ministers and civil servants alike as the bill was discussed and amendments moved.

Bureaucratic process

The bureaucratic process in this case to some extent preceded and to some extent continued in parallel with the legislative process. It began with a learning process when civil servants had to negotiate with BT officials and experts. Jason Crisp of *The Financial Times*, who followed these discussions closely, testified that talks were 'frequent, frantic, often very bad tempered'. Then negotiations with other ministries ensued, especially with the Treasury, which was primarily interested in the huge increases in revenue that privatisation would produce. Inevitably, the Department of Trade and Industry was more concerned with achieving a particular kind of settlement, and one that worked, and negotiations with the Treasury were consequently not always smooth.

Next came consultations with the City, where most of the finance was expected to originate. The DTI and the Treasury were clearly determined not to overprice BT's shares. The 1983 election manifesto had listed British Gas, Rolls-Royce, British Steel and others as future candidates for privatisation: they could not afford the failure of such a major test case as BT. The City financiers, like all potential buyers, had an interest in talking the price down, and this they did assiduously.

Finally, negotiations with outside pressure groups took place. In 1980, the British Telecom Union Campaign was formed with the POEU to the fore. With the help of a public relations company and an advertising agency, it orchestrated a campaign to frustrate the bill, and, when that failed, to soften its impact upon trade union members. The POEU, in its booklet *The Battle for British Telecom*, tells the story of how it put pressure on 800 key opinion makers in industry, and in the programme already referred to (Jones, 1986), John Golding told how the relevant pressure groups were mobilised over rural services, especially the provision of kiosks. The response from the likes of the National Farmers' Union, the local authority associations and the Women's Institutes was so overwhelming that civil servants 'begged' him to call off the campaign because the department was absolutely inundated by resolutions and letters that came from all those traditionally Conservative-supporting bodies. 'But of course we kept the campaign on and ... The ministers caved in and made certain that they protected the rural services as far as it was possible'.

A number of points can be made about the way in which this decision was made.

1. *Result differed from intention*: According to party ideology, the main thrust of privatisation is to reintroduce competition and to spread public ownership of shares. At the end of the three-year process, competition seemed to have taken a back seat. And while nearly two million people helped to produce the £4 billion flotation (within two years BT doubled in price to about £8 billion), the numbers had decreased to under 1.6 million owning only 12.6 per cent of BT stock. The result of all the pressures bearing upon the process therefore produced an outcome substantially different from the original intention.

2. *Complexity*: Given the dense complexity of the process, it is small wonder that the public loses touch with all the various twists and turns through Parliament and the corridors of Whitehall. Nor is it surprising that many governments shrink from major initiatives when such mountains of vested interests have to be moved. Margaret Thatcher's governments were indeed unusual in taking so many major initiatives – trade union reform, abolishing the metropolitan counties, privatisation – and succeeding in pushing so many through.

3. *The limits of majority rule*: The case of BT illustrates that a large majority is no substitute for workable legislation. On occasions even opposition MPs have to be called upon to provide the necessary expertise.

4. *The opportunities for influence and consultation are considerable*: Throughout the legislative and bureaucratic processes there are extensive opportunities for individuals and pressure groups to intervene and make their point.

5. *The professionalism of civil servants*: Civil servants are often accused of being generalists – experts on nothing – but in the case of BT they mastered an immensely technical field with remarkable speed. There is no evidence either that they dragged their heels over the privatisation of BT or did anything other than loyally carry out the bidding of their political masters. However, the irony is that the team which privatised BT dispersed soon afterwards, lured by private sector employers impressed with the relevant know-how the privatisation process had bestowed upon them.

Recent developments at BT

A Channel 4 documentary in March 2001 analysed this first privatisation experiment. BT needed £4 billion in investment and received it threefold via the flotation. Mercury was brought in to compete, with Oftel set up as regulator to keep the playing field level. Phone boxes had been treated with contempt – vandalised, stinking of urine, concreted equipment – and BT decided to renovate them all, which they did to improve customer perceptions. But despite privatisation the monopoly mindset persisted. Ian Vallance, head of BT, tried hard to play the global game and bought up wavebands for the new business. The result was a £39 billion debt and a slump in the share price to less than one-half of what it had been in the mid-1990s: from £15 down to £5.50. But potentially BT still has a big future, with 80 per cent of the nation's homes connected and the potential to become a major player. The present plan is to split BT into four companies and float each one individually, a big gamble indeed.

Millennium Dome project

A Conservative project

The provenance of this idea is to be found in John Major's 1992 administration: to celebrate the new millennium in a way that would capture the imaginations of the British people, rather as the Festival of Britain had done in 1951. The Millennium Commission was set up in 1993 and received substantial funding from the National Lottery. Various ideas were mooted to celebrate the event, some located outside the capital – one in Birmingham being the strongest rival to the London region. Michael Heseltine was keen on an exhibition based on the site of an old gasworks on the Greenwich peninsula on the prime meridian (0 degrees longitude). He became the driving force behind it, being appointed to the Millennium Commission when it was set up in 1994 and continuing in this role after becoming

Deputy Prime Minister in 1995. In 1996, he set up a Cabinet subcommittee to progress the idea and to raise capital from bankers and businessmen. Crick (1997, p. 430) tells how the DPM bullied and twisted arms, holding a series of weekly breakfast meetings to ensure that the project would be embraced by the government. The problem was that financing the project was very problematic, more so than the rejected Birmingham option. However, Heseltine was totally committed to the idea and steamrolled the doubters. In 1997, it seemed that the forthcoming election might imperil the project, so he personally lobbied Blair before the election (Heseltine, 2000, p. 513) and won his agreement to continue with it (should he win the election), subject to a review.

New Labour adopts the Dome

New Labour considered the Dome in an early Cabinet. Blair, it seemed, was uncertain and dithered for a month over a decision. Peter Mandelson, grandson of Herbert Morrison, architect of the 1951 Festival, was the chief proponent of the project but was opposed by Gordon Brown, who scorned such PR approaches and was worried that the Treasury would have to bail out a possible failure. With a week to go, 'the costings were dubious; the sponsorship was absent; the contents were vague when not non existent' (Rawnsley, 2000, p. 54). Moreover, the press was mostly derisive and other ministers were highly sceptical, including Chris Smith, Frank Dobson (who said that the Dome should be 'fired into outer space'), Clare Short and David Blunkett. However, Blair was taken by Mandelson's flamboyant vision of a huge, symbolic, all-inclusive dome to celebrate the 'rebirth of Britain under New Labour'. It seems that the initial doubts of John Prescott had been won over by the regeneration aspects of the scheme. At a pre-Cabinet meeting on 19 June 1997, moreover, he insisted that abandonment of the project at this early stage would make them look 'not much of a government'. When Blair had to leave the meeting early, Prescott took over and faced so much criticism that he dared not take a vote. Instead, 'Tony wants it' was enough for the project to be approved. Blair chose to ignore the Dome's critics in the press, Parliament and Cabinet and to press on with the (destined) national 'folly'.

In a *Guardian* article (13 May 2003) following her resignation as International Development Secretary, Clare Short recalled the decision on the Dome being taken:

We went around the table and everyone spoke. I remember Donald Dewar saying you could have a party and free drink for everyone in the country and still save a lot of money. Then Tony said 'I've got to go' and went out and announced we were going ahead with the dome. John Prescott was left there to sum up and that's how we learned that cabinet government was coming to an end.

Short added that this was too often the way in which bad decisions were taken.

The Dome

The structure was designed by the Richard Rogers Partnership and became the world's largest dome, covering, remarkably, nearly 20 acres. It was divided into six zones for the purposes of the exhibition, including a Learning Zone, a Body Zone, a Talk Zone and a Faith Zone. Mandelson was the first minister to be in charge of the project, Blair's former flatmate Lord Falconer the next in line. Jenny Page, a former civil servant, was made chief executive of the government-owned Millennium Experience Company. In 1997, the first of many public controversies was caused when Stephen Bayley, the somewhat volatile consultant creative director, resigned. Critics fastened onto the lateness of the project and the inaccessibility of the site plus the paucity of displays to fill the vast new arena. Mandelson's visit to Disneyland in January 1998 gave out all the wrong signals. Through the fog of government pronouncements the press delightedly began to discern something decidedly pear-shaped. Mandelson's 'it's going to knock your socks off' merely added fuel to negative expectations. The cost soon escalated from £200 million closer to £1 billion, and the undoubted quality of the Dome's structure – completed, astonishingly, on time – did not silence the critics, many of whom were invited to the opening celebration on New Year's Eve 1999. The evening's performances were rated as good but, by the greatest ill fortune, transport to the Dome broke down and huge crowds of key opinion formers were left waiting for three hours at a freezing East London station during which they sharpened their pens and then dipped them in vitriol for the next day's papers. Even New Labour's spin machine could not save the Dome from a comprehensive panning.

From then on it was downhill. The exhibitions were open to the public for the space of a year, and to meet financial targets twelve million members of

Finding a use for the Millennium Dome continues to prove difficult
Source: Copyright © Chris Riddell. From *The Observer*, 10 September 2000. Reproduced with permission from Guardian Newspapers Limited

the public were expected to pay the £20 entrance fee. However, actual attendance figures were half that, and while most who visited claimed that it was value for money, a vociferous minority insisted that it was not. Rawnsley comments acidly that 'The Dome was the vapid glorification of marketing over content, fashion over creation, ephemera over achievement . . . It was a folie de bombast' (2000, pp. 327–30). Even a Dome supporter, Polly Toynbee in *The Guardian*, had to confess that it was 'a lemon'. Within weeks, the Dome had to be subsidised with a further £60 million of lottery money. In February Jenny Page resigned, to be replaced by a Frenchman from Eurodisney, Pierre-Yves Gerbeau. The press assiduously reported the poor attendance and the breakdowns. In May, the chairman of the Millennium Company resigned. Poor 'Charlie' Falconer – the fall guy once Mandelson had departed – was forced to sustain a false enthusiasm for an unconscionable period. Eventually, the government came to sell the structure but found few

takers. In the end, it gave the building away – in exchange for a share of putative profits – to a company planning to turn it into a venue for rock concerts. A 'vacuous temple to political vanity' (Rawnsley, 2000, p. 331) had lost the nation a sum of money that could have built many schools and hospitals.

What went wrong?

■ *Icon politics*: The government opted for a vanity project with little focus or meaning. Moran (2001) calls this 'icon politics', projects chosen merely for their symbolic significance. Inevitably it was decided by those occupying the inner sanctum of government – it was intended to be Blair's opening manifesto ploy in his re-election campaign.

■ *Entertainment ill-suited to government*: The project was entertainment-based, and governments are not designed or equipped to succeed in such a fickle area. Desperate attempts to please a huge audience almost inevitably turned into banality; whatever the media advisers might have sought to feed to the nation, no amount of spin could change this.

■ *Financial warnings*: From early days, warnings regarding uncertain finances were ignored.

■ *Cabinet doubts* were voiced but overruled because of the iconic significance of the project. Fear of damaging criticism from the Opposition meant that such high-level criticism failed to enter the public domain.

■ *Abandonment* of the project at an early stage might have minimised the damage but the government – Blair to the fore – determined not to admit defeat and to brazen out the hurricane of flak.

All these factors contributed to the digging of an ever deeper hole by the government: a classic case of policy making gone horribly wrong.

Identity cards

This third case study is different because it is an ongoing policy issue which will not be finally resolved for some years yet. This policy saga – for that is what it has become – first entered the public domain in February 2002 when David Blunkett, the then Home Secretary, announced an 'entitlement card' to prevent benefit fraud and deter terrorism. The idea soon attracted vitriolic criticism for its estimated cost of over a billion pounds and its erosion of civil liberties. In consequence the idea was repackaged to be introduced in stages with a full decision on a compulsory scheme delayed until 2013. Many suggested the idea should be dropped, but instead of dropping the scheme after the 2005 election it was submitted to Parliament at the end of June. This time, however, the card was to include biometric information relating to the subject's face, fingerprints and iris; it was passed on its second reading but the government's slimmed majority was further reduced by rebels – mostly from the left-wing Campaign Group – to a mere thirty-one. In *The Guardian* on 28 June 2005 Martin Kettle discussed objections by David Davis, Charles Clarke's Conservative Shadow Home Secretary, who had

suggested that the idea had to pass the test of four questions:

1. Will it work to achieve its stated goals? Certainly it would help prevent benefit and identity fraud but few believe, even in government, that it would deter terrorists, producing an (at best) opaque case for the innovation in the first place. Debates in the Lords during January made the case seem more 'dubious' the longer they continued, according to *The Guardian* on 18 January 2006. In a letter to the same paper on 23 January 2006, the minister in charge, Tony McNulty, argued that the card would be a major blow against financial and benefit fraud: 'linking a unique biometric to personal data means people have control over access to their details.'

2. Is the government capable of introducing such a system? IT-based schemes have turned out to be notoriously difficult to introduce successfully and huge amounts had been wasted by the NHS on new data processing which had proved calamitous, as had the tax credit scheme which had resulted in huge overpayments being claimed back from recipients.

3. Is it cost-effective? Initial estimates of the cost exceeded £1 bn but that soon tripled, with the government's best estimate of the cost to the public of the card – in combination with a passport – being £93 per person. Over half of respondents to an ICM poll supported the scheme at such a price in June 2005. The Home Office calculated the cost at £6 bn over ten years, but a careful study by the LSE placed the total cost at £19 bn or even £24 bn. While rebutting the LSE estimate as absurd, the government resisted giving detailed costings on the grounds that such commercially sensitive information would prevent the public from receiving the best possible deal when contracts were issued. Lord Crickhowell in the Lords debate inevitably accused the government of offering the taxpayer a 'pig in the poke'.

4. Can civil liberties be safeguarded? The Information Commissioner, Richard Thomas, thinks not. He addressed the Home Affairs Select Committee in June 2004 and confessed himself 'increasingly alarmed' by the plan. He did not see a 'sufficient rationale' for recording for the whole population their name, address, date of birth, gender,

Steve Bell's caustic view on Charles Clarke's plans for ID cards
Source: Copyright © Steve Bell. From *The Guardian*, 28 June 2005. Reproduced with permission

nationality and biometric details from finger and eye scans. The idea had 'potential for significant detrimental impact on the day-to-day lives of individuals.'

So, ID cards appear to be too expensive, too riskily experimental, and far too dangerous a violation of civil liberties. But the government – convinced that these judgements will all be proved wrong – was determined to push through a 'flagship' piece of legislation. On 29 March 2006 votes in both Houses appeared to end the conflict between the two Houses. Despite the opposition of the Liberal Democrats, the measure was passed in the House of Lords 287–60. MPs later approved it 301–

84. From 2008 everyone renewing a passport will be issued an ID card and have their details placed on the National Identity Register. Through a legislative compromise, people will have the right, until 2010 not to be given a card; however, they will still have to pay for one and their details placed on the NIR. Anyone seeking a passport after 2010 will be obliged to have an ID Card. Sceptics, however, felt that little now stood in the way of a compulsory scheme for the whole country by that date. Time will tell whether the opposition was informed by the better analysis or whether, as so often with innovations that are initially opposed as the end of civilisation, ID cards become an accepted and necessary element of national life.

BOX 24.3   BRITAIN IN CONTEXT

Policy-making in the USA

Each political system produces different patterns of policy making. To some extent this is a direct reflection of system 'mechanics', but political culture and personalities as well as international factors often play important roles. So we see that in the USA, policy emerges via a route very different from that in the UK. At heart the British Prime Minister dominates the executive, like the President, but as long as his party is behind him, he also dominates the legislature. The US chief executive, however, is separately elected and has responsibility for initiating and implementing policy: on the face of it a more powerful figure. However, the US system is complex with myriad checks and balances.

The President is Head of State, Commander in Chief of the Armed Forces, Chief Appointing Officer, Chief Diplomat and, effectively, Chief Legislator. The President can veto any Congressional bill with which he disagrees; in addition to this he has responsibility for the successful implementation of policy. But these powers are balanced by the sole ability of Congress to declare war, the requirement for many appointments to be confirmed by the Senate, the need for a two-thirds majority to ratify treaties, the power of Congress over the making of new laws and the raising of revenue, the ability of Congress to override the veto with a two-thirds majority, and the ability of Congress to impeach the President for 'high crimes and misdemeanors'.

The President faces substantial foreign policy constraints from the Senate, made even more restrictive after the War Powers Act in 1973 in the wake of the Vietnam War. He has more freedom of action domestically but cannot set interest rates and is dependent on Congress for revenue. For a long time after the Constitution deemed that Congress would check the President, Congress was perceived as the more powerful institution, but in 1933 Roosevelt successfully extended presidential powers in a bid to overcome the problems created by the Depression. Since then the relationship has ebbed and flowed. Presidential success is crucially dependent on the President's ability to negotiate successfully with Congress; he often has to persuade dissident legislators from his *own* party to give him the support he needs to push measures through; party discipline is nowhere near as strong as in the UK. Congress may also, of course, be of a different political complexion, as Clinton found to his cost towards the end of his time in power.

The President appoints Cabinet members to lead departments but shares one much criticised feature of British politics: he tends to rely a great deal on personal aides and advisers. Both Thatcher and Blair were criticised for allowing their 'kitchen cabinets' to assume too much power, as did Nixon, Carter, Reagan and Clinton. George Bush Jr has also attracted some criticism but has perhaps tended to give secretaries of state like Rumsfeld and Rice relatively more room in which to operate. So a constant tension exists between departments and White House advisers as to whom the President listens and whose advice he follows.

The President has two other powerful weapons at his disposal. Firstly, he can appoint to the Supreme Court judges who tend to reflect his political views, thus influencing the context in which laws will be made over the next two to three decades. Secondly, he has unrivalled access to public opinion which he uses to encourage or even bully Congress into passing his laws. Roosevelt, when negotiating with unsympathetic Congressional leaders, used to glance meaningfully at the microphone placed on his desk in the Oval Office – it often did the trick. Public opinion is a constant resource available to the President as voters can be thus mobilised to put pressure on Congress to follow the presidential lead. This explains why presidential ratings are often taken more seriously in the US than those of the Prime Minister in the UK.

Chapter summary

Policy can be defined as either rules and regulations or public expenditure and its distribution. There are various theories about or models of policy making, including the pluralist, corporatist, ruling-class and Whitehall models, plus the rational choice and incrementalist perspectives on decision making. Policy can be seen to pass through three stages: initiation, formulation and implementation. 'Core' decision makers have a constant control of the process, but elements from the 'periphery' are brought in from time to time. The concept of policy networks is useful in analysing policy making. Extra-parliamentary parties and think-tanks can have considerable influence, depending on the issue and the situation. Implementation can be very difficult and result in policy objectives being missed or even reversed. Policy makers face many restraints upon their actions, including timing, coordination and international events.

Discussion points

■ Which model of policy making seems closest to reality?

■ Should there be more popular control over policy making?

■ How persuasive is Lindblom's theory of incrementalism?

■ What lessons can be learned from the process whereby BT was privatised and the Millennium Dome project brought into being?

Further reading

Building on the foundation texts of Lasswell, Simon, Lindblom, Etzioni, Dror and Wildavsky, the field of policy studies has spawned a substantial literature over the past forty years or more. In recent decades, Burch and Wood (1990) and Ham and Hill (1993) have provided good introductions to the denser studies available. Hogwood and Gunn (1984) is well written and interesting, as is Jordan and Richardson (1987). For an up-to-date and penetrating analysis see Smith (1993). The best comprehensive study of policy studies is Wayne Parsons' *Public Policy* (1995), but Peter John's *Analysing Public Policy* (1998) and Michael Hill's *The Policy Process in the Modern State* (2000) are shorter but competent, clear treatments. For an excellent shorter introduction to the topic, Moran's *Politics and Governance in the UK* (2005, pp. 412–50) has not been bettered.

References

Allison, G.T. (1971) *The Essence of Decision: Explaining the Cuban Missile Crisis* (Little, Brown).

Ashbee, E. and Ashford, N. (1999) *US Politics Today* (Manchester University Press).

Bachrach, P.S. and Baratz, M.S. (1970) *Power and Poverty, Theory and Practice* (Oxford University Press).

Baggott, R. (1995) *Pressure Groups Today* (Manchester University Press).

Bulpitt, J. (1983) *Territory and Power in the United Kingdom* (Manchester University Press).

Burch, M. (1979) 'The policy making process', in B. Jones and D. Kavanagh (eds), *British Politics Today* (Manchester University Press).

Burch, M. and Wood, B. (1990) *Public Policy in Britain*, 2nd edn (Martin Robertson).

Butler, Lord of Brockwell (2004) *Review of Intelligence on Weapons of Mass Destruction*, HC898, July.

Castles, F. (1982) *The Impact of Parties* (Sage).

Castles, F. (1989) *The Comparative History of Public Policy* (Oxford University Press).

Crick, M. (1997) *Michael Heseltine* (Hamish Hamilton).

Downs, A. (1957) *An Economic Theory of Democracy* (Harper & Row).

Easton, D. (1965) *A Framework for Political Analysis* (Prentice Hall).

Etzioni, A. (1964) *A Comparative Analysis of Complex Organisations* (Prentice Hall).

Etzioni, A. (1968) *An Active Society: A Theory of Societal and Political Processes* (Free Press).

Franklin, B. (1998) *Tough on Soundbites, Tough on the Causes of Soundbites*, Catalyst paper 3 (Catalyst).

Hague, R., Harrop, M. and Breslin, S. (1998) *Comparative Government and Politics* (Macmillan).

Ham, C. and Hill, M. (1993) *The Policy Process in the Modern Capitalist State* (Harvester Wheatsheaf).

Heseltine, M. (2000) *Life in the Jungle: My Autobiography* (Coronet).

Hill, M.J. (ed.) (1993) *New Agendas in the Study of the Policy Process* (Harvester Wheatsheaf).

Hill, M. (2000) *The Policy Process in the Modern State* (Prentice Hall).

Hogwood, B. (1992) *Trends in British Public Policy* (Open University Press).

Hogwood, B. and Gunn, L.A. (1984) *Policy Analysis in the Real World* (Oxford University Press).

Jessop, B. (1990) *State Theory: Putting Capitalist States in Their Place* (Polity Press).

John, P. (1998) *Analysing Public Policy* (Pinter).

Jones, B. (1986) *Is Democracy Working?* (Tyne Tees TV).

Jordan, G. and Richardson, J.J. (1982) 'The British policy style or the logic of negotiation', in J.J. Richardson (ed.), *Policy Styles in Western Europe* (Allen & Unwin).

Jordan, G. and Richardson, J.J. (1987) *Governing Under Pressure* (Martin Robertson).

Lee, G. (1989) 'Privatisation', in B. Jones (ed.), *Political Issues in Britain Today*, 3rd edn (Manchester University Press).

Lees-Marchment, J. (2001) *Political Marketing and British Political Parties: The Party's Just Begun* (Manchester University Press).

Lindblom, C.E. (1959) 'The science of muddling through', *Public Administration Review*, Vol. 19.

Lindblom, C.E. and Woodhouse, E.J. (1993) *The Policy Making Process*, 3rd edn (Prentice Hall).

Marx, K. and Engels E. (1848) *The Communist Manifesto* (Oxford University Press).

McKay, D. (2001) *American Politics and Society* (Blackwell).

Miliband, R. (1969) *The State in Capitalist Society* (Weidenfeld & Nicolson).

Moran, M. (2001) 'Not steering but drowning: policy catastrophes and the regulatory state', *Political Quarterly*, Autumn, pp. 414–27.

Moran. M. (2005) *Politics and Governance in the UK* (Palgrave).

National Audit Office, The Millennium Dome: report by the Comptroller and Auditor General, HC936 1999–2000, accessible at www.open.gov.uk/nao

Naughtie, J. (2001) *The Rivals* (Fourth Estate).

Parsons, W. (1995) *Public Policy* (Edward Elgar).

Platt, S. (1998) *Government by Task Force*, Catalyst paper 2 (Catalyst).

Rawnsley, A. (2000) *Servants of the People* (Hamish Hamilton).

Rowlands, D. and Pollock, A. (2004) 'Choice and responsiveness for older people in the "patient centred" NHS', *British Medical Journal*, January.

Schmitter, P.C. (1979) 'Still the century of corporatism', in P.C. Schmitter and G. Lembruch (eds), *Trends Towards Corporatist Intermediation* (Sage).

Schnattschneider, E.E. (1960) *The Semisovereign People* (Holt, Reinhart & Winston).

Simpson, D. (1999) *Pressure Groups* (Hodder & Stoughton).

Smith, M. (1993) *Pressure, Power and Policy* (Harvester Wheatsheaf).

Watts, D. (2003) *Understanding US/UK Government and Politics* (Manchester University Press).

Wildavsky, A. (1979) *Speaking the Truth to Power* (Little, Brown).

Wilensky, H. (1975) *The Welfare State and Equality* (University of California Press).

Useful websites

Fabian Society: www.fabian-society.org.uk

Demos: www.demos.co.uk

Catalyst: www.catalystforum.org.uk

10 Downing St: www.number10.gov.uk

Anti-ID Card Group: www.no2id.net

CHAPTER 25

The politics of law and order

Bill Jones

■ To explain the connection between political ideas and the problem of law and order.

■ To chart the extent of the problem and discuss the phenomenon of the 'crime wave' together with claims that it was reversed in the early 1990s.

■ To consider the causes of crime.

■ To examine responses to crime in the form of policing, penal policy, prisons and vigilantism.

■ To explain and analyse the secret security services.

The mood and temper of the public with regard to the treatment of crime and criminals is one of the unfailing tests of the civilization of a country.
Winston Churchill, as Home Secretary, 1911, quoted in Jenkins (2001), p. 180

A society should not be judged on how it treats its outstanding citizens but by how it treats its criminals.

Fyodor Dostoyevsky

Introduction

This chapter examines a political issue that affects everyone: crime and punishment. Opinion surveys show that concern on this topic has been steadily rising throughout the 1980s and 1990s as crime figures have soared and in some cases, for example property crime, even exceeded American levels. Anticipating a general election in 2005, Tony Blair packed his Queen's Speech in autumn 2004 with even more proposals to crack down on crime. This chapter examines the subject within the context of political ideas; assesses the extent of the current problem; discusses some of the probable causes of crime; looks at the contentious issue of policing, sentencing, prisons and crime prevention, including vigilantism; and concludes with a brief examination of the security services and other Home Office issues.

Tony Blair's suggestion that louts should face on-the-spot fines was – and continues to be – controversial
Source: From *The Observer*, 9 July 2000

■ Law, order and political ideas

Ever since humankind began to live together over 9,000 years ago, the question of law and order has been of central concern. Solitary cave dwellers did not need a code of law, but any group of humans living as a community did. Fundamental to such a code was property. From the earliest times this included food, clothes, homes and utensils, joined later by money once it had become a medium of exchange. Also highly important was physical safety – one of the reasons, after all, why people lived together in the first place. The Babylonian king, Hammurabi (d. 1750 BC) established a body of law famously based on the notion of retribution: 'an eye for an eye, a tooth for a tooth'; Islamic ('*sharia*') law, in some respects, tends to perpetuate such principles.

Legal systems in developed Western countries still seek to defend property and the person, but an extremely large variety of considerations have been embodied in pursuit of that elusive concept, 'justice'. Political thinkers have also wrestled with these problems. Aristotle recognised the necessity of law and governments that apply it with wisdom and justice. In the wake of the English Civil War, the philosopher Thomas Hobbes (see Chapter 5) rested his whole justification for the state on its ability to provide physical protection for its citizens. Without such protection, he argued, life would be a brutal process of destructive anarchy. Conservative philosophers have always stressed the need for such protection, arguing that humans are inherently weak and unable to resist the lure of evil without the deterrent of strict state-imposed sanctions. Conservative Party policy still reflects this powerful emphasis: 'The Conservative Party has always stood for the protection of the citizen and the defence of the rule of law' (1992 election manifesto).

Another group of philosophers approach the problem from a different angle. They argue that people are naturally inclined to be law-abiding and cooperative. They only transgress, so the argument runs, when their social environment damages them and makes deviation both inevitable and understandable. Social reorganisation therefore, can alleviate the problem of crime. Foremost among these thinkers was Karl Marx, who attributed most of what was wrong with society to the corrupting and debilitating effect of a vicious capitalist economic system.

A kind of continuum is therefore recognisable: pessimists, who see criminals as reflections of man's innate imperfections; and optimists, who believe that crime has roots in society and can be attacked and remedied by social action. In British politics, the Tories have tended to occupy a position towards the pessimistic end of the spectrum and Labour the optimistic one.

In 1979, Margaret Thatcher made great play of how hers was the party of law and order. Studies showed this benefited her enormously in the election of that year. Moreover, there is reason to believe that most voters tend towards the pessimistic end of the spectrum and respond to tough remedies that hark back to Hammurabi (if not the American Wild West). The Thatcherite analysis – still very influential in the Conservative Party – is that humans are

basically weak and sinful creatures who need all the support of Church, family, school and community to keep them on the straight and narrow. During the 1960s ('that third-rate decade', according to Norman Tebbit) Labour's over-liberal approach tipped the balance of socialisation towards an absence of individual responsibility: parents were encouraged to slough off their responsibility in favour of an insidiously vague concept of 'society', which took the blame for a whole portmanteau of things and destroyed the notion of 'personal accountability', that crucial binding quality in any functioning society. Consequently, children grew up expecting and exercising free licence – 'doing their own thing' in the argot of the time – moving on to become juvenile offenders and then hardened criminals. The *Sunday Telegraph* neatly summarises the Thatcherite argument (15 August 1993):

It is the very beliefs of those theorists [left-wing academics who maintain that crime is caused by social conditions] that are responsible for our present malaise. They preach, in a doctrine which first became prominent during the sixties but stretches back to Rousseau, that man is inherently good, and that he must cast off the chains of conventional behaviour and morality that enslave him.

The unlimited flow of immigrants, the argument continues, caused more tensions and contributed to crime, while the mob rule encouraged by militant trade union leaders further eroded belief in the rule of law.

Labour rejected this view of the world. Their Home Office spokesmen and spokeswomen preferred to concentrate on the roots of crime, which they believed lay in poor economic and social conditions. The first element of this is seen as the huge inequality between rich and poor that the free-enterprise economic system invariably creates. Such social gulfs create anger and frustration: members of the favoured élite are able to progress smoothly through privileged education to highly paid and influential jobs. Meanwhile, poor people face vastly inferior life chances and huge, often insurmountable, challenges if they wish to succeed. They are surrounded by images that equate personal value with certain symbols such as expensive cars and clothes: when they cannot acquire them legally, it is a small step to breaking the law to redress the balance. So the system itself causes crime by encouraging people to want things that they have to steal to acquire. When

DAVID SIMONDS

PARTY GEAR –
YEARS GONE BY

PARTY GEAR –
2003

The killing of two Birmingham teenagers at a New Year's Eve party shocked the nation and highlighted Britain's growing gun culture
Source: Copyright © David Simonds. Reproduced with permission

they do not, the result is often poverty and hopelessness: the breeding ground of crime for successive generations of people at the bottom of the pile. Left-wingers also point to how the law favours the rich and protects their property, imprisoning petty burglars for long stretches yet letting off city fraudsters with suspended sentences or fines.

Interestingly, the positions of both major parties began to converge in the early 1990s. The Tories had long insisted that social conditions were not connected with crime: how else did figures stay stable during the Depression years of the 1930s? However, the massive increase in crime during the 1980s and early 1990s and a series of studies by the Home Office (especially those of Simon Field, who plotted graphs of property crime and consumption in 1900–88, finding a close correlation between unemployment and property crime) encouraged a change of heart. Eventually, the government abandoned this untenable position: on 28 October 1992

Home Office minister Michael Jack accepted that recession had played its part in pushing up the crime figures, saying that downturns in the economy were traditionally accompanied by increases in crime.

For its part, Labour responded to the spate of fearsome juvenile crime in 1993 – including the horrific murder of Jamie Bulger by two young boys – by expressing a tougher line on sentencing and the treatment of young offenders. The two big parties, especially with Kenneth Clarke as Home Secretary and Tony Blair as Shadow Home Secretary ('tough on crime, tough on the causes of crime'), found a surprising amount upon which to agree.

As the 1997 general election approached, both parties targeted crime as a campaign priority, adopting tough postures on handguns and combat knives in the autumn of 1996, for example. Indeed Michael Howard, the populist Conservative Home Secretary, sought to play to the right-wing gallery in his own

BIOGRAPHY

Michael Howard (1941–)

Former Conservative Home Secretary. Educated at Cambridge. Became MP in 1983, minister of local government, Employment and Environment Secretary before Home Secretary 1993–7. Stood in leadership election in 1997 but, after being criticised in a Commons speech by former junior understudy Ann Widdecombe, saw the man he asked to run as his deputy go on to win. Left the Shadow Cabinet in 1999. In 2001 he returned as Shadow Chancellor under Iain Duncan Smith. When this period of leadership came to an undistinguished end, Howard was elected unopposed to take IDS's place. He led his party into the May 2005 election but when Labour won its third term, Howard resigned, leaving the field open for a new generation of younger Conservatives. He never quite lost the negative aura he acquired whilst Home Secretary in 1993–7.

party; what was more surprising was that his Labour shadow, Jack Straw, sought to match him and even exceed him in right-wing zeal, so sensitive had the opposition become to the need to attract floating votes, especially middle-class ones, in order to end eighteen years out of power (see also Reiner, 2006a).

Crime figures and 'reversing' the crime wave

Given that crime is such a sensitive issue, much debate between government and opposition focuses on the interpretation of crime figures. Conservative spokesmen on crime during the eighties and nineties tended to minimise the rate of crime increase: they did not want voters to think there had been no return for all the money spent on law and order since 1979. The party's *Campaign Guide* in 1997 played the international comparison card:

Since 1945 the general trend in crime in Western countries has been upward. However, in the years 1993–5, England and Wales . . . had the largest fall in recorded crime – 8% – of any of the 18 OECD countries . . . In Amsterdam there are . . . 84 murders per million people;

in Stockholm 54 per million; in Berlin 39 per million. The homicide rate for London was 22 murders per million people in 1995.

The 1992 International Crime Survey for England and Wales revealed a lower rate of theft victims than in Germany, Switzerland, Finland, the USA and Australia. Moreover, the same survey showed that in terms of violent assault, the home figures were well below those of (surprisingly) the Netherlands, Germany, the USA and Australia. Some criminologists point out that the 'crime wave' is a statistical concept and like all statistics can be easily misunderstood:

1. It is not the volume but the proportion of certain crimes being reported that has increased in some cases. More people have reported burglaries because many more people now have property insurance as well as telephones.

2. The majority of crime is very trivial, perhaps involving no damage or derisory sums of a few pounds.

3. Britain used to be much more violent than it is today, as the work of E.G. Dunning (1987) from Leicester University has demonstrated. In thirteenth-century Britain, historians estimate that twenty murders were committed for every 100,000 people: seventeen times today's rate.

4. The huge increase in police manpower since 1979 has boosted the ability of the police to record crimes that before might have been omitted.

5. The publicity given to crime figures can mask the fact that Britain is still a country where the average chance of being mugged is slightly less than once every five centuries; or of sustaining an injury from an assault once every century. In this respect, Britain is much safer than Germany, the USA or Australia.

Just when the Conservative government must have been despairing of what to do about crime, statistics in 1993–4 came to the rescue. They showed a drop of 5 per cent on the previous year, and the 1994–5 figures showed a similar decline, although the 1995 figures registered only a 2.4 per cent fall. Michael Howard claimed jubilantly that his get-tough policies were finally winning through and the 1994 party conference – containing grey-haired old ladies who want to bring back the birch – applauded him to the echo. *The Economist* (23 September 1995), however, would not believe a word of it. The right-of-centre journal pointed out the following:

1. Unemployment had been falling, and even official Home Office studies proved a causal connection between levels of unemployment and crime rates.

2. Most crimes are committed by young men aged between 15 and 24; between 1989 and 1993 their number declined from 4.5 million to 4 million.

3. Some police forces have been targeting groups of hardened criminals, e.g. the Met's pre-emptive Bumblebee and Eagle Eye operations. It could be that they have borne some fruit.

4. Better anti-theft devices on cars could also have had a slowing-down effect on vehicle crime, which fell by 10 per cent between 1993 and 1994.

■ The current extent of the problem

A BBC *Panorama* programme on 2 August 1993 revealed how widespread the perception of crime is in the UK. In a study commissioned by the BBC, majorities were found who had been burgled in the previous year and who expected to be burgled again. Crime is ubiquitous and all-pervading. Many people can recall a different era when it was safe to leave a car unlocked for half an hour or more, or to leave doors unlocked at night. Not now. In 1921, a mere 103,000 **notifiable offences** were recorded; by 1979, the number was 2.5 million; by 1993, it had increased to an alarming 5.7 million, a 128 per cent increase in fourteen years. During the mid-1990s the figures began to fall, although the first two years of the new millennium witnessed a slight new upward curve.

According to the Home Office's British Crime Survey, a survey of victims, not reported offences (and widely regarded by criminologists as the most reliable indicator of crime trends), in 1992, 94 per cent of all notified crimes were against property, while 5 per cent were crimes of violence. By 2002 the BCS showed, contrary to recorded figures, a surprising drop back to the levels of the early 1980s.

Figures for 1998 exceeded 5 million but reflected a new way of recording crime that counted every crime suffered by a victim, e.g. a person stealing six cars is now recorded as six offences, not one. In addition, new categories of crime were recorded, including 'possession of drugs' and 'common assault'. This tended to inflate crime figures misleadingly.

Using the 'old rules', the 1998 figures revealed the sixth successive annual fall, although the subsequent increases up to 2002 were relatively small. From there, annual BCS figures showed surprisingly large reductions. Figures for domestic burglary fell by one-fifth during the twelve months from 2003–4 to 2004–5. Vehicle thefts fell by 11 per cent during the same period and violent crime by 7 per cent. The figures recorded by police tend to be less cheering as they are often in conflict with the Home Office's BCS. So, for example, Home Office experts challenge the view that violent crime has really increased and attribute the difference to changes in reporting and recording practices. Hazel Blears, the Home Office minister, added that the pattern of crime recording had changed, with people more likely than before to report low-level scuffles to the police, and the 'increased activity of police on Friday and Saturday nights in city centres.'

Burglary figures, however, matched exactly for domestic burglaries, prompting the assistant director of Home Office research to note that they registered the biggest fall since 1915, bringing overall numbers back to the level of 1981. This means the average risk of being burgled had declined by 2005 to once every 58 years from a high of once every 27 years in 1995. Moreover, apparent increases in sexual crimes were explicable, according to the Home Office, by the fact that a new crime – indecent exposure – had been added to this category. Using BCS figures, the overall reduction in crime since the 1995 peak was a massive and unprecedented 44 per cent.

Clear-up rates

Despite the relative stability of the crime figures, and the recent falls, nobody can afford to be complacent. Moreover, at the end of the 1970s the police cleared up 40 per cent of all crime; within the next two decades the clear-up rate had plummeted to around a quarter. When Labour came to power it pledged to achieve convictions in 1.2 million of the five million annual crimes. However, by October 2002 the pledge had been dropped as figures revealed an even sharper drop in convictions between March 2000 and the following March, when they fell by 80,000 from 1.1 million. Home Secretary David Blunkett set a new date of April 2006 for the 2001 target. More happily, by 2004 the number of detected crimes had increased to 1.4 million, up 2 per cent on the 2003 figure, 3 per cent for violence against the person.

The criminal mind

Fear of crime

Considerable concern has been expressed over the fear of crime that so much lurid publicity engenders. Newspapers know that the public has a morbid interest in crime stories and consequently feed it in order to sell copies. The result is that elderly ladies are terrified to go out even though they are the category least at risk from violent crime. Interviews with 10,000 women for the 1994 British Crime Survey revealed that one in five felt 'very unsafe' when walking out at night, even though fewer than seventy claimed to have been attacked in the past year. Paradoxically, young males living in inner city areas are least afraid yet most likely to be the victims of crime. Indeed, the inner cities seem to be the breeding ground of a great deal of crime, and their working-class denizens are most likely to be the victims. Similarly, a professional person is 50 per cent less likely to be burgled than an unskilled worker.

The position of the inner cities as the 'headquarters of crime' has slipped, however. A report in *The Guardian* (12 December 1992) revealed that more crime was now committed in rural areas (56 per cent) than in urban areas (44 per cent). Nevertheless, the inner areas of the cities are still the most prone to crime. The 1992 BCS revealed that the poorest council estates faced a risk of burglary 2.8 times the average. Figures for 2001–2 showed that, as so often before, a substantial number of people – 67 per cent – believed that crime was rising despite the fact that it declined by 22 per cent during 1997–2001. At the same time figures revealed declining confidence in the police, with less than half believing they do a 'good or excellent job' compared with 64 per cent in 1996. Similarly, confidence in prisons declined from 38 per cent to 26 per cent over the same period. In April 2003, *The Guardian* carried a report on crime

figures from the most recent BCS. It showed that despite a substantial fall in crime a sharp rise had occurred in the number of people believing that crime was on the increase: from 56 per cent in 2001 to 71 per cent in 2002. Jon Simmons, of the Home Office said, 'The public will take some time before their understanding catches up with the current reality.' How long such catching up takes, or indeed if it ever does, given lurid crime reporting practices in the media, is anyone's guess. However, one hopeful indication was a report on 18 January 2006 that fear of crime had fallen by 19 per cent in London, with 62 per cent saying that they felt safe, even at night. According to the sixth annual London survey, more localising of police forces had seemed to bear fruit in reduced crime and anxieties about crime.

In April 2006 the Institute of Public Policy and Research (IPPR) published a report, *Crime-share: the Unequal Impact of Crime*. This revealed that poor and unemployed people are twice as likely to be mugged than the average, twice as likely to be 'very worried' about violent crime, and three times as likely to suffer emotional damage as a result of it. Victims of violent crime, almost half a million, tended to avoid public transport and streets after dark; 32,000 people changed jobs and 180,000 moved homes as a direct result of being attacked. Nick Pearce, director of IPPR, said:

People living in poorer households have less choice about where they live, cannot afford to pay for expensive alarm systems or take taxis home in the evening. They are less able to control the risks they face and often have no option but to expose themselves to greater danger.

Patterns of offending and causes of crime

One longitudinal survey of all people born in 1953 revealed that by the age of 30 one in three men had been convicted of a crime; one in sixteen had been to prison; and, significantly, the 7 per cent who had been convicted six or more times accounted for two-thirds of all offences. The survey also showed that violence was on the increase: one in eight men convicted of an offence had committed a crime of violence by the age of 20. For those born in 1963, the proportion had risen to one in five. Certainly young criminals seem to abound. Most crimes are committed by people aged 14 to 20; over 90 per cent of all 15- to 16-year-old offenders re-offend within four years. On 20 November 1996, the Audit Commission reported on juvenile justice. Its document, *Misspent Youth*, revealed that the 150,000 teenage offenders commit seven million crimes every year, only 19 per cent of which are recorded by police and only 5 per cent cleared up, with a mere 3 per cent resulting in arrest and action. Moreover, there is a demographic 'crime bomb' in the making as the population begins to bulge in the 18- to 20-year-old age group, now the peak age of offending for young men.

Whatever the qualifications one has to apply to crime figures, there is no doubt that they are far too high. All the crime surveys show that the public is highly aware that crime is a ubiquitous threat. As Walter Ellis wrote in the *Sunday Telegraph* (4 July 1993):

For the public . . . crime has become a lottery, a prize draw in which the odds of becoming a victim are shortening every day. To those who have been burgled for the fourth time, or seen their car driven off by a 15-year-old, or been mugged for 50p outside a kebab house the ergonomics of policing are only of passing importance. Ordinary people want to feel safe in their own streets.

Some of the causes of crime have already been touched on. Politicians, it has been shown, argue either that people have become, or have been allowed to become, less law-abiding, more 'evil' even, or that society has become a forcing ground for such deviancy. Causes inevitably reflect political prejudices, but there are other possible causes.

The huge gap between rich and poor

One view is that all forms of private property constitute a form of theft, that all property by rights belongs to everyone. According to this view, everyone who is rich has 'appropriated' their property from others, leading to the position espoused by the American radical Angela Davis: 'The real criminals in this society are not the people who populate the prisons across the state but those who have stolen the wealth of the world from the people.' A less articulate version of this justification was offered by a Liverpudlian youth in a *Weekend World* programme broadcast in December 1987: 'Some people have got jobs, they can go out and buy things they want. But we're on the dole, we haven't got the money so we go out robbing to get the money.' It remains a fact that the gap between rich and poor in Britain over the last twenty years has grown

faster than in any other developed Western country. Recent research has also shown, unsurprisingly maybe, that the closer the juxtaposition of wealth and poverty and the greater the difference, then the greater the stimulus to crime (see Dorling, 2005).

There are now so many more potential crimes

In the old days, family arguments were ignored by police as 'domestics'. Since the law has changed, crimes of violence have registered an increase. Furthermore, the proliferation of consumer goods has increased the opportunity for crime: there are simply more things to steal, especially valuable portable objects.

Young people are faced with a difficult world in which to grow up

1. Many of them are increasingly the products of fragmented families and have lacked the emotional security of a proper home.

2. Long-term unemployment has replaced valuable socialisation with despair. As a consequence young people lose out, as American sociologist Charles Murray (1990) observes, 'acquiring skills and the network of friends and experiences enable them to establish a place for themselves – not only in the workplace but a vantage point from which they can make sense of themselves and their lives' (p. 25).

3. As a consequence of unemployment, youngsters find life infinitely grey and pointless. Crime can seem like the ultimate rebellion and excitement. John Purves, a solicitor who has defended many young joyriders in the northwest and the northeast, explains that it 'provides an escape from their humdrum existences. They are thrilled by the speed of these flying machines and the more dangerous it gets the more excited they become. It's an addiction . . . The press call them "deathriders"; that's the real thrill' (*The Observer*, 25 June 1994).

Growth of an underclass

Charles Murray, quoted above, has written that he thinks the UK is well on the way to developing its own underclass of disaffected poor living in the inner cities, often in council housing and unemployed,

BOX 25.1	IDEAS AND PERSPECTIVES

What really causes crime? Polly Toynbee's view

In 1988 a piece of Home Office research fell on stony ground, out of kilter with the ruling ideology of the times. *Trends in Crime and their Interpretation* plotted crime figures in the last century against the economic cycles, with graphs tracking crime against boom and bust. Its evidence is conclusive: in good times, when *per capita* consumption rises with higher employment, property crime falls. When people have money their need is less great, so burglary and theft trends drop. However, theft rises as soon as consumption falls when the economy dips and people on the margins fall out of work. But that is not the whole picture. Something else happens in good times. People have more money in their pockets, they go out and their consumption of alcohol rises. The result? They hit each other more and personal violence figures rise. Exactly this is happening now with near full employment and soaring drink consumption, creating a rise in assaults, mainly young men hitting each other at night (mainly not very hard, only 14 per cent visited a doctor afterwards).

Source: Polly Toynbee, 'What Really Causes Crime?', *The Guardian*, 12 July 2002.
© Guardian Newspapers Limited 2002, reprinted with permission

eking out their lives on benefits and crime. Any youngster living in such an area finds it very difficult to resist the allure and rewards of crime and the attractions of drugs, easy living and violence.

Values have declined

This view is especially popular with Conservatives, who hark back to a golden age when it was possible to live without fear of crime. Geoff Pearson's book *Hooligan* (1983) disposes of this myth:

Conservatives have enthused about this mythical law abiding society 20 years ago for decades. Twenty years ago, in fact, they were just as worried about crime and disorderly youth as they are now, panicked by hippies in the late sixties and early seventies, by Teds in the fifties and 'Americanised youth' in the forties.

Drugs and crime

Much has been written about the complex connection between drugs and crime. Chris Nuttal, in charge of research at the Home Office, estimates that two-thirds of all property crime is drug-related. On average a heroin addict has to raise £13,500 annually to support the habit, £8,000 more if crack cocaine is also involved. Most of this is raised via shoplifting, and a series of drug tests in different parts of the country have revealed that over three-quarters of those arrested were under the influence of alcohol and two-thirds other drugs. Figures for 2002 revealed that one-third of people blamed drugs

as the main source of crime. In July 2005 the press revealed that a suppressed report on the war on drugs showed it was being lost. Traffickers made so much money out of their trade that seizures of 60–80 per cent were needed to turn the tide; in reality seizures amounted to a mere 20 per cent. An increasingly influential argument has emerged pressing for control of recreational drugs through legalisation, but most politicians shy away from a policy which superficially appears to advocate easier access to dangerous drugs.

Anti-social behaviour

Much has been written about the rise of anti-social behaviour or 'yob culture' of the kind which makes town and city centres unwelcome to families, women on their own or middle-aged people wishing to go to theatres and cinemas. The source of the problem, most agree, is excessive consumption of alcohol and so the further liberalisation of drinking hours which took place in November 2005 was not thought to be an especially intelligent piece of government, though, to be fair, it had minimal impact.

■ Responses to crime

Policing

If, as Hobbes asserted, the prime purpose of government is the preservation of law and order, then the police, in modern society, are at the front line of enforcement: they implement the most important rationale of government.

The police occupy an ambivalent and politically sensitive role in society. According to classic democratic theory they are the neutral instruments of society, acting, as Sir Robert Mark (Commissioner of the Metropolitan Police in the 1970s) observed, 'not . . . at the behest of a minister or any political party, not even the party in government. We act on behalf of the people as a whole.'

However, the police command great power in society, and there are plenty of examples of how they have become the creatures of a particular political ideology or the willing instruments of oppression: Nazi Germany, the USSR, Red China and many regimes in South America and elsewhere. In Britain, the police have traditionally been thought to be a source of national pride, the friendly 'bobby on his beat' being an international symbol of our social stability and consensual style. However, as crime figures rose in the 1970s and the right-wing policies of Thatcherism began to be implemented in the early 1980s, the police became a subject of intense political debate. The Left accused Thatcher of using the police to suppress public reaction to her unpopular and socially divisive policies. The police were also seen as willing accomplices, weighed down with right-wing prejudices such as contempt for the poor, ethnic minorities and women, and riddled with corruption and criminal inefficiencies of the kind that caused miscarriages of justice such as the Guildford Four and the Birmingham Six.

Is there any proof of these left-wing allegations? A report by the Policy Studies Institute (PSI) in the late 1980s revealed widespread racist (of which more below) and sexist attitudes together with frequent drunkenness on duty. Reiner (1993) reports that one of his studies revealed that 80 per cent of officers questioned described themselves as Conservatives, with the remainder equally divided between Labour and Liberals (p. 123). He also cites substantial evidence from the UK and USA supporting the contention that police routinely subscribe to racist views (pp. 125–8). However, these research findings should be qualified: British police seem no worse than similar forces in the USA and Canada; and the same PSI report revealed that the large majority of Londoners were satisfied with the service provided.

The Right preferred to see the police as staunch defenders of society, beleaguered by attacks from the Left and misguided 'do-gooders'. The eccentric former chief constable of Greater Manchester, James Anderton, even believed at one time that the Left planned to undermine the whole edifice of police neutrality in preparation for the totalitarian state they craved (Reiner, 1993). Throughout the 1980s, debate over the police was highly polarised, particularly during the 1984–5 miners' strike, when Labour accused the government of trying surreptitiously to establish a national police system antithetical to the notion of community service and accountability. Towards the end of the decade, however, the manifest failure of the police to stem the increase in crime led to a change of heart on the Right. This was occasioned partly by the publicity given to miscarriages of justice and the spate of lawlessness typified by joyriders operating with apparent impunity while the police seemed to stand idly by. All this helped to create an unprecedented fall in public esteem for the apparatus of law enforcement. Writing in the *Sunday Times* (11 February 1989), journalist Simon Jenkins wrote: 'Crime is the Passchendaele of Whitehall. The more money wasted on fighting it the more is demanded for "just one more push".' Indeed, on the value for money criterion, over the period 1979–93 the police did not come out too well: spending went up by 88 per cent, including 70 per cent increases in pay, yet offences more than doubled while clear-up rates plummeted. In 1993 even the chief of the new National Criminal Intelligence Service described the entire criminal justice system as 'archaic and irrelevant'. The police have defended themselves with vehemence, claiming politicians are asking too much of the thin blue line which lies between the lawless and the law-abiding. They claim the law is slanted too much in favour of the criminal and not the victim and that they are overburdened by paperwork. Indeed, there was something in this latter claim: *The Guardian* reported a case in September 1992 which generated a remarkable 45 tons of paper, and in 2002 a survey revealed that on average policemen and policewomen spent 43 per cent of their time inside the police station and only 17 per cent on patrol.

On 26 June 1993, *The Economist* ran a story that in many parts of London the police had simply 'given up', letting criminals off with a caution rather than face the excessive paperwork and the good chance the criminal will get off with a light sentence. Writing in the *Daily Telegraph* on 20 July 1993, Roger Graef observed: 'The net effect of victims not reporting crimes and police not recording or detecting them is that only two out of every hundred

Stephen Lawrence, a black teenager, was stabbed to death in 1993. The 1999 Macpherson Report accused the police of 'institutional racism'
Source: Courtesy of The Stephen Lawrence Charitable Trust (www.stephenlawrence.org.uk)

crimes are punished in court.' As if to compound these fears, an Audit Commission report leaked to *The Guardian* on 20 September 1993 recommended that police forces should prioritise responses to crime, concentrating on the important ones at the expense of the trivial, handing over the latter to uniformed officers while the CID addressed major crime and criminals.

Race and the police

Police have often been accused of racism, and the 1999 Macpherson Report into the 1993 murder of black student Stephen Lawrence accused the police of 'institutional racism'. In November 2002, research showed that black people are eight times more likely to be stopped and searched by the police than whites. Given this bias, it could be argued, it is hardly surprising that one in six of those in prison is black, while blacks as a group make up a mere 2 per cent in the general population.

Scarman Report

Following the inner city riots in the early 1980s, the Scarman Report urged closer cooperation with local communities and more bobbies on the beat. Some of these recommendations were implemented, and the spirit of Scarman permeated thinking on police policy in the 1980s. However, concern with management structures and value for money led to the production of an even more contentious report in 1993, produced by Sir Patrick Sheehy, a businessman. He recommended abolition of three senior ranks and a number of perks enjoyed by the force. Resistance was fierce and instant – even employing the advocacy of former Prime Minister James Callaghan – and the more unpalatable proposals were shelved. In 2005 the government suggested a series of mergers between police forces, based on a study by the chief inspector of police Dennis O'Connor. Enlarging police authorities would enable them to deal with wider ranges of serious offences but the police bulk at the proposed reduction of authorities from 43 to 12. The police, in early 2006, argued that bigger does not necessarily mean better in terms of efficiency and they resisted the increased centralisation implicit in the plan. When the detailed plans were announced on 25 January 2006 police organisations, not to mention Conservative and Liberal Democrat spokespeople, expressed opposition to the proposed ability of the Home Secretary to intervene in failing authorities and to install management 'hit squads'. The proposals were eventually scaled down.

Police and civil liberties

When Tony Blair included so many items in the 2004 Queen's Speech relating to crime and police powers, many lawyers expressed alarm at the erosion of civil liberties such powers would bring. Lawyers condemned Blunkett's plan to give the police powers to arrest for *all* criminal offences and not just the more important ones, as 'utterly unacceptable and grossly disproportionate' (*The Guardian*, 23 November 2004). This measure was eventually passed into law, opposition to it having been reduced by the fear and outrage occasioned by the July bombings in the London Underground. Blair encountered even more fervent opposition when he sought to give police the right to detain suspects under a new terrorism act for a total of 90 days. This was too much for Labour back-benchers who rejected this clause in November 2005 and reduced the period allowed to 28 days, still far too long according to some civil libertarians, but far too short a time according to policemen who argued more time was required to assemble cases against such offenders.

BOX 25.2 IDEAS AND PERSPECTIVES

Role of the police and analyses of society

In January 2005 the right-leaning think-tank, Civitas, accused British police of being among the 'world's worst'. Their report – *Cultures and Crimes: Policing in Four Nations* – blamed the decline in efficacy on the breakdown of the traditional family and the disappearance of the bobby on the beat: 'the police need to be visible to stop people committing crimes, not driving around in cars', said one of the authors, Norman Dennis. The Association for Chief Police Officers dismissed the report, as did the Home Office which pointed to the massive drop in crime since 1997. On 18 November 2005 Sir Ian Blair, the Metropolitan Police Commissioner, addressed the state of the police in his Dimbleby Lecture (see his interview in *The Guardian*, 16 November 2005). He believed the state of the police was such that a major debate on its future was required. He attributed crime and anti-social behaviour to the decline of social 'glue' which used to be provided by the Church, trade unions and the like; the disappearance of 'agents of social enforcement like park keepers and bus conductors'; and the closing down of long-stay psychiatric wards.

The leading UK authority on the police, Professor Robert Reiner, from the LSE, cast his net for causes a little wider. He argued (in *The Guardian*, 24 November 2005) that:

The supposed golden age of British policing by consent (most of the 20th century but particularly the 1940s and 50s) was a confidence trick. Crime and order were maintained by informal social controls, above all the gradual inclusion of the whole population into common citizenship. However, the police took much of the credit. In myriad individual cases police helped people in distress, although there was also rampant corruption and brutality. But the contribution of policing to the maintenance of overall order was primarily symbolic. Much research evidence shows that policing had little effect on levels of offending.

Reiner sees rocketing crime rates as the consequences of neo-liberalism – unemployment, inequality, poverty – and 'egoistic consumerist culture and declining deference'. He argues that relative inequality breeds crime and violence – 'the rich are a major part of the problem.' Compounding this problem have been the policies pursued by New Labour. Reiner sees the tipping point occurring in the early 1990s when New Labour accepted the 'economic and social framework of Thatcherism', meaning that the second part of Blair's mantra on crime – 'tough on the causes of crime' – was likely to be vestigial; now the police had to try to be 'tough on crime' to substitute for the vanished social cohesion. Reiner believes the police have had some apparent success, though largely through the ameliorative influence of a growing economy, but that the public have continued to feel insecure, partly through the increase in violent crime and in terrorism, a consequence of the government's foreign policy.

Penal policy

Speaking in 1985, Margaret Thatcher told the American Bar Association of the fear of ordinary people that 'too many sentences do not fit the crime'. Given the provenance of her own ideas (see above), it is hardly surprising that she thought sentences should be higher, and indeed between 1984 and 1987 sentences for serious crimes such as armed robbery and rape increased markedly. During that period the average length of custodial sentences

for adult males for using firearms to resist arrest increased by 97 per cent, and for rape by 63 per cent.

However, despite the invariable rhetoric of Conservative candidates during elections and the well-publicised views of Margaret Thatcher, the death penalty for murder was not reintroduced under the Tories despite several attempts by diehard 'hangers'. On 8 June 1988, the vote went 341 votes (in the traditional free vote on this issue) to 218. The truth seems to be that however hard candidates try to milk the alleged two-thirds majority of the public in favour of the death penalty, when they hear the arguments and statistics coolly explained in parliamentary debates they surrender to reason and vote to sustain abolition. The facts show that, at well below 1,000 a year, Britain has a relatively small number of murders (the USA has over 20,000); there is no evidence to suggest that murders have increased since abolition; and reintroduction would impose immense burdens on judges and juries. Cases such as the Guildford Four and the Birmingham Six show how easy it is for innocent people to be found guilty of murder, and once they have been executed it is too late to make amends.

Prisons

Since the Strangeways prison riots in 1990, prisons have been at the centre of an intense debate. Denying a malefactor his or her freedom has been a traditional form of punishment ever since law and order was invented. In the early days conditions in prisons were horrendous, with no sanitation and appalling food. Since then conditions have improved immensely, but denial of freedom is still a very punitive measure.

Some experts argue persuasively that prison is counterproductive. They maintain that prison is merely a place where new crimes are learned and planned and young petty offenders turned into serious criminals – 'the universities of crime' (see Box 25.3). It is sadly true that 60 per cent of prisoners re-offend within two years. These experts also point out that only a small percentage of those locked up – perhaps 10 per cent – are serious offenders: the majority are there for minor offences against property.

The notion of rehabilitation is sometimes overlooked when we discuss prisons. Punishment is seen as the chief rationale – and we punish more extensively by custodial sentences than any other country in Europe: only South Africa and the USA imprison more. The Prison Service costs well over £2 billion a year to run. It costs £37,000 a year to keep someone in prison, much, much more, in most cases, than has been stolen in the first place.

During the 1980s, it became apparent that our prisons were grossly overcrowded: in one case, a maximum prison capacity of 40,000 prisoners was being forced to accommodate, in the mid-1980s, 55,729, many squeezed two or three to a cell and

Wormwood Scrubs, one of Britain's best known, most ancient and most overcrowded prisons
Source: Copyright © Cordaiy Photo Library Ltd/Corbis

BOX 25.3 **EXAMPLE**

Approved training to become a criminal

Prison is a notoriously ineffective way of turning people away from offending.
Paul Cavadino, Director of the National Association for Resettlement of Offenders, April 2003

When Denis was 12, the police found him sitting in a parked stolen car: 'I hadn't nicked it, I had no idea how to drive.' He was sent to an approved school near Dundee, 'a big house which had been converted'. Some of the children were not offenders at all but the victims of abuse: the youngest, who lived in their own cottage, were only five.

'More often than not, we were left to ourselves in the dorms', Denis said. 'There was no counselling, no one to talk to about my experiences, what I had witnessed. Yes we had our activities but there was no love there, no emotional growth. It was an institution, my first prison.'

The fourteen months Denis spent at approved school laid the foundations for what was to follow. He said: 'I learned everything about crime there. I did my first burglary one night when I ran away. I learned how to drive, how to steal a car; how to fight and how to lie and get away with it. It made me what I am, it was where the criminal subculture started.'

After leaving, he went on the run, living rough in squats, before eventually rejoining his mother at her new home near Manchester. 'By then the die was cast. I was a criminal.'

At the age of 15, Denis was arrested for stealing a car and was sent to DC, a detention centre in Nottingham-shire. It was the 'short, sharp shock'. 'They turned us into little tough guys', he said. 'There was circuit training every day, and a lot of physical abuse from the staff. And again, you met all the lads, who'd been to approved school, through the courts system, who were already dreaming of a career in the big time.'

'And the more they tell you you're bad, you're a criminal, the more you accept it and get on with it. At DC, kids were already seeing themselves as gangsters. That's where you made your connections, and found out what families from what areas are into what type of crime, and how to sell your goods.'

'Afterwards, it was like the Vietnam syndrome: you're only drawn to those who've suffered the same trauma, the same experience. So your only pals are the people you met in DC.'

Two months after leaving DC, aged just 15, Denis was in Strangeways for the first time, waiting to be sent for fifteen months to a borstal, convicted of burglary, criminal damage and car theft. 'It was more of the same. You met the lads you'd met in DC, all the same faces.' At 17, after further burglaries, he was back in Strangeways, this time for a year.

Then, for a while, the pattern seemed broken. Denis married and worked as a welder. But it was not easy to build a settled life. 'You were always involved in a bit of "dodge" because you always got phone calls from your pals. The underworld is always there, still thriving.'

He lost one job when a colleague told management he had been to prison. Then his marriage broke up, precipitating a period of drug abuse, and armed robbery seemed like 'a natural progression, the pinnacle of my career.'

Prison education saved him: 'It was a route into myself, I discovered my mind and another world. Up to that point I'd been told by my mother, by the courts, by prison, that I was mad, bad.'

Now preparing to begin a law degree at Bristol University, he has a stark message for Mr Major and Mr Clarke [the then PM and Home Secretary, respectively]. 'They frighten me to death, because they don't have a clue what they are doing. They need to break the circle, stop the abuse. The prisons are where Great Britain hides from its inner self. They are full of the educational system's mistakes, the mental hospitals' mistakes, the courts' mistakes. That's why I want to practise law.'

Source: The Observer, 28 February 1993. © Guardian Newspapers Limited 1993, reprinted with permission

without any proper sanitation. Even the Conservative Home Secretary in the 1980s, William Whitelaw, was moved to describe our prisons as 'an affront to civilised society'. The Strangeways riots, and related riots in other prisons, were to some extent an explosion of pent-up frustration at poor conditions and official indifference. In response came the impressive Woolf Report (600 pages, 204 recommendations) urging a fundamental reform of prison regimes to ensure that they prepared inmates for release by treating them with dignity and respect. The report was endorsed by all three parties in the 1992 general election but has yet to be implemented.

Towards the end of the 1980s the prison population began to decline (45,693 in 1989) as more non-custodial sentences such as community service orders were passed, but this did not mean that all was well. A report by Judge Stephen Tumin, the Chief Inspector of Prisons, discovered that in some prisons inmates had to wait ten days for a shower and even longer for clean underwear. Post-Strangeways changes, moreover, did not stop another serious riot breaking out in September 1993 in Wymott Prison, Lancashire. Here prisoners ran amok, causing £20 million worth of damage to a prison that had been held up as a model regime. Judge Tumin was appointed to investigate, the irony being that in 1991 Tumin had already reported on Wymott, discerning widespread drug taking and the permeation of 'a gangland culture'.

The Labour opposition and the Prison Officers' Association heavily criticised the Conservative government and Michael Howard, then Home Secretary, for concentrating all his efforts not on solving present problems but on seeking to privatise as many prisons as he could in order, according to his critics, to satisfy the right wing of his own party. Certainly, he marked a shift towards a more punitive philosophy, urging less recreation and more sewing of mailbags, arguing that 'prisoners enjoy a standard of comfort which taxpayers would find hard to understand'.

In September 1993, a new programme of prison privatisation was announced: twelve contracts to be awarded for new prisons within two years. Howard declared that the aim was to 'create a private sector able to secure continuing and lasting improvements in standards, quality and cost efficiency across the whole of the prison system'. Despite encouraging experience of private prisons in the USA (see Windlesham, 1993, pp. 280–6), experience in the UK had been mixed. The success of the in-house bid

by Strangeways staff was hailed by the government. But the privately run Wolds Prison had been criticised in April 1992 by the Prison Reform Trust for creating a life for inmates that was 'boring and aimless with evidence of widespread violence and drug abuse'. The contracting-out of court escort services to Group 4 Security (a director of which, embarrassingly, turned out to be Sir Norman Fowler, then chairman of the Conservative Party) became a laughing stock in 1993 when a succession of prisoners escaped. However, despite criticising privatised prisons fiercely in opposition, Labour accepted them as a *fait accompli* once in power and as a cost-effective solution.

The Conservatives were not consistent on prison policy in the 1980s. In the early part of the decade they pandered to their activists by being tough and the prisons filled up; towards the end of the decade they supported non-custodial sentences, but as crime grew relentlessly the gut instinct to get tough again could not be resisted and Michael Howard adopted his 'prison works' approach (see Box 25.4). His policy was much criticised by prison reform groups (but not by police organisations) as likely to increase prison populations by 15,000 new inmates and cost up to £700,000. In April 1996 the prison population stood at 54,974, rising to well over 72,000 by 2002. In December 2002, Home Office projections foresaw a figure of 100,000 by 2006; even the most optimistic projections put the population figure at over 91,000 by 2009 (see Figure 25.1). By August

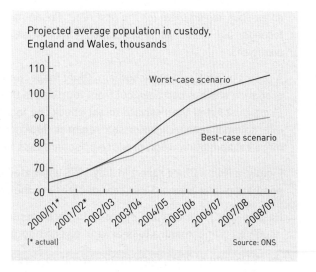

Figure 25.1 Prison populations
Source: From *The Guardian*, 10 December 2002. © Guardian Newspapers Limited 2002, reproduced with permission

BOX 25.4	IDEAS AND PERSPECTIVES

Howard's measures to curb crime

At the 1993 Conservative Party conference in Blackpool, Home Secretary Michael Howard unveiled 'the most comprehensive programme of action against crime' announced in Britain, including abolition of the right to silence for defendants; new measures against terrorism; tougher penalties for persistent young offenders; the building of six new prisons; new powers to evict squatters and for police to stop trespassers; automatic custody for anyone convicted of rape, manslaughter or murder or attempting the offence who is subsequently accused of any of these crimes; a review to toughen sentences in the community; and accepting all sixteen proposals of review on cutting paperwork to let police do more active duties.

Howard told the conference:

There is a tidal wave of concern about crime in this country. I am not going to ignore it. I am going to take action. Tough action.

However, the reaction to Howard's line was not as warm outside the conference chamber as it was within. Lord Justice Woolf threw in a firecracker when he said publicly that these 'get tough' policies would not work and were 'short-sighted and irresponsible'. On 17 October 1993, *The Observer* led with the views of no fewer than seven judges, all of whom attacked the idea asserted by Howard that 'prison works' through taking criminals off the street and providing a deterrent to others.

Lord Ackner said the causes of crime 'lay deep in society, in the deterioration of personal standards, the family and the lack of self-discipline'. Lord Justice Farquharson, chairman of the Judicial Studies Board, said:

I cannot understand why the population of people in prison in this country is greater than in others. I think that's wrong . . . My general philosophy is that you should never impose a prison sentence when you can avoid it. The idea that we are building more and more prisons appals me. I have never believed prison rehabilitates anyone.

Lord Bruce Laughland was even more explicit:

The effectiveness of the deterrent diminishes the more an individual goes to prison. People fear hearing the gates shut behind them for the first time. Prison may satisfy public opinion and the victims' understandable feelings, but it has no rehabilitation effect whatsoever . . . a great deal of dishonesty is contributed by politicians.

A report by Sir David Ramsbotham, Chief Inspector of Prisons, recorded that at one major London prison probation officers had been cut from fourteen to three and the education programme by 55 per cent. *The Economist* noted that Howard might check the fact that 'There are more than 500 pieces of research or international research on prison regimes. Most of them agree that regimes with more education and more rehabilitation work, produce prisoners less likely to reoffend'.

Finally, a Home Office report in July 1998 estimated that it would need a 25 per cent increase in the prison population to achieve a 1 per cent decrease in the crime rate.

Despite being traditionally opposed to harsh sentences, Labour in power seemed to have taken Blair's 'tough on crime' mantra to heart and prison numbers have continued to climb.

On 19 December 2002, Lord Justice Woolf advised judges to sentence burglars for first or second offences to community sentences instead of eighteen months in jail. Part of the motivation was to ease the pressure on prisons and to reduce the re-offending rate.

However, the Lord Chief Justice was virtually contradicted by Sir John Stevens, the Metropolitan Police Commissioner, on 20 January 2003 when he told *The Guardian* that in certain cases of first offences offenders needed to be locked up. He argued that the first time in court rarely reflected the first offence and that 'there comes a time when society has had enough – we need respite from these peoples' activity. I'm sorry, they have to be put in prison.' He also cited US experience, where putting millions in prison seemed to have succeeded in reducing crime rates in the big cities.

2005 UK prisons held 76,897 inmates; the Prison Reform Trust commented that seventy-four of our 142 jails were 'over the certified normal accommodation' level. In October we also learnt that the number had risen to 77,774 of whom 12 per cent were foreign nationals – a result of soaring drug and fraud offences. Charles Clarke, the Home Secretary, admitted that the absolute limit was close; with numbers rising by over 200 a week it has probably, by the time of writing, been exceeded by some distance.

Writing in *The Guardian* on 30 November 2005, Simon Jenkins, himself a relative hardliner on crime, criticised the situation in which we imprisoned half as many people again as France and Germany, including more women and children than any other country in Europe:

The easy soft, do-nothing prison option may appease public opinion. But we do not cure hospital diseases by sacking nurses, or congestion by slashing tyres. Getting tough on crime means finding out what causes crime and trying to redress that. The thirst for revenge that oozes from all fixed sentencing guidelines is medieval. Everything I have read on crime suggests that public protection demands the incarceration of at most a quarter of the present prison population. Britons can't be inherently worse behaved than anyone else in Europe. It is the law that is deficient.

Alternatives to prison

Alternatives to prison are often mooted, but community service orders are often seen by the public as being too mild a corrective for violent young offenders. Indeed, it is young offenders who pose the most intractable problem. It often seems that the problem begins with broken homes, leading to institutionalised children who grow up without any real affection. This often leads to misbehaviour in school with truanting and then petty crime. Once on the elevator of crime and detention centre the child

is lost to the alternative values of the criminal world, where all means to better oneself are acceptable as long as one is not caught. The Audit Commission's report, cited above, judges that money spent on sending second- and third-time offenders through an extended and ineffective court system could be better spent on tackling the problem at an earlier stage before the cycle of decline has set in.

Anti-Social Behaviour Orders (ASBOs)

These new measures were introduced in Jack Straw's 1998 Crime and Disorder Act. They give the police the power to prohibit for a period of two years violent or racist behaviour in local communities. ASBOs are targeted especially at the 'neighbours from hell' and at young troublemakers who can terrorise estates through intimidation and petty crime. They do not require a court appearance but if breached can result in imprisonment for the offender. From a slow beginning their application rose rapidly so that by June 2005 nearly 5,000 had been issued, with almost half on children aged 10–17. Greater Manchester issues the highest number of ASBOs, followed by London and other conurbations. There is no doubt that some ASBOs have solved persistent anti-social behaviour but there are persistent reports of misapplication, as in the case of the 15-year-old boy suffering from Tourette's syndrome, who was abusing neighbours. The civil rights group Liberty feared that in some cases use of the measure 'could lead to vigilantism'.

Respect Agenda

Following his 2005 election victory Tony Blair made much of his 'Respect Agenda': action by government which would serve to reduce yobbish behaviour and increase the amount of respect in society. His 'Respect' Task Force came up with a number of suggestions in January 2006: the eviction from their homes of anti-social neighbours for up to three months; on-the-spot fines for petty offenders; and parenting classes for problem families including a new 'Parenting Academy' to train officials to give advice. Critics argued that it is almost impossible to legislate for more respect and that Blair had overstepped what it is possible for governments legitimately to do. Moreover, say the critics, eviction is simply a sticking-plaster solution: problem families cannot be simply wished away; they still have to live somewhere and their behaviour somehow dealt with.

Other alternatives

Further alternative schemes available include the following:

1. *Caution Plus*: The favoured approach of Northamptonshire diversion unit. The offender is cautioned and agrees to pay compensation to the victim, who has to be met face to face. An 'action plan' is drawn up to prevent further offending. Average cost £640 per case, one-quarter of the present system. Only 35 per cent re-offend after eighteen months.

2. *The Halt Programme*: A Netherlands scheme whereby under-18s can be referred to one of seventy available schemes if they admit guilt and have not been on such a scheme more than twice. Compensation has to be paid and a degree of 'shaming' takes place in which offenders are seen publicly to make amends; for example, shoplifting girls had to clean the floors of the supermarket they had stolen from. The scheme claims a 40 per cent re-offending rate compared with 80 per cent of those prosecuted.

3. *New Zealand family group conferences*: Based on a Maori method of settling disputes whereby instead of a court case, the extended family is convened to discuss the offender's actions; reparation and preventive measures are agreed. Half of victims say they are satisfied with the outcome. In the spring of 2003 Home Secretary David Blunkett announced a new emphasis on restorative justice along the lines pioneered in New Zealand.

4. *Identity chips*: At a Downing Street seminar on crime on 12 October 1999, chief constables told Mr Blair of a scheme to add identity chips to all new electrical goods so that ownership could be traced.

5. *Head Start*: This was the scheme introduced in the 1960s in the USA whereby some 700,000 children in high-crime areas were given two years of nursery education. Studies over the ensuing thirty-year period revealed much higher levels of education and college attendance, lower crime rates, more employment, more home ownership and more stable marriages. Accordingly, the Home Office aimed to spend £200 million on intensive nursery education in UK high-crime areas.

6. *Abortion*: A report in *The Guardian* on 10 August 1999 on a Chicago University study suggested that half of the dramatic drop in the crime rate in the USA was the result of abortion among key groups of women: those separated or unmarried, and those who are poor or from ethnic minorities. Studies reveal that, where such groups had a high rate of abortion, crime dropped off notably in later years. No one suggested that abortion should be adopted as an official anti-crime policy, but the study does suggest how crime is concentrated in certain areas and in certain social groups.

7. *Reducing Offending: Home Office Report, July 1998*: This major report ruled out as effective preventive measures such popular solutions as more police patrols, zero tolerance and merely increasing police numbers. It focused on the utility of targeting repeat offenders, directing patrols to 'hot spot' areas and identifying patterns of crime.

8. *Public opinion*: An ICM poll published in early January 2006 revealed that even victims did not favour retributive forms of punishment. The 'overwhelming majority' of crime victims believe that the best ways to curb non-violent crime are to provide more activities for young people, ensure they are better supervised by their parents, and provide more treatment for drug and mental health problems.

Crime prevention and the vigilante movement

Many experts argue that spending money on preventing crime is more cost-effective than trying to cope with it once it has occurred. Often proposals centre on alerting the community to be more vigilant. Neighbourhood watch areas are now a common feature, numbering over 40,000 nationwide. However, some studies suggest that such schemes merely squeeze crime out of the suburbs and back onto the street. Neighbours have also become a little inured to alarms sounding: to some extent they have become merely another ubiquitous urban noise.

In 1993, the Holme Wood estate in Bradford was assigned a special team to look after its interests: the result was a 61 per cent decrease in burglaries. Much more widespread, however, seems to be a growing reliance on 'do it yourself' policing or, to use its popular name, vigilantism. This issue came dramatically to public attention in 1993. On 10 August, the press reported the case of Alan Hocking, who kidnapped 18-year-old Michael Roberts, whom he suspected of selling LSD to 13-year-olds, and drove him on a nightmare thirty-minute journey before attacking him with a wooden club spiked with nails. Duncan Bond and Mark Chapman were given five-year sentences for kidnapping a well-known local thief in order to teach him a lesson. The huge public response to the sentence helped to reduce it on appeal to six months.

The fear of legal reprisals has not deterred other groups of residents from making their own arrangements when they feel the police have let them down. In St Anne's, a Bristol suburb, a shopkeeper, Norman Guyatt, was so appalled by a brutal daylight robbery of an old couple that he and his two sons and a few others started patrolling the streets in the small hours to detect and report possible burglaries. A sports groundsman, Stan Claridge, now leads the fight against crime in the same area, organising patrols and setting up video cameras in key areas. A local security firm, Knighthawk Security, regularly patrols the streets, being paid a pound a week by each resident. Similar forces patrol Sneyd Park in Bristol and in Merseyside and other urban areas. As a result, crime has dropped in such areas by as much as three-quarters.

There are certainly dangers that vigilantes can dispense arbitrary justice to the wrong people, but the press and public reactions have been largely in favour of self-help so far. Even the police, wary of a movement that is by definition a criticism of their ineffectiveness, have given occasional guarded welcomes to such initiatives, although the Police Federation officially regards private guards as potentially dangerous. In Sedgefield, Co. Durham, the local council has reacted to local crime by setting up its own thirty-strong community force to patrol the streets. The Home Office has responded by exhuming and re-encouraging 'special constables' and uniformed 'town wardens'.

BIOGRAPHY

David Blunkett (1947–)

Born in Sheffield and educated initially in his own city before going to the Royal Normal College for the Blind, Richmond College FE and then Sheffield University, where he studied politics. Worked for the Gas Board and then as a tutor in industrial relations. Became a councillor in 1970, going on to lead Sheffield Council (1980–7) before being elected MP for Sheffield Brightside in 1987. Shadowed Environment and Education before being appointed Secretary of State for Education in 1997, where he was generally reckoned to have had a successful period in office. In 2001 was made Home Secretary, where he became known for being tough on criminals and not overly tender towards asylum seekers. No doubt it was this alleged illiberalism that prompted Sir John Mortimer to declare in March 2003: 'It is so sad to learn, as a lifelong Labour voter, that our Home Secretaries are worse than the Conservative ones.'

■ The security services and related Home Office matters

As well as the law enforcement agencies of the courts, supported by the police, there are the security services, much loved by novelists and screenwriters as sources for their plot lines. People who have worked for these services usually puncture the popular illusion of mystery, excitement and glamour by claiming that such work is mostly routine and often very boring. Most of us, perhaps, would be surprised that defending the state against enemies within or without is not inherently exciting.

Three pieces of legislation authorise the security services:

1. *Security Service Act 1989 (amended in 1996)*: This placed the services under the control of the Home Office and laid out the duties of the Director General.

2. *Intelligence Services Act 1994 (ISA)*: This established the Intelligence and Security Committee,

a Commons Committee that oversees the expenditure, administration and policy of the intelligence and security services.

3. *Regulation and Investigatory Powers Act 2000 (RIPA)*: The Act that set up the Commissioner of Interception, a Commissioner for the intelligence services and a tribunal to hear complaints under the Human Rights Act.

The last two Acts allow warrants to be issued by the Home Secretary to intercept communications, interfere with property and undertake 'intrusive surveillance'.

There are four main elements to the security services: MI5, Special Branch, MI6 and GCHQ.

MI5

The existence of MI5 is well known, but until recently most of its activities were shrouded in secrecy. The most we knew officially was that it was set up in 1909 to counter the activity of German spies in the run-up to the First World War. We now know, since 1993, that it employs 2,000 personnel and has a budget of £150 million per year, most of which is spent on counter-terrorism and the bulk of the rest on counter-espionage. After the end of the Cold War, it was perhaps a little short of things to do and in 1992 it was tasked with gathering intelligence about the IRA. In 1996, it was given the further responsibility of helping to counter 'serious crime'. For most citizens the closest they are likely to get to the agency is if they are vetted for a sensitive post in government. Physically, however, they can now easily see from where this very secret work is controlled: from its headquarters on the banks of the Thames not far from the Houses of Parliament. Political control falls to the Home Secretary.

Special Branch

This is a branch of the police force, ultimately under the Home Secretary, tasked with combating terrorism, espionage, sabotage and subversion. In addition it provides security for important people, watches the ports and airports and makes arrests for MI5. Like MI5, it employs 2,000 personnel but at £20 million per year spends much less.

MI6

MI6 deals with political and economic intelligence abroad. It works mostly through agents attached to British embassies overseas, although it maintains close liaison with the Defence Intelligence Service. It comes under the authority of the Foreign Secretary. From 1994, it has added serious crime to its portfolio of responsibilities, including money laundering and drug smuggling as well as illegal immigration.

Government Communications Headquarters (GCHQ)

This 'listening post' organisation originated from the famously successful code-breaking service based in Bletchley Park during the war. It operates under a treaty signed with the USA in 1947 and seeks to monitor international radio communications utilising communication satellites and listening posts worldwide. Its base in the UK is in Cheltenham and it has over 6,000 employees with an annual budget of £500 million. In 1984, the Thatcher government controversially banned membership of trade unions – allegedly at US request – on security grounds; trade union rights were restored by Labour in 1997.

Apart from the 1994 Act above, the security services are not accountable to Parliament; the Prime Minister is ultimately responsible for their actions, and the respective heads of the services report directly to him. The PM also chairs the Cabinet Committee on the Security and Intelligence Services. One of the six secretariats in the Cabinet Office is concerned with security and intelligence and serves to coordinate relevant information for feeding into Cabinet. This secretariat contains the Coordinator of Intelligence and Security, who is another official in this important area who reports directly to the PM. The Joint Intelligence Committee comprises (among others) the secret service heads; it supplies the Cabinet with security information. The security services do not come under the jurisdiction of any complaints procedure, and they do not need to inform the police of their operations. When security service personnel have had to give evidence in court, they have done so with their identities concealed. Critics point out that those tasked with controlling these services have little time to do so and in practice know very little of what goes on. The Security Commission was established in 1964 and investigates security lapses and shortcomings.

The Home Affairs Select Committee in 1993 asked for the right to investigate the activities of the security services in order to guard against abuses of power. The government went some of the way towards meeting its critics in 1994 when it set up, via the Intelligence Services Act, the Intelligence and Security Committee. This comprises nine members drawn from both Houses of Parliament and is charged with scrutiny of the expenditure, administration and policy of MI5, MI6 and GCHQ. It meets weekly and occasionally issues critical reports like the one (1995) in which the service heads were criticised for not being aware of the adverse effects of the spying activities of CIA agent Aldrich Ames. Critics argue that the new committee has too few powers to be effective: it cannot call witnesses or relevant papers and is able to investigate only that which the security service heads allow.

Transfer of constitutional responsibilities to Lord Chancellor's Department

After the 2001 general election, Tony Blair transferred a number of constitutional functions to the office of his former boss, the Lord Chancellor Lord Irvine. These covered human rights, House of Lords reform, freedom of information, data protection, the crown dependencies (Channel Isles, Isle of Man), royal, hereditary and Church matters, civic honours (city status and lord mayoralties) and the Cenotaph ceremony (an annual service to honour the war dead led by the Queen).

Terrorism Acts

This Act preceded the attack on the World Trade Center, although those horrific events prompted some additional toughening up of the earlier measure. The act defined 'terrorism' as any threat to influence the government of the UK 'for the purpose of advancing a political, religious or ideological cause'. Civil rights campaigners point out that the Act's scope is dangerously wide. Taken with its detailed provisions, it empowers police to make arrests without warrants, enter buildings without court orders (if they reasonably suspect terrorists are to be found within) and prosecute people for holding information likely to be useful to terrorists. People can be stopped at random, and if they refuse to give their names can be sent to prison. Police can also seize any cash that they think 'is intended for the purposes of terrorism' without specific authorisation. The Liberal Democrats in the form of Simon Hughes MP attacked the definition of terrorism as 'far too wide'. In the event of someone being found in possession of something likely to be used for the

purposes of terrorism, then it is up to the accused to prove his or her innocence. In June 2005 the European Commisioner of Human Rights, Alvaro Gil-Robles, published a damning report on Britain's anti-terror laws. He perceived an attitude in which 'human rights are frequently construed as, at best, formal commitments and, at worst, cumbersome obstructions.' He concluded that such rights were not luxuries but 'the very foundation of democratic societies'. Particularly in mind were the long-term detention of terrorist suspects in Belmarsh prison and their treatment while in custody. Then came the July bombings on the London Underground which launched another wave of get-tough initiatives against possible terrorists. In the autumn of 2005 Tony Blair launched yet another Terror Bill which sought to exclude from the UK any people 'glorifying' or inciting terrorist acts, disseminating publications to the same end, or preparing such acts and training others to do so. But the most draconian and controversial measure proposed was the detention of suspects for up to 90 days. Blair and Clarke, his Home Secretary, were warned this was more than their party could accept, but they pressed on regardless and in November 2005 the measure was defeated when 49 Labour MPs refused to support the government. Blair was unrepentant, saying sometimes it was right to lose if the issue was the right course of action. The eventual 28-day period of detention was still longer than most other EU countries had thought wise to impose.

The security services and 'dodgy dossiers' on Iraq

In September 2002, the government published a dossier on Iraqi 'weapons of mass destruction' that embodied a substantial amount of intelligence services information. Later, in February 2003, another dossier was published focusing on the Iraqi regime's concealment of such weapons. Neither dossier was considered convincing at the time, especially when the latter was damagingly revealed to include a plagiarised section of a twelve-year-old PhD thesis, but in the wake of the war, critical scrutiny intensified. In May 2003, it was alleged by a BBC journalist Andrew Gilligan that senior intelligence officers were accusing New Labour's spin-meister, Alastair Campbell, of adding his own material to the September dossier to 'sex it up' to make more compelling the case for a war his master strongly favoured. In the ensuing furious row, which involved the suicide of Dr David Kelly, the MOD officer

BOX 25.5 BRITAIN IN CONTEXT

Crime and punishment

The Economist (23 August 2003) reacted to the news that 11.3 per cent of American boys born in 2001 will go to jail (33 per cent of black boys) with the comment that 'conservative politicians are on their way to creating a criminal class of unimaginable proportions.'

Every society on the planet suffers from problems of crime. Part of this is due to the fact that drugs are, albeit illegally, one of the world's major traded commodities. Crime in the USA has a well-known international profile, as so many Hollywood movies have chosen stories about gangsters, bank robbers or gang violence. Some sociologists have argued that countries with a very high Gini coefficient – relationship of rich to poor – were likely to attract the highest crime rates, as relative differences fuel resentment and – when in the same society – opportunity. Figures available suggest there may be something in such calculations.

The nation with the best rating on this index is Japan with a ratio of richest 10 per cent to poorest 10 per cent of 4.5. The crime rate in Japan is, accordingly, relatively low. The equivalent ratio for the UK is 13.8, placing it fifty-first in the international rankings. The USA comes in at 15.9 and ninety-second. Countries like Brazil and South Africa, both notorious for their crime rates, come even lower down at ratios of 33.1 and 68, respectively: 116th and 117th overall. Murder figures in the USA have been astonishingly high by British or European standards. For many years visitors to New York expected to encounter muggers on every street corner or a Los Angeles blazing with gang warfare.

Crime is still a major problem in the USA with, in 2002, nearly 5,000 cases of aggravated assault in Washington alone, a sexual assault every two minutes somewhere in the country, and forty-two murders for every 100,000 people in Detroit. But then came a rather unexpected fall in crime levels. According to the FBI, the crime rate per 100,000 inhabitants was just under 2,000 in 1960, rose to nearly 6,000 in 1990, but began to fall in the nineties, ending up at about 4,000 in 2004. Why did crime increase?

Professor Robert Reiner, from the LSE (Reiner, 2006b), analyses the changing patterns of crime, noting that similar patterns of crime occurred in the USA and industrialising European countries: an increase during the late eighteenth and early nineteenth centuries during the early industrial revolution followed by 'a long term process of inclusion of the majority of the population in legal, political and, to a lesser extent, economic and social citizenship.' The late twentieth century saw a sharp upturn in crime in these same countries. Reiner identifies two explanations, one favoured by the Left and the other by the Right: the return to a tougher form of capitalism–neo-liberalism, replacing welfarism and causing hardship; and the erosion of social values by the 'permissiveness' of liberalism, expressed most typically during the sixties.

Reiner quotes Currie who attributed the rise to 'great structural inequalities and community fragmentation and weakened ability of parents to monitor and supervise their children – and a great many other things all going on at once, all entwined with each other, and all affecting the crime rate – with the combination having an impact that is much greater than its parts.'

Why did crime fall? Reiner dismisses 'zero tolerance' as other cities in the US experienced similar falls to the home of this approach: New York. He also dismisses the 'enormous expansion of punitiveness, above all the staggering and gross levels of imprisonment' as a major cause. Numbers of US citizens in jail are indeed horrendous – a higher percentage than in any other country: two million are in jail with nearly half of them drawn from the 12 per cent of the population which is black. More likely an explanation for the downturn, he thinks, was the upturn in the economies of these nations which reduced the need for property crime, but he has to conclude: 'The crime drop remains something of a mystery, defying any simple account.'

alleged to be Gilligan's source, many observed that the intelligence services had been involved closely, and unhealthily, in the presentation of what were in essence political arguments. Lord Hutton took extensive evidence in the ensuing inquiry, some of which seemed to support the Gilligan case, but his report surprisingly exonerated government and accused only the BBC, leading to several resignations. The Butler Report on the intelligence services' failure over the non-existent weapons of mass destruction in Iraq also cleared the government of any major wrong-doing but was critical of several areas of poor intelligence; it criticised Blair's description of the Iraq intelligence as 'authoritative' and warned that the country had weapons which could reach British-controlled areas within forty-five minutes. Critics of the government were outraged that the man at the centre of much of the intelligence furore, John Scarlett, was allowed promotion to head of MI5.

Chapter summary

Conservative thinkers have tended to base their law and order policies on a pessimistic view of human nature, while Labour has tended to be more optimistic. However, both views began to converge in the late 1980s and early 1990s. Crime figures suggest a crime wave, but there are many qualifications to bear in mind. It is doubtful whether the Conservatives substantially reversed the crime wave in the early 1990s. It seems likely that crime breeds in poor, rundown areas of big cities. Police attempts to control crime have not been very successful and have received much criticism, even from the Conservatives. Tougher prison sentences are favoured by the Conservatives, but experience suggests that this is no real answer. Vigilante groups have set up in some parts of the country to take the law into their own hands.

The Home Office is the department in charge of the security services, although it has transferred constitutional responsibilities to the Lord Chancellor's Department. The 2000 Terrorism Act has offended those concerned with the defence of human rights.

Discussion points

■ Which analysis of human nature seems closer to the truth, the pessimistic or optimistic version?

■ How reliable are crime figures?

■ Would more widely spread prosperity solve the crime problem?

■ Is vigilantism justified?

■ Should abortion in high-crime areas be encouraged?

Further reading

A slightly longer analysis than the above can be found in Jones (1999). A good, though dated, discussion of the causes of crime can be found in Lea and Young (1984). The best book on the police is still by Robert Reiner (1993), though he has written much on the topic since it came out. On race riots, Michael Keith (1993) is worth a read; and on penal policy, Windlesham (1993) is authoritative and interesting. *The Economist*'s reports on crime are always well informed and well written, as are those of the quality press whenever crime moves to the top of the political agenda.

References

Box, S. (1987) *Recession, Crime and Punishment* (Oxford University Press).

Dorling, D. (2005) 'Prime suspect', in P. Hillyard *et al.*, *Beyond Criminology* (Pluto).

Dunning, E.G., Gaskell, G. and Benewick, R. (eds) (1987) *The Crowd in Modern Britain* (Sage).

IPPR (2006) *Crime-share: the Unequal Impact of Crime* (Institute of Public Policy and Research).

Jenkins, R. (2001) *Churchill* (Pan).

Jones, B. (1999) 'Crime and punishment', in B. Jones (ed.), *Political Issues in Britain Today* (Manchester University Press).

Keith, M. (1993) *Race Riots and Policing* (UCL Press).

Lea, J. and Young, J. (1984) *What is to be Done About Law and Order?* (Penguin).

Mawby, R.I. (1999) *Policing Across the World* (UCL Press).

Murray, C. (1990) *The Emerging British Underclass* (IEA Health and Welfare Unit).

Pearson, G. (1983) *Hooligan: A History of Respectable Fears* (Macmillan).

Reiner, R. (1993) *The Politics of the Police*, 2nd edn (Harvester Wheatsheaf).

Reiner, R. (2006a) 'The social democratic criminology', in T. Newburn and P. Rock (eds), *The Politics of Crime Control* (Oxford University Press).

Reiner, R. (2006b) 'Law and order', in *Current Legal Problems* (published via UCL by Oxford University Press).

Toynbee, P. (2002) 'What really causes crime?' *The Guardian*, 12 June 2002.

Windlesham, Lord (1993) *Responses to Crime*, Vol. 2 (Clarendon Press).

CHAPTER 26

Social policy

Michael Moran

Learning objectives

- To define the nature of social policy.

- To identify the main trends in social commitments undertaken by the state in Britain.

- To examine the main issues and debates within the political system produced by those commitments.

Introduction

Social policy is central to British politics. Guaranteeing **entitlements** to various social services has become a major responsibility of British governments, but the exact range of those guarantees and how they are to be delivered is a source of political debate. Social policy is also of major importance in the distribution of resources in the community. A market economy like that in Britain is known to have great benefits, especially in widening individual choice and producing economic efficiency. It is also recognised to be a source of inequality, often substantial economic inequality. One of the important historical functions of social policy has been to use the power of government to moderate the inequalities produced by the market. If an active social policy of this kind can be combined with a market economy the benefits for society are tremendous – for success would mean that we could have all the great benefits of markets without some of the accompanying drawbacks. And that function helps us to pose two questions addressed in this chapter: how have governments tried to use social policy to moderate the inequalities at different times, and what problems have they encountered with the different methods used?

■ The nature of social policy

The idea of social policy is linked closely to the existence of the **welfare state**. The United Kingdom is a 'welfare state'. In other words, a large part of the responsibility of government has to do with paying for, and in some cases directly providing, welfare services for the population. Many of the welfare policies initiated in Britain made the country an international pioneer: for instance, the foundation of the National Health Service in 1948 established a system of largely free healthcare for everybody paid for mainly out of taxation.

There are two striking features of welfare policy in the United Kingdom. The first is that throughout the twentieth century there was growth in the volume of resources spent on welfare: in the immediate aftermath of the First World War, slightly less than 5 per cent of Gross Domestic Product (a standard measure of national wealth) went on welfare; seventy years later, the figure was approaching 20 per cent of a much larger 'pool' of national wealth. What is more, this advance has continued since the early 1990s: Figure 26.1 shows this growth for an important range of services. But a second feature, summarised in Figure 26.2, puts this history of growth into international perspective. It compares the level of spending on a broad measure of welfare in fifteen members of the the European Union. (It predates the addition of ten new members of the European Union in 2004.) The figure shows that, despite the

long historical growth, welfare spending in the United Kingdom is still comparatively modest when set against the record of some other members of the European Union.

Although the welfare state is commonly spoken of as 'providing services', the reality is that the phrase refers to a wide range of institutions and practices. In the United Kingdom, the most important role of the state lies in raising the resources to pay for welfare. It does this in two rather different ways. First, the direct cost of providing some important services – of which healthcare is the best example – is met largely from the taxes raised by central government. Second, the state plays an important role in administering '**transfer payments**': it raises money in taxes from one group in the community and 'transfers' it to other groups, in the form of payments such as pensions and unemployment benefit. Thus eligibility rules for unemployment and social security benefits are settled within the core executive, but the implementation of those rules is the responsibility of a semi-independent agency (the Benefits Agency) established as part of the last Conservative government's 'Next Steps' programme. (Details of the Next Steps reforms can be found in Chapter 21.)

Notice that while we routinely speak of the welfare state as providing welfare services to the population, hardly anything in the description is about direct provision: it is about funding, and about organising systems of provision. Teachers and

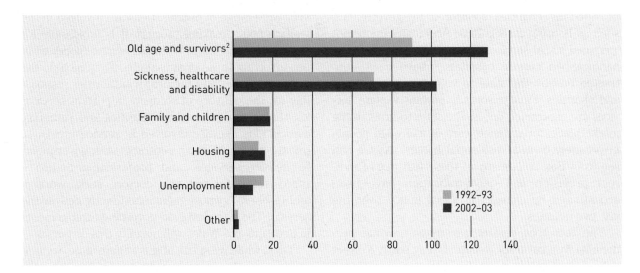

Figure 26.1 The real growth of spending on social protection, 1992–3 to 2002–3[1]
Notes: [1]The figures are for billions of pounds, at 2002–3 prices, i.e. holding constant changes in price levels. [2]Survivors are those whose entitlement derives from their relationship to a deceased person (e.g. widows, widowers and orphans).
Source: Office for National Statistics (2005) *Social Trends*, No. 35, 2005 Edition, p. 110. © Crown Copyright 2005. Crown copyright material is reproduced with the permission of the Controller of Her Majesty's Stationery Office (HMSO)

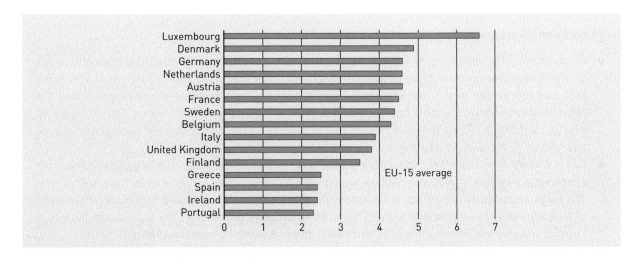

Figure 26.2 How spending in Britain compares internationally: spending on social protection in the UK and other EU members
Note: The figures measure spending per head, in thousands of pounds. The dotted vertical line measures the average for all fifteen EU member states when the data were gathered (before the latest accession of ten new members). When the bar chart is to the right of the line, spending is higher than average – Luxembourg is the leader. When the chart is to the left (as in the case of the UK) spending is below the EU average. The figure should be taken only as an indicator of broad differences: the definition of social spending can often vary greatly between nations.
Source: Office for National Statistics (2005) *Social Trends*, No. 35, 2005 edition, p. 110. © Crown Copyright 2005. Crown copyright material is reproduced with the permission of the Controller of Her Majesty's Stationery Office (HMSO)

healthcare professionals have mostly been paid for out of the public purse, but the role of central government in delivering services is limited. Many social services are actually delivered by the 'local state' – in other words, by local government. But much welfare provision goes beyond the institutions of the state completely. Schooling up to the age of 16, for instance, while long compulsory in Britain, has been provided in many cases by church schools. Low-cost housing for rent has in recent years been provided by charities sponsored by government, such as housing associations. And many important 'personal social services' – such as the care of the handicapped outside hospitals – have been 'contracted out' by the state to voluntary associations and charities. Finally, some important welfare services are contracted out by the state to firms in the marketplace: for instance, care of many old people in privately owned 'residential homes'. As we can see from Box 26.1, many of these features of indirect provision and decentralisation have been accentuated by changes in social policy over the last two decades.

The fact that central government, while predominantly a payer for welfare, is only partly a direct deliverer of services has important consequences for the way welfare policy is made. It means that a very wide range of organisations are involved in the welfare policy-making process. It is impossible for central departments in Whitehall to make policy without involving these organisations. They include the local authorities and the health authorities responsible for the delivery of so many important services 'on the ground'; the many charities and voluntary associations likewise involved in service provision; private firms who have contracts with government to deliver services; and professional bodies – representing, for instance, doctors, social workers and teachers – whose members directly deliver the service. The new devolved governing arrangements in Scotland and Wales will magnify this dispersal.

Thus, while we speak of the welfare state, welfare services are by no means produced only, or even mainly, by the central state machine.

BOX 26.1 IDEAS AND PERSPECTIVES

The old welfare state – and the new

The old welfare state had a number of linked, distinctive features:

- *Universalism*: This meant that the effort was made to give roughly equal levels of service entitlement to everybody in the community, regardless of how rich or poor they were, and regardless of how much they had contributed to the cost of services. The most important example of universalism was the National Health Service, established in 1948: it entitled everybody to register with a doctor (a general practitioner) and to receive the medical care that this general practitioner thought appropriate free, or nearly free, at the point of treatment.
- *Direct delivery of services*: The old welfare state delivered its own services on a large scale. The most spectacular example of that was public housing built for, and rented to, tenants by local authorities. The large, municipally owned council estate without a single owner-occupied house, with conditions of tenancy tightly regulated, and with all services like repairs provided by the local authority, was a familiar sight across Britain for a generation after the end of the Second World War.
- *Public employment*: The agencies that provided services – in health, housing or education – did so by employing their own public servants. Delivery via a private contractor was the exception rather than the rule.
- *Professional domination*: The old welfare state was a 'professional state': the control of policy was in the hands of specialised professionals who made the key decisions about what clients were entitled to. Doctors decided what healthcare patients should receive; teachers decided both the content of the school curriculum and how it should be taught in the classroom.

The new welfare state has modified, although not totally abandoned, these key features:

- *From universalism to 'targeting'*: This has partly revealed itself in the details of benefit provision, notably in the levying of charges and the spread of means testing to establish entitlement to services. But it has also revealed itself, especially since the return of Labour to power in 1997, in a fundamental shift in focus and philosophy. Labour's main concern has been with 'social exclusion': dealing with the minority of the population excluded from work and the full experience of social life by circumstances like poverty, homelessness and drug dependency. Thus the focus of the welfare state has shifted from the provision of social entitlements for the whole population to the management of the social conditions of a minority – principally the poorest.

- *Retreating from direct provision of services*: The most spectacular example has occurred in housing. First, the Conservatives in the 1980s sold off 1.4 million council dwellings to tenants; then both the Conservative and Labour governments set about withdrawing local government from direct provision of housing. Public bodies have been widely displaced by a variety of associations, trusts and private corporate deliverers: thus direct public delivery is now replaced by a mix of quangos and private bodies. Similar, though more limited, changes have taken place in health and education.
- *Decline of public employment*: The new welfare state has increasingly displaced publicly employed servants by delivery through the workforces of private contractors. This is particularly marked in the sphere of personal social care, such as care of the old. While there is no issue of principle in this shift, since there has always been an element of this kind of contracting in welfare delivery, the scale of growth in these modes of service delivery is reshaping the old welfare state into a 'contract state'.
- *Challenge to professional power*: The new welfare state has widely challenged the autonomy and power of professionals. The two biggest areas of change have been in health and education. Since the early 1980s, governments of both party colours have tried to strengthen the hands of managers in the National Health Service at the expense of the clinical autonomy of doctors in the belief that managers, though themselves professionals, are more in tune with what government wants the NHS to deliver. In schools education, two landmark pieces of legislation (in 1988 and 1992) were designed to gain more central control over the content of the curriculum and to gain more control over how teachers actually taught that curriculum in the classroom. The return of Labour to office in 1997 if anything intensified this drive to control the welfare professionals.

■ Why is the welfare state so important?

Welfare spending is by far the largest part of public expenditure in the United Kingdom – as it is in most comparable countries. What is more, this has been the case for many decades and seems likely to continue to be so. Why has the welfare state grown to such an important scale? Four reasons can be identified.

Democratic politics

The welfare state expanded with democracy, because it benefited some of those who were given the vote under democratic politics. Now, the beneficiaries of the welfare state are enormous in number. When we consider the full range of services, from health through education and pensions, we can see that virtually the whole population has a stake in welfare services. Consequently, there are large numbers of votes to be won and lost in the field of welfare policy. What is more, while some of the original motivation for the expansion of welfare services was to help the poor, it has now been demonstrated that many of the services – especially education – also benefit the middle classes (see below). In other words, the educated, prosperous and politically well organised have a big stake in the preservation of many welfare services. This is reinforced by the role of the welfare state as an employer, often of highly educated professionals: for instance, there are over a million people employed in health services in Britain. These occupations amount to a considerable lobby for the preservation of the welfare state.

Political philosophy

Although many of the services of the welfare state are known to benefit the relatively well-off, it is undeniably the case that one motive behind its original development was to provide safeguards against sickness, unemployment and poverty. The philosophies of the political parties that dominated British politics in the twentieth century all in different ways viewed the state as a source of welfare. Before the

Nye Bevan, the charismatic former Welsh miner, set up the NHS in 1948, often described as the 'jewel in the crown' of the welfare state
Source: Copyright © Bettmann / Corbis

First World War, important social policy reforms were introduced by the Liberal government that won office in 1906, and which was dominated by politicians who believed in 'social reform' liberalism – in other words, in using the state as an instrument of social reform. Since the end of the First World War, British politics in Westminster has been dominated by two parties – Labour and Conservative – which in different ways also support welfare provision: the Labour Party because it believes that the purpose of the state is to intervene to ensure that inequalities and deprivations caused by markets are remedied, especially if they affect manual workers and their families; the Conservative Party because, at least until the 1980s, it was dominated by politicians who believed that government had obligations to ensure that the poorest were cared for by the state. Immediately after the Second World War, a reforming Labour government greatly extended the scope of the welfare state. These reforms were accepted, and consolidated, by the Conservative governments in office from 1951 to 1964. In other words, for much of its recent history British politics

has been dominated by two parties that, for different reasons, have been committed to a large welfare state. The parties other than Labour and Conservative that occupy important roles in the new devolved political systems of Scotland and Wales – notably the Scottish National Party and Plaid Cymru in Wales – share this commitment to state welfare.

Despite this constant commitment to welfare, the philosophical form this commitment has taken has changed greatly, especially in the last couple of decades. This shift has affected virtually all parties across the political spectrum, and in particular has reshaped Labour and Conservative policies, mostly in similar ways. The implications of the shift are summarised in Box 26.1. They amount to the development of a consensus about a 'new' welfare state that is replacing the consensus about the 'old' welfare state built during and after the Second World War. The old welfare state was an ambitious, interventionist form of welfare provision. But for the last couple of decades a different philosophy of the welfare state has been increasingly in the ascendant: this 'new' welfare state is more modest in its aims, and more modest also in the extent to which it is prepared to commit to the direct delivery of services. The special ways these new conceptions of welfare have shaped social policy since 1997 are examined later in this chapter (see 'New Labour and the welfare state: from welfare state to work state?').

Economic efficiency

As we shall see shortly, the welfare state has many critics on the grounds that its cost is a 'burden' on the economy. But as Figure 26.2 shows, it is striking how many nations with highly advanced economies have even larger welfare states, on the

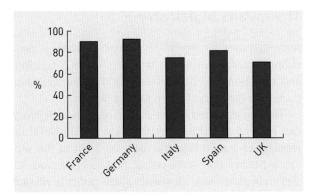

Figure 26.3 The British commitment to education: comparisons across the 'big five' EU economies (percentage of 16–18-year-olds in education or training) *Source*: Calculated from Office for National Statistics (2004) *Regional Trends*, No. 34, 2004 Edition, pp. 31–2. Figures date from 2000. © Crown Copyright 2004. Crown copyright material is reproduced with the permission of the Controller of Her Majesty's Stationery Office (HMSO)

basis of expenditure per head of population. In part, this is because successful economies produce the resources needed to pay for welfare, but it is also because an efficient industrial economy needs the sort of services provided by the welfare state. Industrial economies demand a highly educated workforce. Indeed, one of the commonest criticisms of this part of the British welfare state is that we do not educate or train the population to as high a level as our main competitors (see Figure 26.3). An industrial economy also requires a healthy workforce – which in turn demands efficient healthcare available to all. The most successful economies also function best when workers are willing to be highly adaptable – for instance, to change work practices, and even to accept unemployment, in order to make the best use of the latest technology. Obviously this cooperation is only likely to happen when workers believe that if they lose their jobs through new technology the state will both retrain them for new work and ensure that while unemployed they, and their families, are guaranteed levels of benefit that will keep them out of poverty. In other words, economic success demands generous unemployment and other social security benefits.

Market failure

The United Kingdom is a capitalist economy – which means that the chief mechanism for the production and distribution of goods and services is the marketplace, where exchanges are made for money.

But in many cases markets will fail to produce goods and services or will produce them in insufficient amounts. 'Market failure' is one of the most important reasons for state intervention. Goods and services as different as national defence, street lighting or public parks would be difficult to organise if the state did not compel citizens at large to contribute to their upkeep. Similar problems of collective choice undermine the market in areas of welfare provision. Suppose the state made education entirely voluntary and relied on parents to buy education for their children. Undoubtedly some children would not be educated, because their parents would be unwilling voluntarily to make the necessary economic sacrifices. Likewise, if the long-term sick and disabled had to find the resources to pay for the full cost of their own care, they would simply not be able to raise those resources; there would be great gaps in care for the sick and the disabled if the market alone were left to ensure that funds were available. (Notice that this is not at all the same as saying that the state directly provides those services; it only suggests that government ensures that the resources are available. Whether the services are then delivered by the state, by charities or by private firms is a separate question. And, indeed, the 'new' welfare state sketched earlier has involved precisely such a shift to increased contracting of private deliverers.) The issue of how to deliver welfare services is one of the most important facing policy makers – and is included in the list of key issues that we now examine.

■ Issues in welfare policy

'Welfare policy making' is about choices concerning the welfare services in a community: about their range, about how they should be paid for, about how they should be delivered, and about who should benefit from the welfare state. How to make these choices lies at the heart of most debates about the big issues of welfare policy in Britain.

The level of spending

Although, as we have seen, the welfare state in the United Kingdom is not large by international standards, there has nevertheless been concern about the 'burden' of welfare spending. In part this concern reflects pressures common to all nations that have established generous systems of welfare provision. The expansion of the welfare state across the industrial world took place in the decades after 1945 in a period of international prosperity. In the last twenty years this prosperity has become much less certain, and in most countries questions have been raised about the scope of welfare provision. In the United Kingdom, the problem of the level of provision has been especially severe because the UK economy was, for much of the postwar period, markedly less successful than many other industrial economies in delivering the increased wealth needed to fund welfare services. (We will see in the next chapter, however, that this has been reversed in the last decade: Britain's has become a 'high performing' economy.)

In some areas, difficulties are made more serious by long-term increases in the demand for services. For instance, although the cost of the National Health Service is by international standards modest, the level of spending on health shows a long-term rise – something we will see documented in the next chapter. The pressure of rising costs comes from two areas in particular: constant improvements in medical technology are widening the range of conditions that can be treated; and the ageing of the population is expanding the numbers of people who live to a great, and sickly, old age.

The issue of how much in total to spend on welfare has become particularly important because of changes in the outlook of the Conservative Party, which ruled the country between 1979 and 1997. After Margaret Thatcher became leader in 1975, the influence of those Conservatives who supported large-scale welfare spending declined within the party. Under Mrs Thatcher, and under her successor John Major, welfare spending was viewed in terms of 'opportunity cost': although often desirable, every pound spent on welfare was seen as a resource diverted from productive investment, and therefore from wealth creation. These ambitions to cut the size of the welfare state actually came to little, but they did have two big effects: they altered the balance struck between different welfare programmes and the means of delivering welfare; and they caused major shifts in Labour Party thinking, and thus in the policies pursued by Labour after its return to government in 1997. Above all, as we noted earlier, a historic change has occurred in the basic philosophy of '**universalism**': the principle that welfare services should usually be available as a right to all citizens. The new philosophy, shared by both main parties, is based on selection and targeting, the principle being that welfare services should be available only to those who can demonstrate need.

The means of delivery

Although we often speak of the welfare state as 'providing' welfare services, in fact it is both possible and common for the state to fund services rather than take direct responsibility for delivery.

The issues raised by the means of service delivery can be well illustrated by the case of the National Health Service. In hospital care, for most of the service's history the same public bodies both paid for and delivered care. Hospitals were publicly owned institutions. The reforms in the National Health Service introduced since 1989 are intended to separate the funders of care from the providers. First, the Conservatives introduced a system of 'internal markets': public health authorities could contract with providers – such as hospitals – to supply healthcare on agreed terms. Labour after 1997 disavowed much of the 'market' language, but its policy practice has been in the same direction. For instance in 2004 the government introduced, in the face of substantial opposition from its own back-benchers, a new category of 'Foundation Hospitals' – self-governing trusts which are intended to have more autonomy from central control, and more independence to raise finance in the private marketplace, than was possible under the old NHS. Although the government holds out the possibility of all hospitals acquiring foundation status, at the moment it is reserved for a tiny élite. Only hospitals that have attained the top ranking in the national system of inspection of performance indicators are eligible to apply; at the moment only eleven have actually become foundation hospitals. The government is presently supporting the applications of only twenty-four in all to have foundation status.

This change in the health service is only part of a wider shift in the organisation of service delivery in British government. There has taken place a general shift in the direction of a '**contract state**' – a state where government pays for services but contracts the job of delivery out to a separate body, usually by some sort of competitive system. Some shifts in this direction took place in the National Health Service even before the important reforms of recent years – contracting-out of laundry services in hospitals, for instance, was already well established by the late 1980s. Beyond the particular sphere of welfare, contracting-out has spread to a wide range of services, such as refuse collection in local authorities.

The contrasting arguments surrounding the shift to contracting-out in service delivery illustrate very well what is at issue in the choices between the 'new' and 'old' welfare state summarised in Box 26.1. On the one hand, there is nothing new in principle involved in contracting: as we saw in Chapter 3 the government is a 'customer' for a wide range of services, and there is no obvious dividing line between goods and services that ought to be delivered directly and those that can be 'bought in' from the private sector. It is difficult to imagine anybody seriously defending the proposition that the state should produce everything itself. Competition can extend choice and can create pressures for the delivery of more responsive and more efficient services. On the other hand, the welfare state has been built on the principle of universalism: in other words, on the principle that all citizens should have access to a similar minimum level of service. However, when services are contracted-out with the aim of ensuring that providers compete by offering differing levels and kinds of service, this commitment to universalism is compromised. Whether this is thought objectionable or not depends, as we will see in a few moments, on what philosophy of welfare one believes in. 'Universalism' is also at the centre of another critical issue: funding.

Who should pay?

Britain is fairly unusual in relying on general taxation to provide the lion's share of the money for welfare. In many other European states, for instance, it is common for programmes to be funded out of insurance contributions levied on workers and employers. These contributions are usually obligatory, although they can be voluntary. This is, for instance, one of the commonest ways of paying for the cost of healthcare in Europe. The advantages of an insurance system are twofold. First, the contributions guarantee a stream of income for a welfare programme such as healthcare, whereas in the British system welfare programmes have to compete as best they can against other public spending priorities. (This may be why the British welfare state has tended to spend rather less than the international average.) A second advantage is that in some circumstances insurance systems may encourage more competition and efficiency, because the insurers can be separated from the providers and thus have an incentive to shop around for the most cost-effective forms of delivery. The disadvantage of insurance systems, even of compulsory ones, is that they usually produce inequalities in the service offered. For instance, insurance funds

Patricia Hewitt, the Health Minister, was faced with a NHS deficit of some £800 million in the spring of 2006, despite massive funding by the Labour government
Source: PA Wire / Empics

based on the workplace often end up offering a better deal to the better-paid workers. In discussions about funding the National Health Service in the 1980s, some advocates of reform expressed interest in shifting to an insurance system, although this has never been pursued.

Arguments about the choice between general taxation and insurance to fund welfare make an important assumption – that there is no charge for services at the point of consumption. Indeed, for the most part this is true of major programmes such as school education. However, 'user charges' have always existed for some services, and since the 1980s they have expanded considerably. In healthcare, for instance, in both dental and optical services 'free' services have almost disappeared except for groups exempted on grounds of low income, health condition or age. In 1998, a 'flat rate' fee of £1,000 per annum was introduced for most higher education courses, and from 2006 some universities will charge 'top-up fees' to a maximum of £3,000 per annum. (As a further sign of the decentralisation of the old universal welfare state, however, there is now considerable geographical variation in the incidence of fees: no fees are payable by Scottish students in Scotland; Welsh students in Wales will be exempt from the new 'top-up' system; but all English universities will charge the top-up fee.)

The case for user charges is twofold: charges, even set at modest levels, can raise money that is badly needed; and charges encourage clients to be prudent in making calls on services, whereas if the service is a 'free good' there is the possibility that it will be used (and abused) thoughtlessly. The most important argument against user charges is that charging even a modest amount risks deterring the poorest from using services and thus undermines one of the most important functions of the welfare state.

There is in turn a connection between the issue of charges and the final issue examined here: who should benefit from welfare policy?

Who should benefit?

It is in the nature of universal services – such as schooling, healthcare and pensions – that they are available to everybody who meets the appropriate conditions. Thus, to receive free schooling it is necessary only to be of school age, to receive healthcare only to be judged sick by a doctor, and to receive an old-age pension to have reached the stipulated age and to have an appropriate history of national insurance contributions.

This principle of universalism has created two problems, one concerning efficiency and one concerning equality. The efficiency problem exists because, since resources are limited, it can be argued that it is more efficient to 'target' resources on those in most need. This implies a shift away from universalism in the provision of, for instance, pensions and other benefits to a **selective targeting** on the needy. And, indeed, as we saw above, the British welfare state has persistently drifted away from universalism to selective targeting under governments of both major parties in the last quarter-century. These 'efficiency' issues interact with the concern with equality, for it is obviously a principle of universalism that all, regardless of their personal economic circumstances, should be entitled to a benefit. In some circumstances, this can give the wealthy the same entitlement to

benefits as the poor. Landmark research by Goodin and Le Grand published in the late 1980s (Goodin and Le Grand, 1987) proved highly influential in the long term on exactly this point. (Le Grand is presently a senior adviser in 10 Downing Street.) They demonstrated that services differed greatly in the groups they benefited: for instance, at the most 'pro-poor' end was spending on social housing; while spending on universities and on subsidising rail commuting disproportionately benefited the rich.

There are two broad reasons why welfare spending can, contrary to traditional theories of welfare spending, benefit the rich rather than the poor. First, the rich are usually better able to lobby politically for services that benefit them: that is the lesson, for example, of the history of subsidies to commuter rail services. Second, eligibility for some services is not automatic but depends on achieving success in competition. The most obvious example of this is university education, the overwhelming cost of which is paid for by the state. Even the introduction of fees for students in 1998, and of 'top-up' fees from 2006, makes little difference to the overall importance of state financing. Admission to higher education in all cases depends on demonstrating the capacity to benefit from a university education, and in most cases it rests on success in examinations (chiefly 'A' levels). However, we know that success in academic examinations is closely tied to social class. This explains the pattern in Table 26.1, which shows huge differences in the rates of participation in higher education by social class. What is more, the expansion of higher education in the 1990s widened the gap between the children of the very poorest and the highest-class groups: compare the gap in the table between the top and bottom in 1991–2 and 1997–8. Higher education is one of those areas of public subsidy – another example is opera – that greatly benefits the rich rather than the poor; the introduction of fees only marginally changes this state of affairs: even with top-up fees, the cost of education is hugely subsidised by the state.

Resolving the question of who should benefit from welfare spending depends on arriving at a view about the fundamental purpose of the welfare state. If the point of the welfare state is to ensure that a set of rights are available to all citizens, then there is nothing objectionable in the millionaire having the same rights as, say, an unemployed person, just as we naturally expect the rich and the poor to be treated equally in other spheres – before the courts, for instance. This view can also go with the argument

Table 26.1 Participation rates in higher education by social class, Great Britain (%)

	1991–2	1992–3	1993–4	1994–5	1995–6	1996–7	1997–8
Professional	55	71	73	78	79	82	80
Intermediate	36	39	42	45	45	47	49
Skilled non-manual	22	27	29	31	31	31	32
Skilled manual	11	15	17	18	18	18	19
Partly skilled	12	14	16	17	17	17	18
Unskilled	6	9	11	11	12	13	14
All social classes	23	28	30	32	32	33	34

Source: Office for National Statistics (1999), *Social Trends*, No. 29, 1999 Edition, Table 3.13, p. 61. © Crown Copyright 1999. Crown copyright material is reproduced with the permission of the Controller of Her Majesty's Stationery Office (HMSO)

that spending on the welfare state is principally about ensuring national success and competitiveness rather than equality. If the primary purpose of spending public money on universities, for example, is because we need a large skilled graduate population, it matters not whether the students in universities come from the rich or the poor; it matters only that they are appropriately educated and use their education in the wider economy. On the other hand, if the purpose of the welfare state is to remove or moderate the social inequality created, for instance, by the market system, then the fact that the rich have some of the same benefit entitlements as the poor becomes a real problem.

Labour Party critics fear Blair's education reforms will reintroduce selection into the school system
Source: Copyright © Chris Riddell. From *The Observer*, 11 July 2004. Reproduced with permission from Guardian Newspapers Limited

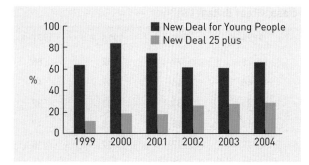

Figure 26.4 The history of New Labour's 'New Deal': percentages of those leaving New Deal programmes who entered 'sustained employment'
Note: 'Sustained employment' means entering employment and remaining off Jobseeker's Allowance for 13 weeks or more. The 'New Deal' for Young People programme (for those aged 18–24) began in January 1998; New Deal '25 plus' – for those aged over 25 – began in July 1998.
Source: Office for National Statistics (2005) *Social Trends*, No. 35, 2005 Edition, p. 58. © Crown Copyright 2005. Crown copyright material is reproduced with the permission of the Controller of Her Majesty's Stationery Office (HMSO)

It is plain, therefore, that a perfectly defensible case can be made for spending programmes that do nothing to lessen social inequality, or that even increase inequality by benefiting the rich. But the 'new' welfare state profiled in Box 26.1 has responded to the recognition that programmes vary greatly in their impact by trying to design and target schemes much more precisely than in the old world of 'universalism'. This stress on targeting is one of the main features, we shall now see, of the social programmes of 'New Labour' since 1997.

■ New Labour and the welfare state: from welfare state to work state?

In many respects the social programmes of New Labour in office have proved highly traditional. In 1997 the new Chancellor imposed on himself a commitment to keep within the spending limits of his Conservative predecessor, and he broadly kept to that commitment. As we shall see in the next chapter, when the brakes came off after 2000, the really big increases were in two highly traditional areas of spending associated with the old 'universal' welfare state: health and education. And despite the imposition of some fees on students in higher education,

Labour has expanded public support for higher education – a service that, as we saw in the last section, does without doubt disproportionately benefit those from better-off families. Nevertheless, there is one powerfully distinctive strand in New Labour's social programme, and it can credibly be claimed as a fundamental shift in how Labour thinks about the welfare state. It involves a turn to labour market intervention as the key to combating social exclusion and poverty.

It is not difficult to see why this turn took place. In Opposition between 1979 and 1997 Labour lived through two great developments in labour markets, both with huge implications for poverty and exclusion. The 1980s and early 1990s were years of the return of mass unemployment; and they were also years when many traditionally secure and comparatively well-paid jobs for manual workers were displaced by low-paid, often casual, employment.

On returning to office in 1997 Labour introduced three key measures in response to this experience:

- It introduced a national minimum wage, backed up by a Low Pay Commission established in 1998. Initially, young workers were exempt from its provisions, but from October 2004 a minimum of £3 per hour was set for 16–17-year-olds. From October 2005 the national minimum for adult workers is set at £5.05 per hour.

- It reshaped the benefit system for the unemployed under the title of the 'New Deal', obliging most claimants to submit to periodic tests of employability, and to take training and education, as a condition of benefit eligibility.

- It introduced a new system of Family Tax Credits for low-income families.

As these measures make clear, the turn to managing the labour market as a form of welfare policy involves a mixture of 'carrots' and 'sticks'. All have been surrounded by controversy. The initial introduction of the national minimum wage was accompanied by claims that it would actually make the lot of the low-paid worse because it would price them out of jobs, leading to more unemployment. There is no evidence that this has happened, though whether this is because the general arguments were false, or because the minimum wage was introduced in an era of strong economic growth and strong demand for labour, is not yet clear. The arguments against the minimum wage probably did, however, influence the government in setting the level initially at a very modest figure.

The 'New Deal' has proved the most controversial of the mix of social programmes introduced by New Labour. As Figure 26.4 shows, measured by capacity to reintegrate young workers in particular to the labour market, it has enjoyed a high measure of success. However, as in the case of the impact of the national minimum wage it is hard to disentangle the effects of the programme itself from the benign circumstances in which it has been introduced: to wit, continuous economic growth and a strong demand for labour. Thus one source of controversy concerns the thorny matter of the actual effects of the programme, and the present imponderable of how it would fare in harder times – when economic growth slows and demand for labour declines. A more fundamental source of controversy concerns the very principles of the programme, notably the principle, for young workers, of linking benefit eligibility to willingness to take part in training and education programmes. Plainly this is a long way from the traditional principles of universal entitlements and – in the terms summarised in Box 26.1 – represents

a substantial shift to the 'new' welfare state. It also carries echoes of more draconian systems linking welfare to willingness to work in other nations, notably parts of the United States.

The third element of the labour market strategy of New Labour is also very much in tune with the 'new' welfare state: the system of tax credits for low-income working families introduced originally in 1999 and subsequently elaborated and extended. The tax credits are intended to boost the income of the poor in work, and they thus fit exactly the philosophy of 'targeting' benefits on precisely identified social groups rather than offering universal benefits. Indeed the 'gainers' among the poor from Labour's social programmes since 1997 have consistently been the working poor. The tax credits are a good example of the 'new' welfare state strategy of trying to be 'smart' in the distribution of benefits so that they have maximum impact on identified 'deserving' groups. There is little partisan controversy over this principle of smart targeting, but a great deal of controversy over the workings of this particular

Tony Blair seems desperate to achieve a legacy comparable with his predecessor Clement Attlee
Source: Copyright © David Simonds. From *The Observer*, 3 August 2003. Reproduced with permission

programme. Smart policy requires smart institutions for effective delivery, and the institutions of welfare delivery in British government have never been notably smart. By 2005 the tax credit scheme was being widely criticised by non-partisan observers, notably in a stinging report from the Parliamentary Ombudsman (Parliamentary and Health Services Ombudsman, 2005). The fundamental problem lay in the design of the scheme, which was unable to adjust to the fluctuations in income common to the low paid. As a result, there was wide overpayment, and then as widespread 'clawbacks' of these overpayments, causing huge short-term, unexpected falls in the total income of the low paid. Although the scheme was subject to widespread criticism from partisan opponents of Labour, both in the Conservative Party and elsewhere, it actually dramatised a problem for all the mainstream parties. All are committed to the kind of smart 'targeting' which the scheme exemplifies; and all therefore have to face up to the formidable difficulties which it revealed of designing systems of rules, and of their implementation, which can solve the problem of making sure that smart targeting does not work stupidly. This is perhaps the single greatest challenge in welfare policy facing not only New Labour but any future governors of the 'new' welfare state.

BOX 26.2 BRITAIN IN CONTEXT

The British social model in comparative context

In the most famous comparative study of the welfare state published in the last two decades (Esping-Andersen, 1990) Britain was assimilated to the category of a residual model, where the state provided a residue of social protection, by comparison with the more expansive systems of middle Europe and Scandinavia. This was always a problematic view of the UK. For instance, it seemed to make little sense of the National Health Service, which had pioneered the provision of healthcare free at the point of treatment for the whole population – a classic case of expansive 'universalism'. Implicitly the UK was being categorised along with the much narrower US 'welfare state'. In the intervening years some of the residualism of the British welfare state has been strengthened, as we have seen in this chapter: that is the story of the increased emphasis on 'targeted' benefits and services. But in other respects the welfare system seems to have become more ambitious, and to have borrowed extensively from other European systems. It has become more ambitious in the scale of resources devoted to services: consider the recent history of spending on health and education documented in this chapter, and in Chapter 27. More important still, the turn to management of the workforce as a key to combating inequality and poverty involves some borrowing from the United States, but it also involves some borrowing from Scandinavia – the historic 'home' of the most ambitious universalist systems. In short, under New Labour the British system of welfare looks distinctive – both from that of the 'residual' welfare systems, like that of the United States, and from many European systems. It is ambitious in its aims, but is combined, as we shall see in the next chapter, with much more emphasis on deregulated labour markets than is characteristic of its big European neighbours.

Chapter summary

In this chapter we have seen that the scale of resources committed to social policy is very large and has been growing for a long time, but it is still comparatively modest by international standards; that the growth of state involvement in the provision of welfare has taken place for a mixture of economic and ideological reasons; and that significant problems of equity and efficiency are raised by the way the welfare state is currently organised. It is a moot point whether the welfare state, set up to help the disadvantaged, actually helps them more than the relatively well-off; and the experience of New Labour shows that efforts to target benefits more selectively on particular groups of the poor face formidable obstacles.

Discussion points

■ Why does Britain seem to be so modest by international standards in the scale of its welfare state?

■ Should welfare policy aim at promoting equality?

■ Can 'targeting' work effectively in the new welfare state?

Further reading

The 'bible' for any beginner studying social policy in Britain should be the annual publication of the Office for National Statistics, *Social Trends*. The reader will notice how often it is the source of the figures in this chapter. At the time of revision, the latest volume was 2005, and it can be downloaded complete at www.statistics.gov.uk/statbase by anyone with a broadband standard Internet connection. An equally important publication, because it gives a historical perspective to contemporary conditions, is the collection edited by Halsey and Webb (2000). Esping-Andersen (1990) sets the British welfare state in an international context (see Box 26.2). Ham (1992) reviews one of the most expensive and contentious sectors. Wilding (1986) reviews and criticises some of the contemporary policy arguments. Mohan (1995) examines a wide range of evidence on distributions and impact. Goodin and Le Grand (1987) examine evidence about the class distributional effect of the welfare state. Deakin (1994) is up to date on recent history. Coates and Lawler (2000) have material on the social policies of New Labour, but Coates (2005) is now more up to date. Finally, Levitas (1998) examines on a broader canvas the social policy ambitions of New Labour.

References

Coates, D. (2005). *Prolonged Labour: The Slow Birth of New Labour in Britain* (Palgrave Macmillan).

Coates, D. and Lawler, P. (eds) (2000) *New Labour into Power* (Manchester University Press).

Deakin, N. (1994) *The Politics of Welfare* (Harvester Wheatsheaf).

Esping-Andersen, G. (1990) *The Three Worlds of Welfare Capitalism* (Polity Press).

Goodin, R. and Le Grand, J. (1987) *Not Only the Poor: The Middle Classes and the Welfare State* (Allen & Unwin).

Halsey, A.H. and Webb, J. (2000). *Twentieth-Century British Social Trends* (Macmillan).

Ham, C. (1992) *Health Policy in Britain* (Macmillan).

Levitas, R. (1998) *The Inclusive Society* (Macmillan).

Mohan, J. (1995) *A National Health Service?* (Macmillan).

Office for National Statistics (1999) *Social Trends*, No. 29, 1999 Edition (HMSO).

Office for National Statistics (2004) *Regional Trends*, No. 34, 2004 Edition (HMSO).

Office for National Statistics (2005) *Social Trends*, No. 35, 2005 Edition (HMSO).

Parliamentary and Health Services Ombudsman (2005) *Tax Credits: Putting Things Right*. HC 124.

Wilding, P. (ed.) (1986) *In Defence of the Welfare State* (Manchester University Press).

Useful websites

Websites are particularly important in this field, as they are in all particular policy fields, because they are likely to be the best source of up-to-date figures and documents about policy. The site of National Statistics itself is a good way of beginning to navigate through the resources available on the websites of individual departments: www.statistics.gov.uk. After that, resources tend to be divided by the different responsibilities for policy fields. Probably the single most important official site is provided by the Department for Work and Pensions: www.dwp.gov.uk. Anyone doing a project on health policy should make as their first point of call www.doh.gov.uk. Anyone wanting to do a project on social policy in the devolved administrations should start with, depending on their interest: www.scotland.gov.uk, www.wales.gov.uk, or for Northern Ireland www.nisra.gov.uk. To compare the UK and Europe, the invaluable resource is 'Eurostat': www.europa.eu.int/comm/eurostat. The issue of social exclusion, to which New Labour has attached so much rhetorical importance, has its own official site provided by the Cabinet Office's Social Exclusion Unit: www.cabinet-office.gov.uk/seu. The most authoritative independent source of statistics and guidance about official statistics is that provided by the outstandingly good Institute of Fiscal Studies: www.ifs.org.uk.

CHAPTER 27

Economic policy

Michael Moran and Bill Jones

Learning objectives

- To identify the nature of economic policy.

- To describe the machinery by which economic policy is made and implemented.

- To examine three key themes in the analysis of recent economic policy – the significance of Thatcherism, the character of New Labour and the importance of Europe in British economic policy.

Introduction

Probably the single most important feature of modern British politics is the extent to which governments are judged by how well they manage the economy. Governments can get lots of things wrong and still win elections if they can deliver what electors perceive as economic success; but no matter how well governments do in other fields, it is almost impossible to be electorally successful if they are economic failures. This simple observation identifies the key place of economic policy in the political system.

■ The nature of economic policy

It may be thought a simple matter to identify 'economic policy': 'policy' consists of the choices made and rejected by government; 'economic' refers to that set of institutions and activities concerned with the production and distribution of goods and services; economic policy therefore consists of those choices made or rejected by government designed to affect the production of goods and services in the community.

This is, it will be plain, a very broad definition. Many activities of government not commonly thought of as 'economic' become so if we rigorously follow this guideline. Thus policy towards the arts – for instance, the provision of subsidised opera and theatre – is directed to influencing the price at which particular artistic services are provided to the community.

A broad definition of economic policy is revealing, for two reasons. First, it alerts us to the fact that

Even in 2006, joining the euro remained an issue for EU enthusiasts
Source: Copyright © Chris Riddell. From *The Observer*, 2 July 2000. Reproduced with permission from Guardian Newspapers Limited

the boundaries of 'economic policy' are moving all the time. For example, in recent years government has increasingly pictured education in economic terms. It conceives the primary purpose of schooling to be the production of one of the community's most valuable economic assets – a competent and educationally adaptable workforce. Thus, to an increasing extent, policy towards schools has been conceived as a facet of economic policy. This is simply reflected in the most recent renaming of the old Department for Education as the Department for Education *and Skills*. One of the primary features of economic policy is therefore that it has wide and constantly changing boundaries.

This connects to a second factor making a 'broad' definition of policy revealing: there is constant struggle and argument over the making and control of policy. British government works in part by a series of conventions that allocate subjects to particular institutions. An issue defined as purely concerned with education, for instance, will be in the domain of the Department for Education and Skills and the teaching profession. Until recently, for example, the content of the school curriculum was thought of as a purely 'educational' matter. But the growing belief that the quality of education, by affecting the quality of the workforce, in turn shapes the fortunes of the economy has introduced economic considerations into arguments about the curriculum and has destroyed the idea that choices about what is to be taught in schools are to be made only by those concerned with education.

This example shows that in economic policy making, arguments about what is and what is not relevant to the economy are of more than definitional significance. They are part of the process by which different groups in government try to gain control over particular areas of decision. The 'boundaries' of economic policy are therefore uncertain and disputed. But if the boundaries are open to argument, there is nevertheless considerable agreement about where the heart of economic policy lies. The most important parts concern the government's own 'housekeeping' and its wider responsibilities for economic management.

Governments have to make choices concerning the raising and distribution of their own resources: they have, in other words, to make choices concerning their budgets in the same way as a firm or a family makes choices. But the choices made by government about how much to spend, where to allocate the money and how to raise it have a special significance. This significance is partly the result of scale: government is the biggest institution in the British economy and has a correspondingly great effect on the rest of society. Decisions by government about how much to spend and how much to tax crucially affect the prosperity or otherwise of the economy at large. But the significance of public spending and taxation choices also lies in their purpose, for they are important instruments that governments can and do use to influence the course of the economy. This connects to a second 'core' aspect of economic policy.

Complementing its role as a major appropriator and distributor of resources in Britain, the government has a second major economic policy responsibility – **'steering the economy'**. The implied comparison with steering a vessel or a vehicle, while not exact, is nevertheless helpful. Like the pilot of a vessel, the government possesses instruments of control that can be manipulated to guide the economy in a desired direction; and like a pilot it has available a variety of indicators telling it how successfully these instruments are working. Among the most important instruments of control used by British government in recent decades are the budgetary instruments to which we have already referred. By varying the total volume of public spending or the level of taxation, government is able to increase or depress the total amount of activity in the economy. By targeting its spending on particular areas – such as education or the inner cities, or as subsidies to particular industries – government can also try to influence specific groups in the economy.

The image of 'steering the economy' was particularly important in the twenty-five years after the end of the Second World War. Margaret Thatcher's administrations, as we have seen in earlier chapters, denied that government could control the economy in the way that was attempted in the past. During the 1980s, 'Thatcherites' asserted that government could only hope to create the right conditions for a freely functioning market economy; competitive forces, for better or worse, would do the rest. Yet the government still does try to 'steer the economy'. It has objectives – such as the control of inflation – which it seeks to achieve, and instruments of control that it uses to that end. After the 1970s, therefore, the direction of economic steering and the instruments of control changed; but all governments in postwar Britain have been engaged in steering the economy.

■ The machinery of economic policy

When we refer to the 'machinery' of something, we are usually speaking of more than the mechanical parts of which it is composed; we also mean the process by which those parts combine in movement. So it is with the machinery of economic policy making: we mean not just the institutions but also the process by which they interact to produce choices.

If we look at a formal organisation chart of British government, we will see that it is hierarchical in nature with elected politicians – ministers – at the top. It would be natural to assume, therefore, that the machinery of economic policy making worked by reserving the power to make policy to a few people at the top of government and reserving the task of carrying out policy to those lower down the hierarchy. But perhaps the single most important feature of policy making is that there is no simple distinction to be made between a few at the top who 'make' policy and a larger number lower down in government who 'implement' or 'execute' policy. More perhaps than in any other area of public affairs, economic policy making and policy implementation are inseparable. Those at the top of government certainly have the potential to make broad decisions about the direction of policy. But the substance of economic policy is determined not only by broad strategic judgements but also by the way large numbers of organisations in both the public and the private sectors translate those into practical reality. The best way of picturing the machinery of economic policy making, therefore, is not as a hierarchy in which a few take decisions that are then executed by those further down the hierarchy but rather as a set of institutions in the centre of the machine that negotiate and argue over policy with a wide range of surrounding bodies in both the public and private sectors.

The centre of the machine

The Treasury

At the centre of the machinery of economic policy making is **the Treasury**. At first glance, the Treasury looks an insignificant institution. It is tiny by the standards of most central departments. What is more, it plays little part in the execution of economic policy. Vital tasks such as administering schemes for financial support of industry and regulating the activities of particular sectors and occupations are carried out elsewhere, notably by the Department of Trade and Industry. The Treasury's importance essentially lies in three features.

First, it is universally recognised as a vital source of policy advice about economic management, not only to its political head, the **Chancellor of the Exchequer**, but also to other senior ministers, notably the Prime Minister. Second, it is, as its name implies, in effect the keeper of the public purse: it is the key institution in decisions about the composition and volume of public spending. This is organised around a virtually continuous cycle of bargaining between the Treasury and the 'spending departments' to fix both the level of spending commitments and the proportionate allocation of resources between competing claimants.

Third, the Treasury shares with the **Bank of England** a large measure of control over policy towards financial markets. These matters include the terms on which the government borrows money and the 'management of sterling' – in other words intervention in foreign exchange markets to influence the rate at which the pound is exchanged for other foreign currencies. Although in most of these activities the Bank of England acts as the agent of government, it only does this in close, virtually continuous, consultation with the Treasury. These responsibilities are especially important because the management of financial markets has since the mid-1970s become a key task of economic policy. And as we will see in a moment, since 1997 the Bank has been given a distinct, semi-independent role in economic management. Consequently the Bank of England should now be placed alongside the Treasury at the core of the machinery of economic policy, despite the fact that it is not a government department, or even located in the area around Westminster where most of the major departments have their headquarters.

The Bank of England

The Bank of England is the nation's 'central bank'. This means that it is a publicly owned institution (although it only became so in 1946) with responsibility for managing the national currency. It also has a more general responsibility to oversee the stability of financial markets. (It used to have direct responsibility for supervision of financial institutions, but that has now been transferred to a separate Financial

The Bank of England, central to the UK's finance governance, was given independence in 1997 to fix interest rates
Source: Copyright © Angelo Hornak/Corbis

BIOGRAPHY

Mervyn King (1948–)

Governor, Bank of England, succeeding Eddie George in 2003. The Bank was dominated for most of its history by 'practical' bankers: either figures who had made a reputation in commercial banking or, like King's predecessor, had made their whole career within the Bank of England. King's appointment signifies the opening up of the Bank to wider influences and makes it look like a 'normal' state regulatory agency. Although he has worked in the Bank since the early 1990s, he had before that a long and distinguished career as an academic economist. But his appointment represented continuity in one important sense: the Bank remains, since the changes introduced by Labour on election in 1997, the most important decision taker about interest rates – and therefore deeply influences the life of everyone in Britain who borrows or lends money, and especially the millions of house mortgage holders.

Services Authority.) It is, as we have already seen, also the Treasury's agent in managing public debt and in interventions to influence levels of interest rates in the economy. The Bank's headquarters are located in the City of London, and this symbolises its distinctive character. Although a public body and part of the core of the machinery of policy making, it retains a tradition of independence. Its Governor, although chosen in effect by the Prime Minister and the Chancellor in combination, is usually a considerable and independent figure, in both the City of London and in international gatherings of other 'central bankers'. Likewise, employees of the Bank are recruited separately from, and paid more than, civil servants.

The Bank's importance in the machinery of economic decision making rests on three factors. First, it plays a major part in the execution of decisions increasingly considered to be the heart of economic policy – those concerning the management of conditions in financial markets. Second, as a result of its continuous and deep involvement with the markets it has an established position as a source of advice about the policy options best suited to the success-

ful management of these markets. Third, under the Labour government elected in 1997 it has acquired new responsibilities for interest rate policy: through a specially constituted Monetary Policy Committee consisting of senior Bank officials and outsiders appointed by the Treasury it controls short-term interest rates with a view to achieving targets for inflation that are laid down by the Treasury.

Describing the Treasury and the Bank of England as the centre of the machinery of economic policy does not amount to the same thing as saying that these two institutions dominate policy. However, it is undoubtedly the case that the two have a continuous role in the discussions about the strategic purposes and daily tactics of economic policy that occupy so much of modern government. No other institution in government specialises in this activity at such a high level.

The Treasury's and the Bank's positions at the centre of the machine are nevertheless shared with others. All governments in modern times have viewed economic policy as a primary responsibility and as a major influence on their chances of re-election. This means that economic management is never far from the minds of senior ministers. Two departmental members of the Cabinet usually occupy Treasury posts: the Chancellor of the Exchequer and the Chief Secretary to the Treasury, whose main responsibility is managing at the highest level the negotiations over expenditure plans between the Treasury and the 'spending' departments. Given the importance of economic policy, prime ministerial participation in consideration of strategy and tactics is now customary.

The Prime Minister

'Prime Minister' here partly means the individual who happens to be the occupant of that position at any particular moment. The Prime Minister is both figuratively and physically close to the machinery of economic policy making: his or her residence and that of the Chancellor adjoin, while the Treasury itself is barely a footstep away from No. 10 Downing Street. However, 'prime ministerial' involvement in economic policy denotes more than the involvement of a particular personality. It happened to be the case in the 1980s that Britain had in Margaret Thatcher an unusually commanding Prime Minister with a particular interest in, and firm grasp of, the mechanics of economic policy. Consequently, she was a central figure in the machinery. However, any modern Prime Minister is likely to be an important part of the machine. The precise position will depend on changing factors: the abilities and interests of a particular individual; the personal relations between the Prime Minister and the Chancellor; and the wider popularity and authority that the Prime Minister can command. After the return of Labour to office in 1997, it was especially complicated because in No. 10 Downing Street there was a Prime Minister with unusual authority because he had delivered landslide general election victories and an unusually strong Chancellor next door who considered himself, and was considered by everybody else, to be at least the second most powerful figure in British government. These complications have grown over the years, notably because of jockeying between the Prime Minister and the Chancellor for authority, and because of the Chancellor's determination to succeed as Prime Minister, preferably as quickly as possible.

Prime ministerial involvement does, however, not consist only of personal intervention. It can also take the form of participation by the staff of the Prime Minister's own office and from institutions closely connected to the Prime Minister, notably the Cabinet Office. Prime ministerial economic advisers can also exert considerable influence: in 1989 the Chancellor, Nigel Lawson, actually resigned over the role performed by Margaret Thatcher's adviser, Sir Alan Walters.

The Cabinet

Prime ministerial participation in the machinery of economic policy making may now be described as 'institutionalised', which means that it is part of the established procedures, irrespective of the capacities and outlook of the individual who at any particular moment happens to occupy No. 10 Downing Street. It is less certain that the same can be said of the Cabinet, a body that was once indisputably a dominant participant. It is true that the Cabinet retains a role irrespective of particular circumstances, such as the style of an individual Prime Minister. Thus the weekly meetings of the Cabinet will always contain agenda items that bear on central parts of economic strategy. But a skilful Prime Minister can often manipulate that agenda to keep economic issues away from the Cabinet. When Mrs Thatcher was first elected in 1979, she recognised that many members of the Cabinet were actually hostile to the policies that she and her Chancellor were pursuing, and for

BIOGRAPHY

Gordon Brown (1951–)

Labour Chancellor of the Exchequer since 1997. Virtually every Chancellor of modern times has been educated at either Oxford or Cambridge University. Brown is the son of a Church of Scotland clergyman and was educated at the University of Edinburgh. This symbolises his unusual character as a Chancellor. A combination of his Scottish power base and internal Labour Party politics have made him the most powerful Chancellor of modern times; he is at least the second most important figure in the New Labour governments and in some eyes is as powerful as the Prime Minister. Under his Chancellorship the Treasury has considerably strengthened its hold over economic policy, and through more detailed control of public spending it has gained increasing influence over the activities of the 'spending departments' like Education and Defence. Following the 2005 general election Brown's control over domestic policy was strengthened, and he became a virtual certainty to succeed Mr Blair as Prime Minister before the next general election.

at least two years the full Cabinet was sidelined in discussions of economic strategy. Only upon her landslide victory in 1983, when the Cabinet was dominated by Thatcher loyalists, could this tactic be relaxed.

But even more important than the manoeuvres of Prime Ministers in marginalising the full Cabinet is the fact that a network of Cabinet committees now does most of its business. This means that while the Cabinet is marginal, cabinet ministers are not – they just exercise their influence over economic policy in committee instead. The Cabinet system retains a particularly important role in deciding public spending. Although the process is dominated by direct bargaining between the Treasury and individual departments, it is still accepted that it is at Cabinet committee level that irreconcilable differences between a department and the Treasury are effectively resolved.

Nevertheless, since the end of the 1970s the extent of collective Cabinet involvement in economic policy making has been uncertain. The importance of individuals remains: after all, three Cabinet members – the Prime Minister, the Chancellor and the Chief Secretary to the Treasury – are all indisputably part of the core machinery. But what may have declined is the collective consideration of strategy and tactics by Cabinet institutions – either in full Cabinet or in committee. Whether this is due to the style of leadership practised by Margaret Thatcher, who dominated her Cabinets in the 1980s, or whether it is due to longer-term changes in the significance of the Cabinet, is at present uncertain; but if it is due to long-term changes it is plainly important; and if due to Margaret Thatcher's leadership style it is also revealing, since it shows that the Cabinet's place in the machinery is dependent on the style of the particular Prime Minister who happens to be in office. We will need to know more than we currently do about the Cabinet relations of Prime Ministers since Mrs Thatcher (Major 1990–7; Blair since 1997) before we can answer this question.

The observation that the Cabinet's role in the machinery is uncertain should not be taken to mean that cabinet ministers and their departments are unimportant. Indeed, since we saw earlier that no simple division can be made between the 'making' of policy and its 'implementation', it follows that departments, in the act of executing policy, in effect also 'make' it by shaping what comes out of the government machine. This is manifestly the case with, for instance, the Department of Trade and Industry, which, in its multitude of dealings with individual firms, industries and sectors, plays a large part in deciding what, in practice, is to be the government's policy towards a wide range of industries.

The machinery of economic policy stretches not only beyond the central institutions like the Treasury to other central departments; it also encompasses what is sometimes called '**quasi-government**' and even institutions that are in the private sector. It is to these matters that we now turn.

Quasi-government

One of the striking features of British government is the small proportion of the 'public sector' that is actually accounted for by what we conventionally think of as the characteristic public institution – the central department headed by a cabinet minister located in central London. Most people who work in the public sector are not 'civil servants', and most of the work of the public sector is done by institutions

that do not have the status of Civil Service departments. This feature has become even more pronounced since the rise of the 'Next Steps' agencies discussed in Chapter 21, but it spreads well beyond the formal reorganisation of central government. We express the importance of this in the language of 'quasi-government'. 'Quangos', as they are sometimes called, have many of the marks of public bodies: they are usually entrusted with the task of carrying out duties prescribed in law; they often draw all, or a proportion of, their funds from the public purse; and the appointment of their leading officers is usually controlled by a minister and his or her department. Yet in their daily operations they normally work with some degree of independence of ministers and are usually less subject than are Civil Service departments to parliamentary scrutiny. There are many reasons why 'quasi-government' is important in the machinery of economic policy, but two are particularly significant. The first is that central government departments simply do not have the resources and knowledge to carry out the full tasks of the public sector; the system would become impossibly overloaded if the effort were made to control everything through a handful of government departments in London. The second reason is that the 'quasi-government' system offers some protection against control by politicians, especially Members of Parliament. It is much harder for a Member of Parliament to scrutinise and call to account an agency than to do the same thing with a Civil Service department headed by a minister.

The importance of quasi-government in understanding economic policy is heightened by a critical transformation in its structure in recent decades. Any reader curious enough could get a good sense of the importance of this transformation simply by looking back at the first edition of this book, written in the late 1980s. There, a single body, the **nationalised corporation**, dominated the description; now, as we shall see in a moment, nationalised corporations have virtually disappeared.

Nationalised corporations were a comparatively standard organisational type. They normally worked under a charter prescribing such matters as the constitution and powers of their governing board. The corporation form has, in the past, been used for activities as different as delivering broadcasting services (the BBC) and mining coal (British Coal). Most nationalised corporations provided goods and services through the market, deriving the bulk of their revenue from sales. But they were also linked to central government. It was common for a corporation to have a 'sponsoring department' in Whitehall. The 'sponsor' was expected to 'speak for' its corporation inside central government, but it was also an instrument for exercising control over the corporation.

The past tense is needed here, because the nationalised corporation has mostly had its day. From 1945 to the end of the 1970s it was a major instrument of government policy – and was itself in turn a major influence over the shape of economic policy. In the 1980s, 'privatisation' reduced the size and significance of the nationalised corporation in the machinery of economic policy. It is important to know about the nationalised corporation because of its historical importance – and because its passing away through 'privatisation' is one of the most important long-term changes in the management of the economy in recent decades.

Britain led the world in privatisation. In the years of Conservative rule between 1979 and 1997, it privatised a comprehensive range of basic industries and services: telecommunications services, gas and electricity services, coal and steel production, water services, rail services – to name only some of the most prominent. But privatisation did not spell the end of public influence over the economy, nor did it spell the end of the importance of quasi-government; it simply replaced the nationalised corporation with an equally important institution of economic control – the **regulatory agency**. Virtually every important publicly owned industry that was privatised is now governed by its own specialised regulatory agency: they include agencies for the privatised telecommunications, gas, electricity and rail industries.

These new agencies have acquired increasingly broad functions since the mid-1980s, when they first appeared. Starting out with a narrow mission to regulate the rate of price increases in privatised industries, they they now have three broad functions:

1. They regulate the terms of competition in industries, including the degree of price competition.

2. They regulate service standards for customers, commonly laying down minimum standards of quality and punctuality.

3. They regulate the social impact of industrial activity, for instance in the interests of ensuring that firms balance the search for profit with the requirement to deliver socially desirable services even when these are not profitable.

Politically the most important feature of the development of a regulated privatised sector is twofold. First, it shows that much of the change in the character of state economic activity since the 1980s involves not a retreat but a change in form and direction. We still have a large state presence in the economy, but it now takes the form of regulation rather than public ownership. Second, it shows that the end of nationalisation has not meant the end of politics: all the three functions summarised above are intensely political, involving as they do highly charged judgements about such matters as the proper rate of profit for a firm and the proper range of its social obligations.

The machinery of economic policy stretches into 'quasi-government', but it also, we shall now see, reaches into the private sector.

BOX 27.1 **FACT**

The new world of regulatory agencies: an example

OFGEM (the Office of Gas and Electricity Markets) was created in 2000. It inherited wide powers arising from the great privatisation programmes carried out in the 1980s, when both electricity supply and generation, and gas supply, were 'privatised': that is, were transformed from public monopolies to privately owned corporations. Separate regulatory bodies were established initially for the gas and electricity industries. The new agency recognises the increasingly integrated nature of energy markets, with general 'utility' companies competing to supply right across the energy sphere. OFGEM regulates a wide range of economic conditions in the markets, such as price and other kinds of competition, and it also regulates the social consequences of market behaviour: for instance, it pays a great deal of attention to the terms under which companies can cut off supply for non-payment of bills.

The private sector

It may seem odd to include privately owned institutions such as business firms in the machinery of policy, but it will become obvious when we realise two things: that economic policy is made in the process of execution, not just by a few people at the top handing down decisions to be routinely carried out elsewhere; and in executing policy the government relies widely on private bodies.

One of the most striking examples of this is provided by the banking system in Britain. Almost all British banks are privately owned, yet without the services provided by the banks any government's economic policies would come to nothing. For instance, the whole payments system, on which the economy depends, is administered by the banks. This includes, for example, the circulation of notes and coins throughout the population and the processing of cheques and other forms of payment. In some of the most technologically advanced sectors of the economy, such as the nuclear power industry, firms in private ownership work in close partnership with government to implement jointly agreed policies.

Box 27.2 highlights some of the main actors in economic policy. It should not be taken as a comprehensive list. It is a sketch designed to show how wide is the range of actors and how far the real world of economic policy making departs from any

simple notion that economic policy is about something as narrow as a 'government' making decisions. The box also helps us to highlight another important feature of economic policy. Look at the entries that have an asterisk attached to them. They have an obvious feature in common: they are all external to the United Kingdom. They stand for the fact that some of the most important policy actors are actually outside Britain. The institutions of the European Union are central to all policy making in Britain, and the 'Europeanisation' of economic policy making is examined in more detail later in this chapter. The World Trade Organisation is the leading forum for the negotiation of trading rules in the world economy, affecting, for instance, what sort of barriers, if any, a country can erect against foreign competition. It also has the power to order compliance with agreements to which member governments have signed up. Foreign multinationals, who appear in our 'private sector' category, are important in all nations. But Britain has been for long the main recipient in the European Union of direct inward investment by foreign multinationals, so they are uniquely important in British economic policy. In recent years, for instance, there has been a considerable revival of car assembly and manufacturing in Britain. Almost all is due to investment by foreign-owned multinationals such as Ford (USA), Toyota and Nissan (Japan) and BMW (Germany).

BOX 27.2　FACT

Actors in economic policy

Public actors
- Prime Minister
- Chancellor of the Exchequer
- Chief Secretary to the Treasury
- Governor of the Bank of England
- Senior Treasury officials
- Economic advisers
- Cabinet Office
- Key Cabinet committees
- Secretary of State, Department of Trade and Industry
- Cabinet
- European Union institutions*

Quasi-government organisations
- Regulatory agencies
- World Trade Organisation*

Private sector
- Business firms
- Banks
- Foreign multinationals*
- Employers' organisations
- Trade Unions

*See text

■ Three themes in economic policy

The Thatcherite revolution

Anybody wanting to make sense of the British economy after the millennium has to come to terms with a revolution in economic thought and practice that started in the 1970s. '**Thatcherism**' is now familiarly used to describe the policies of Margaret Thatcher's Conservative governments, but its impact continues nearly two decades after Margaret Thatcher herself was forced from office. After the Thatcher years there was no turning back; in different ways we are all Thatcherites now.

The origins of Thatcherism lie in the policy failures preceding Margaret Thatcher's election to office in 1979, and the debate prompted by those failures. In the widest historical sense, Thatcherism was a response to a century of British economic decline. In the 1870s, Britain was the world's leading industrial nation; by the 1970s its economy was ailing and it seemed in danger of falling out of the 'premier league' of rich countries. A succession of governments in the 1960s and 1970s had tried to cope with decline by intervening extensively in economic management and by pursuing consensual policies that depended on the agreement of both employers and unions. Thatcherism turned its back on both: it sought to introduce historically different policies that would withdraw the state from economic management; and it sought to replace the consensual and cooperative policy style of British government with a more centralised and directed way of doing things.

The most important features of Thatcherism as economic policy were threefold. The first involved an attempt to change the structure of ownership in the community radically: in the 1980s, the government 'privatised' nearly half of what had been publicly owned in 1979. Second, Thatcherism attempted to change the structure of rewards: it cut the tax bills of the very rich while also reducing the value of many welfare benefits, especially those to the unemployed. The expectation behind this change was that increasing the rewards for success would stimulate enterprise beneficial to all. Making unemployment more unattractive economically would encourage the unemployed to take jobs at lower wage rates, thus reducing both unemployment and the overall pressure of wage demands. Finally, Thatcherism withdrew or reduced subsidies to many industries, compelling the closure of many concerns and the more efficient operation of the rest in the face of international competition.

These changes in substance were accompanied by a change in the style of economic policy making. Precisely because Thatcherism involved an attempt to alter the substance of policy radically, it was compelled to break with the consensual and cooperative approach. Many reforms, such as those bearing on trade unions, were imposed upon groups whose cooperation was usually sought in the past. Many policies – such as obliging inefficient manufacturing to reorganise or to close – were pursued in spite of protests from representatives of manufacturing industry.

This break with consensus and cooperation helps to explain why, despite its domination of economic policy making in the 1980s, judgements about the Thatcherite solution remain deeply divided. The case for Thatcherism can be summarised under three headings. The first is that, however painful the experience of closing down large parts of manufacturing industry may have been, it was only recognition of the inevitable, in conditions where British industries simply were not efficient enough to find markets for goods. Second, a change to a more centralised and directive style of policy making was necessary because the traditional cooperative approach was responsible, at least in part, for the failed policies of the past. Finally, comparison of Britain with other economies shows that Thatcherism is not unique. Across the world governments are, almost regardless of party, introducing economic reforms resembling the Thatcherite programme. This suggests that Thatcherism in Britain was a necessary adjustment to changing patterns in the world economy, without which Britain would lose even its present modest place in the international economic hierarchy.

What is more, comparison of the international record of economic growth before and after Thatcherism suggests that it made a considerable positive difference to the performance of the British economy. Figure 27.1 shows that the United Kingdom, bottom of the usual international league tables in the 1960s and early 1970s, has more recently been near the top. And for a decade now the British economy has been the most successful big economy in the European Union, measured by ability to grow and to create jobs. Many factors other than Thatcherism might account for these patterns, but it seems undeniable that something significant happened to the performance of the British economy

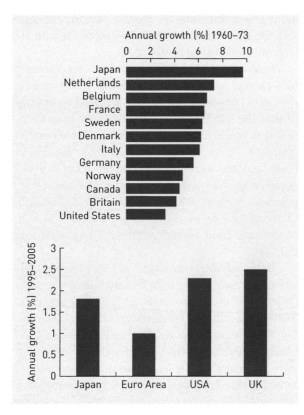

Figure 27.1 From dunce to top of the class: the transformation of British economic performance, 1960–2004

Sources: From *The Economist*, 21 September 1996, for years 1960–73. © The Economist Newspaper Limited 1996. All rights reserved. Reproduced with permission; *International Monetary Fund Survey*, 21 March 2005, p. 77 for years 1995–2005. *Economist* figures are for average increases in manufacturing output; IMF figures are for economic growth per capita

Exchange rates
Up
Reduces inflation. But makes exports more expensive.
Down
Makes exports cheaper. But increases inflation.

Interest rates
Up
Makes borrowing more expensive so reduces amount of money in economy. This reduces inflation. But makes survival for some companies harder, resulting in bankruptcies and unemployment.
Down
Makes it cheaper for business to borrow and thus improves investment. But can cause inflation.

Taxes
Up
More revenue into treasury; anti-inflationary; selective use can discourage undesirable spending, e.g. smoking. But upsets voters.
Down
Pleases voters. But reduces revenue, can be inflationary and increases consumer spending.

Public spending
Up
Increases employment, improves public services, pleases voters. But increases taxation which displeases voters, worries overseas investors.
Down
Reduces taxation which pleases voters. But increases unemployment, public services suffer, voters unhappy.

Employment laws
Favour workers
Unions happy. But business costs increase, loss of competitiveness.
Favour business
Business happy, unions not, costs decrease, competitiveness improves.

Figure 27.2 Steering the economy: some good and bad outcomes

after 1979. (The numbers in Figure 27.1 should be compared with caution: those for 1960–73 are of annual average increases in manufacturing output; those for 1995–2004 are for per head rates of economic growth more generally. But the transformation they record is still remarkable.)

The alternative, critical judgement of Thatcherite economics can be summarised under two headings. First, the most distinctive consequence of Thatcherite economic policies has been to eliminate important parts of manufacturing industry, in a world where the manufacture and sale of finished goods is still the characteristic sign of an advanced industrial economy. In other words, Thatcherism has only hastened what is sometimes called '**deindustrialisation**'. Second, the shift away from a consensual policy style, combined with a deliberate strategy of increasing the rewards to the rich and enterprising,

carries great dangers for social peace and harmony. Governments have a variety of levers which they can pull to make the economy work as they intend but the problem is that for each beneficial effect there is often a harmful one, as Figure 27.2 explains.

New Labour and economic policy

The most striking feature of the economic policy fashioned by the Labour Party to fight the 1997 general election, when it was returned to power, is well known: it largely accepted the great changes in both the conduct of economic management and the structure of the economy introduced by the

Conservatives after 1979. That refashioning created a template which still accounts for the policy of the Labour government nearly ten years later.

The acceptance came in three stages:

1. After Labour's catastrophic general election defeat in 1983, the party moved in stages (chiefly between 1985 and 1989) to accept the main parts of the Thatcherite revolution, notably the big privatisation programme and the Conservatives' reforms of the law on industrial relations.

2. After the election of Tony Blair as leader, he persuaded the party to accept a big symbolic change – the excision from its constitution of the famous 'socialist' Clause Four in place of a new clause that commended 'the enterprise of the market and the rigour of competition'.

3. The third stage was the general election manifesto of 1997, which committed Labour to accepting the level of spending already planned by the Conservatives for its first two years of office and also committed the party not to increase basic or top rates of income tax.

These developments dominated the economic policy of the first Labour government between 1997 and 2001. In order to foster Labour's reputation for 'prudence' – a favourite word of the Chancellor – public spending was kept under tight rein. The object was to reassure both the electorate, and key interests in financial markets. Since the turn of the millennium, however, there have been important changes. They reflect the embedding of Labour in power, notably following its second landslide general election victory in 2001. They also reflect the progress of the economy: in 1997 the economy was already set on a sustained path of economic growth and falling unemployment. As Figure 27.1 showed, the decade after 1995 were years of historically unprecedented success, compared with the performance of other leading capitalist economies, and compared with what had been achieved in Britain in the recent past. After the turn of the millennium

Financial critics of Gordon Brown accuse him of borrowing too much to maintain public finances

Source: Copyright © Chris Riddell. From *The Observer*, 5 December 2004. Reproduced with permission from Guardian Newspapers Limited

Labour's public spending policies therefore changed decisively. Two programmes in particular – health and education – enjoyed a huge boost. In *real* terms (that is, after adjusting for inflation) spending on health and in education nearly doubled between the financial years 1999–2000 and the (planned) spending for 2007–8: education rising from £15 billion to over £31 billion, and health from £45 billion to over £85 billion. (2007–8 is chosen because it is the final year of the present cycle of planned public spending: governments plan spending for a cycle of years rather than for one single financial year. The figures cited here and later, together with the Treasury's reasoning about spending, can be found in HM Treasury, 2005a.)

These figures reflect both the electoral sensitivity of education and health, and also a rather traditional 'old Labour' preoccupation with health and education as central objects of state activity. They also reflect the predominance of these programmes in public spending: as Figures 27.3 and 27.4 show, both the income of government, and its spending obligations, are dominated by a comparatively few budget lines. And while the magnitude of increase for favoured programmes is striking, and represents a substantial historic shift in policy, it does not represent a simple return to old high-spending patterns. The commonest overall measure of the scale of public spending in the context of the whole economy is what is technically called 'Total Managed

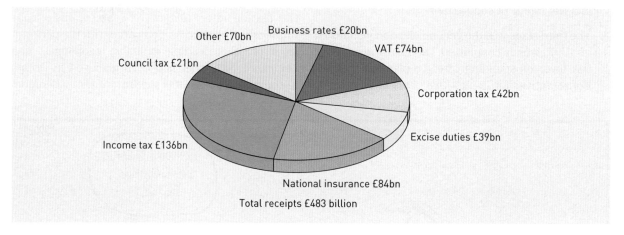

Figure 27.3 Where taxes come from, 2004
Source: HM Treasury (2005a) *Pre-Budget Report 2005 Summary 2005*, <http://prebudget2005.treasury.gov.uk/page08.html>.
© Crown Copyright 2005. Crown copyright material is reproduced with the permission of the Controller of Her Majesty's Stationery Office HMSO)

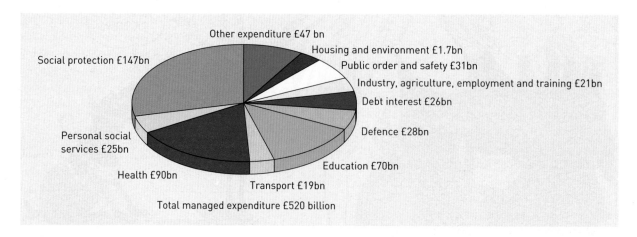

Figure 27.4 Where taxpayers' money is spent, 2004
Source: HM Treasury (2005b) *Pre-Budget Report 2005 Summary 2005*, <http://prebudget2005.treasury.gov.uk/page08.html>.
© Crown Copyright 2005. Crown copyright material is reproduced with the permission of the Controller of Her Majesty's Stationery Office (HMSO)

Expenditure' as a percentage of Gross Domestic Product (a measure of the total size of the economy). At the end of the present round of planned expenditure (2007–8) that figure is forecast to be 42.1 per cent. This is exactly what it was in 1987–8, at the high point of Mrs Thatcher's premiership, when she had just won a third general election victory. It is actually below the level (45.3 per cent) recorded in the last year of the Labour Administration before Mr Blair's (that of James Callaghan, for 1978–9). There are two explanations for the apparent oddity that New Labour has vastly expanded public spending on education and health while keeping the share of public spending in the total economy comparatively low: the economy itself has been growing, thus providing new resources for spending; and tight control has been exercised over other programmes. (For instance, in real terms there is actually a fall in the defence budget between 1999–2000 and 2007–8.)

The impact of Europe

We can see, with the benefit of hindsight, that entry into what was then colloquially called the Common Market in 1973 was momentous for the British economy. It made four big sets of changes:

1. It contributed to a historic shift in trading patterns, with the European Union displacing old trading partners that reflected the trading patterns inherited from the old British Empire.

2. It shifted the location of important economic policy decisions, and in the process caused a big shift in the focus of lobbying by powerful interests from London to Brussels, where the main European Union decision-making institutions are located. This process was given a big boost by the introduction in the 1990s of a single European market in a wide range of goods and services. The introduction of the single market meant that it was necessary to harmonise a wide range of regulations – ranging from the biggest, such as those governing competition rules, to the smallest, such as those governing packaging of materials – at a Community level. Thus the long-term impact of the original entry has been to transform – by Europeanising – the process of economic policy making in Britain.

3. The economic impact of membership of the European Union (as the former Common Market is now known) has in turn had a big effect on the lines of political division within the United Kingdom. Both the major political parties are divided over how the economy of the European Union should develop and over Britain's proper role in that development. Only a minority in both parties now advocate what was a common view only a couple of decades ago – withdrawal of the United Kingdom from the EU. But the internal divisions in the parties mirror a wider debate in Europe about the best way to revitalise the economy of the continent. Broadly, this is a choice between the established European way of doing things and an alternative '**Anglo-Saxon model**', which is very influenced by the United Kingdom in the 1980s and 1990s. The traditional European way involves close regulation of the market economy and a partnership between capital and labour in which organised labour has a big say over policy; the Anglo-Saxon model involves deregulation of markets and a sharp diminution of the influence of organised labour over the making of policy and over the functioning of markets. Although leading politicians in both the Conservative and Labour parties have tended to advocate the Anglo-Saxon model in debates about economic policy within the Union, the Labour government elected in 1997 was more sympathetic than its predecessors to aspects of the traditional regulated European model. This is signified by the Labour government's acceptance of the Social Charter guaranteeing a range of rights in the workplace, which was rejected by its Conservative predecessor.

4. The fourth and final impact of the Union in economic policy involves a historic choice that faces British politicians: whether to take the pound sterling into European monetary union. From 1999, a single currency (the **euro**) existed in twelve states of the Union for all foreign exchange transactions; since the start of 2002, as any reader who has recently holidayed abroad will know, individual national currencies have disappeared to be replaced by the euro for all everyday transactions. (The exceptions are the United Kingdom, Denmark and Sweden; the last held a referendum in 2003 which decided against adopting the euro.) Both major parties in the United Kingdom are internally divided over whether the United Kingdom should participate, although the Labour government remains cautiously inclined to participate while the

Conservative leadership has adopted an increasingly hostile policy. In part the judgement is about economic consequences: about whether the euro will further free the European economy from national barriers and thus lead to a surge in prosperity; or whether it will prove a weak and unstable currency that will undermine economic stability. In part, the judgement is about political consequences: even those politicians most favourable to monetary union believe that there are great dangers in British participation if it is not preceded by a campaign that allays popular fears over the loss of the pound as a symbol and the loss of important economic policy-making powers to the European Central Bank in Frankfurt. If Britain does enter a monetary union, then this chapter's description of the most important institutions in economic policy will have to be drastically revised in future editions to include a range of institutions beyond the borders of the United Kingdom. Since the introduction of the euro, however, the performance of the big economies in the euro-zone – Germany, France, Italy – has been poor, notably by comparison with British economic performance. This has made it increasingly unlikely that any effort will be made to draw the UK into the euro-zone in the near future, if ever.

BOX 27.3   BRITAIN IN CONTEXT

British economic policy in comparative context

The British economy is special. It is historically special: it was the first to make the jump to industrialism, in the industrial revolution. It was the first to experience the long decline away from industrialism; by the 1970s it was the 'sickest' of all the leading capitalist economies. By the turn of the century it was, however, one of the most robust, a star performer in job creation and economic growth, especially compared with the other big economies of the European Union. It did this by taking a unique reform path. It pioneered large-scale privatisation and deregulation, and broke the power of the trade union movement. It abandoned large parts of domestically owned manufacturing industry to world competition. It emerged as a self-conscious example of a distinct model of capitalism, usually called Anglo-Saxon capitalism. Alongside the United States it pointed the way to a deregulated economy where job creation and growth were possible, but apparently at the cost of high levels of job insecurity and high economic inequality. Whatever its merits or otherwise, the British model of economic policy has had one undoubted achievement: it has created an intense debate within the other leading economies of the European Union about the viability of their more regulated models of capitalism. As we saw in Chapter 26, the comparative uniqueness of the British model is also apparent in social policy, and many of the choices and problems in the two domains of policy can be seen to resemble each other when viewed in comparative context.

Chapter summary

Economic policy is probably the most important policy domain with which British government has to deal, if only because failure here is known to be electorally fatal for politicians. But as we have seen in this chapter, shaping economic policy is no simple matter. There are several reasons for this. The boundaries of economic policy are themselves not clear. As a result, the range of actors and institutions involved is wide and constantly changing. It is not possible to govern a modern economy just by issuing policies and expecting them to have an effect. Government has to deal with many institutions over which it has imperfect control, or no control at all. That is true even of many nominally public sector bodies, like regulatory agencies. It is even more true of private sector bodies, which are very important in actually executing policy. And it is perhaps truest of all when these bodies are not even within the formal jurisdiction of British government. That is the case with a wide range of institutions that have cropped up in this chapter: institutions like those of the European Union, bodies concerned with the regulation of the world economy, like the World Trade Organisation, and foreign-owned multinational corporations. To compound uncertainty and instability, British governments are swept along by great economic currents over which they have little control. For a century after 1870 they were swept along by the tide of British economic decline, and since then they have been struggling to adapt to the great tide of European unification. For over a decade from the start of the 1990s the legacy of the Thatcher reforms was an economy which, unusually, performed exceptionally well by international standards, and enjoyed the longest period of sustained economic growth in British history. That long period of growth is now threatened by forces over which the British government has little control: the renewed burst of inflation caused by rising world demand for key commodities, and threats to the security of oil supplies. Whether the British economy is robust enough to shrug off these problems only time will tell.

Further reading

Grant (2002) is the indispensable further reading for this chapter: it is a masterpiece of compression, thoroughness and clarity. It is important to understand British economic policy in the wider context of the workings of market economies in the advanced capitalist world. There now exists a sophisticated but highly accessible comparative account in Coates (2000). Of the large literature on Thatcherism, Gamble (1994) is by far the best. Wright and Thain (1995) is the standard study of public spending. The policies of New Labour are now authoritatively examined in Coates (2005).

References

Coates, D. (2000) *Models of Capitalism: Growth and Stagnation in the Modern Era* (Polity Press).

Coates, D. (2005) *Prolonged Labour: The Slow Birth of New Labour in Britain* (Palgrave Macmillan).

Gamble, A. (1994) *The Free Economy and the Strong State*, 2nd edn (Macmillan).

Grant, W. (2002) *Economic Policy in Britain* (Palgrave).

HM Treasury (2005a) Pre-Budget Report, at http://prebudget2005.treasury.gov.uk

HM Treasury (2005b) *Public Expenditure Statistical Analyses.* Cm 6521.

Wright, M. and Thain, C. (1995) *Treasury and Whitehall: Planning and Control of Public Spending* (Clarendon Press).

Useful websites

The indispensable website for anybody wanting to study economic policy is that provided by the Treasury: www.hm-treasury.gov.uk. The statistics quoted in the figures of this chapter that give 'HM Treasury' as a source are from this site, notably from the 'Economic Tools and Data' pages. An excellent independent source of figures and commentary, especially about public spending, is provided by the web pages of the think-tank, the Institute of Fiscal Studies: www.ifs.org.uk.

CHAPTER 28

British foreign and defence policy under the Blair government

Bill Jones (and Peter Byrd)

Learning objectives

- To explain the nature of foreign policy and, particularly, the 'realist' approach to it.

- To explore the idea of an 'ethical foreign policy' and its viability since 1997.

- To examine foreign policy problems in Sierra Leone, Indonesia and Kosovo.

- To assess defence policy in the post-Cold War world.

- To analyse relations with the USA.

We are the ally of the US not because they are powerful, but because we share their values . . . There is no greater error in international politics than to believe that strong in Europe means weaker with the US. The roles reinforce one another . . . There can be no international consensus unless Europe and the US act together . . . We can help to be the bridge between the US and Europe . . . Europe should partner the US and not be its rival.

Tony Blair, quoted in Gamble (2003)

Introduction

I n this chapter, we study British foreign policy (excluding the European issue) since the election of the Labour government in May 1997 under three headings. The first is the government's 'ethical' foreign policy, introduced as part of the FCO mission statement as early as 12 May 1997, days after the election. The second is the Strategic Defence Review, also announced within days of coming into office, conducted by Secretary of State for Defence George Robertson and completed in July 1998. These two documents constitute not only a statement of foreign and defence policy objectives but also a baseline against which performance in office can be judged. The third heading is the government's relationship with the United States. This is the most familiar theme in foreign policy since the Second World War, although Blair was re-cementing a close relationship that had to some extent atrophied under the Major government.

■ Background

The study of British foreign policy has become increasingly problematical because of the difficulty of defining an arena or 'sphere' of foreign policy that is distinct from domestic policy. The internationalisation of government activity means that there are no longer, if indeed there ever were, clearly defined areas of domestic policy and of foreign policy. In the 1960s, this internationalisation was often characterised by the perceived growth and alleged political influence of the multinational corporation in impacting on national political and economic life. In the 1970s and 1980s, the development of the European Community and of the single market blurred enormously the boundaries between the British polity and a wider European sphere of policy making. Since the 1990s, the favoured term for this process has been 'globalisation', emphasising the consequences of the revolution in information and communications technology on the behaviour of the money and financial markets. The 'global village' predicted in the 1960s appears to have arrived, although some caution is required in interpreting these developments. For instance, the wars fought in former Yugoslavia throughout most of the 1980s were widely reported on our television screens, and commentators have often referred to these horrors taking place only two hours' flying time from Britain and in areas familiar to

British holidaymakers. Nevertheless, at crucial times information about developments on the ground was lacking, air strikes were based on poor information, and the difficulties confronting the Western powers in influencing events were not dissimilar to those confronting the Western allies in 1945.

In this chapter, we again follow the now familiar convention of separating a discussion of developments within the European Union from other areas of foreign policy. In doing this, we assume both that EU policy is the most important sphere of foreign policy and that it is also distinct from other areas of foreign policy in being the best example of the hybridisation of foreign and domestic policy. Practically all departments of government are involved in making European Union policy; the Foreign and Commonwealth Office is not the most important. For instance, policy on British membership of the euro, perhaps the single most important strategic issue facing the government since its election in 1997, has been tightly controlled by the Prime Minister and the Chancellor of the Exchequer. The Chancellor laid down five key criteria to determine the merits of British membership in October 1997, and Foreign Secretary Robin Cook made not a single speech or statement on the euro between the general election campaign and his speech in Tokyo on 6 September 1999. In this speech, Cook argued in much more positive tones for British membership.

Margaret Beckett, as Foreign Secretary, has to meet a constant queue of visiting overseas representatives
Source: Sang Tan / AP / Empics

Two possible reasons may explain Cook's intervention. The first is that he could no longer ignore the warnings from foreign investors in Britain that it would be difficult to sustain investment if Britain remained outside the euro (this might also explain why he chose to speak in Tokyo, given the importance of Japanese investment). The second is that he was exploiting the enhanced prestige of the FCO based on his successful management of the Kosovo issue since March 1999.

■ Ethical foreign policy

On 12 May, Secretary of State Robin Cook identified the goals of Labour's foreign policy in the form of a 'mission statement', adopting in this term one of the key tools of the modern organisation as essential to New Labour's modernising drive. The mission was 'to promote the national interests of the United Kingdom and to contribute to a strong world community'. The pursuit of the mission would bring four benefits to Britain:

1. Security of the UK and the dependent territories (colonies) and peace through the promotion of stability, defensive alliances and arms control.

2. Prosperity through promotion of jobs and trade.

3. Quality of life by protecting the environment and countering drugs, terrorism and crime.

4. Mutual respect by working through international forums and bilateral relationships to 'spread the values of human rights, civil liberties and democracy which we demand for ourselves'.

Despite all the press discussion since 1997 about 'ethical foreign policy', and certainly Robin Cook consistently identified himself with the concept, it is only the fourth element that is, arguably, new or distinctive.

Theorists and analysts have traditionally seen foreign policy as being about the **national interest**. This 'realist' concept of national interest is at the same time familiar and opaque. However, it is normally taken as meaning that foreign policy is focused on a core element of the security of the state within an external environment that is anarchic and potentially hostile and in which power and force are the ultimate determinants of outcome rather than law or rectitude. The state, in short, has to be on its guard. The national interest emphasises the continuity of the state's interests rather than the changing vagaries of governmental aspirations.

This traditional definition of foreign policy is enshrined in Cook's first 'benefit' of his foreign policy objectives. Cook did not abandon the traditional definition of foreign policy; rather, he explicitly sought to widen foreign policy beyond security and prosperity, an objective of foreign policy as old as security, through embracing two other elements. Quality of life and in particular the environment, drugs, terrorism and crime have become increasingly important in foreign policy over the past twenty years or so, in part as a result of the end of the Cold War and the emergence of new foreign policy issues. The Rio Summit of 1992 marked the emergence of the global environment as an important issue for the 'world community' (a term itself founded on acceptance of an ecological perspective on the future of the planet). International terrorism, crime and the drugs trade are older concerns but have been given increased importance by improvements in international communications and the weakening of national territorialities (not to mention the increased energy and deviousness of international criminals).

The novelty of Cook's foreign policy mission, therefore, other than the very notion of a mission, lies in the fourth benefit of mutual respect and human rights. This is the key to the idea of an ethical foreign policy. Cook's claim reversed classical realism's respect for, and non-interference in, the domestic sovereignty of other states. The case for non-interference was based both on rectitude, or legal acceptance of the domestic jurisdiction of states, and on prudence, or the acceptance that, given the nature of the international system, interference in the domestic affairs of other states was foolhardy, ineffective and liable to backfire.

The attempt to formulate and then to prioritise an ethical foreign policy can be evaluated against a number of criteria. First, what does it mean? Is there a distinctive concept of an ethical foreign policy? Second, is an ethical foreign policy an innovation? Third, has British foreign policy since 12 May 1997 met the requirements of a self-consciously articulated ethical foreign policy? We shall examine each of these in turn.

What is an ethical foreign policy?

If foreign policy is based on national interest and is, therefore, by definition selfish or egotistical, is it conceivable for foreign policy to be altruistic or to pursue deliberate self-abnegation? The realist school of foreign policy has argued that the apparent presence of altruism in foreign policy can be explained in one of two ways:

1. Altruism in foreign policy can be promoted within a broadly conceived definition of self-interest. To give an example, a policy of development aid and good neighbourliness can form part of an approach to the international system in which self-interest is promoted along with the general welfare. This idea of 'enlightened' self-interest is quite familiar in other spheres of social life and can be accommodated quite easily into thinking about foreign policy. Security and stability may be enhanced more effectively by promoting the general welfare than by crude assertions of self-interest. From this perspective, foreign policy may contain an element or dimension of altruism while being fundamentally concerned with self-interest.

2. A more extreme realist argument is that the moral or altruistic dimension of foreign policy is a consequence or product of self-interest. Hence, while foreign policy involves the pursuit of selfish interests, states present those interests as if they were really moral or altruistic goals. These doctrines, it is argued, are a mere pretext or camouflage for concealing the self-interest that lurks below. Hence, *status quo* powers may try to preserve their interests by appealing to some higher ethical framework such as respect for law. Rich states may consolidate their economic supremacy by promoting free trade. A recent example might be the support of the established nuclear states, including Britain, for a comprehensive nuclear test ban treaty. This is presented as a general international good, against the objections of emerging nuclear powers, which naturally want to continue testing programmes. These states point to the opposition of states such as Britain to a comprehensive test ban while they were still testing their own current warheads.

Is an ethical foreign policy possible in the light of these objections? To argue that all action in foreign policy is merely based on self-interest is a tenable position, but one that requires the adoption of an unhelpfully broad definition of self-interest. If all action is based on self-interest, then the term 'self-interest' is meaningless. Foreign policy is primarily about self-interest because the anarchic nature of the international system, with the ever-present threat of instability and conflict, demands that foreign policy put the military and economic security interests of the state first. However, much foreign policy activity, such as foreign aid, military assistance to developing countries, international cooperation in education or culture, and support for the Commonwealth, does not fit easily into the realist framework of foreign policy.

Is an ethical foreign policy new?

Foreign policy has always involved a mix of values around a core of national security. Foreign policy has always espoused other values, including those values that could claim to be 'ethical'. The Labour government elected in 1945 proclaimed, at least for a while, that its policy was based on socialist principles. Left-wing back-benchers insisted that Bevin should be true to his claim, on taking office, that 'left can speak unto left'. In the event, the USSR treated Britain like any other Western capitalist state, and its expansion into Eastern Europe made the defensive alliance of NATO inevitable by 1949. In 1997, for a second time, Labour articulated its ethical foreign policy as a radical departure from the policy of its predecessors. The domestic context here is important. The Labour Party and its government strove to project themselves as New Labour, distinct both from Old Labour and also from the sleaze and corruption that, they argued, had become a dominant characteristic of the Conservative government after eighteen years of office. Hence the policy pursued by Cook was not a radical change from earlier foreign policy, although it did contain a stronger emphasis on human rights, but it was important for Cook to promote it as if it were a new and radical departure. It is not merely coincidental, of course, that such policy had significant resonance with a Prime Minister well known for his religious views. Ethical foreign policy is largely about the domestic political aspect of foreign policy rather than the external outputs of policy, which, with some exceptions, show remarkable continuity.

The realist paradigm of foreign policy naturally emphasises continuity in foreign policy and the constraints on the state that make radical shifts of policy difficult, if not impossible. In Britain's case, continuity of policy transcending changes of government can be seen in such obvious spheres as support for NATO, the close relationship with the United States, the Commonwealth, support for nuclear weapons and deterrence, support for membership of the European Community/Union, etc. There is great force in this view of policy as continuity. But governments also exploit foreign policy, and all other aspects of policy, for domestic purposes. Foreign policy is used at home as well as abroad; change and disagreement may thus be articulated. For instance, Conservative governments have emphasised their support for nuclear weapons; Labour governments, while pursuing nuclear policies at least as hawkish as Conservative governments, have, at least until 1997, tried to depoliticise the issue in order to avoid awkward internal problems (Labour has traditionally been much influenced by the Campaign for Nuclear Disarmament).

In 1997, it suited Cook to emphasise the novelty of Labour's ethical foreign policy in order to mark a break with the past and sharply to demarcate New Labour from its Conservative predecessor.

Has policy lived up to being an ethical policy?

The history of foreign policies that proclaim themselves to be ethical or morally superior to their predecessors or the policies of other states is not happy. American foreign policy provides two striking twentieth-century examples. President Woodrow Wilson's Fourteen Points of 1917 sought to replace the tarnished old power politics with a new and ethically superior system of open diplomacy, but their implementation proved not merely to be impossible but also to be destabilising. President Jimmy Carter's foreign policy in 1977 based on human rights was also not only impossible to implement but counterproductive in its consequences. America's foreign relations suffered, and human rights were harmed rather than enhanced. Carter's realist opponents argued that a policy based on human rights rested on a fundamental misunderstanding of what was possible in foreign policy. Cook's ethical foreign policy for some time escaped such a critique. His Conservative critics confined themselves to pointing to the inconsistencies in his policy, for instance stressing human rights in one case while conveniently ignoring them in another.

There are a number of 'test cases' for Cook's approach to foreign policy. Because concepts such as ethical foreign policy are 'essentially contested', these cases should be seen as illustrating rather than proving the argument.

Indonesia and the sale of arms to unstable regions

Indonesia has been a major buyer of British armaments since the end of the conflict with Britain over Malaysia in 1967. Since 1975, it occupied the former Portuguese colony of East Timor in defiance of successive United Nations resolutions. British governments, Labour and Conservative, did not allow the East Timor issue to hinder their harmonious relationship with the Indonesian government. In September 1999, the Indonesian government finally held a referendum on the future of East Timor, precipitating a violent backlash from pro-Indonesian militias when the vote overwhelmingly favoured independence. The British government condemned the tacit support of the Indonesian government for the militias, which murdered and terrorised countless thousands of East Timorese. However, it agreed neither to cancel outstanding deliveries of Hawk military aircraft, despite aircraft already delivered being used by the Indonesian government against helpless civilians, nor to cancel the invitation to the Indonesian government to its major arms export exhibition. When Cook reluctantly suspended further deliveries of the Hawk aircraft, the Secretary of Trade and Industry insisted on supporting other British sales to Indonesia. The government did supply a battalion of Gurkha troops to the multilateral United Nations peacekeeping force sent in to restore order to East Timor, but that aside, it would be difficult to claim that the reaction to the crisis in East Timor (which achieved independence in 2002) met the criteria of an ethical foreign policy based on human rights.

On 21 July 2002, the *Independent on Sunday* published an investigation that showed Britain selling arms to nearly fifty countries where conflict was endemic. These included Israel, Pakistan, Turkey, China, India, Angola and Colombia. The paper commented: 'Under its "ethical" foreign policy the Government bans arms sales to countries already at war, but instead arms manufacturers actively target countries where ethnic conflict is likely to explode.' For example, sales to Turkey in 2000 approached £200 million: 'Amnesty International has accused Turkey of suppressing its Kurdish minority population and of sustained persecution of orthodox Muslim groups, left-wing opponents and human rights activists.'

Sierra Leone

In May 1997, President Kabbah, head of government of Commonwealth member Sierra Leone, was deposed in a military coup. In October, the British government supported the United Nations Security Council in imposing an arms embargo on the illegal government and on the civil war raging in Sierra Leone, which was killing thousands of innocent people. In January 1998, the legitimate government restored itself. This was immediately followed by allegations that Kabbah had been armed and assisted by a British-based security consultancy company, Sandline, in defiance of the UN embargo. Sandline claimed that the FCO had known about its operations. The House of Commons Select Committee on Foreign Affairs investigated the matter, as did an official departmental inquiry chaired by Sir Thomas Legg QC. The outcome of the two inquiries was broadly similar in dismissing the charge of FCO collusion with Sandline. Most attention focused on the High Commissioner to Sierra Leone, Peter Penfold, who had been forced to leave and had set up his office in a hotel room in Conakry in neigbouring Guinea, where the Kabbah government in exile had established itself. Penfold had no secure communications from this temporary base. Legg praised Penfold's support for the restoration of the legitimate government but considered that he had become too close to Sandline, which was working with Kabbah's forces in the interior of Sierra Leone. Penfold responded that he had informed the FCO about Sandline's support for the government and claimed that he understood the arms embargo to apply only to the rebel government and not to forces loyal to former President Kabbah – a position identical to Sandline's.

The impression left by the episode was less one of Britain subverting the arms embargo, or of intervening in support of the legitimate government of Kabbah, than of an ineffectiveness and confusion. Policy making was poorly coordinated between departments and between the FCO and its High Commissioner. Legg found ignorance rather than conspiracy; he concluded that the FCO's knowledge of developments in Africa was patchy, partly as a result of staff dealing with Africa having been reduced from 430 to 328 over the period 1988–98. The government was spared even greater embarrassment over the affair by relief at the restoration of Kabbah to power (with Sandline's help). In any case, when in January 1999 the 'Revolutionary United Front' overthrew President Kabbah for a second time, there

was no effective British response; the only external support for Kabbah came from Nigerian-led military forces operating under the auspices of the Economic Community of West African States.

Can we identify an ethical foreign policy at work in Sierra Leone? The government was concerned by human rights abuses by the opponents of Kabbah and wanted to see his government restored. On the other hand, if there really had been a conspiracy with Sandline to subvert the UN arms embargo, then claims to an ethical foreign policy based on support for the UN would be severely undermined. In the absence of proof of a conspiracy, the best verdict is probably Legg's – poor coordination, poor information and ineffective communications.

Kosovo

Kosovo is the most dramatic example of a major foreign policy issue in which there is a strong ethical dimension arising from the prominence given to human rights. The British intervention in Kosovo has been the most important, and arguably most successful, foreign policy initiative of the Labour government. Throughout the Kosovo crisis in 1999, Britain adopted a clear leadership role within the European Union and the Atlantic Alliance, dragging behind it reluctant alliance partners. In Kosovo, Britain 'punched above its weight' and exercised power within a complex alliance setting. Any study of foreign policy since 1997 must pay attention to Kosovo; the idea of ethical foreign policy also provides a suitable framework for evaluating policy.

Throughout 1998, the situation in Kosovo worsened as the Serbian military and political machine exercised increasingly tight control over the province, in which over 90 per cent of the population was Albanian. NATO repeatedly pushed President Milosevic of Yugoslavia towards an agreement with the Kosovar nationalist opposition. Air strikes were threatened, much as they had been earlier in coercing Milosevic into agreement in Bosnia. Eventually, at Rambouillet in January 1999, an agreement was brokered by NATO between Milosevic and his Kosovar opponents to provide for a degree of self-rule within a larger Serbia. The agreement was short-lived. The Kosovar opposition was tentative in its support for the terms, and Milosevic denounced the terms that his negotiators had secured. On 24 March, without seeking UN support, NATO launched a strategic bombing campaign to force Milosevic back to the table.

The abuse of human rights by Milosevic in Kosovo appears to have been the major consideration in Britain's decision to push NATO into military intervention. Milosevic's behaviour in Kosovo followed similarly aggressive behaviour against Croatia in 1991, followed by the civil war in Bosnia. That had involved widespread ethnic cleansing by the Serbia-backed Croatian Serbs, although there were also human rights violations by the Croat and Bosnian Muslim forces. The Kosovo crisis emerged as the critical test of an ethical foreign policy.

The bombing, code-named Operation Allied Force, lasted until 10 June when, after 34,000 sorties had been flown, President Milosevic signalled that he would accept an allied army in Kosovo and withdraw his own forces. During the air campaign, the war aims of the alliance expanded beyond the Rambouillet settlement to include an international force to be deployed on the ground to guarantee security for the Kosovars. As the scale of the expulsions from Kosovo grew, the British government stated that the removal from power of Milosevic, indicted as a war criminal, had become a necessary guarantee of future stability. Nevertheless, full independence for Kosovo was not a war aim for NATO.

Following Milosevic's acceptance of NATO's terms, a UN Security Council Resolution authorised an armed peacekeeping force (KFOR) in Kosovo. Britain made the largest national contribution (13,000 troops) to KFOR (51,000 in all), which was led by a British commander, General Jackson. In contrast, the British contribution to the air war was minor, on a par with other European allied air forces, militarily ineffective and dwarfed by the American effort. The air war was overwhelmingly American, although European contributions were politically important. The land campaign, which might have involved much heavier armed combat than in fact turned out to be the case, was European-dominated and British-led.

NATO's own analysis of the campaign indicated that the strategic bombing campaign was ineffective in destroying Serb military power, despite progressive escalation from narrowly military targets (air defence systems) to broader military targets (barracks and oil terminals) and eventually to civilian strategic targets (bridges, factories, television stations and power stations). Although it did little harm to Milosevic's position, the air campaign was sustained and hence demonstrated the alliance's resolve. It was continued, despite some members' misgivings and the unintended collateral damage, primarily because the alliance had no other strategy to offer, given American resistance to a land war. The bombing may also have been designed partly to give Milosevic an acceptable pretext for capitulation *vis-à-vis* his own internal opposition.

Why did Milosevic agree to NATO's demands and pull out of Kosovo? The continued resolve of the alliance may have persuaded him that eventually he would be forced to give way and that he could not rule out completely the possibility of a land war. However, the British argument that such a war should be planned and threatened was consistently met by American refusal to contemplate such an outcome. Internal opposition to Milosevic may also have played a part.

The best explanation is probably that Milosevic was urged to back down by the Russians. His Russian allies could not afford to lose cooperation with the West, despite their opposition to the bombing campaign, and needed an end to the war. In an immediate sense, therefore, it was thus the persuasion of an ally rather than the coercion of an enemy that determined the outcome of the war.

The conduct of the war involved complex problems of command and control, with both a national and a NATO chain of command. These parallel chains complicated the conduct of the war. The Cabinet, with a central core of Prime Minister, Foreign Secretary and Defence Secretary, exercised political responsibility for the war. The Chief of the Defence Staff advised them and acted through the recently established Permanent Joint HQ, a tri-service command established for conducting this sort of operation. On the ground in Macedonia, Lieutenant-General Mike Jackson commanded British troops. Parallel with this national chain of command was a NATO political chain of command focused on the North Atlantic Council, within which all seventeen members could, at least in theory, exercise a veto. Military command was vested in the Military Committee and its Supreme Allied Commander Europe, General Wesley Clark. Like Jackson, Clark was both a national and an alliance commander. When Jackson led KFOR into Kosovo, he necessarily exercised many aspects of command without detailed reference to Clark, who was based at Allied Command Europe near Brussels. Moreover, Jackson's own operational preferences reflected the British government's desire to operate land forces in Kosovo as early as possible. The American forces under his command lagged behind in operational readiness and forced him to postpone his advance for twenty-four hours. One result of this delay was that the Russian forces in Bosnia were able to detach a small force to occupy the airport in Kosovo's capital, Priština. When Clark ordered Jackson to remove them, he refused to obey, secure in the knowledge that his authority in the field rested, ultimately, on the support of the British government rather than on Clark as his Supreme Commander.

Was the war fought over Kosovo a humanitarian war fought without selfish interests at stake? There was undoubtedly a humanitarian motive; the failure of the Rambouillet agreement, following months of Serbian oppression in Kosovo, left no doubt that the Kosovars were under imminent threat. Events in Bosnia had already convinced the British government of the lengths to which Milosevic would go in pursuit of Serbian power. Hence the government also viewed Milosevic as a threat to stability throughout the Balkans and considered that such destabilisation would indirectly threaten wider British security interests and the objective of bringing Eastern Europe into closer relations with NATO. In retrospect, the Kosovo war also presents an appalling paradox: if it is the case that the war was fought largely for humanitarian motives, it is also true that the bombing gave the pretext for Milosevic's expulsion of almost one million Kosovars from their homeland, with another half a million or so in hiding from Serb forces in the countryside. In the short run, the war undoubtedly worsened the situation for the Kosovars. The returning Kosovars hoped for full independence, or perhaps union with Albania, not autonomy within Serbia, which was the situation that had existed until 1991, when Milosevic ended their autonomy. Another British war aim, the trial of Milosevic on war crimes, has proved equally difficult to implement. Milosevic was indicted on war crimes in Kosovo in May 2000. When he was deposed as president, the new rulers of Serbia, under intense US pressure, handed the former president over to the International Court in the Hague, where his dogged-self conducted defence against genocide charges ended when he died in prison in March 2006.

Nevertheless NATO's five demands for an end to the war were met:

1. A ceasefire accepted by Milosevic before the bombing campaign ended

2. Withdrawal of Milosevic's troops from Kosovo according to a timetable laid down by NATO

3. Deployment of an international peacekeeping force

4. Return of all refugees

5. A high level of autonomy within Kosovo.

The British government, and its allies, resisted the demands of the Kosovo Liberation Army for an independent Kosovo, preferring weak multinational states in the Balkans to a multiplicity of nation-states. Homogeneous nation-states would, in any case, require further population movements, probably taking the form of 'ethnic cleansing' in a never-ending cycle of misery.

As in the case of President Carter's human rights policy of 1977, it is possible to argue that the war's consequences, as opposed to motives, for human rights were mixed or even counterproductive. The launch of the bombing campaign precipitated the forcible expulsion of the Kosovars from Kosovo. The expulsion campaign was a macabre, larger-scale version of the ethnic cleansing earlier practised by Milosevic. As the bombing continued, the expulsions escalated. After the successful liberation of Kosovo, the refugees were able to return, in many cases only to find burnt-out homes. They have paid a very high price for their right to remain. Unfortunately, but perhaps inevitably, the returning Kosovars began to practise similar tactics against their erstwhile Serb neighbours, about 180,000, precipitating a second exodus of refugees from Kosovo.

Nevertheless, it can be argued that, on balance, the consequences of the war are justified in terms of ethical foreign policy. The war improved the human rights situation for the majority of the population of Kosovo by eventually ending the Serb oppression. If the consequences of the war can be justified in ethical foreign policy, can the conduct of the war? There is a complex debate within the tradition of the 'just war' about strategic bombing and, in particular, the requirements under just war to avoid or at the very least to minimise the risk of unintended (collateral) damage to the innocent. Aerial bombardment tends to be indiscriminate unless the attacker accepts very high risks to himself to aim his bombs with precise accuracy. At the start of the air war, NATO attacked the Serb air-defence systems but thereafter continued to minimise the risk of damage to its own forces by confining itself to high-level bombing from about 14,000 feet. The effect of high-level bombing, together with inadequate ground-level information about Serb deployments, certainly minimised NATO's losses (zero in the case of Britain) but on the other hand increased collateral damage from inaccurate bombing or misinterpreted targets.

Kosovar refugees were themselves bombed and many killed.

Since 1945, the presence of the United Nations in authorising war has emerged as an increasingly important criterion for the just conduct of war. The British government did not seek UN authority for the war in Kosovo, unlike the Falklands War in 1982. Then, and acting outside a NATO framework, the government went to great lengths to ensure the UN's tacit authority. In Kosovo, the British government relied on the multilateral authority of NATO, which knew that the UN Security Council would not back the war because of Russian and Chinese opposition. On the other hand, the Security Council did not oppose the war, and a Security Council resolution established the basis for the settlement of the war.

Dependent Territories

Policy towards the Dependent Territories – the last colonial remnants – also meet the criteria for an ethical foreign policy. In February 1998, Cook announced that the inhabitants of the Dependent Territories, henceforth to be known as Overseas Territories, would gain the right of abode in Britain, which they had lost in the 1981 Nationality Act. Gibraltar and the Falklands had already been awarded this right by the Conservatives in response to Argentine and Spanish territorial claims. For other territories, the restoration was a remarkable human rights concession. The populations concerned are small, and the potential costs to Britain correspondingly small, but given their impoverished nature, the right to migrate and work in Britain was invaluable. At the same time, Cook announced that the government would increase its regulation of the economies of the territories to achieve the highest standards of probity and, in particular, to try to keep out the drugs trade. Policy towards the Overseas Territories demonstrates the familiar situation of generosity being preferred when the real cost of generosity is small. In contrast, Labour did not attempt to extend citizenship rights to the Chinese of Hong Kong before the handover in 1997.

Two other foreign policy issues since 1997 have raised ethical problems. Both arose in an unforeseen way and demanded a response rather than an initiative. Following the volcanic eruption on Montserrat in 1997, the government responded with help for this poor Commonwealth member. It then ran into

criticism of Secretary for Overseas Development Clare Short's complaint that the Montserrat government was rapacious in its demands ('golden elephants') – an error of insensitivity rather than a violation of human rights on Short's part. A second case concerns the arrest in Britain of the former Chilean dictator General Augusto Pinochet in 1998 on charges of torture and human rights abuses at the request of the Spanish legal authorities. The resulting hearings in the courts were a mixed blessing for Cook but, in this example, the driving forces were the Home Office and the Lord Chancellor's Department; the FCO had no effective *locus standi*. The Pinochet case illustrates the problems of coordinating a consistent government external policy between several departments of government rather than a straightforward issue of determining foreign policy.

Where do these cases leave us in evaluating Cook's claim to have conducted an ethical foreign policy? Additional emphasis has been given to an ethical dimension to policy. Policy has been presented at home and abroad in terms of its new ethical dimension, and presentation becomes part of the content of policy to which others react. In Kosovo, the sheer scale of the unfolding humanitarian tragedy of the refugees spurred on the government's determination to see the campaign through to a satisfactory conclusion. But confronted with larger or more distant perpetrators of human rights abuses, such as China or Indonesia or Russia in Chechnya, the government's response has been very similar to that of its predecessors. Practical questions of proximity, other national interests and the size of potential adversaries still count. In the case of China, for instance, the government has not allowed human rights issues to interfere with trade or the arrangements for Hong Kong. The government shares the traditional British view that economic engagement and political dialogue are more effective than enforced isolation or feigned hostility. Blair claimed in his Chicago speech of 22 April 1999 about the 'Doctrine of International Community' that human rights were a necessary basis for international security and overrode traditional conceptions of sovereignty and noninterference in the domestic affairs of other states. This claim remains an aspiration, not yet a determining factor of British foreign policy. What has been achieved since 1997 is a change of emphasis rather than of fundamentals. The subject of ethics will be revisited later in the chapter in connection with the Iraq War.

■ The Strategic Defence Review

Conservative defence policy since 1990 was about managing two external demands: first, the new realities of the post-Cold War world; and, second, increasing pressure for economies. The hopes of the late 1980s that the ending of the Cold War would produce a large 'peace dividend' were not realised. The response to the end of the Cold War came in two phases. In 'Options for Change', June 1990, the government announced a small, general, reduction in defence capabilities with a slight shift of emphasis towards greater flexibility of forces. The main thrust of defence would remain on NATO and on the continental deployment of the army and air force, while the navy would shift emphasis over time away from submarine and antisubmarine warfare towards flexible surface ships. But all capabilities would decline in absolute terms. In July 1994 in the 'Defence Costs Study', known as 'Front Line First', the government announced reductions in support and logistics and some increases in fighting forces, especially for the infantry, together with simplification of commands in recognition of increasing strains on the forces since 1990.

By 1997, defence policy had entered a period of relative stability within ever-declining budgets. Three main defence roles had been identified. Defence role one is the defence of the UK and its territories, even when there is no overt external threat. This core defence capability included the retention of the nuclear deterrent, untargeted in the absence of a nuclear enemy. This 'existential deterrent' (deterrence from mere possession) is similar to the traditional French policy of nuclear dissuasion, in contrast to Britain's previous strategy of deterrence through an overt threat of retaliation. Defence role two is insurance against a major attack on the UK or its allies and encompasses the NATO commitment and NATO force structures. Defence role three is the contribution to wider security interests through the maintenance of peace and stability. This is the extended concept of security including peacekeeping and peace enforcement through the UN and NATO, involving British forces even where no national security interests are immediately at stake. This extended concept of security is the military aspect of the ethical dimension of foreign policy discussed above and indicates continuity rather than change through the 1990s.

Throughout 1990–7, the Labour Party argued for a more comprehensive 'Strategic Defence Review' in which the whole range of security commitments and interests would be analysed, together with actual and potential capabilities. The argument was that the government had reacted to problems in an *ad hoc* way without a clear framework in which resources and commitments could be balanced. Without a framework, Labour argued, the Treasury would dictate defence policy by determining budgets. Certainly, in the period after 1990 defence expenditure measured as a percentage of GDP fell, indeed had been falling since its new Cold War peak of 1986. In the period 1990–8, for instance, it fell by 23 per cent in real terms. By 1998, defence consumed 2.7 per cent of GDP, a low level not reached even during the period of unilateral disarmament under Churchill as Chancellor of the Exchequer in the 1920s.

Immediately upon coming into office, the new Secretary of State for Defence, George Robertson, announced that he would conduct a Strategic Defence Review (SDR) to identify the requirements of defence policy in the uncertainty of the post-Cold War world. The review would be defence-driven rather than Treasury-driven. However attractive this argument appears, the Treasury must play a crucial role in defence policy simply because the claims on defence policy are always greater than the resources available. In the recent past, the influence of the Treasury on defence has never recovered to its role in the 1930s, when it established two of the key elements of strategic thinking: first, that resources had to be deployed cautiously in preparation for a long war and postwar recovery; second, that resources available for the air force should be deployed on air defence rather than on air offence. In any case, Robertson could not reverse the trend of declining defence expenditure, and his review accepted that resources would continue to fall to about 2.4 per cent of GDP by 2002.

Robertson modified the three defence roles identified by his Conservative predecessors into distinct missions. Defence role one he divided into two missions, defence of the UK in a situation of no overt external threat and defence of the Overseas Territories. He confirmed New Labour's revived love affair with nuclear weapons. The only nuclear weapon system available to him, following the Conservative government's decision to abandon the air force's residual nuclear capability of 'free-fall' nuclear bombs, was Trident. Robertson confirmed that the planned Trident fleet of four submarines would be completed to ensure that one submarine would always be on station. However, a stock of only fifty-eight missiles would be leased from the United States, with each submarine deploying only forty-eight warheads on its sixteen missiles, a reduction from the Conservative proposals to deploy ninety-six warheads per submarine. The government would maintain a total of about 200 warheads, a reduction of 70 per cent from the figure in 1990. The post-1990 Conservative governments had shown some interest in the idea of shifting Trident from a weapon of all-out strategic revenge into a more flexible weapon to be used in a limited way, perhaps with a single warhead deployed, against a range of potential nuclear enemies rather than merely Russia. Robertson did not pursue this rather tentative strategy further. By 1998, the cost of the nuclear deterrent had fallen from a peak of over 10 per cent of defence expenditure during the acquisition of Trident to about 3 per cent, a figure very similar to the halcyon days of Polaris in the early 1970s. Trident illustrates how for a medium power such as Britain nuclear weapons are extremely expensive to acquire or modernise but very cheap to operate once deployed.

Defence roles two and three were subject to greater change. The threats to British security now came less from direct military threat from Russia than from a multiplicity of risks around the world arising from instability, escalating local conflicts, etc. Defence role two, defence of Europe from external attack, was broken down into missions to provide defence against strategic attack on NATO and regional conflict within the NATO area. Robertson envisaged NATO continuing to evolve from a purely defensive alliance into an organisation capable of intervening in regional conflicts in Europe through its Rapid Reaction Corps. Defence role three, the promotion of wider security interests, was elaborated into four missions: regional conflicts outside the NATO area (such as the Persian Gulf); support for peace-making and humanitarian intervention; the defence of wider British interests (such as the Five Power Treaty with Malaysia, Singapore, Australia and New Zealand); and defence diplomacy, such as negotiation of arms control agreements.

The ending of the Cold War gave greater prominence to wider security interests at the expense of the traditional balance against the Soviet Union/ Russia but also precipitated new security conflicts both in Eastern Europe and elsewhere. The response to these conflicts in the immediate post-Cold War situation had been President Bush's concept of a New World Order under American leadership. The Gulf War was its early manifestation. The collapse of former Yugoslavia and the deployment of UN and NATO forces in Bosnia on a quasi-permanent basis was the second major example. Robertson's vision was that defence forces would be drawn into various UN and multilateral peacekeeping operations and, beyond that, that a new and closer relationship between foreign policy and defence capability would be forged. Armed forces might be used in a variety of situations in which their role would vary from passive peacekeeping at one end of the spectrum to the enforcement of peace at the other. Peacekeeping could normally rely on lightly armed infantry forces, while peace enforcement might require more heavily armed battlefield forces. Within and without Europe, military force might be called up for a range of tasks in areas of instability.

The main additional requirement for defence was greater mobility and the possibility of deployment in distant theatres of heavily armed forces. In September 1999, this concept bore fruit in the form of 16 Air Assault Brigade, bringing together two existing airborne and airmobile brigades, and, from 2000, with a new fleet of Apache attack helicopters. Throughout the forces there was increased emphasis on flexibility and heavy lift and transport capabilities, controlled by the recently established Joint Permanent Head Quarters as the command structure for combined air/land/sea forces.

Robertson largely confirmed Conservative procurement plans and added one major new project. The order for 386 Challenger 2 tanks would be completed and two armoured divisions established. The major new weapon for the army would be a battlefield helicopter to deploy against armoured forces in the form of the American Apache, to be built under licence in Britain. The Gulf War in 1991 had demonstrated the value of such a capability, at least against a weak opponent and in open desert country, although the American Apache force deployed during the Kosovo war made no impact at all and proved difficult to deploy against the Serbian forces. Robertson committed the government to completion of the full contract for 232 new Eurofighters. This was the weapon that the air force had set its heart on. Since the early 1980s it had lacked a specialist air defence fighter aircraft, relying on the ineffective Tornado F3, which had singularly failed to distinguish itself in the Gulf War. The Eurofighter contract had been subject to constant threats since being developed in the early 1980s with Germany, Italy and

Spain, with the German government in particular perennially hovering on the point of cancellation.

The navy would reduce its declining submarine capability still further to a force of only ten nuclear-powered submarines, plus the four Trident ships. Robertson's major new procurement project, and in one sense the main outcome of the whole review, was the proposal to build two new large aircraft carriers, capable of carrying fifty aircraft, to replace the ageing fleet of three small warfare carriers built in the 1970s. These ships had evolved since the 1970s towards a general air attack role but were too small to carry adequate numbers of aircraft. The two new carriers, together with two new assault ships already on order and the recently completed helicopter carrier *HMS Hero*, would enable rapid deployment of a range of forces by sea. The navy would regain some of its traditional 'blue waters' capability of projecting power globally and flexibly. New naval capabilities complement the army's new emphasis on airmobile forces, in turn supported by heavier forces deployed by sea or by new heavy airlift capabilities.

The rationale for these new capabilities rests on a broad conception of Britain's security interests. What is the case for this? There is no immediate direct military threat to British security other than from the IRA, currently signed up to a ceasefire. However, conflicts in one area may spill over into other areas closer to home. Second, the emphasis on an ethical foreign policy and defence of humanitarian interests requires flexible capabilities. Third, it can be argued that Britain benefits by accepting responsibilities and duties that contribute to a stable world, which is itself a British interest. In the short run, Britain could act, like Japan, as a free rider and obtain the benefits of stability without making a military contribution towards ensuring it, but, the government thinks, influence and prestige would decline if such an attitude were adopted. In short, there is an unquestioned assumption within government that, through punching above its weight, prestige and influence are maximised and hence that responsible behaviour brings its own reward. An activist policy increases influence with the United States and Germany and within NATO. NATO remains, on this analysis, the key to security policy, and Britain plans to remain at the centre of NATO. Command of NATO's Rapid Reaction Corps is one example of this central role. George Robertson's appointment as Secretary-General in October 1999 confirmed it. Implicit in this argument is the failure of the 'emerging security architecture' within Europe, in particular the Organisation for Security and Organisation in Europe, to displace NATO.

Defence forces remain small and overstretched. The end of the Cold War has increased the demands on the forces, not reduced them. In 1998, at the time of publication of the Strategic Defence Review, British forces were deployed in Germany (about 30,000), Cyprus (3,000), Bosnia (4,000+), the Falklands (1,000), the Persian Gulf and Turkey (1,000+), together with smaller forces in Gibraltar, Belize and Brunei, and elsewhere. In addition, 15,000 troops were on peacekeeping operations in Northern Ireland, the most arduous commitment within defence role one. In 1999 to these commitments was added the war in Kosovo (17,000 troops plus air force and navy). Whereas in the early 1990s the greatest pressure within the army had been on infantry battalions, with the government having to increase the number of battalions above the figure set in 1990, the demands from Bosnia and Kosovo were for infantry, plus armour, artillery, engineers, etc. To sustain all Robertson's defence missions demands a very wide range of forces with little possibility of functional specialisation with allies. There is some scope for defence capabilities to be kept at a lower level of readiness, but most forces need to be at a high level of preparedness. Reserve forces can, in theory, make a contribution in such a situation, forming the basis of 'reconstitutive' or even 'regenerative' forces. But while parts, such as medical forces, can be brought relatively easily into active service – and have been in the Gulf, Bosnia and Kosovo – they are very small. The Strategic Defence Review's conclusion was higher levels of preparation but with further reductions in size.

British forces are highly professional and effective but, given high levels of specialisation, also small and expensive, operating without any economies of scale. Under Robertson's plans, they must also be prepared to take on a variety of roles. Given their small size, one particularly awkward question is raised. Can British military power aspire to be a premier-division force capable of fighting a high-intensity war, or are they now a second-division force whose effectiveness is confined to such lower-intensity wars as Bosnia or Kosovo? Forces capable of high-intensity warfare can be deployed on lower-intensity operations, even if their training and equipment are not exactly suited. On the other hand, forces only capable of lower-intensity warfare cannot be used in a high-intensity battle. British forces have clung persistently to the notion that they are small but capable of high-intensity warfare – in the premier division – and unique among other high-intensity forces in also being trained for low-intensity warfare as a result of the Northern Ireland situation and post-colonial wars. Kosovo does not answer the question. The air force participated on a very small scale, and apparently ineffectively, in an American-led high-intensity bombing campaign. On the ground below, the army prepared for a lower-intensity campaign, though one that was overtly coercive and, potentially, of higher intensity. After two years in office, the government made no radical changes to defence policy. The downward pressure on expenditure remains, but there had been progress in establishing more flexible forces, able to operate within tri-service commands both in Europe and outside. Overstretch remains and has increased with the despatch of a Gurkha battalion to East Timor. Uncertainty remains over whether, in the medium term, it is possible to sustain such a varied defence effort with such small forces.

The Defence White Paper in July 2002 reflected the new realities following the 9/11 attacks on the World Trade Center (see below). New weapons were envisaged for the armed forces that would enable them to identify and strike at terrorist enemies within minutes. Geoff Hoon, the Defence Secretary, explained a scenario where very mobile, lightly armed forces would be able to identify the enemy, acquire authority to act and strike in 'near real time'. Apache helicopters armed with Hellfire missiles would be instrumental in this new capacity. Plans to develop a new pilotless reconnaissance aircraft, the Watchkeeper, would be speeded up. Hoon told the Commons:

Terrorism thrives on surprise and one of the key ways to defeat it is to take the fight to the terrorist. We must be able to deal with threats at a distance: hit the enemy hard in his own backyard – not in ours – and at a time of our choosing – not his – acting always in accordance with international law.

The 1998 Strategic Defence Review still provides the main framework for defence policy up to 2015 but, as we have seen, has been flexible enough to accommodate changes. The most logical response to Britain's defence problem is to combine with other EU countries to create a common defence force – together EU defence spending equals about one half of US spending – capable of intervening in places like Kosovo and able to stand up when necessary to the USA. However, the EU is a sensitive subject not

just on the right, and pooling defence efforts across Europe summons up too many demons for too many politicians, and not just in the UK. Some efforts have been made to advance such an idea but none have acquired any real purchase. NATO remains the most cooperative framework involving EU defence forces and perhaps this is because and not despite the US involvement.

Defence overstretch

The Select Committee on Defence, reporting in March 2005, warned that overstretch of resources had reached dangerous levels:

Many frontline units in the army have been experiencing an operational and training cycle whose intensity is unsustainable in the longer term.

MPs also warned that the government may have underestimated the role armed forces may have to play in defending the 'homeland' against international terrorism. Because defence spending had been kept steady at about 2.5 per cent of GDP, a number of measures had been found necessary:

1. Delaying of two new aircraft carriers until the end of the decade or later.

2. Delaying of the Eurofighter (or Typhoon as it is now called) and the Joint Strike Fighter Programme, meaning existing carriers will be at sea without them for a period.

3. Delaying of new helicopters, badly needed by the army and air force.

However, the committee endorsed the decision to merge certain regiments, with some famous single-battalion regiments, like the Black Watch, being merged into bigger regiments.

Cuts continued to achieve economy targets. One journalist, James Meek, reflected in *The Guardian* on 21 January 2004 that the Royal Navy had 900 ships in 1945. Today the number of frigates, destroyers and carriers stands at thirty-six. He went on to question whether even these were needed. Wars fought in recent years had been located in land-locked regions – Afghanistan, Iraq – and even sophisticated high-tech ships like the US Navy's *Cole* had been nearly sunk in 2000 by a few terrorists on a small launch stacked with explosives.

The one aspect of naval renewal which is guaranteed to cause controversy is the replacement of the Trident submarine-borne nuclear deterrent. In November 2005 Defence Secretary John Reid was forced to give a pledge that MPs be allowed to vote on the possible purchase of a replacement from the US with a new weapons system estimated to cost £20–25 bn. Reid agreed to hold the debate in a transparent fashion but insisted: 'I defy anyone here to say we will not need a nuclear weapon in 20–50 years' time.' He added that the UK was not planning to place its deterrent into multilateral disarmament negotiations until the US and Russians did likewise.

An opinion poll in November 2005 showed that when told of the cost of replacement, only 33 per cent declared support and 54 per cent opposed. As long as nuclear weapons continue to proliferate – with Iran being perceived as a dangerous impending candidate – retention of the deterrent is likely to be supported by a majority of Labour MPs, but the issue is highly sensitive and Trident replacement adds, at the time of writing, to the queue of obstacles

placed before Labour's third-term government by its dissenting left wing.

■ Relations with the United States

During the Major government, British relations with the United States deteriorated from the peak of close relations that had characterised Thatcher and Reagan and, to a lesser extent, Thatcher and Bush. The Major–Clinton relationship never established itself. Clinton was slow to forgive Major for his overt and covert support for Bush in the 1992 presidential election. Major resented Clinton's early forays into the Irish problem and pressure in 1994 and 1995 for direct negotiations with Sinn Fein. Other differences emerged. The British government considered Clinton's emphasis on air power in Bosnia, to deter the Serbs, simplistic, especially when the Americans

Blair's critics claim he has given the US total support over Iraq and received nothing in return
Source: Copyright © Chris Riddell. From *The Observer*, 14 November 2004. Reproduced with permission from Guardian Newspapers Limited

were so reluctant to commit ground troops to UNPROFOR, the UN force in Bosnia. In 1993, there were major trade disagreements over farm subsidies in the EC. Clinton's own priorities were domestic rather than foreign, and his foreign policy priorities lay within the North American Free Trade Area and the Pacific Rim.

In contrast, Blair sought a close working relationship with Clinton. At the party level, Clinton and Blair supported each other's election campaigns in 1996 and 1997 and shared similar ideas for a reworking and modernisation of left-of-centre politics – the so-called 'Third Way'.

More specifically, there have been three important areas of cooperation since 1997 in which the two governments committed themselves to working together in a sustained manner. First, they worked together on NATO enlargement, culminating in its first stage in the entry of Poland, Hungary and the Czech Republic in 1999, at the same time avoiding so far as was possible antagonising Russia or weakening Boris Yeltsin's position. There was a recognition of the difficulties confronting Yeltsin and a marked reluctance to interfere in his domestic politics. For instance, the two governments resisted criticism of Russian intervention in Chechnya, despite Blair's emphasis on human rights. In two more specific policy areas effective joint working was established. Blair was prepared to work with Clinton towards a resolution of the Irish problem. He persuaded Clinton to support his strategy of working for a ceasefire to be followed by negotiations towards a political settlement rather than to pursue the usual Democrat policy of a political settlement that would lead to a ceasefire. Clinton then offered the services of former Senator George Mitchell to help bring about an outline political settlement in the April 1998 Good Friday Agreement. When the agreement broke down over the refusal of the IRA to disarm, Mitchell was called back to help to negotiate a new phase of the agreement in November 1999. Mitchell was able to act, remarkably tactfully and skilfully, as an honest broker in a way that Secretary of State Mo Mowlam or her successor Peter Mandelson would not have been able to do.

Blair's remarkably close relationship with Clinton was not shaken in any way by Clinton's declining domestic reputation, despite Blair's own emphasis on a rather moralistic probity and rectitude. When Clinton's close colleague Al Gore was controversially bested by the Texan George W. Bush in 2000, Blair was quickest off the mark in reminding the winner

where his firmest and oldest ally lived. His overtures were well received. It seems that Bush – who makes up his mind over people very quickly – liked the well-spoken British Prime Minister, despite his earlier closeness to the despised Clinton. For Blair, just as it had been for Thatcher, it was automatic that America was central to both British defence and its role in the world. It followed that he felt the EU should join Britain in supporting US foreign policy wherever possible, as he did in his speech in the City on 15 November 2004.

Secret documents briefing US Defence Secretary William Cohen were drawn on in a *Guardian* article of 29 November 1999. In a section that might have embarrassed advocates of the 'ethical foreign policy' and the qualitative break with Conservative practice, Pentagon officials confirmed the closeness of Anglo-US relations:

[Britain] remains our closest partner in political, security and intelligence matters ... Beyond Europe there are few apparent differences between the stated foreign policy goals of Labour and its Conservative predecessor. The government continues to support a strong defence over some objections within the old left of the Labour Party – and is working to keep a military that can deploy with US forces.

Another passage advised Cohen that 'the prime minister has made it clear that NATO will remain the ultimate guarantor of Britain's defence and that emphasis on Europe will not be at the expense of the trans-Atlantic link.' Blair added a new perspective on the relationship between Europe and America at his speech to the Lord Mayor's Banquet on 22 November 1999. He said:

We have a new role – not to look back and try to recreate ourselves as the pre-eminent superpower of 1900, nor to pretend to be the Greeks to America's Romans. It is to use the strengths of our history to build our future not as a superpower but as a pivotal power, *as a power that is at the crux of alliances and international politics which shape the world and its future.*

(author's italics)

The attacks on the World Trade Center, New York, 11 September 2001

When the devastating Osama bin Laden inspired attacks on the twin towers of the World Trade Center occurred, Tony Blair was quick to stand 'shoulder to shoulder' with our American ally. At the Labour Party conference in October 2001, Blair excelled himself with an idealistic speech in which he envisaged a kind of ethical Anglo-US led campaign to make the world better: 'more aid untied to trade'; 'write off debt'; 'encouraging the free trade we are so fond of preaching'. If the world as a community focused on it, 'we could defeat climate change . . . find the technologies that create energy without destroying the planet'. He described Africa as a 'scar on the conscience of the world' that the world could, if it so chose, 'heal'. 'Palestinians', he declared, 'must have justice, the chance to prosper in their own land'. He finished by claiming 'The world community must show as much capacity for compassion as for force'. However, his hopes that the USA would rally to his clarion call were rapidly disappointed: US national interests were paramount for George W. Bush. He had already refused to ratify the hard-won international agreements on climate change signed at Kyoto in 1997. Moreover, he refused to send any representative to the world environment conference in Johannesburg. Tariffs were slapped on European steel products to protect US steel producers, many in regions electorally desirable to the Republicans. And the USA proved unmoved by the continuing refusal of Israel's right-wing government to adopt a conciliatory attitude towards the Palestinians. Progress in resolving this conflict has always been high on the European list of priorities, particularly Britain's.

In the wake of '9/11', Blair made a number of visits to see the President and was, to be fair, received with a warmth denied any other country. But did Blair receive any payoff for his loyalty? Apart from the warmth of his receptions, this was not easy to argue.

It followed, from Blair's declared position, that Britain strongly supported the US war on the Taliban in Afghanistan and deployed troops to assist in the fighting and the subsequent peacekeeping. However, given the paucity of US reciprocation to Blair's overtures for a better world, some domestic critics, and not a small section of the British people (according to opinion polls), were beginning to ask why Blair was behaving so much like George Bush's 'poodle', constantly striving to alter the President's course but when failing arguing that he had been in favour of Washington's line all along. Blair generally ignored these criticisms and maintained his position as Bush's closest and most uncritical ally, insisting that British and American interests were virtually identical in foreign policy terms. Yet this position

BIOGRAPHY

Jack Straw (1946–)

Foreign Secretary 2001–5. Educated at Leeds University, where he became President of the National Union of Students. Called to the Bar in 1972. Served as councillor for Islington, 1971–8; became MP for Blackburn in 1979. Served in a number of senior Shadow roles before becoming Home Secretary in 1997, where his reputation was as a tough though not illiberal minister. In 2001 he was surprised to be appointed Foreign Secretary, usually regarded as the third most important role in government. Straw has proved an effective supporter of Blair's foreign policy, especially over Iraq, but inevitably was overshadowed by his boss over the big issues and on the big occasions. Former ambassador to Washington, Sir Christopher Meyer, in his memoir *DC Confidential*, damned Straw with faint praise in describing him as 'more to be liked than admired'. He was sacked in May 2005.

became very difficult to defend in respect of the threatened war against Iraq.

Britain and the 'Coalition' war with the USA in Iraq, 2002

Anglo-American cooperation in Iraq had been remarkable throughout the 1990s. In the period after the Gulf War of 1991, the British maintained forces in Turkey and Saudi Arabia to enforce the no-fly zones alongside the Americans. Saddam Hussein consistently frustrated the efforts of the United Nations inspectors, UNSCOM, to ensure that Iraq dismantled its biological and atomic military capabilities. In the autumn of 1997 a crisis developed and the government despatched an aircraft carrier to the Gulf. At that time other friendly Arab countries, such as Saudi Arabia, were reluctant to continue to cooperate, and Britain and America alone attempted to pressure Iraq. In February 1998, the UN Secretary-General negotiated a settlement and UNSCOM resumed its work. In July and October 1998 the situation erupted again, and Blair proclaimed that an object of Anglo-American policy was the overthrow of Saddam; Britain and America called on the Iraqi

BOX 28.1 BRITAIN IN CONTEXT

Foreign policy in a changing world

Foreign policy is usually founded on defence policy: the ability of a country both to defend itself from harm and to inflict harm in its own right. As defence policy reflects how much a country feels it can afford to pay on military hardware, foreign policy is also based, at root, on economic power. The USA is the world's only superpower and no country can currently match its expenditure on armaments. It spends over $400 bn a year on defence, a sum which has ratcheted up dramatically since the 9/11 attacks. The US spends as much on defence as the rest of the world combined and twice as much as the EU. In addition to this, US arms technology is years ahead of the rest of the world.

But being a superpower militarily is only one facet of US power. America is aided by the huge advantage of a massive economy which stretches out to every corner of the world and a media industry which mass-markets American values and culture to the same places. And yet the superpower is not and does not feel safe. For years it did, and a strong strand of opinion – isolationism – wished to keep it even safer by avoiding major foreign commitments. Indeed George W. Bush himself, when running for President in 2000, expressed mildly isolationist views. But its huge economic strength and international interests made such objectives unachievable for the USA, especially as some elements in the world, especially fundamentalist Muslims, saw the US as the source of great evil and corruption worldwide.

The attacks by al-Qaeda upon the World Trade Center in 2001 signified the opening of a new war which the US could not avoid as this time the fight had been taken onto American soil – a traumatic development for many Americans. The 'War on Terror' is now the main driver of US foreign policy as it is of UK policy as well. Experience in Vietnam in the sixties and in Iraq since 2003 reveals that mastery of the air and huge military superiority on the ground are no guarantors of successful containment of a determined, irregular enemy armed merely with small arms and suicide bombs.

US foreign policy strategists are highly aware of the changing geopolitical nature of world power. Defending Europe against a predatory USSR used to be its main priority but now the EU is regarded as of waning importance. The new suitors wooed by the USA are all found in Asia. The fastest-rising economic power is China, a country of well over a billion people which has been expanding economically at some 10 per cent a year for the past two decades. It has now left the dark ages of Maoist communism way behind and is beginning to flex its own muscles. It is seen as the major long-term military and economic threat to the USA, already winning manufacturing business from the higher-waged superpower and holding vast sums of US currency which potentially gives it a lever over US economic policy. Bush's visit to India in March 2006 revealed how the US sees the world's biggest democracy – also emerging as an economic superpower in its own right – as a possible counter to China.

In February 2006 Condoleeza Rice announced a major redeployment of diplomatic personnel: sixty-one posts in the 'old' world of the EU were to be dropped while seventy-four new posts were to be established in Asia. The UK also has done something similar: Sir Michael Jay, head of the Diplomatic Service, said on 3 March 2006: 'We are making sure our resources are deployed so the right people are in the right places to promote Britain's interests around the world. Among other things, this means shifting resources from our European to our Asian network.' China too has been readjusting to her nascent superpower status, sending scores of diplomats, inevitably, to the USA but also substantial delegations to other countries where she seeks to increase influence: Pakistan, Japan (despite the appalling historical record) and selected African countries like Angola.

opposition to act. Clinton sought to maximise the urgency and danger of the situation, partly in order to deflect Congress, which was moving towards a vote on impeachment over his domestic misdemeanours. On 16 October 1998, without seeking further UN authority, America and Britain launched massive air strikes against Iraq. On 19 October 1998, the House voted to impeach Clinton. Bombing continued for four days, but it was not clear that Operation Desert Fox secured any military or political objectives (even that of reinforcing Clinton's domestic support).

In the wake of the 'War on Terror' operations against Afghanistan in 2001–2, Bush formulated a startling new foreign policy stance bearing the imprint of his neo-conservative advisers: terror had to be sought out and destroyed *pre-emptively*; rogue states like Iran, Iraq and North Korea represented an 'axis of evil' that had to be combated before it provided terrorists with the weapons that could lay waste to the civilised Western world. The person squarely in George W. Bush's sights was Saddam Hussein, the Iraqi dictator who had ironically survived politically while George Bush senior, who had won the Gulf War, had lost the 1992 election. Hawkish advisers clamoured for a pre-emptive strike. Tony Blair hurried to add his assenting voice together with British support for any planned action. But domestic opinion was divided, with a majority against any action that did not involve sanction from the United Nations. Blair allegedly helped to persuade Bush in August 2002 to appeal to the UN for a resolution requiring Saddam to allow weapons inspectors back in to verify the absence of weapons of mass destruction in his country, as he claimed was the case. The problem was that the inspectors, led by Swede Dr Hans Blix, found no credible 'smoking guns', and without any such evidence public opinion in Europe and to some extent in America was unwilling to endorse an attack by the massive Anglo-US force that had massed in the region. Many argued, correctly, that no proven substantial connection existed between Saddam and the 9/11 attack; that Bush was merely seeking re-election on the back of a successful war; and that the oil corporations, with whom Bush and his team had well-known close connections, were urging war with an eye to controlling Iraq's huge oil reserves.

The doctrine of pre-emption – the idea that the United States or any other nation can attack a nation that is not imminently threatening but may be in the future – is a radical twist on the traditional idea of self-defence. It

appears to be in contravention of international law and the UN charter. And it is being tested at a time of world-wide terrorism, making many countries around the globe wonder whether they will soon be on our – or some other nation's – hit list.

Robert Byrd, Democratic Senator for West Virginia, in one of the few dissenting speeches in the US Senate over Iraq, 12 February 2003

Tony Blair's dilemma was whether to press ahead with his traditional (but apparently slavish) support for the USA or join other European powers in expressing the dissent and unease felt by a section of his own party in both Parliament and the country large enough to bring him down if things went wrong. On 18 March 2003, 139 of his own MPs voted against the proposed action in Iraq, but Blair had the conviction of someone convinced that he was following a morally correct – even unavoidable – foreign policy. He decided to support Bush even without a specific Security Council resolution in favour of military action.

We now learn that before Blair departed for the March 18th debate Downing St had drawn up contingency plans for the withdrawal of British troops from the build-up in the Gulf and also for Blair's resignation should the votes have gone against him. That is how serious it was.

Martin Kettle, *The Guardian*, 14 April 2003

In late March, the 'coalition' – basically US–UK – attack began with British troops assigned to the southern area around Basra. Initial resistance was unexpectedly fierce, but by the time US troops had reached Baghdad the vaunted Republican Guard had melted away and by 9 April troops were in virtual possession of the capital city. With Saddam's power broken, spontaneous demonstrations of Iraqi delight – e.g. demolition of statues and posters of the hated dictator – were eagerly welcomed by politicians in the USA and UK as evidence that the invasion had been justified after all. A poll on 10 April showed Blair's rating as PM having increased by twelve points, and by 15 April support for the war was 63 per cent in favour, 23 per cent against, a near-reversal of the prewar figures.

However, the good news soon ceased, to be replaced by a constant succession of catastrophic suicide bombings, ambushes, kidnappings and assassinations. By January 2006 well over 1,000 US service personnel had been killed and 100 UK ones. Furthermore, Blair was forced to suffer a merciless inquisition over his decision to join the US invasion

As his troubles mounted in 2004, Tony Blair must have regretted his ill-fated decision to invade Iraq alongside the US
Source: Copyright © Chris Riddell. From *The Observer*, 10 October 2004. Reproduced with permission from the Guardian Newspapers Limited

over the row with the BBC concerning the September 2002 intelligence dossier and the suicide of Dr David Kelly. This produced the Hutton Report which cleared the government but not in the eyes of much of the media and public opinion. Later came the diplomatically critical Butler Report into the intelligence leading up to the war. Then, during the run-up to the 2005 election came the claim that the Attorney General, who had advised the government that the invasion was legal, had in fact opposed the war until receiving intensive persuasion by US officials. The political cost of the war was incalculable, with a substantial body of Blair's own party and an even bigger section of public opinion withdrawing their support and trust and pronouncing anathema upon him.

By spring 2006 the damage inflicted on his party and its support in the country had not been repaired, and in the field of foreign policy Blair contemplated a still highly volatile situation in Iraq, Afghanistan, Iran and the wider Middle East; a

NATO alliance split from the divisions caused by the war; and a European split between the pro-USA group (though with fading enthusiasm) led by Blair and a group hostile to Bush led by France and Germany. Blair's determination, however, seemed undimmed. In February 2006 the UK maintained 8,500 troops in southern Iraq and agreed to send 3,500 troops to assist President Karzai subdue the resurgent Taliban. One major purpose of the wars in Afghanistan and Iraq was to fight international terrorism by reaching out to eliminate its sources in the Middle East and nearby. Initially the former military action seemed to achieve some success through removing the Taliban government and installing a democracy which managed a semblance of legitimacy under the pro-Western Hamid Karzai. However, Bin Laden and other al-Qaeda leaders managed to escape the attempts to snare them while the continued insurgency in Iraq, far from eliminating sources of terrorism, has increased its role as a seed-bed for such activity.

JSF programme

If Blair was looking for any reward or payoff for his loyalty, he did not find it in the major British involvement in the huge £144 bn defence contract for the Joint Strike Fighter. Blair found himself lobbying the White House for the third time in a month regarding the cancellation of a £2.4 bn Rolls Royce contract for the development of engines for the new aircraft. Moreover, even deeper resentment was felt in government defence circles at the refusal of the Americans to provide the UK with access to crucial technologies related to the jet. 'We fought shoulder to shoulder alongside them', commented Director General of the CBI Sir Digby Jones; 'This is no way to treat your best friend.'

Certainly, Blair's foreign policy adventures had enabled Britain to 'punch above its weight' through being the proxy for US power and influence, but the risks were stratospheric – his Cabinet colleague Clare Short called him 'reckless' – and by the end of the war, the human cost was all too vividly etched in the lines on his face, his reduced majority and the possibility that he would have to leave the UK's political stage with a flawed and unfulfilled legacy.

Chapter summary

British foreign policy is based upon what it can afford economically and the Strategic Defence Review in the late 1990s did much to adapt defence policy to what could be afforded and what was needed to maintain national security in a rapidly changing world. Labour's attempt to introduce an 'ethical foreign policy' was controversial but was probably justified and successful in terms of the Kosovo crisis. Britain's traditional closeness to US foreign policy was reinforced by Blair when Clinton was president and he was quick to establish close relations with George Bush in 2000. However, the difficulties encountered following the joint invasion of Iraq caused Blair huge political problems at home.

Discussion points

■ Criticise the 'realist' approach to foreign policy.

■ Should Britain have avoided involvement in Kosovo?

■ Does the world need a new form of international government?

■ Is Britain too keen to support the USA in all situations?

■ Was the Iraq war justified?

Further reading

Defence policy is covered well by Keith Hartley in his writings available on the web.

Byrd (1988) is useful for a broad coverage but is now dated. Little and Whickham-Smith's *New Labour's Foreign Policy: a New Moral Crusade?* is more recent and very useful, especially Chapter 1 by Whickham-Smith, but Chapters 2–6 are all acutely analysed and worth reading.

Two key documents are the FCO Mission Statement of 12 May 1997, reported in full in the press the following day and available on the FCO website at www.fco.gov.uk/directory, and the Strategic Defence Review, Cm 3999, July 1998. The most accessible account of the Sandline Affair is in the report of the House of Commons Select Committee on Foreign Affairs (1999) *Sierra Leone* (House of Commons), Paper 116–1. See also Lord Butler's report from 2004 and Sir Christopher Meyer's enjoyably indiscreet memoirs (Meyer, 2005).

References

Butler, Lord (2004) *Review of Intelligence on Weapons of Mass Destruction*, HC 898.

Byrd, P. (1988) *British Foreign Policy Under Thatcher* (Philip Allan).

Carrington, Lord (1988) *Reflect on Things Past* (Collins).

Cook, R. (1997) 'British foreign policy' statement, 12 May.

Economist, 'Fighter jets: keeping secrets', 28 January 2006.

Freedman, C. and Clark, M. (1991) *Britain in the World* (Cambridge University Press).

Gamble, A. (2003) *Between Europe and America: The Future of British Politics* (Palgrave).

Hartley, K. (2002a) 'UK defence policy: an economist's perspective', www.york.ac.uk/depts/econ/research/documents/defence.pdf

Hartley, K. (2002b) 'UK defence policy: a triumph of hope over experience?', www.york.ac.uk/depts/econ/research/documents/ipr.pdf

Kampfner, J. (1998) *Robin Cook* (Gollancz).

Labour Party (1997) *New Labour Because Britain Deserves Better* (Labour Party).

Little, R. and Whickham-Smith, M. (2000) *New Labour's Foreign Policy: a New Moral Crusade?* (Manchester University Press).

Martin, L. and Garnett, J. (1997) *British Foreign Policy: Challenges for the Twenty First Century* (Royal Institute of International Affairs).

Meyer, C. (2005) *DC Confidential* (Weidenfeld & Nicolson).

Owen, D. (1978) *Human Rights* (Jonathan Cape).

Sanders, D. (1990) *Losing an Empire, Finding a Role* (Macmillan).

Wheeler, N.J. and Dunne, T. (1998) 'Good international citizenship: a third way for British foreign policy', *International Affairs*, Vol. 74, No. 4, pp. 847–70.

Useful websites

Amnesty International: www.amnesty.org

Domestic sources of foreign policy: www.apsanet.org/-state

Foreign and Commonwealth Office: www.fco.gov.uk

Ministry of Defence: www.mod.uk

EU common security policy: www.europa.eu.int/pol/cfsp/index-en.htm

NATO: www.nato.int

Organisation for Security and Cooperation in Europe: www.osce.or.at/

CHAPTER 29

Environmental policy

Andrew Flynn

Learning objectives

- To explain the provenance and functions of the Environment Agency, local planning and conservation agencies.

- To elucidate the positions of the main political parties on key features of environmental policy.

- To analyse the role of pressure groups focusing on the environment.

Introduction

The 1990s and the early years of the new millennium have witnessed continual change in the approach of the Labour government to environmental issues, to the administration of environmental policy and to the content of that policy. At the same time, there was a series of unresolved tensions that helped to give British environmental policy its own particular mix and dynamic. These included:

- The environment failed to be a mainstream topic of political debate in the last three general elections of 1997, 2001 and 2005, yet during this time opinion poll evidence shows that the environment/pollution has consistently been among the top five issues that the public believes government should deal with (DEFRA, 2001a). The ten largest environmental groups could claim a reasonably consistent membership among themselves of some 4.5 million people, so far exceeding the membership of political parties (see Chapter 12) and indeed of any other form of social organisation.
- The environment became an increasingly mainstream public policy issue, metamorphosed into sustainable development, and having done so raised further challenges for government in the implementation of policy goals.
- The locus of policy making shifted away from the nation state upwards towards Brussels and downwards to Cardiff and Edinburgh.
- Efforts to secure the integration of policy making and its implementation met countervailing pressures of fragmentation.

For students of politics the challenge raised by environmental issues to existing administrative structures is of enormous interest. So too is the way in which external pressures on bureaucracies, such as those from the European Union (EU), shape the context of environmental policy making and its implementation. But the nature of the challenge posed by environmentalism goes beyond simply studying bureaucratic structures. It involves questions of how governments respond to environmental issues, how societies articulate their environmental concerns and how political parties and pressure groups seek to represent the environment. These questions will be answered during the course of the chapter, but first we address the impact of Europe on British environmental policy, and then consider what environmental policy might be and how it has become part of the broader debate on sustainable development. The third section analyses the impact of devolution on the making and delivery of policy. The fourth section explores the role of key organisations and institutions operating in Britain, since it is they who are responsible for much of the delivery of policy, and the fifth examines the part that political parties and pressure groups play when viewed through the lens of transport and energy policy.

■ The impact of Europe on British environmental policy

Membership of the EU has had a profound influence on the content of British environmental policy and also the way in which it is made (Lowe and Ward, 1998a; Jordan, 2005). These two points are addressed in turn.

Policy content

The European Community first began to take a serious interest in environmental issues in the early 1970s (Lowe and Ward, 1998a, pp. 11–13; Jordan, 2005). Its first Action Programme on the Environment was published in 1973 and aimed to improve people's quality of life, living conditions and surroundings. At this stage the emphasis was very much on

Scientists argue that melting glaciers provide evidence that the world's climate is heating up
Source: NASA / Science Photo Library

trying to ensure that the people within the Community enjoyed similar standards and that environmental regulations were not used by member states as a means of distorting trade. With regard to the latter there was much work on trying to harmonise product standards, a similar burst of activity being associated with the completion of the Single European Market. Throughout the 1970s the environment continued to rise up the European political agenda and was marked by a growing institutionalisation.

An Environment Directorate-General (DGXI) of the Commission was established in 1981, and in 1987 under the Single European Act there was explicitly established a basis for Community action in the environmental field. Until this time environmental legislation had to be justified on the grounds that it was helping to avoid distortions of the market in line with the Community's economic rationale. The EU's responsibilities for environmental protection have been broadened and deepened under the 1993 Treaty on European Union (that amended the Treaty of Rome) and 1997 Treaty of Amsterdam. The former provided a still firmer legal base for EU environmental activities, while the latter has committed the EU as one of its main tasks to promoting sustainable development and a higher quality environment. This involves the EU not only thinking about specific environmental policies but also making sure that environmental concerns are integrated into other policy areas. As we shall see below, Britain has traditionally been regarded as a middle-ranking state with regard to environmental policy. However, in what was clearly designed to give out a quite different message, the Labour government, in hosting its first European Council meeting in Cardiff in June 1998, ensured that there was a reaffirmation of the importance of integrating the environment across the EU's activities.

Articles 174–6 of the Amsterdam Treaty (the latest ratified revision of the founding Treaty of Rome) identified a number of key principles that EU policy should now be based on, including the following:

- *Precautionary principle*: Whereas in the past many decisions have been taken only when there is sufficient supporting evidence to justify a course of action, this principle justifies action to prevent harm to the environment before such evidence is available.

- *Preventative action*: Recognises that it is better to try to stop environmental problems arising at source rather than to deal with them once they have arisen.

- *Polluter pays*: Those who cause pollution should pay for its clean-up rather than those who may be most affected by it.

- *Policy integration*: The environment must play a part in decision making in all policy areas.

The EU's Environmental Action Programmes provide it and the member states with a guide to action, an agenda for change. The Fifth Environmental Action

Programme (5th EAP) running for the period 1992–2000 is entitled *Towards Sustainability* (Commission of the European Communities, 1992). According to one former senior civil servant, it marked the first occasion on which the British government could begin to identify with a European environmental agenda (Sharp, 1998, p. 49). This was a reflection both of the content of the programme and of the way in which ideas in Britain had been developing. The 5th EAP shared the policy principles that were to be found in the Treaty of European Union and suggested that there should be a wider use of policy instruments (e.g. eco-taxes, voluntary agreements with industry) since established command and control measures were no longer sufficient to deal with environmental problems. The document promoted the idea of shared responsibility, that is, the solution to environmental problems was not solely the responsibility of government or the private sector but also needed to include the public, voluntary organisations and the public sector. The 5th EAP also identified five key sectors – agriculture, energy, industry, transport and tourism – where there was a particular need to try to make progress to improve their environmental and economic performance. The linking together of the economy and the environment is an important feature of the way in which the environmental debate has broadened into one on sustainable development, as we shall see below.

The EU's 6th EAP was published in January 2001 and will run until 2012. Its main goal is to decouple economic growth from environmental damage, once again a theme that the UK government has considerable sympathy with, as we shall see below. However, in contrast to the 5th EAP, the 6th is very short on specific commitments or targets. It does reaffirm the 5th EAP's determination to promote shared responsibility for solving environmental problems and of a wish to promote a wider range of policy instruments to achieve goals. There is also less interest than there has been in the past about how goals should be achieved and more attention to the outcomes of policy. A key vehicle for delivery is the identification of thematic strategies, such as air pollution, waste prevention and recycling, the marine environment, the urban environment and soil protection. These themes are in turn underpinned by coordination measures, like implementation (ensuring that member states deliver on policy), integration (promoting sectoral policy complementarity rather than competition), and harnessing the market to achieve environmental goals.

The more modest policy ambitions of the latest EU Environmental Action Plan are a reflection of two key challenges that the EU faces. The first is that earlier Action Plans were able to tackle easier environmental problems. Environmental challenges that have emerged (e.g. climate change) or are still proving difficult to resolve (e.g. the volume and nature of waste production by business and households) do not have straightforward legislative solutions. Tackling waste requires attacking the problem from multiple sources and changing the behaviour of the public – something which is politically sensitive and cannot be secured by traditional forms of regulation alone. Second, the EU is increasingly embracing an economic growth agenda in which environmental issues are clearly less important than they have been in the recent past. Eastward expansion of the EU has further accentuated the growth, rather than the environmental priorities of the EU. In some areas there is a synergy between economic and environmental measures, for example, encouraging more efficient resource use, and where policy progress can be made, but other issues may demand curbs on economic activities, such as tackling climate change.

Policy making

EU law takes precedence over national law and, since in the making of environmental policy there has been a shift away from voting by unanimity to majority voting, Britain, like other EU countries, cannot exercise control over what decisions are made. The environmental field was the fastest-growing EU policy area in the 1980s, and by the mid-1990s John Gummer (1994), a former British Secretary of State for the Environment, had estimated that about 80 per cent of British environmental legislation had its origins in Europe. Not surprisingly, therefore, there have been considerable impacts on the British environmental policy process.

Lowe and Ward (1998a, pp. 26–8) identify three dimensions along which it is possible to assess change in the policy process. The first of these is a challenge to Britain's traditional policy style, that is the management and administration of issues. As an important political issue the environment commands the attention of wide swathes of government in a way in which it did not in the past. In tackling problems such as pollution, Britain's pragmatic approach, in which pollution problems could be dealt with on a case-by-case basis, has been undermined by the elucidation of wide-ranging principles, such as the polluter pays, to govern action. Similarly, regulators had liked to be flexible when dealing with polluters to take account of their circumstances, but that is less possible as European legislation is much more target led, meaning that firms and government must meet preset criteria, so limiting their room for manoeuvre.

Second, there have been changes in the relationships among organisations involved in the policy process. As the focus for policy making has moved from London to Brussels it has opened up the process to environmental groups who have found a more receptive audience for their views. Local government meanwhile may have lost some of its authority, since it is national governments that engage in negotiations and are held responsible by Brussels for the implementation of policy.

Third, and most difficult of all to assess, what has been the impact of Europe on the substance of policy? Although the evidence is somewhat mixed, there is a belief that the EU has meant that Britain has adopted higher standards of environmental protection than it would otherwise have done. What the EU has most certainly done is to help change the terms of the environmental debate in Britain. While in many cases Britain is an adapter rather than an initiator of environmental policy, government thinking is at least now attuned to that of leading nations such as the Netherlands. This is a point that is explored in greater detail below.

■ From environmental policy to sustainable development

It is easy to suggest that environmental policy was 'discovered' in the 1980s and 1990s. Yet many of the most prominent environmental groups were formed well before then, while Britain has long-standing policies to regulate air quality and land use, two components of any environmental policy. So a first question must be whether the environment is really a new policy area or simply older issues recast in a more fashionable light. In part the answer is determined by the way the environment transcends traditional administrative and policy boundaries leading to, for example, the greening of policies in transport and the environment, agriculture and the environment, etc., rather than existing as a separate policy sector. Rather like the environment itself

which is no respecter of borders, environmental policy seemingly knows no policy boundaries. In part also, perceptions of what counts as the environment are culturally and historically constructed. For example, asked 'When people talk about the "environment", which of the following do you think of first?', UK citizens reported pollution in towns and cities (31 per cent) and German citizens protecting nature (27 per cent). Defining the content of environmental policy is, therefore, not easy.

Not surprisingly, therefore, many commentators duck the question of what they regard as environmental policy. It is assumed implicitly that everyone knows what it is and is not. Nevertheless, it is possible to distinguish two popular approaches to defining environmental policy. The first is broad in scope and seeks links to the physical environment: thus environmental policy is 'public policy concerned with governing the relationship between people and their natural environment' (McCormick, 1991, p. 7). Unfortunately this definition is both too narrow, in the sense that it seems to exclude urban areas (as these are difficult to classify as a natural environment), and too general, as it would seem difficult in practice to distinguish it from other policy areas such as rural social policy.

The other approach is much narrower in scope and focuses on 'the use of land and the *regulation* of human activities which have an impact on our physical surroundings' (Blowers, 1987, pp. 278–9, our emphasis). This implies a prescriptive element to policy, as politicians should seek a balance in the use of land between its development, conservation and ecological functions. In practice this involves working through two regulatory systems, that of the land use planning system (responsible for development and conservation) and pollution control (the ecological function). While providing a framework against which to assess changes in environmental policy, the regulatory definition ignores the wider political and social backcloth, including the activities of political parties and new social groups, against which environmental decisions are made.

Neither was it possible to specify that government action on the environment amounted to an environmental policy. Writing at the end of the 1980s, Lowe and Flynn claimed that:

government structures and law relating to environmental protection have been (and largely remain) an accretion of common law, statutes, agencies, procedures and policies. There is no environmental policy other than the sum of these individual elements, most of which have been pragmatic and incremental responses to specific problems and the evolution of relevant scientific knowledge.

Lowe and Flynn (1989), p. 256, emphasis added

However, in 1990 the White Paper *This Common Inheritance* (Cm 1200) was published, the first ever comprehensive statement in Britain of a government's environmental policy. Criticised at the time for its modest proposals, the document nevertheless marks something of a watershed: the environment was a legitimate and high-profile public policy issue. By the end of the decade the terms of the debate had once again shifted. Increasingly simply to think of the environment as a single policy area is to marginalise it. Successive governments have produced detailed statements of their environmental policy, but now they have also sought to integrate the environment with economic and social issues to develop a strategy for sustainable development. So how has such a dramatic shift come about in such a short space of time? Any answer must include at least the following issues: the British government's response to developing agendas in the EU and at the United Nations, the success of pressure groups in the promotion of the environmental agenda, and a growing realisation of the challenges of implementing environmental policy and of the need to ensure that it took account of business and social interests.

■ The sustainable development agenda

One of the classic confrontations of the late twentieth century was that between the environment and the economy. The two were regarded as incompatible: one had either ecological protection and no growth, or economic development and environmental degradation. The notion of sustainable development, and the belief of some that we are moving towards a greener society, integrates the economy and the environment and at one stroke sidesteps much of the traditional debate.

Much of the controversy now is over what is meant by sustainable development, for it has become something of a totem, a concept so powerful that no one should question it. But different interests seek to interpret sustainable development in various ways. As such sustainable development has become an object of contestation within the environmental debate. Originally developed within the ecological sciences, sustainable development was popularised in *Our Common Future* (more commonly known as the Brundtland Report) (World Commission on Environment and Development, 1987) as that which 'meets the needs of the present without compromising the ability of future generations to meet their own needs'. At its minimum this would seem to involve little more than business as usual with a few added-on commitments to environmental protection.

In order to show their commitment to environmental protection and exploit market opportunities, businesses have engaged in such measures as environmental management systems and environmental auditing. Purchasing policies, production processes and waste disposal are all now much more carefully monitored. Eco-labelling schemes now exist in many European countries to show that products are produced to a certain standard and an EU-wide labelling scheme – the Flower – first appeared in 1992.

Governments have shown a willingness to co-ordinate and act to address the issue of sustainable development. The Brundtland Report was endorsed by political leaders at the United Nations Conference on Environment and Development (the Earth Summit) in Rio de Janeiro in 1992. The summit produced the following:

1. The Rio declaration, which established a set of principles for action

2. A programme of action for the next century, Agenda 21

3. A Climate Change Convention to try to reduce the risks of global warming

4. A Biodiversity Convention to protect species and habitats

5. A statement of principles for the conservation of the world's forests.

Each country was charged with taking forward these points. A follow-up, Earth Summit II, was held in New York in June 1997 and began to expose to a wide audience the difficulties that a number of the developed countries were experiencing in putting into practice the ideas they had endorsed some five years earlier in Rio.

More recently the World Summit on Sustainable Development (WSSD), also known as Rio+10, was held from 26 August to 4 September 2002 in

Johannesburg. The sense that Rio had led to tangible achievements heightened the expectations around the Johannesburg summit, but the discussions and outcomes showed clearly the tensions that can emerge between governments and between government and NGOs when they seek to bring together trade, economics, social development and environmental protection. Whilst many activists and governments were dissatisfied at the outcomes, and there were few tangible achievements, business for the first time on the world stage did seek to play the role of full partner with governments and NGOs in delivering on sustainability. What was achieved in the great debates conducted by over 100 heads of government and tens of thousands of citizens? Energy proved to the most contentious issue and little was achieved. More positive were the efforts to promote corporate accountability and sustainable production and consumption, and commitments to improve water quality and sanitation for the world's poor. On globalisation, trade and the environment the primacy of the World Trade Organisation was noted. Perhaps not surprisingly, the value of such set-piece events has been questioned, and Johannesburg may prove to be the last of the great world sustainability summits. Attention is now shifting towards the implementation and monitoring of commitments.

What difference, if any, have these major international conferences had in shaping UK policy development? Following the Rio Conference the former Conservative government put some efforts into delivering its promises on implementing its action programme. After a year-long consultation period it published *Sustainable Development: The UK Strategy* (Cm 2426) in January 1994. The document was largely a restatement of existing policies and ideas but did contain some initiatives to promote new ideas. These included a Panel on Sustainable Development comprising five eminent experts who report directly to the Prime Minister on major strategic issues; a Round Table on Sustainable Development made up of thirty representatives drawn from business, local government, environmental groups and other organisations that seek to build consensus about the ways of achieving sustainable development; and a Going for Green programme to carry the sustainable development message to local communities and individuals. From 2000 the Panel and Round Table was subsumed within a new Sustainable Development Commission chaired by a leading environmentalist, Jonathon Porritt.

The government also published proposals on *Biodiversity: The UK Action Plan* (Cm 2428). Again, the policies were modest and often simply consolidated in one document existing actions but did at least represent a positive step forward. In contrast, parts of local government have been much more innovative in developing sustainability indicators and action programmes, though they remain hamstrung by lack of resources and powers.

When she returned to Britain from the Johannesburg Summit, the then Environment Secretary, Margaret Beckett, announced that she had asked Jonathon Porritt, chair of the Sustainable Development Commission, to convene a group of twelve leading figures from business and local and regional government to discuss how to tackle sustainable consumption and production; the role of business in delivering sustainable development; and renewable energy. Once again, the emphasis appeared to be on awareness raising rather than developing policies for delivery. The direct influence of summits on the development of government policy has, therefore, been rather modest. More important in policy development has been the need to respond to European and domestic agendas.

Many environmentalists argue that a stronger version of sustainable development needs to be put into practice, one in which the state plays a much more positive role in ensuring the equitable distribution of resources through space and time. Attention is switched away from total production to the methods of production of particular goods. A weak version of sustainable development therefore fails to confront the major cause of the ecological crisis, the sheer amount of production and consumption. On this view, sustainable development does not mean no development but much more selective development.

For governments the idea that there should be more selective development is a challenging one as it may alienate voters and their families caught up in those sectors or firms that are seen to be too unsustainable. They have therefore sought to construct defensible policy positions at a point between the weak and strong versions of sustainable development. Shortly after its election to power in 1997 the Labour government announced that it would update the sustainable development strategy of its predecessor. In February 1998 a consultation paper, *Opportunities for Change*, was issued and it was followed by a small number of additional consultation papers on particular aspects of sustainable development, such as business and tourism. A revised sustainable development strategy, *A Better Quality of Life: A Strategy for Sustainable Development for the United Kingdom* (Cm 4345) was published by the government in May 1999.

Interestingly, the government's approach to sustainable development has become ever more interwoven with that of devolution. *A Better Quality of Life* was developed as devolution was coming into force and so would have a limited shelf-life. This is because sustainable development has proved to be a key feature of the responsibilities of the Devolved Administrations. So, in the early 2000s it was increasingly recognised within government that a new UK level strategy would need to be developed that could take account of the impact of devolution on both the formulation and implementation of policy and of the emergence of new issues on the sustainability agenda.

From the outset in developing the new strategy it was recognised that devolution had reshaped the policy context and that it would not be possible to produce a single UK document, like *A Better Quality of Life*, that could embrace both UK policy and that of the Devolved Administrations. Instead, there would be a UK strategy and a UK-wide strategic framework that would cover:

■ 'a shared understanding of sustainable development, a vision of what we are trying to achieve and the guiding principles that we all need to follow to get there;

■ our sustainable development priorities for UK action;

■ our work internationally to help achieve sustainable development; and

■ indicators to monitor and measure performance' (DEFRA, 2004, p. 11)

While the Devolved Administrations and the UK government can recognise the need to work cooperatively to pursue sustainability, there is likely to be an underlying tension as the Administrations will develop their own sustainability strategies 'based on their different responsibilities, needs and views' (DEFRA, 2004, p. 11) and these may not always coincide with one another or with the UK government. At a political level there is a key challenge for government to develop structures or processes that can operate at multiple levels to deliver common goals.

In the spring of 2005 two high-level policy documents on sustainable development were published

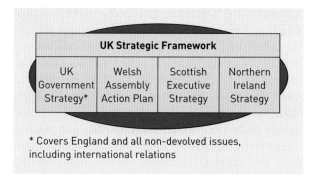

* Covers England and all non-devolved issues, including international relations

Figure 29.1 Hierarchy of UK sustainable development strategies
Source: From the DEFRA (2005a) *Securing the Future – Delivering the UK Sustainable Development Strategy*, Document Cm 6467, p. 15. © Crown Copyright 2005. Crown copyright material is reproduced with the permission of the Controller of Her Majesty's Stationery Office (HMSO)

simultaneously. One is *Securing the Future* (DEFRA, 2005a) which sets out the UK government's sustainability strategy, though much of its content does not apply to Scotland or Wales since they have their own authority in this area. From the perspective of the Devolved Administrations the more important document is *One Future – Different Paths* (DEFRA, 2005b) as this established a strategic framework for their responsibilities and a common agenda with UK government. One official has explained that it is 'the first properly federal document' in the UK, since it says that 'UK policy consists of *One future – different paths* and the documents of the other Devolved Administrations' (which we turn to in the section below). The relationship between the different governments and their key documents is illustrated in Figure 29.1.

Securing the Future recognises that the government's previous sustainable development strategy had largely failed to deliver on its promises, so the latest document concentrates on delivery rather than aspirational commitments. Among the most important areas for delivery are measures to support businesses to be more sustainable through initiatives on sustainable consumption and production and for consumers to adopt more sustainable lifestyles. A core part of the strategy is also devoted to energy and climate change. Also in *Securing the Future* and repeated in *One Future – Different Paths* are a set of principles and priorities that have been agreed by, and apply to, all governments within the UK (Figure 29.2). These principles are important, since they recognise that living within

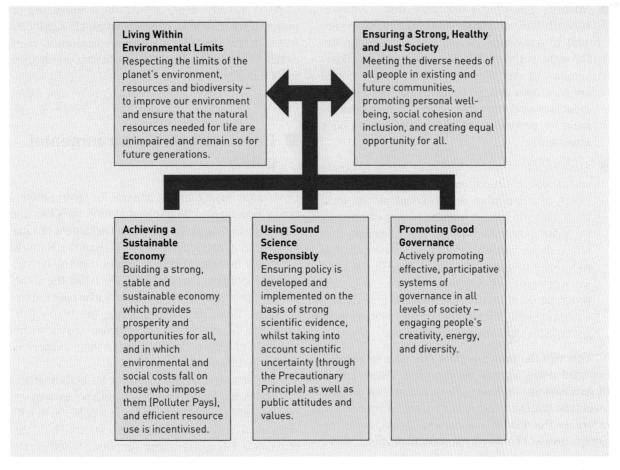

Figure 29.2 UK Sustainable Development Principles
Source: From the DEFRA (2005a) *Securing the Future – Delivering the UK Sustainable Development Strategy*, Document Cm 6467, p. 16. © Crown Copyright 2005. Crown copyright material is reproduced with the permission of the Controller of Her Majesty's Stationery Office (HMSO)

environmental limits and a strong, healthy and just society are underpinned by a vibrant economy, good governance, and the basing of decisions on scientific evidence. If policy is to be sustainable it must respect and progress all five principles and so moves beyond trade-offs between principles (such as the environment and economy) that have often characterised policy in the past.

Along with the principles, the governments have also agreed to four priority policy areas (DEFRA, 2005b):

■ *Sustainable consumption and production*: Sustainable consumption and production is about achieving more with less. This means not only looking at how goods and services are produced, but also the impacts of products and materials across their whole lifecycle and building on people's awareness of social and environmental concerns. This includes reducing the inefficient

use of resources which are a drag on the economy, so helping boost business competitiveness and to break the link between economic growth and environmental degradation.

■ *Climate change and energy*: The effects of a changing climate can already be seen. Temperatures and sea levels are rising, ice and snow cover are declining, and the consequences could be catastrophic for the natural world and society. Scientific evidence points to the release of greenhouse gases, such as carbon dioxide and methane, into the atmosphere by human activity as the primary cause of climatic change. We will seek to secure a profound change in the way we generate and use energy, and in other activities that release these gases. At the same time we must prepare for the climate change that cannot now be avoided. We must set a good example and will encourage others to follow it.

■ *Natural resource protection and environmental enhancement*: Natural resources are vital to our existence and that of communities throughout the world. We need a better understanding of environmental limits, environmental enhancement and recovery where the environment is most degraded to ensure a decent environment for everyone, and a more integrated policy framework.

■ *Sustainable communities*: Our aim is to create sustainable communities that embody the principles of sustainable development at the local level. This will involve working to give communities more power and say in the decisions that affect them; and working in partnership at the right level to get things done. The UK uses the same principles of engagement, partnership, and programmes of aid in order to tackle poverty and environmental degradation and to ensure good governance in overseas communities.

Although the principles and priorities establish a common policy agenda between the different tiers of government, they are pitched at such a general level that the Devolved Administrations retain considerable freedom of manoeuvre. Again, from the perspective of the Devolved Administrations, there is a common perception that having been granted policy responsibility, they would resist policy dictates from Whitehall. So, the agreed principles and priorities had to be broad to secure agreement on them.

The government's sustainable development goal

The goal of sustainable development is to enable all people throughout the world to satisfy their basic needs and enjoy a better quality of life, without compromising the quality of life of future generations.

For the UK Government and the Devolved Administrations, that goal will be pursued in an integrated way through a sustainable, innovative and productive economy that delivers high levels of employment; and a just society that promotes social inclusion, sustainable communities and personal wellbeing. This will be done in ways that protect and enhance the physical and natural environment, and use resources and energy as efficiently as possible.

Source: DEFRA, 2005b

As is already clear, devolution is impacting on policy development in variable but highly significant ways. In the following section we explore in more detail what effects devolution is having on environmental policy.

■ Devolution and environmental policy

Devolution has significant impacts for environmental policy making and its implementation in Wales and especially Scotland. The Scottish Parliament has had far greater powers devolved to it than the National Assembly for Wales: for the former it is the devolution of legislative power and for the latter the ability to exercise responsibility over particular policy areas. Thus, as Table 29.1 shows, while the two legislatures will be concerned with similar topics within the field of environmental policy, their authorities are quite different.

Agriculture, an important topic for both Scotland and Wales, has long been an issue with some devolved responsibilities. Energy, though, is a policy area with significant environmental implications, but this remains a UK government function. Whether the devolution of responsibilities to Wales and Scotland can remain stable is a moot point. The leadership of the Welsh Labour Party has been keen to follow the line laid down by central government that the present powers are sufficient. Others, though, are beginning to look longingly at the greater powers of the Scottish Parliament and how they may help to deal with challenging policy issues. For example, the national paper of Wales, *The Western Mail*, on 16 October 1999 in a special report on the need for integrated transport, argued that devolution is a necessary step:

Solutions appropriate to London or Surrey are not necessarily applicable to Wales, but only some transport powers have been devolved to Cardiff from London. A genuinely integrated Welsh transport policy cannot be drawn up, let alone implemented while London holds the purse strings for railways, and Cardiff for roads.

Before Wales' transport problems can be ironed out, the National Assembly must gain similar controls over railways to its control over roads. Only then can it make balanced decisions on investment and implementation, where money is channelled to whichever solution is the most cost-effective.

Table 29.1 Key environmental responsibilities and powers of the National Assembly for Wales and the Scottish Parliament

	National Assembly for Wales has responsibility for	**Scottish Parliament has legislative powers over**
Transport	Control of the construction of trunk roads in Wales, and the maintenance of existing ones	Passenger and road transport covering the Scottish road network, the promotion of road safety, bus policy, concessionary fares, cycling, taxis and minicabs, some rail grant powers, the Strathclyde Passenger Transport Executive and consultative arrangements in respect of public transport
Planning	Determining policies on town and country planning and issuing guidance to local authorities	Land-use planning and building control
Heritage	Determining and implementing policy on ancient monuments and listed buildings; allowing and encouraging visits to ancient monuments and public buildings owned by Cadw	The natural heritage including countryside issues and the functions of Scottish Natural Heritage; the built heritage including the functions of Historic Scotland
The environment	Funding, directing and making appointments to the Countryside Council of Wales and the Environment Agency (alongside the DETR and MAFF); controlling water quality and river pollution in Wales	The environment including environmental protection, matters relating to air, land and water pollution and the functions of the Scottish Environment Protection Agency; water supplies and sewerage; and policies designed to promote sustainable development within the international commitments agreed by the UK

Although Wales has more limited devolved powers than Scotland, it does have a unique responsibility amongst all levels of UK government to progress sustainable development. Under the Government of Wales Act 1998 the Assembly is legally required to make a scheme setting out how it proposes, in carrying out its work, to promote sustainable development. For any legislature such a responsibility, if taken seriously, is formidable, and for a Welsh bureaucracy that has limited experience of policy making (as opposed to policy delivery) and limited resources the challenge is all the greater. What is already clear is that the Assembly is taking its duty seriously. In its internal operations it is addressing machinery of government and policy appraisal issues to ensure that sustainability is considered across all its work, and also rethinking its external relationships so that it can promote a partnership approach to the delivery of sustainable development.

The greater political commitment to devolution in Scotland than in Wales meant that the Scots had done more preparatory work on how they would progress sustainable development within their parliament. So while no duty for sustainable development was imposed upon the Scottish Parliament in the devolution legislation, Lord Sewell, a former Scottish Office Minister, argued:

In Scotland, we have moved forward rapidly to make sustainable development a mainstream issue for Government, for local authorities, for business and for the people of Scotland. The cross-linking of issues comes naturally to Scotland; there is a genuine interest in Scotland in delivering on the three arms which make up sustainable development: a sound economy, strong social development, built on a real concern for the environment.

In practice, though, early Scottish efforts to mainstream sustainable development were limited. Scotland and Wales have now both prepared their second round of sustainable development strategies. As *Down to Earth*, the first Scottish strategy for sustainable development, put it: 'The Scottish Parliament will choose for itself the form [of sustainable development] which best suits the circumstances of Scotland' (Scottish Office, 1999, p. 5). Whilst the priorities in Edinburgh and Cardiff have not markedly diverged from those in London, and neither should we expect them to, given that Wales and Scotland have signed up to common sustainable development principles and priorities (see above), different emphases are apparent. In its second sustainable development strategy, *Choosing our Future*, the Scottish Executive (2005) makes it clear that its priority is a more environmentally friendly form of economic growth, whilst in Wales the debate has moved on to how the Assembly government might enable people to start *Living Differently* (the title of the second sustainable development scheme, Welsh Assembly Government, 2004) by changing structural factors (such as the organisation of communities) and the leadership provided by the Assembly. However, the Welsh Assembly has to work with fewer levers than the Scottish Executive in seeking to redirect economic or social forces and has the potential to be caught between its own ambitions, the expectations it raises and its ability to shape more sustainable outcomes. For the future, the ways in which the devolved legislatures meet their own policy agendas and contributions to UK-negotiated international environmental agreements, and indeed to the UK sustainable development strategy, will be interesting to observe.

Europe, devolution and policy change

There are two interrelated features that emerge so far from the analysis of policy development in the late 1990s and into the 2000s. The first is that thinking on the environment and sustainability becomes an ever more central concern for government. So, for example, the former Conservative Secretary of State for the Environment John Gummer had shown himself to be a keen advocate of policy reform but his ministerial colleagues did not share his enthusiasm. The Labour government has a much greater commitment to environmental issues across government, for example, reflected in administrative improvements to the machinery of government and the content of policy. It is important, though, to remember that politicians will have highly variable interests in the environment. For instance, the Liberal Democrats have consistently advocated high environmental standards. Meanwhile, the former Conservative Party leader, Michael Howard, made only one speech on the environment and concluded 'there is almost no meaningful debate on the environment. It means that politicians like me can trot up to the odd conference, and make a fine and concerned speech, and go away again perhaps coming back in 12 months time to chuck around a few statistics.' Howard's successor, David Cameron, has made more effort to reposition the Conservatives on the environment and move it towards the centre of the party's concerns by making it a quality of life issue. The

second feature is the changing base of policy. Partly as the result of the process of devolution and the European agenda outlined above, British sustainable development policy has become more attuned to that of its neighbours.

A clear sense of the pace and direction of change can be gained from comparing the development of sustainable development policy in Britain and the Netherlands. The Dutch have dealt seriously with the challenge of the environmental implications of development for a number of years and at the end of the 1980s there was a wide gulf in the thinking of the two nations. Both governments produced documents on their sustainable development strategy in 1994. Britain's as we saw was largely a restatement of existing thinking, while the Dutch engaged in a more fundamental review about the long-term direction of policy. Towards the end of the decade both countries (the Netherlands in February 1998 and Britain in May 1999) once again produced major policy statements. The Dutch remain clear European policy leaders, while Britain remains in the formative stages of its sustainable development thinking (see Table 29.2).

At that time there remained a number of differences of emphasis and some of substance between the two documents that in large part reflect the different social, political and economic circumstances of the two countries. In Britain there is a strong wish to accelerate the rate of economic growth and promote societal renewal, while in the Netherlands there is a more explicit recognition of the need to manage the impacts of industry and consumers on the environment. Within the Netherlands there is also much greater social and political consensus on the principles and content of sustainable development policy. This helps to promote policy continuity and longer-term thinking that are so essential in the promotion of sustainable development. In Britain, meanwhile, while there is much agreement on policy aims between the political parties (partly because they are so broad) there tends to be less agreement on means. Since the major opposition party invariably regards it as a duty to oppose government measures, policy can quickly become politicised as the case of road transport explored below shows.

A key aspect of the sustainability strategy of both countries, and one that is now a central theme of the EU's 6th EAP, is that over time the economy should have less impact on the environment. As the British government put it: 'We have to find a new way forward. We need greater prosperity with less

Table 29.2 Britain and the Netherlands compared in the late 1990s

Feature	Britain	Netherlands
Continuity with previous sustainable development document	Medium – greater emphasis on social issues and that high standards of environmental protection are a prerequisite for future economic growth	High
Overall policy goals	(a) Social progress; (b) effective protection of the environment; (c) prudent use of natural resources; and (d) maintenance of high and stable levels of economic growth and employment	(a) Solve large number of existing environmental problems within one generation (before 2010); (b) prevent continuing economic growth causing new environmental problems
Programme of action	Emphasis on developing indicators to measure progress towards sustainability in the future and of actions that need to be undertaken	Identification of areas where progress is being made towards sustainability and where activity has been inadequate
Responsibility for action	Key actors to progress sustainable development are noted and their role within the overall framework made clear – a scene-setting exercise rather than the allocation of tasks	Target groups (e.g. industry, agriculture, consumers, government) are identified and they are made responsible for progressing the strategy

environmental damage. We need to improve the efficiency with which we use resources' (Cm 4345, para 1.8). While this is a laudable sentiment that is shared by the Dutch – they term it 'decoupling' (i.e. improving economic growth and at the same time reducing pressures on the environment) – they would wish to distinguish between:

■ relative decoupling (when pressure on the environment increases at a slower rate than the economy grows), the position favoured by the British government; and

■ absolute decoupling (when environmental degradation reduces or at least remains constant while the economy grows) (VROM, 1998, p. 16), which is the perspective that the Dutch government advocates.

The approach of the Dutch government is more ambitious than that of the British government, but its emphasis on absolute decoupling has come from its positive experience of breaking the connection between resource use and economic growth. In particular, the Dutch have found that new markets have developed for their industries in, for example, the field of environmental technology, and that promoting the highest possible environmental standards within the EU helps create further markets for their companies in other parts of Europe. While the British government may be sympathetic to the approach pursued by the Dutch, it will obviously impose additional costs on firms who are currently wasteful of resources. Although there is now some data

(DEFRA, 2002) to support claims that the British economy is decoupling, sceptics believe the change largely reflects a switch from coal to gas for electricity generation rather than a shift in resource efficiency. It will be difficult for British environmental technology firms to quickly catch up with their Dutch counterparts and so issues of competitiveness will play a part in the nuancing of British sustainable development policy.

Within both Dutch and UK governments, thinking on the environment has now moved forward a further stage, but once again the Dutch remain a step ahead. Debates in the Netherlands have now begun on how governments should manage the transition towards more sustainable societies. The starting point is the recognition that current fossil fuel-based energy production, intensive farming and transport are unsustainable. Alternative systems must be devised that are environmentally more benign and also beneficial from an economic point of view. The role of government is to help set long-term goals and create a framework in which society can experiment with different means to achieve those goals. In the UK, there is considerable interest in the Dutch approach to innovation and transition, but far less thinking has taken place on the long-term reforms to institutional structures and processes that may be necessary (though considerable restructuring has taken place, as we shall see below). Thus environmental policy goals and mechanisms tend to be rather more cautious than those found in the Netherlands.

■ Central government and its agencies

Department of the Environment, Food and Rural Affairs (DEFRA)

Recurrent themes in the analysis of British institutions for environmental protection are those of integration and fragmentation. As political priorities have changed over time and new problems have arisen, governments have attempted to solve them through a series of organisational fixes. These fixes, though, become ever more contested as the environment becomes a more important political issue and commentators increasingly turn their attention to the principles and processes for organising to protect the environment. The creation of DEFRA, its predecessor the Department of the Environment Transport and the Regions (DETR) and the original Department of the Environment (DoE), illustrate well the pressures on government and the way in which the pendulum of integration and fragmentation can swing back and forth. The challenge to integrate central government functions to adequately cope with the broad nature of environmental decisions does not change, but the political response does.

In an argument that resonates as clearly today as it did when written in 1970, a White Paper on *The Reorganisation of Central Government* (Cmnd 4506, 1970) pointed out that:

It is increasingly accepted that maintaining a decent environment, improving people's living conditions and providing for adequate transport facilities, all come together in the planning of development . . . Because these functions interact, and because they give rise to acute and conflicting requirements, a new form of organisation is needed at the centre of the administrative system.

This new organisation was the Department of the Environment. Headed by a Secretary of State in the Cabinet, it was an amalgamation of the Ministries of Housing and Local Government, Public Building and Works, and Transport. With the benefit of hindsight, however, it is easy to see that while the government may have believed that organisational reform was sufficient to deal with environmental problems, the Department of the Environment was more a re-arrangement of the machinery of government than the creation of a department with new powers. It was never going to work as a department *of* the environment, let alone one *for* the environment, because

the politics of Whitehall had left key environmental issues with other departments. Thus, responsibility for agriculture and the countryside remained with the Ministry of Agriculture, and energy with the then Department of Energy. In 1976, as political priorities shifted under a Labour government, transport was separated from the department.

Ironically the Labour government elected in 1997 thought it politically important to once again bring transport into the DoE and emphasise the role of regional development (moved from the DTI) and create the DETR. Environmentalists such as Friends of the Earth welcomed the merger of the Departments of the Environment and Transport as it was thought a unified department would be able to think in a more integrated manner. Early on, though, there were doubts about whether the new department would be more effective than its predecessors. It did not gain significant new powers, some environment responsibilities still lay with other Whitehall departments, and with devolution Edinburgh and Cardiff now also have a more important part to play than in the past. Nevertheless, there was surprise in some quarters that the department should once again be reorganised following Labour's 2001 election victory. There had been disquiet within government at the performance of the Ministry of Agriculture, Fisheries and Food (MAFF) and its demise was expected. The organisation that emerged, DEFRA, was less well anticipated. Alongside the responsibilities of MAFF, DEFRA has also inherited responsibility for sustainable development, environmental protection and water, rural development, countryside, and energy efficiency. What had been DETR now became the Department of Transport, Local Government and the Regions, though the following year, in 2002, Transport was separated out to reflect its political prominence. DEFRA will clearly be well placed to attempt the 'greening' of agricultural policy, but in many ways the reforms may not be positive for environmental policy. Planning, a key tool, for delivering sustainable development has been transferred to the Office of the Deputy Prime Minister.

The continual repackaging of environment-related responsibilities must raise doubts as to whether bringing together functions does aid integrated policy making. The fundamental tensions between different sectors do not disappear and so what would have been interdepartmental disputes now take place behind the closed doors of one department. In an effort to make sure that the environmental impacts of different policies are incorporated into decision making, the Labour government has built upon the efforts of its Conservative predecessor which had taken two forms. One was to amend the machinery of government and the other was to engage in the environmental appraisal of new policies.

The lead role in formulating the Conservative government's 1990 White Paper *This Common Inheritance* had been taken by the then Department of the Environment, but its content had been debated and a number of compromises made in a Cabinet committee set up to oversee its production. Ministers and senior civil servants involved in the process recognised the value of being able to discuss the environment as a policy issue both within and across departments. The White Paper therefore made two commitments to improving the machinery of government: to retain the Cabinet committee, and the nomination of a green minister in each department who would be responsible for considering the environmental implications of the department's policies and programmes. At the time (1991) the Conservative Secretary of State for the Environment, Michael Heseltine, proclaimed: 'We now have some of the most sophisticated machinery to be found anywhere in the world integrating environment and other policies.' Commentators have subsequently pointed out that the Cabinet committee was downgraded to a ministerial committee and that the committee 'was an ineffective institutional device, mainly due to the continued territorial preoccupation of departments and hostility within the central government machinery towards the . . . DoE, particularly from the "economic" departments' (Voisey and O'Riordan, 1998, p. 159). The Labour government has upgraded the committee to its original Cabinet status, where it is known as the Cabinet Ministerial Committee on the Environment (ENV), but tangible achievements are difficult to detect. Labour has also sought to reinvigorate the green ministers and they now have to report to the ENV Committee and prepare an annual report on their activities. Government has made commitments to put its own house in order. Departments now have to think seriously about introducing environmental management systems and having their performance appraised against eight criteria, including their business travel and water use. As its own contribution to improving the machinery of government, Labour created in 1997 a House of Commons Select Committee on Environmental Audit. The Committee's terms of reference are to evaluate the extent to which the policies and programmes of departments

and non-departmental public bodies contribute to environmental protection and sustainable development. However, in a review of the government's progress on mainstreaming sustainable development across Whitehall, the Environmental Audit Committee (2004) pointed out that few have met the government's ambitions: only a few departmental sustainability strategies have been prepared and these have been treated as one-off exercises with little wider relevance.

Government officials routinely engage in policy appraisal. Since 1991 they have been encouraged to broaden their analysis to take into account environmental issues. However, much of the guidance for officials on how to undertake environmental policy appraisals has been skewed towards economic techniques and may not have received a sympathetic response. The Labour government appears to be making renewed efforts to instil environmental appraisal into the routines of decision making (Environmental Audit Committee, 1998, paras 89–91). Nevertheless, practice within departments appears to be variable, and while they may be becoming more frequent there is little evidence to suggest that environmental appraisals have made much impact on significant policy issues (Environmental Audit Committee, 2004).

The organisational and administrative changes noted above certainly indicate some of the ways in which the environment has been accorded a higher political priority. While the search for policy integration is certainly a desirable objective and may help to achieve higher levels of environmental protection, it should not obscure our gaze from the content of policy. And yet, at times, this seems to have been the consequence of a series of organisational reforms, as we shall see below.

The Environment Agency

The substance of environmental policy presents enormous challenges to decision makers because it defies their conventional time-scales and functional divisions. Thus, where politicians' horizons may normally be bounded by that of elections, the environment forces them to think on a quite different scale, of generations for which they cannot possibly receive any political payback. Meanwhile, organisations like to do things in their own way with the minimum of external interference. But environmental policy cross-cuts traditional divisions of government and raises, for those concerned, the unwelcome possibility of turf disputes about who gets to do what. Faced with these dilemmas, decision makers have shown a greater interest in the organisation of environmental protection as a substitute, or at least an alternative focus, for the more challenging issues surrounding the content of policy. Thus recent years have witnessed a flurry of, perhaps, unprecedented organisational reforms. The result has been some grander thinking on structures than is normal and the creation in 1996 of a large, centralised Environment Agency that may fit less easily into Britain's traditional administrative culture. In the past, small, specialised bodies, with for the most part low public profiles, have tended to be favoured.

Demands for the creation of a unified environment body have been long-standing. Since the mid-1970s the standing Royal Commission on Environmental Pollution had argued for a greater integration of the functions of what were at the time a set of disparate organisations. By the 1980s, increasing support from environmental groups, such as Friends of the Earth, and latterly the Labour and Liberal Democrat parties, helped make questions of integration a topic of policy debate. The late 1980s and early 1990s saw the creation of important new bodies – Her Majesty's Inspectorate of Pollution (HMIP), the National Rivers Authority (NRA) and the Waste Regulatory Authorities (WRAs) – but still this did not quell the clamour for further reform. Within a month of the publication in 1990 of the government's White Paper (Cm 1200) on the environment, *This Common Inheritance*, the opposition parties had issued their own policy documents (*An Earthly Chance* and *What Price Our Planet?* by Labour and the Liberal Democrats respectively), which, in contrast to the Conservatives, committed themselves to major institutional reforms.

Within a year the Conservative government had fallen into line, and in July 1991 John Major, in his first speech on the environment as Prime Minister, argued that 'it is right that the integrity and indivisibility of the environment should now be reflected in a unified agency' and announced the government's intention 'to create a new agency for environment protection and enhancement'.

HMIP, the NRA and the WRAs together form the core of the Environment Agency in England and Wales. The Scottish Environment Protection Agency (the difference in name may be of some significance) has in addition to the three core groups the local authority environmental health officers who dealt with air pollution. In terms of the logic creating a

unified and all-embracing pollution regulation body, the inclusion of such staff makes sense. That it did not happen in England and Wales indicates the way in which organisational design in the public sector is invariably intertwined with political factors. The then Conservative government had a much greater representation in local government in England than it did in Scotland and knew that it would arouse opposition within its own ranks should it take away responsibility for air pollution from English local authorities.

What does the Environment Agency mean for the work of its core groups and what effects might it have on those they regulate? The functions set out in Box 29.1 are derived from its constituent elements. Of these, HMIP was formed in 1987 as the result of interdepartmental disputes, embarrassment at pollution discharges at Sellafield nuclear power station and pressures from the European Commission. It combined what had been distinct inspectorates in industrial air pollution. It was responsible for regulating discharges to air, land or water for some 2,000 industrial processes with the greatest polluting potential.

The NRA was a much larger and higher profile organisation than HMIP. It has gone on to form the largest part of the new agency and its former staff have secured a number of key positions within it. The NRA was created at the same time as the water authorities were privatised, under the Water Act 1989, and it took on the pollution control functions and some of the activities of these authorities. The latter were both guardians of the water environment and also major polluters as dischargers of sewage, that is, acting as both poacher and gamekeeper.

Waste collection and disposal has been a traditional local government activity but one where it has lost out to the twin pressures of integration in environmental protection and for contracting-out of services. The 1990 Environmental Protection Act created three types of waste authority. Waste Collection Authorities (a local authority or a contractor working for the authority) arrange for the collection of household and commercial waste. Its disposal is the responsibility of a Waste Disposal Authority (either a part of local government or a Local Authority Waste Disposal Company). Waste Regulation Authorities, whose staff have been moved from local government to the Environment Agency, are responsible for the safe treatment and disposal of wastes produced by households, mines, quarries and agriculture (so-called controlled waste).

BOX 29.1 **FACT**

Key responsibilities of the Environment Agency and the Scottish Environment Protection Agency

Functions

■ Water resource management – conserve and secure the proper use of water

■ Water quality – prevent and control pollution and monitor the quality of rivers, estuaries, coastal waters and groundwater

■ Integrated pollution control – control discharges to land, air and water for larger and more complex industrial processes

■ Air – SEPA alone – control processes which have a medium pollution risk (in England and Wales this task is undertaken by local authority Environmental Health Officers)

■ Waste regulation – (a) register and monitor those who carry waste for a business; (b) approve management of waste disposal sites.

Achieved by

■ Issuing of abstraction licences

■ Granting of consent to discharge

■ Integrated Pollution Control authorisation by
  – Regulation of the firm
  – Licensing of site operators.

By bringing together in one organisation the control of water pollution, air pollution and commercial waste there is an effort to provide a more integrated approach to environmental management. While structures are important in trying to achieve policy goals, both the English and Welsh agency and the Scottish agency have had to surmount a number of hurdles. It has taken longer than expected to forge them into a cohesive grouping. The professionals who staff them came with different professional priorities, tactics, approaches to regulation and (not to be ignored) career structures. To be seen to be more than the sum of their organisational parts, it has been essential for the agencies to prove their independence from government and of those they regulate. The agencies have not been helped in this regard, as they have received few additional powers from those that their constituent bodies held. It is unlikely that most businesses will have noticed any practical difference in the way in which they are regulated.

Nevertheless, both agencies have tried to promote a different style and this may lead to a change in substance. For example, the Environment Agency has been actively involved in initiatives to promote waste minimisation in business. Waste minimisation

offers a double dividend: a firm reduces its impact on the environment because less material is used in the production process and there is less waste to be disposed of, and at the same time becomes more efficient because it is using its materials more efficiently. Here the Agency is able to act as an educator of business, encouraging it along a more sustainable route. Where business has proved more recalcitrant, the Agency has changed tack and adopted a high-profile name and shame campaign of major polluters, for instance, producing an annual *Spotlight on Business* that highlights environmental performance (see Figure 29.3). Here the Agency has a role as the citizen's friend through its actions to protect the environment.

Throughout its three terms of office Labour has been sensitive to the potential burden that environmental regulation may place on business. It remains an ongoing challenge for the Labour government to follow through the logic of its sustainable development policy with its implication of rigorous and stringent environmental regulation by the Environment Agency. The Agency has recognised that enforcement action is perceived to be weak and has put in place special enforcement teams to target serious pollution offenders. Table 29.3 provides

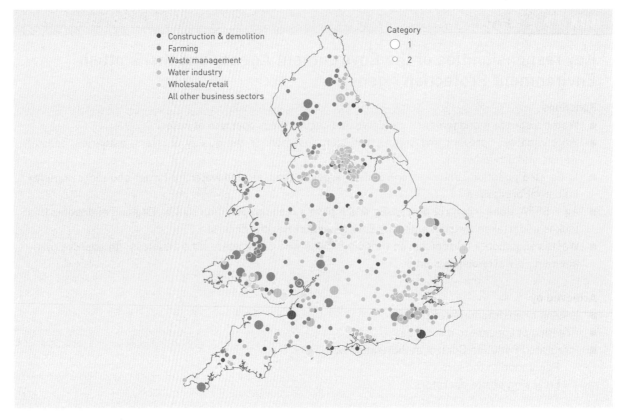

Figure 29.3 Serious pollution incidents in England and Wales by sector
Source: Environment Agency (2005) *Doing the Right Thing: Spotlight on Business Environmental Performance 2004*,
<http://publications.environment-agency.gov.uk/pdf/GEHO0706BLBM-e-e.pdf>. Copyright © 2005 Environment Agency.
All rights reserved. Reproduced with permission

Table 29.3 Successful prosecutions for pollution and waste offences

	2001	2002	2003	2004
Water quality	237	221	171	187
Integrated pollution prevention and control	0	0	1	3
Radioactive substance releases	11	1	3	2
Waste	493	517	433	451
Total	**741**	**739**	**608**	**643**

information on the number of Agency prosecutions for pollution and shows that waste is by far the most important area where offenders can make a substantial living from operating illegally.

The rise in the level of prosecutions in 2004 is a reflection of the growth in the number of serious environmental incidents that the Environment Agency investigated. The number of major – so-called category 1 – incidents was 131 in 2004, an increase on the figure for 2003. However, the seriousness of environmental pollution is not fully reflected by the courts. For example, in 2004 although fines totalled £2.3m and 153 firms were fined over £5,000, the average fine against companies was £8,524 (a figure lower than those for 2003 and 2002).

An additional challenge for both SEPA and the Environment Agency will arise from the way in which they respond to their responsibilities under devolution. Obviously SEPA will continue to look to Edinburgh for guidance and funding, and over time it is possible that its strategy and responsibilities will become still more distinct from those of the Environment Agency. Even in Wales with its more limited devolved responsibilities, the relevant part of the Agency is playing a more active role in trying to formulate a sustainable development strategy for the National Assembly. It is not inconceivable that within a relatively short space of time issues of funding and accountability help to force a separation of the English and Welsh parts of the Agency. These points were considered further above in the section on the implications of devolution for environmental policy.

■ The rural conservation agencies

It is the rural conservation agencies that have the greatest experience of country-specific operations and the fragmentation that it entails. The reforms to the Countryside Agency, English Nature, the Countryside Council for Wales and Scottish Natural Heritage are illustrative of the way in which administrative structures influence environmental policy making and government thinking on the environment. The broad remits and size of the different agencies are illustrated in Table 29.4.

All the conservation bodies can trace their origins back to the 1949 National Parks and Access to the Countryside Act. Under the Act two sets of responsibilities were established. The first was for nature conservation. English Nature, for example (and its predecessor, the Nature Conservancy Council), is based on scientific and technical expertise and draws upon an élite tradition of interest in natural history and the preservation of flora and fauna. The other responsibility was for landscape protection and was the responsibility in England of the Countryside Commission, now superseded by the Countryside Agency with a broader remit for rural development.

Thus was born a perhaps unique organisational division amongst public sector bodies in Europe of separating landscape and nature protection. The divide reflects some of the characteristics of British environmentalism. While English Nature might argue that the public should be excluded from nature reserves on scientific grounds, the Countryside Commission (now the Countryside Agency) tended to favour access. But these are not the only differences between the agencies. English Nature has a much greater executive role through its management of national nature reserves. Both organisations, however, are grant-in-aid bodies, i.e. they are funded from public funds.

The reorganisation of the conservation agencies has taken a different path from that of the pollution control bodies. On the one side, predating devolution, there has been a geographical fragmentation. On the other side there are signs of integration or unification of responsibilities amongst the bodies, although it has taken different forms and been played out over different time-frames. For the conservation agencies the functional integration in 1989 in Wales and Scotland (in which landscape and nature were combined in the Countryside Council for Wales and Scottish Natural Heritage) was not followed in England until 2006. The landscape and recreation functions of the Countryside Agency were joined with English Nature (and DEFRA's Rural Delivery Service) to create Natural England. The Countryside Agency's socio-economic responsibilities have been passed on to the Regional Development Agencies and DEFRA. The remaining functions of the Countryside Agency have been reconstituted as the Commission for Rural Communities, a body that is to act as a rural advocate and expert advisor to government. It is not a situation dictated by organisational logic or adherence to explicit environmental principles. What it represents is the current state of play in an organisational and policy framework that has developed in a largely *ad hoc* and pragmatic manner, and is a vivid testimony to the weakness of the statutory environmental bodies. Judgements on the conservation bodies tend to be harsh but it is difficult to

Table 29.4 Responsibilities and sizes of the rural conservation agencies

Name	Key responsibilities	Number of employees	Budget (£m)
English Nature	Nature conservation	876	85
Countryside Agency	Landscape protection, economic and social development in rural England	600	100
Scottish Natural Heritage	Landscape protection and nature conservation	754	61
Countryside Council for Wales	Landscape protection and nature conservation	660	56

Note: Figures are wherever possible for the financial year 2004/5

differ from that of Lowe and Goyder (1983, p. 67) in writing of the predecessors to the current organisations that they 'have small budgets, little power and limited policy-making initiative, and they are politically marginal'.

Devolution seems to have had a positive impact on the funding of the conservation agencies. The Devolved Administrations may be more sympathetic to the resource claims of CCW and SNH; they are after all their own organisations, and in the case of Scotland there is now the power to reshape SNH if thought necessary. In terms of policy development the situation is less clear cut. Both organisations may also find that they have better links to policy makers and the policy community more generally, enjoy higher status and are more able to shape strategy, and there are examples of innovative policy development, such as Tir Gofal, an all-Wales agri-environment scheme launched in 1989. On the other hand, the bodies for England, Wales and Scotland may become more inward-looking and less able to share good practice. There may be much duplication of effort and an inability to develop the high-level scientific expertise that a unified body with all of its resources would be able to bring to bear. Another difficulty that may loom, especially in Wales, is that the conservation bodies will find themselves competing more directly for resources and influence with well-established and highly thought of economic development agencies. Unless the Scottish Parliament and National Assembly for Wales are able to formulate sustainable development strategies that do genuinely bring together economic and environmental interests, there is a danger that the latter could find themselves marginalised over time.

■ Local government and environmental policy

Traditionally, local councils have played a key and wide-ranging role in the UK's system of environmental regulation. They have had statutory responsibilities for waste, air pollution and planning. To this they have added a non-statutory initiative, Local Agenda 21 (LA21), that stems from the Rio Earth Summit in 1992, and which has recently been superseded by a more recent statutory duty to produce a Community Strategy. The fortunes of local government in each of these areas have been inextricably tied up with the thinking and actions

of government in England, Scotland, Wales and Northern Ireland.

Pollution regulation by local authorities

While the Environment Agency is responsible for emissions from industrial processes scheduled under legislation, district and unitary councils in England and Wales are responsible for those from non-scheduled processes. Scottish councils had held similar powers but these were transferred to SEPA. These responsibilities stem principally from the Public Health Act 1936, the Clean Air Acts of 1956 and 1968 and the Environmental Protection Act 1990. Under the legislation, local authorities control emissions of smoke, dust, grit and odour, and, under the Control of Pollution Act 1974, noise.

As we have seen, however, local authorities play a more important role in waste regulation. Until quite recently local authorities collected, disposed of and were responsible for regulation of the waste that was created in their areas. In England, counties remain responsible for waste regulation (Waste Regulation Authorities). (There is a more confused situation in some metropolitan areas where there can be joint responsibility for disposal and regulation, and the different structures of local government in Wales and Scotland also lead to slightly different arrangements.) Under the Environmental Protection Act 1990, responsibility for the collection of household and some commercial and industrial waste is split between the different tiers of government, but the authorities, in this case largely county councils in England, are required to subject these services to private company bids in a process known as compulsory competitive tendering.

Waste management illustrates well the pressures on local government. The EU has set targets for the reuse and recycling of waste and if these targets are not met then the UK government will be subject to fines. Since waste collection is a local government function then responsibility for meeting the targets will depend upon the actions of local government. For 2005/6 the national target is to recycle 25 per cent of household waste, and English authorities look well set to meet that figure, having achieved a figure of nearly 23 per cent in 2004/5. However, headline figures disguise enormous differences in the recycling rates of different councils. For example, the best-performing councils are likely to be found in rural and semi-rural areas of Eastern England and the East Midlands and the best will be recycling over 50 per cent of the waste that they collect. The lowest recycling rates are to be found in northeast England and London where recycling rates can be below 10 per cent.

Local planning

The planning system is one of the most sophisticated mechanisms for environmental regulation, more specifically for controlling and promoting land use development, in Britain. Although planning decisions are made under the broad supervision of the Office of the Deputy Prime Minister (for England), the Scottish Executive and Welsh Assembly Government, councils are responsible for both drawing up plans and making decisions on proposed developments. Planning law grants wide discretion to councils to control and promote land-use planning, including the content of plans, the granting of planning permission, the enforcement of breaches of control and the pursuit of positive planning. This discretion and decentralisation make for both variability and vitality in local planning.

The planning system has been subject to considerable pressure over the past two decades. Through the 1980s and up to the mid-1990s under the Conservative government planning was regarded as a bureaucratic impediment to the operation of the market. Government reforms were therefore designed to reduce the scope of local authority involvement in the planning process and to remove some of the constraints faced by developers in securing planning approval.

From the mid-1990s, the then Conservative government began tentatively to embrace the environmental agenda and curb its deregulatory instincts. Planning was now heralded as a key means of promoting more sustainable development because of its ability to engage with economic issues (i.e. the development of land), social needs (what is appropriate development for particular communities) and the protection of valued environments. The ongoing challenge that has been faced by the Labour government is, to what extent should the planning system constrain the market? The most contentious debates are taking place in the southeast of England. Here there are major pressures for development, an articulate opposition well able to make their views known through the planning system, and a group of councils who are arguing that if the pressures they face for development are not more actively managed then they will become less sustainable. The touchstone around which these debates are taking place is housing.

The government suggest that new housing development should take place as far as possible on brownfield (i.e. previously developed) sites and has set a target of 60 per cent of new housing to be built on such land. The government's strategy dovetails neatly with the thrust of its sustainability thinking: homes that are new or rebuilt on brownfield sites are likely to be close to existing transport networks, services such as shops, and employment, so reducing people's need to travel. The difficulty that rural conservationists face is that even if 60 per cent of new dwellings could be developed on brownfield sites (and for some councils that is an ambitious target) the numbers projected are such that there will have to be considerable building on greenfield sites. The planned number of new houses is considerable: following the Barker Review commissioned by the Treasury and the Office of the Deputy Prime Minister into housing supply, the government has

---

BOX 29.2   IDEAS AND PERSPECTIVES

Key questions for government

1. Does it accept the housing projections and provide homes accordingly (so-called predict and provide) or seek to manage demand?
2. Does it listen to councils in the southeast who wish to lower the projections that central government wishes to impose on them?
3. Should it make more efforts to redirect new building away from the south of England?
4. Once decisions have been made on house numbers and their location, should it promote dispersed development (share out the misery) or concentrate the development in a limited number of new urban centres or the significant growth of existing ones?

proposed that 200,000 new homes should be built in England each year. Here people's perceptions of what is an acceptable level of development will potentially come into conflict with the demands of the market and raise political and policy challenges for government. For example, the Campaign for the Protection of Rural England, a leading conservation pressure group, has calculated that each year the area of countryside lost to development is 21 square miles (equivalent to the size of Southampton) and housing development accounts for about half of this.

In tackling problems of development and under-development across the UK, the Labour government faces challenges that have beset a number of its predecessors. A central issue is how to resolve the perceived tension in the planning system between promoting sustainable development and encouraging development. In the Planning and Compulsory Purchase Act 2004, the government wishes to make planning decisions speedier and more certain in England by amending the current public inquiry system for major projects, replacing the structure plans produced by county councils with Regional Spatial Strategies produced by the eight English regions. District councils will produce Local Development Frameworks (in Wales they are called local development plans) rather than the local plans they currently prepare. Both regional and local documents will be subject to sustainability appraisals and the planning system will also have to contribute to sustainable development. Environmental groups are concerned that the Act makes the planning system less accountable to local people and too sympathetic to economic interests. In Scotland too there have been calls to improve the speed and certainty of plan decision making. There is, however, a different approach from that of England and Wales where the level of scrutiny attached to a proposed development will vary. For example, national decisions, like major roads, will be decided by Scottish executive ministers. Other decisions will be made by local authorities but there are plans to delegate more decisions to planning officers and give less to elected councillors as currently happens.

The government's approach to planning and waste illustrates well a key tension: on the one side when concerned with service delivery in England the government can appear to be highly prescriptive and concerned with cost or the meeting of targets, and on the other hand, government is keen for local authorities to promote sustainable development in its activities. It is to this area of local government work that we now turn.

Local authority initiatives

Finally, despite, or perhaps more accurately because of, the criticism and restrictions to which local government has been subject, it has become increasingly involved in a series of measures by which it can promote the environment and at the same time promote itself not only as 'green' but as an active organ of government. The UNCED Conference at Rio, where much of Agenda 21 (the global environmental agenda for the next century) was predicated upon local action, provided a convenient means by which local government could repackage much of what it was already doing and have a justification for extending its work still further. There is no clear agreement on what the content of an LA21 should be since it should be tailored to local circumstances. However, the internal issues that a local authority should expect to cover include managing and improving its own environmental performance, integrating sustainable development across its activities, and awareness raising and education. In its dealings with the wider community the authority should consult the public on LA21, engage in partnerships with the business and voluntary sectors, and measure and report on local progress towards sustainable development. According to O'Riordan and Voisey (1998a, p. 154) the UK is probably the most advanced nation in taking forward LA21. The Labour government has recognised the considerable potential for local government in the delivery of sustainable development and encouraged the production of LA21 strategies.

O'Riordan and Voisey are not, however, convinced that much beyond rhetoric and the production of documentation is taking place. There are a number of difficulties, including the task of taking the sustainable message to those groups such as business who may not be sympathetic to it; overcoming public indifference or even antagonism to local government; broadening the agenda from the environment to include social and development issues; and having to work with limited resources. A test of central government's commitment to sustainable development will be to see whether it meets local government requests for more powers and resources to deal with Agenda 21. At a time of budgetary constraints, local government finds that it can do little more than carry out its statutory duties, and yet

BOX 29.3	IDEAS AND PERSPECTIVES

Transport Act 2000 includes possibility of road charges

The Act introduced the politically controversial idea of charging for road use. Local authorities will be given the power to charge motorists for driving into cities, the idea being that such charging will help reduce congestion and provide funds for the improvement of public transport. The legislation is only permissive, entitling local authorities to introduce such schemes if they so choose, subject to government approval. Durham introduced a small-scale scheme in 2002 and London's started in early 2003. Other cities, such as Nottingham and Bristol, are expected to adopt charging schemes if that in London is seen to be a success. The AA is sceptical of the idea, pointing out that motorists 'already pay £8 in tax for every £10 they pay on fuel'.

much that it does or wishes to do in the LA21 field is of a non-statutory nature.

In part in recognition of the weakness of LA21 but also to bind local government more closely into its business community and citizens, the Local Government Act 2000 places a duty on councils in England and Wales to prepare a Community Strategy. The purpose of these strategies is to enhance the quality of life of local communities through action to improve their economic, social and environmental well-being, and contribute to the achievement of sustainable development. This duty was reinforced by a significant new power within the Act that provided for local government to 'do anything which they consider is likely to achieve the promotion or improvement of the economic, the social or the environmental well-being of their area'. In other words, local government now has an explicit responsibility to promote sustainable development. If Community Strategies and the duty to promote well-being are to be translated into practice, local government will have to overcome considerable hurdles. These include engaging councillors and senior managers in a new agenda and thinking in a more integrated and less silo-based manner (a difficulty that is also shared with Whitehall).

■ Pressure groups and government: the case of road transport

Road transport debates and protests illustrate well the changing nature of the environmental movement in Britain, how it can help to change the terms of debate and the challenges that government faces in trying to move policy on to a more sustainable footing (Box 29.3).

Environmental groups

According to McCormick (1991, p. 34), 'Britain has the oldest, strongest, best-organized and most widely supported environmental lobby in the world'. The foundations of the lobby were laid in the late nineteenth century with subsequent bursts of growth in environmental groups in the late 1920s, the late 1950s, the early 1970s, and the late 1980s. The 1970s were distinguished from earlier periods both by the rapid growth of existing groups and by the formation of new ones such as Friends of the Earth (formed in the United States in 1969), Greenpeace (formed in Canada in 1972) and Transport 2000. The new groups made a significant impact upon the lobby by highlighting the international nature of many environmental problems, and providing radical analyses of environmental issues which linked them to contemporary social and economic conditions. New tactics also emerged, with Friends of the Earth and Greenpeace adopting vigorous, high-profile campaigns to draw attention to a broad range of threats to the environment (see Table 29.5).

The success of the environmental lobby in increasing its membership, along with a range of other fund-raising activities, has had a positive effect on its finances. With greater income, groups have been able to employ more staff to monitor more accurately government activities, engage in more lobbying and prepare better critiques of official policy. Campaigns are much more sophisticated than they used to be, making still greater use of the media and, for the more radical groups, there has been a greater

Table 29.5 Membership of selected environmental groups (thousands)

	1971	1981	1991	2002
National Trust	278	1,046	2,152	3,000
National Trust for Scotland	37	105	234	260
Royal Society for the Protection of Birds	98	441	852	1,022
World Wide Fund for Nature	12	60	227	320
Greenpeace	–	30	312	221
Friends of the Earth	1	18	111	119
Campaign for the Protection of Rural England	21	29	45	59

reliance on science and legal evidence to support their positions. The emphasis, therefore, has been for the most part on strengthening traditional styles of lobbying.

Greenpeace has confronted a more difficult situation. Unlike the other groups in the table, its membership peaked in the early 1990s and has since gone into decline. Its membership high coincided with a Conservative government that expressed indifference to the environment, major infrastructure proposals and a growing awareness of global environmental issues. Unless some of these conditions can be replicated – and any proposals for new nuclear power stations may be one possibility – then Greenpeace may have to cope with the challenge of managing membership decline or stability. In some countries the nature of the political system is such that Greenpeace can keep its distance from government and still seek to influence debate. In Britain that is more difficult, and now that many of its concerns have become matters of public policy deliberation, partly as a result of its direct action tactics, it has to decide whether the same tactics are required for the formulation and implementation of policy.

Road building protests

One of the most bitterly contested areas of government policy has been that relating to road transport. The controversy it has excited has led to set-piece confrontations around proposed new developments, spawned a new wave of environmental activism and challenged successive governments' commitment to sustainable development.

Many local road improvement schemes will arouse little if any controversy. The road-building schemes that have aroused national attention, notably those at Twyford Down, Newbury and Honiton, are significant because of their scale and their impact on nationally important environments. They have thus become a focus, sometimes at a symbolic level, for the arguments for and against the road-building programme. The M3 protest at Twyford Down began in the mid-1980s and initially involved a classic local protest: concerned residents engaged in conventional campaigning tactics, such as lobbying and high-profile events (e.g. protest walks) in which they worked closely with national groups, notably Friends of the Earth.

As all legal avenues of protest disappeared a new form of protester appeared who was committed to non-violent direct action. The latter drew much of their inspiration from the American group Earth First! and disdained conventional politics as failing to protect the environment. The initially small group occupied part of the road-building site known as the Dongas, an area of deep hollows, and became known as the Dongas Tribe. Faced with overwhelming odds the Dongas Tribe could not hope to stop the building of the road. Nevertheless, their courage and commitment provoked enormous interest and inspired other protests such as that at Newbury. The Twyford Down campaign was also significant in another respect. As Barbara Bryant, a leading activist, has written:

almost for the first time . . . [the media] had witnessed middle-class Conservative voters, retired military men, elected politicians and a younger, less conventional group, coming together in an alliance against the Government's road building campaign.

Bryant (1996), p. 192

While it is important not to overemphasise the extent to which a coalition did exist (there were undoubted tensions between the different groups), it does mark a point at which diverse interests could come together to oppose a common policy.

There are many similarities between the Twyford Down protest and that at Newbury. Once again legal avenues of campaigning had been exhausted, leaving the protesters to try to disrupt and delay the building programme sufficiently so that there might be a rethink of policy by a new government. The protests against the Newbury bypass began in earnest in late 1995 with the establishment of six protest camps. At the height of the campaign in the spring of 1996 this had mushroomed to twenty-nine. Some of the camps were based in trees, others in tunnels, and led to dramatic media coverage of the evictions of protesters as bailiffs brought in cranes and cherry-picking equipment to dislodge them. Once a site has been cleared for a new road it would be a dramatic event for a government to then halt operations.

Transport protests are now commonplace. Reclaim the Streets, an anti-car pressure group, has organised a number of events in London which have brought traffic to a standstill. In 1996 a street party on a stretch of the M41 was attended by some 7,000 people, at which parts of the road were dug up and trees planted (see Jordan, 1998). A central element to the protest movement now is the extent to which the organisers of different groups seek to link their activities and exchange ideas: a move from competing and exclusive organisations to supportive and overlapping disorganisations.

Government policy and road transport

By helping to raise the profile of transport issues, protesters have played a part in creating a climate in which a new agenda can develop. Faced with a massive forecast for increases in traffic, the former Conservative government committed itself to a large road-building programme in the suitably titled 1989 White Paper *Roads for Prosperity* (Cm 693). Within a few years, though, a number of schemes had been dropped or shelved. The reasons for the change in heart are many but, perhaps, three were key. Firstly, the Treasury, desperate to retain a hold on the public finances, had been alarmed at the burgeoning expenditure on roads. Secondly, early in 1994 the government published its strategy on *Sustainable Development* in which, in the cautious language of civil servants, it acknowledged that unlimited traffic growth was incompatible with its environmental commitments. In other words demand would have to be managed, a key argument of the environmental lobby. Thirdly, later in 1994 saw the publication of two key reports on transport. One was by the influential Royal Commission on Environmental Pollution on *Transport and the Environment* in which it expressed its concern at the implication of current policy on health and the environment. It argued for a halving of the road-building programme and a doubling of the real price of petrol over the decade. The other was by the Standing Advisory Committee on Trunk Road Assessment which concluded that new roads can generate or induce new traffic (i.e. that they may not ease congestion).

The Conservatives' cautious embrace of the need to manage road transport was much more fully embraced by the Labour Party. In government Labour has promoted, through its White Paper *A New Deal for Transport*, the idea of an integrated transport policy to fight congestion and pollution. Essentially, integration means bringing together different types of transport, and ensuring that transport is linked to other policies such as land-use planning. Most attention has focused on three areas: bus quality partnerships to improve services; a strategic rail authority to oversee the privatised companies; and local transport plans. These plans, backed up by the Transport Act 2000, will allow councils to introduce charges on some trunk roads and on trunk road bridges more than 600 metres long. The money raised from such charges would then be invested in public transport improvements. The proposals, though modest given the scale of the traffic problem, and voluntary, have aroused enormous controversy.

Some indication of the pressures on the government came to a head in the second half of 2000. As we have seen, up until this time the government's transport policy had been reasonably ambitious with a cut in the road-building programme and more money for public transport. It was encapsulated in the 1998 White Paper on transport that promised 'radical change'. The government, though, was becoming increasingly sensitive to the charge that it was anti-car or anti-driver, and an indication of the shift in policy came in July 2000 when the government launched its much-heralded ten-year plan for transport. It promised investments of over £180 billion but a third of the money was to go on motorways and trunk roads, so heralding something of a renaissance in road building. However, the ten-year plan fails to address the fundamental transport problems facing the UK – an over-reliance on the car and the growth in road traffic. Shortly after the publication of the ten-year plan, the government was shocked by the widespread protests in the early autumn of 2000 led by lorry drivers and farmers concerned at the increase in costs of vehicle fuel. The support the protests gathered heightened unease within government that it was alienating drivers, a potentially important part of the electorate. In his November 2000 pre-budget report the Chancellor of the Exchequer announced cuts in fuel and vehicle excise duty. Ever since, the government has been conscious that it may be open to the charge that it is over-taxing the motorist.

The wider ramifications of the pressure that Labour perceives on transport are apparent. It is sensitive to the charge that it is anti-car, perhaps one reason why it is making implementation of car reduction policies the responsibility of local and not central government. It may also help us to understand why the government has become more cautious about promoting green taxes for transport. Government policy is now focused on reducing the impacts of the car rather than reducing the need to drive. The difficulties that the Labour government has encountered in tackling car use have spilled over into, and coloured, the government's approach to climate change and energy policy.

■ Climate change and energy policy

Climate change moved to the forefront of international environmental politics with the signing of the Kyoto Protocol in 1997. Industrialised nations, including the European Union and Japan (but not the USA), approved a plan to cut emissions of gases linked to global warming to 5.2 per cent below 1990 levels by 2012. The UK, however, has set itself more stringent targets and is committed to reducing its 1990 greenhouse gas emissions by 12.5 per cent by 2010 (and is on course to do so). At the 2001 general election a stronger manifesto commitment was made to cut carbon dioxide emissions by 20 per cent by 2010. This commitment was later reduced to an aspiration (and looks unlikely to be met, with government figures suggesting that reductions of 15–18 per cent by 2020 are more achievable (DEFRA, 2006)) and the target now is to achieve a 60 per cent reduction by 2050 (and this figure too is in some doubt).

Debates on climate change and energy policy send out numerous mixed messages. While the science of climate change has become ever more certain, governments across the globe have found that tackling the causes of climate change have questioned the basis of fundamental policies and the behaviour of consumers, and thus policies may have

Climate change possibly explains the freak tornado which hit Birmingham in July 2005
Source: PA Wire / Empics

high political costs. For Tony Blair climate change has provided the opportunity to lead international opinion, especially in the UK's role as President of the G8 and of the EU in 2005. Unfortunately the government's efforts at global leadership were undermined by data showing that Britain was finding it difficult to reduce its carbon emissions. Climate change debate in the UK has also proved a mixed blessing for environment groups, as they are now expected to play an increasing part in devising solutions to deep-rooted problems and not simply to raise awareness of the problems.

Nevertheless, there is considerable common ground between groups and government. The government has a target of a 20 per cent reduction in CO_2 emissions by 2010 and commitment to an EU-wide greenhouse gas reduction target of 30 per cent by 2020. The Labour government in its Presidencies of the EU and G8 sought to promote climate change as an international priority. In a speech on 14 September 2004 Tony Blair told his audience of business people that what 'I believe to be the world's greatest environmental challenge [is] climate change.' Finally, the government has developed policies to help the developing world adapt to climate change. All of these commitments are endorsed by environmental groups. The difficulty is in believing that the policies and government commitment are themselves delivering change sufficiently rapidly. In an interesting switch in policy responsibility, government is now saying to environmental groups that policy failures cannot simply be blamed on government and that groups must accept their share of responsibility. One key failing that government is laying at the doors of environment groups is an inability sufficiently to communicate to the public the dangers of climate change. The environmental movement has in part accepted the veracity of the argument and has responded by forming in 2005 a new body, Stop Climate Chaos. This draws together influential environmental groups such as Friends of the Earth, Greenpeace and WWF and development organisations like Oxfam. In explaining the reasoning behind the formation of Stop Climate Chaos, its Director, Asok Sinha, pointed out that 'Individual organizations have done their best, running very good climate or energy campaigns. But the pressure applied didn't bring about the desired changes in policy. Business as usual in terms of campaigning was just not working.' Stop Climate Chaos is modelled on Make Poverty History and Jubilee 2000 and aims to turn climate change from an envir-onmental issue into a moral one (in the way in which poverty and international debt relief have been) so that government can feel that the public wants it to take difficult decisions.

Whether groups and government agree over the outcome of difficult decisions in the area of environmental policy is likely to become an increasingly moot point. In a high-profile energy White Paper published in 2003 (Department of Trade and Industry, 2003), the government managed to secure a wide-ranging consensus embracing environmental groups, the business community and the renewables industry because it promoted a low-carbon energy economy. For the very first time environmental issues, and specifically climate change, were at the core of energy policy, along with maintaining reliable supplies, promoting competition and ensuring affordable domestic energy. An indication of how climate change had moved to the fore of policy making was the government's commitment to a 60 per cent reduction in CO_2 emissions (from 1990 levels) by 2050, to be achieved by greater energy efficiency, combined heat and power (CHP) projects and renewable energy. To environmental groups such as Greenpeace and Friends of the Earth, the White Paper also appeared to signal the demise of the nuclear industry, since it noted that the 'economics of nuclear power makes it an unattractive option for new generating capacity'. One of the most glaring weaknesses of the White Paper was in its treatment of transport. Carbon emissions from road transport had grown by 10 per cent between 1990 and 2000 and could rise by another 9 per cent by 2010, and there is little to suggest how the government might curb the growth in road transport. The matter has not been helped by the Chancellor's reluctance in recent budgets to increase the levy (tax) on fuel above the rate of inflation to give motorists a clear price signal on car use. More worrying still, however, is the case of international air travel (which is not covered by national targets set under the Kyoto Protocol). Carbon dioxide emissions from flights using UK airports could double by 2020 and cancel out the CO_2 savings the government is hoping to make in all other sectors, and the government is reluctant to intervene to discourage air travel.

By the autumn of 2005 it was becoming clear that the government was concerned that its energy policy was being undermined by internal and external factors. Within government there was increasing concern about the growing reliance on sourcing energy from potentially unstable regions of the world, recognition that energy consumption was continuing to grow, that energy efficiency measures were not delivering, and that renewable energy was not making the contribution to energy supply that had been hoped for. In essence, the argument emerging from government was that by 2020 the UK will have decommissioned coal and nuclear plants that together generate over 30 per cent of today's electricity supply. Renewable energy, it was claimed, was incapable of meeting the energy shortfall. In December 2005 Tony Blair announced the terms of reference for a major review of energy policy that put nuclear energy back on the agenda as a means of closing the energy gap (caused by decommissioning existing power stations) and of helping to meet Britain's CO_2 emission reduction targets. Interestingly,

the inclusion of nuclear power in the energy mix was justified on environmental grounds. Malcolm Wicks, the Energy Minister, has argued 'I want as many people as possible to realise it ain't going to be easy to meet our climate change targets. We need a huge step-change to save the planet.' He continued: 'The environmental lobby should at least consider the possibility that the most effective way for energy supply to help us through climate change is nuclear, rather than thinking being green is anti-nuclear' (quoted in *The Guardian*, 23 January 2006). Wicks may be rather optimistic in his hope that environmental groups will support nuclear power. More likely is that any government commitment to nuclear energy will reinvigorate the environmental movement, remove the current mood of introspection and distance groups from government.

BOX 29.4   BRITAIN IN CONTEXT

Shaping Britain's environmental policies

Much of Britain's environmental policy is shaped at the international level, notably because of the key role that the European Union plays. Traditionally Britain has been reluctant to embrace EU environmental initiatives, for example, seeking to water or slow down the drafting of key European directives on Environmental Impact Assessment or Bathing Waters. The British position reached its peak with the Conservative governments of the 1980s and was shaped by a long-standing antipathy towards Europe and a sense that Britain's environment was already well protected and so had little to benefit from engagement with Europe.

Over time, though, it became increasingly apparent that Britain's environment, like that of many of its neighbours, was suffering from long-term degradation and that British insularity might not be the virtue that some had proclaimed. With the election of the Labour government in 1997 there was also a new-found willingness to engage positively with European environmental debates. As UK government has moved from margin to mainstream in discussions of Europe's future there have also been efforts to exercise leadership, notably in relation to climate change.

Whilst Britain has recognised the need for action at the international level to tackle climate change, two of its traditional allies – Australia and the USA – have been much more circumspect. So, as part of the EU, Britain was one of the first countries to sign up to the Kyoto Protocol of 1997. The Protocol sets legally binding targets and a timetable for emission reductions. After initially signing the Protocol, the Australian government in 2002 then rejected it because, according to Prime Minister Howard, 'It is not in Australia's interests to ratify. The Protocol would cost us jobs and damage our industry.' Australia is the world's largest exporter of coal, and burning coal makes a significant contribution to carbon dioxide levels, the main greenhouse gas targeted under the Protocol. The USA, meanwhile, is the largest producer of greenhouse gases in the world and has been a long-standing opponent to Kyoto. It, too, believes that signing the Protocol is not in its national interest as the costs would be too high for its industry, so making it uncompetitive in global markets. Britain, in contrast, over the last thirty years or more has witnessed a dramatic decline in its coal industry (and its use as a source of power) and traditional heavy industrial base. It, therefore, engages with the international politics of climate change from a different perspective.

Environmentalists despair at the failure of George W. Bush to recognise the reality of global warming
Source: Copyright © Chris Riddell. From *The Observer*, 3 July 2005. Reproduced with permission from Guardian Newspapers Limited

Chapter summary

This chapter began by pointing out the forces that make environmental policy a dynamic and changing area. The impact of Europe on the content of British environmental policy and on the policy-making process were then described. It was noted that there has been a considerable shift in thinking on the environment so that it now encompasses a very broad area under the term sustainable development. The role of key organisations in central government was set out and the implications of devolution of responsibilities to Cardiff and Edinburgh explored. The part that local government plays in environmental protection and more generally sustainable development was discussed. Finally, the role of pressure groups was outlined and how they have contributed to the road transport and energy debates and how in turn government policy has changed. The chapter shows that issues related to sustainable development are among the most challenging that any government can face. Not only do they involve all sections of society but also different levels of government. Moreover, a more sustainable society is a long-term goal but policies to achieve that goal often seem to involve short-term political costs. Little wonder, then, that at present policies do not seem to match up to the rhetoric or the scale of the challenge.

Discussion points

■ What is the appropriate contribution of Europe, national government and the devolved administrations to environmental policy?

■ Is sustainable development a meaningful term?

■ Should we try to integrate environmental policy making and its implementation or fragment it among geographically and functionally specialised organisations?

Further reading

The best book on the topic is that by Neil Carter (2001). Two other good general-purpose books on environmental policy and politics are those by Gray (1995) and Connelly and Smith (1999). The former is an edited book with a wide-ranging collection of papers, while the latter is an informative and lively account of contemporary environmental politics. For those interested in studying further how British environmental policy has been shaped by decisions in Europe, the book by Lowe and Ward (1998a) is a very good place to start. One of the better books by an environmental activist with insights into the policy process is that by Bryant (1996). There are now a number of good environmental websites. Aside from the media, these prove a good means of keeping up to date with what is a fast-changing policy area.

References

Blowers, A. (1987) 'Transition or transformation? Environmental policy under Thatcher', *Public Administration*, Vol. 65, No. 3, pp. 277–94.

Bryant, B. (1996) *Twyford Down: Roads, Campaigning and Environmental Law* (E. and F. N. Spon).

Carter, N. (2001) *The Politics of the Environment: Ideas, Activism, Policy* (Cambridge University Press).

Cm 1200 (1990) *This Common Inheritance* (HMSO).

Cm 2426 (1994) *Sustainable Development: The UK Strategy* (HMSO).

Cm 2428 (1994) *Biodiversity: The UK Action Plan* (HMSO).

Cm 4345 (1999) *A Better Quality of Life: A Strategy for Sustainable Development for the United Kingdom* (The Stationery Office).

Cmnd 4506 (1970) *The Reorganisation of Central Government* (HMSO).

Commission of the European Communities (1992) *Towards Sustainability: The Fifth Environmental Action Programme* (CEC).

Connelly, J. and Smith, G. (1999) *Politics and the Environment* (Routledge).

DEFRA (Department for Environment, Food and Rural Affairs) (2001a) *2001 survey of public attitudes to quality of life and to the environment*, at www.defra.gov.uk/environment/statistics/pubatt/download/pdf/survey2001.pdf

DEFRA (Department for Environment, Food and Rural Affairs) (2001b) *Resource use and efficiency of the UK economy*, available on www.defra.gov.uk/environment/statistics/des/waste/research/index.htm

DEFRA (Department for Environment, Food and Rural Affairs) (2002) *Resource Use and Efficiency of the UK Economy*. A report by the Wuppertal Institute, London (DEFRA).

DEFRA (Department for Environment, Food and Rural Affairs) (2004) *Taking it on. Developing UK sustainable development strategy together*, a Consultation Paper (DEFRA).

DEFRA (Department for Environment, Food and Rural Affairs) (2005a) *Securing the Future. Delivering the UK sustainable development strategy*, Cm 6467 (HMSO).

DEFRA (Department for Environment, Food and Rural Affairs) (2005b) *One Future – Different Paths. The UK's shared framework for sustainable development* (HMSO).

DEFRA (Department for Environment, Food and Rural Affairs) (2006) *Climate Change. The UK Programme 2006* (HMSO).

(DTI) Department of Trade and Industry (2003) *Energy White Paper: Our Energy Future – Creating a Low Carbon Economy* (HMSO).

Environment Agency (2005) *Doing the Right Thing: Spotlight on Business Environmental Performance 2004*, <www.publications.environment-agency.gov.uk/pdf/GEHO0706BLBM-e-e.pdf> (HMSO)

Gray, T. (ed.) (1995) *UK Environmental Policy in the 1990s* (Macmillan).

Gummer, J. (1994) 'Europe, what next? Environment, policy and the Community', speech to the ERM Environment Forum organised by the Green Alliance.

House of Commons Environmental Audit Committee (1998) *The Greening Government Initiative*, Vol. 1 (The Stationery Office).

House of Commons Environmental Audit Committee (2004) *The Sustainable Development Strategy: Illusion or Reality?*, Vol. 1 (The Stationery Office).

Jordan, A. (2005) *The Europeanisation of British Environmental Policy* (2nd edn) (Earthscan).

Jordan, J. (1998) 'The art of necessity: the subversive imagination of anti-road protest and Reclaim the Streets', in G. McKay (ed.), *DiY Culture: Party and Protest in Nineties Britain* (Verso).

Lowe, P. and Flynn, A. (1989) 'Environmental politics and policy in the 1980s', in J. Mohan (ed.), *The Political Geography of Contemporary Britain* (Macmillan).

Lowe, P. and Goyder, J. (1983) *Environmental Groups in Politics* (Allen & Unwin).

Lowe, P. and Ward, S. (eds) (1998a) *British Environmental Policy and Europe* (Routledge).

Lowe, P. and Ward, S. (1998b) 'Britain in Europe: themes and issues in national environmental policy', in P. Lowe and S. Ward (eds), *British Environmental Policy and Europe* (Routledge).

McCormick, J. (1991) *British Politics and the Environment* (Earthscan).

Ministerie van Volkshuisvesting Ruimtelkijke Ordening en Milieubeheer (VROM) (Ministry of Housing, Physical Planning and the Environment) (1998) *National Environmental Policy Plan 3* (VROM).

O'Riordan, T. and Voisey, H. (eds) (1998a) *The Transition to Sustainability: the Politics of Agenda 21 in Europe* (Earthscan).

O'Riordan, T. and Voisey, H. (1998b) 'Editorial introduction', in T. O'Riordan and H. Voisey (eds), *The Transition to Sustainability: the Politics of Agenda 21 in Europe* (Earthscan).

Sharp, R. (1998) 'Responding to Europeanisation: a governmental perspective', in P. Lowe and S. Ward (eds), *British Environmental Policy and Europe* (Routledge).

Scottish Office (1999) *Down to Earth – a Scottish perspective on sustainable development*, February 1999 (The Scottish Office Sustainable Development Team).

Scottish Executive (2005) *Choosing Our Future: Scotland's Sustainable Development Strategy* (Scottish Executive Publications).

Voisey, H. and O'Riordan, T. (1998) 'Sustainable development: the UK national approach', in T. O'Riordan and H. Voisey (eds), *The Transition to Sustainability: the Politics of Agenda 21 in Europe* (Earthscan).

VROM (1998) (Ministry of Housing, Spatial Planning and the Environment) (1998) *The Third National Environmental Policy Plan* (NEPP3) (The Hague, VROM).

Welsh Assembly Government (2004) *Starting to Live Differently: The sustainable development scheme of the National Assembly for Wales* (Welsh Assembly Government).

World Commission on Environment and Development (1987) *Our Common Future* (Oxford University Press).

Useful websites

Countryside Agency:
http://www.countryside.gov.uk/index.htm
Countryside Council for Wales:
http://www.ccw.gov.uk
Department for Environment, Food and Rural Affairs:
http://www.defra.gov.uk/
English Nature: http://www.english-nature.org.uk/
Environment Agency:
http://www.environment-agency.gov.uk/
Friends of the Earth: http://www.foe.co.uk/
Greenpeace: http://www.greenpeace.org.uk/
Scottish Environmental Protection Agency:
http://www.sepa.org.uk/
Scottish Executive:
http://www.scotland.gov.uk/topics/?pageid=1
Scottish Natural Heritage: http://snh.org.uk
Welsh Assembly Government:
http://new.wales.gov.uk/topics/sustainable
development/?lang=en

CHAPTER 30

Northern Ireland

Jonathan Tonge

Learning objectives

■ To explore why conflict developed in Northern Ireland. How does history shape today's politics?

■ To assess which explanation of the political problem is the most convincing. Is Northern Ireland an arena of ethnic conflict?

■ To examine what beliefs are held by the political parties. Is there much common ground?

■ To understand why a peace process developed during the 1990s. Did governments, parties or paramilitary groups change their political stances?

■ To assess the prospects for settled devolved government in Northern Ireland, following the ending of armed conflict.

Stormont, Belfast, site of controversial devolved government until 1972 and from 1999–2002
Source: Shout / Alamy

Introduction

The politics of Northern Ireland is based on what at times has appeared to be an intractable problem. The province contains a divided population, split between two main groupings holding different loyalties and identities. The majority of the population in Northern Ireland, a minority in the entire island of Ireland, regard themselves as British. Most wish that Northern Ireland should remain part of the United Kingdom. A sizeable minority within Northern Ireland regard themselves as Irish, and many among this minority would prefer to see the island of Ireland united eventually under a single, Irish authority. As a minimum, this minority advocates a substantial 'Irish dimension' to the governance of Northern Ireland. The central element (although other dimensions were apparent and large numbers of civilians were killed) of the bloodiest conflict in western Europe since the Second World War was the battle for a united independent Ireland waged by the Irish Republican Army (IRA) against British forces, comprising the Army and police, which resisted the challenge to Northern Ireland's place in the United Kingdom. This 'war' persisted from 1970 until 1997.

In 1998, sufficient common ground was found to reach a political accord, the Good Friday Agreement, following almost three decades of violence which arguably had threatened the existence of Northern Ireland. However, the agreement encountered numerous problems. Although one conflict – that of Irish republicans versus the British state – has subsided, the old problem of sectarian tension between Protestants and Catholics remains evident in a society where segregation has increased on some measures.

The broad division between British Unionists and Irish nationalists (see Box 30.1 for definitions of these terms) is reinforced by a religious divide. Unionists are mainly Protestant, while nationalists are predominantly Catholic. Protestants form 45 per cent of the population of Northern Ireland, whilst Catholics comprise 41 per cent. In Scotland and Wales, debates over national identity are resolved through constitutional politics. In Northern Ireland, paramilitary and military solutions were also attempted. Competing explanations of the nature of the Northern Ireland exist. They reflect disputes over the historical origins of the problem and the extent to which the minority nationalist community suffered social, economic and political discrimination.

BOX 30.1 | **FACT**

Important political terms in Northern Ireland

- *Unionist*: British supporter of the political Union of Great Britain and Northern Ireland.
- *Loyalist*: Another term for unionist, although the term loyalist tends to be used to describe working-class unionists, who may emphasise loyalty to certain symbols of Britishness, such as the Crown, the Ulster flag, or the Protestant Faith.
- *Nationalist*: Irish supporter of a united, independent Ireland. The term is generally used to describe those who support peaceful assertions of Irish identity and non-violent political change.
- *Republican*: Again, an Irish supporter of a united, independent Ireland, although the term republican is usually used to describe more militant supporters of progress towards such a goal.

■ The development of Northern Ireland

Historical quarrels

From the eleventh to the eighteenth century, Ireland existed under loose British colonial rule (**colonialism**). The origins of modern problems lay with the conflict between Planter and Gael in the early seventeenth century. The latter were Irish natives, displaced by Scottish Presbyterians undertaking the Plantation of Ulster, the nine-county province in the northeastern quarter of the island. Whilst the Act of Union in 1801 consolidated British sovereignty, Irish nationalism increased after the famine of the 1830s to 1850s. In response, the British government introduced a trio of Home Rule Bills from 1886, designed to provide limited autonomy for Ireland. Each Bill was strenuously opposed by Protestants in Ulster, the descendants of the original Planters. Unyielding in their determination to retain their British Pro-testant identity, they argued that home rule would mean Rome rule. With the overwhelming majority of the native population Catholic, Protestants feared absorption within an increasingly independent Ireland dominated by the Roman Catholic Church. In the south, nationalist sentiment for an independent Ireland increased after the British government executed several leaders of the 1916 Easter Rising, a rebellion against British rule led by the organisation which became known as the IRA.

Division

Compromise provided a settlement, but not a solution. The Government of Ireland Act 1920 divided the country in an attempt to satisfy the desires of both identities. A twenty-six-county state was created in the south, later to become the Republic of Ireland. This was ruled by a parliament in Dublin, which by 1949 was independent. In the northeastern corner of the island, six of the nine counties of the ancient province of Ulster were incorporated into the new administrative unit of Northern Ireland. Exclusion of the remaining three counties, each with a high Catholic population, guaranteed Protestants a substantial majority in the new political unit.

From its outset, Northern Ireland was an insecure state, persistently under threat, real or imagined. Internal dissent came from a dissident Catholic nationalist minority, amounting to one-third of the population. They resented the creation of what they saw as an artificial state, devoid of geographical, historical or political logic. External threats came from the embryonic Irish state in the south. This state adopted a constitution, which, from 1937 until the Good Friday Agreement of 1998, laid claim to Northern Ireland, insisting that the national territory consisted of 'the whole island of Ireland, its islands and the territorial seas'.

Unionist control and reaction

Unionists attempted to secure their statelet through security measures. As early as 1922, a Special Powers Act was enacted, providing the overwhelmingly Protestant security forces in Northern Ireland with vast, arbitrary powers. Although designed to reflect the population balance, the police force, the Royal Ulster Constabulary, averaged only 10 per cent Catholic membership. The auxiliary police force, the B Specials, was exclusively Protestant. Discrimination against Catholics was common, although the amount is disputed. Many Catholics felt alienated by the political system as the Unionist Party held power for fifty years and Unionists controlled 85 per cent of councils, a dominance increased through the process of **gerrymandering**, in which electoral boundaries were devised to maximise Unionist successes.

In an attempt to challenge inequalities, the Northern Ireland Civil Rights Association (NICRA) was formed in 1967. Its demands were:

1. one man, one vote;

2. the end of gerrymandering;

3. legislation against discrimination;

4. introduction of a points system in housing allocations;

5. repeal of the Special Powers Act;

6. disbandment of the B Specials.

Civil rights protests encountered a violent response from the police and loyalists. The moderate Prime Minister of Northern Ireland, Terence O'Neill, was outflanked by hardline Protestant opposition and resigned. Sectarian rioting in summer 1969 led the British government to send in troops to restore order. For a brief 'honeymoon' period, the British Army was welcomed by Catholics. As relations declined, the Irish Republican Army (IRA) revived, attempting through violence to remove the British presence from Ireland. Twenty-five years of conflict followed, with little prospect of resolution until a peace process developed by the mid-1990s, which led to the abandonment of the IRA's armed campaign.

■ Paramilitary violence

The IRA had survived in various forms since the division of Ireland, continuing to launch occasional armed actions for a united Ireland, most visibly, if entirely unsuccessfully, in its 1956–62 border campaign. At the end of that campaign, the organisation was moribund and some within the IRA argued for more left-wing social agitation rather than militarism. The IRA split in 1970 over whether to have mainly peaceful participatory politics or continue with some form of armed struggle. Those favouring the latter formed the Provisional IRA. Members of the new organisation rejected what they saw as the Marxist drift of the IRA of the 1960s. Instead, the Provisional IRA believed in traditional physical force republicanism. This group argued that Catholics in Northern Ireland had been left 'defenceless' against loyalist attacks in the riots of 1969. The Provisionals argued that the British Army had been sent to Northern Ireland to shore up a discriminatory unionist regime. Unionist rule had to be ended and British sovereignty over Northern Ireland also had to go. By 1971, the Provisional IRA had begun to attack the Army and police.

A combination of IRA violence and incompetent or brutal actions of the British Army, including curfews, the introduction of internment (detention without trial) and 'Bloody Sunday', in which the British Army killed 14 civilians, soured relations between the British Army and Catholic population. The British Army, Royal Ulster Constabulary and Ulster Defence Regiment were the main targets

Table 30.1 Deaths arising from 'the Troubles', 1969–97

British Army	445
Royal Ulster Constabulary	201
RUC Reserve	102
Ulster Defence Regiment	197
Royal Irish Regiment	9
Civilians	2,372
Total	3,326

Note: 'Civilians' includes members of paramilitary organisations.
Source: Adapted from Royal Ulster Constabulary (1999) *Royal Ulster Constabulary Chief Constable's Report, 1999.* © Crown Copyright 1999. Crown copyright material is produced with permission of the Controller of Her Majesty's Stationery Office (HMSO)

of the most sustained campaign in the history of the IRA.

The IRA's 'long war' soon replaced its initial belief that a military campaign would enforce an early British withdrawal. The British government attempted to portray IRA members as common criminals. Paramilitary prisoners were no longer treated as prisoners of war. This cessation of special category status led to the republican hunger strikes of 1980–1, in which ten prisoners died. The IRA's military campaign was insufficient to end British rule in Northern Ireland, but it was also difficult to impose an outright military defeat on the IRA. The 'Troubles' claimed over 3,000 victims, mainly civilians (see Table 30.1).

Nearly 60 per cent of deaths were attributable to republican paramilitaries (Darby, 1994). Loyalist paramilitary organisations, namely the Ulster Volunteer Force, Red Hand Commando, Ulster Defence Association and Ulster Freedom Fighters, also carried out numerous killings, many amounting to random assassinations of Catholics. The RUC and the British Army were responsible for a significant number of deaths.

■ Explanations of the problem

Part of the difficulty in finding solutions to the problems of Northern Ireland lay in the lack of agreement over the causes of conflict. Four main competing explanations emerged.

Ethnic or ethno-national explanations

Ethno-national arguments provide the most orthodox modern explanation of the Northern Ireland problem. Two competing ethnic groups want their 'state to be ruled by their nation' (McGarry and O'Leary, 1995, p. 354). Many nationalists see themselves as Irish, associating with the cultural traditions, history and religion of the population of the Irish Republic. As such, nationalists demand, as a minimum, a substantial Irish dimension to political arrangements. Most Unionists see themselves as British and wish to remain so, seeking political arrangements designed to bolster Northern Ireland's place within the United Kingdom (Tables 30.2 and 30.3). They assert their British identity and believe that they have much in common with the people of the British mainland. Northern Ireland's ethnic divisions are reinforced by educational segregation and a low rate of 'mixed' marriages between Catholics and Protestants.

Critics of ethnic conflict explanations argue that identities can change. An increasing number identify

Table 30.2 Preferred long-term policy for Northern Ireland, 2004

Policy	% Protestants	% Catholics
Remain in UK	85	24
United Ireland	5	47
Independent Northern Ireland	6	15
Other	1	3
Don't know	3	11

Source: From ARK (2005) *Northern Ireland Life and Times Survey, 2004* (www.ark.ac.uk/nilt). Reproduced with permission of ARK social and political archive

Table 30.3 Primary national identity in Northern Ireland, 2004

Identity	% Protestants	% Catholics
British	74	12
Irish	2	61
Northern Irish	17	25
Ulster	5	0
Other/Don't know	2	2

Source: From ARK (2005) *Northern Ireland Life and Times Survey, 2004* (www.ark.ac.uk/nilt). Reproduced with permission of ARK social and political archive

themselves as 'Northern Irish' rather than exclusively British or Irish. Perceptions of the conflict as ethno-national may lead to solutions entrenching ethnic blocs through their formal recognition in power-sharing arrangements. The 1998 Good Friday Agreement (see below) was based upon an ethno-national interpretation of the problem.

Colonial explanations

Arguments that Northern Ireland is Britain's last colony are now rare. Traditionally, such views were expressed by Irish republicans, although they found an occasional voice in academia (Miller, 1998). Originally, colonial theories were linked to ideas of imperialism. The British government was seen as exploiting Northern Ireland for financial benefit. Given the cost of the British presence, these arguments have disappeared. Critics of colonial and imperial arguments point to the conditional basis of Britain's claim to Northern Ireland, based on the consent of its people. The British government insists it has 'no selfish, strategic or economic interest' in Northern Ireland. It claims that partition is an acknowledgement of the reality of divisions on the island, not an assertion of British self-interest. The Secretary of State for Northern Ireland can act as a colonial governor by, for example, suspending the Northern Ireland Assembly, but such acts are undertaken reluctantly by British governments when local political agreement is impossible, as has generally been the case in the history of Northern Ireland.

Religious or ethno-religious explanations

When sectarianism was rife during the early years of the Troubles, it was common to perceive the Northern Ireland problem in terms of two warring religious communities. As people fled from areas increasingly dominated by members of the 'other' religion, perceptions of inter-communal conflict grew. Sectarianism persists, but the killings in Northern Ireland have not occurred because of theological differences between Catholics and Protestants. The conflict was never a holy war over matters such as the virgin birth. Political problems remain despite a reduction in the numbers identifying themselves as members of either religion. Nonetheless, religion is still an important marker and sectarian conflict persists. Thus Bruce's argument (1986, p. 249) continues to be supported by some:

The Northern Ireland conflict is a religious conflict. Economic and social differences are also crucial, but it was the fact that the competing populations in Ireland adhered and still adhere to competing religious traditions which has given the conflict its enduring and intractable quality.

Economic factors

Economic explanations of the problem centre on the impact of inequalities endured by the working-class loyalist and nationalist populations in Northern Ireland, whose deprivation means that they may have little stake in élite-level political accommodations such as the Good Friday Agreement. Despite political reforms and workforce monitoring, unemployment among Catholics remains twice as high as that found among Protestants. Nationalist deprivation and the discrimination endured by that community fuelled the rebirth of the IRA in the 1970s. Nowadays, working-class Protestants also claim to be the victims of deprivation and have protested against recent perceived concessions to nationalists. Economic explanations are subject to criticism. Variations in levels of unemployment may be attributable to skills differentials, rather than discrimination. Identity may be more important than discrimination. Identity may be more important than wealth or status. Economic parity might have only a marginal impact on the differences in constitutional aspirations held by Unionists and nationalists.

■ The political parties: the rise of the Democratic Unionist Party and Sinn Fein

The main political parties in Northern Ireland are divided into two main groupings, Unionist and nationalist. Unionist parties attract almost exclusively Protestant support; nationalist parties gain their support from Catholics. Unionist parties have as their central cause the maintenance of Northern Ireland's position within the United Kingdom. They believe in the legitimacy of Northern Ireland as a distinct political, economic and cultural entity. Unionist parties prefer cross-border activity to be located in the economic rather than the political sphere.

Although Unionists remain the majority, the total vote for the two nationalist parties in Northern

Table 30.4 Election results in Northern Ireland since 1997

Election	First preference party vote share (%)			
	DUP	UUP	SF	SDLP
Pre-GFA				
1997 Westminster	13.6	32.7	16.1	24.1
1997 Council	15.6	27.9	16.9	20.7
Post-GFA				
1998 Assembly	18.1	21.3	17.6	22.0
1999 European	28.4	17.6	17.4	28.2
2001 Westminster	22.5	26.8	21.7	21.0
2001 Council	21.4	22.9	20.7	19.4
2003 Assembly	25.7	22.7	23.5	17.0
2004 European	31.9	16.5	26.3	15.9
2005 Westminster	33.7	17.7	24.3	17.5
2005 Council	29.6	18.0	23.2	17.4

Ireland has been growing, now reaching over 40 per cent. Recent election results are shown in Table 30.4. Since the Good Friday Agreement (GFA), there has been a rapid growth in support for the Democratic Unionist Party (DUP).

Founded in 1971, the DUP has been led throughout its existence by the Reverend Ian Paisley. Many within the party fuse politics and the Free Presbyterian religion. Support for the DUP is much more widely based than this fundamentalist group. The DUP offers strident forms of political and cultural unionism, based upon expressions of Protestant Britishness. The DUP opposed the 1998 Good Friday Agreement (GFA) as a potential sell-out of the Union and claimed it was part of a process of concessions to republicans. As confidence in the Agreement among Protestants collapsed, the party's fortunes soared. The DUP supports devolved government and power sharing for Northern Ireland, but refused to share power with Sinn Fein pending fully verifiable decommissioning of the weapons of the IRA. The DUP opposed the early release of paramilitary prisoners and changes to policing which arose from the GFA.

The DUP's electoral gains have been at the expense of the Ulster Unionist Party (UUP) which had been the dominant party electorally in Northern Ireland since the formation of the state. Traditionally regarded as more moderate than the DUP, the pro-GFA leadership of the UUP had to contend with internal party divisions and increasing disenchantment with the GFA. The UUP's eclipse was highlighted in 2005 when the party leader, David Trimble, lost his Westminster seat. Trimble's replacement, Sir Reg Empey, faces an uphill task in reviving the party.

To most non-Unionists, the peace and political processes were the end game of Gerry Adams's strategy of leading the IRA away from violence, climaxed by the IRA's formal abandonment of its armed campaign in 2005, well short of a united Ireland. Many Unionists were more wary, seeing the IRA's approach as tactical. These Unionists continued to be unimpressed by their own apparent constitutional victory in keeping Northern Ireland in the United Kingdom. Opposition to the agreement and to the UUP's supposed 'pushover unionism', involving gains for nationalists, became a useful marketing device for the DUP. The party perceived the replacement of the overwhelmingly Protestant Royal Ulster Constabulary by the Police Service of Northern

BIOGRAPHY

Ian Paisley (1926–)

Unchallenged leader of the DUP, the Reverend Ian Paisley has been MP for North Antrim since 1970 and an MEP since 1979. Paisley founded his political party and his Church. Although often criticised as outdated, Paisley remains the most popular political figure in Northern Ireland. Regarded as a demagogue by detractors, Paisley is seen by some supporters as a leader 'chosen by God to protect Ulster' (Connolly, 1990, p. 104). Unyielding in opposition to Irish republicanism, Paisley insists that his politics stem from his Free Presbyterian religion. Paisley was vociferous in his criticism of the peace process and critical of the UUP's participation in negotiations. Having achieved his aim of the DUP displacing the UUP as unionism's primary representative, the question begged was whether Paisley would lead his party back into a Northern Ireland Executive in which Sinn Fein, shorn of the IRA, was the largest nationalist party.

Dr Ian Paisley gave some signs that he might be prepared to make a deal with Sinn Fein; in the end, he kept his cards close to his chest
Source: Copyright © Martin Rowson. From *The Guardian*, 20 May 2005. Reproduced with permission

Ireland – recruiting on a 50–50 Catholic–non-Catholic basis to correct the religious imbalance – as one example of a concession to nationalists. Others included reductions in police and army numbers, the removal of some symbols of Britishness and the re-routing of Protestant Orange Order parades away from nationalist areas by the Parades Commission.

Sinn Fein (SF) has become the larger nationalist party in Northern Ireland, at the expense of its rival, the Social Democratic and Labour Party (SDLP). A welfare adjunct to the IRA in the 1970s, Sinn Fein revived as a political organisation and electoral force in the early 1980s, providing a political outlet for the military campaign of the IRA and eventually becoming the dominant element of modern republicanism. The link between Sinn Fein and the IRA provided a strategy based on a 'ballot paper in one hand and

an Armalite in the other', according to Sinn Fein's Director of Publicity, Danny Morrison, in 1981. Sympathy for IRA hunger strikers assisted Sinn Fein in the early 1980s. Sinn Fein justified 'armed struggle' to end British rule in Northern Ireland. It asserted that the partition of Ireland was unjust, as it was never supported by a majority of Irish citizens. Sinn Fein won three-quarters of the seats in the last all-Ireland elections held in 1918. The party challenged the legitimacy of Northern Ireland and argued for self-determination for the Irish people as a single unit.

In recent years, Sinn Fein has adopted a much more pragmatic republicanism, softening its demands or making them less immediate. The previous non-cooperation with state institutions and earlier strident demands for rapid British withdrawal have been superseded by a softer tone and more participatory politics. In 1986, Sinn Fein recognised the hitherto 'partitionist' Irish Republic. In 1992, Sinn Fein's policy document, *Towards a Lasting Peace in Ireland*, suggested that British *indications* of withdrawal might provide sufficient basis for negotiation. The party came into closer contact with the northern state through, for example, participation in local councils and began to concentrate more on change within Northern Ireland, with an 'equality agenda' for nationalists, covering issues such as housing, human rights and policing.

In 1998, Sinn Fein's members voted overwhelmingly to change the party's constitution to allow elected party representatives to take their seats in a devolved Northern Ireland Assembly at Stormont. Given that Provisional Sinn Fein had formed in 1970 in direct opposition to such a development, the U-turn was remarkable. Sinn Fein came to accept that a united Ireland could only be achieved in the long term, and not through violence.

Formed in 1970, the SDLP offered a moderate

constitutional nationalism from its outset. Its membership is overwhelmingly Catholic. Founded following civil rights agitation, the party attempted to replace the old, abstentionist Nationalist Party with a more dynamic brand of left-wing politics. Always in favour of Irish unity, the SDLP emphasises the need for an 'agreed Ireland'. The party accepted the need for the consent of Unionists for fundamental constitutional change, a stance now tacitly accepted by Sinn Fein. The SDLP also stresses the importance of two other political relationships: north–south cooperation between representative bodies in Northern Ireland and the Irish Republic, alongside east–west cooperation between the London (east) and Dublin (west) governments. Much of the SDLP's thinking was reflected in the 1998 Good Friday Agreement.

■ The search for political agreement

Since 1972, Northern Ireland has been governed by direct rule from Westminster, with exceptional periods of power-sharing (Table 30.5). Until the peace process, all political initiatives appeared doomed to failure; the main such initiatives are listed in Table 30.5. Unionists would not countenance any initiative containing a substantial all-Ireland dimension, while nationalists would not support any set of arrangements in which the Irish government had little say.

Case study 1: the Sunningdale Agreement 1973

The agreement finalised at Sunningdale in December 1973 provided a political blueprint for Northern Ireland and its relationships to the Westminster and

BIOGRAPHY

Gerry Adams (1949–)

President of Sinn Fein since 1983, Gerry Adams was instrumental in changing Sinn Fein from an IRA support network to a developed political party. A former IRA member from a traditional republican family, Adams was MP for West Belfast from 1983 to 1992 and regained the seat in 1997. As early as 1980, Adams acknowledged that the IRA could not win by military means alone. This perception meant that Adams sought broader nationalist support, which arrived in the peace process. Adams steered his party towards a revisionist, less fundamental republicanism, Sinn Fein became a strong electoral force and Adams encountered relatively few internal critics, although the party's IRA links made Unionists cautious. Adams transformed Sinn Fein to such dramatic effect that it was prepared to assist in the governance, rather than destruction, of Northern Ireland. By 2005, Adams completed the republican journey away from violence by playing the lead role in persuading the IRA to declare an end to its 'armed struggle'.

Table 30.5 Main political initiatives, 1973–98

Sunningdale Agreement leading to power sharing	1973: collapsed 1974
Constitutional Convention	1975: ended 1976
Constitutional Conference	1980: ended 1981
Northern Ireland Assembly	1982: collapsed 1986
New Ireland Forum	1983: ended 1984
Anglo-Irish Agreement	1985: ended 1998
Good Friday Agreement	1998: institutions suspended 2002

Dublin governments. The model of the Sunningdale Agreement endured, to the extent that the deputy leader of the SDLP, Seamus Mallon, described the 1998 Good Friday Agreement as 'Sunningdale for slow learners'. The Sunningdale Agreement created devolved power-sharing government for Northern Ireland. Unionists, nationalists and the non-aligned Alliance Party shared responsibilities in an executive, presiding over an elected assembly. A Council of Ireland was attached to the assembly. This comprised a consultative forum of elected representatives from the north and south of Ireland and a council of ministers from both countries.

Although the agreement contained a declaration that there could be no change in the constitutional status of Northern Ireland without the consent of the majority of its population, the Irish dimension was too strong for many Unionists. In the February 1974 general election, eleven of the twelve Unionists elected opposed the Sunningdale Agreement. Still reeling from the loss of their parliament two years earlier, many Unionists also objected to power sharing, arguing that majority rule was more democratic. In May 1974, the power-sharing executive collapsed, finally defeated by a strike by Protestant workers.

Stalemate

A weak attempt to revive the concept of power sharing was made through the Northern Ireland Constitutional Convention in 1975. This foundered owing to the absence of consensus over what powers should be shared and the extent of Irish involvement. In 1980, the new Conservative government under Margaret Thatcher tentatively mooted the prospect of a return to some form of devolved administration. Early political initiatives made little impact. A Constitutional Conference failed to find common ground between the political parties. 'Rolling devolution' began in 1982. This attempted to coax the political groupings into cooperating with each other in return for a steady return of power to a devolved administration and a new Northern Ireland Assembly. The lack of an all-Ireland dimension was deemed unsatisfactory by the SDLP and Sinn Fein. Both nationalist parties boycotted the assembly, which became a mere 'talking shop' for the Unionist parties and the Alliance Party (Bew and Patterson, 1985, p. 132).

Adamant that no purely internal settlement was possible, the SDLP attempted to forge a consensus among constitutional nationalists through the New Ireland Forum. Political parties in the Republic of Ireland deliberated on the best common approach to the future of the North. After a year's deliberation, the 1984 Forum Report proposed three alternative models:

1. A united, independent Ireland

2. A confederal Ireland, in which Britain and Ireland were linked by loose overarching political ties

3. Joint authority over Northern Ireland, to be held by the British and Irish governments.

Margaret Thatcher's rejection of each suggestion was characteristically brusque: 'that is out . . . that is out . . . that is out'.

Case study 2: the Anglo-Irish Agreement 1985

Despite the rejection of the New Ireland Forum, an accord between the British and Irish governments was reached the following year in the Anglo-Irish Agreement. The agreement was important in confirming that the Irish Republic would have at least have a limited say in the affairs of Northern Ireland, irrespective of Unionist opposition. It was the culmination of Anglo-Irish cooperation promised by Margaret Thatcher and the Irish Taioseach (Prime Minister) Charles Haughey in 1980. They pledged to look at the 'totality of relationships between the two islands'. Registered as an international treaty with the United Nations, the agreement:

1. guaranteed no change in the constitutional status of Northern Ireland without the consent of the majority;

2. accepted that no majority for change existed;

3. allowed the Republic of Ireland a consultative role in Northern Ireland.

A permanent intergovernmental conference was established, which allowed the Irish government to assist on political, security, legal and cooperative measures in Northern Ireland. As with the Irish dimension of the Sunningdale Agreement a decade earlier, Unionists opposed the Anglo-Irish Agreement. Unlike Sunningdale, however, the new agreement was difficult to boycott as it effectively bypassed political parties due to its intergovernmental framework. Frustrated by failure to achieve power sharing, the British government was now prepared to allow the Irish government to 'put forward views and proposals' concerning matters that 'are not the responsibility of a devolved administration in Northern Ireland'. As no such devolved administration existed, some saw this as a wide remit.

'Ulster Says No' was the rallying cry of Unionist opposition. A protest rally at Belfast City Hall attracted 100,000 people. Although fifteen Unionist MPs resigned, the impact of this protest was muted when only fourteen were returned at subsequent by-elections. Unionists also resigned from public bodies, but to little avail. Meanwhile, the SDLP welcomed the all-Ireland dimension and the bolstering of constitutional nationalism. The party was concerned with growing support for Sinn Fein, a process temporarily reversed after the agreement. For constitutional nationalists, the Anglo-Irish Agreement offered greater parity of esteem for the nationalist minority and gave Dublin a representative role on behalf of the nationalist community.

■ The peace process

As numerous political initiatives foundered, many wondered whether violence would ever end. Yet a carefully constructed process developed, involving a series of private and public initiatives (Table 30.6). The creation of a peace process depended on numerous factors. They included:

■ Moderation of republican politics, encouraged by private initiatives undertaken by Gerry Adams and by the more public dialogue between Sinn Fein and the SDLP

■ Changes in Unionism, including an increased acceptance of an all-Ireland dimension to any solution

■ Acknowledgement of the aspirations and identity of both communities by the British government, allied to measures to reduce discrimination

Table 30.6 A chronology of the peace process

1985	Sinn Fein President Gerry Adams liaises privately with the Catholic Church to persuade Irish nationalist parties to construct a 'pan-nationalist' approach. The Anglo-Irish Agreement gives the Irish government consultative rights over policy for Northern Ireland
1988	'Hume–Adams' talks begin, between the SDLP and Sinn Fein
1990	The Brooke initiative, communicating with the IRA, begins
1993	Downing Street Declaration
1994	Paramilitary ceasefires
1995	Framework Documents published
1996	Mitchell Commission Report
	Forum elections
	IRA cessation of violence ended
1997	IRA cessation of violence restored
	Multi-party talks begin
1998	Good Friday Agreement
	Referendums in Northern Ireland and the Irish Republic confirm support for the Agreement
	Elections to the Northern Ireland Assembly
	First and Deputy First Ministers elected by Assembly members
1999	Devolved powers awarded to the Northern Ireland Assembly and executive. Power sharing with an Irish dimension established
2002	Political institutions suspended for the fourth time, as Unionists demand disbandment of the IRA. Direct rule is reintroduced
2003	Ian Paisley's Democratic Unionist Party and Gerry Adams' Sinn Fein emerge as the largest unionist and nationalist parties respectively in elections to the (suspended) Northern Ireland Assembly. A restoration of devolution may require agreement between the supposedly militant political representatives of the two rival ethnic blocs
2005	The IRA announces an end to its armed campaign and decommissions its weapons

Which way to follow the peace process?
Source: Copyright © Oliver Kugler. From *The Guardian*, 22 February 2005

■ Constitutional change from the Irish government

■ External pressure, notably from the USA, but also from other peace processes (see below).

Nationalist dialogue

The tortuous road to peace began with Sinn Fein's search for inclusive dialogue and an end to the IRA's armed struggle. This began with private moves by Gerry Adams, unauthorised initially by the IRA, to establish an alliance of all the major nationalist parties in Ireland (pan-nationalism) to press the case for Irish self-determination and the right of all the people on the island of Ireland to determine their own future free from British 'interference' (Moloney, 2002). The culmination of the initiative of Adams was the replacement of the armed, militant and conspiratorial themes of republicanism by a political discourse (Arthur, 2002). The intermittent talks between Gerry Adams and John Hume, leader of the SDLP, commencing in 1988, were an attempt by the latter to persuade republicans that:

■ Britain was neutral on whether Northern Ireland should remain in the United Kingdom.

■ A united Ireland, or national self-determination, could only be achieved through the allegiance of both traditions.

■ Violence was an impediment to such allegiance.

Hume received a sympathetic ear from Adams in his attempts to persuade Sinn Fein that nationalists

were not opposing a colonial aggressor. Instead, Hume asserted, it was the opposition of 900,000 Unionists within Northern Ireland to a united Ireland that was the problem. The dialogue was assisted by a declaration in 1990 by the Secretary of State for Northern Ireland, Peter Brooke, that Britain had no 'selfish, strategic or economic interest in Northern Ireland'. Brooke pursued public and private approaches towards peace. The former, based on cross-party talks, achieved little. The latter involved a secret line of communication to the IRA, known as the Back Channel (Mallie and McKittrick, 1996). This line of communication had developed in the 1980s with a Catholic priest, Father Alec Reid, acting as an intermediary, conveying to Gerry Adams and *vice versa* (Moloney, 2002).

Secret communication was followed by public political initiatives. The British and Irish governments produced the Downing Street Declaration, or Joint Declaration for Peace, in December 1993. This attempted:

1. to satisfy Unionists by restating guarantees that there could be no change in the status of Northern Ireland without the consent of the majority;

2. to interest nationalists by supporting the right of the Irish people to self-determination, provided that consent was given in both parts of the island to political arrangements.

An IRA cessation of violence was announced in 1994, reciprocated soon afterwards by loyalist paramilitary groups. The IRA believed that it might advance its own cause via an unarmed strategy, owing to the presence of a strong nationalist coalition. This embraced Sinn Fein, the SDLP and the Irish government.

Case study 3: the Good Friday Agreement 1998

By Easter 1998, exhaustive multi-party negotiations had reached their conclusion in the Good Friday Agreement. This established:

1. A 108-seat devolved Northern Ireland Assembly, presided over by an executive

2. A North–South ministerial council, presiding over a minimum of twelve areas of cross-border cooperation

3. A British–Irish council, linking developed institutions throughout Britain and Ireland

4. A British–Irish Intergovernmental Conference, to promote British–Irish cooperation.

These formal institutional measures were accompanied by others of equal importance in selling the agreement. For the paramilitary groups, the agreement offered the release of prisoners within two years. Nationalists were offered a commission on policing, and a human rights commission was also established. Unionists were offered the repeal of the Irish Republic's constitutional claim to Northern Ireland. The Good Friday Agreement possessed key themes attempted in the Sunningdale Agreement a quarter of a century earlier:

1. **Devolution**: Successive British governments desired a return of devolution to Northern Ireland. The Labour government placed the return of such powers within a wider restructuring of the United Kingdom, with devolution also awarded to Scotland and Wales.

2. **Consociationalism**, or power sharing: This was seen as necessary in a divided society to prevent domination by one community. The executive comprised Unionist and nationalist representation. The First and Deputy First Minister were elected with cross-community support. Key decisions required weighted majorities or parallel consent, i.e. support from Unionists and nationalists.

3. **Cross-borderism**: There was an all-Ireland dimension, by which ministers from the Northern Ireland Assembly would meet with those of the Irish government to develop and implement new cross-border bodies. Nationalists hoped for political 'spillover' from economic cooperation. Potential areas of cooperation included transport, agriculture and relations with the EU.

4. **Intergovernmentalism**: Anglo-Irish cooperation would continue through a series of institutional mechanisms, concentrating on matters not devolved to the new assembly.

There were some important differences from the Sunningdale Agreement. The Good Friday Agreement linked Britain and Ireland's governments and newly devolved institutions, in a very loose confederation. More importantly, however, the agreement was inclusive. Earlier agreements had attempted to marginalise groups associated with paramilitary activity. Now there was an effort to bring such groups into the political mainstream, not least through the 'carrot' of prisoner releases. The 1999 Patten Report on policing led to the creation of the Police Service of Northern Ireland (PSNI) to replace the Royal Ulster Constabulary. The new policing service was supposed to offer changes in culture, ethos and composition, designed to end claims of bias.

The referendums on the Good Friday Agreement, held in May 1998, confirmed its inclusivity, yielding some unusual allies in Northern Ireland. The UUP, SDLP and Sinn Fein all advocated support for the agreement, opposed by the DUP, although the UUP was divided; 71 per cent of Northern Ireland's voters and 94 per cent of those in the Irish Republic endorsed the agreement. The majority in favour within the Unionist community was nonetheless slight (only 57 per cent of Protestants voted in favour of the deal in the referendum, and there was only a very narrow pro-agreement Unionist majority in the assembly elections in June 1998).

In 1999, devolved powers were awarded to a Northern Ireland executive and Assembly for the first time in twenty-five years. The Northern Ireland Assembly enjoyed a substantial primary legislative role, although it did not possess tax-varying powers, and security matters remained reserved or excepted powers, retained at Westminster. However, uncertainty over the quantity of IRA weapons decommissioned and allegations of continued IRA activity undermined fragile Unionist confidence. By 2002, a majority of Protestants opposed the GFA. Although support for devolved government *per se* remained high, the Agreement floundered amid unproven claims of an IRA 'spy ring' at Stormont. It later transpired that a Sinn Fein member charged with 'spying', Denis Donaldson, had been working for British intelligence since 1985. Republicans argued that no spy ring had ever existed as the IRA's war was effectively already over; Unionists argued that further information was needed to solve the mystery. The Director of Public Prosecutions decided it was in the 'public interest' – although the public felt exactly the opposite – for no further information to be revealed. Not for the first time, the politics of Northern Ireland were cloaked in mystery, which merely added to the impressions of excessive secrecy, 'dirty tricks' by security agencies and a generally dysfunctional polity. It was also apparent that elements within the republican leadership, belonging to the IRA and Sinn Fein, were under the control of the British for many years prior to the peace process. Infiltration of the IRA and Sinn Fein hastened the demise of the republican 'armed struggle'.

The Assembly and Executive were suspended indefinitely amid the 'spying' furore of 2002. The institutions had an uncertain future, one in which cooperation between the DUP and Sinn Fein, the biggest parties in the Assembly since the 2003 elections to a mothballed institution, will be needed if devolution is to be restored. Although Assembly committees had undertaken useful work, the Executive 'coalition' was a dysfunctional body, in which party fiefdoms were more important than a sense of the collective.

Towards a durable peace

The Provisional IRA's announcement, in 2005, of the abandonment of its armed campaign, appeared to finally signal the end of conflict. The organisation pledged to place its arms beyond use and it appeared that the vexed question of decommissioning might finally be resolved.

Hitherto, the peace process had not produced a perfect peace and the political process suffered a number of setbacks. Given that conflict resolution was designed to end 800 years of enmity, such imperfections were inevitable. Between 1994/5 and 2001/2, there were 2,262 shooting and bombing incidents (Table 30.7).

A total of 1,313 persons were charged with terrorist or serious public order offences in the first four years after the Good Friday Agreement (Police Service of Northern Ireland, 2002). The death toll did drop dramatically, although over 100 people were killed by what was (sometimes loosely) termed

Table 30.7 Security-related incidents in Northern Ireland, 1995–2002

Year	Shooting incidents	Bombing incidents
1995/6	65	0
1996/7	140	50
1997/8	245	73
1998/9	187	123
1999/2000	131	66
2000/1	331	177
2001/2	358	318

Source: Police Service of Northern Ireland (2000), *Report of Chief Constable 2001–02*. © 2002 Crown copyright material is produced with permission of the Controller of the HMSO

political violence in the first six years after the Good Friday Agreement was brokered.

'Dissident' loyalist and republican groups emerged, and the ceasefires of the main loyalist paramilitary groups, the Ulster Defence Association (UDA) and Ulster Volunteer Force (UVF), were temporarily declared invalid by the Secretary of State in 2001 and 2005 respectively. The 'Real IRA' (RIRA) believed that Sinn Fein and the Provisional IRA had betrayed republican principles by entering an assembly and managing British rule in Northern Ireland. In conjunction with another tiny group of republican ultras, the Continuity IRA, the RIRA responded by committing one of the worst atrocities of the 'Troubles', killing twenty-nine people in a bomb attack at Omagh in 1998. Punishment beatings and shootings increased after the paramilitary ceasefires as the 'mainstream' paramilitary organisations strove to maintain authority within their communities. IRA members were involved in the most infamous of these, the killing of Robert McCartney in early 2005, the international outcry hastening the formal ending of the republican armed campaign. The McCartney killing came only weeks after the IRA was blamed by the police for the largest bank robbery in British and Irish history, at the Northern Bank in Belfast.

Sectarianism, if anything, increased, reflected in persistent, mainly low-level conflict at interface areas where nationalist and loyalist territory lay adjacent, resulting in an increase in the number of 'peace walls'. Feuding among loyalist paramilitary groups led to more than a dozen deaths between 2000 and 2005. Sinn Fein refused to join the Policing Board overseeing the new Police Service of Northern Ireland, arguing that the Patten Report had not been fully implemented. The refusal of Sinn Fein ministers in government to back the state's own police force emphasised the abnormality of Northern Ireland politics, although Sinn Fein's position appeared likely to change. Protestant disenchantment with supposedly pro-nationalist changes to policing and parades led to serious rioting in 2005. The peace process created a new set of problems, such as how to deal with unsolved killings, how to treat former paramilitaries still 'on the run' and how to treat victims, via inquiries (such as the Bloody Sunday inquiry into killings by the British Army in 1972) or, possibly, some form of truth and reconciliation commission, as used in South Africa.

BOX 30.2   BRITAIN IN CONTEXT

Northern Ireland in context: the international dimension

The international importance of Northern Ireland has declined in recent years. Until the mid-twentieth century its significance was as a site of British Empire. From the Second World War until 1990, Northern Ireland had some geographical value as an Atlantic outpost for the United Kingdom during the Cold War. The international significance of Northern Ireland since 1990 has been as a site of a relatively successful peace process, one which has virtually eradicated a prolonged conflict, even if the accompanying political process has been subject to difficulty.

Although Northern Ireland has been described as a place apart and does indeed contain unique features, the attempts at creating a consociational political agreement (such as the Good Friday Agreement) to manage a divided society are familiar elsewhere, Belgium and the Netherlands providing nearby examples. Consociational deals allow the political leaderships of ethnic blocs to manage and reduce conflict by giving rival communities places in government without domination by the majority community (through the use of proportionality and vetoes) and allowing different communities some autonomy. Globally, however, the record of consociational settlements is at best moderate (Horowitz, 2001). Those sceptical of consociational approaches advocate that peace and reconciliation measures are developed mainly within civic society rather than among political élites.

The Northern Ireland peace process may have developed mainly within the island, as various actors changed their political stances. However, external factors were also important. The end of the Cold War reduced Northern Ireland's strategic value to the British government and created greater space for tacit declarations of British neutrality on the future of the Province. Meanwhile Sinn Fein's movement from left-wing politics post-Cold War removed (exaggerated) fears of republicans turning Ireland into a socialist republic. Peace processes elsewhere have impacted upon developments in Northern Ireland. Perhaps most notably, the negotiating styles of the African National Congress in the South African process impacted upon republicans.

The US President from 1992 to 2000, Bill Clinton, adopted a more proactive stance on Northern Ireland than had hitherto been the case with US administrations. Clinton's facilitation of US entry visas for leading republicans helped Sinn Fein and the IRA realise the potential benefits of peace. Clinton's deployment of Senator George Mitchell as a peace negotiator proved instrumental in developing multi-party agreement. Clinton's personal role in the negotiations is disputed, but the President's even-handed activism provided a positive contribution to the development of the peace process.

Arguably above all else, the hostility towards international terrorism post-9/11 made a return to violence by republicans untenable. Fund-raising for armed republicanism became much more difficult, due to a combination of antipathy and tough legislative measures by the US government. Continuing activity by IRA members in 2004–5, including the largest bank robbery in British and Irish history and the murder of a Belfast Catholic, Robert McCartney, an act which led to a high-profile anti-IRA campaign which reached the White House, isolated those republicans still reluctant to follow purely constitutional routes.

Alternatives to the Good Friday Agreement?

Alternatives to the Good Friday Agreement suffer from insufficiency of consensus. The alternatives to devolved power sharing, linked to an Irish dimension, that have been offered are:

1. *Direct rule from Westminster*: Few see direct rule as a solution. At best, direct rule produces reforms rather than resolution of the problem. Direct rule indicates a lack of consensus over the future of Northern Ireland. If significant powers were transferred to local government in Northern Ireland, consensus 'from below' might develop, but beyond this, direct rule has little potential for transformation of the conflict.

2. *Full integration into the United Kingdom*: This is favoured by some Unionists on the grounds that it would end uncertainty over the future of the province. Supporters argue that this would assist in the reduction of violence. Detractors point out that the suggestion takes no account of the Irish identity of the minority population in Northern Ireland. The conflict may further polarise British versus Irish identities and increase violence.

3. *Joint British–Irish authority*: A sharing of power in Northern Ireland would require both traditions to accept that exclusive sovereignty cannot be exercised by a single government. Joint authority might be acceptable to many nationalists. Unionists would reject joint authority, not least because it would be seen as an interim settlement towards a full abdication of British sovereignty. A prolonged absence of devolution might nonetheless lead to nudges from the British government in the direction of a form of direct rule with increased input from the Irish government.

4. *United Ireland*: Favoured by republicans, the absorption of Northern Ireland into a thirty-two county independent Irish Republic would almost certainly be met by armed resistance from loyalists. War might ensue throughout the entire island.

5. *Independent Northern Ireland*: Such an option has declined in its limited popularity. This proposal would end rule by the British government and rule out control from Dublin. It was attractive to some working-class loyalists sceptical of the value of the British link. Catholics, outnumbered in such a new state, would be fearful.

6. *Repartition*: Any redrawing of the border would be beset by practical difficulties, although such an outlandish proposal was considered as an option of last resort by Conservative governments in the 1970s and 1980s. It would be impossible to reshape without leaving a vulnerable minority Protestant community in the counties allocated to the Republic. Catholics in what remained of Northern Ireland might be equally unhappy.

7. *European authority*: Some commentators have expressed interest in the possibilities raised by membership of the European Union (Boyle and Hadden, 1994). Substantial aid from the European Union has boosted Northern Ireland's economy. It has been hoped that membership of the European Union held by Britain and Ireland might produce one or more of the following:

   ■ the transfer of citizenship loyalties towards a new European identity;

   ■ the withering of the importance of the border as a range of cross-border institutions develop, promoted by European trade initiatives;

   ■ the emergence of a Europe of the Regions, replacing exclusive national loyalty with pooled sovereignty.

   Thus far, none of these possible developments has displaced traditional affiliations.

8. *Demographic change*: Higher Catholic birth rates have led to speculation that Catholics might form a majority in Northern Ireland during the first half of this century. This raised the possibility that the population might vote the state of Northern Ireland out of existence. Either possibility is unlikely. Sufficient Catholics support the Union to ensure that a large Catholic majority would be required to end British control.

9. *Devolution from below*: Grand executive coalition and consociationalism would be abandoned in favour of giving more powers to local councils. The advantage would be that all parties cooperate at the local level in Northern Ireland and that 'blocking' minority or parallel consent rules might not be required. The disadvantage is that it would be difficult to coordinate the governance of Northern Ireland. How, for example, could budget priorities for the entire province be determined?

Chapter summary

The formal ending by the Provisional IRA of its thirty-five-year war in 2005 marked the final stage of the peace process in Northern Ireland. With the conflict finally over, a return of devolved government appears probable, although this will not occur until the DUP, as Northern Ireland's largest party, is prepared to accept the constitutional *bona fides* of Sinn Fein.

Notwithstanding post-GFA stalemate, seismic changes have occurred in the politics of Northern Ireland. The 'sound of breaking ice' could be heard in the forging and aftermath of the Agreement (O'Leary and McGarry, 1996). Unionists and republicans engaged in a fragile shared governance from 1999 to 2002 and it remained possible that political institutions might be restored. Much of the peace and political processes were based upon careful choreography (see Dixon, 2001). From the mid-1980s onwards, leading republicans developed an exit strategy from an unwinnable war while, until many years later, publicly defending the legitimacy of armed struggle. While for some time publicly refusing to talk to 'terrorists', the British government privately encouraged political change within republicanism, offering limited gains designed to prevent the republican movement splitting. Having infiltrated the IRA and Sinn Fein at senior levels, the British government knew the strengths and weaknesses of the republican movement. Although the IRA could still be a devastating force, blowing up Canary Wharf in London and Manchester city centre in 1996, its war had run its course without military victory. Given that the British–Irish conflict might be regarded as having an 800-year history, the emergence of an armed campaign by a 'new' IRA cannot be entirely discounted, but it is maybe more unlikely than at any previous stage of Irish history.

The peace process was to some extent a 'pre-cooked deal', as the British government and the combined forces of Irish nationalism came to an agreed formula for Irish self-determination sufficient to end the IRA's armed campaign and bring about a political agreement (Moloney, 2002, p. 254). Change on the republican side ended the boycotting of Northern Ireland's political institutions. The aspiration of a united Ireland remains, but politics and electoralism are preferred to 'armed struggle', even though the shift towards Irish unity under the Good Friday Agreement is slight and conditional upon demographic gains. The modern dynamic of republicanism lies closer to in the production of more (nationalist) babies and votes for Sinn Fein than in the planting of bombs. As such, the outworking of the Adams-led changes to the republican movement were designed to stand down the Provisional IRA.

Aspects of the Good Friday Agreement and related changes were nonetheless unpalatable to a section of Unionism. Opposition to the Good Friday Agreement was a useful electoral tactic for the DUP, as sporadic alleged IRA activity reduced Unionist confidence in the deal. The removal of the IRA from the equation in 2005 raises prospects of a more durable agreement, although a fevered imagination is still required to envisage a Paisley–Adams axis at the head of a Northern Ireland government. The Good Friday Agreement risks joining the list of unsuccessful political initiatives that led to the application of the label 'failed political entity' to Northern Ireland. Nonetheless, an overhaul of the agreement or continuing direct rule from Westminster will not see a return to substantial armed conflict. Armed republicanism and loyalist paramilitary activity are unlikely to disappear entirely, but there is little appetite for a return to the previous conflict. A greater problem is that of continuing sectarianism, fuelled by Unionist disenchantment at what many see as the erosion of Protestant-Britishness within Northern Ireland.

A new politics has emerged, based upon republican movement towards constitutional methods and Unionist recognition of the Irishness of the minority, accompanied by an acceptance of the need for an Irish dimension to political arrangements. Political thawing has been accompanied by greater economic prosperity. A new politics of Northern Ireland, less concerned with traditional constitutional politics and involving cross-community social issues, may yet emerge. Nonetheless it remains fragile and uncertain, amid religious residential segregation and continuing sectarian tensions.

Discussion points

■ Why has power sharing been so difficult to achieve in Northern Ireland?

■ Is a consociational political deal the only option for Northern Ireland?

■ To what extent is the Northern Ireland problem one of religious sectarianism?

■ To what extent does the Good Friday Agreement legitimise sectarianism?

■ Have republicans and Unionists changed their political strategies in recent years?

■ Should the Irish Republic be given a substantial say in the affairs of Northern Ireland?

■ Is the Good Friday Agreement a good deal for Unionists?

■ What factors enabled a peace process to develop?

■ Did IRA violence achieve any of the goals held by the organisation?

■ Why do Unionists wish to remain British?

■ Has Sinn Fein remained true to republican principles?

■ Which explanation of the Northern Ireland problem is the most realistic?

■ Should the DUP share power with Sinn Fein?

■ Was the IRA defeated?

Further reading

For those unfamiliar with – even bewildered by – the complex politics of Northern Ireland, Tonge's *Northern Ireland: Conflict and Change* (2002), Aughey and Morrow's *Northern Ireland Politics* (1996), and Wichert's *Northern Ireland since 1945* (1999) provide useful guides.

Important considerations of the Good Friday Agreement are now emerging. These include Arthur Aughey's *The Politics of Northern Ireland: Beyond the Belfast Agreement* (2005) and the provocatively titled *The Failure of the Northern Ireland Peace Process* by Gary Peatling

(2005). Tonge's (2005) *The New Northern Irish Politics?* assesses the extent of political change, whilst his (2006) volume entitled *Northern Ireland* also examines aspects of the conflict. Students must also read the excellent collection of essays in Rick Wilford's edited volume, *Aspects of the Belfast Agreement* (2001). Paul Dixon outlines how much of the peace process was choreographed in *Northern Ireland: the Politics of War and Peace* (2001). For informative analyses of consociational aspects of the deal and comparisons of the Northern Ireland peace process with similar processes elsewhere, students should read John McGarry's edited book *Northern Ireland and the Divided World* (2001). Coakley's edited work, *Changing Shades of Orange and Green* (2002), offers illuminating accounts of the dynamics of party and ideological change from politicians and academics.

An outstanding, pre-Good Friday Agreement, scholarly work is provided by McGarry and O'Leary (1995). This goes further than the seminal study of Whyte (1990) in proposing solutions. *The Politics of Antagonism* (1996), by the same authors, is also an essential read. Another high-quality account is offered by Bew *et al.* (2002). Readers might also choose Mitchell and Wilford's edited book, *Politics in Northern Ireland* (1999). Bruce (1986) and Bruce (1994) offer useful studies of loyalism, and *Unionist Politics and the Politics of Unionism since the Anglo-Irish Agreement* (2001) by Feargal Cochrane ought to be read. Changes within the republican movement are detailed in Moloney's excellent revelatory work *A Secret History of the IRA* (2002) and these developments are the subject of a lucid and fair-minded analysis in English's work, *Armed Struggle* (2003). Developments in republicanism are also discussed in Henry Patterson's *The Politics of Illusion: A Political History of the IRA* (1997) and Brendan O'Brien's *The Long War: the IRA and Sinn Fein* (1999). Brian Feeney's 2002 study, *Sinn Fein: A Hundred Turbulent Years*, draws a number of pertinent conclusions. Maillot (2004) provides a sympathetic view of Sinn Fein. Murray and Tonge (2005) cover developments within Sinn Fein and the SDLP. Highly readable accounts of the peace process are provided by Coogan (1995) and Mallie and McKittrick (1996).

References

ARK (2005) *Northern Ireland Life and Times Survey, 2004* (www.ark.ac.uk/nilt).

Arthur, P. (2002) 'The transformation of republicanism', in J. Coakley (ed.) *Changing Shades of Orange and Green* (University College Dublin).

Arthur, P. and Jeffery, K. (1998) *Northern Ireland since 1968* (Blackwell).

Aughey, A. (2005) *The Politics of Northern Ireland: Beyond the Belfast Agreement* (Routledge).

Aughey, A. and Morrow, D. (eds) (1996) *Northern Ireland Politics* (Longman).

Bairner, A. (1996) 'Paramilitarism' in A. Aughey and D. Morrow (eds) (1996) *Northern Ireland Politics* (Longman).

Bew, P. and Patterson, H. (1985) *The British State and the Ulster Crisis* (Verso).

Bew, P., Gibbon, P. and Patterson, H. (2002) *Northern Ireland 1921–2002: Political Forces and Social Classes* (Serif).

Boyle, K. and Hadden, T. (1994) *Northern Ireland: The Choice* (Penguin).

Bruce, S. (1986) *God Save Ulster: The Religion and Politics of Paisleyism* (Oxford University Press).

Bruce, S. (1994) *At the Edge of the Union* (Oxford University Press).

Coakley, J. (2002) *Changing Shades of Orange and Green: Redefining the Union and the Nation in Contemporary Ireland* (University College Dublin).

Cochrane, F. (2001) *Unionist Politics and the Politics of Unionism since the Anglo-Irish Agreement*, 2nd edn (Cork University Press).

Connolly, M. (1990) *Politics and Policy-Making in Northern Ireland* (Prentice Hall).

Coogan, T.P. (1995) *Ireland's Ordeal 1966–1995 and the Search for Peace* (Hutchinson).

Darby, J. (1994) 'Legitimate targets: a control on violence?' in A Guelke (ed.), *New Perspectives on the Northern Ireland Conflict* (Avebury).

Dixon, P. (2001) *Northern Ireland: the Politics of War and Peace* (Palgrave).

English, R. (2003) *Armed Struggle* (PanMacmillan).

Feeney, B. (2002) *Sinn Fein. A Hundred Turbulent Years* (O'Brien Press).

Horowitz, D. (2001) 'The Northern Ireland Agreement: Clear, Consociational and Risky', in J. McGarry (ed.) *Northern Ireland and the Divided World* (Oxford University Press).

Maillot, A. (2004) *New Sinn Fein* (Routledge).

Mallie, E. and McKittrick, D. (1996) *The Fight for Peace* (Heinemann).

McCullagh, M. and O'Dowd, L. (1986) 'Northern Ireland: the search for a solution', *Social Studies Review*, March.

McGarry, J. (ed.) (2001) *Northern Ireland and the Divided World* (Oxford University Press).

McGarry, J. and O'Leary, B. (1995) *Explaining Northern Ireland* (Blackwell).

Miller, D. (ed.) (1998) *Rethinking Northern Ireland* (Longman).

Mitchell, P. and Wilford, R. (eds) (1999) *Politics in Northern Ireland* (Westview Press).

Moloney, E. (2002) *A Secret History of the IRA* (Penguin).

Murray, G. (1998) *John Hume's SDLP* (Hurst).

Murray, G. and Tonge, J. (2005) *Sinn Fein and the SDLP* (Hurst).

O'Brien, B. (1999) *The Long War: The IRA and Sinn Fein* (O'Brien Press).

O'Leary, B. and McGarry, J. (1996) *The Politics of Antagonism* (Athlone).

Patterson, H. (1997) *The Politics of Illusion: A Political History of the IRA* (Serif).

Peatling, G. (2005) *The Failure of the Northern Ireland Peace Process* (Irish Academic Press).

Police Service of Northern Ireland (2002) *Report of the Chief Constable 2001–02* (PSNI).

Porter, N. (1996) *Rethinking Unionism* (Blackstaff).

Royal Ulster Constabulary (1999) *Royal Ulster Constabulary Chief Constable's Report, 1999* (Royal Ulster Constabulary).

Tonge, J. (2002) *Northern Ireland: Conflict and Change* (Pearson).

Tonge, J. (2005) *The New Northern Irish Politics* (Palgrave).

Tonge, J. (2006) *Northern Ireland* (Polity).

Whyte, J. (1990) *Interpreting Northern Ireland* (Blackwell).

Wichert, S. (1999) *Northern Ireland since 1945* (Longman).

Wilford, R. (ed.) (2001) *Aspects of the Belfast Agreement* (Oxford University Press).

Useful websites

Conflict achive on the Internet: cain.ulst.ac.uk

Northern Ireland Life and Times Survey:
   www.ark.ac.uk

Northern Ireland Assembly:
   www.ni-assembly.gov.uk

Northern Ireland Executive: www.nics.go.uk

SDLP: www.sdlp.ie

Ulster Unionist Party: www.uup.org

Democratic Unionist Party: www.dup.org.uk

Sinn Fein: www.sinnfein.ie

Progressive Unionist Party: www.pup.org

Alliance Party of Northern Ireland:
   www.allianceparty.org

Northern Ireland Unionist Party: www.niup.org

United Kingdom Unionist Party: www.ukup.org

Police Service of Northern Ireland:
   www.psni.police.uk

Grand Orange Lodge of Ireland:
   www.grandorange.org.uk

Republican Sinn Fein: www.iol.ie/~saoirse

Northern Ireland Political Collection, Linenhall
      Library: www.bl.uk/collections/northern.html

CHAPTER 31

Britain and European integration

Simon Bulmer

Learning objectives

- To offer a brief overview of Britain's postwar relationship with the European integration process.

- To give an introduction to the institutions and policy process of the European Union.

- To explain the policy activities of the EU and give an idea of their impact upon Britain.

- To review developments in European policy under the Blair government.

- To highlight a key characteristic of British politics, namely the existence of a multi-level form of government.

Introduction

Should the United Kingdom sign up to the European Union's Constitutional Treaty? Should the UK adopt the euro, the common currency used by twelve member states of the European Union (EU)? Should the UK give up the rebate that it receives on its otherwise high contributions to the EU budget? Can the Conservative Party overcome ongoing splits regarding its policy towards the EU? These are some of the key current political questions relating to Britain's relationship with European integration. These questions arise from the UK's accession, in 1973, to what is now known as the European Union (EU). In the subsequent period, the UK's political system has become increasingly interlinked with, and affected by, the institutions and policies associated with the European integration process. Very few areas of British policy have escaped some impact from the EU. Similarly, almost all political forces and institutions have been affected in some way by European integration. This chapter is designed to explain how Britain fits in with the political processes of the EU. It will reveal an increasingly multi-level form of government: linking local authorities, the devolved executives and assemblies, Whitehall/Westminster and the EU level in Brussels. It will also reveal some of the continuing flashpoints in Britain's relationship with the EU.

Tony Blair, Jack Straw and José Manuel Barroso at the EU Commission
Source: Reuters / Yves Herman

■ Britain and European integration: the context

For Britain and the rest of Europe the period following the Second World War brought major change. However, how Britain responded was distinctive. Unlike several of their western European counterparts on the continent, British governments did not see a need to make a significant departure from the traditional foreign policy role as a world power. The result has been a relationship with the European Union characterised by semi-detachment and by internal political division within and between the political parties (George, 1998; Baker and Seawright, 1998).

For Britain, the postwar global context had changed significantly. Although emerging as one of the victorious allies, the UK effectively lost its status as a world power. The USA was to occupy the leadership role in the international economy and, politically, in the Western hemisphere. For Britain the new situation had two effects. First, it had to manage the 'descent from power' in its foreign policy and adapt to being a medium-sized power. Second, it had to recognise that it no longer occupied the central role in the postwar economic order. Of course, these patterns can look all too clear when viewed with the benefit of hindsight. However, politicians had to contend with the day-to-day challenges of government as well as with electoral needs. In addition, there were other pressing issues, in particular popular pressures for the development of the welfare state and demands on the part of the colonies for independence. Above all, having emerged from the Second World War as one of the victorious powers, Britain was not presented with an immediate need to make a major change to foreign policy. Hence successive governments did not confront the issue of reorienting British foreign policy to a new European-centred focus. For these and other reasons, governments led by both major parties were reluctant to participate in new forms of European integration that seemed to challenge national sovereignty. The nation-state was still an object of pride.

The postwar experience of continental Europe was rather different. By continental Europe, we mean first of all Western Europe but excluding Spain and Portugal (as rather isolated dictatorships until the mid-1970s) as well as the Scandinavian countries, which had different traditions. The six member states that were to form the core of European integration until 1973 shared two particular experiences that encouraged them to develop a new form of co-operation. First, they had all had their prestige undermined by virtue of national defeat: whether at the hands of Hitler's Germany or, as in the case of Germany and Italy, at the hands of the Allies. Second, in various ways they had all suffered from the excesses of state power, with the Nazi regime the most extreme manifestation of this. These six states were France, Germany, Italy, Luxembourg, the Netherlands and Belgium.

For these countries – unlike Britain – the nation-state had been discredited, resulting in powerful political forces for new forms of inter-state cooperation. These new forms of cooperation were needed for three reasons. First, the six states all confronted the task of economic reconstruction but sought to solve particular economic policy issues in new ways. Second, most of the states bordered West Germany and sought an innovative way of constraining German power. Third, the Cold War created a geopolitical division through the centre of Europe and a need to organise against the perceived threat of communism. The consequence was that key continental political leaders, predominantly from the centre-right, developed supranational integration as a specific form of cooperation between states. Thus this supranational form of European integration and the first of the three European Communities were born.

Supranationalism not only involves a commitment on the part of member states to work together but, unlike other European or international organisations, also places formal constraints on national autonomy. Moreover, supranationalism expresses itself in a distinctive institutional structure: in a body of law that takes precedence over national law; in a dense network of institutions located chiefly in Brussels; and in a pattern of government that penetrates national (i.e. British) politics and policies to a unique extent.

Before looking at the present-day interaction of Britain and the EU, we need a brief examination of the course of integration from the early 1950s in order to appreciate the current situation.

A range of European organisations was set up in the immediate postwar period, as well as the North Atlantic Treaty Organisation (NATO), the transatlantic organisation concerned with the defence of Western Europe. The first of the supranational organisations was the European Coal and Steel Community (ECSC). This was proposed in the Schuman Plan of 1950 and was a French attempt to place the German (and French) 'industries of war' under supranational control, thus facilitating the reconstruction of the two industries in a way that would not threaten peace and indeed would form the basis for Franco-German reconciliation. This Franco-German plan was adopted by the Six, and the ECSC came into operation in 1952. The resultant Franco-German relationship has been a peaceful one, but it followed eighty years of recurrent hostilities. It has been the bedrock of supranational integration.

Despite some setbacks in the mid-1950s, the Six agreed in 1957 to extend the supranational approach. Two new communities were set up in the Treaties of Rome and came into operation in 1958. These were the European Atomic Energy Community and the European Economic Community (EEC). Of the three European Communities, it is the EEC that has been the most prominent. In 1967 the three communities merged their institutions, and from this time they were known collectively as the European Community/ies (EC). When the Maastricht Treaty came into effect in November 1993, the current term – European Union – was adopted.

The early British response to supranational integration had been one of complete detachment. But by 1961 two factors had prompted the UK government, under Conservative Prime Minister Harold Macmillan, to apply for membership. These were:

1. The stronger economic performances of those states in the three communities;

2. Britain's declining foreign policy influence, as highlighted by the decolonisation process and the Suez Crisis of 1956, when Britain failed to reverse the actions of a small country – Egypt – in nationalising the Suez Canal.

This first application and a subsequent one made by the Labour government of Harold Wilson in 1967 were unsuccessful because they were blocked by the French President, Charles de Gaulle. He feared that Britain might compete with France for leadership of the EC. He also halted the supranational development of the EC through the 1965 'empty chair crisis', which had the consequence of stopping the scheduled introduction of majority voting in the Council of Ministers. Under this voting system – the formal provision in the treaties for some policy areas – individual member governments could be overruled, thereby challenging their **sovereignty**. During the 1960s the EC stagnated politically owing to the other states' opposition to de Gaulle's policies. However,

circumstances changed in 1969 with his resignation. A relaunch of integration was undertaken and it was as part of this that enlargement returned to the agenda.

Eventually, after successful terms of membership had been negotiated, the first enlargement took place in 1973 (with the UK, Ireland and Denmark acceding). At home the British government presented the EC as an organisation that posed little major threat to sovereignty. In other words, final and absolute authority would remain in the UK and not be challenged from outside. In the House of Commons, the decision to approve the terms of membership was highly contested. Edward Heath's Conservative government was reliant on support from rebel Labour MPs, who rejected their party's line of opposing the terms negotiated. Sovereignty was a key point of conflict during the debates. However, it is important to remember that this assumption about sovereignty was true only in terms of the way the EC had developed in the 1960s. In fact, under the formal rules set down in the treaties there was considerable provision for sovereignty to be challenged. When member states started to wish to return to the formal rules, and in particular to majority voting in the Council of Ministers (see below), the UK was less at ease because sovereignty was challenged.

The stagnation of integration that had started in the mid-1960s continued in many respects throughout the 1970s. Apart from enlargement there were some isolated advances, in particular the establishment of the European Monetary System (EMS) in 1979. However, it was in the 1980s that the integration process advanced in a striking way, through both widening and deepening. The EC was widened by virtue of two southern enlargements: in 1981 to encompass Greece, and in 1986 with the accession of Spain and Portugal. Deepening came about in the form of the Single European Act (SEA), which took effect in 1987.

The SEA was the first major set of revisions to the original treaties of the 1950s. Most prominently, the SEA contained a commitment to accelerate economic integration. It was designed in part to put into practice an agreement reached in 1985 to create a single European market: the basis for reinvigorating the competitiveness of the European economy. However, the SEA also strengthened the supranational institutions in order to speed up decision making.

The renewed dynamism of the SEA brought with it a more widespread revival of momentum. The links between EC policies led to pressures for initiatives in other spheres, for instance the proposals for monetary union (EMU). These developments formed one of the dynamics for a further exercise of treaty revision, in the Treaty on European Union (or, more popularly, the Maastricht Treaty), which was signed in February 1992. The other source of dynamics arose from the dramatic changes in the map of European politics at the end of 1989. The end of the Cold War, as well as the reunification of Germany in October 1990, reopened some of the fundamental issues that the integration process had sought to address at the start of the 1950s. What should now be regarded as 'Europe'? Who was to be responsible for ensuring the economic prosperity and democratic stability of this 'new' Europe? How should Europe's international role be defined? What should Germany's role be in the 'new' Europe? Should the institutions of the EC be reformed in anticipation of much greater membership in the future? Hence, all these kinds of question became intertwined with the existing questions, such as how to proceed to EMU.

The Maastricht Treaty represented an attempt at a revised structure for European integration. This treaty had a number of key aspects:

- It set out the blueprint for European Monetary Union (EMU), including a single European currency.

- It sought to strengthen social policy provision through the Social Chapter.

- It made the process of policy making more supranational.

- It formally created the European Union, comprising three pillars: the existing economic and social pillar; foreign policy; and cooperation on justice and home affairs (see below).

In the meantime, four non-members had begun to reassess their relationship with the integration process in the aftermath of the Cold War. For Austria, Finland, Sweden and Norway, traditionally 'neutral' states, the new international circumstances reduced the incompatibility between their neutrality and the EU's orientation. In addition, the single market programme was creating particular concerns for them, as the EU's economic rules were affecting them but they had no real say in decision making. The solution was to apply for membership. These states successfully negotiated terms and joined in January 1995, thus enlarging the EU. Membership was enlarged only to fifteen states because Norway rejected membership in a referendum.

Since the momentum generated in the mid-1980s, the integration process has barely paused for breath. Even while the Maastricht timetable for the single currency was moving ahead, the fifteen governments began in 1996 to review further treaty reform. This process culminated in the Amsterdam Treaty of 1997, which came into effect in 1999. This treaty tried to bring improvements to the functioning of the EU across a range of its policies, for example through institutional reforms, and placed emphasis on developing an 'area of freedom, justice and security' in the EU. In 2001, further reforms were agreed in the Treaty of Nice, although largely confined to institutional and decision-making matters ahead of the anticipated enlargement. A further – and the largest – round of enlargement took place as of May 2004 when ten member states joined the EU: Cyprus, the Czech Republic, Estonia, Hungary, Latvia, Lithuania, Malta, Poland, the Slovak Republic and Slovenia (see Figure 31.1). Although none of these states is of the size of the UK, and most are quite small, this enlargement has had a significant impact upon the character of the EU. Bringing in new democracies (as well as Cyprus and Malta), the EU now has a more diverse set of interests (see Table 31.1 for details on countries, accession dates and populations). France and Germany seem to have lost some of their traditional role as the motor of integration. The general pattern of intermittent institutional reform as well as enlargement together led the member governments to believe that the existing treaties and institutional structure were no longer 'up to the job'. Consequently a process of constitutional review was set in motion in December 2001, culminating in the twenty-five states approving the 'Treaty establishing a Constitution for Europe' in 2004. This treaty will discussed further below, but it should be noted that it has not been ratified as yet, so is not taken as the basis of the outline of the institutions and policies in what follows.

■ The EU's institutions and decision making

The European Union has five key institutions with which the student of British politics should be familiar. These are the European Commission, the Council of Ministers, the European Council, the

Figure 31.1 Map of European Union in 2006 showing seats of government near here

European Parliament (EP) and, finally, the European Court of Justice (ECJ).

The European Commission

The Commission acts as the 'civil service' of the EU. However, it also has a fair amount of autonomy. This is what sets the Commission apart from the secret-

ariats of other international organisations. This autonomy finds particular expression in two of its functions. First, it is the initiator of policy. This means that the Commission does not have to await instructions or guidelines from ministers but can propose legislation on its own initiative. Second, it is the 'conscience of the European Community'. This means that the Commission is supposed to develop

Table 31.1 Member state indicators in the EU of 25

Member state	Accession date[a]	Population 2004 (millions)	Votes in Council	MEPs 2004–7	In Euro?
Austria	1995	8.1	10	18	√
Belgium	1952	10.4	12	24	√
Cyprus	2004	0.7	4	6	
Czech Republic	2004	10.2	12	24	
Denmark	1973	5.4	7	14	
Estonia	2004	1.4	4	6	
Finland	1995	5.2	7	14	√
France	1952	59.9	29	78	√
Germany	1952	82.5	29	99	√
Greece	1981	11.0	12	24	√
Hungary	2004	10.1	12	24	
Ireland	1973	4.0	7	13	√
Italy	1952	57.9	29	78	√
Latvia	2004	2.3	4	9	
Lithuania	2004	3.4	7	13	
Luxembourg	1952	0.5	4	6	√
Malta	2004	0.4	3	5	
Netherlands	1952	16.3	13	27	√
Poland	2004	38.2	27	54	
Portugal	1986	10.5	12	24	√
Slovakia	2004	5.4	7	14	
Slovenia	2004	2.0	4	7	
Spain	1986	42.3	27	54	√
Sweden	1995	9.0	10	19	
United Kingdom	1973	59.7	29	78	
Total EU		**456.8**	**321**	**732**	

[a] Accession to the EC/EU or, for founder members, to the European Coal and Steel Community.

ideas that transcend national interests, although the proposals have to be practical if they are to be sure of success. Its other functions include helping to construct agreement on policy between member governments, ensuring that they put such agreements into legal effect and overseeing some of the detailed running of particular policies, for example the Common Agricultural Policy (CAP).

The Commission has a permanent staff establishment of some 25,000. This sounds large but, as the European Commission itself points out, is 'fewer than the number of staff employed by a typical medium-sized council in Europe'. At the head of

the Commission are twenty-five commissioners, one from each member state and one each in charge of a policy area (see photos). The Commission officials are organised into twenty-six directorates-general (DGs) as well as nine 'services'. The DGs may be seen as the equivalent of ministries in Whitehall: they are responsible for individual policy areas, such as agriculture, while the 'services' include central tasks such as interpreting.

The commissioners are appointed by national governments. One of the commissioners acts as president: at present it is José Manuel Barroso, a former Portuguese prime minister, who holds office

European Commission 2004–09

Source: Courtesy of the European Communities, 2006

NA-60-04-244-EN-P

for the period 2004–9. The Commission president is a potentially important figure who can set the tone for the work of the EU. That was the case under Jacques Delors, who served several terms lasting from 1985 to December 1994. During this period the Commission acted as an important force for deepening integration. Delors's successor, Jacques Santer, was much less successful and indeed he and the entire team of commissioners were forced to resign after the Commission became wrapped up in accusations of mismanagement. President Barroso has placed the emphasis in his work programme on improving the competitiveness of the European economy. The current UK Commissioner is Peter Mandelson, a key associate of Tony Blair and former minister in the Labour government. His responsibility is the important one of EU world trade policy, an area where the Commission has relatively strong powers. Like Commission officials, the commissioners are supposed to reflect the European interest rather than that of their country of origin. However, they tend to maintain a strong interest in their home country – something that is especially likely with Mandelson, given his strong relations with Tony Blair.

The Council of Ministers

The Council of Ministers is the main decision-making organ of the EU. It comprises ministers from each of the twenty-five member states. It meets almost 100 times each year but does so in nine different guises depending on the subject matter under discussion. Thus the Council of Agriculture and Fisheries Ministers or the Council of Economic and Financial Affairs Ministers (Ecofin) bring together the twenty-five national government ministers with responsibility for the respective policy area. Together with the General Affairs and External Relations Council (of foreign ministers), these are the three principal formations in which the Council meets. A formation that has been meeting increasingly frequently is the Justice and Home Affairs Council, which deals with issues such as visas, immigration and asylum from outside the EU as well as combating terrorist atrocities such as those in Madrid in 2004 and London in 2005. All ministers from the policy-based departments of Whitehall meet in one Council formation or other, including, from 1998, defence ministers.

The work of the Council is principally to take the many policy decisions of a political nature, agree the EU's budget, legislate and conclude international agreements with non-EU states or other international organisations. This work requires considerable preparation. Three agencies are worth mentioning in this connection. The preparation of the work of the Council is largely undertaken by officials of national governments in conjunction with counterparts in the Commission. The main forum for preparation is the Committee of Permanent Representatives (COREPER) and its related working groups. COREPER meetings are attended either by national civil servants or by diplomats who are based in the permanent representations, effectively member states' embassies in Brussels to the EU. It is in such meetings that the agenda is prepared for the forthcoming meetings of the Council of the EU. Given their heavy domestic schedules, meetings of the ministers can thus be confined to either rubber-stamping matters agreed in COREPER or to thrashing out the politically contentious issues.

The second agency is the presidency of the Council of Ministers. The presidency is held by each member state on a rota basis for a six-month term. The presidency is responsible for chairing Council and COREPER meetings. More generally, it serves the function of trying to put together packages of agreements across a range of policy areas that have a sufficient balance to satisfy the interests of all member states. The UK held the presidency in the second half of 2005. A six-month period is very short for the officials of a member state to master their brief. This is where the third agency comes in, namely the permanent secretariat of the Council. It has some 2,500 staff, including a contingent of translators and interpreters. Its key officials are able to provide continuity between the rotating presidencies.

What is distinctive about the EU, when compared with other international organisations, is the provision for the member governments to take decisions by weighted majority voting. Under majority voting, each member state is assigned a weighting to its vote, based roughly on the size of the country concerned. Such a system means that the British government may be overruled, but it still has to give effect to the legislation agreed by the majority. Thus the importance of majority voting is that it is a clear way in which national sovereignty may be lost. In reality, and despite Treaty provision, little use was made of majority voting until the mid-1980s and the passage of the SEA. The Maastricht and Amsterdam treaties extended provision still further. The Nice Treaty radically changed the way in which majority voting is carried out. The prevailing rules are now as follows

Source: Reuters / Yves Herman

(see Table 31.1 for details of the number of votes assigned to each member state):

A qualified majority is reached

■ if a majority of member states (in some cases a two-thirds majority) approve, *and*

■ if a minimum of 232 votes is cast in favour – which is 72.3 per cent of the total.

In addition, a member state may ask for confirmation that the votes in favour represent at least 62 per cent of the total population of the Union. If this is found not to be the case, the decision will not be adopted. This last condition has been included because the enlargement of 2004 brought in a series of small to medium-sized countries. The consequence was that a large number of small states could in principle outvote a small number of large states. The population rule is designed to ensure that an adequate majority of both states *and* of the EU's population approves legislation.

The European Council

The European Council, established in 1974, has developed into an important institution covering all activities of the European Union created by the Maastricht Treaty. It is broadly comparable with the Council of Ministers, except that it comprises the heads of government (in France's case, the President), the twenty-five foreign ministers and two commissioners. It meets at least twice per year, often four times. It has initiated some of the key EC/EU developments, such as the European Monetary System, the SEA, the Maastricht Treaty and the Amsterdam Treaty and the launch of the single currency on 1 May 1998. Given its composition, the European Council is best placed to provide leadership for strategic initiatives. Equally, however, its meetings may become media events, resulting in little substantive progress. Sessions of the European Council represent an opportunity for Tony Blair to play a part in EU policy making. Rivalry between

Hands up if you 'don't' think European agricultural subsidies need reforming: Prime Minister Tony Blair and French President Jacques Chirac clash at the June 2005 European Council
Source: Copyright © Chris Riddell. From *The Observer*, 12 June 2005. Reproduced with permission of Guardian Newspapers Limited

Tony Blair and French President Jacques Chirac over a range of issues – including different approaches to economic reform, the future of the EU and reform of agricultural budgetary policy – formed the background to disagreements between them at the June 2005 European Council (see cartoon).

The European Parliament

The EP comprises 732 members (or MEPs) since enlargement of the EU to twenty-five member states. MEPs are elected every five years by EU citizens in elections organised within the member states. The most recent elections were in June 2004. The UK results of those elections, in which the UK Independence Party made a strong showing, are set out in Table 31.2. Once elected, the seventy-eight UK MEPs and their counterparts from the other twenty-four states sit in transnational parliamentary groups rather than in national groups. The current

affiliations are set out in Table 31.2. A small number of British MEPs are non-attached, for example Robert Kilroy-Silk, the former television chat-show host. He was elected in the East Midlands on the UK Independence Party ticket but subsequently fell out with his colleagues and is now non-attached. Leaving aside these exceptions, the main British political parties have had to come to terms with cooperating with their counterparts, often from different political traditions, in the other member states. Of the major parties, this challenge has been the greatest for the Conservative Party, which has not always been at ease with continental counterparts from strongly pro-European Christian Democratic parties. Indeed, David Cameron's main move in European policy after election was to seek to end the Conservatives' association with the more pro-European (Christian Democratic) European People's Party, although it was unclear at the time of writing what the exact outcome will be.

Table 31.2 UK results in the 2004 European elections and EP group membership

Party	No. of MEPs	Name of party group in EP
Conservative	27	EPP-ED (26), one non-attached
Labour	19	Socialist Group in EP
UK Independence	12	Independence/Democracy Group (10), two non-attached
Liberal Democrat	12	Alliance of Liberals and Democrats
Green	2	Group of the Greens/European Free Alliance
Scottish National Party	2	Group of the Greens/European Free Alliance
Plaid Cymru	1	Group of the Greens/European Free Alliance
Democratic Unionist Party	1	Non-attached
Sinn Fein	1	European United Left/Nordic Green Left
Ulster Unionist Party	1	EPP-ED
Total	78	

Notes: EPP-ED–Group of the European People's Party (Christian Democrats) and European Democrats in the European Parliament. Party group affiliation reflects the situation in early 2006

Directly elected for the first time in 1979, the Parliament has suffered from a number of weaknesses, although these have gradually been addressed through reform measures. The principal weakness was its lack of powers. Until the mid-1980s, its powers were largely limited to offering (non-binding) opinions on legislation, the theoretical power to sack the Commission (never formally effected, but the Commission resigned in 1999 following a report by experts appointed by the Parliament) and the right to scrutinise the work of the Commission and Council.

The first steps towards enhancing these powers came in the 1970s, when the EP gained important influence over the EC budget. Then, from 1987, the implementation of the SEA introduced a new legislative role for the EP in certain policy areas. Its powers were further developed in the Maastricht Treaty by the introduction of a new co-decision power. Co-decision means that the EP is placed on an equal footing with the Council, and has the ultimate power to reject an item of legislation altogether. This is the most common procedure (of several) for the EP's involvement, its scope having been extended in the Amsterdam Treaty. The EP has significant powers in respect of agreements between the EU and third countries as well as the power of veto over the accession of new member states.

Nevertheless, the EP's public profile remains weak. The EP's work is not particularly suited to television, not least because a multilingual institu-

tion lacks the cut and thrust of the House of Commons. A further problem hampering the EP is the complex situation regarding its seat. Its plenary sessions are normally in Strasbourg; its committee meetings are in Brussels; its secretariat is based in Luxembourg. This split-site, three-country operation scarcely helps the EP to gain a clear profile. And the logistical arrangements seem to confirm the sceptical citizen's concern about the EU's remoteness and incomprehensibility. The EP's strong committee system is little known to those outside the EU policy-making 'network' but is actually central to its work. The EP remains the only directly elected parliament of any international organisation and potentially represents a competing focus for democratic legitimacy alongside national parliaments such as Westminster.

Indicative of the EP's problems with its profile is the turnout at European elections (see Table 31.3). When the sixth set of direct elections was held in 2004, EU-wide turnout was only 45.6 per cent, a figure strikingly lower than for national elections. The EC/EU average turnout has declined with every election, as the table shows. In the UK, turnout had been at the bottom end of the scale and in 1999 was only 24 per cent, but it increased to 38.9 per cent in 2004 when, however, there were considerably lower turnouts in several of the new member states. Low turnout figures do not give MEPs a strong claim to represent the country compared with the national government, elected on a much bigger turnout.

Table 31.3 Turnout in European elections (%)

Country	Year of election					
	1979	1984	1989	1994	1999	2004
Austria	na	na	na	67.7 (1996)	49.4	42.4
Belgium	91.6	92.2	90.7	90.7	91.0	90.8
Denmark	47.1	52.3	46.1	52.9	50.5	47.9
Finland	na	na	na	60.3 (1996)	31.4	41.1
France	60.7	56.7	48.7	52.7	46.8	42.8
Germany	65.7	56.8	62.4	60.0	45.2	43.0
Greece	78.6 (1981)	77.2	79.9	71.2	75.3	63.4
Ireland	63.6	47.6	68.3	44.0	50.2	59.7
Italy	85.5	83.9	81.5	74.8	70.8	73.1
Luxembourg	88.9	87.0	87.4	88.5	87.3	90.0
Netherlands	57.8	50.5	47.2	36.0	30.0	39.3
Portugal	na	72.2 (1987)	51.1	35.5	40.0	38.8
Spain	na	68.9 (1987)	54.8	59.1	63.0	45.1
Sweden	na	na	na	41.6 (1996)	38.8	37.8
UK	31.6	32.6	36.2	36.4	24.0	38.9
Cyprus	na	na	na	na	na	71.2
Czech Republic	na	na	na	na	na	28.3
Estonia	na	na	na	na	na	26.9
Hungary	na	na	na	na	na	38.5
Latvia	na	na	na	na	na	41.3
Lithuania	na	na	na	na	na	48.3
Malta	na	na	na	na	na	82.4
Poland	na	na	na	na	na	20.9
Slovakia	na	na	na	na	na	17.0
Slovenia	na	na	na	na	na	28.3
EC/EU average	63	61	58.5	56.8	49.8	45.6

Notes: na denotes not applicable, as the states had not yet joined the EC/EU.
Some member states have compulsory voting requirements, for instance Belgium and Luxembourg.
Election data for Germany prior to the 1994 election are for West Germany.
Dates in parentheses relate to the first direct elections held in the state concerned after their accession to the EC/EU.
Source: From the European Parliament website (www.elections2004.eu.int/ep-election/sites/en/results1306/turnout_ep/turnout_table.html), accessed 5 October 2005. Reproduced with permission of the European Communities

The UK elects seventy-eight MEPs: seventy-five from the British mainland by a closed regional list system, and three from Northern Ireland using a single-constituency proportional representation (PR) method. The closed regional list system of PR was introduced with the 1999 elections. The regional lists correspond to the boundaries of the English regions, as well as the Scottish and Welsh devolved institutions.

The European Court of Justice and EU law

Consideration of the ECJ enables attention to be drawn to three important characteristics of the EU. First, the significance of EU law and the treaties must not be underestimated. Within the UK, particularly in the absence of a formal, written constitution, it is difficult to appreciate continental traditions. A number of major developments in European integration have come about as a result of pathbreaking rulings by the ECJ in interpreting what the treaties 'meant'. Moreover, as the treaty basis of the EU widens, so a gradual constitutionalisation is taking place at the European level. It would not be too far-fetched to argue that the constitutional law of the EU is bringing about a 'quiet revolution' in British constitutional practice.

A second important feature is to point out the existence of a body of EU law. What is distinctive about European law is that, in principle, it has primacy over national law. Moreover, it may be directly applicable in not requiring the enactment of national legislation. It may also have direct effect, meaning that EU law entails rights and obligations that may be tested before national courts. These features of EU law are of fundamental importance to understanding the formal way in which EU membership challenges national sovereignty. In a 1990 ruling (the *Factortame* case), the ECJ effectively 'disapplied' British legislation because it did not comply with EU law (see Chapter 23). This case clearly demonstrated the principle that Parliament is no longer sovereign. In practical terms, however, large parts of criminal law are unaffected by the EU.

The third feature is simply to draw attention to the ECJ itself. It comprises twenty-five judges – one from each member state – and is based in Luxembourg. It acts in a number of ways: interpreting the treaties, enforcing the law and so on. Nugent (1994, p. 234) summarises its role thus:

The Court of Justice has played an extremely important part in establishing the EU's legal order . . . whether it is acting as an international court, a court of review, a court of appeal, or a court of referral . . . the Court is also frequently a maker of law as well as an interpreter of law.

The ECJ is assisted by the Court of First Instance, which deals with less important cases. Neither of these Luxembourg-based courts is to be confused with the European Court of Human Rights. Based in Strasbourg, it is associated with the Council of Europe, a quite different organisation from the EU that is concerned with human rights and democracy.

Other bodies and interest groups

There are a number of other EU institutions. These include the Court of Auditors, which scrutinises EU expenditure. The Economic and Social Committee is consulted on much legislation and acts as a kind of 'parliament of interests'. Its importance has been overshadowed somewhat in recent years by virtue of the increased power of the EP. Additionally, the Maastricht Treaty created a Committee of the Regions. This institution enhanced the involvement of the regions, particularly in those EU policy areas with spatial aspects, such as regional policy. Also important is the European Central Bank (ECB) based in Frankfurt, Germany. It is responsible for setting the interest rate for all those states fully participating in the single currency, the euro. Although the UK is not a participant, the ECB's interest rate decisions have an impact on the thinking of the Bank of England. If the UK were to join the euro, the ECB would take over key functions of the Bank of England.

The final main category of participants in decision making is the vast array of interest groups lobbying the EU institutions. There are over 500 such groups, which bring together interest groups from the member states. One of the principal such organisations is the Committee of Professional Agricultural Organisations (COPA), which comprises most of the national-level farmer organisations, including the UK's National Farmers' Union. The extensive nature of European lobbying demonstrates another way in which the EU has penetrated UK politics, for it is now necessary for all British interest groups potentially affected by EU decisions to have some means of lobbying the relevant institutions, especially the Commission. Moreover, it is not normally feasible or effective for a UK interest group to lobby the Commission. The Commission has limited staffing resources and prefers only to consult groups representative of the EU as a whole. In this way it can consult one interest group rather than twenty-five national ones. However, what is also true is that UK interest groups still lobby national government on EU policies. Nevertheless, this strategy may not suffice, particularly given that the UK government may be overruled in the Council of Ministers through a majority vote.

A final further observation on lobbying at the EU level concerns local government and the regions. It has now become the rule for the English regions and the devolved authorities in Scotland and Wales to have a European office of some kind. Some local authorities have their own such office. In the case of those parts of the UK eligible to receive aid from the EU's funds, it is essential for local authorities to have effective contacts with the Commission. There is, in consequence, a significant impact on local authority activity in the UK. Of course, local authorities are not normally regarded as interest groups. However, in their relations with the EU authorities, this is the best kind of parallel to make for their activities.

EU decision making

There are many different patterns for EU decision making. However, it is important to give some kind of impression of the interaction of the agencies outlined above. Necessarily this requires some simplification. What follows sets out the decision-making process in the economic and social policy domains of the EU (the so called EC 'pillar' of the EU). Proposals normally originate from the Commission, which will usually have consulted with interested parties beforehand. The proposals are then sent to the Council of Ministers. There, deliberations take place initially at the specialist level among officials of the national governments, usually under the umbrella of COREPER. However, the proposal is simultaneously sent to the EP and the Economic and Social Committee. The latter submits an opinion on the proposal to the Council. However, the former will make its views known through one of several procedures (principally consultation or co-decision), depending on the legal basis of the proposal. It is during this phase that a second stage of lobbying takes place through two channels: EU-level groups lobby the EP, and national groups will lobby 'their'

national government. The final stage of the process is when the Council reaches its decision, taking into account the advice received and in accordance with the prevailing voting method for the policy area under consideration. A schematic presentation of decision making is set out in Figure 31.2.

EU decision making and the impact upon British politics

As has been seen, decision making can follow several paths. Moreover, its characteristics are not especially familiar to the broader British public. Why is this so?

1. The procedure is remote by virtue of being centred on Brussels.

2. The constitutional–legal principles are different from those familiar in the UK.

3. The EU's policy responsibilities are wide. This means that it is easy to present the EU as 'interfering' with accepted British practice, even though this interference will probably have been sanctioned by a British minister.

4. The EU remains largely concerned with economic issues, and its predominant mode of governing, in the absence of a large budget, is through acting as a regulator. Thus it sets the framework for economic activities (for instance, through competition policy); it regulates particular sections of the economy (for instance, agriculture and telecommunications); and it seeks to ensure that economic interests do not work against those of society at large (for instance, through environmental policy and equal opportunities policy). This regulatory mode of governing tends to be very much a matter for technical bargaining between governments, the EU institutions and interest groups. It is conducted away from the public eye.

5. Even for those specialising in the politics of the EU, the multiplicity of possible procedures makes decision making difficult to penetrate.

All these characteristics have important ramifications for British politics because the UK and the EU are interlocked systems of government. The institutional and policy-making apparatus in Brussels has a significant impact upon the way in which the UK is governed (see Table 31.4). We review this impact – sometimes known as Europeanisation – in summary form.

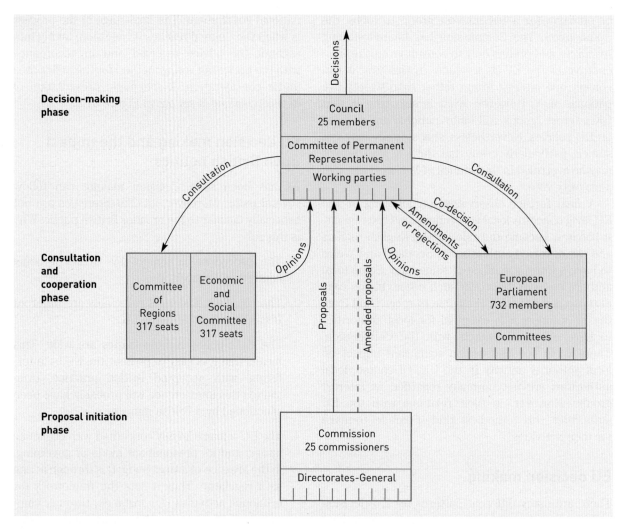

Figure 31.2 The Union's proposal and decision-making process

■ A significant amount of draft legislation emanates from the EU – chiefly from the Commission – and must be reviewed by government officials to establish how it affects UK interests.

■ Officials from across the whole of central government, including the devolved authorities beyond London, must define a position and present it at meetings of both officials, and ultimately ministers, from the EU (Bulmer and Burch, 1998, 2000). As part of this they may have to develop new skills: in foreign languages or in the different type of negotiating that takes place in the EU. It is no good trying to negotiate as if in Whitehall or Westminster when the rules of the EU game are quite different. In 1998, for instance, Council data revealed that there had been 3,139 meetings of officials within its working groups.

■ In order to respond to the challenge of the EU, all Whitehall ministries have set up coordinating offices to have some oversight over the impact

Table 31.4 EU decision-making bodies attended by UK ministers and officials

Institution	UK participant	Number of formations
European Council	Prime Minister, Foreign Secretary, advisers	1
Council of the EU	Minister, advisers	9
Working groups	Officials, usually from Whitehall	200 +

of European policy upon their responsibilities. The key ministerial players are the Foreign and Commonwealth Office, the Treasury, the Department of the Environment, Food and Rural Affairs, the Department of Trade and Industry and the Cabinet Office, whose European Secretariat acts as a troubleshooter where differences arise between ministries. The head of this secretariat acts as the Prime Minister's adviser at meetings of the European Council.

■ Ministers are also involved in this process: the Prime Minister through participation in European Council sessions, the Foreign Secretary, the Chancellor and most other members of the Cabinet and their junior ministers. There are nearly 100 ministerial meetings in the EU each year.

■ Later in the decision-making process, these same ministries as well as other bodies from employers to local government have to ensure that they have mechanisms in place to implement or adhere to European law. If they do not do so, the full force of the law may be applied to their cost through the national court system in the same way as for purely domestic legislation.

■ Parliamentarians have had to adapt their own procedures in both Houses to try to ensure that they can make an effective input into decision making at the EU level. The European Scrutiny Committee of the House of Commons seeks to hold the government to account. However, this is a difficult task, since the government participates directly within EU policy-making, whereas Parliament does not. Following devolution, members of the Scottish Parliament, Welsh Assembly and Northern Ireland Assembly have sought to address these issues too.

■ Members of the European Parliament can serve as a separate channel of democratic input from regional constituencies into the EU policy process.

■ Sub-national government has also had to adapt: the devolved authorities in Scotland, Wales, Northern Ireland (when operational) and, increasingly, the English regions, plus local authorities across the UK. This adaptation is especially important since some parts of the UK have been eligible over the years for substantial financial support for regional and social development, notably Northern Ireland, Merseyside, the Highlands and Islands, South Yorkshire and Cornwall. The most active authorities set up an office in Brussels for lobbying or intelligence gathering.

■ Political parties must adapt. They need to find ways to 'play the European game'. Unless they are pursuing a deliberately non-cooperative policy, like the UK Independence Party for example, they will most likely seek out allies among their continental counterparts. Why? Because in an EU of twenty-five states joint initiatives or action stand a much greater chance of success in EU negotiations. This is the dilemma that faces the new Conservative leader, David Cameron. He wants Conservative MEPs to leave the more pro-European European People's Party but risks losing influence within the EP as a result.

■ Interest groups have to get to grips with a multi-level lobbying strategy where their interests are affected by the EU. Farmers and industrialists may go beyond lobbying in conjunction with their EU counterparts and set up their own offices in Brussels to ensure that their voice is heard. The same is true for the largest companies. An alternative approach is to engage the services of lobbying consultants in Brussels.

■ More problematically, UK public opinion on European issues has to be taken account of. The difficulty is that many members of the public regard the EU as remote until some threat to the British way of life is perceived, such as the abolition of the pound if the government were to join EMU. UK public opinion is among the least positive about the European integration process, as indicated in successive Eurobarometer polls (available on line at http://europa.eu.int/comm/public_opinion/index_en.htm).

The result of this impact is the emergence of multi-level government and politics in the UK. Whether it is central government, Parliament or interest groups, they must ensure both that they are well equipped to know what the EU is doing and that their voice is heard in the EU's decisions.

■ The key policy areas

The integration process has involved an ever-widening portfolio of policies. The initial concern of integration was with the coal and steel industries, in the ECSC. By contrast, the EEC had a much wider policy impact. It comprised a large range of policies and, as they were put into operation, so the policy areas began to penetrate the activities of the member states, resulting in the 'Europeanisation' of national policies. From the 1970s, the member states also dealt with a handful of policy issues outside the formal treaties. The best example of this was the foreign policy cooperation procedure, created in 1970. Subsequently, such issues as combating international terrorism were treated in this way. With the end of the Cold War, the home affairs area became more salient to the member states because of fears of large-scale immigration from the east and of criminal gangs exploiting opportunities in a new borderless European market. The Maastricht Treaty sought to give these activities a clearer basis through treaty status but with separate arrangements for decision making. The treaty introduced institutional arrangements based on a temple (see Figure 31.3).

In this 'architecture' of a temple, all the collective activities of the member states were placed under the 'roof' of the European Union. The existing economic treaties form a supranational EC 'pillar' within the European Union. However, the EU is supported by two other pillars, which comprise activities conducted in an intergovernmental manner. One of these pillars formalises foreign policy cooperation, now known as the Common Foreign and Security Policy (CFSP), in the EU. The other pillar comprised Justice and Home Affairs (JHA) cooperation. Following the Amsterdam Treaty the third pillar is confined to the areas of police cooperation and judicial cooperation such as over extradition. The institutional structures of the CFSP and JHA pillars are dominated by governments, normally voting by unanimity and thus with no formal threat to sovereignty. Links with supranational institutions such as the Commission and EP are more limited in these areas of policy. Similarly, decisions taken in these two pillars do not have the status of European law.

We now turn to the activities encompassed by the European Union as a whole but begin with those of the long-standing EC pillar. The three long-standing policies associated with the EC pillar have been the common market between the member states, the Common Agricultural Policy (CAP) and a common commercial policy with the outside world.

The common market

The idea of creating a common market between the member states was to provide a stimulus to economic efficiency. A common market would allow consumers to choose between the most price-competitive producers from within the market. At the same time, producers would be able to produce their goods and services for a market larger than their own state, thereby becoming able to generate economies of scale. How, then, does it correspond to what has happened in the European context?

As set out in the EEC Treaty, the European common market provided essentially for three developments. These were the removal of tariffs on trade between member states; the free movement of goods, persons, services and capital; and harmonising legislation that affects the operation of the common market. The first of these three was achieved without major difficulty in mid-1968, one year ahead of the treaty schedule. However, other barriers to trade proved much more resistant to change. Member states used different technical requirements and a host of national measures to protect domestic producers. For example, German law defined very strictly what ingredients were permitted in beer. Beer including ingredients other than those could not be sold in Germany, so German law formed a barrier to trade. This kind of situation was pervasive.

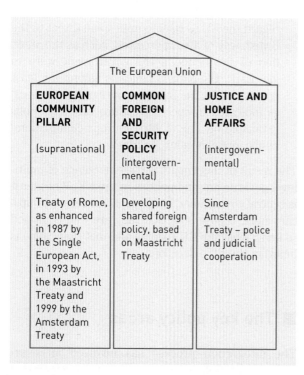

Figure 31.3 The architecture of the European Union

As a result of such barriers, the EC's progress towards achieving a true common market was, in reality, poor. However, this policy was revived by the single-market programme, endorsed and accelerated by the SEA. As a result, most of the legislation needed to create a common (or internal) market had been agreed by the deadline of 31 December 1992. The UK government of Margaret Thatcher was one of the main proponents of the single-market programme, for it was consistent with the Conservatives' support for opening up markets and introducing more competitive economic conditions. Linked to the common market is competition policy, which aims to ensure that fair business practices prevail in trade between member states. The internal market and competition policy have very substantial effects on the day-to-day activities of businesses in the UK. This is reflected not least in the fact that the UK's fellow member states in the EU represent its most important trading partners (over half of both imports to, and exports from, the UK). In more recent times, the single market has been regarded as a key element in the EU's response to the challenge of globalisation.

The Common Agricultural Policy

The CAP was introduced in the 1960s. Although it now represents a small share of EU GDP and of EU employment, agriculture was more important in 1958. In fact the EU became more 'agricultural' with eastern enlargement in 2004, since some of the new states – for instance Poland – have a large farming sector. 2003 statistics for the present twenty-five states show agriculture representing 5.2 per cent of the civilian working population and generating 1.6 per cent of EU GDP. Agriculture has also been of greater electoral importance on the continent than in the UK. Reflecting the interests of the then six member states, the CAP was created as a high-cost, protectionist policy that in crude terms favoured the interests of farmers over those of consumers. Its high costs derived from its price-setting policy, which aimed to cover the costs even of small, inefficient farmers. It was protectionist because it worked on the basis of 'Community preference'; lower-cost producers from the world market were denied free access.

Prior to 1973, the UK had a different type of agricultural policy. It was expensive for the taxpayer but ensured cheap food supplies to consumers. Adaptation to the CAP proved controversial in the UK because food prices rose following accession. In addition, the lack of a large agricultural sector meant that Britain did not receive much revenue from a large expenditure component of the modest EC budget. This in turn created a further imbalance, for the UK found itself becoming a major net contributor to the EC budget, alongside Germany. The costs of the CAP, along with the budgetary imbalance, led to Margaret Thatcher's demands, in the early 1980s, for the UK to have its 'own money back'. This dispute, which soured Britain's relations with the EC, also slowed progress on some other policies until the matter was resolved. That occurred in 1984 with the creation of a budget rebate to reflect the inequity Britain faced under the system. From about that time a period of agricultural reforms began, aimed at reducing the policy's cost and making it more in step with the liberalisation of world trade. Successive UK governments – Conservative and Labour alike – have argued strongly for reducing CAP expenditure and increased agricultural efficiency. More recently, as part of its engagement with the campaign to 'make poverty history', British criticism has also been directed at the way in which the CAP hampers exports by some of the world's poorest states.

Today, Britain can scarcely be considered to have its own agricultural policy, for it is largely determined at EU level. This situation was displayed most graphically with the BSE crisis in 1996. National solutions to the eradication of 'mad cow disease' were an insufficient policy response; in a single market the other member states needed assurances that there were no risks to their consumers, and a ban on the export of British beef was imposed.

The common commercial policy

The common commercial policy formed the external counterpart to creating a common internal European market. Hence, as internal tariffs were removed, so a common external tariff was created. This means that the EU is a powerful bloc in international trade negotiations. The UK government now has very limited powers in trade policy. The government's main involvement is in ensuring that the policy of the EU is consistent with British wishes. In the international trade negotiations conducted in the World Trade Organization, the bargaining with states such as Japan and the USA is conducted by representatives of the EU rather than by the individual member states.

Economic and Monetary Union (EMU)

Economic and monetary policy received considerable attention in the Maastricht Treaty, although EMU had already been on the EC's agenda in the early 1970s; indeed, it was due to have been completed by 1980! However, the 1973 oil crisis and upheaval in the international monetary system put a stop to that. In 1979, the more modest European Monetary System was introduced to stabilise currency fluctuations, but without UK membership of the all-important exchange rate mechanism (ERM). Participating countries kept their national currencies. The British government was opposed to membership on the grounds that it would constrain domestic economic policy. However, in October 1990, John Major, then Chancellor of the Exchequer, convinced Margaret Thatcher to join. Membership ended in September 1992 on 'Black Wednesday', when turmoil in the foreign exchanges forced the pound to leave. The domestic consequence was that the Conservatives were seen as losing their reputational advantage over Labour for safely running the economy.

The Maastricht Treaty included a commitment to proceeding to EMU by 1999 at the latest. Nevertheless, John Major negotiated an opt-out of this policy, meaning that the UK did not accede to a single currency even though the other member states agreed in May 1998 to proceed to the third (final) stage in 1999. The Labour government adopted a slightly different policy. In the 1997 election campaign, the Labour Party committed itself to entering EMU but only after receiving authorisation in the Cabinet, in Parliament and in a popular referendum. In the autumn of 1997, Chancellor Gordon Brown announced the government's policy of having no constitutional objections to membership but making accession dependent upon five economic tests (see Bulmer, 2000, pp. 246–7; also further discussion below). In the meantime, the euro (denoted by the symbol €) replaced national currencies in the twelve participating states (see Table 31.1 for the members).

Other policies

Social and regional policies came to be significant activities by the 1990s. Both these policies were of negligible significance in the original EEC Treaty. In the early 1970s, a concern to give the EC more of a 'social' role led to various policy proposals. The European Regional Development Fund was set up in 1975 to provide assistance to poorer areas in the EC. The European Social Fund was developed as a means of supporting projects such as employment training or retraining in areas of economic underdevelopment or economic restructuring. The UK was a substantial recipient of aid from these funds but they are now being refocused on the poorer states of central and eastern Europe following the 2004 enlargement. Both policies gained additional emphasis at the time of the SEA, for the EC developed an explicit interest in 'cohesion'. This term referred to a commitment to ensure that the poorer member states – at that time principally those of southern Europe – were neither socially nor regionally disadvantaged by completion of the internal market. With the commitment to EMU in the Maastricht Treaty, a new Cohesion Fund was created to assist economically weaker member states. Collectively, the above funds are usually referred to as the Structural Funds.

Social policy measures had been limited until the mid-1980s, when a new direction was taken with the EC's attempts to ensure that the labour force did not suffer deteriorating workplace conditions as a result of the more competitive single market. Conservative governments in the UK resisted most of these developments and secured an opt-out of the principal one, namely the Maastricht Treaty's Social Chapter. However, the Labour Party opposed this opt-out and signed up to the Social Chapter after assuming office.

All these economic and social policies are run with a – by national standards – very modest EC budget. For 2005, it amounted to €117 billion (or £79 billion). This is only 1 per cent of EU GNP and is therefore a very small instrument for achieving any major policy impact. CAP spending, at its peak approaching three-quarters of the EC budget, is now down to approximately half of overall expenditure. However, the budget is insufficient for the EU to manage the macro-economy. The main public expenditure and fiscal powers remain with member states even in the era of EMU.

Other policies with major impacts on the UK include environmental, transport and technology policy. In addition, there are the activities in the other two pillars of the European Union. In the 1990s, the Home Office underwent the Europeanisation process that other Whitehall ministries had experienced much earlier. This development arose from the Maastricht Treaty onwards, when combating international crime and increasing international cooperation on immigration and asylum became

EU matters. Further impulses to this policy area came in response to the al-Qaeda terror attacks on American targets on 11 September 2001 and subsequently on European ones. In the area of foreign policy cooperation, the member states have extremely well-developed procedures. UK foreign policy can no longer be seen in isolation from the collective activities of the member states. However, it is certainly not possible to refer to a common European foreign policy as yet, for there are still occasions when member states break ranks. In the 1980s the UK government did this on several occasions, preferring to follow American foreign policy instead (George, 1998). Occasional high-profile divisions between member states over foreign policy continue to demonstrate that the EU has some way to go before it can claim to have a truly 'common' foreign and security policy. The most recent divisions came in 2002–3 over Iraq (see Box 31.4).

The Maastricht Treaty extended cooperation into the security domain, but the Conservative government regarded defence policy to be the preserve of NATO. Initially, this seemed also to be the policy of the Blair government, for instance as expressed in the negotiation of the Amsterdam Treaty. In October 1998, however, it floated the idea of giving the EU a defence identity. Subsequently, it was agreed among other things that the EU should, by 2003, be able to mobilise 60,000 troops at two months' notice (see Deighton, 2002). The EU has subsequently developed its military capacity so that it can act in support of its foreign policy declarations where NATO action is not appropriate. For example, it has deployed forces in the Congo and took over NATO responsibilities in Bosnia from December 2004.

In conclusion, the impact of the EU upon UK public policy has been very considerable.

■ Britain and the EU in the new millennium: continuing controversy or new consensus?

Supranational integration has provoked opposition or division in the UK ever since the 1950 Schuman Plan. It has been the cause of major political divisions within both parties. In this section, we examine those divisions and whether the Blair government has been able to build a new consensus on EU membership.

1. Already at the time of negotiating the terms of British membership and in the subsequent parliamentary ratification of the European Communities Act (1971–2), divisions emerged within both parties. Divisions within the Conservative Party meant that the Heath government's whips had to rely on pro-European Labour MPs refusing to vote against the accession legislation to secure the necessary votes to achieve membership. Within the opposition Labour Party, divisions created serious problems for maintaining party unity: Harold Wilson's compromise position of advocating a referendum on membership resulted in the resignation of the deputy leader, Roy Jenkins.

2. The 1975 referendum, which was called by Harold Wilson's government with a view to resolving domestic disputes concerning EC membership, was a device aimed at limiting the damage arising from serious splits within the governing Labour Party (see above).

3. The defection in 1981 of four senior Labour politicians to found the Social Democratic Party (SDP) was in part the result of frustration at Labour's then policy of withdrawal from the EC.

4. Three senior Conservative ministers were casualties of divisions relating to supranational integration: Nigel Lawson on membership of the ERM (1989); Nicholas Ridley over German power in the EC (1990); and Sir Geoffrey Howe over the direction of Mrs Thatcher's policy.

5. At the end of 1990, Margaret Thatcher was ousted as party leader as a result of matters brought to a head by a European disagreement concerning the development of proposals for EMU.

6. During 1992–3, the government of John Major found great difficulty in maintaining the necessary party unity to secure the ratification of the Maastricht Treaty. The Labour Party was not opposed to the treaty but opposed Britain's opt-out of the Social Chapter and made ratification very difficult for Major's government. The treaty was finally approved on 23 July 1993, but only after the Conservative government had made the issue a vote of confidence, with the threat of a general election hanging over its rebels (see Baker *et al.*, 1994).

7. Subsequently, in December 1994, nine of the critics of the Maastricht Treaty from the

Conservative back benches voted against the government on a European issue and had the party whip withdrawn, thus technically removing John Major's parliamentary majority.

8. During 1996–7, the Major government played an obstructionist role in the negotiations on a review of the Maastricht Treaty. This tactic was pursued because of its small electoral majority and the need to avoid divisions within the party. Eventually, the other fourteen EU governments deferred further negotiation until the British general election had taken place. It was the Labour government which signed the Amsterdam Treaty that ensued from this process.

9. In 1996, the BSE crisis led to a major row with EU partners. Other member states were concerned about the spread of 'mad cow disease' among their cattle, about the possible transmission of the disease to humans, and about the loss of confidence in their domestic beef markets. In consequence, an export ban was imposed on the UK. The Major government blocked much EU decision making for one month in 1996 as a protest, creating considerable diplomatic tension (Westlake, 1997).

The Conservative Party had entered the 1997 election with fundamental divisions over European policy. This issue and the loss of its reputation for good economic management – something that could be traced back to mishandling membership of the European exchange rate mechanism – raised serious questions about the Conservatives' ability to govern. The Labour Party was more united on European issues, and Tony Blair promised a more constructive engagement with the EU. The Blair government was able to notch up some achievements in its first term (see Bulmer, 2000, Deighton, 2001, and Smith, 2005, for fuller details). This broad pattern has continued in subsequent terms, but problem areas remain.

■ It played a constructive role in the negotiations leading to the Amsterdam Treaty.

■ It conducted a reasonably successful presidency of the EU's Council of Ministers in 1998.

■ Internally, Blair initiated an internal European policy review designed to raise the profile of European business in Whitehall and the UK's impact on the EU stage (see Bulmer and Burch, 2005).

■ Strengthened defence cooperation emerged as an area of emphasis for British diplomacy in the EU and contributed to increasing collaboration between member states in this domain.

■ In the economic domain, the government placed emphasis on increasing the European economy's competitiveness, promoting in particular a process of policy exchange and comparison designed to get more Europeans into jobs. This process also made a mark at EU level.

■ It has been a strong advocate of successive enlargements of the EU. During its presidency in 2005 the UK government oversaw agreement on holding talks about eventual Turkish membership, although this process is likely to take ten years or more.

■ In discussion on the future organisation of the EU, the Labour government arguably became the first since membership in 1973 to engage constructively with discussion concerning the EU's constitution. This debate took place within the so-called Convention on the Future of Europe. The Convention was invited by the European Council to draw up a constitution for a post-enlargement EU. Successive reforms through the Amsterdam and Nice Treaties had adjusted the existing apparatus but it was felt that a new blueprint was needed. This process led the twenty-five governments to agree in 2004 on a Constitutional Treaty, but it has not yet been ratified and its prospects currently look uncertain (see Box 31.1).

■ During the British presidency of the EU in the second half of 2005, Tony Blair's government tried once again to reform the EU budget over the medium term. British policy, announced by Blair at the European Parliament in June 2005, was to improve the budget's focus on modernising the EU to meet the competitiveness challenges posed by globalisation. Other member states attacked the continuation of the British budgetary rebate. New member states from central and eastern Europe resented any British attempts to limit the amount of structural funds they would receive. At a summit in Brussels in December 2005 a compromise was reached: very modest reform, structural aid to eastern Europe, a mid-term review of the budget, and a reduction in the British rebate.

The Blair government has certainly built a more consensual position on European policy. However, Blair's own pro-European ambitions have not been

BOX 31.1 FACT

A constitution for Europe?

A Convention on the Future for Europe was set up in 2001 and met during the period 2002–3. It was presided over by the former French President, Valéry Giscard d'Estaing. A number of British MPs, MEPs and ministerial representatives – notably Peter Hain, the Minister for Europe, participated in the exercise along with counterparts from other states. The tasks it faced were:

- How to organise the division of responsibilities between the Union and the Member States?
- How to better define the respective tasks of the European institutions?
- How to ensure the coherence and effectiveness of the Union's external action?
- How to strengthen the Union's legitimacy?

The convention submitted a **Draft Treaty** establishing a Constitution for Europe to the European Council. The latter body set up an Inter-Governmental Conference to convert the treaty into something acceptable to all governments. This was accomplished in June 2004.

According to the Foreign Office's ten-point summary of the 2004 Constitutional Treaty, it:

- Consolidates existing Treaties into a single text;
- Creates a President of the European Council and a Union Minister for Foreign Affairs;
- Introduces a new system of double majority voting from November 2009: decisions by QMV will need support of 55 per cent of countries, representing 65 per cent of EU population;
- Extends Qualified Majority Voting to 15 areas;
- Makes it explicit that Member States can leave the EU if they wish;
- Includes a new role for national Parliaments to opine on Commission proposals in draft (a 'subsidiarity mechanism');
- Makes Qualified Majority Voting (QMV) the norm for JHA issues but includes an emergency brake mechanism for criminal procedural law;
- Carries over UK Protocol so UK can opt-in where it wants to for immigration, asylum and civil justice issues;
- Incorporates the Charter of Fundamental Rights;
- Otherwise, existing Treaties are largely carried over unchanged.

Ratification commenced from 2004 but, with several states having ratified, the process came to a stop in May/June when referendums in France and then the Netherlands rejected the Constitutional Treaty. In June 2005 the European Council called for a period of reflection. It remains unclear whether the treaty will be revived or whether it has to be abandoned because of the lack of any prospect of a yes vote in France and the Netherlands. In official terms the process has been paused for 'reflection'.

Sources: Based on information from the following websites, accessed 7 October 2005: http://europa.eu.int/constitution/futurum/index_en.htm and http://www.fco.gov.uk/

fulfilled in two respects. First, the original intention following election in 1997 had been to make the case for joining the single currency, but it remains unfulfilled. In summer 2003 the Treasury published a report based on the five economic tests announced by Chancellor Gordon Brown in the autumn of 1997. The Chancellor sought to keep this policy decision as firmly under Treasury control as possible but the Cabinet wanted greater involvement. The report deemed that not all five tests had been met and a decision was deferred. It is not expected that the government will pursue the idea of joining the euro during the current parliament. If and when the Labour government does advocate membership, it has committed itself to securing approval of the policy in a referendum.

The second major failing is that the government has failed to make an effective 'case for the EU' in the eyes of the public. It has launched initiatives at EU level but domestic public opinion has become less supportive of the EU. Other areas of tension with EU partners have also remained, although these are pretty much a product of divergent British national interests. Problems over CAP reform have already been mentioned. Another major area of recurrent tension is on foreign and security policy. While the Labour government has favoured strengthening the EU's capacity, there have been recurrent tensions where the UK has found the pulls of European policy at odds with Anglo-American relations. During the Iraq crisis in 2002–3, the government found itself torn between the very hostile attitude of the Bush Administration to Iraq on the one hand and the wish of its EU partners to pursue all avenues of diplomacy on the other.

The Conservative Party under successive leaders (William Hague, Iain Duncan Smith and Michael Howard) remained divided on European policy. However, latterly the party has succeeded in downplaying European policy: a smart tactical move, given its internal divisions. However, it is now much less clear what Conservative policy on the EU amounts to. In consequence, where the Conservatives seek to criticise the government's European policy, their approach is open to the accusations of being haphazard and lacking in alternatives. Perhaps policy will become clearer under the new leader, David Cameron. The Liberal Democrats, by contrast, have a much more coherent (and positive) European policy. The Scottish National Party and Plaid Cymru have had to give thought to European policy because of their wish to articulate a vision of Scotland/Wales in Europe within the devolved assemblies.

■ The UK, the EU and multi-level government

Traditionally, British politicians have come to see the EU as a threat: more power for the EU means less power for British MPs and ministers. Although a minority of Conservative politicians currently seem to wish to question the desirability of EU membership, the vast majority of the political élite is signed up to it. Indeed, under the Blair government there

has been some attempt to go beyond the traditional perception of the EU as a threat. Moreover, it is important to see the links between the changing domestic landscape of constitutional change and the EU context. Devolution within the UK, changes in the electoral system (greater use of proportional representation), parliamentary reform measures and incorporation of human rights principles: these developments are bringing the British political system closer to its continental counterparts. These developments are also promoting the development of a multi-level system of government. And they may have helped the Blair government to feel more at ease than its predecessors in debates about the EU constitution.

Following devolution to Scotland and Wales in mid-1999, the issue of agriculture offered some indications of UK politics in an increasingly interlocked pattern of government. With farmers concerned about the emergence of a crisis with falling incomes for livestock, the question arose as to which level of government was appropriate to solve the problem. Should the new devolved authorities in Scotland and Wales offer financial support in light of their responsibilities for agriculture? How would the UK Department of Food, Rural Affairs and Agriculture (DEFRA) fit in, with its responsibilities for presenting a single voice in the EU and for agriculture in England? And what of the CAP, which limits the scope for action at odds with European policy? The result was a need to achieve a mutually compatible solution for all three levels: to get an agreed situation within the UK and to secure the approval of the EU (for a detailed account, see Bulmer *et al.*, 2002, Chapter 5). This pattern has already extended into other policy areas, including regional policy, the environment and fisheries. And as Whitehall and Westminster become used to sharing power downwards to Cardiff, Edinburgh and – depending on the peace process – Belfast, the ability to share it upwards with the EU may become less fraught in the future. At the same time, changes may come about in the way we identify with the different levels of government that impact upon us (see Box 31.2). After thirty years of EU membership, Britain has perhaps reduced its fixation with the indivisible, sovereign nation-state, although this view is not shared in the Conservative Party. Combined with domestic devolution, European integration has brought about a multi-level form of British government that is more in line with the practice of democracy in other member states (see Box 31.3).

BOX 31.2 IDEAS AND PERSPECTIVES

UK, the EU and the sense of identity

The Economist on 6 November 1999 made a useful contribution to the debate over the future of relation-ships between Britain and the EU. It published the results of a MORI poll, which suggested that British people have already assumed the future is likely to be more European, whatever the Eurosceptics might say or wish. Tables 31.5, 31.6 and 31.7 reveal nearly half of the citizens of the four national elements of

Table 31.5 Influence:
In 20 years' time, which of these bodies, if any, do you expect to have most influence over your life and the lives of your children? (%)

	Britain	England	Scotland	Wales
My local council	13	14	5	7
Scottish Parliament/Welsh Assembly/my regional assembly	13	9	46	26
Westminster Parliament	22	23	8	25
European Parliament/European Union	44	46	31	37
Don't know	8	8	10	6

Source: From *The Economist*, 6 November 1999. Copyright © The Economist Newspaper Limited 1999. All rights reserved. Reproduced with permission

Table 31.6 Regional identification:
Which two or three of these, if any, would you say you most identify with?

	Britain	England	Scotland	Wales
This local community	41	42	39	32
This region	50	49	62	50
England/Scotland/Wales	45	41	72	81
Britain	40	43	18	27
Europe	16	17	11	16
Commonwealth	9	10	5	3
The global community	8	9	5	2
Don't know	2	2	1	0

Source: From *The Economist*, 6 November 1999. Copyright © The Economist Newspaper Limited 1999. All rights reserved. Reproduced with permission

Table 31.7 Flag identification:
Which of these flags, if any, do you identify with? (%)

	Britain	England	Scotland	Wales
United Kingdom (Union Jack)	83	88	49	55
England (Cross of St George)	33	38	2	3
Scotland (Cross of St Andrew)	23	18	75	8
Wales (Welsh Dragon)	26	24	12	85
European Union (12 stars)	21	23	5	7
United States (Stars and Stripes)	23	26	7	<1
Don't know	2	2	0	1

Source: From *The Economist*, 6 November 1999. Copyright © The Economist Newspaper Limited. All rights reserved. Reproduced with permission

▶

the UK assuming that it will be the EU that will exert the most influence over their lives and those of their children within twenty years. Interestingly, though, only 16 or 17 per cent most identified (in the autumn of 1999) with the EU, and most looked for such an allegiance to either their local community, region, country or the composite, 'Britain'.

When it came to flags, the EU flag attracted one-fifth support, while the Union Flag was the favourite, with the Welsh dragon doing just as well in Wales itself. Significantly, perhaps, over a fifth of Britons identified with the US flag.

Another significant question related to the entity that would be likely to offer the most support in a crisis. Figure 31.4 shows that the USA easily exceeds the EU as the likely source of support, suggesting that loyalties to the EU are still heavily tempered by distrust and insecurity. Similarly, Figure 31.5 suggests that the USA is also seen as the more appropriate template for economic policy and political progress.

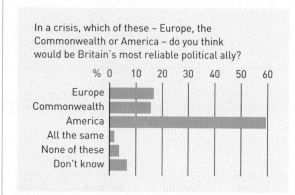

Figure 31.4 Britain's most reliable political ally?
Source: From *The Economist*, 6 November 1999. © The Economist Newspaper Limited 1999. All rights reserved. Reproduced with permission

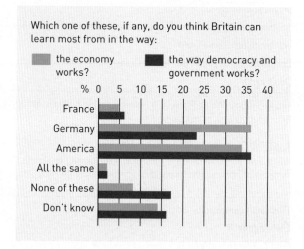

Figure 31.5 Who can Britain learn from?
Source: From *The Economist*, 6 November 1999. © The Economist Newspaper Limited 1999. All rights reserved. Reproduced with permission

---

BOX 31.3 IDEAS AND PERSPECTIVES

Key concepts in European integration

Supranationalism
Supranationalism refers to the characteristics that make the EU and its institutions unique among international organisations. These include the autonomy from national governments granted to specific institutions (the Commission, the EP, the Court of Justice); the primacy of EC law over national law; and the possibility of the Council of Ministers taking decisions by a majority vote. Supranationalism implies the placing of constraints upon national sovereignty. The EP, the Commission and the ECJ are often referred to as the supranational institutions of the EU.

Intergovernmentalism
Intergovernmentalism implies the primacy of the governments in decision making. Although possessing the supranational attributes outlined above, the EU was frequently described as intergovernmental in

character from the mid-1960s to the mid-1980s. This was because the supranational institutions lost prestige following the 1965 'empty chair' crisis, and majority voting was not practised in the Council of Ministers. Since the strengthening of the supranational institutions in the SEA, it has become less fashionable to use the term 'intergovernmentalism' to characterise the EU. In reality, there are elements of both supranationalism and intergovernmentalism in the EU, and the balance between them has varied over time. UK governments have consistently favoured intergovernmentalism over supranationalism because it represents much less of a threat to sovereignty, although the Blair government has departed from this position to some extent. The Council of Ministers and the European Council, which are composed of government ministers, are often referred to as the intergovernmental institutions of the EU. The two new 'pillars' of integration introduced by the Maastricht Treaty are essentially intergovernmental in nature.

Sovereignty

Because of its long-established territorial integrity, British (and especially English) politicians have been reluctant to see the limitations of the nation-state in assuring British welfare and security. Moreover, a lengthy constitutional tradition has embedded the notion of parliamentary sovereignty in the thinking of the political élite. As a consequence of these two features, UK governments have been particularly unwilling to cede sovereignty (i.e. autonomy and power) to the EU. Many of the main disputes between Britain and its EU partners about the development of European integration have their origins in different notions of sovereignty.

Subsidiarity

This term has come into use from the late 1980s onwards. Essentially it means that the EU should perform only those tasks that the member states governments (or sub-national governments) are unable to carry out themselves.

Federalism

Federalism entails a clear constitutional ordering of relations between the EU and the member states, together with constitutional guarantees. The UK's lack of a formal written constitution, together with an aversion to giving up sovereignty, has resulted in federalism being used inaccurately to denote everything that is disliked about moves towards closer integration. This was symbolised during the Maastricht debates by British politicians' references to the 'F word'.

BOX 31.4　BRITAIN IN CONTEXT

Should British foreign policy align with the EU or the US?

This controversy has been a long-standing one. The EU is committed to a Common Foreign and Security Policy and even cooperation in defence matters, but the UK's 'special relationship' with the US at times results in hard choices being necessary. European policy over Iraq in 2002–3 was one such hard choice.

In the immediate aftermath of the 9/11 terrorist attacks in the US the EU had stood united in solidarity with the Americans. It also supported the US's intervention in Afghanistan, which was seen as a regime offering support to al-Qaeda terrorists.

The US Administration of George W. Bush undertook insufficient consultation of his European allies with regard to his next wish in the 'war on terror'. He wanted to topple the regime of Saddam Hussein in Iraq on the basis that it had not given up its weapons of mass destruction, raising the (highly contested) possibility of offering material support for al-Qaeda. This neglectful transatlantic diplomacy, together with tensions between British and French leaders, resulted in a division opening up between EU member states. The UK along with a number of other states – including Spain, Italy and some of the members due to join in 2004 – supported Bush's decision to take military action in Iraq. Other states, notably France and Germany, wished for lengthier consideration of the issue in the United Nations Security Council. Split down the middle, but with Blair as the principal ally of the American Administration, the EU's efforts to present a common position collapsed. US Defence Secretary Donald Rumsfeld spoke of the division between 'old Europe' (meaning France, Germany and other opponents of invasion) and 'new Europe' (the USA's supporters). This episode damaged the credibility of the EU as a foreign policy actor and has damaged relations between the major leaders in the EU (Blair, Chirac and Schröder), with wider effects on relations between the larger states.

Although the EU was divided, it must be pointed out that, on many policy external issues, the UK *is* aligned with the EU. And the Iraq issue was highly controversial, as shown by the divisions in British public opinion.

Chapter summary

■ The UK's relationship with European integration has been troublesome but has arguably become less so over the period since membership. Its distinctive wartime experience, history of territorial integrity, distinctive form of parliamentary government, island mentality and former great power status are among the factors explaining late engagement with European integration. Joining at the third attempt, acceding to a community whose shape had been influenced by other states, and doing this in 1973 at the time of an international economic recession: these were not factors conducive to making EC/EU membership a painless matter. In fact, these circumstances merely added to the existing political divisions concerning membership. The UK is still somewhat apart from some of the longer-standing member states by virtue of not having adopted the euro as its currency (and by not actively pursuing this option at present) as well as stepping aside from some other practices, for instance by retaining border controls. However, as an advocate of a European Security and Defence Policy and of taking all efforts to make the EU competitive in the global economy, Britain under Blair has reduced its semi-detached appearance.

■ The institutions and policy process of the EU add a layer of governance above the UK itself. In distinction to national political systems, that of the EU has evolved considerably since accession in 1973. Institutional reform has been undertaken, new policies have been introduced, and the membership has grown from the original six states to twenty-five. The EU is a dynamically changing organisation and an awareness of its activities is crucial to understanding UK politics.

■ Each of these developments has posed challenges for the UK: both the negotiation of the changing EU arrangements and their subsequent impact within the UK political system. To the extent that they have occurred at times where UK governments have been especially divided on the European issue, the developments have made the headlines in British politics, notably over the Maastricht Treaty. At the same time the EU is an opportunity structure for British governments. It can provide a framework for resolving policy problems that transcend national boundaries or where a larger-sized body gives greater influence on the world stage. For example, Mrs Thatcher saw the opportunity of exporting her domestic liberalisation and deregulation agenda and successfully advocated the single market programme in the mid-1980s.

- The Blair government came to office with a manifesto commitment to a policy of constructive engagement with the EU. In its first term it was successful in this aim. It made several proposals – on security/defence and European competitiveness – that shaped the EU's own agenda. The second term was much more problematic because the decision to intervene in Iraq split the EU and created tensions with counterparts in France and Germany, although the UK was not isolated as in the past. These divisions tended to overshadow the Labour government's European policy in its second term. In its third term Blair's government had modest success during the 2005 presidency of the EU. Chancellor Gordon Brown has been less of an enthusiast for the EU in the period since 1997, and it remains to be seen what European policy will be like under his leadership, on the assumption that he is the successor to Blair.

- Combined with domestic devolution, the EU's development has highlighted the increasingly multi-level form of governance that UK politics has become.

- Challenges remain ahead. The Constitutional Treaty remains as a potential source of problems for the Labour government, should ratification recommence, as it would be a very difficult task for Labour to secure a majority in a popular referendum on this matter. The Conservative Party remains Eurosceptic; will David Cameron change this policy? For its part, the EU is more in line with successive UK governments' wishes than at any time since accession. The old Franco-German bedrock of integration is subsiding. In an EU of twenty-five it is difficult for two states to play that role. The French and German economies have performed relatively weakly of late and this means that those states are less influential in debates on economic reform than in the past. Some of the central and eastern European states favour the more neo-liberal economic policies of the UK. As a result, the UK is arguably more in the mainstream of EU thinking than at any time in the past. And yet the public is unconvinced. In the meantime, other actors – sub-national government, industry and the trade unions – pursue a more practical approach of engagement with the EU. For them, the EU is one of several levels of government with which they have to work. Whether politics and public opinion can attain this pragmatic outlook remains an open question.

Discussion points

- Why has the UK had such an uneasy relationship with European integration?

- What are the distinctive features of supra-nationalism, and why have they created controversy in UK politics?

- Can British governments solve policy problems in isolation, or do they need to seek collective solutions through the EU?

- From the perspective of British politics, is the European Union best seen as a threat or an opportunity?

- Which level of government do you think has most influence over your life (see Table 31.5)?

- Should the UK align its foreign policy with partners in the EU or with the United States?

Further reading

An important source of information on the EU is its own publications, many of which can be obtained free of charge from the London offices of the European Commission or European Parliament. Many of the publications are also now available on the EU's websites, which offer a wealth of information. Among the useful books on the history, institutions and policies of the EU are McCormick (2005), Nugent (2006), Dinan (2004) and Magnette (2005). Bainbridge with Teasdale (2004) is a useful reference book on EU matters. George (1998) and John Young (2000) provide good accounts of the UK's European policy over the time up to the early Blair period, while Hugo Young (1998) offers a more biographical account by focusing on the role of key figures from Churchill to Blair. George (1992), although dated, offers a more interpretative study that not only covers UK policy but also traces its main-springs to party politics, Parliament and other factors arising from British domestic politics. Geddes (2003) offers a useful overview of the intersections between the UK and the EU; for a chapter-length overview, see Allen (2005). For accounts of European policy making in Britain, see Armstrong and Bulmer (2003); also Forster and Blair (2002). Bulmer and Burch (1998, 2000, 2005) offer assessments that focus particularly on the impact of the EU on the work of British central government. For the impact on political forces – the parties, industry, trade unions and the media – see Baker and Seawright (1998). For a more detailed review of the European policy of the Blair government, see Bulmer (2000), Deighton (2001) or Smith (2005). Finally, for a study of the Europeanisation of British politics see Bache and Jordan (2006).

References

Allen, D. (2005) 'The United Kingdom: a *Europeanized* government in a *non-Europeanized* polity', in S. Bulmer and C. Lequesne (eds), *The Member States of the European Union* (Oxford University Press).

Armstrong, K. and Bulmer, S. (2003) 'The United Kingdom: between political controversy and administrative efficiency', in W. Wessels, A. Maurer and J. Mittag (eds), *Fifteen into One: The European Union and Member States* (Manchester University Press).

Bache, I. and Jordan, A. (eds) (2006) *The Europeanization of British Politics* (Palgrave).

Bainbridge, T. with Teasdale, A. (2004) *The Penguin Companion to European Union*, 3rd edn (Penguin).

Baker, D. and Seawright, D. (eds) (1998) *Britain For and Against Europe: British Politics and the Question of European Integration* (Clarendon Press).

Baker, D., Gamble, A. and Ludlam, S. (1994) 'The parliamentary siege of Maastricht 1993: Conservative division and British ratification', *Parliamentary Affairs*, Vol. 47, No. 1.

Bulmer, S. (2000) 'European policy: fresh start or false dawn?', in D. Coates and P. Lawler (eds), *New Labour in Power* (Manchester University Press).

Bulmer, S. and Burch, M. (1998) 'Organizing for Europe: Whitehall, the British state and European Union', *Public Administration*, Vol. 76, No. 1.

Bulmer, S. and Burch, M. (2000) 'The Europeanisation of British central government', in R.A.W. Rhodes (ed.), *Transforming British Government*, Vol. 1, *Changing Institutions* (Macmillan).

Bulmer, S. and Burch, M. (2005) 'The Europeanization of UK government: from quiet revolution to explicit step-change?', *Public Administration*, Vol. 83, No. 4.

Bulmer, S., Burch, M., Carter, C., Hogwood, P. and Scott, A. (2002) *British Devolution and European Policy-Making: Transforming Britain into Multi-Level Governance* (Palgrave).

Deighton, A. (2001) 'European Union policy', in A. Seldon (ed.), *The Blair Effect: The Blair Government 1997–2001* (Little, Brown).

Deighton, A. (2002) 'The European security and defence policy', *Journal of Common Market Studies*, Vol. 40, No. 4.

Dinan, D. (2004) *Europe Recast* (Palgrave).

Forster, A. and Blair, A. (2002), *The Making of Britain´s European Policy* (Longman).

Geddes, A. (2003) *European Union and British Politics* (Palgrave).

George, S. (ed.) (1992) *Britain and the European Community* (Clarendon Press).

George, S. (1998) *An Awkward Partner: Britain in the European Community*, 3rd edn (Oxford University Press).

Magnette, P. (2005) *What is the European Union? Nature and Prospects* (Palgrave).

McCormick, J. (2005) *Understanding the European Union*, 3rd edn (Palgrave).

Nugent, N. (1994) *The Government and Politics of the European Union*, 3rd edn (Macmillan).

Nugent, N. (2006) *The Government and Politics of the European Union*, 6th edn (Palgrave).

Smith, J. (2005) 'A missed opportunity? New Labour's European policy 1997–2005', *International Affairs*, Vol. 81, No. 4.

Westlake, M. (1997) 'Keynote article: "Mad cows and Englishmen" – the institutional consequences of the BSE crisis', in N. Nugent (ed.), *The European Union 1996: Annual Review of Activities* (Blackwell Publishers), pp. 11–36.

Young, H. (1998) *This Blessed Plot: Britain and Europe from Churchill to Blair* (Macmillan).

Young, J. (2000) *Britain and European Unity 1945–1999*, 2nd edn (Macmillan).

Useful websites

The Europa server – the gateway to all EU sites:
http://www.europa.eu.int/

The European Parliament:
http://www.europarl.eu.int/

The European Parliament's UK site:
www.europarl.org.uk

The European Commission:
http://www.europa.eu.int/comm/

The European Commission's UK office:
http://www.cec.org.uk/

The Council of the EU: http://ue.eu.int/en/

The European Court of Justice: http://curia.eu.int/

The European Central Bank: http://www.ecb.int/

Debate on the European constitution:
http://europa.eu.int/constitution/futurum/
index_en.htm

The Foreign and Commonwealth Office's site
(select topic 'Britain in Europe'):
http://www.fco.gov.uk/

The Treasury's site on the euro:
http://www.euro.gov.uk/

The European Movement in Britain:
http://www.euromove.org.uk/

The campaign for an independent Britain:
http://www.bullen.demon.co.uk/

UACES – the University Association for
Contemporary European Studies
(the UK's leading association for study of the EU):
http://www.uaces.org/

Sources of reporting on the EU:
http://www.euobserver.com/
http://www.euractiv.com/

CHAPTER 32

Labour in government: an assessment

Dennis Kavanagh

Learning objectives

- To assess the record of Labour in power since its election in May 1997.
- To examine the major policy initiatives undertaken by Blair's administration.
- To evaluate the criticisms made of the government's record to date.
- To evaluate the Conservative opposition.

Introduction

The return of a Labour government in 1997 brought to an end the longest period of one-party government for over a century and the longest period during which the opposition party had remained out of office. Obviously the new Labour ministers were inexperienced – only one had served in a Cabinet before. But for much of the 1992 parliament, and certainly from the time Tony Blair became leader in July 1994, Labour was regarded as a government in waiting among the media, Whitehall and even many Conservatives. Preparations for government, including contacts between senior civil servants and shadow ministers, were pretty advanced before the new government came to office. There was ample goodwill and even high expectations among much of the media, the European Union, and business and City circles. This concluding chapter assesses Labour's record since its election to power in May 1997.

■ 'New Labour' for a 'new Britain'?

No previous Labour government has achieved two full terms, let alone three. When there have been two terms, either the first or the second term has been short-lived because of a small parliamentary majority (1950–1, 1964–6, 1974–9) or absence of a majority at all (February–October 1974). Previous Labour governments had also been beset by economic crises – rising inflation and balance of payments problems, devaluation of the pound, incomes policies, public spending cuts and a squeeze on living standards. These policies in turn created divisions in the movement at large and confrontations between a Labour government and the annual party conference and trade unions. So far, the government has avoided economic downturns or major conflicts with conference and the unions.

Tony Blair's rhetoric before becoming Prime Minister promised much (for example, a 'new Britain') but on close inspection was often vague, except for the five key pledges in 1997 (see Box 32.1). Spending promises for the immediate future would depend on the achievement of savings within departmental budgets, to be made via a comprehensive spending review, and economic growth. Crucially, in opposition Gordon Brown, the Shadow Chancellor, and Blair had accepted the spending programmes of the Conservative government for the first two years of a new Labour government and also accepted the existing rates of income tax. They were determined to kill off accusations that Labour would be a tax-and-spend government: they had to demonstrate that they could

be trusted with people's money. Both men feared a repetition of the Conservatives' 1992 charges that the party would impose higher taxes. But they also believed that prudent economic management required such policies. Brown and Blair considered that globalisation limited the economic discretion of national governments of both left and right. Low inflation, lower rates of income tax, business-friendly policies and a tight cap on public spending were all necessary. The policy had costs: for much of the first term public services were denied resources essential to make improvements. The Institute of Fiscal Studies calculated that real growth (i.e. allowing for inflation) in public spending went up by only 1.4 per cent, while tax receipts increased by 4 per cent. This built a 'war chest' to spend in the second term.

Blair promised that Labour's second term would be about delivery. The party's plea in the 2001 election was, reasonably enough, that it needed another term to achieve its reforms. Investment (what used to be called more public spending) and reform together would 'transform' services, particularly health and education. However, two linked (in the minds of Bush and Blair, at least) events – the attacks on the Twin Towers in September 2001 and the war in Iraq and its fallout – slowed progress and weakened Blair politically. But over the course of the second term the government introduced foundation hospitals, extended the NHS internal market, brought in tuition fees, and announced plans to set up an independent supreme court replacing the law lords, to take effect in 2009. And thanks to continued economic stability it was able to invest heavily

Labour's key election pledges

1997

1. Cut class sizes to thirty or under for five-, six- and seven-year-olds by using money saved from the assisted places scheme.
2. Fast-track punishment for persistent young offenders by halving the time from arrest to sentencing.
3. Cut NHS waiting lists by treating an extra 100,000 patients as a first step by releasing £100 million saved from NHS red tape.
4. Remove 250,000 people aged under 25 from benefits and get them into work by using money from a windfall levy on the privatised utilities.
5. No rise in income tax rates; cut VAT on heating to 5 per cent; and keep inflation and interest rates as low as possible.

2001

1. Mortgages as low as possible.
2. 10,000 extra teachers and higher standards in schools.
3. 20,000 extra nurses and 10,000 extra doctors in a reformed NHS.
4. 6,000 extra police.
5. Raise minimum wage to £4.20 per hour and retain pensioners' winter fuel payout.

2005

1. Your family better off.
2. Your child achieving more.
3. Your children with the best start.
4. Your family treated better and fairer.
5. Your community safer.
6. Your country's borders protected.

in services. There were some improvements (e.g. cutting hospital waiting lists) but surveys reported public dissatisfaction with the results.

Few Prime Ministers have had such advantages as Tony Blair in May 1997 or 2001. To the 179 Labour majority in the House of Commons he could add a divided and discredited Conservative opposition, his own record high levels of popularity, according to the opinion polls, his authority in the Labour Party, which was perhaps the least ideologically divided in memory, and a more favourable set of economic indicators than most new governments inherit. Remarkably, many of these factors lasted until the 2001 general election and for much of the 2001 parliament. The enduring popularity of Blair and his government, or, alternatively, their huge leads in the opinion polls over their Conservative counterparts, were without precedent.

Within days, the government granted the Bank of England control over interest rates, handing it to a Monetary Policy Committee. This body was given an inflation target of 2.5 per cent per year and was to set interest rates at a level that would hit the inflation target. Some critics objected to the omission of a target for unemployment, and others complained that politicians, who are democratically accountable, should not relinquish the power to set interest rates. But markets were more likely to trust bankers and non-politicians to handle interest rates. Gordon Brown announced his strategy in his 1997 Budget: first, over the economic cycle the government would borrow only to invest and current spending would be met from taxation; and second, public debt would be held at a prudent and stable level. He was also constrained by his pledge not to raise marginal rates of income tax, and he had to

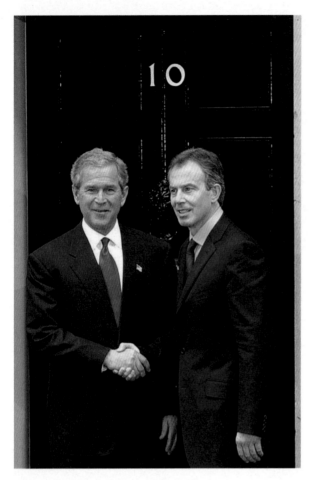

George W. Bush ushers Tony Blair into No. 10 for talks
Source: Empics Sports Photo Agency

turn to indirect taxes if he was to raise revenue. He proceeded to implement an excess profits tax on the profits of the privatised utilities to provide for public spending, notably on Welfare to Work.

For its first term, the government continued John Major's achievement of falling and subdued levels of inflation, declining unemployment and, eventually, low interest rates (inflation met the target of 2.5 per cent and unemployment was halved to less than a million, a twenty-year low of less than 4 per cent). Professional judgements from the IMF and OECD have often been glowing in their praise of the economy. Brown's forecasts for economic growth, derided by a number of commentators, proved to be correct until 2005. Labour increased its lead as the party of economic competence over the Conservatives (still suffering from memories of the recession in the early 1990s, and the débâcle of withdrawal from the ERM in September 1992). This economic record and approval of it was crucial to Labour's

successful election campaigns in 2001 and 2005. Departments have had to pledge improvements in services (e.g. cutting hospital waiting times, reducing school truancy and improving train punctuality) in return for the extra money; the deal was reflected in so-called 'public service agreements' (PSAs) between each department and the Treasury.

Gordon Brown's 2002 Budget, with its tax and spending increases, was a defining episode in the second administration. It can be seen as a return to the good/bad days of tax and spend of social democracy because it placed spending on public services ahead of tax cuts for the first time in over twenty years. It certainly enthused the Labour Party, and the polls reported record levels of approval for a Chancellor and a Budget. Labour activists were less impressed with the insistence that the extra investment must go hand in hand with reform – involving greater use of the private sector and adoption of more flexible working practices. Public spending rose from 39.8 per cent of GDP in 2002 to 41.8 per cent in 2005/6. This may be compared with an average of 47 per cent across EU states.

The government has also continued with and in some respects strengthened the Conservatives' managerial devices across the public sector of market testing, targets, league tables, performance indicators and performance-related pay. Poorly performing local education authorities have been 'named and shamed', and the approach was extended to hospitals and health authorities. This central control ('control freakery') has led to claims that these techniques depress staff morale and add to already severe problems of staff recruitment and retention. Moreover, they may be self-defeating, as service workers on the front line often know more about effective service delivery than bureaucrats in London or the regional headquarters. The NHS, with a structure essentially laid down over fifty years ago, is a perfect example of this problem – Labour's 1997 pledge to cut waiting lists by 100,000 meant that in order to meet the political targets, medical staff had to ignore more pressing cases. Political diktats were substituted for medical judgements. In 2002, the health minister, Alan Milburn, moved to greater decentralisation, giving more independence to so-called 'foundation' hospitals.

On the European Union, the Blair government, like John Major's, started off promising a fresh start and a more constructive relationship. The government incorporated the Social Chapter (see Chapter 31), but on the question of British entry to the

> ### BOX 32.2 FACT
>
> ## Labour's conditions for entering the euro
>
> 1. A settled and sustained period of convergence between the UK and continental European economies.
> 2. Good for investment.
> 3. Good for employment.
> 4. Good for the City of London.
> 5. European economies demonstrate sufficient flexibility to adapt to a common monetary policy.

single currency – crucial for a state that was bidding to be influential in the EU – Tony Blair proved to be as cautious as John Major. However, he began the process of preparing for British entry – *if* it is carried in a referendum. The Blair–Brown conditions, holding a referendum before entry, and entry only if it would satisfy British interests, were essentially no different from those of John Major (see Box 32.2). Commentators thought that Blair supported entry in principle but was constrained by the hostility of public opinion (for most of the past five years, polls reported that it was running heavily against) and of the Murdoch press, particularly the *Sun* and *The Times*. He was also constrained by the doubts of his Chancellor; at an early stage Brown decided that the case for entry had to be made on economic grounds and formulated five tests. It was no surprise when he announced in 2003 that only one and a half of the five had been satisfied; prospects of a referendum have receded. Supporters of the project complained that Blair and other supporters have failed to give a positive lead on the case for British entry and that in the vacuum anti-EU voices have shaped public opinion.

No other British government has produced such a far-reaching programme of constitutional reform as Labour did in the period 1997–2005, and it forms a sharp contrast to the indifference (or conservatism) of the Thatcher and Major governments. Scottish and Welsh devolution proposals were implemented swiftly, and within just over two years the Scottish Parliament and the Welsh Assembly were up and running. Other reforms (see Chapter 15) included:

- Direct election of a London mayor and assembly
- Tackling the anomalous position of the Lord Chancellor as a member of the Cabinet and head of the judiciary and creating a supreme court

- Proportional representation for Scottish, Welsh, London and European elections
- A Human Rights Act, incorporating the European Convention on Human Rights
- Freedom of information
- The abolition of voting rights of hereditary peers.

Question marks hang over the successor arrangements for the House of Lords, both its powers and its composition, and the role and financing of local government. In the wake of the allegations in March 2006 that Labour had been 'trading' peerages for undeclared loans to the party, the government has offered to hold all-party talks on reform of the Lords and has promised a paper on local government finance for late 2006. But it has not fulfilled its 2001 promise of an assessment on the working of the various PR systems introduced since 1997 and, since the northeast referendum decisively rejected the idea of an elected assembly, the prospects of elected regional assemblies for England have virtually disappeared.

The government, largely in response to the growing awareness of terrorism since 2001, has taken measures that have upset advocates of the rule of law. The Criminal Justice Act (2003) removed the right to trial by jury in certain cases and limited the right to silence. The Terrorism Act (2000) limited the presumption of innocence, although the House of Lords in 2004 overturned the Home Secretary's detention of terrorist suspects in Belmarsh prison. The introduction of identity cards in 2006 and the Prevention of Terrorism Act (2005) erode rights to privacy and the right not to be punished unless a court decides there has been a breach of law. Civil rights lawyers and commentators have protested vigorously against the erosion of human rights.

Tony Blair faced dark times when he was accused of offering honours to wealthy people who loaned large sums to the Labour Party
Source: Empics Sports Photo Agency

Critics have argued that the constitutional changes are *ad hoc*, that they lack any guiding vision, and Blair has rarely spoken about the constitution. This is probably true, but it reflects the British tradition of incremental change. Many of the measures, e.g. devolution, freedom of information and ridding the Lords of hereditary peers, were traditional Labour aims. The reforms are broadly pluralistic, have eroded civil liberties and move Britain closer to the constitutional model in most EU states. But the political pluralism is subject to limits, including the closed list system for voting in the European, Scottish and Welsh elections, ruling out a directly elected second chamber and a freedom of information act that has been widely dismissed as being in some respects more restrictive than the *status quo ante*. The London-based Labour leadership also threw its resources behind Alun Michael in the party election for First Minister in Wales, relying on the votes of trade unions in the process, and in 2000 campaigned hard to defeat Ken Livingstone as a

Labour candidate for London mayor. No other Prime Minister has been as keen to make appointments to the House of Lords: in his first three years alone, Blair made more appointments than Mrs Thatcher did in eleven years, feeding allegations of 'Tony's cronies'. These features lend support to the claims that Blair's management of the Labour party and his government is often too 'top down'.

More active party members showed their resentment of Millbank – the location of the party headquarters for the first term (now in Victoria Street) but a codeword for the Blair leadership. Alun Michael was forced to stand down as Welsh First Minister and was replaced by his deputy, Rhodri Morgan, who had been opposed by Blair during the party's election for its candidate for the post. Ken Livingstone was defeated in an electoral college ballot – widely regarded as fixed to defeat him – as the party candidate for London mayor. He then decided to run as an independent and won an overwhelming victory against Labour's Frank Dobson, who was inevitably dubbed Blair's 'stooge'. Livingstone attracted the votes of many Labour supporters and in January 2004 was readmitted to the party.

For all its promises of a fresh beginning, any new government inherits many of its predecessor's problems and commitments. This is seen in Northern Ireland with the continuing search for peace and devolution to a power-sharing executive in the province; in the first two years it probably took up more of Blair's time than any other issue. The 1998 Good Friday Peace Agreement linked the creation of a power-sharing executive, containing Sinn Fein, and an elected assembly, these two to move in tandem with decommissioning of paramilitary weapons. The package was approved by over 70 per cent of the Northern Ireland electorate in 1998. Blair has involved both the Irish government and the US President in the process. Although the killing has been sharply reduced and the IRA has signalled its intentions to disarm, there is still terror in the neighbourhoods of both communities and the executive has been suspended twice as Ian Paisley's Democratic Unionists refused to share power with Sinn Fein in the absence of stronger evidence of IRA decommissioning. An imperfect peace still holds – just.

In spite of the large House of Commons majorities in 1997 and 2001, there was no relaxation in central control of the party or calls for self-discipline among Labour MPs. But these have become less successful over time. In the first term there were dissenting votes on proposals over asylum, cuts in benefits for single parents, freedom of information and the 75p increase in the state pension in 2000. In the second term Labour MPs were more rebellious, largely because the government's bills offended many traditional Labour instincts. During the summer and autumn of 2002, MPs and much of the party membership made clear their opposition to any Anglo-American attack on Iraq without prior UN consent. The 139 Labour MPs who voted against the decision to go to war was the largest revolt on government benches in modern times, and Robin Cook, the Leader of the House of the Commons, resigned in protest. There were also substantial revolts over bills for foundation hospitals, tuition fees and tackling suspected terrorists. The dissent has continued into the third term, notably over ID cards, a ban on smoking and the schools bill in 2006 which Blair carried only thanks to Conservative support.

Party critics, not just confined to the left wing, complained that the government has gone too far in appealing to middle England, symbolically associated with the editorial tone and readership of the *Daily Mail*, and is ignoring its core vote in the north, the working class, manufacturing and trade unions. However, if Labour's rhetoric has been addressed to 'middle England', many measures were also directed to its core supporters. The extra rights for the unions in 'Fairness at Work', the minimum wage, the Social Chapter, increases in child benefit, the minimum income guarantee for pensioners, increased spending on health and education, and Gordon Brown's redistributive budgets have long been demanded by the Left. It is most unlikely that a Thatcher or even a Major government would have introduced any of the above. The Conservatives have accepted much of the above, as well as the Monetary Policy Committee of the Bank of England and the constitutional changes. In the new century, Labour, like Thatcher in the 1980s, has dominated the agenda, or what is sometimes called the middle ground in politics.

Advocates of the New Labour project, as noted in Chapter 12, realised that as long as Labour's core vote was concentrated among the declining sections of the electorate (the poor and the working class) then the party was unlikely to hold power again. To win general elections, Labour had to build a broader base of votes, in particular among the middle class, home-owners and traditionally non-Labour voters in the southeast. Blair did this by offering reassurance; his government would not threaten their economic

BIOGRAPHY

John Prescott (1938–)

Labour Deputy Prime Minister. Educated at Ruskin College and Hull University. Served as a steward in the merchant navy before becoming an official in the Seamen's Union. Leader of Labour group in European Parliament 1976–9. Deputy Leader since 1994 and Deputy PM since 1997. Between 1997 and 2001 held the post of Secretary for the Environment, Transport and the Regions. Criticised for poor performance on transport. Since 2001 has been First Secretary of State, heading another 'giant' department. His support for elected regional assemblies in England has been scuppered since the northeast voted decisively against. Has been a voice for trade unions and working class in Labour, but since revelations in 2006 of his affair with his diary secretary he has become something of a figure of fun and is no longer expected to play a key role in any Blair–Brown transition.

interests and would not be redistributive at their cost. In the 1997 general election this project was remarkably successful. Labour gained nearly one-fifth of its vote from 1992 Conservative and Liberal Democratic voters and a further one-sixth from those who had been too young to vote or who had abstained in 1992. In all, a third of the party's support came from people who had not voted for it in 1992. This coalition of voters largely held in 2001 and, to a lesser extent, in 2005.

From his election as leader in 1994 and into his first term as Prime Minister, Blair attached importance to cooperation with the Liberal Democrats. He calculated that Labour's chances of winning a general election in 1996 or 1997 would be greatly assisted if the two parties cooperated. Indeed, each party gained around twenty seats in the 1997 election due to tactical anti-Conservative voting (and gained again in 2001). Cooperation in government, including appointing the Jenkins Commission on proportional representation, and a joint Cabinet committee that included Liberal Democrat MPs, continued. A second incentive was the longer-term project of winning at least two terms in office, making Labour the natural party of government in the

---

BOX 32.3   **IDEAS AND PERSPECTIVES**

Verdict on Blair's Labour government

Blair came to power in 1997 promising a 'New Britain'. He commenced the third term promising a 'New Europe'. The first has not happened, and the second will not fully transpire in his political lifetime. Had Blair's mastery of persuasion and presentation extended to policy-making and governing, the net 'Blair effect' might have been considerable: as it stands, the Blair effect on 2001–5 will be remembered as much for its opportunities lost as for its achievements.

Source: Seldon and Kavanagh (eds) (2005), pp. 428–9

---

twenty-first century, just as the Conservatives had been in the twentieth. Blair reasoned that divisions between Liberals and Labour had greatly aided Conservative election victories in the past. Finally, Blair had a project of reshaping the centre-left. For much of the first term, he had much in common with the Liberal Democrats, not least on Europe and constitutional reform. Critics in the Labour party suspected that Blair wished to shed his more left-wing members while embracing the Liberal Democrats in a Progressive alliance. After 2001, however, this project faded out; Kennedy withdrew his party from the joint Cabinet committee and cooperation has little support among other senior party members. In its opposition to the Iraq war and tuition fees and in their appeal for a 50 per cent top rate of income tax, the Liberal Democrats had more in common with Blair's left-wing critics in his own party. As noted, voters' perceptions of the Liberal Democrats as being as much on the left as Labour has helped the party to attract the votes of disillusioned Labour supporters.

■ Blair and abroad

As we noted in Chapter 19, international affairs are taking up more of a Prime Minister's time. Apart from his involvement in major wars, Blair set himself the tasks of exercising leadership in the EU, bringing peace to the Middle East and tackling the problems of poverty and governance in Africa. Britain held the six-month Presidency of the EU and it remains to be seen how successful it will be in calling for economic reforms in the EU. The same applies to the Africa Commission and the attempt to increase aid to that continent and improve govern-

ance and reduce corruption. In 1999 in a speech in Chicago he spelt out his philosophy of the international community and the case for 'humanitarian intervention', i.e. for the community to act against regimes which were a threat to international peace and abusing the human rights of their population. This was part of his case for going to war in Iraq and earlier intervening in Kosovo on the grounds that Serbia was threatening genocide against the Albanian Muslims. The British interventions have always been as a subordinate partner to the US. The support has helped the US to claim that its military action has been helped by 'a coalition of the willing', but Blair's critics claim that he seems to have exercised little leverage on the US, and his support for the US over Iraq harmed British relations with Germany and France.

However unfairly, the Blair record will probably be dominated by Iraq and the doubtful legality of the case for going to war in March 2003. Blair insisted from the outset that he would stand 'shoulder to shoulder' with President Bush in removing Saddam Hussein in Iraq. Aware of the substantial public and party opposition to going to war without a UN Security Council mandate, Blair persuaded Bush to try for this. Although Saddam had defied a number of UN resolutions, the Security Council did not accept that these justified war. Labour was the only social democratic party to support the war and Blair joined right-wing governments in Australia, Spain and Italy in supporting Bush. Such company was troubling for many in the party. The war divided the EU, the Labour party, and the public.

The speedy victory brought the government only a short-lived respite. The continued insurgency, reports of mistreatment of Iraqi prisoners, the death of Dr David Kelly, and growing doubts about the integrity of the intelligence about Iraq's alleged

Blair is exonerated by the 2004 Hutton Report into Dr David Kelly's death, but there were still no signs of the WMD
Source: Copyright © Chris Riddell. From *The Observer*, 1 November 2004. Reproduced with permission from Guardian Newspapers Limited

weaponry all damaged Blair and the government. Post-mortems revealed that Blair and his staff had exaggerated the thin evidence that Saddam had 'weapons of mass destruction' (WMD) and claims that Saddam could launch them at 45 minutes' notice. The issue, and associated question of Blair's trustworthiness, was a factor in the 2005 general election and turned a number of Labour and Muslim supporters from voting for the party.

■ Public and social services

Dissatisfaction with the state of public services and hopes that Labour would bring about substantial improvements had been important in promoting voters' disillusion with the Conservatives in 1997. In its second term, Labour set itself the goal of making big improvements in public services, particularly health, education and transport. For its first term of office, it could and did claim that it needed more time to turn things around and that it had to cope with problems inherited from the outgoing Tory government. All governments say this during their first term of office. But as late as the 2005 general election opinion polls reflected the voters' disappointment at the scale of progress, although surveys also showed that voters still trusted Labour more than the Conservatives to improve the services.

Probably because of ministers' obsession with headlines, the government has often frittered goodwill with so many initiatives, a practice now dismissed as 'initiativitis'. The late Hugo Young, *The Guardian*'s magisterial columnist, wrote 'Seldom has any government seemed more self promoting than Tony Blair's, forever making the grandest claims for itself' (27 January 2000). Yet his overall conclusion on 8 February was still favourable: 'The real record, if one takes the long view, is not bad. What is bad is the perception.' As Education Secretary (1997–2001), David Blunkett was notorious for sending circulars on an almost daily basis to head teachers. In education, the government could point to achievements in the primary sector – reducing class sizes for 7- and 8-year-olds (although the sizes increased for older children) and the literacy and numeracy targets. Over the first term education received a smaller share of GDP than it did under John Major's government, but the increase in funding in the second term meant that spending per pupil nearly doubled between 1997 and 2006. The government has tried to extend parental choice and diversity among providers by creating city academies and specialist schools, but Blair's attempt to take this further by increasing the independence of schools in his 2006 education bill is strongly opposed in his own party (nearly eighty MPs voted against or abstained on the vote). Improvements in standards have slowed down after early progress: more than a quarter of children leave primary school with inadequate reading and numeracy skills.

The government was guilty of neglecting transport in its first term. House of Commons Select Committees, with Labour majorities, criticised John Prescott's DETR for confusing action with announcing working parties rather than tackling congestion. (The critique applied more widely across departments.) Rail crashes at Paddington and Hatfield – and the resultant crippling of large parts of the network – catapulted transport up the agenda. The accidents highlighted the poor state of the infrastructure – which critics linked to long-term failure to invest in public services. But it also showed how unintegrated Labour transport plans were: the original intention was to reduce travel on congested roads and expand public transport. Unfortunately, much of the latter was in a poor state. Funding has been substantially increased, although initiatives like congestion charging in London and road charging (the M6 toll road) have come from outside Whitehall.

The extra funds for health have provided extra doctors, nurses, health treatment units and better technology, and reduced deaths from coronaries and cancer and waiting times. But critics argue that the NHS is an inefficient structure – too centralised and not responsive enough to the wishes and needs of patients – and that much of the infusion of funds has been wasted because the reforms have been too timid. Indeed studies show that much of the extra funding has been swallowed up in extra salaries and wages for NHS staff, the employment of more administrators, and more expensive drugs. The improvement in output has been very modest. The

service still performs poorly on many indicators in comparison with European states, even controlling for costs, although waiting times for treatment for these have been impressively reduced. In the 2005 general election the Conservatives exploited public concerns over MRSA and the number of deaths occurring because of patient infections caused by poor hygiene in hospitals. The NHS was no longer the envy of the world. In 2002 it was announced that patients who had been waiting for lengthy periods for certain operations could be treated privately or be treated abroad and the costs borne by the NHS. It is true that most EU states spend a higher share of their GDP on health than Britain does. But they also have a greater mix of public and private finance, the last via social insurance schemes. Ministers point to a paradox: surveys show that people overwhelmingly express satisfaction with their NHS treatment but majorities still express dissatisfaction about the service in general. Ministers suggest that this paradox is explained by media 'scare' stories. At the end of the 2005–6 financial year a number of health authorities were running deficits and having to lay off staff.

On the social justice front the minimum wage has been introduced and, contrary to Conservative warnings, has not led to the loss of jobs. The same is true for the acceptance of the EU's Social Chapter. Poverty among children and pensioners has also fallen. But research shows that progress in social mobility has stopped and in spite of Brown's redstributive measures inequalities in wealth and income have actually increased. In spite of the expansion of higher education there has been no increase in the proportion of children from families in lower social classes going to so-called élite universities. Supporters of the government claim that globalisation has intensified the forces which exacerbate inequalities and that without Labour's efforts the inequalities would be even greater.

■ Sleaze and spin

Sleaze had been a potent factor in the decline and ejection of the Major government and the election of a supposedly squeaky-clean new Labour administration. But Labour has been caught up in its own scandals, appearing to be doing favours for businesses that donate to the party coffers, and to have too cosy a relationship with business. The case involving

Bernie Ecclestone, the F1 entrepreneur and generous party donor, and the exemption he gained from the ban on TV tobacco advertisements, was the first of a number of such cases. Blair has also granted peerages to a number of large party donors. There is nothing new about this but Labour came to office with expectations and claims that it would restore probity to public life ('purer than pure'). The government, aware that polls suggest that it is seen as being as sleazy as the previous Conservative government and concerned about voter apathy, has tried and so far failed to restore trust in the political process (Oborne, 2005). Indeed, the revelations in March 2006 about the £13.9 million of undeclared loans and the links with Labour nominations for peerages placed Blair further in the mire. Other senior party figures, including Gordon Brown, John Prescott and the party Treasurer, hurriedly declared that they had not known about the loans.

The government has also suffered from its excessive 'spinning' of stories and exaggerated claims of alleged success (Box 32.4). This feature has led to a virtual war with sections of the press, notably over the suggestion by a government special adviser, Jo

---

BOX 32.4 **IDEAS AND PERSPECTIVES**

Mandelson and Short on Labour spin

Once in office, New Labour's 'spin machine' went into action and, having promised less than we thought we could do, we started hyping more than we were actually achieving, with the consequence that the major transformations in British society that the government had put under way were lost in a fog of charge and countercharge, with the media assuming the role of Her Majesty's Opposition.

Peter Mandelson, *The Guardian*, 17 May 2002

We have a Prime Minister so focused on presentation that there is inadequate consideration of the merits of policy.

Source: Clare Short, *The Guardian*, 7 September 2003

BOX 32.5 **IDEAS AND PERSPECTIVES**

Blair–Brown rivalry

The rivalry between these two big beasts – the architects of new Labour – has dominated the government and been fuelled by aides (called 'tribes' by insiders) who brief the media and authors on their man's behalf. To date there have been a dozen books on one or other of the two.

Allegedly, the rivalry dates back to a so-called 'accord' the two men made in 1994 in which Brown agreed not to contest the party leadership in return for Blair, if he became leader, granting him control of social and economic policy and – this is disputed – standing aside during his second term as Prime Minister. Over time it appears that Blair has come to regard Brown as unhelpful if not an obstacle to his plans to enter the single currency and reform public services. Relations between the two virtually broke down in 2004 when Brown, according to a book written with the cooperation of his aides (Peston, 2005), charged Blair with breaking a promise to stand aside.

Blair's initial plans to fight the 2005 general election without much help from Brown had to be abandoned when surveys showed that Brown and the economy were assets to the party while Blair had lost much of his sheen with voters (Kavanagh and Butler, 2005). Brown was recalled to play a central role in the campaign and a grateful Blair announced that Brown would stay on as Chancellor after the election.

Even though Blair had announced in autumn 2004 that the next general election would be his last as leader of the party, and Brown is widely regarded as certain to succeed, suspicion between two men remains.

Moore, on the day of the attack on the Twin Towers, that it was a 'good day' to release unflattering (for ministers) news. In 2002, in a change of tack, No. 10 introduced a new 'openness'. The lobby briefings have been made more transparent. Blair now appears before the House of Commons Liaison Committee, and his press conferences are now broadcast, and Alastair Campbell has departed.

■ Labour's third term

The first year of Labour's third term illustrates the relevance of the old adage about the importance of events. The first six months started off well, with the success of London's bid to host the 2012 Olympics, collapse of the EU constitution and with it the need to call a potentially embarrassing UK referendum, and uncertainty over who would be the new leader of the Opposition.

But since then, things have gone badly wrong and the afterglow of the election triumph seems but a distant memory. By 2006, Labour appeared to share the fate of most long-term governments, as they suffer from:

■ loss of direction

■ failures in policy

■ disunity over policy

■ declining support for the Prime Minister and calls for a change of leader

■ a resurgent opposition.

By 2006 there were many parallels with the third-term Conservative government under Thatcher in 1990. Between March and May 2006 a series of events greatly damaged the standing of the Labour government and Blair. And they reflected on two claims which Labour had constantly made for itself since 1997 – trustworthiness and integrity, and competence.

Blair finds loss of public trust makes his job so much more difficult
Source: Copyright © Chris Riddell. From *The Observer*, 31 August 2003. Reproduced with permission from Guardian Newspapers Limited

Labour became even more associated with the label sleaze that had so damaged the last Conservative government. The Metropolitan Police force investigated claims that the party had been involved in a 'sale of peerages', or the nomination for honours to wealthy individuals who had made substantial donations or loans to party funds. The party treasurer Jack Dromey claimed that these had been authorised by Number 10 and bypassed him. There soon followed the lurid press coverage of John Prescott's affair with a junior civil servant in his office and protests that he was keeping his salary and rent-free houses even though his duties were greatly reduced.

But there were also growing doubts about the government's competence. In spite of the record infusion of funds a number of hospitals reported debts at the end of the financial year and were dismissing medical staff and closing wards in an effort to balance the books. Blair removed Charles Clarke from his post as Home Secretary following revelations that over 1,000 foreign criminals had been released from prison at the end of their sentences without being considered for deportation. Amid mounting concern about the performance of the immigration and prison services, Clarke's successor John Reid claimed that his department was 'not fit for purpose'. These cases followed well-documented policy fiascos over computer failures, costs of poor computer procurement, failures of the Child Support Agency and overpayment of tax credits.

Reviewing the above and other cases, Simon Jenkins in *The Guardian* (24 May 2006) wondered: 'Is British government collapsing?' He claimed that the system was at fault and ministers, with their interest in short-term fixes and initiatives, made it worse.

The voters delivered their verdict in the May 2006 local elections when the party lost ground and the Conservatives made significant gains. Opinion polls placed the Conservatives ahead of Labour and with their highest share of support since 1993, Blair's standing at an all-time low, and Labour actually trailing on its traditionally strong issues like education and health.

■ Questions for the future

Looking to the future, a number of questions remain:

- Membership of the EU single currency appears to have slipped off the agenda and the expected Brown succession may make British entry to the EU single currency even less likely. Brown, based on his own experience and success at the Treasury, takes British sovereignty in economic policy making seriously. What will be the impact on British domestic politics of remaining out of the single currency?

- The ambitious spending programme for the public services is due to slow down sharply in 2007–8, except for health. But the growth for health will also slow down and by early 2006 a number of hospital trusts were already in debt and making staff redundant. If economic growth is not delivered, how much extra tax or extra borrowing will the government accept to maintain the spending?

- How will Labour strike a balance between its commitment to maintaining low income taxes and tight controls on public spending and improving public services? How will it balance its traditional interest in redistribution to the less well-off and maintaining the support of middle England?

- The Liberal Democrats have also changed their leader, from Charles Kennedy to Sir Menzies Campbell. Like the Conservatives they are also reviewing their policies. Will the party shift from its high-tax policy of 2005 and where will it position itself on the political spectrum – remain on the left or move even further to the left? And if no party has a clear majority of seats after the next general election, are the Liberal Democrats prepared to enter a coalition and will they be even-handed between Conservative and Labour?

- Security issues, in the wake of 9/11 and the London bombings in 2005, are now a major concern of government. They are linked in some minds with the need for greater control of immigration and asylum and, in striking the balance between security and civil liberties, have exacerbated tensions between the judiciary and ministers. In December 2004 the law lords ruled against the British government's indefinite detention of suspected terrorists without trial at Belmarsh prison. How will this balance resolve itself in the coming years?

- Will constitutional reform lead to a new style of politics, one involving more power sharing between parties and pluralism?

■ Will the widely expected handover from Blair to Brown take place and if so when? And what will it mean for the future direction of the New Labour project? Brown as much as Blair has been an architect of achievements so far. But he will be eager to make his own mark. He is widely seen as being more committed to an agenda of social justice, redistribution (via tax credits and child-care policies), and central control of services. Blair is thought to be more concerned about retaining the support of Labour's new middle-class supporters and for more consumer choice and a greater role for the private sector in the public services. But Brown has also promoted the Private Finance Initiative (in which the private sector finances public works such as hospitals and the London Underground) and is a strong advocate of reforms which will increase Britain's economic competitiveness to cope in a global economy.

■ New Labour's record to date

An assessment of a government's record (see Table 32.1) is not like a school report. Different policy areas impact on one another, e.g. the success of the economy affects the level of resources available to invest in services, the level of unemployment affects the size of the welfare budget, and so on. And many circumstances, particularly international, are largely outside a government's control, e.g. Iraq, the July 2005 bombs in London, or bird flu. Governments, it has been said, are first of all reactors before they are initiators, and inheritors before they are choosers. Labour ministers have not been modest in pointing to achievements and pledges kept, while – probably to disarm critics – asking for more time, not least for their ten-year plans in many fields. Brown's stewardship of the economy and the constitutional changes are two undoubted achievements. But on public services and Europe it is a case of wait and see.

Some commentators complain that the Blair government lacks an ideological compass, that it is too pragmatic, driven by press headlines and the opinion polls. Others have criticised (or praised) it for being Thatcherite in its acceptance of the Conservative governments' trade union measures, backing of a more market-oriented economy and attempts to introduce more choice and competition in health and education. Blair is bored by such discussion. He says that he is interested in what works and wants to combine the best of the free market and the public sector. What is undeniable, however, is that Brown's redistributive budgets are a break with Thatcherism.

To date, the Blair government's accomplishments hardly bear comparison with those of the 1945–50

Table 32.1 Assessment of the government's record (1997–2006)

Positive policy	Indifferent / Poor policy
Constitutional reform – although it might have gone further	Exaggerated promises (e.g. 1999 to be the 'year of delivery')
Economic growth and stability, and the rise in employment (e.g. through the 'New Deal')	Poor productivity. Mixed record of improvements for record increases in public spending. Reform has been slow and limited
Some redistribution of income and reduction of poverty (via the minimum wage, family tax credit reforms, etc.)	Indecision on the euro
Northern Ireland (with the 1998 Good Friday Agreement, and the Assembly established)	Lack of strategic clarity in some areas (e.g. transport and the role intended for local government)
Command of 'centre ground' in politics and historic third successive general election victory	Loss of opportunity radically to restructure the second chamber and introduce PR
Modernisation of the Labour Party (although sceptical and critical forces remain)	Concern with 'managing' the mass media to neglect of policy and forfeited reputation for trust and honesty
Continuation by a Labour government of the enterprise culture without losing social/communal values	Too much centralisation and obsession with meeting 'targets' (e.g. priority to cutting NHS waiting lists at cost of other clinical goals, excessive paperwork for teachers). Poor delivery, particularly in Home Office matters

Source: Based in part on Seldon (ed) (2001), p. 59

Table 32.2 Policy battleground in the 2005 general election

Q. Which issue is the most important in your decision on how to vote and which party is putting forward the best policies on the following?

Policy	Most important (%)	Party with best policies (%)		
		Labour	Cons.	Lib. Dem.
Health service	21	41	29	12
Law and order	16	32	37	9
Education	15	38	26	15
Tax and public services	13	37	29	13
Economy generally	13	45	26	10
Asylum and immigration	8	28	38	10
Fight against terrorism	3	38	26	9
Europe	3	36	26	12

Source: ICM Research, 14 April 2005

Labour government (including recovery from a six-year war, extending public ownership to most utilities, achieving full employment, establishing the NHS, and granting independence to India and other colonies), or Thatcher's first government (trade union reforms, privatisation, creation of a more market-oriented economy, restoring the authority of the government).

For much of its time in office the greater part of the government's popularity, vision and strategy has rested with Blair. Except for a spell in 2004, when it appeared that he was on the point of resigning, he has been as dominant as Mrs Thatcher ever was. He has done more than any Prime Minister in the twentieth century to reform both his party and No. 10, with the aim of facilitating the type of leadership he believes is necessary. His dominance was shown over Iraq, where he defied not only public opinion but also much of his party in going to war without United Nations approval. Of course, no Prime Minister can do it alone. Apart from the interest groups and civil servants, he needs able ministers to deliver the improvements that voters are looking for (Table 32.2). Although Gordon Brown has so far attracted plaudits for his management of the economy, Peter Riddell in *The Times*, as early as 16 October 2001, pointed to the lack of genuine modernisers in the departments: 'this is, in many ways, a rather second-rate administration. The talent is spread very thin.' At the time he had Estelle Morris, David Blunkett, Stephen Byers and Alan Milburn in front-line departments – Education, Home Office, Transport and Health, respectively. At the outset

of the 2001 parliament, Blair told the four that he intended to keep them in post for the duration of the parliament. Continuity would probably have been in the interests of good government. But politics intervened and none lasted the course.

■ The Conservative opposition

In the early hours of 6 May 2005 Michael Howard was the third Conservative leader in succession to announce his resignation after a general election defeat. When David Cameron succeeded him some months later he was the party's fourth leader in the eight years since John Major had stepped down. The party's traumas have now continued for over ten years.

Even politicians desperate to gain and hold on to power agree that an effective opposition is a vital part of good democratic government. It forces government to explain itself and deters foolish policy ventures lest they be ridiculed in the eyes of the voters. But it also provides voters with an alternative if and when they decide 'to vote the rascals out'. Tony Blair has been fortunate – but Parliament and the country perhaps less so – that the Conservative opposition he has faced since 1997 has been unimpressive. William Hague, elected to the leader's job in 1997, was only 36 years of age. He proved able and sharp at the despatch box but could not convince the wider electorate that he was a plausible Prime Minister. He also proved inconsistent on policy,

BOX 32.6 BRITAIN IN CONTEXT

Governments face common problems

In the twenty-first century Britain faces challenges similar to those in her relatively large and economically advanced EU neighbours. They include:

- A lack of trust in political rulers and falling participation in political parties and elections
- Reconciling the growing popular demand for better health, education and pensions – the first two overwhelmingly provided and financed by the state – with fears of a tax backlash as voters resent paying higher taxes (including council tax)
- Combining the idea of an active state, in the sense of spending money and regulating business and public and private behaviour, with encouragement of enterprise and free choice
- Striking a balance between measures to protect people (particularly against the threat of terrorism) and the defence of liberty
- Balancing a liberal economic order (including competition, economic incentives, and efficiency even where this entails reducing the size of the workforce) with the social and economic consequences of inequality and the emergence of an underclass.

There is now a growing tendency for a state to study and try to learn from policy successes in other states. Lessons are diffused through academic studies, think-tanks, conferences of policy makers and analyses from bodies like the World Bank and OECD. The decision to grant independence to the Bank of England in 1997 was based in part on US experience. There has been some convergence in economic policies in part because of globalisation (see Chapter 2) and Britain's membership of the EU. The Labour government's welfare to work programme, pension reform, student loans, and Blair's drive to introduce more consumer choice and diversity in provision of health and education have drawn on policies in other EU states. France and Germany, it is often noted, do not have waiting lists for hospital appointments.

In the 1980s some states borrowed from some of Thatcher's economic policies; more recently Britain has been more of a borrower. Note that Labour's virtual trebling of health spending since 1997 was to bring Britain in line with levels of spending in comparable EU states.

But Britain's political stability over the past decade makes it different from some of its neighbours. By 2009/10 Labour is likely to have been in government for 12–13 years, whereas in recent years there have been major changes in Germany, Spain and Italy and in 1998 in the USA. And it has been one-party government with a clear majority of seats in the legislature. In Italy and Germany the changes of government took time to achieve because the majority was so small and the coalitions so complicated.

---

appearing at first to embrace a 'caring Conservatism' and then veering into a more populist agenda.

Hague resigned promptly after the 2001 Tory general election defeat and several candidates entered the competition for his replacement, including Michael Howard, Kenneth Clarke and Michael Portillo (the former right-winger now reinvented in the media as the new prophet of a more liberal Conservatism). The MPs chose Clarke and Iain Duncan Smith, former captain in the Scots Guards whose days as an MP had been characterised by the leading role he took in the rebellion against the Maastricht Treaty in 1992, to go forward for the decisive vote of the party members. The man most likely to win voter support, Clarke, had little chance and Duncan Smith was overwhelmingly elected by the ageing party membership. All three successors to Major had been on the right or centre-right of the party.

The arrival of the 39-year-old David Cameron seems to have revived the party. The resignation of Michael Howard gave opportunities to young talent, notably Cameron and George Osborne, sometimes spoken of as the Blair and Brown of the Conservative party. Although Cameron authored the party's manifesto for the 2005 general election, he has promised a fresh start and warned the party that it has to change fundamentally in order to convince people that it is in touch with modern Britain. Supporters say that his ambition is to do for the Conservative party what Blair did for Labour a decade ago, namely forge a 'New Conservatism', one that will win elections.

This project seems to involve an acceptance of much of Blair's agenda, particularly those parts to which some of the Labour party object, e.g. giving more independence to state schools and higher tuition fees for universities. In the contest for the party leadership he rejected his rival David Davis's call for income tax cuts, on the grounds that it would be irresponsible to do so four or five years ahead of a general election. Moreover, he claims that economic stability and funding public services properly are higher priorities than tax cuts and has pledged to match Labour's planned spending on health and education. He also wants to break with the normal adversarial approach of the political opposition and in March 2006 backed Blair's schools bill which many Labour MPs voted against; the bill would not have passed without Conservative support. Much of the Cameron effect in the first few months has been about demonstrating a more voter-friendly personality and style, and within his first few weeks he gained a favourable press. He wants to convince voters that the party has changed, that it has moved to the centre ground, and surveys suggest that he has had some success. He has abandoned the idea of 'patient passports' in the NHS, restoring grammar schools or a return to the 11+exam, and taking steps which might be seen as encouraging the middle class to opt out of public services. He has emphasised the need for business to follow more environmentally friendly policies and for policies to combat world poverty. Early surveys showed him doing better when faced by Gordon Brown rather than Tony Blair.

Yet success in changing the party's image (in October 2002 the party chairman, Teresa May, admitted to Conference that it was seen as the 'nasty party') will depend on policies, and the review of policy will not be complete under 2007. Already some on the party's right wing are complaining that Cameron's convergence with New Labour policies will deny 'true' Conservatives a meaningful choice.

Looking ahead to the next general election in 2009/10, the Conservatives may gain from the mood of time for change after what will be some twelve years of Labour rule. But it will have to overcome the government's superior reputation for managing the economy and the public services, prevent disillusioned Labour voters defecting to the Liberal Democrats, and gain a large enough majority over Labour of the popular vote to offset the anti-Conservative bias of the electoral system.

Chapter summary

This chapter has examined the impact made by Blair's government since it came to power in May 1997, including its major legislative initiatives and policies and achievements in terms of constitutional changes and the sound management of the economy. It also discussed Blair's objectives, tight party discipline and the growing pockets of dissent within the party and the new Conservative challenge.

Discussion points

- How has Iraq affected Tony Blair's authority in the Labour party and the country?

- In what respects has the Blair premiership been (a) a success, and (b) a failure?

- To what extent have the constitutional changes been problematic?

Further reading

On Tony Blair, see Rentoul (2001) and Seldon (2005), and on the government's record see Seldon and Kavanagh (2005). Gould (1998) is excellent on the provenance and evolution of New Labour.

References

Gould, P. (1998) *The Unfinished Revolution* (Little, Brown).

Kavanagh, D. and Butler, D. (2005) *The British General Election of 2005* (Palgrave)

Ludlam, S. and Smith, M. (eds) (2003) *Governing as New Labour: Politics and Policy under Blair* (Palgrave).

Oborne, P. (2005) *The Rise of Political Lying* (The Free Press).

Peston, R. (2005) *Brown's Britain* (Little, Brown).

Rentoul, J. (2001) *Tony Blair* (Little, Brown).

Seldon, A. (ed.) (2001) *The Blair Effect* (Short Books).

Seldon, A. (2005) *Blair* (Little, Brown).

Seldon, A. and Kavanagh, D. (eds) (2005) *The Blair Effect 2001–5* (Cambridge University Press).

Toynbee, P. and Walker, D. (2001) *Did Things Get Better?* (Penguin).

Toynbee, P. and Walker, D. (2005) *Better or Worse?* (Penguin).

Waging wars: foreign policy and terrorism

Simon Jenkins

In March 2006 the Prime Minister set out on a world tour to declare his new vision of British foreign policy. It was dominated by one theme, the war on terrorism, viewed through the prism of five more specific wars that Tony Blair had fought during his term of office, in Kosovo, Sierra Leone, Afghanistan and Iraq (twice). The last time he had set out a British *casus belli* was in Chicago in 1999, when he propounded the concept of a just war in a modern age. Britain's duty was, wherever possible, to make the world a better place. The United Nations' 'principle of non-interference' no longer applied. It was overruled by genocide, ethnic cleansing and 'regimes based on minority rule'. This unilateral 'doctrine of international community' was to be realised by militarising the humanitarian imperative. With the realists (and the Treasury and Foreign Office) tugging at his sleeve, Blair did qualify his bold phraseology. Before going to war, Britain's case must be strong, diplomacy should be tried first, there should be a clear strategy, Britain's interests must be at stake and armed force must be likely to win. These plodding provisos did not restrain Blair's zest for war.

Seven years on humanitarianism had acquired a harder edge. Terrorism ruled, and Blair's foreign policy was seen as a global 'values' crusade. Britain must be proactive and pre-emptive, not reactive and defensive, said the Prime Minister in March 2006. It should seek international support and build new institutions, but if Britain shirked the fight, it 'risks chaos threatening our very stability.' The crusade to introduce democracy worldwide, said Blair, was 'utterly determinative of our future here in Britain'. Hence wars in Iraq, Afghanistan and, by implication, Iran, not to mention putative aggression against Sudan, Burma, Zimbabwe and North Korea. 'In their

salvation lies our own security.' Pre-emptive war had become a matter of national survival.

This was astonishing from a modern British Prime Minister. As international relations, let alone international law, it was alarming rubbish. There was certainly an argument to be had over the future treatment of developing countries suffering varying degrees of 'failure'. This could even be defined as 'ultimately a battle about modernity'. Blair's readiness to call a totalitarian spade a spade was refreshing and his criticism of those unwilling to do so out of diplomatic delicacy was fair. But there is a world of difference between a cold and a hot 'battle' over modernisation, between disagreement and war. It is one thing to wish another man were more like oneself and quite another to feel at risk because he is not.

The Blair thesis that anyone who does not run their country like Britain, or on Western democratic lines, 'threatens our values and national security' was little short of demented. It was impossible to analyse Blair's remarks as implying anything other than sabre-rattling belligerence. It was extremely dangerous since the highly questionable doctrine of pre-emptive war, as demonstrated in Iraq, leads states into horrors of dissembling intelligence and deceiving their peoples. It is illegal and it is usually disastrous. Blair seemed quite unaware of this.

Blair's foreign policy in the early twenty-first century seemed to be based on a schoolboy howler. Terrorism is not, as Blair kept calling it, an ideology. It is a weapon, like a gun or a bomb. It can kill people and destroy property but it cannot win arguments or topple governments. It can only gain publicity and spread fear. Given the West's sensitivity to media coverage, the weapon can be potent in scaring those fearful of (other people's) bombs. But it is a weapon that most armies use. NATO in 1999 claimed the bombing of Belgrade would terrify the Serbs into submission. Britain and America used airborne terrorism in the assault on Baghdad in 2003, even describing it in terrorist jargon as 'shock and awe'. But if peoples persistently decline to be terrified into changing their policy or way of life, the terrorist weapon is mere senseless destruction.

There is no such thing as global terrorism any more than there is global bombing. Nor did it serve any diplomatic purpose for Blair to tar Muslim fundamentalism with the terrorist brush. Many (though not most) Muslims did not live in democracies and strongly disagreed with Blair's claim to superior 'values'. They rejected the West's loose morality and would doubtless like to see it come to nought. They thought that the UN was set up after the Second World War to protect such differences between peoples. Yet the overwhelming majority even of fundamentalist Muslims would emphatically reject the use of violence to express that difference. They are not terrorists by virtue of disagreeing with Blair, any more than they were a threat to Western security as he claimed.

Blair's obsession was with the al-Qaeda network, though he appeared ignorant of the dozen or so books available on the subject, all of which depicted it as at best a small and desperately inchoate network of gangsters. Its leader, Osama bin Laden, was undoubtedly a menace and his appeal to disaffected Muslim youths dangerous. But he was neither representative of evangelical Islam nor a substantive military or political force. Cells in various countries can kill people in his name, though relatively few deaths have been attributable to the organisation after the horror of 9/11. Since then al-Qaeda has never deployed anything more dangerous than a bomb. Even if it did, it would not 'threaten Western values'. The chief threat came from the West's own response, notably in America and Britain, where Blair and his Home Secretary, Charles Clarke, seemed eager to portray criminal acts as victories against Western civilisation. They, not the terrorists, delivered the most determined assault on British civil rights and values in half a century, an assault that was entirely self-inflicted.

To grant such apocalyptic status to a loose criminal network invited anyone with a grudge against the West to join in – or at least offer rhetorical support. Blair's attempt to bond al-Qaeda, Saddam Hussein, Iran's mullahs, Afghanistan's Taliban and the Palestinian Hamas into some giant global conspiracy both was inaccurate and distorted any coherent British strategy towards the Muslim world. Among other things it ignored the importance of distinguishing secular and hierocratic Muslim regimes. To claim that Britain must 'go to war for its salvation' against any bomb-maker who writes al-Qaeda on a laptop was ridiculous.

There is no good reason to question the sincerity of Blair's motives, merely their relevance and perhaps their sanity. Indeed had he and George W. Bush been less idealistic and more scheming in Iraq they might have been more competent. As it was, they so believed in the sanctity of their war that they could not see the mayhem they sowed wherever they put their boots in the sand. At the start of 2006 Blair showed the depth of his self-delusion by sending 5,000 British troops to south Afghanistan, where they could not possibly curb the opium trade or establish peace and democracy among the re-emergent Taliban. As for the claim that these wars may be tough in the short term but will 'deliver Islam for democracy' in the long term, Blair appeared to have read no history.

What was most curious in Blair's outlook was his seeming lack of faith in the robustness of Western democracy. It had seen off the two ideological challenges in the twentieth century, state fascism and state communism. To equate al-Qaeda with such titanic forces was plain silly. As Lord Guthrie, formerly Blair's chief of defence staff, pointed out, far tougher terrorist campaigns had been met and overcome in the past without 'declaring war' on an entire -ism (Guthrie, 2005). Blair's claim that terrorism had found a chink in the West's defences for Muslim extremists to exploit was simply incredible. It suggested a Nixonian paranoia so immured behind bodyguard, bomb shelters, machine guns and security briefings as to have lost touch with reality. Even if Muslim extremism were a real threat to the West, to imagine that it can be countered by the military conquest of nations was fantasy. Most people would like to see their own values propagated, but to claim that they must conquer or die was jihadist rather than democratic.

As he neared the end of his term Blair's interest in foreign affairs became messianic, not unlike that of his heroine, Margaret Thatcher. Much that he championed was good. His admiration for most things American and his loathing for dictatorship and oppression were sound. His quest for fairer trade and a more realistic approach to aid was forlorn but sincere. The search for a new sense of 'international community' was often put cogently. But such a community could only come into being if pursued through example and persuasion, not through war. Success lay in propagating culture and capitalism, through the interpenetration of peoples and religions and the liberation of market forces. Because such intercourse was not couched in the language of a medieval crusader, Blair seemed unwilling to recognise it. Indeed he dismissed it as 'benign inactivity'. Such dismissal showed how limited was his political vision.

The West's attempt – or rather that of a Labour Prime Minister and a Republican President – to impose its values on various distant states through armed force at the start of the new century was an aberration doomed to failure. As Francis Fukuyama pointed out in a celebrated recantation, it betrayed the neo-conservative cause as much as the liberal one (Fukuyama, 2006). It was so obviously cruel, costly and counter-productive as to be almost beyond debate. Yet the mistake towered over what seemed certain to be the last period of Blair's rule. It tainted all he did and qualified all his achievements. It was a true nemesis.

References

Fukuyama, F. (2006) *After the Neocons: Where the Right Went Wrong* (Profile Books).

Guthrie, C. (2005) in Reid, A., *Taming Terrorism – It's Been Done Before* (Policy Exchange).

Glossary

Active minority: that minority of the population which participates to a high degree in political life.

Adversarial politics: a theory popularised by (among others) Prof. S.E. Finer in the 1970s which portrayed politics at Westminster as a gladiatorial combat between Labour and the Conservatives with disastrous consequences for the national interest.

Affiliated: the way in which an organisation associates itself with a political party by paying a fee and gaining influence in the party's affairs. In Britain, a number of trade unions are affiliated to the Labour party; members pay the 'political levy' which makes them affiliated members of the party.

Alignment: a situation when the electorate is divided into reliable and stable support for the various parties. The British electorate was said to be aligned in both class and partisan terms from 1945 to 1970.

Anglo-Saxon model: a form of economic organisation dominant especially in the United States and the United Kingdom which stresses the importance of free markets over state controls.

Authority: the acceptance of someone's right to be obeyed.

Back-bencher: the name given to all MPs who are not members of the government or the Opposition Front Bench.

Bank of England: the institution concerned with the government's management of all financial markets, and after the Treasury the most important institution in economic policy.

Better Quality Services: the Blair government's rebranding of market testing. Designed to identify the 'best supplier' of a service, BQS obliges departments and agencies to review their systems and consider the possibility of competitive tendering. However, provided real quality improvements can be achieved through internal reviews, there is no compulsion to put services out to tender.

Bicameral legislature: a legislature that consists of two houses. Most Western industrialised countries have a bicameral legislature, with the second or Upper House having a more limited role than the Lower, perhaps being composed of appointed rather than elected members, although in a few countries, most notably the United States, both are of more or less equal significance.

Bi-polarity: often used to describe the division of the world between the communist east and the capitalist west after the Second World War, but applicable to any international system in which there are two dominant centres of power.

Block vote: the system under which affiliated trade unions cast votes at Labour Party conferences and in party elections. Unions cast votes on the basis of the numbers of members paying the political levy. These votes may or may not reflect the views of union members.

Bottom-up: the idea that power in the Labour party is dispersed throughout the party, with the final say in the choices of policy and party organisation being vested in the annual conference.

Broadsheets: large-format newspapers, which aim at the better-educated and more affluent readers, with a particular interest in influencing the opinion-formers.

Budgetary instruments of control: those measures that can have an impact on the way in which the economy works, like increasing tax or benefits.

Butskellism: a 'consensus' Keynesian approach to economic policy adopted by post-war Labour and Conservative governments, including full employment, the welfare state and the mixed economy. The term was coined by *The Economist* from the names of R.A. Butler, Conservative Chancellor 1951–5, and Hugh Gaitskell, his Labour predecessor.

Cabinet: the Cabinet consists of the leading members of the government, chosen by the Prime Minister. It is the place where major decisions are taken or ratified and where disagreements within government are resolved.

Cabinet committees: Cabinet committees are appointed by the Prime Minister and are composed of cabinet ministers (sometimes with junior ministers) to consider items of government business. Some are standing committees, some are *ad hoc*, to deal with specific problems or issues.

Cabinet government: the view that collective government survives and that the Prime Minister is not the dominant force within government. Decisions are taken by a group of colleagues after discussions in Cabinet according to this view.

Capital expenditure: expenditure on long-term projects such as buildings, large items of equipment, etc.

Capitalism: an economic and political system in which property and the means of production and distribution are in private ownership (rather than in the hands of the state) and goods are produced for private profit.

Cause or promotion groups: these groups promote some particular cause or objective, perhaps the protection of some vulnerable section of society, or seek to express the attitudes and beliefs of members. They tend to concentrate on a single issue.

Chancellor of the Exchequer: the political head of the Treasury, and with the Prime Minister the most important elected politician concerned with economic policy.

Charisma: a natural attraction as a quality of leadership.

Charterism: rebranded *Service First* by the Blair government, the Citizen's Charter and its offshoots have the objective of enhancing the quality of public service delivery while emphasising the rights of service users, as 'clients', 'customers' and 'consumers'.

Civil law: the law governing the rights of individuals and their relationships with each other rather than the state.

Civil servants: servants of the Crown, other than holders of political or judicial offices, who are employed in a civil capacity and whose remuneration is paid wholly and directly out of moneys voted by Parliament.

Civility: respect for authority and tolerance of opposing/different points of view.

Class: distinctions made between people on the basis of their social origins, education and occupation.

Cold War: the state of hostility between nations or alliances without actual fighting. Usually applied to USA-USSR relationships after 1945.

Collective responsibility: all members of the government are collectively responsible for its decisions. Members, whatever their private reservations, must be prepared to defend government policy. If unable to do so, they must resign or be dismissed.

Colonialism: the extension or retention of power by one nation over another.

Committee of the Whole House: a sitting of the House of Commons presided over by the Chairman of Ways and Means (Deputy Speaker) which hears the Budget speech and debates the committee stage of important bills, especially those affecting the constitution. It deals with matters where, in principle, any member should be allowed to participate.

Common law: the body of law, distinct from statute law, based on custom, usage and the decisions of the law courts in specific cases brought over time.

Communism: an economic and political system which aimed at the abolition of capitalism, the establishment of the dictatorship of the proletariat and the eventual 'withering away' of the state.

Community charge (poll tax): a flat-rate local tax introduced to replace the rates by the Thatcher government. It was intensely unpopular because of its perceived unfairness, in that the amount paid was not related to income. It was a factor in Mrs Thatcher's downfall.

Competition state: refers to a state intervening to open up society and economy to international market norms.

Compulsory Competitive Tendering (CCT): an aspect of market testing applied to services such as hospital catering and refuse collection. The aims were to improve efficiency and customer responsiveness and to break the power of public sector unions.

Confederation: a loose binding of states.

Consensus: an agreement. In British politics it describes the general continuity and overlap between economic, social, defence and foreign policies of post-war Labour and Conservative governments.

Conservation: care and protection of natural resources.

Consociationalism: power-sharing among political élites, designed to stabilise society.

Constitution: the system of laws, customs and conventions which defines the composition and powers of organs of the state, and regulates their relations with each other and with the citizens. Constitutions may be written or unwritten, codified or uncodified.

Constitutional: doing things according to agreed written or legal authority within the state.

Constitutional monarchy: while the monarch is the titular head of state invested with considerable legal powers, these powers are exercised almost without exception on 'advice' (i.e. by ministers); and the monarch has a largely symbolic role.

Contract state: the system where the state, instead of delivering services by its own institutions, contracts with private institutions for their delivery.

Conventions: unwritten rules of constitutional behaviour; generally agreed practices relating to the working of the political system, which have evolved over time.

Core executive: the group of people and institutions in Whitehall around the Cabinet and Prime Minister who decide most key policies. They include No. 10 staff, the Cabinet Office and senior civil servants, particularly those in the Treasury.

Corporatism: the tendency of the state to work closely with relevant groups in the making of policy. It developed as the state became increasingly interventionist in economic and social affairs.

Cosmopolitan: here meaning a world free from national interests and prejudices.

Council tax: the local tax introduced by the Major government in 1993 to replace the poll tax. It is a property-based tax with reductions and exemptions for a number of categories of residents.

Criminal law: law determining the acts and circumstances amounting to a crime or wrong against society as defined by the terms of law.

Criminalisation: an attempt (in Northern Ireland) to portray and treat convicted members of paramilitary organisations as common criminals.

Cross-borderism: links, in the Irish context, between Northern Ireland and the Irish Republic, mainly in the economic sphere.

Dealignment: a situation when there is a weaker relationship between occupational class and party support and when a declining percentage of the electorate identify with a party.

Decommissioning: removal from use of paramilitary arms in N. Ireland.

Deference: a propensity to believe that people who have good education or connections with well-established families have more right to be in positions of authority than those who lack these characteristics.

Deindustrialisation: the process by which manufacturing industries decline and close.

Democracy: a political system in which a government is removable by the people, and in which they should be the ultimate decider of who should govern, thus enabling all adults to play a decisive part in political life.

Democratic: a form of decision making in which the wishes of the adult population are claimed to be of decisive importance.

Democratic deficit: the argument that reforms to the management of public services have reduced the accountability of government and diminished the democratic rights available to the citizen.

Department (also known as ministry): the principal organisation of central government, responsible for providing a service or function, such as social security or defence, and headed (usually) by a secretary of state or minister.

Dependency culture: the growth in the sense of dependence by users on the welfare services.

Deviant voting: voting for a party other than the party normally supported by the class to which one belongs.

Devolution: creating government institutions that exercise power locally rather than centrally.

Direct rule: ruling an area directly from the capital of a country rather than through a local or regional government.

Disclaim: under the 1963 Peerage Act, a hereditary peer can give up his or her title (and thus, until 1999, the right to sit in the Lords) without affecting the claim of the next heir.

Divine right: the belief that monarchs derive their power and position from God and that Parliament is dependent on the will of the monarch.

Dominant values: those ideas about the way in which life should be led held by the group in society traditionally exercising most power.

Ecological Modernisation: Maarten Hajer (a leading ecological theorist) sees ecological modernisation as pulling together several 'credible and attractive story-lines': a sustainable development in place of 'defining growth'; a preference for anticipation rather than cure; equating pollution with inefficiency; and treating environmental regulation and economic growth as mutually beneficial.

Ecology: an approach to politics centred around the importance of the environment.

Election pacts: an arrangement made at either national or local level between two parties for a mutual withdrawal of candidates in the hope of maximising their strength *vis-à-vis* a third party.

Electoral college: the body that, in the USA, is legally responsible for the election of the President. In Britain it is best known as the process by which the Labour party elects its leader, with the unions, the constituency parties and the parliamentary Labour Party having one-third of the vote each.

Electoral quota: the average number of electors per constituency. There are separate electoral quotas for England, Wales, Scotland and Northern Ireland. Parliament decides the number of constituencies in each part of the United Kingdom and the *Boundary Commission* is then responsible for drawing constituency boundaries as near the electoral quota as possible.

Electoral register: the list of those entitled to vote. It is compiled on a constituency basis by the Registrar of Electors, an official of the local authority, through forms distributed to homes and by door-to-door canvassing. Although it is supposed to be 100 per cent accurate, there are doubts about its comprehensiveness, an issue highlighted by the poll tax.

Electoral system: a set of rules enabling voters to determine the selection of the legislature and/or the executive. Electoral systems have several often incompatible aims: to produce a legislature that is proportional to the distribution of votes; to produce a government that represents the majority of voters; and to produce strong, stable and effective government.

Emerge: the process by which leaders of the Conservative Party were chosen prior to the adoption of a system of elections in 1965. The new leader would 'emerge' following secret discussions between leading members of the party, with the monarch's private secretary acting as a go-between.

Enabling authorities: the idea that local councils should cease to be solely concerned with the provision of services but should enable those services to be provided by a mixture of in-house and external organisations.

Entitlements: legal rights to welfare services and benefits.

Entrenchment: the idea that the constitution is protected in some way against amendment by a temporary majority in the legislature. There may be provision for judicial review, i.e. that courts can review the constitutionality of statutes.

Environmentalism: the belief that protection of the environment is a political issue of central importance.

Equality: the belief that people should all be treated in the same way and have the same rights.

Equality of opportunity: the idea that there should be no legal or formal barriers to advancement in the world between citizens.

Euro: the short name for the single European currency which since 2002 has been the only currency used in most member states of the European Union. Whether Britain abolishes sterling and joins the euro-zone will be the most important issue in British politics in the near future.

European Council: the European Council is made up of all the heads of government of the member states of the European Union.

Europeanisation: a term with a number of meanings, including the impact of membership of the European Union on British society and politics; the European Union expanding its boundaries through enlargement; the development of institutions of governance at the European level; adapting national and sub-national systems of governance to Europe-wide institutions and Europe-wide norms; a political project aiming at a unified and politically stronger Europe; and the development of a sense of identity with Europe, the EU, etc.

Eurosceptic: a person with the view that the process of European integration has been moving too fast.

Euroscepticism: a shorthand expression for a set of complex feelings that sees closer economic and political integration in Europe as damaging to national independence. Commonly associated with, but by no means confined to, sections of the Conservative party in the UK.

Executive: the body in a political system responsible for the day-to-day running of the state.

Executive agencies: an office performing a function of government, subordinate to but not wholly controlled by the parent department. They perform the *executive* as opposed to the *policy-making* functions of government.

Fascism: the right-wing nationalist ideas espoused by Mussolini and adapted by Hitler as the basis of his own Nazi ideology.

Feminism: the advocacy of women's rights on the grounds of equality of the sexes.

Financial institutions: institutions such as pension funds and insurance companies, identified as the largest holders of shares in British companies.

Financial Management Initiative: a general initiative to enable managers in the Civil Service to identify their objectives and the resources available, to provide methods of measuring performance while clearly identifying responsibilities for performance.

First past the post: the name given to the electoral system used in Britain and a few other Commonwealth countries such as Canada, in which the country is divided into single-member parliamentary constituencies and the winner is the candidate with the largest number of votes, irrespective of whether he or she gains an absolute majority. This can often produce highly disproportionate election results.

Fiscal: relating to public revenue, e.g., taxes.

Flexible constitution: a constitution with no formal method of amendment. The British constitution is amended either by an ordinary Act of Parliament or by a change in convention.

Free market: a doctrine that believes that the economy operates best when it is subject to the 'laws' of supply and demand and when government interferes and regulates as little as possible. The capitalist market system is the best supplier of goods and services and allocator of rewards; the role of government is minimal and is restricted to those things that only it can do, such as national defence and internal law and order.

Front bench: the leaders of the main parties in Parliament, derived from the fact that the leadership groups sit on the front benches of Parliamentary seats in the Chamber.

Front-bencher: the name given collectively to members of the government, who sit on the front bench on their side of the House, and to members of the Shadow Cabinet, who sit opposite.

Full employment: a political and economic doctrine which advocates that everyone seeking work should be able to find a job within their capacities at a wage that would enable them to live an adequate life.

Functional chamber: a legislative body composed of representatives of various interests in society, such as business, trade unions, the churches and so on.

G8: The seven major world economies – G7 (The United States, Japan, Germany, UK, France, Italy and Canada) plus Russia.

Gerrymandering: the practice of rigging electoral boundaries or affecting the social composition of electoral districts to ensure the success of the governing party, whatever level of support it receives. The term derives from Elbridge Gerry, Governor of Massachusetts, who in 1812 drew a congressional district shaped like a salamander so as to maximise the advantage for his party.

Glasnost: the Russian word for freedom of expression, popularised by Mikhail Gorbachev.

Globalisation: the process by which the world is made more interconnected and interdependent, through interregional, transnational and global networks and flows. Especially relevant to the production and marketing of goods which is increasingly organised on a worldwide scale.

Golden Age: the period from 1832 to 1867 when, some commentators claim, there was a balance between the executive and the legislature and when Parliament was a significant influence on government policy and actions.

Governance: the act or manner of governing within or across territorial jurisdictions.

Hegemony: the dominant military and economic state that uses its power to force a world order conducive to its own interests.

Hereditary peers: a member of the aristocracy whose title has been inherited from the nearest relative. Very few peerages are inheritable through the female line.

Home rule: the transfer of independence by a sovereign parliament to former territories.

Hung council: a council in which no party has an overall majority of seats and where business may be conducted by a minority administration or as a result of an agreement between two or more parties.

Identifiers: voters who have a continuing relationship with a party and consider themselves partisans who identify with its beliefs and policies.

Ideology: a system of beliefs embodying political, social and economic ideas and values.

Imperialism: the policy of acquiring power over other countries, usually neighbouring ones, by political and economic exploitation.

Industrial Revolution: the period in the late eighteenth and early nineteenth centuries when mass production techniques were invented and introduced into what became known as factories.

Industrialism: Jonathan Porritt's term for the present attitude of political parties to unlimited production and consumption.

Inequality: differences in wealth and opportunity between different groups in society.

Inflation: the increase in the amount of money in circulation producing rising prices and falls in value.

Influence: the ability to have some bearing on the outcome of a decision.

Inner city: the areas that surround the centres of cities, usually comprising older housing in poor condition and acting as 'reception' areas for immigrant groups.

Integration: full unity of one territory with another. The cooperative process whereby countries move closer together on economic and other areas of policy.

Interest: a stake, or a reason for caring about the outcome of a particular decision.

Interest groups: *see* Sectional or interest groups.

Intergovernmentalism: primacy of national governments in decision making.

Internal market: when an artificial separation between users and providers is invented to try to introduce some of the discipline of the free market into a public service.

International regimes: sets of rules, norms and decision-making procedures that coordinate state activity in particular policy areas.

Internationalism: the view that foreign policy should be based on the idea of cooperation between countries all over the world.

Issue voting: voting on the basis of issues presented at an election rather than on the basis of class or party preference.

Joint authority: the sharing of rule among governments.

Joint sovereignty: ruling an area jointly between two countries, both recognising equal rights to and responsibilities for it.

Judicial review: the ability of the courts to declare illegal any government action that they deem to be unauthorised by the terms of law.

Judiciary: the body in a political system responsible for interpreting and enforcing laws.

Keynesian/Keynesianism: named after the economic theories and prescriptions for government action of John Maynard Keynes (1883–1946). These advocated a role for vigorous government action to stimulate economic growth through high levels of spending and the control of aggregate demand in order to avoid slumps and booms.

Law lords: lords of appeal in ordinary are senior judges who have been given a life peerage so that they can carry out the judicial work of the Lords. There are currently 12 law lords.

Legislature: the body in a democracy responsible for discussing and creating laws.

Legitimacy: the right to govern.

Liberalisation: literally to make freer or less restrictive, as in 'liberalisation of trade'.

Liberty: freedom from slavery, captivity or any other form of arbitrary control.

Life peers: since the 1958 Life Peerages Act, most peers have been created for their lifetime only. Until 1999, life peers constituted around one-third of the nominal membership of the Lords.

Lobby: the general term used to describe the activities of pressure groups, so called because lobbyists seek to waylay MPs as they pass through the lobby of the Commons. It also refers to the off-the-record briefings given by government spokespeople to journalists.

Lords spiritual: the Archbishops of Canterbury and York and the 24 most senior diocesan bishops of the Church of England who sit in the Lords until they cease to hold their post.

Lords temporal: all those peers who are not lords spiritual.

Majoritarian: electoral systems such as the alternative vote which require that the winning candidate receives an absolute majority (over 50 per cent) of the total vote. Although each winning candidate can claim a *mandate* from his or her electors, it does not prevent disproportionality and other problems.

Mandate: the idea that winning the general election gives the government the authority to put its policies, either as stated in the campaign or as required by circumstances, into effect. It can also mean that the government is expected to put its manifesto into action, that it has made a binding contract with the electors.

Mandatory reselection: the process by which sitting Labour MPs have to face a reselection meeting of the constituency Labour Party to determine whether they will be reselected as candidates for the next election. It was one of the reforms achieved by the Bennite left in the 1980s and is gradually being abandoned.

Manifesto: a document issued by a political party containing a list of policy pledges which will be implemented if the party wins the election.

Manipulation: the ability to influence someone else involved in a decision.

Market failure: instances where the workings of supply and demand in markets fail to provide goods or services that the community desires or needs.

Market testing: the idea that activities provided by government organisations should be tested for cost and effectiveness by subjecting in-house provision to competitive bids from outside bodies.

Means of delivery: the method whereby a particular service is provided.

Media: the collective name for the press, radio and television. Sometimes called the Fourth Estate, to represent its powerful position in the political system.

Mercantilism: the doctrine that state power and security were enhanced by a favourable balance of trade. Popular in Britain between the mid-16th and the mid-18th centuries, when policy was directed to reducing imports and increasing national self-sufficiency at the expense of free trade.

Ministerial responsibility: ministers are responsible to Parliament for their ministerial conduct, the general work of their departments and the actions or omissions of their officials.

Ministry: *see* Department.

Mixed economy: the existence of a substantial public sector in the economy alongside a substantial private one. An economic system combining public ownership (most commonly of certain infrastructure industries and services) with the private ownership of the rest of the economy.

Modernising Government: White Paper published in March 1999, which encapsulates a range of managerial and service delivery themes with a focus on updating and modernising the basic functioning of the government machine. The White Paper and the subsequent implementation programme contained many modish concepts including 'government direct', 'joined-up government' and 'information-age government'.

Monetarism: an economic doctrine adopted by the Thatcherite wing of the Conservative Party which emphasises the control of the money supply as the way to defeat inflation – seen as the main job of the government – rather than ensuring full employment.

Motion of no confidence: a motion tabled (usually by the Leader of the Opposition) stating that 'This House has no confidence in Her Majesty's Ministers'. If passed, the government must, by convention, resign or request a dissolution of Parliament.

Multilateral: agreements between two or more states.

Multilateralism: attempting to solve international problems through collective approaches.

Multinational companies/firms: organisations that operate in a wide range of companies/firms across several national boundaries, shifting economic activity around them in order to exploit the best conditions for producing profit.

Multi-polar: an international system where there are more than two dominant powers, or no dominant powers at all.

National identity: a shared sense by a group of people – usually citizens of a state – as to their own history and character.

National interest: the calculation by its government of what constitutes the best course of action for a nation in international affairs.

Nationalisation: the act of transferring a part of the economy to state ownership, usually by establishing a nationalised corporation. Usually associated with the post-war 'socialist' political device of placing sections of the economy under the control of the government, so that privately owned assets such as buildings, equipment etc., or shares in a company are transferred by law from private into public ownership.

Nationalised corporations: the legal form taken by most publicly owned industries, and until recently the most important form of quasi-government (see below) concerned with economic policy.

Nationalism: the belief that one's country is worth supporting strongly in most situations.

Natural rights: the belief that everyone is born with certain basic rights regarding freedom, citizenship and law.

Negative constitutionalism: a belief in a constitution serving as a constraining mechanism, giving precedence to enduring principles over the transient will of the majority.

Neo-liberalism: in this usage refers to the doctrine which advocates individual autonomy and market principles over state control.

New Labour: the summary label to describe the economic policies devised by the Labour Party in the 1990s to ensure a departure from traditional ('old') Labour economic policies.

'New magistracy': the tendency of governments since 1979 to put functions into the hands of non-elected bodies such as quangos, including health service trusts, responsible for spending large amounts of money with little public accountability.

Next Steps: stemming from the Ibbs, or Next Steps, Report in 1988, a programme of managerial and structural reform which transformed the Civil Service through the creation of new executive agencies to carry out central government services and functions.

Notifiable offences: those offences that are sufficiently serious to be tried by a judge.

Occupational class: the method of assigning individuals to class groups on the basis of their occupational classification – manual working class, and so on.

Oligarchy: a political system in which power is exercised by a group or committee of people.

One member, one vote (OMOV): the process of reform in the Labour Party by which party members vote as individuals instead of having their views represented by unions, constituency parties, etc.

Order: the degree of calm and law-abidingness present in society.

Pacificism: opposition to the conduct of war.

Paramilitaries: groups of supporters for a cause who accept violence as a method, accept military discipline and often wear neo-military dress.

Paramilitary groups: armed organisations not recognised by the state.

Parliamentary lobby: a small group of political journalists from the main media outlets who are given privileged access to ministers and other government spokespeople. They receive highly confidential briefings and in return do not reveal their sources of information.

Parliamentary sovereignty: the doctrine that Parliament is the supreme law-making body in the United Kingdom, with absolute *legal* right to make any law it chooses, subject only to those restrictions imposed by the membership of the EU, itself an expression of parliamentary sovereignty. The sovereignty of Parliament is subject to a host of practical and political limitations.

Participatory democracy: a political system in which everyone is allowed and encouraged to take part in making decisions.

Partisan dealignment: the declining number of voters over the past three decades who are identifying with political parties.

Perestroika: the Russian word for reconstruction, popularised by Mikhail Gorbachev.

Permissive: the alleged characteristic of Labour social policy in the 1960s when it was first believed that anything goes and that 'doing your own thing' was good.

Photo opportunity: a media event where politicians pose for photographs but refuse to answer questions from journalists and where the public is excluded, a technique perfected by Mrs Thatcher.

Pluralism: a political system in which power is diffused into several different centres within society and thus there are competing centres of power and authority rather than one in which the state is dominant. Pluralists argue that power is and should be dispersed in society, thus ensuring that freedom is maintained.

Pluralist: a form of political decision making in which a variety (a plurality) of interests are held to contest outcomes.

Plurality: electoral systems (especially 'first past the post') that require only that the winning candidate has more votes that his or her nearest rival rather than an absolute majority. Such systems tend to produce disproportionate results.

Policy cycle: the process of policy initiation, formulation and implementation.

Political demands: the requirements made upon political systems by the societies they regulate.

Policy directorate: in 2001 Blair combined the No. 10 Policy Unit and some members of the private office into a directorate and it advises him on policy. Since June 2005 the two groups have been reconstituted.

Political entrepreneurship: the activity of promoting political causes, interests or groups in the political marketplace.

Political participation: the act of taking part in politics.

Political party: an organised group of people sharing common policy preferences and a general ideological position. It seeks to possess or share political power, usually by nominating candidates for election and thus seeking a place in the legislature.

Political recruitment: the process by which citizens are recruited into high participation in political life.

Polluted: made unclean, corrupt or defiled.

Positive constitutionalism: a belief in a constitution serving as a mechanism through which the will of the people is paramount.

Power: the ability to make someone do as one wishes.

'Power corrupts': the notion that the ability to get people to behave in a certain way will eventually be abused for selfish ends by the holders of power.

Pragmatism: the belief that problems should be solved on their unique merits rather than according to some pre-ordained ideological pathway.

Prerogative: prior or exclusive privilege often associated with rank or position.

Press barons: newspaper proprietors who have been raised to the peerage either out of gratitude for services rendered to the governing party or because of the hope that they will omit to bite the hand that feeds it.

Pressure group: a body possessing both formal structure and common interests which seeks to influence government at the national, local and international level without normally seeking election to representative bodies.

Primary, secondary and tertiary sectors: the three levels of the economy corresponding to the activities of producing raw materials, producing manufactured goods and delivering services.

Prime ministerial government: the view most associated with Richard Crossman and John Mackintosh that the Prime Minister has become dominant, almost a President, and that the Cabinet has become part of the 'dignified' aspects of the system.

Private bill: a bill brought forward by an individual, company or public body outside Parliament to effect a change in the law of particular interest or benefit to the person or persons promoting it.

Private member's bill: a public bill promoted by a member of the Commons who is not a minister. They have a variety of purposes; several pass into law each year, though most fail. The opposition of the government is usually fatal.

Private sector: the part of the economy that is the product of market forces alone.

Privatisation: the process of transferring state-owned enterprises to the private sector, mainly by the sale of shares. The term also refers to other aspects of the reduction of the economic role of the state, such as liberalisation policies to encourage greater reliance on the market including deregulation of business, contracting out of services and the opening of the public sector generally to market forces.

Professional politicians: the small minority of citizens who devote their whole life to politics, and who make a livelihood from it.

Promotion groups: *see* Cause or promotion groups.

Proportional representation (PR): a system of election that attempts to relate votes cast for the various parties to the number of seats won in the legislature. There are various forms of PR, with widely differing consequences.

Psephology: the study of voting behaviour as shown in elections and opinion polls. The word derives from the

Greek word *psephos*, a pebble. Classical Athenians voted by putting a pebble into one of two jars, one for the 'yes' votes, the other for the 'no' votes. It was a form of direct democracy.

Public bills: bills that must relate to a matter of public (general) interest and be introduced by an MP or a peer. Any bill proposed by the government, regardless of its content or intent, is a public bill.

Public corporations: organisations set up to run enterprises and provide services within the public sector or state sector. They include nationalised industries such as coal, gas and electricity and bodies such as the BBC.

Public sector: that part of the economy which is in state ownership and is funded substantially by money originating from taxation of some kind.

Public-Private Partnerships: a range of initiatives designed to bring about greater collaboration between the public and private sectors in the provision of services. The Private Finance Initiative, introduced to facilitate the funding of major public sector capital projects using private funds, is a prime example of public-private partnership.

Quango: a quasi-autonomous non-governmental organisation, independent (at least in theory) from the department that created it, nominally under the control of the minister who appoints its members, sets its budget and establishes its aims, and with little responsibility to Parliament. Quangos are public bodies which advise on or administer activities and which carry out their work at arm's length from government.

Quasi-government: those public institutions that are not formally part of the government but carry out a function central to it.

Rates: a form of local taxation based upon the notional value of a property which was used until replaced by the community charge or poll tax.

Rationality: a belief that the exercise of reason is superior to other ways of finding the truth.

Reactionary: right-wing policies held to be harsh and unfeeling. Strictly speaking support for the *status quo ante* (that which previously existed).

Realignment: a fundamental change in party structure and voting support for the various parties. An example is the wholesale desertion of the American Republican Party by black voters to the Democratic Party in the 1920s.

Referendum: a ballot in which the people at large decide an issue by voting 'yes' or 'no', although multi-outcome referenda are possible. The matter may be referred to the people by the government, perhaps because it is unable to make a decision, the law or the constitution may require such a reference, or there may be a mechanism by which the people can demand a referendum. Britain's only national referendum, that of 1975 over continued membership of the EC, was *advisory* only.

Regionalisation: the process of interconnection and interaction between groupings of states and societies. The basis for regionalisation may be common history, geographical proximity or common interests.

Regulatory agency: an institution that specialises in a given regulatory task, such as the regulation of competition generally, or of competitive conditions in a single industry or sector, such as the railway industry.

Representation: the notion that those who are governed should be involved in the process of government.

Representative government: government whereby decisions are taken by representatives who are (normally) elected by popular vote. The people do not take decisions directly.

Responsibility: the accountability of government to the people.

Responsible government: the view that government should be held accountable for its actions, initially to the people's representatives and ultimately to the people themselves.

Restructuring the welfare state: changing the balance in spending between different services.

Revenue expenditure: day-to-day expenditure by local authorities on items such as salaries, office supplies and heating.

Rigid constitution: a constitution that contains a provision that it can only be changed by a process different from and more complex than that required for the passage of ordinary legislation. The best-known example is that of the United States.

Royal prerogative: powers that legally are in the hands of the Crown, having been accepted by the courts over time as rightfully belonging to the monarch in his or her capacity as ruler. Most prerogative powers are now exercised by ministers (particularly the Prime Minister) who 'advise' the monarch as to their use.

Rule of law: the idea that human activity should be controlled within a framework of agreed rules.

Secondary sector: *see* Primary, secondary and tertiary sectors.

Sectional or interest groups: these groups represent the interests (particularly economic) of their members. They include business, labour and professional organisations and often have close links with political parties.

Select committee: a committee chosen by the House to work according to specific terms of reference. It may be given special powers to investigate, examine and report its findings to Parliament. Some are concerned with the working of Parliament itself; others scrutinise the activities of the executive.

Selective targeting: the rejection of universalism (see below) in favour of restricting availability of benefits and services to those deemed to be in need by some standard test.

Service sector: *see* Tertiary sector.

Shared responsibility: the solution to environmental problems is the responsibility of government, business, citizens, voluntary organisations and the public sector.

Social capital: The networks and norms of reciprocal trust built up through interpersonal connections. When people associate with one another through voluntary associations they develop better skills of social interaction, treat cooperation as normal and come to rely upon and trust each other.

Social imperialism: an idea involving abandoning the principles of free trade in order to protect British industries and building closer ties with the white dominions of New Zealand, South Africa and Australia, in order to create a closed imperial market. The Tariff Reform Movement under Joseph Chamberlain advocated an elaborate system of imperial preferences, that is, a system of bilateral tariff concessions granted to each other by Britain and the white dominions. The Imperial Conference in 1917 formally approved such a system, but it was not until the 1930s that imperial preference developed to any great extent.

Socialism: an economic system in which everyone benefits from the labour of others.

Soundbite: a brief quote that is intended to make the maximum possible political impact. Research indicates that most listeners and viewers can absorb information for some thirty seconds, a theory that has influenced politicians on both sides of the Atlantic.

Sovereignty: autonomy over national decision making. The ultimate legal authority in a state.

Special relationship: the close feeling between US and British governments based on common culture and alliance in warfare.

Spin doctor: a party official or public relations consultant whose job is to influence the media and put the best possible construction on events, by getting the party or candidate's message over by any possible means.

Standing committee: usually a small group of MPs reflecting party strength in the Commons which takes the committee stage of bills that have received their second reading. They scrutinise the bills and can propose amendments to the House.

State: A commonly governed group of people all living within a defined territory.

Statist-corporatism: is often used to descibe practices in authoritarian and some democratic states and refers

to a process by which the state uses officially-recognised organisations as a tool for policy-makung and restricting public participation in the political process, thus limiting the power of civil society.

Statute law: those laws deriving their authority from Acts of Parliament and subordinate (delegated) legislation made under authority of the parent Act. Statute law overrides common law.

Steering the economy: the dominant image used to describe the business of economic management as conducted by government.

Subsidiarity: the general aim of the principle of subsidiarity is to guarantee a degree of independence for a lower authority in relation to a higher body or for a local authority in respect of a central authority. It therefore involves the sharing of powers between several levels of authority, a principle which forms the institutional basis for federal states. When applied in an EU context, the principle means that the member states remain responsible for areas which they are capable of managing more effectively themselves, while the Community is given those powers which the member states cannot discharge satisfactorily.

Subvention: government subsidy.

Suffrage: the right to vote. The extension of the suffrage was a gradual process, culminating in 1969 when 18-year-olds were enfranchised. The suffrage is unusually wide in this country, including British subjects, resident Commonwealth citizens and citizens of the Irish Republic who have been resident for three months.

Supply-side economics: provided the political and theoretical foundation for a remarkable number of tax cuts in the United States and other countries during the 1980s. Supply-side economics stresses the impact of tax rates on the incentives for people to produce and to use resources efficiently.

Supranationalism: the character of authority exercised by European Union bodies that takes precedence over the autonomy of the member states.

Sustainable development: the capability of the current generation to ensure it meets the need of the present without compromising the ability of future generations to meet their own needs.

Sustainable economy or sustainable growth: one in which resources are used more efficiently so that pressures on the environment do not increase as the economy grows.

Swing: the way in which the switch of voters from one party to another on a national or constituency basis can be calculated. It is worked out by adding the rise in one party's vote to the fall in the other party's and then dividing by two.

Tabloids: small format newspapers, usually aimed at the bottom end of the market with an informal style, use of large and often sensational headlines and many photographs.

Tertiary (or service) sector: *see* Primary, secondary and tertiary sectors.

Thatcherism: the economic, social and political ideas and particular style of leadership associated with Margaret Thatcher, Prime Minister from 1979 to 1990. It was a mixture of neo-liberal beliefs in the free market and neo-conservative social attitudes and beliefs about the limited role of government.

The Treasury: the most important department of government concerned with economic policy.

Theological: based upon the science of religion.

Think-tanks: the name give to specialist organisations that frequently research and publish on policy and ideological matters.

Toleration: accepting the legitimacy of views with which one does not necessarily agree.

Top-down: the term used to denote power residing in the leading figures of an organisation, control over organisation being exercised by those figures over the ordinary members.

Transfer payments: a method of transferring money from one group of citizens to another: for instance, taxing those in work and transferring the money raised to the unemployed in the form of unemployment benefits.

Transnationalisation: the process whereby politics and other social relations are conducted across and perhaps regardless of national boundaries. There are transnational corporations, such as Wal-Mart, transnational communities, such as religious communities, transnational structures, for example, of finance, and transnational problems like drug trafficking.

Tripartism: a variant of *corporatism* in which economic policy is made in conjunction with business and labour groups to the exclusion of Parliament and other interests.

Turnout: the measure, usually expressed as a percentage, of registered voters who actually vote. The average turnout in postwar elections has been around 75 per cent, generally lower than in most other EU countries.

Tyranny: a political system in which power is exercised harshly without any consideration for the citizenry.

Ulsterisation: the return to frontline policing by the Royal Ulster Constabulary, replacing the British Army, undertaken in the mid 1970s, to maintain the image of normality.

Unicameral legislature: legislatures made up of one chamber are to be found mainly in smaller countries such as Israel and New Zealand or in smaller states in federal systems, such as Nebraska in the United States.

Unitary authorities: a local government structure in which all services are provided by a single-tier authority as opposed to a structure in which powers and functions are divided between two tiers.

Universalism: the principle that welfare services should be freely available to all citizens.

U-turn: a fundamental change of policies or philosophy by a political party or leader. The term is used to describe Heath's abandonment in 1971/2 of the free-market policies on which he was elected in 1970.

Washington Consensus: formerly a list of policy prescriptions that were influential in US policy-making circles in the late 1980s and early 1990s. The three big ideas at the heart of the concept were macro-economic discipline, a market economy, and openness to the world (at least in respect of trade and FDI).

Welfare mix: phrase invented by Michael Rose to explain his analysis of how welfare services are provided through a wide variety of sources.

Welfare state: the system of comprehensive social security and health services which was based on the Beveridge Report of 1942 and implemented by the post-war Labour government. Often referred to as 'cradle to grave' security.

Welfarism: the idea that the government should take some responsibility for the health and well-being of its citizens.

Whip: this term has several meanings: (a) parliamentary business managers found in all parties, responsible for maintaining party discipline and ensuring a maximum turnout in the division lobbies; (b) the summons to vote for an MP's party, with the importance of the issue indicated by a one-, two- or three-line whip, sent out weekly to members of the parliamentary party; (c) membership of an MP's party – withdrawal of the whip means that the MP concerned is no longer recognised as a member in good standing.

Working peers: peers that are created on the nomination of the political parties to strengthen their representation in the Upper House. This is particularly important to the Labour party, which traditionally was supported by few hereditary peers.

Index

Note: Terms where the page references are in **bold** may be found in the Glossary